The
Computer
Desktop
Encyclopedia

ALAN FREEDMAN

The Computer Desktop Encyclopedia

amacom

American Management Association

New York • Atlanta • Boston • Chicago • Kansas City • San Francisco • Washington, D.C.
Brussels • Mexico City • Tokyo • Toronto

Library of Congress Cataloging-in-Publication Data

Freedman, Alan
        Computer desktop encyclopedia / Alan Freedman.
            p.   cm.
        ISBN 0-8144-0012-4 (pbk. and CD-ROM). — ISBN 0-8144-0010-8 (pbk.)
        1. Computers—Dictionaries.   I. Title.
    QA76.15.F732   1996
    004'.03—dc20   96-724
                                                                         CIP

Printing number

10   9   8   7   6   5   4   3   2

To my mother,
who had the vision to send me
to "automation school" in 1960

ILLUSTRATIONS: Peter Felperin, Alan Freedman, Irma Lee Morrison,
Eric Jon Nones, Joseph D. Russo
EDITORIAL/PRODUCTION: Irma Lee Morrison
COPY EDITING: Mary McCann
BOOK DESIGN & TYPOGRAPHY: Cedar Waxwing Design, Rosemont, NJ
PUBLISHING SOFTWARE: PageMaker 5.0
PRINTER: HP LaserJet 4+, PCL Driver
FONTS: Garamond, Arial and Courier

A Note from the Author

The purpose of *Computer Desktop Encyclopedia* is to provide a meaningful definition of every important computer concept, term and buzzword used in the world of computers from micro to mainframe. Major hardware and software products are included as well as backgrounders on the companies that make them. Many historical photos of the first computers and electronic devices are in this book to remind us of the extraordinary acceleration of the technology of our era. All of this has come about in little over a hundred years, since the harnessing of electricity. It is a good idea to stop and smell the roses as we race towards the newest and the fastest.

It is also the purpose of this book to make sense out of this industry in general. As impossible a task as that may be, I have been trying for the past 15 years. What started out as a 300-term compendium for my computer seminars has now become my life's work. And, for that, I am very grateful, because I am interested in all the facets of this industry. I am lucky to have had a wide variety of experience in this field, and I am very lucky to have expert professionals who have been willing to help.

The degree of technical explanation chosen for each term is based on the term. Fundamental terms are explained for the lay person. More technical terms are explained with other technical terms, because, at some point, we have to assume a base knowledge without starting from scratch. However, all the terms used in this book are defined in the book.

I hope you find this book helpful and enjoyable. If there are concepts or products you feel should be included in the next edition, please let me know. Chances are they may have already been added to our floppy and CD-ROM versions, which are updated more frequently; however, I would love to hear from you and review your suggestions. Please write, fax, e-mail or call. Thank you very much for purchasing *Computer Desktop Encyclopedia.*

Alan Freedman

The Computer Language Company Inc.
U.S. Mail: P.O. Box 265
FedEx, UPS: 5521 State Park Road
Point Pleasant, PA 18950
215 297-5999 fax 8424
E-mail: freedman@computerlanguage.com

Acknowledgments

It woud be impossible to put a book like this together without the help of hundreds of technical engineers and public relations people who work for the hardware and software companies that make up this industry. In addition, many readers of my of current and previous editions of *The Computer Glossary* have contributed terms, suggestions and comments. For all of you that have willingly helped me, I thank you very much for your assistance. For those of you who made the experience akin to pulling teeth, well, thank you too. I appreciate your help.

I'd like to give a special acknowledgement to the following professionals who have continued to help me year after year. Thanks again to:

Thom Drewke, Technical Directions
James J. Farrell, III, Motorola, Inc.
Max B. Fetzer, Envirotronics
Lynn S. Frankel, Byrd Press
Peter Hermsen, Open Market, Inc.
Terry O'Donnel, Adobe Systems
Gary Saxer, Quarterdeck Office Systems
Jim Stroh, LXD Inc.
David Wallace, Dun & Bradstreet Software
Paul and Jan Witte, Originetics

I would like to thank the staff at AMACOM who paved the way for this book to be published, especially *Weldon Rackley, Tony Vlamis, Steve Arkin* and *Lydia Lewis*. Thanks for believing in me and for your continued support over the years.

Most of all, an extra special thank you to *Irma Lee Morrison*, my wife and partner. Your contribution has always been the most significant, because you are truly my inspiration. I love you dearly Irmalee.

Basic Concepts and Vocabulary
The entries in the following list are the fundamental terms for the topics indicated. Review them and use them as a springboard to other concepts and terms.

Fundamentals
analog
digital
binary
hardware
software
bit
byte
data
computer
computer system
operating system
application software
system software
chip
PC
bus
local bus

Graphics & Multimedia
graphics
paint program
drawing program
CAD
MPC
CD
CD-ROM
CD-R
virtual reality

Communications
communications
modem
LAN
client
server
client/server
client/server development system
enterprise networking
peer-to-peer communications
gateway
router
hub
Ethernet
Token Ring
OSI
online services
NetWare
V.34
TCP/IP
Internet
World Wide Web
Yahoo
information superhighway

Application Development
information system
field
record
file
database
DBMS
data administration
data dictionary
functional specification
systems analysis & design
system development cycle
prototyping
DSS
OLAP database
Systemantics

Programming
programming language
source language
machine language
assembly language
high-level language
object-oriented programming

Advanced Concepts
multitasking
multiprocessing
SMP
MPP
virtual memory
virtual machine
RISC
computer architecture
pipeline processing
memory protection
address modes
relocatable code
standards & compatibility

Interesting Stuff
RTFM
flame
salary survey
hot topics
space/time
object technology
software vendors
hardware vendors
boss screen
emoticons
Easter Egg
2000 time problem
how to spoof your technical friend
holographic storage

Use Acronyms...

Most of the terms in this book are defined by their acronymns, not their formal names. If you cannot find a multi-word term in the book, TRY ITS ACRONYM!

A:

The designation for the first floppy disk drive in a PC.

A20

The address line in a PC that points beyond one megabyte. For downward compatibility with 8086/8088s, this line is gated in 286s and up and is controlled by circuitry on the motherboard. When disabled, it keeps the machine in Real Mode (under 1MB). When enabled, the CPU can address beyond 1MB (Protected Mode).

AA

(Auto Answer) See *modem.*

AAUI

(Apple AUI) Apple's version of the Ethernet AUI connector.

abacus

One of the earliest counting instruments. Similar devices go back to the Greek and Roman days. It uses sliding beads in columns that are divided in two by a center bar. The top is "heaven," where each of two beads is worth 5 when moved to the center bar. The bottom is "earth," where each of five beads is worth 1 when moved toward the center.

ABAP/4

The Development Workbench part of SAP's R/3 software suite. See *R/3.*

ABC

(Atanasoff-Berry Computer) The first electronic digital computer. Completed in 1942 by Iowa State Professor John Atanasoff and graduate student Clifford Berry, it embodied the input, memory and arithmetic unit of future computers.
John Mauchly, cobuilder of the ENIAC, visited Atanasoff in 1940 and corresponded with him. Although Eckert and Mauchly are considered the creators of the first electronic digital computer, Atanasoff and Berry are acknowledged contributors. In 1990, nearly 50 years after his invention, 87-year-old Atanasoff was awarded the National Medal of Technology.

ABC Computer
(Photo courtesy of Charles Babbage Institute, University of Minnesota.)

ABCD
See *CompTIA.*

abend
(ABnormal END) Also called a *crash* or *bomb*, it occurs when the computer is presented with instructions or data it cannot recognize or the program is reaching beyond its protective boundary. It is the result of erroneous software logic or hardware failure.

When the abend occurs, if the program is running in a personal computer under a single-task (one program at a time) operating system, such as DOS, the computer locks up and has to be rebooted. Multitasking operating systems with memory protection halt the offending program allowing remaining programs to continue.

If you consider what goes on inside a computer, you might wonder why it doesn't crash more often. A large mainframe's memory can easily contain over one billion storage cells (bits). Within every second, millions of these cells change their state from uncharged to charged to uncharged. If only one cell fails, the computer can abend.

ABI
(Application Binary Interface) A specification for a particular hardware platform and operating system. It is one step beyond the application program interface (API), which defines the calls from the application to the operating system. The ABI defines the API plus the machine language for a particular CPU family. An API does not ensure runtime compatibility, but an ABI does, because it defines the machine language, or runtime, format.

For example, the PowerOpen Environment is an ABI that specifies the machine language of the PowerPC CPU family and the function calls made by the application to a PowerOpen-compliant operating system.

ablative WORM
An optical disk technology in which the creation of the bit permanently alters the recording material, and the data cannot be changed.

abort
(1) To exit a function or application without saving any data that has been changed.
(2) To stop a transmission.

above the line
See "IBM COBOLs" in *COBOL.*

ABR
(AutoBaud Rate detect) The analysis of the first characters of a message to determine its transmission speed and number of start and stop bits.

absolute
In programming, a mathematical function that always returns a positive number. For example, ABS(25-100) yields 75, not -75.

absolute address
An explicit identification of a memory location, peripheral device, or location within a device. For example, memory byte 107,443, disk drive 2 and sector 238 are absolute addresses. The computer uses absolute addresses to reference memory and peripherals. See *base address* and *relative address.*

absolute path
Same as *full path.*

ABI (Application Binary Interface)

A specification for a particular hardware platform and operating system. It is one step beyond the application program interface (API), which defines the calls from the application to the operating system. The ABI defines the API plus the machine language for a particular CPU family. An API does not ensure runtime compatibility, but an ABI does, because it defines the machine language, or runtime, format.

For example, the PowerOpen Environment is an ABI that specifies the machine language of the PowerPC CPU family and the function calls made by the application to a PowerOpen-compliant operating system.

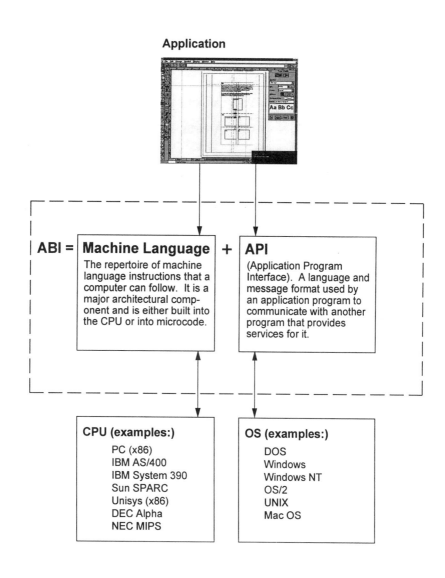

Application

ABI = | **Machine Language** + **API**

The repertoire of machine language instructions that a computer can follow. It is a major architectural component and is either built into the CPU or into microcode.

(Application Program Interface). A language and message format used by an application program to communicate with another program that provides services for it.

CPU (examples:)

PC (x86)
IBM AS/400
IBM System 390
Sun SPARC
Unisys (x86)
DEC Alpha
NEC MIPS

OS (examples:)

DOS
Windows
Windows NT
OS/2
UNIX
Mac OS

absolute vector

In computer graphics, a vector with end points designated in absolute coordinates. Contrast with *relative vector.*

absolute zero

The theoretical temperature at which molecular activity ceases. It is -273.15 degrees Celsius and -459.67 degrees Farhrenheit.

abstract class

Also called an *abstract superclass,* in object technology, it is a class created as a master structure. No objects of an abstract class are created, rather subclasses of the abstract class are defined with their own variations, and the subclasses are used to create the actual objects.

abstract data type

A user-defined data type in object-oriented programming. See *abstraction* and *object-oriented programming.*

abstraction

In object technology, determining the essential characteristics of an object. Abstraction is one of the basic principles of object-oriented design, which allows for creating user-defined data types, known as objects. See *object technology* and *encapsulation.*

abstract superclass

See *abstract class* and *superclass.*

AC

(Alternating Current) The common form of electricity from power plant to home/office. Its direction is reversed 60 times per second in the U.S.; 50 times in Europe. Contrast with *DC.*

AC adapter

Same as *power adapter.*

accelerator

A key combination used to activate a task. See *accelerator board* and *graphics accelerator.*

accelerator board

An add-in board that replaces the existing CPU with a higher performance CPU. See *graphics accelerator.*

acceptance test

A test performed by the end user to determine if the system is working according to the specifications in the contract.

access

To store data on and retrieve data from a disk or other peripheral device. See *access arm, access method* and *Microsoft Access.*

access arm

access arm

The mechanical arm that moves the read/write head across the surface of a disk similar to a tone arm on a phonograph. The access arm is directed by instructions in the operating system to move the read/write head to a specific track on the disk. The rotation of the disk positions the read/write head over the required sector.

ACCESS.bus

A serial bus that is expected to become popular in the 1996 timeframe. It allows multiple devices to be daisy chained together using a four-wire cable and connector similar to a phone jack. It runs at 125Kbits/sec and is designed to hook up several slower-speed peripherals such as a mouse, keyboard and modem.

access charge

The charge imposed by a communications service or telephone company for the use of its network.

access code

(1) An identification number and/or password used to gain access into a computer system.

(2) The number used as a prefix to a calling number in order to gain access to a particular telephone service.

access denied

The system is unable to retrieve the file you are requesting. This often means that the file you want to open is already open in another application. It may also mean that the file has been purposefully made unavailable. See *hidden file*.

access line

The line from a customer site to a telephone company's central office.

access method

A software routine that is part of the operating system or network control program which performs the storing/retrieving or transmitting/receiving of data. It is also responsible for detecting a bad transfer of data caused by hardware or network malfunction and correcting it if possible.

Tape Access Methods

With tapes, the *sequential* access method is always used for storing data, which places the next block of data after the previous one.

Disk Access Methods

For disks, *indexed* access methods are widely used to keep track of records and files. The index is a table of contents for each file or each record within the file. The sequential method is also used when retrieval of individual records is not required. The *indexed sequential method*, or ISAM, combines both methods by providing an index that is kept in sequential order. For fastest retrieval, the *direct* access method uses a formula to convert the record's identifying field, such as account number, into a physical storage address.

Communications Access Methods

Communications access methods, such as IBM's TCAM and VTAM, transfer data between a host computer and remote terminals. These routines prepare the data for transmission by placing the data into frames with appropriate control codes. These methods reference layers 3, 4 and 5 of the OSI model.

LAN access methods, such as CSMA/CD (Ethernet) and token passing (Token Ring), transfer data to and from connected computers on the network. These methods reference layers 1 and 2 of the OSI model.

access server

See *communications server*.

access time

(1) Memory access time is how long it takes for a character in memory to be transferred to or from the CPU. In a personal computer, fast RAM chips have an access time of 70 nanoseconds or less.

(2) Disk access time is an average of the time it takes to position the read/write head over the requested track. Fast personal computer hard disks have access times of 18 milliseconds or less. Mainframe disks can be less than one millisecond. This is a common speed measurement, but disk performance is influenced by channel speed (transfer rate), interleaving and caching.

accounting machine

An early office machine used to compute and prepare invoices and payroll, etc., using magnetic stripe ledger cards or punched cards.

account number

The number assigned to an employee, customer, vendor or product for identification. Although it may contain only numeric digits, it is often stored as a character field, so that parts of the account number can be searched independently. For example, the number could contain a territory code, and records could be selected by state or region.

accumulator

A hardware register used to hold the results or partial results of arithmetic and logical operations.

ACD

(Automatic Call Distribution) The routing of an incoming telephone call to the next available operator.

ACE

(Advanced Computing Environment) An open standard based on UNIX and Windows NT introduced in 1991 by MIPS Computer Systems and others. Although later disbanded, its purpose was to provide users a migration path from x86 PCs to MIPS RISC machines.

ACF

(Advanced Communications Function) An official product line name for IBM SNA programs, such as VTAM (ACF/VTAM), NCP (ACF/NCP), etc.

ACK

(ACKnowledgment code) The communications code sent from a receiving station to a transmitting station to indicate that it is ready to accept data. It is also used to acknowlege the error-free receipt of transmitted data. Contrast with *NAK*.

acknowledgement code

See *ACK*.

ACM

(Association for Computing Machinery, 1515 Broadway, New York, NY 10036, 212/869-7440) A membership organization founded in 1947 dedicated to advancing the arts and sciences of information processing. In addition to awards and publications, ACM also maintains special interest groups (SIGs) in the computer field.

acoustic coupler

A device that connects a terminal or computer to the handset of a telephone. It contains a shaped foam bed that the handset is placed in, and it may also contain the modem.

Acrobat

Document exchange software from Adobe Systems, Inc., Mountain View, CA, that converts a DOS, Windows, UNIX or Macintosh document into a proprietary file format for viewing on other machines. Documents are converted to Acrobat's Portable Document Format (PDF) format that are displayed on the target machine with an Acrobat reader, which is free of charge.

Fonts are either embedded within the PDF document, or to save space, the Acrobat reader can simulate the page layout with only two fonts. The style will differ, but the sizes and weights of the characters will reproduce correctly to maintain the same positioning of the text on the page.

Acrobat Exchange lets you view, print, annotate and collate electronic documents. It includes the PDF Writer driver for creating PDF files from most applications and also lets users add bookmarks and hypertext links to their documents. Acrobat Distiller is used to convert PostScript files into the PDF Format and allows for the creation of thumbnails.

ACS

(Asynchronous Communications Server) A communications server that manages a pool of modems. It directs outgoing messages to the next available modem and directs incoming messages to the appropriate workstation.

active addressing

A technology that improves passive matrix LCD screens. Rather than having a transistor attached to each pixel on the back of the screen, the transistors are on chips on the motherboard. The resulting display looks almost as good as active matrix without the high cost. This emerging technology is expected in 1995 or 1996. See *LCD*.

active hub

The central connecting device in a network that regenerates signals. Contrast with *passive hub* and *intelligent hub*. See *hub*.

active matrix

An LCD technology used in flat panel computer displays. Using a transistor for each pixel, it produces a high quality display and eliminates the submarining associated with passive matrix screens. See *LCD*.

active star

See *active hub*.

ACTOR

An object-oriented programming language for PCs from The Whitewater Group Inc., Evanston, IL. It runs under Windows and has a Pascal-like syntax to ease the transition to object-oriented languages.

actuator

A mechanism that causes a device to be turned on or off, adjusted or moved. The component that moves the head assembly on a disk drive or an arm of a robot is called an actuator.

Ada

A high-level programming language developed by the U.S. Department of Defense along with the European Economic Community and many other organizations. It was designed for embedded applications and process control but is also used for logistics applications. Ada is a Pascal-based language that is very comprehensive. Ada was named after Augusta Ada Byron (1815-1852), Countess of Lovelace and daughter of Lord Byron. She was a mathematician and colleague of Charles Babbage, who was developing his Analytical Engine. Some of her programming notes for the machine have survived, giving her the distinction of being the first documented programmer in the world.
The following Ada program converts Fahrenheit to Celsius:

```
with Text_IO;
procedure Convert is
package Int_IO is new Text_IO.Integer_IO(Integer);
Fahrenheit : Integer;
begin
 Text_IO.Put_Line("Enter Fahrenheit");
 Int_IO.Get(Fahrenheit);
 Text_IO.Put("Celsius is ");
 Int_IO.Put((Fahrenheit-32) * 5 / 9);
 Text_IO.New_Line;
end Convert;
```

ADABAS

A DBMS from Software AG, Reston, VA, for IBM mainframes, VAXes, various UNIX platforms and OS/2 PCs. It is an inverted list DBMS with relational capabilities. A 4GL called NATURAL, text retrieval, GIS processing, SQL and distributed database functions are also available. Introduced in 1969, it was one of the first DBMSs.

ADAPSO

See *ITAA.*

adapter

A device that allows one system to connect to and work with another. Display adapters and network adapters are really controllers, not adapters. See *host adapter* and *expansion bus.*

adaptive bridge

A network bridge that remembers destination addresses in order to route subsequent packets more quickly. Most bridges are this type.

adaptive compression

A data compression technique that dynamically adjusts the algorithm used based on the content of the data being compressed.

adaptive equalization

A transmission technique that dynamically adjusts its modulation method based on the quality of the line.

adaptive routing

The ability to select a new communications path to get around heavy traffic or a node or circuit failure.

adaptor

An alternate spelling of adapter.

ADB

(Apple Desktop Bus) The Macintosh communications port for keyboards, mice, trackballs, graphics tablets and other input devices.

ADC

See *A/D converter.*

ADCCP

(Advanced Data Communications Control Procedure) An ANSI communications protocol that is similar to the SDLC and HDLC protocols.

A/D converter

(Analog to Digital Converter) A device that converts continuously varying analog signals from instruments that monitor such conditions as movement, temperature, sound, etc., into binary code for the computer. It may be contained on a single chip or can be one circuit within a chip. See *modem* and *codec.* Contrast with *D/A converter.*

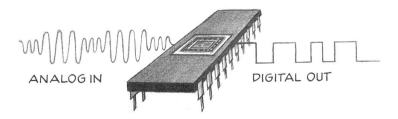

ANALOG IN   DIGITAL OUT

AD/Cycle

(Application Development/Cycle) SAA-compliant software from IBM that provides a system for managing systems development. It provides a structure for storing information about all phases of an information system including systems analysis and design, database design and programming.

adder

An elementary electronic circuit that adds the bits of two numbers together.

add-in, add-on

Refers to hardware modules, such as printed circuit boards, that are designed to be plugged into a socket within the computer.

address

(1) The number of a particular memory or peripheral storage location. Like post office boxes, each byte of memory and each disk sector has its own unique address. Programs are compiled into machine language, which references actual addresses in the computer.
(2) As a verb, to manage or work with. For example, "the computer can address 2MB of memory."

addressable cursor

A screen cursor that can be programmed to move to any row or column on the screen.

address bus

An internal channel from the CPU to memory across which the addresses of data (not the data) are transmitted. The number of lines (wires) in the address bus determines the amount of memory that can be directly addressed as each line carries one bit of the address. For example, the 8088 CPU has 20 address lines and can address 1,048,576 bytes. The 68020 has 32 address lines and can address four gigabytes.

Various swapping and switching techniques can be added to the hardware that allow a computer to use more memory than is directly addressable by its address bus. See *EMS*.

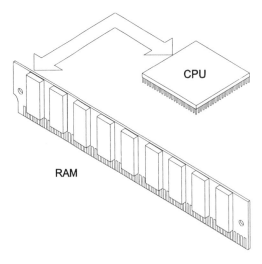

CPU

RAM

Address Bus

address mode

The method by which an instruction references memory. An *indexed address* is modified by the contents of an index register before execution. An *indirect address* points to another address. Ultimately, in order to do any actual processing, the instruction must derive *real,* or *absolute addresses,* where the required data is located.

address register

A high-speed circuit that holds the addresses of data to be processed or of the next instruction to be executed.

address resolution

Obtaining a physical address that is ultimately needed to perform an operation. All instructions executing at the machine level require a physical memory, storage or network node address when referencing the actual hardware. Machine addresses are derived using table lookups and/or algorithms.

In a network, a "where is?" request is broadcast onto the network, and the logical address (name) is turned into a physical address (machine number), either by the recipient node or by a router that maintains a list of address translations.

address resolution protocol

See *ARP.*

address space

A computer's address space is the total amount of memory that can be addressed by the computer. For example, the 486 can address 4GB of physical memory and 64TB of virtual memory.

A program's address space is the actual memory used by the program when running. It may refer to physical memory (RAM chips) or to virtual memory (disk) or to a combination of both.

address translation

Transforming one address into another. For example, assemblers and compilers translate symbolic addresses into machine addresses. Virtual memory systems translate a virtual address into a real address.

ADE

(Application Development Environment) An IBM approach for developing applications that will run in all SAA environments. The development software is client/server based, and the main functions reside in the host.

ADF

(Application Development Facility) An IBM programmer-oriented mainframe application generator that runs under IMS.

ad hoc query

A non-standardized inquiry. An ad hoc query is composed to answer a question when the need arises.

ADMD

(ADministrative Management Domain) A public e-mail service. See *X.400.*

administrator

See *data administrator, database administrator, network administrator* and *system administrator.*

Adobe

(Adobe Systems, Inc., Mountain View, CA) Founded in 1982 by Dr. John Warnock, Adobe helped pioneer desktop publishing with its fonts and applications.

Initially developed for the Macintosh, Adobe's PostScript fonts have become the industry standard among graphics and printing service bureaus. Adobe PhotoShop and Adobe Type Manager are examples of world-class software that spearheaded the industry.

In 1995, Adobe acquired Aldus Corporation, makers of PageMaker, turning Adobe into the preeminent desktop publishing software company.

Adobe fonts

See *PostScript*.

Adobe Illustrator

A full-featured drawing program for Windows and Macintosh from Adobe Systems, Inc., Mountain View, CA. It provides sophisticated tracing and text manipulation capabilities as well as color separations. Included is Adobe Type Manager and a selection of Type 1 fonts. Illustrator was originally developed for the Mac and includes more features. The Windows versions comes with Adobe Type Align and Adobe Streamline, for tracing bitmaps.

Adobe Photoshop

A popular image editor for the Macintosh and Windows from Adobe Systems, Inc., Mountain View, CA. The original Mac versions were the first to bring affordable image editing down to the personal computer level in the late 1980s. Photoshop has become a standard in image editing.

Adobe Type Align

Software from Adobe Systems, Inc., Mountain View, CA, that is used to align text to different shapes; for example, wrapping text around a circle or along the borders of an irregular or multi-sided object.

Adobe Type Manager

A PostScript font utility for the Macintosh and Windows from Adobe Systems, Inc., Mountain View, CA. It scales Type 1 fonts into screen fonts and prints them on non-PostScript dot matrix and HP laser printers. For printing fonts, current versions of ATM download font bitmaps to the printer. Earlier versions sent a bitmap of the entire page of text to the printer.

ATM technology is built into OS/2 and NeXTstep, and was originally developed to provide WYSIWYG screen fonts for the Mac. Since Windows does not render PostScript fonts on screen, ATM is widely used to do so. Both work together. Under Windows, ATM scales Type 1 fonts, while Windows 3.1 scales TrueType fonts. See *PostScript*.

ADP

(1) (Automatic Data Processing) Synonymous with data processing (DP), electronic data processing (EDP) and information processing.

(2) (Automatic Data Processing, Inc., Roseland, NJ) A nationwide computer services organization that specializes in payroll processing.

ADPCM

(Adaptive Differential PCM) An advanced PCM technique that converts speech to 32 or 16 Kbits/sec. Instead of coding an absolute measurement at each sample point, it codes the difference between samples and can dynamically switch the coding scale to compensate for variations in amplitude and frequency.

ADP system

(Automatic Data Processing system) Same as *computer system*.

ADSL

(Asymmetrical Digital Subscriber Line) A telephone line that handles high-speed data such as interactive TV and video on demand. Asymmetrical means uneven transmission rates: from customer to telephone company up to 640Kbps; from telco to customer at 1.544Mbs (T1) and higher.

The ANSI-standard Discrete Multitone (DMT) and AT&T's Carrierless Amplitude and Phase Modulation (CAP) are the two modulation techniques used for ADSL. See *HDSL*.

ADT

(Asynchronous Data Transfer) A transmission technique used in ISDN PBXs that dynamically allocates bandwidth. See also *abstract data type* and *tool* (as in application development tool).

Advanced Revelation

An application development system for DOS and OS/2 from Revelation Technologies, Inc., Stamford, CT. It provides strong text handling with the variable-length structures of its DBMS. It includes the R/BASIC programming language and supports SQL, DB2, Oracle and other databases. The Windows counterpart is called OpenInsight and uses the BASIC+ language.

AdvanceNet

HP's early network strategy that included OSI, SNA and various networking standards along with its proprietary networking. In the mid 1980s, HP moved from proprietary networking to open standards.

ADW

(Application Development Workbench) An integrated CASE-based application development system from Sterling Software, Atlanta, GA (formerly KnowledgeWare). It integrates a variety of PC-based tools for designing and developing client/server, AS/400 and IBM mainframe applications. In early 1994, KnowledgeWare reported that it shipped its 100,000 unit of ADW.

AFE

(Apple File Exchange) A Macintosh utility that converts data files between Mac and PC formats. It also includes a file translator between IBM's DCA format and MacWrite; however, MacLink Plus Translators can be used for additional capability.

AFIPS

(American Federation of Information Processing Societies Inc.) An organization founded in 1961 dedicated to advancing information processing in the U.S. It was the U.S. representative of IFIP and umbrella for 11 membership societies. Dissolved in 1990 and superseded by FOCUS.

AFM file

(Adobe Font Metrics file) A file that contains font metric information for a Type 1 PostScript font. See *PFA file, PFB file* and *PostScript*.

AFP

(AppleTalk Filing Protocol) A client/server protocol used in AppleTalk communications networks. In order for non-Apple networks to access data in an AppleShare server, their protocols must translate into the AFT language.

AFS

A distributed file system for large, widely-dispersed UNIX networks from Transarc Corporation, Pittsburgh, PA. It is noted for its ease of administration and expandability and stems from Carnegie-Mellon's Andrew File System.

After Dark

A popular screen saver program for Macs and PCs from Berkeley Systems, Inc., that allows the user to develop custom animations. After Dark popularized the "flying toaster" display in 1989.

agent

A software routine that waits in the background and performs an action when a specified event occurs. For example, agents could transmit a summary file on the first day of the month or monitor incoming data and alert the user when a certain transaction has arrived. Agents are also called *intelligent agents*. When used with PDAs, they are often called *personal agents*. See *workflow*.

AI

(Artificial Intelligence) Devices and applications that exhibit human intelligence and behavior including robots, expert systems, voice recognition, natural and foreign language processing. It also implies the ability to learn or adapt through experience. In the future, everything we now know and think about a computer will change. By the turn of the century, you should be able to converse with the average computer. Future systems will ask you what help you need and automatically call in the appropriate applications to aid you in solving your problem.

In the 1990s, the AI buzzword will be abused to the hilt as it will refer to any and all advancements. However, the acid test of AI was defined in the 1940s by the English scientist, Alan Turing, who said, "A machine has artificial intelligence when there is no discernible difference between the conversation generated by the machine and that of an intelligent person."

Note: The term intelligence refers to processing capability; therefore, every computer is intelligent. But, artificial intelligence implies human-like intelligence. An ironic twist in terminology.

Shakey the Robot

Developed in 1969 by the Stanford Research Institute, Shakey was the first fully-mobile robot with artificial intelligence. Shakey is seven feet tall and was named after its rather unstable movements.
(Photo courtesy of The Computer Museum, Boston.)

AIIM

(Association for Information and Image Management) A membership organization that promotes and advances the development of systems that store, retrieve, integrate and manage images of documents. Founded in 1943, it provides periodicals, industry studies, educational programs and expositions. Address: 1100 Wayne Ave., Suite 1100, Silver Spring, MD 20910, 301/587-8202.

AIM

(Apple/IBM/Motorola) The alliance of Apple, IBM and Motorola, which developed the PowerPC chip, Taligent, Kaleida, etc. See *Apple*.

AIX

(Advanced Interactive eXecutive) IBM's version of UNIX, which runs on PCs (386 and up), RS/6000 workstations and 390 mainframes. It is based on AT&T's UNIX System V with Berkeley extensions.

alarm filtering

In network management, the ability to pinpoint the device that has failed. If one device in a network fails, others may fail as a result and cause alarms. Without alarm filtering, the management console reports all deteriorating devices with equal attention.

ALC

(Assembly Language Coding) A generic term for IBM mainframe assembly languages.

Aldus

The software company that pioneered desktop publishing with its PageMaker program for the Macintosh. Aldus is now part of Adobe Systems, Inc., Mountain View, CA.

Aldus Persuasion

A desktop presentation program for the Mac from Adobe Systems, Inc., Mountain View, CA. It is used to create output for overheads, handouts, speaker notes and film recorders and provides sophisticated transition features (fades, gravel, swipes, etc.).

algebraic expression

One or more characters or symbols associated with algebra; for example, A+B=C or A/B.

ALGOL

(ALGOrithmic Language) A high-level compiler language that was developed as an international language for the expression of algorithms between people and between people and machines. ALGOL-60 (1960) was simple and widely used in Europe. ALGOL-68 (1968) was more complicated and scarcely used, but was the inspiration for Pascal.

The following example changes Fahrenheit to Celsius:

```
fahrenheit
begin
  real fahr;
  print ("Enter Fahrenheit ");
  read (fahr);
  print ("Celsius is ", (fahr-32.0) * 5.0/9.0);
end
finish
```

algorithm

A set of ordered steps for solving a problem, such as a mathematical formula or the instructions in a program. The terms algorithm and logic are synonymous. Both refer to a sequence of steps to solve a problem. However, an algorithm implies an expression that solves a complex problem rather than the overall input-process-output logic of typical business programs.

alias

(1) An alternate name used for identification, such as for naming a field or a file.

(2) A phony signal created under certain conditions when digitizing voice.

aliasing

In computer graphics, the stair-stepped appearance of diagonal lines. See *anti-aliasing*.

ALL-IN-1

Office systems software from Digital for the VAX series. It provides a menu to all of Digital's office systems programs, including word processing, appointment calendars and e-mail systems.

allocate

To reserve a resource such as memory or disk. See *memory allocation*.

all points addressable

See *APA*.

ALOHA

A type of TDMA transmission system developed by the University of Hawaii used for satellite and terrestrial radio links. In the traditional ALOHA system, packets are transmitted as required, and, like Ethernet's CSMA/CD method, collisions can occur. A "Slotted ALOHA" system triggers transmission starts by a clock and reduces the number of collisions.

Alpha

A family of advanced RISC-based, 64-bit CPUs from Digital. The first model introduced in early 1992 was the 150MHz 21064-AA, considered equivalent to a Cray-1 on a single chip. Alpha AXP computer systems use the Alpha CPU and run under Windows NT, OpenVMS and Digital's OSF/1 operating systems.
The Alpha 21164 CPU, introduced in 1994, continues to blaze trails for high-speed microprocessors. The 21164 has 9.3 million transistors and executes 1.2 BIPS. It comes in 266MHz and 300MHz versions.

alpha channel

The high-order eight bits in a 32-bit graphics pixel used as a separate layer to mask an area for editing or creating special effects (textures, montages, etc.).

Alpha Four, Five

A database program from Alpha Software Corporation, Burlington, MA, that is noted for its ease of use. Alpha programs read and write dBASE files directly. Alpha Four for DOS provides scripts for customizing applications. Alpha Five for Windows includes Xbasic, a BASIC-like programming language that incorporates database commands.

alphageometric

See *alphamosaic*.

alphamosaic

A very-low-resolution display technique that uses elementary graphics characters as part of its character set.

alphanumeric

The use of alphabetic letters mixed with numbers and special characters as in name, address, city and state. The text you're reading is alphanumeric.

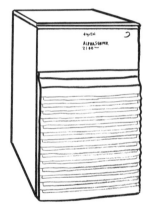

AlphaServer 2100
The AlphaServer 2100 holds up to four CPUs, 2GB of memory and 500GB of storage. It is capable of 1,200 TPS (transactions per second).

alpha test
The first test of newly developed hardware or software in a laboratory setting. The next step is *beta testing* with actual users.

Altair 8800
A microcomputer kit introduced in late 1974 from Micro Instrumentation and Telemetry Systems (MITS). It sold for $400 and used an 8080 microprocessor. In 1975, it was packaged with the Microsoft MBASIC interpreter written by Paul Allen and Bill Gates. Although computer kits were advertised earlier by others, an estimated 10,000 Altairs were sold, making it the first commercially successful microcomputer.

Altair 8800
Computer
(Photo courtesy of
The Computer
Museum, Boston)

alternate routing
The ability to use another transmission line if the regular line is busy.

alternating current
See *AC.*

AlterNet
See *UUNET.*

alt key
A keyboard key that is pressed with a letter or digit key to command the computer. For example, in Windows, holding down the alt key and pressing F displays the File menu. Pressing Alt-Tab toggles between applications.

Alto
The personal computer from Xerox that pioneered the mouse/icon/desktop environment. Developed at PARC, it was the progenitor of Xerox's Star and Apple's Lisa and Mac. Designed in 1973 with 128K RAM, 608x808 screen, 2.5MB removable hard disk and built-in Ethernet. About 1,000 Altos were in use by 1979.

Alto Computer
The first graphical user interface created for business purposes was working more than 10 years before the Macintosh was introduced. *(Photo courtesy of Xerox Corporation.)*

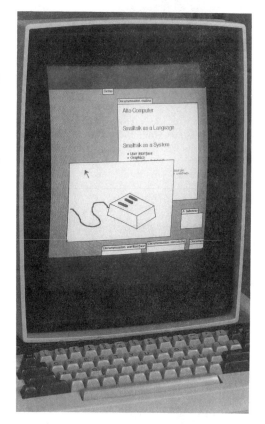

ALU

(Arithmetic Logic Unit) The high-speed CPU circuit that does calculating and comparing. Numbers are transferred from memory into the ALU for calculation, and the results are sent back into memory. Alphanumeric data is sent from memory into the ALU for comparing. The results are tested by GOTOs; for example, IF ITEMA EQUALS ITEMB GOTO UPDATE ROUTINE.

An ALU in the Early Days
This was an arithmetic logic unit you could admire. The equivalent electronics of the ALU in Honeywell's Datamatic 1000 could fit on the head of a pin today. *(Photo courtesy of Honeywell, Inc.)*

AM

(Amplitude Modulation) A transmission technique that blends the data signal into a carrier by varying (modulating) the amplitude of the carrier. See *modulate*.

Am386, Am486

Low-power, 386- and 486-compatible CPU chips from AMD (Advanced Micro Devices).

ambient

Surrounding. For example, ambient temperature and humidity are atmospheric conditions that exist at the moment.

AMD

(Advanced Micro Devices, Inc., Sunnyvale, CA) A manufacturer of x86-compatible CPUs. AMD has become a competitor to Intel and its chips are used by many PC makers, including Compaq. Chips with the Am386 and Am486 logo are made by AMD.

Amdahl

(Amdahl Corporation, Sunnyvale, CA) A computer manufacturer founded in 1970 by Gene Amdahl, chief architect of the IBM System/360. In 1975, Amdahl installed its first IBM-compatible mainframe, the 470/V6. Although not the first to make IBM-compatible mainframes, it succeeded where others failed. Amdahl offers a full range of IBM-compatible mainframes as well as application development software and midrange UNIX servers.

Dr. Amdahl left the company to form Trilogy in 1979 and later Andor Corporation, a manufacturer of products for large IBM mainframe installations.

Dr. Gene M. Amdahl

In 1975, Dr. Amdahl stands beside the computer he designed in 1950. The Wisconsin Integrally Synchronized Computer (WISC) was constructed in 1952. *(Photo courtesy of Dr. Gene M. Amdahl)*

America Online

An online information service that provides conferencing, news, e-mail, education, technical support forums, more than 70,000 software files and access to a large variety of databases, including National Geographic and PC World magazine. Software for DOS, Windows, Mac and Apple II provides navigation through the system. See *online services*.

AMI BIOS

A popular PC-compatible BIOS from American Megatrends, Inc., Norcross, GA.

Amiga

A personal computer series from Commodore that runs under the AmigaDOS operating system. Amigas use the 68000 CPU family and feature the Workbench graphical user interface. The Amiga 500 was geared for home use with built-in speech synthesis, stereo sound and color graphics. The Amiga 2000 was designed for office applications, CAD and desktop publishing. The Amiga 3000 and 4000 improved performance with the 68030 and 68040 CPUs respectively. Although Commodore went into bankruptcy in 1994, the technology was purchased and Amigas are expected once again. See *Commodore*.

Ami Pro

See *Word Pro*.

amp

(AMPere) A unit of electrical current in a circuit. *Volts* measure the force or pressure behind the current. *Watts* are a total measurement of power derived from multiplying amps times volts.

amplitude

The strength or volume of a signal, usually measured in decibels.

amplitude modulation

See *AM*.

AMPS

(Analog Mobile Phone System) The non-digital cellular mobile phone system as originally introduced. AMPS is the cellular equivalent of POTS.

analog

A representation of an object that resembles the original. Analog devices monitor conditions, such as movement, temperature and sound, and convert them into analogous electronic or mechanical patterns. For example, an analog watch represents the planet's rotation with the rotating hands on the watch face. Telephones turn voice vibrations into electrical vibrations of the same shape. Analog implies continuous operation in contrast with digital, which is broken up into numbers.

Advantages and Disadvantages Of Analog Techniques

Traditionally, audio and video recording has been analog. Sound, which is continuously varying air vibrations, is converted into analogous electrical vibrations. Video cameras scan their viewing area a line at a time and convert the infinitely varying intensities of light into analogous electrical signals.

The ability to capture the subtle nature of the real world is the single advantage of analog techniques. However, once captured, modern electronic equipment, no matter how advanced, cannot copy analog signals perfectly. Third and fourth generations of audio and video recordings show marked deterioration.

By converting analog signals into digital, the original audio or video data can be preserved indefinitely and copied over and over without deterioration. Once continuously varying analog signals are measured and converted into digital form, they can be stored and transmitted without loss of integrity due to the accuracy of digital methods.

The key to conversion is the amount of digital data that is created from the analog signal. The shorter the time interval between samples and the more data recorded from that sample, the more the digital encoding reflects the original signal.

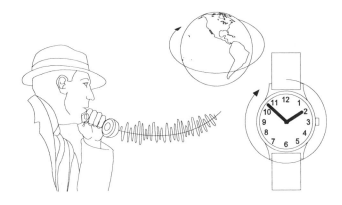

Analog Concepts
There are countless analog systems in use. The world turns and so do the hands on a watch. The telephone converts air waves into analogous electrical waves. In time, telephones will all be converted to digital.

analog channel

In communications, a channel that carries voice or video in analog form as a varying range of electrical frequencies. Contrast with *digital channel*.

analog computer

A device that processes infinitely varying signals, such as voltage or frequencies. A thermometer is a simple analog computer. As the temperature varies, the mercury moves correspondingly. Although special-purpose, complex analog computers are built, almost all computers are digital. Digital methods provide programming flexibility.

analog monitor

A video monitor that accepts analog signals from the computer (digital to analog conversion is performed in the display adapter). It may accept only a narrow range of display resolutions; for example, only VGA or VGA and Super VGA, or it may accept a wide range of signals including TV. See *multisync monitor* and *RGB monitor*. Contrast with *digital monitor*.

analysis

See *systems analysis & design*.

analyst

See *systems analyst* and *business analyst*.

analytical database engine

Software that provides multiple views into a database of numerical information. The data is maintained in a non-redundant database, and the views are displayed in a traditional spreadsheet interface. See *spreadsheet* and *TM/1*. See also *OLAP database*.

Analytical Engine

A programmable calculator designed by British scientist Charles Babbage in the mid 1830s. Although it was never completed due to a lack of funds and constant redesign, it was a major advance because it contained the principles of the stored program computer.
Babbage's colleague and close friend, Augusta Ada Byron, the Countess of Lovelace and daughter of the poet Lord Byron, explained the machine's concepts to the public. Her programming notes have survived making her the first official computing machine programmer in the world. The Ada programming language was named after her. See *Difference Engine*.

Analytical Engine
(Photo courtesy of Charles Babbage Institute, University of Minnesota)

anchor

In desktop publishing, a format code that keeps a graphic near or next to a text paragraph. If text is added, causing the paragraph to move to a subsequent page, the graphic image is moved along with it. See also *hypertext anchor*.

AND, OR & NOT

The fundamental operations of Boolean logic. AND is true if both inputs are true, OR is true if any input is true, and NOT is an inverter; the output is always the opposite.

AND, OR and NOT are implemented as switches (transistors) that open and close. When wired in a certain fashion (series, parallel, etc.), the AND, OR and NOT gates generate the outputs as shown in the following truth tables. Combinations of ANDs, ORs and NOTs make up circuits, and circuits make up electronic systems. See *Boolean search, chip* and *gate*.

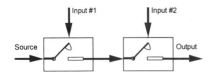

An AND Gate

An AND gate is wired in series. Both switches must be pulsed to complete the circuit from source to output.

An OR Gate

An OR gate is wired in parallel. It only takes one switch to close to produce output.

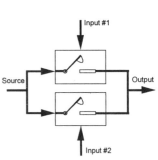

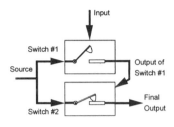

A NOT Gate

The NOT uses two kinds of switches, one normally open, the other normally closed. If there is no input pulse, there is always output as you can see in the diagram above.

If there is input, switch #1 closes causing switch #2 to open, blocking the flow to the output.

ANDF

(Architecture Neutral Distributed Format) See *OSF*.

angstrom

A unit of measurement equal to .1 nanometer, which is approximately 1/250 millionth of an inch. Ten angstroms equal one nanometer. Angstroms are used to measure the wavelengths of light and the elements in a chip.

ANI

(Automatic Number Identification) A telephone service that provides the telephone number of the incoming call. ISDN supports ANI by carrying the calling telephone number in the D channel.

animated graphics

Moving diagrams or cartoons. Often found in computer-based courseware, animated graphics take up far less disk space than video images.

anisotropic

Refers to properties, such as transmission speed, that vary depending on the direction of measurement. Contrast with *isotropic*.

anode

In electronics, a positively charged receiver of electrons that flow from the negatively charged *cathode*.

anomaly

Abnormality or deviation. It is a favorite word among computer people when complex systems produce output that is inexplicable.

anonymous FTP

An FTP site on the Internet that contains files that can be downloaded by anyone. The anonymous FTP directory is isolated from the rest of the system and will generally not accept uploads from users.

ANSI

(American National Standards Institute, 11 West 42 St., New York, NY 10036, 212/642-4900) A membership organization founded in 1918 that coordinates the development of U.S. voluntary national standards in both the private and public sectors. It is the U.S. member body to ISO and IEC. Information technology standards pertain to programming languages, EDI, telecommunications and physical properties of diskettes, cartridges and magnetic tapes.

ANSI character set

The ANSI-standard character set that defines 256 characters. The first 128 are

ASCII, and the second 128 contain math and foreign language symbols, which are different than those on the PC. See *extended ASCII*.

ANSI.SYS

A DOS driver used for screen control (cursor movement, clearing the screen, etc.) and as a keyboard macro processor to assign commands to a function key or reassign awkwardly placed keys. Some early applications require ANSI.SYS, but generally new applications do not. See *CONFIG.SYS*.

ANSI terminal

A display terminal that follows commands in the ANSI standard terminal language. Uses escape sequences to control the cursor, clear the screen and set colors, for example. Communications programs support the ANSI terminal mode and often default to this terminal emulation for dial-up connections to online services and BBSs.

answer only modem

A modem capable of answering a call, but not initiating one.

anti-aliasing

Smoothing the jagged appearance of diagonal lines in a bitmapped image. The pixels that surround the edges of the line are changed to varying shades of gray or color in order to blend the sharp edge into the background. This technique is also called dithering, but when it is applied to diagonal and curved lines, it is called anti-aliasing.

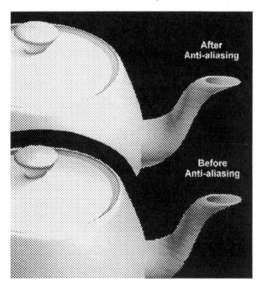

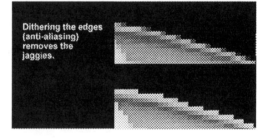

Anti-aliasing
The teapot was a famous first example of anti-aliasing, which was programmed at the University of Utah. *(Teapot courtesy of Computer Sciences Department, University of Utah.)*

Antifuse

A PLD technology from Actel Corporation that works the opposite of typical programmable chip methods. Instead of creating open circuits (blowing the fuse), connections are made between elements.

antivirus

A program that detects and removes a virus.

ANVIL

A family of CADD/CAM software packages from Manufacturing and Consulting Services Inc., Scottsdale, AZ. ANVIL products include 2 1/2-D and 3-D mechanical engineering systems for PCs, workstations, minis and mainframes.

any key

The message "press any key" means that you must press a key on the keyboard to continue. It doesn't matter which one you press: a letter key, return key, the space bar, etc.

AOCE

(Apple Open Collaboration Environment) Extensions to the Macintosh System 7 operating system from Apple that provide a technology framework for sharing services across a multiplatform enterprise. PowerTalk and PowerShare are the first AOCE products.

AOL

See *America Online.*

APA

(All Points Addressable) Refers to an array (bitmapped screen, matrix, etc.) in which all bits or cells can be individually manipulated.

APCUG

(Association of Personal Computer User Groups) A non-profit organization dedicated to fostering communication among and between user groups and between user groups and vendors. Address: Suite 700, 1730 M St. N.W., Washington, DC 20036.

aperture card

A punched card that holds a frame of microfilm.

API

(Application Program Interface) A language and message format used by an application program to communicate with the operating system or other system program such as a database management system (DBMS). APIs are implemented by writing function calls in the program, which provide the linkage to a specific subroutine for execution. See *ABI* and *interface.*

PROGRAMS TALK TO EACH OTHER!

APIC

(Advanced Programmable Interrupt Controller) An Intel chip that provides symmetric multiprocessing (SMP) for its Pentium systems. It can support up to 60 processors. See *OpenPIC.*

APL

(A Programming Language) A high-level mathematical programming language noted for its brevity and matrix generation capabilities. Developed by Kenneth Iverson in the mid 1960s, it runs on micros to mainframes and is often used to develop mathematical models. It is primarily an interpreted language, but compilers are available.

APL uses unique character symbols and, before today's graphical interfaces, required special software or ROM chips to enable the computer to display and print them. APL is popular in Europe.

APM

(Advanced Power Management) An API from Intel and Microsoft for battery-powered computers that lets programs communicate power requirements to slow down and speed up components.

Apollo

Formerly Apollo Computer, Inc., this maker of high-performance workstations became a division of HP in 1989. Founded in 1980, it pioneered networked workstations.

app

See *application*.

APPC

(Advanced Program-to-Program Communications) A high-level communications protocol from IBM that allows one program to interact with another program across the network. It supports client/server and distributed computing by providing a common programming interface across all IBM platforms. It provides commands for managing a session, sending and receiving data and transaction security and integrity (two-phase commit).

APPC software is either part of, or optionally available, on all IBM and many non-IBM operating systems. Since APPC has only supported SNA, which utilizes the LU 6.2 protocol for session establishment, APPC and LU 6.2 have been considered synonymous. In time, APPC is expected to support other industry protocols, such as TCP/IP.

In the past, APPC commands have differed across platforms. However, the CPI-C interface defines a standard set of APPC verbs.

app code

(APPlication code) Instructions in a program that actually process data.

append

To add to the end of an existing structure.

Apple

(Apple Computer, Inc., Cupertino, CA) A manufacturer of personal computers and the industry's most fabled story. Founded in a garage by Steve Wozniak and Steve Jobs and guided by Mike Markkula, Apple blazed the trails for the personal computer industry. Today, Apple makes more personal computers than any other single company.

Apple was formed on April Fool's Day in 1976. After introducing the Apple I at the Palo Alto Homebrew Computer Club, 10 retail stores were selling them by the end of the year.

In 1977, it introduced the Apple II, a fully-assembled computer with 4K RAM for $1,298. Its open architecture encouraged third-party vendors to build plug-in hardware enhancements. This, plus sound and color graphics, caused Apple IIs to become the most widely used computer in the home and classroom. They were also used in business primarily for the innovative VisiCalc software that was launched on it.

In 1983, Apple introduced the Lisa, the forerunner of the Macintosh. Lisa was aimed at the corporate market, but was soon dropped in favor of the Mac. As a graphics-based machine, the Mac was successful as a low-cost desktop publishing system. Although praised for its ease of use, its slow speed, small screen and closed architecture didn't excite corporate buyers.

Since the advent of the Mac II in 1987, that has changed. Macs offer large screens, open architecture and color. Numerous entry-level and high-speed models have been added and widely accepted.

In 1991, Apple surprised the industry by announcing an alliance with IBM to integrate Macs into IBM enterprise networks and to develop new hardware and software together. For details, see *Apple-IBM alliance.*

The first product of this alliance was the PowerMac, introduced by Apple in 1994. The PowerMac is the next generation of Macintoshes, which uses the PowerPC chip and runs traditional Mac applications as well as DOS and Windows applications. All Mac applications will eventually be ported to the native PowerPC architecture. The PowerMacs offer a high-speed computing environment for the 1990s.

The Primary Founders of Apple
The two Steves pioneered the microcomputer revolution. Together, Jobs' marketing charisma (left) and Wozniak's engineering ability helped create one of the most legendary computer companies in the world.
(Photo courtesy of Apple Computer.)

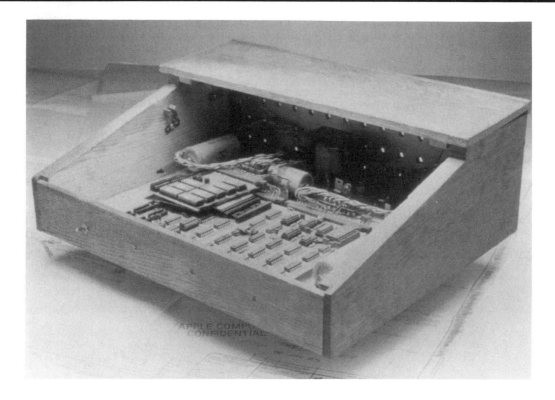

The First Apple
The Apple I. Humble beginnings! *(Photo courtesy of Apple Computer.)*

Apple Desktop Bus
See *ADB*.

Apple File Exchange
See *AFE*.

Apple-IBM alliance
In 1991, Apple and IBM agreed to do the following:

(1) To better integrate Macs into IBM enterprise networks.

(2) To develop the PowerPC, a single-chip version of IBM's RS/6000 architecture, with IBM and Motorola.

(3) To develop PowerOpen, an industry standard operating system that runs AIX and Mac applications on the PowerPC.

(4) To form Taligent, Inc., to develop and license an object-oriented operating system for the PowerPC, Motorola 68xxx and Intel x86 families with compatibility with AIX, OS/2 and System 7.

(5) To form Kaleida Labs, Inc. to develop and license multimedia software, tools and scripting languages for a diverse variety of computers and consumer electronic gear.

The Results

(1) More integration of Apple products into IBM shops has taken place. IBM routers can optionally run Apple's communications protocols to connect to Apple networks. IBM and Apple designed a Token Ring adapter for the Macintosh.

(2) By the end of 1995, over two million PowerPC chips were shipped in PowerMacs and certain models of IBM's RS/6000 workstations. The PowerPC inspired Intel to speed up design and production of its next-generation chips.

(3) PowerOpen is no longer an operating system, but a specification for compliance for a UNIX-based operating system on the PowerPC. This is intended to bring about shrink-wrapped UNIX software for the PowerPC (see *PowerOpen*).

(4) Hewlett-Packard became part of the Apple-IBM ownership of Taligent in 1994, but the operating system has been put on hold. In the meantime, it has delivered its CommonPoint application frameworks and development tools for AIX, OS/2, HP-UX and the PowerMac (see *Taligent*).

(5) Kaleida introduced its ScriptX multimedia technology in early 1995.

Apple II

The personal computer family from Apple that pioneered the microcomputer revolution and has been widely used in schools and home. It uses the 8-bit 6502 microprocessor running at 1MHz, an 8-bit bus and runs under Apple's DOS or ProDOS operating system. AppleSoft BASIC is built into ROM and always available.

With a Z80 microprocessor board plugged in, Apple IIs can run CP/M programs, such as dBASE II.

As of the end of 1992, the Apple IIe and a IIe card for the Mac LC are the only Apple II models still in the product line.

APPLE II AND II+

Introduced in 1977, the Apple II came with 4K RAM and hooked up to a TV and cassette tape recorder. A floppy disk was available in 1978. In 1979, an enhanced II+ came with 48K of RAM. Screen resolution is 280x192x6.

APPLE IIe AND IIc

In 1983, the "e"nhanced Apple IIe was introduced with four cursor keys (not two) and 128K of RAM. In 1984, the IIc portable was launched with a sleek design, but limited expandability.

Apple IIe

The Apple IIe and VisiCalc, the first spreadsheet, became a marriage that launched the desktop computer into the business world.

APPLE IIGS
Introduced in 1986 and discontinued in 1992, the IIGS is faster and adds enhanced graphics and sound (GS). It runs standard Apple II software, but requires GS software to use its enhancements. Specs: 2.8MHz 16-bit 65C816 CPU, 320x200x256 screen, 15 sounds, AppleTalk.

APPLE III
Yes, there was an Apple III, introduced in 1980 and intended for business users. It was not 100% compatible with the II and never caught on.

Apple key
The original name of the Command key.

Apple menu
The menu at the top left side of a Macintosh screen that is always available to provide access to desk accessories.

AppleScript
A comprehensive command language used for automating tasks that is part of the System 7 operating system from Apple, starting with System 7 Pro. AppleScript provides a command line interface to the Macintosh similar to the way DOS commands are used in a PC.

AppleShare
Software from Apple that turns a Macintosh into a file server. It works in conjunction with the Mac operating system and can coexist with other Macintosh applications in a non-dedicated mode.

AppleShare PC
Software for PCs from Apple that allows a PC to connect to an AppleTalk network. It requires a LocalTalk PC Card from Apple for ISA PCs, or a LocalTalk Card from DayStar Communications for Micro Channel PCs.

AppleSoft BASIC
Apple's version of BASIC that comes with Apple II models. It is installed in firmware and is always available.

applet
A small application, such as a utility program or a limited-function spreadsheet or word processor.

AppleTalk
Apple's local area network architecture introduced in 1985. It supports Apple's proprietary LocalTalk access method as well as Ethernet and Token Ring. The AppleTalk network manager and the LocalTalk access method are built into all Macintoshes and LaserWriters.
With other products from Apple and third parties, AppleTalk can run in PCs, VAXs and UNIX workstations. Since AppleTalk is patterned after the OSI model, it is a routable protocol that contains a network layer (OSI layer 3).

AppleTalk Filing Protocol
See *AFP*.

AppleWorks
An integrated software package for Apple IIs from Claris Corporation. Introduced in 1983 by Apple, it combines word processing, file management, spreadsheet,

business graphics and communications.

application

(1)A specific use of the computer, such as for payroll, inventory and billing. For a list of major application software categories, see *application software*.

(2)Same as *application program* and *software package*.

application binary interface

See *ABI*.

application centric

Focusing on the application as the foundation or starting point. In an application-centric system, the program is loaded first, which in turn is used to create or edit a particular type of data structure (text, spreadsheet, image, etc.). Contrast with *document centric*. See *component software*.

application developer

An individual that develops a business application and usually performs the duties of a systems analyst and application programmer.

application development environment

The combination of hardware and software used to develop an application. See *application development system* and *ADE*.

application development language

Same as *programming language*.

application development system

A programming language and associated utility programs that allow for the creation, development and running of application programs. Many database management systems (DBMSs) include a complete application development system along with a query language, report writer and the capability to interactively create and manage database files.

An application development system may also provide a full-scale application generator or various degrees of automatic application generation. An application development system that does not include its own database provides links to other databases via SQL, ODBC and other interfaces.

A client/server application development system is one in which the end product runs on a local area network. A two-tiered system splits the software between client and server. A three-tiered system splits the software between client, application server and database server. The application server provides the business logic in this case. See *client/server development system* and *application generator*.

Application Development Workbench

See *ADW*.

Application Error

In Windows 3.1, an error message that occurs when a program crashes. When that happens, a dialog box asks you if you want to close the application or ignore it. If you press IGNORE and can continue to function, save your data and reload your application. Generally, pressing IGNORE will do nothing, so you will have to select CLOSE. When you do, you will get a dialog box that tells you that you have a General Protection Fault and which program module caused the problem.

A General Protection Fault means that the program has erroneously led the computer outside of its address space or that it is trying to execute instructions that are not valid. This is a problem with the application itself, and there is nothing you can do about it, so click on CLOSE to quit the program.

It is often suggested that once you get a General Protection Fault in Windows 3.1, you should save all data in your other active applications and exit and reload Windows. Some applications can crash, be terminated and you can go on your merry way with your other applications. Others cause damage to Windows settings that will affect other applications during this session.

If selecting CLOSE locks up the computer, or if the computer locks up at any time during this process, press Ctrl-Alt-Del. If the computer is still locked up, turn it off and back on again to reboot. Then reload Windows.

application framework

(1) The building blocks of an application.

(2) A class library that provides the foundation for programming an object-oriented application.

application generator

Software that generates application programs from descriptions of the problem rather than by traditional programming. It is at a higher level and easier to use than a high-level programming language. One statement or descriptive line may generate a huge routine or an entire program. However, application generators always have limits as to what they can be used for. Generators used for complex program development allow if-then-else programming to be expressed along with the simpler descriptive entries.

The goal with application generators and computer-aided software engineering (CASE) has always been to create a program by describing it, not programming it. The problem with such high-level systems is that either the resulting code is too slow or certain functions simply cannot be performed at all. As a result, commercial programs are rarely written in these languages; they are used for business information systems and often only for creating prototypes that are later reprogrammed in COBOL or C.

As computers run faster, they are capable of absorbing the excess code generated by higher-level products. In time, it is expected that the machine efficiency demanded of today's hardware may not be as critical and higher-level development tools may become the norm, relegating lower-level languages to a handful of highly-skilled and very highly-paid individuals. See *application development system*.

application layer

In communications, the interaction at the user or application program level. It is the highest layer within the protocol hierarchy. See *OSI model*.

application notes

Instructions and recommendations from the vendor provided in addition to the normal reference manuals.

application package

A software package that is created for a specific purpose or industry.

application partitioning

Separating an application into components that run on clients and multiple servers in a client/server environment. Programming languages and development systems that support this architecture, known as *three-tier client/server*, may allow the program to be developed as a whole and then separated into pieces later.

Development systems are differentiated by their ability to perform partitioning as a mainstream function in a high-level language or with visual programming (drag & drop) versus having to write chunks of code in C.

Application partitioning is an important capability for migrating legacy systems onto client/server environments. In many business applications, there is a lot of processing that should be done centrally in a server and not in each client machine. Such programs are either too demanding and process intensive for the client or they represent proprietary business logic that should not be replicated all over the enterprise. The centralized mainframe has always made a lot of sense for many applications. Partitioning the logic onto multiple servers emulates this approach in a client/server environment.

Who's Doing It?
Application partitioning can always be accomplished by writing 3GL code. However, with today's push for rapid application development (RAD), writing in a traditional programming language takes time. Newer client/server development systems such as Forte and DYNASTY provide application partitioning at the 4GL level, and it is being included in upgrades to existing development systems.
The OSF's Distributed Computing Environment (DCE) standard is expected to become popular for three-tier client/server, because it provides a standard for accessing programs and databases no matter where they are located.

application processor
A computer that processes data in contrast with one that performs control functions, such as a front end processor or database machine.

application program
Any data entry, update, query or report program that processes data for the user. It includes the generic productivity software (spreadsheets, word processors, database programs, etc.) as well as custom and packaged programs for payroll, billing, inventory and other accounting purposes. For a list of major application software categories, see *application software*. Also see *program*. Contrast with *system program*.

application program interface
See *API*.

application program library
Application programs used by an organization.

application programmer
An individual who writes application programs in a user organization. Most programmers are application programmers. Contrast with *systems programmer*.

application server
(1) A server in a LAN that contains applications shared by network clients. It functions as a remote disk drive for storing applications.

(2) A server in a LAN that contains the business processing in a client/server environment. In this case, the client provides the user interface, and a third machine may be used to store the data. See *three-tiered client/server*.

application sharing
A data conferencing capability that lets two or more users interactively work on the same application at the same time. The application is loaded and running in only one machine; however, keystrokes are transmitted from and screen changes are transmitted to the other participants. Application sharing provides the same capability as remote control software. See *application viewing* and *T.120*.

application software

Following are the major categories of application software (software packages). See *system software* for a list of system software categories. Integrated software packages and application suites usually contain the first five applications.

Integrated packages and application suites generally contain these kinds of programs:	**Database Programs (Data Management)** Create and edit master and transaction records. Interactive editing of data. Ask questions, summarize, sort, print reports. **Word Processing** Create and edit text files. Replaces all typewriter functions. Some programs provide rudimentary desktop publishing. **Spreadsheet** Create and edit rows and columns of numbers for budgets and financial reports. What if analysis? Multidimensional spreadsheets provide different slices, or views, of data quickly. Advanced financial planning systems provide goal seeking as well as statistical calculations. **Presentation Graphics** Create slide shows, do freehand drawing and turn numbers into 2-D and 3-D business graphics. **Communications and Electronic Mail** Send and receive data and mail via modem or over the network.
	Desktop Publishing Merge text and graphics and provide complete control over page layout for printing. More precision than word processing programs. Disk output is accepted directly by many printers. **PIM (Personal Information Manager)** Organize random information for fast retrieval. Includes such features as a telephone list with automatic dialing, calendar, scheduler and tickler. **Project Management** Keep track of a project and determine the impact of changes. The "critical path" is computed, which monitors all tasks that will slow down the entire project if delayed. **CAD (vector graphics)** Create drawings for illustration and industrial design. **Imaging (raster graphics)** Scan documents and paint pictures into TV-like images. **Diagramming Program** Create drawings of interconnected symbols, such as network diagrams and organization charts. When symbols are moved, the lines stay connected. **Contact Manager** Keep track of prospects, names, addresses, appointments. Similar to a PIM, but specialized for sales activities. **Infoware** Online dictionaries, books and other references with hypertext links.

Mathematical
Create, run and print complex mathematical equations.

Scientific
Analyze real-world events by simulating them mathematically. Supercomputers are widely used for this.

Vertical Markets
Data entry, query, update and report programs custom tailored for an industry such as banking and insurance. Either off-the-shelf or custom programmed, vertical market software is the most specialized type of information system available.

Multimedia (Games and education)
Multimedia adds graphics, sound and video for interactive games, encyclopedias and other references and educational courseware of all kinds.

See *system software* for a list of system software categories.

applications programmer
See *application programmer*.

application suite
A set of applications designed to work together. In the Windows environment, the application suite is the successor to the integrated package, except that the individual applications are stand alone and can be purchased separately. Although Windows provides integration features such as cut and paste and compound document creation, the suites provide additional tools to move data from one application more easily into another. In addition, common functions such as spell checking can be installed once and shared among all programs.

application viewing
A data conferencing capability that lets two or more users view the same application at the same time. All users may be able to highlight different parts of the document, spreadsheet or database, but only the user at the machine where the application is loaded can actually edit it. See *application sharing* and *T.120*.

APPN
(Advanced Peer-to-Peer Networking) Extensions to IBM's SNA communications that provide the necessary flexibility to enable direct communication between users anywhere on the network. Features includes improved administration, intermediate node routing and dynamic network services. APPN makes use of LU 6.2 protocols and is implemented in an SNA Node Type 2.1.

Approach
A relational database from Lotus that is also part of Lotus' SmartSuite set. It provides the ability to graphically create Windows applications using industry standard database formats, such as dBASE and Paradox. It includes macros and the ability to attach programming statements to data, providing a way to automate many kinds of applications.

AppWare
A client/server development system from Novell that supports Windows and Mac clients. It includes Novell's Visual AppBuilder visual programming tool, which is used to create applications by linking pre-built Application Loadable Modules (ALMs) together. ALMs communicate with each other over a "software bus" known as the AppWare Bus.

Foundation libraries for Windows, Mac, OS/2, NT, Solaris, HP and UnixWare were originally created to provide cross-platform portabilty. However, in late 1994, Novell dropped the libraries, while continuing with Visual AppBuilder for Windows and Macintosh.

APT

(Automatic Programmed Tools) A high-level programming language used to generate instructions for numerical control machines.

Arago

A dBASE IV-compatible DBMS and compiler (Arago Quicksilver) originally developed by WordTech Systems. In 1992, the technology was acquired by Borland.

arbitration

A set of rules for allocating machine resources, such as memory or peripheral devices, to more than one user or program.

ARC, ARC+Plus

(1) PC compression programs from System Enhancement Associates, Inc., Clifton, NJ. ARC was one of the first compression utilities to become popular in the early 1980s. ARC+Plus provides enhanced features and speed.

(2) The ARC extension was previously used by PKWARE Inc. in its PKARC program.

(3) (Advanced RISC Computing) An open system specification based on the MIPS R3000 and R4000 CPUs. It includes EISA and TURBOchannel buses.

Archie

(ARCHIvE) An Internet utility used to search for file names. There are approximately 30 computer systems throughout the Internet, called "Archie servers," that maintain catalogs of files available for downloading from various FTP sites. Periodically, Archie servers search FTP sites throughout the Internet and record information about the files they find. If you do not have Archie, some Internet hosts let you log on via Telnet as user "archie." See *FTP*.

Archistrat Client
The cabinets of the Archistrat computers are as different as their internal architecture.

Archistrat computer

An upgradable computer system from the Archistrat division of The Panda Project, Boca Raton, FL. It is designed to accomodate future technologies by using a high-bandwidth backplane (up to 256 bits on the servers) which CPU and peripheral boards plug into. Boards use the Compass connector from the Archistrat Technologies division, which also makes the VSPA chip package. Archistrat shipped its first Intel-based systems at the end of 1995.

architecture

See *computer architecture, network architecture* and *software architecture*.

archive

(1) To copy data onto a different disk or tape for backup. Archived files are often compressed to maximize storage media.

(2) To save data onto the disk.

archive attribute

A file classification that indicates whether the file has been updated since the last backup.

ARCNET

(Attached Resource Computer NETwork) The first local area network (LAN) introduced in 1968 by Datapoint Corporation. It connects up to 255 nodes in a star topology at 2.5 Mbits/sec over twisted pair or coax. A 20 Mbits/sec version was introduced in 1989. Although not as popular as Ethernet and Token Ring, alot of ARCNET networks were sold due to their lower-cost adapters. Gateways can connect ARCNET to mini and mainframe networks.

ARCNET is a data link protocol and functions at the data link and physical levels of the OSI model (1 and 2). It uses the token passing access method. See *data link protocol* and *OSI model.*

Ardis

(Advanced National Radio Data Service) A joint venture of IBM and Motorola that provides wireless data transmission in the 800MHz FM band. It covers most U.S. metropolitan areas with over 1,000 base stations.

areal density

The number of bits per square inch of storage surface. It typically refers to disk drives, where the number of bits per inch times the number of tracks per inch yields the areal density. The areal density of disk storage devices has increased dramatically since IBM introduced the RAMAC, the first hard disk computer in 1956.

The RAMAC had an areal density of 2000 bits per square inch. Current-day disk drives have areal densities of several hundred million bits per square inch. IBM has set records with magnetic disk areal densities of over 500 million bits per square inch and has demonstrated in its laboratories magnetic disks with one billion bits per square inch and optical disks with 2.5 billion bits per square inch.

It is expected that by the year 2000, areal densities of disk drives will range from 10 to 30 billion bits per square inch. See *holographic storage* and *atomic force microscope.*

arg

See *argument.*

argument

In programming, a value that is passed between programs, subroutines or functions. Arguments are independent items, or variables, that contain data or codes. When an argument is used to customize a program for a user, it is typically called a *parameter.*

arithmetic coding

A statistical data compression method that converts strings of data into single floating point numbers between 0 and 1.

arithmetic expression

(1) In mathematics, one or more characters or symbols associated with arithmetic, such as 1+2=3 or 8*6.
(2) In programming, a non-text expression.

arithmetic logic unit

See *ALU.*

arithmetic operators

Symbols for arithmetic functions: + add, - subtract, * multiply, / divide. See *precedence.*

arithmetic overflow

The result from an arithmetic calculation that exceeds the space designated to hold it.

arithmetic underflow

The result from an arithmetic calculation that is too small to be expressed properly. For example, in floating point, a negative exponent can be generated that is too large (too small a number) to be stored in its allotted space.

ARP

(Address Resolution Protocol) A low-level TCP/IP protocol used to obtain a node's physical address when only its logical IP address is known. An ARP request with the IP address is broadcast onto the network. The node with that IP address sends back its hardware address so that packets can be transmitted.

Reverse ARP, or RARP, is used by a diskless workstation to obtain its logical IP address. Responding to a RARP broadcast from the workstation, a RARP server sends back the IP address.

ARPANET

(Advanced Research Projects Agency NETwork) The research network funded by DARPA (originally ARPA) and built by BBN, Inc., in 1969. It pioneered packet switching technology and was the original backbone and testbed for the now-gigantic Internet. In 1983, the military communications part of it was split off into MILNET.

ARQ

(Automatic Repeat reQuest) A method of handling communications errors in which the receiving station requests retransmission if an error occurs.

array

An ordered arrangement of data elements. A vector is a one dimensional array, a matrix is a two-dimensional array. Most programming languages have the ability to store and manipulate arrays in one or more dimensions. Multi-dimensional arrays are used extensively in scientific simulation and mathematical processing; however, an array can be as simple as a pricing table held in memory for instant access by an order entry program. See *subscript*.

Item	Amount	Item	Amount	Item	Amount	Item	Amount
0001	016.54	0002	005.44	0003	159.95	0004	249.95

Price list in one-dimensional array

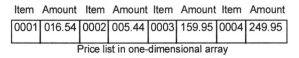

Jan	Feb	Dec	Jan	Feb	Dec	Jan	Feb	Dec
24484	09880	77855	58254	11876	37665	24484	09843	30387

Sales figures in two-dimensional array

array element

One item in an array.

array processor

A computer, or extension to its arithmetic unit, that is capable of performing simultaneous computations on elements of an array of data in some number of dimensions. Common uses include analysis of fluid dynamics and rotation of 3-D objects, as well as data retrieval, in which elements in a database are scanned simultaneously. See *vector processor* and **math coprocessor**.

ART

(Automated Reasoning Tool) A general expert system written in LISP that is used with various AI techniques for different applications.

artifact

Some distortion of an image or sound caused by a limitation or malfunction in the graphics hardware or software.

artificial intelligence

See *AI*.

artificial language

A language that has been predefined before it is ever used. Contrast with *natural language*.

artificial life

An evolving computer science that models the behavior of biological systems. The models are used to study evolution as well as to apply the algorithms to a variety of problems in such fields as engineering, robotics and drug research.

ART-IM

An expert system from Inference Corporation, El Segundo, CA. Inference's CBR Express reasoning shell sits on top of ART-IM.

AS

(Application System) An IBM mainframe 4GL that runs under MVS. It was originally designed for non-computer people and includes commands for planning, budgeting and graphics. However, a programmer can also produce complex applications. It also provides computer conferencing.

AS/400

(Application System/400) An IBM minicomputer series introduced in 1988 that runs under the OS/400 operating system. It is IBM's midrange series of computer systems used primarily for business applications, most of which are written in RPG III.

The AS/400 was designed to supersede the System/36 and System/38, IBM's prior midrange computers. The AS/400 is an enhanced version of the System/38, which includes an integrated relational database management system. Since System/38 programs can be run without change in the AS/400, System/38s were readily exchanged for AS/400s. However, in order to run System/36 applications, the programs have to be recompiled. As a result, many System/36s still exist as of late 1994.

In 1994, IBM introduced the AS/400 Advanced System/36, a PowerPC-based version of the AS/400 that natively runs the System/36 SSP operating system and its applications. Future AS/400s are expected to run both SSP and OS/400.

The AS/400 serves in a variety of networking configurations: as a host or intermediate node to other AS/400s and System/3x machines, as a remote system to mainframe-controlled networks and as a network server to PCs.

ascender

The part of lowercase b, d, f, h, k, l, and t, that extends above the body of the letters.

ASCII

(American Standard Code for Information Interchange) Pronounced "ask-ee." A binary code for text as well as communications and printer control. It is used for most communications and is in the built-in character code in most minicomputers and all personal computers.

ASCII is a 7-bit code providing 128 character combinations, the first 32 of which are control characters. Since the common storage unit is an 8-bit byte (256 combinations) and ASCII uses only 7 bits, the extra bit is used differently depending on the computer.

For example, the PC uses the additional values for foreign language and graphics symbols (see ASCII chart below). In the Macintosh, the additional values can be user-defined. In the Mac version of this database, the PC symbols are designed into the font used for the definitions. See *ASCII chart* and *hex chart*.

ASCII file

A file that contains data made up of ASCII characters. It is essentially raw text just like the words you're reading now. Each byte in the file contains one character that conforms to the standard ASCII code. Program source code, DOS batch files, macros and scripts are written as straight text and stored as ASCII files.

ASCII text files become a common denominator between applications that do not import each other's formats. If both applications can import and export ASCII files, you can transfer your files between them.

All text editors (Notepad, DOS Editor, Brief, etc.) and a few word processors, such as XyWrite, create ASCII files. Every other application generates its own format for storing data. It may use ASCII text for names and addresses, but it contains proprietary codes that conflict with ASCII control codes.

For example, if you display a non-ASCII file in an ASCII editor, you get garble on screen. Sometimes it beeps or the characters seem to fly by very fast. It's because the ASCII editor is picking up proprietary codes that are coincidentally the same as ASCII returns, line feeds and bells (see ASCII chart on next page).

ASCII file, ASCII text file, text file and TXT file are synonymous. Contrast with *graphics file* and *binary file*.

ASCII protocol

The simplest communications protocol for text. It transmits only ASCII characters and uses ASCII control codes. It implies little or no error checking.

ASCII sort

The sequential order of ASCII data. In ASCII code, lower case characters follow upper case. True ASCII order would put the words DATA, data and SYSTEM into the following sequence:

        DATA   SYSTEM   data

Ashton-Tate

A software company founded in 1980 by Hal Lashlee and George Tate to market dBASE II, which was created by Wayne Ratliff (see *dBASE*). The company developed and acquired other products, including Framework, MultiMate and dBASE Mac. Borland acquired Ashton-Tate in 1991 and dispensed with all products except dBASE.

ASIC

(Application Specific Integrated Circuit) A custom chip designed for a specific application. It is designed by integrating standard cells from a library. ASIC design is faster than designing a chip from scratch, and design changes can be made more easily.

ASCII Character Codes (decimal notation)

STANDARD ASCII
The first 32 characters (0-31) are control codes

0	NUL	Null
1	SOH	Start of heading
2	STX	Start of text
3	ETX	End of text
4	EOT	End of transmit
5	ENQ	Enquiry
6	ACK	Acknowledge
7	BEL	Audible bell
8	BS	Backspace
9	HT	Horizontal tab
10	LF	Line feed
11	VT	Vertical tab
12	FF	Form feed
13	CR	Carriage return
14	SO	Shift out
15	SI	Shift in
16	DLE	Data link escape
17	DC1	Device control 1
18	DC2	Device control 2
19	DC3	Device control 3
20	DC4	Device control 4
21	NAK	Neg. acknowledge
22	SYN	Synchronous idle
23	ETB	End trans. block
24	CAN	Cancel
25	EM	End of medium
26	SUB	Substitution
27	ESC	Escape
28	FS	Figures shift
29	GS	Group separator
30	RS	Record separator
31	US	Unit separator
32	SP	Blank space (Space bar)

33	!	81	Q
34	"	82	R
35	#	83	S
36	$	84	T
37	%	85	U
38	&	86	V
39	'	87	W
40	(	88	X
41	)	89	Y
42	*	90	Z
43	+	91	[
44	,	92	\
45	-	93	]
46	.	94	^
47	/	95	_
48	0	96	`
49	1	97	a
50	2	98	b
51	3	99	c
52	4	100	d
53	5	101	e
54	6	102	f
55	7	103	g
56	8	104	h
57	9	105	i
58	:	106	j
59	;	107	k
60	<	108	l
61	=	109	m
62	>	110	n
63	?	111	o
64	@	112	p
65	A	113	q
66	B	114	r
67	C	115	s
68	D	116	t
69	E	117	u
70	F	118	v
71	G	119	w
72	H	120	x
73	I	121	y
74	J	122	z
75	K	123	{
76	L	124	|
77	M	125	}
78	N	126	~
79	O	127	▨
80	P		

EXTENDED ASCII
(IBM PC)

128	Ç	174	«	220	▄
129	ü	175	»	221	▌
130	é	176	░	222	▌
131	â	177	▒	223	▀
132	ä	178	▓	224	α
133	à	179	│	225	β
134	å	180	┤	226	Γ
135	ç	181	╡	227	π
136	ê	182	╢	228	Σ
137	ë	183	╖	229	σ
138	è	184	╕	230	µ
139	ï	185	╣	231	τ
140	î	186	║	232	Φ
141	ì	187	╗	233	Θ
142	Ä	188	╝	234	Ω
143	Å	189	╜	235	δ
144	É	190	╛	236	∞
145	æ	191	┐	237	φ
146	Æ	192	└	238	ε
147	ô	193	┴	239	∩
148	ö	194	┬	240	≡
149	ò	195	├	241	±
150	û	196	─	242	≥
151	ù	197	┼	243	≤
152	ÿ	198	╞	244	⌠
153	Ö	199	╟	245	⌡
154	Ü	200	╚	246	÷
155	¢	201	╔	247	≈
156	£	202	╩	248	°
157	¥	203	╦	249	•
158	₧	204	╠	250	·
159	ƒ	205	═	251	√
160	á	206	╬	252	η
161	í	207	╧	253	²
162	ó	208	╨	254	▪
163	ú	209	╤	255	
164	ñ	210	╥		
165	Ñ	211	╙		
166	ª	212	╘		
167	º	213	╒		
168	¿	214	╓		
169	⌐	215	╫		
170	¬	216	╪		
171	½	217	┘		
172	¼	218	┌		
173	¡	219	█		
174	«	220	▄		
175	»	221	▌		

askSam

A text management system for PCs from askSam Systems, Perry FL. It holds unstructured text as well as standard data fields. The product is noted for its flexible text retrieval and hypertext capabilities.

ASM

(1) (Association for Systems Management) An international membership organization founded in 1947 with over 10,000 administrative executives and specialists in information systems. It sponsors conferences in all phases of administrative systems and management and serves business, education, government and the military. Address: 24587 Bagley Rd., Cleveland, OH 44138, 216/243-6900.

(2) File extension for assembly language source programs.

ASMP

(ASymmetric MultiProcessing) A multiprocessing design in which each CPU is assigned a particular program or part of a program that it executes for the duration of the session. Contrast with *SMP*, in which all the CPUs function as a single resource pool and take on whatever tasks need to processed next. See *MPP*.

ASN.1

(Abstract Syntax Notation.1) The rules for defining data structures transmitted over an OSI network.

ASP

(Association of Shareware Professionals) A trade organization for shareware founded in 1987. Author members submit products to ASP, which are approved, virus checked and distributed monthly via CD to member vendors and BBSs. CDs are periodically made available to the public. Address: 545 Grover Road, Muskegon, MI 49422, 616/788-5131.

aspect ratio

The ratio of width to height of an object.

ASPI

(Advanced SCSI Programming Interface) An interface from Adaptec, Inc., Milpitas, CA, that provides a common language between drivers and SCSI host adapters. See *CAM*.

assembler

Software that translates assembly language into machine language. Contrast with *compiler*, which is used to translate a high-level language, such as COBOL or C, into assembly language first and then into machine language.

assembly language

A programming language that is one step away from machine language. Each assembly language statement is translated into one machine instruction by the assembler. Programmers must be well versed in the computer's architecture, and, undocumented assembly language programs are difficult to maintain. It is hardware dependent; there is a different assembly language for each CPU series.

In the past, control programs (operating systems, database managers, etc.) were written in assembly language to maximize the machine's performance. Today, C is often used instead. Like assembly language, C can manipulate the bits at the machine level, but it is also portable to different computer platforms. There are C compilers for most computers.

Although often used synonomously, assembly language and machine language are not the same. Assembly language is turned into machine language. For example, the assembly instruction COMPARE A,B is translated into COMPARE contents of memory bytes 2340-2350 with 4567-4577 (where A and B happen to be located). The physical binary format of the machine instruction is specific to the computer it's running in.

Assembly languages are quite different between computers as is evident in the example below, which takes 16 lines of code for the mini and 82 lines for the micro. The example changes Fahrenheit to Celsius.

HP 3000

```
begin
intrinsic  read,print,binary,ascii;
array buffer(0:17);
array string(0:3);
byte array b'string(*) = string;
integer ftemp, ctemp, len;
  move buffer:= "Enter Fahrenheit ";
  print (buffer,-30,%320);
  len:=read (string,-4);
  ftemp:= binary(b'string,len);
  ctemp:= (ftemp-32) * 5 / 9;
  len:= ascii(ctemp,1-,b'string);
  move buffer:= "Celsius is ";
  move buffer(14) := string, (-len);
  print (buffer,-32,%0);
end
```

PC (Intel x86)

```
cseg     segment para public 'CODE'
         assume  cs:cseg,ds:cseg
start:
         jmp     start1
msgstr   db      'Enter Fahrenheit '
crlf     db      13,10,'$'
nine     db      9
five     db      5
outstr   db      'Centrigrade is $'
start1:  push    ds
         push    cs
         pop     ds
         mov     dx,offset cseg:msgstr
         mov     ah,9
         int     21h
sloop:
cent:    call    getnumb
         test    ax,ax
         je      exit
         push    ax
         mov     dx,offset cseg:outstr
         mov     ah,9
         int     21h
         pop     ax
         sub     ax,32
         jns     c1
         push    ax
         mov     dl,'-'
         mov     ah,6
         int     21h
         pop     ax
         neg     ax
c1:      mul     five
         div     nine
         call    putval
         mov     dx,offset cseg:crlf
         mov     ah,9
         int     21h
```

```
        jmp     sloop
exit:   pop     ds
        mov     ah,4ch
        int     21h
getnumb:
        xor     bx,bx
llp:    mov     dl,0ffh
        mov     ah,1
        int     21h
        cmp     al,0dh
        je      llr
        sub     al,'0'
        jb      llr
        cmp     al,'9'
        ja      llr
        xor     ah,ah
        shl     bx,1
        add     ax,bx
        shl     bx,1
        shl     bx,1
        add     bx,ax
        jmp     llp
llr:    mov     dx,offset cseg:crlf
        mov     ah,9
        int     21h
        mov     ax,bx
        ret
putval: xor     bx,bx
        push    bx
        mov     bx,10
llg:    xor     dx,dx
        div     bx
        add     dx,'0'
        push    dx
        test    ax,ax
        jne     llg
bloop:  pop     dx
        test    dx,dx
        je      endx
        mov     ah,6
        int     21h
        jmp     bloop
endx:   ret
cseg    ends
        end     start
```

assignment statement

In programming, a compiler directive that places a value into a variable. For example, **counter=0** creates a variable named counter and fills it with zeros. The VARIABLE=VALUE syntax is common among programming languages.

associating files

See *file association*.

Association for Computing Machinery

See *ACM*.

Association for Systems Management

See *ASM*.

Association of Shareware Professionals

See *ASP*.

associative storage

Storage that is accessed by comparing the content of the data stored in it rather than by addressing predetermined locations.

ASSP

(Application Specific Standard Part) An ASIC chip originally designed for one customer and then released to the general public.

AST

(AST Research, Inc., Irvine, CA) A PC manufacturer founded in 1980 by Albert Wong, Safi Quershey and Tom Yuen (A, S and T). It offers a complete line of PCs and sells through its dealer channel. AST was initially known for its line of add-in memory boards for the PC, including the Rampage and SixPak Plus boards. Since then, it has become a major PC player with revenues of more than two billion in 1994. In 1993, AST acquired Tandy Corporation's PC manufacturing facilities.

asymmetric modem

A full-duplex modem that transmits data in one direction at one speed and simultaneously in the other direction at another speed. For example, data flows at high-speed in one direction while acknowledgement is returned at low speed in the other. Contrast with *ping pong*.

asymmetric multiprocessing

See *ASMP*.

asymmetric system

(1) A system in which major components or properties are different.
(2) In video compression, a system that requires more equipment to compress the data than to decompress it.

asynchronous

(1)Unsynchronized events, for example, the time interval between event A and B is not the same as B and C.
(2) Able to initiate a transmission at either end.
(3) In SNA, refers to independent events rather than concurrent events. For example, if one user sends mail to a party who is not available, the ability to forward the mail at a later time is considered asynchronous.
(4) Starting the next I/O operation before the current one is completed.
(5) In SCSI, the acknowledgment of each byte of data transferred.
Contrast with *synchronous*.

asynchronous communications server

See *ACS*.

asynchronous I/O

Overlapping input and output with processing. Both the hardware and the software must be designed for this capability. The peripherals must be able to run independent of the CPU, and the software must be designed to manage it.

asynchronous protocol

A communications protocol that controls an asynchronous transmission, for example, ASCII, TTY, Kermit and Xmodem. Contrast with *synchronous protocol*.

Asynchronous Protocol Specification
See *X.445*.

asynchronous transfer mode
See *ATM*.

asynchronous transmission
The transmission of data in which each character is a self-contained unit with its own start and stop bits. Intervals between characters may be uneven. It is the common method of transmission between a computer and a modem, although the modem may switch to synchronous transmission to communicate with the other modem. Also called start/stop transmission. Contrast with *synchronous transmission.*

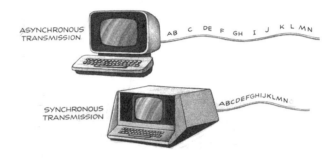

ASYNCHRONOUS TRANSMISSION

AB C DE F GH I J K L MN

SYNCHRONOUS TRANSMISSION

ABCDEFGHIJKLMN

AT
(Advanced Technology) IBM's first 286-based PC, introduced in 1984. It was the most advanced machine in the PC line and featured a new keyboard, 1.2MB floppy and 16-bit data bus. AT-class machines run considerably faster than XTs (8088-based PCs). See *PC.*

IBM AT
The fastest PC in 1984. Users were amazed at the extraordinary speed with which files could be accessed and copied on its 20MB hard disk.

AT&T
(American Telephone & Telegraph Company) The largest long distance communications carrier in the U.S. Once the largest corporation in America, it was relieved of its operating telephone companies on January 1, 1984, by Federal court order. It has gone through a major change from the world's largest monopoly to a competitive enterprise. Its early ventures into the PC market were modest, but in 1991, AT&T acquired NCR, a seasoned computer company, which it later renamed AT&T GIS.
In 1995, AT&T announced its intension to break up the company again, only this time, on its own volition. It plans to create three independent companys, one for telecommunications, another for manufacturing of telecom equipment, and the third is AT&T GIS, which will be on its own once again.

AT&T GIS

(AT&T Global Information Solutions, Dayton, OH) Formerly the NCR
Corporation, AT&T GIS is a major manufacturer of computers and financial
terminals. It was founded in 1884 when John Henry Patterson purchased National
Manufacturing Company of Dayton, Ohio, and renamed it National Cash Register.
It became the leading cash register company and, by 1911, had sold its one
millionth machine.

Starting in the 1930s, NCR made accounting machines that posted customer
accounts and became successful in the banking and retail industries, in which it has
remained ever since.

In 1957, it introduced the "304" transistorized computer. It accepted data from
NCR cash registers and banking terminals via paper tape. The 304 was very reliabile
and widely accepted.

NCR computer lines have included the Century series (1960s), Criterion series
(1970s) and the V and I series (1980s). Starting in 1982 with the UNIX- and
Motorola 68000-based Tower series, NCR embraced open systems and industry
standards. In 1990, the x86-based System 3000 series was introduced, a complete
line from laptops to massively parallel machines running DOS, Windows and OS/2
at the low end and UNIX at the high end.

In 1991, NCR was acquired by AT&T and operates as a wholly-owned subsidiary.
It was renamed AT&T GIS in January 1994. The NCR name remains on ATM and
POS terminals as well as microelectronics and business forms. Computer systems
use the AT&T name. In 1995, AT&T announced its plan to return AT&T GIS to
an independent company once again.

ATA

(AT Attachment) The interface specification for IDE drives. ATA is often not
mentioned on advertising specs for computer systems with IDE drives, but it is the
formal engineering name for the IDE interface. The ATA interface is also used for
PCMCIA solid state disks.

ATA-2, sometimes called Fast ATA, defines higher transfer rates supported by
Enhanced IDE, the second generation of IDE. ATAPI (ATA Packet Interface)
defines the specification for CD-ROMs and tape drives. See *Enhanced IDE* and
QIC-157.

Following are the transfer rates for the various ATA modes.

	Mode	Maximum Transfer Rate (MBytes/sec)
ATA	Mode 0	4
ATA-2	Mode 1	6
ATA-2	Mode 2	8
ATA-2	Mode 3	11
ATA-3	Mode 4	16
ATA-3	Mode 5	22

ATAPI

(AT Attachment Packet Interface) See *ATA*.

Atari

(Atari Computer, Sunnyvale, CA) A video game manufacturer founded in 1972 by
Nolan Bushnell. It became famous for "Pong," a Ping-Pong-like game that was
viewed over a TV. In 1976, Atari was sold to Time Warner and then in 1984 to Jack
Tramiel and investors. Shortly thereafter, it introduced the 520ST, the first model
in its ST line of personal computers built with a MIDI interface. The STs evolved
into the Falcon, and in 1993, the Falcon line was spun off, and the company went

back to its roots. It currently offers the Jaguar line of hand-held and CD-ROM based video games.

ATASPI

(ATA Software Programming Interface) A programming interface and Enhanced IDE manager from Future Domain Corporation for Enhanced IDE devices. It supports the IDE hard disk interface (ATA) and Enhanced IDE CD-ROM and tape interface (ATAPI) and provides improved 32-bit performance under DOS and Windows 3.1.

AT Attachment

See *ATA*.

AT bus

Refers to the 16-bit bus introduced with the IBM AT. It was the early term for what is today called the "ISA bus."

AT class

Refers to second-generation PCs that use the 286 CPU and the 16-bit AT (ISA) bus. In the mid 1980s, AT class machines were the high-speed PCs of the day.

AT command set

A series of machine instructions used to activate features on an intelligent modem. Developed by Hayes Microcomputer Products, Inc., and formally called the Hayes Standard AT Command Set, it is used entirely or partially by most every modem manufacturer. AT is a mnemonic code for ATtention, which is the prefix that initiates each command to the modem. See *Hayes Smartmodem*.

ATE

(Automatic Test Equipment) Machines that test electronic systems, primarily chips. See *EDA* and *DTA*.

AT interface

See *AT bus*. See also *ATA*.

AT keyboard

An 84-key keyboard provided with the PC AT. It corrected the non-standard placement of the PC's return and left shift keys. See *PC keyboard* and *Enhanced keyboard*.

ATM

(1) (Asynchronous Transfer Mode)
(2) (Automatic Teller Machine)
(3) See *Adobe Type Manager*.

(1) (Asynchronous Transfer Mode) A high-speed cell-switching network technology for LANs and WANs that handles data and realtime voice and video. It combines the high efficiency of packet switching used in data networks, with the guaranteed bandwidth of circuit switching used in voice networks. ATM is defined in the Broadband ISDN (BISDN) standard.
When implemented by the telephone companies, ATM will provide "bandwidth on demand" by charging customers for the amount of data they send rather than fixed-cost digital lines (DS1, DS3, etc.) that often go underutilized. Unlike leased lines, which are point to point, ATM can switch data to any ATM node worldwide.
ATM data rates are scalable starting as low as 1.5 Mbps with intermediate speeds of 25, 51 and 100 Mbps to high speeds of 155, 622 Mbps and up into the gigabit range.

ATM is currently used in LANs connecting high-speed workstations, but adapters for personal computers are available, and the prices are dropping. It is expected that ATM will become widely used for both LANs and WANs.

The Ubiquitous ATM
Could we live without them?

ATM works by chopping all traffic into 53-byte cells, or packets. The fixed-length packet allows very fast switches to be built, and the small packet size ensures that voice and video frames can be inserted into the stream often enough for realtime transmission.

ATM can also encompass frame relay traffic by breaking up frame relay's variable-length frames into ATM cells. ATM provides network services at the same level as Ethernet and Token Ring (OSI layers 1 and 2).

For an excellent booklet called "Asynchronous Transfer Mode: Bandwidth for the Future," which explains many technical details of ATM, contact Advanstar Marketing Services, Cleveland, OH, 800/598-6008, fax 216/891-2726. See *ATM Forum.*

(2) (Automatic Teller Machine) A banking terminal that accepts deposits and dispenses cash. Stand alone or online to a central computer, ATMs are activated by inserting a cash or credit card that contains the user's account number on a magnetic stripe.

ATM Forum

A membership organization founded in 1991 to promote ATM networking technology. It works with ANSI and the ITU to set standards. Its first specification in 1992 defined the User-Network Interface (UNI). Technical committees work on various projects in order to accelerate standards. Address: 480 San Antonio Rd., Suite 100, Mountain View, CA 94040, 415/962-2585 (fax 415/941-0849).

ATM.INI

A Windows configuration file that contains the locations of installed Type 1 fonts. It contains the path to both the PFB and PFM files.

AT motherboard

A motherboard that uses the same form factor as the original IBM AT. Most PCs today use the smaller baby AT motherboards, which are approximately 9x10" in size. In 1995, Intel introduced the successor to the baby AT board, called the ATX, which includes built-in multimedia. PCs are expected to migrate to ATX over time. See *ATX.*

atom

In list processing languages, a single element in a list.

atomic

Indivisible. An atomic operation, or atomicity, implies an operation that must be performed entirely or not at all. For example, if machine failure prevents a transaction to be processed to completion, the system will be rolled back to the start of the transaction. See *two-phase commit.*

atomic force microscope

A device used to detect atoms in a molecule. In 1992, IBM demonstrated a prototype atomic force microscope for recording data. Its pyramid-shaped tip was heated by a laser and pressed against the surface of a disk to form an indentation (a bit). Such a device might be capable of storing 30 billion bits per square inch in the future.

attached processor

An additional CPU connected to the primary CPU in a multiprocessing environment. It operates as an extension of the primary CPU and shares the system software and peripheral devices.

attachment unit interface

See *AUI*.

attenuation

Loss of signal power in a transmission.

attribute

(1) In relational database management, a field within a record.
(2) For printers and display screens, a characteristic that changes a font, for example, from normal to boldface or underlined, or from normal to reverse video.
(3) See *file attribute*.

At Work

An operating environment from Microsoft designed for office equipment such as telephones, copiers and fax machines. It comprises a realtime operating system with a simple graphical user interface for office machines, a communications capability that provides secure transmission plus the ability to print or display a document at a remote device exactly the same as it was created. At Work provides an interface for desktop Windows applications in a PC to control At Work devices.

ATX

A motherboard specification from Intel that supersedes the widely-used baby AT form factor. It rotates the CPU and memory 90 degrees, allowing full-length boards in all sockets. It supports multimedia (built-in audio and video) and the USB (Universal Serial Bus). The ATX power supply blows air over the processor chip rather than pulling air through the chassis.

audio

The range of frequencies within human hearing (approx. 20Hz at the low to a high of 20,000Hz).
Traditional audio devices are analog, because they handle sound waves in an analogous form. Radios maintain the audio signal as rippling waves from antenna to speaker. Sound waves are "carved" into plastic phonograph records, and audio tape records sound as magnetic waves.
Audio is processed in a computer by converting the analog signal into a digital code using various techniques, such as PCM.

audio adapter

Same as *sound card*.

audio board

Same as *sound card*.

audio CD

The music compact disc (CD) format that has replaced the phonograph record. Starting in the early 1990s, certain stereo amplifiers and receivers have come on the market without a phono input, making the definitive statement that analog phonograph records are history! See *CD* and *Red Book*.

audio conferencing

See *audioconferencing*.

audioconferencing

An audio communications session among several people that are geographically dispersed. It is provided by a conference function in a PBX or multiline telephone or by the telephone companies. See *videoconferencing* and *data conferencing*.

audio response

See *voice response*.

audiotex

A voice response application that allows users to enter and retrieve information over the telephone. In response to a voice menu, users press the keys or answer questions to select their way down a path of choices. It is used for obtaining the latest financial quotes as well as for ordering products. It is also built into interactive systems that allows databases to be changed. See *VIS*.

audiotext

Same as *audiotex*.

audiovisual

Audio and/or video capability.

audit

An examination of systems, programming and datacenter procedures in order to determine the efficiency of computer operations.

audit software

Specialized programs that perform a variety of audit functions, such as sampling databases and generating confirmation letters to customers. It can highlight exceptions to categories of data and alert the examiner to possible error. Audit software often includes a non-procedural language that lets the auditor describe the computer and data environment without detailed programming.

audit trail

A record of transactions in an information system that provides verification of the activity of the system. The simplest audit trail is the transaction itself. If a person's salary is increased, the change transaction includes the date, amount of raise and name of authorizing manager.

A more elaborate audit trail can be created when the system is being verified for accuracy; for example, samples of processing results can be recorded at various stages. Item counts and hash totals are used to verify that all input has been processed through the system.

AUI

(Attachment Unit Interface) The network interface used with standard Ethernet, which uses a thick coaxial cable. On the adapter card, it is a 15-pin socket. A transceiver, which taps into the Ethernet cable, plugs into the socket.

authentication

Verifying the identity of a user that is in the process of logging onto or has already logged onto a network. See *IP spoofing, password* and *digital signature.*

authentication token

A security device given to authorized users who keep them in their possession. To log onto the network, the card may be read directly like a credit card, or it may display a changing number that is typed in as a password. See *SecurID card.*

authoring program

Software that allows for the development of tutorials and CBT programs.

authorization code

An identification number or password that is used to gain access to a local or remote computer system.

Authorware Professional

A popular multimedia authoring program from Macromedia that is widely used for creating interactive learning programs on Windows and Macintosh. See *Macromedia.*

auto

(AUTOmatic) Refers to a wide variety of devices that perform unattended operation.

auto answer

A modem feature that accepts a telephone call and establishes the connection. See *auto dial.*

auto attendant

A voice store and forward system that replaces the human operator and directs callers to the appropriate extensions or voice mailboxes.

auto baud detect

A modem feature that detects the highest speed of the called modem and switches to it.

autobaud rate

See *ABR.*

auto bypass

The ability to bypass a terminal or other device in a network if it fails, allowing the remaining devices to continue functioning.

AutoCAD

A full-featured CAD program from AutoDesk Inc., Sausalito, CA, that runs on PCs, VAXs, Macs and UNIX workstations. Originally developed for CP/M machines, it was one of the first major CAD programs for personal computers and became an industry standard. There are countless third-party add-on packages that are available for AutoCAD, and many graphics applications import and export AutoCAD's DXF file format.

autocoder

An IBM assembly language for 1960s-vintage 1400 and 7000 series computers.

auto dial

A modem feature that opens the line and dials the telephone number of another computer to establish connection. See *auto answer*.

AUTODIN

(AUTOmatic DIgital Network) The worldwide communications network of the U.S. Defense Communications System.

AUTOEXEC.BAT

(AUTOmatic EXECute BATch) A DOS batch file that is executed when the computer is started. The file contains DOS commands that initialize operating system settings, load RAM-resident programs and/or automatically call in a specific application program. In Windows 95 as well, AUTOEXEC.BAT will be executed if found. The OS/2 counterpart is STARTUP.CMD.

autoflow

Wrapping text around a graphic image or from one page to the next.

auto line feed

A feature that moves the cursor or print head to the next line when a CR (carriage return) is sensed. PCs put a LF (line feed) after the CR and do not use this feature. The Mac uses only a CR for end of line and requires it.

AutoLISP

An AutoCAD language used to create customized menus and routines.

auto logon

Performing the complete log-on sequence necessary to gain entry into a computer system without user intervention.

automata theory

An open-ended computer science discipline that concerns an abstract device called an "automaton," which performs a specific computational or recognition function. Networks of automata are designed to mimic human behavior.

automatic data processing

Same as *data processing*.

automatic feature negotiation

The ability of a modem to determine and adjust to the speed, error control and data compression method of the modem at the other end of the line.

automation

The replacement of manual operations by computerized methods. Office automation refers to integrating clerical tasks such as typing, filing and appointment scheduling. Factory automation refers to computer-driven assembly lines.

automounting

Making remote files available to a client at the time the file is accessed. Remote directories are associated with a local directory on the client ahead of time, and the mounting takes places the first time a remote file is opened by the client.

auto redial

A modem, fax or telephone feature that redials a busy number a fixed number of times before giving up.

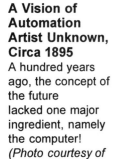

A Vision of Automation Artist Unknown, Circa 1895
A hundred years ago, the concept of the future lacked one major ingredient, namely the computer!
(Photo courtesy of Rosemont Engineering.)

auto reliable
A modem feature that enables it to send to a modem with or without built-in error detection and compression.

auto resume
A feature that lets you stop working on the computer and take up where you left off at a later date without having to reload applications. Memory contents are stored on disk or kept active by battery and/or AC power.

autosave
Saving data to the disk at periodic intervals without user intervention.

autosizing
The ability of a monitor to maintain the same rectangular image size when changing from one resolution to another.

autostart routine
Instructions built into the computer and activated when it is turned on. The routine performs diagnostic tests, such as checking the computer's memory, and then loads the operating system and passes control to it.

autotrace

A routine that converts a raster graphics image into a vector graphics image. It scans the bitmap and turns the dark areas into vectors (lines). Once a bitmap has been turned into vectors, individual components of the drawing can be scaled independently.

This process usually creates many more vectors than if the picture were drawn in a drawing program in the first place. In order to faithfully reproduce the original, the conversion routine will generate a vector for the slightest deviation in a line. However, extraneous vectors can be deleted afterwards.

A/UX

Apple's version of UNIX for the Macintosh. It is based on AT&T's UNIX System V with Berkeley extensions.

auxiliary memory

A high-speed memory bank used in mainframes and supercomputers. It is not directly addressable by the CPU, rather it functions like a disk. Data is transferred from auxiliary memory to main memory over a high-bandwidth channel. See *auxiliary storage*.

auxiliary storage

External storage devices, such as disk and tape.

availability

See *high availability*.

AVC

(Audio Visual Connection) Multimedia software from IBM that works in conjunction with IBM's Audio Capture and Video Capture boards for the PS/2. It allows users to integrate sound and pictures into applications and includes an authoring language.

AV drive

(Audio Visual drive) A hard disk drive that is optimized for audio and video applications. Transferring analog high-fidelity audio and video signals onto a digital disk and playing them back at high performance levels requires a drive that can sustain continuous reads and writes without interruption. AV drives are designed to postpone thermal recalibration when reading and writing so that long data transfers will not be interrupted, and frames will not be lost.

AVI

(Audio Video Interleaved) A Windows multimedia video format from Microsoft. It interleaves standard waveform audio and digital video frames (bitmaps) to provide reduced animation at 15 fps at 160x120x8 resolution. Audio is 11,025Hz, 8-bit samples.

avionics

The electronic instrumentation and control equipment used in airplanes and space vehicles.

Award BIOS

A PC-compatible BIOS from Award Software, Inc., Los Gatos, CA. By 1991, over 20 million Award BIOSs have been installed.

awk

(Aho Weinberger Kernighan) A UNIX programming utility developed in 1977 by

Aho, Weinberger and Kernighan. Due to its unique pattern-matching syntax, it is often used in data retrieval and data transformation. DOS versions are also available.

Axiant

An application development system from Cognos for client/server environments. Built on Cognos' PowerHouse 4GL, it supports Windows and Macintosh clients and a variety of databases and UNIX servers. Cognos' Impromptu query language and PowerPlay EIS/DSS system are components. Also included is the WATCOM/SQL database.

AXP

A family of computer systems from Digital that use the Alpha CPU chip. This series is expected to take Digital throughout the 1990s and beyond.

azimuth

The trajectory of an angle measured in degrees going clockwise from a base point. A disk azimuth alignment test checks for the correct positioning of the read/write head to the track.

B

B:
The designation for the second floppy disk drive in a PC.

B1
The computer system security level required by the Department of Defence (DOD). See *NCSC.*

baby AT
Refers to a commonly-used motherboard in PCs or a case that holds the board. See *AT motherboard.*

Bachman tools
A variety of systems design, database administration and system performance measurement products from Bachman Information Systems, Inc., Burlington, MA.

backbone
In communications, the part of a network that handles the major traffic. It often employs the highest-speed transmission paths in the network and may also run the longest distance. Smaller networks are attached to the backbone.
A backbone can span a large geographic area or be as small as a backplane in a single cabinet. See *collapsed backbone.*

backdoor
See *trapdoor.*

back-end CASE
CASE tools that generate program code. Contrast with *front-end CASE.*

back end processor
Same as *database machine.*

backfile conversion
Scanning older documents that reside in a file cabinet. Service bureaus specialize in this conversion process.

background
(1) The non-interactive processing in the computer. See *foreground/background.*
(2) The base, or backdrop color. In order to distinguish any image on screen, whether text or graphics, there must be a contrasting background color.

background ink
A highly reflective OCR ink used to print the parts of the form not recognized by a scanner.

background noise
An extraneous signal that has crept into a line, channel or circuit.

background processing
Processing in which the program is not visibly interacting with the user. Most personal computers use operating systems that run background tasks only when foreground tasks are idle, such as between keystrokes. Advanced multitasking operating systems let background programs be given any priority from low to high.

backing storage
Same as *auxiliary storage.*

backlit

An LCD screen that has its own light source from the back of the screen, making the background brighter and characters appear sharper.

BackOffice

A suite of network server software products from Microsoft that includes Windows NT Server, SQL Server, Systems Management Server (SMS), SNA Server and Mail Server.

backplane

(1) The reverse side of a panel or board that contains interconnecting wires.
(2) A printed circuit board, or device, containing slots or sockets for plugging in boards or cables. See *bus*.

backsolver

See *solver*.

backspace

(1) To move the screen cursor one column to the left, deleting the character that was in that position. A backspace to the printer moves the print head one column to the left.
(2) To move to the previous block on a magnetic tape.

back up

To make a copy of important data onto a different storage medium for safety.

backup

Additional resources or duplicate copies of data on different storage media for emergency purposes. See *backup types*.

backup & recovery

The combination of manual and machine procedures that can restore lost data in the event of hardware or software failure. Routine backup of databases and logs of computer activity are part of a backup & recovery program. See *checkpoint/restart*.

backup copy

A disk, tape or other machine readable copy of a data or program file. Making backup copies is a discipline most computer users learn the hard way— after a week's work is lost.

backup disk

A disk used to hold duplicate copies of important files. Floppy disks and disks cartridges are used for backup disks.

backup power

An additional power source that can be used in the event of power failure. See *UPS*.

backup tape

See *tape backup*.

backup types

The selection of files for backup purposes.

Full Backup
Backs up all selected files.

Differential Backup
Backs up selected files that have been changed. This is used when only the latest version of a file is required.

Incremental Backup
Backs up selected files that have been changed, but if a file has been changed for the second or subsequent time since the last full backup, the file doesn't replace the already-backed-up file, rather it is appended to the backup medium.
This is used when each revision of a file must be maintained for backup.

Backus-Naur form

Also known as Backus normal form, it was the first metalanguage to define programming languages, developed by John Backus and Peter Naur in 1959.

backward chaining

In AI, a form of reasoning that starts with the conclusion and works backward. The goal is broken into many subgoals or sub-subgoals which can be solved more easily. Known as top-down approach. Contrast with *forward chaining*.

backward compatible

Same as *downward compatible*.

Bad command or file name

A DOS error message that means DOS does not understand the command you entered, or it cannot find the program you asked it to run.

bad font

A scalable font that is poorly programmed. If a font programmer does not follow the rules when coding a Type 1 or TrueType font, problems can occur when the rasterizer (RIP) tries to convert it into bitmaps for display or printing.

bad sector

A segment of disk storage that cannot be read or written due to a physical problem in the disk. Bad sectors on hard disks are marked by the operating system and bypassed. If data is recorded in a sector that becomes bad, file recovery software, and sometimes special hardware, must be used to restore it.

BAK file

(BAcKup file) A DOS and OS/2 file extension for backup files.

BAL

(1) (Basic Assembly Language) The assembly language for the IBM 370/3000/4000 mainframe series.
(2) (Branch And Link) An instruction used to transfer control to another part of the program.

ballistic gain

A trackball or mouse feature that changes cursor travel relative to hand speed. The faster the ball is moved, the farther the cursor is moved.

baloon help

On-screen help displayed in a cartoon-style dialogue box that appears when the pointer (cursor) is placed over the object in question.

balun

(BALanced UNbalanced) A device that connects a balanced line to an unbalanced line; for example, a twisted pair to a coaxial cable. A balanced line is one in which both wires are electrically equal. In an unbalanced line, such as a coax, one line has different properties than the other.

Balun
The left unit shows a BNC connector for attaching coaxial cable. The right one shows the connection for a pair of wires. *(Photo courtesy of Black Box Corporation.)*

band
(1) The range of frequencies used for transmitting a signal. A band is identified by its lower and upper limits; for example, a 10MHz band in the 100 to 110MHz range.
(2) A contiguous group of tracks that are treated as a unit.
(3) A rectangular section of a page that is created and sent to the printer. See *band printing*.
(4) The printing element in a band printer.

band pass filter
An electronic device that prohibits all but a specific range of frequencies to pass through it.

band printer
A line printer that uses a metal band, or loop, of type characters as its printing mechanism. The band spins horizontally around a set of hammers. When the desired character is in front of the selected print position, the corresponding hammer hits the paper into the ribbon and onto the character in the band. This is not to be confused with *band printing*, which is a method for sending output to the printer.

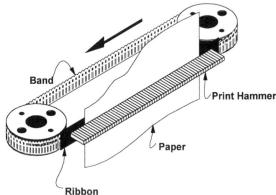

Band Printer Mechanism

Band

Print Hammer

Paper

Ribbon

band printing
Printing a page by creating the output in several rectangular sections, or bands, rather than the entire page. It enables a printer with limited memory to print a full page of text and graphics. Most dot matrix printers and some laser printers benefit from this approach. This is not to be confused with *band printer*, which is hardware.

bandwidth
The transmission capacity of a computer channel, communications line or bus. It is

expressed in cycles per second (Hertz), the bandwidth being the difference between the lowest and highest frequencies transmitted. The frequency is equal to or greater than the bits per second. Bandwidth is also often stated in bits or bytes per second. See *video bandwidth*.

bank

An arrangement of identical hardware components.

bank switching

Engaging and disengaging electronic circuits. Bank switching is used when the design of a system prohibits all circuits from being addressed or activated at the same time, requiring that one unit be turned on while the others are turned off.

BAPC

(Business Applications Performance Corporation) A nonprofit organization founded in 1991 that develops benchmarks for PC software.

bar chart

A graphical representation of information in the form of bars. See *business graphics*.

bar code

The printed code used for recognition by a scanner. Traditional one-dimensional bar codes use the bar's width as the code, but encode just an ID or account number. Two-dimensional bar codes, such as PDF417 from Symbol Technology, are read horizontally and vertically. PDF417 holds 1,800 characters in an area the size of a postage stamp. See *UPC*.

One-Dimensional Bar Code

Two-Dimensional Bar Code
This PDF417 bar code image developed by Symbol Technology contains the entire Gettysburg address. (Photo courtesy of Symbol Technology, Inc.)

barrel distortion

A screen distortion in which the sides bow out. Contrast with *pincushioning*.

barrel printer

Same as *drum printer*.

base

(1) A starting or reference point.
(2) In a bipolar transistor, the line that activates the switch. Same as *gate* in a CMOS transistor.
(3) A multiplier in a numbering system. In a decimal system, each digit position is worth 10x the position to its right. In binary, each digit position is worth 2x the position to its right.

base address

The starting address (beginning point) of a program or table. See *base/displacement* and *relative address*.

base alignment

The alignment of a variety of font sizes on a baseline.

baseband

A communications technique in which digital signals are placed onto the transmission line without change in modulation. It is usually limited to a few miles and does not require the complex modems used in broadband transmission. Common baseband LAN techniques are token passing ring (Token Ring) and CSMA/CD (Ethernet).

In baseband, the full bandwidth of the channel is used, and simultaneous transmission of multiple sets of data is accomplished by interleaving pulses using TDM (time division multiplexing). Contrast with *broadband* transmission, which transmits data, voice and video simultaneously by modulating each signal onto a different frequency, using FDM (frequency division multiplexing).

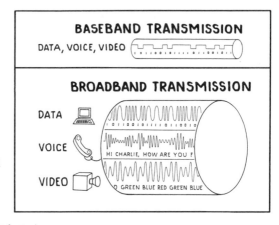

base/displacement

A machine architecture that runs programs no matter where they reside in memory. Addresses in a machine language program are displacement addresses, which are relative to the beginning of the program. At runtime, the hardware adds the address of the current first byte of the program (base address) to each displacement address and derives an absolute address for execution.

All modern computers use some form of base/displacement or offset mechanism in order to to run multiple programs in memory at the same time.

base font

The default font used for printing if none other is specified.

baseline

The horizontal line to which the bottoms of lowercase characters (without descenders) are aligned. See *typeface*.

baselining tool

A network monitor that analyzes communications usage in order to establish routine traffic patterns.

BASIC

(Beginners All purpose Symbolic Instruction Code) A programming language developed by John Kemeny and Thomas Kurtz in the mid 1960s at Dartmouth College. Originally developed as an interactive, mainframe timesharing language, it has become widely used on small computers.

BASIC is available in both compiler and interpreter form. As an interpreter, the language is conversational and can be debugged a line at a time. BASIC is also used as a quick calculator.

BASIC is considered one of the easiest programming languages to learn. Simple programs can be quickly written on the fly. However, BASIC is not a structured language, such as Pascal, dBASE or C, and it's easy to write spaghetti code that's difficult to decipher later.

The following BASIC example converts Fahrenheit to Celsius:

```
10 INPUT "Enter Fahrenheit "; FAHR
20 PRINT "Celsius is ", (FAHR-32) * 5 / 9
```

basic encoding rules
See *BER.*

BASIC in ROM
A BASIC interpreter stored in a read only memory chip that is available to the user at all times.

Basic Rate
See *ISDN.*

batch
A group, or collection, of items.

batch data entry
Entering a group of source documents into the computer.

batch file
(1) A file containing data that is processed or transmitted from beginning to end.
(2) A file containing instructions that are executed one after the other. See *BAT file* and *shell script.*

batch file transfer
The consecutive transmission of two or more files.

batch job
Same as *batch program.*

batch operation
Some action performed on a group of items at one time.

batch processing
Processing a group of transactions at one time. Transactions are collected and processed against the master files (master files updated) at the end of the day or some other time period. Contrast with *transaction processing.*

Batch and Transaction Processing
Information systems typically use both batch and transaction processing methods. For example, in an order processing system, transaction processing is the continuous updating of the customer and inventory files as orders are entered.
At the end of the day, batch processing programs generate picking lists for the warehouse. At the end of some period, batch programs print invoices and management reports.

(See illustration on following page.)

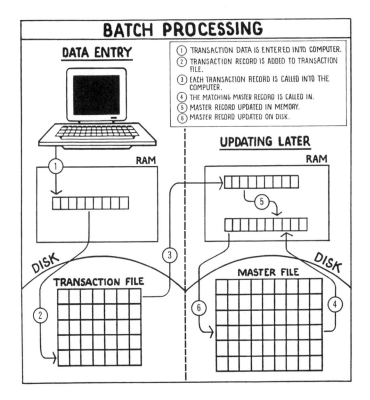

BATCH PROCESSING

DATA ENTRY

① TRANSACTION DATA IS ENTERED INTO COMPUTER.
② TRANSACTION RECORD IS ADDED TO TRANSACTION FILE.
③ EACH TRANSACTION RECORD IS CALLED INTO THE COMPUTER.
④ THE MATCHING MASTER RECORD IS CALLED IN.
⑤ MASTER RECORD UPDATED IN MEMORY.
⑥ MASTER RECORD UPDATED ON DISK.

UPDATING LATER

RAM   RAM

DISK   DISK

TRANSACTION FILE   MASTER FILE

batch program

A non-interactive (non-conversational) program such as a report listing or sort.

batch session

Transmitting or updating an entire file. Implies a non-interactive or non-interruptible operation from beginning to end. Contrast with *interactive session.*

batch stream

A collection of batch processing programs that are scheduled to run in the computer.

batch system

See *batch processing.*

batch terminal

A terminal that is designed for transmitting or receiving blocks of data, such as a card reader or printer.

batch total

The sum of a particular field in a collection of items used as a control total to ensure that all data has been entered into the computer. For example, using account number as a batch total, all account numbers would be summed manually before entry into the computer. After entry, the total is checked with the computer's sum of the numbers. If it does not match, source documents are manually checked against the computer's listing.

BAT file

(BATch file) A file of DOS or OS/2 commands that are executed one after the other. It has a .BAT extension and is created with a text editor. Batch files are commonly used to save typing the same commands over again to perform a routine task, such as backing up files.

batteries

See *lead acid, lithium ion, nickel cadmium, nickel hydride* and *zinc air.*

baud

(1) The signalling rate of a line. It's the switching speed, or number of transitions (voltage or frequency changes) that are made per second. Only at low speeds are bauds equal to bits per second; for example, 300 baud is equal to 300 bps. However, one baud can be made to represent more than one bit per second. For example, the V.22bis modem generates 1200 bps at 600 baud.

(2) Commonly (and erroneously) used to specify bits per second for modem speed; for example, 1200 baud means 1200 bps. See previous paragraph.

baudot code

Pronounced "baw-doh." One of the first standards for international telegraphy developed in the late 19th century by Emile Baudot. It uses five bits per character.

baud rate

A redundant reference to baud. Baud is a rate.

Bay Networks

(Bay Networks, Inc., Santa Clara, CA) A communications products company that is the merger in late 1994 of SynOptics Communications, Inc., Santa Clara, CA, and Wellfleet Communications, Inc., Billerica, MA. At the time of the merger, SynOptics was number #1 in hubs, and Wellfleet was number #2 in routers.

The Bay name comes from Santa Clara being located in the California Bay area and Billerica, located in Massachusetts, which is known as the Bay State.

bayonet connector

A plug and socket that uses a connecting mechanism to lock them together. One part is pushed into the other and turned. BNC and ST connectors are examples of bayonet connectors.

BBS

(Bulletin Board System) A computer system used as an information source and message system for a particular interest group. Users dial into the BBS, review and leave messages for other users as well as communicate to other users on the system at the same time. BBSs are often used to distribute shareware. Software vendors use BBSs to obtain customer feedback and distribute updates and program fixes. A BBS may provide access to running an application via a technique known as a *door.*

The floppy disk and CD-ROM versions of this book contain the national list of BBSs from Boardwatch Magazine as well as a list of BBS list keepers.

BCD

(Binary Coded Decimal) The storage of numbers in which each decimal digit is converted into binary and is stored in a single character or byte. For example, a 12-digit number would take 12 bytes. See *numbers.*

	256 + 4	
Binary	00000001	00000100

	2	**6**	**0**
BCD	00000010	00000110	00000000

Binary Versus BCD

Two methods are used to store the number 260 in the above example. The binary method stores it as a 16-bit binary number. BCD stores it as three separate bytes, each holding one decimal digit. Notice that the 1 in the left byte of the binary example is 256. The 256 is actually the ninth bit starting from the rightmost bit in the right byte.

BCS

(1) (The Boston Computer Society, 101a 1st Avenue, Waltham, MA 02154, 617/252-0600) A nonprofit membership organization founded in 1977 by Jonathan Rotenberg. With over 28,000 members, it is the world's largest personal computer association. Services include user and special interest groups, a subscription to BCS publications, access to the Resource Center, public-domain software and shareware.
(2) (Binary Compatibility Standard) See *ABI*.
(3) (The British Computer Society) Address: 13 Mansfield St., London, England W1M 0BP.

BDE

See *Borland Database Engine*.

BDOS error

See *read error* and *write error*.

beaconing

A continuous signalling of error conditions on a LAN.

bead

(1) A small programming subroutine. A sequence of beads that are strung together is called a *thread*.
(2) The insulator surrounding the inner wire of a coaxial cable.

BeBox

A multimedia personal computer from Be, Inc., a startup run by Jean Louise Gassee, former head of R&D at Apple. The BeBox is expected to ship in 1996 with dual PowerPC processors and a proprietary operating system. It should cost between $1500 and $3000, depending on configuration.

behavior

In object technology, the processing that an object can perform.

BEL

See *bell character*.

Bell 103

An AT&T standard for asynchronous 300 bps full-duplex modems using FSK modulation on dial-up lines.

Bell 113

An AT&T standard for asynchronous 300 bps full-duplex modems using FSK modulation on dial-up lines. The 113A can originate but not answer calls, while the 113D can answer but not originate.

Bell 201

An AT&T standard for synchronous 2400 bps full-duplex modems using DPSK modulation. Bell 201B was originally designed for dial-up lines and later for leased lines. Bell 201C was designed for half-duplex operation over dial-up lines.

Bell 202

An AT&T standard for asynchronous 1800 bps full-duplex modems using DPSK modulation over four-wire leased lines as well as 1200 bps half-duplex operation over dial-up lines.

Bell 208

An AT&T standard for synchronous 4800 bps modems. Bell 208A is a full-duplex modem using DPSK modulation over four-wire leased lines. Bell 208B was designed for half-duplex operation over dial-up lines.

Bell 209

An AT&T standard for synchronous 9600 bps full-duplex modems using QAM modulation over four-wire leased lines or half-duplex operation over dial-up lines.

Bell 212

An AT&T standard for asynchronous 1200 bps full-duplex modems using DPSK modulation on dial-up lines.

bell character

The control code used to sound an audible bell or tone in order to alert the user (ASCII 7, EBCDIC 2F).

Bell compatible

A modem that is compatible with modems originally introduced by the Bell Telephone System.

Bellcore

(BELLCOmmunications REsearch) The research and development organization created at divestiture and jointly owned by the regional Bell telephone companies (RBOCs). It is also involved in communications issues of the U.S. government regarding national security and emergency preparedness.

Bell Labs

The research and development center of AT&T and one of the most renowned scientific laboratories in the world.

Bell System

AT&T and the Bell Telephone Companies before divestiture. See *divestiture* and *RBOC*.

benchmark

A test of performance of a computer or peripheral device. The best benchmark is the actual set of application programs and data files that the organization will use. Running benchmarks on a single user computer is reasonably effective; however, benchmarking a multiuser system is complicated. Unless the user environment can be duplicated closely, the benchmark may be inaccurate. See *Linpack, Dhrystones, Whetstones, Khornerstones* and *SPECmark*.

benign virus

A prank virus that does not destroy programs or data, but displays a message on screen either randomly or on a certain date to proclaim something such as "Peace on Earth" or "Happy Birthday to ..."

The Real Bell
Alexander Graham Bell was born in Scotland in 1847 and died in 1922. His famous sentence "Watson, come here, I want to see you," were the first words to travel over a wire, ringing the birth of electronic communications. *(Photo courtesy of AT&T.)*

Bento

A data structure used to store embedded documents in an OpenDoc compound document. Bento, which stands for lunch box in Japanese, provides a "container" to hold the data and a format for defining its contents.

BER

(1) (Basic Encoding Rules) One method for encoding information in the OSI environment. For example, it defines how Boolean data is coded.
(2) (Bit Error Rate) The average number of bits transmitted in error.

Berkeley extensions

See *BSD UNIX.*

Bernoulli Box

A removable disk drive for personal computers from Iomega Corporation, Roy, UT. It uses a type of floppy disk technology that provides hard disk speeds and a very reliable and transportable storage medium. The first Bernoulli Box in 1983 used a 10MB, 8" cartridge. In 1987, 20MB 5.25" cartridges were introduced and later 44MB and 90MB. The MultiDisk 150 drive accepts 35, 65, 90, 105 and 150MB cartridges. In 1994, the 230MB disk was introduced that is backward compatible to the 44MB disks. Bernoulli drives use the SCSI interface.

Unlike a hard disk in which the read/write head flies over a rigid disk, the Bernoulli floppy is spun at high speed and bends up close to the head. Upon power failure, a hard disk must retract the head to prevent a crash, whereas the Bernoulli floppy naturally bends down. See *Bernoulli principle* and *Zip disk.*

Bernoulli principle

The Swiss scientist, Daniel Bernoulli (1700-1782), demonstrated that, in most cases, the pressure in a fluid (air, water, gas, etc.) decreases as the fluid moves faster. This explains in part why a wing lifts an airplane and why a baseball curves.

Beta

The first home VCR format, called Betamax. Developed by Sony, it uses 1/2" tape cassettes. Beta Hi-fi added CD-quality audio, and SuperBeta improved the image. Today, VHS is the standard 1/2" VCR format, although Sony still makes Beta players.

beta test

A test of hardware or software that is performed by users under normal operating conditions. See *alpha test.*

betaware

Software in beta test that has been provided to a large number of users in advance of the formal release.

BeyondMail

A Windows-based mail program from Banyan Systems Inc., Westboro, MA, that works with Banyan's own Intelligent Messaging and Novell's MHS messaging systems. It includes a variety of pre-formatted message forms that can be programmed to access ODBC-compliant databases directly. It provides message distribution into selected folders, automatic filtering and forwarding and a tickler. An optional calendaring module is available.

Bezier curve

In computer graphics, a curve that is generated using a mathematical formula which assures continuity with other Bezier curves. It is mathematically simpler, but more difficult to blend than a b-spline curve. Within CAD and drawing programs, Bezier curves are typically reshaped by moving the handles that appear off of the curve.

BFT

(Binary File Transfer) An extension to the fax protocol that allows transmission of raw text instead of an image of the text document. The ability to transfer actual data similar to a common data modem provides a true e-mail capability via fax boards. A page of text (without graphics) is also transmitted faster that a bitmap of the page and is displayed at normal printer resolution at the receiving side.

bias

The voltage used to control or stabilize an electronic circuit.

BI bus

A proprietary high-speed bus used in the VAX series.

BICSI

(Building Industry Consulting Services International) A membership organization devoted to advancing its members in the field of distributing low-level electronics within a building. It publishes the Telecommunications Distribution Methods Manual and coordinates the testing for the RCDD (Registered Communications Distribution Designer), which is a certificate for excellence in telecommunications distribution design in commercial, campus and multi-family buildings.

bidirectional

The ability to move, transfer or transmit in both directions.

bidirectional printer

A printer that prints alternate lines from right to left.

bi-endian

The ability to switch between big endian and little endian ordering. For example, the PowerPC is a bi-endian CPU.

BIFF

(Binary Interchange File Format) A spreadsheet file format that holds data and charts, introduced with Excel Version 2.2.

bifurcate

To divide into two.

Big Blue

A nickname for IBM coined from the blue covers on most of its earlier mainframes.

big endian

The order of bytes in a word in which the most significant byte or digits are placed leftmost in the structure. This is the way humans deal with normal arithmetic. However, some CPUs are built using the little endian method, which is just the opposite and places the least significant digits on the left. Since numbers are calculated by the CPU starting with the least significant digits, little endian numbers are already set up for the required processing order.

A bi-endian machine, such as the PowerPC, is built to handle both types of byte ordering.

In the following example, the decimal number 23,041 (equivalent to 5A01 in hex) is shown in the big endian byte order and little endian byte order.

Big endian	Little endian
(Motorola 680x0)	(Intel x86)
5A01	015A

billion

One thousand times one million or 10 to the 9th power. See *giga* and *nanosecond.*

bill of materials

The list of components that make up a system. For example, a bill of materials for a house would include the cement block, lumber, shingles, doors, windows, plumbing, electric, heating and so on. Each subassembly also contains a bill of materials; the heating system is made up of the furnace, ducts, etc. A bill of materials "implosion" links component pieces to a major assembly, while a bill of materials "explosion" breaks apart each assembly or subassembly into its component parts.

The first hierarchical databases were developed for automating bills of materials for manufacturing organizations in the early 1960s.

bin

(BINary) A popular directory name for storing executable programs, device drivers, etc. (binary files).

binaries

Executable programs in machine language.

binary

Meaning two. The principle behind digital computers. All input to the computer is converted into binary numbers made up of the two digits 0 and 1 (bits). For example, when you press the "A" key on your personal computer, the keyboard generates and transmits the number 01000001 to the computer's memory as a series of pulses. The 1 bits are transmitted as high voltage; the 0 bits are transmitted as low. The bits are stored as charged and uncharged memory cells in the computer. On magnetic disk and tape, the bits are stored as positively and negatively charged spots. Display screens and printers convert the binary numbers into visual characters.

The electronic circuits that process these binary numbers are also binary in concept. They are made up of on/off switches (transistors) that are electrically opened and closed. The current flowing through one switch turns on (or off) another switch, and so on. These switches open and close in nanoseconds and picoseconds (billionths and trillionths of a second).

A computer's capability to do work is based on its storage capacity (memory and disk) and internal transmission speed. Greater storage capacities are achieved by making the memory cell or magnetic spot smaller. Faster transmission rates are achieved by shortening the time it takes to open and close the switch. In order to increase computer performance, we keep improving binary devices.

How Binary Numbers Work

Binary numbers are actually simpler than decimal numbers as they use only the digits 0 and 1 instead of 0 through 9.

In decimal, when you add 9 and 1, you get 10. But, if you break down the steps you find that by adding 9 and 1, what you get first is a result of 0 and a carry of 1. The carry of 1 is added to the digits in the next position on the left. In the following example, the carry becomes part of the answer since there are no other digits in that position.

```
carry - 1
        9
      + 1
       10
```

The following example adds 1 ten times in succession. Note that the binary method has more carries than the decimal method. In binary, 1 and 1 are 0 with a carry of 1.

Binary	Decimal	Binary	Decimal
0	0	101	5
+ 1	+ 1	+ 1	+ 1
1	1	110	6
+ 1	+ 1	+ 1	+ 1
10	2	111	7
+ 1	+ 1	+ 1	+ 1
11	3	1000	8
+ 1	+ 1	+ 1	+ 1
100	4	1001	9
+ 1	+ 1	+ 1	+ 1
101	5	1010	10

binary code

A coding system made up of binary digits. See *BCD, data code* and *numbers.*

binary coded decimal

See *BCD.*

binary compatible

Refers to any data, hardware or software structure (data file, machine code, instruction set, etc.) in binary form that is 100% identical to another. It most often refers to executable programs.

binary field

A field that contains binary numbers. It may refer to the storage of binary numbers for calculation purposes, or to a field that is capable of holding any information, including data, text, graphics images, voice and video. See *BLOB.*

binary file

(1) An executable program in machine language ready to run.
(2) A file that contains binary numbers.

binary file transfer

See *BFT.*

binary format

(1) Numbers stored in pure binary form in contrast with *BCD* form. See *binary numbers.*
(2) Information stored in a binary coded form, such as data, text, images, voice and video. See *binary file, binary field* and *BLOB.*
(3) A file transfer mode that transmits any type of file without loss of data.

binary notation

The use of binary numbers to represent values.

binary numbers
Numbers stored in pure binary form. Within one byte (8 bits), the values 0 to 255 can be held. Two contiguous bytes (16 bits) can hold values from 0 to 65,535.

binary search
A technique for quickly locating an item in a sequential list. The desired key is compared to the data in the middle of the list. The half that contains the data is then compared in the middle, and so on, either until the key is located or a small enough group is isolated to be sequentially searched.

binary synchronous
See *bisync.*

binary tree
A data structure in which each node contains one parent and no more than two children.

binary values
The maximum number of numeric combinations in a binary structure. The floppy disk and CD-ROM versions of this book contain a chart of binary numbers up to 1,099,511,627,776.

bind
(1) In programming, to link or assign one routine or address to another. The operation is accomplished by setting pointers or indexes to the appropriate locations in memory or disk or by copying codes from one variable into another. See *binding time* and *linkage editor.*
(2) In a network, to establish the connection between the network protocol and the transport protocol. Data flows from the application to the transport protocol to the network driver and then onto the network. Binding the protocols creates the pathway.

bindery
A NetWare file used for security and accounting in NetWare 2.x and 3.x. A bindery pertains only to the server it resides in and contains the names and passwords of users and groups of users authorized to log in to that server. It also holds information about other services provided by the server to the client (print, modem, gateway, etc.).
NDS (NetWare Directory Service) is the bindery counterpart in NetWare 4.x, but NDS is global oriented, manages multiple servers and provides a naming service, which the bindery does not. Bindery emulation software enables NetWare 2.x and 3.x clients to access services on NetWare 4.x servers. See *NDS.*

bindings
A set of linkages or assignments. See *bind.*

binding time
(1) In program compilation, the point in time when symbolic references to data are converted into physical machine addresses.
(2) In programming languages, when a variable is assigned its type (integer, string, etc.). Traditional compilers and assemblers provide early binding and assign types at compilation. Object-oriented languages provide late binding and assign types at runtime when the variable receives a value from the keyboard or other source.

biomechanics
The study of the anatomical principles of movement. Biomechanical applications on

the computer employ stick modeling to analyze the movement of athletes as well as racing horses.

bionic

A machine that is patterned after principles found in humans or nature; for example, robots. It also refers to artificial devices implanted into humans replacing or extending normal human functions.

BIOS

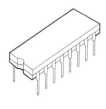

(Basic Input Output System) Detailed instructions that activate peripheral devices. Although BIOSs have been around for more than 30 years, today, the term generally refers to the BIOS in a PC, which holds certain fundamental parts of the operating system. A PC's BIOS has traditionally been stored in a permanent ROM chip and is often referred to as the ROM BIOS. Increasingly, the PC's BIOS is built into a flash memory chip, which can be updated in place by installing the latest version of the routines just like one updates a software application.

The motherboard contains a system BIOS, and expansion cards often have their own BIOSs. The system BIOS includes routines for the keyboard, screen, disk, parallel and serial port and for internal services such as time and date. It accepts requests from the device drivers in the operating system as well as from application programs. It also contains an autostart routine that tests the system on startup and prepares the computer for operation. It searches for BIOSes on the plug-in boards and sets up pointers (interrupt vectors) in memory to access BIOS routines. It then loads the operating system and passes control to it.

System BIOSs prior to 1990 may not be compatible with new software and peripherals. In order to use devices such as 3.5" diskettes, 101-key keyboards, IDE and Enhanced IDE drives as well as provide compatibility with Windows, NetWare and other applications, you can upgrade an older PC with a new BIOS. The following firms specialize in BIOS upgrades:

UNICORE SOFTWARE   800/800-BIOS
1538 Turnpike St.
N. Andover, MA 01845

UPGRADES, ETC.   800/955-3527
2432-A Palma Drive
Ventura, CA 93003

bipolar

A category of high-speed microelectronic circuit design, which was used to create the first transistor and the first integrated circuit. The most common variety of bipolar chip is TTL (transistor transistor logic). Emitter coupled logic (ECL) and integrated injection logic (I2L) are also part of the bipolar family.

Today, bipolar and CMOS are the two major transistor technologies. Most all personal computers use CMOS, and even large mainframes that have traditionally used bipolar have given way to CMOS designs. CMOS uses far less energy than bipolar.

However, bipolar transistors are still widely used for high radio frequency (RF) applications that reach into the gigahertz range, which CMOS technology cannot handle.

The bipolar transistor works by pulsing a line called the *base*, which allows current to flow from the *emitter* to the *collector*, or vice versa depending on the design.

bipolar transmission

A digital transmission technique that alternates between positive and negative signals. The 1s and 0s are determined by varying amplitudes at both polarities while non-data is zero amplitude.

BIPS

(Billion Instructions Per Second) See *MIPS*.

biquinary code

Meaning two-five code. A system for storing decimal digits in a four-bit binary number.

birefringence

Using a crystal to split light into two frequencies that travel at different speeds and at right angles to each other. It's used to filter out a color in an LCD display.

bis

Second version. It means twice in Old Latin, or encore in French. Ter means three. For example, V.27bis and V.27ter are the second and third versions of the V.27 standard.

B/ISDN

(Broadband/ISDN) See *ISDN* and *ATM*.

bison

The Free Software Foundation's version of yacc.

bistable circuit

Same as *flip-flop*.

bisync

(BInary SYNChronous) A major category of synchronous communications protocols used in mainframe networks. Bisync communications require that both sending and receiving devices are synchronized before transmission of data is started. Contrast with *asynchronous* transmission.

bisynchronous

See *bisync*.

bit

(BInary digiT) The smallest element of computer storage. It is a single digit in a binary number (0 or 1). The bit is physically a transistor or capacitor in a memory cell, a magnetic spot on disk or tape or a high or low voltage pulsing through a circuit.

Groups of bits make up storage units in the computer, called characters, bytes, or words, which are manipulated as a group. The most common is the byte, made up of eight bits and equivalent to one alphanumeric character.

Bits are widely used as a measurement for transmission. Ten megabits per second means that ten million pulses are transmitted per second. A 16-bit bus means that there are 16 wires transmitting the bit at the same time.

Measurements for storage devices, such as disks, files and databases, are given in bytes rather than bits. See *space/time*.

The Bits and Bytes

The Bit   0   1   **The Byte**

The smallest element of computer storage and transmission is the binary digit, or bit, based on the binary numbering system. The 0s and 1s are charged and uncharged cells in memory or magnetic spots of positive and negative polarity on disk and tape.

Eight binary digits make up the standard unit of storage called a byte. A byte is always eight bits.

The Spot Gets Smaller...

Bits on magnetic disk

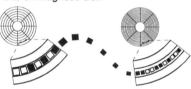

Bits on magnetic tape

The smaller the bit, the higher the storage capacity.

The Switch Opens/Closes Faster...

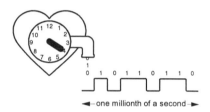

0 1 0 1 1 0 1 1 0

◄— one millionth of a second —►

0 1 0 1 0 1 0 1 1 1 0 0 1 0 1 1 0 1 0

Bits and Bytes
The language of the
21st century!

bitblit

See *bitblt*.

bitblt

(**BIT**BLock Transfer) In computer graphics, a hardware feature that moves a rectangular block of bits from main memory into display memory. It speeds the display of moving objects (animation, scrolling) on screen.

A hardware bitblt provides fastest speed, but bitblts are also implemented in software even in non-graphics systems. For example, text scrolls faster when it is copied as a contiguous block (bitblt) to the next part of the window rather than processing every character on every line. See *stretch blt*.

bit cell

A boundary in which a single bit is recorded on a tape or disk.

bit density

The number of bits that can be stored within a given physical area.

bit depth

(1) The number of bits used to hold a pixel. Also called *color depth* and *pixel depth*, the bit depth determines the number of colors that can be displayed at one time. Digital video requires at least 15 bits, while 24 bits produces realistic TV-like colors.

Color depth	Total number of colors
4-bits	16
8-bits	256
15-bits	32,768
16-bits	65,536
24-bits	16,777,216
32-bits	16,777,216 + alpha channel

(2) Bit depth can refer to any coding system that uses numeric values to represent something. The depth, or number of bits, determines how many discrete items can be represented.

bite

See *byte*.

bit error rate

See *BER*.

bit flipping

Same as *bit manipulation*.

bit level device

A device, such as a disk drive, that inputs and outputs data bits. Contrast with *pulse level device*.

bit manipulation

Processing individual bits within a byte. Bit-level manipulation is very low-level programming, often done in graphics and systems programming.

bitmap

A binary representation in which a bit or set of bits corresponds to some part of an object such as an image or font. For example, in monochrome systems, one bit represents one pixel on screen. For gray scale or color, several bits in the bitmap represent one pixel or group of pixels. The term may also refer to the memory area that holds the bitmap.

A bitmap is usually associated with graphics objects, in which the bits are a direct representation of the picture image. However, bitmaps can be used to represent and keep track of anything, where each bit location is assigned a different value or condition.

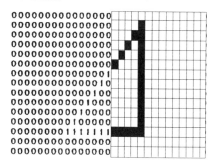

A Monochrome Bitmap
The left half of this diagram shows the bits in the bitmap, and the right half depicts what would show on screen. In monochrome systems, one bit is used to represent one pixel. Images that are scanned into the computer are turned into bitmaps, and bitmaps can be created in a paint program.

bitmap file
See *BMP*.

bitmapped font
A set of dot patterns for each letter and digit in a particular typeface (Times Roman, Helvetica, etc.) for a specified type size (10 points, 12 points, etc.). Bitmapped typefaces are either purchased in groups of pre-generated point sizes, or, for a wide supply of fonts, font generators allow the user to create a variety of point sizes. Bitmapped fonts take up disk space for each point size. Contrast with *scalable font*. See *font* and *font generator*.

bitmapped graphics
The raster graphics method for generating images. Contrast with *vector graphics* and *character graphics*.

BITNET
A worldwide communications network founded in 1981 that primarily serves higher education and research. It uses the NJE protocol for e-mail, file transfers and short messages. Well known for its LISTSERV software for managing electronic mailing lists, BITNET was for many years the world's largest computer-based, higher-education network. It is gradually being supplanted by the Internet.

bit-oriented protocol
A communications protocol that uses individual bits within the byte as control codes, such as IBM's SDLC. Contrast with *byte-oriented protocol*.

bit parallel
The transmission of several bits at the same time, each bit travelling over a different wire in the cable.

bit pattern
A specific layout of binary digits.

bit plane
A segment of memory used to control an object, such as a color, cursor or sprite. Bit planes may be reserved parts of a common memory or independent memory banks each designed for one purpose.

bit rate
The transmission speed of binary coded data. Same as *data rate*.

bit serial
The transmission of one bit after the other on a single line or wire.

bit slice processor
A logic chip that is used as an elementary building block for the computer designer. Bit slice processors usually come in 4-bit increments and are strung together to make larger processors (8 bit, 12 bit, etc.).

bit specifications
Everything in the digital world is measured in bits and bytes. Bits are a measurement of different components and functions depending on what is being referenced. Following are the most common. See also *binary values*.

(1) The size of the computer's internal word, or registers, which is the amount of data the CPU can compute at the same time. If the clock rates are the same (50MHz, 100MHz, etc.) and the basic architectures are equal, a 32-bit computer works twice as fast internally as a 16-bit computer.

(2) The size of the computer's data bus, which is the pathway over which data is transferred between memory and the CPU and between memory and the peripheral devices. If the bus clock rates are equal, a 16-bit bus transfers data twice as fast as an 8-bit bus.

(3) The size of the address bus, which determines how much memory the CPU can address directly. Each bit doubles the number, for example, 20-bits addresses 1,048,576 bytes; 24-bits addresses 16,772,216 bytes.

(4) The number of colors that can be displayed at one time. This is called *bit depth, color depth* and *pixel depth*. Unless some of the memory is used for cursor or sprite movement, an 8-bit display adapter generates 256 colors; 16-bit, 64K colors; 24-bit, 16.8 million colors. See *alpha channel* and *bit depth*.

Bit specifications, such as 64-bit and 128-bit, refer to the display adapter's architecture, which affects speed, not the number of colors. See *64-bit graphics accelerator* and *128-bit graphics accelerator*.

(5) The quality of sound based on the number of bits in the samples taken. A 16-bit sample yields a number with 65,536 increments compared to 256 in an 8-bit sample. See *8-bit sample* and *16-bit sample*.

bit stream
The transmission of binary signals.

bit stuffing
Adding bits to a transmitted message in order to round out a fixed frame or to break up a pattern of data bits that could be misconstrued for control codes.

bit twiddler
Same as *hacker*.

bit wise
See *bitwise* and *bit manipulation*.

bitwise

Dealing with bits rather than larger structures such as a byte. Bitwise operators are programming commands or statements that work with individual bits. See *bit manipulation*.

BIX

(Byte Information eXchange, 1030 Massachusetts Ave., Cambridge, MA 02138, 800/695-4775, 617/491-3393) An online database of computer knowledge from BYTE magazine, designed to help users fix problems and obtain info on hardware and software products. See *online services*.

bixie

See *BICSI*.

Black Apple

An early Apple II+ with a black case and external audio controls. Bell and Howell sold them in a training kit.

black box

A custom-made electronic device, such as a protocol converter or encryption system. Yesterday's black boxes often become today's off-the-shelf products.

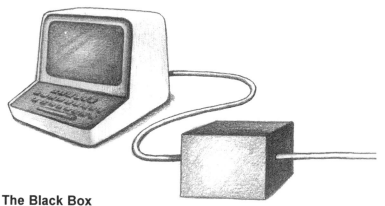

The Black Box
A black box doesn't have to look like a box. It can be any contraption that is custom made for an application.

Black Box Corporation

(Black Box Corporation, Pittsburgh, PA) An organization that specializes in communications and LAN products. It offers expert services, custom solutions and hard-to-find products.

blank character

A space character that takes up one byte in the computer just like a letter or digit. When you press the space bar on a personal computer keyboard, the ASCII character with a numeric value of 32 is created.

blank squash

The removal of blanks between items of data. For example, in the expression **CITY + ", " + STATE**, the data is concatenated with a blank squash resulting in DALLAS, TX rather than DALLAS   TX.

bleed

Printing at the very edge of the paper. Many laser printers, including all LaserJets up to the 11x17" 4V, cannot print to the very edge, leaving a border of approximately 1/4". In commercial printing, bleeding is generally more expensive, because wider paper is often used, which is later cut to size.

Blenheim shows

The Blenheim Group is a major producer of trade shows and organizes more than 40 information technology expositions around the world. Annual attendance is over 600,000 for all shows according to Blenheim's news release in 1994. PC EXPO is its largest computer show. For more information, contact The Blenheim Group PLC, One Executive Drive, Fort Lee, NJ 07024, 800/829-3976.

blip

A mark, line or spot on a medium, such as microfilm, that is optically sensed and used for timing or counting purposes.

blit

See *bitblt*.

blitting

Using a bitblt to transfer data.

BLOB

(Binary Large OBject) A database field that holds any digitized information. This is one method of storing multimedia objects (audio, video) in a DBMS, since it holds any binary data. However, most relational DBMSs are better suited to small fields typical of transaction data, such as name, amount, etc. The object-oriented DBMS is more efficient for managing the storage of long, linear amounts of data. See *object-oriented DBMS*.

block

(1) A group of disk or tape records that is stored and transferred as a single unit.
(2) A group of bits or characters that is transmitted as a unit.
(3) A group of text characters that has been marked for moving, copying, saving or other operation.

block device

A peripheral device that transfers a group of bytes (block, sector, etc.) of data at a time such as a disk. Contrast with *character device*.

block diagram

A chart that contains squares and rectangles connected with arrows to depict hardware and software interconnections. For program flow charts, information system flow charts, circuit diagrams and communications networks, more elaborate graphical representations are usually used.

Block diagram of a computer

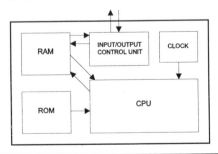

blocking factor
The number of records in a block.

block move
The ability to mark a contiguous segment of text or data and move it.

blow
To write code or data into a PROM chip by blowing the fuses of the 0 bits. The 1 bits are left alone.

blow up
Same as *crash*, *bomb* or *abend*.

blue laser
A type of laser capable of writing bits with up to five times greater density than the infrared lasers commonly used. In 1993, IBM demonstrated a recording density of 2.5 billion bits per square inch on a magneto-optic disk. It is expected that blue lasers will be commercially used in a few years.

Blue Lightning
IBM's clock tripling version of the 486. The first model released at the end of 1993 is a 25MHz 486 with an internal speed of 75MHz.

blue screen
See *color key*.

BMP
(Bit MaP) A Windows and OS/2 raster graphics format that may be device dependent or independent. Device independent BMP files (DIB files) are coded for translation to a wide variety of displays and printers.

BNC connector

(British Naval Connector) A commonly used connector for coaxial cable. The plug looks like a tiny tin can with the lid off and two short pins sticking out on the upper edge on opposite sides. After insertion, the plug is turned, tightening the pins in the socket.

board
See *printed circuit board* and *BBS*.

board level
Electronic components that are mounted on a printed circuit board instead of in a cabinet or finished housing.

Bob
See *Microsoft Bob*.

BOC
(Bell Operating Company) One of 22 telephone companies that was formerly part of AT&T and now part of one of the seven regional Bell telephone companies.

BOCOEX
(BOston COmputer EXchange) See *computer exchange*.

body type

The typeface and size commonly used for text in paragraph copy. Typically 10 points.

BOF

(Beginning Of File) The status of a file when it is first opened or when an instruction or command has reset the file pointer.

boilerplate

A common phrase or expression used over and over. Boilerplate is stored on disk and copied into the document as needed.

boldface

Characters that are heavier and darker on printed output and brighter than normal on a display screen.

boldface attribute

A code that turns normal characters into boldface characters on a printer or display screen.

boldface font

A set of type characters that are darker and heavier than normal type. In a boldface font, all characters have been designed as bold characters.

bomb

Same as *abend* and *crash*.

BOMP

(Bill Of Materials Processor) One of the first DBMSs used for bill of materials explosion in the early 1960s from IBM. A subsequent version, DBOMP, was used in manufacturing during the 1970s.

Booch

An object-oriented analysis and design method developed by Grady Booch, chief scientist of Rational Software. See *object references* and *Rational Rose*.

books

See *how to find a good computer book*.

Boolean data

Yes/no or true/false data.

Boolean expression

A statement using Boolean operators that expresses a condition which is either true or false.

Boolean logic

The "mathematics of logic," developed by English mathematician George Boole in the mid 19th century. Its rules govern logical functions (true/false). As add, subtract, multiply and divide are the primary operations of arithmetic, AND, OR and NOT are the primary operations of Boolean logic. *(See illustrations on pages 84 and 85.)*

Boolean operator

One of the Boolean logic operators such as AND, OR and NOT.

Boolean search

A search for specific data. It implies that any condition can be searched for using the Boolean operators AND, OR and NOT. For example, the English language request: "Search for all Spanish and French speaking employees who have MBAs, but don't work in Sales." is expressed in the following dBASE command:

```
list for degree = "MBA" .and.
  (language = "Spanish" .or. language = "French")
    .and. .not. department = "Sales"
```

**You Need Help
to Get Started**

boot

Causing the computer to start executing instructions. Personal computers contain built-in instructions in a ROM chip that are automatically executed on startup. These instructions search for the operating system, load it and pass control to it. Starting up a large computer may require more button pushing and keyboard input. The term comes from "bootstrap," since bootstraps help you get your boots on, booting the computer helps it get its first instructions. The term is often used erroneously for application software. You might hear for example, "let's boot WordPerfect," whereas the correct usage is "load WordPerfect." See *cold boot, warm boot* and *clean boot*.

bootable disk

A disk that contains the operating system in a form ready to load into the computer. It often refers to a floppy disk that contains the operating system in its boot sectors. If a hard disk personal computer does not find a bootable floppy disk in the primary floppy drive at startup (A: in a PC), it boots from the hard disk.

It's a good idea to make a bootable disk for your personal computer in case the hard disk doesn't boot some day. That way, you'll be able to start the computer and access important data.

boot drive

A disk drive that contains the operating system.

boot failure

The inability to locate and/or read the operating system from the designated disk.

boot record

See *boot sector*.

boot ROM

A memory chip that allows a workstation to be booted from the server or other remote station.

boot sector

An area on disk (usually the first sectors in the first disk partition) reserved for the operating system. On startup, the computer looks in the boot sectors for the operating system, which must be loaded first.

bootstrap

See *boot*.

boot virus

A virus written into the boot sectors of a floppy disk. If the floppy is booted, it

Boolean Logic

If you really want to know what goes on inside a computer chip, you can trace the flow of current through a circuit yourself. Start with the rules for the fundamental building blocks known as **AND**, **OR** and **NOT**.

AND accepts two inputs and one output. If both inputs are true (1), the output is true (1). **OR** requires only one input to be true in order to produce output. **NOT** reverses the input. If a 1 comes in, a 0 goes out, and vice versa. These **AND**, **OR** and **NOT** rules are created in silicon by wiring transistors in different patterns (series, parallel, etc.). Look at the diagrams for these gates, and see if you follow how the opening and closing of switches causes these rules to be satisfied.

AND
A pulse on the input line causes the switch to close, allowing current to flow from the electrical source to the output.

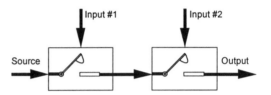

OR
A pulse on the input line causes the switch to close, allowing current to flow from the electrical source to the output.

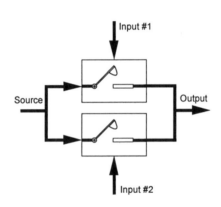

NOT
A pulse on the input line causes switch #1 to close. Current goes through switch #1 to switch #2, which works the opposite of switch #1. It is normally closed, but when pulsed, it opens. Since, it is open, the output is 0. A 1 creates a 0. If there is no pulse on the input line, the **NOT** generates output because switch #2 is normally closed, and current flows

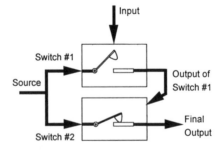

The transistors make up gates (**AND** gates, **OR** gates, etc.), and gates make up circuits. Circuits make up a logical device, such as a CPU. (See *The Formation of One Transistor*)

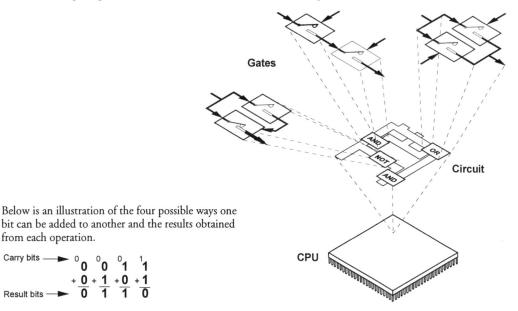

Gates

Circuit

CPU

Below is an illustration of the four possible ways one bit can be added to another and the results obtained from each operation.

Carry bits ⟶

$$
\begin{array}{cccc}
0 & 0 & 0 & 1 \\
\mathbf{0} & \mathbf{0} & \mathbf{1} & \mathbf{1} \\
\mathbf{+0} & \mathbf{+1} & \mathbf{+0} & \mathbf{+1} \\
\hline
\mathbf{0} & \mathbf{1} & \mathbf{1} & \mathbf{0}
\end{array}
$$

Result bits ⟶

The following illustrations will allow you to trace the flow of electricity through a half-adder circuit, a fundamental circuit that simply adds one bit to another. There are two outputs from this circuit, the result bit and the carry bit.

Trace the current throught the following example, which adds a 0 and a 1. The 1 is represented by the dark line (flow of current), the 0 by no line (no current). If it makes sense to you, try to simulate the flow of current through the circuit path that is empty.

See how the **AND**, **OR** and **NOT** gates react to their inputs.

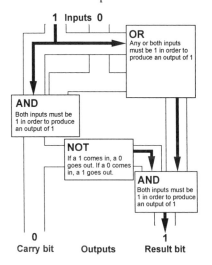

Try This!
(a) Start with any two inputs (0 and 1, 1 and 1, or 0 and 0). If a bit is zero, draw nothing. If it is a 1, draw a line to the first **OR** and **AND** gate.

(b) Determine the output of the **AND**. Draw a line if it is a 1, or nothing if it is a 0, to the **NOT** and to the carry result.

(c) Determine the output from the **NOT** to the second **AND** gate.

(d) Determine the output of the second **AND** gate, and that is the result bit.

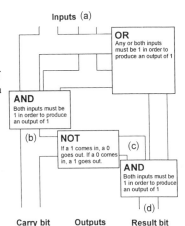

infects the system. For example, the Michelangelo virus, which destroys data on March 6th, Michelangelo's birthday, infects a computer if the virus diskette is left in the drive and booted inadvertently when the computer is turned back on.

Borland

(Borland International, Inc., Scotts Valley, CA) A software company, founded in 1983 by Philippe Kahn, that is noted for its database and language products. Borland's Sidekick was the first PC desktop accessory program, which popularized TSRs for DOS applications.

Its Turbo Pascal moved Pascal out of the academic halls into a commercial product, and its Turbo C became an industry standard for DOS. Borland's C++ is widely used for developing Windows applications.

With Borland's acquisition of Ansa's Paradox in 1987 and Ashton-Tate's dBASE in 1991, it became the leader in PC database software. In 1994, it sold its Quattro Pro spreadsheet to WordPerfect and introduced dBASE for Windows. In early 1995, Kahn resigned as president and CEO, remaining as chairman. See *Borland Database Engine*.

Philippe Kahn
(Photo courtesy of Borland International.)

Borland C++

An ANSI C and C++ compiler from Borland for DOS and Windows applications. It is Turbo C-compatible and its debugger supports Windows programs written in Microsoft C. It includes application frameworks for Windows (ObjectWindows) and DOS (Turbo Vision). Borland C++ for OS/2 is also available.

Borland Database Engine

Software from Borland that runs on a Windows client and unifies database access across multiple platforms. It is packaged separately as well as with dBASE for Windows and Paradox for Windows. It allows dBASE and Paradox applications, as well as C++ applications written to the IDAPI programming interface, to access local dBASE and Paradox files and to access remote Oracle, Sybase, Informix and Interbase servers. It also provides an ODBC socket to connect an ODBC driver for remote access to any ODBC-compliant database (DB2, Btrieve, etc.).

boss screen

A fake business-like screen that can be quickly popped up over a game when the boss walks in. Boss screens are typically used with DOS games as there is no standard way to switch applications under DOS. With Windows, a user can easily press Alt-Tab and switch between Solitaire and programming as in the following example.

Boston Computer Exchange
See *computer exchange*.

Boston Computer Society
See *BCS*.

Boundary Routing
3Com's trade name for remote office routing, which it pioneered. See *remote-office router*.

Bourne shell
See *UNIX*.

bpi
(Bits Per Inch) The measurement of the number of bits stored in a linear inch of a track on a recording surface, such as on a disk or tape.

BPR
(Business Process Reengineering) See *reengineering*.

B protocol
A file transfer protocol from CompuServe. Quick B is a faster version only for downloading. Later versions of B will automatically select Quick B.

bps
(Bits Per Second) The measurement of the speed of data transfer in a communications system.

braces
Symbols used in programming and other technical references to mark the beginning and end of a contained area. They are the { and } characters.

brains
A computer's "brains" are its central processing unit. See *CPU*.

branch
(1) Same as *goto*.
(2) A connection between two blocks in a flowchart or two nodes in a network.

braze
To solder using metals with a very high melting point, such as with an alloy of zinc and copper.

BRB
Digispeak for "be right back."

Breadboard
(Photo Courtesy of 3M Company.)

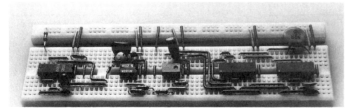

breadboard
A thin plastic board full of holes used to hold components (transistors, chips, etc.) that are wired together. It is used to develop electronic prototypes or one-of-a-kind systems.

break

To temporarily or permanently stop executing, printing or transmitting.

break key

A keyboard key that is pressed to stop the execution of the current program or transmission.

breakout box

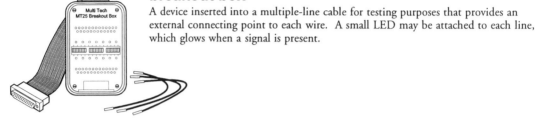

A device inserted into a multiple-line cable for testing purposes that provides an external connecting point to each wire. A small LED may be attached to each line, which glows when a signal is present.

breakpoint

The location in a program used to temporarily halt the program for testing and debugging. Lines of code in a source program are marked for break points. When those instructions are about to be executed, the program stops, allowing the programmer to examine the status of the program (registers, variables, etc.). After inspection, the programmer can step through the program one line at a time or cause the program to continue running either to the end or to the next break point, whichever comes first.

BRI

See *ISDN.*

bridge

(1) To cross from one circuit, channel or element over to another.
(2) A device that connects two LAN segments together, which may be of similar or dissimilar types, such as Ethernet and Token Ring. Bridges are inserted into a network to improve performance by keeping traffic contained within smaller segments.

Bridges maintain address tables of the nodes on the network through experience. They learn which addresses were successfully received through which output ports by monitoring which station acknowledged receipt of the address.

Bridges work at the data link layer (OSI layer 2), whereas routers work at the network layer (layer 3). Bridges are protocol independent; routers are protocol dependent. Bridges are faster than routers because they do not have to read the protocol to glean routing information. See *transparent bridge, repeater, router, gateway* and *hub.*

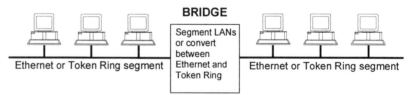

BRIDGE

| Ethernet or Token Ring segment | Segment LANs or convert between Ethernet and Token Ring | Ethernet or Token Ring segment |

bridge router

A communications device that provides the functions of a bridge and router. See *bridge* and *router.*

bridgeware

Hardware or software that converts data or translates programs from one format into another.

Brief

A text editor for PC programming from Borland. It provides automatic indentation and the ability to edit different parts of a source program at the same time.

Briefcase

In Windows 95, a system folder used for synchronizing files between two computers, typically a desktop and laptop computer. Files to be worked on are placed into a Briefcase, which is then transferred to the second machine via floppy, cable or network. The Briefcase is then brought back to the original machine after its contents have been edited on the second machine, and a special update function replaces the original files with the new ones.

brightness

The light level on a display screen. Contrast with *contrast*.

British Telecom

The telephone and communications carrier that provides services in Great Britain and Northern Ireland. It used to be a division of the British Post Office.

broadband

(1) A technique for transmitting data, voice and video over long distances. Using high frequency transmission over coaxial cable or optical fibers, broadband transmission requires modems for connecting terminals and computers to the network. Using the same FDM (frequency division multiplexing) technique as cable TV, several streams of data can be transmitted simultaneously. Contrast with *baseband*.

(2) High-speed transmission. The term is commonly used to refer to high-speed networks in general, typically at T1 rates and above. Used in this context, it has no bearing on broadband versus baseband technologies as described in definition (1) above. It is thus broadband versus lower-speed transmission, which is sometimes referenced as narrowband and wideband.

broadband ISDN

See *ISDN*.

broadcast

To disseminate information to several recipients simultaneously.

broadcast storm

Excessive tranmission of address resolution requests in a network. It can occur when multiple routers come online or synchronize themselves simultaneously, each trying to identify all the connected nodes in the network. Broadcast storms can be lessened by properly designing and balancing the number of nodes on each network segment.

Brooklyn Bridge

A PC file transfer program from Fifth Generation Systems, Baton Rouge, LA, that transfers data between laptops and desktop computers.

brouter

(Bridging ROUTER) See *bridge router*.

browse
(1) To view the contents of a file or a group of files. Browser programs generally let you view data by scrolling through the documents or databases. In a database program, the browse mode often lets you edit the data. See *Web browser*.
(2) To view and edit a flow chart of a system created in a program specialized for visual system design or to view and edit a class hierarchy of objects in an object-oriented programming language.
(3) In Windows 3.1, the Browse button lets you view the file names in your disk directories. Clicking on the names of the drives and directories switches you to those locations.

browser
A program that lets you look through data. See *Web browser* and *browse*.

BSC
(Binary Synchronous Communications) See *bisync*.

BSD socket
A communications interface in UNIX first introduced in BSD UNIX. See *UNIX socket*.

BSD UNIX
(Berkeley Software Distribution UNIX) A version of UNIX developed by the Computer Systems Research Group of the University of California at Berkeley from 1979 to 1993. BSD enhancements, known as the "Berkeley Extensions," include networking, virtual memory, task switching and large file names (up to 255 chars.). BSD's UNIX was distributed free, with a charge only for the media. USL code is contained in most BSD versions, and users require a valid USL license in such cases. Bill Joy ran the group until 1982 when he co-founded Sun Microsystems, bringing 4.2BSD with him as the foundation of SunOS. The last BSD version released by BSD is 4.4BSD.
BSDI (Berkeley Software Design, Inc.) a private company founded in 1991 and headquartered in Falls Church, VA, continues to develop BSD code. In 1993, BSDI offers a complete version of BSD's NET 2 for x86 machines, which contains no USL code and includes some GNU and other utilities. Other platforms are forthcoming.

b-spline
In computer graphics, a curve that is generated using a mathematical formula which assures continuity with other b-splines.

BT
See *British Telecom*.

BTA
(Business Technology Association, 12411 Wornall Road, Kansas City, MO 64145, 816/941-3100) A membership association of office equipment dealers founded in 1994. It is a merger of NOMDA (National Office Machine Dealers Association), founded in 1926, with LANDA and AIMED (LAN Dealers Association and Affiliated Independent Mailing Equipment Dealers). Publications, training seminars and conferences are provided for members.

BTAM
(Basic Telecommunications Access Method) IBM communications software used in bisynch, non-SNA mainframe networks. Application programs must interface directly with the BTAM access method.

BT font

(BitsTream font) Refers to fonts from Bitstream Inc., Cambridge, MA. See *FaceLift* and *FontWare*.

BTLZ

(British Telecom Lempel Ziv) A data compression algorithm based on the Lempel-Ziv method that can achieve up to 4x the throughput of 2400 and 9600 bps modems.

BTOS

Burroughs' version of CTOS.

B-tree

(Balanced-tree) A technique for organizing indexes. In order to keep access time to a minimum, it stores the data keys in a balanced hierarchy that continually realigns itself as items are inserted and deleted. Thus, all nodes always have a similar number of keys.

B+tree is a version of B-tree that maintains a hierarchy of indexes while also linking the data sequentially, providing fast direct access and fast sequential access. IBM's VSAM uses this.

Btrieve

A file manager from Novell that accompanies its NetWare operating systems. It allows for the creation of indexed files, using the b-tree organization method. Btrieve functions can be called from within many common programming languages. See *Xtrieve*.

BTW

Digispeak for "by the way."

bubble

A bit in bubble memory or a symbol in a bubble chart.

bubble chart

A chart that uses bubble-like symbols often used to depict data flow diagrams.

Bubble Jet

Canon's ink jet printer technology.

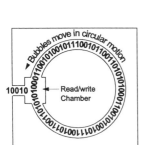

bubble memory

A solid state semiconductor and magnetic storage device suited for rugged applications. It is about as fast as a slow hard disk and holds its content without power.

It is conceptually a stationary disk with spinning bits. The unit, only a couple of square inches in size, contains a thin film magnetic recording layer. Globular-shaped bubbles (bits) are electromagnetically generated in circular strings inside this layer. In order to read or write the bubbles, they are rotated past the equivalent of a read/write head.

bubble sort

A multiple-pass sorting technique that starts by sequencing the first two items, then the second with the third, then the third with the fourth and so on until the end of the set has been reached. The process is repeated until all items are in the correct sequence.

bucket

Another term for a variable. It's just a place to store something.

buckyballs

A type of carbon, identified in 1985, that has potential as a superconductor. It is one of a group of "buckminsterfullerenes," named after R. Buckminster Fuller, because of its molecular similarity to his geodesic domes.

buffer

A reserved segment of memory used to hold data while it is being processed. In a program, buffers are created to hold some amount of data from each of the files that will be read or written. A buffer may also be a small hardware memory bank used for special purposes.

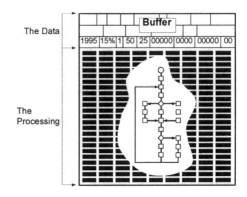

buffer flush

The transfer of data from memory to disk. Whenever you command your application to save the document you're working on, the program is actually flushing its buffer (writing the contents of one or more reserved areas of memory to the hard disk).

Go Flush Your Cold Buffer!

Try this one out on your colleagues. A cold buffer is a reserved area of memory that contains data, which hasn't been updated for a while. Cold buffers are flushed at periodic intervals. More importantly, this phrase sounds as strange as they get. Better yet, try "go flush your cold buffer into your SCSI DASD" (pronounced scuzzy dazdy). Be sure to say this without cracking a smile, and expect quite a grin from a systems professional. If your friend doesn't understand this phrase, be sure to recommend a good computer dictionary!

buffer pool

An area of memory reserved for buffers.

bug

A persistent error in software or hardware. If the bug is in software, it can be corrected by changing the program. If the bug is in hardware, new circuits have to be designed.

Although the derivation of bug is generally attributed to the moth that was found squashed between the points of an electromechanical relay in a computer in the 1940s, the term was already in use in the late 1800s. See *software bug*. Contrast with *glitch*.

A Note from the Author

On October 19, 1992, I found my first "real bug." When I fired up my laser printer, it printed blotchy pages. Upon inspection, I found a bug lying belly up in the trough below the corona wire. The printer worked fine after removing it!

bug compatible

A hardware device that contains the same design flaws as the original.

bulk storage

Storage that is not used for high-speed execution. May refer to auxiliary memory, tape or disk.

bulletin board

See *BBS*.

Bull HN

(Bull HN Information Systems Inc., Billerica, MA) The American subsidiary of the French company, Compagnie des Machines Bull (CMB), founded in 1932. The HN stands for Honeywell and NEC, which were partners in joint development that had varying amounts of ownership until 1991.

CMB has been a major computer company in Europe with partnerships and alliances throughout the world. Honeywell, a temperature control company founded in 1927, became one of the first computer companies in the U.S. when it created its computer division in 1957. It later acquired GE's computer division. When Honeywell withdrew from the computer business, Bull took over the activities of its American partner.

Today, Bull offers networking and integration services and a range of computer systems from workstation to mainframe. A complete line of PCs is also available through the Zenith Data Systems subsidiary, which CMB acquired in 1989.

bump file

(BuMP file) See *BMP*.

bump mapping

In computer graphics, a technique for simulating rough textures by creating irregularities in shading.

BUNCH

(Burroughs, Univac, NCR, Control Data and Honeywell) IBM's competitors after RCA and GE got out of the computer business.

bundle

To sell hardware and software as a single product or to combine several software packages for sale as a single unit. Contrast with *unbundle*.

bunny suit

The protective clothing worn by an individual in a clean room that keeps human bacteria from infecting the chip-making process. The outfit makes people look like oversized rabbits.

Bunny Suit
(Photo courtesy of Hewlett-Packard Company.)

burn in

To test a new electronic system by running it for some length of time. Weak components often fail within the first few hours of use.

burster

A mechanical device that separates continuous paper forms into cut sheets. A burster can be attached to the end of a collator, which separates multipart forms into single parts.

burst mode

A high-speed transmission mode in a communications or computer channel. Under certain conditions, the system sends a burst of data at higher speed. For example, a multiplexor channel may suspend transmitting several streams of data and send one high-speed transmission using the entire bandwidth.

bursty

Refers to data that is transferred or transmitted in short, uneven spurts. LAN traffic is typically bursty. Contrast with *streaming data.*

bus

A common pathway, or channel, between multiple devices. Buses are generally hardware, although software can be designed and linked via a so called "software bus."

The computer's internal bus is known as the local bus, or processor bus. It connects the CPU to its main memory and to other buses. In a PC, the local bus connects to the ISA, EISA and Micro Channel buses, which run at slow speeds compared to the CPU. It also connects to the higher-speed PCI and VL-bus buses, which are also called *local buses.* Examples of other computer buses used in the industry are NuBus, TURBOchannel, VMEbus, MULTIBUS and STD bus.

A computer bus provides parallel data transfer; for example, a 16-bit bus transfers two bytes at a time over 16 wires, a 32-bit bus uses 32 wires, etc. The bus is comprised of two parts: the address bus and the data bus. Addresses are sent over the address bus to signal a memory location, and the data is transferred over the data bus to that location.

Another common use of a bus is a network bus. For example, Ethernet uses a serial bus, which is a common cable connecting all stations. Data is transmitted serially (one bit after the other) over the cable. A data packet, which contains the address of the destination station, is broadcast to all nodes at the same time, and the recipient computer responds by accepting it.

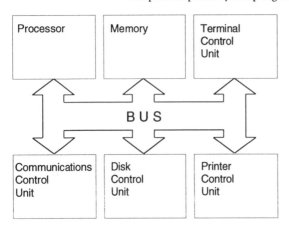

Why Is It Called a Bus?
The term was coined after a real bus, because a bus stops at all the bus stops on the route. The same goes for an electronic bus. All signals on the bus go to all stations or devices connected to it.

bus bridge

A device that connects two similar or dissimilar busses together, such as two VMEbuses or a VMEbus and a Futurebus. This is not the same as a communications bridge, which connects network segments together. See *bridge*.

bus card

An expansion board (card) that plugs into the computer's expansion bus.

bus extender

(1) A board that pushes a printed circuit board out of the way of surrounding boards for testing purposes. It plugs into an expansion slot, and the expansion board plugs into the bus extender.

(2) A device that extends the physical distance of a bus. See *repeater*.

(3) A device that increases the number of expansion slots. It is either an expansion board containing multiple expansion slots, or an expansion board that cables to a separate housing that contains the slots and its own power supply.

business analyst

An individual who analyzes the operations of a department or functional unit with the purpose of developing a general systems solution to the problem that may or may not require automation. The business analyst can provide insights into an operation for an information systems analyst.

Business Basic

A version of the BASIC programming language derived from the original Dartmouth BASIC created by Kemeny and Kurtz. It was first developed by MAI Systems Corporation with later versions known as Thoroughbred Basic from Thoroughbred Software International, Inc., Somerset, NJ, and BBxPROGRESSION/4 from Basis International, Ltd, Irvine, CA.

business graphics

Numeric data represented in graphic form. While line graphs, bar charts and pie charts are the common forms of business graphics, there are dozens of others types. The ability to generate business graphics is often included in spreadsheet and presentation graphics programs.

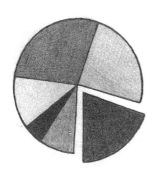

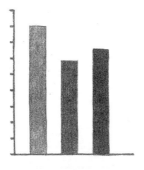

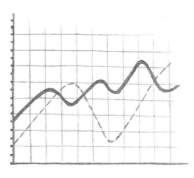

PIE CHART   BAR CHART   GRAPH

business logic

The part of an application program that performs the required data processing of the business. It refers to the routines that perform the data entry, update, query and report processing, and more specifically to the processing that takes place behind the scenes. A client application is made up of a user interface and the business logic. A server application may be mostly business logic.

Both client and server applications also require communications links to the network, but they, like the user interface, are not part of the business logic.

business machine

Any office machine, such as a typewriter or calculator, that is used in clerical and accounting functions. The term has traditionally excluded computers and terminals.

business process reengineering

See reengineering.

bus mastering

A bus design that allows add-in boards to process independently of the CPU and to be able to access the computer's memory and peripherals on their own.

bus mouse

Bus Connector

PS/2 Connector

A mouse that plugs into an expansion board. It takes up an expansion slot whereas a serial mouse takes up a serial port. The choice depends on how many devices must be connected to each type of socket.

The connector on the mouse cable of a bus mouse looks like the PS/2 mouse connector commonly used to hook up an external mouse on a laptop, but the pin configurations are different and not compatible as shown in the diagram.

Butterfly keyboard

A nickname for IBM's TrackWrite keyboard that folds into its case for travelling.

Butterfly Switch

A parallel processing topology from BBN Advanced Computers Inc., Cambridge, MA, that mimics a crossbar and provides high-speed switching of data between nodes. It can also be used to create a hypercube topology.

button

(1) A knob, such as on a printer or a mouse, which is pushed with the finger to activate a function.

(2) A simulated button on screen that is "pushed" by moving the cursor onto it and clicking the mouse.

On-screen Button
The button on the left is in its normal state. The one on the right has been depressed. When a button is clicked, it simulates the physical depression of a real button by offsetting the icon a few pixels and switching the shadow lines from the right and bottom to the top and left edges.

buying a personal computer

See *how to select a personal computer.*

bypass

In communications, to avoid the local telephone company by using satellites and microwave systems.

byte

The common unit of computer storage from micro to mainframe. It is made up of eight binary digits (bits). A ninth bit may be used in the memory circuits as a parity bit for error checking.

A byte holds the equivalent of a single character, such as the letter A, a dollar sign or decimal point. For numbers, a byte can hold a single decimal digit (0 to 9), two numeric digits (packed decimal) or a number from 0 to 255 (binary numbers).

Byte Specifications

The primary specifications of hardware are rated in bytes; for example, a 40-megabyte (40M or 40MB) disk holds 40 million characters of instructions and data. A one-megabyte (1M or 1MB) memory allows one million characters of instructions and data to be stored internally for processing.

With database files and word processing documents, the file size is slightly larger than the number of data characters stored in it. Word processing files contain embedded codes for layout settings (margins, tabs, boldface); therefore, a 100,000-byte document implies slightly less than 100,000 characters of text (approx. 30 pages). Database files contain codes that describe the structure of the records, thus, a 100,000-byte database file holds somewhat less than 100,000 characters of data. Unlike data and text, a 100,000-byte graphics file is not indicative of the size of the image contained in it. There are many graphics standards, and the higher the image quality, the more bytes are needed to represent it. A low-resolution graphics file can take as little as 8,000 bytes, while high-resolution files can take 100,000 or more bytes per picture.

byte addressable

A computer that can address each byte of memory independently of the others. In today's computers, all of memory is usually byte addressable, which is why memory is used for processing. Units (fields) of data can be worked on independently. Contrast with *word addressable.*

Byte Information Exchange

See *BIX.*

byte ordering

See *big endian.*

byte-oriented protocol

A communications protocol that uses control codes made up of full bytes. The bisynchronous protocols used by IBM and other vendors are examples. Contrast with *bit-oriented protocol.*

C

C

A high-level programming language developed at Bell Labs that is able to manipulate the computer at a low level like assembly language. During the last half of the 1980s, C has become the language of choice for developing commercial software. C can be compiled into machine languages for almost all computers. For example, UNIX is written in C and runs in a wide variety of micros, minis and mainframes. C is programmed as a series of functions that call each other for processing. Even the body of the program is a function named "main." Functions are very flexible, allowing programmers to choose from the standard library that comes with the compiler, to use third party functions from other C suppliers, or to develop their own.

Compared to other high-level programming languages, C appears complicated. Its intricate appearance is due to its extreme flexibility. C was standardized by ANSI (X3J11 committee) and ISO in 1989. See *Turbo C, Borland C++, Microsoft C* and *Visual C++*.

The following C example converts fahrenheit to centigrade:

```
main()    {
    float fahr;
    printf("Enter Fahrenheit ");
    scanf("%f", &fahr);
    printf("Celsius is %f\n", (fahr-32)*5/9);
        }
```

The Origin of C

C was developed to allow UNIX to run on a variety of computers. After Bell Labs' Ken Thompson and Dennis Ritchie created UNIX and got it running on several PDP computers, they wanted a way to easily port it to other machines without having to rewrite it from scratch. Thompson created a language called B, a simpler version of a language called BCPL, itself a version of CPL. Later, in order to improve B, Thompson and Ritchie created C.

C:

A designation for the primary hard disk in a PC.

C++

An object-oriented version of C created by Bjarne Stroustrup. C++ has become popular because it combines traditional C programming with OOP capability. Smalltalk and other original OOP languages did not provide the familiar structures of conventional languages such as C and Pascal. See *Borland C++* and *Visual C++*.

C2

The minimum security level defined by the National Computer Security Center. See *NCSC*.

CA

(Computer Associates International, Inc., Islandia, NY) The world's largest diversified software vendor offering more than 350 applications from micro to mainframe. Founded in 1976 by Charles Wang and three associates, its first product was CA-SORT, an IBM mainframe utility. In personal computers, it was originally known for SuperCalc, one of the first spreadsheets. With 1994 revenues exceeding two billion dollars, CA is concentrating heavily in the Windows market. CA has acquired several software companies with well-known products, all of which are now titled with the CA- designation.

Charles Wang
(Photo courtesy of Computer Associates International, Inc.)

CAB file

(CABinet file) A file format from Microsoft used to hold compressed files on its distribution disks. The Windows 95 Extract program is run at the command line to decompress the files.

cable

A flexible metal or glass wire or group of wires. All cables used in electronics are insulated with a material such as plastic or rubber.

cable categories

The following categories are based on their transmission capacity. The majority of new wiring installations use Category 5 UTP wire in order to be able to run or upgrade to the faster network technologies that will require it. Categories 1 through 5 are based on the EIA/TIA-568 standard.

Category	Cable type	Application
1	UTP	Analog voice
2	UTP	Digital voice1 Mbps data
3	UTP, STP	16 Mbps data
4	UTP, STP	20 Mbps data
5	UTP, STP	100 Mbps data
6	Coax	100 Mbps+data
7	Fiber optic	100 Mbps+data

cable matcher

Same as *gender changer*.

cable modem

A modem used to connect a computer to a cable TV system that offers online services.

cabletext

A videotex service that uses coaxial cable. See *videotex*.

cable types

See *cable categories*.

cache

Pronounced "cash." A dedicated bank of high-speed memory or a reserved section of regular memory used to improve performance. The cache provides a temporary storage area for instructions and data that is closer to the CPU's speed. The larger the cache, the faster the performance, since there is a greater chance that the instruction or data required next is already in the cache.

Memory Caches

A memory cache, or CPU cache, is a memory bank that bridges main memory and the CPU. It is faster than main memory and allows instructions to be exececuted and data to be read at higher speed. Instructions and data are transferred to the cache in blocks, using some kind of look-ahead algorithm. The more sequential the instructions and data, the more the cache improves performance.

A level 1 cache is built into the chip. Level 2 is a group of memory chips on the motherboard. Increasing a Level 2 cache may speed up some

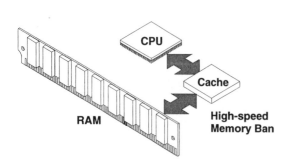

CPU

Cache

RAM

High-speed Memory Ban

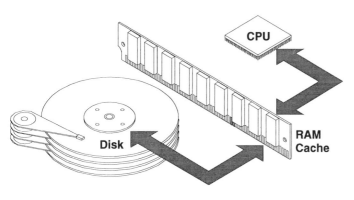

applications and amount to nothing on others. Both types are used together. In PCs, the cache is static RAM (SRAM), while main memory is dynamic RAM (DRAM).

Disk Caches
A disk cache is a section of main memory or memory on the controller board that bridges the disk and the CPU. When the disk is read, a larger block of data is copied into the cache. If subsequent requests for data can be satisfied in the cache, a much slower disk access is not required.

If the cache is used for writing, data is queued up at high speed and then written to disk during idle machine cycles by the caching program. If the cache is built into the hardware, the disk controller figures out when to do it.

DOS and Windows 3.x use the SmartDrive caching program. Windows 95 uses Vcache. See *write back cache* and *write through cache*.

cache coherency
Managing a cache so that data is not lost or overwritten. For example, when data is updated in a cache, but not yet transferred to its target memory or disk, the chance of corruption is greater. Cache coherency is obtained by well-designed algorithms that keep track of the cache. It is even more critical in symmetric multiprocessing (SMP) where memory is shared by multiple processors.

caching controller
A disk controller with a built-in cache. See *cache*.

CA-Clipper
An application development system from Computer Associates. Originally a dBASE compiler, it has become a complete stand-alone development environment with many unique features. Clipper was originally developed by Nantucket Corporation.

CA-Cricket Presents
A desktop presentation program for the Macintosh from Computer Associates. It provides the ability to create output for overheads, handouts, speaker notes and film recorders.

CAD
(Computer-Aided Design) Using computers to design products. CAD systems are high-speed workstations or personal computers using CAD software and input devices such as graphic tablets and scanners. CAD output is a printed design or electronic input to CAM systems (see *CAD/CAM*).

CAD software is available for generic design or specialized uses, such as architectural, electrical and mechanical design. CAD software may also be highly specialized for creating products such as printed circuits and integrated circuits.

CAD systems are often turnkey systems which are put together by vendors that may develop or integrate software into standard or optimized hardware. Except in a few cases, CAD systems rely extensively on graphics. See *graphics, CADD*, and *CAE*.

CAD
The layout of the circuitry within the chip is designed by computers, which accounts for the dramatic explosion in computer technology over the past decade. Look up *chip* for an explanation of how the chip is made.

CADAM

A full-featured IBM mainframe CAD application, which includes 3-D capability, solid modeling and numerical control. Originally developed by Lockheed for internal use, it was distributed by IBM starting in the late 1970s. In 1989, IBM purchased the Lockheed subsidiary, CADAM, Inc.

CA-DATACOM/DB

A relational database management system (DBMS) from Computer Associates that runs on PCs, IBM minis and mainframes. There are many options and add-ons that support the product all under the CA-DATACOM umbrella, such as CA-DATACOM/CICS Services and CA-DATACOM/SQL Option.

CA-dBFast

A dBASE-compatible application development system from Computer Associates. It provides over 200 language extensions to dBASE allowing dBASE or xBASE programs to be converted to Windows applications.

CAD/CAM

(Computer-Aided Design/Computer-Aided Manufacturing) The integration of CAD and CAM. Products designed by CAD are direct input into the CAM system. For example, a device is designed and its electronic image is translated into a numerical control programming language, which generates the instructions for the machine that makes it.

CADD

(Computer-Aided Design and Drafting) CAD systems with additional features for drafting, such as dimensioning and text entry.

CADKEY

An integrated 2-D drafting and 3-D design system for PCs from CADKEY, Inc., Manchester, CT. It offers a total design solution with solids creation and built-in DXF and IGES translators. Over 200 manufacturing systems link to CADKEY through its CADL programming language.

CAE

(1) (Computer-Aided Engineering) Software that analyzes designs which have been created in the computer or that have been created elsewhere and entered into the computer. Different kinds of engineering analyses can be performed, such as structural analysis and electronic circuit analysis.
(2)(Common Application Environment) Software development platform that is specified by X/Open.

CA-Easytrieve

An application development system for IBM mainframes, DOS and OS/2 from Computer Associates. It includes 4GL query and reporting capabilities and can access many IBM mainframe and PC database formats. UNIX and Windows versions forthcoming. Easytrieve was originally developed by Pansophic Systems.

CAI

(1) (Computer-Assisted Instruction) Same as *CBT*.
(2) See *CA*.

CA-IDMS

A relational DBMS from Computer Associates that runs on minis and mainframes. IDMS (Integrated Data Management System) was developed at GE in the 1960s and marketed by Cullinane, later renamed Cullinet and then acquired by CA in 1989. There are a variety of CA-IDMS products, such as CA-IDMS/R for the relational DBMS, CA-IDMS/DDS for its distributed version and so on.

CA-Ingres

The original version of CA-OpenIngres from Computer Associates. See *CA-OpenIngres*.

Cairo

The code name for an object-oriented version of Windows NT to be released after Windows NT is established.

CAL

(1) (Computer-Assisted Learning) Same as *CBT*.
(2) (Conversational Algebraic Language) A timesharing language from the University of California.

calculated field

A numeric or date field that derives its data from the calculation of other fields. Data is not entered into a calculated field by the user.

calculator

A machine that provides arithmetic capabilities. It accepts keypad input and displays results on a readout and/or paper tape. Unlike a computer, it cannot handle alphabetic data.

CA-Librarian

A version control system for IBM mainframes from Computer Associates. Librarian's master files can be simultaneously accessed on shared disks by different operating systems. Librarian was originally developed by ADR, Inc.

call

(1) In programming, a statement that requests services from another subroutine or program. The call is physically made to the subroutine by a branch instruction or some other linking method which is created by the assembler, compiler or interpreter. The routine that is called is responsible for returning control to the calling program after it has finished processing.
(2) In communications, the action taken by the transmitting station to establish a connection with the receiving station in a dial-up network.

call by reference

In programming, a call to a subroutine that passes addresses of the parameters used in the subroutine.

call by value

In programming, a call to a subroutine that passes the actual data of the parameters used in the subroutine.

call control

Also called *call processing*, it is the controlling of telephone and PBX functions. It includes connecting, disconnecting and transferring the call, but it does not affect the content of the call. Contrast with *media control*.

call distributor

A PBX feature that routes incoming calls to the next available agent or operator.

called routine

In programming, a program subroutine that performs a task and is accessed by a call or branch instruction in the program.

calling program

In programming, a program that initiates a call to another program.

calling routine

In programming, a program subroutine that initiates a call to another program routine.

Call Level Interface

See *CLI*.

CALS

(Computer-Aided Acquisition and Logistics Support) A DOD initiative for electronically capturing military documentation and linking related information.

CAM

(1) (Computer-Aided Manufacturing) The automation of manufacturing systems and techniques, including numerical control, process control, robotics and materials requirements planning (MRP). See *CAD/CAM*.
(2) (Common Access Method) An ANSI standard interface that provides a common language between drivers and SCSI host adapters. It is primarily supported by Future Domain and NCR. See *ASPI*.
(3) (Content Addressable Memory) Same as *associative storage*.

camera ready

Printed material that serves as original artwork for commercial printing. Camera-ready material is photographed, and the films are made into plates for the printing presses. Camera ready implies high-resolution text and graphics. See *resolution* and *high-resolution*.

Canadian Standards Association

See *CSA*.

candela

A unit of measurement of the intensity of light. An ordinary wax candle generates one candela. See *lumen*.

canned program

A software package that provides a fixed solution to a problem. Canned business applications should be analyzed carefully as they usually cannot be changed much, if at all.

canned routine

A program subroutine that performs a specific processing task.

canonical synthesis

The process of designing a model of a database without redundant data items. A canonical model, or schema, is independent of the hardware and software that will process the data.

CA-OpenIngres

A relational database management system (DBMS) from Computer Associates that runs on Windows NT, OS/2, VAXs and most UNIX platforms. CA-OpenIngres is an enhanced version of Ingres, one of the first heavyweight DBMSs and noted for its advanced features. For example, Ingres was the first major DBMS to include triggers and stored procedures.

Ingres was originally developed by Relational Technology, founded in 1980 to market a commercial version of "INteractive Graphics and REtrieval System," which was developed at the University of California at Berkeley in the early 1970s. The company was renamed Ingres Corporation, then later acquired by the Ask Group and eventually Computer Associates.

CA-OpenRoad

A client/server development system from Computer Associates that runs on Windows, X terminal and OS/2 clients. It supports the major SQL databases including CA-OpenIngres. CA-OpenRoad was originally Windows 4GL from Ingres, but supported only the Ingres database.

CAP

See *ADSL*.

capacitor

An electronic component that holds a charge. It comes in varying sizes for use in power supplies. It is also constructed as microscopic cells in dynamic RAM chips.

Capacitors

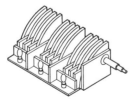

CA-Panvalet

A version control system for IBM mainframes from Computer Associates that keeps track of source code, JCL and object modules. Panvalet was originally developed by Pansophic Systems. CA-PAN/LCM is a similar product for PCs, which also provides interfaces to mainframe systems, such as CA-Panvalet and CA-Librarian.

capstan

On magnetic tape drives, a motorized cylinder that traps the tape against a free-wheeling roller and moves it at a regulated speed.

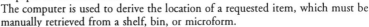

CAPSTANS

capture buffer

A reserved memory area for holding an incoming transmission.

CAR

(Computer-Assisted Retrieval) Systems that use the computer to keep track of text documents or records stored on paper or on microform. The computer is used to derive the location of a requested item, which must be manually retrieved from a shelf, bin, or microform.

CA-RAMIS

A fourth-generation retrieval language for IBM mainframes and PCs from Computer Associates. Originally developed by Mathematica, RAMIS was later acquired by Martin Marietta Data Systems, On-Line Software, then CA in 1991. The earliest version of RAMIS was one of the first database packages with a non-procedural language for IBM mainframes.

card

See *printed circuit board, magnetic stripe, punched card* and *HyperCard.*

CardBus

The successor to the PC Card-16. See *PCMCIA.*

card cage

A cabinet or metal frame that holds printed circuit cards.

card column

A vertical column that is used to represent a single character of data by its pattern of punched holes. The common IBM card contains 80 card columns.

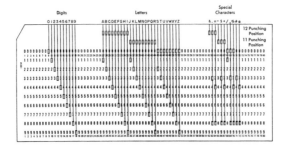

Card Column
(Photo courtesy of International Business Machine Corporation.)

card image

The representation of punched cards in which each hole in the card is represented by a bit on tape or disk.

cardinal number

The number that states how much or how many. In "record 43 has 7 fields," the 7 is cardinal. Contrast with *ordinal number*.

card punch

(1) An early peripheral device that punches holes into cards at 100 to 300 cards per minute.

(2) Same as *keypunch machine*.

card reader

(1) A peripheral device that reads magnetic stripes on the back of a credit card.

(2) An early peripheral device that reads punched cards at 500 to 2,000 cards/minute. The code is detected by light patterns created by the holes in the card.

card services

Software that manages PCMCIA cards. See *PCMCIA*.

CA-Realizer

An application development system for Windows and OS/2 from Computer Associates. It is based on a superset of BASIC and includes visual tools and the ability to incorporate routines written in C, Pascal and other languages. Realizer was originally developed by Within Technologies.

caret

An up-arrow (^) symbol used to represent a decimal point or the control key. For example, ^Y means Ctrl-Y. It is Shift-6 on the keyboard.

carpal tunnel syndrome

The compression of the main nerve to the hand due to scarring or swelling of the surrounding soft tissue in the wrist (area formed by carpal bones on top and muscle tendons below). Caused by trauma, arthritis and improper positioning of the wrist, it can result in severe damage to the hands. Wrist supports that keep the wrist in a neutral position can help to prevent injury. See *RSI* and *Wrist Pro*.

carriage

A printer or typewriter mechanism that holds the platen and controls paper feeding and movement.

carriage return

See *return key*.

carrier

An alternating current that vibrates at a fixed frequency, used to establish a boundary, or envelope, in which a signal is transmitted. Carriers are commonly used in radio transmission (AM, FM, TV, microwave, satellite, etc.) in order to differentiate transmitting stations. For example, an FM station's channel number is actually its carrier frequency. The FM station merges (modulates) its audio broadcast (data signal) onto its carrier and transmits the combined signal over the airwaves. At the receiving end, the FM tuner latches onto the carrier frequency, filters out the audio signal, amplifies it and sends it to the speaker.
Carriers can be used to transmit several signals simultaneously. For example,

multiple voice, data and/or video signals can travel over the same line with each residing in its own carrier vibrating at a different frequency.

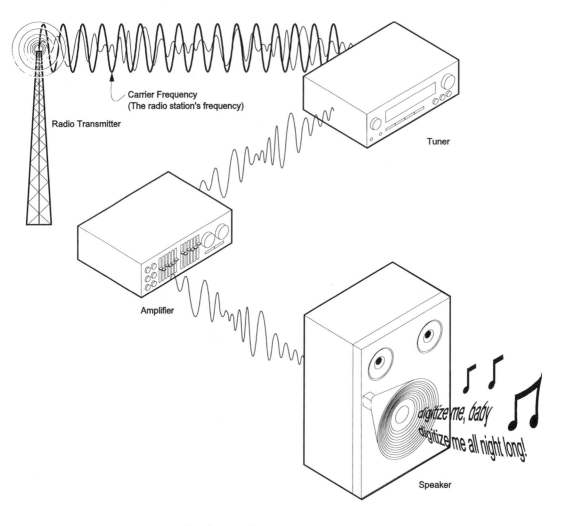

Carrier Frequency
(The radio station's frequency)

Radio Transmitter

Tuner

Amplifier

Speaker

digitize me, baby
digitize me all night long!

carrier based

A transmission system that generates a fixed frequency (carrier) to contain the data being transmitted.

carrier detect

A signal that indicates a connection has been made by sensing a carrier frequency on the line. See *RS-232* and *modem*.

carrier frequency

A unique frequency used to "carry" data within its boundaries. It is measured in cycles per second, or Hertz. See *carrier* and *FDM*.

Carterfone decision

The FCC decree in 1968 that permitted users to connect their own telephone equipment to the public telephone system.

cartridge

A removable storage module that contains disks, magnetic tape or memory chips. Cartridges are inserted into slots in the drive, printer or computer. See *data cartridge, font cartridge* and *cassette*.

CAS

(1) (Communications Application Specification) Intel's fax/modem protocol that allows personal computers to exchange data with fax machines. Introduced in 1988, Intel provides both the boards and the chips.

(2) (Column Address Strobe) A clock signal in a memory chip used to instruct the circuits when to input and output data.

cascade

A connected series of devices or images. It often implies that the second and subsequent device takes over after the previous one is used up. For example, cascading tapes in a dual-tape backup system means the second tape is written after the first one is full. In a 286 or higher PC, a second IRQ chip is cascaded to the first, doubling the number of interrupts.

CASE

(Computer-Aided Software Engineering or Computer-Aided Systems Engineering) Software that is used in any and all phases of developing an information system, including analysis, design and programming. For example, data dictionaries and diagramming tools aid in the analysis and design phases, while application generators speed up the programming phase.

CASE tools provide automated methods for designing and documenting traditional structured programming techniques. The ultimate goal of CASE is to provide a language for describing the overall system that is sufficient to generate all the necessary programs. See also *case statement*.

case-based reasoning

An AI problem solving technique that catalogs experience into "cases" and matches the current problem to the experience. Such systems are easier to maintain than rule-based expert systems, because changes require adding new cases without the complexity of adding new rules. It is used in many areas including pattern recognition, diagnosis, troubleshooting and planning.

case cracker

A tool used to "crack" open the cases of various laptop computers. The early Macintosh cases and many laptop cases are designed to snap together. The spatula-like ends of the case cracker make it easier to pry open the case without damaging it.

case sensitive

Distinguishing lower case from upper case. In a case sensitive language, "abc" is considered different data than "ABC."

case statement

In programming, a variation of the if-then-else statement that is used when several ifs are required in a row. The following C example tests the variable KEY1 and performs functions based on the results.

```
switch (key1)   {
    case '+':  add();  break;
    case '-':  subtract();  break;
    case '*':  multiply();  break;
    case '/':  divide();  break;
            }
```

cash memory
See *cache*.

cassette
A removable magnetic tape storage module that contains a supply reel and a takeup reel. See *cartridge* and *data cassette*.

Cassette
Cassettes such as this are widely used for recording analog sound.

casting
In programming, the conversion of one data type into another.

cat
(conCATenate) A UNIX command that displays the contents of a file.

catalog
A directory of disk files or files used in an application. Also any map, list or directory of storage space used by the computer.

Category 3, 5, etc.
See *cable categories*.

CA-Telon
An application generator from Computer Associates that generates COBOL and PL/I code for IBM mainframes and COBOL code for AS/400s. Development can be performed on mainframes or PCs. Telon was originally developed by Pansophic Systems.

cathode
In electronics, a device that emits electrons, which flow from the negatively charged cathode to the positively charged *anode*. Cathodes are used in CRTs and in diodes.

cathode ray tube
See *CRT*.

CATV
(Community Antenna TV) The original name for cable TV, which used a single antenna at the highest location in the community. Now refers to cable TV.

CAU
(Controlled Access Unit) An intelligent hub from IBM for Token Ring networks. Failed nodes are identified by the hub and reported via IBM's LAN Network Manager software.

CAV

(Constant Angular Velocity) A recording technique that rotates the disk at a constant speed. The number of bits in each track is the same, but their density varies because the inner tracks have smaller circumferences than the outer tracks. This method wastes the most amount of disk space. The CLV and ZBR techniques maximize the space on the disk better than CAV. See *CLV* and *ZBR*.

CAVE

(Computer Automatic Virtual Environment) A virtual reality system that uses projectors to display images on the walls and ceilings rather than requiring the participant to wear goggles. Contrast with *HMD*.

CA-Visual Objects

An object-oriented client/server development system from Computer Associates that is used to develop Windows applications. It provides an Xbase language, visual programming tools and supports a variety of SQL databases. It comes with the Watcom SQL database for testing and includes a compiler for generating Windows EXEs and DLLs.

CB

(Citizen's Band) The frequency band for public radio transmission in the 27 MHz range.

CBEMA

(Computer and Business Equipment Manufacturers Association, 311 First St., N.W., Washington, DC 20001, 202/737-8888) A membership organization founded in 1916 composed of over 25 manufacturers and suppliers. It is concerned with the development of standards for data processing and business equipment in the U.S. and abroad.

CBR

(1) (Computer-Based Reference) Reference materials accessible by computer in order to help people do their jobs quicker. For example, this database on disk!
(2) (Constant Bit Rate) A uniform transmission rate. For example, voice traffic requires a CBR.
(3) See *case-based reasoning*.

CB simulator

See *computer conferencing*.

CBT

(Computer-Based Training) Using the computer for training and instruction. CBT programs are called *courseware* and provide interactive training sessions for all disciplines. It uses graphics extensively, as well as CD-ROM and LaserDisc. CBT courseware is developed with authoring languages, such as Adroit, PILOT and Demo II, which allow for the creation of interactive sessions.

CBX

(Computerized Branch eXchange) Same as *PBX*.

CCA

(1) (Common Cryptographic Architecture) IBM encryption software for MVS and DOS applications.
(2) (Compatible Communications Architecture) A Network Equipment Technology protocol for transmitting asynchronous data over X.25 networks.

(3) (Communications Control Architecture) The U.S. Navy network that includes an ISDN backbone called BITS (Base Information Transfer System).

CCC/Harvest

A software configuration management (SCM) system for client/server environments from Softool Corporation, Goleta, CA. It supports all the major UNIX platforms and Windows, OS/2 and NT clients. Other products from Softool include CCC/Manager for VAXes and CCC/LCM for mainframes.

CCD

(Charge Coupled Device) An electronic memory made of a special type of MOS transistor that can store charges in a sequential fashion. CCDs can be charged by light as well as by electricity and are thus used to store images in scanners as well as digital video and still cameras.

CCFL

(Cold Cathode Flurorescent Lamp) Same as *CCFT.*

CCFT

(Cold Cathode Fluorescent Tube) A type of light source for a backlit screen. It weighs more and uses more power than other backlights.

CCIA

(Computer and Communications Industry Association, 666 11th St., N.W., Washington, DC 20001, 202/783-0070) A membership organization composed of over 60 hardware and software vendors, service bureaus, leasing and repair companies. It represents their interests in domestic and foreign trade, and, working with the NIST, keeps members advised of regulatory policy.

CCIE

(Cisco Certified Internetwork Expert) A certification for competency in internetworking devices and concepts and Cisco routers specifically. It is administered by Cisco Systems, San Jose, CA, as well as Drake testing centers throughout the U.S. and Canada.

CCIS

(Common Channel Interoffice Signaling) A telephone communications technique that transmits voice and control signals over separate channels. Control signals are transmitted over a packet-switched digital network, providing faster connects and disconnects and allowing data, such as calling number, to be included. See *CCS (2).*

CCITT

See *ITU.*

cc:Mail

A widely-used messaging system from Lotus that runs on PC LANs. Originally developed by cc:Mail, Inc., Mountain View, CA, Lotus acquired the company in 1991. Mail-enabled applications that are written to the VIM programming interface can use the cc:Mail system.

CCP

(Certificate in Computer Programming) The award for successful completion of an examination in computer programming offered by ICCP.

CCS

(1) (Common Communications Support) SAA specifications for communications,

which includes data streams (DCA, 3270), application services (DIA, DDM), session services (LU 6.2) and data links (X.25, Token Ring).

(2) (Common Channel Signaling) An integral part of ISDN known as "Signaling System 7," which advances the CCIS method for transmitting control signals. It allows call forwarding, call waiting, etc., to be provided anywhere in the network.

(3) (Common Command Set) The de facto instruction set between a SCSI-1 adapter and a hard disk.

(4) (Continuous Composite Servo) A technique for aligning the read/write head over a track in an optical disk by sensing special tracking grooves in the disk.

(5) (100Call Seconds) A unit of measurement equal to 100 seconds of conversation. One hour = 36 CCS.

CCW

(Continuous Composite Write) A magneto-optic disk technology that emulates a WORM (Write Once Read Many) disk. It uses firmware in the drive to ensure that data cannot be erased and rewritten.

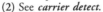

CD

(1) (Compact Disc)

(2) See *carrier detect.*

(1) (Compact Disc) A digital audio disc that contains up to 72 minutes of hi-fi stereo sound. The disc is a plastic platter 4.75" in diameter, recorded on one side, with individual selections playable in any sequence. The CD was introduced in 1982.

Sound is converted into digital code by sampling the sound waves 44,056 times per second and converting each sample into a 16-bit number. It requires approximately 1.5 million bits of storage for each second of stereo hi-fi sound.

Other forms of CDs, such as CD-ROM, CD-I and Video CD, all stem from the audio CD, which is also known as Compact Disc-Digital Audio (CD-DA).

The Books
Documentation for various CD formats are found in books commonly known by the color of their covers.

```
Red Book       - Audio CDs (CD-DA)
Yellow Book    - CD-ROM
Orange Book    - Write-once (Photo CD, CD-R)
Green Book     - CD-I
White Book     - Video CD
```

What Happened to the Phonograph?
The audio CD was introduced in the U.S. in 1983. Three years later, sales of CDs and CD players exceeded sales of LPs and turntables.

Unlike phonograph records, in which the platter contains "carved sound waves," CDs are recorded in digital form as microscopic pits (binary code) covered by a clear, protective plastic layer. Instead of a needle vibrating in the groove, a laser shines onto the pits and the reflections are decoded. Audio CDs, as well as CD-ROMs, use a spiral recording track just like the phonograph record.

Digital sound is so clear because the numbers are turned into sound electronically. There's no needle pops and clicks as there are with phonograph records (there's also no tape hiss if the original recording was digital). In addition, the CD can handle a wider range of volume (dynamic range), providing more realism. A soft whisper can be interrupted by a loud cannon blast. If a phonograph record were recorded with that much dynamic range, the needle would literally jump out of the groove.

CDA

(Compound Document Architecture) A compound document format from Digital that creates hot links between documents.

CD audio

Same as *CD* and *DAD*.

CDC

See *Control Data*.

CD caddy

A plastic container that holds a CD-ROM disc. The caddy is inserted into the disc drive.

CD-DA

See *CD*

CDDI

(Copper Distributed Data Interface) A version of FDDI that uses UTP (unshielded twisted pair) wires rather than optical fiber. The term is a trademark of Crescendo Communications, Sunnyvale, CA. ANSI's standard for FDDI over UTP is officially TP-PMD (Twisted Pair-Physical Media Dependent).

CD-E

(CD-Erasable) An erasable CD-ROM technology that is expected in 1996. CD-E drives will read and write CD-E disks and also read existing CD-ROM and CD-R disks. See also *CDE*.

CDE

(1) (Common Desktop Environment) A graphical user interface for open systems. It is based on Motif with elements from HP, IBM and others. Originally developed by COSE, it is now governed by the X/Open organization. See also *CD-E*.
(2) (Cooperative Development Environment) A client/server application development system from Oracle Corporation that includes BPR, CASE, 4GL, 3GL and end-user tools. The core programs are Oracle Forms for creating the user screens, Oracle Reports for reporting, Oracle Graphics for generating business graphics and Oracle Browser and Oracle Data Query for queries. Oracle Procedure Builder provides drag and drop application partitioning, and Oracle Transparent Gateway provides access to non-Oracle databases.
(3) (Computer Desktop Encyclopedia) What you are reading at this very moment.

cdev

(Control Panel DEVice) Customizable settings in the Macintosh Control Panel that pertain to a particular program or device. Cdevs for the mouse, keyboard and startup disk, among others, come with the Mac. Others are provided with software packages and utilities.

CDF

(Central Distribution Frame) A connecting unit (typically a hub) that acts a central distribution point to all the nodes in a zone or domain. See *MDF*.

CDFS

(CD-ROM File System) The file system that handles CD-ROMs in Windows 95. It is the 32-bit version of the 16-bit MSCDEX.EXE used in DOS/Windows 3.1.

CD-I

(Compact Disc-Interactive) A compact disc format developed by Philips and Sony that holds data, audio, still video and animated graphics. It provides up to 144 minutes of CD-quality stereo, 9.5 hours of AM-radio-quality stereo or 19 hours of monophonic audio.

CD-I includes an operating system standard as well as proprietary hardware methods for compressing the data further in order to display video images. CD-I discs require a CD-I player and will not play in a CD-ROM player. The standard specification for the CD-I format is contained in a document entitled the Green Book. See *CD, CD-ROM, DVI.*

CDIF

(CASE Data Interchange Format) An EIA standard for exchanging data between CASE tools. See *PCTE.*

CDIP

(Sidebrazed Ceramic DIP) A high-qualty ceramic DIP that typically uses gold-plated leads attached by brazing.

CDMA

(Code Division Multiple Access) A spread spectrum technique that converts analog signals into digital for transmission over the cellular network. It provides up to 35 times the capacity of the analog network. Qualcomm, Inc., San Diego, CA, has several patents on products using its CDMA implementation. See *FDMA, TDMA* and *CDPD.*

CDP

(Certificate in Data Processing) The award for the successful completion of an examination in hardware, software, systems analysis, programming, management and accounting, offered by ICCP.

CDPD

(Cellular Digital Packet Data) A type of digital transmission using the cellular network. Based on IBM's CelluPlan II, it moves data at 19.2Kbps over ever-changing unused intervals in the voice channels. It is being implemented by IBM, AT&T (through McCaw Cellular) and most major telephone companies. See *FDMA, TDMA* and *CDMA.*

CD-R

(CD-Recordable) A recordable CD-ROM technology using a disc that can be written only once. The CD-R drives that write the CD-R discs are also called one-off machines. CD-R discs are used for beta versions and original masters of CD-ROM material as well as a means to distribute a large amount of data to a small number of recipients.

CD-R discs are also used for archiving data. Their advantage over WORM drives is that the discs can be read on any CD-ROM drive. Most CD-R drives can also be used as a regular CD-ROM reader. The recording process takes from 20 minutes to an hour per disc depending on the speed of the drive. While this may be suitable for archiving or small distributions, large numbers of CD-ROMs are duplicated on a pressing machine from a master plate derived from the original CD-R recording.

A CD-R Disk
This diagram shows the multiple layers of a CD-R disk. In standard CD-ROM drives as well as CD-R recorders, the laser beam shines up into the disk from the bottom to create the pit. The pits create changes in the binary code, which is read by sensing the reflections (non pits) of the laser beam that is shined into it.

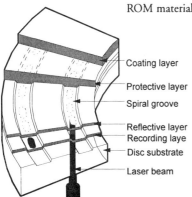

Coating layer
Protective layer
Spiral groove
Reflective layer
Recording laye
Disc substrate
Laser beam

CDRAM

(Cache **DRAM**) A high-speed DRAM memory chip developed by Mitsubishi that includes a small SRAM cache.

CD recorder

See *CD-R.*

CD-ROM

(Compact Disc Read Only Memory) A compact disc format used to hold text, graphics and hi-fi stereo sound. It's like an audio CD, but uses a different track format for data. The audio CD player cannot play CD-ROMs, but CD-ROM players usually play audio CDs and have output jacks for a headphone or amplified speakers.

CD-ROMs hold in excess of 650MB of data, which is equivalent to about 250,000 pages of text or 20,000 medium-resolution images.

A CD-ROM drive (player, reader) connects to a controller card, which is plugged into one of the computer's expansion slots. Earlier drives used a proprietary interface and came with their own card, requiring a free expansion slot in the computer. Today, most CD-ROMs use the SCSI interface and can be daisy chained to an existing SCSI controller. Increasingly, CD-ROM drives are built with the IDE interface, which allows them to connect to the same Enhanced IDE controller that the hard and floppy disks are attached to.

Earlier CD-ROM drives transferred data at 150KB per second. Double, triple and quad-speed drives provide 2x, 3x and 4x the 150KB transfer rate. Six-speed drives increase transfer to 900KB. For full-motion video, at least double speed is required. Access times run from a slow half second to under 200 milliseconds.

Audio and data reside on separate tracks and cannot be heard and viewed together on earlier drives that are not CD-ROM XA compliant. Unlike other optical disks, CD-ROMs, as well as audio CDs, use a spiral recording track just like the "ancient" phonograph record. See *CD-ROM XA, CD-I* and *DVI.* See also *SIGCAT Foundation.*

CD-ROM audio cable

A cable used to send audio CD sound into the computer's sound system. When playing audio CDs, CD-ROM drives output analog sound to both a headphones jack and external connector, just like a CD player. Unlike the digital sound on a CD-ROM disk, which is passed via the computer's bus to the sound card, the CD-ROM audio cable passes analog sound to the sound card.

MPC Level 2 defines a four-pin cable, which is expected to become a standard. However, cards and drives have used different connectors, with from three to six pins. Finding the right cable has been a problem. Earlier drives have no connector. One advantage of a multimedia upgrade kit is that it includes the card, drive and the right cable.

In lieu of this connection, a stereo cable from the headphones jack of the drive to the AUDIO IN of the sound card can always be used.

CD-ROM changer

A CD-ROM player that houses several CD-ROMs, although only one is playable at one time. CD-ROM changers, also called CD-ROM jukeboxes, come in as many varieties just like audio CD players. They can hold from six to 200 or more discs. In order to have access to multiple CD-ROMs simultaneously, it is necessary to have several CD-ROM drives; for example, two or three SCSI drives chained together. In this case, each drive is identified by its own drive letter or name and multiple CD-ROMs can be open and active simultaneously.

CD-ROM Extensions

The software required to use a CD-ROM drive on a PC running DOS. It allows

CD-ROM drives to be addressed like a hard disk and take the next available drive letter; for example, drive D: in a system with one hard disk. Microsoft's CD-ROM Extensions are in the file MSCDEX.EXE. CORELCDX.COM is the file name for Corel's version. The installation program for a CD-ROM drive installs the CD-ROM driver and MSCDEX.EXE.

Windows 95 includes the CD-ROM File System (CDFS), which is a 32-bit version of MSCDEX.EXE. If MSCDEX.EXE is found when installing, it is replaced with CDFS.

CD-ROM jukebox

See *CD-ROM changer*.

CD-ROM XA

(CD-ROM eXtended Architecture) A CD-ROM enhancement introduced in 1988 by Philips, Sony and Microsoft that lets text and pictures be narrated by allowing concurrent audio and video. It provides up to 9.5 hours of AM-quality stereo or 19 hours of monophonic audio. CD-ROM XA drives are required for Kodak's Photo CD discs.

CD-ROM XA functions as a bridge between CD-ROM and CD-I, since CD-ROM XA discs will play on a CD-I player. CD-ROM XA uses a standard CD-ROM player, but requires a CD-ROM XA controller card in the computer. See *CD-I* and *DVI*.

CDTV

(Commodore Dynamic Total Vision) A multimedia and video game technology from Commodore that has been superseded by the CD32 system. It also plays audio CDs.

CDV

(1) (Compressed Digital Video) The compression of full-motion video for high-speed, economical transmission.

(2) (CD Video) A small videodisc (5" diameter) that provides five minutes of video with digital sound plus an additional 20 minutes of audio. Most LaserDisc players can also play CDVs.

CeBIT

The world's largest information technology show hosted in Hannover, Germany. In 1994, 3570 exhibitors from Germany and 2,280 exhibitors from 53 other countries drew 675,000 attendees. The 1995 schedule is March 8-15.

CEbus

(Consumer Electronics bus) An EIA standard for a control network.

Ceefax

A teletext service of the British Broadcasting Corporation.

CEG

(Continous Edge Graphics) A VGA RAMDAC chip from Edsun Labs that adds anti-aliasing on the fly. It can also calculate intermediate shades, thus providing thousands of colors on an 8-bit board that normally generates only 256 colors.

cell

(1) An elementary unit of storage for data (bit) or power (battery).
(2) In a spreadsheet, the intersection of a row and column.

Cello
An Internet utility that lets you browse through the World Wide Web.

cell relay
A transmission technology that uses small fixed-length packets (cells) that can be switched at high speed. It is easier to build a switch that switches fixed-length packets than variable ones. ATM uses a type of cell relay technology.

centering cone
A short plastic or metal cone used to align a 5.25" floppy disk to the drive spindle. It is inserted into the diskette's center hole when the drive door is closed.

centimeter
A unit of measurement that is 1/100th of a meter or approximately 4/10ths of an inch (0.39 inch).

centralized processing
Processing performed in one or more computers in a single location. All terminals in the organization are connected to the central computers. Contrast with *distributed computing* and *decentralized processing*.

central office
The telephone switching facility that interconnects subscribers' telephone lines to each other and to intra and intercity trunk lines.

central processing unit
See *CPU*.

CENTREX
PBX services provided by a local telephone company. Switching is done in the telephone company's central office. Some services do the switching at the customer's site, but control it in the central office.

Centronics
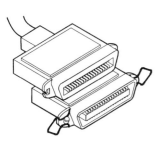
A standard 36-pin parallel interface for connecting printers and other devices to a computer. It defines the plug, socket and signals used and transfers data asynchronously up to 200 Kbytes/sec.
The plug (1.5" wide, 1/8" thick) has 18 contacts each on the top and bottom. The socket contains one opening with matching contacts.
This de facto standard was developed by Centronics Corporation, maker of the first successful dot matrix printers. The printer was introduced in 1970, and the company was bought by Genicom Corporation in 1987. See *printer cable*.

CEO
(Comprehensive Electronic Office) Office software from Data General introduced in 1981. It includes word processing, e-mail, spreadsheets, business graphics and desktop accessories.

CERDIP
(CERamic DIP) A type of DIP that uses two ceramic layers epoxied together.

CERN
(Conseil Europeen pour la Recherche Nucleaire - European Laboratory for Nuclear Research) The research center where the World Wide Web was developed. Located in Geneva, Switzerland, it was originally created to link research information. A complete Web server software package is available at no charge from CERN.

Certificate in Computer Programming
See *CCP*.

certification
See *CCP, NetWare certification, Microsoft Certified Professional, CompTIA* and *CCIE*.

CFG file
(ConFiGuration file) A file that contains startup information required to launch a program or operating system. Same as *INI file*.

CGA
(Color/Graphics Adapter) An IBM video display standard that provided low-resolution text and graphics. It was the first graphics standard for the IBM PC and has been superseded by EGA and VGA. CGA requires a digital RGB Color Display monitor. See *PC display modes*.

CGI
(1) (Computer Graphics Interface) A device independent graphics language for display screens, printers and plotters that stemmed from GKS.
(2) (Common Gateway Interface) The programming interface for executing programs on Web (HTTP) servers. CGI defines the structure for passing data from the server to the server's gateway program, which does the processing, and returning the results from the gateway program to the HTTP server back to the requesting client.

CGM
(Computer Graphics Metafile) A standard format for interchanging graphics images. CGM stores images primarily in vector graphics, but also provides a raster format. Earlier GDM and VDM formats have been merged into CGM. There are many non-standard varieties of CGM in use.

chad
A piece of paper that is punched out on a punched card, paper tape or on the borders of continuous forms. A chadded form is when the holes are cut completely through. A chadless form is when the chads are still attached to one edge of the hole.

chained list
A group of items in which each item contains the location of the next item in sequence.

chaining
Linking items or records to form a chain. Each link in the chain points to the next item.

chain printer
A line printer that uses character typefaces linked together in a chain as its printing mechanism. The chain spins horizontally around a set of hammers. When the desired character is in front of the selected print position, the corresponding hammer hits the paper into the ribbon and onto the character in the chain.

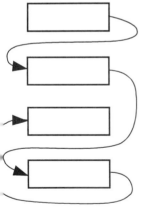

Chained List

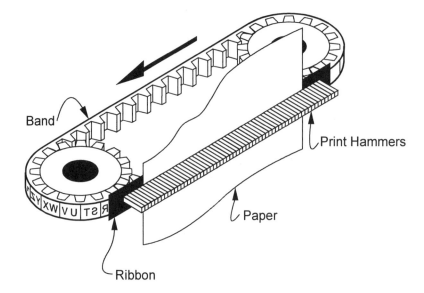

Chain Printer Mechanism

Band

Print Hammers

Paper

Ribbon

change control
See *version control.*

change file
A transaction file used to update a master file.

change management
See *version control* and *configuration management.*

channel
(1) A high-speed metal or optical fiber pathway between the computer and the control units of the peripheral devices. Channels are used in mainframes and high-end machines. Each channel is an independent unit that can transfer data concurrently with other channels as well as the CPU. For example, in a 10-channel computer, 10 streams of data are being transmitted to and from the CPU at the same time. In contrast, the bus in a personal computer serves as a common, shared channel between all devices. Each device must wait for its turn on the bus.
(2) In communications, any pathway between two computers or terminals. It may refer to the physical medium, such as coaxial cable, or to a specific carrier frequency (subchannel) within a larger channel or wireless medium.

channel bank
A multiplexor that merges several low-speed voice or data lines into one high-speed (typically T1) line and vice versa.

channel program
Instructions executed by a peripheral channel. The channel executes the channel program independently of the CPU, allowing concurrent operations to take place in the computer.

chaos
The science that deals with the underlying order of the seemingly random nature of the universe. See *fractals.*

character

(1) A single alphabetic letter, numeric digit, or special symbol such as a decimal point or comma. A character is equivalent to a byte; for example, 50,000 characters take up 50,000 bytes.

(2) The term character is also used to describe command-driven systems. For example, in the phrase "it supports Mac, Windows and character interfaces," character refers to the line-at-a-time text entry used with dumb terminals.

character based

Same as *text based*.

character cell

A matrix of dots used to form a single character on a display screen or printer. For example, an 8x16 cell is made up of 16 rows each containing eight dots. Character cells are displayed and printed contiguously; therefore the design of each letter, digit or symbol within the cell must include surrounding blank space.

character code

Same as *data code*.

character data

Alphanumeric data or text. Contrast with *numeric data*.

character device

A peripheral device that transfers data one byte at a time at a time, such as a parallel or serial port. Contrast with *block device*.

character field

A data field that holds alphanumeric characters. Contrast with *numeric field*.

character generator

(1) Circuitry that converts data characters into dot patterns for a display screen.
(2) A device that creates text characters that are superimposed onto video frames.

character graphics

A set of special symbols strung together like letters of the alphabet to create elementary graphics and forms, as in the following example:

Character Graphics

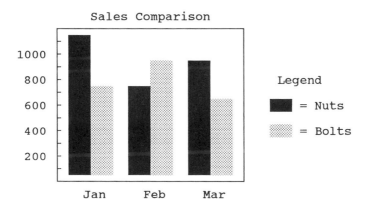

121

characteristic

In logarithms and floating point, the number that indicates where the decimal point is placed.

Character Map

A Windows utility that displays all the characters in a particular font. See *Win Typing special characters*.

character mode

Same as *text mode*.

character-oriented protocol

See *byte-oriented protocol*.

character pitch

The measurement of the number of characters per inch. See *cpi*.

character printer

A printer that prints one character at a time, such as a dot matrix or daisy wheel printer. See *printer*.

Character Printer

character recognition

The ability of a machine to recognize printed text. See *OCR* and *MICR*.

character set

A group of unique symbols used for display and printing. Character sets for alphabet-based languages, such as English and Spanish, generally contain 256 symbols, which is the number of combinations one byte can hold. Except for special fonts, such as Dingbats, Wingdings and the Greek Symbol font, the symbols are the same for the first 128 characters. The letters may have different styling due to their typeface, but an M still looks like an M with each character set, for example.

The second 128 characters differ depending on the font/character set chosen. See *ASCII chart* for the actual characters in the PC-8 character set, which was defined for the original IBM PC. See *extended ASCII*.

character string

A group of alphanumeric characters. Contrast with *numeric data*.

character terminal

A display screen without graphics capability.

Charisma

A presentation graphics program for Windows from Micrografx. It includes a comprehensive media manager that helps manage large libraries of image, sound and video clips.

charting program

Software used to create business graphics, charts and diagrams. See *business graphics* and *diagramming program.*

chat mode

A communications option that lets users type messages back and forth to each other. Each keystroke is transmitted as it is pressed. See *Internet Relay Chat.*

Cheapernet

See *Ethernet.*

check bits

A calculated number used for error checking. The number is derived by some formula from the binary value of one or more bytes of data. See *parity checking, checksum* and *CRC.*

check box

A small box on screen that simulates the equivalent symbol on a paper form. When the box is clicked, the box displays an X or a checkmark to indicate that option has been selected.

check digit

A numeric digit used to ensure that account numbers are correctly entered into the computer. Using a formula, a check digit is calculated for each new account number, which then becomes part of the number, often the last digit.

When an account number is entered, the data entry program recalculates the check digit and compares it to the check digit entered. If the digits are not equal, the account number is considered invalid.

checkpoint/restart

A method of recovering from a system failure. A checkpoint is a copy of the computer's memory that is periodically saved on disk along with the current register settings (last instruction executed, etc.). In the event of any failure, the last checkpoint serves as a recovery point.

When the problem has been fixed, the restart program copies the last checkpoint into memory, resets all the hardware registers and starts the computer from that point. Any transactions in memory after the last checkpoint was taken until the failure occurred will be lost.

check sum

See *checksum.*

checksum

A value used to ensure data is transmitted without error. It is created by adding the binary value of each alphanumeric character in a block of data and sending it with the data. At the receiving end, a new checksum is computed and matched against the transmitted checksum. A non-match indicates an error.

Just as a check digit tests the accuracy of a single number, a checksum tests a block of data. Checksums detect single bit errors and some multiple bit errors, but are not as effective as the CRC method.

Chicago

The original code name for Windows 95.

chicklet keyboard

A keyboard with small, square keys not suitable for touch typing.

child

(1) In database management, the data that is dependent on its parent. See *parent-child*.

(2) A component that is subordinate to a higher-level component. See *child menu, child program* and *child window*.

child menu

A secondary or submenu that is displayed on screen when a certain option in the "parent" menu is selected.

child program

A secondary or subprogram called for and loaded into memory by the main program. See *parent program*.

child window

A secondary window on screen that is displayed within the main overall window of the application.

chip

An integrated circuit. Chips are squares or rectangles that measure approximately from 1/16th to 5/8th of an inch on a side. They are about 1/30th of an inch thick, although only the top 1/1000th of an inch holds the actual circuits. Chips contain from a few dozen to several million electronic components (transistors, resistors, etc.). The terms *chip, integrated circuit* and *microelectronic* are synonymous.

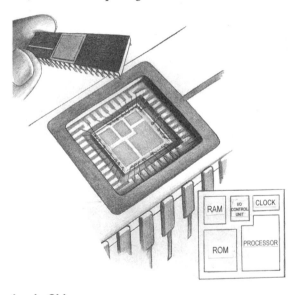

Types of Chips by function

Logic Chip

A single chip can perform some or all of the functions of a processor. A microprocessor is an entire processor on a single chip. Desktop and portable computers use one microprocessor for their CPU while larger computers may employ several types of microprocessors as well as hundreds or thousands of specialized logic chips.

Memory Chip

Random access memory (RAM) chips contain from a couple of hundred thousand to several million storage cells (bits). They are the computer's working storage and require constant power to keep their bits charged. Firmware chips, such as ROMs,

PROMs, EPROMs, and EEPROMs are permanent memory chips that hold their content without power.

Computer on a Chip

A single chip can contain the processor, RAM, ROM, I/O control unit, and a timing clock. It is used in myriads of consumer and industrial products.

Analog/Digital and DSP

A single chip can perform the conversion between analog and digital signals. A programmable CPU called a *DSP* (digital signal processor) is also used in many analog/digital conversions. It contains fast instructions sequences commonly used in such applications.

Special Purpose Chip

Chips used in low-cost consumer items (watches, calculators, etc.) as well as higher-cost products (video games, automobile control, etc.) may be designed from scratch to obtain economical and effective performance. Today's ASIC chips can be quickly created for any special purpose.

Logic Array and Gate Array

These chips contain logic gates which have not been tied together. A final set of steps applies the top metal layer onto the chip stringing the logic gates together into the pattern required by the customer. This method eliminates much of the design and fabrication time for producing a chip.

Bit Slice Processor

Bit slice chips contain elementary electronic circuits that serve as building blocks for the computer architect. They are used to custom-build a processor for specialized purposes.

How the Chip came about

Revolution

In 1947, the semiconductor industry was born at AT&T's Bell Labs with the invention of the *transistor* by John Bardeen, Walter Brattain and William Shockley. The transistor, fabricated from solid materials that could change their electrical conductivity, would eventually replace all the bulky, hot, glass vacuum tubes used as electronic amplifiers in radio and TV and as on/off switches in computers. By the late 1950s, the giant first-generation computers were giving way to smaller, faster and more reliable transistorized machines.

Evolution

The original transistors were discrete components; each one was soldered onto a circuit board to connect to other individual transistors, resistors and diodes. Since hundreds of transistors were made on one round silicon wafer and cut apart only to be reconnected again, the idea of building them in the required pattern to begin with was obvious. In the late 1950s, Jack Kilby of TI and Robert Noyce of Fairchild Semiconductor created the *integrated circuit*, a set of interconnected transistors and resistors on a single chip.

Since then, the number of transistors that have been put onto a single chip has increased exponentially, from a handful in the early 1960s to millions by the late 1980s. Today, a million transistors take up no more space than the first transistor.

The "Doctors"
(Photo courtesy of AT&T.)

A byproduct of miniaturization is speed. The shorter the distance a pulse travels, the faster it gets there. The smaller the elements in the transistor, the faster it switches. Transistor speeds are measured in billionths and trillionths of a second. A Josephson junction transistor has been able to switch in 50 quadrillionths of a second.

Logic and Memory

In first- and second-generation computers, internal main memory was made of such materials as tubes filled with liquid mercury, magnetic drums and magnetic cores.

As integrated circuits began to flourish in the 1960s, design breakthroughs allowed memories to also be made of semiconductor materials. Thus, logic circuits, the "brains" of the computer, and memory circuits, its internal workspace, were moving along the same miniaturization path.

By the end of the 1970s, it was possible to put a processor, working memory (RAM), permanent memory (ROM), a control unit for handling input and output and a timing clock on the same chip. Within 25 years, the transistor on a chip grew into the computer on a chip. When the awesome UNIVAC I was introduced in 1951, you could literally open the door and walk inside. Who would have believed the equivalent electronics would some day be built into your watch.

Tube, Transistor, Chip
(Photo courtesy of AT&T.)

The Making of a Chip

Computer circuits carry electrical pulses from one point to another. The pulses flow through transistors (on/off switches) that open or close when electrically activated. The current flowing through one switch effects the opening or closing of another and so on. Transistors are wired together in patterns of Boolean logic. Logic gates make up circuits. Circuits make up CPUs and other electronic systems.

From Logic to Plumbing

Circuits were originally designed by humans. Today, they reside in circuit libraries, and designers pick and choose ready-made modules (standard cells) from a menu. Computers make computers. The computer converts the logical circuit design into transistors, diodes and resistors. From there the whole thing is turned into a plumber's nightmare that connects several million components together. After inspection by technicians, the electronic images are transferred to machinery that creates glass, lithographic plates, called *photomasks*.

Reviewing the "Plumbing"
(Photo courtesy of Elxsi Corporation.)

The photomask is the actual size of the chip, replicated many times to fit on a round silicon wafer, which is generally 6 to 8" in diameter. The transistors are built by creating subterranean layers in the silicon, and a different photomask is created to isolate each layer to be worked on.

Chips Are Just Rocks

The base material of a chip is usually silicon, although materials such as sapphire and gallium arsenide are also used. Silicon is found in quartz rocks and is purified in a molten state. It is then chemically combined (doped) with other materials to alter its electrical properties. The result is a silicon crystal ingot up to eight inches in diameter that is either positively (p-type) or negatively charged (n-type). *Wafers*, about 1/30th of an inch thick, are cut from this "crystal salami."

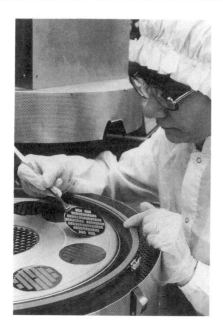

**Inspecting
Wafers**
*(Photo courtesy
of AT&T.)*

Building the Layers

Circuit building starts out by adhering a layer of silicon dioxide insulation on the wafer's surface. The insulation is coated with film and exposed to light through the first photomask, hardening the film and insulation below it. The unhardened areas are etched away exposing the silicon base below. By shooting a gas under heat and pressure into the exposed silicon (diffusion), a sublayer with different electrical properties is created beneath the surface. Through multiple stages of masking, etching, and diffusion, the sublayers on the chip are created. The final stage lays the top metal layer (usually aluminum), which interconnects the transistors to each other and to the outside world.

Each chip is tested on the wafer, and bad chips are marked for elimination. The chips are sliced out of the wafer, and the good ones are placed into packages (DIPs, PQFPs, etc.). The chip is connected to the package with tiny wires, then sealed and tested as a complete unit.

Chip making is extremely precise. Operations are performed in a "clean room," since air particles can mix with the microscopic mixtures and easily render a chip worthless. Depending on the design complexity, more chips can fail than succeed.

The Future

There is a never-ending thirst for putting more circuits onto a chip. In order to miniaturize elements of a transistor even more, the photomasks have to be made with x-rays, which are narrower than light. Circuit patterns will eventually be etched directly onto the chip, eliminating the photographic process entirely. Just as integrated circuits eliminated cutting apart the transistors only to be reconnected again, eventually *wafer scale integration* will eliminate cutting apart the chips only to be tied together with other chips. All the computer circuitry will be built on one chip.

As we're trying to make the chip wider, we're also trying to make it deeper. Instead of adding more circuits across the surface, we are experimenting building with overlapping layers. Within the next 10 years, today's multi million-dollar supercomputer will fit within a cubic inch.

The Test Floor
(Photo courtesy of VLSI Corporation.)

The Designing of a Chip

IF (A+B) **AND** (C+D) OCCUR
OR
IF (A+B) **AND** (D+E) OCCUR
THEN
F AND G **AND** (H+I) IS...

1. All fundamental circuits are designed by people using the rules of Boolean logic (**AND, OR** and **NOT**). After they have been designed, they reside in disk libraries in the computer system waiting to be selected by the designer.

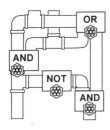

2. The chip designer selects the appropriate circuits from the library and the computer generates the physical circuit paths that resemble a "plumber's nightmare".

3. The "plumbing" is refined by a designer.

4. The final results are further inspected to ensure that all the components are aligned properly.

5. The "plumbing" is turned into several photomasks that will transfer the design of the elements of every transistor onto the chip.

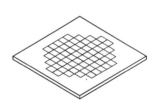

The Making of a Chip

1. Silicon, the raw material of chips, is refined from quartz rocks and purified. It is fabricated into salami-like ingots from three to five inches in diameter.

silicon

1

wafer

2. The ingots are sliced into wafers approximately 1/30th of an inch thick, covered with an oxide insulation layer and then coated with film.

1/30"   film

2

3. A design is transferred onto the wafer by exposing it to ultraviolet light through a mask. Wherever light strikes the film, the film is hardened along with the insulation layer beneath it.

4. The wafer is subjected to an acid that ethics out the unhardened insulation layer exposing the silicon below.

5. The next step is an implantation process that forces chemicals into the exposed silicon under pressure, creating electrically altered elements below the surface.

exposed
hardened film   insulation

silicon below

3   4   5

Through a series of masking, etching and implantation steps (**3**, **4**, **5**), each element for every transistor is created at the same time. Millions of transistors are created together, one step at a time.

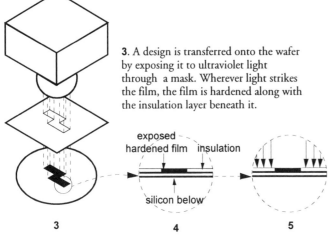

6. The finished wafer is tested and the bad chips are marked for disposal. The wafer is sliced into chips, and the good ones are placed into their final spider-like package. Tiny wires bond the chip to the package's "feet". Each chip is then tested individually. The nimber of chips that make it through to the very end can be less then the number that don't.

finished wafer

The Formation of one Transistor

These steps are performed on every transistor in every chip in the wafer at the same time.

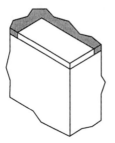 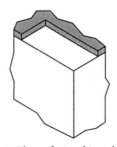 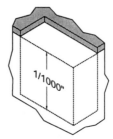

1. The film and insulation layer become hardened when exposed to light. The dark area is the exposed, hardened part; the light area is unexposed.

2. The wafer is subjected to acid, which etches out the unhardened film and insulation area exposing the silicon area beneath it.

3. Under pressure, chemicals are implanted into the silicon creating a sublayer element that is electrically altered from the rest of the silicon.

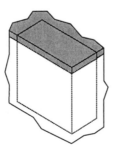 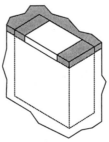 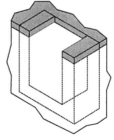

4. The wafer is recovered with insulation and film.

5. The next design is transfered by photomask onto the wafer.

6. A new hole is opened up, and chemicals are implanted to create an element within the sublayer.

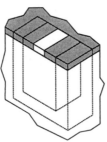 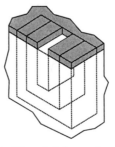 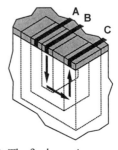

7. "The patient is sewed up once more," and another design is transferred onto the wafer.

8. The third element is created by the same etching and implantation process.

9. The final stage is to tunnel through the insulation again and adhere the aluminum pathways that carry the current to and from the transistor. Line **A** is the triggering line. The signal that activates the transistor comes over this line. Line **B** has a constant source of electricity. When a pulse comes in on line **A**, the middle sublayer becomes electrically conductive (switch is closed) allowing current to travel from **B** to **C**.

The Hierarchy

The transistors make up gates (**AND** gates, **OR** gates, etc.), and gates make up circuits. Circuits make up a logical device, such as a CPU.

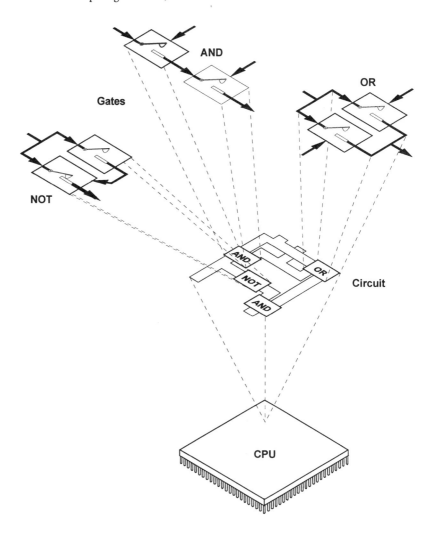

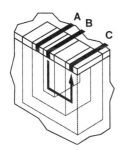

Line **A** is the triggering line. The signal that activates the transistor comes over this line. Line **B** has a constant source of electricity. When a pulse comes in on line **A**, the middle sublayer becomes electrically conductive (switch is closed) allowing current to travel from **B** to **C**.

chip card
See *smart card* and *memory card.*

chip carrier
(1) The package that a chip is mounted in.
(2) A chip package with connectors on all sides. See *leaded chip carrier* and *leadless chip carrier.*

chip set
See *chipset.*

chipset
A group of chips designed to work as a unit to perform a function. For example, a modem chipset contains all the primary circuits for transmitting and receiving. A PC chipset contains the system, memory and bus controllers. Combine the chipset on the motherboard with the clock, CPU and memory, and you have a complete computer. Today, an entire PC chipset can be made to fit on a single chip.

chirp
See *CHRP.*

Chkdsk
A DOS utility that tests the status of the disk file.

CHMOS
(High-density CMOS) A chip with a high density of CMOS transistors.

Chooser
A Macintosh desk accessory that allows the user to select a printer, file server or network device, such as a network modem.

chroma
Color.

chroma key
See *color key.*

chromatic dispersion
The spreading of light rays within an optical fiber, which causes decreased bandwidth.

CHRP
(Common Hardware Reference Platform) A common specification for PowerPCs that allows them to run a variety of operating systems, including the Mac OS, AIX, OS/2, Solaris and NT. It defines ports and sockets commonly found on both PCs and Macs. It also defines the bootstrap ROM, a Level 2 cache and a ROM SIMM socket compatible with the Macintosh.

CICS
(Customer Information Control System) A TP monitor from IBM that was originally developed to provide transaction processing for IBM mainframes. It controls the interaction between applications and users and lets programmers develop screen displays without detailed knowledge of the terminals used. It provides terminal routing, password security, transaction logging for error recovery and activity journals for performance analysis.

CICS has also been made available on non-mainframe platforms including the RS/6000, AS/400 and OS/2-based PCs.

CICS commands are written along with and into the source code of the applications, typically COBOL, although assembly language, PL/I and RPG are also used. CICS implements SNA layers 4, 5 and 6.

CICS programmer

A programmer versed in CICS commands as well as in the programming language used to develop the application.

CIDR

(Classless Inter-Domain Routing) A method for reducing the burden on routing tables in the Internet. It provides a subnetwork for Internet service providers by combining a number of Class C addresses into one. See *IP address*.

CIE model

(Commission Internationale de l'Eclairage model) A color model defined in 1931 that represents all possible colors in a three-dimensional color space. All of the variants of CIE (CIELAB, CIELUV, CIEXYZ, etc.) use values of lightness, red-green and yellow-blue to represent a color. The CIE Chromaticity Diagram is a two-dimensional drawing of this model.

CIF

(Common Intermediate Format) A video format that transmits 36.45 Mbits/sec at 30 frames/sec. See *QCIF* and *H.261*.

CI Labs

(Component Integration Labs, Sunnyvale, CA) The vendor consortium that manages OpenDoc.

CIM

(1) (Computer-Integrated Manufacturing) Integrating office/accounting functions with automated factory systems. Point of sale, billing, machine tool scheduling and supply ordering are part of CIM.

(2) (CompuServe Information Manager) See *CompuServe*.

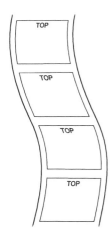

cine-oriented

A film-image orientation like that of movie film, in which the tops of the frames run perpendicular to the outer edge of the medium. Contrast with *comic-strip oriented*.

Cinepak

A video compression/decompression algorithm from SuperMac Technologies, Sunnyvale, CA, that is used to compress movie files. It is widely used on the Macintosh and is included in Windows 95.

CIO

(Chief Information Officer) The executive officer in charge of all information processing in an organization.

ciphertext

Data that has been coded (enciphered, encrypted, encoded) for security purposes.

CIR

(Committed Information Rate) In a frame relay network, the minimum speed maintained between nodes.

circuit

(1) A set of electronic components that perform a particular function in an electronic system.

(2) Same as *communications channel.*

circuit analyzer

(1) A device that tests the validity of an electronic circuit.

(2) In communications, same as *data line monitor.*

circuit board

Same as *printed circuit board.*

circuit breaker

A protective device that opens a circuit upon sensing a current overload. Unlike a fuse, it can be reset.

circuit card

Same as *printed circuit board.*

circuit cellular

The transmission of data over the cellular network using a voice channel and modem similar to using land-based modems. Contrast with *packet cellular.* See *wireless.*

circuit switching

The temporary connection of two or more communications channels. Users have full use of the circuit until the connection is terminated. Contrast with *message switching,* which stores messages and forwards them later, and contrast with *packet switching,* which breaks up a message into packets and routes each packet through the most expedient path at that moment.

Circuit switching is used by the telephone company for its voice networks in order to guarantee steady, consistent service for two people engaged in a telephone conversation.

CIS

(1) (CompuServe Information Service) See *CompuServe.*

(2) (Card Information Structure) A data structure on a PCMCIA card that contains information about the card's contents. It allows the card to describe its configuration requirements to its host computer.

CIS B

(CompuServe Information Service B) A proprietary communications protocol from CompuServe that is used for transferring files. See *B protocol.*

CISC

(Complex Instruction Set Computer) Pronounced "sisk." The traditional architecture of a computer which uses microcode to execute very comprehensive instructions. Instructions may be variable in length and use all addressing modes, requiring complex circuitry to decode them. Contrast with *RISC.*

Cisco

(Cisco Systems, Inc., San Jose, CA) Founded in 1984, Cisco is a major manufacturer of networking equipment, including routers, bridges, Ethernet and ATM switches, dial-up access servers and network management software. Starting in 1993, Cisco acquired several companies, including Crescendo Communications (CDDI networking), Newport Systems Solutions (software-based routers), Kalpana (Ethernet switches) and LightStream Corporation (ATM switches).

CL/1

(Connectivity Language/1) A database language from Apple that lets a Macintosh access an SQL-based database in another computer. CL/1 applications communicate with the CL/1 client program in the Mac, and the client program communicates with the CL/1 server program in the host computer.

cladding

The plastic or glass sheath that is fused to and surrounds the core of an optical fiber. It keeps the light waves inside the core and adds strength to it. The cladding is covered with a protective outer jacket.

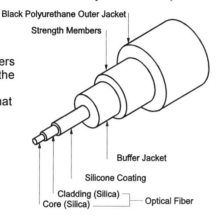

Black Polyurethane Outer Jacket
Strength Members

Cladding
The cladding covers the inner core of the fiber which is the actual pathway that the light travels through.

Buffer Jacket
Silicone Coating
Cladding (Silica)
Core (Silica) ──── Optical Fiber

clamping ring

The part of a 5.25" floppy disk drive that presses the disk onto the spindle. It is usually part of the centering cone.

Clarion

A family of application development systems for DOS and Windows from TopSpeed Corporation, Pompano Beach, FL. It provides a comprehensive set of tools for development, including a screen builder, 4GL and application generator. It includes a compiler that is known for generating fast executables. It also includes a data dictionary and drivers for popular databases. TopSpeed Corporation was formerly Clarion Software Corporation.

Claris

(Claris Corporation, Santa Clara, CA) A software subsidiary of Apple that was separated from the corporation (although mostly owned by it) in 1988 and then bought back in 1990.

Claris CAD

A full-featured 2-D CAD program for the Macintosh from Claris Corporation that is noted for its ease of use. It provides an easy-to-learn path into CAD, while offering most features found in CAD programs.

ClarisWorks

An integrated software package for the Mac and Windows from Claris. It includes a word processor, spreadsheet, database and drawing program. Without using OpenDoc or OLE, ClarisWorks provides its own form of compound document creation that lets you, for example, insert a spreadsheet into your text document.

class

In object-oriented programming, a user-defined data type that defines a collection of objects that share the same characteristics. A class member (object) is an "instance" of the class. Concrete classes are designed to be "instantiated." Abstract classes are designed to pass on characteristics through inheritance.

Class A, B

See *FCC Class.*

class library

An object-oriented programming classes suplied by third parties; for example, a GUI library.

CLCC

(Ceramic Leaded Chip Carrier) See *leaded chip carrier*.

clean boot

Booting the computer without loading anything but the main part of the operating system.

clean room

A room in which the air is highly filtered in order to keep out impurities.

ClearCase

A software configuration management (SCM) system for client/server environments from Atria Software, Inc., Natick, MA. It supports all the major UNIX platforms as well as Windows NT.

clear memory

To reset all RAM and hardware registers to a zero or blank condition. Rebooting the computer may or may not clear memory, but turning the computer off and on again guarantees that memory is cleared.

clear to send

See *CTS*.

CLI

(Call Level Interface) A database programming interface from the SQL Access Group, an SQL membership organization. SAG's CLI is an attempt to standardize the SQL language for database access. Microsoft's ODBC conforms to the CLI, but adds its own extensions. Under CLI, SQL statements are passed directly to the server without being recompiled.

click

To select an object by pressing the mouse button when the cursor is pointing to the required menu option or icon.

click and drag

Using a pointing device, such as a mouse, to latch onto an icon on screen and move it to some other location. When the screen pointer is over the icon of the object, the mouse button is clicked to grab it. The button is held down while the object is moved ("dragged") to its destination. Then the mouse button is released.

ClickNet

A network diagramming program for Windows from PinPoint Software Corporation, San Jose, CA. It keeps the lines connected to the objects when they are moved and also allows a database to be linked to diagram objects for equipment and network documentation. More than 2,300 predefined images and 80 management reports are included.

clickstream

The trail of mouse clicks and keystrokes made by a user in the act of performing a particular operation on the computer.

client

(1) A workstation or personal computer in a client/server environment. See *client/server* and *fat client*.

(2) One end of the spectrum in a request/supply relationship between programs. See *X Window* and *OLE*.

Client Platforms (CPU & OS)

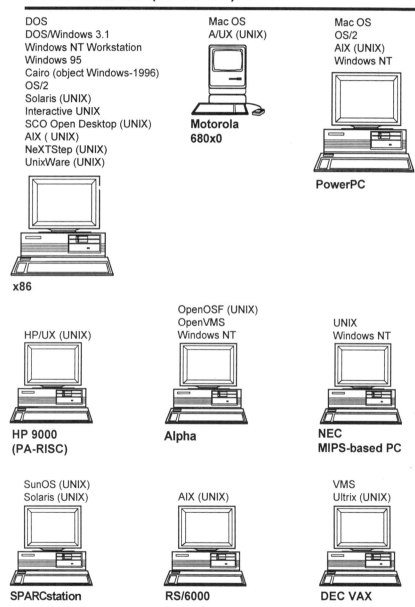

DOS
DOS/Windows 3.1
Windows NT Workstation
Windows 95
Cairo (object Windows-1996)
OS/2
Solaris (UNIX)
Interactive UNIX
SCO Open Desktop (UNIX)
AIX (UNIX)
NeXTStep (UNIX)
UnixWare (UNIX)

x86

Mac OS
A/UX (UNIX)

**Motorola
680x0**

Mac OS
OS/2
AIX (UNIX)
Windows NT

PowerPC

HP/UX (UNIX)

**HP 9000
(PA-RISC)**

OpenOSF (UNIX)
OpenVMS
Windows NT

Alpha

UNIX
Windows NT

**NEC
MIPS-based PC**

SunOS (UNIX)
Solaris (UNIX)

SPARCstation

AIX (UNIX)

RS/6000

VMS
Ultrix (UNIX)

DEC VAX

137

client application

An application running in a workstation or personal computer on a network. See also *OLE*.

client-client-server

An Apple architecture that allows users with remote devices, such as laptops and PDAs, to have easy access to their desktop machines (clients) as well as to the servers.

client/server

An architecture in which the client (personal computer or workstation) is the requesting machine and the server is the supplying machine. Servers can be high-speed microcomputers, minicomputers or even mainframes. The client provides the user interface and may perform some or all of the application processing.

A database server maintains the databases and processes requests from the client to extract data from or update the database. An application server provides additional business processing for the clients.

Client/server architecture is the equivalent of a mainframe system on a network of smaller computers. The network operating system (NOS) together with the DBMS (database management system) and TP monitor (transaction monitor) are responsible for the integrity and security of the system and must provide the same degree of robustness as mainframes for mission critical applications.

Client/server means that the server is used for more than just a remote disk drive. Simply downloading files from or sharing databases on a server is not true client/server architecture. Take a look at the following examples.

NON-CLIENT/SERVER

In non-client/server architecture, the server is nothing more than a remote disk drive. The user machine does all the processing. If many users routinely perform lengthy searches, this can bog down the network, because each client has to pass the entire database over the net. At 1,000 bytes per record, a 10,000 record database requires 10MB of data be transmitted.

TWO-TIER CLIENT/SERVER

In two-tier client/server, processing is done in both machines. An SQL request is generated from the database counterpart in the client and is transmitted to the database management system (DBMS) in the server. The DBMS seaches for the data locally and transmits back only the mathing records. If only 50 records met the criteria, only 50K would be sent over the network. In a LAN with heavy traffic, this method is required.

THREE-TIER CLIENT/SERVER

There are many business applications in which various components of the operation lend themselves to central processing in a server. Such programs may be too demanding of the user's PC, or they may be proprietary programs that should not be replicated throughout the enterprise. In addition, keeping the application in one machine makes administration easier.

Three-tier client/server is when one or more application servers are used. The client machine provides the user interface, the application server(s) provide shared processing, and the database server(s) process the queries and updates. See *client/server development system*.

Client/Server

Non-client/server
Entire database is passed over network (client does searching).

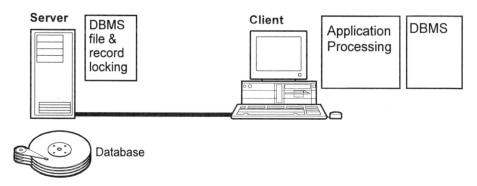

Database

Two-tier client/server
Only the results of the database search are passed to the client.

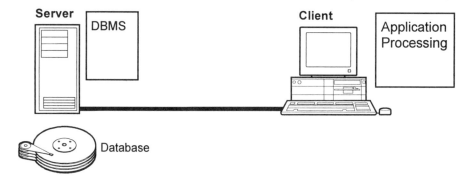

Database

Three-tier client/server
Separate server does some of the business logic.

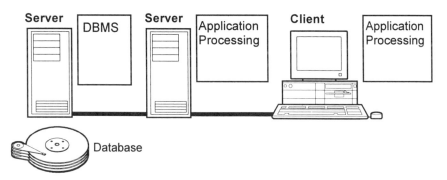

Database

client/server architecture

A network and application design that divides processing between clients and servers. See *client/server*.

client/server development system

An application development system used to create applications for a client/server environment. A comprehensive system generally includes a GUI builder for creating one or all of the major GUIs: Windows, Mac and Motif, a fourth-generation language for creating the business logic, an interpreter and/or compiler and debugging tools. It provides support for many of the major database management systems (Oracle, Sybase, Informix, etc.), and it may include its own DBMS.

For enterprise-wide client/server development, a system may allow for application partitioning, which separates parts of the application onto different machines. Such systems support the major server environments (UNIX, NetWare, etc.) in order to accomodate the dispersion of business logic onto multiple computers. It may also include software configuration management capabilities that provide version control and bug tracking.

Almost any language can be used to develop the client front ends in a client/server application. For example, Visual Basic is very popular for such purposes. However, a client/server system implies that client-to-server connections and application partitioning are written at a higher level than a 3GL programming language. It implies that there is little or no "tweaking" to make things happen. See *client/server* and *application partitioning*.

Following is a list of client/server development tools in alphabetical order. PowerBuilder, SQLWindows and Oracle's CDE are widely used. DYNASTY and Forte are a new breed of enterprise-wide tools, and dBASE and Paradox for Windows have moved into client/server with the addition of the Borland Database Engine.

Application Development Workbench
Axiant
CA-Visual Objects
C/S ELEMENTS
dBASE for Windows/Borland Database Engine

Delphi Client/Server
DYNASTY
Enfin/Object Studio
ESL for Windows
ESL Workbench

Forte
INFORMIX-New Era
JAM
ObjectPro
ObjectView

OMNIS
Oracle CDE (Oracle Forms, Oracle Reports, etc.)
Paradox for Windows/Borland Database Engine
Passport
PowerBuilder

Progress
SQLWindows
Superbase
Team Enterprise Developer
UNIFACE

Unify VISION
Visual Basic
Windows 4GL/CA-OpenRoad

client/server environment

A networking environment that is made up of clients and servers running applications designed for client/server architecture. See *client/server.*

client/server network

(1) A communications network that uses dedicated servers. In this context, the term is used to contrast it with a *peer-to-peer network*, which allows any client to also be a server.
(2) A network that is processing applications designed for client/server architecture. See *client/server.*

client/server protocol

A communications protocol that provides a structure for requests between client and server in a network. It refers to OSI layer 7.

clip art

A set of canned images used to illustrate word processing and desktop publishing documents.

clipboard

Reserved memory used to hold data that has been copied from one application in order to be inserted into another.

Clipper

(1)See *CA-Clipper.*
(2) A family of 32-bit RISC microprocessors from Intergraph Corporation, Huntsville, AL.
(3) An encryption chip endorsed by the U.S. government for general use that would let authorities unscramble the data if needed.

clipping

Cutting off the outer edges or boundaries of a word, signal or image. See *scissoring.*

clipping level

A disk's ability to maintain its magnetic properties and hold its content. A high-quality level range is 65-70%; low quality is below 55%.

clobbering memory

Erroneously writing into an area of memory that contains instructions and data that are still being worked on. See *memory* and *memory allocation.*

clock

An internal timing device. Following are the different varieties of clocks:

CPU Clock

Uses a quartz crystal to generate a uniform electrical frequency from which digital pulses are created and used. See *clock*

Realtime Clock
A time-of-day clock that keeps track of hours, minutes and seconds and makes this data available to the programs.

Timesharing Clock
A timer set to interrupt the CPU at regular intervals in order to provide equal time to all the users of the computer.

Communications Clock
In a synchronous communications device, a clock maintains the uniform transmission of data between the sending and receiving terminals and computers.

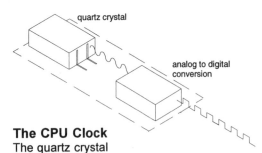

quartz crystal

analog to digital conversion

clock/calendar
An internal time clock and month/year calendar that is kept active with a battery. Its output allows software to remind users of appointments, to determine the age of a transaction and to activate tasks at specified times.

clock doubling
Doubling the internal processing speed of a CPU while maintaining the original clock speed for I/O (transfers in/out of the chip). Intel popularized the technique with its Speed Doubler chips. See *486* and *clock tripling*.

The CPU Clock
The quartz crystal generates continuous waves, which are converted into digital pulses.

clock pulse
A signal used to synchronize the operations of an electronic system. Clock pulses are continuous, precisely spaced changes in voltage. See *clock speed*.

clock speed
The internal heartbeat of a computer. The clock circuit uses fixed vibrations generated from a quartz crystal to deliver a steady stream of pulses to the CPU. A faster clock will speed up internal processing provided the computer's circuits can handle the increased speed. For example, the same processor running at 100MHz is twice as fast internally as one running at 50MHz.

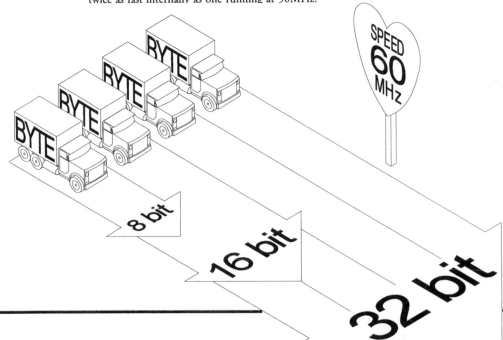

clock tripling

Tripling the internal processing speed of a CPU while maintaining the original clock speed for I/O (transfers in/out of the chip). See *DX4*.

clone

A device that works like the original, but does not necessarily look like it. It implies 100% functional compatibility.

closed

With regard to a switch, closed is "on." Open is "off."

closed architecture

A system whose technical specifications are not made public. Contrast with *open architecture*.

closed shop

An environment in which only data processing staff is allowed access to the computer. Contrast with *open shop*.

closed system

A system in which specficiations are kept proprietary to prevent third-party hardware or software from being used. Contrast with *open system*.

cloud

See *network cloud*.

cluster

Some number of disk sectors (typically two to 16) treated as a unit. The entire disk is divided into clusters, each one a minimum unit of storage. Thus, a 30-byte file may use up 2,048 bytes on disk if the disk cluster is four 512-byte sectors. See *lost cluster*.

cluster controller

A control unit that manages several peripheral devices, such as terminals or disk drives.

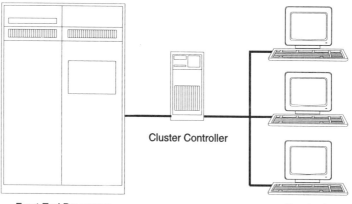

Front End Processor   Cluster Controller   Terminals

CLUT

(Color Look Up Table) A hardware or software table that contains color mixing information (intensity of red, green and blue) for each color in a palette or series of palettes.

CLV

(Constant Linear Velocity) A recording technique that rotates the disk at varying speeds. By changing speed depending on which track is being accessed, the density of bits in each track can be made uniform. This allows the outer tracks to hold more data than the inner tracks and fully utilizes the space on the disk. CLV is used on CDs, CD-ROMs and LaserDiscs. Contrast with *CAV.* See *ZBR.*

CM

See *configuration management.*

CM/2

(Communications Manager/2) A communications program for OS/2 from IBM that provides cross platform connectivity. It provides terminal emulation to IBM mainframes, AS/400s and VAXes and supports APPN and APPC protocols.

CMC

(Common Messaging Calls) A programming interface specified by the XAPIA as the standard messaging API for X.400 and other messaging systems. CMC is intended to provide a common API for applications that want to become mail enabled.

CMI

(Computer-Managed Instruction) Using computers to organize and manage an instructional program for students. It helps create test materials, tracks the results and monitors student progress.

CMIP

(Common Management Information Protocol) Pronounced "C-mip." A network monitoring and control standard from ISO. CMOT (CMIP over TCP) is a version that runs on TCP/IP networks, and CMOL (CMIP over LLC) runs on IEEE 802 LANs (Ethernet, Token Ring, etc.).

CMIS

(Common Management Information Services) Pronounced "C-miss." An OSI standard that defines the functions for network monitoring and control.

CMM

See *SEI.*

CMOL

See *CMIP.*

CMOS

(Complementary MOS) Pronounced "C moss." A type of integrated circuit widely used for processors and memories. It uses PMOS and NMOS transistors in a complementary fashion that results in less power to operate. The term is used loosely to refer to the CMOS RAM in a PC.

CMOS RAM

(1) A small, battery-backed memory bank in a personal computer that is used to hold time, date and system information such as drive types. In a PC, if disk drives are added, removed or changed, the parameters in the CMOS memory must be updated in order for the operating system to recognize the new devices.
To edit the data in the CMOS RAM, you have to gain access to a built-in setup program, which is done either immediately at boot time by pressing a key such as DEL or F1, or by pressing some key combination, such as Ctrl-Alt-Esc. If there is

no on-screen message that tells you what key to press when you reboot the computer, refer to your system manual (RTFM!). See *hard disk configuration*.
(2) Memory made of CMOS chips. Due to their low power requirement, they are increasingly being used for main memory in portable computers.

CMOS setup
See *hard disk configuration*.

CMOT
See *CMIP*.

CMS
(1) (Conversational Monitor System) Software that provides interactive communications for IBM's VM operating system. It allows a user or programmer to launch an application from a terminal and interactively work with it. The CMS counterpart in MVS is called TSO. Contrast with *RSCS*, which provides batch communications for VM.
(2) (Call Management System) An AT&T call accounting package for its PBXs.
(3) (Color Management System) A system for defining and maintaining consistent colors from the creation of documents and images to the final printing process.

CMYK
(Cyan Magenta Yellow blacK) A color model used for printing. In theory, cyan, magenta and yellow (CMY) can print all colors, but inks are not pure and black comes out muddy. Black ink is required for quality printing. See *colors* and *RGB*.

CNA
See *NetWare certification*.

CNC
(Computerized Numerical Control) See *numerical control*.

CNE, CNI
See *NetWare certification*.

CO
(Central Office) A local telephone company switching station that covers a geographic area such as a town or part of a city.

coax
Same as *coaxial cable*.

coax adapter
Same as *3270 emulator*. The board is sometimes called a coax adapter because of its coaxial cable connection to the IBM cluster controller.

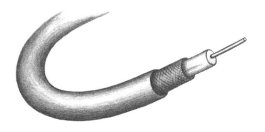

coaxial cable
A high-capacity cable used in communications and video, commonly called co-ax. It contains an insulated solid or stranded wire surrounded by a solid or braided metallic shield, wrapped in a plastic cover. Fire-safe teflon coating is optional.
Although similar in appearance, there are several types of coaxial cable, each designed with a different width and impedance for a particular purpose (TV, baseband, broadband). Coax provides a higher bandwidth than twisted wire pair. See *cable categories*.

COBOL

(COmmon Business Oriented Language) A high-level programming language that has been the primary business application language on mainframes and minis. It is a compiled language and was one of the first high-level languages developed. Formally adopted in 1960, it stemmed from a language called Flowmatic in the mid 1950s. COBOL is a very wordy language. Although mathematical expressions can also be written like other programming languages (see example below), its verbose mode is very readable for a novice. For example, **multiply hourly-rate by hours-worked giving gross-pay** is self-explanatory. COBOL is structured into the following divisions:

Division name	Contains
IDENTIFICATION	Program identification.
ENVIRONMENT	Types of computers used.
DATA	Buffers, constants and work areas.
PROCEDURE	The processing (program logic).

The following COBOL example converts a Fahrenheit number to Celsius. To keep the example simple, it performs the operation on the operator's terminal rather than a user terminal.

```
IDENTIFICATION DIVISION.
    PROGRAM-ID.  EXAMPLE.

ENVIRONMENT DIVISION.
    CONFIGURATION SECTION.
    SOURCE-COMPUTER.   IBM-370.
    OBJECT-COMPUTER.   IBM-370.

DATA DIVISION.
    WORKING-STORAGE SECTION.
    77 FAHR  PICTURE 999.
    77 CENT  PICTURE 999.

PROCEDURE DIVISION.
    DISPLAY 'Enter Fahrenheit ' UPON CONSOLE.
    ACCEPT FAHR FROM CONSOLE.
    COMPUTE CENT = (FAHR- 32) * 5 / 9.
    DISPLAY 'Celsius is ' CENT UPON CONSOLE.
    GOBACK.
```

IBM COBOLs

In 1994, IBM dropped support of OS/VS COBOL, which conforms to ANSI 68 and ANSI 74 standards and limits a program's address space to 16 bits. IBM's VS COBOL II (1984) and COBOL/370 (1991) conform to ANSI 85 standards and provide 31-bit addressing, which allows programs to run "above the line."
COBOL/370 is more compliant with AD/Cycle, has more string, math and date functions, including four-digit years, allows development through a PC window and provides enhanced runtime facilities.

CODASYL

(COnference on DAta SYstems Languages) An organization devoted to the development of computer languages. Founded in 1959, it is made up of individuals and institutions that contribute their own time and effort. COBOL is a product of CODASYL. For information, contact Jan Prokop, 29 Hartwell Avenue, Lexington, MA 02173, 617/863-5100.

code

(1) A set of machine symbols that represents data or instructions. See *data code* and *machine language*.
(2) Any representation of one set of data for another. For example, a parts code is an abbreviated name of a product, product type or category. A discount code is a percentage.
(3) To write a program. See *source code* and *line of code*.
(4) To encode for security purposes. See *encryption*.

codec

(1) (COder-DECoder) An electronic circuit that converts audio or video into digital code (and vice versa) using techniques such as pulse code modulation and delta modulation. A codec is an A/D and D/A converter.
(2) (COmpressor/DECompressor) A hardware circuit or software routine (software codec) used to compress and decompress digitized audio, video or images. A single codec may include the functions of A/D and D/A conversion as well as compression and decompression. See *video codec*.

code generator

See *application generator* and *macro recorder*.

code page

In DOS 3.3 and higher, a table that sets up the keyboard and display characters for various foreign languages.

coder

(1) A junior, or trainee, programmer who writes simple programs or writes the code for a larger program that has been designed by someone else.
(2) Person who assigns special codes to data.

CodeView

A Microsoft debugger for programs written with Microsoft C and CodeView-compatible compilers. Like other modern debuggers, it links source and object program letting the programmer step through the source code as the program is executed.

COFF

(Common Object File Format) A UNIX System V machine language format.

Cognos

(Cognos Inc., Ottawa, Canada) A software company that specializes in application development and 4GL tools. Founded in 1969 as a consulting firm, its PowerHouse 4GL was introduced in the late 1970s for midrange systems. Products include the PowerPlay EIS/DSS system, Impromptu report and query language and Axiant client/server development system.

COGO

(COordinate GeOmetry) A programming language used for solving civil engineering problems.

Coherent

A version of UNIX for 386s and up from Mark Williams Co., Northbrook, IL, that supports a variety of office applications off the shelf. It includes a C compiler, over 200 utilities and the Bourne and Korn shells. It uses minimal system resources.

COLD

(Computer Output to LaserDisc) Archiving large volumes of transactions on optical media. Instead of printing large paper reports or producing microfilm or microfiche, data is stored on optical disks. The advantage of COLD over COM (Computer Output Microfilm) for high-volume, archival storage is that optical disks can be directly accessed just like a hard disk.

cold boot

Starting the computer by turning power on. Turning power off and then back on again clears memory and many internal settings. Some program failures will lock up the computer and require a cold boot to use the computer again. In other cases, only a warm boot is required. See *boot, warm boot* and *clean boot*.

ColdFire

A 680x0 CPU architecture from Motorola that has been specialized for embedded systems. It is faster and smaller than previous 680x0 chips and also contains fewer instructions. ColdFire is targeted for use in consumer electronics devices.

cold start

Same as *cold boot*.

collapsed backbone

A network configuration in which a high-speed bus within a single equipment cabinet is used as the backbone.

collating sequence

The sequence, or order, of the character set built into a computer. See *ASCII chart* and *EBCDIC chart*.

collator

(1) A punched card machine that merges two decks of cards into one or more stacks. (2) A utility program that merges records from two or more files into one file.

collector

One side of a bipolar transistor. When the base is pulsed, current flows from the emitter to the collector, or vice versa depending on the design. See *drain*.

collision detection

See *CSMA/CD*.

color bits

The number of bits associated with each pixel that represent its color. See *bit depth*.

color calibration

The matching of colors to a base color, such as a Pantone color, or from one device to another; for example, screen and printer output.

color cycling

In computer graphics, a technique that simulates animation by continuously changing colors rather than moving the objects. Also called color lookup table animation.

color depth

Same as *bit depth*.

color graphics

The ability to display graphic images in colors.

color key

A technique for superimposing a video image onto another. For example, to float a car on the ocean, the car image is placed onto a blue background. The car and ocean images are scanned together. The ocean is made to appear in the resulting image wherever background (blue) exists in the car image. The ocean is cancelled wherever the car appears (no background).

color map

See *CLUT*.

color model

The method used to represent color for display and printing. See *RGB, CIE, CMYK, HSV, HLS* and *YIQ*.

color monitor

See *monitor*.

color printer

A printer that prints in color using dot matrix, electrophotographic, Cycolor, electrostatic, ink jet or thermal-transfer techniques. See *printer*.

colors

The perception of the different wavelengths of light. It is possible to create almost all visible colors using two systems of primary colors. Transmitted colors use red, green and blue (RGB), and reflected colors use cyan (light blue), magenta (purplish-red), yellow and black (CMYK). Color displays use RGB (colors are added to create white) and color printing uses CMYK (colors are subtracted to create white).

color separation

Separating a picture by colors in order to make negatives and plates for color printing. Full color requires four separations: cyan, magenta, yellow and black (CMYK). See *OPI* and *DCS*.

color space

A 3-D model of the three attributes of a color, which are hue, value and saturation (chroma).

color space conversion

Changing one color signal into another. It typically refers to converting YUV analog video into digital RGB video.

column

A vertical set of data or components. Contrast with *row*.
(See illustration on next page).

column move

Relocating a rectangular block of characters within a text document or a column in a spreadsheet.

columns

See *column*.

COM

(1) (Common Object Model) An object, or ORB, standard from Digital and Microsoft announced in late 1993. It is based on Microsoft's OLE2 (second generation of OLE), whose underlying structure is called Component Object Model.

Columns
of
text
on a
character-based
display
screen.

REPORT COLUMNS

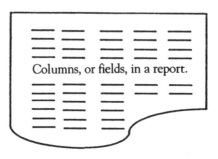

Columns, or fields, in a report.

COLUMNS OF PIXELS

Columns
of dots
in a
graphics
system.
(Raster graphics
or
dot matrix).

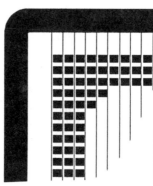

MAGAZINE COLUMNS

TABBED COLUMNS

EXPENSES	Planned	Actual
Rent	2,300.00	2,300.00
Electric	450.00	562.23
Gas	100.00	87.46
Water	50.00	43.23
Phone	1100.00	1457.99
Salaries	12,330.00	12,765.32
Auto	1200.00	1,371.09
Garage	225.00	225.00
Entertainment	1500.00	1,093.44
Travel	2500.00	2,788.40
Fees	6000.00	2850.00
Commissions	22,000.00	17,844.34
Advertising	5000.00	7,488.21
Miscellaneous	5000.00	2,389.20
TOTAL	59,755.00	53,265.91

NAME	STREET	BALANCE
Jones, Jennifer A.	10 West Main Ave.	0000208.49
Russo, George C.	23 East Benton St.	0000107.49
Morrison, Emil T.	1240 Parkway East	0001005.77
Fernandez, Joseph R.	39 Gate Drive	0003484.49

Columns of data
cells in a spreadsheet
or fields in a
database.

COM is not CORBA compliant; however, interoperability between COM and CORBA is expected.

(2) (Computer Output Microfilm) Creating microfilm or microfiche from computer output. A COM machine can be online or stand-alone (transfer via tape/disk). It receives print-image output from the computer and creates a film image of each page. Additional graphics (lines, logos, etc.) can be added.

(3) See *COM port* and *dot com*.

COM1

In a PC, the logical name assigned to the first serial port. Two serial ports, or COM ports, are provided on a PC to connect a mouse and modem. Typically the mouse is on COM1, and the modem on COM2, but this is not mandatory. Any serial device can be connected to either serial port.

The COM1 and COM2 names are used to inform the operating system of the physical connections that have been made. The term originated before the days of the mouse, when the serial port was primarily used for modem COMmunications. DOS versions up to 3.2 support COM1 and COM2. Version 3.3 supports up to COM4, and OS/2 supports eight COM ports. Contrast with *LPT1*.

COM2

In a PC, the logical name assigned to the second serial port. See *COM1*.

COMDEX

(COMputer Dealers EXposition) A trade show originally intended for PC manufacturers, developers, dealers and distributors. However, large numbers of end users attend. Sponsored by SOFTBANK COMDEX Inc., COMDEX/Fall in Las Vegas is the largest U.S. computer show. It is housed in both major convention centers as well as in several large hotels. It takes over the city.

Shuttle buses escort attendees between sites. Waiting in line for a bus can become a welcome relief after walking the massive corridors of COMDEX. COMDEX Las Vegas is exhausting, and fascinating.

COMDEX was originally developed by The Interface Group, which was acquired by the Japanese SOFTBANK Corporation in 1995. The first COMDEX/Fall in 1979 had 157 exhibitors and 4,000 attendees. In 1994, over 2,200 exhibitors drew 200,000 attendees.

COMDEX/Spring has been held in Chicago and Atlanta. It began in 1981 with 237 exhibitors and more than 11,000 attendees. In 1995 Atlanta drew 1,100 exhibitors and more than 100,000 exhibitors.

SOFTBANK COMDEX is located at 300 First Avenue, Needham, MA 02194. For more information, call 617/433-1500.

Comensa

A datacenter control system from MAXM Systems Corporation, Vienna, VA, used to monitor a variety of minicomputers and mainframes. It can set off audio alarms if problems occur.

COM file

(1) (COMmand file) An executable DOS or OS/2 program that takes up less than 64K and fits within one segment. It is an exact replica of how it looks in memory. See *EXE file*.

(2) A VMS file containing commands to be executed.

comic-strip oriented

A film-image orientation like a comic strip, in which the tops of the frames run parallel with the edge of the film. Contrast with *cine-oriented*.

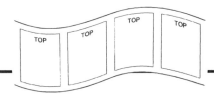

comma delimited

A record layout that separates data fields with a comma and usually surrounds character data with quotes, for example:

```
"Pat Smith","5 Main St.","New Hope","PA","18950"
"K. Jones","34 E. 88 Ave.","Syosset","NY","10024"
```

command

Instruction for the computer. See *command-driven, menu-driven* and *function.*

COMMAND.COM

The command processor in DOS and Windows 95. COMMAND.COM displays the DOS prompt and executes the DOS commands you type in. The COMMAND.COM in Windows 95 has been expanded to accomodate long file names.

command-driven

A program that accepts commands as typed-in phrases. It is usually harder to learn, but may offer more flexibility than a menu-driven program. Once learned, command-driven programs may be faster to use, because the user can state a request succinctly. Contrast with *menu-driven.*

command interpreter

Same as *command processor.*

Command key

On Apple keyboards, a key with the outline of an Apple, a propeller, or both. It is pressed along with another key to command the computer.

command language

A special-purpose language that accepts a limited number of commands, such as a query language, job control language (JCL) or command processor. Contrast with *programming language,* which is a general purpose language.

command line

In a command-driven system, the area on screen that accepts typed-in commands.

command mode

An operating mode that causes the computer or modem to accept commands for execution.

command processor

A system program that accepts a limited number of user commands and converts them into the machine commands required by the operating system or some other control program or application. COMMAND.COM is the command processor that accompanies DOS. See *4DOS.*

command queuing

The ability to store multiple commands and execute them one at a time.

command set

Same as *instruction set.*

command shell

Same as *command processor.*

comment

A descriptive statement in a source language program that is used for documentation.

comment out

To disable lines of code in a program by surrounding them with comment-start and comment-stop characters.

commercial software

Software that is designed and developed for sale to the general public.

Commodore

(Commodore Business Machines, Inc., West Chester, PA) In 1977, Commodore introduced the PET computer and launched the personal computer industry along with Apple and Radio Shack. In 1982, it introduced the Commodore 64 (64K RAM) and later the Commodore 128. These were popular home computers, and over 10 million were sold.

In 1985, the Amiga series was introduced, which continued to offer advanced imaging and video capabilities at affordable prices. A line of IBM-compatible PCs were also introduced, but the Amiga series was Commodore's mainstay until May of 1994, when the company went into bankruptcy. Escom, AG, a German computer manufacturer and retail organization, purchased the Commodore technology and is expected to manufacture and sell Amigas once again.

Commodore 128

common carrier

A government-regulated organization that provides telecommunications services for public use, such as AT&T, the telephone companies, ITT, MCI and Western Union.

Common Desktop Environment

See *CDE*.

Common Gateway Interface

See *CGI*.

Common Ground

Document exchange software from No Hands Software, Inc., Belmont, CA, that converts a Windows or Macintosh document into a proprietary file format for viewing on other machines. The viewer allows multiple documents to be displayed at the same time. No Hands calls its file format "Digital Paper."

Common OS API

A specification for a standard UNIX programming interface (API) which was defined in 1993 by all major UNIX vendors, including Sun, HP, IBM, DEC, Novell and SCO. It led to Spec 1170, which is governed by the X/Open consortium.

CommonPoint

See *Taligent*.

comm port

May refer to any serial communications port or specifically to the serial ports on a PC. See *COM1*.

comm program

See *communications program*.

communications

The electronic transfer of information from one location to another. *Data communications* refers to digital transmission, and *telecommunications* refers to analog and digital transmission, including voice and video.

The Protocol

The way communications systems "talk to" each other is defined in a set of standards called *protocols*. Protocols work in a hierarchy starting at the top with the user's program and ending at the bottom with the plugs, sockets and electrical signals. See *communications protocol* and *OSI* .

Personal Computer Communications Take Several Forms

Via Modem

Data can be transferred between two distant personal computers by using modems, a telephone line and a communications program in each computer.

Between Two Computers

Data can be transferred between two local computers by cabling them together with a null modem cable and a file transfer program in each computer.

Remote Terminal

Personal computers can act like a remote terminal to a mini or mainframe. For example, a 3270 emulation board, such as Attachmate's Irma board, plugs into a personal computer and turns it into an IBM mainframe terminal.

Network

Personal computers can be part of a local area network (LAN), in which databases and printers are shared among users. If the LAN interconnects with mini and mainframe networks, then personal computers can communicate with larger computers.

Increasingly, LANs of personal computers are running applications previously delegated to minis and mainframes. These applications are designed as "client/server" applications, which duplicate the integrity, security and transaction processing requirements of the larger computers.

Minicomputer Communications

Minicomputer communications systems control as many as several hundred terminals connected to a single computer system. They support a variety of low-speed dial-up terminals and higher-speed local terminals. With larger minicomputers, the communications processing is handled in separate machines, called *communications controllers*.

Minicomputers are designed with communications in mind. The communications programs and operating systems are often integrated and provide simpler operation than mainframes.

Minicomputers can connect to a mainframe by emulating a mainframe terminal, in which case, the mainframe thinks it's talking to another user terminal. Minicomputers can connect directly to some LANs, or to all LANs via a gateway, which converts the protocols.

Mainframe Communications

Mainframe systems can control several thousand remote terminals. They support a variety of low-speed dial-up terminals and high-speed local terminals.

Large mainframes use separate machines, called *communications controllers* or *front end processors*, to handle the communications processing. These machines take the data from the mainframes and package it for transmission over the network. They also strip the communications codes from the incoming messages and send pure data to the mainframes for processing.

Mainframes set the standards for communications. It's usually up to the mini and micro vendors to provide compatibility with the mainframe systems.

Analog vs Digital Communications

The most common form of long-distance communications has been the telephone system, which, up until a few years ago, transmitted only voice frequencies. This technique, known as *analog* communications, has been error prone, because the electronic frequencies get mixed together with unwanted signals (noise) that are nearby.

In analog telephone networks, amplifiers are placed in the line every few miles to boost the signal, but they cannot distinguish between signal and noise. Thus, the noise is amplified along with the signal. By the time the receiving person or machine gets the signal, it may be impossible to decipher it.

In a *digital* network, only two (binary) distinct frequencies or voltages are transmitted. Instead of amplifiers, repeaters are used, which analyze the incoming signal and regenerate a new outgoing signal. Any noise on the line is filtered out at the next repeater. When data is made up of only two signals (0 and 1), it can be more easily distinguished from the garble. Digital is simple!

The First Analog Communications (1876)
"Mr. Watson, come here. I want to see you."
(Photo courtesy of AT&T.)

Communication Program

Communications programs allow users to connect to remote computers, online services and bulletin boards (BBSs) via modem. Comm programs include a variety of file transfer protocols as shown in window (1) below. In order to transmit a file, both sender and receiver must use the same communications protocol. Zmodem is one of the most popular general-purpose protocols. Parity, data bits and stop bits are additional settings that must be the same on both sides. A phonebook (2) is included for numbers that are frequently dialed. Clicking on a name sends commands to the modem to dial the recipient's telephone number. The upload and download functions manage the transmission according to the rules of the protocol.

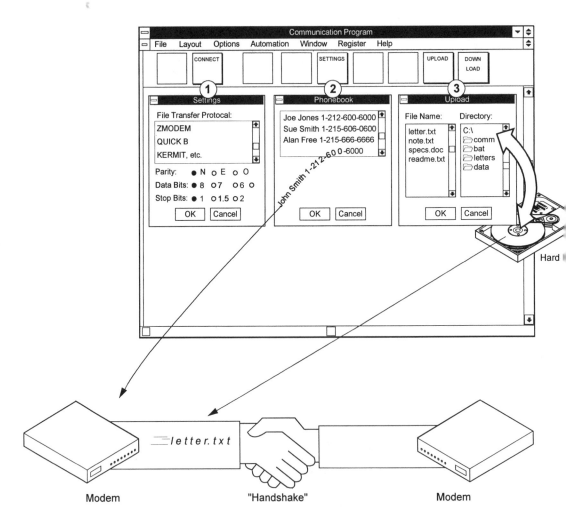

Communications Act

The establishment of the Federal Communications Commission (FCC) in 1934, the regulatory body for interstate and foreign telecommunications. Its mission is to provide high-quality services at reasonable cost to everyone in the U.S. on a nondiscriminatory basis.

communications channel

Also called a *circuit* or *line*, it is a pathway over which data is transferred between remote devices. It may refer to the entire physical medium, such as a telephone line, optical fiber, coaxial cable or twisted wire pair, or, it may refer to one of several carrier frequencies transmitted simultaneously within the line as in broadband transmission (see *broadband*).

communications controller

A peripheral control unit that connects several communications lines to a computer and performs the actual transmitting and receiving as well as various message coding and decoding activities.

Communications controllers are typically nonprogrammable units designed for specific protocols and communications tasks. Contrast with *front end processor*, which can be programmed for a variety of protocols and network conditions.

communications network

The transmission channels interconnecting all client and server stations as well as all supporting hardware and software.

communications parameters

The basic settings for modem transmission, which include bit rate (2400 bps, 9600 bps, etc.), parity (none, even, odd), number of data bits (7 or 8) and number of stop bits (typically 1). See *N-8-1*.

communications program

Software that manages the transmission of data between computers and terminals. In personal computers, it manages transmission to and from the computer's serial port. It includes several communications protocols and can usually emulate dumb terminals for hookup to minis and mainframes.

In a file server, the communications program is called the *network operating system* (NetWare, LANtastic). In mini and mainframe networks, the programs that support communications are called *access methods, network control programs* and *TP monitors*. See *front end processor*.

communications protocol

Hardware and software standards that govern transmission between two stations. On personal computers, communications programs offer a variety of protocols (Kermit, Xmodem, Zmodem, etc.) to transfer files via modem.

On LANs, data link protocols such as Ethernet, Token Ring and FDDI provide the access method (OSI layers 1 and 2) that moves packets from station to station, and higher level protocols, such as NetBIOS, IPX and TCP/IP (OSI layers 3, 4 and 5) control and route the transmission.

The following conceptual exchange is at the data link level (Zmodem, Ethernet, etc.), which ensures that a block of data is transferred between two nodes without error.

The Data Link Protocol

Are you there? **Yes, I am.** Are you ready to receive? **Yes, I am.** Here comes the message—bla, bla, bla— did you get it? **Yes, I did.** Here comes the next part—bla, bla, bla— did you get it? **No, I didn't.** Here it comes again— bla, bla, bla— did you get it? **Yes, I did.** There is no more. Goodbye. **Goodbye.**

communications satellite

A radio relay station in orbit 22,300 miles above the equator. It travels at the same rate of speed as the earth (geosynchronous), so that it appears stationary. It contains many communications channels that receive analog and digital signals from earth stations. All signals are transmitted within a carrier frequency. The signals are amplified and transmitted back to earth, covering either a small geographical area (spot beam) or almost a third of the earth's surface. In the latter case, private data is often encrypted.

communications server

A computer that provides communications services to external terminals or personal computers. It controls a pool of modems and provides outside line connection from a computer to remote terminals or from a LAN to remote users. It also lets remote users dial up a central computer or LAN. When used in a LAN to connect portable computers, it is usually called a *remote access server*. Sometimes gateways are called communications servers.

compact disc

See *CD*.

COMPACT II

A high-level numerical control programming language used to generate instructions for numerical control (machine tool) devices.

compandor

(COMpressor/exPANDOR) A device that improves the signal for AM radio transmission. On outgoing transmission, it raises the amplitude of weak signals and lowers the amplitude of strong signals. On incoming transmission, it restores the signal to its original form.

companies

See *hardware vendors*, *software vendors*, *vendors* and *online services*.

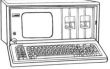

Compaq Portable
This machine put Compaq on the map real fast. Its portability (or luggability), its incredible reliability and its true IBM PC compatibility made it a huge success.

Compaq

(Compaq Computer Corporation, Houston, TX) A leading PC manufacturer founded in 1982 by Rod Canion, Bill Murto and Jim Harris. In 1983, it shipped 53,000 PC-compatible COMPAQ Portables, which resulted in $111 million in revenues and an American business record. The Portable's success was due to its rugged construction, ability to run all PC software and its semi-portability (it weighed 30 pounds!).

In 1984, it introduced its DESKPRO desktop computers and achieved a computer-industry sales record in its second year. In 1986, it was the first to offer a 386-based machine. Throughout its history, Compaq has been well respected for its computer products.

comparator

A device that compares two quantities and determines their equality.

compare

A fundamental computer capability. By comparing one set of data with another, the computer can locate, analyze, select, reorder and make decisions. After comparing, the computer can indicate whether the data were equal or which set was numerically greater or less than the other. See *ASCII chart* and "The 3 C's" in *computer*.

Compass connector

An input/output connector from the Archistrat Technologies division of The Panda Project, Boca Raton, FL, that provides up to 132 contacts per linear inch and up to 1,100 per square inch. Each pin is split into quarters like the four points of a compass.

compatibility

See *standards & compatibility*.

compatibility mode

A feature of a computer or operating system that allows it to run programs written for a different system. Programs often run slower in compatibility mode.

compilation

Compiling a program. See *compiler*.

compiler

(1) Software that translates a high-level programming language (COBOL, C, etc.) into machine language. A compiler usually generates assembly language first and then translates the assembly language into machine language.

The following example compiles program statements into machine language:

Source code	Assembly Language	Machine language
IF COUNT=10	Compare A to B	Compare 3477 2883
GOTO DONE	If equal go to C	If = go to 23883
ELSE	Go to D	Go to 23343
GOTO AGAIN		
ENDIF		

Actual machine code
1001010100010100010100
1010101001010100100010
1010010101000101001010

(2) Software that converts a high-level language into a lower-level representation. For example, a help compiler converts a text document embedded with appropriate commands into an online help system. A dictionary compiler converts terms and definitions into a dictionary lookup system.

compiler language

See *high-level language* and *compiler*.

compile time

The time it takes to translate a program from source language into machine language. Link editing time may also be included in compile time.

complement

The number derived by subtracting a number from a base number. For example, the tens complement of 8 is 2. In set theory, complement refers to all the objects in one set that are not in another set.

Complements are used in digital circuits, because it's faster to subtract by adding complements than by performing true subtraction. The binary complement of a number is created by reversing all bits and adding 1. The carry from the high-order position is eliminated. The following example subtracts 5 from 8.

Decimal Subtraction	Binary Equivalent	Subtraction by Adding the complement
8	1000	1000
-5	-0101	+1011
3	0011	0011

component

One element of a larger system. A hardware component can be a device as small as a transistor or as large as a disk drive as long as it is part of a larger system. Software components are routines or modules within a larger system.

component software

Software routines that are designed to work together and cooperate with each other. For years, this has been a dream of the software community, but it is slowly materializing. Object technology has formalized the building of self-contained program modules that interact with each other. In time, more and more programs may be built by combining components.

In addition, the industry is moving towards document-centric processing in which a compound document contains text, images and video. It requires that different applications can be called on instantly to work on each piece of the document with no more effort than moving the cursor to the appropriate data structure that is on screen.

In many cases, users do not really need full-blown applications to do simple tasks such as text editing and spreadsheet computations. It is expected that smaller software components that provide a handful of functions may eventually replace the monster applications that do everything. Through transport mechanisms such as OpenDoc, CORBA and OLE, it is hoped that these components can seamlessly interoperate in a heterogeneous environment. See *OpenDoc, CORBA* and *OLE*.

COM port

A serial communications port on a PC. See *COM1* and *serial port*.

composite video

The video-only (no audio) part of a TV signal. Used on early personal computers for TV hookup, it mixes red, green, blue and sync signals like a standard TV and is not as crisp as separate red, green and blue cables (RGB).

compound document

A single document that contains a combination of data structures such as text, graphics, spreadsheets, sound and video clips. The document may embed the additional data types or reference external files by pointers of some kind. SGML and HTML are examples of compound document formats.

OLE and OpenDoc are examples of object-oriented compound document architectures. They allow the user to edit each of the data objects by automatically calling in the application that created them.

compress

To compact data to save space. See *data compression*.

compression

See *data compression*.

compression ratio

The measurement of compressed data. For example, a file compressed into 1/4th of its original size can be expressed as 4:1, 25%, 75% or 2 bits per byte.

compressor
(1) A device that diminishes the range between the strongest and weakest transmission signals. See *compandor*.
(2) A routine or program that compresses data. See *data compression*.

Compsurf
A NetWare utility that performs a high-level hard disk format. NetWare servers require their own proprietary format.

CompTIA
(Computing Technology Industry Association, 450 East 22nd St., Lombard, IL 60148, 708/268-1818) Formerly ABCD:The Microcomputer Industry Association, it is a membership organization of resellers, distributors and manufacturers dedicated to business ethics and professionalism, founded in 1982. It sets voluntary guidelines and is involved with many issues including product returns, frieght and warranty claims and price protection.
It also provides certification for computer service technicians, known as A+, which is administered by Drake testing centers throughout the U.S. and Canada.

CompuServe
An online information service that provides conferencing, news, e-mail and access to a huge number of technical support forums, software files and databases.
CompuServe provides access to Internet e-mail and newsgroups, and FTP capability via the CompuServe Information Manager (CIM). The CIM software also makes it easier to navigate the system rather than using a generic communications program. See *online services*.

compute
To perform mathematical operations or general computer processing. See *computer (The 3 C's)*.

compute bound
Same as *process bound*.

computer
A general-purpose machine that processes data according to a set of instructions that are stored internally either temporarily or permanently. The computer and all equipment attached to it are called *hardware*. The instructions that tell it what to do are called *software*. A set of instructions that perform a particular task is called a program, or *software program*.

What a Computer Does

The instructions in the program direct the computer to input, process and output as follows:

Input/Output
The computer can selectively retrieve data into its main memory (RAM) from any peripheral device (terminal, disk, tape, etc.) connected to it. After processing the data internally, the computer can send a copy of the results from its memory out to any peripheral device. The more memory it has, the more programs and data it can work with at the same time.

Storage
By outputting data onto a magnetic disk or tape, the computer is able to store data permanently and retrieve it when required. A system's size is based on how much disk storage it has. The more disk, the more data is immediately available.

Calculate, Compare and Copy (The 3 C's)

The following examples show a similar sequence of events. Data is read from the disk and written into memory (RAM). Once in memory, it can be processed by calculating, comparing and copying.

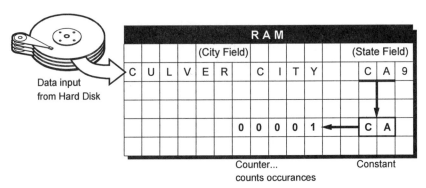

Data input
from Hard Disk

Counter...
counts occurances

Constant

Finding Things All searches (queries) in the computer are accomplished by **comparing**. The example above counts all the California records in the database by comparing each record with "CA." Every record in the database is read into memory. The memory locations that the STATE field falls into are compared with a constant in the program that contains the letters C and A. If they are equal, then a 1 is added to the California counter (**calculating**). After the first record is compared, the second record is written into the same memory locations, and the field is compared again, and this process is performed over and over until all the records in the database have been searched.

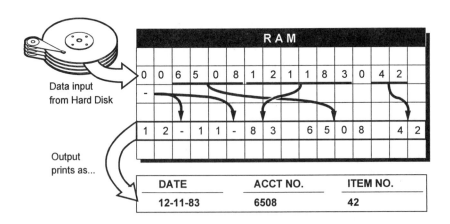

Data input
from Hard Disk

Output
prints as...

DATE	ACCT NO.	ITEM NO.
12-11-83	6508	42

Displaying and Printing Data is stored as contiguous fields in the database. There are no blanks between the fields for human readability. The data is displayed and printed the way we like to see it by writing the data into memory and **copying** the characters into the desired order. The date in this example is printed through a "picture," which is a set of characters that serves as a filter. Each character in the date is **compared** to each character in the picture, and the character that is copied as output is determined by the rules. Pictures can be implemented in software or in hardware.

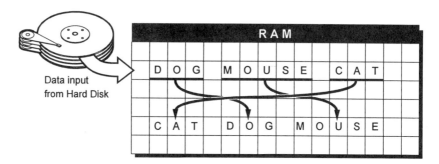

Sorting Sorting, or resequencing, data in the computer is accomplished by **comparing** each item of data with the others and **copying** it into the appropriate order. Of course, there's a ton of **calculating** going on to keep track of what is being compared. In the early to mid 1960s, when most databases were stored on magnetic tape, the speed of a vendor's sort program was a powerful marketing feature. All transactions had to be sorted into, for example, customer file sequence in order to be processed. In today's online systems, data is often indexed. Instead of sorting the rather lengthy data records, the much smaller indexes are sorted.

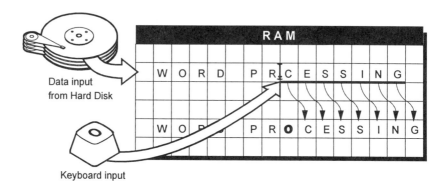

Editing The magic of word processing is really nothing more than **copying** the text in memory. In this example, if you want to insert a character into an existing line, the remaining characters are simply copied one memory location (byte) to the right so there is room for the additional letter. Deleting is just the opposite. Copying in reverse. As in all data processing, there is alot of **calculating** and **comparing** going on to keep track of where the text is stored in memory.

Processing:	Once the data is in the computer's memory, the computer can process it by
(The 3 C's*)	calculating, comparing and copying it.

Calculate
The computer can perform any mathematical operation on data by adding, subtracting, multiplying and dividing one set with another.

Compare
The computer can analyze and evaluate data by matching it with sets of known data that are included in the program or called in from storage.

Copy
The computer can move data around to create any kind of report or listing in any order.

By calculating, comparing and copying, the computer accomplishes all forms of data processing. For example, records are sorted into a new order by comparing two records at a time and copying the record with the lower value in front of the one with the higher value.

The computer finds one customer out of thousands by comparing the requested account number to each record in the file. The dBASE query statement: SUM SALARY FOR TITLE = "NURSE" causes the computer to compare the title field in each record for NURSE and then add (calculate) the salary field for each match.

In word processing, inserting and deleting text is accomplished by copying characters from one place to another.

Remember The 3 C's
If you wonder whether the computer can solve a problem, identify your data on paper. If it can be calculated, compared and copied on paper, it can be processed in the computer.

The Stored Program Concept

The computer's ability to call in instructions and follow them is known as the *stored program concept.*

Instructions are copied into memory from a disk, tape or other source before any data can be processed. The computer is directed to start with the first instruction in the program. It copies the instruction from memory into its control unit circuit and matches it against its built-in set of instructions. If the instruction is valid, the processor carries it out. If not, the computer comes to an abnormal end (abend, crash).

The computer executes instructions sequentially until it finds a GOTO instruction that tells it to go to a different place in the program. It can execute millions of instructions per second tracing the logic of the program over and over again on each new set of data it brings in.

As computers get faster, operations can be made to overlap. While one program is waiting for input from one user, the operating system (master control program) directs the computer to process data in another program. Large computers are designed to allow inputs and outputs to occur simultaneously with processing. While one user's data is being processed, data from the next user can be retrieved into the computer.

It can take hundreds of thousands of discrete machine steps to perform very routine tasks. Your computer could easily execute a million instructions to put a requested record on screen for you.

Generations of Computers

First-generation computers, starting with the UNIVAC I in 1951, used vacuum tubes, and their memories were made of thin tubes of liquid mercury and magnetic drums.

Second-generation systems in the late 1950s replaced tubes with transistors and used magnetic cores for memories (IBM 1401, Honeywell 800). Size was reduced and reliability was significantly improved.

Third-generation computers, beginning in the mid 1960s, used the first integrated circuits (IBM 360, CDC 6400) and the first operating systems and DBMSs. Online systems were widely developed, although most processing was still batch oriented using punched cards and magnetic tapes.

Starting in the mid 1970s, the fourth generation brought us computers made entirely of chips. It spawned the microprocessor and personal computer. It introduced distributed processing and office automation. Query languages, report writers and spreadsheets put large numbers of people in touch with the computer for the first time.

The fifth generation ought to become visible by the mid 1990s with the more widespread use of voice recognition, natural and foreign language translation, optical disks and fiber optic networks. Higher-speed machines combined with more sophisticated software will enable the average computer to talk to us with reasonable intelligence by the 21st century.

Computers Come in Many Sizes

Computers are as small as a chip or as large as a truck. The difference is in the amount of work they do within the same time frame. Its power is based on many factors, including word size and the speed of its CPU, memory and peripherals. Following is a rough guide to system cost:

Computer system type (Bits show word size)	Approximate range In 1996 US $
Computer on a chip (chip only)(4, 8, 32, 16-bit)	$2 - 75
Microprocessor (chip only)(4, 8, 16, 32, 64-bit)	$5 - 1000
Personal computer client (16, 32, 64-bit)	$800 - 15,000
Personal computer server (32, 64-bit)	$6,000 - 30,000
Workstation (32, 64-bit)	$10,000 - 100,000
Minicomputer server (32, 64-bit)	$15,000 - 250,000
Mainframe (32, 64-bit)	$150,000 - 3,000,000
Supercomputer (64-bit)	$1,000,000 - 40,000,000

computer architecture

The design of a computer system. It sets the standard for all devices that connect to it and all the software that runs on it. It is based on the type of programs that will run (business, scientific) and the number of them run concurrently.

It specifies how much memory is needed and how it is managed (memory protection, virtual memory, virtual machine). It specifies register size and bus width (16-, 32-, 64-bit) and how concurrency is handled (channels, bus mastering, parallel processing).

Its native language instruction set stipulates what functions the computer performs and how instructions are written to activate them. This determines how programs will communicate with it forever after.

The trend toward large, complicated instruction sets has been reversed with RISC computers, which use simpler instructions. The result is a leaner, faster computer, but requires that the compilers generate more code for complex functions that used to be handled in hardware.

Fault tolerant operation influences every aspect of computer architecture, and computers designed for single purposes, such as array processors and database machines, require special designs.

computer-assisted learning

See *CBT*.

Computer Associates

See *CA*.

computer-based training

See *CBT*.

computer conferencing

An interactive communications session by computer among several people that are geographically dispersed. Users communicate by typing on the keyboard, and the text appears on the screens of the participants. It is provided by software in a host computer or in a BBS. See *videoconferencing* and *data conferencing*.

computer cracker

A person who gains illegal entrance into a computer system.

computer designer

A person who designs the electronic structure of a computer.

computer exchange

A commodity exchange through which the public can buy and sell used computers. After a match, the buyer sends a check to the exchange and the seller sends the equipment to the buyer. If the buyer accepts it, the money is sent to the seller less commission. Commissions usually range from 10 to 20%. Following are the major exchanges in the U.S.

American Computer Exchange (AmCoEx)
800/786-0717   FAX 404/250-1399

Boston Computer Exchange (BoCoEx)
617/542-4414   FAX 617/542-8849

National Computer Exchange (NaComEx)
212/614-0700   FAX 212/777-1290

The Newman Group
313/426-3200   FAX 313/426-0777

computer graphics

See *graphics*.

computer language

A programming language, machine language or the language of the computer industry.

computer literacy

Understanding computers and related systems. It includes a working vocabulary of computer and information system components, the fundamental principles of computer processing and a perspective for how non-technical people interact with technical people.
It does not deal with how the computer works (digital circuits), but does imply knowledge of how the computer does its work (calculate, compare and copy). It requires a conceptual understanding of systems analysis & design, application programming, systems programming and datacenter operations.
To be a computer literate manager, you must be able to define information requirements effectively and have an understanding of decision support tools, such as query languages, report writers, spreadsheets and financial planning systems. To be truly computer literate, you must understand "standards & compatibility" in this database. If you can't sleep at night, it's a guaranteed cure for insomnia!

Computer Museum

(The Computer Museum, Boston, MA) A museum dedicated to computers that provides an historical display of computing devices as well as hands-on exhibits of a wide variety of applications geared to kids and adults. You can run the world's largest personal computer (as big as a house) and literally walk through its components.

The Computer Museum is funded by several computer companies as well as private individuals. The Museum Store sells a unique variety of computer games, books, jewelry and artifacts. Open daily in the summer from 10am to 6pm; winters from 10am to 5pm, Tuesday thru Sunday, holidays excluded. Address: 300 Congress St., Boston, MA 02210, 617/423-6758. Call 800/370-CHIP for group rates and reservations.

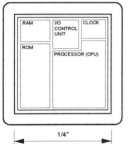

computer on a chip

A single chip that contains the processor, RAM, ROM, clock and I/O control unit. It is used for myriads of applications from automobiles to toys.

computer power

The effective performance of a computer. It can be expressed in MIPS (millions of instructions per second), clock speed (10Mhz, 16Mhz) and in word or bus size, (16-bit, 32-bit). However, as with automobile horsepower, valves and cylinders, such specifications are only guidelines. Real power is whether it gets your job done quickly.

A software package is "powerful" if it has a large number of features.

Computer Press Association

See *CPA*.

computer readable

Same as *machine readable*.

Computer Recycling Center

(Computer Recycling Center, Inc.) A non-profit organization that channels old computer equipment to schools and other non-profit organizations. Founded by Mark Hass, it maintains a warehouse and technical support for the equipment it receives. It accepts incomplete systems, parts and pieces as well as software. Address: 1245 Terra Bella Ave., Mountain View, CA 94043, 415/428-3700. See *how to donate old equipment*.

computer science

The field of computer hardware and software. It includes systems analysis & design, application and system software design and programming and datacenter operations. For young students, the emphasis in typically on learning a programming language or running a personal computer with little attention to information science, the study of information and its uses.

If students were introduced to data administration, DBMS concepts and transaction and master files, they would have a better grasp of an organization's typical information requirements.

computer security

See *security*.

Computer Select

A CD-ROM service from Information Access Company, Foster City, CA, that provides articles and abstracts from over 140 computer-related periodicals. It includes over 75,000 hardware, software and communications products and 11,000 manufacturer's profiles. Subscribers receive a CD-ROM every month with articles from the preceding 12 months. Computer Select was originally developed by the Computer Library division of the Ziff-Davis Publishing Company.

Computer System

A computer system is made up of a CPU, the peripherals that connect to it and an operating system. Although this hardware diagram more readily depicts a mainframe or minicomputer system, it could also be a multiuser microcomputer. Eliminate all but one terminal and one modem, and the components are the same as a desktop computer.

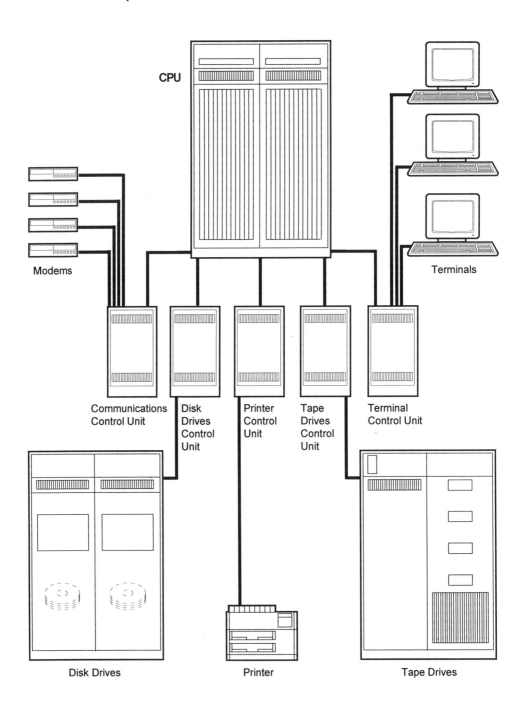

computer services

Data processing (timesharing, batch processing), software development and consulting services. See *service bureau*.

computer system

The complete computer made up of the CPU, memory and related electronics (main cabinet), all the peripheral devices connected to it and its operating system. Computer systems fall into ranges called *microcomputers* (personal computers), *minicomputers* and *mainframes*, roughly small, medium and large.

Computer systems are sized for the total user workload based on (1) number of terminals required, (2) type of work performed (interactive processing, batch processing, CAD, engineering, scientific), and (3) amount of online data required. Following are the components of a computer system and their significance:

Component	Significance
Machine language	Compatibility with future hardware/software
Operating system	Performance and future hardware/software compatibility
Clock speed (MIPS rate)	Performance
Number of terminals	Number of concurrent users
Memory capacity	Performance
Disk capacity	Amount of available information
Communications	Access to inhouse and external information
Programming languages	Compatibility with future hardware
Fail-safe design	Reliability

How Systems Relate

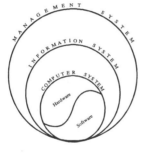

computer telephone integration

See *CTI*.

Computex

A Taiwanese trade show for PC manufacturers and PC component buyers promoted by the China External Trade Development Council. For information, call Taiwan 886-2-725-5200, FAX 886-2-757-6653.

COMSAT

(COMmunications SATellite Corporation) A private communications satellite company created by Congress in 1962 that provides communications capacity to carriers such as AT&T and MCI. In 1965, it launched Early Bird, the first commercial satellite to transmit signals from a geosynchronous orbit. See *INTELSAT* and *INMARSAT*.

The Early Bird, 1965
(Photo courtesy of Communications Satellite Corporation.)

concatenate

To link structures together. Concatenating files appends one file to another. In speech synthesis, units of speech called phonemes (k, sh, ch, etc.) are concatenated to produce meaningful sounds.

concentrator

A device that joins several communications channels together. It is similar to a multiplexor except that it does not spread the signals back out again on the other end. The receiving computer performs that function.

concurrency

Simultaneous operation within the computer. See *multiprocessing, multitasking, multithreading, SMP* and *MPP*.

concurrency control

In a DBMS, managing the simultaneous access to a database. It prevents two users from editing the same record at the same time and is also concerned with serializing transactions for backup and recovery.

Concurrent DOS

An early multiuser DOS-compatible operating system from Digital Research. See *Multiuser DOS*.

concurrent operation

See *multitasking, multiprocessing* and *parallel processing*.

conditional branch

In programming, an instruction that directs the computer to another part of the program based on the results of a compare. In the following (simulated) assembly language example, the second line is the conditional branch.

```
COMPARE FIELDA with FIELDB
GOTO MATCHROUTINE if EQUAL.
```

High-level language statements, such as IF THEN ELSE and CASE, are used to express the compare and conditional branch.

conditioning

Extra cost options in a private telephone line that improve performance by reducing distortion and amplifying weak signals.

conductor

A material that can carry electrical current. Contrast with *insulator*.

conferencing

Same as *teleconferencing*.

CONFIG.SYS

A DOS and OS/2 configuration file. It resides in the root directory and is used to load drivers and change settings at startup. Install programs often modify CONFIG.SYS in order to customize the computer for their particular use. Windows 95 will execute the lines in CONFIG.SYS if it contains drivers that Windows 95 found no counterpart for when it was installed.

configuration

The makeup of a system. To "configure" is to choose options in order to create a custom system. "Configurability" is a system's ability to be changed or customized.

configuration file

A file that contains information about a specific user, program, computer or file.

configuration management

(1) In a network, a system for gathering current configuration information from all nodes in a LAN.

(2) In software development, a system for keeping track of large projects. Although version control, which maintains a database of revisions, is part of the system, a full-blown software configuration management system (SCM system or CM system) automatically documents all components used to build executable programs. It is able to recreate each build as well as to recreate earlier environments in order to maintain previous versions of a product. It may also be used to prevent unauthorized access to files or to alert the appropriate users when a file has been altered.

Increasingly, parts of version control and configuration management are being added to application development systems.

Examples of stand-alone configuration management systems are PVCS, the CCC products from Softool and ClearCase.

connectionless

In communications, the inclusion of source and destination addresses within each packet so that a direct connection or established session between nodes is not required. Transmission within a local area network (LAN) is typically connectionless. Each data packet sent contains the address of where it is going. Contrast with *connection oriented*.

Connection Machine

A family of parallel processing computers from Thinking Machines Corporation, Cambridge, MA, that contain from 4K to 64K processors. They can be set up as hypercubes or other topologies and require another computer as a front end. Used for such applications as signal processing, simulation and database retrieval.

connection oriented

In communications, requiring a direct connection or established session or circuit between two nodes for transmission. Transmission within a wide area network (WAN) is typically connection oriented. Once established, the circuit, whether physical or virtual, is dedicated to that single transmission until the session is completed. Contrast with *connectionless*.

connectivity

(1) Generally, the term refers to communications networks or the act of communicating between computers and terminals.

(2) Specifically, the term refers to devices such as bridges, routers and gateways that link networks together.

connector

(1) Any plug, socket or wire that links two devices together.

(2) In database management, a link or pointer between two data structures.

(3) In flowcharting, a symbol used to break a sequence and resume the sequence elsewhere. It is often a small circle with a number in it.

connect time

The amount of time a user at a terminal is logged on to a computer system. See *online services* and *service bureau*.

console

(1)A terminal used to monitor and control a computer or network.

(2)Any display terminal.

constant

In programming, a fixed value in a program. Minimum and maximum amounts, dates, prices, headlines and error messages are examples.

constant bit rate

See *CBR*.

constant ratio code

A code that always contains the same ratio of 0s to 1s.

consultant

An independent specialist that may act as an advisor or perform detailed systems analysis and design. They often help users create functional specifications from which hardware or software vendors can respond.

contact

A metal strip in a switch or socket that touches a corresponding strip in order to make a connection for current to pass. Contacts may be made of precious metals to avoid corrosion.

contact manager

Software that keeps track of sales prospects. It holds names and addresses and is used for appointments similar to a personal information manager (PIM), but is specialized for sales reps that make repetitive contact with a large number of prospective customers.

container

See *OLE*.

contention

A condition that arises when two devices attempt to use a single resource at the same time. See *CSMA/CD*.

contention resolution

Deciding which device gains access to a resource first when more than one wants it at the same time.

context sensitive help

Help screens that provide specific information about the condition or mode the program is in at the time help is sought.

context switching

Switching between active applications. It often refers to a user jumping back and forth between several programs in contrast with repeated task switching performed by the operating system. However, the terms context switching and task switching are used synonymously.

contextual search

To search for records or documents based upon the text contained in any part of the file as opposed to searching on a pre-defined key field.

contiguous

Adjacent or touching. Contrast with *fragmentation*.

continuity check

A test of a line, channel or circuit to determine if the pathway exists from beginning to end and can transmit signals.

continuous carrier

In communications, a carrier frequency that is transmitted even when data is not being sent over the line.

continuous forms

A roll of paper forms with perforations for separation into individual sheets after printing. See *pin feed* and *burster*.

contrast

The difference between the lightest and darkest areas on a display screen. Contrast with *brightness*.

control block

A segment of disk or memory that contains a group of codes used for identification and control purposes.

control break

(1) A change of category used to trigger a subtotal. For example, if data is subtotalled by state, a control break occurs when NJ changes to NM. See also *Ctrl-Break*.

control character

See *control code*.

control code

One or more characters used as a command to control a device. The first 32 characters in the ASCII character set are control codes for communications and printers. There are countless codes used to control electronic devices. See *escape character*.

Control Data

(Control Data Systems, Inc., Arden Hills, MN) One of the first computer companies. Founded in 1957, Bill Norris was its first president and guiding force. Its first computer, the 1604, was introduced in 1957 and delivered to the U.S. Navy Bureau of Ships.

For more than 30 years, the company was widely respected for its high-speed computers used heavily in government and scientific installations. Using the CYBER trade name, Control Data produced a complete line from workstations to mainframes. It also manufactured supercomputers.

In 1992, it spun off its military involvement into an independent company called Ceridian Corporation, and Control Data Corporation became Control Data Systems. Soon after, it ceased R&D of its proprietary computers. While providing maintenance for its installed base, it currently specializes in systems integration of UNIX-based computers from HP, Sun and Silicon Graphics, which includes custom software, consulting services and facilities management.

William C. Norris
(Photo courtesy of Control Data Systems, Inc.)

control field

Same as *key field*.

control key

Abbreviated "ctrl" or "ctl." A keyboard key that is pressed with a letter or digit key to command the computer; for example, holding down control and pressing U, turns on underline in some word processors. The caret (shift-6) symbol represents the control key: ^Y means control-Y.

controller

An electronic circuit board or system that controls a peripheral device. See *control unit*.

controller card

See *expansion board* and *control unit (2)*.

control network

A network of sensors and actuators used for home automation and industrial control.

control panel

A software routine that changes the computer's environment settings, such as keyboard and mouse sensitivity, sounds, colors and communications and printer access. It is a desk accessory in the Macintosh and a system program in Windows. Control panels are also provided by the vendors of display adapters and other peripherals to allow the user to customize the device.

control parallel

Same as *MIMD*.

control program

Software that controls the operation of and has highest priority in a computer. Operating systems, network operating systems and network control programs are examples. Contrast with *application program*.

Control Program Facility

See *CPF*.

control total

Same as *hash total*.

control unit

(1) Within the processor, the circuitry that locates, analyzes and executes each instruction in the program.
(2) Within the computer, a *control unit*, or *controller*, is hardware that performs the physical data transfers between memory and a peripheral device, such as a disk or screen, or a network.
Personal computer control units are contained on a single plug-in expansion board, called a controller or adapter (disk controller, display adapter, network adapter, etc.). In large computers, they may be contained on one or more boards or in a stand-alone cabinet.
In single chip computers, a built-in control unit accepts keyboard input and provides serial output to a display.

control variable

In programming, a variable that keeps track of the number of iterations of a process. Its value is incremented or decremented with each iteration, and it is compared to a constant or other variable to test the end of the process or loop.

conventional memory

In a PC, the first 640K of memory. The next 384K is called the UMA (upper memory area). The term may also refer to the entire first megabyte (1024K) of RAM, which is the memory that DOS can directly manage without the use of additional memory managers. See *DOS memory manager*.

conventional programming

Writing a program in a traditional procedural language, such as assembly language or a high-level compiler language (C, Pascal, COBOL, FORTRAN, etc.).

convergence

(1) The intersection of red, green and blue electron beams on one CRT pixel. Poor convergence decreases resolution and muddies white pixels.

(2) See *digital convergence*.

conversational

An interactive dialogue between the user and the computer.

conversion

(1) Data conversion is changing data from one file or database format to another. It may also require code conversion between ASCII and EBCDIC.

(2) Media conversion is changing storage media such as from tape to disk.

(3) Program conversion is changing the programming source language from one dialect to another, or changing application programs to link to a new operating system or DBMS.

(4) Computer system conversion is changing the computer model and peripheral devices.

(5) Information system conversion requires data conversion and either program conversion or the installation of newly purchased or created application programs.

converter

(1) A device that changes one set of codes, modes, sequences or frequencies to a different set. See *A/D converter*.

(2) A device that changes current from 60Hz to 50Hz, and vice versa.

cooperative multitasking

Same as *non-preemptive multitasking*.

cooperative processing

Sharing a job among two or more computers such as a mainframe and a personal computer. It implies splitting the workload for the most efficiency.

coordinate

Belonging to a system of indexing by two or more terms. For example, points on a plane, cells in a spreadsheet and bits in dynamic RAM chips are identified by a pair of coordinates. Points in space are identified by sets of three coordinates.

Copland

The code name for the next generation Macintosh operating system. It is a major upgrade that provides preemptive multitasking, multithreading, better crash protection and the ability to customize the user interface. Copland is expected in 1996.

copper

(Cu) A reddish-brown metal that is highly conductive and widely used for electrical wire. When a signal "runs over copper," it means that a metal wire is used rather than a glass wire (optical fiber).

coprocessor

A secondary processor used to speed up operations by handling some of the workload of the main CPU. See *math coprocessor* and *graphics coprocessor*.

copy

To make a duplicate of the original. In digital electronics, all copies are identical, which is, of course, both a blessing and a curse. The blessing is that data can be maintained and remanufactured accurately forever. The curse is that anyone can

duplicate copyrighted material and send it around the world in seconds.
The text in this database takes up about two and a half megabytes. During the
course of writing and updating it, the text has been copied hundreds of times,
causing billions of bits to be transmitted between disk and memory. Just to show
that things aren't entirely perfect, a character does get garbled every once in a while.
We'll have to settle for 99.9999% instead of 100%!

copy buster

A program that bypasses the copy protection scheme in a software program and
allows normal, unprotected copies to be made.

copy protection

Resistance to unauthorized copying of software. Copy protection was never a serious
issue with mainframes and minicomputers, since vendor support has always been
vital in those environments.

In the early days of floppy-based personal computers, many copy protection methods
were used. However, with each scheme introduced, a copy buster program was
developed to get around it. When hard disks became the norm, copy protection was
abolished. In order to manage a hard disk, files must be easily copied from one part
of the disk to another.

This is a constant dilemma for software vendors as well as the publishing and
broadcasting industries that transmit their content via digital means. Every recipient
of a digitally-distributed medium has the ability to reproduce a perfect copy of the
original.

The only copy protection system that works is the hardware key, which is a plug and
socket that is attached to the computer's parallel port with a unique serial number
that the software identifies. Hardware keys are used to protect high-priced software,
but users are generally not fond of them, because it requires unplugging the printer
cable, inserting the hardware key, and plugging back the printer.

A system similar to the hardware key designed into the personal computer from day
one should have been established. Perhaps some day a solid state software capsule
with a digital signature will plug into the computer. In the meantime, anyone who
can figure out an economical way to prevent unauthorized duplication of digital
material that does not interfere with managing a hard disk or the quality of the
original transmission will become the country's first trillionaire!

CORBA

(Common Object Request Broker Architecture) The communications component
of the Object Management Architecture (OMA) from the Object Management
Group (OMG). It is software that handles the communication of messages to and
from objects in a distributed, multi-platform environment.

The concept behind CORBA is to provide a standard way to execute program
modules in a distributed environment no matter what language the routines are
written in or what platform they reside in. It enables complex systems to be built
across an entire enterprise. For example, three-tier client/server applications can be
constructed using CORBA-compliant ORBs. CORBA is suited for widely disbursed
networks, where an event occurring in one location requires services to be performed
in another.

In CORBA, the client makes a request to a common interface known as the Object
Request Broker or ORB. The ORB directs the request to the appropriate server that
contains the object and redirects the results back to the client. The required object
might also be located on the same machine as the client.

The first version of CORBA addressed source code portability across different platforms, and implementations such as IBM's SOM/DSOM, Sun's DOE and HP's DOMF were designed to this specification. In late 1994, the CORBA 2 specification was introduced to support interoperability between ORBs, so that an ORB from one vendor can communicate directly to an ORB from another.

core

A round magnetic doughnut that represents one bit in a core storage system. A computer's main memory used to be referred to as core. See *core storage*.

core dump

Same as *memory dump*.

CorelDRAW

A suite of Windows graphics applications from Corel Corporation, Ottawa, Ontario. CorelDRAW was originally a drawing program introduced in 1989, which became popular due to its speed and ease of use. As of CorelDRAW 5, it is a complete suite of applications for image editing, charting and presentations as well as desktop publishing, with the inclusion of Corel VENTURA.

CorelFlow

A flowcharting program for Windows from Corel Corporation, Ottawa, Ontario. It includes more than 2,000 shapes, photos and pieces of clip art as well as over 100 TrueType fonts.

CorelRAID

Software from Corel Systems Corporation, Ottawa, Ontario, that creates RAID arrays on a Novel 3.11 server using an ASPI-compatible SCSI host adapter and three or more SCSI disks.

CorelSCSI

A SCSI driver from Corel Systems Corporation, Ottawa, Ontario, that supports a wide variety of SCSI devices, including removable media, juke boxes, digital cameras and WORM drives and translates them into the ASPI standard. See *PowerSCSI!*.

Corel VENTURA

A Windows desktop publishing program from Corel Corporation, Ottawa, Ontario. It is a full-featured program suited for producing books and other long documents. It is designed to import data from other graphics and word processing programs and includes several graphics functions from CorelDRAW.
Corel VENTURA was formerly Ventura Publisher, which was developed by a company that was acquired by Xerox. The early versions were available for DOS, Windows, OS/2 and the Macintosh. In 1993, Corel acquired it, made substantial improvements to it and includes it in its CorelDRAW suite. Corel VENTURA is also available stand alone.

co-resident

A program or module that resides in memory along with other programs.

core storage

A non-volatile memory that holds magnetic charges in ferrite cores about 1/16th" diameter. The direction of the flux determines the 0 or 1. Developed in the late 1940s by Jay W. Forrester and Dr. An Wang, it was used extensively in the 1950s and 1960s. Since it holds its content without power, it is still used in specialized

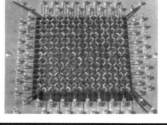

Core Storage
Core storage is why the internal workspace of the computer is called memory. Like magnetic disks, magnetic cores hold their content without power.
(Photo courtesy of The MITRE Corporation Archives.)

applications in the military and in space vehicles.

In 1956, IBM paid Dr. Wang $500,000 for his patent on core memories, which he used to expand his company, Wang Laboratories.

Core System

The first proposed standard for computer graphics, developed by the Graphics Standards Planning Committee of SIGGRAPH and used in the late 1970s and early 1980s. Its objectives were portability of programs between computers and the separation of modeling graphics from viewing graphics. Almost all features of the Core System were incorporated into the ANSI-endorsed GKS standard.

corona wire

A charged wire in a laser printer that draws the toner off the drum onto the paper. It must be cleaned when the toner cartridge is replaced.

correlation

In statistics, a measure of the strength of the relationship between two variables. It is used to predict the value of one variable given the value of the other. For example, a correlation might relate distance from urban location to gasoline consumption. Expressed on a scale from -1.0 to +1.0, the strongest correlations are at both extremes and provide the best predictions. See *regression analysis*.

corrupted file

A data or program file that has been altered accidentally by hardware or software failure, causing the bits to be rearranged and rendering it unreadable.

corruption

Altering of data or programs due to viruses, hardware or software failure or power failure. See *data recovery*.

CorStream

A network operating system from Artisoft, Inc., Tucson, AZ, makers of LANtastic. CorStream is a version of Novell's NetWare 4.x combined with an Artisoft NLM, which turns a PC into a high-speed LANtastic server. LANtastic clients communicate with CorStream as if it was another LANtastic server.

COS

(Corporation for Open Systems International) A not for profit R&D consortium founded in 1986, dedicated to assuring acceptance of a worldwide open network architecture. It is made up of manufacturers and user organizations that provide development, service, and support of systems that conform to international standards, including OSI and ISDN. Address: 1750 Old Meadow Road, Suite 400, McLean, VA 22102, 703/883-2700.

COSE

(Common Open Software Environment) Pronounced "cozy." An alliance of major UNIX vendors dedicated to standardizing open systems. In 1993, its first specification was the CDE (Common Desktop Environment), a user interface based on Motif. COSE has since disbanded, and CDE is now governed by X/Open.

cosine

See *sine*.

cost-based query optimizer

Software that optimizes an SQL query for the fastest processing, based on the size of the file and other variables.

cost/benefits analysis

The study that projects the costs and benefits of a new information system. Costs include people and machine resources for development as well as running the system. Tangible benefits are derived by estimating the cost savings of both human and machine resources to run the new system versus the old one. Intangible benefits, such as improved customer service and employee relations, may ultimately provide the largest payback, but are harder to quantify.

counter

(1) In programming, a variable that is used to keep track of anything that must be counted. The programming language determines the number of counters (variables) that are available to a programmer.

(2) In electronics, a circuit that counts pulses and generates an output at a specified time.

Courier

```
A monospaced typeface originating from the typewriter that is
commonly used for letters.  It is still considered by many to be
the "appropriate" typeface for business correspondence. This
paragraph is Courier.
```

courseware

Educational software. See *CBT*.

covert channel

A transfer of information that violates a computer's built-in security systems. A covert storage channel refers to depositing information in a memory or storage location that can be accessed by different security clearances. A covert timing channel is the manipulation of a system resource in such a way that it can be detected by another process.

CP

See *copy protection*, *CPU* and *control program*.

CPA

(Computer Press Association, 529 18th Ave., San Francisco, CA 94121, 415/750-9281) An organization founded in 1983 that promotes excellence in computer journalism. Comprised of approximately 300 members (1992), its annual awards honor outstanding journalism in print, broadcast and electronic media.

CPE

(Customer Premises Equipment) Communications equipment that resides on the customer's premises.

CPF

(Control Program Facility) The IBM System/38 operating system that included an integrated relational DBMS.

CPGA

(Ceramic PGA) See *PGA*.

cpi

(1) (Characters Per Inch) The measurement of the density of characters per inch on tape or paper. A printer's CPI button switches character pitch.

(2) (Counts Per Inch) The measurement of the resolution of a mouse/trackball as flywheel notches per inch (horizontal and vertical flywheels rotate as the ball is

moved). Notches are converted to cursor movement.

(3) (CPI) (Common Programming Interface) See *SAA* and *CPI-C*.

CPI-C

(Common Programming Interface for Communications) A general-purpose
communications interface under IBM's SAA. Using APPC verbs as its foundation, it
provides a common programming interface across IBM platforms. See *APPC*.

CP/M

(Control Program for Microprocessors) A single user operating system for the 8080
and Z80 microprocessors from Digital Research. Created by Gary Kildall, CP/M
had its heyday in the early 1980s.

CP/M was an unsophisticated program that didn't instill confidence in users, yet it
was a major contributor to the personal computer revolution. Because the industry
never standardized on a CP/M disk or video format, software publishers had to
support dozens of screen displays and floppy disk formats. This chaos helped IBM
set the standard with its PC.

Although IBM asked Kildall to provide the operating system for its new PC, he
didn't agree to certain demands. IBM went to Microsoft, which purchased an
operating system from another company and turned it into DOS. DOS was
modeled after CP/M.

CPM

(Critical Path Method) A project management planning and control technique
implemented on computers. The critical path is the series of activities and tasks in
the project that have no built-in slack time. Any task in the critical path that takes
longer than expected will lengthen the total time of the project.

cps

(Characters Per Second) The measurement of the speed of a serial printer or a data
transfer between devices. CPS is equivalent to bytes per second. See also *Microsoft
Certified Professional*.

CPU

(Central Processing Unit) The computing part of the computer. Also called the
processor, it is made up of the control unit and ALU.

A personal computer CPU is a single microprocessor chip. A minicomputer CPU is
contained on one or more printed circuit boards. A mainframe CPU is made up of
several boards.

The CPU, clock and main memory make up a computer. A complete computer
system requires the addition of control units, input, output and storage devices and
an operating system.

**From the Mainframe
Point of View**
Computer professionals
involved with mainframes
and minicomputers often
refer to the whole
computer as the CPU, in
which case, CPU refers
to the processor,
memory (RAM) and I/O
architecture (channels or
buses).

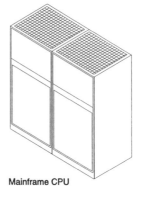

Mainframe CPU

Microcomputer CPU

CPU bound

Same as *process bound*.

CPU cache

See *cache*.

CPU chip

Same as *microprocessor*.

CPU speed

See *MHz*.

CPU time

The amount of time it takes for the CPU to execute a set of instructions and generally excludes the waiting time for input and output.

CR

(Carriage Return) The return key or the actual code that is generated when the key is pressed (decimal 13, hex 0D). See *return key*.

CRAM

(Card RAM) A magnetic card mass storage device made by NCR in the 1960s. In order to read or write data, a card was pulled out of the cartridge and wrapped around a rotating drum.

crash

See *abend* and *head crash*.

crash recovery

The ability to automatically correct a hardware, software or line failure.

Cray

(Cray Research, Inc., Eagan, MN) A supercomputer manufacturer founded in 1972 by Seymour Cray, a leading designer of large-scale computers at Control Data. In 1976, Cray shipped its first computer to Los Alamos National Laboratory. The CRAY-1 was a 75MHz, 64-bit machine with a peak speed of 160 megaflops, making it the world's fastest vector processor.

The company has since launched many different models from entry-level to high-end supercomputers that are used in industrial, technical and commercial applications, including the X-MP, Y-MP, C90, T90, J90 and T3E series. Cray also incorporates its unique architecture in its CS6400 line of SPARC and Alpha-based machines. All Cray computers use the UNIX operating system.

In 1989, Seymour Cray left Cray Research to found Cray Computer Corporation in Colorado Springs, CO. He developed the Cray-3, an incredibly fast gallium arsenide-based computer that ran at a 1GHz clock rate. With the Cray-4 sitting in the wings, the company was unable to attract customers for the new products and closed its doors in 1995.

In 1996, Cray Research was acquired by SGI (Silicon Graphics, Inc.).

Seymour Cray
(Photo courtesy of Cray Research, Inc.)

CRC

(Cyclical Redundancy Checking) An error checking technique used to ensure the accuracy of transmitting digital data. The transmitted messages are divided into predetermined lengths which, used as dividends, are divided by a fixed divisor. The remainder of the calculation is appended onto and sent with the message. At the receiving end, the computer recalculates the remainder. If it does not match the transmitted remainder, an error is detected.

CRC cards

(Class Responsibility Collaboration card) An object-oriented design method that uses ordinary 3x5 index cards. Developed by Ward Cunningham at Textronix, a card is made for each class containing responsibilities (knowledge and services) and collaborators (interactions with other objects). The cards provide an informal, intuitive way for group members to work on object design together.

For a book on CRC cards that provides a clear introduction to object concepts and modeling, read "Using CRC Cards" by Nancy Wilkinson, published by SIGS BOOKS, ISBN 1-884842-07-0.

Creative Labs

(Creative Labs, Inc., Milpitas, CA) A manufacturer of sound cards and products that was founded in 1988 by Sim Wong Hoo. It introduced the Game Blaster stereo sound board in 1988, and in 1989, the Sound Blaster card, which has become a de facto standard. In 1991, it launched the Sound Blaster Multimedia Upgrade Kit.

Cricket Presents

See *CA-Cricket Presents*.

crippleware

Demonstration software with built-in limitations; for example, a database package that lets only 50 records be entered.

criteria range

Conditions for selecting records; for example, "Illinois customers with balances over $10,000."

CR/LF

(Carriage Return/Line Feed) The end of line characters used in standard PC text files (ASCII 13 10). In the Mac, only the CR is used; in UNIX, the LF.

crop marks

Printed lines on paper used to cut the form into its intended size.

cross assembler

An assembler that generates machine language for a foreign computer. It is used to develop programs for computers on a chip or microprocessors used in specialized applications, which are either too small or are incapable of handling the development software.

crossbar switch

See *crosspoint switch*.

cross compiler

A compiler that generates machine language for a foreign computer. See *cross assembler*.

crossfoot

A numerical error checking technique that compares the sum of the columns with the sum of the rows.

crosshatch

A criss-crossed pattern used to fill in sections of a drawing to distinguish them from each other.

crossover cable

Same as *null modem cable*.

crosspoint switch

Also known as a crossbar or NxN switch, it is a switching device that provides for a fixed number of inputs and outputs. For example, a 32x32 switch is able to keep 32 nodes communicating at full speed to 32 other nodes.

Cross System Product

See *CSP*.

cross tabulate

To analyze and summarize data. A common example is summarizing the details from database records and placing them into a spreadsheet. The following example places the details of order records into summary form.

Transactions being cross tabbed

Date	Customer	Quantity
1- 7-93	Smith	7
1-13-93	Jones	12
2- 5-93	Gonzales	4
2-11-93	Fetzer	6
3-10-93	Smith	12
3-22-93	Gonzales	15

Results of cross tab

Customer	Jan	Feb	Mar	Total
Smith	7	12		19
Jones	12			12
Gonzales		4	15	9
Fetzer			6	6
Total	19	10	27	56

crosstalk

(1) In communications, interference from an adjacent channel.

(2) (Crosstalk) Communications programs for DOS and Windows from Attachmate Corporation, Bellevue, WA. Crosstalk products were originally developed by Microstuf, Inc., later merged with DCA and then later merged with Attachmate. It was one of the first personal computer communications programs, originating in the CP/M days. Crosstalk includes user-definable menus and a scripting language called CASL (Crosstalk Application Script Language).

CRT

(Cathode Ray Tube) A vacuum tube used as a display screen in a video terminal or TV. The term more often refers to the entire monitor rather than just the tube itself. Years ago, CRT was the popular term for the display screen. Today, monitor is the preferred term. See *VGA* and *monitor*.

crunch

(1)To process data. See *number crunching*.
(2)To compress data. See *data compression*.

cryogenics

Using materials that operate at very cold temperatures. See *superconductor*.

cryptography

Conversion of data into a secret code for security purposes. Same as *encryption*.

crystal

A solid material containing a uniform arrangement of molecules. See *quartz crystal.*

crystalline

The solid state of a crystal. Contrast with *nematic.*

c/s

See *client/server.*

CSA

(1) (Canadian Standards Association) The Canadian counterpart of U.S. Underwriters Laboratory.

(2) (Client Server Architecture) See *client/server.*

(3) (CallPath Services Architecture) An IBM standard that integrates applications with the telephone system, designed for use with AT&T, Northern Telecom and other PBX vendors.

CSE

(Certified Systems Engineer) See *Microsoft Certified Professional.*

C/S ELEMENTS

An object-oriented client/server development system from Neuron Data, Palo Alto, CA, that is used to develop applications for all the major GUIs, including Windows, OS/2, Motif and Mac. It supports more than 40 platforms and provides links to its rule-based NEXPERT expert system.

C shell

See *UNIX.*

CSIC

(Customer Specific Integrated Circuit) Pronounced "C-sick." Custom-developed chips from Motorola.

CSLIP

(Compressed SLIP) A version of SLIP that compresses the data for transmission.

CSMA/CD

(Carrier Sense Multiple Access/Collision Detection) The LAN access method used in Ethernet. When a device wants to gain access to the network, it checks to see if the network is free. If it is not, it waits a random amount of time before retrying. If the network is free and two devices attempt access at exactly the same time, they both back off to avoid a collision and each wait a random amount of time before retrying.

CSP

(1) (Cross System Product) An IBM application generator that runs in all SAA environments. CSP/AD (CSP/Application Development) programs provide the interactive development environment and generate a pseudo code that is interpreted by CSP/AE (CSP/Application Execution) software in the running computer. For AS/400 applications, CSP/AD generates compiled code. For the PS/2, EZ-PREP and EZ-RUN are the CSP/AD and CSP/AE counterparts.

(2) (Certified Systems Professional) The award for successful completion of an ICCP examination in systems development.

CSTA

(Computer Supported Telephony Application) An international standard interface between a network server and a telephone switch (PBX) established by the European Computer Manufacturers Association (ECMA).

CSU
See *DSU/CSU.*

CSV
(Comma Separated Value) Same as *comma delimited.*

CT
See *Microsoft Certified Professional.*

CTI
(Computer Telephone Integration) Combining data with voice systems in order to enhance telephone services. For example, automatic number identification (ANI) allows a caller's records to be retrieved from the database while the call is routed to the appropriate party. Automatic telephone dialing from an address list is an outbound example.

CTIA
(1) See *CompTIA.*
(2) (Cellular Telecommunications Industry Association) A membership organization founded in 1984 that is involved with regulatory and public affairs issues in the cellular phone industry. Address: 1250 Connecticut Ave., N.W., Washington, DC 20036, 202/785-0081.

Ctl
See *control key.*

CTO
(Chief Technical Officer) The executive responsible for the technical direction of an organization.

CTOS
An operating system that runs on Unisys' x86-based SuperGen series (formerly the B-series). It was originally developed by Convergent Technologies, which was acquired by Unisys. Designed for network use, its message-based approach allows program requests to be directed to any station in the network.

Ctrl
See *control key.*

Ctrl-Alt-Del
In a PC, holding down the CTRL and ALT keys and pressing the DEL key reboots the system.

Ctrl-Break
In a PC, holding down the CTRL key and pressing the BREAK key cancels the running program or batch file. Same as *Ctrl-C.*

Ctrl-C
In a PC, holding down the CTRL key and pressing the C key cancels the running program or batch file. Same as *Ctrl-Break.*

Ctrl-S
In a PC, holding down the CTRL key and pressing the S key pauses and continues the running program.

CTS

(1) (Clear To Send) The RS-232 signal sent from the receiving station to the transmitting station that indicates it is ready to accept data. Contrast with *RTS*. See also *carpal tunnel syndrome*.

CUA

(Common User Access) SAA specifications for user interfaces, which includes OS/2 PM and character-based formats of 3270 terminals. It is intended to provide a consistent look and feel across platforms and between applications.

CUI

(Character-based User Interface) A user interface that uses the character, or text, mode of the computer and typically refers to typing in commands. Contrast with *GUI*.

CUL

Digispeak for "see you later."

Curie point

The temperature at which the molecules of a material can be altered when subjected to a magnetic field. In optical material, it is approximately 200 degrees Celsius. See *magneto-optic*.

current

(1)Present activities or the latest version or model.
(2)The flow of electrons within a wire or circuit, measured in amps.
(3) (Current) A Windows PIM from IBM that includes a calendar, address book, phone dialer, outliner, word processor and Gantt charts for project tracking. It was revised by its developer, Jensen-Jones Inc., Red Bank, NJ, into a new package called Commence.

current directory

The disk directory the system is presently working in. Unless otherwise specified, commands that deal with disk files refer to the current directory.

current loop

A serial transmission method originating with teletype machines that transmits 20 milliAmperes of current for a 1 bit and no current for a 0 bit. Today's circuit boards can't handle 20mA current and use optical isolators at the receiving end to detect lower current. Contrast with *RS-232*.

cursive writing

Handwriting.

cursor

(1) A movable symbol on screen that is the contact point between the user and the data. In text systems, it is a blinking rectangle or underline. On graphic systems, it is also called a pointer, and it usually changes shape (arrow, square, paintbrush, etc.) when it moves into a different part of the screen. See also *database cursor*.
(2)A pen-like or puck-like device used with a digitizer tablet. As the tablet cursor is moved across the tablet, the screen cursor moves correspondingly. See *digitizer tablet*.

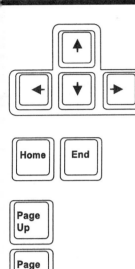

cursor keys

The keys that move the cursor on screen, which include the up, down, left and right arrow, home, end, PgUp and PgDn keys. In addition to cursor keys, a mouse or tablet cursor also moves the cursor.

custom control

A software routine that adds some enhancement or feature to an application. Custom controls are written to provide as little as a few graphical interface improvements to as much as providing full imaging, spreadsheet and text editing extensions to the application. Depending on the development system, custom controls are either linked into the application when it is written or maintained as independent executable files that are called at runtime. DLLs, VBXs and OCXs are examples.

customized toolbar

A toolbar that can be custom configured by the user. Buttons can be added and deleted as required.

cut & paste

To move or copy a block of text or graphics from one document to another. To perform the operation, do the following: (1) Highlight the text or graphics with the mouse and select Cut or Copy from the EDIT menu, (2) switch to the receiving document, (3) click in the location you want the information to go into, and (4) select Paste from the EDIT menu.

CUT mode

(Control Unit Terminal mode) A mode that allows a 3270 terminal to have a single session with the mainframe. Micro to mainframe software emulates this mode to communicate with the mainframe. Contrast with *DFT mode*.

cut-through switch

A switching device that begins to output an incoming data packet before the packet is completely received. Contrast with *store-and-forward switch*.

cyber

(1) From cybernetics, a prefix attached to everyday words to add an electronic or online connotation.
(2) (CYBER) An early family of computers from Control Data that ranged from workstations to supercomputers.

cybercafe

The high-tech equivalent of the coffee house. However, instead of playing chess or having heated political discussions, you browse the Internet and other online services and discuss the latest technology. CD-ROMs, games and other "cyber" stuff is available. They started in New York and are now to be found around the world.

cybercop

A criminal investigator of online fraud or harassment.

cybernetics

The comparative study of human and machine processes in order to understand their similarities and differences. It often refers to machines that imitate human behavior. See *AI* and *robot*.

cyberpunk

A futuristic, online delinquent: breaking into computer systems; surviving by high-tech wits. The term comes from science fiction novels such as "Neuromancer" and "Shockwave Rider."

cyberspace

Coined by William Gibson in his novel "Neuromancer," it is a futuristic computer network that people use by plugging their minds into it! The term is now used to refer to the Internet or to the online or digital world in general. See *Internet* and *virtual reality*.

cycle

(1) A single event that is repeated. For example, in a carrier frequency, one cycle is one complete wave.

(2) A set of events that is repeated. For example, in a polling system, all of the attached terminals are tested in one cycle. See *machine cycle* and *memory cycle*.

cycles per second

The number of times an event or set of events is repeated in a second. See *Hertz*.

cycle stealing

A CPU design technique that periodically "grabs" machine cycles from the main processor usually by some peripheral control unit, such as a DMA (direct memory access) device. In this way, processing and peripheral operations can be performed concurrently or with some degree of overlap.

cycle time

The time interval between the start of one cycle and the start of the next cycle.

Cycolor

A printing process from Mead Imaging that prints full tonal images like photographs. It uses a special film coated with light-sensitive microcapsules, called cyliths, that contain leuco dyes. The film is exposed to the color image that is being printed, resulting in a latent image of hard and soft cyliths. The latent image donor film is transferred onto a special Cycolor paper by being squeezed together through pressure rollers, thus releasing the dyes from the film onto the paper. The paper is then briefly heated, and the result is a full-color image that resembles a photograph.

Cylinder
The cylinder is the aggregate of the same track number on every platter used for recording.

cylinder

The aggregate of all tracks that reside in the same location on every disk surface. On multiple-platter disks, the cylinder is the sum total of every track with the same track number on every surface. On a floppy disk, a cylinder comprises the top and corresponding bottom track. When storing data, the operating system fills an entire cylinder before moving to the next one. The access arm remains stationary until all the tracks in the cylinder have been read or written.

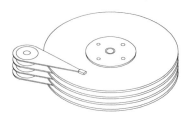

multi-platter hard disk

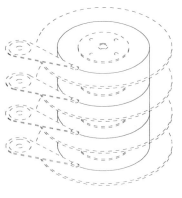

cylinder

D

D&B Software

(Dun & Bradstreet Software, Atlanta, GA; The Dun & Bradstreet Corporation) A software and consulting organization formed in 1990 as a merger of Management Science America (MSA) and McCormack & Dodge. It is one of the largest software companies in the world.

MSA was originally founded in 1963 to provide textile consulting services. Under the leadership of John Imlay, who rejoined the company in 1970 as Chairman and CEO, MSA grew rapidly in business applications software and was the first to enter the international marketplace in 1979.

McCormack & Dodge began as a packaged financial software firm in 1969 and later introduced the first integrated environment for mainframe business applications. In 1983, it was acquired by The Dun & Bradstreet Corporation.

Imlay directed the merger and headed the new company in the development of client-server versions of its mainframe software until his retirement in 1993.

John P. Imlay, Jr.
Under Imlay's leadership, Management Science America grew rapidly and entered the international marketplace in 1979. *(Photo courtesy of Dun & Bradstreet Software.)*

D4

A framing format for T1 transmission that places 12 T1 frames into a superframe. See *ESF*.

DA

See *desk accessory* and *data administrator*.

DAC

(1) See *D/A converter*.
(2) (Discretionary Access Control) A security control that does not require clearance levels. See *NCSC*.

D/A converter

(Digital to Analog Converter) A device that converts digital pulses into analog signals. Contrast with *A/D converter*. See *DSP* and *ladder DAC*.

DAD

(1) (Database Action Diagram) Documentation that describes the processing performed on data in a database.
(2) (Digital Audio Disc) Same as *CD*.

daemon

Pronounced "demon." A UNIX program that executes in the background ready to perform an operation when required. It is usually an unattended process initiated at startup. Typical daemons are print spoolers and e-mail handlers or a scheduler that starts up another process at a designated time. The term comes from Greek mythology meaning "guardian spirit." Same as *agent*.

daisy chain

Connected in series, one after the other. Transmitted signals go to the first device, then to the second and so on.

daisy wheel

An earlier print mechanism that used a plastic or metal hub with spokes like an old-fashioned wagon wheel minus the outer rim. At the end of each spoke is the carved image of a type character.

When the required character spins around to the print hammer, the image is banged into a ribbon and onto paper. The mechanism is then moved to the next location. Daisy wheel printers print typewriter-like quality from 10 to 75 cps and have been superseded by dot matrix and laser printers.

Daisy Wheel
In the early 1980s, daisy wheel printers cost $3,000 and more, 10 times what a small laser printer costs today. They clicked and clacked to produce near typewriter-quality output. Daisy wheel printers were popular because you could "change the fonts" by changing wheels.

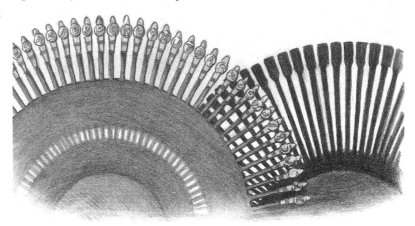

DAL

(Data Access Language) A database interface from Apple that allows the Mac to access DAL-supported databases on Macs or non-Apple computers. It is a superset of SQL. Database vendors license the specs and translate DAL calls to their database engines.

damping

A technique for stabilizing an electronic or mechanical device by eliminating unwanted or excessive oscillations.

Dan Bricklin's demo programs

See *Demo II.*

dark current

The current that flows in a photodetector when it is not receiving any light. It may increase as the temperature rises.

darkened datacenter

Unattended datacenter operation. With printers distributed throughout the enterprise and the use of tape and optical libraries that automatically mount the appropriate disk and tape volume, the datacenter increasingly does not require human intervention.

dark fiber

Unused transmission capacity in a fiber optic trunk.

Darlington circuit

An amplification circuit that uses two transistors coupled together.

DARPA

(Defense Advanced Research Projects Agency) See *ARPANET.*

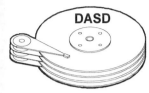

DAS

See *FDDI*.

DASD

(Direct Access Storage Device) Pronounced "dazdee." A peripheral device that is directly addressable, such as a disk or drum. The term is used in the mainframe world.

Dashboard

A Windows utility from Starfish Software, Scotts Valley, CA, that provides a centralized control panel for launching applications, finding files and viewing system resources. Dashboard was originally developed by HP, then acquired by Borland.

DAT

(1) (Digital Audio Tape) A digital recording technology that uses a helical scan read/write head and 4mm magnetic tape. Although initially a CD-quality audio format, the DDS (Digital Data Storage) specification, developed by Sony and HP in 1988, defined a format and quality level for DAT tapes so that they could be used by computers. DAT cassettes have capacities in the gigabyte range.

DAT cassettes provide the most data storage in the smallest tape module on the market. DAT tape library systems hold from a handful up to several thousand cassettes. See *tape backup*.

(2) (Dynamic Address Translator) A hardware circuit that converts a virtual memory address into a real address.

DAT Read/Write Mechanism
DAT uses a helical scan mechanism like videotape where the tracks are angled on the tape. Just like your VCR, the tape is pulled out of the cassette and wrapped around the head at the correct angle.

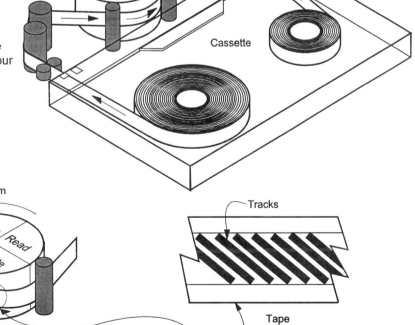

data

(1) Technically, raw facts and figures, such as orders and payments, which are processed into information, such as balance due and quantity on hand. However, in common usage, the terms data and information are used synonymously.

The amount of data versus information kept in the computer is a tradeoff. Data can be processed into different forms of information, but it takes time to sort and sum transactions. Up-to-date information can provide instant answers.

A common misconception is that software is also data. Software is executed, or run, by the computer. Data is "processed." Software is "run."

(2) Any form of information whether in paper or electronic form. In electronic form, data refers to files and databases, text documents, images and digitally-encoded voice and video.

(3) The plural form of datum.

data abstraction

See *abstraction.*

Data Access Language

See *DAL.*

data acquisition

(1) The automatic collection of data from sensors and readers in a factory, laboratory, medical or scientific environment.

(2) The gathering of source data for data entry into the computer.

data administration

The analysis, classification and maintenance of an organization's data and data relationships. It includes the development of data models and data dictionaries, which, combined with transaction volume, are the raw materials for database design. The data administration organization often includes database administration. However, data administration functions provide the overall management of data as an organizational resource. Database administration is the technical design and management of the database.

Data Is Complex
The flow of data/information within a company is complex since the same data is viewed differently as it moves from one department to the other.

For example: When a customer places an order, the order becomes a commission for sales, a statistic for marketing, an order to keep track of in order processing, an effect on cash flow for financial officers, picking schedules for the warehouse, and production scheduling for manufacturing.

Users have different requirements for interrogating and updating data. Operations people need detail, management needs summaries. Database design must take this into consideration.

data administrator

A person who coordinates activities within the data administration department. Contrast with *database administrator.*

data analyst

See *data administrator.*

data bank

Any electronic depository of data.

database

A set of related files that is created and managed by a database management system (DBMS). Today, DBMSs can manage any form of data including text, images, sound and video. Database and file structures are always determined by the software. As far as the hardware is concerned, it's all bits and bytes.

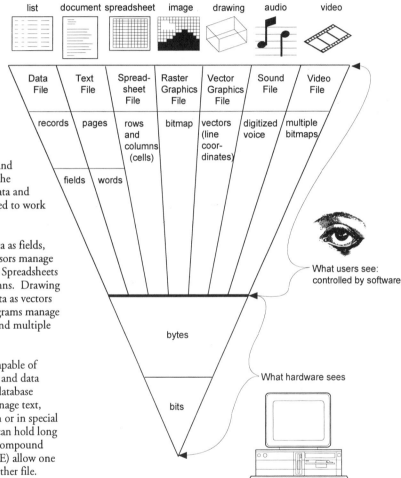

The Software Provides the Structure

The hardware "sees" only bits and bytes, but the software creates the file formats and manages the data and information the way people need to work with it.

Database programs manage data as fields, records and files. Word processors manage data as words, lines and pages. Spreadsheets manage data as rows and columns. Drawing and paint programs manage data as vectors and bitmaps. Multimedia programs manage data as digitized sound waves and multiple sequences of bitmaps.

Increasingly, applications are capable of managing multiple file formats and data types. For a number of years, database programs have been able to manage text, either in fields of limited length or in special fields, called *memo* fields, that can hold long and varying amounts of text. Compound documents (OpenDoc and OLE) allow one file to be embedded within another file.

In time, the concept of individual applications as we know them today may go by the wayside. If file formats become more standardized, instead of applications, functions will be packaged (text tools, database tools, spreadsheet tools, etc.) that work with multiple file formats.

DATABASE 2
See *DB2.*

database administrator
A person responsible for the physical design and management of the database and for the evaluation, selection and implementation of the DBMS.
In small organizations, the database administrator and data administrator are one in the same; however, when the two responsibilities are managed separately, the database administrator's function is more technical.

database analyst
See *data administrator* and *database administrator.*

database cursor
A record pointer in a database. When a database file is selected and the cursor is opened, the cursor points to the first record in the file. Using various commands, the cursor can be moved forward, backward, to top of file, bottom of file and so forth.

database designer
See *data administrator* and *database administrator.*

database driver
A software routine that accesses a database. It allows an application or compiler to access a particular database format.

database engine
Same as *database manager.*

database machine
A computer system designed for database access. Database machines never caught on until the early 1990s when massively parallel processors (MPPs) from companies such as Teradata, now part of AT&T, nCube, Thinking Machines and Kendall Square Research, proved the concept. Using hundreds and even thousands of microprocessors with database software designed for parallelism, database machines can scan large files much faster than a mainframe.
Dramatic performance increases have been documented. For example, a large financial organization reduced 30 days worth of month-end analysis and reporting to a single day. In other cases, queries have been speeded up by a factor of 100. Database machines using MPP architecture are expected to grow in popularity for decision support systems in large organizations.

database management system
See *DBMS.*

database manager
(1) With personal computers, software that allows a user to manage multiple data files (same as *DBMS*). Contrast with *file manager*, which works with one file at a time.
(2) Software that provides database management capability for traditional programming languages, such as COBOL, BASIC and C, but without the interactive capabilities.
(3) The part of the DBMS that stores and retrieves the data.

database program
A software application that allows for the management of data and information

structured as fields, records and files. Database programs provide a way of creating and manipulating the electronic equivalent of a name and address card that can hold large amounts of information.

Because all data is structured into a one record per subject or transaction format, it allows for powerful query capabilities, in which you can select records based on any of their content. A database program is the heart of a business information system and provides mainly file creation, data entry, update, query and reporting functions. The traditional term for a database program is a database management system (DBMS). It is also called a data management system. For more details on the features of a DBMS, see *DBMS*. Also see *application software* for a breakdown of all major software applications.

User Interaction with a Database Program

The database programs available on personal computers let you perform all the following tasks interactively on one file at a time. However, as soon as you want data in one file to automatically update another, programming has to be done. That's where the faint of heart take their leave, and the hackers take over. Following are the common tasks you need to perform to create and work with a database file.

Create a File and Set the Index Order
Each field in a record is defined by name, type and length. In order to keep the file in sequence, one or more fields are defined as key fields, upon which indexes are created and maintained. The index is updated whenever new records are added or existing records are deleted or any data in a key field changes.

Create Data Entry Forms
Data entry is accomplished by designing a form to display each record. Data entry forms contain field validation. You decide what data can go in and what must stay out of these fields.

Update/Edit
In a single-user, one-file-at-a-time application, there is nothing to predefine here. Changing data is just a matter of opening the file and selecting the EDIT mode. However, in a multiuser system, security must be administered and audit trails must be programmed.

View/Query
You can browse an entire file or just selected records. Selected records are usually created as a temporary file that can be saved or abandoned. The temporary file may be sorted into a new sequence if desired.

The ease with which a query can be composed determines how much users will ask their own questions or rely on their IS staff to create them. Getting data from two files; for example, customers and orders, or vendors and purchases, requires knowledge of how to link the files for the query. Most database programs have a JOIN function, which creates a new file with data from two existing files. Once a query description has been composed, it can be saved for use again.

Report
Reports provide details and summaries in a more elaborate fashion than queries. They have page and column headers and can be sorted into order by multiple fields; for example, county within city within state. Once a report description has been composed, it can be saved for use again.

Modify Structure
From time to time, it is necessary to add or delete fields, change their lengths or possibly their names. This function is similar to creating the record structure in the first place, except that you are editing the structure rather than defining it from scratch.

database publishing

Using desktop publishing to produce reports of database contents.

databases

See *online services.*

database server

A computer in a LAN dedicated to database storage and retrieval. The database server is a key component in a client/server environment. It holds the database management system (DBMS) and the databases. Upon requests from the client machines, it searches the database for selected records and passes them back over the network.

A database server and file server may be one in the same, because a file server often provides database services. However, the term implies that the system is dedicated for database use only and not a central storage facility for applications and files. See *client/server.*

database trigger

See *trigger.*

data bits

The number of bits used to represent one character of data. When transmitting ASCII text via modem, either seven or eight bits may be used. Most other forms of data require eight bits.

data bus

An internal pathway across which data is transferred to and from the processor. The expansion slots in personal computers are connected to the data bus.

data carrier

(1) Any medium such as a disk or tape that can hold machine readable data.
(2)A carrier frequency into which data is modulated for transmission in a network.

data cartridge

A removable magnetic tape module that is used for data storage. The QIC cartridge uses a wheel inside the drive that presses the tape against a passive roller in the cartridge. A tension belt is attached to the roller that presses against and moves the supply and takeup reel.

DAT and 8mm cartridges are like audio cassettes with a supply reel of magnetic tape and a takeup reel. Half-inch cartridges have a supply reel of magnetic tape that is threaded onto a supply reel inside the drive. See *data cassette.*

data cassette

A removable magnetic tape module that contains a supply reel and a takeup reel similar to audio tape used in cars and home tape players. The D/CAS (Data CASsette) drive uses an upgraded version of audio tape for data storage. DAT and 8mm drives each use a different size cassette, which are also called data cartridges. See *data cartridge.*

Data Cell

An IBM mass storage device made in the 1960s that used 3 x 15" tape strips which were extracted out of a cartridge and wrapped around a rotating drum for reading. More than 100 of these units were installed worldwide, but the tapes were very susceptible to wear. See *RACE* and *CRAM.*

datacenter

The department that houses the computer systems and related equipment, including the data library. Data entry and systems programming may also come under its jurisdiction. A control section is usually provided that accepts work from and releases output to user departments.

data circuit-terminating equipment

See *DCE*.

data code

(1) A digital coding system for data in a computer. See *ASCII* and *EBCDIC*.
(2) A coding system used to abbreviate data; for example, codes for regions, classes, products and status.

data collaboration

See *data conferencing*.

data collection

Acquiring source documents for the data entry department. It comes under the jurisdiction of the data control or data entry department. See *data acquisition*.

datacom

(DATA COMmunications) See *communications* and *CA-DATACOM/DB*.

data communications

Same as *communications*.

data communications equipment

See *DCE*.

data compression

Encoding data to take up less storage space. Digital data is compressed by finding repeatable patterns of binary 0s and 1s. The more patterns can be found, the more the data can be compressed. Text can generally be compressed to about 40% of its original size, and graphics files from 20% to 90%. Some files compress very little. It depends entirely on the type of file and compression algorithm used.

There are numerous compression methods in use. Two major technologies are Huffman coding and Lempel-Ziv-Welch (LZW), representing examples of the statistical and dictionary compression methods.

When a compression algorithm is packaged for use for a specific platform and file format, it is called a *codec* (compressor/decompressor). ADPCM, PCM and GSM are examples of codecs for sound, and Indeo, Cinepak and MPEG are examples of codecs for video.

In the DOS/Windows world, Pkzip is the most widely-used compression application. See *Pkzip abc's*.

Lossless versus Lossy
When text and financial data are compressed, they must be decompressed back to a perfect original, bit for bit. This is known as *lossless compression*. However, audio and video can be compressed to as little as 5% of its original size using *lossy compression*. Some of the data is actually lost, but the loss is not noticeable to the human ear and eye.

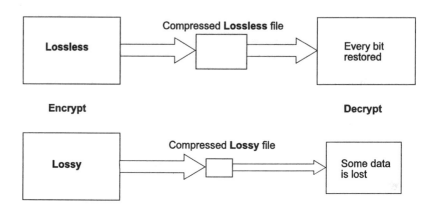

data conferencing
Sharing data interactively among several users in different locations. Data conferencing is made up of whiteboards and application sharing. A whiteboard is the electronic equivalent of the chalkboard or flip chart. Participants at different locations simultaneously write and draw on an on-screen notepad viewed by everyone.

Application sharing is the same as remote control software, in which multiple participants can interactively work in an application that is loaded on only one user's machine. Application viewing is similar to application sharing; however, although all users can see the document, only one person can actually edit it.

Whiteboards and application sharing are often used in conjunction with an audio or videoconferencing connection. An audio-only connection can be a separate telephone call or be transmitted with the data using simultaneous voice and data (SVD) modems.

data control department
The function responsible for collecting data for input into a computer's batch processing operations as well as the dissemination of the finished reports. The data entry department may be under the jursidiction of the data control department or vice versa.

DATA/DAT
(DATA/Digital Audio Tape) A DAT format for data backup that can be divided into as many as 254 partitions allowing for updating in place. See *tape backup*.

data declaration
Same as *data definition (1)*.

data definition

(1) In a source language program, the definitions of data structures (variables, arrays, fields, records, etc.).

(2) A description of the record layout in a file system or DBMS.

data description language

See *DDL.*

data dictionary

A database about data and databases. It holds the name, type, range of values, source, and authorization for access for each data element in the organization's files and databases. It also indicates which application programs use that data so that when a change in a data structure is contemplated, a list of affected programs can be generated.

The data dictionary may be a stand-alone system or an integral part of the DBMS. Data integrity and accuracy is better ensured in the latter case.

data dipper

Software in a personal computer that queries a mainframe database.

data division

The part of a COBOL program that defines the data files and record layouts.

DataEase

A relational DBMS for PCs from DataEase International, Inc., Trumbull, CT. It provides a menu-driven interface for developing applications without programming and is noted for its ease of use.

data element

The fundamental data structure in a data processing system. Any unit of data defined for processing is a data element; for example, ACCOUNT NUMBER, NAME, ADDRESS and CITY. A data element is defined by size (in characters) and type (alphanumeric, numeric only, true/false, date, etc.). A specific set of values or range of values may also be part of the definition.

Technically, a data element is a logical definition of data, whereas a field is the physical unit of storage in a record. For example, the data element ACCOUNT NUMBER, which exists only once, is stored in the ACCOUNT NUMBER field in the customer record and in the ACCOUNT NUMBER field in the order records. *Data element, data item, field* and *variable* all describe the same unit of data and are used interchangeably.

data encryption

See *encryption, DES* and *RSA.*

data entry

Entering data into the computer, which includes keyboard entry, scanning and voice recognition. When transactions are entered after the fact (batch data entry), they are just stacks of source documents to the keyboard operator. Deciphering poor handwriting from a source document is a judgment call that is often error prone. In online data entry operations, in which the operator takes information in person or by phone, there's interaction and involvement with the transaction and less chance for error.

data entry department

The part of the datacenter where the data entry terminals and operators are located.

data entry operator

A person who enters data into the computer via keyboard or other reading or scanning device.

data entry program

An application program that accepts data from the keyboard or other input device and stores it in the computer. It may be part of an application that also provides updating, querying and reporting.

The data entry program establishes the data in the database and should test for all possible input errors. See *validity checking, table lookup, check digit* and *intelligent database*.

data error

A condition in which data on a digital medium has been corrupted. The error can be as little as one bit.

In DOS, the message "Data error on drive x" means that an area of the disk is unreadable. Press R to retry. Most likely, you'll have to press A to stop (abort). If the data or program is critical and there's no backup, use a utility program to try to reconstruct the damaged area.

data file

A collection of data records. This term may refer specifically to a database file that contains records and fields in contrast to other files such as a word processing document or spreadsheet. Or, it may refer to a file that contains any type of information structure including documents and spreadsheets in contrast to a program file.

data flow

(1) In computers, the path of data from source document to data entry to processing to final reports. Data changes format and sequence (within a file) as it moves from program to program.

(2) In communications, the path taken by a message from origination to destination and includes all nodes through which the data travels.

data flow diagram

A description of data and the manual and machine processing performed on the data.

data fork

The part of a Macintosh file that contains data. For example, in a HyperCard stack, text, graphics and HyperTalk scripts reside in the data fork, while fonts, sounds, control information and external functions reside in the resource fork.

data format

Same as *file format*.

Data General

(Data General Corporation, Westboro, MA) A computer manufacturer founded in 1968 by Edson de Castro. In 1969, it introduced the Nova, the first 16-bit mini with four accumulators, a leading technology at the time. During its early years, the company was successful in the scientific, academic and OEM markets. With its 32-bit ECLIPSE family of computers and its Comprehensive Electronic Office (CEO) software, Data General gained entry into the commercial marketplace in the early 1980s.

In 1989, the company introduced its AViiON line of UNIX-based servers that use the Motorola 88000 CPU, and more powerful models continue to be introduced. Data General's CLARiiON line of fault-tolerant (RAID) storage systems, introduced

Edson D. de Castro
(Photo courtesy of Data General Corporation.)

in 1992, are available for UNIX-based IBM and Sun computer systems.
The "Eagle project," DG's development of its ECLIPSE and first 32-bit computer, was chronicled in Tracy Kidder's Pulitzer-prize winning novel, "Soul of a New Machine," published by Little, Brown and Company, ISBN 0-316-49170-5.

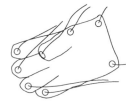

data glove

A glove used to report the position of a user's hand and fingers to a computer. See *virtual*

datagram

A TCP/IP message unit that contains internet source and destination addresses and data.

DataHub

A database administration tool for DB2 and other database environments from IBM. It functions as a control center for accessing databases located throughout the enterprise.

data independence

A DBMS technique that separates data from the processing and allows the database to be structurally changed without affecting most existing programs. Programs access data in a DBMS by field and are concerned with only the data fields they use, not the format of the complete record. Thus, when the record layout is updated (fields added, deleted or changed in size), the only programs that must be changed are those that use those new fields.

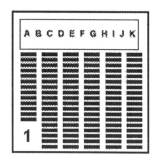

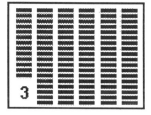

Data Independence Deals with Space

Program #1 reads the whole record and reserves space for all of its fields (A through K). If the file is converted to a new format, the program must be changed. Program #2 calls the DBMS to deliver just the fields it uses (D G H K). It still reserves space for the data, but unless a field it uses has been resized, it is not affected by any other file modifications. Program #3 is fully independent of the data structure. It calls for data by field name, and the DBMS allocates the right amount of space at runtime.

data integrity

The process of preventing accidental erasure or adulteration in a database.

Data Interchange Format

See *DIF.*

data item

A unit of data stored in a field. See *field.*

data legibility

The clear readability of data in a decision support system (DSS). One of the keys to a successful DSS is its ability to provide understandable answers to queries, which conform to the user's business model and use recognizable field and table names.

data library

(1) The section of the datacenter that houses offline disks and tapes. Data library personnel are responsible for cataloging and maintaining the media.
(2) A directory on a server that contains files for downloading. BBSs and online services sometimes call these sections data libraries.

data line

An individual circuit, or line, that carries data within a computer or communications channel.

data line monitor

In communications, a test instrument that analyzes the signals and timing of a communications line. It either visually displays the patterns or stores the activity for further analysis.

data link

In communications, the physical interconnection between two points (OSI layers 1 and 2). It may also refer to the modems, protocols and all required hardware and software to perform the transmission.

data link escape

A communications control character which indicates that the following character is not data, but a control code.

data link protocol

In communications, the transmission of a unit of data from one node to another (OSI layer 2). It is responsible for ensuring that the bits received are the same as the bits sent. Following are the major categories:

Asynchronous Transmission

Originating from mechanical teletype machines, asynchronous transmission treats each character as a unit with start and stop bits appended to it. It is the common form of transmission between the serial port of a personal computer or terminal and a modem. ASCII, or teletype, protocols provide little or no error checking. File transfer protocols, such as Zmodem and Ymodem, provide data link services as well as higher-level services, collectively known as transport services.

Synchronous Transmission

Developed for mainframe networks using higher speeds than teletype terminals, synchronous transmission sends contiguous blocks of data, with both sending and receiving stations synchronized to each other. Synchronous protocols include error checking. Examples are IBM's SDLC, Digital's DDCMP, and the international HDLC.

LANs

Developed for medium to high transmission speeds between stations, LANs typically use collision detection (CSMA/CD) or token passing methods for transmitting data between nodes. Common examples are Ethernet, Token Ring and MAP.
The IEEE 802 specification for LANs breaks the data link layer into two sublayers: the LLC (Logical Link Control) and MAC (Media Access Control). The LLC provides a common interface point to the MAC layers, which specify the access method used.

data management

Refers to several levels of managing data. From bottom to top, they are:

(1) The part of the operating system that manages the physical storage and retrieval of data on a disk or other device. See *access method.*
(2) Software that allows for the creation, storage, retrieval and manipulation of files interactively at a terminal or personal computer. See *file manager* and *DBMS.*
(3) The function that manages data as an organizational resource. See *data administration.*
(4) The management of all data/information in an organization. It includes data administration, the standards for defining data and the way in which people perceive and use it.

data management system

See *DBMS.*

data manipulation

Processing data.

data manipulation language

A language that requests data from a DBMS. It is coded within the application program such as COBOL or C.

data migration

See *HSM.*

data mining

Exploring detailed business transactions. It implies "digging through tons of data" to uncover patterns and relationships contained within the business activity and history. See *OLAP database, DSS, EIS* and *data warehouse.*

data model

A description of the organization of a database. It is often created as an entity relationship diagram. Today's modeling tools allow the attributes and tables (fields and records) to be graphically created. The SQL code that defines the data structure (schema) in the database is automatically created from the visual representation.

Data Modeling

Data modeling is the creation of the table structures and the relationships between them. The layout of all the table relationships in the database is called a *schema* (pronounced "skeema"). Each different view of the database for an individual user, group or department is called a *subschema.*

The following diagram is an example of a state-of-the-art CASE tool. It allows the database to be modeled graphically, and it eliminates writing the database descriptions in the SQL data definition language. The ouput of this model is the SQL code required to create the database.

The ERwin modeling program from Logic Works, Princeton, NJ, stands for Entity Relationship for Windows (an entity is a table). It can generate schemas for PowerBuilder WATCOM SQL databases as well as the DB2, Oracle, Ingres, Sybase, INFORMIX, SQLbase, Rdb and NetWare SQL databases. It can also be used to manage existing databases more effectively by viewing them graphically. ERwin can read all the existing schemas of the databases it supports and turn them into flow charts as in the example below.

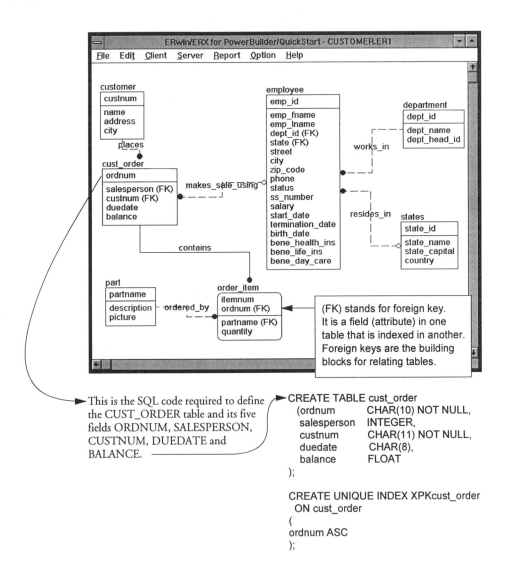

This is the SQL code required to define the CUST_ORDER table and its five fields ORDNUM, SALESPERSON, CUSTNUM, DUEDATE and BALANCE.

```
CREATE TABLE cust_order
    (ordnum        CHAR(10) NOT NULL,
     salesperson   INTEGER,
     custnum       CHAR(11) NOT NULL,
     duedate       CHAR(8),
     balance       FLOAT
);

CREATE UNIQUE INDEX XPKcust_order
    ON cust_order
    (
    ordnum ASC
);
```

data modem
A modem used for sending data and not faxes. See *modem* and *fax/modem*.

data module
A sealed, removable storage module containing magnetic disks and their associated access arms and read/write heads.

data name
The name assigned to a field or variable.

data network
A communications network that transmits data. See *communications*.

data packet
One frame in a packet-switched message. Most data communications is based on dividing the transmitted message into packets. For example, an Ethernet packet can be from 64 to 1518 bytes in length.

data parallel
Same as *SIMD*.

DataPhone
An AT&T trade name for various equipment and services. See *DDS*.

data processing
The capturing, storing, updating and retrieving data and information. It may refer to the industry or to data processing tasks in contrast with other operations, such as word processing.

Data Processing Management Association
See *DPMA*.

data processor
(1) A person who works in data processing.
(2) A computer that is processing data, in contrast with a computer performing another task, such as controlling a network.

data projector
A video machine that projects output from a computer onto a remote screen. It is bulkier than a flat LCD panel, but is faster for displaying high-speed animation.

Data Propagator
An IBM query language that maintains consistency between DB2 and IMS/ESA DB databases. When data is changed in the IMS database, it is automatically changed in the DB2 database.

DataPropagator
A database administration tool for DB2 and other database environments from IBM. It is used to keep relational databases in sync throughout the enterprise.

data pump
A circuit that transmits pulses in a digital device. It typically refers to the chipset in a modem that generates the bits based on the modem's modulation techniques.

data rate
(1) The data transfer speed within the computer or between a peripheral and

computer.

(2) The data transmission speed in a network.

data recovery

Restoring data that has been physically damaged or corrupted on a disk or tape. Disks and tapes can become corrupted due to viruses, bad software, hardware failure as well as from power failures that occur while the magnetic media is being written.

data representation

How data types are structured; for example, how signs are represented in numerical values or how strings are formatted (enclosed in quotes, terminated with a null, etc.).

data resource management

Same as *data administration*.

data set

(1) A data file or collection of interrelated data.

(2) The AT&T name for modem.

data set ready

See *DSR*.

data sharing

See *data conferencing*.

data sheet

A page or two of detailed information about a product.

data signal

Physical data as it travels over a line or channel (pulses or vibrations of electricity or light).

data sink

A device or part of the computer that receives data.

data source

A device or part of the computer in which data is originated.

data stream

The continuous flow of data from one place to another.

data striping

See *disk striping*.

data structure

The physical layout of data. Data fields, memo fields, fixed length fields, variable length fields, records, word processing documents, spreadsheets, data files, database files and indexes are all examples of data structures.

data switch

A switch box that routes one line to another; for example, to connect two computers to one printer. Manual switches have dials or buttons. Automatic switches test for signals and provide first-come, first-served switching.

data system

Same as *information system*.

data tablet
Same as *digitizer tablet*.

data terminal ready
See *DTR*.

data terminating equipment
See *DTE*.

data transfer
The movement of data within the computer system. Typically, data is said to be transferred within the computer, but it is "transmitted" over a communications network. A transfer is actually a copy function since the data is not automatically erased at the source.

data transfer rate
Same as *data rate*.

data transmission
Sending data over a communications network.

data transparency
The ability to easily access and work with data no matter where it is located or what application created it.

data type
A category of data. Typical data types are numeric, alphanumeric (character), dates and logical (true/false). Programming languages allow for the creation of different data types.

When data is assigned a type, it cannot be treated like another type. For example, alphanumeric data cannot be calculated, and digits within numeric data cannot be isolated. Date types can only contain valid dates.

data warehouse
A database designed to support decision making in an organization. It is batch updated and structured for fast queries and summaries. The majority of data warehouses contain over 10GB of data, some as much as 50GB and more. The amounts are expected to grow rapidly as more organizations expand their ability to support them. See *OLAP database*, *DSS* and *EIS*.

data word
See *word*.

date math
Calculations made upon dates. For example, March 30 + 5 yields April 4.

datum
The singular form of data; for example, one datum. It is rarely used, and data, its plural form, is commonly used for both singular and plural.

daughter board
A small printed circuit board that is attached to or plugs into a removable printed circuit board.

dazdee
See *DASD*.

DB

See *database, decibel* and *DB connector.*

DB2

(DATABASE 2) A relational DBMS from IBM that was originally developed for its mainframes. It is a full-featured SQL language DBMS that has become IBM's major database product. Known for its industrial strength reliability, IBM has made DB/2 available for all of its own platforms as well as others.

DB2/2, also known as DB2 for OS/2, runs on PCs using OS/2. DB2/400 and DB2/6000 run on AS/400s and RS/6000s. DB2 for HP-UX runs on HP 9000 workstations and computers, and DB2 for Solaris runs on Sun computers.

DB2/2

The OS/2 version of DB2 from IBM. Also called DB2 for OS/2, it is a 32-bit DBMS that replaced OS/2's earlier 16-bit Database Manager. See *DB2.*

DB2/400

The AS/400 version of DB2 from IBM. See *DB2.*

DB2/6000

The RS/6000 version of DB2 from IBM. See *DB2.*

DB-9, DB-15, DB-25, DB-37, DB-50

See *DB connector* and *plugs and sockets.*

DBA

See *database administrator.*

dBASE

A relational database management (DBMS) and application development system for DOS and Windows from Borland. dBASE was the first sophisticated database program for personal computers and has been widely used since the early 1980s. dBASE file formats are de facto standards.

Starting with dBASE for Windows and then Visual dBASE, it became a client/server development system with the inclusion of the Borland Database Engine. dBASE has automatic links to the Engine's IDAPI interface, allowing dBASE applications to access remote database servers (see *Borland Database Engine*).

dBASE provides a Pascal-like, interpreted programming language and fourth-generation commands for interactive use. The following dBASE 3GL example converts Fahrenheit to Celsius:

```
INPUT "Enter Fahrenheit " TO FAHR
? "Celsius is ", (FAHR - 32) * 5 / 9
```

The following dBASE 4GL example opens the product file and displays green items:

```
use products
list for color ='GREEN'
```

C. Wayne Ratliff
Ratliff created the first successful DBMS for personal computers, dBASE II. *(Photo courtesy Ratliff Software Productions.)*

Evolution of dBase dBASE II was the first comprehensive relational DBMS for personal computers. Originally named Vulcan, dBASE II was created by Wayne Ratliff to manage a company football pool. It was modeled after JPLDIS, the DBMS at Jet Propulsion Labs in Los Angeles.

Renamed dBASE II when Hal Lashlee and George Tate formed Ashton-Tate to market it (Ashton-Tate was acquired by Borland in 1991), dBASE became a huge success within a couple of years.

dBASE spawned the "Xbase" industry, which includes Clipper, FoxBase, FoxPro and other products that provide a dBASE-like programming language and support the dBASE file formats.

dBase II, III & IV

Introduced in 1981, dBASE II was the original command-driven dBASE for CP/M machines and later for PCs. In 1984, dBASE III was a major upgrade for PCs only. It added menus, more programming commands and handled larger databases. Two years later, dBASE III PLUS introduced new menus and features, including the ability to store queries and relational views. In 1988, dBASE IV was another major upgrade with support for SQL. dBASE IV was also ported to UNIX, Sun and VAX computers.

Visual dBase

In 1994, dBASE 5.0 for Windows added objects and visual programming to dBASE and provided connectivity to a variety of SQL databases using the Borland Database Engine. It runs dBASE III and dBASE IV DOS applications in a compatibility window, and its Component Builder converts DOS screen and report formats into dBASE for Windows files. Version 5.5 was renamed Visual dBASE in 1995. See *Borland Database Engine.*

dBASE compiler

Software that converts dBASE source language into machine language. The resulting programs execute on their own like COBOL or C programs and do not run under dBASE. See *CA-Clipper, Force* and *Quicksilver.*

dBASE Mac

A Macintosh DBMS from Ashton-Tate that never caught on because it was incompatible with dBASE.

DB9

DB25

DB15 VGA

DB connector

A family of plugs and sockets widely used to hook up communications and computer devices. DB connectors come in 9, 15, 25, 37 and 50-pin sizes. The DB connector defines the physical structure of the connector, not the purpose of each line. DB-9 and DB-25 connectors are commonly used for the serial ports (mouse, modem, etc.) on a PC. A DB-25 socket is the parallel port on a PC (see *printer cable*).
A high-density DB-15 connector is used for the VGA port on a PC, which has 15 pins in the same shell as the DB-9 connector. See *plugs and sockets.*

DB/DC

(DataBase/Data Communications) Refers to software that performs database and data communications functions.

DBF file

The dBASE data file extension. dBASE II and dBASE III files both use DBF, but are not compatible.

DBMS

(DataBase Management System) Software that controls the organization, storage, retrieval, security and integrity of data in a database. It accepts requests from the application and instructs the operating system to transfer the appropriate data. DBMSs may work with traditional programming languages (COBOL, C, etc.) or they may include their own programming language for application development. DBMSs let information systems be changed more easily as the organization's requirements change. New categories of data can be added to the database without disruption to the existing system. Adding a field to a record does not require changing any of the programs that do not use the data in that new field.

Major Features of a DBMS

Data Security

The DBMS can prevent unauthorized users from viewing or updating the database. Using passwords, users are allowed access to the entire database or subsets of it called *subschemas*. For example, in an employee database, some users may be able to view salaries while others may view only work history and medical data.

Data Integrity

The DBMS can ensure that no more than one user can update the same record at the same time. It can keep duplicate records out of the database; for example, no two customers with the same customer number can be entered.

Interactive Query

Most DBMSs provide query languages and report writers that let users interactively interrogate the database and analyze its data. This important feature gives users access to all management information as needed.

Interactive Data Entry and Updating

Many DBMSs provide a way to interactively enter and edit data, allowing you to manage your own files and databases. However, interactive operation does not leave an audit trail and does not provide the controls necessary in a large organization. These controls must be programmed into the data entry and update programs of the application.

This is a common misconception about personal computer DBMSs. Complex business systems can be developed in dBASE and Paradox, etc., but not without programming. This is not the same as creating lists of data for your own record keeping.

Data Independence

With DBMSs, the details of the data structure are not stated in each application program. The program asks the DBMS for data by field name; for example, a coded equivalent of "give me customer name and balance due" would be sent to the DBMS. Without a DBMS, the programmer must reserve space for the full structure of the record in the program. Any change in data structure requires changing all application programs.

Database Design

A business information system is made up of subjects (customers, employees, vendors, etc.) and activities (orders, payments, purchases, etc.). Database design is the process of organizing this data into related record types. The DBMS that is chosen is the one that can support the organization's data structure while efficiently processing the transaction volume.

Organizations may use one kind of DBMS for daily transaction processing and then move the detail to another DBMS better suited for random inquiries and analysis. Overall systems design decisions are performed by data administrators and systems analysts. Detailed database design is performed by database administrators.

Hierarchical, Network and Relational Databases

Information systems are made up of related files: customers and orders, vendors and purchases, etc. A key DBMS feature is its ability to manage these relationships. Hierarchical databases link records like an organization chart. A record type can be owned by only one owner. In the following example, orders are owned by only one customer. Hierarchical structures were widely used with early mainframe systems; however, they are often restrictive in linking real-world structures.

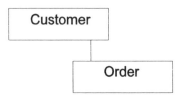

In network databases, a record type can have multiple owners. In the example below, orders are owned by both customers and products, reflecting their natural relationship in business.

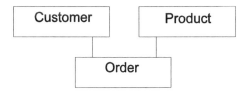

Relational databases do not link records together physically, but the design of the records must provide a common field, such as account number, to allow for matching. Often, the fields used for matching are indexed in order to speed up the process.

In the following example, customers, orders and products are linked by comparing data fields and/or indexes when information from more than one record type is needed. This method is more flexible for ad hoc inquiries. Many hierarchical and network DBMSs also provide this capability.

Intelligent Databases

All DBMSs provide some data validation; for example, they can reject invalid dates or alphabetic data entered into money fields. But most validation is left up to the application programs.

Intelligent databases provide more validation; for example, table lookups can reject bad spelling or coding of items. Common algorithms can also be used such as one that computes sales tax for an order based on zip code.

When validation is left up to each application program, one program could allow an item to be entered while another program rejects it. Data integrity is better served when data validation is done in only one place. Mainframe DBMSs are increasingly becoming intelligent. Eventually all DBMS will follow suit.

Multimedia Databases

The world of information is made up of data, text, pictures and voice. Many DBMSs manage text as well as data, but very few manage both with equal proficiency. Throughout the 1990s, DBMSs will begin to integrate all forms of information. Eventually, it will be common for a database to handle data, text, graphics, voice and video with the same ease as today's systems handle data.

The relational DBMS is not suited to storing multimedia data, because there are so many different types of sound and video formats. Although a relational DBMS may provide a BLOB (binary large object) field that holds anything, extensive use of this field can strain the processing.

An object-oriented database is often better suited for multimedia. Using the object model, an object-oriented DBMS can store anything or refer to anything. For example, a video object can reference a video file stored elsewhere on some other hard disk and launch the video player software necessary to play it.

The DBMS

The database managment system, or DBMS, is the software that manages the database. It allows for the creation of tables and the processing against those tables. Most all DBMSs today are actually RDBMSs (relational database management systems), which means that they can manage relationships between tables.

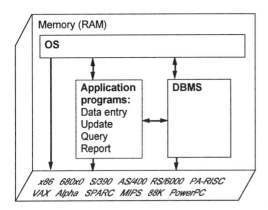

The DBMS is used to create tables by defining the individual elements of data that reside in them. These data fields are called *attributes* in relational terminology. In order to process the data entry, update, query and report transactions, the application "talks to" the DBMS in the SQL language. For example, the DBMS accepts SQL Join commands to search for data that resides in two or more tables and produces a duplicate, combined file.

The DBMS uses the operating system's file services to actually store and retrieve the data from the disk. Like application software, it must interface with the operating system.

Interfacing with the DBMS adds another linkage that locks the application into a particular environment. Moving an application to a different computer system requires that a version of the current DBMS also be available on the new platform. Otherwise, changing DBMSs means recompiling the applications for the new DBMS and possibly hand tailoring the SQL code, as each DBMS provides extensions to SQL, creating its own dialect.

Personal Computer Databases
Using databases such as dBASE or Paradox for developing personal address and inventory files is relatively easy. However, when files have to be linked, and audit trails have to be established, the job becomes more difficult. Thousands of applications have been developed in dBASE and Paradox, but not without programming in the dBASE and Paradox programming languages.

The major DBMSs used in mainframes, minis and client/server environments
DB2
Oracle
Ingres
NetWare SQL
SQL Server
SQLbase
SYBASE
INFORMIX
Rdb
WATCOM

Widely-used DBMSs for single user or file server use
dBASE
Paradox
Access
Approach
Alpha Four
Fifth Dimension (Mac)

Mission Critical Features:
DBMSs used in an enterprise must be robust enough to handle power and hardware failures as well as be capable of preventing the database from being corrupted by errant application programs.

Two-phase commit
In a distributed database environment, where multiple databases, each in a different location, are updated from one transaction, two-phase commit is a feature that keeps the databases in sync in the event of a hardware or network failure. All DBMSs involved in the transaction first confirm that the transaction was received and is recoverable (stored on disk). Then each DBMS is told to commit the transaction (do the actual updating).

Triggers and stored procedures
Triggers are SQL procedures that are executed when a record is added or deleted. it is used to maintain *referential integrity*, which means for example, that a customer record cannot be deleted if there are orders for that customer still in the database. Stored procedures are SQL programs that are stored in the database which are called for directly from the client or by a database trigger. When the SQL procedure is stored in the database, it does not have to replicated in each client.

DBOMP

(DataBase Organization and Maintenance Processor) An early DBMS that was derived from BOMP.

DBS

(Direct Broadcast Satellite) A one-way TV broadcast service direct from a satellite to a small 18" dish antenna. Although DBS service exists in other countries, the first DBS satellite in the U.S. was launched in December 1993 by Hughes Communications and Hubbard Broadcasting with a combined investment of $1 billion.

DBS service began in 1994, offering every household in the country a cable-like TV service for the first time. Although satellite service has been available for years, expensive, large dishes and receivers are required, and viewers have to know what programming is on which satellite before changing channels. With DBS, you change channels like cable TV.

The Hughes DirecTv subsidiary uses 11 of the 16 transponders and Hubbard's U.S. Satellite Broadcasting uses five. Transmission is a highly-compressed digital signal.

DB to DB adapter

A device that connects one type of DB connector to another. For example, a DB to DB adapter is used to connect a 9-pin mouse to a 25-pin serial port.

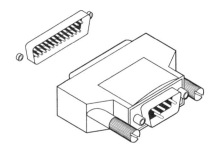

DB to DB Adapter
This male DB-9 to female DB-25 adapter is commonly used to attach a 9-pin plug on a mouse cable to a 25-pin serial port.

dBXL

A dBASE III PLUS-compatible DBMS from WordTech Systems, Inc., Orinda, CA, that features a menu-driven option for interactive use. See *Arago*.

DC

(1) (Direct Current) An electrical current that travels in one direction and used within the computer's electronic circuits. Contrast with AC.
(2) (Data Communications) See *DB/DC*.

DC2000

See *QIC*.

DCA

(1) (Document Content Architecture) IBM file formats for text documents. DCA/RFT (Revisable-Form Text) is the primary format and can be edited. DCA/FFT (Final-Form Text) has been formatted for a particular output device and cannot be changed. For example, page numbers, headers and footers are placed on every page.
(2) (Distributed Communications Architecture) A network architecture from Unisys.
(3) (Digital Communications Associates, Inc., Alpharetta, GA) A manufacturer of communications products, known for its famous "Irma" board. In late 1994, DCA merged with and became part of Attachmate Corporation of Bellevue, WA. See *Irma board*.

D/CAS

(Data/CASsette) A tape backup technology that uses an upgraded version of the common audio tape cassette. It can hold as much as 600MB of data.

DCC

(1) (Digital Compact Cassette) A digital tape format that uses a variation of the common analog audio cassette. DCC tape players also play analog tape cassettes.
(2) (Distributed Call Center) An automatic call distribution (ACD) system from Teloquent Communications, Billerica, MA, that runs on standard PCs and uses public ISDN lines.

DCE

(1) (Data Communications Equipment or Data Circuit-terminating Equipment) A device that establishes, maintains and terminates a session on a network. It may also convert signals for transmission. It is typically the modem. Contrast with *DTE*.
(2) (Distributed Computing Environment) See *OSF*.

DCI

(Display Control Interface) An Intel/Microsoft programming interface for full-motion video and games in Windows. It allows applications to take advantage of video accelerator features built into the display adapter. DCI requires updated display drivers and the DCI DLL from Microsoft. DCI has been superseded by DirectDraw in Windows 95.

DCL

(1) (Digital Command Language) Digital's standard command language for the VMS operating system on its VAX series.
(2) (Data Compression Library) A set of compression routines that allow realtime compression and decompression of data. See *PK software*.
(3) (Data Control Language) A language used to gain access to or manage a database.

DC/OSx

(DataCenter/OSx) Pyramid Technology's UNIX operating system that runs on its Nile series of SMP machines. DC/OSx is the first SMP implementation on UNIX System V Release 4.

DCS

(1) (Distributed Communications System) A telephone system that puts small switches close to subscribers making local loops shorter and maximizing long lines to the central office.
(2) (Digital Cross-connect System) A high-speed data channel switch that accepts separate instructions for switching independently of the data travelling through it.
(3) (Desktop Color Separation) A graphics format for color separation that uses five Encapsulated PostScript (EPS) files, one for each of the CMYK colors, and one master file, which links the other four and contains a preview image.
(4) (Distributed Control System) A process control system that uses disbursed computers throughout the manufacturing line for control.
(5) (Document Control Software) A menu-driven query system from Workgroup Technologies for Oracle databases on PCs and Sun stations.

DCT

(Discrete Cosine Transform) An algorithm, similar to Fast Fourier Transform, that converts data (pixels, waveforms, etc.) into sets of frequencies. The first frequencies in the set are the most meaningful; the latter, the least. For compression, latter frequencies are stripped away based on allowable resolution loss. The DCT method is used in the JPEG and MPEG compression.

DD

(Double Density) The designation for low-density diskettes, typically the 5.25" 360K and 3.5" 720K floppies. See *double density*. Contrast with *HD*.

D/DAT

See *DATA/ DAT*.

DDBMS

(Distributed Database Management System) See *distributed database*.

DDC

See *VESA Display Data Channel.*

DDCMP

(Digital Data Communications Message Protocol) Digital's proprietary, synchronous data link protocol used in DECnet.

DDE

(Dynamic Data Exchange) A message protocol in Windows that allows application programs to request and exchange data between them automatically.

DDL

(1) (Data Description Language) A language used to define data and their relationships to other data. It is used to create the data structure in a database. Major database management systems (DBMSs) use a SQL data description language.
(2) (Document Description Language) A printer control language from Imagen that runs on the HP LaserJet series.
(3) (Direct Data Link) The ability of a supplier to directly interrogate a customer's inventory database in order to manage scheduling and shipping more efficiently. Pioneered by Ford Motor Co. in 1988, Ford lets suppliers check stock levels in assembly plants throughout North America.

DDM

(Distributed Data Management) Software in an IBM SNA environment that allows users to access data in remote files within the network. DDM works with IBM's LU 6.2 session to provide peer-to-peer communications and file sharing.

DDP

(Distributed Data Processing) See *distributed processing.*

DDS

(1) (Dataphone Digital Service) An AT&T private line digital service with data rates from 2400 bps to 56Kbps. Private analog lines can be connected to DDS lines.
(2) (Digital Data Service) A private line digital service from a non-AT&T carrier.
(3) (Digital Data Storage) A DAT format for data backup. It is a sequential recording method; data must be appended at the end of previous data. See *tape backup.*

deadlock, deadly embrace

A stalemate that occurs when two elements in a process are each waiting for the other to respond. For example, in a network, if one user is working on file A and needs file B to continue, but another user is working on file B and needs file A to continue, each one waits for the other. Both are temporarily locked out. The software must be able to deal with this.

deallocate

To release a computer resource that is currently assigned to a program or user, such as memory or a peripheral device.

deblock

To separate records from a block.

debug

To correct a problem in hardware or software. Debugging software is finding the errors in the program logic. Debugging hardware is finding the errors in circuit design.

debugger

Software that helps a programmer debug a program by stopping at certain breakpoints and displaying various programming elements. The programmer can step through source code statements one at a time while the corresponding machine instructions are being executed.

DEC

(Digital Equipment Corporation) The trade name for Digital's products (DECmate, DECnet, etc.). Many people refer to the company as DEC.

decay

The reduction of strength of a signal or charge.

decentralized processing

Computer systems in different locations. Although data may be transmitted between the computers periodically, it implies limited daily communications. Contrast with *distributed computing* and *centralized processing*.

decibel

(dB) The unit that measures loudness or strength of a signal. dBs are a relative measurement derived from an initial reference level and a final observed level. A whisper is about 20 dB, a normal conversation about 60 dB, a noisy factory 90 dB and loud thunder 110 dB. 120 dB is the threshold of pain.

decimal

Meaning 10. The universal numbering system that uses 10 digits. Computers use binary numbers because it is easier to design electronic systems that can maintain two states rather than 10.

decision box

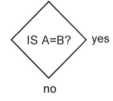

A diamond-shaped symbol that is used to document a decision point in a flowchart. The decision is written in the decision box, and the results of the decision branch off from the points in the box.

decision instruction

In programming, an instruction that compares one set of data with another and branches to a different part of the program depending on the results.

decision making

Making choices. The proper balance of human and machine decision making is an important part of a system's design.

It is easy to think of automating tasks traditionally performed by people, but it is not that easy to analyze how decisions are made by an experienced, intuitive worker. If an improper analysis of human decision making is made, the wrong decision making may be placed into the machine, which can get buried in documentation that is rarely reviewed. This will become an important issue as AI applications proliferate. From a programming point of view, decision making is performed two ways: algorithmic, a precise set of rules and conditions that never change, or heuristic, a set of rules that may change over time (self-modify) as conditions occur. Heuristic techniques are employed in AI systems.

decision support system

See *DSS* and *EIS.*

decision table

A list of decisions and their criteria. Designed as a matrix, it lists criteria (inputs) and the results (outputs) of all possible combinations of the criteria. It can be placed into a program to direct its processing. By changing the decision table, the program is changed accordingly.

decision tree

A graphical representation of all alternatives in a decision making process.

deck

The part of a magnetic tape unit that holds and moves the tape reels. See also *DEC.*

declaration

In programming, an instruction or statement that defines data (fields, variables, arrays, etc.) and resources, but does not create executable code.

DECmate

A family of computer systems from Digital specialized for word processing. Introduced in 1981, DECmates use the PDP-8 architecture.

DECmcc

(DEC Managment Control Center) Digital's network management software for DECnet and TCP/IP. DECmcc Management Stations for VMS and ULTRIX support X Window and provide color-coded alarms.

DECnet

Digital's communications network, which supports Ethernet-style LANs and baseband and broadband WANs over private and public lines. It interconnects PDPs, VAXs, PCs, Macs and workstations. In DECnet philosophy, a node must be an intelligent machine and not simply a terminal as in other systems. See *DNA.* DECnet/DOS allows DOS machines to function as end nodes in DECnet networks, and DECnet/OSI is the implementation of DECnet Phase V that supports OSI and provides compatibility with DECnet Phase IV and TCP/IP.

decoder

A hardware device or software program that converts a coded signal back into its original form.

decollator

A device that separates multiple-part paper forms while removing the carbon paper.

decompiler

A program that converts machine language back into a high-level source language. The resulting code may be very difficult to maintain as variables and routines are named generically: A0001, A0002, etc. See *disassembler.*

decompress
To restore compressed data back to its original size.

decrement
To subtract a number from another number. Decrementing a counter means to subtract 1 or some other number from its current value.

DECstation
(1) A series of RISC-based single-user workstations from Digital, introduced in 1989, that run under ULTRIX.
(2) A PC series from Digital introduced in 1989.
(3) A small computer system from Digital, introduced in 1978, used primarily for word processing (DECstation 78).

DECsystem
(1) A series of RISC-based, 32-bit computers from Digital that run under ULTRIX. Introduced in 1989, the 5400 model is a Q-bus system; the 5800 model uses the XMI bus.
(2) A series of mainframes from Digital that were introduced from 1974 through 1980 and were the successor to the 36-bit PDP-10 computers.

DECtalk
A voice synthesizing system from Digital that accepts serial ASCII text and converts it into audible speech. It is used in Touch-tone telephone response systems as well as for voice-output for visually handicapped users.

DECwindows
Digital's windowing architecture, based on X Window, Version 11. It is compatible with X Window while adding a variety of enhancements.

dedicated channel
A computer channel or communications line that is used for one purpose.

dedicated service
A service that is not shared by other users or organizations.

de facto standard
A widely-used format or language not endorsed by a standards organization.

default
The current setting or action taken by hardware or software if the user has not specified otherwise.

default directory
Same as *current directory*.

default drive
The disk drive used if no other drive is specified.

default font
The typeface and type size used if none other is specified.

defragger
Also called an *optimizer program*, it is a software utility that defragments a disk.

defragment

To reorganize the disk by putting files into contiguous order. Because the operating system stores new data in whatever free space is available, data files become spread out across the disk if they are updated often. This causes extra read/write head movement to read them back. Periodically, the hard disk should be defragmented to put files back into order.

degausser

A device that removes unwanted magnetism from a monitor or the read/write head in a disk or tape drive.

de jure standard

A format or language endorsed by a standards organization.

delay line

A communications or electronic circuit that has a built-in delay. Acoustic delay lines were used to create the earliest computer memories. For example, the UNIVAC I used tubes of liquid mercury that would slow down the digital pulses long enough (a fraction of a second) to serve as storage.

delete

To remove an item of data from a file or to remove a file from the disk. See *undelete*.

delimiter

A character or combination of characters used to separate one item or set of data from another. For example, in comma delimited records, a comma is used to separate each field of data.

deliverable

The measurable result or output of a process.

DEL key

(DELete key) The keyboard key used to delete the character under the screen cursor or some other currently-highlighted object.

Dell

(Dell Computer Corporation, Austin, TX) A PC manufacturer founded in 1984 by Michael Dell. Originally selling under the "PCs Limited" brand, Dell was the first to legitimize mail-order PCs by providing quality telephone support. Dell made the Fortune 500 in 1991, and its fiscal 1994 revenues exceeded three billion dollars.

Delphi

(1) An online information service that provides access to a wide variety of databases, files and shopping. It is the first major online service to provide full Internet access, not just for electronic mail. Internet tools such as Archie, Veronica, Gopher and World Wide Web browsers are available to the user logged on to Delphi. See *online services*.

(2) An application development system for Windows from Borland, introduced in 1995. Based on the object-oriented Object Pascal language, it includes visual programming tools and generates executable programs (.EXE files). It includes the Borland Database Engine, which allows access to dBASE, Paradox and ODBC databases. Delphi also uses Visual Basic controls (VBXs). The Delphi Client/Server upgrade supports major client/server databases such as Oracle, Sybase and INFORMIX.

(3) (Delphi Consulting Group, Boston, MA) An organization that specializes in

electronic document management systems. Founded by Tom Koulopoulos, it provides consulting services, publications and inhouse and public seminars on the subject.

delta modulation

A technique that is used to sample voice waves and convert them into digital code. Delta modulation typically samples the wave 32,000 times per second, but generates only one bit per sample. See *PCM*.

DEMA

(Association for Input Technology and Management, 101 Merritt 7, Norwalk, CT 06851, 203/846-3777) An organization devoted to the advancement of managers in data entry technologies. Founded in 1976 as the Data Entry Management Association, it sponsors educational courses and conferences.

demand paging

Copying a program page from disk into memory when required by the program.

demand processing

Same as *transaction processing*.

demodulate

To filter out the data signal from the carrier. See *modulate*.

Demo II

Officially "Dan Bricklin's Demo II," it is a demonstration, authoring and prototyping program for DOS from Lifeboat Software, Shrewsbury, NJ. It is used to create courseware and slide shows and simulate interactive user interfaces for prototyping. The Windows version of Demo II is demo-It!. Dan Bricklin designed the original VisiCalc spreadsheet.

demon

See *daemon*.

demoware

Demonstration software that shows some or all of the features of a commercial product. See *crippleware*.

demultiplex

To reconvert a transmission that contains several intermixed signals back into its original separate signals.

density

See *packing density* and *bit density*.

departmental computing

Processing a department's data with its own computer system. See *distributed computing*.

dependent segment

In database management, data that depends on data in a higher level for its full meaning.

dequeue

Pronounced "d-q." To remove an item from a queue. Contrast with *enqueue*.

DES

(Data Encryption Standard) A NIST-standard encryption technique that scrambles data into an unbreakable code for public transmission. It uses a binary number as an encryption key with 72 quadrillion possible combinations. The key, randomly chosen for each session, is used to create the encryption pattern for transmission. See *RSA*.

descenders

The parts of the lower case characters g, j, p, q and y that fall below the line. Sometimes these characters are displayed and printed with shortened descenders in order to fit into a smaller character cell, making them difficult to read.

descending sort

Arranging data from high to low sequence (Z to A, 9 to 0).

descriptor

(1) A word or phrase that identifies a document in an indexed information retrieval system.
(2) A category name used to identify data.

deserialize

To convert a serial stream of bits into parallel streams of bits.

DesignCAD

A family of 2-D and 3-D CAD programs from American Small Business Computers, Pryor, OK, for DOS, Windows and Mac, noted for their ease of use. DesignCAD 3-D for Windows includes such features as texture mapping, reflection mapping with up to eight light sources and keyframe animation.

Designer

A full-featured Windows drawing program from Micrografx, Inc., Richardson, TX. It creates its own proprietary file formats (DRW, DS4 and DSF) and supports PIC files compatible with other Micrografx products. Designer is a very sophisticated vector illustration program providing many of the features of a CAD program. When originally introduced, it was the first Windows program to provide almost all of the design tools found in the Macintosh drawing programs of the time.

Designer/2000

See *Developer/2000*.

desk accessory

In the Macintosh, a program that is always available from the Apple menu no matter what application is running. With System 7, all applications can be turned into desk accessories.

desk checking

Manually testing the logic of a program.

DeskJet

A family of popular desktop ink-jet printers for PCs from HP.

DESKPRO

A Compaq trade name for its PCs.

desktop

(1) An on-screen representation of a desktop. The windowing capabilities built into graphical user interfaces (GUIs) provide a "virtual desktop," in which the user views an infinite desktop full of documents. Both the Macintosh and Windows use this metaphor, but the Mac more closely simulates a real desktop.

(2) A buzzword attached to applications traditionally performed on more expensive machines that are now on a personal computer (desktop publishing, desktop mapping, etc.).

desktop accessory

Software that simulates an object normally found on an office desktop, such as a calculator, notepad and appointment calendar. See *TSR*.

desktop application

See *desktop accessory*.

desktop computer

A computer that is small enough to reside on a desktop. It either refers to personal computers (PCs, Macs, Amigas, PowerPCs, etc.) or to workstations from Sun, IBM, HP, Digital and others.

desktop conferencing

See *videoconferencing* and *data conferencing*.

Desktop Management Interface

See *DMI*.

desktop manager

The part of a GUI that displays the desktop and icons, allows programs to be launched from the icon and files to be visually dragged & dropped (copied, deleted, etc.). The desktop manager combined with the window manager make up the GUI. The desktop manager is included with the Mac and Windows. In OSF/Motif and Open Look, products such as IXI's X.desktop and Visix Software's Looking Glass add this capability.

desktop mapping

Using a desktop computer to perform digital mapping functions.

desktop media

The integration of desktop presentations, desktop publishing and multimedia (coined by Apple).

desktop organizer

See *desktop accessory*.

desktop presentations

The creation of presentation materials on a personal computer, which includes charts, graphs and other graphics-oriented information. It implies a wide variety of special effects for both text and graphics that will produce output for use as handouts, overheads and slides as well as sequences that can be viewed on screen. Advanced systems generate animation and control multimedia devices.

desktop publishing

Abbreviated "DTP." Using a personal computer to produce high-quality printed output or camera-ready output for commercial printing. It requires a desktop publishing program, high-speed personal computer, large monitor and a laser printer.

DTP packages provide the ultimate in page layout capabilities, including magazine style columns, rules and borders, page, chapter and caption numbering as well as precise typographic aligment. A key feature is its ability to manage text and graphics on screen WYSIWYG style. The program can flow text around graphic objects in a variety of ways.

Text and graphics may be created in the DTP program, but few of them have full-featured text and graphics capability. Usually, the work is created in word processing, CAD, drawing and paint programs and then imported into the publishing system.

A laser printer may be used for final text output, but it cannot print line art and shaded drawings respectably unless its resolution is 1000 dpi or greater. Imagesetters, at resolutions of 1270 and 2540 dpi, can accept file formats from popular DTP packages and generate high-quality camera ready material.

Since DTP has dramatically brought down the cost of high-end page makeup, it is often thought of as "the" way to produce inhouse newsletters and brochures. However, creating quality material takes experience. Desktop publishing is no substitute for a graphics designer who knows which fonts to use and how to lay out the page artistically.

DeskWriter

A family of popular desktop ink-jet printers for the Macintosh from HP. Color models are also available.

DESQview

A multitasking, windows environment for DOS from Quarterdeck Office Systems, Santa Monica, CA. It runs multiple DOS text and graphics programs in resizable windows. Calendar, notepad, calculator and communications utilities are also available.

DESQview 386 includes the widely-used QEMM-386 expanded memory manager and utilizes the virtual machine capability of the 386. DESQview was a very popular switching environment for DOS before Windows 3.0 became so popular.

DESQview/X

A version of DESQview that runs DOS, Windows and X Window applications locally or remotely on other DESQview/X PCs or X workstations. QEMM-386 and Adobe Type Manager are included. There are several ways DESQview/X can be implemented.

It adds X Windows to a PC network, allowing each DOS machine to run multiple applications on different PCs in the network. As an integration product, it allows DOS and Windows apps to run in an X Window network under UNIX or any other X-based environment. In a stand-alone DOS machine, it adds a graphical and customizable interface to DESQview.

Optional DESQview/X Motif and X11 toolkits allow Motif and X applications to be recompiled to a DOS machine.

destructive memory

Memory that loses its content when it is read, requiring that the circuitry regenerate the bits after the read operation.

detail file

Same as *transaction file*.

developer's toolkit

A set of software routines and utilities used to help programmers write an application. In graphical interfaces, it provides the tools for creating resources, such as menus, dialog boxes, fonts and icons. It provides the means to link the new application to its operating environment (OS, DBMS, protocol, etc.). See *development system, client/server development system* and *GUI builder*.

Developer/2000

A client/server application development system for Windows and the Macintosh from Oracle Corporation. Formerly the Cooperative Development Environment, the core programs are Oracle Forms for creating the user screens, Oracle Reports for reporting, Oracle Graphics for generating business graphics and Oracle Browser and Oracle Data Query for queries. Oracle Procedure Builder provides drag and drop application partitioning, and Oracle Transparent Gateway provides access to non-Oracle databases. Oracle's Designer/2000 is the data modeling and CASE counterpart for Windows.

development cycle

See *system development cycle*.

development system

(1) A programming language and related components. It includes the compiler, text editor, debugger, function library and any other supporting programs that enable a programmer to write a program. See *developer's toolkit* and *application development system*. For a list of popular client/server development tools, see *client/server development system*.

(2) A computer and related software for developing applications.

development tool

Software that assists in the creation of new software. Compilers, debuggers, visual programming tools, GUI builders, application generators are examples. See *developer's toolkit*. For a list of popular client/server development tools, see *client/server development system*.

device

(1) Any electronic or electromechanical machine or component from a transistor to a disk drive. Device always refers to hardware.

(2) In semiconductor design, it is an active component, such as a transistor or diode, in contrast to a passive component, such as a resistor or capacitor.

device adapter

Same as *interface adapter*.

device address

See *address, I/O address* and *port address*.

device control character

A communications code that activates a function on a terminal.

device dependent

Refers to programs that address specific hardware features and work with only one type of peripheral device. Contrast with *device independent*. See *machine dependent*.

device driver

See *driver*.

device independent

Refers to programs that work with a variety of peripheral devices. The hardware-specific instructions are in some other program (OS, DBMS, etc.). Contrast with *device dependent*. See *machine independent*.

device level

(1) In circuit design, refers to working with individual transistors rather than complete circuits.
(2) Refers to communicating directly with the hardware at a machine language level.

device name

A name assigned to a hardware device that represents its physical address. For example, LPT1 is a DOS device name for the parallel port.

DFT mode

(Distributed Function Terminal mode) A mode that allows a 3270 terminal to have five concurrent sessions with the mainframe. Contrast with *CUT mode.*

DG

See *Data General.*

DGIS

(Direct Graphics Interface Standard) A graphics interface for PC display adapters from Graphic Software Systems, Beaverton, OR. It is primarily used with TI's 340x0 graphics chip and custom drivers are licensed to video board manufacturers.

DG/UX

(Data General UNIX) A UNIX-based operating system developed by Data General. It supports symmetric multiprocessing and is generally used with the Tuxedo TP monitor for transaction processing.

DHCP

(Dynamic Host Configuration Protocol) Software included in Windows NT and 95 that assigns IP addresses (TCP/IP) to stations in the network. The assignments are made by the DHCP server software that runs under Windows NT Server. A Windows 95 client calls the server to obtain the address. See *WINS.*

Dhrystones

A benchmark program that tests a general mix of instructions. The results in Dhrystones per second are the number of times the program can be executed in one second. See *Whetstones.*

DIA

(Document Interchange Architecture) An IBM SNA format used to exchange documents from dissimilar machines within an LU 6.2 session. It acts as an envelope to hold the document and does not set any standards for the content of the document, such as layout settings or graphics standards.

Diablo emulation

A printer that accepts the same commands as the Diablo printer.

diacritical

A small mark added to a letter that changes its pronunciation, such as the French cedilla (Ç).

diagnostic board

An expansion board with built-in diagnostic tests that reports results via its own readout. Boards for PCs, such as Landmark's KickStart and UNICORE's POSTcard, have their own POST system and can test a malfunctioning computer that doesn't boot.

diagnostics
(1) Software routines that test hardware components (memory, keyboard, disks, etc.). In personal computers, they are often stored in ROM and activated on startup.
(2) Error messages in a programmer's source code that refer to statements or syntax that the compiler or assembler cannot understand.

diagnostic tracks
The spare tracks on a disk used by the drive or controller for testing purposes.

diagramming program
Software that allows the user to create flow charts, organization charts and similar diagrams. It is similar to a drawing program, but specialized for creating interconnected diagrams. It comes with a palette of predefined shapes and symbols and usually keeps the lines connected between them if they are edited and rearranged.
Examples of general flowcharting programs are ABC FlowCharter, Visio, CorelFlow and allClear. Network diagram-specific programs that can link an equipment database to the objects in the diagram are ClickNet and netViz.

DIALOG
An online information service that contains the world's largest collection of databases. Address: 3460 Hillview Ave., Palo Alto CA 94304, 415/858-2700. See *online services*.

dialog box
A small, on-screen window displayed in response to some request. It provides the options currently available to the user.

dial-up line
A two-wire line as used in the dial-up telephone network. Contrast with *leased line*.

dial-up network
The switched telephone network regulated by government and administered by common carriers.

dial-up services
See *online services*.

diazo film
A film used to make microfilm or microfiche copies. It is exposed to the original film under ultraviolet light and is developed into identical copies. Copy color is typically blue, blue-black or purple.

DIB
(1) (Directory Information Base) Also called *white pages*, a database of names in an X.500 system.
(2) (Device Independent Bit map) See *BMP*.

dibit
Any one of four patterns from two consecutive bits: 00, 01, 10 and 11. Using phase modulation, a dibit can be modulated onto a carrier as a different shift in the phase of the wave.

DIBOL

(DIgital coBOL) A version of COBOL from Digital that runs on the PDP and VAX series.

DID

(Direct Inward Dialing) The ability to make a telephone call directly into an internal extension within a company without having to go through the operator.

die

The formal term for the square of silicon containing an integrated circuit. The popular term is chip.

dielectric

An insulator (glass, rubber, plastic, etc.). Dielectric materials can be made to hold an electrostatic charge, but current cannot flow through them.

DIF

(1) (Data Interchange Format) A standard file format for spreadsheet and other data structured in row and column form. Originally developed for VisiCalc, DIF is now under Lotus' jurisdiction.

(2) (Display Information Facility) An IBM System/38 program that lets users build custom programs for online access to data.

(3) (Document Interchange Format) A file standard developed by the U.S. Navy in 1982.

(4) (Dual In-line Flatpack) A type of surface mount DIP with pins extending horizontally outward.

Difference Engine

An early calculator designed by Charles Babbage and subsidized by the British government. It used rods and wheels, which was tried before by other designers. It was started in 1821 and abandoned in 1833. Although never completed, it did improve the precision of Britain's machine-tool industry. Babbage later turned his attention to the Analytical Engine. In 1991, the National Museum of Science and Technology built a working model of the Difference Engine.

In 1879, Babbage's son reassembled a section of the Difference Engine from parts. In 1995, Christie's auction in London auctioned off the section to the Power House Museum in Sydney for $282,000. See *Analytical Engine*.

The Difference Engine
(Photo courtesy of Smithsonian Institution.)

Differential Analyzer

An analog computational device built to solve differential equations by Vannevar Bush (MIT, 1930s). Less than a dozen were built, but they were effective in calculating ballistics tables in World War II. The machine took up an entire room and was programmed by changing camshaft-like gears with screwdriver and wrench. See illustration on following page.

Differential Analyzer
Programming with a screwdriver and wrench is a far cry from today's calculating machines. *(Photo courtesy of The MIT Museum.)*

differential backup

See *backup types.*

differential configuration

The use of individual wire pairs for each electrical signal for high immunity to noise and crosstalk. Contrast with *single-ended configuration.*

differential PCM

See *DPCM.*

diffusion

A semiconductor manufacturing process that infuses tiny quantities of impurities into a base material, such as silicon, to change its electrical characteristics.

digispeak

In online communications, the use of acronyms to make a shorthand out of common phrases. For example, BTW for "by the way" and IMHO for "in my humble opinion." People are doing so much typing these days that they welcome shortcuts, and the shortcuts are turning into a new language.

digit

A single character in a numbering system. In decimal, digits are 0 through 9. In binary, digits are 0 and 1.

digital

Traditionally, the use of numbers and comes from digit, or finger. Today, digital is synonymous with computer. See also *Digital Equipment.*

digital audio

Sound waves that have been digitized and stored in the computer. Common digital audio formats are audio CDs (CD-DA "Red Book") and WAV files. Although also in digital form and stored in the computer, MIDI is not considered digital audio.

digital audio disc
Same as *CD*.

digital audio tape
See *DAT*.

digital camera
A video camera that records its images in digital form. Unlike traditional analog cameras that convert light intensities into infinitely variable signals, digital cameras convert light intensities into discrete numbers.

It breaks down the picture image into a fixed number of pixels (dots), tests each pixel for light intensity and converts the intensity into a number. In a color digital camera, three numbers are created, representing the amount of red, green and blue in each pixel.

Cameras used today for TV production are digital in design and record their initial field of view as a digital image, using charge coupled devices (CCDs). However, after a microprocessor processes the image, it is converted into analog form for recording on analog tape recorders. The analog method is still much more economical for routine video recording and playback.

In time, it is expected that TV recording will be all digital from start to finish.

digital channel
A communications path that handles only digital signals. All voice and video signals have to be converted from analog to digital in order to be carried over a digital channel. Contrast with *analog channel*.

digital circuit
An electronic circuit that accepts and processes binary data (on/off) according to the rules of Boolean logic.

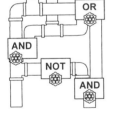

Digital Plumbing!
A digital circuit can be conceptualized as a mass of plumbing: the circuit paths are the pipes, the transistors are the valves, and the electricity is the water. Imagine opening a valve, and the water that passes through it and down a pipe will eventually reach a second valve, causing it to turn on, allowing water in another pipe to flow through the second valve, which will reach another valve, and so on. A resistor can be viewed as a large pipe that narrows into a pipe with a smaller diameter, a capacitor as a storage tank, and a diode as a one-way valve, allowing water to flow in only one direction.

digital computer
A computer that accepts and processes data that has been converted into binary numbers. All common computers are digital. Contrast with *analog computer*.

digital convergence
The integration of computers, communications and consumer electronics. Data and text were converted into digital form for the very first computers years ago, however since the advent of audio CDs and, increasingly, digital video, it becomes apparent that all forms of information, both for business and entertainment, can be managed together.

With one coaxial cable or optical fiber into everyone's home, music, movies, video games and all sorts of interactive programs can be requested on demand similar to the way people routinely select news, files and information from online services, such as CompuServe and PRODIGY, via modem.

The Digital VideoDisc (DVD) is expected to be a major convergence product. It is a video medium that should eventually replace LaserDiscs and VHS tapes for recorded movies as well as become the primary video vehicle for personal computers. When DVDs evolve into erasable DVDs, they will replace videotapes entirely and provide a single medium for home movies, home theater as well as computer use.

Digital Darkroom

A Macintosh graphics editing program from Silicon Beach Software, Inc., for enhancing black & white photographs. Version 2.0 supports color overlays for colorizing gray scale images.

digital data

Data in digital form. All data in the computer is in digital form.

digital domain

The world of digital. When something is done in the digital domain, it implies that the original data (images, sounds, video, etc.) has been converted into a digital format and is manipulated inside the computer's memory.

digital effects

Special sounds and animations that have been created in the digital domain. Synthetic sounds and reverberation, morphing and transitions between video frames (fades, wipes, dissolves, etc.) are examples.

Digital Equipment

(Digital Equipment Corporation, Maynard, MA) A major computer manufacturer, commonly known as DEC or Digital. It was founded in 1957 by Kenneth Olsen, who headed the company until he retired in 1992. Digital pioneered the minicomputer industry with its PDP series.

Its early success came from the scientific, process control and academic communities; however, after the VAX was announced in 1977, Digital gained a strong foothold in commercial data processing. The VAX evolved into a complete line from desktop to mainframe, using the same VMS operating system in all models and causing Digital to achieve substantial growth in the 1980s.

Over the years, Digital has been widely recognized for its high-quality systems. Its strategy for the 1990s and beyond is to embrace open systems with its powerful, RISC-based Alpha architecture introduced in 1992. In addition, Digital has a large services business that provides full project life cycle support from installation to maintenance for Digital and non-Digital products.

Kenneth H.Olsen
Olsen pioneered the minicomputer industry with his PDP computer series. He ran Digital for 35 years until his retirement in 1992. *(Photo courtesy of Digital Equipment Corporation.)*

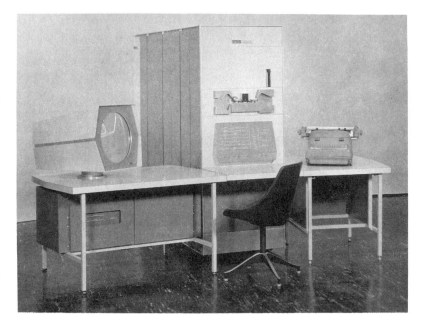

The First "Mini" Computer
This PDP-1 was Digital's first computer, which was a breakthrough in 1959. Digital spearheaded the minicomputer industry with its PDP series.
(Photo courtesy of Digital Equipment Corporation.)

digital mapping
Digitizing geographic information for a geographic information system (GIS).

digital monitor
A video monitor that accepts a digital signal from the computer and converts it into analog signals to illuminate the screen. Common examples are MDA, CGA and EGA monitors. Contrast with *analog monitor*.

digital nonlinear editing
See *nonlinear video editing*.

digital PABX
See *digital PBX*.

Digital Paper
(1) A non-erasable storage material from ICI Electronics used for tape and disk archival storage. It uses a polyester film coated with a reflective layer on top of which is adhered a dye polymer layer that is sensitive to infrared light. A laser burns pits into the film as close as half a micron apart. Capacities are about one Gbyte on a 5.25" disk and 600 GBytes on a 2,400 foot tape reel.
(2) A text file format that maintains the page and style layout of the original document. See *Common Ground*.

digital PBX
(digital Private Branch Exchange) A modern PBX that uses digital methods for switching in contrast to older PBXs that use analog methods.

digital radio
The microwave transmission of digital data via line of sight transmitters.

digital recording
See *digital video*, *digital nonlinear editing* and *magnetic recording*.

Digital Research

(Digital Research, Inc., Monterey, CA) A software company founded in 1976 by Gary Kildall that spearheaded the microcomputer revolution with its CP/M operating system. DRI's products include the GEM windows environment, FlexOS realtime operating system and DR DOS, a DOS-compatible operating system with advanced features.

In 1991, DRI was acquired by Novell, Inc., Provo, UT, makers of the widely-used NetWare operating systems.

digital signal

An electronic signal transmitted as binary code either as on/off pulses or as high and low voltages. See also *DS*.

digital signal processing

See *DSP*.

digital signature

An electronic signature that cannot be forged. It is a coded message that accompanies the data that is transmitted over a network. Digital signatures ensure that senders are who they say they are. See *RSA* and *DSS*.

Digital SVD

See *DSVD*.

digital video

Video recording in digital form. In order to edit video in the computer or to embed video clips into multimedia documents, a video source must originate as digital (digital camera) or be converted to digital. Frames from analog video cameras and VCRs are converted into digital frames (bitmaps) using frame grabbers or similar devices attached to a personal computer.

Uncompressed digital video signals require huge amounts of storage and bandwidth. High-ratio realtime compression schemes, such as MPEG, are essential for handling digital video in today's computers. See *MPEG, DVD, digital nonlinear editing* and *HDTV*.

Digital VideoDisc

See *DVD*.

digital video effects

Visual effects performed by computer that create a more interesting transition from one scene to another rather than just switching scenes. They include fading or dissolving the frame, wiping one frame over another, flipping the frame and simulating a camera lens opening and closing (iris effect).

digital watermark

A pattern of bits embedded into a file used to identify the source of illegal copies. For example, if a digital watermark is placed into a master copy of an audio CD, then all copies of that CD are uniquely identified. If a licensee were to manufacture and distribute them in areas outside of its authorized territory, the watermark provides a trace.

The watermark developer has to find creative ways of altering the file without disturbing it for the user. It is extremely difficult to embed a watermark within an ASCII file, which is just raw text. But it is somewhat easier to alter a few bits within digital audio samples without making a noticeable difference on playback.

digitize

To convert an image or signal into digital code by scanning, tracing on a graphics tablet or using an analog to digital conversion device. 3-D objects can be digitized by a device with a mechanical arm that is moved onto all the corners.

digitizer tablet

Digitizer Tablet
Digitzer tablets are also called *graphics tablets*. The puck-like object used for drawing and menu selection is technically called a cursor, or tablet cursor, but not a mouse. Drawings created on tablets are stored as mathematical line segments, the collection of which is called a *display list*.

A graphics drawing tablet used for sketching new images or tracing old ones and for selecting from menus. The user makes contact with the tablet with a pen-like or puck-like device called a cursor (mistakenly called a mouse), which is connected to the tablet by a wire. For sketching, the user draws with the tablet cursor and the screen cursor "draws" a corresponding image. When tracing an image on the tablet, a series of x-y coordinates (vector graphics) are created, either as a continuous stream of coordinates, or as end points. Menu selection is accomplished by a tablet overlay or by a screen display. The tablet cursor selects an item by making contact with it on the overlay, or by controlling the screen cursor. See *mouse*.

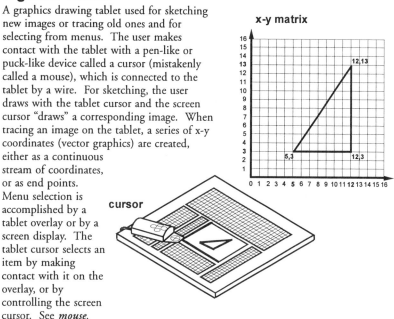

x-y matrix

cursor

dimension

One axis in an array. In programming, a dimension statement defines the array and sets up the number of elements within the dimensions.

dimensioning

In CAD programs, the management and display of the measurements of an object. There are various standards that determine such things as tolerances, sizes of arrowheads and orientation on the paper.

Dimensioning Examples

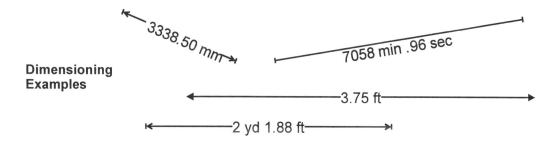

3338.50 mm

7058 min .96 sec

3.75 ft

2 yd 1.88 ft

Keyboard:
5 Pin Din

DIN connector

(Deutsches Institut fur Normung - German Standards Institute) A plug and socket used to connect a variety of devices; for example, the PC keyboard uses a five-pin DIN. Full-size DIN plugs look like an open metal can a half inch in diameter with pins inside in a circular pattern. The smaller Mini-DIN plugs have a 5/16ths of an inch diameter.

Dingbats

A group of typesetting and desktop publishing symbols from International Typeface Corporation that include arrows, pointing hands, stars and circled numbers. They are formally called ITC Zapf Dingbats.

DIN Connectors
DIN connectors are commonly used for keyboard and mouse ports on desktop and laptop computers.

diode

An electronic component that acts primarily as a one-way valve. As a discrete component or built into a chip, it is used in a variety of functions. It is a key element in changing AC into DC. They are used as temperature and light sensors and light emitters (LEDs). In communications, they filter out analog and digital signals from carriers and modulate signals onto carriers. In digital logic, they're used as one-way valves and as switches similar to transistors.

DIP

(Dual In-line Package) A common rectangular chip housing with leads (pins) on both long sides. Tiny wires bond the chip to metal leads that wind their way down into spider-like feet that are inserted into a socket or are soldered onto the board.

The DIP
The DIP chip package is commonly used to hold small chips, such as main memory, cache memory, A/D and D/A converters. PGA packages are another type of packaging commonly used to hold larger chips, such as high-end CPUs.

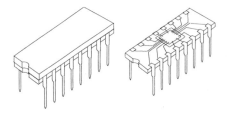

DIP switch

(Dual In-line Package switch) A set of tiny toggle switches built into a DIP, which is mounted directly on a circuit board. The tip of a pen or pencil is required to flip the switch on or off.
Remember! Open is "off." Closed is "on."

The tip of a pencil is often used to flip a DIP switch.

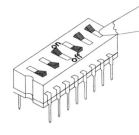

Switches on the DIP
DIP switches provide an inexpensive way to select options on a hardware device and will probably be used for years to come. However, as personal computers become more sophisticated, plug-in boards increasingly contain programmable chips. Instead of opening the case, pulling the board and figuring out which switch to flip, settings are changed using a software control panel.

Dir

(DIRectory) A CP/M, DOS and OS/2 command that lists the file names on the disk.

direct access

The ability to go directly to a specific storage location without having to go through what's in front of it. Memories (RAMs, ROMs, PROMs, etc.) and disks are the major direct access devices. See *DASD*.

direct access method

A technique for finding data on a disk by deriving its storage address from an identifying key in the record, such as account number. Using a formula, the account number is converted into a sector address. This is faster than comparing entries in an index, but it only works well when keys are numerically close: 100, 101, 102, etc.

direct broadcast satellite

See *DBS*.

direct-connect modem

A modem that connects to a telephone line without the use of an acoustic coupler.

direct current

See *DC*.

DirectDraw

A graphics display system for Windows 95. It is expected to coexist with the Windows GDI interface and provide high-speed rendering of games, full-motion video and 3-D objects on screen. It takes advantage of hardware features on the display adapter that speed up video and 3-D. See *video accelerator*.

direct memory access

See *DMA*.

Director

A popular multimedia authoring program for Windows and Macintosh from Macromedia. Runtime versions can be run, edited and switched between Windows and Mac platforms. Director was initially introduced as MacroMind Director for the Mac in 1989, and it has been the de facto standard for Macintosh multimedia authoring. Before the Windows authoring version was introduced, a Windows player was available to run the Mac programs. See *Macromedia*.

directory

A simulated file folder on disk. Programs and data for each application are typically kept in a separate directory (spreadsheets, word processing, etc.). Directories create the illusion of compartments, but are actually indexes to the files which may be scattered all over the disk.

directory management

The maintenance and control of directories on a hard disk. Usually refers to menuing software that is easier to use than entering commands.

Directory Server Agent

See *DSA*.

directory service

In a messaging system, it is a directory of names and addresses of every mail

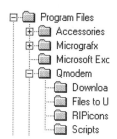

recipient on the network. When sent a user name as a query, it returns the logical mail address (mailbox) of that user. A directory service usually differs from a network naming service in that a directory service returns a logical address, whereas a naming service returns the physical address of a node. Sometimes, either term refers to either function.

directory tree

A graphic representation of a hierarchical directory as in the example on the left.

dirty power

A non-uniform AC power (voltage fluctuations, noise and spikes), which comes from the electric utility or from electronic equipment in the office.

disable

To turn off a function. Disabled means turned off, not broken. Contrast with *enable*.

disassembler

Software that converts machine language back into assembly language. Since there is no way to easily determine the human thinking behind the logic of the instructions, the resulting assembly language routines and variables are named and numbered generically (A001, A002, etc.). Disassembled code can be very difficult to maintain. See *decompiler*.

disaster recovery

A plan for duplicating computer operations after a catastrophe occurs, such as a fire or earthquake. It includes routine off-site backup as well as a procedure for activating necessary information systems in a new location.

disc

An alternate spelling for disk. Compact discs and videodiscs are spelled with the "c." Most computer disks are spelled with a "k."

discrete

A component or device that is separate and distinct and treated as a singular unit.

discrete component

An elementary electronic device constructed as a single unit. Before integrated circuits (chips), all transistors, resistors and diodes were discrete. They are widely used in amplifiers and other devices that use large amounts of current. They are also still used on circuit boards intermingled with the chips.

Discrete Components

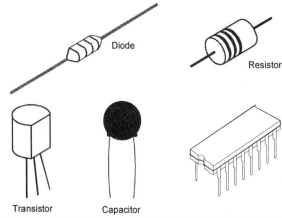

Diode

Resistor

In a chip, there can be millions of transistors, capacitors and other electronic components. However, they cannot handle the power load of discrete components.

Transistor   Capacitor

discrete cosine transform

See *DCT*.

discretionary hyphen

A user-designated place in a word for hyphenation. If the word goes over the margin, it will split in that location.

dish

A saucer-shaped antenna that receives, or transmits and receives, signals from a satellite.

disk

A direct access storage device. See *floppy disk, hard disk, magnetic disk, optical disk* and *videodisc.*

disk array

Two or more disk drives combined in a single unit for increased capacity, speed and/ or fault tolerant operation. See *RAID.*

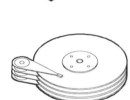

disk based

(1) A computer system that uses disks as its storage medium.
(2) An application that retrieves data from the disk as required. Contrast with *memory based.*

disk cache

See *cache.*

disk cartridge

A removable disk module that contains a single hard disk platter or a floppy disk.

disk controller

A circuit that controls transmission to and from the disk drive. In a personal computer, it is an expansion board that plugs into an expansion slot in the bus. See *hard disk.*

Diskcopy

A DOS and OS/2 utility used to copy entire floppy disks track by track.

disk crash

See *head crash.*

disk drive

A peripheral storage device that holds, spins, reads and writes magnetic or optical disks. It may be a receptacle for disk cartridges, disk packs or floppy disks, or it may contain non-removable disk platters like most personal computer hard disks.

disk dump

A printout of disk contents without report formatting.

disk duplicator

A device that formats and makes identical copies of floppy disks for software distribution. Simple units contain two floppy disks and require manual loading, elaborate units have automatic loading and may also attach the labels.

disk emulator

A solid state replication of a disk drive.

diskette

Same as *floppy disk*.

disk failure

See *head crash, data error* and *General failure reading drive x.*

disk farm

A very large number of hard disks. As more years of computer processing history pile up within the enterprise, databases are reaching staggering proportions. For example, thirty years of sales figures for companies with thousands of products in hundreds of locations result in multiple gigabytes of data. It is not uncommon to need a terabyte disk farm, which would require 500 two-gigabyte drives.

disk file

A set of instructions or data that is recorded, cataloged and treated as a single unit on a disk. Source language programs, machine language programs, spreadsheets, data files, text documents, graphics files and batch files are examples.

disk format

The storage layout of a disk as determined by its physical medium and as initialized by a format program. For example, a 5.25" 360KB floppy vs a 3.5" 1.44MB floppy or a DOS disk vs a Mac disk. See *low-level format, high-level format, DOS format* and *file format.*

diskless workstation

A workstation without a disk. Programs and data are retrieved from the network server.

disk management

The maintenance and control of a hard disk. Refers to a variety of utilities that provide format, copy, diagnostic, directory management and defragmenting functions.

disk memory

Same as *disk.* In this lexicon, disks and tapes are called storage devices, not memory devices.

disk mirroring

The recording of redundant data for fault tolerant operation. Data is written on two partitions of the same disk, on two separate disks within the same system or on two separate computer systems.

disk operating system

See *DOS.*

disk optimizer

A utility program that defragments a hard disk. See *defragment.*

disk pack

An early removable hard disk module used in minis and mainframes that contained two or more platters housed in a dust-free container. For mounting, the bottom of the container was removed. After insertion, the top was removed.

Disk Packs
Disk drives used to be huge washing machine-like devices. These were the kinds of removable disk modules that were used in them.

disk parameters
See *hard disk configuration*.

disk partition
A subdivision of a hard disk. The maximum size of a disk partition depends on the operating system used.

disk striping
The spreading of data over multiple disk drives to improve performance. Data is interleaved by bytes or by sectors across the drives. For example, with four drives and a controller designed to overlap reads and writes, four sectors could be read in the same time it normally takes to read one. Disk striping does not inherently provide fault tolerance or error checking. It is used in conjunction with various other methods. See *RAID*.

DISOSS
(DIStributed Office Support System) An IBM mainframe centralized document distribution and filing application that runs under MVS. Its counterpart under VM is PROFS. It allows for e-mail and the exchange of documents between a variety of IBM office devices, including word processors and PCs. DISOSS uses the SNADS messaging protocol.

dispatcher
Same as *scheduler*.

dispersed intelligence
Same as *distributed intelligence*.

displacement
Same as *offset*. See *base/displacement*.

display
(1)To show text and graphics on a video or flat panel screen.
(2) A screen or monitor.

display adapter
An expansion board that plugs into a desktop computer that converts the images created in the computer to the electronic signals required by the monitor. It determines the maximum resolution, maximum refresh rate and the number of colors that can be sent to the monitor. The monitor must be equally capable of

handling its highest resolution and refresh. The VGA card is the common display adapter for the PC.

The display adapter converts the characters or graphic patterns (bitmaps) within the computer's memory into signals used to refresh the display screen. Display adapters also contain their own memory, which is used to build the images before they are displayed.

In earlier digital systems (CGA, EGA, etc.), the display adapters generated digital signals for the monitor. The monitor then did the conversion from digital to analog. In today's analog systems (VGA, Macintosh, etc.), the display adapter creates the analog signals that are sent to the monitor.

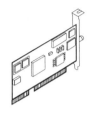

It's Real Straightforward

Graphics adapter, graphics board, graphics card, graphics controller, video display adapter, video display board, video display card, video display controller, video adapter, video board, video card, video controller, display board, display card, display controller, VGA adapter, VGA board, VGA card and VGA controller are other terms for the display adapter.

By the way, a video graphics board is something different. It is a video capture board that accepts analog NTSC video from a videotape player (VCR) or camera. Increasingly, NTSC video is being integrated with computers, so the terminology might even get a tad more confusing!

display attribute
See *attribute*.

display board, display card
Same as *display adapter*.

display cycle
In computer graphics, the series of operations required to display an image.

display device
See *display screen* and *display adapter*.

display element
(1) In graphics, a basic graphic arts component, such as background, foreground, text or graphics image.
(2) In computer graphics, any component of an image.

display entity
In computer graphics, a collection of display elements that are manipulated as a unit.

display font
Same as *screen font*.

display frame
In computer graphics, a single frame in a series of animation frames.

display list
In computer graphics, a collection of vectors that make up an image stored in vector graphics format.

display list processor
In computer graphics, an engine that generates graphic geometry (draws lines, circles, etc.) directly from the display list and independently of the CPU.

display modes
See *PC display modes.*

Display PostScript
The screen counterpart of the PostScript printer language that translates elementary commands in an application to graphics and text elements on screen. It is designed for inclusion in an operating system to provide a standard, device-independent display language.

display resolution
See *how to select a PC display system.*

display screen
A surface area upon which text and graphics are temporarily made to appear for human viewing. It is typically a CRT or flat panel technology.

display terminal
See *video terminal.*

DisplayWrite
A full-featured IBM word processing program for PCs that stems from the typewriter-oriented DisplayWriter word processing system first introduced in 1980. See *XyWrite.*

distributed computing
The use of multiple computers in an organization rather than one centralized system. Most all large organizations have computers dedicated to departmental use. Distributed computing implies that they are networked together, not just decentralized systems without any communications between them. In addition, client/server applications continue to disburse more and more computers througout the enterprise. Distributed computing used to be called *distributed processing.* See *client/server.*

Distributed Computing Environment
See *OSF.*

distributed database
A database physically stored in two or more computer systems. Although geographically dispersed, a distributed database system manages and controls the entire database as a single collection of data. If redundant data is stored in separate databases due to performance requirements, updates to one set of data will automatically update the additional sets in a timely manner. See *replication.*

distributed data processing
See *distributed processing.*

distributed file system
Software that keeps track of files stored across multiple networks. It converts file names into physical locations.

distributed function
The distribution of processing functions throughout the organization.

distributed intelligence
The placing processing capability in terminals and other peripheral devices. Intelligent terminals handle screen layouts, data entry validation and other pre-

processing steps. Intelligence placed into disk drives and other peripherals relieves the central computer from routine tasks.

distributed logic

See *distributed intelligence*.

Distributed Management Environment

See *DME*.

distributed processing

The first term used to describe the distribution of multiple computers throughout an organization in contrast to a centralized system. It started with the first minicomputers. Today, distributed processing is called *distributed computing*. See also *client/server*.

distribution disk

A floppy disk or CD-ROM used to disseminate files in a software package.

dithering

Simulating more colors and shades in a palette. In a monochrome system that displays or prints only black and white, shades of grays can be simulated by creating varying patterns of black dots. This is how halftones are created in a monochrome printer.

In color systems, additional colors can be simulated by varying patterns of dots of existing colors. Dithering cannot produce the exact same results as having the necessary color depth (levels of gray or colors), but it can make shaded drawings and photographs appear much more realistic.

Dithering is also used to create a wide variety of patterns for use as backgrounds, fills and shading, as well as for creating anti-aliasing effects.

Dithering

The picture below on the left is an original photograph. It is printed in this book as a halftone. The picture was scanned into the computer and printed on a laser printer (middle). The picture on the right is the zoomed-in view and shows the actual dot patterns of the rectangular section marked in the middle picture.

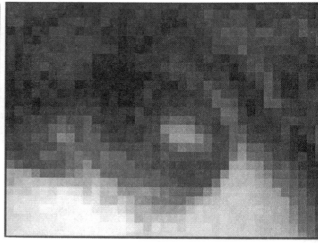

divide overflow

A program error in which a number is accidentally divided by zero or by a number that creates a result too large for the computer to handle.

DIX standard

(DEC-Intel-Xerox standard) An earlier Ethernet standard which has been superseded by IEEE 802.3. Network protocols often use the Ethernet frame from this specification.

DL/1

(Data Language 1) The database language in IMS.

DLC

(1) (Data Link Control) See *data link* and *OSI*.
(2) (Data Link Control) The protocol used in IBM's Token Ring networks.
(3) (Digital Loop Carrier) See *loop carrier*.

DLC chip

Any one of several Intel-compatible CPUs from Cyrix Corporation. See *486DLC*.

DLL

(Dynamic Link Library) An executable program module that performs some function. DLLs are not launched directly by users. When needed, they are called for by a running application and loaded to perform a specific function. DLLs are generally written so that their routines are shared by more than one application at the same time (see *reentrant code*).

In the DOS world, there was never a solid way to dynamically link and share routines at runtime. ISRs and TSRs were created for this purpose, but they were not formally sanctioned by Microsoft and often caused conflict.

Windows, on the other hand, uses DLLs as a standard way of linking and sharing functionality. There are many DLLs that come with Windows that applications depend on and call for as required (look in your \WINDOWS\SYSTEM directory for the .DLL extension). Applications may also include their own DLLs, which are usually stored in the application directory.

Trouble in Windows City

A commonly-shared DLL, such as VBRUN300.DLL, which is the Visual Basic runtime module, may be placed into the \WINDOWS\SYSTEM directory by an application's install program. Some install programs simply overwrite the DLL on top of an existing one without checking that it may be a more recent version of the routine that another application depends on. Thus, installing one application fouls up another. Although Microsoft has published guidelines, there is no way to enforce compliance with this system.

DLT

(Digital Linear Tape) A magnetic tape used for backing up data. The tape is 1/2" wide and provides transfer rates faster than most tape technologies. Cartridges provide storage up to 20GB. Originally popular in the UNIX world, DLT migrated to PCs and Macs in the mid 1990s.

DLUR/DLUS

(Dependent LURequester/Server) SNA enhancements that enable traditional host connections, such as host to terminal and host to printer, to run over an APPN network. It supports LU sessions other than 6.2. See *LU*.

DLUS

See *DLUR/DLUS*.

DMA

(Direct Memory Access) Specialized circuitry or a dedicated microprocessor that transfers data from memory to memory without using the CPU. Although DMA may periodically steal cycles from the CPU, data is transferred much faster than using the CPU for every byte of transfer.

On PCs, there are eight DMA channels commonly used as follows. Most sound cards are set to use DMA channel 1.

DMA	Used for
0	8-bit transfer
1	8-bit transfer
2	Floppy disk controller
3	8-bit transfer
4	Cascaded from 0-3
5	16-bit transfer
6	16-bit transfer
7	16-bit transfer

DME

(Distributed Managment Environment) A network monitoring and control protocol defined by the Open Software Foundation. See *OSF.*

DMF

(Distribution Media Format) A floppy disk format that Microsoft uses to distribute its software. DMF floppies compress more data (1.7MB) onto the 3.5" diskette, and the files cannot be copied with normal DOS and Windows commands. A utility that supports the DMF format must be used.

DMI

(Desktop Managment Interface) A management system for PCs developed by the Desktop Management Task Force (initiated by Intel). DMI provides a bi-directional path to interrogate all the hardware and software components within a PC. When PCs are DMI-enabled, their hardware and software configurations can be monitored from a central station in the network.

A memory-resident agent resides in the background. When queries are made to the agent, it responds by sending back data contained in MIFs (Management Information Files) and/or activating MIF routines. Static data in a MIF would contain items such as model ID, serial number, memory and port addresses. A MIF routine could report errors to the management console as they occur, or it could read ROM or RAM chips and report their contents, as well.

DMI is a complete management system but can co-exist with SNMP and other management protocols. For example, when an SNMP query arrives, DMI can fill out the SNMP MIB with data from its MIF. A single workstation or server can serve as a proxy agent that would contain the SNMP module and service an entire LAN segment of DMI machines.

Data-only MIFs can be created by anyone using a text editor, but it is envisioned that all hardware and software vendors will eventually include at least a data-only MIF with their products.

TOP MANAGEMENT INTERFACE LAYER (API): Calls to DMI from console software, such as Intel's LANdesk and Novell's NMS.

MIDDLE SERVICE LAYER: DMI agent in each client machine (TSR, DLL, etc.)

BOTTOM COMPONENT INTERFACE LAYER: Accesses the MIF and provides calls from component back to the console.

DMPL

(Digital Microprocessor Plotter Language) A vector graphics file format from Houston Instruments that was developed for plotters. Most plotters support the DMPL or HPGL standards.

DMS

(Document Management System) See *document management.*

DMT

See *ADSL.*

DMTF

(Desktop Management Task Force) Initiated by Intel in 1992, it created the DMI interface. See *DMI.*

DNA

(Digital Network Architecture) Introduced in 1978, DNA defines Digital's protocols, formats and control of message exchange over a network. DECnet is the implementation of this architecture.

DNS

(Domain Naming System) Software that lets users locate computers on the Internet by host name. The DNS server maintains a database of host names and IP addresses. In this hypothetical example, when a name such as **mycompany.com** is presented, DNS returns the IP address **167.93.8.51**. See *WINS.*

docking station

A base station for a laptop that includes a power supply and expansion slots as well as monitor and keyboard connectors. See *port replicator.*

docs

Short for documents or documentation.

DocuComp

A Windows program from Mastersoft, Inc., Scottsdale, AZ, that compares two documents and highlights the differences. It is typically used to keep track of revisions of documents where several authors have been involved.

document

(1)Any paper form that has been filled in.
(2) A word processing text file.
(3) In the Macintosh, any text, data or graphics file created in the computer.

documentation

The narrative and graphical description of a system. Documentation for an information system includes:

Operating Procedures

1. Instructions for turning the system on and getting the programs initiated (loaded).
2. Instructions for obtaining source documents for data entry.
3. Instructions for entering data at the terminal, which includes a picture of each screen layout the user will encounter.
4. A description of error messages that can occur and the alternative methods for handling them.

5. A description of the defaults taken in the programs and the instructions for changing them.
6. Instructions for distributing the computer's output, which includes sample pages for each type of report.

System Documentation

1. Data dictionary - Description of the files and databases.
2. System flow chart - Description of the data as it flows from source document to report.
3. Application program documentation - Description of the inputs, processing and outputs for each data entry, query, update and report program in the system.

Technical Documentation

1. File structures and access methods
2. Program flow charts
3. Program source code listings
4. Machine procedures (JCL)

document centric

Focusing on the document as the foundation or starting point. In a document-centric system, the document is retrieved and automatically calls the appropriate software required to work with it. Contrast with *application centric*. See *component software*.

document collaboration

See *data conferencing*.

document exchange software

Software that allows document files to be viewed on other computers that do not have the original application that created it. The software comes in two parts. The first component converts the document into a proprietary format for distribution. The second is a viewer program that displays the files, and viewers are generally free. Unlike file viewers that rely on the fonts installed in the computer to display file contents accurately, document exchange systems carry the fonts over within the file format to the viewing machine. The fonts are only used for displaying the document, however, not for general use by the system. The viewers may allow sections of the document to be copied to the clipboard.

The three major products to date are Adobe's Acrobat, Farallon's Replica and No Hands Software's Common Ground.

document handling

A procedure for transporting and handling paper documents for data entry and scanning.

document image management

See *document imaging*.

document image processing

See *document imaging*.

document imaging

The online storage, retrieval and management of electronic images of documents. The main method of capturing images is by scanning paper documents.

Document imaging systems replace large paper-intensive operations. Documents can be shared by all users on a network and document routing can be controlled by the computer (workflow). The systems are often simpler to develop and implement than traditional data processing systems, because users are already familiar with the paper documents that appear on screen.

Document images are created in raster graphics format, and although a small amount of text (key words) may be associated with the document in order to index it, the meaning of the document content is known only to the human viewer, not the computer. Like microfilm, signatures and other original markings remain intact.

Document Imaging Takes Storage Space

When a page of text is scanned, it takes up much more storage space than if the individual characters were typed in. When data is entered on the keyboard, each character uses one byte of storage. When it is scanned, the piece of paper is turned into a digital picture, which is an image of dots. The white space on the paper also takes up storage.

Depending on the resolution required for the printed text, a scanned page can take 50 times as much storage as the raw ASCII characters of typed-in data.

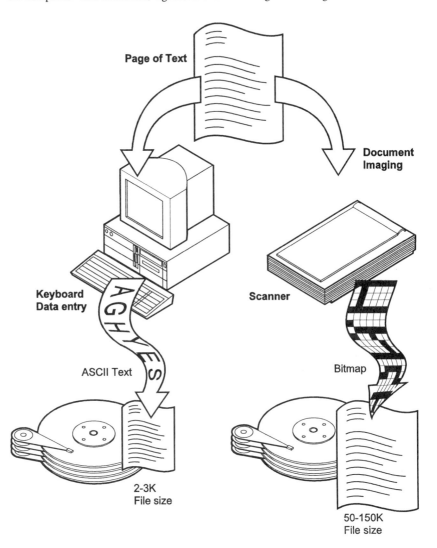

Page of Text

Document Imaging

Keyboard Data entry

Scanner

ASCII Text

Bitmap

2-3K File size

50-150K File size

document management

The capture and management of documents within an organization. The term used to imply the management of documents after there were scanned into the computer. Today, the term has become an umbrella under which document imaging, workflow, text retrieval and multimedia fall.

The trend towards designing information systems as document centric, where the document becomes the focus, not the application that created it, is expected to bring document management to the forefront of computing.

document management system

Software that manages documents for electronic publishing. It typically supports SGML and a variety of standard document formats. A document management system allows text fragments to be written by different authors, then combined in the database and searched and compiled for different versions of a publication. It also may include a workflow component that lets the appropriate users have access to the documents. See *workflow*.

document mark

In micrographics, a small optical blip on each frame on a roll of microfilm that is used to automatically count the frames.

document processing

Processing text documents, which includes indexing methods for text retrieval based on content. See *document imaging*.

document publishing software

See *document exchange software* and *desktop publishing*.

document sharing

See *data conferencing*.

document viewer

See *file viewer* and *document exchange software*.

docuterm

A word or phrase in a text document that is used to identify the contents of the document.

Dolby AC-3

See *5.1 channel*.

Dolch

(Dolch Computer Systems, Fremont, CA) A manufacturer of high-end, ruggedized portable PCs for industrial use. It introduced the first portable active matrix PC, the first portable 386, 486, Pentium and dual Pentium, and in 1994, the first videoconferencing-equipped portable.

In 1976, Volker Dolch founded Dolch Logic Instruments, which became the largest supplier of logic analyzers in Europe. In 1987, he sold the company and arranged a management buy-out of its American division.

do loop

A high-level programming language structure that repeats instructions based on the results of a comparison. In a DO WHILE loop, the instructions within the loop are performed if the comparison is true. In a DO UNTIL loop, the instructions are bypassed if the comparison is true. The following DO WHILE loop prints 1 through 10 and stops.

```
COUNTER = 0
DO WHILE COUNTER < 10
   COUNTER = COUNTER + 1
   ? COUNTER
ENDDO
```

domain

(1) In database management, all possible values contained in a particular field for every record in the file.

(2) In communications, all resources under control of a single computer system. In a LAN, a domain is a subnetwork comprised of a group of clients and servers under the control of one security database. Dividing LANs into domains improves performance and security.

(3) In magnetic storage devices, a group of molecules that makes up one bit.

(4) In a hierarchy, a named group that has control over the groups under it, which may be domains themselves.

(5) In the Internet, addresses are cataloged by type of organization, or domain. See *Internet address*.

domain naming system

See *DNS*.

dominant carrier

A telecommunications services provider that has control over a large segment of a particular market.

dongle

Same as *hardware key*.

door

(1) In a BBS system, a programming interface that lets an online user run an application program in the BBS.

(2) See *drive door*.

doorway mode

In a communications program, a mode that passes function, cursor, ctrl and alt keystrokes to the BBS computer in order to use the remote application as if it were on the local machine.

dopant

An element diffused into pure silicon in order to alter its electrical characteristics.

doping

Altering the electrical conductivity of a semiconductor material, such as silicon, by chemically combining it with foreign elements. It results in an excess of electrons (n-type) or a lack of electrons (p-type) in the silicon.

DOS

(1) (Disk Operating System) Pronounced "dahss." A generic term for operating system.

(2) Disk Operating System) A single-user operating system for the PC. It is the most widely used operating system in the world. The version provided by IBM is called PC-DOS to distinguish it from MS-DOS, the version for non-IBM PCs. All versions of DOS and MS-DOS have been developed by Microsoft with IBM participating in varying degrees. The more recent versions of DOS are developed independently.

Except for DOS 6, both versions are almost identical. Microsoft's MS-DOS 6 and IBM's PC-DOS 6 provide different versions of the utilities, although all commands and primary functions are the same.

As Windows 95 and Windows NT become more widely used, DOS will eventually fade into history, although chances are that DOS programs will be running well into the 21st century.

IBM's DOS 6

IBM's DOS 6, which was formally introduced as PC-DOS 6.1, is somewhat different than Microsoft's DOS 6. All the fundamental DOS commands are the same, but PC-DOS 6.1 includes direct support for pen-based computing and the PCMCIA card. For the first time, PC-DOS became available from IBM as a retail product, not just for IBM systems. Several utilities are different than MS-DOS 6. For example, PC-DOS 6.1 includes an enhanced text editor with split screens and macros, an unattended program scheduler, an antivirus monitor that takes only 5K and claims fewer false alarms, a more comprehensive backup utility that includes tape and backup scheduling, and a full-screen Undelete for both DOS and Windows that lets you preview your files before you delete them. For years, the terms MS-DOS and PC-DOS differentiated Microsoft's version from IBM's version, but the term DOS is generally used for both. Up until DOS 6, they had been identical for practical purposes. See *DOS 7*.

DOS 7

In early 1995, IBM released PC-DOS 7 with enhanced memory management and virus protection. It includes the Stacker data compression program as well as utilites to enhance mobile computing.

Novell, which was the first to release a DOS 7, is no longer planning new DOS versions.

The DOS included in Windows 95 is often called DOS 7, which is an enhanced version of DOS 6. It is unlikely that Microsoft will introduce a DOS 7 independently of Windows.

DOS batch file

A batch file is a file of DOS commands that are "batch" processed. That is, each command in a batch file is executed by DOS until the end of the file is reached. See CD-ROM version for information about how to create batch files.

DOS box

The DOS compatibility mode. When a DOS application is running under Windows or OS/2, it is running in a DOS box. The "box" is actually one instance of the Intel x86 Virtual 8086 Mode, which simulates an independent, fully functional PC environment. See *Virtual 8086 Mode*.

DOS environment

A reserved area in DOS for holding values used by DOS and other applications. The values stored in this area are called "environment variables" and are created with the Set command.

DOS extender

Software that is combined with a DOS application to allow it to run in extended memory (beyond 1MB). Some DOS extenders work with 286s and up, others require a 386 minimum. To gain access to extended memory, it runs the application in Protected Mode. When the application requests DOS services, the DOS extender either handles them itself or, with functions such as disk accesses, resets the machine to Real Mode, lets DOS service the request and then switches back into Protected Mode.

DOS-extended programs can run by themselves in a DOS machine, but the VCPI specification was developed to enable them to run cooperatively with DESQview and other VCPI-compliant applications. The DPMI spec was developed for compliance with Windows 3.0.

If an XMS driver is present, DOS extenders will use XMS to allocate memory.

DOS external command

A separate utility program that comes with DOS, such as Format, Diskcopy, XCopy, Tree, Backup and Restore, but is not resident within DOS, such as Copy and Dir.

DOSmark

A unit of performance based on Ziff-Davis' PC Labs tests. It rates a PC's ability to run DOS applications, which is a composite of CPU, memory, disk and video tests. See *Winmark*.

DOS memory manager

Software that expands DOS' ability to manage more than one megabyte of memory or to manage its first megabyte more effectively. Since the early days of DOS, third party memory managers, such as QEMM and 386MAX, have used every trick in the book to move TSRs and drivers out of the lower 640K and into the 384K upper memory area (UMA).

Starting with DOS 5, DOS includes its own memory managers. HIMEM.SYS manages extended memory, and EMM386.EXE manages expanded memory.

DOS on Mac Card

A PC add-in card for the Macintosh from Reply Corporation, San Jose, CA. It includes a 486 CPU and installs into the Mac's PDS slot, providing true PC operation within the Macintosh. It is similar to Apple's PowerMac 6100, which has a built-in 486.

DOS prompt

The message DOS displays when ready to accept user input. The default prompt (C>, D>...) displays the current drive and doesn't say which directory you're in. Since this can be changed, PCs are usually configured with the **prompt pg** line in the AUTOEXEC.BAT file, which creates a prompt that includes the the current directory name, such as C:\BUDGETS>.

DOS Shell

A menu-driven user interface that accompanies DOS, starting with DOS 4.01. It is an optional interface to COMMAND.COM, which requires commands be typed in.

DOS system file

A DOS file that contains the fundamental part of DOS (the kernel). See *MSDOS.SYS*.

DOS text file

A text file that does not contain any proprietary coding schemes. Batch files and source language programs are examples. It contains only ASCII characters and has a CR/LF (carriage return/line feed) code at the end of each line. Text files are read by text editors as well as word processors with "ASCII" or "text" input options.

DOS/V

A Japanese version of DOS that supports two-byte-long characters for handling the Kanji character set. It can switch between English and Japanese and is geared for 286s and up with VGA graphics. Backed by IBM Japan and the OADG. In Japan, NEC is the major personal computer vendor with its PC-9801 series.

DOS/VSE

See *VSE*.

DOS wild cards

Wild cards are symbols that let you reference groups of related files. As in card games, wild cards take on any value. DOS wild cards are the "*" and "?." The asterisk takes the value of any number of characters; for example, **dir gloss*** would find GLOSS1, GLOSS10 and GLOSSARY.

The question mark matches any single character. For example, **dir ?gloss** would find 1GLOSS, 2GLOSS and XGLOSS. Note that ***gloss** is not valid for this.

DOS/Windows

Generally means Windows 3.x as these versions require DOS to operate. Sometimes the term will refer to both DOS and Windows 3.x applications, which are 16-bit programs, in contrast to 32-bit Windows 95, Windows NT and OS/2 applications. Windows 95 includes an enhanced version of DOS, which some call DOS 7.

dot

(1) A tiny round, rectangular or square spot that is one element in a matrix, which is used to display or print a graphics or text image. See *dot matrix.*
(2) A period; for example, V dot 22 is the same as V.22.

dot addressable

The ability to program each individual dot on a video display, dot matrix printer or laser printer.

dot chart

Same as *scatter diagram.*

dot com

Refers to a commercial Internet address, which ends with a period and the word "com" (.com). For example, the Internet addresses for the CompuServe and America Online online services are **compuserve.com** and **aol.com**. See *Internet address.*

dot gain

An increase in size of each dot of ink when printed due to temperature, ink and paper type.

dot matrix

A pattern of dots that forms character and graphic images on printers. Although ink jet and laser printers print in dots, and monitors display dots as well, the term generally refers to images created with serial dot matrix printers. The more dots per square inch, the higher the resolution. See *dot matrix printer.*

Dot Matrix Printing Mechanism
Dot matrix printers print columns of dots in a serial fashion. The more dot hammers (pins), the better looking the printed results.

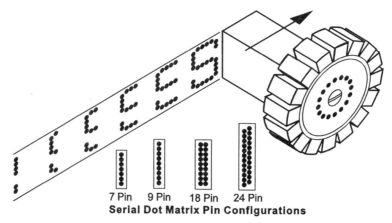

7 Pin   9 Pin   18 Pin   24 Pin
Serial Dot Matrix Pin Configurations

dot matrix printer

A printer that uses hammers and a ribbon to form images out of dots. The common desktop dot matrix printer uses one or two columns of dot hammers that are moved serially across the paper. The more dot hammers used, the higher the resolution of the printed image. 24-pin dot matrix printers produce typewriter-like output. Dot matrix printers are still widely used to print name and address labels, diskette labels and multiple-part forms. Unlike sheet-fed laser and ink jet printers, the tractor and sproket mechanism of a dot matrix printer accepts thicker material than plain paper.

Dot Matrix Printer

Dot matrix printers fitted with a tractor feed are commonly used for printing continuous multipart forms and mailing and diskette labels. The tractor feed contains a sprocket that grabs the perforated holes at both sides of the form and pulls it through uniformly.

dot pitch

The distance between a red (or green or blue) dot and the closest red (or green or blue) dot on a color monitor (typically from .28 to .51mm; large presentation monitors may go up to 1.0mm). The smaller the dot pitch, the crisper the image. A .28 dot pitch means dots are 28/100ths of a millimeter apart. A dot pitch of .31 or less provides a sharp image, especially on text.

Dot pitch measurements between conventional tubes and Sony's Trinitron tubes are roughly, but not exactly equivalent. Sony's CRTs use vertical stripes, not dots, and its measurement is the distance between stripes, not the diagonal distance between dots.

double buffering

A programming technique that uses two buffers to speed up a computer that can overlap I/O with processing. For example, data in one buffer is being processed while the next set of data is read into the second buffer.

When video is displayed on screen, the data in one buffer is being filled while the data in the other is being displayed. Full-motion video is speeded up when the function of moving the data between buffers is implemented in a hardware circuit rather than being performed by software. See *video accelerator*.

Data is being read into this buffer

➤ **488598932938200320**

while data in this buffer is being processed.

4885994880000488048840MR88900032342

double click

To press the mouse button twice in rapid succession.

double density

Twice the capacity of the prior format. Yesterday's double density can be today's low density (see *DD*).

double precision

Using two computer words instead of one to hold a number used for calculations, thus allowing twice as large a number for more arithmetic precision. Contrast with *single precision*.

double sided disk

A floppy disk that is recorded on both of its sides. See *DS/DD* and *DS/HD*.

DoubleSpace

A realtime compression technique built into DOS 6 and removed in 6.21.

double strike

Printing a character twice in order to darken the image.

double twist

Same as *supertwist*.

double word

Twice the length of a single computer word. A double word is typically 32 bits long. See *word*.

down

Refers to a computer that fails to operate due to hardware or software failure. A communications line is down when it is unable to transfer data.

downlink

A communications channel from a satellite to an earth station. Contrast with *uplink*.

download

To transmit a file from one computer to another. When conducting the session, download means receive, upload means transmit. It implies sending a file rather than interacting in a conversational mode.

Downloading a file from a personal computer that has a modem is accomplished by (1) using a communications program to dial up another computer or online service, and (2) by selecting a file transfer protocol common to both systems.

Once you connect to an online service, you will be prompted through a variety of options. You have to select a file to download and then select a protocol to use, such as Zmodem, Ymodem or CIS B, for example. You have to choose one that your communications program supports. Zmodem is usually the best choice.

If you are on a LAN, downloading a file from a network server to your local machine is accomplished by performing standard copy procedures in the Mac or on a Windows PC or by using the DOS copy command. You would reference the network hard disk as the source and your local hard disk as the destination. On a PC, network drives are usually identified as K:, L: or with some other letter higher up in the alphabet. In UNIX, you would use the UUCP or FTP utilities.

downloadable font

Same as *soft font*.

downsizing

Converting mainframe and mini-based systems to personal computer LANs.

downtime

The time during which a computer is not functioning due to hardware or system software failure. That's when you truly understand how important it is to have reliable hardware.

downward compatible

Also called backward compatible. Refers to hardware or software that is compatible with earlier versions. Contrast with *upward compatible*.

DP
See *data processing* and *dot pitch*.

DPCM
(Differential PCM) An audio digitization technique that codes the difference between samples rather than coding an absolute measurement at each sample point. See *ADPCM*.

dpi
(Dots Per Inch) The measurement of printer resolution. A 300 dpi printer means 90,000 dots are printable in one square inch (300x300). 400 dpi generates 160,000 dots; 500 dpi yields 250,000 dots.

DPMA
(Data Processing Management Association, 505 Busse Highway, Park Ridge, IL 60068, 708/825-8124) A membership organization founded in 1951 with over 40,000 managers of DP installations, programmers, systems analysts and research specialists. It founded the CDP examinations, now administrated by the ICCP. Offers many educational programs and seminars, in addition to sponsoring student organizations around the country interested in DP.

DPMI
(DOS Protected Mode Interface) A DOS extender specification for 286s and up that allows DOS extended programs to cooperatively run under Windows 3.x. Developed by Microsoft, it keeps a DOS-extended application from crashing the computer and usurping Windows' control. It is not compatible with VCPI, the first DOS extender standard, but Windows 3.1 is more tolerant of VCPI applications than Windows 3.0.

XMS Versus VCPI/DPMI
XMS, VCPI and DPMI all deal with extended memory. However, XMS allows data and programs to be stored in and retrieved from extended memory, whereas the VCPI and DPMI interfaces allow programs to "run" in extended memory.

DPPX
(Distributed Processing Programming EXecutive) An operating system for the 8100, now defunct. DPPX/370 is a version allowing users to migrate to 9370s.

DPS
Minicomputer series from Bull HN.

DPSK
(Differential Phase Shift Keying) A common form of phase modulation used in modems. It does not require complex demodulation circuitry and is not susceptible to random phase changes in the transmitted waveform. Contrast with *FSK*.

DQDB
(Distributed Queue Dual Bus) The protocol used to control access to an IEEE 802.6 queued packet synchronous exchange (QPSX) network, used for metropolitan area networks (MANs). This architecture allows for both circuit and packet switching and supports data, voice and video traffic. Using fixed length cell relay technology, DQDB is suited to volatile network traffic.

Drafix
A 2-D and 3-D CAD packages for PCs and Atari STs from Foresight Resources

Corporation, Kansas City, MO. It features professional functions and provides constant on-screen information during drawing.

draft mode

The highest-speed, lowest-quality printing mode.

drag

To move an object on screen in which its complete movement is visible from starting location to destination. The movement may be activated with a stylus, mouse or keyboard keys.

To drag an object with the mouse, point to it. Press the mouse button and hold the button down while moving the mouse. When the object is at its new location, release the mouse button.

drag & drop

The ability to execute a function graphically without typing in a command. For example, in the Macintosh, selecting a floppy disk icon and dragging it onto the trashcan icon causes the floppy to be ejected.

drag lock

The ability to lock onto a screen object so that it can be dragged with the mouse without continuously holding down the mouse (or trackball) button.

drain

One side of a field effect transistor. When the gate is pulsed, current flows from the source to the drain, or vice versa depending on the design. See *collector*.

DRAM, D-RAM

See *dynamic RAM*.

DRAW

(Direct Read After Write) Reading data immediately after it has been written to check for recording errors.

drawing program

A graphics program used for creating illustrations. It maintains an image in vector graphics format, which allows all elements of the picture to be isolated, moved and scaled independently from the others.

drawing program

Drawing programs create vector graphic images that are built with independent elements, such as squares, rectangles, circles and ellipses, that are tied together as a group. Using a drawing program, the dog's collar is drawn as an independent entity that can be removed from the dog's neck (left). If the dog were scanned into or "painted" into the computer with a paint program, isolating the collar would leave a blank rectangle in the picture (right).

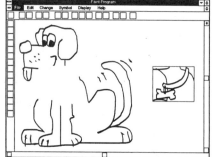

Drawing programs and CAD programs are similar; however, drawing programs usually provide a large number of special effects for fancy illustrations, while CAD programs provide precise dimensioning and positioning of each graphic element in order that the objects can be transferred to other systems for engineering analysis and manufacturing.

Examples of popular drawing programs for Windows are Adobe Illustrator, Macromedia Freehand, Designer and CorelDRAW. Adobe Illustrator and Macromedia Freehand are also available for the Macintosh. Contrast with *paint program*. See *diagramming program*.

DRDA

(Distributed Relational Database Architecture) An IBM architecture for distributing data across multiple heterogeneous platforms. It also serves as a protocol for access to these databases from IBM and non-IBM platforms. DRDA uses LU 6.2 as its transport protocol.

DRDBMS

(Distributed Relational **DBMS**) A relational DBMS that manages distributed databases. See *distributed database*.

DR DOS

See *Novell DOS*.

DRI

See *Digital Research*.

dribbleware

Software that is publicly displayed and previewed well in advance of its actual release. Dribbleware is one stage beyond vaporware.

drift

Change in frequency or time synchronization of a signal that occurs slowly.

drill down

To move from summary information to the detailed data that created it.

drive

(1) An electromechanical device that spins disks and tapes at a specified speed. Also refers to the entire peripheral unit such as *disk drive* or *tape drive*.

(2)To provide power and signals to a device. For example, "this control unit can drive up to 15 terminals."

drive bay

A cavity for a disk drive in a computer cabinet.

drive door

A panel, gate or lever used to lock a disk in a disk drive. In a 5.25" floppy drive, the drive door is the lever that is turned down over the slot after inserting the disk.

drive mapping

A letter or name assigned to a disk or tape drive. In a PC, the basic drive mappings are A: and B: for the floppy disk and C: for the primary hard disk. Additional drive mappings are assigned by the operating system based on the next available letter (D:, E:, etc.).

In PC networks, drive mappings reference remote drives and directories. For example, on your local machine, you might assign drive K: to be the root directory of drive C: on another machine in the network.

driver

(1) Also called a *device driver*, a program routine that links a peripheral device to the operating system. It is written by programmers who understand the detailed knowledge of the device's command language and characteristics. It contains the precise machine language necessary to activate the device and perform the functions requested by the application.

When a new hardware device is added to the computer, such as a sound card, scanner or CD-ROM drive, its driver must be installed in order to run it. The operating system calls the driver, and the driver "drives" the device. Routines that perform internal functions, such as memory managers and disk caches, are also called drivers.

In a PC, fundamental drivers that manage such components as the keyboard, floppy and non-SCSI hard disks, are included in the system BIOS chip. Additional drivers are loaded at boot time from commands in the CONFIG.SYS file.

Drivers Can Drive You Crazy!

If it seems that the solution to every problem is to update a driver, that is often the case. The driver is the link between the operating system and the peripheral device. If the peripheral is changed, the driver must also be changed. If a bug is found in the driver, a new version is often released to solve it. New drivers are made available on various bulletin boards for downloading.

In Windows, one of the most erratic conditions is the display driver used with the particular display adapter installed. In Windows, everything you see on screen is the result of the display driver drawing the screen according to the commands that Windows issues to it. A display driver is extremely difficult to program and is error prone simply due to its complex nature.

There Used to Be Even More Drivers

The effort required to support different brands of peripheral devices was one of the major reasons DOS gave way to Windows. For example, in the DOS world, in order to provide complete control over the printing of a document, each application provides its own printer drivers for the most popular printers.

With Windows and the Macintosh, the printer driver is installed by the operating system, not by each application. From then on, all applications gain access to the printer through the operating system and its one driver for that printer.

(2) A driver is also a hardware device that provides signals or electrical current to activate a transmission line or display screen. See *line driver*.

The Windows Display Driver

This diagram shows the part the driver plays when a Windows application wants to display something on screen. The application calls the GDI (Graphics Device Interface) in Windows and tells it to do something. GDI in turn sends commands to the driver supplied with the display adapter to actually draw the image. The display adapter draws the image in the display adapter's memory, which is simultaneously being sent to the monitor.

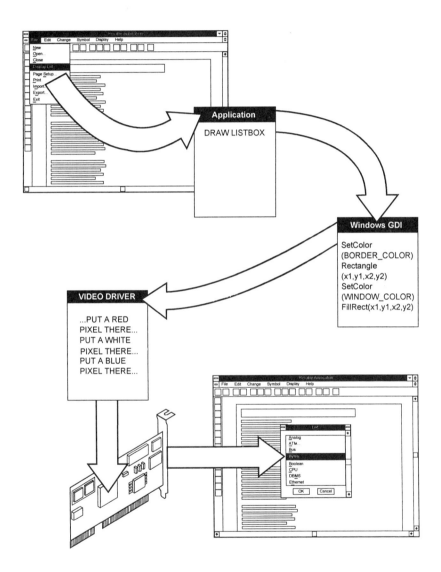

DriveSpace

Microsoft's disk compression that replaces the DoubleSpace technology previously used. It is included starting with MS-DOS 6.22.

drop cap

In typography, a large first letter that drops below the first line, as shown at the beginning of this sentence. It's purpose is generally to visually locate, or reinforce the start point of a block of text.

drop-down menu

See *pull-down menu*.

drop in

An extraneous bit on a magnetic medium that was not intentionally written, due to a surface defect or recording malfunction.

drop out

(1) On magnetic media, a bit that has lost its strength due to a surface defect or recording malfunction.
(2) In data transmission, a momentary loss of signal that is due to system malfunction or excessive noise.

droupie

(Data gROUPIE) A person who likes to spend time in the company of programmers and data processing professionals.

drum

See *magnetic drum*.

drum plotter

A graphics plotter that wraps the paper around a drum. The drum turns to produce one direction of the plot; the pen moves to provide the other.

drum printer

A line printer that uses formed character images around a cylindrical drum as its printing mechanism. There is a band of characters for each print position. When the desired character for the selected print position has rotated around to the hammer line, the hammer hits the paper from behind and pushes it into the ribbon and onto the character.

drum scanner

A type of scanner used to capture the highest resolution from an image. Photographs and slides are taped onto a clear cylinder that is rotated during scanning. For transparencies, light is directed from the center of the cylinder. For opaque items, a reflective light source is used.

The drum scanner's photomultiplier tube is more sensitive than the CCDs used in flatbed and sheet-fed scanners and can produce resolutions exceeding 8,000 dpi. Contrast with *flatbed scanner, sheet-fed scanner* and *hand-held scanner*.

dry plasma etching

A method for inscribing a pattern on a wafer by shooting hot ions through a mask to evaporate the silicon dioxide insulation layer. Dry plasma etching replaces the wet processing method that uses film and acid for developing the pattern.

drystone

See *Dhrystones*.

DS

(Digital Signal) A classification of digital circuits. The DS technically refers to the rate and format of the signal, while the T designation refers to the equipment providing the signals. In practice, "DS" and "T" are used synonymously; for example, DS1 and T1, DS3 and T3.

North America, Japan, Korea, etc.

Service	VoiceChannels	Speed
DS0	1	64 Kbps
DS1	24	1.544 Mbps (T1)
DS1C	48	3.152 Mbps (T1C)
DS2	96	6.312 Mbps (T2)
DS3	672	44.736 Mbps (T3)
DS4	4032	274.176 Mbps (T4)

Europe (ITU)

Service	Voice Channels	Speed (Mbps)
E1	30	2.048
E2	120	8.448
E3	480	34.368
E4	1920	139.264
E5	7680	565.148

Sonet Circuits

Service		Speed (Mbps)
STS-1	OC1	51.84 (28 DS1s or 1 DS3)
STS-3	OC3	155.52 (3 STS-1s)
STS-3c	OC3c	155.52 (concatenated)
STS-12	OC12	622.08 (12 STS-1s, 4 STS-3s)
STS-12c	OC12c	622.08 (12 STS-1s, 4 STS-3c's)
STS-48	OC48	2488.32 (48 STS-1s, 16 STS-3s)

DS1

See *DS*.

DSA

(1) (Directory Server Agent) An X.500 program that looks up the address of a recipient in a Directory Information Base (DIB), also known as white pages. It accepts requests from the Directory User Agent (DUA) counterpart in the workstation.

(2) (Digital Signature Algorithm) The algorithm used in the Digital Signature Standard (DSS).

(3) (Digital Storage Architecture) A disk controller standard from Digital.

(4) (Digital Signal Analyzer) A Tektronix oscilloscope that samples high-frequency signals.

(5) (Distributed Systems Architecture) A Bull HN network architecture.

DS/DD

(Double Sided/Double Density) Refers to floppy disks, such as the 5.25" 360KB PC format and 3.5" 720KB PC and 800KB Mac formats.

DS/HD

(Double Sided/High Density) Refers to floppy disks, such as the 5.25" 1.2MB PC format and 3.5" 1.44MB PC and Mac formats.

DSOM

See *SOM.*

DSP

(1) (Digital Signal Processor) A special-purpose CPU used for digital signal processing (see below). It provides extra fast instruction sequences, such as shift and add and multiply and add, commonly used in math-intensive signal processing applications.

(2) (Digital Signal Processing) A category of techniques that analyze signals from sources such as sound, weather satellites and earthquake monitors. Signals are converted into digital data and analyzed using various algorithms such as Fast Fourier Transform.

Once a signal has been reduced to numbers, its components can be isolated, analyzed and rearranged more easily than in analog form. DSP is used in many fields including biomedicine, sonar, radar, seismology, speech and music processing, imaging and communications.

In sound cards, DSP chips are used to compress and decompress audio formats as well as to assist with recording and playback and speech synthesis. Other audio uses are the DSP chips in stereo amplifiers, which are programmed to simulate concert hall and cinema effects for home theater and music listening.

DSR

(Data Set Ready) An RS-232 signal sent from the modem to the computer or terminal indicating that it is able to accept data. Contrast with *DTR.*

DSS

(1) (Decision Support System)
(2) (Digital Signature Standard)

(1) (Decision Support System) An information and planning system that provides the ability to interrogate computers on an ad hoc basis, analyze information and predict the impact of decisions before they are made.

DBMSs let you select data and derive information for reporting and analysis. Spreadsheets and modeling programs provide both analysis and "what if?" planning. However, any single application that supports decision making is not a DSS. A DSS is a cohesive and integrated set of programs that share data and information. A DSS might also retrieve industry data from external sources that can be compared and used for historical and statistical purposes.

An integrated DSS directly impacts management's decision-making process and can be a very cost-beneficial computer application. See *EIS* and *OLAP database.*

(2) (Digital Signature Standard) A National Security Administration standard for authenticating an electronic message. See *RSA* and *digital signature.*

DSS & EIS

DBMSs used for transaction processing are not always as efficient for handling ad hoc queries. As more years pile up in a computerized organization, there is more transaction data to wade through. When managers need historical data, it takes forever to get it.

Large enterprises have a big enough job handling their current year's worth of information, let alone history. Retailers with millions of customers and hundeds of thousands of products have enormous transaction and master tables. Managers and executives want multidimensional views of their data. Product summaries by region, by year, by type. The relational database doesn't accomodate these kinds of searches easily.

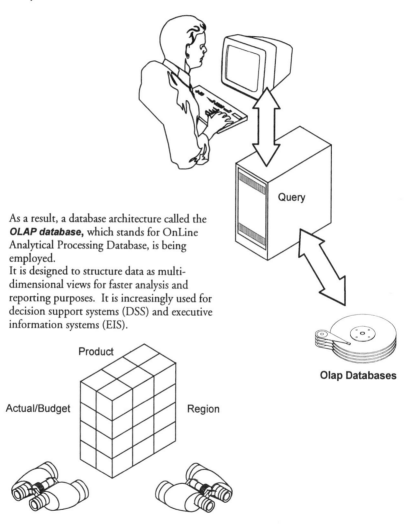

Query

As a result, a database architecture called the **OLAP database,** which stands for OnLine Analytical Processing Database, is being employed.
It is designed to structure data as multi-dimensional views for faster analysis and reporting purposes. It is increasingly used for decision support systems (DSS) and executive information systems (EIS).

Olap Databases

Product

Actual/Budget

Region

Multidimensional Views

DSTN

(Double layer STN) A type of passive matrix display technology that uses an extra display layer as a compensating layer between the STN display and rear polarizer. It produces an almost-pure black and white display with little color tinge and maintains its image better than STN in temperature extremes. See *FSTN* and *LCD*.

DSU/CSU

(Digital (or Data) Service Unit/Channel Service Unit) A pair of communications devices that connect an inhouse line to an external digital circuit (T1, DDS, etc.). It is similar to a modem, but connects a digital circuit rather than an analog one.

The CSU terminates the external line at the customer's premises. It also provides diagnostics and allows for remote testing. If the customer's communications devices are T1 ready and have the proper interface, then the CSU is not required, only the DSU.

The DSU does the actual transmission and receiving of the signal and provides buffering and flow control. The DSU and CSU are often in the same unit. The DSU may also be built into the multiplexor, commonly used to combine digital signals for high-speed lines.

```
              Customer side       |     T1 provider

Multiplexor <--> DSU <--> CSU <--------> T1 line

    Multiplexor <--> DSU/CSU <--------> T1 line

    Multiplexor/DSU <--> CSU <--------> T1 line

        Multiplexor/DSU/CSU <--------> T1 line
```

DSVD

(Digital Simultaneous Voice and Data) An all-digital technology for concurrent voice and data (SVD) transmission over a single analog telephone line. DSVD is endorsed by Intel, Hayes, U.S. Robotics and others and has been submitted to the ITU for possible standardization. DSVD modems became available in the first half of 1995. See *SVD*.

DSX-1

(Digital Signal Cross-connect Level 1) A standard that defines the voltage, pulse width and plug and socket for connecting DS-1 (T1) signals.

DTA

(Design and Test Alliance) A group of ATE and EDA vendors, chip makers and systems houses dedicated to improving testing of complicated electronic systems.

DTD

See *SGML*.

DTE

(Data Terminating Equipment) A communications device that is the source or destination of signals on a network. It is typically a terminal or computer. Contrast with *DCE*.

DTMF

(Dual Tone Multi Frequency) The formal name of touch tone (pushbutton) technology found on telephone keypads.

DTP

See *desktop publishing*.

DTR

(Data Terminal Ready) An RS-232 signal sent from the computer or terminal to the modem indicating that it is able to accept data. Contrast with *DSR*.

DTS

(1) (Digital Termination Service) A microwave-based, line-of-sight communications provided directly to the end user.
(2) (DeskTop Server) A motorola 68000-based network server from Banyan.
(3) (Developer Technical Support) The tech-support group for developers at Apple.

DUA

(Directory User Agent) An X.500 routine that sends a request to the Directory Server Agent (DSA) to look up the location of a user on the network.

dual boot

A computer configuration that allows it to be started with either one of two different operating systems. The dual boot feature is contained in one of the operating systems.

dual in-line package

See *DIP*.

dual Pentium

A PC with a motherboard that contains two Pentium CPUs. Such machines are designed for use with an operating system that supports symmetric multiprocessing (SMP), such as Windows NT. See *SMP*.

dual-scan LCD

A technique used to improve passive matrix color screens. The screen is divided into halves, and each half is scanned simultaneously, thereby doubling the number of lines refreshed per second. It provides a sharper appearance, but still does not approach the richness of active matrix.

dumb terminal

A display terminal without processing capability. It is entirely dependent on the main computer for processing. Contrast with *smart terminal* and *intelligent terminal*.

dump

To print the contents of memory, disk or tape without any report formatting. See *memory dump*.

duplex channel

See *full-duplex*.

duplexed system

Two systems that are functionally identical. They both may perform the same functions, or one may be standby, ready to take over if the other fails.

Duplicate file name or file not found

A DOS error message that means you are referencing a file that does not exist or that you are renaming a file to a file name that already does exist.

duplicate keys

Identical key data in a file. Primary keys, such as account number cannot be duplicated, since no two customers or employees should be assigned the same number. Secondary keys, such as date, product and city, may be duplicated in the file or database.

DVCR

(Digital VideoCassette Recorder) A digital VCR that is able to decode compressed digital video signals on playback. DVCRs are expected in the 1996-1997 timeframe. See *D-VHS*.

DVD

(Digital VideoDisc) The next-generation video CD and high-capacity CD-ROM. It has been agreed that the two competing technologies, the MultiMedia CD (MMCD) from Sony and Philips and the Super Density (SD) format from Toshiba, Time Warner and others, will be merged into one.

Expected in 1996 is a double-sided, double-layered CD with capacity in the 9-10GB range. It uses MPEG-2 compression and provides visual quality between VHS tape and LaserDisc. The target video length is 135 minutes, which covers most films. This is not a guaranteed amount, because the data rate varies depending on how much action takes place on screen.

DVD is expected to obsolete LaserDiscs and VHS videotape as well as become the digital movie medium for personal computers.

D-VHS

(Data-VHS) A VHS videocassette recorder that is able to store data from a digital satellite system (DSS). A D-VHS machine is a modified S-VHS VCR. See *DVCR.*

DVI

(Digital Video Interactive) An Intel compression technique for data, audio and full-motion video. On a CD-ROM, it provides up to 72 minutes of full-screen video, 2½ hours of half-screen video, 40,000 medium-resolution or 7,000 high-resolution images. It compresses full-motion video at ratios greater than 100 to 1 and still images at 10 to 1.

DVI uses standard storage devices, but requires a DVI controller board in the personal computer. Developed by RCA's Sarnoff Research labs in Princeton, Intel acquired it in 1988. Software-only versions of DVI are also forthcoming. See *CD, CD-ROM, CD-I.*

Dvorak keyboard

A keyboard layout designed in the 1930s by August Dvorak, University of Washington, and his brother-in-law, William Dealey. 70% of words are typed on the home row compared to 32% with qwerty, and, more words are typed using both hands. In eight hours, fingers of a qwerty typist travel 16 miles, but only one for the Dvorak typist.

DVST

(Direct View Storage Tube) An early graphics screen that maintained an image without refreshing. The entire screen had to be redrawn for any change.

DWCFGMG.SYS

The software driver that adds Plug and Play capability to older DOS machines.

dweeb

A very technical person. Dweebs sometimes call sales people "slime," anybody interested in technology for profit rather than the art of it.

DX

In an Intel 386 CPU, DX, or 386DX, refers to the full 386, which contains a 32-bit data path, in contrast to the slower 386SX, which uses a 16-bit data path. In an Intel 486 CPU, DX, or 486DX, refers to the full 486, which contains the math coprocessor, in contrast to the 486SX, which does not have the coprocessor.
This is a prime example of the careless naming so common in this industry. People have been thoroughly confused by the DX and SX designations, because they have entirely different meanings depending on whether they refer to a 386 or a 486. See *386* and *486.*

DX2

A 486 with a clock-doubled CPU. Clock doubling doubles the internal speed of the CPU without requiring any changes in the chip's external connections. For example, the 486DX2/66 has an internal speed of 66MHz, while its external bus from the CPU to RAM runs at 33MHz. The 486DX2/50 has an internal speed of 50MHz and 25MHz externally. Intel calls the DX2 a "Speed Doubler" chip.
Note that the 486DX2/66 is often tagged as simply a 486/66. Since there is no full DX 66MHz 486, the DX2 designation is often dropped. This is not true of the 486/50. The 486DX/50 is a true 50MHz machine internally and externally, while the 486DX2 is only 50MHz internally. See *iCOMP.*

DX2 CPU	Internal	External
486DX2/66	66MHz	33MHz
486DX2/50	50MHz	25MHz
486DX/50	50MHz	50MHz

DX4 CPU	Internal	External
486DX4/75	75MHz	25MHz
486DX4/100	100MHz	33MHz

DX4

A 486 with a clock-tripled CPU. Clock tripling triples the internal speed of the CPU without requiring any changes in the chip's external connections. DX4s come in 75MHz and 100MHz versions that access RAM at 25MHz and 33MHz respectively. See *DX2* and *iCOMP* for speed comparisons.

DXF file

(Document EXchange Format file) An AutoCAD 2-D graphics file format. Many CAD systems import and export the DXF format for graphics interchange.

dyadic

Two. Refers to two components being used.

dye diffusion

See *thermal dye diffusion.*

dye polymer recording

An optical recording technique that uses dyed plastic layers as the recording medium. WORM disks typically use a single layer, and erasable disks use two layers: a top retention layer and a bottom expansion layer. A bit is written by shining a laser through the retention layer onto the expansion layer, which heats the area and forms a bump that expands into the retention layer. The retention layer bumps are the actual bits read by the unit. To erase a bit, another laser (different wavelength) strikes the retention layer and the bump subsides.

dye sublimation

See *thermal dye transfer.*

dynamic

Refers to operations performed while the program is running. The expression, "buffers are dynamically created," means that space was created when actually needed, not reserved beforehand.

dynamic address translation

In a virtual memory system, the ability to determine what the real address is at the time of execution.

dynamic binding

Also called *late binding*, it is the linking of a routine or object at runtime based on the conditions at that moment. Contrast with *early binding*. See *binding time* and *polymorphism*.

dynamic compression

The ability to compress and decompress data in realtime; for example, as it's being written to or read from the disk.

Dynamic Data Exchange

See *DDE.*

dynamic link

The connection established at runtime from one program to another.

dynamic link library

A set of program routines that can be called at runtime as needed. See *DLL.*

dynamic memory allocation

Allocating memory as needed without having to specify a fixed amount beforehand. All advanced operating systems perform dynamic memory allocation to some extent.

dynamic network services

Realtime networking capabilities, such as adaptive routing, automatically reconfiguring the network when a node is added or deleted and the ability to locate any user on the network.

dynamic node addressing

A network technology that dynamically assigns machine addresses to nodes upon startup. For example, when a station is turned on in an AppleTalk network, it identifies itself to the network. If its number has been taken in the meantime by another node, it creates a new one using a random number generator.

dynamic RAM

The most common type of computer memory, also called D-RAM ("dee-RAM") and

DRAM. It usually uses one transistor and a capacitor to represent a bit. The capacitors must be energized hundreds of times per second in order to maintain the charges. Unlike firmware chips (ROMs, PROMs, etc.) both major varieties of RAM (dynamic and static) lose their content when the power is turned off. Contrast with *static RAM.*

In memory advertising, dynamic RAM is often erroneously stated as a package type; for example, "DRAMs, SIMMs and SIPs on sale." It should be "DIPs, SIMMs and SIPs," as all three packages typically hold dynamic RAM chips.

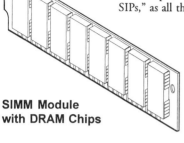

**SIMM Module
with DRAM Chips**

dynamic range
A range of signals from the weakest to the strongest.

dynamic SQL
See *embedded SQL.*

DYNASTY
An application development system for enterprise client/server environments from Dynasty Technologies, Inc., Naperville, IL. Introduced in 1993, it is a repository-driven system that supports Windows, Mac and Motif clients and NT, OS/2 and major UNIX servers and databases. It provides partitioning for creating three-tier applications. DYNASTY generates C and SQL code.

DYNIX/ptx
Sequent Computer's UNIX-based operating system that runs on its Symmetry series of x86 symmetric multiprocessing (SMP) servers.

dynlink
See *dynamic link.*

E

E

See *exponent*.

E1

The European counterpart to T1, which transmits at 2.048 Mbits/sec. See *DS* for chart.

EAM

(Electronic Accounting Machine) Same as *tabulating equipment*.

early binding

In programming, the assignment of types to variables and expressions at compilation time. Also called *static binding* and *static typing*. Contrast with *dynamic binding*. See *binding time*.

EAROM

(Electrically Alterable ROM) Same as *EEPROM*.

earth station

A transmitting/receiving station for satellite communications. It uses a dish-shaped antenna for microwave transmission.

Earth Station

Easel

(Easel Corporation, Burlington, MA) A software tools company founded in 1981. Easel has two lines of client/server tools: one based on its ESL technology which includes ESL Workbench for OS/2 and ESL for Windows. The other is its object-oriented Object Studio based on Smalltalk. Sometimes, the name Easel, by itself, is used to refer to the Easel Renovator screen scraper, now called ESL Renovator.

Easel Workbench

See *ESL Workbench*.

Easter Egg

An undocumented function hidden in a program. Easter Eggs are secret "goodies" that are found by accident or word of mouth. For example, in Windows 3.1, to see the names of the people who worked on the project, open the About Program Manager dialog box (Help, About) and double click on the Windows icon at the upper left while holding down Ctrl and Shift. Click OK, then open the box again.

Ctrl-Shift Double click again and note the dedication. Click OK and repeat once more.

East West Foundation

(55 Temple Place, Boston, MA 02111, 617/542-1234) A non-profit public charity that funnels old computer equipment to schools and other public service organizations in the U.S. and abroad. Founded by Alex Randall, East West maintains a warehouse and technical support for equipment and accepts incomplete systems, parts and pieces as well as software. See *how to donate old equipment*.

EasyCAD 2

A full-featured PC CAD program from Evolution Computing, Tempe, AZ, that is known for its ease of use. EasyCAD users can migrate to FastCAD, which looks almost identical on screen, but provides multiple windows and is designed for high-speed operations.

easy to learn and use

Easy to learn refers to software that is well designed and capable of being used right away. If you make the program work with little problem, it's easy to learn.

Easy to learn implies easy to use right away, but it does not imply easy to use after you're familiar with it. The menus that coddled you in the beginning can become tiresome when used constantly. Advanced programs have a macro recorder that lets you store a series of menu selections and execute them automatically.

Easytrieve

See *CA-Easytrieve*.

EBCDIC

(Extended Binary Coded Decimal Interchange Code) Pronounced "eb-suh-dick." The binary code for text as well as communications and printer control from IBM. This data code originated with the System/360 and is still used in IBM mainframes and most IBM midrange computers. It is an 8-bit code (256 combinations) that stores one alphanumeric character or two decimal digits in a byte.

EBCDIC and ASCII are the two codes most widely used to represent data.

EBL

(Extended Batch Language) A shareware programming language by Frank Canova that allows for more complex programming in DOS batch files.

ECC memory

(Error-Correcting Code memory) A memory system that tests for and corrects errors on the fly. It uses circuitry that generates checksums to correct errors greater than one bit.

ECCO

A Windows PIM from Arabesque Software, Bellevue, WA. ECCO provides a phone book, calendar, to-do list, outlining and notetaking. It is noted for its tightly integrated and sophisticated functions.

ECF

(Enhanced Connectivity Facilities) IBM software that allows DOS PCs to query and download data from mainframes as well as issue mainframe commands. It also allows printer output to be directed from the PC to the mainframe. It uses the SRPI interface and resides in the PC (client) and mainframe (server). Applications issue SRPI commands to request services.

echo

(1) Same as *echoplex*.
(2) A DOS and OS/2 screen command that displays messages and turns off/on screen responses.

echo cancellation

A high-speed modem technique that isolates and filters out unwanted signals caused by echoes from the main transmitted signal. This permits full-duplex modems to send and receive on the same frequency.
Telephone networks often use echo cancellers in addition to or in place of echo suppressors. Network-based echo cancellation can interfere with modems that do their own, such as V.32, so a method is provided for those modems to disable network echo cancellers.

echo check

In communications, an error checking method that retransmits the data back to the sending device for comparison with the original.

echoplex

A communications protocol that transmits the received data back to the sending station allowing the user to visually inspect what was received.

echo suppressor

A communications technique that turns off reverse transmission in a telephone line, thus effectively making the circuit one way. It is used to reduce the annoying effects of echoes in telephone connections, especially in satellite circuits.

ECL

(Emitter-Coupled Logic) A variety of bipolar transistor that is noted for its extremely fast switching speeds.

ECLIPSE

A series of 32-bit minicomputers from Data General. The development of the initial 32-bit ECLIPSE MV/8000 was the subject of Tracy Kidders' best-selling book, "Soul of a New Machine" published in 1981 by Little, Brown and Company.

ECMA

(European Computer Manufacturers Association) An organization devoted to international standards. Address: Rue du Rhone 114, CH-1204 Geneva, Switzerland.

ECNE

See *NetWare certification*.

ECP

(Enhanced Capabilities Port) See *IEEE 1284*.

ED

(1) (Extra High Density) Refers to 2.88M floppy disks.
(2) (EDitor) An early UNIX line editor that contained functionality later incorporated into vi.

EDA

(1) (Electronic Design Automation) Using the computer to design and simulate the performance of electronic circuits on a chip. See *ATE*.

(2) (Electronic Document Authorization) Authorizing certificates used to identify public keys for encrypting data under the RSA method.

EDA/SQL

(Enterprise Data Access/SQL) Software from Information Builders, Inc., New York, that provides a common interface between a wide variety of SQL programs and SQL databases. It also allows queries on data from different types of databases at the same time.

edge concentrator

A device that connects a LAN to a high-speed backbone or switch such as an ATM switch.

edge connector

The protruding part of an expansion board that is inserted into an expansion slot. It contains a series of printed lines that go to and come from the circuits on the board. The number of lines (pins) and the width and depth of the lines are different on the various interfaces (ISA, EISA, PCI, Micro Channel, etc.).

Edge Connector

edge path adapter

See *EPA*.

EDI

(Electronic Data Interchange) The electronic communication of business transactions, such as orders, confirmations and invoices, between organizations. Third parties provide EDI services that enable organizations with different equipment to connect. See *X12, Tradacoms* and *EDIFACT.*

EDIFACT

(Electronic Data Interchange For Administration Commerce and Transport) An ISO standard for EDI that is proposed to supersede both X12 and Tradacoms standards to become the worldwide standard.

e-disk

(Emulated-disk) Same as *RAM disk*.

edit

To make a change to existing data. See *update*.

editable PostScript

A file of PostScript commands that can be edited by a word processor or other program. This allows PostScript documents to be changed without requiring the use of the application that originally created it.

edit checking

Same as *validity checking*.

edit instruction

A computer instruction that formats a field for display or printing. Using an edit mask, it inserts decimal points, commas and dollar signs into the data.

edit key

A key combination or function key that changes the program into edit mode when pressed.

edit mask

A pattern of characters that represent formatting codes through which data is filtered for display or printing. See *picture*.

edit mode

An operational state in a program that allows existing data to be changed.

editor

See *text editor* and *linkage editor*.

edit program

(1) A data entry program that validates user input and stores the newly created records in the file.
(2) A program that allows users to change data that already exists in a file. See *update*.

edit routine

A routine in a program that tests for valid data. See *validity checking*.

EDL

See *nonlinear video editing*.

Edlin

An archaic text editor used in DOS. The OS/2 counterpart is SSE.

EDMS

(Electronic Document Management System) See *document management*.

EDO RAM

(Extended Data Out RAM) A type of dynamic RAM chip with performance that approaches static RAM. It increases speed by overlapping certain internal operations and is expected to become popular in the 1995-1996 timeframe.

EDP

(Electronic Data Processing) The first name used for the computer field.

EDRAM

(Enhanced **DRAM**) A high-speed DRAM chip developed by Ramtron International Corporation, Colorado Springs, CO. It allows overlap of a read at the trailing end of a write operation to obtain its speed.

EDSAC

(Electronic Delay Storage Automatic Calculator) Developed by Maurice Wilkes at Cambridge University in England and completed in 1949, it was one of the first stored program computers and one of the first to use binary digits. Its memory was 512 36-bit words of liquid mercury delay lines, and its input and output were provided by paper tape. The EDSAC could do about 700 additions per second and 200 multiplications per second. It was in routine use at the University until 1958.

edu

An Internet address domain name for an educational organization. See *Internet address*.

education

Teaching concepts and perspectives. Computer education includes computer systems and information systems. Contrast with *training*.

edutainment

Educational material that is also entertaining.

EEPROM

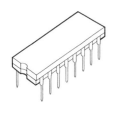

(Electrically Erasable Programmable Read Only Memory) A memory chip that holds its content without power. It can be erased, either within the computer or externally and usually requires more voltage for erasure than the common +5 volts used in logic circuits. It functions like non-volatile RAM, but writing to EEPROM is slower than writing to RAM.

EEPROMs are used in devices that must keep data up-to-date without power. For example, a price list could be maintained in EEPROM chips in a point of sale terminal that is turned off at night. When prices change, the EEPROMs can be updated from a central computer during the day. EEPROMs have a lifespan of between 10K and 100K write cycles. See *flash memory*.

eesa

See *EISA* and *ESA/370*.

EFF

(Electronic Frontier Foundation) An organization founded in 1990 by Mitchell Kapor and John Perry Barlow dedicated to raising public awareness of the opportunities and challenges posed by computing and telecommunications. Address: 155 Second St., Cambridge, MA 02141, 617/864-0665.

e-forms

(Electronic-FORMS) See *forms software*.

EFT

(Electronic Funds Transfer) The transfer of money from one account to another by computer.

EGA

(Enhanced Graphics Adapter) An IBM video display standard that provides medium-resolution text and graphics. It supports previous display modes and requires a digital RGB Enhanced Color Display or equivalent monitor. EGA was superseded by VGA. See *PC display modes*.

EGP

(Exterior Gateway Protocol) A protocol that broadcasts TCP/IP addresses to the gateway in another network.

EHLLAPI

See *HLLAPI.*

EIA`

(Electronic Industries Association, 2001 Pennsylvania Ave., N.W., Washington, DC 20006, 202/457-4900) A membership organization founded in 1924 as the Radio Manufacturing Association. It sets standards for consumer products and electronic components. In 1988, it spun off its Information & Telecommunications Technology Group into a separate organization called the TIA.

EIA-232, 422, 423, 449, 485

See *RS-232, RS-422, 423, 449* and *RS-485.*

EIA-568

An EIA standard for telecommunications wiring in a commercial building. See *cable categories.*

EIDE

See *Enhanced IDE.*

Eiffel

An object-oriented programming language developed by Bertrand Meyer, Interactive Software Engineering Inc., Goleta, CA. It runs on DOS, OS/2 and most UNIX platforms. The Eiffel compiler generates C code, which can be modified and recompiled with a C compiler.

ISA

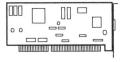

EISA

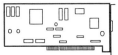

PCI

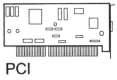

L-bus

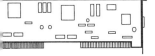

Micro Channel

EIS

(Executive Information System) An information system that consolidates and summarizes ongoing transactions within the organization. It should provide management with all the information it requires at all times from internal as well as external sources. Increasingly, EISs are providing some of the "what if?" manipulation functions of a DSS (decision support system); however, a DSS provides true modeling capabilities. See *DSS.*

EISA

(Extended ISA) Pronounced "ee-suh." A PC bus standard that extends the 16-bit ISA bus (AT bus) to 32 bits and provides bus mastering. ISA cards can plug into an EISA slot. It was announced in 1988 as a 32-bit alternative to the Micro Channel that would preserve investment in existing boards. EISA is also used in various workstations from HP and others.

EISA still runs at the slow 8MHz speed of the ISA bus in order to accomodate all the ISA cards that may be plugged into it. PCI and VL-bus local buses provide independent data paths and higher speeds than EISA.

EL

See *electroluminescent.*

electricity

The flow of electrons in a circuit. The speed of electricity is the speed of light (approximately 186,000 miles per second). In a wire, it is slowed due to the resistance in the material.

Its pressure, or force, is measured in *volts* and its flow, or current, is measured in *amperes.* The amount of work it produces is measured in *watts* (amps X volts).

electrode

A device that emits or controls the flow of electricity.

electroluminescent

A flat panel display that provides a sharp, clear image and wide viewing angle. It contains a powdered or thin film phosphor layer sandwiched between an x-axis and a y-axis panel. When an x-y coordinate is charged, the phosphor in that vicinity emits visible light. Phosphors are typically amber, but green is also used.

Electroluminescent Screen

Electroluminescent screens were the first portable screens that provided a wide viewing angle. They have been superseded by active matrix LCD screens. *(Diagram courtesy of Planar Systems, Inc.)*

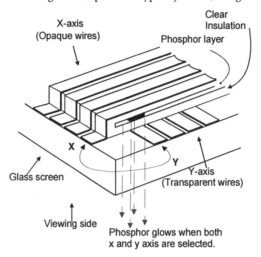

electrolyte

In a rechargeable battery, the material that allows electricity to flow from one plate to another by conducting ions.

electromagnet

A magnet energized by electricity. A coil of wire is wrapped around an iron core. When current flows in the wire, the core generates an energy called magnetic *flux*.

electromagnetic interference

See *EMI*.

electromagnetic radiation

The energy that exists in all things, including humans, which incorporates cosmic rays, gamma rays, x-rays, ultraviolet light, visible light, infrared light and radar.

electromagnetic spectrum

The range of electromagnetic radiation in our known universe, which includes visible light as outlined below. Parts of the radio spectrum are still unassigned, but will eventually be used for some commercial communications purpose.

electromechanical

The use of electricity to run moving parts. Disk drives, printers and motors are examples. Electromechanical systems must be designed for the eventual deterioration of moving parts.

electromotive force

The pressure in an electric circuit measured in volts.

electron

An elementary particle that circles the nucleus of an atom. Electrons are considered to be negatively charged.

Electromagnetic Spectrum

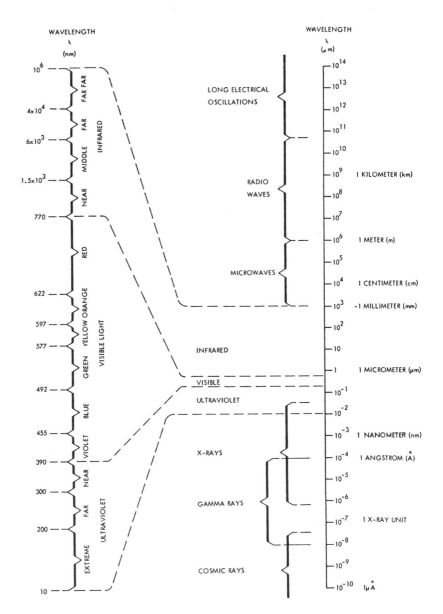

electron beam

A stream of electrons, or electricity, that is directed towards a receiving object.

electron gun

A device that shoots a fine beam of electrons onto the phosphor screen of a CRT.

electronic

The use of electricity in intelligence-bearing devices, such as radios, TVs, instruments, computers and telecommunications. Electricity used as raw power for heat, light and motors is considered electrical, not electronic.

Although coined earlier, "Electronics" magazine (1930) popularized the term. The magazine subheading read "Electron Tubes - Their Radio, Audio, Visio and Industrial Applications." The term was derived from the electron (vacuum) tube.

electronic circuit

See *circuit* and *digital circuit.*

electronic commerce

Doing business online. It includes purchasing products via online services and the Internet as well as electronic data interchange (EDI), in which one company's computer queries and transmits purchase orders to another company's computer.

electronic forms

See *forms software.*

Electronic Frontier Foundation

See *EFF.*

electronic mail

Also called *e-mail,* it is the transmission of memos and messages over a network. Users can send mail to a single recipient or broadcast it to multiple users. Sophisticated systems prompt recipients for a reply if they haven't responded within a certain time frame. With multitasking workstations, mail can be delivered and announced while the user is working in an application. Otherwise, mail is sent to a simulated mailbox in the network server or host computer, which must be interrogated.

An electronic mail system requires a messaging system, which provides the store and forward capability, and a mail program that provides the user interface with its send and receive functions. See *messaging system* and *EDI.*

Electronic Mail versus Fax

Fax documents are scanned images and are thus treated like pictures even if they contain only text. E-mail messages are raw ASCII text, which can be edited immediately in any text editor or word processor that imports ASCII text (most do).

In order to edit the text in a fax, the images of the characters have to be turned into ASCII text by an OCR (optical character recognition) program, which is highly error prone. If all you want to do is read a message, either method works well. However, if you are sending a text document that will be edited and used in a desktop publishing program, e-mail will save your recipient from having to retype it all over again.

E-mail Versus Fax

When a message is typed into the computer, it is stored as ASCII text. When it is transmitted, the recipient can edit it immediately. When a message is faxed, the text is scanned and turned into a bitmap. In order to edit that text, the bitmapped image must be run through an OCR program in the computer to turn it back into raw text again.

electronic messaging

See *electronic mail* and *messaging system.*

electronic money

See *e-money.*

electronic prepress

The use of computers to prepare camera-ready materials up to the actual printing stage. It includes drawing, page makeup and typesetting, all performed electronically rather than by drafting or mechanical cut and paste methods.

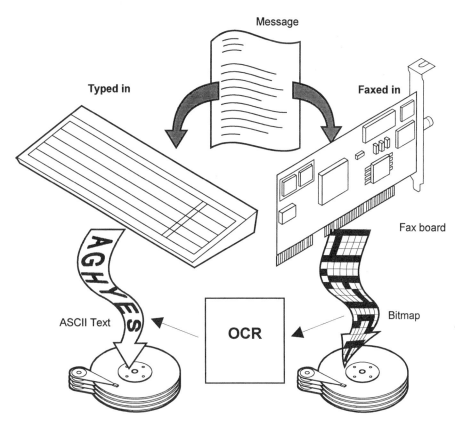

Electronic mail versus Fax

An e-mail file contains the same characters as a text document that is typed into the computer. When a fax is captured by the computer, its file is the same as a scanned image. Optical character recognition (OCR) is used to convert the bitmapped images into raw ASCII text.

electronic publishing

Providing information in electronic form to readers or subscribers via an online service. It also includes the publication of databases on CD-ROM. See *information utility, Internet* and *hot topics.*

electronic switch

An on/off switch activated by electrical current.

electrophotographic

The printing technique used in copy machines and laser printers. A negative image made of dots of light is painted onto a photosensitive drum or belt that has been electrically charged. The light comes from a laser, LEDs or liquid crystals that shutter a light source.

Wherever light is applied, the drum becomes uncharged. A toner (dry ink) is applied and adheres to the charged areas of the drum. The drum transfers the toner to the paper, and pressure and heat fuse the toner and paper permanently.

Some electrophotographic systems use a positive approach in which the toner is attracted to the laser-produced latent image.

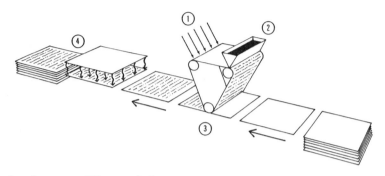

Electrophotographic Process
(1) The belt or drum is charged. (2) The toner, which is dry ink, is adhered to the charged areas. (3) The toner is transferred onto the paper. (4) The toner is fused onto the paper.

electrosensitive printer

A dot matrix printer that burns away dots on the outer silver coating of a special black paper.

electrostatic

Stationary electrical charges in which no current flows.

electrostatic plotter

A plotter that uses a special paper that is charged as it passes by a line of electrodes. Toner is then applied to the charged paper. Models print in in black and white or color, and some handle paper up to six feet wide.

electrostatic printer

Same as *electrostatic plotter*.

elegant program

A program that is simple in design and uses the least amount of computer resources (memory, disk, etc.).

elevator

Also called a *thumb*, it is a square box that slides within a scroll bar. The elevator is dragged up and down to position the text or image on screen.

elevator seeking

A disk access technique that processes multiple requests in a priority based upon which ones are closest to the current position of the read/write head.

ELF

(Extemely Low Frequency) See *low radiation*.

elite

A typeface that prints 12 cpi.

em

In typography, a unit of measure equal to the width of the capital letter M in a particular font.

EMA

(1) (Enterprise Management Architecture) Digital's stategic plan for integrating network, system and application management. It provides the operating environment for managing a multi-vendor network.
(2) (Electronic Mail Association, 1555 Wilson Blvd., Arlington, VA 22209, 703/875-8620) A membership organization founded in 1983 with over 250 vendor and user companies involved in electronic messaging and information exchange.

Concerns include marketing e-mail within the corporation, privacy, security, interconnection and standards.

EMACS

(Editor MACroS) A UNIX text editor developed at MIT that is used for writing programs. It provides a wide variety of editing features including multiple windows.

e-mail

See *electronic mail.*

e-mail address

See *Internet address.*

EMBARC

(EMBARC Communications Service, Boyton Beach, FL) A Motorola subsidiary that provides wireless broadcasting of mail and news to mobile computers that have a Motorola NewStream, SkyTel SkyStream, PCMCIA NewsCard or similar receiver. EMBARC stands for Electronic Mail Broadcast to a Roaming Computer. It uses a 930-931MHz channel licensed to Motorola and can handle long messages of 30,000 characters and more.

embedded command

(1) A command inserted within text or other codes.
(2) In word processing, a command within the text that directs the printer to change fonts, print underline, boldface, etc. The command is inserted when the user selects a layout change. Commands are often invisible on screen, but can be revealed if required.

embedded controller

Controller circuitry built into a device or on the main system board in contrast with a removable card or module.

embedded SQL

SQL statements that are written into a high-level programming language such as C or Pascal. In a preprocessing stage, the SQL code is converted into function calls, which may be optimized to provide the fastest results. If the programmer knows exactly what the query is going to do, and the query does not change, it is called *static SQL.* If the query requires user input at runtime, it is called *dynamic SQL.* If the client program passes the SQL statements directly to the database server without any intermediate step, it is called *passthrough SQL.*

embedded system

A specialized computer used to control a device such as an automobile, appliance or space vehicle. Operating system and application functions are often combined in the same program.

EMF

(1) (ElectroMagnetic Field) See *electromagnetic radation.*
(2) (Enhanced MetaFile) The 32-bit version of the Windows Metafile (WMF) format. The original WMF format is simple and cannot completely replicate images created by sophisticated graphics programs. The EMF format enhances the structure and solves most of these deficiencies of the WMF format.

EMI

(ElectroMagnetic Interference) Electromagnetic waves that eminate from an electrical device. It often refers to both low-frequency waves from electromechanical devices and high-frequency waves (RFI) from chips and other electronic devices. Allowable limits are governed by the FCC.

emitter

One side of a bipolar transistor. See *collector*.

emitter-coupled logic

See *ECL*.

EMM

(Expanded Memory Manager) Software that manages expanded memory (EMS). In XTs and ATs, expanded memory boards must also be used. In 386s and up, the EMM converts extended memory into EMS.

EMM386.EXE

A memory manager that accompanies DOS and Windows starting with DOS 5 and Windows 3.0. It turns extended memory into expanded memory (EMS) for applications that use it and/or it allows drivers and TSRs to be stored in the upper memory area (UMA) between 640K and 1M. EMM386.EXE is loaded by a **device=** line in the CONFIG.SYS file.

In Windows 95, EMM386.EXE can still be used to load 16-bit drivers and TSRs into upper memory. However Win 95 provides its own memory manager that supports EMS memory for DOS applications that run windowed rather than full screen.

e-money

(Electronic money) The consumer equivalent of electronic funds transfer (EFT), which has taken place in the commercial banking and financial industries for years. E-money covers a variety of online financial transactions that transfer funds from bank accounts, debit cards and credit cards for paying bills, investing and shopping.

emoticon

(EMOTional ICON) Also called a *smiley*, it is an expression of emotion typed into a message using standard keyboard characters. The following examples are viewed sideways. Tilt your head down toward your left shoulder.

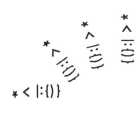

Santa Claus

Smiley:	Meaning:
:)	original smiley face
:-)	smile
:-(	frown
;-)	wink
:-D	big smile
:-O	mouth open in amazement
:-Q	tounge hanging out in nausea
:-{)	smile (user has moustache)
:-{)}	moustache and beard
8-)	smile (user wears glasses)
(-:	smile (user left handed or Australian)
:*)	red nosed smile, suggesting inebriation
*<l:{)}	Santa Claus!
@:{)===	sikh with turban and long beard

For an extensive list of more than 650 emoticons, read "Smileys" by David Sanderson, published by O'Reilly & Associates, Inc., ISBN 1-56592-041-4.

EMS

(1) (Expanded Memory Specification)
(2) (Electronic Message Service)
(3) (Enterprise Messaging Server)

EMS Memory

DOS can only address the first megabyte of memory. When EMS is used, a 64K chunk of the upper memory area (UMA) is reserved for the EMS page frame, which serves as a window into the EMS memory bank. An expanded memory manager, such as EMM386.EXE, turns extended memory into EMS memory and remaps the requested 64K page into the page frame area, which DOS can reach.

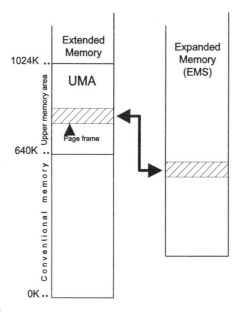

(1) (Expanded Memory Specification) The first technique to allow DOS to go beyond its one megabyte memory limit. It lets DOS address up to 32MB of RAM by bank switching segments of EMS memory into a 64KB chunk of upper memory (UMA), known as the page frame.

In older XTs and ATs, EMS is installed by plugging in an EMS memory board and adding an EMS driver. In 386s and up, extended memory is turned into EMS memory by a software memory manager. All modern memory managers, such as EMM386 (DOS 5 and up), QEMM and 386MAX, can dynamically allocate expanded memory as needed, but the 64KB page frame must be reserved at startup if EMS is to be used at any time during the session. In order to use EMS, the application is either written to use it directly (Lotus 1-2-3 Ver. 2.x, AutoCAD, etc.) or the application is run in an environment that uses it, such as DESQview. Windows does not use EMS, but supports it for DOS applications that require it.

Expanded versus Extended

Expanded memory (EMS) and extended memory are not the same. EMS can be installed in XT-class machines and up, whereas extended memory requires at least a 286. EMS broke the 1MB memory barrier in the early days, but since Windows and DOS-extended applications also break the 1MB barrier and use regular contiguous memory beyond 1MB (extended memory), EMS is only used for older DOS applications.

EMS History and Versions

In 1984, Lotus, Intel and Microsoft introduced EMS (LIM EMS), which addressed up to 8MB. By Version 3.2, it was widely-supported, but limited to one 64K page frame (four 16K pages) only in upper memory (UMA). AST, Quadram and Ashton-Tate later introduced Enhanced EMS (EEMS), letting the page frame take the full 1M address space (64 16K pages), allowing programs such as DESQview to multitask large applications within conventional memory.

In 1987, Lotus, Intel and Microsoft introduced Version 4.0, increasing memory to 32MB and incorporating the EEMS standard.

(2) (Electronic Message Service) The part of the radio spectrum assigned to electronic messaging over digital satellite circuits.

(3) (Enterprise Messaging Server) Original name for Microsoft's Exchange Server. See *Microsoft Exchange.*

EMS emulator

Before the 386, it referred to software for 8086/88s and 286s that simulated EMS memory in extended memory or disk. It was a low-cost alternative to an EMS board, but was slower.

Starting with the 386, it refers to a memory manager (EMM) that creates EMS out of extended memory. Technically, the 386 is really not emulating anything. The

386 can map any memory to any other memory, thus it is merely mapping memory according to the EMS specification.

EMS memory manager

See *EMM* and *EMS emulator*.

emulation mode

An operational state of a computer when it is running a foreign program under emulation.

emulator

A device that is built to work like another. A computer can be designed to emulate another model and execute software that was written to run in the other machine. A terminal can be designed to emulate various communications protocols and connect to different networks. The emulator can be hardware, software or both.

en

In typography, a unit of measure equal to one half the width of an em. An en is typically the width of one numeric digit.

enable

To turn on. Contrast with *disable*.

Enable/OA

An integrated software package for PCs from Enable Software, Inc., Ballston Lake, NY. It is noted for being a very comprehensive package rivaling many stand-alone programs. Version 4.0 also runs under UNIX.

**Emulators
Are Copycats**

Encapsulated PostScript

See *EPS*.

encapsulation

(1) In communications, a method for transmitting multiple protocols within the same network. The frames of one type of protocol are carried within the frames of another. For example, SNA's SDLC frames can be encapsulated within TCP/IP and transmitted over a TCP/IP network.
(2) In object technology, making the data and processing within the object private, which allows the internal implementation of the object to be modified without requring any change to the application that uses it. This is also known as *information hiding*. See *object technology*.

Encina

A UNIX-based TP monitor from Transarc Corporation, Pittsburgh, PA, that is layered over OSF's Distributed Computing Environment (DCE). IBM's CICS/6000 TP monitor is based on Encina, and IBM acquired Transarc in 1994. Encina and Novell's Tuxedo are the major TP monitors in the UNIX client/server environment.

encipher

To encode data for security purposes. See *encryption*.

encode

(1)To assign a code to represent data, such as a parts code.
(2) Same as *encipher* or *encrypt*. See *encryption*.

Encore

(Encore Computer Corporation, Ft. Lauderdale, FL) A computer company founded in 1983 that specializes in multiprocessing and realtime systems. Its Motorola

88110-based Infinity line provides SMP systems and massively parallel systems scalable to 2,048 CPUs running UMAX V, Encore's version of UNIX System V.
Encore uses mainframe-like channels and architecture for high I/O speed between processors. Its realtime computers stem from Gould's computer division that it acquired in 1989. Also from Gould comes Reflective Memory technology, a high-speed bus that allows multiple memories to be read and written simultaneously.

encryption

Using cryptography to encode data for security purposes for transmission over a public network. The original text, or plaintext, is converted into a coded equivalent called ciphertext via an encryption algorithm. The ciphertext is decoded (decrypted) at the receiving end with the use of a decryption key.

Secret versus Public Key

There are two methods of encrypting data. The traditional method uses a secret key, such as the DES standard. Both sender and receiver use the same key. This is the fastest method, but transmitting the secret key to the recipient in the first place is not secure.

The second method is public-key cryptography, such as RSA, which uses both a private and a public key. Each recipient has a private key that is kept secret and a public key that is published for everyone. The sender looks up the recipient's public key and uses it to encrypt the message. The recipient uses the private key to decrypt the message.

If speed is an issue, the public-key method can be used to send the secret key followed by the message encrypted with the secret key. See *DES* and *RSA*.

Secret Key

Secret key encryption uses **one key**. The problem is maintaining the secrecy of the key and sending it to a new user.

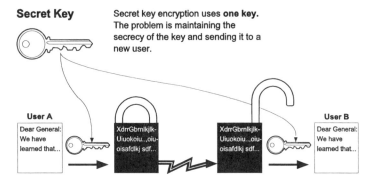

Public Key

Public key encryption uses a **two-part key**. One part is made public and published for everyone to see, and the other is kept secret and used only by the originating user and recipient of the message.

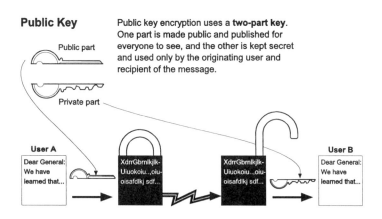

endian

See *big endian*.

end key

A keyboard key commonly used to move the cursor to the bottom of the screen or file or to the next word or end of line.

endless loop

A series of instructions that are constantly repeated. It can be caused by an error in the program or it can be intentional; for example, a screen demo on continuous replay.

end points

In vector graphics, the two ends of a line (vector). In 2-D graphics, each end point is typically two numbers representing coordinates on x and y axes. In 3-D, each end point is made up of three numbers representing coordinates on x, y and z axes.

2,18

73,1

end user

Same as *user*.

Energy Star

Power conservation requirements set forth by the Environmental Protection Agency of the U.S. Government. In order to display the Energy Star logo, devices (PCs, monitors, printers, etc.) must use less than 30 watts of power when inactive.

Enfin

A client/server development system based on the Smalltalk language. It is now part of the Object Studio environment. See *Object Studio*.

engine

(1)A specialized processor, such as a graphics processor. Like any engine, the faster it runs, the quicker the job gets done. See *graphics engine* and *printer engine*.

(2)Software that performs a primary and highly repetitive function such as a database engine, graphics engine or dictionary engine.

"This is a computing device that really looks like an engine!" *(Difference Engine photo courtesy of Smithsonian Institution.)*

engineering cylinder

See *diagnostic tracks.*

engineering drawing sizes

A - 8 1/2 x 11
B - 11 x 17
C - 17 x 22
D - 22 x 34
E - 34 x 44

Enhanced IDE

An extension to the IDE hardware interface that supports more devices and increased transfer rates. Enhanced IDE, or EIDE, supports multiple channels, each able to connect two devices, the ATA-2 interface, which increases transfer rates to 11MB/sec, and hard disks greater than 528MB. It also supports the ATAPI interface, which connects CD-ROMs, tape drives and optical disks.

Starting in 1994, almost all PCs were shipped with Enhanced IDE BIOSs, host adapters and drives. Many motherboards provide primary and secondary IDE channels for up to four devices total. See *IDE, ATA* and *hard disk.*

Enhanced keyboard

An IBM 101-key keyboard that superseded the PC and AT keyboards. It has a separate cursor key cluster located between the original numeric/cursor keypad and the letter keys. Most PC keyboards use this design or something very similar to it.

enhancement

Any improvement made to a software package or hardware device.

ENIAC

(Electronic Numerical Integrator And Calculator) The first operational electronic digital computer developed for the U.S. Army by John Eckert and John Mauchly at the University of Pennsylvania. Completed in 1946, it was decimal-based, used 18,000 vacuum tubes, took up 1,800 square feet and performed 5,000 additions/second. Today, the equivalent technology is used in a watch.

The First Operational Digital Computer
What an awesome sight this must have been in 1946. The electrical power used could supply a thousand computers today. *(Photo courtesy of The Moore School of Electrical Engineering, University of Pennsylvania.)*

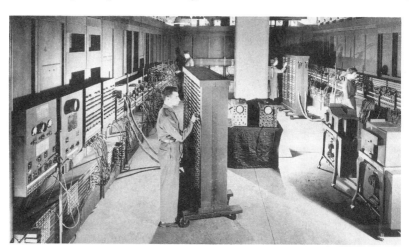

enqueue

Pronounced "n-q." To place an item in a queue. Contrast with *dequeue*.

enquiry character

In communications, a control character that requests a response from the receiving station.

ENS

(Enterprise Networking Services) A variety of networking services from Banyan that have been separated from its VINES network operating system and made available on other platforms such as NetWare, Windows NT and AIX. They include the VINES Streettalk directory, network management and electronic mail services.

enter key

See *return key*.

enterprise

The entire organization. See *enterprise networking*.

enterprise data

Centralized data that is shared by many users throughout the organization.

enterprise model

A model of how an organization does business. Information systems are designed from this model.

enterprise network

A geographically-dispersed network under the jurisdiction of one organization. It often includes several different types of networks and computer systems from different vendors.

enterprise networking

The networking infrastructure in a large enterprise with multiple computer systems and networks of different types is extraordinarily complex. Due to the myriads of interfaces that are required, much of what goes on has little to do with the real data processing of the payroll and orders. An enormous amount of effort goes into planning the integration of disparate networks and systems and managing them, and, planning again for yet more interfaces as marketing pressures force vendors to develop new techniques that routinely change the ground rules.

Application Development and Configuration Management

There are a large number of programming languages and development tools for writing today's client/server applications. Each development system has its own visual programming interface for building GUI front ends and its own fourth-generation language (4GLs) for doing the business logic. Programmers are always learning new languages to meet the next generation.

Traditional programming has given way to programming for graphical user interfaces and object-oriented methods, two technologies with steep learning curves for the traditional programmer.

Programming managers are responsible for maintaining legacy systems in traditional languages while developing new ones in newer languages and tools for the client/server environment. They must also find ways to keep track of all the program modules and ancillary files that make up an application when several programmers work on a project. Stand-alone version control and configuration management programs handle this, and parts of these systems are increasingly being built into the development systems themselves (see *configuration management*).

Database Management

Like all software, a database management system (DBMS) must support the hardware platform and operating system it runs in. In order to move a DBMS to another platform, a version must be available for the new hardware and operating system. The common database language between client and server is SQL, but each DBMS vendor implements its own rendition of SQL, requiring a special SQL interface to most every DBMS.

For certain kinds of applications, relational databases (RDBMSs) are giving way to object-oriented databases (OODBMSs) or unified databases that are both relational and object oriented. This puts a new slant on learning about data structures and the way they are processed.

Database administrators must select the DBMS or DBMSs that efficiently process the daily transactions and also provide sufficient horsepower for decision support. They must decide when and how to split the operation into different databases, one for daily work, the other for ad hoc queries. They must also create the structure of the database by designing the record layouts and their relationships to each other.

Operating Systems

Network Operating Systems

Operating systems are the master control programs that run the computer system. Single-user operating systems, such as DOS, Windows and Mac, are used in the clients, and multiuser network operating systems, such as NetWare, Windows NT and all the variations of UNIX, are used in the servers.

The operating system sets the standard for the programs that run under it. The choice of operating system combined with the hardware platform determines which ready-made applications can be purchased to work on it.

On the Intel x86 platform, there are more choices for operating environments than ever before. However, just as the PC begins to mature into manageable bedlam, the PowerPC emerges to challenge the sacrosanct standard and offer us even more choices.

Systems programmers and IS managers must determine when newer operating systems make sense and plan how to integrate them into existing environments.

Communications Protocols

Communications protocols determine the format and rules for how the transmitted data is framed and managed from the sending station to the receiving station. IBM's SNA, Digital's DECnet, Apple's AppleTalk, Novell's IPX/SPX, UNIX's TCP/IP and Microsoft's NetBEUI are the major ones. Exchanging data and messages between Macs, PCs, minis, mainframes and UNIX workstations means that network managers increasingly are designing networks for a multiprotocol environment.

LANs

Transmission from station to station within a LAN is performed by the LAN access method, or data link protocol, such as Ethernet and Token Ring. As traffic expands within an organization, higher bandwidth is required, causing organizations to plan for Fast Ethernet, switched Ethernet, FDDI and CDDI. At the same time, ATM continues to make inroads as the be-all-end-all networking topology.

Repeaters, bridges, routers, gateways, hubs and switiches are the devices used to extend, convert, route and manage traffic in an enterprise network. Increasingly, one device takes on the job of another (a router does bridging, a hub does routing). Vendor offerings are dizzying.

Network traffic is becoming as jammed as the Los Angeles freeways. Network administrators have to analyze current network traffic in light of future business plans and increasing deployment of multimedia image, sound and video files. They have to determine when to increase network bandwidth while maintaining existing networks, which today have become the technical lifeblood of an enterprise.

WANs

Transmitting data to remote locations requires the use of private lines or public switched services offered by local and long distance carriers. Connections can be as simple as dialing up via modem or by leasing private lines, such as T1 and T3. Switched 56, frame relay, ISDN, SMDS and ATM offer a variety of switched services in which you pay for the digital traffic you use.

Laptop use has created a tremendous need for remote access to LANs. Network administrators have to design LANs with a combination of remote access and remote control capability to allow mobile workers access to their databases and processing functions.

Network Management

Network management is the monitoring and control of LANs and WANs from a central management console. It requires network management software, such as IBM's NetView and HP's OpenView. The Internet's SNMP has become the de facto standard management protocol, but there are many network management programs and options. For example, there are over 30 third-party add-ons for HP's popular OpenView software.

Systems Management

Systems management includes a variety of functions for managing computers in a networked environment, including software distribution, version control, backup & recovery, printer spooling, job scheduling, virus protection and performance and capacity planning. Network management may also fall under the systems management umbrella.

Electronic Mail

Electronic mail requires a store and forward system so that mail can be safely kept in a "mailbox" until it is retrieved. Although messages and attached files are transmitted using standard transport protocols, the mail system is a high-level application with its own messaging protocols. The major ones are IBM's SNADS, the international X.400, Novell's MHS, the Internet's SMTP, Lotus' cc:mail and Microsoft Mail.

Formats

Word processors, DBMSs, spreadsheets, drawing and paint programs generate files in their own proprietary data format. For example, there are more than 75 graphics formats alone. Moving files from one application to another requires conversion (exporting and importing) from one format to another. Dealing with multiple formats and multimedia is why object-oriented databases are being evaluated. They can support any kind of text, picture, sound and video format that exists today or that comes tomorrow.

In Summary...Happy Computing!

entity

In a database, anything about which information can be stored; for example, a person, concept, physical object or event. Typically refers to a record structure.

entity relationship model

A database model that describes the attributes of entities and the relationships among them. An entity is a file (table). Today, ER models are often created graphically, and software converts the graphical representations of the tables into the SQL code required to create the data structures in the database. See page 204.

entity type

In a database, a particular kind of file; for example, a customer or product file.

entropy

In data compression, a measure of the amount of non-redundant, non-compressible information in an object.

entry

The input of an item or set of items at a terminal. See *data entry*.

entry point

In programming, the starting point of the instructions in a subroutine.

enumerate

To count or list one by one. For example, an enumerated data type defines a list of all possible values for a variable, and no other value can then be placed into it.

envelope

(1) A range of frequencies for a particular operation.
(2) A group of bits or items that is packaged and treated as a single unit.

environment

A particular configuration of hardware or software. "The environment" refers to a hardware platform and the operating system that is used in it. A programming environment would include the compiler and associated development tools. Environment is used in other ways to express a type of configuration, such as a networking environment, database environment, transaction processing environment, batch environment, interactive environment and so on. See *platform*.

environment variable

A stored value used by DOS and applications. It is set with the DOS Set command. For example, **set temp=c:\dos** sets the TEMP environment variable to the C:\DOS directory.

EOF, EOL, EOM, EOT

(End Of File, End Of Line, End Of Message, End Of Transmission)

EPA

(Edge Path Adapter) A device that converts packets from an Ethernet or Token Ring LAN to the cell structure of an ATM network and vice versa.

epitaxial layer

In chip making, a semiconductor layer that is created on top of the silicon base rather than below it. See *molecular beam epitaxy*.

epoch date

The starting point from which time is measured as the number of days, minutes, etc., from that time.

EPP

(1) (Enhanced Parallel Port) See *IEEE 1284*.
(2) (Ethernet Packet Processor) A chip from Kalpana, Inc., Santa, Clara, CA, that doubles speed of Ethernet transmission to 20Mbits/sec.

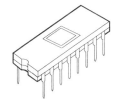

EPROM

(Erasable Programmable ROM) A programmable and reusable chip that holds its content until erased under ultraviolet light. EPROMS have a lifespan of a few hundred write cycles. EPROMS are expected to eventually give way to flash memory. See *EPROM programmer*.

EPROM programmer

A device that writes instructions and data into EPROM chips. Some earlier units were capable of programming both PROMs and EPROMs.

EPS

A PostScript file format that contains PostScript code for the document as well as optional preview images in TIFF, Windows Metafile or Macintosh PICT formats. The PostScript code drives a PostScript printer directly, and the preview formats allow the image to be manipulated on screen. DOS and OS/2 files use an EPS extension.

Epson emulation

Compatible with Epson dot matrix printers. The command set in the Epson MX, RX and FX printers has become an industry standard. Useful codes are:

ASCII Value	Command
12	Form feed
27 48 8	LPI
27 50 6	LPI
15	Condensed on
18	Condensed off
27 81 1	Double width on
27 81 0	Double width off
27 69	Emphasized on
27 70	Emphasized off
27 83 1	Subscript on
27 83 0	Superscript on
27 84	Sub/super off
27 45 1	Underline on
27 45 0	Underline off

EPSS

(Electronic Performance Support System) A computer system that provides quick assistance and information without requiring prior training to use it. It may incorporate all forms of multimedia delivery as well as AI techniques such as expert systems and natural language recognition.

EQ

(EQual to) See *relational operator*.

equalization

In communications, techniques used to reduce distortion and compensate for signal loss (attenuation) over long distances.

equation

An arithmetic expression that equates one set of conditions to another; for example, $A = B + C$. In a programming language, assignment statements take the form of an equation. The above example would assign the sum of B and C to the variable A.

ERA

(Electrically Reconfigurable Array) A programmable logic chip (PLD) technology from Plessey Semiconductor that allows the chip to be reprogrammed electrically.

erase

See *delete*.

erase head

In a magnetic tape drive, the device that erases the tape before a new block of data is recorded.

Ergonomics
(Photo courtesy of Hewlett-Packard Company.)

ergonomics

The science of people-machine relationships. An ergonomically-designed product implies that the device blends smoothly with a person's body or actions.

Erlang

A unit of traffic use that specifies the total capacity or average use of a telephone system. One Erlang is equivalent to the continuous usage of a telephone line. Traffic in Erlangs is the sum of the holding times of all lines divided by the period of measurement.

ER model

See *entity relationship model.*

error checking

(1)Testing for accurate transmission of data over a communications network or internally within the computer system. See *parity checking* and *CRC.*
(2) Same as *validity checking.*

error control, error detection & correction

See *error checking* and *validity checking.*

error-free channel

An interface (wire, cable, etc.) between devices that is not subject to external interference; specifically not the dial-up telephone system.

error handling

Routines in a program that respond to errors. The measurement of quality in error handling is based on how the system informs the user of such conditions and what alternatives it provides for dealing with them.

error messages

Various DOS and Windows error messages are listed individually in this book by the message that is displayed when they occur.

error rate

The measurement of the effectiveness of a communications channel. It is the ratio of the number of erroneous units of data to the total number of units of data transmitted.

Erwin

(Entity Relationship for WINdows) An data modeling program for Windows from Logic Works, Princeton, NJ. It allows the database schemas to be build graphically and turns the graphs into the appropriate SQL code for creating PowerBuilder, DB2, Oracle, Sybase and other databases.

ES

See *expert system.*

ES/3090

A high-end IBM mainframe that incorporates the ESA/370 enhancements.

ES/9000

The IBM System/390 computer line introduced in late 1990 that uses 31-bit addressing with maximum memory capacities from 256MB to 9GB. It's 18 models (Model 120 to Model 960) offered the widest range of power in a single introduction at one time with prices ranging from $70K to $23M. Vector processing is optional on high-end water-cooled and certain air-cooled models. See *System/390*.

ESA/370

(Enterprise System Architecture/370) IBM enhancements that increase the performance of high-end 4381 and 3090 mainframes. Introduced in 1988, it increases virtual memory from 2GB to 16TB and adds techniques for managing it more effectively. This architecture is built into System/390 ES/9000 computers.

ESA/390

(Enterprise System Architecture/390) Extensions to ESA/370 for the System/390 series. It includes MVS/ESA, VM/ESA and VSE/ESA operating systems.

Esc

See *escape character* and *escape key*.

escape character

A control character often used to precede other characters to control a printer or other device. For example, escape, followed by &l10, sets the LaserJet to landscape mode. In ASCII, escape is decimal 27, hex 1B; in EBCDIC, it is hex 27.

escape key

A keyboard key commonly used to exit a mode or routine, or cancel some function.

escape sequence

(1) A machine command that starts with an escape character. Printers are often commanded by escape sequences. See *escape character*.
(2) In a modem, a unique sequence of characters that precedes a command. It allows modem commands (dial, hang up, etc.) to be transmitted with the data. See *TIES* and *Hayes Smartmodem*.

ESCON

(Enterprise Systems CONnection) An IBM System/390 fiber optic channel that transfers 10 Mbytes/sec up to 5.6 miles. An ESCON Director is the coupling device that provides 8-16 ports (Model 1) or 28-60 ports (Model 2).

ESD

(1) (Electronic Software Distribution) Distributing new software and upgrades via the network rather than individual installations on each machine. See *ESL*.
(2) (ElectroStatic Discharge) Sparks (electrons) that jump from an electrically-charged object to an approaching conductive object.
(3) (Entry Systems Division) The IBM division that conceived and developed the original IBM PC.

ESDI

(Enhanced Small Device Interface) A hard disk interface that transfers data in the one to three MByte/sec range. ESDI was the high-speed interface for small computers for a while, but has been superseded by IDE and SCSI drives. See *hard disk*.

ESDL

(Electronic Software Distribution and Licensing) The combination of ESD and ESL.

ESDS

(Entry Sequence DataSet) A VSAM structure that stores records one after the other without regard to content. Records are retrieved by address. Contrast with *KSDS*.

ESF

(1) (Extended SuperFrame) An enhanced T1 format that allows a line to be monitored during normal operation. It uses 24 frames grouped together (instead of the 12-frame D4 superframe) and provides room for CRC bits and other diagnostic commands.

(2) (External Source Format) A specification language for defining an application in IBM's CSP/AD application generator.

ESL

(Electronic Software Licensing) Software that keeps track of the number of active users per application in order to comply with the multiuser licensing contracts that have been purchased.

ESL for Windows

A client/server development system for Windows from Easel Corporation. It is a native Windows version of Easel's Workbench product which is primarily an OS/2 development system with Windows runtime support. ESL for Windows includes ESL QuickStep, a source code project manager.

ESL Renovator

A screen scraper from Easel Corporation that is used to turn character-based mainframe and mini screens into Windows front ends.

ESL Workbench

A client/server development system for OS/2 from Easel Corporation that also provides Windows runtime capability. ESL Workbench is geared for developing very large applications. Subsequently, Easel introduced a native Windows development system, called ESL for Windows. Starting with Version 4.0, ESL Workbench provides international language capability, which instantly switches menus and messages to Spanish, German, etc.

ESP

(1) (Enhanced Service Provider) An organization that adds value to basic telephone service by offering such features as call-forwarding, call-detailing and protocol conversion.

(2) (E-tech Speedy Protocol) A proprietary protocol of E-Tech Research used in its modems.

(3) (Electronic Still Photography) Digitizing and transmitting images over a telephone line.

(4) (Emulex SCSI Processor) A proprietary chip used in Emulex's SCSI disk controller.

ESS

(1) (Electronic Switching System) A large-scale computer used to switch telephone conversations in a central office.

(2) (Executive Support System) See *EIS*.

(3) (Electronic SpreadSheet) See *spreadsheet*.

Ethernet

A local area network (LAN) developed by Xerox, Digital and Intel (IEEE 802.3). It is the most widely used LAN access method. Token Ring is next. Ethernet connects up to 1,024 nodes at 10 Mbps over twisted pair, coax and optical fiber. Faster Ethernets have been developed. 100BaseT and 100VG-AnyLAN transmit at 100 Mbps rather than 10, and switched Ethernet gives each pair of users that want to communicate with each other a dedicated 10 Mbps channel. See *100BaseT, 100VG-AnyLAN* and *switched Ethernet*.

Ethernet uses the CSMA/CD technology which employs a broadcast method. When a station is ready to send, it transmits its data packets onto the network, which is common to all nodes. All stations "hear" the data. The station that matches the destination address in the packet is the one that responds, while the others do nothing.

Standard Ethernet (10Base5), also called *Thick Ethernet* and *ThickNet*, uses a thick coax cable that can run as far as 1,640 feet without using repeaters. Attachment is made by clamping a transceiver onto the thick coax, which contains another cable that is connected to the adapter card via a 15-pin socket (AUI port).

Thin Ethernet (10Base2), also called *ThinNet* and *CheaperNet*, uses a thinner, less-expensive coax that is easier to connect but has a limitation of 607 feet per segment. ThinNet uses T-type BNC connectors, and the transceivers are built into the adapter cards.

Twisted pair Ethernet (10BaseT) uses economical telephone wiring and standard RJ-45 connectors, often taking advantage of installed wires in a building. Fiber Optic Ethernet (10BaseF) is impervious to external radiation. Both 10BaseT and 10BaseF use a star topology and connect to a central hub.

Ethernet is a data link protocol and functions at the data link and physical levels of the OSI model (1 and 2). See *data link protocol* and *OSI model*.

Ethernet	Segment type	Max. Length	Devices	Topology
10Base5	"Thick"	1,640 ft.	100	bus
10Base2	"Thin"	607 ft.	30	bus
10BaseT	Twisted pair	328 ft.	2	star
10BaseF	Fiber Optic	1.2 mi.	2	star

Ethernet adapter

An Ethernet network adapter. See *network adapter*.

Ethernet address

A unique number assigned to each Ethernet network adapter. It is a 48-bit number maintained by the IEEE. Hardware vendors obtain blocks of numbers that they can build into their cards.

EtherTalk

Macintosh software from Apple that accompanies its Ethernet Interface NB Card and adapts the Mac to Ethernet networks.

EtherWave

An Ethernet system from Farallon Computing, Inc., Alameda, CA, that provides network adapters that daisy chain 10BaseT wire from machine to machine. Regular 10BaseT systems require a central hub that connects all machines. To add a station to the network when a hub is out of ports requires adding a hub. EtherWave allows connecting seven daisy-chained EtherWave PCs to a single hub port.

E-time

See *execution time*.

Eurocard

A family of European-designed printed circuit boards that uses a 96-pin plug rather than edge connectors. The 3U is a 4x6" board with one plug; the 6U is a 6x12" board with two plugs; the 9U is a 14x18" board with three plugs.

even parity

See *parity checking*.

Ethernet

There are three popular types of Ethernet in use. Thick Ethernet is the original Ethernet and uses a thick coaxial cable. Each station is connected to a transceiver which clips onto the cable. Thin Ethernet uses a thinner coaxial cable which attaches to each station with a T-type BNC connector. The most popular Ethernet is 10Base-T or twisted pair Ethernet. Each station is wired into a central hub. See previous page for maximum lengths and number of devices that can be attached to each type of Ethernet.

Thick Ethernet

15 pin
AUI
connector

Transceiver

Thin Ethernet

BNC
connector

BNC T-connector

10BaseT

RJ45
connector

Hub
with RJ45 connectors

event driven

An application that responds to input from the user or other application at unregulated times. It's driven by choices that the user makes (select menu, press button, etc.). Contrast with *procedure oriented.*

EVGA

(Extended VGA) See *VGA.*

eWorld

An online service from Apple aimed at the consumer market. Introduced in 1994 initially for Macintoshes, Windows capability was later added.

Exabyte

(Exabyte Corporation, Boulder, CO) The world's largest independent tape drive manufacturer. Its high-capacity 8mm tape drives, which were first introduced in 1987, are sold direct and through OEMs. The 8mm cassettes hold from 2.5 to 20GB. Tape library systems hold from 500GB to over one terabyte. With acquisitions made in 1993, Exabyte also makes QIC and DAT drives.

examinations

See *CCP, NetWare certification* and *Microsoft Certified Professional.*

Excel

A full-featured spreadsheet for PCs and the Macintosh from Microsoft. It can link many spreadsheets for consolidation and provides a wide variety of business graphics and charts for creating presentation materials.

Exception error 12

A DOS error message that means DOS does not have enough room to handle hardware interrupts. Increasing the number of stacks in the STACKS= command in the CONFIG.SYS file may solve the problem.

exception report

A listing of abnormal items or items that fall outside of a specified range.

exclusive NOR, exclusive OR

See *NOR* and *OR.*

executable

A program in machine language that is ready to run in a particular computer environment.

execute

To follow instructions in a program. Same as *run.*

execution time

The time in which a single instruction is executed. It makes up the last half of the instruction cycle.

executive

Refers to an operating system or only to the operating system's kernel.

executive information system

See *EIS.*

EXE file

(EXEcutable file) A runnable program in DOS, OS/2 and VMS. In DOS, if a program fits within 64K, it may be a COM file.

exhibitions

See *trade shows*.

exit

(1)To get out of the current mode or quit the program.
(2) In programming, to get out of the loop, routine or function that the computer is currently in.

expanded memory

See *EMS*, *EMM* and *expanded storage*.

expanded storage

Auxiliary memory in IBM mainframes. Data is usually transferred in 4K chunks from expanded storage to central storage (main memory).

expand the tree

To display the sublevels of a hierarchical tree.

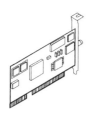

expansion board

(1) A printed circuit board that plugs into an expansion slot. All the boards (cards) that plug into a personal computer's bus are expansion boards, such as display adapters, disk controllers and sound cards.
(2) See *bus extender*.

expansion bus

(1) The computer's bus comprised of a series of receptacles or slots into which expansion boards (video display, disk controller, etc.) are plugged.
(2) Sometimes refers to *bus extender (3)*.

expansion card

Same as *expansion board*.

expansion slot

A receptacle inside a computer or other electronic system that accepts printed circuit boards. The number of slots determines future expansion. In personal computers, expansion slots are connected to the bus.

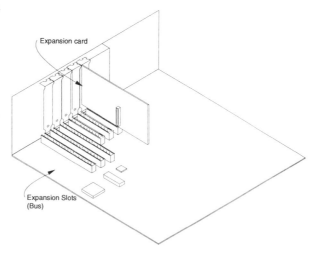

Expansion card

Expansion Slots
(Bus)

ExperLogo

A Macintosh version of Logo from ExperTelligence, Inc., Goleta, CA. It contains more functions similar to LISP than most versions of Logo.

expert system

An AI application that uses a knowledge base of human expertise for problem solving. Its success is based on the quality of the data and rules obtained from the human expert. In practice, expert systems perform both below and above that of a human.

It derives its answers by running the knowledge base through an inference engine, which is software that interacts with the user and processes the results from the rules and data in the knowledge base.

Examples of uses are medical diagnosis, equipment repair, investment analysis, financial, estate and insurance planning, vehicle routing, contract bidding, production control and training. See *EPSS*.

Expert System

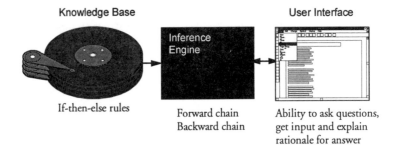

Knowledge Base

Inference Engine

User Interface

If-then-else rules

Forward chain
Backward chain

Ability to ask questions, get input and explain rationale for answer

expireware

Software with a built-in expiration date, either by date or number of uses.

explode

(1) To break down an assembly into its component pieces. Contrast with *implode*.
(2) To decompress data back to its original form.

exponent

The number written above the line and to the right of a number that indicates the power of a number, or how many zeros there are in it. For example 10 to the 3rd power indicates three zeros. The number 467,000 can be stated as 467 x 10 to the 3rd. On a screen or printout, the number is expressed as 467E3. See *floating point*.

exponential growth

Extremely fast growth. On a chart, the line curves up rather than being straight. Contrast with *linear*.

exponential smoothing

A widely-used technique in forecasting trends, seasonality and level change. Works well with data that has a lot of randomness.

export

To convert a data file in the current application program into the format required by another application program.

expression

In programming, a statement that describes data and processing. For example, VALUE=2*COST and PRODUCT="HAT" AND COLOR="GRAY".

extended application

A DOS application that runs in extended memory under the control of a DOS extender.

extended ASCII

The second half of the ASCII character set (characters 128 through 255). Extended ASCII symbols are different for each font. The standard font in DOS uses extended ASCII for foreign language letters as well as characters that make up simple charts and diagrams (see *ASCII chart*). The Macintosh allows extended ASCII characters to be user defined.

The extended ASCII characters in most Windows fonts are defined by ANSI for foreign languages, and the Character Map utility can be used to view them.

extended maintenance

On-call service that is ordered for periods in addition to the primary period of maintenance.

extended memory

In Intel 286s and up, it is standard memory above one megabyte. Extended memory is used directly by Windows and OS/2 as well as DOS applications that run with DOS extenders. It is also used under DOS for RAM disks and disk caches. Contrast with expanded memory (EMS), which is specialized memory above one megabyte. Memory boards can usually be set up as a mix of the two. See *EMS, XMS* and *DOS extender*.

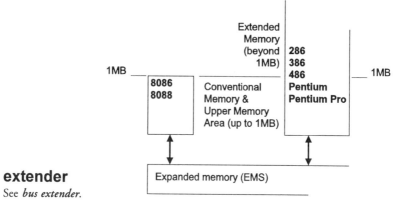

extender

See *bus extender*.

extensible

Capable of being expanded or customized. For example, with extensible programming languages, programmers can add new control structures, statements or data types.

extension

A DOS, Windows and OS/2 file category. Extensions are file types, or file categories, that are added to the end of DOS, Windows 95 and OS/2 file names. The extension is separated from the file name with a dot such as LETTER.DOC. An extension can have up to three letters or digits. Executable files use .EXE, .COM and .BAT extensions; for example, NOTEPAD.EXE is the text editor that comes with Windows.

All programs and most data files use extensions. However, some word processing files do not, in which case you could create your own filing system; for example, CHAP1.NOV and CHAP2.NOV could be chapters in a novel. See *graphics formats*. See also *Macintosh extension*.

Ext.	Type of file
906	Calcomp plotter
ABC	Computer Desktop Encyclopedia configuration
AD	After Dark image
AFM	Type 1 font metrics
AG4	Access G4 document imaging
AI	Adobe Illustrator graphics,
	Encapsulated PostScript header
ARC	ARC, ARC+ compressed
ASC	ASCII file
ASM	Assembly source code
ATT	AT&T Group IV fax
AVI	Microsoft movie format
BAK	Backup
BAS	BASIC source code
BAT	DOS, OS/2 batch file
BIN	Driver, overlay
BMP	Windows & OS/2 bitmap
C	C source code
CAB	Microsoft compressed format for distribution
CAL	Windows calendar,
	SuperCalc spreadsheet,
	CALS raster and vector formats
CAP	Ventura Pub. captions
CAL	CALS raster and vector formats
CDR	Corel Draw vector graphics
CFG	Configuration
CGM	CGM vector graphics
CHP	Ventura Pub. chapter
CHK	DOS Chkdsk chained file
CIF	Ventura Pub. chapter info.
CIT	Intergraph scanned image
COB	COBOL source code
CLP	Windows clipboard
CMP	LEAD Technologies raster graphics
COM	Executable program
CPI	DOS code page
CPL	Windows control panel applets
CPP	C++ source code
CPR	Knowledge Access raster graphics
CSV	Comma delimited
CUT	Dr. Halo raster graphics
DAT	Data
DB	Paradox table
DBF	dBASE database
DBT	dBASE text
DBX	DATABEAM raster graphics
DCA	IBM text
DCS	Color separated EPS format
DCT	Dictionary
DG	Autotrol vector graphics
DGN	Intergraph vector graphics
DIB	Windows DIB raster graphics

DIC	Dictionary	INF	Setup information
DIF	Spreadsheet	INI	Initialization
DLL	Dynamic link library		
DOC	Document (Multimate, Word...)	JPG	JPEG (JFIF) raster graphics
DOX	MultiMate V4.0 document	JT	JT Fax
DPI	Pointline raster graphics		
DRV	Driver	KFX	Kofax Group IV fax
DRW	Designer vector graphics (Version 2.x, 3.x)		
DS4	Designer vector graphics (Version 4.x)	LBL	dBASE label
DSF	Designer vector graphics (Version 6.x)	LBM	Deluxe Paint graphics
DWG	AutoCAD vector format	LIB	Function library
DX	Autotrol document imaging	LZH	LHARC compressed
DXF	AutoCAD vector format		
		MAC	MacPaint raster graphics
ED5	EDMICS raster graphics (DOD)	MAP	Linkage editor map
EPS	Encapsulated PostScript	MCS	MathCAD format
ESI	Esri plot file (vector)	MDB	Access database
EXE	Executable program	MET	OS/2 Metafile
FAX	Various fax formats	MEU	Menu items
FDX	Force index	MDX	dBASE IV multi-index
FLC	AutoDesk animation	MID	MIDI sound file
FLD	Hijaak thumbnail folder	MIL	Same as GP4
FLI	AutoDesk animation	MMM	Macromind animation format
FLT	Graphics conversion filter	MOV	QuickTime for Windows movie
FMT	dBASE Screen format	MRK	Informative Graphics markup file
FNT	Windows font	MSG	Message file
FON	Windows bitmapped font	MSP	Microsoft Paint raster graphics
	Telephone file		
FOR	FORTRAN source code	NDX	dBASE index
FOT	Windows TrueType font info.	NG	Norton Guides text
FOX	FoxBase compiled program	NLM	NetWare NLM program
FM3	Format info for 1-2-3 Version 3		
FRM	dBASE report layout	OAZ	OAZ Fax
		OBJ	Object module
G4	GTX RasterCAD (raster into vector)	OVL	Overlay module
GCA	IBM MO:DCA - GOCA vector graphics	OVR	Overlay module
GED	Arts & Letters graphics	OZM	Sharp Organizer memo bank
GEM	GEM vector graphics	OZP	Sharp Organizer telephone bank
GIF	CompuServe raster graphics		
GP4	CALS Group IV - ITU Group IV	PAS	Pascal source code
GRF	Micrografx Charisma vector graphics	PCL	HP LaserJet series
GRP	Windows ProgMan Group	PCD	Photo CD raster graphics
GX1	Show Partner raster graphics	PCM	LaserJet cartridge info.
GX2	Show Partner raster graphics	PCT	PC Paint raster graphics,
			Macintosh PICT raster & vector graphics
HLP	Help text	PCW	PC Write document
HPL	HP Graphics language	PCX	PC Paintbrush raster graphics
HYC	WordPerfect hypen list	PDF	Portable Document Format (Acrobat)
			Printer driver
ICA	I BM MO:DCA - IOCA raster graphics		Printer description (QuarkXpress)
ICO	Windows icon	PDV	PC Paintbrush printer driver
IDE	Development environment configuration	PFA	Type 1 font (ASCII)
IDX	FoxBase index	PFB	Type 1 font (encrypted)
IFF	Amiga	PFM	Windows Type 1 font metrics
IGF	Inset Systems (Hijaak)	PGL	HPGL 7475A plotter (vector graphics)
	raster & vector graphics	PIC	Various vector formats:
IL	Icon library (hDC Computer)		Lotus 1-2-3,
IMG	GEM Paint raster graphics		Micrografx Draw,

	Mac PICT format,	TGA	TARGA raster graphics
	IBM Storyboard raster graphics	TIF	TIFF raster graphics
PIF	Windows info. for DOS programs,	TMP	Temporary
	IBM Picture Interchange	TTC	TrueType font compressed
PIX	Inset Systems raster & vector graphics	TTF	TrueType font
PM	PageMaker graphics/text	TXT	ASCII text
PMx	PageMaker document (x=ver.)		
PPD	PostScript printer description	USP	LaserJet portrait font
PRD	Microsoft Word printer driver	USL	LaserJet landscape font
PRG	dBASE source code		
PRN	XyWrite printer driver	VGR	Ventura Pub. chapter info.
PRN	Temporary print file	VOC	Sound Blaster sound
PRN	PostScript file	VUE	dBASE relational view
PRS	WordPerfect printer driver		
PRT	Formatted text	WAV	Windows sound
PS	PostScript page description	WKQ	Quattro spreadsheet
PTx	PageMaker template (x=ver.)	WKS	Lotus 1-2-3 ver. 1a spreadsheet
P10	Tektronix Plot10 plotter (vector graphics)	WK1	Lotus ver. 2.x
		WK3	Lotus ver. 3.x & Windows
QLC	ATM font info.	WK4	Lotus ver. 4.x
		WMF	Windows Metafile
RAS	Sun raster graphics	WPD	Windows printer description
RIA	Alpharel Group IV raster graphics	WPG	WordPerfect raster & vector graphics
RIB	Renderman graphics	WPM	WordPerfect macro
RIC	Roch FaxNet	WPS	Microsoft Works document
RIX	RIX virtual screen	WRI	Windows Write document
RLC	CAD Overlay ESP (Image Systems)	WRK	Symphohony spreadsheet
RLE	Compressed (run length encoded)		
RND	AutoShade format	XBM	X Bitmap image
RNL	GTX Runlength raster graphics	XFX	JetFax
RTF	Microsoft text/graphics	XLC	Excel chart
R8P	LaserJet portrait font	XLS	Excel spreadsheet
R8L	LaserJet landscape font	XPM	X Pixelmap image
SAM	Ami Pro document	ZIP	PKZIP compressed
SBP	IBM Storyboard graphics/Superbase text	ZOO	Zoo compressed
SC	Paradox source code		
SCx	C oloRIX raster (x=res.)	$$$	Temporary
SCM	ScreenCam movie		
SCR	dBASE screen layout		
SCR	Script		
SCR	Windows screen saver		
SCT	Lotus Manuscript screen capture text		
SET	Setup parameters		
SFP	LaserJet portrait font		
SFL	LaserJet landscape font		
SFS	PCL 5 scalable font		
SLD	AutoCAD slide		
SND	Aristosoft sound		
SPD	Speedo scalable font		
STY	Ventura Pub. style sheet		
SYL	SYLK format (spreadsheets)		
SYS	DOS, OS/2 driver		
TAL	Adobe Type Align shaped text		
TDF	Speedo typeface definition		
TFM	Intellifont font metrics		

extent
Contiguous space on a disk reserved for a file or application.

external command
(1) In DOS and OS/2, a function performed by a separate utility program that accompanies the operating system. Contrast with *internal command.* See *DOS external command.*

(2) A user-developed HyperCard command. See *XCMD.*

external function
A subroutine that is created separately from the main program. See *XFCN.*

external interrupt
An interrupt caused by an external source such as the computer operator, external sensor or monitoring device, or another computer.

external modem
A self-contained modem that is connected via cable to the serial port of a computer. It draws power from a wall outlet. The advantage of an external modem is that a series of status lights on the outside of the case display the changing states of the modem (off-hook, carrier detect, transmitting, etc.). In varying degrees, the communications program informs the user as well. However, having the indicators visible on the unit may be more helpful if a problem occurs. Contrast with *internal modem.*

external reference
In programming, a call to a program or function that resides in a separate, independent library.

external sort
A sort program that uses disk or tape as temporary workspace. Contrast with *internal sort.*

external storage
Storage outside of the CPU, such as disk and tape.

EXTRA!
Terminal emulation software from Attachmate Corporation, Bellevue, WA. It is used with 3270 and 5250 emulators to gain access to a mainframe or mini from a personal computer. Versions for Windows and Mac are available.

extremely low frequency
See *low radiation.*

F

f

See *farad* and *femto*.

F1 key

Function key number one. There are 12 function keys on a PC keyboard. F1 is used for retrieving help in Windows and in most DOS applications.

fabless

(FABricationLESS) A semiconductor vendor that does not have inhouse manufacturing facilities. Although it designs and tests the chips, it relies on external foundries for their actual fabrication. See *foundry*.

FaceLift

A font scaler for Windows and WordPerfect from Bitstream Inc., Cambridge, MA, that provides on-the-fly font scaling for Bitstream's own Speedo fonts. FaceLift for Windows also supports Type 1 fonts. FaceLift for WordPerfect lets users create a wide variety of custom fonts, including outlines, shadows and fill scaling, for the DOS version of WordPerfect.

facilities management

The management of a user's computer installation by an outside organization. All operations including systems, programming and the datacenter can be performed by the facilities management organization on the user's premises.

facsimile

See *fax*.

factorial

The number of sequences that can exist with a set of items, derived by multiplying the number of items by the next lowest number until 1 is reached. For example, three items have six sequences (3x2x1=6): 123, 132, 231, 213, 312 and 321.

failover

Maintaining an up-to-date copy of a database on an alternate computer system for backup. The alternate system takes over if the primary system becomes unusable. See *replication*.

fail safe

Same as *fault tolerant*.

fail soft

The ability to fail with minimum destruction. For example, a disk drive can be built to automatically park the heads when power fails. Although it doesn't correct the problem, it minimizes destruction.

FAMOS

(Floating gate Avalanche-injection Metal Oxide Semiconductor) A type of EPROM.

fan

A device that uses motor-driven blades to circulate the air in a computer or other electronic system. Today's CPUs run extremely hot, and large computer cabinets use two and three fans to reduce temperature. See *FanCard*.

fan-fold paper

Same as *continous forms*.

fan in

To direct multiple signals into one receiver.

fan out

To direct one signal into multiple receivers. See *port multiplier*.

FAQ file

(Frequently Asked Questions file) A documentation file that contains the most commonly asked questions about a subject. FAQ files are widely used on the Internet.

farad

A unit of electrical charge that is used to measure the storage capacity of a capacitor. In microelectronics, measurements are usually in microfarads or picofarads.

far pointer

In an Intel x86 segmented address, a memory address that includes both segment and offset. Contrast with *near pointer*.

Fast

An asynchronous communications protocol used to quickly transmit files over high-quality lines. Error checking is done after the entire file has been transmitted.

FastCAD

A full-featured PC CAD program from Evolution Computing, Tempe, AZ, known for its well-designed user interface. It requires a math coprocessor. Users with less sophisticated requirements can start out with FastCAD's baby brother, EasyCAD.

FastDisk

A Windows 3.1 driver that speeds up disk accesses by running in 32-bit mode, bypassing DOS and the BIOS and communicating directly with the disk controller. It works on Western Digital and compatible controllers or on other controllers with upgraded drivers from the manufacturer. To turn this feature on and off, select 386 Enhanced in Control Panel, then click Virtual Memory, Change, Use 32-Bit Disk Access. See *WinDisk*.

Fast Ethernet

Generally refers to high-speed 100BaseT Ethernet, but may also include 100VG-AnyLAN. See *100BaseT* and *100VG-AnyLAN*.

Fast Fourier Transform

See *FFT*.

FAT

(File Allocation Table) The part of the DOS and OS/2 file system that keeps track of where data is stored on disk. When the disk is high-level formatted, the FAT is recorded twice and contains a table with an entry for each disk cluster.
The directory list, which contains file name, extension, date, etc., points to the FAT entry where the file starts. If a file is larger than one cluster, the first FAT entry points to the next FAT entry where the second cluster of the file is stored and so on to the end of the file. If a cluster becomes damaged, its FAT entry is marked as such and that cluster is not used again.

fatal error

A condition that halts processing due to read errors, program bugs or anomalies.

fat binary

A Macintosh executable program that contains machine language in one file for both the Macintosh and PowerMac machines (680x0 and PowerPC CPUs). Software distributed in this format will run native on whichever Mac architecture it is loaded on.

FatBits

A MacPaint option in the "Goodies" menu that lets a user edit an image a pixel at a time.

fat client

A client machine in a client/server environment that performs most or all of the application processing with little or none performed in the server. Contrast with *thin client* and *fat server*. See *two-tier client/server*.

father file

See *grandfather, father, son*.

fat server

A server in a client/server environment that performs most or all of the application processing with little or none performed in the client. The counterpart to a fat server is a thin client. Contrast with *fat client*. See *two-tier client/server*.

Fat Client

fault resilient

See *high availability*.

fault tolerant

The ability to continue non stop when a hardware failure occurs. A fault tolerant system is designed from the ground up for reliability by building multiples of all critical components, such as CPUs, memories, disks and power supplies into the same computer. In the event one component fails, another takes over without skipping a beat.

Many systems are designed to recover from a failure by detecting the failed component and switching to another computer system. These systems, although sometimes called fault tolerant, are more widely known as *high availability* systems, requiring that the software resubmits the when the second system is available.

True fault tolerant systems are the most costly, because redundant hardware is wasted if there is no failure in the system. On the other hand, fault tolerant systems provide the same processing capacity after a failure as before, whereas high availability systems often provide reduced capacity.

Tandem and Stratus are the two major manufacturers of fault-tolerant computer systems for the transaction processing (OLTP) market. Stratus computers are used by long distance carriers for 800 routing and other out-of-band services.

fax

(FACSimile) Originally called telecopying, it is the communication of a printed page between remote locations. Fax machines scan a paper form and transmit a coded image over the telephone system. The receiving machine prints a facsimile of the original. A fax machine is made up of a scanner, printer and modem with fax signalling.

Groups 1 and 2, used in the 1970s and 1980s, transmit at six and three minutes per page respectively. Group 3 transmits up to 9,600 baud using data compression at less than one minute per page. This speed increase led to the extraordinary rise in usage in the late 1980s, resulting in today's most universal form of electronically-transmitted mail.

Group 3 resolution is 203x98 dpi in standard mode and 203x196 dpi in fine mode. Higher-speed Group 4 machines rely on all-digital (ISDN) networks which may not be prevalent until the mid 1990s. See *electronic mail.*

fax board

Fax transmission on an expansion board. It uses software that generates fax signals directly from disk files or the screen and transmits a sharper image than a fax machine, which gets its image by scanning. Incoming faxes are printed on the computer's printer.

fax logging

Automatically storing copies of incoming and outgoing faxes onto some storage medium.

fax/modem

A combination fax board and data modem available as an external unit that plugs into the serial port or as an expansion board for internal installation. It includes a fax switch that routes the call to the fax or data modem. Most all modems today are fax/modems.

fax switch

A device that tests a phone line for a fax signal and routes the call to the fax machine. When a fax machine dials a number and the line answers, it emits an 1,100Hz tone to identify itself. Some devices handle voice, fax and data modem switching and may require keying in an extension number to switch to the modem.

FCB

(File Control Block) The first method used to handle files in DOS. Early applications that remain compatible with DOS 1.0 and use this approch.

FCC

(Federal Communications Commission) The regulatory body for U.S. interstate telecommunications services as well as international service originating in the U.S. It was created under the U.S. Communications Act of 1934, and its board of commissioners is appointed by the President.

FCC Class

An FCC certification of radiation limits on digital devices. Class A certification is for business use. Class B, for residential use, is more stringent in order to avoid interference with TV and other home reception. See Part 15, Subpart B, of the Federal Register (CFR 47, Parts 0-19).

FCFS

First come, first served.

fci

(Flux Changes per Inch) The measurement of polarity reversals on a magnetic surface. In MFM, each flux change is equal to one bit. In RLL, a flux change generates more than one bit.

F connector

A coaxial cable connector used to connect antennas, TVs and VCRs. It is easily recognized: the plug's inner wire is stripped bare and sticks out of the connector looking somewhat unfinished. The plug's shell contains threads on the inside and is screwed into the threaded socket.

F Connector

FD

(Floppy Disk) For example, FD/HD refers to a floppy disk/hard disk device.

FDDI

(Fiber Distributed Data Interface) An ANSI standard token passing network that uses optical fiber cabling and transmits at 100 Mbits/sec up to two kilometers. FDDI is used for MANs and LANs and includes its own network management standard called STM (Station Management). The TP-PMD (CDDI) version will run over copper (UTP), although limited to distances of typically 50 to 100 meters. FDDI provides network services at the same level as Ethernet and Token Ring (OSI layers 1 and 2).

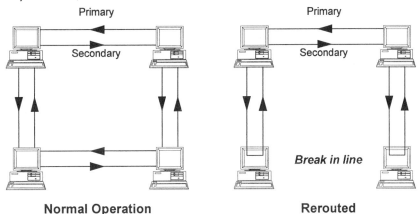

Normal Operation   **Rerouted**

An FDDI Dual Counter-Rotating Ring

FDDI provides an optional "dual counter-rotating ring" topology that contains primary and secondary rings with data flowing in opposite directions. If the line breaks, the ends of the primary and secondary rings are bridged together at the closest node to create a single ring again.

SAS or DAS

Stations can be configured as Single Attached Stations (SAS) connected to concentrators, or as Dual Attached Stations (DAS), connected to both rings. Groups of stations are typically wired to concentrators connected in a hierarchical tree to the main ring. Large networks may be configured as a "dual ring of trees," in which the dual ring provides the backbone to which multiple hierarchies of concentrators are attached.

FDDI provides a ten-fold jump in speed over 10 Mbps Ethernet and 16Mpbs Token Ring and allows high-resolution images to be quickly transmitted. See *TP-PMD* and *CDDI*.

FDDI II adds circuit-switched service to this normally packet-switched technology in order to support isochronous traffic such as realtime voice and video.

**An FDDI
Primer**

For a copy of a 456-page book on FDDI called "The Fiber Optic LAN HANDBOOK," contact Codenoll Corporation, 1086 N. Broadway, Yonkers, NY 10701, 914/965-6300.

FDISK

A utility program in DOS and Windows 95 that is used to partition a hard disk, which is necessary before high-level formatting.

FDM

(Frequency Division Multiplexing) A technology that transmits multiple signals simultaneously over a single transmission path, such as a cable or wireless system. Each signal travels within its own unique frequency range (carrier), which is modulated by the data (text, voice, video, etc.). Television uses FDM and transmits several TV channels from the same antenna. The TV tuner locks onto a particular frequency (channel) and filters out the video signal. Contrast with *TDM*. See also *WDM*.

FDMA

(Frequency Division Multiple Access) The technology used in the analog cellular telephone network that divides the spectrum into 30KHz channels. See *TDMA*, *CDMA* and *CDPD*.

FD:OCA

(Formatted Data:Object Content Architecture) An SAA-compliant (CCS) specification for formatting data in fields.

FDSE

(Full-Duplex Switched Ethernet) A type of switched Ethenet that uses full-duplexed network adapters and provides a 20 Mbps bi-directional transmission between nodes. It is expected that by 1995, most network adapters will have built-in full duplex capability and can be used in a switched environment.
FDSE improves network throughput from server to server as well as in video conferencing, both of which benefit from full-duplexed, bi-directional transmission.

FDX

See *full-duplex*.

FEA

(Finite Element Analysis) A mathematical technique for analyzing stress, which breaks down a physical structure into substructures, called finite elements. The finite elements and their interrelationships are converted into equation form and solved mathematically.
Graphics-based FEA software can display the model on screen as it is being built and, after analysis, display the object's reactions under load conditions. Models created in popular CAD packages can often be accepted by FEA software.

feasibility study

The analysis of a problem to determine if it can be solved effectively. The operational (will it work?), economical (costs and benefits) and technical (can it be built?) aspects are part of the study. Results of the study determine whether the solution should be implemented.

feature connector

See *VGA feature connector*.

feature negotiation

See *automatic feature negotiation*.

FEC

See *forward error correction.*

federal regulations

See *NCSC* and *Computer Security Act.*

female connector

A receptacle into which the male counterpart of the connector is plugged.

femto

One quadrillionth or 10 to the -15th power.

femtosecond

One quadrillionth of a second. See *space/time.*

FEP

See *front end processor.*

ferric oxide

(Fe^{2}O^3) An oxidation of iron used in the coating of magnetic disks and tapes.

ferromagnetic

The capability of a material, such as iron and nickel, to be highly magnetized. See *FRAM.*

ferromagnetic RAM

See *FRAM.*

FET

(Field Effect Transistor) The type of transistor used in CMOS and other types of MOS circuits. The transistor works by pulsing a line called the *gate,* which allows current to flow from the *source* to the *drain,* or vice versa depending on the design.

fetch

To locate the next instruction in memory for execution by the CPU.

FF

See *form feed.*

FFT

(Fast Fourier Transform) A class of algorithms used in digital signal processing that break down complex signals into elementary components.

fiber bundle

A set of adjacent optical fibers running in parallel and adhered together. It is used for transmitting light to brighten an area as well as transmitting whole images, but is not used for modern digital communications.

Fiber Channel

A type of transmission path used as an internal computer channel as well as a network medium. It works with existing interfaces, such as IPI, SCSI and HiPPI. In a LAN, it can be used as a high-speed backbone. Speeds range up to 100 MBytes/sec using optical fiber.

Fiber Distributed Data Interface

See *FDDI*.

fiber loss

The amount of attenuation of signal in an optical fiber transmission.

fiber optic

Communications systems that use optical fibers for transmission. Fiber-optic transmission became widely used in the 1980s when the long-distance carriers created nationwide systems for carrying voice conversations digitally over optical fibers.

Eventually, all transmission systems may become fiber optic-based. Also, in time, the internals of computers may be partially or even fully made of light circuits rather than electrical circuits. See *FDDI*, *Fiber Channel* and *optical fiber*.

fiber-optic connectors

There are several types of connectors used to connect pairs of optical fibers. The most popular are the ST and SMA connectors, which connect one optical fiber. The ST connector uses a bayonet mount, and the SMA connector uses a threaded mount.

The MIC and SC connectors each handle a pair of cables and the design of the plug and socket ensures that the polarity is maintained (transmit and receive cables are in correct order). The SC connector provides a strong connection that is hard to pull apart.

Attaching a fiber-optic connector to an optical fiber is a bit of an art. The end has to be cut in a special way and carefully polished in order to let the maximum light pass through. Most class time on the subject is "hands on."

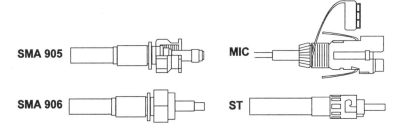

Fibonacci numbers

A series of whole numbers in which each number is the sum of the two preceding ones: 1, 1, 2, 3, 5, 8, 13, etc. It is used to speed up binary searches by dividing the search into the two lower numbers; for example, 13 items would be divided into 5 and 8 items; 8 items would be divided into 5 and 3.

fiche

Same as *microfiche*.

fiddy

See *FDDI*.

FidoNet

An E-mail protocol that originated from the Fido BBS created by Tom Jennings in 1984. Over 10,000 FidoNet nodes are in use. Users must have their networks active for one universal hour in the early morning, and the software must adhere to the FTSC-001 specification. The FidoNet address format is zone:local net/node; for example, Boardwatch Magazine's address is 1:104/555.

field

A physical unit of data that is one or more bytes in size. A collection of fields make up a record. A field also defines a unit of data on a source document, screen or report. Examples of fields are NAME, ADDRESS, QUANTITY and AMOUNT DUE.

The field is the common denominator between the user and the computer. When you interactively query and update your database, you reference your data by field name.

There are several terms that refer to the same unit of storage as a field. A *data element* is the logical definition of the field, and a *data item* is the actual data stored in the field. For each data element, there are many fields in the database that hold the data items.

In the following example, for the data elements Product description and Product no., there are fields in the database that hold the data items manilla folder, pencil, rubber band, and so forth.

Data Elements

	Product description	Product No.	
	FIELD	FIELD	

Data Items

manilla folder	O-3994
pencil	O-4387
rubber band	O-8993-2
copy paper	CP200-1
paper clip	P-4993
envelope	P-100-50

field engineer

A person who is responsible for hardware installation, maintentance and repair. Formal training is in electronics, although many people have learned on the job.

field name

An assigned name for a field (NAME, ADDRESS, CITY, STATE, etc.) that will be the same in every record.

field separator

A character used to mark the separation of fields in a record. See *comma delimited* and *tab delimited.*

field service

See *field engineer.*

field squeeze

In a mail merge, a function that eliminates extra blank spaces between words when fixed-length fields are inserted into the document text. See *line squeeze.*

field template
See *picture*.

FIF
(Fractal Image Format) A graphics file format from Iterated Systems, Inc., Norcross, GA, that stores fractal images with compression ratios as high as 2,500:1.

FIFO
(First In-First Out) A storage method that retrieves the item stored for the longest time. Contrast with *LIFO*.

fifth-generation computer
A computer designed for AI applications. Appearing in the late 1990s, these systems will represent the next technology leap.

file
A collection of bytes stored as an individual entity. All data on disk is stored as a file with an assigned file name that is unique within the directory it resides in.

To the computer, a file is nothing more than a series of bytes. The structure of a file is known to the software that manipulates it. For example, database files are made up of a series of records. Word processing files, also called documents, contain a continuous flow of text.

Following are the major types of files stored in a computer system. Except for ASCII text files, all files contain proprietary information contained in a header or interspersed throughout the file.

Type	Contents
data file (table)	data records
document	text
spreadsheet	rows and columns of cells
image	rows and columns of bits
drawing	list of vectors
audio	digitized sound waves
MIDI	MIDI instructions
video	digital video frames
batch file	text
source program	text
object program	
(EXE & COM file)	machine language

file and record locking
A first-come, first-served technique for managing data in a multiuser environment. The first user to access the file or record prevents, or locks out, other users from accessing it. After the file or record is updated, it is unlocked and available.

file association
(1) The relationship between the file and the application that created it. In the DOS/Windows world, the association is made by the file extension.
(2) The relationship of one file to another based on the data it contains.

file attribute
A file access classification that allows a file to be retrieved or erased. Typical attributes are read/write, read only, archive and hidden.

file find
A utility that searches all directories for matching file names.

file format

The structure of a file. There are hundreds of proprietary formats for database, word processing and graphics files. See *graphics formats* and *record layout*.

file grooming

Cleaning up the files on a computer system. It includes deleting temporary and backup files as well as defragmenting the disk.

file handle

A temporary reference assigned by the operating system to a file that has been opened. The handle is used to access the file throughout the session.

file layout

Same as *record layout*.

file maintenance

(1)The periodic updating of master files. For example, adding/deleting employees and customers, making address changes and changing product prices. It does not refer to daily transaction processing and batch processing (order processing, billing, etc.).
(2) The periodic reorganization of the disk drives. Data that is continuously updated becomes physically fragmented over the disk space and requires regrouping. An optimizing program is run (daily, weekly, etc.) that rewrites all files contiguously.

FileMaker II

A Macintosh file manager from Claris. It is a popular program for general data management and provides a variety of statistical functions, fast search capabilities and extensive reporting features.

FileMan

(1) Public-domain MUMPS software that provides a stand-alone, interactive DBMS as well as a set of utilities for the MUMPS programmer.
(2) Nickname for Windows' file manager, which is precisely named "File Manager."

file manager

(1) Software that manages data files. Often erroneously called database managers, file managers provide the ability to create, enter, change, query and produce reports on one file at a time. They have no relational capabilty and usually don't include a programming language.
(2) Software used to manage files on a disk. It provides functions to delete, copy, move, rename and view files as well as create and manage directories. The file manager in Windows 3.x is aptly named "File Manager."

file name

A name assigned by the user or programmer that is used to identify a file.

FileNet

A document imaging system from FileNet Corporation, Costa Mesa, CA. Introduced in 1985, FileNet is the most widely-used, high-end workflow system. It runs on PCs, Sun and Digital workstations and also offers an RS/6000 document server running UNIX and Oracle.

File Not Found

A DOS error message that means DOS cannot locate the file you have specified. Use the Dir command to check its spelling. It may be also be in another directory.

file protection

Preventing accidental erasing of data. Physical file protection is provided on the storage medium by turning a switch, moving a lever or covering a notch. On 1/2" tape, a plastic ring in the center of the reel is removed (no ring-no write). In these cases, writing is prohibited even if the software directs the computer to do so. Logical file protection is provided by the operating system, which can designate a single file as read only. This method allows both regular (read/write) and read only files to be stored on the same disk volume. Files can also be designated as hidden files, which makes them invisible to most software programs.

Protecting Floppies
In order to prevent a floppy disk from being erased or written over by the program or user when it's in the machine, do the following:

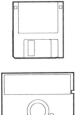

3.5" Diskettes
Looking at the back of the disk with the metal circle in the middle and the metal door at the top, slide the square, plastic window (bottom right) downward uncovering a hole through the disk.

5.25" Diskettes
Cover the small, square side notch with a label. If you don't have the reflective, self-adhesive label that came with the disk, use any Avery or similar type of stick-on label.
The method is exactly the opposite for both disks: uncover the 3.5", cover the 5.25". Of course!

file protect ring

A plastic ring inserted into a reel of magnetic tape for file protection.

file recovery program

Software that recovers disk files that have been accidentally deleted or damaged.

file server

A high-speed computer in a LAN that stores the programs and data files shared by users on the network. Also called a network server, it acts like a remote disk drive. See *database server*.

file sharing protocol

A communications protocol that provides a structure for file requests (open, read, write, close, etc.) between stations in a network. If file sharing is strictly between workstation and server, it is also called a client/server protocol. It refers to layer 7 of the OSI model.

file size

The length of a file in bytes. See "Byte Specifications" in the term *byte*.

file spec

(file SPECification) A reference to the location of a file on a disk, which includes disk drive, directory name and file name. For example, in DOS and OS/2, c:\wordstar\books\chapter is a file spec for the file CHAPTER in the BOOKS subdirectory in the WORDSTAR directory on drive C.

file system

(1) A method for cataloging files in a computer system. See *hierarchical file system*.
(2) A data processing application that manages individual files. Files are related by customized programming. Contrast with *relational database*.

file transfer program

A program that transmits files from one computer to another. Such programs; for example, Travelling Software's LapLink and the Interlink utility that comes with DOS 6, allow the user to control both computers from one machine. See *FTP*.

file transfer protocol

A communications protocol used to transmit files without loss of data. A file transfer protocol can handle all types of files including binary files and ASCII text files. Common examples are Xmodem, Ymodem, Zmodem and Kermit.

file viewer

Software that displays the contents of a file as it would be normally displayed by the application that created it. A single file viewer program is generally capable of displaying a wide variety of document, database and spreadsheet formats. Examples of file viewers for Windows are Symantec's Norton File Viewer, Phoenix Technologies' Eclipse Find and Systems Compatibility's Outside In. See *document exchange software*.

fill

(1) In a paint program, to change the color of a bordered area.
(2) In a spreadsheet, to enter common or repetitive values into a group of cells.

fill pattern

(1) A color, shade or pattern used to fill an area of an image.
(2) Signals transmitted by a LAN station when not receiving or transmitting data in order to maintain synchronization.

fill scaling

The ability to change a fill pattern from light to dense. For example, if polka dots were used, the fill pattern could range from thick dots widely separated to very thin dots tightly packed together.

film recorder

A device that takes a 35mm slide picture from a graphics file, which has been created in a CAD, paint or business graphics package. It generates very high resolution, generally from 2,000 to 4,000 lines.
It typically works by recreating the image on a built-in CRT that shines through a color wheel onto the film in a standard 35mm camera. Some units provide optional Polaroid camera backs for instant previewing. Film recorders can be connected to personal computers by plugging in a controller board cabled to the recorder.

filter

(1) A process that changes data, such as a sort routine that changes the sequence of items or a conversion routine (import or export filter) that changes one data, text or graphics format into another. See also *image filter*.
(2) A pattern or mask through which only selected data is passed. For example, certain e-mail systems can be programmed to filter out important messages and alert the user. In dBASE, **set filter to file overdue**, compares all data to the matching conditions stored in OVERDUE.

financial planning language

A language used to create data models and command a financial planning system.

financial planning system

Software that helps the user evaluate alternatives. It allows for the creation of a data model, which is a series of data elements in equation form; for example, **gross profit**

= **gross sales - cost of goods sold**. Different values can be plugged into the elements, and the impact of various options can be assessed (what if?).

A financial planning system is a step above a spreadsheet by providing additional analysis tools; however, increasingly, these capabilities are being built into spreadsheets. For example, sensitivity analysis assigns a range of values to a data element, which causes that data to be highlighted if it ever exceeds that range. Goal seeking provides automatic calculation. For example, by entering **gross margin** = 50% as well as the minimums and maximums of the various inputs, the program will calculate an optimum mix of inputs to achieve the goal (output).

Finder

The part of the Macintosh operating systems that keeps track of icons, controls the Clipboard and Scrapbook and allows files to be copied. Finder originally managed one application at a time and was superseded by MultiFinder, which managed multiple applications. Later, MultiFinder was incorporated into Finder.

finger

A UNIX command widely used on the Internet to find out if a particular user is currently logged on. Some systems provide additional information such as voice number and the last time the user logged on. The person being "fingered" must have placed his or her profile on the system.

finger mouse

Same as *touchpad.*

fingerprint reader

A scanner used to identify a person's fingerprint for security purposes. After a sample is taken, access to a computer or other system is granted if the fingerprint matches the stored sample. A PIN may also be used with the fingerprint sample.

finite element

See *FEA.*

finite state machine

See *state machine.*

Fingerprint Reader
(Photo courtesy of Identix, Inc.)

firewall

A network node set up as a boundary to prevent traffic from one segment to cross over to another. Firewalls are used to improve network traffic as well as for security purposes. A firewall may be implemented in a router or it may be a device specialized for such purposes.

FireWire

A serial bus developed by Apple and Texas Instruments that allows for the connection of up to 63 devices at speeds ranging as high as 400 Mbits/sec. Also known as P1394, the FireWire is expected to become a replacement for SCSI, providing a single plug and play interface technology for all peripheral devices, including printers.

firmware

A category of memory chips that hold their content without electrical power and include ROM, PROM, EPROM and EEPROM technologies. Firmware becomes "hard software" when holding program code.

first-generation computer
A computer that used vacuum tubes as switching elements; for example, the UNIVAC I.

fixed disk
A non-removable hard disk such as is found in most personal computers. Programs and data are copied to and from the fixed disk.

fixed-frequency monitor
A monitor that accepts one type of video signal, such as VGA only. Contrast with *multiscan monitor*.

fixed head disk
A direct access storage device, such as a disk or drum, that has a read/write head for each track. Since there is no access arm movement, access times are significantly improved.

fixed length field
A constant field size; for example, a 25-byte name field takes up 25 bytes in each record. It is easier to program, but wastes disk space and restricts file design. Description and comment fields are always a dilemma. Short fields allow only abbreviated remarks, while long fields waste space if lengthy comments are not required in every record. Contrast with *variable length field.*

fixed length record
A data record that contains fixed length fields.

fixed point
A method for storing and calculating numbers in which the decimal point is always in the same location. Contrast with *floating point.*

FK
See *foreign key.*

Fkey
(Function key) A Macintosh command sequence using command, shift and option key combinations. For example, Fkey 1 (command-shift 1) ejects the internal floppy.

F keys
See *function keys.*

flag
(1) In communications, a code in the transmitted message which indicates that the following characters are a control code and not data.
(2) In programming, a "yes/no" indicator built into certain hardware or created and controlled by the programmer.
(3) A UNIX command line argument. The symbol is a dash. For example, in the command **head -15 filex**, which prints the first 15 lines of the file FILEX, the -15 flag modifies the Head command.

flame
To communicate emotionally and/or excessively via electronic mail. In other words, "online cursing." See *netiquette.*

flame bait

A subject posted to an Internet newsgroup that is designed to produce an emotional reaction and start a flame war.

flame war

In an Internet newsgroup, an ongoing tirade of contrasting opinions about a topic.

flash BIOS

A PC BIOS that is stored in flash memory rather than in a ROM. Flash BIOSs can be updated in place, whereas ROM BIOSs must be replaced with a newer chip. See *BIOS*.

flash disk

A solid state disk made of flash memory. It emulates a standard disk drive in contrast with flash memory cards, which require proprietary software to make them function.

flash memory

A memory chip that holds its content without power, but must be erased in fixed blocks rather than single bytes. Block sizes typically range from 512 bytes up to 256KB. The term was coined by Toshiba for its ability to be erased "in a flash." Derived from EEPROMs, flash chips are less expensive and provide higher bit densities. Flash is also becoming an alternative to EPROMS, because it can be easily updated.

Flash memory is used in PCMCIA memory cards, PCMCIA flash disks and other types of solid state disks, embedded controllers and smart cards. It typically has a lifespan of 100K write cycles, but newer chips can be written a million times.

If flash memory or a derivative technology can be made to erase one byte at a time, it may lead to a non-volatile RAM some day.

To receive the "Focus On Flash" newsletter on the flash memory market, contact M-Systems, 556 Mowry Avenue, Suite 103, Fremont, CA 94536, 510/505-9081 (fax 9084).

Flashpoint

A screen scraper from Sterling Software, Atlanta, GA (formerly KnowledgeWare), that is used to turn a character-based mainframe screen into a Windows front end.

flat address space

A memory that is addressed starting with 0. Each susequent byte is referenced by the next sequential number (0, 1, 2, 3, 4, etc.) all the way to the end of memory. This is normal addressing in contrast to segmented addressing, which addresses memory in blocks. Contrast with *segmented address space*.

flatbed plotter

A graphics plotter that draws on sheets of paper that have been placed in a bed. The size of the bed determines the maximum size sheet that can be drawn.

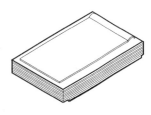

flatbed scanner

A scanner that provides a flat, glass surface to hold pages of paper, books and other objects for scanning. The scan head is moved under the glass across the page. Sheet feeders are usually optionally available that allow multiple sheets to be fed automatically. Contrast with *sheet-fed scanner, hand-held scanner* and *drum scanner*.

flat file

A stand-alone data file that does not have any pre-defined linkages or pointers to locations of data in other files. This is the type of file used in a relational database;

however, the term is often used to refer to a type of file that has no relational capability, exactly the opposite. This business can drive you nuts!

flat panel display

A thin display screen that uses any of a number of technologies, such as LCD, electroluminscent or plasma. Used today in laptops to reduce size and weight, they will eventually supersede CRTs.

flat screen

(1) A display screen in which the CRT viewing surface is flatter than most CRTs, which are slightly rounded. The flat screen provides less distortion at the edges. (2) See *flat panel display*.

flat shading

In computer graphics, a technique for computing a one-tone shaded surface to simulate simple lighting.

FLC file

An animation file format from AutoDesk, Inc., Sausalito, CA, that is commonly known as a "flick" file. It uses the .FLC file extension and provides a 640x480 resolution. An earlier .FLI format provides 320x200 resolution. Both FLC and FLI files provide animated sequences, but not sound. FLI and FLC formats were introduced respectively with Autodesk's Animator and Animator Pro programs for DOS.

flexible disk

Same as *floppy disk* and *diskette*.

flicker

A fluctuating image on a video screen. See *interlaced*.

flick file

See *FLC file*.

FLI file

See *FLC file*.

flip-flop

An electronic circuit that alternates between two states. When current is applied, it changes to its opposite state (0 to 1 or 1 to 0). Made of several transistors, it is used in the design of static memories and hardware registers.

flippy board

A PC expansion board that connects to both ISA/EISA and Micro Channel buses. ISA/EISA connectors are on one edge of the board; MCA on the other.

float

In programming, a declaration of a floating point number.

Flat Panel
The flat panel display has allowed the laptop to flourish. In time, even desktop screens will use flat panel technology.

Mantissa	Exponent		Actual value
6508	0	=	6508
6508	1	=	65080
6508	-1	=	650.8

floating point

A method for storing and calculating numbers in which the decimal points do not line up as in fixed point numbers. The significant digits are stored as a unit called the mantissa, and the location of the radix point (decimal point in base 10) is stored in a separate unit called the exponent. Floating point methods are used for calculating a large range of numbers quickly.

Floating point operations can be implemented in hardware (math coprocessor), or they can be done in software. In large sysems, they can also be performed in a separate floating point processor that is connected to the main processor via a channel.

floating point processor

An arithmetic unit designed to perform floating point operations. It may be a coprocessor chip in a personal computer, a CPU designed with built-in floating point capabilities or a separate machine, often called an *array processor*, which is connected to the main computer.

floppy disk

A reusable magnetic storage medium. It is the primary method for distributing personal computer software. It's also used to transfer data between users, although local area networks can eliminate much of this "sneakernet."

Also called a diskette, the floppy is a flexible disk, similar to tape, with both surfaces used for magnetic recording. The disk drive grabs the floppy's center and spins it inside its housing, and the read/write head makes contact with the surface through an opening in the floppy's envelope, case or cartridge.

Floppies are much slower than hard disks, because they spin at 300 rpm, at least one tenth the rotation of a hard disk, and they are at rest until a data transfer is requested. In order of last to first developed, the major types are:

External format	Capacity	Creator
3.5" rigid case	400KB - 2.8MB	Sony
5.25" flexible envelope	100KB - 1.2MB	Shugart
8" flexible envelope	100 - 500KB	IBM

Although floppy disks look the same, what's recorded on them determines their capacity and compatibility. Each new floppy must be "formatted," which records the sectors on the disk that will hold the data. Many 3.5" disk drives can read DOS disks as well as their native format. See *format program* and *magnetic disk*.

The 3.5" Microfloppy Diskette

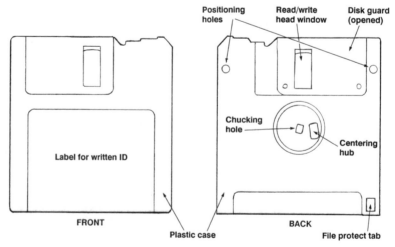

Positioning holes   Read/write head window   Disk guard (opened)

Chucking hole   Centering hub

Label for written ID

FRONT   BACK

Plastic case   File protect tab

FLOPS

(FLoating point Operations Per Second) A unit of measurement of floating point calculations. For example, 100 megaflops is 100 million floating point operations per second.

Floptical

A type of floppy disk that records data magnetically, but uses grooves in the disk to optically align the head over the tracks. The original 3.5" drive from Insite Peripherals, San Jose, CA, reads and writes 21MB Floptical and standard 1.44MB diskettes. The technology never caught on, but a 120MB version is expected from Compaq, 3M and Matsushita-Kotobuki Electronics, which is also compatible with standard diskettes.

flowchart

A graphical representation of the sequence of operations in an information system or program. Information system flow charts show how data flows from source documents through the computer to final distribution to users. Program flow charts show the sequence of instructions in a single program or subroutine. Different symbols are used to draw each type of flow chart.

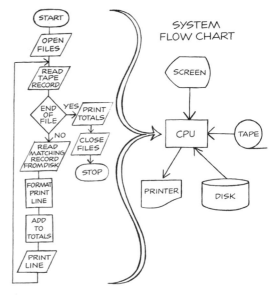

flowcharting program

See *diagramming program.*

flow control

(1) In communications, the management of transmission between two devices. It is concerned with the timing of signals and enables slower-speed devices to communicate with higher-speed ones. There are various techniques, but all are designed to ensure that the receiving station is able to accept the next block of data before the sending station sends it. See *xon-xoff.*

(2) In programming, the if-then and loop statements that make up the program's logic.

flush

To empty the contents of a memory buffer onto disk.

flush center

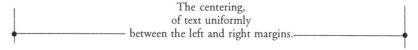

The centering,
of text uniformly
between the left and right margins.

flush left

The alignment of text uniformly to the left margin. All text is typically set flush left as is this paragraph.

flush right

The alignment of text uniformly to the right
margin while the left margin is
set ragged left.

flux

The energy field generated by a magnet.

flux transition

The change of magnetic polarity from 0 to 1 or 1 to 0 on a magnetic disk or tape.

FM

(1) (Frequency Modulation) A transmission technique that blends the data signal into a carrier by varying (modulating) the frequency of the carrier. See *modulate*.
(2) (Frequency Modulation) An earlier magnetic disk encoding method that places clock bits onto the medium along with the data bits. It has been superseded by MFM and RLL.

FM synthesis

A MIDI technique that simulates the sound of musical instruments. It uses operators, typically four of them, which create wave forms or modulate the wave forms. FM synthesis does not create sound as faithfully as wave table synthesis, which uses actual samples of the instruments.

Fn key

(FuNction key) A keyboard key that works like a shift key to activate the second function on a dual-purpose key, typically found on laptops to reduce keyboard size. It is different than the function keys F1, F2, etc.

FOCA

(Font Object Content Architecture) See *MO:DCA*.

FOCUS

(1) A DBMS from Information Builders, Inc., New York, that runs on PCs, mainframes and minis. It allows relational, hierarchical and network data structures and can access a variety of databases, including standard IBM mainframe files, DB2, IMS, IDMS and others. It includes a fourth-generation language and a variety of decision support facilities.
(2) (Federation On Computing in the U.S.) The U.S. representative of IFIP. Address: IEEE Computer Society, 1730 Mass. Ave. N.W., Washington, DC 20036, 202/371-0101.

FOIA

(Freedom Of Information Act) A U.S. Government rule that states that public information shall be delivered within 10 days of request.

FOIRL

(Fiber Optic Inter Repeater Link) An IEEE standard for fiber optic Ethernet. FOIRL and 10BaseF are compatible, but FOIRL is an earlier standard generally used to extend a backbone beyond the 328 foot limitation of 10BaseT. FOIRL is limited to .6 miles distance per segment, whereas 10BaseF segments can extend to 1.2 miles. 10BaseF is a more comprehensive standard for complete fiber-based installations.

folder

In the Macintosh and Windows 95, a simulated file folder that holds data, applications and other folders. A folder is the same as a DOS directory, and a folder within a folder (subfolder) is the same as a DOS subdirectory. Folders were popularized on the Mac and later adapted to UNIX and Windows.

foldering

Using folders to store and manipulate documents on screen.

Folio

(1) Text management software for PCs from Folio Corporation, Provo, UT, that provides storage, retrieval and hypertext capability for text databases. It can import text from over 40 file formats. Folio files are called *Infobases*.
(2) (folio) In typography, a printed page number. For example, folio 3 could be the 27th physical page in a book.

FON file

(FONt file) In Windows 3.1 and 95, a file that contains a font used for on-screen displays (menus, buttons, etc.) by Windows and Windows applications as well as by DOS applications running under Windows. Most .FON files contain bitmapped fonts. Contrast with *TTF file*.

font

A set of type characters of a particular typeface design and size. Usually, each typeface (Times Roman, Helvetica, Arial, etc.) is made available in four variations: normal weight, bold, italic and bold italic. Thus, for bitmapped fonts, which are fully generated ahead of time, four fonts would be required for each point size used in each typeface. For scalable fonts, which are generated in any point size on the fly, only four fonts would be required for each typeface.
Fonts come built into the printer, as plug-in cartridges or as soft fonts, which reside on the computer's hard disk or a hard disk built into the printer. See *bitmapped font* and *scalable font*.

font cartridge

A set of bitmapped or outline fonts for one or more typefaces contained in a plug-in module for the printer. The fonts are stored in a ROM chip within the cartridge. Contrast with *soft font* and *internal font*.

font characteristics

Font selection in an HP LaserJet is made by sending a coded command to the printer with the following criteria:

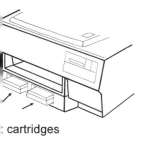

cartridges

Code:	Characteristic:
Typeface	Design (Courier, Times Roman, etc.)
Orientation	Portrait or landscape
Symbol set	Country or special characters
Spacing	Proportional or fixed width
Pitch	Characters per inch (fixed spacing)
Point size	Height of characters
Style	Upright or italic
Stroke weight	Light, medium or bold appearance

font compiler

Same as *font generator*.

font editor

Software that allows fonts to be designed and modified.

font family

A set of fonts of the same typeface in assorted sizes, including bold, italic and bold italic variations.

font generator

Software that converts an outline font into a bitmap (dot pattern required for a particular font size). Font generation is not linear, simply expanding a letter to any size. As fonts get bigger, their characteristics must change in order to make them attractive.

Font generation is used to create bitmapped fonts, which are fully generated and stored on disk before use. Contrast with *font scaler*, which generates the font in any point size the instant it is needed for display or printing.

font manager

See *font scaler*.

font metric

Typographic information (width, height, kerning) for each character in a font.

font number

An identification number assigned to a font. A program references the font by this number.

font rasterizer

See *font scaler*.

font scaler

Software that converts scalable fonts into bitmaps on the fly as required for display or printing. Examples are TrueType, Adobe Type Manager and Bitstream's Facelift. See *scalable font* and *font generator*.

font style

A typeface variation (normal, bold, italic, bold italic).

font utility

Software that provides functions for managing fonts, including the ability to download, install, design and modify fonts.

Fontware

A font generator for various DOS applications from Bitstream Inc., Cambridge, MA, which includes a library of typeface outlines in normal, italic, bold and bold italic weights. FontWare has been discontinued in favor of newer scalable font technogies. See *font scaler*.

font weight

The thickness of characters (light, medium or bold).

foo

A popular name for a temporary file, function or variable, or example of same. Often used in conjunction with "bar," from "fubar" (Fouled Up Beyond All Recognition).

footer

In a document or report, common text that appears at the bottom of every page. It usually contains the page number.

footnote

Text that appears at the bottom of a page, which adds explanation. It is often used to give credit to the source of information. When accumulated and printed at the end of a document, they are called *endnotes*.

footprint

The amount of geographic space covered by an object. A computer footprint is the desk or floor surface it occupies. A satellite's footprint is the earth area covered by its downlink.

Force

A dBASE compiler from Sophco, Inc., Boulder, CO, that combines C and dBASE structures. It is noted for generating very small executable programs.

foreground/background

The priority assigned to programs running in a multitasking environment. In a multiuser environment, foreground programs have highest priority, and background programs have lowest. Online users are given the foreground, and batch processing activities (sorts, updates, etc.) are given the background. If batch activities are given a higher priority, terminal response times may slow down considerably.

In a personal computer, the foreground program is the one the user is currently working with, and the background program might be a print spooler or communications program.

foreign key

In relational database, it is a field in one table that is indexed in another. Foreign keys provide the building blocks for relating tables. For example, in a customer order table, the salesperson field might contain an employee number. That field would be a foreign key in the table, because the employee table would be indexed on employee number.

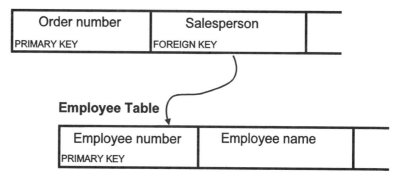

ForeRunner

A family of ATM adapters from Fore Systems, Warrendale, PA.

Forest & Trees

A data analysis program for PCs from Trinzic Corporation, Portsmouth, NH, that integrates data from a variety of applications. It provides a control room interface that lets users monitor important business information.

Fore Systems

(Fore Systems, Inc., Warrendale, PA) A manufacturer of ATM switches and network adapters. Fore is the pioneer in ATM adapters for LANs and is a market leader in ATM products.

fork

(1) In UNIX, to make a copy of a process for execution.
(2) In the Macintosh, a part of a file. See *data fork* and *resource fork*.

form

(1) A paper form used for printing.
(2) A screen display designed for a particular application.

format

The structure, or layout, of an item.
Screen formats are the layout of fields on the screen.
Report formats are the columns, headers and footers on a page.
Record formats are the fields within a record.
File formats are the structure of data and program files, word processing documents and graphics files (display lists and bitmaps) with all their proprietary headers and codes. See *format program, disk format* and *style sheet*.

format program

Software that initializes a disk. There are two formatting levels. The low-level initializes the disk surface by creating the physical tracks and storing sector identification in them. Low-level format programs lay out the sectors as required by the particular drive technology used (IDE, SCSI, etc.).
The high-level format creates the indexes used by the operating system (Mac, DOS, etc.) to keep track of data stored in the sectors.
Floppy disk format programs perform both levels on a diskette.

formatted text

Text that contains codes for font changes, headers, footers, boldface, italics and other page and document attributes. Word processors create formatted text, but all the major ones use their own coding systems. See *ASCII file*.

form factor

The physical size of a device.

form feed

Advancing a printer form to the top of the next page. It is done by pressing the printer's form feed (FF) button or by sending the form feed code (ASCII 12) to the printer from the computer.

forms software

(1) Workflow software used to create on-screen data entry forms and provide e-mail routing and tracking of the resulting electronic documents.
(2) Program development tools that build applications by designing the on-screen forms for data entry, update and so on. The forms are generally designed with visual programming tools that allow fields, buttons and logos to be drawn directly on screen. The business logic is either selected via menus and/or written in behind each field or button with lines of 4GL or 3GL programming code.

formula

(1) An arithmetic expression that solves a problem. For example, (fahrenheit-32)*5/9 is the formula for converting Fahrenheit to Celsius.
(2) In spreadsheets, an algorithm that identifies how the data in a specific number of

cells is to be calculated. For example, **+C3*D8** means that the contents of cell C3 are to be multiplied by the contents of cell D8 and the results are to be placed where the formula is located.

form view

A screen display showing one item or record arranged like a preprinted form. Contrast with *table view*.

for statement

A high-level programming language structure that repeats a series of instructions a specified number of times. It creates a loop that includes its own control information. The following BASIC and C examples print "Hello" 10 times:

```
BASIC                    C
for x = 1 to 10          for (x = 0;  x < 10;  x++)
print "hello"            printf ("hello\n");
next x
```

Forte

An application development system for enterprise client/server environments from Forte Software, Inc., Oakland, CA. Introduced in 1994, it is a repository-driven system that supports Windows, Mac and Motif clients and all the major UNIX servers as well as VMS. It supports Oracle, Sybase and Rdb databases and provides partitioning for creating three-tier applications. Testing and debugging is done in an interpreted mode while production programs are compiled into C++ code.

FORTH

(FOuRTH-generation language) A high-level programming language created by Charles Moore in the late 1960s as a way of providing direct control of the computer. Its syntax resembles LISP, it uses reverse polish notation for calculations, and it is noted for its extensibility.

It is both compiler and interpreter. The source program is compiled first and then executed by its operating system/interpreter. It is used in process control applications that must quickly process data acquired from instruments and sensors. It is also used in arcade game programming as well as robotics and other AI applications. The following polyFORTH example converts Fahrenheit to Celsius:

```
: CONV ( n) 32 - 5 9 * / . ." Celsius
: USER_INPUT  ." Enter Fahrenheit " CONV ;
```

FORTRAN

(FORmula TRANslator) The first high-level programming language and compiler, developed in 1954 by IBM. It was originally designed to express mathematical formulas, and although it is used occasionally for business applications, it is still the most widely used language for scientific, engineering and mathematical problems. FORTRAN IV is an ANSI standard, but FORTRAN V has various proprietary versions. The following FORTRAN example converts Fahrenheit to Celsius:

```
WRITE(6,*) 'Enter Fahrenheit '
READ(5,*) XFAHR
XCENT = (XFAHR - 32) * 5 / 9
WRITE(6,*) 'Celsius is ',XCENT
STOP
END
```

forum

An information interchange regarding a specific topic or product that is hosted on an online service or BBS. It can include the latest news on the subject, a conferencing capability for questions and answers by participants as well as files for downloading fixes, demos and other related material.

forward chaining

In AI, a form of reasoning that starts with what is known and works toward a solution. Known as bottom-up approach. Contrast with *backward chaining*.

forward compatible

Same as *upward compatible*.

forward error correction

A communications technique that can correct bad data on the receiving end. Before transmission, the data is processed through an algorithm that adds extra bits for error correction. If the transmitted message is received in error, the correction bits are used to repair it.

FOT file

(FOnt TrueType file) A TrueType font file in Windows that points to the location of the TTF file, which contains the actual mathematical outlines of the font. See *TTF file*.

foundry

A semiconductor manufacturer that makes chips for third parties. It may be a large chip maker that sells its excess manufacturing capacity or one that makes chips exclusively for other companies. As of 1995, it costs at least a billion dollars to construct a high-production semiconductor manufacturing plant that produces standard chips. See *fabless*.

fountain fill

In computer graphics, a painted area that smoothly changes its color or pattern density. A radial fountain fill starts at the center of an area and radiates outward.

fourth-generation computer

A computer made up almost entirely of chips with limited amounts of discrete components. We are currently in the fourth generation.

fourth-generation language

Also known as a *4GL*, it is a computer language that is more advanced than traditional high-level programming languages. For example, in dBASE, the command **List** displays all the records in a data file. In second- and third-generation languages, instructions would have to be written to read each record, test for end of file, place each item of data on screen and go back and repeat the operation until there are no more records to process.

First-generation languages are machine languages; second-generation are machine dependent assembly languages; third-generation are high-level programming languages, such as FORTRAN, COBOL, BASIC, Pascal, and C.

Although many languages, such as dBASE, are called fourth-generation languages, they are actually a mix of third and fourth. The dBASE List command is a fourth-generation command, but applications programmed in dBASE are third-generation. The following example shows the difference between dBASE third- and fourth-generation syntax to open a customer file and display all names and addresses on screen.

dBASE 3GL	dBASE 4GL
| ```
use customer
do while .not. eof
? name, address
skip
enddo
``` | ```
use customer
list name, address
``` |

Query language and report writers are also fourth-generation languages. Any computer language with English-like commands that doesn't require traditional input-process-output logic falls into this category.

Many fourth-generation language functions are also built into graphical interfaces and activated by clicking and dragging. The commands are embedded into menus and buttons that are selected in an appropriate sequence.

FoxBASE+

A dBASE III PLUS-compatible DBMS for the Macintosh from Microsoft. Originally developed by Fox Software for the PC, FoxBASE gained a reputation for its speed and compatibility.

FoxPro

A dBASE IV-compatible DBMS from Microsoft for PCs. An enhanced version of FoxBASE, FoxPro includes windowing, SQL and QBE interfaces and "Rushmore" technology for fast queries on large databases.

FPGA

(Field Programmable Gate Array) A programmable logic chip with a high density of gates.

fps

(1) (Frames Per Second) See *frame*.
(2) (FPS) (Floating Point Systems, Inc., Beaverton, OR) A supercomputer manufacturer.

FPU

(Floating Point Unit) A computer circuit that handles floating point operations.

Fractal Design Painter

See *Painter*.

fractals

A lossy compression method used for color images. It provides ratios of 100:1 or greater and is especially suited to natural objects, such as trees, clouds and rivers. It turns an image into a set of data and an algorithm for expanding it back to the original.

The term comes from "fractus," which is Latin for broken or fragmented. It was coined by IBM Fellow and doctor of mathematics Benoit Mandelbrot, who expanded on ideas from earlier mathematicians and discovered similarities in chaotic and random events and shapes.

fractional T1

A service that provides less than full T1 capacity. One or more 64 Kbits/sec channels are provided.

FRAD

(Frame Relay Assembler/Dissassembler) A communications device that formats outgoing data into the format required by a frame relay network. It strips the data back out at the other end. It is the frame relay counterpart to the X.25 PAD.

fragmentation

The non-contiguous storage of data on disk. As files are updated, new data is stored in available free space, which may not be contiguous. Fragmented files cause extra head movement, slowing disk accesses. A disk maintenance, or optimizer, program is used to rewrite and reorder all the files.

FRAM

(1) (Ferroelectronic RAM) A non-volatile semiconductor memory that retains its content without power for up to 10 years.
(2) (Ferromagnetic RAM) A non-volatile memory that records microscopic bits on a magnetic surface.

frame

(1) In computer graphics, one screenful of data or its equivalent storage space.
(2) In communications, a fixed block of data transmitted as a single entity. Also called a *packet*.
(3) In desktop publishing, a movable, resizable box that holds a graphic image.
(4) In AI, a data structure that holds a general description of an object, which is derived from basic concepts and experience.

frame buffer

An area of memory used to hold a frame of data. A frame buffer is typically used for screen display and is the size of the maximum image area on screen. It is a separate memory bank on the display adapter that holds the bitmapped image while it is being "painted" on screen. Sophisticated graphics systems are built with several memory planes, each holding one or more bits of the pixel.

frame grabber

A device that accepts standard TV signals and digitizes the current video frame into a bitmap image.

FrameMaker

A desktop publishing program from Frame Technology Corporation, San Jose, CA, that runs on UNIX platforms, Macintosh and Windows. It is noted for its large number of advanced features, including full text and graphics editing capabilities. Optional viewers let documents run on machines without FrameMaker, providing a way to distribute hypertext-based help systems. In late 1995, Frame was acquired by Adobe.

frame relay

A high-speed packet switching protocol used in wide area networks (WANs). It has become popular for LAN to LAN connections across remote distances, and services are provided by all the major carriers. Frame relay is faster than traditional X.25 networks, because it was designed for today's reliable circuits and performs less rigorous error detection.
Frame relay provides for a granular service up to DS1 rates of 1.544 Mbps and is suited for data and image transfer. Because of its variable-length packet architecture, it is not the most efficient technology for realtime voice and video.

framework

(1) In object-oriented programming, a generalized subsystem design for building

applications. It consists of abstract classes and their object collaboration as well as concrete classes. While object-oriented programming supports software reuse, frameworks support design reuse.

(2) (FrameWork) One of the first integrated software packages for PCs that included a programming language. It was developed by Ashton-Tate, later acquired by Borland.

framing bit

Same as *start bit* and *stop bit*.

free-form database

A database system that allows entry of text without regard to length or order. Although it accepts data as does a word processor, it differs by providing better methods for searching, retrieving and organizing the data.

free-form language

A language in which statements can reside anywhere on a line or even cross over lines. It does not imply less syntax structure, just more freedom in placing statements. For example, any number of blank spaces are allowed between symbols. Most high-level programming languages are free-form.

FreeHand

See *Macromedia FreeHand*.

Freelance Graphics

A presentation graphics program for Windows from Lotus that is also part of Lotus' SmartSuite set of applications.

Freeman Reports

A series of technical reports on data storage devices from Ray Freeman of Freeman Associates, Inc., Santa Barbara, CA. They provide exhaustive detail about the disk and tape industry and include up-to-date data on the technology, capacities, purposes, market share and future trends.

Free Software Foundation

A non-profit organization founded in 1985 by Richard Stallman, dedicated to eliminating restrictions on copying and modifying programs by promoting the development and use of freely redistributable software. Its GNU computing environment, X Windows and other programs are available for a transaction charge. Address: 675 Mass. Ave., Cambridge, MA 02139, 617/876-3296, Internet: gnu@prep.ai.mit.edu. See *League for Programming Freedom*.

freeware

Software distributed without charge. Ownership is retained by the developer who has control over its redistribution, including the ability to change the next release of the freeware to payware. See *shareware* and *public domain software*.

freeze-frame video

Video transmission in which the image is changed once every couple of seconds rather than 30 times per second as is required in full-motion video.

frequency

The number of oscillations (vibrations) in an alternating current within one second. See *frequency response, audio* and *carrier*.

frequency range

In a communications system, the range of frequencies from the lowest to the highest. In a high-fidelity audio system, this would be typically from 20Hz to 20,000Hz.

frequency response

In an audio system, the accuracy of sound reproduction. A totally flat response means that there is no increase or decrease in volume level across the frequency range. Measured in decibels (dB), this would be plus or minus 0 dB from 20Hz to 20,000Hz. A high-end audio system can deviate by +/- 0.5 dB, but a CD-ROM drive should not be off by more than +/- 3 dB.

friction feed

A mechanism that allows cut paper forms to be used in a printer. The paper is passed between the platen and a roller that presses tightly against it. Contrast with *tractor feed.*

frob

To manipulate and adjust dials and buttons for fun. From the term "frobnicate," of course.

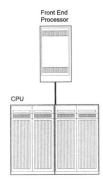

Front End Processor

CPU

front-end CASE

CASE tools that aid in systems analysis and design. Contrast with *back-end CASE.*

front end processor

A computer that handles communications processing for a mainframe. It connects to the communications lines on one end and the mainframe on the other. It transmits and receives messages, assembles and disassembles packets and detects and corrects errors. It is sometimes synonymous with a communications controller, although the latter is usually not as flexible.

frontware

Same as *screen scraper.*

FSK

(Frequency Shift Keying) A simple modulation technique that merges binary data into a carrier. It creates only two changes in frequency: one for 0, another for 1.

FSN

(Full-Service Network) A communications network that provides shopping, movies on demand and access to databases and a variety of online, interactive services. Telephone, cable and TV companies are positioning themselves to provide FSN services that are expected to evolve throughout the 1990s.

FSR

(Free System Resource) In Windows, the amount of unused memory in a 64K block (128K for Version 3.1) reserved for managing current applications. Every open window takes some space in this area. See *Windows memory limitation.*

FSTN

(Film Compensated STN) A type of passive matrix display technology that uses a film as as a compensating layer between the STN display and rear polarizer. It produces an almost-pure black and white display with little color tinge and weighs less than DSTN technology. Most laptops today employ FSTN technology in their LCD screens. See *DSTN* and *LCD.*

FT-1

See *fractional T1*.

FTAM

(File Transfer Access and Management) A communications protocol for the transfer of files between systems of different vendors.

FTP

(File Transfer Protocol/File Transfer Program) In a TCP/IP network (Internet, UNIX, etc.), a set of commands used to log onto the network, list directories and copy files. It can also convert between the ASCII and EBCDIC character codes. See *anonymous FTP* and *TFTP*.

FTP site

A computer system on the Internet that maintains files for downloading. See *anonymous FTP*.

FTS 2000

(Federal Telecommunications System 2000) A digital fiber-optic network providing voice, video, e-mail and high-speed data communications for the U.S. government. AT&T and Sprint are the major equipment providers.

FTX

(Fault Tolerant UNIX) Stratus Computer's version of UNIX System V for its XA/R fault tolerant computer systems.

FUD factor

(Fear Uncertainty Doubt factor) A marketing strategy used by a dominant or privileged organization that restrains competition by not revealing future plans.

full backup

See *backup types*.

full-duplex

Transmitting and receiving simultaneously. In pure digital networks, this is achieved with two pairs of wires. In analog networks or in digital networks using carriers, it is achieved by dividing the bandwidth of the line into two frequencies, one for sending, the other for receiving.

full featured

Hardware or software that provides capabilities and functions comparable to the most advanced models or programs of that category.

full-height drive

A 5.25" disk drive that measures 3.25" in height. It was the size of first-generation drives in desktop computers, but high-capacity hard drives are still made in this size. A full-height drive bay allows for the installation of one full-height drive or two half-height drives. Contrast with *half-height drive*.

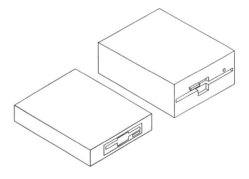

full-motion video

Video transmission that changes the image 30 frames per second (30 fps). Motion pictures are run at 24 fps, which is the minimum frequency required to eliminate the perception of moving frames and make the images appear visually fluid to the eye.

TV video generates 30 interlaced frames per second, which is actually transmitted as 60 half frames per second.

Video that has been digitized and stored in the computer can be displayed at varying frame rates, depending on the speed of the computer. The slower the computer, the more jerky the movement. Contrast with *freeze-frame video*.

full path

A path name that includes the drive (if required), starting or root directory, all attached subdirectories and ending with the file or object name. Contrast with *relative path*. See *path*.

full project life cycle

A project from inception to completion.

full-screen mode

A programming capability that allows data to be displayed in any row, column or pixel location on screen. Contrast with *teletype mode*.

full-service network

See *FSN*.

fully populated

A circuit board whose sockets are completely filled with chips.

function

In programming, a self-contained software routine that peforms a job for the program it is written in or for some other program. The function performs the operation and returns control to the instruction following the calling instruction or to the calling program. Programming languages provide a set of standard functions and may allow programmers to define others. For example, the C language is built entirely of functions.

functional decomposition

Breaking down a process into non-redundant operations. Structured programming uses functional decomposition to break down an application into component pieces that can be worked on by different teams of programmers.

Functional Decomposition
This is a very simple example of breaking down a program into components. In a real program, there may be dozens if not hundreds of individual modules.

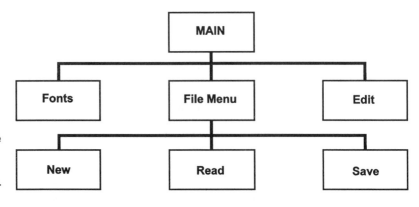

functional specification

The blueprint for the design of an information system. It provides documentation for the database, human and machine procedures, and all the input, processing and output detail for each data entry, query, update and report program in the system.

function call

A request by a program to use a subroutine. The subroutine can be large and perform a significant amount of processing, or it can be as small as computing two numbers and returning the result. When applications are running, they make millions of function calls to the operating system.

A function call written in a program states the name of the function followed by any values or parameters that have to be passed to it. When the function is called, the operation is performed, and the results are returned as variables or pointers with new values.

The function may be written within the program, be part of an external library that is combined with the program when it is compiled or be contained in another program, such as the operating system or DBMS.

function keys

A set of keyboard keys used to command the computer (F1, F2, etc.). F1 is often the help key, but the purpose of any function key is determined by the software currently running.

function library

A collection of program routines. See *function*.

function overloading

In programming, using the same name for two or more functions. The compiler determines which function to use based on the type of function, arguments passed to it and type of values returned.

function prototyping

In programming, formally defining each function in the program with the number and types of parameters passed to it and its return values. The compiler can then report an error if a function is not written to conform to the prototype.

fuse

(1)A protective device that is designed to melt, or blow, when a specified amount of current is passed through it. PROM chips are created as a series of fuses that are selectively blown in order to create the binary patterns of the data or machine language.

(2)To bond together.

fusible link

A circuit line in a PROM chip or similar device that is designed to be blown apart. See *PROM programmer*.

Futurebus+

An IEEE standard multisegment bus that can transfer data at 32, 64, 128 and 256-bits and can address up to 64 bits. Clock speeeds range from 25 to 100MHz. At 100MHz and 256 bits, it transfers 3.2 Gbytes/sec.

fuzzy computer

A specially-designed computer that employs fuzzy logic. Using such architectural components as analog circuits and parallel processing, fuzzy computers are designed for AI applications.

fuzzy logic

A mathematical technique for dealing with imprecise data and problems that have many solutions rather than one. Although it is implemented in digital computers which ultimately make only yes-no decisions, fuzzy logic works with ranges of values, solving problems in a way that more resembles human logic.

Fuzzy logic is used for solving problems with expert systems and realtime systems that must react to an imperfect environment of highly variable, volatile or unpredictable conditions. It "smoothes the edges" so to speak, circumventing abrupt changes in operation that could result from relying on traditional either-or and all-or-nothing logic.

Fuzzy Computer
Well, isn't it?

Fuzzy logic was conceived by Lotfi Zadeh, former chairman of the electrical engineering and computer science department at the University of California at Berkeley. In 1964, while contemplating how computers could be programmed for handwriting recognition, Zadeh expanded on traditional set theory by making membership in a set a matter of degree rather than a yes-no situation.

fuzzy logician

An individual who is involved in developing fuzzy logic algorithms.

fuzzy search

An inexact search for data that finds answers that come close to the desired data. It can get results when the exact spelling is not known or help users obtain information that is loosely related to a topic.

FWIW

Digispeak for "for what it's worth."

FYI

Digispeak for "for your information."

G

G
See *giga*.

gain
The amount of increase that an amplifier provides on the output side of the circuit.

GAL
(Generic Array Logic) A programmable logic chip (PLD) technology from Lattice Semiconductor.

gallium arsenide
An alloy of gallium and arsenic compound (GaAs) that is used as the base material for chips. It is several times faster than silicon.

game port
An I/O connector used to attach a joy stick. It is typically a 15-pin socket on the back of a PC. See *serial port*.

gamma
The relationship between the input and output of a device, expressed as a number, with 1.0 being a perfect linear plot (the output is increased in the exact same proportion as the input).

gamma correction
An adjustment to the light intensity of a scanner, monitor or printer. It generally refers to the adjustment of the brightness of a display screen in order to compensate for a CRT's irregularity. A gamma correction plot is a curve, not a straight line as is the standard brightness control. Gamma correction is also used to make the monitor display images more closely in appearance with the laser printer that creates the output.

gang punch
To punch an identical set of holes into a deck of punched cards.

Gantt chart
A form of floating bar chart usually used in project management to show resources or tasks over time.

Gantt Chart
This Gantt chart depicts the system development cycle of an information system.

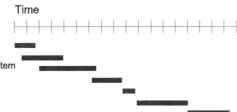

gap
(1)The space between blocks of data on magnetic tape.
(2) The space in a read/write head over which magnetic flux (energy) flows causing the underlying magnetic tape or disk surface to become magnetized in the corresponding direction.

gapless
A magnetic tape that is recorded in a continuous stream without interblock gaps.

garbage collection

A routine that searches memory for program segments or data that are no longer active in order to reclaim that space.

gate

(1) An open/closed switch.
(2) A pattern of transistors that makes up an AND, OR or NOT Boolean logic gate. See *gate array*.
(3) In a field effect transistor (CMOS), the line that activates the switch. Same as *base* in a bipolar transistor.

gate array

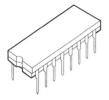

A type of chip that contains unconnected logic elements, which are typically two-input NAND gates. NAND gates can be interconnected to provide all the Boolean operations required for digital logic. The chip is completed by designing and adhering the top layers which provide the interconnecting pathways. This final masking stage is less costly than designing the chip from scratch.

gated

Switched "on" or capable of being switched on and off.

gateway

(1) A computer that performs protocol conversion between different types of networks or applications. For example, a gateway can connect a personal computer LAN to a mainframe network. An electronic mail, or messaging, gateway converts messages between two different messaging protocols. See *bridge*.
(2) (Gateway) (Gateway 2000, N. Sioux City, SD) A PC manufacturer founded in 1985 by Ted Waitt and Mike Hammond. With fiscal 1994 revenues of nearly three billion dollars, it is one of the largest direct marketers of PCs in the U.S. Gateway first sold peripherals to owners of Texas Instrument computers. In 1987, it began to offer complete systems and has continued to drive down the cost of quality PCs by mail.

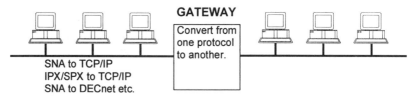

GATEWAY
Convert from one protocol to another.

SNA to TCP/IP
IPX/SPX to TCP/IP
SNA to DECnet etc.

gather write

To output data from two or more noncontiguous memory locations with one write operation. See *scatter read*.

GatorBox

A gateway from Cayman Systems, Inc., Cambridge, MA, that interconnects LocalTalk and Ethernet networks and supports TCP/IP and NFS protocols. It also functions as a router to connect AppleTalk-based computers on a LAN with remote AppleTalk devices.

gauss

A unit of measurement of magnetic intensity.

Gaussian distribution

A random distribution of events that is often graphed as a bell-shaped curve. It is used to represent a normal or statistically probable outcome.

Gaussian noise

In communications, a random interference generated by the movement of electricity in the line. Also called white noise.

GB, Gb

See *gigabyte* and *gigabit*.

Gbits/sec

(GigaBITS per SECond) Billion bits per second.

GBps, Gbps

(GigaBytes Per Second, GigaBits Per Second) Billion bytes per second. Billion bits per second.

G-byte

See *gigabyte*.

GCOS

A Bull HN operating system used in its minis and mainframes (formerly Honeywell's product).

GCR

(1) (Group Code Recording) An encoding method used on magnetic tapes and Apple II and Mac 400K and 800K floppy disks.
(2) (Gray Component Replacement) A method for reducing the amount of printing ink used. It substitutes black for the amount of gray contained in a color, thus black ink is used instead of the three CMY inks. See *UCR* and *dot gain*.

GD&R

Digispeak for "grinning, ducking and running," said after a snide remark. Another variation is GD&WVVF, which stands for "grinning, ducking and walking very, very fast."

GDDM

(Graphical Data Display Manager) Software that generates graphics images in the IBM mainframe environment. It contains routines to generate graphics on terminals, printers and plotters as well as accepting input from scanners. Programmers use it for creating graphics, but users can employ its Interactive Chart Utility (ICU) to create business graphics without programming.
GDDM/graPHIGS is a programming environment that combines graphics capability with a user interface similar to the Presentation Manager in OS/2.

GDI

(Graphics Device Interface) The graphics display system in Microsoft Windows. When an application needs to display or print, it makes a call to a GDI function and sends it the parameters for the object that must be created. GDI in turn "draws" the object by sending commands to the screen and printer drivers, which actually render the images. See *Driver*.
The DirectDraw interface is expected for Windows 95, which adds a faster mechanism for displaying games, full-motion video and 3-D objects on screen.

GDM

See *CGM*.

GE

(Greater than or Equal to) See *relational operators*.

GEM

(Graphics Environment Manager) A graphical user interface from Digital Research similar to the Mac/Windows environment. It is built into ROM in several Atari computers. The DOS version of Ventura Publisher came with a runtime version.

gender changer

A coupler that reverses the gender of one of the connectors in order that two male connectors or two female connectors can be joined together.

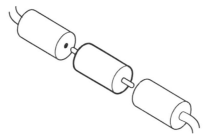

Gender Changer
The unit in the middle is the gender changer.

General failure reading drive x

A DOS error message. The full message is

General failure reading drive X
Abort, Retry, Fail?

This usually means that an unformatted floppy is being used. Press A to Abort, format the floppy and try again.
You'll also get this if you try to read a high-density disk in a low-density drive. High-density disks require high-density drives.

General Fault

See *GPF*.

generalized program

Software that serves a changing environment. By allowing variable data to be introduced, the program can solve the same problem for different users or situations. For example, the electronic versions of this database could be programmed to read in a different title and thus be used for any type of dictionary.

General Magic

(General Magic, Inc., Sunnyvale, CA) A spinoff of Apple Computer in 1990. Its mission is to create new personal intelligent communications products and services by developing and licensing technology to a wide variety of manufacturers and service providers. It has formed an alliance with large organizations such as AT&T, Sony, Philips and Motorola in order to reach the widest possible audience. See *Telescript* and *Magic Cap*.

General MIDI

A standard set of 128 sounds for MIDI sound cards and devices (synthesizers, sound modules, etc.). By assigning instruments to specific MIDI patch locations, General MIDI provides a standard way of communicating MIDI sound.
MIDI's small storage requirement makes it very desirable as a musical sound source for multimedia applications compared to digitizing actual music. For example, a three-minute MIDI file may take only 20 to 30K, whereas a WAV file (digital audio) could consume up to several megabytes depending on sound quality.

General Protection Fault
See *GPF.*

general-purpose computer
Refers to computers that follow instructions, thus virtually all computers from micro to mainframe are general purpose. Even computers in toys, games and single-function devices follow instructions in their built-in program. In contrast, computational devices can be designed from scratch for special purposes (see *ASIC*).

general-purpose controller
A peripheral control unit that can service more than one type of peripheral device; for example, a printer and a communications line.

general-purpose language
A programming language used to solve a wide variety of problems. All common programming languages (FORTRAN, COBOL, BASIC, C, Pascal, etc.) are examples. Contrast with *special-purpose language.*

generator
(1) Software that creates software. See *application generator* and *macro generator.*
(2) A device that creates electrical power or synchonization signals.

Generic CADD
A full-featured CADD package for DOS from AutoDesk, Inc., Sausalito, CA, that offers levels for beginner, intermediate and advanced users. It was originally developed by Generic Software of Bothell, WA.

GEnie
(General Electric Network for Information Exchange) An online information service from GE Information Services that provides business information, news and access to special interest groups. See *online services.*

Genifer
A dBASE application generator from Bytel Corporation, Berkeley, CA, that creates dBASE source code.

genlock
(generator lock) Circuitry that synchronizes video signals for mixing. In personal computers, a genlock display adapter converts screen output into an NTSC video signal, which it synchronizes with an external video source.

GEO
See *geosynchronous.*

geographic information system
See *GIS.*

GeoPort
A serial port from Apple designed for voice and video applications. With an adapter, it can be used to dial an analog phone. Standard on various Macintosh models, GeoPort provides a 2 Mbps bandwidth, suitable for very high-quality videoconferencing. The GeoPort is endorsed by Versit.

geostationary, geosynchronous
Earth aligned. Refers to communications satellites that are placed 22,282 miles

above the equator and travel at the same speed as the earth's rotation, thus appearing stationary. Contrast with *LEO*.

GeoWorks Ensemble

A graphical operating environment for DOS from GeoWorks, Inc., Berkeley, CA, that includes word processing, drawing, communications, card file and calendar applications. It provides complete DOS file management and simulates file folders like the Macintosh. Users can launch all applications from within Ensemble. GeoWorks Pro includes the Quattro Pro spreadsheet.

germanium

(Ge) The material used in making the first transistors. Although still used in very limited applications, germanium was replaced by silicon years ago.

gesture recognition

The ability to interpret simple hand-written symbols such as check marks and slashes.

get

(1) In programming, a request for the next record in an input file. Contrast with *put*.
(2) An FTP command to copy a file or to display the contents of a text file.

Gflops

See *gigaflops*.

ghost

(1) A faint second image that appears close to the primary image on a display or printout. In transmission, it is a result of secondary signals that arrive ahead of or later than the primary signal. On a printout, it is caused by bouncing print elements as the paper passes by.
(2) To display a menu option in a dimmed, fuzzy typeface, indicating it is not selectable at this time.

GHz

(GigaHertZ) One billion cycles per second. High-speed radio frequency applications transmit in the gigahertz range. See *RF*.

GIF

(Graphics Interchange Format) A popular raster graphics file format developed by CompuServe that handles 8-bit color (256 colors) and uses the LZW method to achieve compression ratios of approximately 1.5:1 to 2:1.

GIF files include a color table which includes the most representative 256 colors used in the image. For example, a picture of the forest would include a color table with mostly greens. This method provides excellent realism in an 8-bit image. In addition, GIF file sizes are based on the actual number of colors used. Thus images with fewer colors take up less space in the computer.

GIF89 is a more sophisticated version of GIF87 and allows one of the colors to be made transparent, taking on the background color of the underlying page or window.

giga

Billion. Abreviated "G." It often refers to the precise value 1,073,741,824 since computer specifications are usually binary numbers. See **binary values** and **space/time**.

gigabit

One billion bits. Also Gb, Gbit and G-bit. See *giga* and *space/time*.

gigabyte

One billion bytes. Also GB, Gbyte and G-byte. See *giga* and *space/time*.

gigaflops

(GIGAFLoating point OPerations per Second) One billion floating point operations per second.

gigahertz

See *GHz*.

GIGO

(Garbage In Garbage Out) "Bad input produces bad output." Data entry is critical. All possible tests should be made on data entered into a computer.

"Garbage In, Gospel Out"
An alternate meaning. Many people have complete faith in computer output!

GIS

(1) (Geographic Information System) A digital mapping system used for exploration, demographics, dispatching and tracking.
(2) (Generalized Information System) An early IBM mainframe query and data manipulation language.

GKS

(Graphical Kernel System) A device-independent graphics language for 2-D, 3-D and raster graphics images. It allows graphics applications to be developed on one system and easily moved to another with minimal or no change. It was the first true standard for graphics applications programmers and has been adopted by both ANSI and ISO.

glare filter

A fine mesh screen that is placed over a CRT screen to reduce glare from overhead and ambient light.

glitch

A temporary or random hardware malfunction. It is possible that a bug in a program may cause the hardware to appear as if it had a glitch in it and vice versa. At times it can be extremely difficult to determine whether a problem lies within the hardware or the software.

global

Pertaining to an entire file, database, volume, program or system.

global variable

In programming, a variable that is used by all modules in a program.

glossary

A term used by Microsoft Word and adopted by other word processors for the list of shorthand, keyboard macros created by a particular user.

glue chip

A support chip that adds functionality to a microprocessor, for example, an I/O processor or extra memory.

GM

See *General MIDI*.

GMR

(Giant Magnetoresistive) See *magnetoresistive*.

GMTA

Digispeak for "great minds thing alike."

GNU

(Gnu's Not UNIX) A project sponsored by the Free Software Foundation that is developing a complete software environment including operating system kernel and utilities, editor, compiler and debugger. Many consultants and organizations provide support for GNU software.

go

A command used on a BBS or online service to switch the user to a particular forum or section. For example, typing **go macintosh** might switch you to a section that specializes in Macintosh computers or software. Like any command language, you have to know what words to enter.

goal seeking

The ability to calculate a formula backward to obtain a desired input. For example, given the goal **gross margin = 50%** as well as the range of possible inputs, goal seeking attempts to obtain the optimum input.

GOCA

(Graphics Object Content Architecture) See *MO:DCA*.

gooey

See *GUI*.

gooey builder

See *GUI* builder.

Gopher

A program that searches for file names and resources on the Internet and presents hierarchical menus to the user. As users select options, they are moved to different Gopher servers on the Internet. Where links have been established, Usenet news and other information can be read directly from Gopher. See *Veronica, Archie, Jughead, WAIS* and *World Wide Web*.

Gopherspace

The collective information made available on Gopher servers throughout the Internet.

GOSIP

(Government Open Systems Interconnection Profile) A U.S. government mandate that after August 15, 1990, all new network procurements must comply with OSI. Testing is performed at the NIST, which maintains a database of OSI-compliant commercial products. GOSIP also allows TCP/IP protocols to be used.

Since broad adoption of OSI standards never came to fruition, GOSIP evolved into POSIT (Profiles for Open Systems Internetworking Technologies), which is a set of non-mandatory standards that acknowledge the widespread use of TCP/IP.

goto

(1) In a high-level programming language, a statement that directs the computer to go to some other part of the program. Low-level language equivalents are *branch* and *jump*.

(2) In dBASE, a command that directs the user to a specific record in the file.

(3) In word processing, a command that directs the user to a specific page number.

goto-less programming

Writing a program without using goto instructions, an important rule in structured programming. A goto instruction points to a different part of the program without a guarantee of returning. Instead of using goto's, structures called subroutines or functions are used, which automatically return to the next instruction after the calling instruction when completed.

Gouraud shading

In computer graphics, a technique developed by Henri Gouraud that computes a shaded surface based on the color and illumination at the corners of polygonal facets.

gov

An Internet address domain name for a governmental agency. See *Internet address*.

GPCmark

See *PLB*.

GPF

(1) (General Protection Fault) The Windows 3.1 error name for a program that has crashed. In Windows 3.0, it was called an Uninterruptible Application Error. See *Application Error*.

(2) (GUI Programming Facility) An OS/2 application generator from GPF Systems, Inc., Moodus, CT.

GPI

(Graphical Programming Interface) A graphics language in OS/2 Presentation Manager. It is a derivative of the GDDM mainframe interface and includes Bezier curves.

GPIB

(General Purpose Interface Bus) An IEEE 488 standard parallel interface used for attaching sensors and programmable instruments to a computer. It uses a 24-pin connector. HP's version is the HPIB.

gppm

(Graphics Pages Per Minute) The measurement of printer speed based on printing graphics, which takes considerably longer to print than text. A gppm rating is more meaningful to the graphics designer than ppm (pages per minute), which usually rates the speed of printing text.

GPS

(Global Positioning System) A series of continuously-transmitting satellites used for identifying earth locations. By triangulation from three satellites, a hand-held receiving unit can pinpoint wherever you are on earth.

With GPS, the "James Bond" style of on-screen mobile map reading is a reality. Units combined with CD players, which read the map data, are available for installation in the car.

Car Navigation Using GPS
Using a portable CD-ROM player to read Naviken electronic maps and a GPS satellite receiver to get its bearings, Sony's NVX-F160 puts you on the map. It can calculate your current position to within 100 to 700 feet, and it can also direct you to the nearest restaurant and hotel. *(Photo courtesy of Sony Corporation.)*

GPSS

(General Purpose Simulation System) A programming language for discrete event simulation, which is used to build models of operations such as manufacturing environments, communications systems and traffic patterns. Originally developed by IBM for mainframes, PC versions are available, such as GPSS/PC by Minuteman Software and GPSS/H by Wolverine Software.

grabber

See *frame grabber* and *screen grabber*.

grabber hand

An on-screen pointer that is shaped like a hand and is used to select objects on screen.

graceful degradation

A system that continues to perform at some reduced level of performance after one of its components fails.

graceful exit

The ability to get out of a problem situation in a program without having to turn the computer off.

grade

The transmission capacity of a line. It refers to a range or class of frequencies that it can handle; for example, telegraph grade, voice grade and broadband.

gradient

A color spread from light to dark to shade an object or give it a sense of depth. It is also used to create a colorful background.

Gradient
This is an example of a typical gradient.

GRAFCET

(GRAPHe de Commande Etape-Transition - stage transition command graph) A PLC specification and programming language.

GrafPort

See *graphics port (2)*.

grammar checker

Software that checks the grammar of a sentence. It can check for and highlight incomplete sentences, awkward phrases, wordiness and poor grammar.

Grammatik

A popular grammar checking program for DOS, Windows, Macintosh and UNIX from WordPerfect Corporation, Orem, Utah. U.S. Government versions check for usage according to the Government Printing Office and other military and civilian guides. In 1993, WordPerfect acquired Reference Software of San Francisco, developers of Grammatik.

grandfather, father, son

A method for storing previous generations of master file data that are continuously updated. The son is the current file, the father is a copy of the file from the previous cycle, and the grandfather is a copy of the file from the cycle before that one.

granularity

The degree of modularity of a system. The more granularity (grains or granules), the more customizable or flexible the system.

graph

A pictorial representation of information. See *business graphics*.

graphical user interface

See *GUI*.

graphic character

A printable symbol that includes digits and letters.

graphics

Called *computer graphics*, it is the creation and manipulation of picture images in the computer. It is defined here as *graphics*, to keep it next to the other entries that begin with "graphics."

A graphics computer system requires a graphics display screen, a graphics input device (tablet, mouse, scanner, camera, etc.), a graphics output device (dot matrix printer, laser printer, plotter, etc.) and a graphics software package; for example, a CAD, drawing or paint program.

Vector Graphics and Raster Graphics

Two methods are used for storing and maintaining pictures in a computer. The first method, called vector graphics (also known as object-oriented graphics), maintains the image as a series of points, lines, arcs and other geometric shapes.

The second method, called raster graphics, resembles television, where the picture image is made up of dots.

Understanding these two methods and how they intertwine in today's graphics systems is essential for mastering computer graphics. When you create an image on the computer, you may not know which method is used, but when you try to manipulate that image, it will become obvious.

Vector Graphics for CAD and Drawing

Vector graphics is the method employed by computer-aided design (CAD) and drawing packages. As you draw, each line of the image is stored as a vector, which is two end points on an x-y matrix. For example, a square becomes four vectors, one for each side. A circle is turned into dozens or hundreds of tiny straight lines, the number of which is determined by the resolution of the drawing. The entire image is commonly stored in the computer as a list of vectors, called a display list.

A vector graphics image is a collection of graphic elements, such as lines, squares, rectangles and circles. Although grouped together, each element maintains its own integrity and identity and can always be selected and erased or resized independent of all the others.

Vector graphics can be transmitted directly to x-y plotters that "draw" the images from the list of vectors. Older CAD systems used vector screens that also drew the vectors. Today, all monitors are raster graphics displays made up of dots, and the vectors are "rasterized" into the required dot patterns by hardware or software.

Raster Graphics for Imaging and Painting

Raster graphics is the TV-like method that uses dots to display an image on screen. Raster graphics images are created by scanners and cameras and are also generated by paint packages. A picture frame is divided into hundreds of horizontal rows, with each row containing hundreds of dots, called pixels.

Unlike TV, which uses one standard (NTSC) for the country, there are dozens of raster graphics standards. Also, unlike TV, which records and displays the dots as infinitely variable shades and colors (analog), computer graphics have a finite number of shades and colors (digital).

When you scan an image or paint an object into the computer, the image is created in a reserved area of memory called a bitmap, with some number of bits corresponding to each dot (pixel). The simplest monochrome bitmap uses one bit (on/off) for each dot. Gray scale bitmaps (monochrome shades) hold a number for each dot large enough to hold all the gray levels. Color bitmaps require three times as much storage in order to hold the intensity of red, green and blue.

The image in the bitmap is continuously transmitted to the video screen, dot for dot, a line at a time, over and over again. Any changes made to the bitmap are instantly reflected on the screen.

Papyrus of the 21st Century
The graphics tablet and other input devices such as the mouse are the drawing tools of the 21st century.

Graphics

Drawing creates vector graphics...

Scanning and painting create raster graphics...

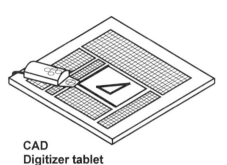

**CAD
Digitizer tablet**

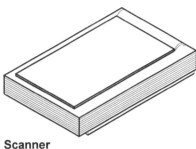

Scanner

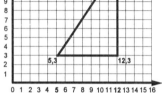

The Display List

The display list is a collection of all the vectors in a CAD drawing. The advantage of vector graphics is that each element within the image is created and maintained as an independent object that can be scaled and manipulated separately. Vector graphics file formats also generally store text and bitmaps, creating what is known as a metafile, a file that contains other files.

The Bitmap

When you scan a picture or create one in a paint program, the software gen-erates a matrix of dots, or pixels, called a bitmap. This raster graphics imaging technique, somewhat similar to tele-vision, uses one or more bits to rep-resent each pixel. The more bits per pixel, the more different colors can be displayed. Unlike vector images, objects within a raster graphics image cannot be independently scaled and manipulated. However an autotrace program can convert bitmaps into vectors.

Color depth (bit depth)

2 colors = 1 bit
16 colors = 4 bits
256 colors = 8 bits
65K colors = 16 bits
16M colors = 24 bits

Since colors are designated with numbers, changing red to green is simply searching for the red number and replacing it with the green number. Animation is accomplished by continuously copying new sequences from other areas in memory into the bitmap, one after the other.

Raster graphics images may take up more space on disk than their vector graphics counterpart, because storage for each pixel is required even if it's part of the background. A small object in vector graphics format will take up only a few vectors in the display list file.

graphics accelerator

A high-performance display adapter for graphical user interfaces that has line drawing and pixel block move functions (bitblt) built into hardware. For example, in Windows, such boards speed up the display of fonts and images and provide faster scrolling.

Windows applications will display and scroll faster on a slower PC with a graphics accelerator than on a faster PC without one. See *Winmark*.

graphics adapter, graphics board, graphics card

Same as *display adapter*.

graphics based

The display of text and pictures as graphics images; typically bitmapped images. Contrast with *text based*.

graphics coprocessor

A programmable chip that performs much of the processing required to display graphics on a video screen. It frees the computer from such tasks as drawing dots, circles, lines and rectangles by accepting commands to perform these operations and executing them on the video adapter's coprocessor rather than the computer's CPU. As technology changes, what is true today is not true tomorrow. As CPUs get faster, offloading graphics operations to the coprocessor becomes less and less important.

Coprocessor vs Accelerator

A graphics coprocessor is good for CAD work, especially if not running under Windows. On the other hand, a graphics accelerator is good for Windows and other GUIs, which require a lot of blitting and text drawing. An advantage of a graphics coprocessor is that it is programmable and can be updated as required with new graphics operations, whereas the graphics accelerator is fixed and cannot be changed. This is not a disadvantage in Windows, since Windows requires limited functions to draw the screen.

graphics engine

(1) Hardware that performs graphics processing tasks independently of the computer's CPU. See *graphics accelerator* and *graphics coprocessor*.
(2) Software that accepts commands from an application and builds images and text that are directed to the graphics driver and hardware. Macintosh's QuickDraw and Windows' GDI are examples.

graphics file

A file that contains only graphics data. Contrast with *text file* and *binary file*.

graphics formats

There is a wide variety of graphics formats in use today. The following list contains most of them. The formats are in order by extension name under raster or vector category. Some formats appear in both categories because they can hold both raster and vector images.

Raster Graphics Formats (Bitmaps)

AI   Adobe Illustrator
AG4 Access G4 document imaging
ATT   AT&T Group IV

BMP Windows & OS/2

CAL CALS Group IV
CIT   Intergraph scanned images
CLP   Windows Clipboard
CMP Photomatrix G3/G4 scanner format
CMP LEAD Technologies

CPR Knowledge Access
CT   Scitex Continuous Tone
UT   Dr. Halo

DBX DATABEAM
DX   Autotrol document imaging

ED5   EDMICS (U.S. DOD)
EPS   Encapsulated PostScript

FAX   Fax

GED Arts & Letters
GIF   CompuServe
GP4 CALS Group IV - ITU Group IV
GX1 Show Partner
GX2 Show Partner

ICA   IBM IOCA (see *MO:DCA*)
ICO   Windows icon
IFF   Amiga ILBM
IGF   Inset Systems (HiJaak)
IMG GEM Paint

JPG   JPEG JFIF

KFX Kofax Group IV

MAC MacPaint
MIL   Same as GP4 extension
MSP Microsoft Paint

PCD PhotoCD
PCL HP LaserJet
PCX PC Paintbrush
PIX   Inset Systems (HiJaak)

RAS Sun
RIA   Alpharel Group IV document imaging
RLE Various RLE-compressed formats
RNL GTX Runlength

SBP IBM StoryBoard

TGA Targa

TIF   TIFF

WPG WordPerfect image

Vector Graphics Formats

906   Calcomp plotter

CAL CALS subset of CGM
CGM Computer Graphics Metafile
CLP   Windows clipboard

DG   Autotrol
DGN Intergraph drawing format
DRW Micrografx Designer 2.x, 3.x
DS4 Micrografx Designer 4.x
DXF AutoCAD
DWG AutoCAD

EPS   Encapsulated PostScript
ESI   Esri plot file (GIS mapping)

GCA IBM GOCA
GEM GEM proprietary
G4   GTX RasterCAD - scanned images into vectors
       for AutoCAD

IGF   Inset Systems (HiJaak)

MCS MathCAD
MET OS/2 metafile
MRK Informative Graphics markup file

P10   Tektronix plotter (PLOT10)
PCT   Macintosh PICT drawings
PGL   HP plotter
PIC   Variety of picture formats
PIX   Inset Systems (HiJaak)
PLT   HPGL Plot File (HPGL2 has raster format)

RLC   Image Systems "CAD Overlay ESP" vector files
       overlaid onto raster images

WMF Windows Metafile
WPG WordPerfect graphics

graphics interface

See *graphics language* and *GUI*.

graphics language

A high-level language used to create graphics images. The language is translated into images by software or specialized hardware. See *graphics engine*.

graphics mode

A screen display mode that displays graphics. Contrast with *text mode* and *character mode*.

graphics port

(1) A socket on the computer for connecting a graphics monitor.
(2) Also called *GrafPort*, it is a Macintosh graphics structure that defines all the characteristics of a graphics window.

graphics primitive

An elementary graphics building block, such as a point, line or arc. In a solid modeling system, a cylinder, cube and sphere are examples.

graphics processor

Same as *graphics engine*.

graphics program

See *paint program, drawing program, presentation graphics, image editor* and *image processing*.

graphics tablet

Same as *digitizer tablet*.

graphics terminal

A terminal or personal computer that displays graphics.

graPHIGS

See *GDDM*.

The First Teletypewriter
Elisha Gray's printing telegraph was an outstanding success and catapulted Gray and Barton into the mainstream of electronic communications. *(Photo courtesy of Graybar.)*

Graybar

(Graybar, Clayton, MO) An international distributor of electrical and voice and data communications equipment. In 1869, the company was founded in Cleveland as Gray and Barton by Elisha Gray and Enos Barton. The company initially manufactured Gray's telegraph equipment, the most successful of which was his printing telegraph.
Gray and Barton was later renamed Western Electric Company when Western Union, its major customer, became an investor. Although Elisha Gray and Alexander Graham Bell had battled in the courts over patent rights to the telephone, and Bell had won, Western Electric became the manufacturer of Bell's telephones. Western Electric also supplied electrical products to the telephone companies as well as to other organizations as the electrical business flourished in the country.
In 1926, Western Electric spun off its electrical distribution as Graybar Electric Company. Graybar also sold telephone equipment to non-Bell companies. In 1929, Graybar was the first large company to be bought out by its own employees.
In the mid 1980s, after the breakup of AT&T, Graybar added more voice communications suppliers and got heavily involved in data communications. Today, it handles tens of thousands of products from more than 250 major suppliers.

A Greeked Page
Greeked pages
show the overall
layout of the text,
but not the
individual letters.

gray scale
A series of shades from white to black. The more shades, or levels, the more realistic an image can be recorded and displayed, especially a scanned photo. Scanners differentiate typically from 16 to 256 gray levels.
Although compression techiques help reduce the size of graphics files, high-resolution gray scale requires huge amounts of storage. At a printer resolution of 300 dpi, each square inch is made up of 90,000 pixels. At 256 levels, it takes one byte per pixel, or 90,000 bytes per square inch of image. See *halftone*.

greek
To display text in a representative form in which the actual letters are not discernible, because the screen resolution isn't high enough to display them properly. Desktop publishing programs let you set which font sizes should be greeked.
The term comes from typography and graphic design, in which Greek or Latin letters and words are placed into layouts to hold the position for and represent the real text that was forthcoming.

Green Book
See *CD-I*.

green PC
An energy-saving personal computer or peripheral device. Green computers, printers and monitors go into a low-voltage "suspend mode" if not used after a certain period of time. Many contemporary CPUs can run at variable clock rates and can idle at very low speeds, to save current. When input is detected, they revert to full-power. The green concept includes using less packaging materials, recycling toner cartridges, providing a return location for used batteries, distributing multi-disk software on a CD-ROM and sending e-mail rather than paper mail.

grep
(Global Regular Expression and Print) A UNIX pattern matching utility that searches for a string of text and outputs any line that contains the pattern.

ground
An electrically conductive body, such as the earth, which maintains a zero potential (not positively or negatively charged) for connecting to an electrical circuit.

ground current
The current found in a ground line. It may be caused by imbalanced electrical sources; for example, the ground line in a communications channel between two computers deriving power separately.

ground fault
The temporary current in the ground line, caused by a failing electrical component or interference from an external electrical source such as a thunderstorm.

ground loop
An unwanted ground current flowing back and forth between two devices that are grounded at two or more points.

ground noise injection
An intentional insertion of unwanted noise by a power supply into the ground line.

Workflow versus Workgroup (Groupware) Computing

Workgroup computing, also known as groupware, focuses on the information being processed and enhancing the user's ability to share information within workgroups.

Workflow, on the other hand, emphasizes the importance of the process, which acts as a container for the information. In this way, workflow combines rules, which govern the tasks performed, and coordinates the transfer of the information required to support these tasks. This is a *"process-centered"* model as opposed to an *"information-centered"* model.

Workgroup Model:
"Information Centered"

Workflow Model:
"Process Centered"

(Diagram courtesy of Delphi Consulting Group, Inc., Boston, MA.)

groupware

Software designed for use in a network that serves a group of users working on a related project. Groupware is an evolving concept that is more than multiuser software, which allows access to the same data. Groupware provides a mechanism that helps several users coordinate and keep track of an on-going project. Groupware could be thought of as the document counterpart of database management systems (DBMSs). DBMSs have been around for years and have enabled multiple users (groups) to access a central or distributed database. DBMSs typically deal with the highly structured data found in relational databases, whereas groupware tends to deal with less structured data such as text documents and images. Groupware also includes e-mail, group scheduling and threaded discussions. A variety of software products are expected under the groupware umbrella, all of which are designed to support teamwork.

Lotus Notes is often considered the first major groupware product, because it combines e-mail, document sharing and replication with an environment for developing applications designed for group collaboration.

GroupWise

Formerly WordPerfect Office, it is a groupware package from Novell that provides e-mail and group calendar and scheduler for a variety of client platforms. It also includes a text-to-speech converter that lets users listen to their mail remotely via telephone.

GSM

(Global System for Mobile Communications) A digital cellular phone system based on TDMA that is widely deployed in Europe and throughout the world. There is controversy over GSM. It produces a deafening sound for hearing aid wearers and is known to interfere with electronic devices. An Australian newspaper claimed a motorist set off his airbag with his cellphone, and most interesting, GSM phones are supposedly able to reset taxi meters to zero in Paris.

GSOS

(GSOperating System) A graphical operating system for the Apple IIGS that also accepts ProDOS applications.

GT

(Greater Than) See *relational operator*.

guard band

A frequency that insulates one signal from another. In an analog telephone line, the low band is 0-300; the high band is 3300-4000Hz.

GUI

(Graphical User Interface) A graphics-based user interface that incorporates icons, pull-down menus and a mouse. The GUI has become the standard way users interact with a computer. The three major GUIs are Windows, Macintosh and Motif. In a client/server environment, the GUI resides in the user's client machine. See *desktop manager, window manager* and *Star*. Contrast with *CUI*.

GUI accelerator

See *graphics accelerator*.

GUI builder

Visual programming software that lets a user build a graphical user interface by dragging and dropping elements from a toolbar onto the screen. It may be a stand-alone program or part of an application development system or client/server development system. See *application development system* and *client/server development system.*

GUI painter

Same as *GUI builder*.

gulp

Some number of bytes!

gutter

In typography, the space between two columns.

GVPN

(Global Virtual Private Network) A service from cooperating carriers that provides international digital communications for multinational companies.

GVS

(Global VideoPhone Standard) The technology behind AT&T's VideoPhones. GVS transmits at 10 frames per second, a third the rate of regular TV. The GVS technology is licensed to other manufacturers.

GW-BASIC

(Gee Whiz-BASIC) A BASIC interpreter that accompanied MS-DOS in versions prior to 5.0. See *QBasic*.

H

h

(Hexadecimal) A symbol that refers to a hex number. For example, 09h has a numeric value of 9, whereas 0Ah has a value of 10. See chart in *hex* definition.

H&J

(Hyphenation and Justification) The alignment of the right margin in a document. Hyphenation breaks up words that exceed the margin. Justification aligns text uniformly at the right margin while spacing text evenly between both margins.

H.261

The ITU standard compression algorithm for the H.320 videoconferencing standard. The algorithm can be implemented in hardware or software and uses intraframe and interframe compression. It is designed to transmit over one or more 64 Kbps ISDN channels (Px64).

H.320

An ITU standard for videoconferencing over digital lines. Using the H.261 compression method, it allows H.320-compliant videoconferencing room and desktop systems to communicate with each other over ISDN, switched digital and leased lines. A counterpart standard for data conferencing is T.120.

H.322

An ITU standard for videoconferencing over LANs that can guarantee bandwidth. It is expected to be completed by early 1996.

H.323

An ITU standard for videoconferencing over shared-media LANS such as Ethernet and Token Ring. It is expected to be completed by early 1996.

H.324

An ITU standard for videoconferencing over analog telephone lines (POTS) using modems. It is expected to be completed by the end of 1995 or early 1996.

hack

Program source code. You might hear a phrase like "nobody has a package to do that, so it must be done through some sort of hack." This means someone has to write some code to solve the problem. There's no pre-written package to do it. The purist would say that doing a hack means writing in languages such as assembly language and C, which are low level and highly detailed. The more liberal person would say that writing any programming language counts as hacking.

hacker

A person who writes programs in assembly language or in system-level languages, such as C. Although it may refer to any programmer, it implies very tedious "hacking away" at the bits and bytes.

The term has become widely used for people that gain illegal entrance into a computer system. This use of the term is not appreciated by the vast majority of honest hackers. See *hack* and *computer cracker*.

HAL

(1) (Hardware Abstraction Layer) The translation layer in Windows NT that resides between the NT kernel and I/O system and the hardware itself. Its purpose is to be able to port NT to another platform only by designing a new HAL layer for that platform. In practice, parts of the kernel may also have to be changed to optimize NT to a new platform.

(2) (Heuristic/ALgorithmic) The computer in the film "2001," which takes over command of the spaceship. Each of the letters in H-A-L coincidentally precede the letters I-B-M.

half-adder

An elementary electronic circuit in the ALU that adds one bit to another, deriving a result bit and a carry bit.

half-duplex

The transmission of data in both directions, but only one direction at a time. Two-way radio was the first to use half-duplex, for example, while one party spoke, the other party listened. Contrast with *full-duplex*.

half-height drive

A 5.25" disk drive that takes up half the vertical space of first-generation drives in desktop computers. Measuring 1 5/8" in height, it is commonly used for 5.25" floppy disks and hard disks. Contrast with *full-height drive*.

half-inch tape

A magnetic tape format that has been in use for more than 30 years. Second-generation computers used 7-track, half-inch tape in open reels that were mounted on the drive and threaded by hand. Third-generation computers used 9-track tape reels for a long time, and this format still exists.

Half-inch reel-to-reel tape evolved into half-inch, self-threading tape cartridges that contain magnetic tape with 18 or 36 parallel tracks. They are also available in tape libraries that hold hundreds and thousands of cartridges with an automated system for moving them to the read station.

Storage Technologies, Louisville, CO, is expected to introduce a helical scan version of the half-inch cartridge that will increase capacities from 800MB into the multiple gigabyte range. Both types of cartridges can be mixed in its tape library. See *7-track, 9-track, 3480, 3490* and *tape library*.

halftone

In printing, the simulation of a continuous-tone image (shaded drawing, photograph) with dots. All printing processes, except for Cycolor, print dots. In photographically-generated halftones, a camera shoots the image through a halftone screen, creating smaller dots for lighter areas and larger dots for darker areas.

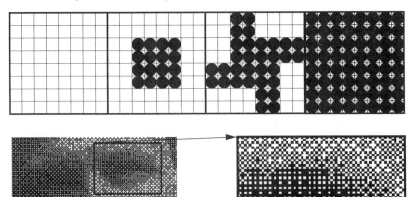

Digitally-composed printing prints only one size of dot. In order to simulate varying size halftone dots in computer printers, dithering is used, which creates clusters of dots in a "halftone cell." The more dots printed in the cell, the darker the gray. As the screen frequency gets higher (more lines per inch), there is less room for dots in the cell, reducing the number of gray levels that can be generated.

This tradeoff is a compromise in a 300 dpi printer, since realistic gray-scale printing reduces the resolution; for example, the 8x8 halftone cell required to create 64 grays results in a coarse 38 lpi resolution (300 dpi/8). In high-resolution imagesetters, the highest screen frequencies can be used with ample gray scale.

hammer

In a printer, the mechanism that pushes the typeface onto the ribbon and paper or pushes the paper into the ribbon and typeface.

Hamming code

A communications error correction method that intersperses three check bits at the end of each four data bits. At the receiving station, the check bits are used to detect and correct one-bit errors automatically.

hand coding

Writing in a programming language. Hand coding in assembly language or in a third-generation language, such as COBOL or C, is the traditional way programs have been developed. In contrast, visual programming tools allow full applications or parts of an application to be developed without writing lines of programming code.

hand-held scanner

A scanner that is moved across the image to be scanned by hand. Hand-held scanners are small and less expensive than their desktop counterparts, but rely on the dexterity of the user to move the unit across the paper. Trays are available that keep the scanner moving in a straight line. Contrast with *flatbed scanner, sheet-fed scanner* and *drum scanner.*

handle

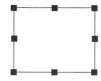

(1) In computer graphics, a location on an image that can be grabbed for reshaping. It is usually a tiny square.

(2) A temporary name or number assigned to a file, font or other object. For example, an operating system may assign a sequential number to each file that it opens as a way of identifying and keeping track of it.

(3) A nickname used when conferencing on a bulletin board, like a "CB handle" used by a truck driver.

handler

A software routine that performs a particular task. For example, upon detection of an error, an error handler is called to recover from the error condition.

handoff

Switching a cellular phone transmission from one cell to another as a mobile user moves into a new cellular area. The switch takes place in about a quarter of a second so that the caller is generally unaware of it.

handset

The part of the telephone that contains the speaker and the microphone.

handshaking

Signals transmitted back and forth over a communications network that establish a valid connection between two stations.

hang

To have the computer freeze or lock up. When a personal computer hangs, there is often no indication of what caused the problem. The computer could have crashed, or it could be something simple such as the printer running out of paper.

hanging paragraph

Also called *hanging indent*, it is a paragraph in
which the first line is set to the left
margin, but all subsequent lines are
indented as is this paragraph.

hard boot

Same as *cold boot*.

Hardcard

An earlier family of hard disks from Plus Development Corporation, Milpitas, CA, that housed the disk drive and controller electronics on a single expansion board that plugged into a PC. Its advantage was that it did not take up a drive bay as many early PCs had little cabinet room.

hard coded

Software that performs a fixed number of tasks or works with only a fixed number of devices. For example, a program could be written to work with only two types of printers. Hard coded solutions to problems are usually the fastest to program and often run the fastest, but are not as easy to change.

hard copy

Printed output. Contrast with *soft copy*.

hard disk

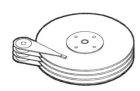

The primary computer storage medium, which is made of one or more aluminum or glass platters. Each side of the platter is coated with a ferromagnetic material. Older hard disks held as little as five megabytes. Today's hard disks can hold several gigabytes.

Desktop computers use disks from 1.5" to 5" in diameter. Minicomputer and mainframe disks range up to 12" in diameter, but are increasingly becoming as compact as the desktop drives.

Hard disks provide fast retrieval because they rotate at high speed, from 3,000 to over 7,000 rpm. In order to preserve the battery in laptops, the hard disk can be optionally turned off after some specified amount of time.

Fixed hard disks are permanently sealed in the drive. Removable hard disks are encased in a cartridge that can be moved between computers with the same kinds of drives.

Hard disks are usually low-level formatted from the factory, which records the original sector identification on them. See *floppy disk, magnetic disk* and *format program*.

To understand more about the parameters you have to enter into your PC when you add a new hard disk, see *hard disk configuration*.

Types of Hard Disks

Interface Type	Encoding Method*	Typical Transfer Rate (Bytes/sec)	Storage Capacities
ST506	MFM	625K	5M - 100M
ST506 RLL	RLL	937K	30M - 200M

IDE ATA	RLL	3-4M	40M - 1G
Enhanced IDE:			
ATA-2**	RLL	6-11M	500M - 1G
ATA-3**	RLL	16-22M	1G - 8G
ESDI	RLL	1-3M	80M - 2G
SCSI-1	RLL	1-5M	20M - 1.5G
SCSI-2	RLL	1-40M	40M - 9G
SMD	RLL	1-4M	200M - 2G
IPI	RLL	10-25M	200M - 3G

* Most disks use RLL, but the encoding method is not prescribed by all interfaces.
** For Enhanced IDE (ATA) data transfer rates and modes, see *ATA*.

Hard Disk Measurements

Capacity is measured in bytes, and speed is measured in bytes per second (transfer rate) and in milliseconds (access time). Fast personal computer hard disk access times range from 9 to 14ms; in larger computers as fast as 1ms.

hard disk configuration

Following are the parameters stored in a PC's CMOS RAM that describe the configuration of the hard disks in the system. SCSI hard disks are usually not identified in the CMOS RAM.

TYPE: There are 46 hard disk types, numbered 1 to 46, that include all the required parameters below. Since they cover earlier drives that only go up to 152MB, the user-configurable Type 47 is usually chosen and the remaining parameters are entered manually.

CYLINDERS: Number of cylinders.
HEADS: Number of read/write heads.
WPCOM: Write precomensation starting track.
LANDING ZONE: Cylinder used for parking heads.
SECTORS: Number of sectors per track.
CAPACITY: Total capacity derived from above parameters:
(heads X cylinders X sectors X 512)

For sources of hard disk parameters, see *hard disk references* below.

hard disk references

Following are some sources for obtaining hard disk parameters. Most new drives have the number of cylinders, heads and sectors printed directly on their housing. Many earlier drives do not. Listings of hard drive parameters are available from many bulletin boards as well.

"Pocket PCRef" is a handy pocket reference that also contains DOS commands, printer commands and other useful references and specifications for the support person.

"Pocket PCRef" by Thomas Glover & Millie Young
Sequoia Publishing, Inc., Littleton, CO
ISBN 0-9622359-7-0

"Hard Drive Bible"
Corporate Systems Center, Sunnyvale, CA
408/737-7312

"Hard Disk Technical Guide"
"Hard Disk Encyclopedia" (3 volumes)
Micro House, Boulder, CO, 800/926-8299

"DrivePro"
Hard disk installation and setup utility
includes hard disk and controller info.
Micro House, Boulder, CO, 800/926-8299

hard drive

The mechanism that reads and writes a hard disk. The terms hard drive and hard disk are used interchangeably.

hard error

(1) A permanent, unrecoverable error such as a disk read error. Contrast with *soft error.*
(2) A group of errors that requires user intervention and includes disk read errors, disk not ready (no disk in drive) and printer not ready (out of paper).

hard hyphen

A hyphen that always prints. Contrast with *soft hyphen.*

hard return

A code entered into a text document by pressing the return (enter) key. DOS and OS/2 text files use a CR/LF (carriage return/line feed) pair, but this is not standard (WordPerfect uses only an LF). The Macintosh uses a CR and UNIX uses an LF. A hard return is sometimes represented by a symbol on screen, such as the < in WordStar, but it usually remains invisible until revealed in an expanded screen mode. Contrast with *soft return.*

hard sectored

A sector identification technique that uses a physical mark. For example, hard sectored floppy disks have a hole in the disk that marks the beginning of each sector. Contrast with *soft sectored.*

hard space

A special space character that acts like a letter or digit, used to prevent multiple-word, proper names from breaking between lines.

hardware

Machinery and equipment (CPU, disks, tapes, modem, cables, etc.). In operation, a computer is both hardware and software. One is useless without the other. The hardware design specifies the commands it can follow, and the instructions tell it what to do. See *instruction set.*

Hardware Is
"Storage and Transmission"

The more memory and disk storage a computer has, the more work it can do. The faster the memory and disks transmit data and instructions to the CPU, the faster it gets done. A hardware requirement is based on the size of the databases that will be created and the number of users or applications that will be served at the same time. How much? How fast?

Software Is
"Logic and Language"

Software deals with the details of an ever-changing business and must

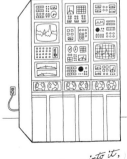

*if you bump into it,
it's hardware*

process transactions in a logical fashion. Languages are used to program the software. The "logic and language" involved in analysis and programming is generally far more complicated than specifying a storage and transmission requirement.

hardware failure

A malfunction within the electronic circuits or electromechanical components (disks, tapes) of a computer system. Contrast with *software failure*.

hardware interface

An architecture used to interconnect two pieces of equipment. It includes the design of the plug and socket, the type, number and purpose of the wires and the electrical signals that are passed across them. See *bus, local bus, ISA, VL-bus, RS-232, PCI, IDE, SCSI* and *channel*.

hardware interrupt

An interrupt caused by some action of a hardware device, such as the depression of a key or mouse movement. See *IRQ* and *interrupt*.

hardware key

Also called a "dongle," it is a copy protection device supplied with software that plugs into a computer port, typically the parallel port on a PC. The software sends a code to that port, and the key responds by reading out its serial number, which verifies its presence to the program. The key hinders software duplication, because each program is tied to a unique number, which is difficult to obtain, and the key has to be programmed with that number.
The key also acts as a pass-through to the printer or other peripheral. Multiple hardware keys can be used, each plugged in one after the other.

hardware monitor

A device attached to the hardware circuits of a computer that reads electronic signals directly in order to analyze system performance.

hardware platforms

Each hardware platform, or CPU family, has a unique machine language. All software presented to the computer for execution must be in the binary coded machine language of that CPU. Following is a list of the major hardware platforms in existence today.

Platform	Developed by/usage
x86	Intel, most PCs
680x0	Motorola, mostly Apple Mac
VAX	Digital's mini series, VMS OS
S/370	IBM mainframe architecture
AS/400	IBM midrange, formerly System/38
S/36	old IBM mini, System/36
Tandem	fault tolerant systems, Non-Stop
Unisys	Unisys mainframes
CDC	CDC mainframes and midrange
Wang	VS midrange

PDP/11	PDP was Digital's 1st mini
	PDP/11 chips still sold

RISC chips

88000	Motorola, DG, Encore
MIPS	SGI, Pyramid, Tandem, NEC, Siemens
SPARC	Sun and SPARC-licened clones
PA-RISC	HP workstations, minis
Alpha	Digital's newest series
PowerPC	Apple, IBM, Motorola, newest PC
i860	Intel, Stratus systems

hardware scaling

Enlarging a video frame by performing the operation within the circuits of the display adapter. Putting the function in a chip speeds up the process. See *video accelerator*.

hardware vendors

Following are the major hardware manufacturers in the computer industry and their past two year's performance. See also *software vendors*.

In 1994, the following companies collectively generated 225 billion dollars in sales and employed nearly one million people.

Revenues from Major Hardware Vendors

Year	Company	Sales (000,000)	Profit	Employees (000)

Computer System Manufacturers:

1994	IBM	64,052	3,021	243
1993		62,716	(8,101)	267
1992		65,096	(4,965)	308
1994	HP	24,991	1,599	98
1993		20,317	1,177	96
1992		16,427	549	93
1994	DEC	13,451	(2,156)	78
1993		14,371	(251)	94
1992		14,027	(2,796)	114
1994	Compaq	10,866	867	14
1993		7,191	462	11
1992		4,132	213	10
1994	Apple	9,189	310	15
1993		7,977	87	15
1992		7,087	530	15
1994	Unisys	7,400	101	46
1993		7,743	565	49
1992		8,422	(361)	54
1994	Sun	4,690	196	13
1993		4,309	157	13
1992		3,628	173	13

1994 Dell	3,475	149	6		1994 Western	1,540	73	7
1993	2,014	102	5		1993 Digital	1,225	(25)	7
1992	890	51	3		1992	940	(73)	7
1994 Gateway	2,701	96	5		1994 Maxtor	1,153	(258)	6
1993	1,732	66	4		1993	1,443	46	9
1992	1,107	70	18		1992	1,039	7	8

Semiconductor Manufacturers

1994 AST	2,369	54	7		1994 Motorola	22,245	1,560	132
1993	1,412	(54)	5		1993	16,983	1,022	120
1992	951	69	4		1992	13,341	453	107
1994 Tandem	2,108	170	8		1994 Intel	11,521	2,288	33
1993	2,031	(518)	10		1993	8,782	2,295	30
1992	2,058	(41)	11		1992	5,922	1,067	26
1994 Amdahl	1,639	75	6		1994 Rockwell	11,205	634	72
1993	1,681	(580)	6		1993 Int'l.	10,840	562	77
1992	2,554	(7)	9		1992	10,995	(1,036)	79
1994 Silicon	1,482	141	4		1994 Texas	10,315	691	56
1993 Graphics	1,091	95	4		1993 Instruments	8,523	472	59
1992	867	(118)	4		1992	7,470	247	61
1994 Data General	1,121	(88)	6		1994 National	2,295	264	22
1993	1,078	(60)	7		1993 Semiconductor	2,014	130	23
1992	1,127	(63)	7		1992	1,726	(120)	27
1994 Intergraph	1,041	(70)	9		1994 Advanced	2,135	305	12
1993	1,050	(116)	10		1993 Micro Devices	1,648	229	12
1992	1,182	8	10		1992	1,531	245	12

1994 Cray Research	922	56	5
1993	895	61	5
1992	798	(15)	5
1994 Wang Labs	855	23**	5
1993	1,247	(197)	4
1992	1,910	(357)	13

** excluding one-time adjustment

Drive Manufacturers

1994 Seagate	3,500	225	53
1993	3,044	195	43
1992	2,889	63	43
1994 Conner	2,365	110	10
1993	2,152	(445)	9
1992	2,273	121	13
1994 Quantum	2,131	3	3
1993	1,697	94	2
1992	1,128	47	18
1994 Storage	1,625	41	10
1993 Technology	1,405	(78)	10
1992	1,521	15	10

hardware virtual memory

Virtual memory management built into a chip. Although virtual memory can be performed by software only, it is far more efficient to do it in hardware. See *DAT* and *PMMU.*

hardwired

(1) Electronic circuitry that is designed to perform a specific task. See *hard coded.*
(2) Devices that are closely or tightly coupled. For example, a hardwired terminal is directly connected to a computer without going through a switched network.

harmonic distortion

In communications, frequencies that are generated as multiples of the original frequency due to irregularities in the transmission line.

Harvard Graphics

Popular presentation graphics programs for DOS and Windows from Software Publishing Corporation, Mountain View, CA. Its DOS version was one of the first business graphics packages to allow for the creation of columnar and free form text charts.

hash total, hash value

A method for ensuring the accuracy of processed data. It is a total of several fields of data in a file, including fields not normally used in calculations, such as account number. At various stages in the processing, the hash total is recalculated and compared with the original. If any data has been lost or changed, a mismatch signals an error.

HASP

(Houston Automatic Spooling Program) A mainframe spooling program that provides task, job and data management functions.

Hayes compatible

Refers to modems controlled by the Hayes command language. See *AT command set.*

Hayes Smartmodem

A family of intelligent modems for personal computers from Hayes Microcomputer Products, Inc., Atlanta, GA. Hayes developed the intelligent modem for first-generation personal computers in 1978, and its command language (Hayes Standard AT Command Set) for modem control has become an industry-standard.

The Intelligent Modem

An intelligent modem has a command state and an online state. In the command state, it accepts instructions. In the online state, it dials, answers, transmits and receives.

Once connected, it performs the handshaking with the remote modem, which is similar to the opening exchange of a telephone call. The called party says "hello," the calling party says "hello, this is..." After this, the real conversation begins. If the modem's speaker is on, you can hear the whistles and tones used in the handshake. Once the handshake is completed, you are online with the other computer, and data can be transmitted back and forth.

An important part of the Hayes standard is the escape sequence, which tells the modem to switch from online to the command state. It usually consists of three plus signs in sequence (+++) with a Hayes-patented, one-second guard time interval before and after it, which prevents the modem from mistaking a random occurrence of the escape sequence. The escape sequence and guard time interval can be programmed in the modem's Status registers.

To issue an escape sequence, hold down the shift key and press + + +. Pause one second before and after the sequence. The modem will return the OK result code, indicating it is ready to accept commands.

HC

See *high color*.

HD

(1) (High Density) The designation for high-density diskettes; for example, the 5.25" 1.2MB and 3.5" 1.44MB floppies. Contrast with *DD*.
(2) (Hard Disk) For example, FD/HD refers to a floppy disk/hard disk device such as a controller.

HDA

(Head Disk Assembly) The mechanical components of a disk drive (minus the electronics), which includes the actuators, access arms, read/write heads and platters.

HDCD

(1) (High Density CD) See *DVD*.
(2) (High Definition Compatible Digital Processing) A digital processing technique from Pacific Microsonics that increases fidelity on audio CDs. It uses a 20-bit master instead of 16 bits and stores the additional data in a subchannel that is processed on HDCD-equipped players. Some of the additional data is included in the regular recording which is audible on standard audio CD players.

HDD

(Hard Disk Drive) See *hard disk*.

HDLC

(High-level Data Link Control) An ISO communications protocol used in X.25 packet switching networks. It provides error correction at the data link layer. SDLC, LAP and LAPB are subsets of HDLC.

HDSL

(High bit rate Digital Subscriber Line) A technology for transmitting at T1 and higher data rates over regular telephone lines. A typical HDSL transmission is 784Kbps in each direction. HDSL uses a coding method that was derived from ISDN. See *ADSL*.

HDTV

(High Definition TV) A high-resolution TV standard. Japan was the first to develop HDTV and currently broadcasts an 1125-line signal picked up on 36" to 50" TV sets that cost about $10,000. Both Japan and Europe's HDTV use traditional analog signalling.
The U.S. is currently developing a single HDTV standard from specifications by various proponents, and the goal is to have it working by the 1996 Olympics. The technology will be all-digital with a resolution anywhere from 787 to 1200 lines. The refresh rate will be similar to the current NTSC 60 half-frames per second, or perhaps 60 full frames.
The current TV standard (NTSC) is a 525-line analog signal. HDTV will be transmitted on separate channels concurrently with the NTSC signals.

HDX

See *half-duplex*.

head

See *read/write head* and *HDA*.

head crash

The physical destruction of a hard disk. Misalignment or contamination with dust can cause the read/write head to collide with the disk's recording surface. The data is destroyed, and both the disk platter and head have to be replaced.

The read/write head touches the surface of a floppy disk, but on a hard disk, it hovers above its surface at a distance that is less than the diameter of a human hair. It has been said that the read/write head flying over the disk surface is like trying to fly a jet plane six inches above the earth's surface.

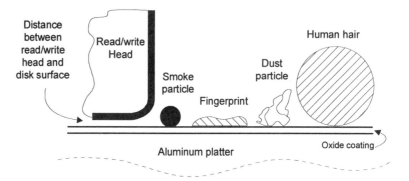

head disk assembly

See *HDA*.

head end

The originating point in a communications system. In cable TV, the head end is where the cable company has its satellite dish and TV antenna for receiving incoming programming. In online services, the head end is the service company's computer system and databases.

header

(1) The first record in a disk or tape file. It may be used for identification only (name, date of last update, etc.), or it may describe the structural layout of the contents, as is common with many document and database formats.

(2) In a document or report, common text printed at the top of every page.

(3) In communications, the first part of the message, which contains controlling data, such as originating and destination stations, message type and priority level.

(4) Any caption or description used as a headline.

header label

A record used for file identification that is recorded at the beginning of the file.

head skew

The offset distance from the start of the previous track so that the head has time to switch from top of platter to bottom of platter and be at the start of the new track. See *cylinder skew*.

heap

In programming, the common pool of free memory available to the program.

heartbeat

See *MHz*.

heat sink

A material that absorbs heat.

helical scan

A recording method used on videotape and digital audio tape (DAT) that runs the tracks diagonally from top to bottom in order to increase the storage capacity.

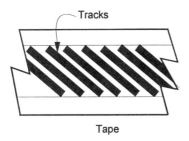

Tracks

Tape

help

On-screen instruction regarding the use of a program. On PCs, pressing F1 is the de facto standard for getting help. With graphics-based interfaces (Mac, Windows, etc.), clicking a "?" or HELP button gets help. See *context sensitive help*.

help compiler

Software that translates text and compiler instructions into an online help system.

help desk

A source of technical support for hardware or software. Help desks are staffed by people that can either solve the problem directly or forward the problem to someone else. Help desk software provides the means to log in problems and track them until solved. It also provides the management information regarding support activities.

henry

A unit of measurement of the strength of a magnetic field in an inductor. See *inductor*.

Hercules Graphics

A video display standard for PCs from Hercules Computer Technology Inc., Berkeley, CA, that provides monochrome graphics and text with a resolution of 720x348 pixels. IBM's first PC monochrome display did not provide graphics, and Hercules introduced its display adapter to fill the void in 1982. It quickly became a de facto standard incorporated into all monochrome display boards.

Hertz

The frequency of electrical vibrations (cycles) per second. Abbreviated "Hz," one Hz is equal to one cycle per second. In 1883, Heinrich Hertz detected electromagnetic waves. See *MHz*.

heterogeneous

Not the same. Contrast with *homogeneous*.

heterogeneous environment

Hardware and system software from different vendors. Increasingly, organizations use computers, operating systems and databases from a variety of vendors. Contrast with *homogeneous environment*.

heuristic

A method of problem solving using exploration and trial and error methods. Heuristic program design provides a framework for solving the problem in contrast with a fixed set of rules (algorithmic) that cannot vary.

Hewlett-Packard

See *HP*.

hex

(HEXadecimal) Hexadecimal means 16. The base 16 numbering system is used as a shorthand for representing binary numbers. Each half byte (four bits) is assigned a hex digit as follows:

Dec	Hex	Binary	Dec	Hex	Binary	Dec	Hex	Binary
0	0	0000	6	6	0110	10	A	1010
1	1	0001	7	7	0111	11	B	1011
2	2	0010	8	8	1000	12	C	1100
3	3	0011	9	9	1001	13	D	1101
4	4	0100				14	E	1110
5	5	0101				15	F	1111

In a hex number, each digit position has a value 16 times greater than the one to its right. Two hex digits make up one byte; for example, A7h (h means hex) is equivalent to decimal 167 (10x16 + 7x1). See *hex chart*.

	A		7
4096	256	16	1

The hex number A000 (pronounced "A thousand") is equivalent to 40,960 in decimal (4096x10); however, for PC addressing, hex addresses are interpreted uniquely (see *paragraph*).

$, h and H

Sometimes a $ is used to represent hex values as well as upper and lower-case H; for example, $3E0, 3E0h and 3E0H are the same hex number.

hexadecimal

See *hex*.

HFS

(Hierarchical File System) The file system used in the Macintosh. See *hierarchical file system*.

HGC

See *Hercules Graphics*.

HHOK

Digispeak for "ha ha only kidding."

Hi-8

A video recording and playback system that uses 8mm video cassettes and the S-video technology.

ASCII Character Codes (hexadecimal notation)

STANDARD ASCII				EXTENDED ASCII	
The first 32 characters (0-31) are control codes				(IBM and compatible pcs)	

00	NUL	Null	21	!	51	Q	80	Ç	AE	«	DC	▄
01	SOH	Start of heading	22	"	52	R	81	ü	AF	»	DD	▌
02	STX	Start of text	23	#	53	S	82	é	B0	░	DE	▐
03	ETX	End of text	24	$	54	T	83	â	B1	▒	DF	▀
04	EOT	End of transmit	25	%	55	U	84	ä	B2	▓	E0	α
05	ENQ	Enquiry	26	&	56	V	85	à	B3	│	E1	β
06	ACK	Acknowledge	27	'	57	W	86	å	B4	┤	E2	Γ
07	BEL	Audible bell	28	(	58	X	87	ç	B5	╡	E3	π
08	BS	Backspace	29	)	59	Y	88	ê	B6	╢	E4	Σ
09	HT	Horizontal tab	2A	*	5A	Z	89	ë	B7	╖	E5	σ
0A	LF	Line feed	2B	+	5B	[	8A	è	B8	╕	E6	μ
0B	VT	Vertical tab	2C	,	5C	\	8B	ï	B9	╣	E7	τ
0C	FF	Form feed	2D	–	5D	]	8C	î	BA	║	E8	Φ
0D	CR	Carriage return	2E	.	5E	^	8D	ì	BB	╗	E9	Θ
0E	SO	Shift out	2F	/	5F	_	8E	Ä	BC	╝	EA	Ω
0F	SI	Shift in	30	0	60	`	8F	Å	BD	╜	EB	δ
10	DLE	Data link escape	31	1	61	a	90	É	BE	╛	EC	∞
11	DC1	Device control 1	32	2	62	b	91	æ	BF	┐	ED	φ
12	DC2	Device control 2	33	3	63	c	92	Æ	C0	└	EE	ε
13	DC3	Device control 3	34	4	64	d	93	ô	C1	┴	EF	∩
14	DC4	Device control 4	35	5	65	e	94	ö	C2	┬	F0	≡
15	NAK	Neg. acknowledge	36	6	66	f	95	ò	C3	├	F1	±
16	SYN	Synchronous idle	37	7	67	g	96	û	C4	─	F2	≥
17	ETB	End trans. block	38	8	68	h	97	ù	C5	┼	F3	≤
18	CAN	Cancel	39	9	69	i	98	ÿ	C6	╞	F4	⌠
19	EM	End of medium	3A	:	6A	j	99	Ö	C7	╟	F5	⌡
1A	SUB	Substitution	3B	;	6B	k	9A	Ü	C8	╚	F6	÷
1B	ESC	Escape	3C	<	6C	l	9B	¢	C9	╔	F7	≈
1C	FS	Figures shift	3D	=	6D	m	9C	£	CA	╩	F8	°
1D	GS	Group separator	3E	>	6E	n	9D	¥	CB	╦	F9	•
1E	RS	Record separator	3F	?	6F	o	9E	₧	CC	╠	FA	·
1F	US	Unit separator	40	@	70	p	9F	ƒ	CD	═	FB	√
			41	A	71	q	A0	á	CE	╬	FC	η
20	SP	Blank space	42	B	72	r	A1	í	CF	╧	FD	²
		(Space bar)	43	C	73	s	A2	ó	D0	╨	FE	■
			44	D	74	t	A3	ú	D1	╤	FF	
			45	E	75	u	A4	ñ	D2	╥		
			46	F	76	v	A5	Ñ	D3	╙		
			47	G	77	w	A6	ª	D4	╘		
			48	H	78	x	A7	º	D5	╒		
			49	I	79	y	A8	¿	D6	╓		
			4A	J	7A	z	A9	⌐	D7	╫		
			4B	K	7B	{	AA	¬	D8	╪		
			4C	L	7C	|	AB	½	D9	┘		
			4D	M	7D	}	AC	¼	DA	┌		
			4E	N	7E	~	AD	¡	DB	█		
			4F	O	7F	⌂						
			50	P								

hidden file

A file classification that prevents a file from being accessed. It is usually an operating system file; however, utility programs let users hide files to prevent unauthorized access.

hierarchical

A structure made up of different levels like a company organization chart. The higher levels have control or precedence over the lower levels. Hierarchical structures are a one to many relationship; each item having one or more items below it.

hierarchical communications

A network controlled by a host computer that is responsible for managing all connections. Contrast with *peer-to-peer communications*.

hierarchical file system

A file organization method that stores data in a top-to-bottom organization structure. All internal access to the data starts at the top and proceeds throughout the levels of the hierarchy.

Most all operating systems use hierarchical file systems to store data and programs, including DOS, OS/2, Windows NT and 95, UNIX and the Macintosh. See *root directory, path* and *HFS*.

hierarchical storage management

See *HSM*.

hierarchy

A structure that has a predetermined ordering from high to low. In object technology, the hierarchy is a ordering of objects.

high availability

Also called *RAS* (reliability, availability, serviceability) or *fault resilient*, it refers to a multiprocessing system that can quickly recover from a failure. It also implies servicing a component in the system without shutting down the entire operation. This is not the same as fault tolerant, in which redundant components are designed for continuous processing without skipping a heartbeat. See *hot fix*.

high-capacity CD-ROM

See *DVD*.

high color

The ability to generate 32,768 colors (15 bits) or 65,536 colors (16-bit). 15-bit color uses five bits for each red, green and blue pixel. The 16th bit may be a color, such as XGA with 5-red, 6-green and 5-blue, or be an overlay bit that selects pixels to display over video input. See *true color*.

high definition TV

See *HDTV*.

high density

Refers to increased storage capacity of bits and/or tracks per square inch. See *HD*.

high-density CD-ROM

See *DVD*.

high DOS memory

Same as *UMA*.

high-level format

A set of indexes on the disk that the operating system uses to keep track of the data stored on the disk. See *format program*.

high-level language

A machine-independent programming language, such as FORTRAN, COBOL, BASIC, Pascal and C. It lets the programmer concentrate on the logic of the problem to be solved rather than the intricacies of the machine architecture such as is required with low-level assembly languages.

There are dramatic differences between high-level languages. Look up the terms C, BASIC and COBOL, and review the sample code. What is considered high level depends on the era. There were assembly languages thirty years ago that were easier to understand than C.

highlight

To identify an area on screen in order to select, move, delete or change it in some manner.

highlight bar

The currently-highlighted menu item. Choice is made by moving the bar to the desired item and pressing enter or clicking the mouse. The bar is a different color on color screens or reverse video on monochrome screens.

high memory

(1) The uppermost end of memory.
(2) In PCs, it refers to either memory in the upper part of the first megabyte (between 640K and 1M), called the *Upper Memory Area*, or *UMA*, or to memory above 1M, called *extended memory*. It may also refer to the 64K area between 1024K and 1088K, called the *High Memory Area*, or *HMA*. Real straightforward, isn't it? See *PC memory, UMA, HMA* and *extended memory*.

High-Performance Computing

A federal initiative to enhance U.S. computing capability that includes a T3-speed network linking agencies, private companies and schools to supercomputer centers.

High-Performance Routing

See *HPR.*

high resolution

A high-quality image on a display screen or printed form. The more dots used per square inch, the higher the quality. To display totally realistic images including the shades of human skin requires about 1,000x1,000 pixels on a 12" diagonal screen. Desktop laser printers print respectable text and graphics at 300 dpi, but typesetting machines print 1,270 and 2,540 dpi. At 600 dpi, laser printers can produce excellent text for camera-ready reproduction. Going beyond 600 dpi does not generally make much improvement with text unless the text is very small (6-8 points). On the other hand, photographs and shaded drawings require more than 600 dpi resolution for quality reproduction in a book or journal.

High Sierra

The first CD-ROM standard that later evolved into ISO 9660. It was named for an area near Lake Tahoe where the format was developed in 1985.

high tech

Refers to the latest advancements in computers and electronics as well as to the social and political environment and consequences created by such machines.

HiJaak

A graphics file conversion and screen capture program for PCs from Inset Systems Inc., Brookfield, CT. It supports a wide variety of raster and vector graphics formats as well as fax boards. It also handles conversion between PC and Mac formats.

HIMEM.SYS

An extended memory manager that is included with DOS and Windows, starting with DOS 5 and Windows 3.0. It allows programs to cooperatively allocate extended memory in 286 and higher PCs. HIMEM.SYS is an XMS driver. In Windows 95, HIMEM.SYS is automatically loaded at startup.

hints

Font instructions that make a character uniform and legible at small point sizes and lower resolutions. They also ensure that serifs and accents appear in proper proportion. When there are not enough pixels in the print or display image, smaller fonts can sometimes translate into patterns that are not recognizable as the characters they represent. Hints ensure that both sides of an H, for example, must be of uniform width and that certain elements of the character cannot be left out. Hints are not necessary when printing at 600 dpi or more, but are required when printing characters 13 points or less at 300 dpi. When displaying those same characters on a screen with a 96 dpi or lower resolution, hints are also needed.

HIPO

(Hierarchy plus Input-Process-Output) Pronounced "hy-po." An IBM flow-charting technique that provides a graphical method for designing and documenting programs.

HiPPI

(HIgh Performance Parallel Interface channel) An ANSI-standard high-speed communications channel that uses a 32-bit or 64-bit cable and transmits at 100 or 200 Mbytes/sec. It is used as a point-to-point supercomputer channel or, with a crosspoint switch, as a high-speed LAN.

hi res

Same as *high resolution*.

histogram

A chart displaying horizontal or vertical bars. The length of the bars are in proportion to the values of the data items they represent.

history

A user's input and keystrokes entered within the current session. A history feature keeps track of user commands and/or retrieved items so that they can be quickly reused or reviewed.

HKEY

See *Windows 95 Registry*.

HLLAPI

(High Level Language Application Program Interface) An IBM programming interface that allows a PC application to communicate with a mainframe application. The hardware hookup is handled via normal micro to mainframe 3270 emulation. An extended version of the interface (EHLLAPI) has also been defined.

HLS

(Hue Lightness Saturation) A variation of the HSV color model. The H and L in

HLS correspond to the H and V in the HSV model. However, the saturation component is measured differently; for example, pure green in HLS is 120,1,0.5 compared to an HSV of 120,1,1. See *HSV*.

HMA

(High Memory Area) In PCs, the first 64K of extended memory from 1024K to 1088K, which can be accessed by DOS. It is managed by the HIMEM.SYS driver. It was discovered by accident that this area could be used by DOS, even though it was beyond the traditional one-megabyte barrier.

HMD

(Head Mounted Display) Typically refers to the stereoscopic goggles worn by participants of a virtual reality system. Contrast with *CAVE*.

HMOS

(High-density MOS) A chip with a high density of NMOS transistors.

hog

A program that uses an excessive amount of computer resources, such as memory or disk, or takes a long time to execute.

Hollerith machine

Herman Hollerith
A rather dapper young man for the father of modern data processing.
(Photo courtesy of Library of Congress.)

The first automatic data processing system. It was used to count the 1890 U.S. census. Developed by Herman Hollerith, a statistician who had worked for the Census Bureau, the system used a hand punch to record the data in dollar-bill-sized punched cards and a tabulating machine to count them.

It was estimated that, with manual methods, the 1890 census wouldn't be completed until after 1900. With Hollerith's machines, it took two years and saved five million dollars.

Hollerith formed the Tabulating Machine Company and sold his machines throughout the world for a variety of accounting functions. In 1911, his company was merged into the company that was later renamed IBM.

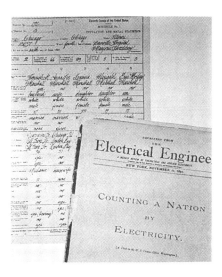

What a Novel Concept?
The date on this issue of ***Electrical Engineer*** was November 11, 1891. The page at the top is a census form filled out by one of the census takers.

Hollerith's Keypunch Machine

All 60 million Americans were counted by punching holes into a card from the census forms. *(Photo courtesy of International Business Machines Corporation.)*

Hollerith's Tabulating Machine

The card was placed in the press, the handle was pushed down, and the data was tabulated on the dials. Then the appropriate lid opened up on the sorting box, and the punched card was dropped in. *(Photo courtesy of Smithsonian Institution.)*

High Tech, 1890 Style
The beginning of data processing made the August 30, 1890 cover of Scientific American. The binary concept. A hole or no hole! *(Photo courtesy of Scientic American Magazine.)*

holographic storage

A future technology that records data as holograms that fill up the entire mass of a tiny optical cylinder no bigger than one millimeter in diameter by one centimeter in length. The hologram is created by two lasers. One laser is beamed through a matrix of LCD shutters that are opened or closed based on the binary pattern of the page of data that is going to be stored. Using an LCD matrix of 1,000 pixels on each side, the page could be a million bits.

A reference laser is angled into the data laser intersecting it at the mouth of the cylinder. If the angle and/or frequency is changed, another hologram can be created overlapping and filling the same space as the first hologram. In fact, 10,000 holograms (pages) can be stored in one tiny cylinder.

The data is read by directing the reference laser back into the cylinder, causing a reflection into a matrix of CCD sensors, the same size as the LCD matrix. Although research in this area stems back to the 1960s, it is expected that holographic storage will begin to make inroads around the turn of the century. In the space of one of today's disk drives, holographic storage could hold 50 million images or 10 billion pages of text. By the time this technology is commercially feasible, computers may be fast enough to use it. See *PRISM*.

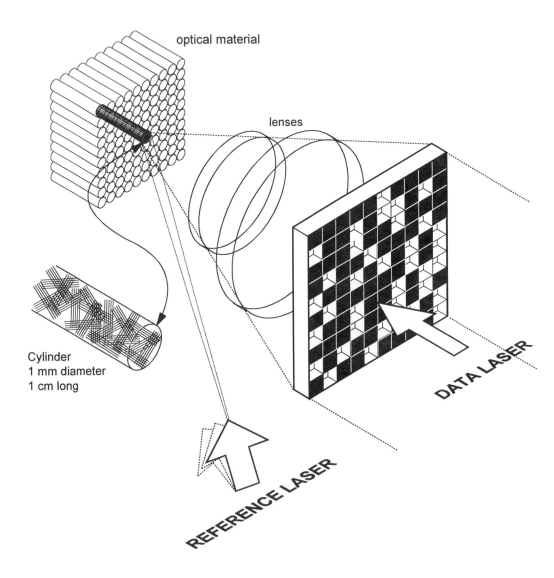

optical material

lenses

Cylinder
1 mm diameter
1 cm long

DATA LASER

REFERENCE LASER

Holographic Storage
The intersection of the data laser and the reference laser at the mouth of the cylinder creates the holographic page (hologram).

home brew

Products that are developed at home by hobbyists.

home button

An icon that represents the beginning of a file or a set of basic or starting functions.

home computer

In the 1980s, a home computer was the lowest-priced computer of the time, such as an Apple II, Commodore 64 or 128, Tandy Color Computer or Atari ST. Today, the term generally refers to a PC or Mac.

home key

A keyboard key used to move the cursor to the top of the screen or file or to the previous word or beginning of line. See *home button*.

home page

A foundation, or starting, page on the World Wide Web. Home pages are used as tables of contents and indexes to other resources on the Web or to other Internet servers. See *World Wide Web* and *URL*.

home run

A single wire that begins at a central distribution point (hub, PBX, etc.) and runs to its destination (workstation, telephone, etc.) without connecting to anything else.

homogeneous

The same. Contrast with *heterogeneous*.

homogeneous environment

Hardware and system software from one vendor; for example, an all-IBM or all-Digital shop. Contrast with *heterogeneous environment*.

Honeywell

The Information Systems division of the Honeywell temperature control company was one of the first major computer companies in the US. Honeywell's computers were extremely advanced from the very beginning and gained a solid reputation. In the early 1960s, the Honeywell 200 series gave IBM a run for its money, because it outperformed the 1401 and could run its programs via emulation.

Honeywell eventually took over GE's computer business and then Bull took over Honeywell. The famous Honeywell name unfortunately only remains as the "H" in Bull HN. See *Bull HN*.

The Honeywell Datamatic
In the late 1950s, the Datamatic was a very sophisticated computer. *(Photo courtesy of Honeywell Inc.)*

hook

In programming, instructions that provide breakpoints for future expansion. Hooks may be changed to call some outside routine or function or may be places where additional processing is added.

hooked vector

A trapped interrupt in a PC. The pointer for a particular interrupt in the interrupt vector table has been modified to jump to a new routine to service that interrupt.

hookemware

Free software that contains a limited number of features designed to entice the user into purchasing the more comprehensive version.

hop count

The number of gateways and routers in a transmission path. Each hop slows down transmission since the gateway or router must analyze or convert the packet of data before forwarding it to its destination.

hopper

A tray, or chute, that accepts input to a mechanical device, such as a disk duplicator.

horizontal market software

Software packages, such as word processors and spreadsheets, that are used in all industries (banking, insurance, etc.). Such products are also called *productivity software*. Contrast with *vertical market software*.

horizontal resolution

The number of elements, or dots, on a horizontal line (columns in a matrix). Contrast with *vertical resolution*.

horizontal scaling

In multiprocessing, adding more computer systems to the environment. Contrast with *vertical scaling*.

horizontal scan frequency

The number of lines illuminated on a video screen in one second. For example, a resolution of 400 lines refreshed 60 times per second requires a scan rate of 24KHz plus overhead (time to bring the beam back to the beginning of the next line). Same as horizontal sync frequency in TV. Contrast with *vertical scan frequency*.

horizontal software

See *horizontal market software*.

horizontal sync

See *horizontal scan frequency*.

HOS

(Higher Order Software) A design and documentation technique used to break down an information system into a set of functions that are mathematically correct and error free. It uses a rigid set of rules for the decomposition of the total system into its elementary components. The resulting specifications are complete enough to have machine language programs generated directly from them.

host

A central computer or server in a network. It used to refer to only large centralized mainframes or timesharing computers. The term is still used in that manner, but it can also refer to any computer that functions as the source of information or services. It can be a server in a network (source of sharable programs and data) as well as a desktop PC that functions as a host to its peripherals (source of electrical power and commands). See *host adapter*.

host adapter

Also called a controller, it is a device that connects one or more peripheral units to a computer. It is typically an expansion card that plugs into the bus. IDE drives and SCSI peripherals are examples of peripheral interfaces that call their controllers host adapters. See *host*.

host based

A communications system that is controlled by a central computer system.

host mode

A communications mode that allows a computer to answer an incoming telephone call and receive data without human assistance.

hot fix

To repair a component in the middle of its operation. For example, some SCSI drives can automatically move the data in sectors that are becoming hard to read to spare sectors without even the SCSI host adapter being aware of it, let alone the operating system or the user. See *hot swap*.

HotJava

A Web browser from Sun Microsystems that supports the Java programming language, also developed by Sun. HotJava executes Java programs embedded directly within Web documents.

hotkey

The key or key combination that causes some function to occur in the computer, no matter what else is currently running. It is commonly used to activate a memory resident (TSR) program.

hot link

A predefined connection between programs so that when information in one database or file is changed, related information in other databases and files are also updated. See *hypertext, hypergraphic, compound document* and *OLE*.

hot potato routing

In communications, rerouting a message as soon as it arrives.

hot spot

Hot spot

(1) An icon or part of a larger image used as a hyperlink to another document or file. When the hot spot is selected by clicking on it, the linked material is searched and displayed.

(2) The exact part of an icon or screen pointer that is sensitive to selection. A hot spot may be part of a larger image. For example, an image may have several hot spots, one for each of its components. When clicked, a greater explanation of the component is produced. Where hot spots begin and end determine how easy they are to select.

The screen pointer also has a hot spot, which is a small number of pixels that make contact with the icon's hot spot. For example, the tip of an arrow or finger pointer or the crosspoint of an X-shaped pointer may be the pointer's hot spot.

(3) A network node that is processing at its maximum or is backlogged due to an excessive number of transactions.

hot swap

To pull out a component from a system and plug in a new one while the power is still on and the unit is still operating. Redundant systems can be designed to swap drives, circuit boards, power supplies, virtually anything that is duplexed within the computer. See *warm swap* and *hot fix*.

hot topics

Following is a synopsis of the latest trends in the computer industry.

The Information Superhighway

Due to the Clinton/Gore administration's interest in the information superhighway, starting in late 1993, books on the Internet flooded the shelves of bookstores. However, the Internet was never intended to be the sum total of an information superhighway. It was cited merely as a model for an information superhighway. Nevertheless, the Internet has all of a sudden, become synonymous with the "i-way" or "infobahn."

The real superhighway concept is meant to modernize the telecommunications infrastructure in the U.S. so that everyone has access to information and educational materials no matter what their station in life. Right now, there is a monthly service fee to get onto the Internet, and you have to have a personal computer. This is clearly not a service for everyone.

The delivery of an information superhighway for the masses is more realistically in the hands of the telephone and cable companies, because they are already wired into everyone's home and are capable of delivering multimedia content.

Entertainment may be more of a driving force than information and education as video-on-demand and all variety of interactive services converge into this new frontier of online delivery. With deals being made daily by cable and telephone companies, video providers and TV networks, major companies are positioning themselves for what they believe to be a huge consumer market.

One thing is certain, some pretty large investments are going to go down the tubes until it all settles down and mom, pop and the kids decide what they do and don't want, what they will and won't watch and, more to the point, what they will and won't pay for. See *information superhighway* and *Internet*.

Multimedia

Multimedia means a lot of different things to people, but the bottom line is that the integration of pictures, voice and video with traditional text is a major force that will bring changes in hardware and software for years to come. Multimedia pushes the hardware to extremes. Typing a page of text uses three to five thousand bytes of storage, but scanning that same page and treating it as an image can take 50 thousand bytes or more.

Online help in the form of video clips promises improved productivity, but a few minutes of video can eat up an entire hard disk. Audio messages, while not as storage intensive, require considerably more capacity than text. Thus, multimedia not only impacts the production of CD-ROM drives, sound cards, speakers and a whole variety of imaging and video software, but larger storage capacities and faster networks must also meet the demand of ever-increasing multimedia files.

While CD-ROMs hold 650 megabytes of data, they are as slow as floppy disks. We are already seeing CD-ROMs with huge databases crammed to the limit. New standards for increased capacity, faster speeds, network servers, carousel and juke box drives are options. But, ideally the single user would like a 10 gigabyte hard disk to store a dozen CD-ROMs on it and run them at high speed. The drive should also cost $1000. At current prices as low as 30 cents per megabyte, it won't be too long before it will. See *DVD* and *holographic storage*.

Although CD-ROMs are hot, videoconferencing is another multimedia application that is starting to gain alot of attention. Having been around for a decade in the form of room systems for group conferencing between remote locations, desktop videoconferencing is expected to explode over the next several years. See *videoconferencing*.

Client/Server and Downsizing

Switching applications from minicomputer and mainframes to LANs of desktop computers has been the trend for the past six or seven years. Minis and mainframes may still be used as servers to the desktop machines, but dumb terminals to a single, central computer architecture is no longer in vogue for implementing most new information systems.

Many organizations are migrating to client/server LANs in stages, placing new information systems on the LANs and planning to convert legacy systems as necessary. The primary reasons for downsizing are cost/performance, increasingly favoring LANs, the variety of applications available for desktop machines and the wide variety of sources for hardware. However, organizations have a huge investment in legacy systems, and downsizing must be carefully analyzed.

As desktop hardware becomes faster and as desktop operating systems and LAN networking software become more stable, providing the industrial strength required to perform online transaction processing 24 hours a day, more and more legacy systems will be converted to client/server architecture.

Other factors necessitate the conversion as well. Many legacy systems were programmed years ago with the original programmers either long gone or nearing retirement. Old systems can be extremely difficult to maintain, and outsourcing the programming to keep the systems current is expensive. Many older information systems were developed to handle a two-digit year and assume a '19' prefix. When we reach the year 2000, our software has to handle a four-digit year. After a while, it's just time for a change.

Just to throw a fly in the ointment, there is also a great possibility that by the year 2010 or 2015, there will be a push to go back to the central mainframe concept. The mainframe may have 1,000 processors in it, but reigning in all the complexity from the desktop back into the glass-enclosed datacenter may not be such a bad idea. With transmission capacities as high as they will be tomorrow, a dumb terminal back to an intelligent, centralized switching system may provide better network management and system administration than the client/server architecture that's so hot right now and growing increasingly more complex every day.

The universe works in cycles.

Networking

Just as most organizations have gone through round one in networking their desktop computers together for information sharing and electronic mail, the demands of client/server applications, multimedia and realtime video are forcing them to plan round two.

Passing image and video files, especially realtime video, over a network places greater demands on network throughput. As networks expand, monitoring and controlling their routine operation become more difficult. Tying together heterogeneous networks from different departments, subsidiaries and divisions is a daunting task for network administrators and IS managers.

The network has becoming the information backbone of the entire organization and will continue to be the most complex of all operations to manage. See *enterprise networking* and *ATM*.

The PowerPCs

The PowerPC chips from IBM and Motorola offer the first major threat to the x86 architecture, which has been the mainstay of the PC industry. Although Intel has done a commendable job enhancing the x86 line, with Pentium CPUs over a hundred times faster than the first 8088 chip, the x86 architecture suffers from an ancestry that evolved from a calculator chip.

The joint venture of IBM, Apple and Motorola has produced RISC-based PowerPC chips that have been designed in the 1990s for the 21st century. The first implementation of the PowerPC is the Power Macintosh line that runs the Macintosh operating system with sizable performance increases. The PowerMacs also run DOS and Windows applications via emulation with upcoming models expected to provide exceptional speed.

IBM has introduced its PowerPC-based PCs, which run AIX, Windows NT and eventually OS/2. Other vendors are expected to follow.

With all new hardware, many take a wait and see attitude. Nevertheless, the PowerPC has caused Intel to announce future CPU designs earlier than it might have, and the competition between Intel and Motorola is definitely heating up. See *PowerPC* and *PowerMac*.

Objects

Just like plugging an expansion board into an expansion slot, objects and object-oriented programming are designed to make software components equally interchangeable. The ability to plug together software routines that can be purchased from a wide variety of sources and have them work together across a distributed environment holds enormous promise for software developers and users. Standardizing an object format that will run across all platforms is perhaps as impossible as standardizing on any other area in computing. Therefore, it remains to be seen how bumpy the road to success will be in this area. See *objects* and *object-oriented programming*.

housekeeping

A set of instructions that are executed at the beginning of a program. It sets all counters and flags to their starting values and generally readies the program for execution.

how to choose an accounting package

The following article was written by and is reprinted with permission of Mr. Frank Arbaugh, 213 Pinecrest Lane, Lansdale, PA 19446, a consultant in accounting systems for small businesses in the greater Philadelphia area.

How to choose Accounting Software

The right accounting package should (1) give you the information you need for management, tax estimation and tax preparation, and (2) enable you to easily input the figures. Management needs are usually balance sheets and P & L statements. There also may be a need for cash flow analysis, receivable/payable management and identifying profit or loss on a job by job basis (job costing).

Tax estimation/preparation functions should enable you to prepare quarterly state and federal estimated tax returns. The system should also give you annual figures that can easily be used for tax preparation, both state and federal. Much of this will depend on you and your accountant's ability to set up your chart of accounts properly. Sometimes there are conflicts between management and tax needs when setting up the accounts, but they can be resolved in time.

Most accounting software has provisions for recurring entries, math calculators (debits must equal credits), and the ability to add accounts during data entry. The issue of whether you account on a cash or accrual basis must be analyzed. Most packages do not support your invoicing if you are on a cash basis. Each package has its good and bad points in these areas.

Job costing is not a traditional accounting function. It is an additional entry that keeps track of the costs involved with a certain activity or job. Some accounting packages support it directly while others can be adapted for it.

Accounting software imposes certain demands on you or your bookkeeper. If you have a manual system, you learned which journals to keep what records in, and perhaps at the end of the month you posted them all to the general ledger. There may not have been much thought about the impact of each transaction on management information or even tax strategies. But electronic accounting forces you to deal with these issues from the start, when you set up your chart of accounts, and on a daily basis when you enter and disburse each transaction.

You now will be generating the financial statements and reports, and the overall structure and disbursements will determine the usefulness and validity of these reports and statements. The bottom line is that management must understand and participate in the setup and daily use of these systems to be sure that they serve the needs defined above.

Bookkeeping, tax strategies through your accountant as well as management needs must be closely coordinated for best results. Perhaps people who have never communicated before will get to know each other! The good part is that no tax deductions should slip away because of a lack of documentation.

How do you choose the right package? You should have identified your needs through discussions with your accountant and bookkeeper, which may be one in the same. However, you are playing Russian roulette if you expect them to make this selection for you. You will lose a golden learning opportunity if you don't take this responsibility yourself or share it equally. Prices for accounting software packages start at $30 and range upwards to $10,000 and more, but price is not a measure of how well any system will meet your needs. Even the least expensive one takes effort to install and set up properly. If the software costs $300 or more, it might have more features than a small business will ever need.

Installing an accounting package is an on-going process. Don't expect to get everything right or the way you want it the first time. It is also not recommended that you drastically change your chart of accounts midyear, since the validity and usefulness of the figures are greatly determined by consistency. Once you make a decision on what account to disperse a particular expense to, you should not change that during the same accounting period.

Nobody can make a specific recommendation without looking at your needs. However, I have personally had considerable experience with the following accounting packages. For individuals, I have found Moneycounts and Quicken to offer the most features for the cost. For small business, the business version of Moneycounts, Quickbooks and One Write Plus should be considered. If you have more than one person working on your books, inventory, purchasing, etc., consider Pacioli 2000. It is multiuser and network ready right out of the box.
There are dozens of good accounting packages on the market. All of them have their strengths and weaknesses. To be truly proficient in any of them, you must use one for at least a year.

Sales people and consultants can help but keep in mind their perspectives and motivations. Remember that no matter how expert somebody is, that person can only know a handful of software packages well. No one individual can know them all; there are too many, and each one is complex with nuances and subtleties that take time to master.

Talk to other people who have similar accounting needs. Try and understand the similarities and differences between their business and yours. How long have they been using the package and has enough time transpired to point up problems? They have to go through at least one fiscal year to know what's going on. Make the effort up front. You don't want to switch accounting packages year every year, since this may invalidate annual comparison of figures. Computer magazines have in-depth reviews of accounting software, but keep in mind that reviews are written by editors, not long-time users of the software. They view products generically, not from your perspective.

If your invoicing or inventory needs are unique, you might consider custom software or a combination of packaged and custom software. This is an expensive process but can be very rewarding, since you will get the system that you truly need.
Even if you don't require customized software, if you obtain the assistance of a

consultant that will help you through the installation of an existing software package, you will have less frustration, and you will reach your goals more quickly. Good luck!

how to convert files

There are dozens of file formats for word processing documents, database files, graphics, spreadsheets and so on. If a file was created in one application and you want to use it in another, you can either import the file or use a conversion program.

Converting Text Files

Most word processing programs provide an Import function, which provides built-in conversion for various document formats. Simply select Import from the File or Import menu and choose the document type you want to input.

If your word processor does not import the document type you need, you can usually use the ASCII file format as a common denominator; however, you will need the word processing program that created the original document.

If both word processing programs import and export ASCII files, convert your original document into an ASCII file using the source word processor. Look for Export in the File or Export menu. Select ASCII file or Text File. After creating an ASCII file of the source document, use the destination word processor and import that file using the Import option, again for an ASCII file or Text File. Note that all format commands (bold, italics, headers, footers, etc.) will generally be lost between conversion.

Converting Database Files

Most database programs provide an Import function, which provides built-in conversion for various record formats. Simply select Import from the File or Import menu and choose the database type you want to input.

If your database program does not import the file type you need, you can usually use the ASCII file format as a common denominator; however, you will need the database program that created the original file.

If both database programs import and export ASCII files, convert your original file into an ASCII file using the source database program. Look for Export in the File or Export menu. Select ASCII file or Text File. There are generally two types of ASCII files that can be created: comma delimited and SDF.

Comma delimited separates each field with a comma and puts quotes around text fields, for example:

```
"Harry Bacon","123 Main","El Paso","TX"
"Mary Katz",4 W. 3rd St.","New York","NY"
```

The SDF, or standard data format, creates contiguous fixed fields:

```
Harry Bacon    123 Main      El Paso     TX
Mary Katz      4 W. 3rd St.  New York    NY
```

Each field in a comma delimited or SDF format follows in the order of its original placement. In your destination database program, create a new database file with the same structure as the original, using the same order as the original. Then import the ASCII file into that structure. You can always modify the structure after you have imported the data into it.

Converting Images and Drawings

Most paint, drawing, word processing, desktop publishing and presentation graphics programs provide an Import function, which provides built-in conversion for various image and drawing formats. Simply select Import from the File or Import menu and choose the graphics file type you want to input.

If your program does not import the file type you need, you can convert one image or drawing format into another using an independent graphics conversion program, such as Inset System's popular HiJaak.

Note that image formats, or raster graphics formats, such as PCX, BMP, TIFF, GIF, etc. cannot be converted into drawing formats, or vector graphics formats, such as WMF, DXF, DRW, CGM, etc., but vector formats can be turned into raster images (for more on rasters and vectors, see *graphics* and *graphics formats*).

Windows programs can usually import BMP and WMF files, which are the standard Windows graphics formats. BMP is a raster graphics format (image) and WMF is a vector graphics format (drawing).

how to donate old equipment

There are organizations that channel old computer equipment to the less fortunate. The National Cristina Foundation maintains a database of organizations that support the handicapped. The East-West foundation provides a warehouse and support for equipment sent to schools and other public service organizations in the U.S. and around the world. The Computer Recycling Center maintains a warehouse and support for machines intended for schools and non-profit organizations. Millions of devices become "obsolete" every day in our high-tech society. Don't throw them out! They might be very useful for those less fortunate. Contact:

National Cristina Foundation
591 West Putnam Ave.
Greenwich, CT 06830
800/274-7846

East West Foundation
55 Temple Place
Boston, MA 02211
617/542-1234

Computer Recycling Center, Inc.
1245 Terra Bella Ave.
Mountain View, CA 94043
415/428-3700

how to download a file

See *download*.

how to find a file

It is easy to forget which directory/folder you saved a file in. The file find capability searches directories for a file or category of files.

In Windows 95, select FIND from the Start menu.

In Windows 3.1, in File Manager, select SEARCH from the FILE menu.

In DOS, the /s switch is used with the Dir command. For example, to search for all files beginning with XYZ, you would type: `dir \xyz* /s`

how to find a good computer book

Good computer books are worth their weight in gold, because the online help in most applications leaves a lot to be desired. Unfortunately, while millions are spent programming software, considerably less money is allocated to documenting it. Worse yet, the documentation is usually last minute, rushed and never read by anyone but the unfortunate user of the software. That's why having auxiliary documentation in the form of books is extremely helpful.

How to find a good book is simple. Get two or three on the same subject. Today, software applications are often the culmination of decades worth of functions and features that includes everything everyone ever wanted in the program. It is rare to find a single author equally competent in all areas of the program, and you won't know that when you browse the book in the bookstore, only when you're stuck later on. If you have more than one book, your chances are greater that your question will be answered.

In lieu of direct technical support from the software vendor or from your organization's help desk or IS department, several books on the subject is your best bet.

how to install a PC peripheral

Installing an additional peripheral device into the ISA bus on a DOS or Windows 3.1 PC can be simple or very frustrating. If you add a first or even second device to a basic system, you may have no conflicts, but as you add more, the chances are greater for a conflict. Each device uses one or more resources of the computer, and two devices cannot generally share the same one. If the CD-ROM, sound card, scanner, etc., that you add uses the same setting as an existing board, you have to figure out where the conflict is and choose another resource.

ISA, EISA and Micro Channel Buses

The ISA bus was the original PC bus and does not have any advanced installation features. PCs that use the EISA and Micro Channel buses still have configuration problems, but they have two advantages. First, when a board is added, a setup program is run to install the board, and conflicts are identified ahead of time. Although the user still has to participate under this "plug and tell" capability, it is better than the "plug and hope" offered by ISA-bus cards.

Secondly, the boards are configurable by software, which eliminates the need to set switches or jumpers on the boards themselves. If you have to change a setting, you don't have to pull the board out of the socket in order to do it. You run the setup program and select the configuration option.

PCI, PCMCIA and Plug and Play

PCI cards and PCMCIA cards (PC Cards) are better yet. They assign most resources automatically. But the best is Plug and Play. When all PCs run Windows 95, which supports Plug and Play, and all peripherals are built for Plug and Play, resource conflicts will become history.

The Resources

The PC uses several resources to transfer signals to a peripheral device, and the settings associated with these resources are often arbitrary.

1. IRQ
2. I/O address (port address)
3. Memory address

Most peripherals use an IRQ and an I/O address. Many use a memory address. When you install a new board in your PC, you MUST read the installation manual in order to find out what the initial settings are and how to change them if necessary. If a new board uses the same setting as an existing board, it won't work properly or at all. Or, it will work and the old one won't, or both won't work.

Keep a List

If you plan on installing several peripherals, it is IMPERATIVE that you write down the resources used for each board you install when you install it. It will save you much time later. Utility programs, such as MSD.EXE, which comes with Windows, Quarterdeck's Manifest (QEMM386) and Helix's Discover (NETROOM), will help you identify most current settings, but not all of them.

Make a chart like the one below and keep it handy:

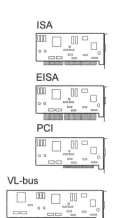

ISA

EISA

PCI

VL-bus

Micro Channel

Device	IRQ	I/O	Memory address
COM1			
COM2			
LPT1			
scanner			
CD-ROM			
etc:			

IRQ (Interrupt Request)

An interrupt is a method of signalling the computer for attention. There are 16 IRQ lines in a PC, but only 15 are usable, because one line (IRQ 2) is used to connect the first bank of eight to the second bank (the early XTs had only eight lines).

If the device uses an interrupt, it must use a unique IRQ line. IRQ settings are changed by setting DIP switches or changing jumpers on the board itself or by running a setup program. Just be sure that no two devices use the same interrupt number.

Some expansion boards are preset to one IRQ. If two such boards are preset to the same number and cannot be changed with DIP switches, jumpers or software, they cannot co-exist in the same PC.

Following are the standard IRQ settings. If a second parallel port (LPT2) is not used, IRQ 5 is available. IRQ 9 is also often available, and IRQs 10, 11, 12 and 15 are "up for grabs."

IRQ	Assignment	IRQ	Assignment
0	System timer		
1	Keyboard	8	Realtime clock
2	Connects to IRQ 9	9	VGA, 3270 emulation**
3	COM2, COM4	10	**
4	COM1, COM3	11	**
5	LPT2**	12	**
6	Floppy disk	13	Math coprocessor
7	LPT1	14	Hard disk
		15	**

** For general use. "The battleground."

I/O Address

The I/O address, or port address, is one way a peripheral device is identified, or addressed, from another. The addresses are numbered in hex; for example:

    280h
    290h
    2A0h

Like IRQs, they are set with DIP switches or jumpers on the board, or preferably by a software setup program. If you change settings, you may have to identify that change elsewhere, such as by changing a parameter in a **device=** line in the CONFIG.SYS file. Read the manual for your new device. There is no other source for that kind of information.

If you change I/O addresses and still have a problem, try an address that is one or two numbers apart on the list. For example, if one board is set to 280h and another at 290h, change 280h to 270h or 260h and try again. For details on this architecture, see *PC I/O addressing*.

The default I/O addresses for the parallel and serial ports are:

Port	PC	PS/2
LPT1	378h	3BCh
LPT2	278h	378h
LPT3	3BCh	278h
COM1	3F8h	
COM2	2F8h	
COM3	2E8h	
COM4	2E0h	

Memory Address

A peripheral device often requires a block of upper memory (between 640K-1M) for transferring data, which must be reserved for its exclusive use. Some common devices, such as VGA video, use fixed areas in upper memory that are automatically reserved. With other devices, you have to find an unused block in this area (for a diagram, see *PC memory map*).

This is why you will usually find a number of memory addresses to select, typically in the C800h to F000h range (800-960K) so that you can find an unused block without conflict (hopefully). Addresses are given in hexadecimal as a beginning address or as a beginning and ending address, for example:

CC00		CC00-CEFF
CE00	or	CE00-D0FF
D000		D000-D2FF

When a block is chosen, it is also necessary to inform your memory manager not to load other drivers or TSRs into it. This may be done by a setup program or you may have to do it yourself by adding an "exclude" to the line in CONFIG.SYS that loads the memory manager. For example, EMM386.EXE is the memory manager in DOS 5 and Windows. To exclude the E800-EFFF block, the x= parameter is added to the **device=** line as follows:

```
device=emm386.exe noems x=e800-efff
```

For other memory managers, such as QEMM and 386MAX, a similar "exclude" parameter is also used.

If you use Windows, an "exclude" line is also added to the [386Enh] section in the SYSTEM.INI file; for example:

```
EMMExclude=e800-efff
```

If you later change the board to another memory area, both CONFIG.SYS and SYSTEM.INI must be updated.

DMA
Yet Another!

Although not as frequently used as IRQs and I/O addresses, some peripheral devices, such as sound cards, use the PC's DMA channels to transfer data directly from memory to memory without going through the CPU. Like everything else, there is no standard assignment for DMA channels, and they can conflict.

There are eight DMA channels commonly used as follows. Most sound cards are set to use DMA channel 1.

DMA	Used for
0	8-bit transfer
1	8-bit transfer
2	Floppy disk controller
3	8-bit transfer
4	Cascaded from 0-3
5	16-bit transfer
6	16-bit transfer
7	16-bit transfer

RTFM!

Summary
You **MUST READ** the installation manual that comes with your peripheral. Each type of board is configured differently. The first time you install a new board, fill out the chart suggested above. It will save you headaches later! See *Plug and Play.*

how to install a program

Most professional install programs make installation of your application fairly easy. All you should have to do is just insert the next disk when prompted. If there is a "Custom" installation option, you will have to know something about the application in order to pick and choose the features and modules you want. Otherwise, just select the "Express" or "Normal" installation, and the install program will install what most users require.

Following are the general routines for installing DOS, Windows 3.1, Windows 95 and Macintosh applications.

DOS

To install a DOS application, do the following:

1. Insert floppy disk #1 into the appropriate floppy disk drive.
2. At the DOS prompt,

   type **a:install** or **b:install.**

3. If the install program is written by amateurs, you will have to default to the floppy drive first and then load the install program; for example, if you're using the B: drive, you would type:

   b:install

4. The install program should prompt you through all the necessary steps, including when to insert the next floppy (if applicable). It will create a subdirectory for you, also allowing you to choose your own name for it.
   The install program may have to make changes in your AUTOEXEC.BAT and CONFIG.SYS files. If asked whether the install program should make certain changes now or let you do it later, let the program do it.

   After installation, you are usually returned to the DOS prompt. You load your DOS program by typing in the name of an .EXE, .COM or .BAT file. The installation manual will tell you what the name is. Note that you can generally run a DOS install program from within Windows by loading it from the Run command in the File menu. Type **a:install** or **b:install** on the command line.

Windows 3.1

To install a Windows application under Windows 3.1, do the following:

1. Insert floppy disk #1 into the appropriate floppy disk drive.
2. At Program Manager, select Run from the File menu and

   type **a:setup** or **b:setup** or
   type **a:install** or **b:install**

3. The install program should prompt you through all the necessary steps, including when to insert the next floppy (if applicable). It will create a subdirectory for you, also allowing you to choose your own name for it.

After installation, you are returned to Program Manager. There is generally a new group window on screen that contains the icon of the new application. Click on that icon to launch the program.
4. Windows 3.1 installation programs may modify your WIN.INI, SYSTEM.INI, AUTOEXEC.BAT and CONFIG.SYS files. If these files are changed, the old files are generally renamed and kept on the disk.

Windows 95

To install a Windows application under Windows 95, do the following:

1. Insert floppy disk #1 into the appropriate floppy disk drive.
2. From the Start button, select SETTINGS, then CONTROL PANEL. Double click on ADD/REMOVE PROGRAMS. Click INSTALL and follow the instructions.
3. The install program should prompt you through all the necessary steps, including when to insert the next floppy (if applicable). It will create a folder for you and place the application in the Programs section of the Start menu.
4. Windows 95 installation programs should not modify the WIN.INI, SYSTEM.INI, AUTOEXEC.BAT and CONFIG.SYS configuration files. They will however make a change in the Windows 95 Registry. They will at least install the uninstall program in the Registry so that you can remove the application later if you wish by selecting the ADD/REMOVE PROGRAMS controlpanel.

Macintosh

To install a Macintosh application, do the following:

1. Insert floppy disk #1 into the floppy disk drive.
2. When the floppy disk window appears, there is usually an icon that says "Double Click on Me." Double click on the icon to start the install.
3. The install program should prompt you through all the necessary steps, including when to insert the next floppy (if applicable). It will create a new folder for you, also allowing you to choose your own name for it.

how to make backups

Backups are copies of documents, spreadsheets, databases and images on the hard disk that have been placed onto an external storage medium such as floppy disk or tape. Backups should be made routinely because the hard disk can self destruct (see *head crash*). There is definitely more paranoia about this than the number of incidents, but they do happen, so it is wise to make backups.

Using a Copy Command or Function
There are two ways to back up files onto external storage media. The first is to copy the individual files using a copy command or function. In DOS, you would use the Copy or Xcopy commands. In Windows or the Mac, you would dragg the file icon with a mouse from the graphical representation of the hard disk to that of the desired floppy. Copying files works best for copying a small number of files or if you are sure that the all the required files fit on the target storage medium. To fit more files onto a single diskette, you can compress files before you copy.

Using a Backup Command or Utility
The second way to back up files is to use a backup program or backup command. The advantage of this method is that you can copy any number of files as long as you have enough blank floppy disks. When a floppy disk is full and only a part of the file has been copied, the backup program copies the remaining part of the file to the next disk. When restoring files, the backup program deals with these overlapping files, which normal copy commands cannot.
In addition, backup programs support tape backup units, something that copy

commands do not generally do. They also compress files automatically to save space. DOS provides its own Backup and Restore commands, but if you use Backup to back up your files onto floppies and then switch to a different computer, the Restore command from a different DOS version won't restore your files. As of DOS 6, separate backup utilities are included with DOS that make the job easier. However, third-party backup utilities provide more versatility than both the commands and utilities included with DOS.

Another advantage of using a backup utility is that you can make a full copy of your entire disk directory, not just your data files, but the software too. This is especially helpful as you add more and more applications to your system. If your disk crashed, reinstalling everything would take quite some time. However this works best when you use high-capacity tapes or optical disks for backup. Routine copying onto multiple floppies is a nuisance.

Remember, it's your data (documents, spreadsheets, databases, images, etc.) that is most critical. As long as it is still popular, you can always obtain another copy of the software. But you cannot purchase copies of your data from anybody. See *backup types*.

how to protect a floppy

See *file protection*.

how to select a PC display system

The display adapter and monitor you use can make a big difference in your computing enjoyment. The factors to consider are:

1. Monitor size and resolution
2. Number of colors
3. Refresh rate
4. Graphics and video acceleration

MONITOR SIZE AND RESOLUTION

Monitor size and resolution depend on the applications you run on your computer. The standard resolutions are 640x480, 800x600, 1024x768, 1280x1024 and 1600x1200. For example, 640x480 means that there are 640 columns and 480 rows of pixels on screen. The higher the resolution, the more pixels and the more viewing area.

Some display adapter generate all these resolutions, while many go only as high as 1024x768. The monitor must be capable of handling the highest resolution you wish to use.

The shift from DOS to Windows through the first half of the 1990s has caused a significant increase in monitor size and resolutions. While 640x480 is fine for DOS character-based screens, a 17" monitor at 800x600 is much more enjoyable for Windows applications. Running Windows on a 20" or 21" monitor at 1024x768 is better yet.

Number of Colors:
The standard number of colors that are displayed are 16, 256, 65K and 16M. The jumps are large, from 256 to 65 thousand to 16 million. The number of colors is known as the color depth, or bit depth. Sometimes a display adapter will offer a hybrid 15-bit color depth.

Number of Colors	Color Depth	Commonly Known as
16	4-bit	Standard VGA
256	8-bit	Super VGA
32K	15-bit	High Color
65K	16-bit	High Color
16M	24-bit	True Color

To display multimedia applications, you need at least 65K colors, or 32K colors if your adapter supports it. The most realistic photographs and full-motion video will be achieved with 16M colors, but 65K is more than adequate. For standard business applications, such as word processing and spreadsheets, either 16 or 256 colors will suffice.

Refresh Rate:
The refresh rate is the number of times per second the image is painted onto the screen. Refresh is necessary, because the phosphors hold their glow for just a fraction of a second. The higher the refresh rate, the more rock solid the image will appear on screen. The higher the better. Look for a refresh of at least 70Hz.

Graphics and Video Acceleration:
Placing drawing functions into the circuits of the display adapter speeds up displaying images on screen. After Windows became popular, vendors added graphics acceleration to their cards, which put various screen drawing functions into the hardware. Today, any display adapter worth its salt has built-in graphics accleration.
The latest trend in hardware-supported features is video acceleration, which puts several full-motion video functions into the chips. Look for these features if you plan on running alot of multimedia movies. See *video accelerator*.

It's a Tradeoff
The more colors, resolution and refresh, the harder the display adapter has to work and the more expensive they are to purchase. In addition, if you don't need the highest capacities of a card, don't purchase it, because another card can deliver what you need for less money.
The higher the settings, the slower the adapter operates. Whenever there's a faster adapter that runs 16 million colors at yet a higher resolution, it's always a breakthrough.

For Example
Following is an example of adapter specifications. The numbers are from Number Nine Visual Technology's 9FX Motion 771, which is a medium to high-end display adapter that includes video acceleration. Number Nine is widely praised for its high-quality adapters and makes many models both above and below the Motion 771.
Notice how the the colors decrease as the resolution increases. Also notice that it takes more memory (VRAM) on the display adapter to achieve higher resolutions and higher colors at the same time.

Resolution:	640	800	1024	1152	1280	1600
	x	x	x	x	x	x
VRAM	480	600	768	864	1024	1200
2MB Colors	16M	16M	65K	65K	256	256
Refresh	150	150	150	150	100	83
4MB Colors	16M	16M	16M	16M	65K	65K
Refresh	150	150	150	150	100	83

how to select a personal computer
The most important thing in selecting a personal computer is that you obtain the performance and storage capacity from your system that you need as well as the technical support from your dealer that you require. The primary decision criteria are:

1. PC versus Mac
2. DOS versus Windows
3. Ergonomics
4. Desktop versus Laptop
5. Where to buy

PC versus Mac

The first decision is whether to purchase a PC or a Macintosh. It is, afterall, a PC and Mac personal computer world. Although Apple has only about 10% of the business, it is also only one company. The rest of the personal computer market is made up of countless PC vendors from thousands of mom and pop shops to the big companies such as Compaq, IBM, Dell and Gateway. Thus, Apple continues to hold its own in a largely PC world.

The advantage of the Mac is that it is easier to use compared to Windows and DOS machines. The Macintosh infrastructure is much more solid. Applications for both the PC and the Mac are increasingly becoming more feature laden and more complicated as a result. With the Mac, you can spend more time learning your application and less time configuring your computer.

It is also considerably easier to upgrade a Mac than a PC. Adding a second or third peripheral to a PC can be a royal pain. Adding one to a Mac usually means "just plug in it." However, PCs are getting easier to upgrade with Windows 95, which assists in the installation and supports the Plug and Play standard. When Plug and Play boards are universal, which is expected in the 1996-1997 timeframe, then the PC may be as easy to upgrade as the Mac.

The disadvantage of the Mac is compatibility. Although, major applications, such as Word, Excel and PageMaker, run on both Mac and Windows, there are many applications that are not available on both platforms. Processing data created on the other platform may require conversion. If your company supports PCs and Macs, support personnel have most likely determined the appropriate applications and utilities that make file transfer between both platforms straightforward. If not, you may have problems.

Another disadvantage is that there are decidedly more applications for Windows than there are for the Mac. However this disadvantage is slowly dwindling, because Power Macintoshes run DOS and Windows applications at respectable speeds, and future models will run them even faster.

DOS versus Windows

If you've settled on a PC, then the type of applications you will run determines the system size. If you running only a vertical market application (doctor, dentist, retailer, etc.) that is still DOS based, you can get by with a minimal PC (see requirements below). However, almost all applications are being rewritten for Windows, and almost all DOS productivity programs (spreadsheets, word processors, etc.) have long since had their last revision as a DOS program.

If you are running Windows, you need a fast and large machine. Windows applications take enormous amounts of disk space these days, from 20 to 50 megabytes. In some cases as much as 100. You may not be entering a lot of data, but you could use up 200 to 400 megabytes of disk just by installing a dozen applications. In addition, if you want to keep a half dozen or more applications open at the same time, you need plenty of memory (RAM).

Future Windows applications will be even more demanding than current ones. If you can afford it, get the faster machine. Follwing are recommended PC configurations.

Recommended System for DOS

CPU	486/25
Bus	ISA
RAM	4MB
Hard disk	340MB
Monitor	15"
Resolution	640x480

Recommended System for Windows

	Word processing, database, spreadsheets	CAD, imaging desktop publishing
CPU	486/66	Pentium/133
Bus	ISA	ISA/PCI
RAM	8-16MB	32-64MB
Hard disk	800MB	2-4GB
Monitor	17"	21"
Resolution	800x600	1024x768, 1280x1024

Multimedia for	
loading programs	2x CD-ROM
games/video/interaction	4x CD-ROM, sound board and speakers

Yes, It Can Be Slower

You can always get by with a slower machine. It's all a matter of your patience waiting for something to happen. Your experience level has nothing to do with the power of the machine you deserve. You will get used to the fastest PC on the market in 10 minutes. Then, if you go to a slower machine, you will understand why speed is so much of an issue in this business.

Ergonomics

The most important parts of your PC are the ones you come in contact with. The keyboard, mouse and screen are the devices you touch and see. In the highly-competitive PC world, these are also the areas where vendors can skimp to offer a lower price. Keyboards cost $15 to $100. There is a difference. After eight hours of typing, you'll find out what it is. Check out the newer angled keyboards. They offer a more natural position for your hands if you do alot of typing.

The mouse is another device that can vary widely in cost and design. One can be far more comfortable than another. Trackballs are also an alternative that many prefer over the mouse.

Lastly, display systems, which are made up of the display adapter (the card that plugs into the PC) and the monitor, vary widely in cost and quality.

The Windows desktop simulates an office desktop, but when is the last time you worked at a desk that was one foot wide? Running Windows on a 14" monitor is limiting. You cannot see an entire document unless you run at a resolution that makes everything very small. A 17" monitor is much better, and a 21" monitor is even better yet.

A small, inexpensive monitor can cost as little as $200. A high-quality 21" monitor can cost as much as $2500 and more. A low-end display adapter for $35 is not the same as the thousand-dollar high-resolution card used for professional CAD, desktop publishing and color imaging work. There is a difference. See *how to select a PC display resolution.*

Desktop versus Laptop

If you have a requirement for a computer in more than one location, a laptop can be an economical alternative. It can function as a desktop computer by attaching a full-size monitor and keyboard.

The caveat with laptops is that they are not as expandable as desktops. On a destop PC, if you need more hard disk, you can add another or swap your current one for a larger one. On laptops, the hard disk may not be upgradable at all. If it is, there may be a limited number of options, and it will usually cost at least twice that of a desktop drive, so plan ahead.

A docking station may provide one or two expansion slots for expandability, but you will have to duplicate docking stations and peripherals if you need them in both locations. Laptops with PCMCIA slots also offer flexibility for expansion.

In addition, the display resolution on a laptop is built into the motherboard. Even if you attach a large monitor, you cannot upgrade to a higher resolution unless you have a docking station with another VGA adapter installed in it and the laptop is built to switch to an external adapter. For a list of laptop features, see *laptop*.

Where to buy

The best price to pay for a personal computer and the best place to buy it often has more to do with the support you need than the equipment you purchase. If you don't need support, shop for the best price from local dealers, superstores and the mail-order houses.

Most components in PCs are highly reliable, but there are always exceptions. Hard and floppy drives come from a handful of vendors, but there are dozens of motherboard manufacturers. Look for OS/2 and Novell certification, a good sign of compatibility. Get customer referrals.

If you use your computer all day, or if you keep it on 24 hours as some do, opt for the brand name. The power supply in the no-name clone might give way in a year or so. An option is to buy the no-name clone and put in a better power supply, such as one from PC Power and Cooling, Carlsbad, CA.

If you're new to computers, look for local dealers that specialize in hand holding for the novice. There is usually a dealer nearby that caters to the beginner. You may pay a few hundred dollars more for your system, but it may be well worth it, saving you time and frustration later.

The superstores are also a good source for computers, but the amount of support you get will vary. Remember, you can always pay a consultant by the hour to help you if you don't know any sympathetic hackers.

The mail-order houses are another good source with quality machines, but you will have to rely on technical support by phone. Ironically, the more successful the direct sales organization, the worse its phone support becomes, if only temporarily. A disadvantage of mail order is that you will have to ship back your unit if you can't fix it by phone. Look for mail-order firms with on-site support administered by a national repair organization.

Caution # 1 - The Small Business

The small business looking to automate its accounting is going to need more help. Don't be fooled by the prices of hardware and off-the-shelf software. The small company often has information requirements as complicated as a much larger one. There are countless custom-designed applications that have cost $5,000 to $25,000, running on $1,500 PCs, because no off-the-shelf software package could fit the bill.

It's tempting to think a $100 software package can do the accounting for your entire company, and the fact is, in many cases, it very well can. But, even if you understand your detailed information requirements, matching them with the marketing blurbs on a package cover is not simple. You generally do not find the software's limitations until after you are up and running.

Determining the best accounting software for your particular needs is not something most PC vendors want to get involved with. To do the job right, it can take hours, days or weeks of analysis depending on your business and what you want to computerize. You may want to use the services of a software consulting firm or an independent consultant.

Caution #2 - The Bleeding Edge

Even if you can easily afford the newest technology, it's not always a good idea to be the first on the block to have it. Wait a bit. Ask around. When the bugs are finally fixed, and that can take several months, you may be a lot better off. Good luck and happy computing.

how to spoof your technical friend

To have a light-hearted joke with your technical colleagues, take the highest clock rate of an Intel CPU chip and triple or quadruple it. Then, simply say "did you hear about Intel's 400MHz Pentium? They've kept it a secret, but they're shipping it now!" Expect a "wow" reaction, or "that's impossible!"

Be careful. You have to stay on top of the numbers. Years ago, a 100MHz chip sounded unbelievable. Today, workstation chips are reaching 300MHz speeds. It is expected that within a few years after the turn of the century, we will achieve 1GHz clock rates. See also *buffer flush* and *Stringy Floppy*.

how to transfer a file

Within the Same Machine From one Application to Another

The ability to transfer a file from one application to another within the same machine depends on the import and export capabilities of the application. All full-featured applications accept a variety of foreign files.

Graphics applications (drawing programs, desktop publishing, image editing, etc.) are typically designed to import and export a wide variety of file formats. Just look at the import/export menus.

Some word processing and database programs can detect different document and database types when you open a file. Other programs have to be explicity told the type of file it is. If you're not sure, look for import/export menus or read the import/export section in the manual or online help.

From One Computer to Another Using a File Transfer Program

File transfer programs provide the simplest method for transferring files between computers. For remote transfer, you need a modem and the file transfer program on both machines. The modems do not have to come from the same vendor, but the file transfer programs do. However, if the remote computer does not already have the program installed, the transfer program can usually install itself on the remote computer after you connect to it, using its remote install procedure.

In a file transfer program, the transfer protocols are built in requiring no selection by the user, and the entire operation is set up to send and receive. You can view on screen the directories of both the local and remote machines.

For transfer between local machines, file transfer programs come with special cables to connect both computers via the serial or parallel ports. See *DOS Interlink*.

From One Computer to Another Using a Communications Program

Files can be transferred using general-purpose communications programs. The programs do not have to be the same in both machines. In order to transfer a file remotely, both machines need modems, which can come from different vendors. The user in the receiving computer sets the communications program to Auto Answer. The user in the sending computer uses the communications program to dial up the modem of the receiving machine. Both users must agree on a file transfer protocol, the most common today being Zmodem. When a connection is made, the sending computer selects Upload and identifies the file or files to be sent. The receiving computer selects Download. When the transfer is complete, each user selects "hang up."

If the machines are side by side, instead of using a modem, connect a null modem cable between the serial ports of both machines. Since there are no modems and telephone lines to dial, the transfer is made by selecting Upload and Download (send and receive) in the respective communications programs.

From an Online Service

Online services allow for downloading files, and each one provides its own method for doing so. If you are connected to the service via your own general-purpose communications program, you have to find the forum of interest and then select Download from a menu of options. You can search for file names if you do not know the name. You will also be asked to select a file transfer protocol. Zmodem is always a good choice.

Many online services provide their own software to help you select options and navigate their databases. If you are using such a program, such as CompuServe's WinCIM, a series of menus makes it easier to search for and download the files you need.

HP

(Hewlett-Packard Company, Palo Alto, CA) The second largest computer company in the U.S. HP was founded in 1939 by William Hewlett and David Packard in a garage behind the Packard's California home. Its first product, an audio oscillator for measuring sound, was the beginning of a line of electronics that made HP an international supplier of electronic test and measurement instruments. Walt Disney Studios, HP's first big customer, purchased eight oscillators to develop and test a new sound system for the movie "Fantasia."

HP entered the computer field in 1966 with the 2116A, the first of the HP 1000 series designed to gather and analyze the data produced by HP instruments. HP 1000 computers are used for CIM applications, such as process monitoring and control, alarm management and machine monitoring.

In 1972, HP branched into business computing with the 3000 series, a multiuser system that became well known for its high reliability, especially for that time. The successful 3000 family has continued to be one of HP's major computer series. Also in 1972, HP introduced the first scientific handheld calculator, the HP-35, obsoleting the slide rule and ushering in a new age of pocket-sized calculators. In 1982, the first HP 9000 workstation was introduced.

HP's first personal computer was the Touchscreen 150, a non-standard MS-DOS personal computer that gained only modest acceptance. In 1985, it introduced its first completely IBM-compatible PC, the 286-based Vectra. As of the 1990s, the Vectra has become a very successful part of HP's business.

In 1984, HP revolutionized the printer market with its desktop LaserJet printer, which has set the standard for the industry. HP continues its leadership in this area with routine advances in resolution, speed and price.

In 1986, it introduced Precision Architecture, a RISC-based architecture for its 3000 and 9000 series product lines, which has proven very successful. In 1989, HP acquired Apollo Computer, a workstation manufacturer, and combined technologies to become a formidable contender in this field. In 1994, HP was the second largest workstation vendor after Sun.

HP sells over 10,000 different products in the electronics and computer field and has gained a worldwide reputation for its quality engineering.

Hewlett & Packard
This picture of William R. Hewlett and David Packard was taken in 1964, two years before they introduced their first computer. *(Photo courtesy of Hewlett-Packard Company.)*

HP's First Product

So many of today's giants started out with a simple product. This audio oscillator launched the company that is today a 25-billion dollar international enterprise. *(Photo courtesy of Hewlett-Packard Company.)*

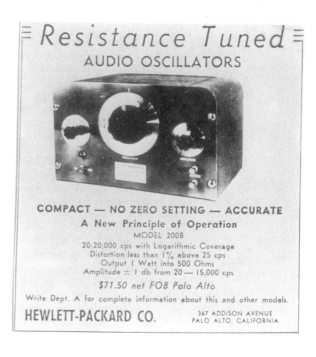

≡ *Resistance Tuned* ≡
AUDIO OSCILLATORS

COMPACT — NO ZERO SETTING — ACCURATE

A New Principle of Operation

MODEL 200B

20-20,000 cps with Logarithmic Coverage
Distortion less than 1% above 25 cps
Output 1 Watt into 500 Ohms
Amplitude ± 1 db from 20 — 15,000 cps

$71.50 net FOB Palo Alto

Write Dept. A for complete information about this and other models.

HEWLETT-PACKARD CO.   367 ADDISON AVENUE
PALO ALTO, CALIFORNIA

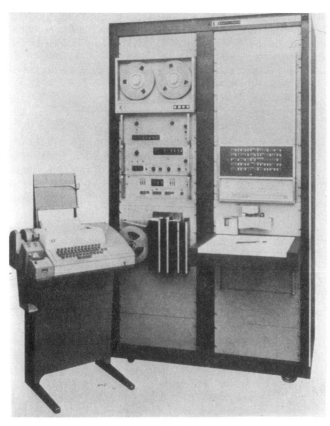

HP's First Computer

In 1966, the 2116A computer was introduced to gather and analyze data from HP instruments. *(Photo courtesy of Hewlett-Packard Company.)*

HP 1000

A family of realtime computers from HP introduced in 1966. They are sensor-based computers used extensively in laboratory and manufacturing environments for collecting and analyzing data.

HP 3000

A family of business-oriented computers from HP. These midrange computers set a standard for reliability and rugged engineering when they were introduced in 1972. Today's 900 models use HP's PA-RISC architecture, are compatible with the original 3000s and run the MPE/iX operating system. Over the years, HP 3000s have migrated from the central computer architecture to client/server, in which intelligent workstations and PCs have replaced the dumb terminal.

HP 9000

A family of high-performance UNIX workstations and business servers from HP all running the HP/UX operating system. The series 700 are workstation clients and the series 800 and model T500 are servers. The T500 is a multiprocessing mainframe class computer that can contain up to 12 CPUs. All current models use HP's PA-RISC architecture.

The earlier series 300 and 400 were based on Motorola 680x0 CPUs, and the series 500 and 600 were predecessors to current models.

HPC

See *High-Performance Computing*.

HPFS

(High Performance File System) The file system, introduced with OS/2 Version 1.2, that handles larger disks (2TB volumes; 2GB files), long file names (256 bytes) and can launch the program by referencing the data as in the Macintosh. It coexists with the existing FAT system.

HPGL

(Hewlett-Packard Graphics Language) A vector graphics file format from HP that was developed as a standard plotter language. Most plotters support the HPGL and DMPL standards.

HPIB

(Hewlett-Packard Interface Bus) HP's version of the IEEE 488 standard GPIB.

HP PA-RISC

(Hewlett-Packard Precision Architecture-RISC) A proprietary RISC architecture from HP introduced in 1986 that is incorporated into all new models of its 3000 and 9000 computer families.

HPR

(High-Performance Routing) Extensions to IBM's APPN networking that improve routing performance and reliability. HPR is designed to eliminate congestion on network backbones.

HP-UX

HP's version of UNIX that runs on its 9000 family. It is based on SVID and incorporates features from BSD UNIX along with several HP innovations.

HP-VUE

A Motif-based graphical user interface used in HP workstations. Parts of HP-VUE are used in COSE's CDE (Common Desktop Environment).

HREF

(Hypertext REFerence) The mnemonic used to assign a hypertext address to an HTML document. The **HREF**= is followed by the name or URL of the target document. The HREF resides within a hypertext anchor. See *hypertext anchor*.

HS

(High Speed) See *modem*.

HSB

(Hue Saturation Brightness) See *HSV*.

HSL

(Hue Saturation Lightness) See *HLS*.

HSM

(Hierarchical Storage Management) The automatic movement of files from hard disk to slower, less-expensive storage media. The typical hierarchy is from magnetic disk to optical disk to tape. HSM software constantly monitors hard disk capacity and moves data from one storage level to the next based on age, category and other criteria as specified by the network or system administrator. HSM often includes a system for routine backup as well.

Data Migration
A data migration path in an HSM system might be from high-speed hard disk to slower speed optical disk to offline tape. In time, optical disks will almost surely replace magnetic media, but there will still be a need to take data off premises for protection against fire and accidents.

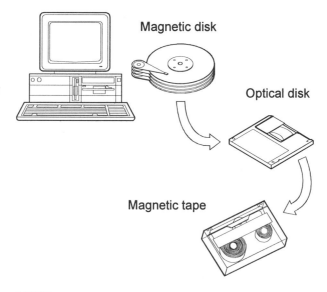

Magnetic disk

Optical disk

Magnetic tape

HSSI

(High-Speed Serial Interface) A standard for a serial connection with transmission rates up to 52 Mbps. It is often used to connect to T3 lines.

HST

(1) An asymetrical modem protocol from U.S. Robotics that includes error control and compression and transmits from 4800 to 14400 bps in one direction and from 300 to 400 bps in the other. HST was the first reliable, high-speed modem protocol before the V.32bis and V.42 standards became widely used.
(2) (Hubble Space Telescope) Launched in April 1990, it views star material some 10 to 12 billion light years from earth.

HSV

(Hue Saturation Value) A color model that uses a cylindrical coordinate system structured as an inverted hexcone (six-sided pyramid). The hue, or H, is measured by the angle around the vertical axis in degrees with red at 0, yellow 60, green 120, cyan 180, blue 240 and magenta 300. The saturation, or S, is the amount of color from 0 to 1 or 0 to 100%. The value, or V, is the amount of light from black to white (0 to 1 or 0 to 100%). For example, pure green would be H=120, S=1 and V=1. See *HLS*.

HTML

(HyperText Markup Language) A standard for defining documents with hypertext links. HTML is a subset of SGML (Standard Generalized Markup Language) and is used to establish links between documents on the World Wide Web.
HTML 2.0 was defined by the Internet Engineering Task Force (IETF) with a basic set of features for all Web documents, including interactive forms capability. NetScape has added features such as blinking text and custom backgrounds, which has become a de facto HTML 3.0. The NetScape formats are expected to be incorporated into the formal HTML 3.0 when finalized by the IETF. See *VRML*.

HTTP

(HyperText Transport Protocol) The client/server protocol used on connect to servers on the World Wide Web. Addresses of Web sites begin with an **http://** prefix. See *URL*.

hub

A central connecting device in a network that joins communications lines together in a star configuration. Passive hubs are just connecting units that add nothing to the data passing through them. Active hubs, also sometimes called *multiport repeaters*, regenerate the data bits in order to maintain a strong signal, and intelligent hubs provide added functionality.
Hubs are required in twisted pair Ethernet (10BaseT) and Token Ring networks. In Token Rings, the hub is called a MAU (Multi-station Access Unit). Multiple media hubs interconnect different types of Ethernets (twisted pair, coax and optical fiber). Hubs can provide bridging between LAN types; for example, Ethernet, Token Ring and FDDI. Switching hubs provide Ethernet and ATM switching.
Hubs have become very intelligent, modular and customizable, allowing for the insertion of bridging, routing and switching modules all within the same unit. A hub can even host a CPU board and network operating system, turning the hub into a file server or some type of network control processor that performs LAN emulation or other complex function as networks grow.

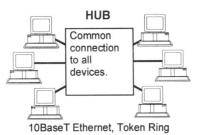

10BaseT Ethernet, Token Ring

hub ring

A flat ring pressed around the hole in a 5.25" floppy disk for rigidity. The drive's clamping ring presses the hub ring onto the spindle.

hue

In computer graphics, a particular shade or tint of a given color.

Huffman coding

A statistical compression method that converts characters into variable length bit strings. Most-frequently-occurring characters are converted to shortest bit strings; least frequent, the longest. Compression takes two passes. The first pass analyzes a block of data and creates a tree model based on its contents. The second pass compresses the data via the model. Decompression decodes the variable length strings via the tree. See *LZW*.

hybrid circuit

See *hybrid microcircuit*.

hybrid computer

A digital computer that accepts analog signals, converts them to digital and processes them in digital form. It is used in process control and robotics.

hybrid file

Sometimes refers to a graphics file that contains vector graphics and raster graphics (bitmapped) images. See *metafile*.

hybrid microcircuit

An electronic circuit composed of different types of integrated circuits and discrete components, mounted on a ceramic base. Used in military and communications applications, it is especially suited for building custom analog circuits including A/D and D/A converters, amplifiers and modulators. See *MCM*.

Hybrid Microcircuits
The picture shows a variety of hybrid circuits. The tiny, square white spots are the actual chips. *(Photo courtesy of Circuit Technology, Inc.)*

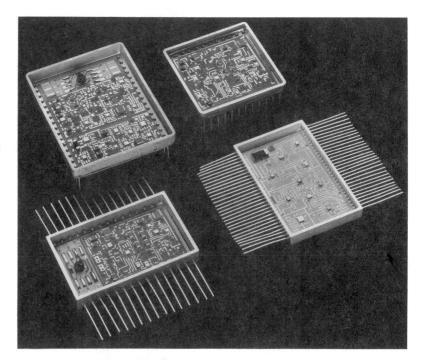

hybrid network
In communications, a network made up of equipment from multiple vendors.

Hydra
(1) (Hybrid Document Reproduction Apparatus) A printer, photocopier, scanner and fax built into one machine.
(2) A device that converts analog signals to ISDN Basic Rate Interface (BRI).
(3) A utility from the Austin Mac Developer's Association that tests Macintosh graphics card performance.

Hyperaccess
A PC communications program from Hilgraeve, Inc., Monroe, MI, that provides data compression, has its own script language and supports a variety of terminals and protocols.

HyperCard
An application development system from Apple that runs on the Macintosh and Apple IIGS. Using visual tools, users build "stacks" of "cards" that hold data, text, graphics, sound and video with hypertext links between them. The HyperTalk programming language allows complex applications to be developed. Third-party compilers can compile HyperCard stacks into executable programs, eliminating the need to have HyperCard running in order to execute the stacks.
HyperCard used to be more popular with many commercial and shareware stacks being developed routinely. Today Apple includes only a runtime version with its Macs, not the full development version, which is available from Claris.
HyperCard's visual programming approach was brought to PCs with Brightbill-Robert's HyperPad and Asymetrix's ToolBook.

hypercube
A parallel processing architecture made up of binary multiples of computers (4, 8, 16, etc.). The computers are interconnected so that data travel is kept to a minimum. For example, in two eight-node cubes, each node in one cube would be connected to the counterpart node in the other.

hypergraphic
A linkage between related information by means of a graphic image. It is the graphics counterpart of hypertext. Instead of clicking on a word, you click on an icon to jump to the related section, document or file. See *hypertext* and *hot spot*.

hyperlink
A predefined linkage between one object and another. See *hypertext* and *hypergraphic*.

hypermedia
The use of data, text, graphics, video and voice as elements in a hypertext system. All the various forms of information are linked together so that a user can easily move from one to another.

HyperPAD
An application development system for PCs from Brightbill-Roberts & Company, Ltd., Syracuse, NY. It is a HyperCard-like program that works in text mode and includes the PADtalk scripting language.

HyperScript
An advanced macro (scripting) language that is provided with the WINGZ spreadsheet.

HyperTalk

The programming language used in HyperCard.

hypertext

A linkage between related text. For example, by selecting a word in a sentence, information about that word is retrieved if it exists, or the next occurrence of the word is found. The concept was coined by Ted Nelson as a method for making the computer respond to the way humans think and require information.

In the electronic versions of this database, you can hypertext to the definition of any term used within the definitions by clicking on it or highlighting it with the mouse. See *hypergraphic*.

hypertext anchor

In an HTML document, the format codes used to define a hypertext link to another document. The hypertext anchor is embedded into the text. It begins with an <A and ends with a </A>. The text or icon between the <A and </A> becomes the hyperlink's hot spot.

hyperware

Hypertext products.

hyphenation

Breaking words that extend beyond the right margin. Software hyphenates words by matching them against a hyphenation dictionary or by using a built-in set of rules, or both. See *discretionary hyphen*.

hyphenation dictionary

A word file with predefined hyphen locations.

hyphenation zone

The distance from the right margin within which a word may be hyphenated.

hyphen ladder

Hyphens on two or more consecutive lines, which causes distraction to the reader.

hypotenuse

In a right triangle, the side opposite the right angle. See *sine*.

hysteresis

The lag between making a change, such as increasing or decreasing power, and the response or effect of that change.

Hz

(HertZ) See *Hertz*.

I750

A programmable compression chip from Intel that supports a variety of techniques including DVI, MPEG and JPEG.

i860

A RISC-based, 64-bit processor from Intel that uses a 64-bit data bus, has built-in floating point and 3-D graphics capability and contains over one million transistors. It can be used as a stand-alone CPU or to accelerate performance in existing systems.

IAB

See *Internet*.

IAC

(InterApplication Communications) The interprocess communications capability in the Macintosh starting with System 7.0. Many IAC events take place behind the scenes. For example, when you drag and drop an object onto an icon, the Finder may send an IAC message to the application, or an application may send a message to another application, to perform a function.

IANAL

Digispeak for "I am not a lawyer, but..."

IAW

Digispeak for "in accordance with."

IBI

(Information Builders, Inc., New York) IBI is the creator of the FOCUS database management system and the EDA/SQL middleware. See *FOCUS* and *EDA/SQL*.

IBM

(International Business Machines Corporation, Armonk, NY) The world's largest computer company. It started in New York in 1911 when the Computing-Tabulating-Recording Company. (CTR) was created by a merger of The Tabulating Machine Company (Hollerith's punched card company in Washington, DC), International Time Recording Company (time clock maker in NY state), Computing Scale Company (maker of scales and food slicers in Dayton, Ohio), and Bundy Manufacturing (time clock maker in Poughkeepsie, NY). CTR started out with 1,200 employees and a capital value of $17.5 million.

In 1914, Thomas J. Watson, Sr., became general manager. During the next 10 years, he dispensed with all non-tabulating business and turned it into an international enterprise renamed IBM in 1924. Watson instilled a strict, professional demeanor in his employees that set IBMers apart from the rest of the crowd.

IBM achieved spectacular success with its tabulating machines and the punched cards that were fed them. From the 1920s through the 1960s, it developed a huge customer base that was ideal for conversion to computers.

IBM launched its computer business in 1953 with the 701 and introduced the 650 a year later. By the end of the 1950s, the 650 was the most widely used computer in the world with 1,800 systems installed. The 1401, announced in 1959, was its second computer winner, and by the mid 1960s, an estimated 18,000 were in use.

In 1964, it announced the System/360, the first family of compatible computers ever developed. The 360s were enormously successful and set a standard underlying IBM mainframes to this day.

During the 1970s and 1980s, IBM made a variety of incompatible minicomputer systems, including the System/36 and System/38. Its highly-successful AS/400, introduced in 1988, provides a broad family of compatible machines in this segment.

In 1981, IBM introduced the PC into a chaotic personal computer field and set the standard almost overnight. IBM is still one of the largest PC manufacturers, but the majority of PC sales come from the PC industry at large, from companies such as Packard Bell, HP, Compaq and Dell to mom and pop shops by the thousands. Although just like everyone else, IBM includes Windows on its PCs, it continues to promote its OS/2 operating system for PC desktops and servers. OS/2 Warp, released in late 1994, is highly praised, but to date has not gained the increase in market share IBM hoped for.

Thomas J. Watson, Sr.
This photo was taken in 1920 before Watson renamed the company IBM. *(Photo courtesy of International Business Machines Corporation.)*

Although IBM is a company with over 60 billion dollars in sales, the early 1990s were gut-wrenching years. IBM experienced major losses in 1992 and 1993, due mainly to slowing sales of high-profit mainframes as companies worldwide began to implement client/server systems with smaller computers. IBM also reduced PC prices to become more competitive, further reducing margins. To meet the challenges of the 1990s, IBM reduced its staff by more than 150,000 employees.

In 1991, IBM startled the industry by teaming up with Apple and Motorola to produce the PowerPC chip, a single-chip version of IBM's RS/6000 workstations (see *Apple-IBM alliance*). The first PowerPC models were introduced in new RS/6000s in 1993 and in stand-alone PowerPC-based PCs in 1995. IBM is consolidating its CPU architecture by moving its AS/400 line to the PowerPC as well.

In 1995, IBM surprised us once again with the purchase of Lotus Development Corporation, publishers of Lotus 1-2-3 and the popular Notes groupware for Windows and OS/2.

As to the future, IBM was king of the hill for decades, and although some have enjoyed seeing it humbled, if only temporarily, IBM is not a company to be underestimated. IBM sells an enormous number of mainframes, minicomputers, workstations and personal computers, and more dollar value of software than anybody else in the world.

In addition, with all the push to distributed client/server systems, the bulk of the data in most large enterprises still resides in IBM mainframes. As more computers are distributed into the enterprise, many organizations are finding that client/server implementations on PCs are not a panacea. A more centralized architecture with mainframes as servers may be an effective way to manage the ever-increasing complexity. The universe runs in cycles. More surprises are in store.

IBM Office, London, 1935
"Dayton Money Making Machines" were sold all across the world. IBM became an international enterprise in the late 1930s. *(Photo courtesy of International Business Machines Corporation.)*

IBM-Apple alliance

See *Apple-IBM alliance.*

IBMBIO.COM

See *IBMDOS.COM.*

IBM-compatible PC

A personal computer that is compatible with the IBM PC and PS/2 standards. Although this term is still used, it had more validity in the early days when PC makers were trying to copy the IBM PC, and many PCs were not compatible. Today, PCs conform to standards that, although originally set by IBM, have been modified over time by the PC industry at large.

IBMDOS.COM

One of two hidden system files that make up IBM's PC-DOS. The other is IBMBIO.COM. These two system files are loaded into memory when the computer is booted. They process the instructions in CONFIG.SYS, then load COMMAND.COM and finally process the instructions in AUTOEXEC.BAT. The MS-DOS counterparts of these system files are IO.SYS and MSDOS.SYS.

IBM mainframes

Following is a list of the different series of mainframes IBM has offered over the years. All of the series in this list stem from the original System/360 architecture introduced in 1964. For information about a series, look up the individual term.

Year Intro.	Series name	(model numbers)
1964	System/360	(20 to 195)
1970	System/370	(115 to 168)
1977	303x series	(3031, 3032, 3033)
1979	43xx series	(4300 to 4381, ES/4381)
1980	308x series	(3081, 3083, 3084)
1986	3090 series	(120 to 600, ES/3090)
1986	9370 series	(9370, ES/9370)
1990	System/390	(ES/9000, 120 to 9X2)
1994	System/390	(Parallel Enterprise Server)

IBM Mainframe
This ES/9000 mainframe is behind the proverbial glass-enclosed datacenter. *(Photo courtesy of International Business Machines Corporation.)*

IBM minicomputers

Following is a list of the different series of minicomputers IBM has offered over the years. For information about a series, look up the individual term.

Year Intro	Series name	Year Intro	Series name
1969	System/3	1983	System/36
1975	System/32	1985	System/88
1976	Series/1	1988	AS/400
1977	System/34	1990	RS/6000
1978	System/38	1993	RS/6000 (PowerPC based)
1978	8100	1995	AS/400 (PowerPC based)

IBM PC

Starting on the next page is a list of early IBM PCs as well as PS/2 models whose model numbers do not convey CPU size and speed. Other models of IBM personal computers conform to common numbering systems used by the PC industry; for example, 486/33 and 486/66. Also included in the list are the popular ThinkPad notebooks. For information about PCs, look up *PC*.

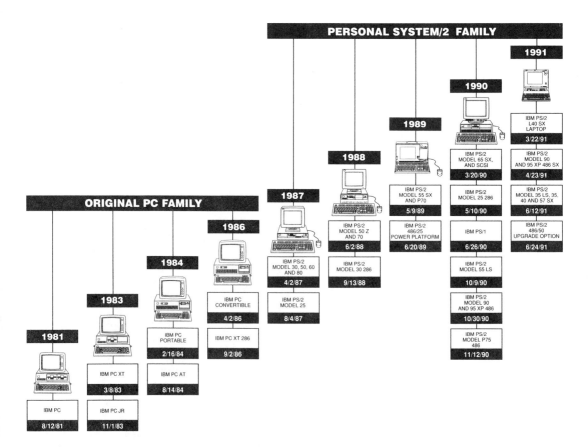

The First 10 Years

This illustration describes the models introduced during the first 10 years of the IBM Personal Computer and IBM Personal System series. *(Illustration courtesy of International Business Machines Corporation.)*

First Generation PC Models

Model	Year Intro.	CPU, Features
PC	1981	8088, No. 1 (floppy only)
XT	1983	8088, slow hard disk
XT 286	1986	286, slow hard disk
XT/370	1983	8088, 370 emulation
AT	1984	286, medium-speed hard disk
3270 PC	1983	8088, 3270 emulation
PCjr	1983	8088, floppy-based home use
PC Portable	1984	8088, floppy-based portable
Convertible	1986	8088, microfloppy laptop

Second Generation PS/2 Models

PS/2 models use the Micro Channel bus architecture unless otherwise noted below.

Model	Year Intro.	CPU Features
25	1987	8086, PC bus (limited expansion)
30	1987	8086, PC bus
30-286	1988	286, ISA bus
35 LS	1991	386SX, ISA bus, diskless
35 SX	1991	386SX, ISA bus
L40 SX	1991	386SX, ISA bus, laptop
40 SX	1991	386SX, ISA bus
N45 SL		386SL notebook
50	1987	286
50 Z	1988	286, faster 50
N51 SX	1992	386SX, notebook
N51 SLC	1992	386SLC, notebook
55 SX	1989	386SX
55 LS	1990	386SX, diskless
56 SLC	1992	386SLC
56 SX	1992	386SX, upgradeable
57 SLC	1992	386SLC
57 SX	1991	386SX, 2.88MB floppy
CL57 SX	1992	386SX, notebook, active matrix
60	1987	286
65	1990	386SX
70	1988	386
70 486	1989	486
P70	1989	386 portable
P75 486	1990	486 portable, 22 lbs.
76	1994	486SX & DX, OS/2, SCSI
76i	1994	486SX, OS/2, IDE drive
77	1994	DX4, OS/2, SCSI, ECC memory
77i	1994	DX4, OS/2, IDE drive, ECC memory
80	1987	386, tower
90	1990	486, XGA, SCSI, upgradable
90	1992	486DX2/66
95	1990	486, tower
90 SX	1991	486SX
95 SX	1991	486SX, tower

ThinkPad 760

The 760 has been extremely popular due to its 12.1" diagonal screen, the largest flat panel screen on a laptop to date.

Thinkpad Notebook Computers

300	1992	386SL/25
350	1993	486SL/25, PCMCIA slot
350C	1993	486SL/25, PCMCIA, passive color
360CSE	1995	486DX2/50, passive color
360CE	1995	486DX2/50, active matrix
500	1993	486SLC2 50/25, PCMCIA, 3.8 pounds
700	1992	486SLC/25
700C	1992	486SLC/25, active matrix color

701C	1995	486DX2/50 or DX4/100, act. matrix , TrackWrite, sound, 4 pounds
710T	1993	486SLC/25, pen-based
720	1993	486SLC2 50/25, PCMCIA slot
720C	1993	486SLC2 50/25, PCMCIA, active color
750Cs	1994	486SL/33, PCMCIA, dual scan passive, removable hard disk, sound
755CSE	1994	DX4/100, dual scan passive, sound
755CE	1994	DX4/100, act. matrix, sound
755CD	1994	DX4/100, act. matrix, sound, CD-ROM
760CD	1995	P90, 12.1" active matrix, CD-ROM

IBM PC Company

A subsidiary of the IBM Corporation located in Raleigh, NC, that is involved with all aspects of IBM PCs.

IBM workstation

See *RS/6000.*

IC

See *integrated circuit* and *information center.*

I-CASE

(Integrated CASE) CASE systems that generate applications code directly from design specifications. Features include support for rapid prototyping, modeling the data and processing and drawing logic diagrams.

Solitaire

IC card

See *PC card* and *memory card.*

ICCP

Character Map

(Institute for Certification of Computer Professionals, 2200 E. Devon Ave., Des Plaines, IL 60018, 708/299-4227) An organization founded in 1973 that offers industry certification and provides worldwide test centers. The Associate Computer Professional exam is open to all. The Certified Computer Programmer (CCP), Certified Data Processor (CDP) and Certified Systems Professional (CSP) require job experience (academic credit may substitute).

ICE

Media Player

(1) (In-Circuit Emulator) A chip used for testing and debugging logic circuits typically in embedded systems. The chip emulates a particular microprocessor and contains breakpoints and other debugging functions. See *ROM emulator.*
(2) (Ice) A Lotus 1-2-3 add-on program from Baler Software Corporation, Rolling Meadows, IL, that adds extensions to Lotus macros. It is used for developing customized macro-driven 1-2-3 programs.

icon

Write

A small, pictorial, on-screen representation of an object (file, program, disk, etc.) used in graphical interfaces. For example, to delete a file in the Macintosh, the file icon is moved onto the wastebasket icon.

Icons

These icons represent some of the programs that come with Windows 3.1.

iconic interface

A user interface that uses icons.

ICR

(Intelligent Character Recognition) The ability to recognize hand printing.

IDA

(Intelligent Drive Array) A high-performance hard disk interface from Compaq that controls a disk array via the EISA bus.

IDAPI

(Independent Database API) The programming interface to the Borland Database Engine. IDAPI calls are made from dBASE, Paradox and C++ applications to access data in one of the supported databases. See *Borland Database Engine*.

IDC

(International Data Corporation, Framingham, MA) The largest market research, analysis and consulting firm in the information field. Founded in 1964, it provides annual briefings and in-depth reports on all aspects of the industry.

IDE

(1) (Integrated Drive Electronics)
(2) (Integrated Development Environment)
(1) (Integrated Drive Electronics) A type of hardware interface widely used to connect hard disks to a PC. IDE is popular due to its lower cost and is increasingly being used to connect CD-ROMs and tape drives. Starting out with 40MB capacities years ago, IDE hard disks up to 1GB are now common and cost as little as 30 cents per megabyte (mid 1995). Prices are expected to drop, and capacities are expected to increase.

IDE drives connect via a 40-line flat ribbon cable to an expansion board called a host adapter, which plugs into an expansion slot in the PC. Each cable connects up to two drives. The original IDE host adapter supported two drives, but Enhanced IDE (EIDE) adapters provide a second channel for two more disk, tape or CD-ROM drives.

Since the controller electronics are contained in the IDE drive itself, the host adapter is a simple circuit board. For example, a $20 Enhanced IDE host adapter can control four drives, two floppies, two serial ports, a parallel port and a game port, essentially all the primary input/output on a PC except for keyboard and monitor. Some motherboards have a built-in IDE host adapter and 40-pin connector that the cable plugs directly into.

Technically, the IDE interface is defined by the ATA (AT Attachment) specification. ATA-2, or Fast ATA, defines the faster transfer rates used in Enhanced IDE, and ATAPI defines the IDE standard for CD-ROMs and tape drives. See *hard disk* and *Enhanced IDE*.

(2) (Integrated Development Environment) A set of programs run from a single user interface. For example, programming languages often include a text editor, compiler and debugger, which are all activated and function from a common menu.

IDE controller

The term generally refers to an IDE host adapter, the plug-in card used to attach IDE drives. Since an IDE drive contains both the controller and the drive, the term technically refers to the controller built into the drive housing, not the interface to the computer. However, this distinction would only be critical for a very technical person such as a disk drive design engineer. See *IDE host adapter*.

IDE host adapter

An expansion board that plugs into a PC, which is used to connect either two or four IDE hard disks. It generally also provides control for two floppy disks, two serial ports, a parallel port and a game port. Sometimes, the IDE host adapter is built onto the motherboard. See *enhanced IDE*.

IDE Drive
The IDE drive contains the controller and drive electronics.

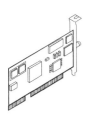

IDE Host Adapter
Since the controller is built into the IDE drive, the IDE host adapter is a very simple circuit board. It generally also provides the floppy disk control and the serial, parallel and game ports.

idle character

In data communications, a character transmitted to keep the line synchronized when there is no data being sent.

idle interrupt

An interrupt generated when a device changes from an operational state to an idle state.

idle time

The duration of time a device is in an idle state, which means that it is operational, but not being used.

IDMS

See *CA-IDMS*.

IE

See *information engineering*.

IEC

(International Electrotechnical Commission) An organization that sets international electrical and electronics standards founded in 1906 and headquartered in Geneva. It is made up of national committees from over 40 countries. Contact is via ANSI in New York.

IEEE

(Institute of Electrical and Electronic Engineers, 345 E. 47th St., New York, NY 10017, 212/705-7900) A membership organization that includes engineers, scientists and students in electronics and allied fields. Founded in 1963, it has over 300,000 members and is involved with setting standards for computers and communications.

The Computer Society of the IEEE has over 100,000 members and holds meetings and technical conferences on computers. Address: 1730 Mass. Ave. N.W., Washington, DC 20036, 202/371-0101.

IEEE 1284

An IEEE standard for an enhanced parallel port that is compatible with the Centronics parallel port commonly used on PCs. The standard also defines the type of cable that must be used in order to increase distances up to 30 feet and sustain the higher transfer rates.

There are several modes of operation. The EPP (Enhanced Parallel Port) mode provides high-speed transfer to 500 Kbytes/sec compared to about 150 Kbytes/sec for Centronics. It also allows multiple devices to be daisy chained from one port. A higher-speed ECP (Enhanced Capabilities Port) mode, originally developed by Microsoft and HP, provides speeds up to 2Mbytes/sec in each direction. Nibble and byte modes provide slower bi-directional transfer.

IEEE 488

See *GPIB*.

IEEE 802

IEEE standards for networking. See "LANs" under *data link protocol*.

802.1	Covers network management and related topics
802.2	Specifies data link layer for the following access methods:
802.3	CSMA/CD, Ethernet
802.4	Token passing bus, MAP

802.5	Token passing ring, Token Ring
802.6	DQDB, Metropolitan Area Network
803.12	Demand priority, 100VG-AnyLAN

IEF

(Information Engineering Facility) A fully-integrated set of CASE tools from TI that runs on PCs and MVS mainframes. It generates COBOL code for PCs, MVS mainframes, VMS, Tandem, AIX, HP-UX and other UNIX platforms.

IETF

See *Internet.*

I/E time

See *instruction cycle.*

IEW

(Information Engineering Workbench) CASE software from Sterling Software, Atlanta, GA (formerly KnowledgeWare), that runs on DOS PCs and generates COBOL, CICS and IMS code for MVS mainframes.

IFIP

(International Federation of Information Processing, 16 Place Longemalle, CH-1204 Geneva, Switzerland, 41 22 28 2649) A multinational affiliation of professional groups concerned with information processing, founded in 1960. There is one voting representative from each country (U.S. representative is FOCUS).

I-frame

A key frame used in MPEG compression. See *MPEG.*

IFS

(Installable File System) An OS/2 feature that supports multiple file systems. Different systems can be installed (UNIX, CD-ROM, etc.) just like drivers are installed for new peripherals.

IFSHLP.SYS

See *IFSMgr.*

IFSMgr

(Installable File System ManaGeR) The driver that provides the 32-bit file system for Windows for Workgroups and Windows 95. It also uses a "helper" file called IFSHLP.SYS which, among other things, translates 16-bit to 32-bit calls. See *installable file system.*

if-then-else

A high-level programming language statement that compares two or more sets of data and tests the results. If the results are true, the THEN instructions are taken; if not, the ELSE instructions are taken. The following is a BASIC example:

```
10   IF ANSWER = "Y"   THEN PRINT "Yes"
20   ELSE PRINT "No"
```

In certain languages, THEN is implied. All statements between IF and ELSE are carried out if the condition is true. All instructions between ELSE and ENDIF are carried out if not true. The following dBASE example produces the same results as above:

```
IF ANSWER = "Y"
   ? "Yes"
  ELSE
   ? "No"
ENDIF
```

IGES

(Initial Graphics Exchange Specification) An ANSI graphics file format that is system independent and also intended for human interpretation. It evolved out of the Air Force's Integrated Computer Automated Manufacturing (ICAM) program in 1979. For more on IGES and PDES, contact: IGES Organization, National Institute of Standards & Technology, Building 220, Room A-353, Gaithersburg, MD 20899, 301/921-3691.

IHV

(Independent Hardware Vendor) An organization that makes electronic equipment. It implies a company that specializes in a niche area, such as display adapters or disk controllers, rather than a computer systems manufacturer. Contrast with *ISV*. See *VAR* and *systems integrator*.

IIA

(1) (Information Industry Association) A trade organization that includes members from all aspects of the information field. Its purpose is to conduct active government relations that safeguard the interests of a healthy, competitive information industry. IIA sponsors seminars and conferences and provides newsletters, newspapers and books. Address: 555 New Jersey Ave. N.W., Washington, DC 20001, 201/639-8262.
(2) (Information Interchange Architecture) IBM formats for exchanging documents between different systems.

illustration program

Same as *drawing program*.

IMA

(Interactive Multimedia Association, 3 Church Circle, Annapolis, MD 21401, 410/626-1380) A trade association founded in 1988 originally as the Interactive Video Industry Association. The IMA provides an open process for adopting existing technologies and is involved in subjects such as networked services, scripting languages, data formats and intellectual property rights..

image

A picture (graphic). See also *system image*.

image editing

Changing or improving graphics images either interactively using a paint program or by using software routines that alter contrast, smooth lines or filter out unwanted data. See *image filter* and *anti-aliasing*.

image editor

Software that allows scanned images to be altered and enhanced. Image editors have a full set of painting tools as well as a variety of image filters that can can be applied to all or a portion of the image. Examples of full-featured image editors are Adobe Photoshop, Picture Publisher and Fractal Design Painter. High-end image editors are sometimes called *photo illustration software*. See *image filter*.

image filter

A routine that changes the appearance of an image or part of an image by altering the shades and colors of the pixels in some manner. Filters are used to increase brightness and contrast as well as to add a wide variety of textures, tones and special effects to a picture.

image processing

(1)The analysis of a picture using techniques that can identify shades, colors and relationships that cannot be perceived by the human eye. It is used to solve identification problems, such as in forensic medicine or in creating weather maps from satellite pictures and deals with images in raster graphics format that have been scanned in or captured with digital cameras.

(2) Any image improvement, such as refining a picture in a paint program that has been scanned or entered from a video source.

imagesetter

A machine that accepts PostScript input and generates output for the printing process; for example a film-based paper that is photographed or the actual film for making the printing plates. Input comes from the keyboard, or via disk, tape or modem. Earlier machines handled only text and were called *phototypesetters*. Modern imagesetters use lasers to generate the image directly onto the film. Older machines passed light through a spinning font photomask, then through lenses that created the point size and onto film. Others created images on CRTs and exposed the film.

The typesetter was originally the only machine that could handle multiple fonts and text composition such as kerning. Today, desktop laser printers are used for many typesetting jobs and are quickly advancing in resolution, although the 1270 and 2540 dpi resolutions of the imagesetter combined with the high-quality of film still provide the finest printing for photographs and halftones.

imaging

Creating a film or electronic image of any picture or paper form. It is accomplished by scanning or photographing an object and turning it into a matrix of dots (raster graphics), the meaning of which is unknown to the computer, only to the human viewer. Scanned images of text may be encoded into computer data (ASCII or EBCDIC) with page recognition software (OCR). See *micrographics, image processing* and *document imaging*.

imaging model

A set of rules for representing images.

imaging system

See *document imaging, image processing* and *image enhancement*.

IMHO, IMO

Digispeak for "in my humble opinion" and "in my opinion."

immediate access

Same as *direct access*.

impact printer

A printer that uses a printing mechanism that bangs the character image into the ribbon and onto the paper. See *printer* for examples.

impedance

The resistance to the flow of alternating current in a circuit.

implementation

(1) Computer system *implementation* is the installation of new hardware and system

software.

(2) Information system *implementation* is the installation of new databases and application programs and the adoption of new manual procedures.

implode

To link component pieces to a major assembly. It may also refer to compressing data using a particular technique. Contrast with *explode*.

import

To convert a file in a foreign format to the format of the program being used.

Impromptu

A Windows query and reporting tool from Cognos with support for a large variety of databases. It is capable of generating cross tabs for spreadsheets such as Excel, Lotus for Windows and Quattro Pro for Windows.

Improv

A multidimensional Windows spreadsheet from Lotus that allows for easy switching to different views of the data. Data is referenced by name as in a database rather than the typical spreadsheet row and column coordinates. Improv was originally developed for the NeXt computer.

IMS

(Information Management System) An IBM hierarchical DBMS for mainframes under MVS. It was widely implemented throughout the 1970s and continues to be used. IMS/DC is its transaction processing component (like CICS) that handles the details of communications and SNA networking. IMS/DC is also used to access DB2 databases.

imux

See *inverse multiplexor*.

in band

Inside the primary frequency or system. See *signaling in/out of band*.

incident light

In computer graphics, light that strikes an object. The color of the object is based on how the light is absorbed or reflected by the object.

in-circuit emulator

See *ICE*.

Incorrect DOS version

A DOS error message that means the command you are using belongs to another version of DOS. Somehow an earlier or later version of a command is on your hard disk. Commands from one DOS version often do not work in other versions.

increment

To add a number to another number. Incrementing a counter means adding 1 to its current value.

incremental backup

See *backup types*.

incremental spacing

See *microspacing*.

IND$FILE

An IBM mainframe program that transfers files between the mainframe and a PC functioning as a 3270 terminal.

indent

To align text some number of spaces to the right of the left margin. See *hanging paragraph*.

Indeo

A video compression/decompression algorithm from Intel that is used to compress movie files.

index

(1) In data management, the most common method for keeping track of data on a disk. Indexes are directory listings maintained by the OS, DBMS or the application. An index of files contains an entry for each file name and the location of the file. An index of records has an entry for each key field (account no., name, etc.) and the location of the record.

(2) In programming, a method for keeping track of data in a table. See *indexed addressing*.

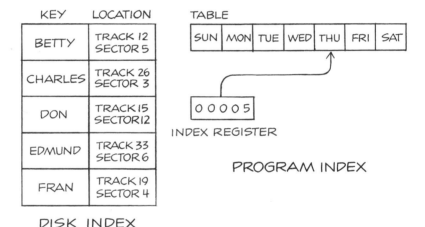

DISK INDEX

PROGRAM INDEX

indexed addressing

A technique for referencing memory that automatically increments the address with the value stored in an index register. See *subscript (2)*.

indexed sequential

See *ISAM*.

index hole

A small hole punched into a hard sectored floppy disk that serves to mark the start of the sectors on each track.

indexing

(1) Creating indexes based on key data fields or key words.

(2) Creating timing signals based on detecting a mark, slot or hole in a moving medium.

index mark

A physical hole or notch, or a recorded code or mark, that is used to identify a starting point for each track on a disk.

index register

A high-speed circuit used to hold the current, relative position of an item in a table (array). At execution time, its stored value is added to the instructions that reference it.

indirect addressing

An address mode that points to another pointer rather than the actual data. This mode is prohibited in RISC architecture.

inductance

The magnetic field that is generated when a current is passed through an inductor.

induction

The process of generating an electric current in a circuit from the magnetic influence of an adjacent circuit as in a transformer or capacitor.

Electrical induction is also the principle behind read/write heads on magnetic disks. To create (write) the bit, current is sent through a coil that creates a magnetic field which is discharged at the gap of the head onto the disk surface as it spins by. To read the bit, the magnetic field of the bit "induces" an electrical charge in the head as it passes by the gap.

inductor

A coil of wire that generates a magnetic field when current is passed through it. The strength of the magnetic field is measured in henrys. When the current is removed, as the magnetic field disintegrates, it generates a brief current in the opposite direction of the original.

industrial strength

Refers to software that is designed for high-volume, multiuser operation. It implies that the software is robust and that there are built-in safeguards against system failures. For example, an industrial-strength operating system runs its applications in protected address spaces and does not lock up or stop if one of them crashes. Industrial-strength features in a DBMS are referential integrity and two-phase commit.

The term is used to refer to any solid, sound program that has been thoroughly tested in live user environments for extensive periods, whether system software (OS, DBMS, etc.) or application software (order entry, desktop publishing, etc.).

inference engine

The processing program in an expert system. It derives a conclusion from the facts and rules contained in the knowledge base using various artificial intelligence techniques.

INF file

(INFormation file) A Windows file that contains installation information. The SETUP.INF file is used to install Windows itself, and other INF files are used for installing other programs and hardware devices.

infix notation

The common way arithmetic operators are used to reference numeric values. For example, A+B/C is infix notation. Contrast with *Polish notation* and *reverse Polish notation*.

infobahn

(INFOrmation BAHN) A nickname for the information superhighway. It comes from the German "Autobahn," or automobile superhighway.

Infobase

A database created in Folio. See *Folio*.

infopreneur

A person who is in business to gather and disseminate electronic information.

InfoPump

Software from Trinzic Corporation, Palo Alto, CA, that is used to synchronize data in different types of databases by moving the data and converting it to the destination format. It supports Lotus Notes documents, ASCII files, mainframe file formats and most of the popular databases. A Windows-based client component controls the InfoPump Server. Data movement can be performed on a scheduled or event-driven basis.

informate

To dispense information, as coined by Harvard Professor Shoshana Zuboff.

information

The summarization of data. Technically, data are raw facts and figures that are processed into information, such as summaries and totals. But since information can also be raw data for the next job or person, the two terms cannot be precisely defined. Both terms are used synonymously and interchangeably.

As office automation and data processing merge, it may be more helpful to view information the way data is defined and used, namely: data, text, spreadsheets, pictures, voice and video. Data are discretely defined fields. Text is a collection of words. Spreadsheets are data in matrix (row and column) form. Pictures are lists of vectors or frames of bits. Voice is a continuous stream of sound waves. Video is a sequence of frames.

Future databases will routinely integrate all these forms of information.

information appliance

A type of future home or office device that can transmit to or plug into common public or private networks. Envisioned is a "digital highway," like telephone and electrical power networks.

information center

The division within the IS department that supports end-user computing. Responsible for training users in applications and solving related personal computer problems.

information collaboration

See *data conferencing*.

information engineering

An integrated set of methodologies and products used to guide and develop information processing within an organization. It starts with enterprise-wide stategic planning and ends with running applications.

information hiding

Keeping details of a routine private. Programmers only know what input is required and what outputs are expected. See *encapsulation* and *abstraction*.

information highway

See *information superhighway*.

information industry

(1) Organizations that publish information via online services or through distribution by diskette or CD-ROM.
(2) All computer, communications and electronics-related organizations, including hardware, software and services.

Information Industry Association

See *IIA*.

information management

The discipline that analyzes information as an organizational resource. It covers the definitions, uses, value and distribution of all data and information within an organization whether processed by computer or not. It evaluates the kinds of data/information an organization requires in order to function and progress effectively. Information is complex because business transactions are complex. It must be analyzed and understood before effective computer solutions can be developed. See *data administration*.

information processing

Same as *data processing*.

information requirements

The information needed to support a business or other activity. Requirements are typically defined as lists of detailed items as well as summarized data from business transactions, such as orders and purchases, and master records, such as customers and vendors. How frequently this information must be made available is also part of the requirement.

Information requirements (the what and when) are turned into functional specs (the how) of an information system by systems analysts. The information is defined as a collection of data elements that are obtained by running query and report programs against a particular database or group of databases. The data and information that is stored in the databases in the first place is also derived from the information requirements. See *functional specification*.

information resource management

See *Information Systems* and *information management*.

information science

See *information management*.

information service

Any information retrieval, publishing, timesharing or BBS facility. See *online services*.

Information Services

See *Information Systems*.

information sharing

See *data conferencing*.

information superhighway

The telecommunications infrastructure within the U.S. that will allow access to government, industry and educational data banks for all people. While many envision a single high-speed link to and from every house in America, this is not feasible for many years. What is already happening is an interlinking of existing capabilities via local telephone, cable TV, satellite and online service providers. Also, rather than one type of receiver, many types of devices will hook into this superhighway, including TVs with the appropriate adapters, personal computers and PDAs (personal digital assistants).

The Internet has become synonymous with the information superhighway, because it provides an enormous source of information that is available to the public. However, universal, dial-up access to the Internet is not without charge, and it was never designed to be a high-speed link into everyone's home. It may serve as a backbone for the information superhighway, or it may serve only as a prototype for a real information superhighway in the future.

Various bills for altering U.S. communications laws have been proposed that allow telephone and cable companies to enter each other's markets. Some telephone companies have already ventured into new markets, challenging existing laws. Stay tuned!

information system

A business application of the computer. It is made up of the database, application programs, manual and machine procedures and encompasses the computer systems that do the processing.

The database stores the subjects of the business (master files) and its activities (transaction files). The application programs provide the data entry, updating, query and report processing. The manual procedures document how data is obtained for input and how the system's output is distributed. Machine procedures instruct the computer how to perform the batch processing activities, in which the output of one program is automaticaly fed into another program.

The daily processing is the interactive, realtime processing of the transactions. At the end of the day or other period, the batch processing programs update the master files that have not been updated since the last cycle. Reports are printed for the cycle's activities.

The periodic processing of an information system is the updating of the master files, which adds, deletes and changes the information about customers, employees, vendors and products.

Relationships Between Systems

	Structure (is)	Function (does)
Management System	1. PEOPLE 2. MACHINES	Sets organization's goals and objectives, strategies and tactics, plans, schedules and controls

Information System	1. DATABASE
	2. APPLICATION
	    PROGRAMS
	3. PROCEDURES
		Defines data structures
		Data entry, updating,
		    queries and reporting
		Defines data flow

Computer System	1. CPU 2. PERIPHERALS 3. OPERATING SYSTEM	Processes (The 3 C's) Store and retrieve Manages computer system

Sample Master Records (subjects)

Key Field				Fields			
Employee Number	Name	Address	Date of hire	Date of birth	Title	Job Class	Pay Rate
Customer Number	Name	Bill to	Ship to	Credit Limit	Date 1st Order	Sales to date	YTD Sales
Vendor Number	Name	Address	Terms	Quality Rating	Shipping History		
Product Number	Description	Quantity On hand	Location	Primary Vendor	Secondary Vendor		

Records

Master Files

Master files contain information about the subjects of the system, such as employees, assets, customers, vendors, products and general ledger accounts. The master file contains a **record** for each subject. Each item of data or information about the subject is stored in a **field**.

In relational database terminology, files are called **tables**, because the data is structured in tabular form (rows and columns). Records are called **rows** or **tuples**, and fields are called **attributes**. In practice, file and table, record and row, and field and attribute are used synonymously.

There is *always* a key field.

Records are identified by number, such as employee number and customer number. The field that the number is stored in is called a **key field.**

In order to be able to look up an individual customer or employee record immediately, the key field for that record must be indexed. An index is a list of account numbers and pointers to where the individual records are stored in the database. It is 100 times faster to compare index items once they have been read into memory than it is to read and compare each record in the database. The DBMS keeps the index up-to-date whenever a record is added or deleted.

Sample Daily Transactions (actions)

Transaction Files

Transaction files contain the detailed records of the activity of the organization. Data entered into these records is used to update the records in the master file.

Any action that changes the master file must be recorded as a transaction. These are the detail records that must be kept to provide an audit trail as well as history for decision support and executive infor-mation.

	Key							
Payroll	Employee Number	Today's Date	Hours Worked					
Order	Customer Number	Today's Date	Quantity	Product Number				
Payment	Customer Number	Today's Date	Invoice Number	Amount Paid	Check Number			
Purchase	PO Number	Today's Date	Dept.	Authorized Agent	Vendor Number	Quantity	Product Number	Due Date
Receipt	PO Number	Today's Date	Quantity	Product Number				

Maintenance (periodic transactions)

Pay Raise	Employee Number	Today's Date	Transaction Type	New rate	Management Authorization
Credit Limit Change	Customer Number	Today's Date	New limit	Management Authorization	
Product Description Change	Product Number	Today's Date	New descripton	Management Authorization	

Create the Master File

When a new information system is implemented, the first tables to be created are the subject tables (master files). Master records from the old system can be converted to the new database via a conversion program or a conversion function in the DBMS. If history from the old system is required in the new one, then transaction data also has to be brought over.

Every information system is designed to accomodate maintenance transactions, which periodically update the database. Address changes, pay rate changes and credit limit changes are examples. They also provide an audit trail of management authorization (who authorized the increase?) which is archived for historical purposes.

Databases developed for personal use with a database package, such as dBASE and Paradox, do not automatically generate an audit trail. You can edit the data any way you wish. In an enterprise application, all activity that updates the database is recorded and maintained as transaction history.

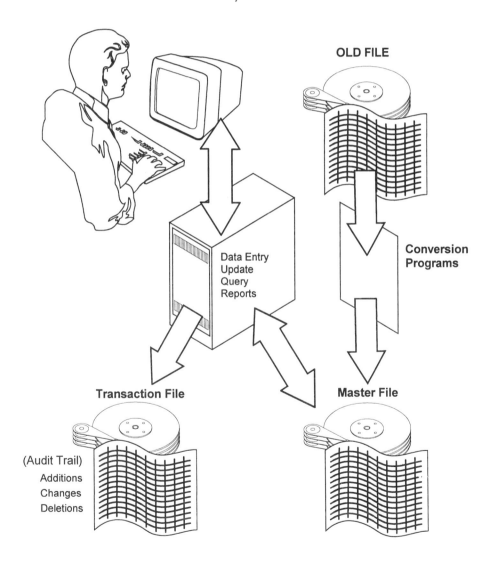

Transaction Processing & Batch Processing

The transaction processing in an enterprise is the daily work of a computer. Also called *online transaction processing*, or *OLTP*, it means that the database is updated as soon as a transaction is received. A sales order depletes inventory immediately, a sale of stock updates the last close for that stock, a pledge adds to the fund raising balance the instant it's made.

Transaction processing keeps the business records up-to-date the moment transactions are keyed into or transmitted to the system.

An information system is made up of batch processing as well. Batch processing is updating or searching an entire table from beginning to end. Any month-end report is a batch job. Printing payroll checks is a batch job. Adding records to a database by typing in stacks of paper documents is also batch processing.

There are still jobs too large for transaction processing. For example, most telephone bills are batch processed. Telephone calls are collected until month end, then sorted into telephone number sequence and matched against the customer table for updating with all the other customers at the same time.

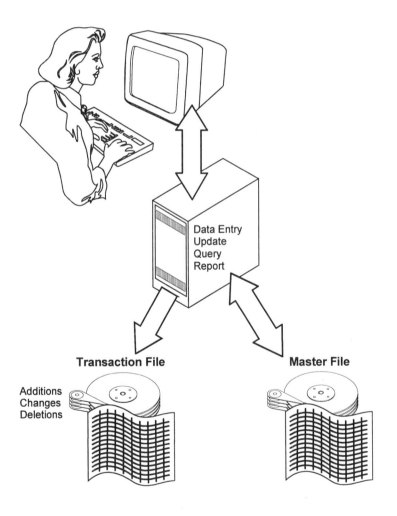

Data Entry
Update
Query
Report

Transaction File

Additions
Changes
Deletions

Master File

Information Systems

The formal title for a data processing, MIS, or IS department. Other titles are Data Processing, Information Processing, Information Services, Management Information Systems, Management Information Services and Information Technology.

Information Technology Association of America

See *ITAA*.

information theory

The study of encoding and transmitting information. From Claude Shannon's 1938 paper, "A Mathematical Theory of Communication," which proposed the use of binary digits for coding information.

information utility

(1) A service bureau that maintains up-to-date databases for public access.
(2) A central source of information for an organization or group.

information warehouse

The collection of all databases in an enterprise across all platforms and departments.

information warfare

Creating havoc by disrupting the computers that manage stock exchanges, power grids, air traffic control and telecommunications.

INFORMIX

A relational database management system (DBMS) from Informix Software, Inc., Menlo Park, CA, that runs on most UNIX platforms, including SCO UNIX for x86 machines and NetWare. Development tools from Informix include INFORMIX-4GL, a fourth-generation language, and INFORMIX-New Era, a client/server development system for Windows clients that supports INFORMIX and non-INFORMIX databases.

Info Select

A popular personal information manager (PIM) for PCs from Micro Logic Corporation, Hackensack, NJ, that includes automatic phone dialing via modem. It is noted for its exceptional ease of use and ability to store random information and instantly retrieve it in a very useful manner. It is based on an earlier product called Tornado designed by Paul Mendelsohn and Micro Logic's Jim Lewis.

infowar

See *information warfare*.

infoware

Information sold electronically, such as the electronic versions of this database.

InfoWindow

The trade name for IBM display screens.

infrared

An invisible band of radiation at the lower end of the electromagnetic spectrum. It starts at the middle of the microwave spectrum and goes up to the beginning of visible light. Infrared transmission requires an unobstructed line of sight between transmitter and receiver. It is used for wireless transmission between computer devices as well as most all hand-held remotes for TVs, video and stereo equipment. Contrast with *ultraviolet*. See *SIR*.

infrastructure

The fundamental structure of a system or organization. The basic, fundamental architecture of any system (electronic, mechanical, social, political, etc.) determines how it functions and how flexible it is to meet future requirements.

Ingres

See *CA-OpenIngres*.

in hardware

Refers to logic that has been placed into the electronic circuits of the computer.

inheritance

In object-oriented programming, the ability of one class of objects to inherit properties from a higher class.

inhouse

An operation that takes place on the user's premises.

INI file

(INItialization file) A file that contains startup information required to launch a program or operating system. Same as *CFG file*. See *WIN.INI* and *SYSTEM.INI*.

INIT

(INITiate) A Macintosh routine that is run when the computer is started or restarted. It is used to load and activate drivers and system routines. Many INITs are memory resident and may conflict with each other like TSRs in the PC environment.

initialization string

Same as *setup string*.

initialize

To start anew, which typically involves clearing all or some part of memory or disk.

ink jet

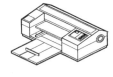

A printer mechanism that sprays one or more colors of ink onto paper and produces high-quality printing like that of a laser printer.

The continuous stream method produces droplets that are aimed onto the paper by electric field deflectors.

The drop-on-demand method uses a set of independently controlled injection chambers, the newest of which use solid ink developed by Exxon in 1983. Solid ink liquefies quickly when heated and solidifies instantly when it reaches the paper.

Ink Jet Printing Process
This diagram shows the flow of ink in a single nozzle ink jet system. *(Diagram courtesy of Dataquest, Inc.)*

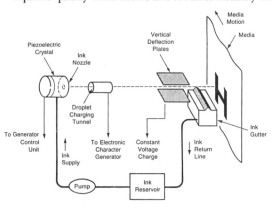

INMARSAT

(INternational MARitime SATellite) An international organization involved in providing satellite communications to and from ships and offshore rigs. It is represented in the U.S. and partially owned by COMSAT.

innoculate

To store characteristics of an executable program in order to detect a possible unknown virus if the file is changed.

i-node

(Identification NODE) An individual entry in a directory system that contains the name of and pointer to a file or other object.

input

(1) Data that is ready for entry into the computer.
(2) To enter data into the computer.

input area

A reserved segment of memory that is used to accept data from a peripheral device. Same as *buffer*.

input device

A peripheral device that generates input for the computer such as a keyboard, scanner, mouse or digitizer tablet.

input/output

See *I/O*.

input program

Same as *data entry program*.

input queue

A reserved segment of disk or memory that holds messages that have been received or job control statements describing work to be done.

input stream

A collection of job control statements entered in the computer that describe the work to be done.

inquiry program

Same as *query program*.

insert mode

A data entry mode that causes new data typed on the keyboard to be inserted at the current cursor location on screen. Contrast with *overwrite mode*.

Ins key

(INSert key) A keyboard key that is used to switch between insert and overwrite mode or to insert an object at the current cursor location.

in software

Refers to logic in a program. For example, "that routine is done in software."

installable file system

A file system that can be added to an operating system that is designed to handle multiple file systems. Multiple file systems allow different types of file structures to be accessed. See *IFSMgr*.

installation conflicts

See *how to install a PC peripheral*.

installation spec

Documentation from an equipment manufacturer that describes how a product should be properly installed within a physical environment.

a:install

a:setup

**Install
Commands**
DOS and Windows programs are generally run by typing the command a:install or a:setup, assuming the floppy is in the A: drive.

install program

Also called a *setup program*, it is a program that prepares an application (software package) to run in the computer. It creates a default directory or folder on the hard disk and copies the files from the distribution diskettes to the hard disk. It decompresses them if they are distributed in a compressed format.

Install programs may analyze the computer's current environment and/or ask the user to identify components in order to link in the appropriate software drivers required to display and print properly.

An install program may also be used to activate new hardware by setting or resetting parameters in an updatable memory (flash memory, EEPROM, etc.) on the expansion board. It is often used to identify resource requirements when installing a new peripheral, such as IRQs and I/O addresses (see *how to install a PC peripheral*). During installation, a component of the install, or setup, program is often copied to and left on the hard disk to allow the user to make additional changes to the application or hardware at a later time. See *how to install a program* and *CMOS RAM*.

instance

(1) A single copy of a running program. Multiple instances of a program mean that the program has been loaded into memory several times.

(2) In object-oriented programming, a member of a class; for example, "Lassie" is an instance of the class "dog." When an instance is created, the initial values of its instance variables are assigned.

instance variable

In object-oriented programming, the data in an object.

instantiate

In object-oriented programming, to create an object of a specific class. See *instance*.

instant print

The ability to use the computer as a typewriter. Each keystroke is transferred to the printer.

instruction

(1) A statement in a programming language.
(2) A machine instruction.

instruction cycle

The time in which a single instruction is fetched from memory, decoded and executed. The first half of the cycle transfers the instruction from memory to the instruction register and decodes it. The second half executes the instruction.

instruction mix

The blend of instruction types in a program. It often refers to writing generalized benchmarks, which requires that the amount of I/O versus processing versus math instructions, etc., reflects the type of application the benchmark is written for.

instruction register

A high-speed circuit that holds an instruction for decoding and execution.

instruction set

The repertoire of machine language instructions that a computer can follow (from a handful to several hundred). It is a major architectural component and is either built into the CPU or into microcode. Instructions are generally from one to four bytes long.

instruction time

The time in which an instruction is fetched from memory and stored in the instruction register. It is the first half of the instruction cycle.

insulator

A material that does not conduct electricity. Contrast with *conductor*.

int

A programming statement that specifies an interrupt or that declares an integer variable. See *interrupt* and *integer*.

int 13

A DOS interrupt used to activate disk functions, such as seek, read, write and format.

int 14

A DOS interrupt used to activate functions on the serial port (COM1, COM2, etc.). See *NASI*.

int 21

A multipurpose DOS interrupt used for various functions including reading the keyboard and writing to the console and printer. It was also used to read and write disks using the earlier File Control Block (FCB) method.

integer

A whole number. In programming, the integer function would yield 123 from 123.898.

Integer BASIC

Apple's version of BASIC for the Apple II that handles only fixed point numbers (non-floating point). Due to its speed, many games are written in it.

integrated

A collection of distinct elements or components that have been built into one unit.

integrated CASE

See *I-CASE*.

integrated circuit

The formal name for chip.

integrated injection logic

A type of bipolar transistor design known for its fast switching speeds.

integrated software package

Software that combines several applications in one program, typically database management, word processing, spreadsheet, business graphics and communications. Such programs (Microsoft Works, AppleWorks, etc.) provide a common user interface for their applications plus the ability to cut and paste data from one to the other.

User interfaces, such as found on the Macintosh and Windows, provide this capability with all applications written for their environments.

integrator

In electronics, a device that combines an input with a variable, such as time, and provides an analog output; for example, a watt-hour meter.

integrity

See *data integrity*.

Intel

(Intel Corporation, Santa Clara, CA) A leading manufacturer of semiconductor devices founded in 1968 by Bob Noyce and Gorden Moore in Mountain View, CA. A year later it introduced its first product, a 64-bit bipolar static RAM chip. By 1971, its very successful memory chips began to obsolete magnetic core storage. Intel is known for its x86 microprocessor family, but it also developed the first microprocessor in 1971. In response to a calculator chip order from Japanese manufacturer Busicom, Intel engineer Marcian E. "Ted" Hoff decided it would make more sense to design a general-purpose machine. The resulting 4004 chip was the world's first microprocessor.

Over the years, Intel has developed a wide variety of chips and board-level products, including the MULTIBUS bus used in industrial applications. Intel started with 12 people and its first year revenues were less than three thousand dollars. In 1994, it had 33,000 employees with revenues of 11.5 billion.

Intellect

A natural language query program from Trinzic Corporation, Palo Alto, CA, that runs on IBM mainframes and other computers. It was originally developed by Artificial Intelligence Corporation, which merged into Trinzic.

Intellifont

A scalable font technology from Agfa CompuGraphic. Intellifont typefaces are built into LaserJet IIIs and 4s (see *LaserJet*). The Intellifont for Windows font scaler creates matching screen fonts for Windows from Intellifont and compatible typefaces.

intelligence

Processing capability. Every computer is intelligent, which is more than can be said for all humans!

intelligent agent

See *agent*.

intelligent controller

A peripheral control unit that uses a built-in microprocessor for controlling its operation.

Better Watch Out
Intelligence
Is Everywhere.

intelligent database

A database that contains knowledge about the content of its data. A set of validation criteria are stored with each field of data, such as the minimum and maximum values that can be entered or a list of all possible entries. See *DBMS (Intelligent Databases)*.

intelligent form

A data entry application that provides help screens and low levels of AI in aiding the user to enter the correct data.

intelligent hub

A central connecting device in a network that performs a variety of processing functions such as network management, bridging, routing and switching. Contrast with *passive hub* and *active hub*. See *hub*.

Intelligent Messaging

A messaging system from Banyan Systems Inc., Westboro, MA, that runs on NetWare and VINES servers and incorporates Banyan's popular Streettalk directory service. It includes a basic mail program, which can be upgraded to Banyan's more advanced BeyondMail system.

intelligent modem

A modem that responds to commands and can accept new instructions during online transmission. It was originally developed by Hayes.

intelligent paper

Same as *intelligent form*.

intelligent terminal

A terminal with built-in processing capability, but no local disk or tape storage. It may use a general-purpose CPU or may have specialized circuitry as part of a distributed intelligence system. Contrast with *dumb terminal*.

IntelliSense

Features in Microsoft applications that help the user by making decisions automatically. By analyzing activity patterns, the software can derive the next step without the user having to explicitly state it. Automatic typo correction and suggesting shortcuts also fall under the IntelliSense umbrella.

Intel motherboard

A motherboard manufactured by Intel. Not only does Intel make the CPU chips, it makes motherboards and other printed circuit boards as well as complete systems, which have been sold under third party logos. It is expected that Intel will introduce systems into the marketplace with the Intel logo.

INTELSAT

(INternational TELecommunications SATellite) An international organization involved in launching and operating commercial satellites. It was created in 1964 with only 11 countries participating. Today, over 100 nations have ownership. It is represented in the U.S. and partially owned by COMSAT.

inter

To cross over boundaries; for example, internetwork means from one network to another. Contrast with *intra*.

interactive

Back-and-forth dialog between the user and a computer.

interactive fiction

An adventure game that has been created or modified for the computer. It has multiple story lines, environments and endings, all of which are determined by choices the player makes at various times.

interactive session

Back-and-forth dialogue between user and computer. Contrast with *batch session*.

interactive TV

Two-way communications between the TV viewer and service providers. Using phone lines, cable, optical fiber or satellite, services include home shopping, movies on demand, interactive participation in live broadcasts as well as access to news, databases and other networks.

Current analog TV sets can be connected to boxes that add dial out capability via modem and phone line as well as handle digital signals interleaved with the incoming analog signals. As cable systems become more digital, more interactive programming will be provided. See *digital convergence*.

Interactive UNIX

A UNIX-based operating system from SunSoft that runs on x86 machines. It has been widely used to connect character-based terminals or process control devices, such as bar code readers in a supermarket, to a central computer.

interactive video

The use of CD-ROM and videodisc controlled by computer for an interactive education or entertainment program. See *CD-ROM* and *videodisc*.

InterBase

A relational DBMS from Borland that runs on UNIX workstations and VAXes, designed to handle online complex processing (OLCP). It can be a peer-to-peer or client/server system and uses SQL plus its own data manipulation language.

interblock gap

Same as *interrecord gap*.

interface

The connection and interaction between hardware, software and the user.

Hardware interfaces are the plugs, sockets, wires and the electrical pulses travelling through them in a particular pattern. Also included are electrical timing considerations. Examples are RS-232 transmission, the Ethernet and Token Ring network topologies and the IDE, ESDI, SCSI, ISA, EISA and Micro Channel interfaces.

Software, or programming, interfaces are the languages, codes and messages programs use to communicate with each other and to the hardware. Examples are the applications that run under the Mac, DOS and Windows operating systems as well as the SMTP e-mail and LU 6.2 communications protocols.

User interfaces are the keyboards, mice, commands and menus used for communication between you and the computer. Examples are the command lines in DOS and UNIX and the Mac, Windows and Motif graphical interfaces.

Interfacing is a major part of what engineers, programmers and consultants do. Users "talk to" the software. The software "talks to" the hardware and other software. Hardware "talks to" other hardware. All this is interfacing. It has to be designed, developed, tested and redesigned, and with each incarnation, a new specification is born that may become yet one more de facto or regulated standard.

Format & Function Every interface implies a structure. Electrical signals are made up of voltage levels, frequencies and duration. The data passed from one device or program to another has a precise format (header, body, trailer, etc.).

Every interface implies a function. At the hardware level, electronic signals activate functions; data is read, written, transmitted, received, analyzed for error, etc. At the software level, instructions activate the hardware (access methods, data link protocols, etc.). At higher levels, the data transferred or transmitted may itself request functions to be performed (client/server, program to program, etc.).

Language & Programming An interface is activated by programming language commands. The complexity of the functions and the design of the language determine how difficult it is to program.

User Interface, Protocol, API and ABI The design of the interaction between the user and the computer is called a *user interface*. The rules, formats and functions between components in a communications system or network is called a *protocol*. The language and message formats between routines within a program or between software components is called an *API*. The specification for an operating system working in a specific machine environment is called an *ABI*.

All the above interactions are interfaces. Regardless of what they're called, they all create rules that must be precisely followed in a digital world.

User Interface

The user talks to the computer via the commands, mouse movements, menus and buttons in the user interface.

Application Programming Interface

Applications talk to the operating system via the application programming interface, or API. It is the set of rules for the parameters that are passed back and forth between the programs.

Application Binary Interface

All software must be translated into the mach-ine language of the computer it is running in. The specification for the binary machine lan-guage of a particular computer system combined with the API for the operating system is known as the application binary interface, or ABI.

Protocol

A protocol is a programming interface for com-munications. It defines the rules for the formats and functions of each layer of the communications system. See *OSI Model* for an understanding of these layers.

interface adapter

In communications, a device that connects the computer or terminal to a network.

interframe coding

In video compression, coding only the differences between frames. See *intraframe coding*.

interlaced

Illuminating a CRT by displaying odd lines and then even lines (every other line first; then filling in the gaps). TV signals are interlaced and generate 60 half frames (30 full frames) per second. Computer display systems may also be interlaced, but usually only at the highest resolution.

Rather than send every line of information to the screen (non-interlaced), interlacing sends half the information in the same time frame, thus requiring less-complicated and less-expensive circuits.

TV's constant animation has always provided acceptable viewing using the interlaced method, although reading a still image on TV is not all that pleasing. Interlaced screens used on computers can provide an annoying flicker that causes headaches and eye strain (see below).

interlaced   non-interlaced

Where's the Flicker?
When you purchase a video display adapter and monitor, the interlaced vs non-interlaced issue comes up when you get into the highest resolution mode. For example, most VGA adapters and monitors support the following three resolutions: 640x480, 800x600 and 1024x768. Advanced models support 1280x1024 and higher.

The lower resolutions (640x480 and 800x600) are usually non-interlaced, but the highest mode 1024x768 or 1280x1024 may be interlaced. When you start up under DOS, you are always at the lowest, non-interlaced 640x480 resolution. It's only when you get into Windows or AutoCAD that the high-resolution drivers, supplied with the graphics adapter, are able to activate the higher modes.

An interlaced resolution does not cause flicker like a badly-synchronized movie projector. Rather it provides a faint overall flutter that is often very noticeable on the entire screen and especially on tiny, complex graphic elements such as buttons and icons.

A related issue is the vertical scan frequency, or the number of times the entire screen is refreshed per second. Since the refresh rate may go down as resolution goes up, this is another consideration. The number can range from 45 to over 100; however, 60 is the smallest refresh

generally tolerable, and 70 and higher is recommended.
For CAD and destop publishing, a non-interlaced 1280x1024 or higher
resolution with a 70Hz refresh rate on a 21" monitor is recommended.
Depending on the size of the page you are working with, a non-interlaced
1024x768 resolution on a 17" screen may suffice.

The high resolutions required to see full pages and facing pages of text
provide enough strain on the eyes. Interlaced screens and low refresh rates
only add to the burden.

Interleaf

Desktop publishing software for DOS and a variety of UNIX-based computers from
Interleaf, Inc., Waltham, MA. A Windows NT version is expected in 1995. Interleaf
is a full-featured program that supports a large number of document and image types.
It is used for creating compound documents as well as extremely long documents
(hundreds of thousands of pages).
It includes built-in word processing and graphics tools and provides a number of
optional components for enhanced document control and workgroup operation.
Interleaf used to be known as Interleaf TPS (Technical Publishing Software). In 1990,
it became Interleaf5, later Interleaf6, etc.
Interleaf RDM (Relational Document Manager) is another product that provides
distribution and tracking of documents. Interleaf WorldView provides runtime
viewing with customizable searches for Interleaf and other document types.

interleave

See *sector interleave* and *memory interleaving*.

interlock

A device that prohibits an action from taking place.

intermediate language

Same as *pseudo language*.

intermediate node routing

Routing a message to non-adjacent nodes; for example, if three computers are
connected in series A—B—C, data transmitted from A to C can be routed through B.

intermittent error

An error that occurs sporadically, not consistently. It is the most difficult type of
problem to diagnose and repair.

internal bus

A data pathway between closely-connected components, such as between the CPU and
memory. See *local bus*.

internal command

In DOS and OS/2, a command, such as Copy, Dir and Rename, which may be used at
all times. Internal commands are executed by the command processor programs
COMMAND.COM in DOS and CMD.EXE in OS/2. The command processor is
always loaded when the operating system is loaded. Contrast with *external command*.

internal font

A set of characters for a particular typeface that is built into a printer. Contrast with
font cartridge and *soft font*.

internal interrupt

An interrupt that is caused by processing, for example, a request for input or output or an arithmetic overflow error. Contrast with *external interrupt.*

internal modem

A modem that plugs into an expansion slot within the computer. Unlike an external modem, an internal modem does not provide a series of display lights that inform the user of the changing modem states. The user must rely entirely on the communications program. Contrast with *external modem.*

internal sort

Sorting that is accomplished entirely in memory without using disks or tapes for temporary files.

Internal stack failure

A DOS error message that means DOS has gotten completely confused. Turn off the computer and restart.

internal storage

Same as *memory.*

Internaut

A person that uses the Internet.

**Look up
World Wide Web**
The Web is the hottest part of the Internet these days. Look up the term for a diagram of how documents are linked via the Web.

internet

(1) A large network made up of a number of smaller networks.
(2) (Internet) "The" Internet is made up of more than 100,000 interconnected networks in over 70 countries, comprised of academic, commercial, government and military networks. Originally developed for the military, the Internet became widely used for academic and commercial research. Users have access to unpublished data, journals and BBSs for every subject known to humankind. Today, the Internet is being commercialized into a worldwide information highway.

The recent surge in growth is twofold. As the major online services (CompuServe, BIX, America Online, etc.) connected to the Internet for e-mail exchange, the Internet began to function as a central hub for e-mail outside of the Internet community. A member of one online service could now send mail to a member of another online service using the Internet as a gateway. The Internet glued the world together for electronic mail.

Secondly, the World Wide Web facility on the Internet links documents around the world, providing an information exchange of unprecedented proportion. With the advent of graphics-based Web browsers, originally Mosaic and now NetScape Navigator and Internet Explorer, this wealth of information has been made easily available to users with PCs and Macs rather than only scientists and hackers at UNIX workstations.

Today, the online services also provide full Internet access. DELPHI was the first, and all the others followed suit. Now you can download files from the Internet and access the World Wide Web via your account. In addition, independent Internet access providers have seemingly risen out of the woodwork to offer individuals and organizations access to the Internet. Many have been overwhelmed by the flood of business, which often results in too many busy signals when trying to log on and poor customer support.

The backbone of the Internet was originally a series of high-speed links between major supercomputer sites and educational and research institutions within the U.S. and throughout the world. A major part of it was the NFSNet, managed by the U.S. National Science Foundation. In 1995, commercial Internet providers (ISPs), such as MCI, Sprint and UUNET, began to deploy their own backbones. Smaller

ISPs hook into these backbones to provide lines for their subscribers.

Internet computers use the TCP/IP communications protocol. There are over 10 million hosts on the Internet, a host being a mainframe, mini or workstation that directly supports the Internet Protocol (the IP in TCP/IP). The Internet is connected to all types of computer networks worldwide via gateways that convert TCP/IP into other protocols.

Although most new users interact with the Internet via their Web browsers, for years, command-line UNIX utilities have been used. For example, an FTP (File Transfer Protocol) program allows files to be downloaded, and the Archie utility provides listings of these files. Telnet is a terminal emulation program that lets you log onto a computer in the Internet and run a program. Gopher provides hierarchical menus describing Internet files (not just file names), and Veronica lets you make more sophisticated searches on Gopher sites.

The IAB, or Internet Activities Board is the governing body for the Internet. Its Internet Research Task Force (IRTF) explores new technologies which it refers to the Internet Engineering Task Force (IETF). The IETF works on the specifications of new standards.

It Has Gone Commercial

There has been more activity, excitement and hype over the Internet than any other new computer or communications topic. Using the World Wide Web, thousands of companies, from conglomerates to mom and pop shops, are trying to figure out how to make the Internet a worldwide shopping mall. Will it succeed, or will too much traffic cause it to bog down like the Los Angeles freeway? Stay tuned!

Getting Started?

For a list of good books on the Internet, see *Internet references*.

Internet access

See *Internet address* and *PDIAL*.

Internet access provider

An organization that provides access to the Internet. Dial-up customers are billed a fixed rate per month or by hourly usage or both. The major online services (CompuServe, America Online, etc.) have all become Internet access providers. Access providers may also offer leased line services for companies that want dedicated high-speed access to the Internet (56Kbps, T1, etc.). See *PDIAL*.

Internet address

The format for addressing a message to an Internet user is

    recipient@location.domain

For example, the address of the Free Software Foundation is **gnu@prep.ai.mit.edu**, which means transmitting to the GNU mailbox via nodes PREP, AI and MIT. The suffix at the end is the domain, or host classification, in this case EDU (see below).

Internet Domains
com - business (commercial)
edu - educational and research
gov - government
mil - military agency
net - gateway or host
org - non-profit organization

Via CompuServe If you are a CompuServe subscriber, you can access the Internet by adding the `internet:` prefix to the Internet address. For example, to send mail from CompuServe to the Free Software Foundation address mentioned above, you would address the message to:

`internet:gnu@prep.ai.mit.edu`

To reach a CompuServe user from the Internet, change the comma in the CompuServe account number to a period. For example, if the CompuServe number is 71022,1560, the Internet e-mail address is **`71022.1560@compuserve.com`**.

To Send Mail to Other Services If you know your recipients' "online names" and which services they use, you can send messages directly to their mailboxes via the Internet. For example, if the recipient's e-mail name is lmorrison, you would address the message to the following services. If the name is "l morrison," remove the blanks.

lmorrison@aol.com	America Online
morrison@genie.geis.com	GEnie
lmorrison@mcimail.com	MCI Mail
lmorrison@prodigy.com	PRODIGY
lmorrison@delphi.com	DELPHI

To Obtain an Internet Address To obtain an Internet network address and reserve a domain name, organizations must register with the InterNIC Registration Service. See *InterNIC*. See also *IP address* for information about the physical structure of an Internet address.

Internet Engineering Task Force

See *Internet*.

Internet gateway

A computer system that converts messages back and forth between TCP/IP and other protocols. Internet gateways connect the Internet to all the other communications networks in the world.

Internet Protocol

See *Internet* and *TCP/IP*.

Internet references

A well-written and excellent book for people getting started on the Internet is "Internet Slick Tricks" by Alfred and Emily Glossbrenner, published by Random House, ISBN 0-679-75611-6.

Another book by Alfred Glossbrenner, but more in depth is "Internet 101," published by McGraw-Hill, ISBN 0-07-024054-X. While aimed at the college market, this is a must-have for anyone interested in the Internet. Glossbrenner is a superb author.

To learn what information is available on the Internet, read "Internet Yellow Pages" by Harley Hahn and Rick Stout, published by Osborne McGraw-Hill, ISBN 007-882023-5.

Joshua Eddings' "How the Internet Works," published by Ziff-Davis Press, ISBN 1-56276-192-7, provides a delightful and colorful guide to the inner-workings of the Internet.

Internet Relay Chat

Computer conferencing on the Internet. There are hundreds of IRC channels on every subject conceivable from more than 60 countries. To get a list of active channels, type **/list**. To join a channel named #HOTSTUFF, type **/join #hotstuff**. After you join a channel, your messages are broadcast to everyone listening to that channel. See *MUD*.

InterNet Router

Macintosh software from Apple that internetworks different access methods (LocalTalk, EtherTalk, TokenTalk, etc.) and can reside in any network station. Each Router can connect up to eight networks with a maximum of 1,024 networks and 16 million nodes.

Internet service provider

Generally synonymous with *Internet access provider*. However, sometimes service provider means offering dedicated high-speed leased lines, whereas access provider means offering dial-up accounts.

Internet Talk Radio

Audio coverage of news events digitized into Internet files at the National Press Building in Washington, DC. ITR files are distributed to FTP sites for users with computers that have sound capabilities.

Internet utility

Software used to search the Internet for specific information. See *Archie, Gopher, Veronica, WAIS* and *WWW*.

internetwork

To go between one network and another.

InterNIC

(NFSnet Network Information Center) The source for Internet information and registration. It was formed in 1993 by agreements with the National Science Foundation, General Atomics, AT&T and Network Solutions Inc.
Internet network addresses and domain names are assigned by InterNIC Registration Services, which is administered by Network Solutions Inc. of Herndon, VA.
For general information about InterNIC services, call the automated hotline at 619/455-4600. Send an e-mail request to **info@is.internic.net**.

interoperable

The ability for one system to communicate or work with another.

Interpedia

(INTERnet encycloPEDIA) A public domain encyclopedia that is expected to be created for and maintained on the Internet. It is currently in the planning stages.

interpolate

To estimate values that lie between known values.

Interpress

A page description language from Xerox used on the 2700 and 9700 page printers (medium to large-scale laser printers). Ventura Publisher provides output in Interpress.

interpret

To run a program one line at a time. Each line of source language is translated into machine language and then executed.

interpreter

A high-level programming language translator that translate and runs the program at the same time. It translates one program statement into machine language, executes it, then proceeds to the next statement. This differs from regular executable programs that are presented to the computer as binary-coded instructions. Interpreted programs remain in the same source language format the programmer wrote in: as text files, not machine language files.

Interpreted programs run slower than their compiler counterparts. Whereas the compiler translates the entire program before it is run, interpreters translate a line at a time while the program is run. However, it is very convenient to write an interpreted program, since a single line of code can be tested interactively.

Interpreted programs must always be run with the interpreter. For example, in order to run a BASIC or dBASE program, the BASIC or dBASE interpreter must be in the target computer.

If a language can be both interpreted and compiled, a program may be developed with the interpreter for ease of testing and debugging and later compiled for production use.

interpretive language

A programming language that requires an interpreter to run it.

interprocess communication

See *IPC.*

interrecord gap

The space generated between blocks of data on tape, created by the starting and stopping of the reel.

Interrecord Gaps
The gaps between the records are larger than the data if single records are written at one time. Usually, several records are written as a block to maximize space.

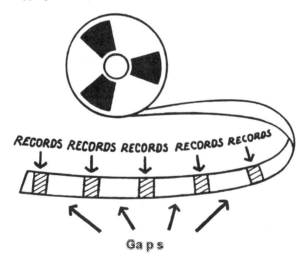

RECORDS RECORDS RECORDS RECORDS RECORDS

Gaps

interrogate

(1)To search, sum or count records in a file. See *query.*
(2)To test the condition or status of a terminal or computer system.

interrupt

A signal that gets the attention of the CPU and is usually generated when I/O is required. For example, hardware interrupts are generated when a key is pressed or when the mouse is moved. Software interrupts are generated by a program requiring disk input or output.

An internal timer may continually interrupt the computer several times per second to keep the time of day current or for timesharing purposes.

When an interrupt occurs, control is transferred to the operating system, which determines the action to be taken. Interrupts are prioritized; the higher the priority, the faster the interrupt will be serviced.

interrupt-driven

A computer or communications network that uses interrupts.

interrupt mask

An internal switch setting that controls whether an interrupt can be processed or not. The mask is a bit that is turned on and off by the program.

interrupt priorities

The sequence of importance assigned to interrupts. If two interrupts occur simultaneously, the interrupt with the highest priority is serviced first. In some systems, a higher-priority interrupt can gain control of the computer while it's processing a lower-priority interrupt.

interrupt vector

In the PC, one of 256 pointers that reside in the first 1KB of memory. Each vector points to the routine in the BIOS or in memory that handles the interrupt.

intersect

In a relational database, to match two files and produce a third file with records that are common in both. For example, intersecting an American file and a programmer file would yield American programmers.

intra

Within a boundary; for example, intraoffice refers to operations that take place within the office. Contrast with *inter*.

intraframe coding

Compressing redundant areas within a video frame. See *interframe coding*.

intranet

An inhouse Web site that serves the employees of the enterprise. Although intranet pages may link to the Internet, an intranet is not a site accessed by the general public. Using programming languages such as Java, client/server applications can be built on intranets. Since Web browsers that support Java run under Windows, Mac and UNIX, such programs also provide cross-platform capability.

Intranets use the same communications protocols and hypertext links as the Web and thus provide a standard way of disseminating information internally and extending the application worldwide at the same time.

Invalid directory

A DOS error message that means you entered the name of a non-existant directory.

Invalid drive specification

A DOS error message. If you get this message on a valid drive such as C:, it may mean that your hard disk has become corrupted.

Invalid file name or file not found

A DOS error message. You have probably used an invalid character in a DOS file name, or you have used wild cards when they are not applicable. For example, type *.* will produce this error, because you cannot Type more than one file at a time.

Invalid media type

A DOS error message that means DOS doesn't recognize the format of the drive being referenced. The disk has been corrupted in some manner and is not readable. You will also get this message if you low-level formatted a new disk, performed the Fdisk procedure, but forgot to high-level format it with the Format command.

invalid parameter

A DOS error message that means DOS doesn't understand the command line. It indicates that a switch is used incorrectly. If you're typing path names, be sure to use a backslash (\), not a forward slash (/). The forward slash is used to enter parameters.

inverse multiplexor

In communications, a device that breaks up a high-speed transmission into several low-speed transmissions and vice versa. It is used to transmit LAN and videoconferencing traffic over lower-speed digital channels. For example, to transmit Ethernet over a T3 link, the 10Mbps Ethernet channel would be inverse multiplexed into multiple 64Kbps channels of the T3 line. A 336Kbps videoconferencing transmission could be split into six 56Kbps channels to transmit over a Switched 56 service. Contrast with *multiplexor*.

inverse video

Same as *reverse video*.

inverted file

In data management, a file that is indexed on many of the attributes of the data itself. For example, in an employee file, an index could be maintained for all secretaries, another for managers. It's faster to search the indexes than every record. Inverted file indexes use lots of disk space; searching is fast, updating is slower.

inverted list

Same as *inverted file*.

inverter

(1) A logic gate that converts the input to the opposite state for output. If the input is true, the output is false, and vice versa. An inverter performs the Boolean logic NOT operation.
(2) A circuit that converts DC current into AC current. Contrast with *rectifier*.

invoke

To activate a program, routine, function or process.

I/O

(Input/Output) Transferring data between the CPU and a peripheral device. Every transfer is an output from one device and an input into another.

I/O address

(1) On PCs, a three-digit hexadecimal number (2AB, 2A0, etc.) used to identify and signal a peripheral device (serial port, parallel port, sound card, etc.). Address assignments must be unique, otherwise conflicts will occur. There are usually a small number of selectable addresses on each controller card. See *how to install a PC peripheral* and *PC I/O addressing*.
(2) The identifying address of a peripheral device.

I/O area

A reserved segment of memory used to accept data from an input device or to accumulate data for transfer to an output device. See *buffer*.

I/O bound

Refers to an excessive amount of time getting data in and out of the computer in relation to the time it takes for processing it. Faster channels and disk drives improve the performance of I/O bound computers. See *I/O intensive*.

IOCA

(Image Object Content Architecture) See *MO:DCA*.

IOCS

(Input Output Control System) An early, rudimentary IBM operating system (1950s). It was a set of I/O routines for tapes and disks. Today's counterpart in the PC is the BIOS.

I/O device

Same as *peripheral device*.

I/O intensive

Refers to an application that reads and/or writes a large amount of data. The performance of such an application depends on the speed of the computer's peripheral devices and can cause a computer to become I/O bound. See *I/O bound*.

I/O interface

See *port* and *expansion slot*.

ion deposition

A printing technology used in high-speed page printers. It is similar to laser printing, except instead of using light to create a charged image on a drum, it uses a printhead that deposits ions. After toner is attracted to the ions on the drum, the paper is pressed directly against the drum fusing toner to paper.
Quality approaches that of a laser printer; however, the ink has not been embedded as deeply, and the paper can smear more easily.

I/O processor

Circuitry specialized for I/O operations. See *front end processor*.

IOS

(Integrated Office System) See *office automation*.

I/O statement

A programming instruction that requests I/O.

IO.SYS

See *MSDOS.SYS*.

IP

(1) (Internet Protocol) The IP part of the TCP/IP protocol, which routes a message across networks. See *TCP/IP, datagram* and *IP address*.
(2) See *image processing*.

IP address

(Internet Protocol address) The physical address of a TCP/IP packet uses 32 bits to contain a network address and host address, known as the *netid* and *hostid*. The 32 bits are divided differently according to the class of the address, which is based on the number of hosts that can be attached to the network. Thus, the more bits used for host address, the fewer remain for the network address. The addresses support the following number of networks and hosts.

Class	Networks	Hosts
A	128	16M
B	16K	65K
C	16M	256

Network addresses are supplied to organizations by the InterNIC Registration Service. See *InterNIC*. See also *CIDR* and *URL*.

IPC

(InterProcess Communication) The exchange of data between one program and another either within the same computer or over a network. It implies a protocol that guarantees a response to a request. Examples are OS/2's Named Pipes, Windows' DDE, Novell's SPX and Macintosh's IAC.

IPCs are performed automatically by the programs. For example, a spreadsheet program could query a database program and retrieve data from one of its databases. A manual example of an IPC function is performed when users cut and paste data from one file to another using the clipboard.

IPDS

(Intelligent Printer Data Stream) An IBM format for sending full pages of text and graphics from a mainframe or mini to a laser printer.

IPI

(Intelligent Peripheral Interface) A high-speed hard disk interface used with minis and mainframes that transfers data in the 10 to 25 MBytes/sec range. IPI-2 and IPI-3 refer to differences in the command set that they execute. See *hard disk*.

IPL

(Initial Program Load) Same as *boot*.

IPng

(IP Next Generation) An enhanced Internet Protocol developed by the Internet Engineering Task Force (IETF). IPng improves data security and increases the Internet address from four to 16 bytes, providing for an unlimited number of networks and systems.

ips

(Inches Per Second) The measurement of the speed of tape passing by a read/write head or paper passing through a pen plotter.

IP spoofing

Inserting the IP address of an authorized user into the transmission of an unauthorized user in order to gain illegal access to a computer system. Routers and other firewall implementations can be programmed to identify this discrepancy. See *firewall*.

IPX

(Internet Packet EXchange) A NetWare communications protocol used to route messages from one node to another. IPX packets include network addresses and can be routed from one network to another. An IPX packet can occasionally get lost when crossing networks, thus IPX does not guarantee delivery of a complete message. Either the application has to provide that control or NetWare's SPX protocol must be used.

IPX provides services at layers 3 and 4 of the OSI model (network and transport layers). See *SPX*.

IR

(1) (Industry Remarketer) Same as *VAR* or *VAD*.
(2) See *infrared.*

IRC

See *Internet Relay Chat.*

IrDA

(InfraRed Data Association, P.O Box 3883, Walnut Creek, CA, 510/943-6546) A membership organization founded in 1993 for the purpose of developing wireless transmission systems between computers that use infrared frequencies. With IrDA ports, a laptop or PDA can exchange data with a desktop computer or use a printer without a cable connection. As of mid 1995, IrDA products began to appear. For example, the HP LaserJet 5P is one of the first printers with a built-in IrDA port. IrDA is a point-to-point transmission just like a TV remote control. The IrDA SIR (IrDA Serial IR) low-speed connection has a maximum data rate of 115.2Kbits/sec and uses an encoder/decoder attached to the serial port or to a low-cost UART chip. Higher rates of 1.15 and 4Mbits/sec, which require a Communications Controller circuit, are backward compatible with IrDA SIR.

IRG

See *interrecord gap.*

IRIX

See *Silicon Graphics.*

IRM

(Information Resource Management) See *Information Systems* and *information management.*

Irma

A trade name for a variety of desktop computer to host communications products from Attachmate Corporation, Bellevue, WA. Irma is not an acronym; it is the lady's name.

Irma 3 Convertible

A 3270 emulator from Attachmate Corporation, Bellevue, WA. It is the third generation of the Irma board, the first 3270 emulator. Convertible stands for its dual bus (ISA and Micro Channel) compatibility.

Irma board

The first 3270 emulator for PCs. Introduced in 1982, it was the first product to provide PC to IBM host connectivity. Irma was originally spelled all caps (IRMA) and was developed by Digital Communications Associates (DCA), which later merged with and became part of Attachmate Corporation. See *Irma 3 Convertible.*

Irmalan

A family of gateway programs from Attachmate Corporation, Bellevue, WA, that allow PCs connected to NetWare, NetBIOS and VINES networks to access an SNA host. Irmalan gateways support IEEE 802.2, SDLC (via modem) and DFT environments.

Irma software

A family of terminal emulation software products from Attachmate Corporation, Bellevue, WA, that provide desktop to host connectivity. Irma Suite is a collection of the following products.

Irma for the Mainframe provides Windows, Mac, DOS, NT and OS/2 client connectivity to IBM mainframes via modem, LAN and 3270 emulator.
Irma for the AS/400 provides Windows client connectivity to the AS/400 via modem, LAN and twinax card.
Irma for Open Systems provides Telnet and LAT support on a Windows client to VAX, HP and UNIX hosts as well as online services via LAN and modem.

iron oxide

The material used to coat the surfaces of magnetic tapes and lower-capacity disks.

IRQ

(Interrupt ReQuest) A hardware interrupt on a PC. Eight lines (0-7 on 8086/88s) and 16 lines (0-15 on 286s and up) accept interrupts from devices such as a scanner and network adapter. Unless specifically programmed to interact together, two devices cannot use the same line. If a new expansion board is preset to the IRQ used by an existing board, one of them must be changed. See *how to install a PC peripheral*.

Starting with the 286, the PC uses two 8259A controller chips to handle the IRQs. The chips are cascaded together. IRQ 2 connects to IRQ 9 of the second chip. All the IRQs except for 10, 11, 12 and 15 are preassigned.

If a second parallel port is not used, IRQ 5 is available. IRQ 9 is also often available as most VGA cards do not require an IRQ. Thus IRQs 5, 9, 10, 11, 12 and 15 are arbitrarily used for scanners, SCSI boards, CD-ROM controllers, sound boards and any other peripheral that can be attached to a PC. They become the "IRQ battleground."

IRQ Assignment

0	System timer	8	Realtime clock
1	Keyboard	9	VGA, 3270 emulation**
2	Connects to IRQ 9	10	**
3	COM2, COM4	11	**
4	COM1, COM3	12	**
5	LPT2**	13	Math coprocessor
6	Floppy disk	14	Hard disk
7	LPT1	15	**

** For general use. "The battleground."

ISA

EISA

PCI

VL-bus

Micro Channel

IRTF

See *Internet*.

IS

See *Information Systems*.

ISA

(1) (Industry Standard Architecture) Pronounced "eye-suh." An expansion bus commonly used in PCs. It accepts the plug-in boards that control the video display, disks and other peripherals. Most PC expansion boards on the market are ISA boards.

ISA was originally called the *AT bus*, because it was first used in the IBM AT, extending the original bus from eight to 16 bits. Most ISA PCs provides a mix of 8-bit and 16-bit expansion slots. Contrast with *EISA* and *Micro Channel*. See *local bus*.

(2) (Interactive Services Association) A trade group for the online industry originally founded in 1981 as the Videotex Industry Association (VIA). Members are online services, service bureaus and hardware and software companies, all providing

products for users with a computer and modem. Address: 8403 Colesville Road, Silver Spring, MD 20910, 301/495-4955.

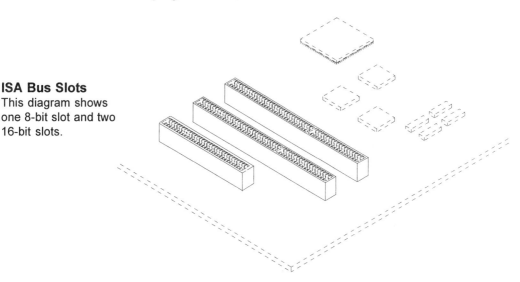

ISA Bus Slots
This diagram shows one 8-bit slot and two 16-bit slots.

ISAM

(Indexed Sequential Access Method) A common disk access method that stores data sequentially, while maintaining an index of key fields to all the records in the file for direct access. The sequential order would be the one most commonly used for batch processing and printing (account number, name, etc.).

ISDN

(Integrated Services Digital Network) An international telecommunications standard for transmitting voice, video and data over digital lines running at 64 Kbps. The telephone companies commonly use a 64 Kbps channel for digitized, two-way voice conversations. ISDN service is becoming widely available in the U.S., but there are still areas where it is not. It is expected to be fully nationwide in a couple of years.

ISDN uses 64 Kbps circuit-switched channels, called B channels, or "bearer" channels, to carry voice and data. It uses a separate D channel, or "delta," channel for control signals. The D channel is used to signal the telephone company computer to make calls, put them on hold and activate features such as conference calling and call forwarding. It also receives information about incoming calls, such as the identity of the caller.

ISDN's basic service is called Basic Rate Interface, or BRI. BRI is made up of two 64 Kbps B channels and one 16 Kbps D channel (2B+D). The total data rate of 128 Kbps is four and a half times the bandwidth of a V.34 modem (28.8 Kbps). Multiple BRI channels can be multiplexed together to build higher speed lines up to 384 Kbps.

ISDN's high-speed service is called Primary Rate Interface, or PRI. In the U.S., it provides 23 B channels and one 64 Kbps D channel (23B+D), which is equivalent to the 24 channels of a T1 line. In Europe, PRI includes 30 B channels and one D channel, equivalent to an E1 line.

Connecting an ISDN Device
Connecting ISDN to a personal computer requires a network terminator (NT1) and ISDN terminal adapter. The NT1 is a permanent connection that plugs into the two-wire ISDN line from the telephone company and provides four-wire output to the ISDN adapter.

The ISDN terminal adapter, like a modem, plugs into the serial port or into an expansion slot of the computer. ISDN adapters may include an analog modem and automatically switch between analog and digital depending on the type of call.

Broadband ISDN

A second-generation ISDN standard, known as Broadband ISDN or BISDN, uses fiber optic cables for speeds of 155 Mbps and higher. BISDN's bottom three layers of implementation comprise ATM (asynchronous transfer mode), which is gaining ground as a networking technology for LANs and WANs.

ISDN terminal adapter

A device that adapts a computer to a digital ISDN line. Like a modem, it plugs into the serial port of the computer or into an expansion slot. It may also include a regular data or fax/modem and switch automatically between analog and digital depending on the type of call. An ISDN terminal adapter is also called an *ISDN modem.*

IS-IS

(Intermediate System to Intermediate System) An ISO protocol that provides dynamic routing between routers.

ISO

(International Standards Organization, U.S. member body: ANSI, 1430 Broadway, New York, NY 10018) An organization that sets international standards, founded in 1946 and headquartered in Geneva. It deals with all fields except electrical and electronics, which is governed by the older International Electrotechnical Commission (IEC), also in Geneva. With regard to information processing, ISO and IEC created JTC1, the Joint Technical Committee for information technology. It carries out its work through more than 160 technical committees and 2,300 subcommittees and working groups and is made up of standards organizations from more than 75 countries, some of them serving as secretariats for these technical bodies.

ISO 13346

A standard format for a rewritable optical disk from the International Standards Association. It specifies the logical format of the disk so that removable cartridges can be interchanged among different platforms.

ISO 9000

A standard for quality in the manufacturing and service industries from the International Standards Association. ISO 9000 defines the criteria for what should be measured. ISO 9001 covers design and development. ISO 9002 covers production, installation and service, and ISO 9003 covers final testing and inspection. ISO 9000 certification does not guarantee product quality. It ensures that the processes that develop the product are performed in a quality manner. Initially popular in Europe, ISO 9000 certification began to increase in the U.S. in 1993. In the computer field, hardware vendors were the first to seek certification. Certification requires exacting documentation and demonstrations in practice over time. The process can take up to a year.

ISO 9660

A standard format for a CD-ROM from the International Standards Association. Evolving from the High Sierra format, it specifies the logical format of the disk. The physical format for a CD-ROM is defined in the Yellow Book.

isochronous

Time dependent. Realtime voice, video and telemetry are examples of isochronous data.

isochronous Ethernet

See *IsoENET*.

IsoENET

(ISOchronous EtherNET) National Semiconductor's enhancement to Ethernet for handling realtime voice and video. IsoENET adds a 6Mbps synchronous channel, made up of 96 64Kbps ISDN subchannels, to the 10Mbps Ethernet standard.

isometric view

In computer graphics, a rendering of a 3-D object that eliminates the distortion of shape created by true perspective. In isometric views, all lines on each axis are parallel to each other, and the lines do not converge. Such drawings are commonly used in technical illustrations because of their clarity, simplicity and speed of creation.

Isometric Versus Perspective
The cube on the left is in perspective, the way the eye sees real objects. The cube on the right is isometric, which shows a more accurate view of each side.

isotropic

Refers to properties, such as transmission speed, that are the same regardless of the direction that is measured. Contrast with *anisotropic*.

ISPF

(Interactive System Productivity Facility) IBM mainframe software that executes interactive user interfaces on 3270 terminals. It is created with ISPF's PDF (Program Development Facility) software.

ISR

(Interrupt Service Routine) Software routine that is executed in response to an interrupt.

ISV

(Independent Software Vendor) A person or company that develops software. It implies an organization that specializes in software only and is not part of a computer systems or hardware manufacturer. Contrast with *IHV*.

IT

(Information Technology) Same as *Information Systems*.

ITAA

(Information Technology Association of America, 1616 N. Fort Myer Dr.,

Arlington, VA 22209, 703/522-5055) Formerly Association of Data Processing Service Organizations (ADAPSO). A membership organization founded in 1960 that defines performance standards, improves management methods and monitors government regulations in the computer services field.

iteration

One repetition of a sequence of instructions or events. For example, in a program loop, one iteration is once through the instructions in the loop.

iterative operation

An operation that requires successive executions of instructions or processes.

I-time

See *instruction time*.

ITSEC

See *NCSC*.

ITU

(International Telecommunications Union) Formerly the CCITT (Consultative Committee for International Telephony and Telegraphy), it is an international organization founded in 1865 and headquartered in Geneva that sets communications standards. The ITU is comprised of over 150 member countries. The Telecommunications Standards Section (TSS) is one of four organs of the ITU. Any specification with an ITU-T or ITU-TSS designation is an ITU standard.

IV

See *interactive video*.

IVDS

(Interactive Video and Data Services) The wireless implementation of interactive TV. In 1994, an additional part of the VHF television spectrum (218-219 MHz), which was divided into 1450 licenses, was auctioned to the highest bidders by the U.S. government. Organizations that own these licenses will be able to provide interactive television services to subscribers in their jurisdictions. See *interactive TV*.

Iverson notation

A set of symbols developed by Kenneth Iverson for writing statements in APL.

IVR

(Interactive Voice Response) See *voice response*.

iWARP

A systolic-array microprocessor from Intel that was originally funded by DARPA and developed by Carnegie-Mellon.

i-way

See *information superhighway*.

IXC

(IntereXchange Carrier) An organization that provides interstate communications services, such as AT&T, MCI and Sprint.

IZE

A PC text management system from Persoft, Inc., Madison, WI, noted for its flexible searching. Key words can be entered manually or can be created from a list or condition, such as the name between "Dear" and a comma.

J

J

A high-level mathematical programming language developed by Kenneth Iverson, the author of APL. J is the successor to APL and runs on a variety of platforms, including DOS, Windows, OS/2 and the Macintosh. The Windows version can be used as a calculating engine for Visual Basic, in which Visual Basic is used to write the file handling and user interface portions, and J is used to program the math.

jack

A receptacle into which a plug is inserted.

jacket

A plastic housing that contains a floppy disk. The 5.25" disk is built into a flexible jacket; the 3.25" disk uses a rigid jacket.

Jacquard loom

An automated loom that transformed the 19th century textile industry and became the inspiration for future calculating and tabulating machines. Developed by the French silk-weaver, Joseph-Marie Jacquard (1752-1834), it used punched cards to control its operation.

Although punched cards were used in earlier looms and music boxes, Jacquard's loom was a vast improvement and allowed complex patterns to be created swiftly. The loom was inspiration to Charles Babbage and, later, to Herman Hollerith.

The Jacquard Loom
(Photo courtesy of Smithsonian Institution.)

JAD

(Joint Application Development) An approach to systems analysis and design introduced by IBM in 1977 that emphasizes teamwork between user and technician. Small groups meet to determine system objectives and the business transactions to be supported. They are run by a neutral facilitator who can move the group toward well-defined goals. Results include a prototype of the proposed system.

jaggies

The stairstepped appearance of diagonal lines on a low-resolution graphics screen. The following example on the left demonstrates the "jaggies." The one on the right is in higher resolution.

JAM

(JYACC Application Manager) An application development system for client/server environments from JYACC, Inc., New York. It supports Windows, Mac and Motif clients and most all UNIX servers and VMS. It supports over 20 databases and includes its own database (JDB) for prototyping. JAM/CASE allows CASE information to be moved into JAM. JAM/TPi integrates JAM with the Tuxedo and Encina TP monitors.

Japanese PC market

NEC has over half the market with its PC-98 series. Apple has the next largest share with approximately 14%. The remainder is divided among Fujitsu, IBM, Epson, Toshiba and others. A Japanese version of Windows is available.

Java

A programming language for World Wide Web applications from Sun Microsystems. Java was modeled after C++, and Java programs are embedded into HTML documents. The first Web browsers to run Java applications are Sun's HotJava and Netscape's Navigator 2.0.

Javelin Plus

A spreadsheet for DOS that can simulate multidimensional views of data. Introduced in 1985 by Javelin Software, it was more a modeling program than a spreadsheet and was the forerunner of today's OLAP databases, which are inherently designed for multiple dimensions. It was later acquired by Information Resources, Inc. and Javelin Plus 3.5 in 1993 was the last version marketed. The technology, along with IRI's Express software, was acquired by Oracle in 1995.

JCL

(Job Control Language) A command language for mini and mainframe operating systems that launches applications. It specifies priority, program size and running sequence, as well as the files and databases used.

JEDEC

(Joint Electronic Device Engineering Council) An international body that sets integrated circuit standards.

JEIDA

(Japanese Electronic Industry Development Association) A Japanese trade and standards organization. JEIDA joined with PCMCIA to standardize the PC card in 1991. The PC Card specifications JEIDA 4.1 and PCMCIA 2.0 are the same.

JES

(Job Entry Subsystem) Software that provides batch communications for IBM's MVS operating system. It accepts data from remote batch terminals, executes them on a priority basis and transmits the results back to the terminals. The JES counterpart in VM is called RSCS.

JetForm

Forms software for DOS, Windows and Mac from JetForm Corporation, Waltham, MA. JetForm provides on-screen forms creation, routing and tracking for workflow systems.

jewel box, jewel case

A plastic container used to package an audio CD or CD-ROM disc.

JFIF

See *JPEG*.

jiff

See *GIF*.

jitter

A flickering transmission signal or display image.

J-lead

See *SOJ*.

job

A unit of work running in the computer. A job may be a single program or a group of programs that work together.

job categories

See *salary survey*.

job class

The descriptive category of a job that is based on the computer resources it requires when running.

job control language, job management language

See *JCL*.

job processing
Handling and processing jobs in the computer.

job queue
The lineup of programs ready to be executed.

job scheduling
In a large computer, establishing a job queue to run a sequence of programs over any period of time such as a single shift, a full day, etc.

job stream
A series of related programs that are run in a prescribed order. The output of one program is the input to the next program and so on.

join
In relational database management, to match one table (file) against another based on some condition creating a third table with data from the matching tables. For example, a customer table can be joined with an order table creating a table for all customers who purchased a particular product.

The default type of join is known as an "inner" join. It produces a resulting record if there is a matching condition. For example, matching shipments with receipts would produce only those shipments that have been received. On the other hand, an "outer" join using that example would create a record for every shipment whether or not it was received. The data for received items would be attached to the shipments, and empty, or null, fields would be attached to shipments without receipts.

Join
This example joins the sales table with the product table to produce the results table. The match is on product number.

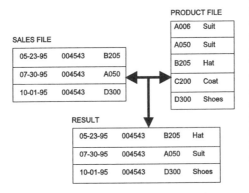

Josephson junction
An ultra-fast switching technology that uses superconductor materials, originally conceived by Brian Josephson. Circuits are immersed in liquid helium to obtain near-absolute zero degrees required for operation. A Josephson junction has been observed to switch in as little as 50 femtoseconds.

joule
A unit of energy equal to 10,000,000 ergs. Surge protectors are often given joule ratings, but this refers only to the amount of energy they can absorb, not what gets through.

journal
Same as *log*.

journaled file system

A file system that contains its own backup and recovery capability. Before indexes on disk are updated, the information about the changes is recorded in a log. If a power or other system failure corrupts the indexes as they are being rewritten, the operating system can use the log to repair them when the system is restarted.

journaling

Keeping track of events by recording them in a journal, or log.

JOVIAL

(Jules' Own Version of the International Algebraic Language) An ALGOL-like programming language developed by Systems Development Corp. in the early 1960s and widely used in the military. Its key architect was Jules Schwartz.

joy stick

A pointing device used to move an object on screen in any direction. It employs a vertical rod mounted on a base with one or two buttons. Joy sticks are used extensively in video games and in some CAD systems.

JPEG

(Joint Photographic Experts Group) An ISO/ITU standard for compressing still images that is becoming very popular due to its high compression capability. Using discrete cosine transform, it provides lossy compression (you lose some data from the original image) with ratios up to 100:1 and higher.

It depends on the image, but ratios of 10:1 to 20:1 may provide little noticeable loss. The more the loss can be tolerated, the more the image can be compressed. Compression is achieved by dividing the picture into tiny pixel blocks, which are halved over and over until the ratio is achieved.

JPEG is implemented in software and hardware, with the latter providing sufficient speed for realtime, on-the-fly compression. C-Cube Microsystems introduced the first JPEG chip.

JPEG++ is an extension to JPEG from Storm Technology, Mountain View, CA, that allows picture areas to be selectable for different ratios. For example, the background could be compressed higher than the foreground image.

JPEG uses the JPEG File Interchange Format, or JFIF. File extensions are .JPG or .JFF. M-JPEG and MPEG are variations of JPEG used for full-motion digital video. See *MPEG*.

JRP

(Joint Requirements Planning) Systems planning performed cooperatively by a team of users and technicians. Functions should be prioritized and related to the organization's goals and business opportunities.

JTC1

(Joint Technical Committee 1) See *ISO*.

Jughead

An Internet utility used to search for a key word throughout all levels of a Gopher menu. With Jughead, you do not have to jump from one menu level to the next.

jukebox

A storage device for multiple sets of CD-ROMs, tape cartridges or disk modules. Using carousels, robot arms and other methods, a jukebox physically moves the storage medium from its assigned location to an optical or magnetic station for reading and writing. Access between modules usually takes several seconds.

Julian date

The representation of month and day by a consecutive number starting with Jan. 1. For example, Feb. 1 is Julian 32. Dates are converted into Julian dates for calculation.

jump

Same as *goto*.

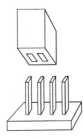

jumper

The simplest form of an on/off switch. It is just a tiny, plastic-covered metal block which is pushed onto two pins to close that circuit. It is used to select myriads of functions on a printed circuit board or on a peripheral device. For example, on a PC, jumpers are used to select I/O addresses and IRQs. On an IDE drive, a jumper selects between master and slave. A jumper can be used in place of a more costly DIP switch.

junction

The point at which two elements make contact. In a transistor, a junction is the point where an N-type material makes contact with a P-type material.

justification

In typography, the alignment of text evenly between left and right margins. Contrast with *ragged right*.
Note that the text in following paragraph is justified. Compare it to the paragraph above in the entry "jumper," which is flush left.

The simplest form of an on/off switch. It is just a tiny, plastic-covered metal block which is pushed onto two pins to close that circuit. It is used to select myriads of functions on a printed circuit board or on a peripheral device. For example, on a PC jumpers are used to select I/O addresses and IRQs. On an IDE drive, a jumper selects between master and slave. A jumper can be used in place of a more costly DIP switch.

justify

(1) To shift the contents of a field or register to the right or left.
(2) To align text evenly between left and right margins.

K

K
See *kilo*.

K&R C
(Kernighan and Ritchie C) A version of C defined by Brian Kernighan and Dennis Ritchie that preceded the ANSI standard.

K5
The code name for a Pentium-class CPU chip from Advanced Micro Devices, Inc., (AMD). It is expected to be available in early 1996.

Kaleida
(Kaleida Labs, Inc., Mountain View, CA) A joint venture of IBM and Apple that is developing multimedia software. See *ScriptX*.

KB, Kb
See *kilobyte* and *kilobit*.

Kbits/sec
(KiloBITS per SECond) Thousand bits per second.

KBps, Kbps
(KiloBytes Per Second, KiloBits Per Second) Thousand bytes per second. Thousand bits per second.

K-byte
See *kilobyte*.

Kerberos
A security system developed at MIT that authenticates users. It does not provide authorization to services or databases; it establishes identity at logon, which is used throughout the session.

Kermit
An asynchronous file transfer protocol developed at Columbia University, noted for its accuracy over noisy lines. Several extensions exist, including SuperKermit, a full-duplex, sliding window version. Kermit is popular on minis and mainframes and can also handle byte-oriented transfers over 7-bit ASCII systems.

kernel
The fundamental part of a program, typically an operating system, that resides in memory at all times and provides the basic services. It is the part of the operating system that is closest to the machine and may activate the hardware directly or interface to another software layer that drives the hardware. See *microkernel*.

kerning
In proportional spacing, the tightening of space between letters to create a visually appealing flow to the text. Letter combinations, such as WA, MW and TA, are routinely kerned for better appearance. See *tracking*.

VA   VA

Fixed Spacing   Proportional Spacing   Kerned Letters

Kerr effect

A change in rotation of light reflected off a magnetic field. The polarity of a magneto-optic bit causes the laser to shift one degree clockwise or counterclockwise.

key

(1) A keyboard button.

(2) Data that identifies a record. Account number, product code and customer name are typical key fields used to identify a record in a file or database. As an identifier, each key value must be unique in each record. See *sort key*.

(3) A numeric code used by an algorithm to create a code for encrypting data for security purposes.

keyboard

A set of input keys. On terminals and personal computers, it includes the standard typewriter keys, several specialized keys and features outlined below. See *PC keyboard, AT keyboard* and *Enhanced keyboard.*

Enter (Return) Key

In text applications, it ends a paragraph or short line. In data applications, it signals the end of the input for that field or line.

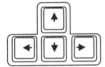

Cursor Keys

The four arrow keys move the cursor on screen. They are used in conjunction with shift, alt and control to move the cursor in bigger jumps; for example, CONTROL UP ARROW might scroll the screen. Some earlier keyboards didn't have cursor keys, in which case, control or alt was used with some letter key.

Control, Alt, Command and Option Keys

Used like a shift key, these keys are held down while another key is pressed to command the computer in a variety of ways.

Escape Key

Commonly used to exit or cancel the current mode such as exiting from a menu. Also used to clear an area or repeat a function such as redrawing the screen.

Numeric Lock

Locks a combination number/cursor keypad into numeric mode only.

Home and End Keys

Commonly used to move the cursor to the extreme left or right side of the current line. Often used in conjunction with shift, control and alt; for example, CONTROL HOME and CONTROL END usually move the cursor to the beginning and end of file.

Page Up and Page Down Keys

Used to move the cursor up and down a page, screen or frame. Often used in combination with shift, control and alt.

Function Keys

Used to call up a menu or perform a function, they are located in a cluster on the left side or in a row across the top of the keyboard (labelled F1, F2, etc.). Often used with the shift, control and alt keys providing 40 separate functions with F1 through F10.

Backspace Key
Used to delete the character to the left of the cursor (erase typos) and may be used with the shift, control and alt keys to erase segments of text. The extra-wide, typewriter-style key is preferred.

Delete Key
Used to erase the character at the current cursor location. Used in conjunction with the shift, control and alt keys, it is used to erase any segment of text, such as a word, sentence or paragraph.

Insert Key
Usually a toggle switch to go back and forth between insert and overwrite mode. Also used to "paste" a segment of text or graphics into the document at the current cursor location.

Repeating Keys
Most computer keys repeat when held down, a phenomenon first-time computer users must get used to. If you hold a key down that is used to command the computer, you'll be entering the command several times.

Audible Feedback
Keyboards may cause a click or beep to be heard from the computer when keys are pressed. This is done to acknowledge that the character has been entered. It should be adjustable for personal preference.

All Keyboards Are Not Equal
Keyboard quality is critical for experienced typists. The feel (tension and springiness) varies greatly. Key placement is important. Older keyboards and new laptop keyboards may have awkward return and shift key placements.

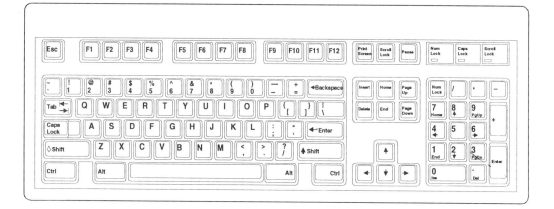

keyboard buffer
A memory bank or reserved memory area that stores keystrokes until the program can accept them. It lets fast typists continue typing while the program catches up.

keyboard connector
On a PC, there are two types of keyboard connectors. The standard PC uses a 5-pin DIN plug and socket. PS/2s and laptops use a smaller 6-pin mini DIN plug and socket. See *PS/2 connector*.

keyboard controller

A circuit that monitors keystrokes and generates the required data bits when pressed.

keyboard enhancer

Same as *macro processor*.

keyboard interrupt

A signal that gets the attention of the CPU each time a key is pressed. See *interrupt*.

keyboard processor

See *keyboard controller* and *keyboard enhancer*.

keyboard template

A plastic card that fits over the function keys to identify each key's purpose in a particular software program.

key cap

A replaceable, top part of a keyboard key. To identify commonly-used codes, it can be replaced with a custom-printed key cap.

key click

An audible feedback provided when a key is pressed. It may be adjustable by the user.

key command

A key combination (Alt-G, Ctrl-B, Command-M, etc.) used as a command to the computer.

key driven

Any device that is activated by pressing keys.

key entry

Data entry using a keyboard.

key field

See *key (2)*.

keyframe

In computer graphics animation, a frame that indicates the beginning or end of an object in motion.

keyframe animation

Animating a graphics object by creating smooth transitions between various keyframes.

key in

To enter data by typing on a keyboard.

keypad

A small keyboard or supplementary keyboard keys; for example, the keys on a calculator or the number/cursor cluster on a computer keyboard.

TELEPHONE KEYPAD

CALCULATOR KEYPAD

keypunch

To punch holes in a punched card. Although punched cards are obsolete, some people still say "keys are punched" on a keyboard.

keypunch department

Same as *data entry department*.

keypunch machine

A punched-card data entry machine. A deck of blank cards is placed into a hopper, and, upon operator command, the machine feeds one card to a punch station. As characters are typed, a series of dies at the punch station punch the appropriate holes in the selected card column.

The First Keypunch Machine
The data for 60 million Americans were punched into Hollerith punched cards from the information recorded by the census takers. The cards were then "automatically" counted. Look up *Hollerith machine* for more pictures of this early process.
(Photo courtesy of International Business Machines Corporation.)

key telephone system

An inhouse telephone system that is not centrally connected to a PBX. Each telephone has buttons for outside lines that can be dialed directly without having to "dial 9."

key-to-disk machine

A stand-alone data entry machine that stores data on magnetic disk for computer entry.

key-to-tape machine

A stand-alone data entry machine that stores data on magnetic tape for computer entry. Introduced by Mohawk Data Sciences in the mid 1960s, it was the first advancement in data entry since the card keypunch. Mohawk's stock went from $2 to $200 in a couple of years.

key word

(1) A word used in a text search.
(2) A word in a text document that is used in an index to best describe the contents of the document.
(3) A reserved word in a programming or command language.

Khornerstones

A benchmark program that tests CPU, I/O and floating point performance.

KHz

(KiloHertZ) One thousand cycles per second. See *horizontal scan frequency*.

kicks

See *CICS*.

killer app

An application that is exceptionally useful or exciting. When new operating systems are on the horizon, people wish for one or two killer apps that run under the new system in order to justify the migration effort and expense. Otherwise known as rationale.

kilo

Thousand. Abbreviated "K." It often refers to the precise value 1,024 since computer specifications are usually binary numbers. For example, 64K means 65,536 bytes when referring to memory or storage (64x1024), but a 64K salary means $64,000. The IEEE uses "K" for 1,024, and "k" for 1,000. See *binary values* and *space/time*.

kilobit

One thousand bits. Also Kb, Kbit and K-bit. See *kilo* and *space/time*.

kilobyte

One thousand bytes. Also KB, Kbyte and K-byte. See *kilo* and *space/time*.

Kinetics FastPath

A gateway from the Kinetics division of Excelan, Inc., that connects LocalTalk and PhoneNet systems and LaserWriters to VAXs, UNIX-based computers, PCs and other Ethernet-based hosts. It supports AppleTalk, TCP/IP and DECnet protocols.

kiosk

A small, self-standing structure such as a newstand or ticket booth. Unattended multimedia kiosks dispense public information via computer screens. Either a keyboard, touch screen or both are used for input.

kludge

Also spelled "kluge" and pronounced "klooj." A crude, inelegant system, component or program. It may refer to a makeshift, temporary solution to a problem as well as to any product that is poorly designed or that becomes unwieldy over time.

knowledge acquisition

The process of acquiring knowledge from a human expert for an expert system, which must be carefully organized into IF-THEN rules or some other form of knowledge representation.

Kiosk

knowledge base

A database of rules about a subject used in AI applications. See *expert system*.

knowledge based system

An AI application that uses a database of knowledge about a subject. In time, it is expected that everyday information systems will increasingly become knowledge based and provide users with more assistance than they do today. See *expert system*.

knowledge domain

A specific area of expertise of an expert system.

knowledge engineer

A person who translates the knowledge of an expert into the knowledge base of an expert system.

KnowledgeMan

An application development system for DOS, OS/2, VMS and UNIX environments from Micro Data Base Systems, Inc., Lafayette, IN. It includes an RDBMS, object-based 4GL programming and integrated functions, allowing, for example, database queries to update spreadsheets or results to be embedded in text documents.

knowledge representation

A method used to code knowledge in an expert system, typically a series of IF-THEN rules (IF this condition occurs, THEN take this action).

Korn shell

See *UNIX*.

KSDS

(Keyed Sequence DataSet) A VSAM structure that uses an index to store records in available free space. Retrieval is by key field or by address. Contrast with *ESDS*.

KSR terminal

(Keyboard Send Receive terminal) Same as *teleprinter*. Contrast with *RO terminal*.

L

L1 cache, L2 cache

See *cache*.

label

(1) In data management, a made-up name that is assigned to a file, field or other data structure.

(2) In spreadsheets, descriptive text that is entered into a cell.

(3) In programming, a made-up name used to identify a variable or a subroutine.

(4) In computer operations, a self-sticking form attached to the outside of a disk or tape in order to identify it.

(5) In magnetic tape files, a record used for identification at the beginning or end of the file.

label prefix

In a spreadsheet, a character typed at the beginning of a cell entry. For example, in 1-2-3, a single quote (') identifies what follows as a descriptive label even if it's a number.

ladder DAC

(ladder Digital to Analog Converter) Circuitry used to convert digital sound back into analog form for amplification. An individual resistor is associated with each bit of the digital sample, typically 16 bits. The resistors are weighted to the mathematical value of the bit they represent. The 16-bit sample is read, passed to all 16 resistors at the same time, and the sum total of the current passing through the resistors represents the analog value of the digital sample.

Ladder DACs represent a parallel conversion of the sample. See *1-bit DAC*.

LAN

(Local Area Network) A communications network that serves users within a confined geographical area. It is made up of servers, workstations, a network operating system and a communications link.

Servers are high-speed machines that hold programs and data shared by all network users. The workstations, or clients, are the users' personal computers, which perform stand-alone processing and access the network servers as required (look up the term *client/server* for more information on this concept).

Diskless and floppy-only workstations are sometimes used, which retrieve all software and data from the server. A printer can be attached to a workstation or to a server and be shared by network users.

Small LANs can allow each workstation to function as a server, allowing all users access to data on all machines. These peer-to-peer networks are often simpler to install and manage, but dedicated servers provide better performance and can handle higher transaction volume. Multiple servers are used in large networks.

The controlling software in a LAN is the network operating system, such as NetWare, UNIX and Appletalk, which resides in the server. A component part of the software resides in each client and allows the application to read and write data from the server as if it were on the local machine.

The message transfer is managed by a transport protocol such as IPX, SPX and TCP/IP. The physical transmission of data is performed by the access method (Ethernet, Token Ring, etc.) which is implemented in the network adapters that plug into the machines. The actual communications path is the cable (twisted pair, coax, optical fiber) that interconnects each network adapter. See *MAN, WAN, bridge, router, gateway* and *hub*.

LAN Software (Client)

This page shows the typical system software that is resident and running in memory in a desktop computer (client) within a local area network. The system software components are required to the counterpart software in the server.

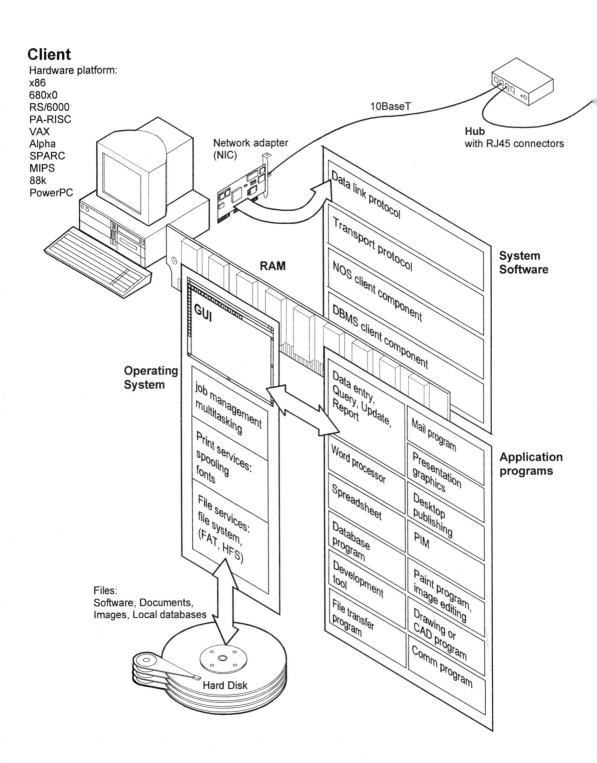

Client

Hardware platform:
x86
680x0
RS/6000
PA-RISC
VAX
Alpha
SPARC
MIPS
88k
PowerPC

10BaseT

Network adapter
(NIC)

Hub
with RJ45 connectors

Data link protocol

Transport protocol

NOS client component

DBMS client component

**System
Software**

RAM

GUI

**Operating
System**

job management
multitasking

Print services:
spooling
fonts

File services:
file system,
(FAT, HFS)

Data entry,
Query, Update,
Report

Mail program

Word processor

Presentation
graphics

Spreadsheet

Desktop
publishing

Database
program

PIM

Development
tool

Paint program,
image editing

File transfer
program

Drawing or
CAD program

Comm program

**Application
programs**

Files:
Software, Documents,
Images, Local databases

Hard Disk

This diagram depicts the typical system software components that are resident and running in memory in a server in a local area network.

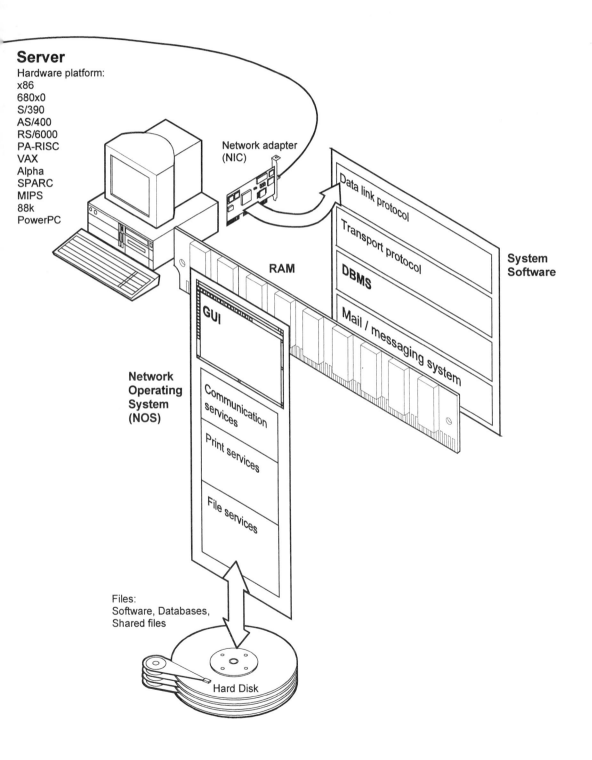

Server

Hardware platform:
x86
680x0
S/390
AS/400
RS/6000
PA-RISC
VAX
Alpha
SPARC
MIPS
88k
PowerPC

Network adapter
(NIC)

Data link protocol

Transport protocol

DBMS

Mail / messaging system

System
Software

RAM

GUI

Network
Operating
System
(NOS)

Communication
services

Print services

File services

Files:
Software, Databases,
Shared files

Hard Disk

LAN Hardware

OSI LAYER 4 (Transport layer) and above

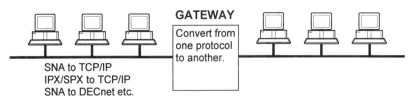

GATEWAY

Convert from one protocol to another.

SNA to TCP/IP
IPX/SPX to TCP/IP
SNA to DECnet etc.

OSI LAYER 3 (Network layer)

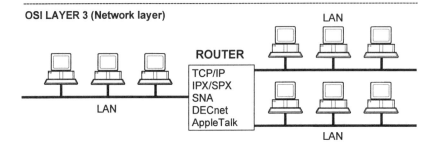

LAN

ROUTER

TCP/IP
IPX/SPX
SNA
DECnet
AppleTalk

LAN

LAN

LAN

OSI LAYERS 1 & 2 (Data link layers)

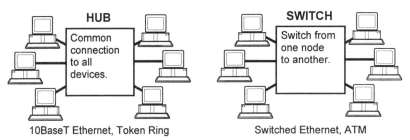

HUB

Common connection to all devices.

10BaseT Ethernet, Token Ring

SWITCH

Switch from one node to another.

Switched Ethernet, ATM

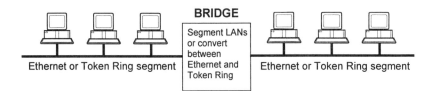

BRIDGE

Segment LANs or convert between Ethernet and Token Ring

Ethernet or Token Ring segment

Ethernet or Token Ring segment

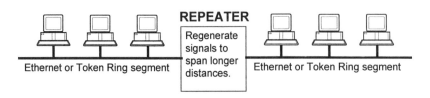

REPEATER

Regenerate signals to span longer distances.

Ethernet or Token Ring segment

Ethernet or Token Ring segment

LAN adapter
Same as *network adapter*.

LAN administrator
See *network administrator*.

LAN analyzer
See *network analyzer*.

LANDA
(**LAN** Dealers Association) An association that merged with NOMDA to become the Business Technology Association. See *BTA*.

landing zone
A safe non-data area on a hard disk used for parking the read/write head.

Landmark rating
A widely-used PC performance test from Landmark Research International, Clearwater, FL, that measures CPU, video and coprocessor speed. CPU speed is rated as the clock speed required in an AT-class machine that would provide equivalent performance. In 1995, Landmark was acquired by Quarterdeck Office Systems.

landscape
A printing orientation that prints data across the wider side of the form. Contrast with *portrait*.

landscape monitor
A monitor that is used to display facing text pages. It is wider than it is high.

LAN Emulation
The ability to support communications protocols, such as IP, IPX, AppleTalk and DECnet, on an ATM network as well as to connect Ethernet, Token Ring and FDDI LANs to ATM networks. The processing is done in a LAN Emulation driver in the client station and in LAN Emulation servers that reside in an ATM network.

LanguageAccess
An SAA-compliant query language from IBM that translates a user's English-language request into SQL language for QMF. QMF retrieves the data.

language processor
Language translation software. Programming languages, command languages, query languages, natural languages and foreign languages are all translated by software.

LAN Manager
(1) A network operating system from Microsoft that runs as a server application under OS/2 and supports both DOS, Windows and OS/2 clients. It uses the Microsoft File Sharing protocol (SMB) for file sharing, the NetBEUI protocol for its transport mechanism and uses Named Pipes for interprocess communication (IPC). See *LAN Server*.
LAN Manager for Windows NT is a different product. It adds network management and services to Windows NT, which includes peer-to-peer networking.
(2) Same as *network administrator*.

LAN Network Manager
IBM Token Ring network management software. LAN Station Manager is the workstation counterpart that collects data for LAN Network Manager.

LAN Requester

LAN Server software that resides in the workstation.

LANRover

A remote access server from Shiva Corporation, Burlington, MA, that provides modem and ISDN access to remote users on a network. The LANRover is a proprietary device that connects to the LAN and supports the PPP protocol as well as standard dial-up ANSI terminal connections.

LAN segment

A section of a local area network that is used by a particular workgroup or department and separated from the rest of the LAN by a bridge, router or switch. Networks are divided into multiple segments for security and to improve traffic flow by filtering out packets that are not destined for the segment.

LAN Server

(1) A network operating system from IBM that runs as a server application under OS/2 and supports both DOS, Windows and OS/2 clients. Originally based on LAN Manager when OS/2 was jointly developed by IBM and Microsoft, Version 3.0 runs under IBM's own OS/2 Version 2.0.

Version 3.0 provides disk mirroring, CID capability and Network Transport Services/2 (NTS/2) for concurrent access to NetWare servers. Options are Lan Server for the Macintosh for Mac client access and System Performance/2 (SP/2), a series of network management utilities.

(2) (LAN server) Generically, a file server in a network.

LAN station

(1) A workstation in a local area network.
(2) See *LAN Network Manager*.

LANtastic

A popular peer-to-peer LAN operating system for DOS, Windows and OS/2 from Artisoft, Inc., Tucson, AZ. It supports Ethernet, ARCNET and Token Ring adapaters as well as its own twisted-pair adapater at two Mbits/sec. Artisoft also makes Ethernet adapters. Included are e-mail and chat functions. Voice mail and conversation are optional.

Simply LANtastic is an entry-level version designed for easy installation and use. It is available as software only or with network adapters that eliminate common cabling problems for first-time users.

Multiple protocols are supported starting with LANtastic 6.0, allowing a LANtastic client station to access a NetWare, LAN Manager, LAN Server or Windows NT server. See *CorStream*.

LAN Workplace

A family of software products from Novell that allows DOS, Windows, Macintosh and OS/2 clients in a NetWare environment to access resources on a TCP/IP network. LAN Workplace for DOS can also encapsulate NetWare protocols and run NetWare-dependent applications entirely within a TCP/IP network.

LAP

(Link Access Procedure) An ITU family of error correction protocols originally derived from the HDLC standard and used on X.25 packet networks.

LAP-B (LAP-Balanced)	Used in current X-25 networks.
LAP-D (LAP-D channel)	Used in the data channel of an ISDN transmission.

LAP-M (LAP-Modem)	Defined in ITU V.42, which uses some of the LAPD methods and adds additional ones.
LAP-X (LAP-Half-dupleX)	Used for ship to shore transmission.

LapLink

A PC file transfer program from Traveling Software, Inc., Bothell, WA, that transfers data between laptops and desktop computers. LapLink Mac transfers files between PCs and Macs.

laptop computer

A portable computer that has a flat screen and usually weighs less than a dozen pounds. It uses AC power and/or batteries. Most have connectors for an external monitor and keyboard transforming them into desktop computers.

Laptop Features

Keyboard
Keyboard layout is often sacrificed. The Home, End, PageUp and PageDn keys may not be dedicated keys, requiring that you hold down the Fn key in conjunction with them. This is cumbersome.
Function keys and cursor keys are often made smaller. There's only one rule— test drive the keyboard carefully.

Screen Quality
Monochrome LCD screens translate colors into shades of gray. The more shades, the better the representation of full-color images. Passive matrix LCD screens provide a subdued color. Active matrix LCD screens are sharp and rich, but are costly and use more power. Double scan passive matrix is better than passive matrix, but not as sharp as active matrix.

Screen Resolution & Acceleration
Without a docking station or expansion slot capability, you cannot improve the built-in display resolution. If you want higher resolution when you hook it up to your desktop monitor, it may not be there. In addition, Windows needs fast graphics. If a high-speed graphics accelerator is not built into your display, you will experience slower Windows performance.

External Display & Keyboard Connectors
Connect a full-size CRT and keyboard for home/office. Even if you like your laptop keyboard, you may want to use an external keyboard with your external monitor, because the laptop screen usually doesn't lie back flat to get out of the way from straight-on viewing of the external monitor.
A full-size keyboard can be connected through the external keyboard connector on most laptops. Keyboards can be attached to earlier laptops with an adapter via the serial or parallel port.

Built-in Pointing Device
There are a wide variety of pointing devices built into laptops, including trackballs and tracksticks, but each one has a different feel. Try it first. The best option is always an external mouse port that lets you connect your favorite desktop mouse if the built-in device becomes cumbersome.

Built-in Modem
Saves carrying an external modem or PC Card modem.

Expansion
Expansion is critical on a laptop. Early laptops had no expansion at all.
Some laptops connect to an optional docking station that provides one or more expansion slots for expandability, but only when they are used as desktop machines.

Some laptops provide interchangeable hard disks and screens.
The PCMCIA PC Card slot has become the major expansion vehicle on a laptop. Laptops with one or two PC Card slots can be expanded with a modem, network adapter, a removable hard disk and other devices as they are developed.

Auto Resume
Lets you return to the computer and pick up where you left off without having to reload your applications.

Dual Display
Using an external monitor and laptop display at the same time. For presentations with a data projector, it may be difficult to look at a projected image off in the distance.

Nickel Hydride Battery
Provides about 20% more power per pound than nickel cadmium and doesn't have its associated memory problem. Recharge life may be shorter, however. Lithium ion and lithium polymer batteries provide even longer life.

Removable Hard Disk
A removable hard drive is the best bet. If you run out of space, you can replace the old disk with a larger or a second one.

Multimedia
Multimedia laptops are increasingly becoming commonplace. With built-in sound, speakers and CD-ROMs, you have a mobile desktop. If you add these devices later as separate items, you will have a lot to lug around.

Weight
Seven pounds doesn't sound like much until you lug it around all day. Some subnotebooks use an external floppy disk to reduce poundage. Also, check the transformer weight (also called the AC adapter or power adapter). They never mention this in the ads, but it can add one or two pounds. On long trips, you will probably keep the transformer in your travelling case. Some laptops are finally getting around to building in a lightweight unit, requiring you to carry only the powercord.

The First Laptops
The Radio Shack Model 100 (below) and the Toshiba T-1000 (right) were the first truly lightweight computers.

Type	Weight in pounds
Laptop	4-18
Notebook	4-7
Subnotebook	2-4
Pocket	1

laser

(Light Amplification from the Stimulated Emission of Radiation) A device that creates a very uniform light that can be precisely focused. It generates a single wavelength or narrow band of wavelengths and is used in applications such as communications, printing and disk storage. Unlike the transmission of electricity, transmission of light pulses over optical fibers is not affected by nearby electrical interferences. See *LED*.

The Laser Discovery

In 1957, the laser was conceived by Gordon Gould, a graduate student in physics at Columbia University. When Gould filed for patents in 1959, he found that Columbia professor Charles Townes and Arthur Schawlow of Bell Labs had already filed for them. The year before, AT&T had, in fact, demonstrated a working laser at Bell Labs. In 1977, after years of litigation, a court awarded Gould rights to the first of three patents and later to all of them. He finally reaped millions in royalties.

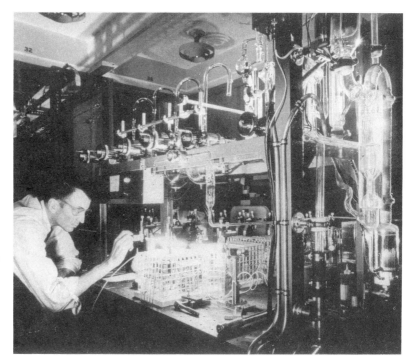

Developing the Laser

This photo of the development of the helium-neon laser was taken at AT&T's Bell Laboratories in 1964. *(Photo courtesy of AT&T.)*

LaserDisc

A 12" diameter optical disk used for full-motion video. Various videodisc systems were introduced in the 1970s, but only LaserVision from Philips survived. LaserDiscs have been used for interactive training as well as for home theater, where its superior resolution is noticeable on larger screens. However, for the most part, CD-ROMs have replaced LaserDiscs for training, and it is expected that DVDs will replace the LaserDisc for movies.

Movies use the CLV (constant linear velocity) format, which records the signal on a continuous, spiraling track. Each side contains 108,000 frames and one hour of video. The signal density is uniform, and the player varies the speed of the disc. For fast direct access for interactive training and games, the CAV (constant angular velocity) format is used. Tracks are concentric circles, each containing one video frame. There are 54,000 frames and 30 minutes of video per side.

Early LaserDiscs recorded analog sound. Today, most LaserDiscs contain analog and digital soundtracks, and newer players default to the digital sound if available. Some players let the user select the soundtrack, allowing multiple languages and other annotations to be included on the same disc.

LaserJet

A family of desktop laser printers from HP. Introduced in 1984 at $3,495, the first LaserJet revolutionized the desktop laser printer market. LaserJets print at 300 dpi and starting with the LaserJet 4, at 600 dpi. Third-party enhancements, such as the WinJet, increase resolution to 1200 dpi. PCL is the printer command language. LaserJets accept bitmapped fonts from plug-in cartridges and, except for the original model, from the computer (soft fonts). Built-in Intellifont scalable fonts were included starting with the LaserJet III (PCL Version 5). The III also overcame previous limitations by being able to print portrait and landscape fonts on the same page and white text on a black background.

PostScript capability became available starting with the Series II in the form of plug-in cartridges from HP and others. Native PostScript models were introduced with the LaserJet 4.

In 1994, HP launched the HP Color LaserJet, capable of printing 16.7 million colors (24 bit) at 300 dpi with a list price of $7295 plus $799 for optional PostScript. It prints color in a single pass at 2 ppm or 10 ppm for black only. It supports an enhanced PCL 5 language as well as PostScript Level 2.

Laserjet Specifications

	Model	Year Intro	Speed (ppm)	Input paper capacity	Built in fonts	Cartridges	Printer RAM	Engine
300 dpi	x LaserJet	1984	8	100	2	1	128K-2M	CX
	x PLUS	1985	8	100	2	1	512K-2M	CX
	x 500 PLUS	1986	8	500	2	1	512K-2M	CX
	x 2000 (1)	1987	20	500	34	3	1½-5½M	LPB20
	x Series II	1987	8	200	6	2	512K-4M	SX
	x IID *dss	1989	8	400	22	2	640K-4M	SX
	x IIP	1989	4	50	14	1	512K-4.5	LX
	x IIP+	1991	slightly faster than IIP					LX
	x III	1990	8	200	22f	2	1-5M	SX
	x IIID *dss	1990	8	400	22f	2	1-5M	SX
	x IIIP	1991	4	50	22f	1	1-5M	LX
	x IIIsi *ds	1991	17	1000	30f	2	1-17M	NX
	4L	1993	4	100	26sf	0	1-2M	
	4ML	1993	4	100	80sf	0	4M	
600 dpi	x 4	1992	8	350	45sf	1	2-32M	EX
	4+ *ds	1994	12	350	45sf	1	2-66M	EX
	x 4P	1993	4	250	45sf	1	2-22M	PX II
	x 4MP	1993	4	250	80sf	1	6-26M	PX II
	x 4M	1992	8	350	80sf	1	6-26M	EX
	4M+ *ds	1994	12	350	80sf	1	6-38M	EX
	4si *ds	1993	17	1000	45sf	2	2-34M	LPB-NX
	4siMX *ds	1993	17	1000	80sf	2	10-26M	LPB-NX
	4V *11x17	1994	17	350	45sf	-	4-68M	LPB-NX
	4MV *11x17	1994	17	350	80sf	-	12-44M	LPB-NX
	5P *IrDA	1995	6	350	45sf	-	2-50M	HP
	5MP *IrDA	1995	6	350	45sf	-	3-50M	HP
Color 300 dpi	Color LJ	1994	2	250	45sf	-	8-72M	
	mono		10					

x = No longer made as of Aug. 1995
 *ds = double sided printing optional
 *dss = double sided printing standard
*11x17 = prints 11x17" paper
*IrDA = includes wireless port
26sf = 26 Intellifont scalable fonts
45sf = 45 scalable fonts: 35 Intellifont, 10 TrueType
80sf = 80 scalable fonts: 35 Intellifont, 10 TrueType, 35 Type 1
22f = 14 bitmapped fonts, 8 Intellifont
30f = 14 bitmapped fonts, 16 Intellifont

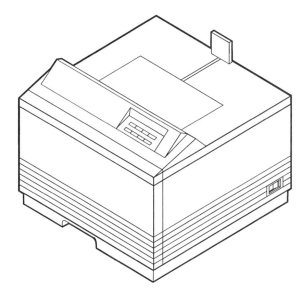

LaserMaster

(LaserMaster Corporation, Eden Prarie, MN) A manufacturer of high-resolution
PostScript printers and add-in boards. See *WinJet*.

laser printer

A printer that uses the electrophotographic method used in copy machines to print a
page at a time. A laser "paints" the dots of light onto a photographic drum or belt.
The toner is applied to the drum or belt and then transferred onto the paper.
Desktop printers use cut sheets like a copy machine. Large printers may use rolls of
paper.

In 1975, IBM introduced the first laser printer, the high-speed model 3800. Later,
Siemens introduced the ND 2 and Xerox introduced the 9700. These self-contained
printing presses are online to a mainframe or offline, accepting print image data on
tape reels or disk packs. Large-scale machines provide collating and stacking, and
some models can print on very wide paper.

In 1984, HP introduced the LaserJet, the first desktop laser printer, which propelled
desktop publishing. The desktop laser printer has made the daisy wheel printer
obsolete, and it competes directly with the dot matrix printer.

Although high-resolution color laser printers are also available, less expensive desktop
versions will become widely used throughout the 1990s.

Note: All large-scale printers that print a page at a time do not use a laser. Some use
ion deposition, which creates the image with electricity rather than light.

LaserWriter

A family of 300 dpi desktop laser printers from Apple introduced in 1985. All models handle bitmapped fonts, and, except for the SC models, include PostScript, built-in AppleTalk connections, as well as RS-232 ports for connecting PCs via Diablo emulation.

LAT

(Local Area Transport) A communications protocol from Digital for controlling terminal traffic in a DECnet environment.

LATA

(Local Access and Transport Area) The geographic region set up to differentiate local and long distance telephone calls. Any telephone call between parties within a LATA is handled by the local telephone company.

latch

An electronic circuit that maintains one of two states. See *flip-flop*.

late binding

Same as *dynamic binding*.

latency

The time between initiating a request for data and the beginning of the actual data transfer. On a disk, latency is the time it takes for the selected sector to come around and be positioned under the read/write head. Channel latency is the time it takes for a computer channel to become unoccupied in order to transfer data. Network latency is the delay introduced when a packet is momentarily stored and then forwarded.

latent image

An invisible image typically of electrical charges. For example, in a copy machine, a latent image of the page to be copied is created on a plate or drum as an electrical charge.

launch

To cause a program to load and run.

LAWN

(Local Area Wireless Network) A transmitter/receiver from O'Neill Communications, Inc., Princeton, NJ, that connects devices using radio transmission.

layer

(1) In computer graphics, one of several on-screen "drawing boards" for creating elements within a picture. Layers can be manipulated independently, and the sum of all layers make up the total image.
(2) In communications, a protocol that interacts with other protocols to provide all the necessary transmission services. See *OSI*.

layout setting

A value used to format a printed page. Margins, tabs, indents, headers, footers and column widths are examples.

lazer

See *laser*.

lazy write

Refers to the effect caused by using a write back cache. Data is written to the cache first and, later, during idle machine cycles or at some specified time, is written to disk if it is a disk cache or to memory if it is a CPU cache.

LBRV

(Low Bit Rate Voice) A voice sampling technique that analyzes each 15-30 millisecond speech segment independently and converts it into a 30-byte frame.

LC

(Low cost Color) See Macintosh.

LCC

See *leaded chip carrier*.

LCD

(Liquid Crystal Display) A display technology that uses rod-shaped molecules (liquid crystals) that flow like liquid and bend light. Unenergized, the crystals direct light through two polarizing filters, allowing a natural background color to show. When energized, they redirect the light to be absorbed in one of the polarizers, causing the dark appearance of crossed polarizers to show. The more the molecules are twisted, the better the contrast and viewing angle.

Because it takes less power to move molecules than to energize a light-emitting device, LCDs replaced LEDs in digital watches years ago. The LCD was developed at RCA's Sarnoff Research Center in Princeton, NJ in 1963.

Passive Display (TN and STN)

Called "passive matrix" when used for computer screens. Called "passive display" when used for digital readouts, icons, etc. All active electronics (transistors) are outside of the display screen. Passive display provides a sharp image for monochrome screens, but is more subdued for color. Submarining is common. Passive display types are:

Types of Passive Display LCDs

TN (TWISTED NEMATIC - 90 DEGREE TWIST)
Low-cost displays for consumer products and instruments. Black on gray/silver background.

STN (SUPERTWISTED NEMATIC- 180-270 DEGREE TWIST)
Used extensively on laptops for mono and color displays. DSTN and FSTN provide improvements over straight STN.
180 degree - green/blue on yellow background
270 degree - blue on white/blue background

DUAL SCAN STN
Improves STN display by dividing the screen into two halves and scanning each half simultaneously and doubling the number of lines refreshed. Not as sharp as active matrix.

ACTIVE ADDRESSING
Improves STN display by addressing pixels differently. Eliminates submarining and less expensive than active displays, but not as sharp. Expected in 1996 timeframe.

Active Display (TFT)

Typically used for laptop color screens, thus called "active matrix" displays. Transistors are built into each pixel within the screen. For example, 640x480 color VGA screen requires 921,600 transistors; one for each red, green and blue dot. Provides a sharp, clear image with good contrast and eliminates submarining, but fabrication costs are high. Uses a 90° (TN) twist. Also called TFT LCD (thin film transistor LCD).

Reflective vs Backlit
Reflective screens used in many consumer appliances and some lightweight laptops require external light and only work well in a bright room or with a desk lamp. Backlit and sidelit screens have their own light source and work well in dim lighting.

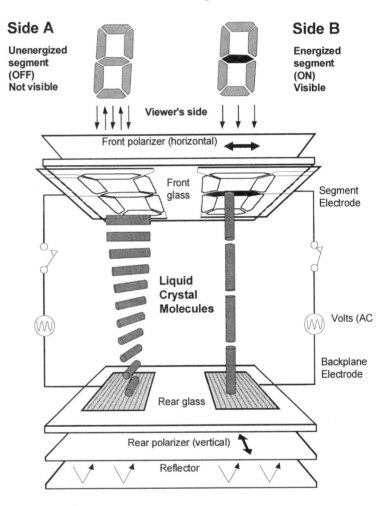

Twisted-Nematic Liquid Crystal Display
The layer of liquid crystals between the front and rear glass is 3/10,000ths of an inch thick.

Side A shows a light gray segment (background). The light source from the viewer's side shines through the front polarizer and glass, down the crystals, through the rear glass and rear polarizer. It bounces off the reflector, back up the rear polarizer, rear glass, crystals, front glass and front polarizer to the viewer. In the normal state, the liquid crystals are induced to lay parallel with their polarizing plates.

Side B shows a dark segment (crossed polarizers). When the segment is energized, the liquid crystal molecules turn perpendicular to the polarizing plates. Light shines through the front polarizer and glass, down the crystals to where it is absorbed by the rear polarizer.

Backlit displays use a translucent reflector and shine a light source behind it. This transflective display makes the background brighter, and the characters appear sharper.

LCD panel

Also called a projection panel, it is a data projector that accepts computer output and displays it on a see-through liquid crystal screen that is placed on top of an overhead projector. Some laptops are built with an LCD screen that you can remove from the computer, take the back off and use as a projection panel.

LCD printer

An electrophotographic printer that uses a single light source directed by liquid crystal shutters.

LE

(Less than or Equal to) See *relational operator*.

lead acid

A rechargeable battery technology widely used in portable gardening tools, but has been used in some portable computers. It uses lead plates and an acid electrolyte. It provides the least amount of charge per pound of the rechargeable technologies. See *nickel cadmium, nickel hydride* and *zinc air*.

leaded chip carrier

A square chip housing with pin connectors on all four sides (provides more I/O paths than a DIP). Contrast with *leadless chip carrier*.

leader

(1) A length of unrecorded tape used to thread the tape onto the tape drive.
(2) A dot or dash used to draw the eye across the printed page, such as in a table of contents.

leading

In typography, the vertical spacing between lines of type (between baselines). The name comes from the early days of typesetting when the space was achieved with thin bars of lead.

leading edge

(1) The edge of a punched card or document that enters the reading station first.
(2) In digital electronics, a pulse as it changes from a 0 to a 1.
(3) In programming, a loop that tests a condition before the loop is entered.
(4) (Leading Edge Products, Inc., Westborough, MA) A PC manufacturer founded in 1980. Its Model M (for Mitsubishi) in 1982 was the first PC-compatible from overseas. Korean Daewoo Corporation supplied it with products since 1984 and acquired it in 1989.

leading zeros

Zeros used to fill a field that do not increase the numerical value of the data. For example, all the zeros in 0000006588 are leading zeros.

leadless chip carrier

A square chip housing with flat contact connectors on all four sides (provides more I/O paths than a DIP). Contrast with *leaded chip carrier*.

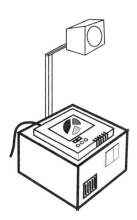

LCD Panel
An LCD panel requires an overhead projector as its light source.

487

leaf

In database management, the last node of a tree.

League for Programming Freedom

An organization of professors, students and businessmen who believe that software copyrights and patents jeopardize the industry. They are dedicated to "bringing back the freedom to write programs." Address: 1 Kendall Square, P.O. Box 9171, Cambridge, MA 02139.

leapfrog test

A storage diagnostic routine that replicates itself throughout the storage medium.

leased line

A private communications channel leased from a common carrier. It can be ordered in pairs, providing a four-wire channel for full-duplex transmission (dial-up system provides only two-wire lines). To improve line quality, it can also be conditioned. Leased lines are a huge business. According to Vertical Systems Group, Dedham, MA, worldwide 1994 leased line revenues were $35 billion. In that same year, frame relay revenues were $250 million and ATM was $35 million, although both of these technologies are expected to grow rapidly.

leased line modem

A high-speed modem used in private lines. It may have built-in lower speeds for alternate use in dial-up lines.

least significant digit

The rightmost digit in a number.

LEC

(1) (Local Exchange Carrier) An organization that provides local telephone services (RBOCs, GTE, etc.).
(2) (LAN Emulation Client) A software driver that runs in a network client to provide LAN emulation in an ATM network.

LED

(Light Emitting Diode) A display technology that uses a semiconductor diode that emits light when charged. It usually gives off a red glow, although other colors can be generated. It is used in readouts and on/off lights in myriads of electronic appliances. It was the first digital watch display, but was superseded by LCD, which uses less power.

LED printer

An electrophotographic printer that uses a matrix of LEDs as its light source rather than a laser.

left click

To press the left button on the mouse.

legacy card

In a PC, an expansion card that does not have the ISA Plug and Play capability built into it. Up until late 1994, all cards were legacy cards.

legacy LAN

A LAN topology, such as Ethernet or Token Ring, that has a large installed base or has been in existence for a long time.

legacy system
A mainframe or minicomputer information system that has been in existence for a long time.

Lempel Ziv
A data compression algorithm that uses an adaptive compression technique. See *LZW.*

LEN
(Low Entry Networking) In SNA, peer-to-peer connectivity between adjacent Type 2.1 nodes, such as PCs, workstations and minicomputers. LU 6.2 sessions are supported across LEN connections.

LEO
(Low-Earth Orbit) A type of communications satellite that orbits no higher than 500 miles above the earth. It differs from the geosynchronous, or GEO, satellite, which is 22,282 miles high. The GEO appears stationary, because it rotates at earth speed. The LEO rotates around the globe in a couple of hours, but its shorter distance supports low-power, hand-held transmitters.

letter quality
The print quality of an electric typewriter. Laser printers, ink jet printers and daisy wheel printers provide letter quality printing. 24-pin dot matrix printers provide near letter quality (NLQ), but the characters are not as dark and crisp.

level 1 cache, level 2 cache
See *cache.*

lexicographic sort
Arranging items in alphabetic order like a dictionary. Numbers are located by their alphabetic spelling.

Lexmark
(Lexmark International, Inc., Lexington, KY) A manufacturer of desktop printers. Lexmark was a division of IBM that was spun off into an independent company in 1991. IBM retained minor ownership and continues to make large line printers used in datacenters. Lexmark makes IBM's dot matrix printers, keyboards, typewriters and related supplies.
Lexmark makes its own printer engines and was the first to bring a 600 dpi laser printer to market as well as a true 1,200 dpi printer. Lexmark laser printers thus far offer quality at lower prices.

LF
See *line feed.*

LHARC
A popular freeware compression program developed by Haruyasu Yoshizaki that uses a variant of the LZW (LZ77) dictionary method followed by a Huffman coding stage. It runs on PCs, UNIX and other platforms as its source code is also free.

librarian
(1) A person who works in the data library.
(2) See *CA-Librarian.*

library
(1) A collection of programs or data files.
(2) A collection of functions (subroutines) that are linked into the main program

when it is compiled.

(3)See *data library*.

library function

A subroutine that is part of a function library. Same as *library routine*.

library management

See *version control*.

library routine

A subroutine that is part of a macro or function library.

LIFO

(Last In First Out) A queueing method in which the next item to be retrieved is the item most recently placed in the queue. Contrast with *FIFO*.

ligature

Two or more typeface characters that are designed as a single unit (physically touch). Fi, ffi, ae and oe are common ligatures.

light bar

Same as *highlight bar*.

light emitting diode

See *LED*.

light guide

A transmission channel that contains a number of optical fibers packaged together.

light pen

A light-sensitive stylus wired to a video terminal used to draw pictures or select menu options. The user brings the pen to the desired point on screen and presses the pen button to make contact.

Screen pixels are constantly being refreshed. When the user presses the button, allowing the pen to sense light, the pixel being illuminated at that instant identifies the screen location.

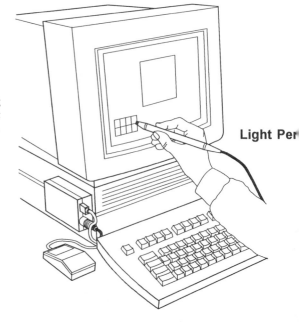

Light Pen

LightShip

A family of client/server tools for analyzing data from multidimensional databases from Pilot Software, Cambridge, MA, a pioneer in the OLAP database field. LightShip includes tools for financial modeling, budgeting and consolidation of large databases. It provides Windows-based point-and-click reporting, a full programming language for advanced users, and support for all the popular databases.

light source

In computer graphics, the implied location of a light source in order to simulate the visual effect of a light on a 3-D object. Some programs can compute multiple light sources.

lightwave

Light in the infrared, visible and ultraviolet ranges, which falls between x-rays and microwaves. Wavelengths are between 10 nanometers and one millimeter.

lightwave system

A device that transmits light pulses over optical fibers at extremely high speeds (Gbits/sec range). Many intercity telephone trunks have been converted to lightwave systems.

lightweight protocol

A communications protocol designed with less complexity in order to reduce overhead. For example, it uses fixed-length headers because they are faster to parse than variable-length headers. To ensure compatibility, it eliminates optional subsets of the standard so that both sides are always equipped to deal with each other.

li-ion

See *lithium ion.*

limited distance modem

Same as *short-haul modem.*

Linda

A set of parallel processing functions added to languages, such as C and C++, that allows data to be created and transferred between processes. It was developed by Yale professor David Gelernter, when he was a 23-year old graduate student.

line

(1) In text-based systems, a row of characters.
(2) In graphics-based systems, a row of pixels.
(3) Any communications channel.

Lines
The exploding communications field in 1883. This photo was taken at Broadway and Courtlandt Streets in New York. *(Photo courtesy of AT&T.)*

line adapter

In communications, a device similar to a modem, that converts a digital signal into a form suitable for transmission over a communications line and vice versa. It provides parallel/serial and serial/parallel conversion, modulation and demodulation.

line analyzer

A device that monitors the transmission of a communications line.

linear

Sequential or having a graph that is a straight line.

linear address space

See *flat address space*.

linear editing

See *linear video editing*.

linear programming

A mathematical technique used to obtain an optimum solution in resource allocation problems, such as production planning.

linear video

Continuous playback of videotape or videodisc. It typically refers to analog video technology.

linear video editing

Editing analog videotape. Before digital editing (nonlinear video editing), video sequences were edited by inserting new frames and reconstructing the balance of the tape by adding the remainder of the frames. Contrast with *nonlinear video editing*.

line concentration

See *concentrator*.

line conditioning

See *conditioning*.

line dot matrix printer

A line printer that uses the dot matrix method. See *printer*.

line drawing

A graphic image outlined by solid lines. The mass of the drawing is imagined by the viewer. See *wire frame*.

line driver

In communications, a device that is used to extend the transmission distance between terminals and computers that are connected via private lines. It is used for digital transmission and is required at each end of the line.

line editor

An outmoded editing program that allows text to be created and changed one line at a time. The Edlin editor included with DOS is an example.

line feed

(1) A character code that advances the screen cursor or printer to the next line. The line feed is used as an end of line code in UNIX. In DOS and OS/2 text files, the

return/line feed pair (ASCII 13 10) is the standard end of line code.
(2) A printer button that advances paper one line when depressed.

line frequency

The number of times each second that a wave or some repeatable set of signals is transmitted over a line. See *horizontal scan frequency*.

line level

In communications, the signal strength within a transmission channel, measured in decibels or nepers.

line load

(1) In communications, the percentage of time a communications channel is used.
(2) In electronics, the amount of current that is carried in a circuit.

line number

(1) A specific line of programming language source code.
(2) On display screens, a specific row of text or row of dots.
(3) In communications, a specific communications channel.

line of code

A statement in a source program. In assembly language, it usually generates one machine instruction, but in a high-level language, it may generate a series of instructions.
Lines of code are used to measure the complexity of a program. However, comparisons are misleading if the programs are not in the same language or category. For example, 20 lines of code in COBOL might require 200 lines of code in assembly language.

line of sight

An unobstructed view from transmitter to receiver.

line printer

A printer that prints one line at a time. Line printers are usually connected to mainframes and minicomputers. See *printer*.

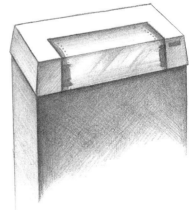

Line Printer

line segment

In vector graphics, same as *vector*.

line speed

See *data rate*.

line squeeze

In a mail merge, the elimination of blank lines when printing names and addresses that contain no data in certain fields, such as title, company and second address line. See *field squeeze*.

Without line squeeze	With line squeeze
Pat Smith 10 South Main Bearcat, OR 80901	Pat Smith 10 South Main Bearcat, OR 80901

link

(1) In communications, a line, channel or circuit over which data is transmitted.
(2) In data management, a pointer embedded within a record that refers to data or the location of data in another record.
(3) In programming, a call to another program or subroutine.

linkage editor

A utility program that links a compiled or assembled program to a particular environment. It formally unites references between program modules and libraries of subroutines. Its output is a load module, a program ready to run in the computer.

link edit

To use a linkage editor to prepare a program for running.

linked list

In data management, a group of items, each of which points to the next item. It allows for the organization of a sequential set of data in noncontiguous storage locations.

linker

See *linkage editor*.

Link Support Layer

See *LSL*.

Linpack

A package of FORTRAN programs for numerical linear algebra that is commonly used to create benchmark programs for testing a computer's floating point performance.

Linux

A freeware version of a clone of the UNIX System V Release 3.0 kernel that runs on x86 machines. It is available on programming BBSs and on the Internet.

LIPS

(Logical Inferences Per Second) The unit of measurement of the thinking speed of an AI application. Humans do about 2 LIPS. In the computer, one LIPS equals from 100 to 1,000 instructions.

liquid crystal display

See *LCD*.

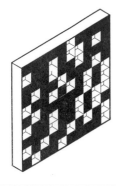

liquid crystal shutters

A method of directing light onto the drum in an electrophotographic printer. A matrix of liquid crystal dots function as shutters that are opened and closed. See *LCD*.

Lisa

The first personal computer to include integrated software and use a graphical interface. Modeled after the Xerox Star and introduced in 1983 by Apple, it was ahead of its time, but never caught on due to its $10,000 price and slow speed. The Macintosh came out a year later and a much lower price offering most of the Lisa's capabilities.

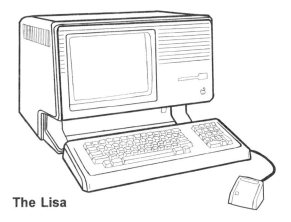

The Lisa

LISP

(LISt Processing) A high-level programming language used in non-numeric programming. Developed in 1960 by John McCarthy, its syntax and structure is very different than traditional programming languages. For example, there is no syntactic difference between data and instructions.

LISP, available in both interpreter and compiler versions, is used extensively in AI applications as well as in compiler creation. The language can be modified and expanded by the programmer. Many varieties of LISP have been developed, including versions that perform calculations efficiently. The following Common LISP example converts Fahrenheit to Celsius:

```
(defun convert ()
  (format t "Enter Fahrenheit ")
  (let ((fahr (read)))
   (format t "Celsius is <126>D"
     (truncate (*(-fahr 32)
        (/ 5 9)))))))
```

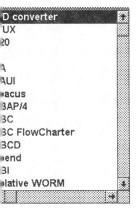

List Box

list

(1) An arranged set of data, often in row and column format.
(2) In fourth-generation languages, a command that displays/prints selected records. For example, in dBASE, **list name address** displays all names and addresses in the current file.

list box

An on-screen display of text items in a scrollable window. For example, the DOS and Windows versions of this database use a list box for the index of terms.

listing

Any printed output.

list processing

Processing non-numeric data.

list processing language

A programming language, such as LISP, Prolog and Logo, used to process lists of data (names, words, objects). Although operations such as selecting the next to first, or next to last element, or reversing all elements in a list, can be programmed in any language, list processing languages provide commands to do them. Recursion is also provided, allowing a subroutine to call itself over again in order to repetitively analyze a group of elements.

literal

In programming, any part of an instruction that remains unchanged when translated into machine language, such as an output message.

lithium ion

A rechargeable battery technology that provides more than twice the charge per pound as nickel hydride. Although used in camcorders and other devices, Toshiba introduced the first lithium ion notebook in the U.S. in late 1993.
Lithium polymer technology may provide twice as much power as lithium ion and be able to keep a notebook powered all day long, but this technology is not expected to appear until at least 1996.

little endian

See *big endian*.

liveware

People.

LLC

(Logical Link Control) See "LANs" under *data link protocol*.

LLCC

See *leadless chip carrier*.

load

(1) To copy a program from some source, such as a disk or tape, into memory for execution. See *boot*.
(2) To fill up a disk with data or programs.
(3) To insert a disk or tape into a drive.
(4) In programming, to store data in a register.
(5) In performance measurement, the current use of a system as a percentage of total capacity.
(6) In electronics, the flow of current through a circuit.

load balancing

The fine tuning of a computer system, network or disk subsystem in order to more evenly distribute the data and/or processing across available resouces.

loaded

Brought into the computer and ready to go. See *load*.

loaded line

A telephone line from customer to central office that uses loading coils to reduce distortion.

loader, loading routine

A program routine that copies a program into memory for execution.

load high

In a PC, to load drivers and TSRs into the upper memory area between 640KB and 1MB. The DOS Loadhigh command is used in the AUTOEXEC.BAT file.

loading coil

A device used in local telephone loops (exceeding 18,000 ft.) that boosts voice-grade transmission. It often adds noise to high-speed data transmission and must be removed for such traffic.

load module

A program in machine language form ready to run in the computer. It is the output of a link editor.

load sharing

Sharing the workload in two or more computers.

lobe length

In a Token Ring network, the length of cable between the MAU and the workstation.

local area network

See *LAN*.

local bus

A pathway between the CPU, memory and peripheral devices that runs at the speed of the CPU. In a PC, the VL-bus (VESA bus) and PCI bus tap into the CPU's local bus to provide faster data transfer than the traditional ISA bus. Since 1994, ISA and EISA motherboards have been built with VL-bus or PCI buses, or both, and contain extra slots to accomodate VL-bus and/or PCI expansion boards.

Starting with the 386, PCs have been built with two buses. The CPU accesses its memory chips via a 32-bit (64 on the Pentium) internal path, known as the local bus, at the full clock speed of the CPU (25MHz, 33MHz, etc.). However, it has traditionally accessed its peripheral devices more slowly; over a 16-bit ISA bus at 8MHz. Even the inherently-faster 32-bit EISA bus runs slow in order to accomodate ISA boards, which plug into it.

The VL-bus runs at up to 40MHz, and PCI runs at 33MHz. Although these buses are called *local buses*, in high-speed machines, such as 50MHz 486s and Pentiums, this nomenclature is technically erroneous, since they run slower than the local buses of those CPUs. However, faster VL-bus and PCI bus speeds are expected.

Bus Speed Comparisons

Bus type	Width	Speed	Total rate
ISA	16 bits	8MHz	16MB
EISA	32 bits	8MHz	32MB
VL-bus	32 bits	25MHz	100MB
VL-bus	32 bits	33MHz	132MB
PCI	32 bits	33MHz	132MB
PCI	64 bits	33MHz	264MB

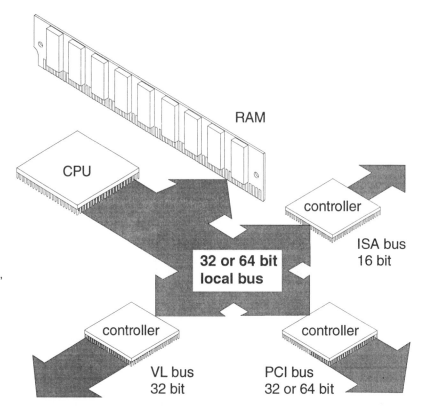

RAM

Local Bus
The peripheral controller cards plug into slots on the ISA, PCI and VLbus buses (disk controller, display adapter, serial port, parallel port, SCSI controller, scanner card, CD-ROM card, sound card, etc.).

CPU

controller

32 or 64 bit local bus

ISA bus
16 bit

controller

controller

VL bus
32 bit

PCI bus
32 or 64 bit

local bypass
An interconnection between two facilities without the use of the local telephone company.

local console
A terminal or workstation directly connected to the computer or other device that it is monitoring and controlling.

local drive
A disk or tape drive connected to the user's computer. Contrast with *network drive*.

local loop
A communications line between a customer and the telephone company's central office. See *loop carrier*.

local memory
The memory used by a single CPU or allocated to a single program or function.

local resource
A peripheral device, such as a disk, modem or printer, that is directly connected to a user's personal computer. Contrast with *remote resource*.

local storage
The disk storage used by a single CPU.

LocalTalk

A LAN access method from Apple that uses twisted pair wires and transmits at 230,400 bps. It runs under AppleTalk and uses a daisy chain topology that can connect up to 32 devices within a distance of 1,000 feet. Third party products allow it to hook up with bus, passive star and active star topologies.

Apple's LocalTalk PC Card lets a PC gain access to an AppleTalk network.

local variable

In programming, a variable used only within the routine or function it is defined in.

lock manager

Software that provides file and record locking for multiple computer systems or processors that share a single database.

lockup

Refers to a computer's inability to respond to user input. See *abend*.

log

A record of computer activity used for statistical purposes as well as backup and recovery.

logic

The sequence of operations performed by hardware or software. Hardware logic is made up of circuits that perform an operations. Software logic (program logic) is the sequence of instructions in a program. See *algorithm*.

Note: Logic is not the same as logical. See *logical vs physical* and *logical expression*.

logical

(1)A reasonable solution to a problem.

(2)A higher level view of an object; for example, the user's view versus the computer's view. See *logical vs physical*.

logical data group

Data derived from several sources. Same as *view*.

logical drive

An allocated part of a physical drive that is designated and managed as an independent unit. For example, drives C:, D: and E: could represent three physical drives or one physical drive partitioned into three logical drives.

logical expression

An expression that results in true or false. Same as *Boolean expression*.

logical field

A data field that contains a yes/no, true/false condition.

logical lock

The prevention of user access to data that is provided by marking the file or record through the use of software. Contrast with *physical lock*.

logical operator

One of the Boolean logical operators (AND, OR and NOT).

logical record

A reference to a data record that is independent of its physical location. It may be physically stored in two or more locations.

Logical Unit

See *LU* and *LU 6.2*.

logical vs physical

High-level versus low-level. Logical implies a higher view than the physical. Users relate to data logically by data element name; however, the actual fields of data are physically located in sectors on a disk. For example, if you want to know which customers ordered how many of a particular product, your logical view is customer name and quantity. Its physical organization might have customer name in a customer file and quantity in an order file cross referenced by customer number. The physical sequence of the customer file could be indexed, while the sequence of the order file could be sequential.

A message transmitted from Phoenix to Boston logically goes between two cities; however, the physical circuit could be Phoenix to Chicago to Philadelphia to Boston. When you command your program to change the output from the video screen to the printer, that's a logical request. The program will perform the physical change of address from, say, device number 02 to device number 04.

logic analyzer

(1) A device that monitors computer performance by timing various segments of the running programs. The total running time and the time spent in selected progam modules is displayed in order to isolate the the least efficient code.

(2) A device used to test and diagnose an electronic system, which includes an oscilloscope for displaying various digital states.

logic array

Same as *gate array* or *PLA*.

logic bomb

A program routine that destroys data; for example, it may reformat the hard disk or insert random bits into data files. It may be brought into a personal computer by downloading a corrupt public-domain program. Once executed, it does its damage right away, whereas a virus keeps on destroying.

logic chip

A processor or controller chip. Contrast with *memory chip*.

logic circuit

A circuit that performs some processing or controlling function. Contrast with *memory*.

logic controller

See *PLC*.

logic diagram

A flow chart of hardware circuits or program logic.

logic error

A program bug due to an incorrect sequence of instructions.

logic gate

A collection of transistors and electronic components that make up a Boolean logical operation, such as AND, NAND, OR and NOR. Transistors make up logic gates. Logic gates make up circuits. Circuits make up electronic systems.

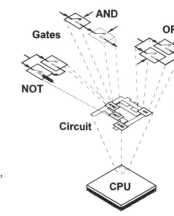

logic operation

An operation that analyzes one or more inputs and generates a particular output based on a set of rules. See *AND, OR & NOT* and *Boolean logic*.

logic-seeking printer

A printer that analyzes line content and skips over blank spaces at high speeds.

login

Same as *logon*.

Logo

A high-level programming language noted for its ease of use and graphics capabilities. It is a recursive language that contains many list processing functions that are in LISP, although Logo's syntax is more understandable for novices. Logo's graphics language is called turtle graphics, which allows complex graphics images to be created with a minimum of coding. The turtle is a triangular-shaped cursor, which is moved on screen with commands that activate the turtle as if you were driving it, for example, go forward 100 units, turn right 45 degrees, turn left 20 degrees.

Stemming from a National Science Foundation project, Logo was created by Seymour Papert in the mid 1960s along with colleagues at MIT and members of Bolt Beranek & Newman. Originally developed on large computers, it has been adapted to most personal computers.

The following Object Logo example converts Fahrenheit to Celsius:

```
convert
local [fahr]
print " Enter Fahrenheit
make "fahr ReadWord
print " Celsius is
print (:fahr - 32) * 5 / 9
end
```

log off

To quit, or sign off, a computer system.

logoff

The process of quitting, or signing off, a computer system. To *log off* is the verb.

log on

To gain access, or sign in, to a computer system. If access is restricted, it requires users to identify themselves by entering an ID number and/or password. Service bureaus often base their charges for the time between logon and logoff.

logon

The process of gaining access, or signing in, to a computer system. To *log on* is the verb. If access is restricted, it requires users to identify themselves by entering an ID number and/or password. Service bureaus often base their charges for the time between logon and logoff.

logout

Same as *logoff.*

long

In programming, an integer variable. In C, a long is four bytes and can be signed (-2G to +2G) or unsigned (4G). Contrast with *short*.

long card

In PCs, a full-length controller board that plugs into an expansion slot. Contrast with *short card.*

Short Card

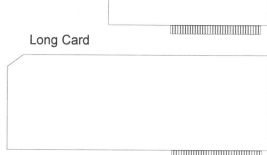

Long Card

long file names

File names that exceed the common eight plus three (8.3) character limitation used in DOS and Windows 3.1. UNIX, Mac and Windows 95 support long file names.dos

long-haul

In communications, modems or communications devices that are capable of transmitting over long distances.

long lines

In communications, circuits that are capable of handling transmissions over long distances.

LONWORKS

A control network from Echelon Corporation, Palo Alto, CA, that uses Echelon's NEURON CHIP (made by Motorola and Toshiba) and LONTALK protocol. Each NEURON CHIP uses a 48-bit number for identification. Control modules that contain the NEURON CHIP and transceivers for transmitting via RS-485, twisted pair, coax and AC power lines are available on credit card-sized boards.
The LONBUILDER development system is used to create applications, which are written into PROM chips. LONWORKS software, as well as programming interfaces for DOS and Windows, provide node installation and network management.

look and feel

Generally refers to the user interface of a program, especially with regard to its similarity to other programs. This issue has been and will continue to be hotly contested in the courts, because some programs look and function like others, and the original developer sometimes gets upset about it.
Oddly enough, programming languages have never been copyrighted or patented, which allows a developer to write a compiler that translates an language identical to one already in use. However, when a vendor sells a software package that looks and feels like another, it is subject to litigation, and look and feel cases have been won in the U.S. courts.

lookup

A data search performed within a predefined table of values (array, matrix, etc.) or within a data file.

loop

In programming, a repetition within a program. Whenever a process must be repeated, a loop is set up to handle it. A program has a main loop and a series of minor loops, which are nested within the main loop. Learning how to set up loops is what programming technique is all about.

The following example prints an invoice. The main loop reads the order record and prints the invoice until there are no more orders to read. After printing date and name and addresses, the program prints a variable number of line items. The code that prints the line items is contained in a loop and repeated as many times as required.

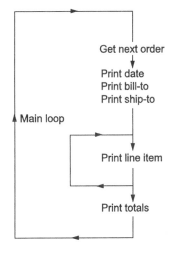

Get next order

Print date
Print bill-to
Print ship-to

Main loop

Print line item

Print totals

Loops are accomplished by various programming structures that have a beginning, body and end. The beginning generally tests the condition that keeps the loop going. The body comprises the repeating statements, and the end is a GOTO that points back to the beginning. In assembly language, the programmer writes the GOTO, as in the following example that counts to 10.

```
        MOVE    "0" TO COUNTER
LOOP    ADD     "1" TO COUNTER
        COMPARE COUNTER TO "10"
        GOTO    LOOP IF UNEQUAL
        STOP
```

In high-level languages, the GOTO is generated by the interpreter or compiler; for example, the same routine as above using a WHILE loop.

```
COUNTER = 0
DO WHILE COUNTER <> 10
COUNTER = COUNTER + 1
ENDDO
STOP
```

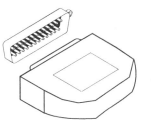

loopback plug

A diagnostic connector that directs the sending line back into the receiving line for test purposes.

loop carrier

In telephone communications, a system that concentrates a number of analog or digital lines from a remote termination station into the central office. It normally converts analog voice into digital at the remote station; however, it can be adapted to provide ISDN service to a customer.

loosely coupled

Refers to stand-alone computers connected via a network. Loosely coupled computers process on their own and exchange data on demand. Contrast with *tightly coupled.*

lo-res

See *low resolution.*

lossless compression

Compression techniques that decompress data 100% back to original. Contrast with *lossy compression.*

lossy compression

Compression techniques that do not decompress data 100% back to original. Images and audio samples may be able to afford small losses of resolution in order to increase compression. Contrast with *lossless compression.*

lost cluster

Disk records that have lost their identification with a file name. This can happen if a file is not closed properly, which can sometimes occur if the computer is turned off without formally quitting an application.

Lotus

(Lotus Development Corporation, Cambridge, MA) A major software company founded in 1981 by Mitch Kapor. It achieved outstanding success by introducing the first spreadsheet for the IBM PC (see *Lotus 1-2-3*). Over the years, it has developed a variety of applications and has helped set industry standards. In 1990, it acquired Samna Corporation, developers of the popular, Windows-based Ami word processors. In 1995, Lotus was acquired by and is a wholly owned subsidiary of IBM.

Lotus 1-2-3

The most widely-used spreadsheet application with over 20 million copies installed worldwide. It runs on DOS, Windows, Macintosh, Sun, VAX, OS/2, UNIX and IBM mainframe platforms. Major development effort centers on Windows, OS/2 and DOS. Starting with Version 3.0, it provides 3-D and dynamic linking capabilities.

Mitchell D. Kapor
(Photo courtesy of Kapor Enterprises, Inc.)

The first 1-2-3 (DOS) shipped in January 1983 under a well-organized marketing campaign. It was the first innovative spreadsheet for the IBM PC. The 1-2-3 stood for the integration of spreadsheet, database and graphics. Its ability to function like a simple database was unique, and turning data into a chart with a single keystroke was dazzling for its time. The program's user interface was also easier to use than other programs.

Lotus Notes

A groupware program from Lotus that runs in a client/server environment under Windows, OS/2 and various UNIX platforms. Notes provides e-mail and outbound fax capability, document sharing and replication and a development environment for workflow applications.

Notes allows multiple users throughout an organization to share and edit documents. Files can be attached to Notes documents so that images and other types of data can be included. Notes keeps the documents in sync. When a change is made to a document, those changes are replicated in other Notes servers at different locations. Notes is also popular for its threaded discussion capability, in which a running log of comments and opinions about a subject is maintained.

As of Release 3, a Windows PC can be a Notes server, and it supports any VIM-compliant e-mail system such as cc:Mail.

In 1994, programming interfaces were introduced to add multimedia capability. Phone Notes lets users access Notes functionality via telephone and listen to Notes databases via text-to-speech facilities. It allows voice annotations to be embedded into Notes databases as well. Video Notes lets video be embedded.

Lotus Notes Visual Programmer

Also known as Notes ViP, it is a graphical development system for Windows from Lotus that is used to create custom Lotus Notes applications.

low density

Refers to an earlier version of a storage device with less bits per inch than today's version. See *DD* and *double density*.

lower CASE

See *back-end CASE*.

low frequency

An electromagnetic wave that vibrates in the range from 30 to 300,000 Hertz.

low-level format

The sector identification on a disk that the drive uses to locate sectors for reading and writing. See *format program*.

low-level language

A programming language that is very close to machine language. All assembly languages are low-level languages. Contrast with *high-level language*.

low radiation

Refers to video terminals that emit less VLF (Very Low Frequency) and ELF (Extremely Low Frequency) radiation. This level of radiation cannot be shielded by office partitions. It must be cancelled out from the CRT. Health studies on this are not conclusive and are very controversial. See *MPR II*.

low resolution

A low-grade display or printing quality due to a lower number of dots or lines per inch.

lpi

(Lines Per Inch) The number of lines printed in a vertical inch.

lpm

(Lines Per Minute) The number of lines a printer can print or a scanner can scan in a minute.

LPT1

In a PC, the logical name assigned to parallel port #1. The parallel port is typically used for the printer. A second parallel port, if installed, is assigned to LPT2. Contrast with *COM1*.

LQ

See *letter quality*.

LRC

(Longitudinal Redundancy Check) An error checking method that generates a parity bit from a specified string of bits on a longitudinal track. In a row and column format, such as on magnetic tape, LRC is often used with VRC, which creates a parity bit for each character.

LSAPI

(Licensing Service API) A programming interface from Microsoft that allows a licensing server to track applications in use for managing multiuser software licenses.

LSI

(Large Scale Integration) Between 3,000 and 100,000 transistors on a chip. See *SSI, MSI, VLSI* and *ULSI*.

LSI-11

A family of board-level computers from Digital that uses the micro version of the PDP-11. Introduced in 1974, it was the first to use the Q-bus.

LSL

(Link Support Layer) A common interface for network drivers. It provides a common language between the transport layer and the data link layer and allows different transport protocols to run over one network adapter or one transport protocol to run on different network adapters.

Instead of directly calling a particular data link protocol, the transport protocol calls the LSL library. Thus, any LSL-compliant network driver can provide data link services in that protocol stack. LSL is part of UNIX System V. It is also the basis of Novell and Apple's ODI specification. See *ODI* and *STREAMS*.

LT

(Less Than) See *relational operator*.

LU

(Logical Unit) In SNA, one end of a communications session. The complete LU to LU session is defined by session type. Common types are:

1	Host to 3770 RJE terminal
2	Host to 3270 mainframe terminal
3	Host to 3270 printer
6.2	Program-to-program
7	Host to 5250 midrange terminal

LU 6.2

An SNA protocol that establishes a session between two programs. It allows peer-to-peer communications as well as interaction between programs running in the host with PCs, Macs and midrange computers.

Before LU 6.2, processing was done only in the mainframe. LU 6.2 allows processing to take place at both ends of the communications, necessary for today's distributed computing and client/server environment. See *APPC* and *CPI-C*.

lumen

A unit of measurement of the flow (rate of emission) of light. A wax candle generates 13 lumens; a 100 watt bulb generates 1,200. See *candela*.

Lumena

A PC paint program from Time Arts, Inc., Santa Rosa, CA, that provides sophisticated, special effects. It accepts and generates NTSC video output and requires a video graphics board.

luminance

The amount of brightness, measured in lumens, that is given off by a pixel or area on a screen. It is the black/gray/white information in a video signal.

LUN

(Logical Unit Number) The physical number of a device in a daisy change of drives. See *SCSI*.

LZW

(Lempel-Ziv-Welch) A widely-used dictionary compression method that stems from two techniques introduced by Jacob Ziv and Abraham Lempel. LZ77 scans a fixed length block of data and creates pointers back to data when it repeats. LZ78 scans the data and creates a dictionary of repeating phrases. Pointers are created to those phrases.

M

Mac "Classic"

M

See *mega.*

M1

The code name for a Pentium-class CPU chip from Cyrix Corporation. It is expected to be available in volume by mid 1995.

Mac

(1) See *Macintosh.*
(2) (MAC) (Mandatory Access Control) A security control that requires clearance levels. See *NCSC.*
(3) See *MAC layer.*

MacAPPC

LU 6.2-compliant software from Apple Computer that allows a Macintosh to be a peer to an IBM APPC application.

Mac clone

A non-Apple Power Macintosh. In late 1994, Apple began to license its operating system and hardware technologies to third-parties so that they could build PowerPC-based Macintoshes. The first models appeared in the spring of 1995. Radius and Power Computing were two of the first companies.

Many have argued that if Apple had licensed its technology years ago, Macintosh ownership would be much larger than it is today, which is approximately 10% of the personal computer market. Stay tuned!

MacDFT

Software that provides 3270 emulation for the Macintosh from Apple. It accompanies Apple's TwinAx/Coax board and supports CUT and DFT modes and DFT multiple sessions under SNA.

MacDraw Pro

A Macintosh drawing program from Claris Corporation that is an enhanced version of the original MacDraw from Apple and includes full on-screen slide presentation capability. It is used for illustrations and elementary CAD work. MacDraw files are a subset of the Claris CAD file format.

Mach

A UNIX-like operating system developed at Carnegie-Mellon University. It is designed with a microkernel architecture that makes it easily portable to different platforms.

machine

Any electronic or electromechanical unit of equipment. A machine is always hardware; however, "engine" refers to hardware or software.

machine address

Same as *absolute address.*

machine code

Same as *machine language.*

machine cycle

The shortest interval in which an elementary operation can take place within the processor. It is made up of some number of clock cycles.

machine dependent

Refers to software that accesses specific hardware features and runs in only one kind of computer. Contrast with *machine independent*. See *device dependent*.

machine independent

Refers to software that runs in a variety of computers. The hardware-specific instructions are in some other program (operating system, DBMS, etc.). Contrast with *machine dependent*. See *device independent*.

machine instruction

An instruction in machine language. Its anatomy is a verb followed by one or more nouns:

OP CODE   OPERANDS (one or more)
(verb)   (nouns)

The op code is the operation to be performed (add, copy, etc.), while the operands are the data to be acted upon (add a to b). There are always machine instructions to INPUT and OUTPUT, to process data by CALCULATING, COMPARING and COPYING it, and to go to some other part of the program with a GOTO instruction. See *hardware platforms* and *computer*.

machine language

The native language of the computer. In order for a program to run, it must be presented to the computer as binary-coded machine instructions that are specific to that CPU model or family. Although programmers are sometimes able to modify machine language in order to fix a running program, they do not create it. Machine language is created by programs called *assemblers, compilers* and *interpreters*, which convert the lines of programming code a human writes into the machine language the computer understands.

Machine language tells the computer what to do and where to do it. When a programmer writes: **total = total + subtotal**, that statement is converted into a machine instruction that tells the computer to add the contents of two areas of memory (where TOTAL and SUBTOTAL are stored).

A programmer deals with data logically, "add this, subtract that," but the computer must be told precisely where this and that are located.

Machine languages differ substantially. What may take one instruction in one machine can take 10 instructions in another. See *hardware platforms, assembly language* and *interpreter*.

machine readable

Data in a form that can be read by the computer, which includes disks, tapes and punched cards. Printed fonts that can be scanned and recognized by the computer are also machine readable.

Machine Language

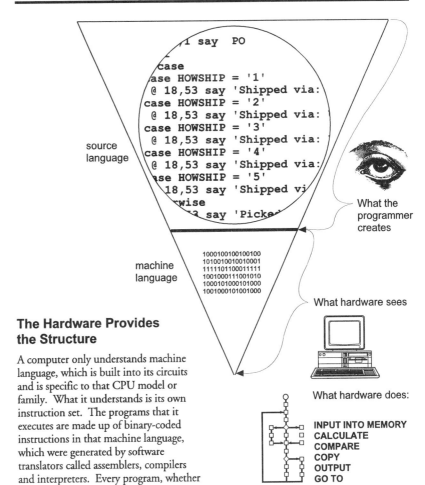

```
      /I say  PO
    /case
   /ase HOWSHIP = '1'
  / @ 18,53 say 'Shipped via:
 |  case HOWSHIP = '2'
 |  @ 18,53 say 'Shipped via:
 |  case HOWSHIP = '3'
 |   @ 18,53 say 'Shipped via:
 \  case HOWSHIP = '4'
  \ @ 18,53 say 'Shipped via:
   \se HOWSHIP = '5'
    \18,53 say 'Shipped vi
     \wise
      \3 say 'Picke
```

source language

machine language

```
1000100100100100
1010010010010001
1111101100011111
1001000111001010
1000101000101000
1001000101001000
```

What the programmer creates

What hardware sees

What hardware does:

INPUT INTO MEMORY
CALCULATE
COMPARE
COPY
OUTPUT
GO TO

The Hardware Provides the Structure

A computer only understands machine language, which is built into its circuits and is specific to that CPU model or family. What it understands is its own instruction set. The programs that it executes are made up of binary-coded instructions in that machine language, which were generated by software translators called assemblers, compilers and interpreters. Every program, whether it is a business application programmed inhouse or a commercial program purchased outside, must be available in the machine language of the computer you want to run it on, or you can't use it.

Programmers write in a programming language, which may be close to the machine or many levels removed from it. The goal for the business organization is to describe the problem, not the logic of how it must be programmed. The goal is achieved somewhat in the form of application generators and CASE (computer-aided software engineering) tools, but the great majority of programs are written in exacting detail by the programmer.

Macintosh

A series of 32-bit personal computers from Apple introduced in 1984. It uses the Motorola 68000 CPU family and an operating system that simulates a user's desktop on screen. The Mac's graphics-based user interface has provided a measure of consistency and ease of use that is unmatched. The Macintosh family is the largest non-IBM compatible personal computer series in use.

Introduced in 1984 as a floppy-based computer with 128K of memory, its "high-rise" cabinet and built-in 9" monochrome screen were unique. This design is retained in the Classic model, while the rest of the line is now clothed in traditional cabinetry.

In 1994, Apple introduced the PowerMacs, the next generation of Macintoshes, which use the PowerPC CPU chip. PowerMacs run native PowerPC applications and emulate traditional Macintosh 680x0 applications as well as DOS and Windows applications.

Mac "Classic"   **PowerMac**

Macintosh extension

Additional software functions for the Macintosh, which include drivers and other enhancements to the operating system. In System 7, system extensions reside in the Extensions folder. Mac extensions are the counterpart to the CONFIG.SYS file for DOS.

Macintosh Toolbox

Software routines that perform the graphical user interface functions in the Macintosh. Apple is licensing the Mac Toolbox to vendors developing a version of PowerOpen for the PowerPC. This is the first time Apple has licensed the Toolbox. See *MAS*.

Macintosh user interface

The method of operating a Macintosh, which was originally developed by Xerox and introduced on the Xerox Star in 1981. It uses a graphics-based screen that places familiar objects on a two-dimensional desktop. Programs, files, folders and disks are represented by small pictures (icons). An object is selected by moving a mouse over the real desktop, which correspondingly moves a pointer on the screen desktop. When the pointer touches an icon, the object is selected by clicking the mouse button.

A hierarchical file system is provided that lets a user "drag" a document icon into and out of a folder icon. Folders can also contain other folders. To delete a document, its icon is literally dragged into a trash can icon.

The Macintosh always displays a row of menu titles at the top of the screen. The full menu appears as if it were pulled down from the top of the screen when selected. With the mouse button held down, the option within the menu is selected by pointing to it and releasing the button.

Unlike the PC world, which, before Windows, left the design of the user interface up to the software developer, Macintosh developers always conform to the Mac interface. As a result, users feel more comfortable with new programs from the start. In operation, the operating system and applications are almost indistinguishable, and Apple keeps technical jargon to a minimum.

Early Mac applications had little regard for experienced typists, forcing them to use the mouse instead of well-designed keyboard commands. Subsequent versions offer both methods and have greatly improved.

The Macintosh style has been adapted to many environments, including Windows, OS/2 and Motif.

MacIRMA

A 3270 emulator board for the Macintosh from Attachmate Corporation, Bellevue, WA. It is the Macintosh counterpart of the IRMA board, the first 3270 emulator for PCs. See *Irma software*.

MAC layer

(Media Access Control layer) The protocol that controls access to the physical transmission medium on a LAN. The MAC layer is built into the network adapter. Common MAC layer standards are the CSMA/CD architecture used in Ethernet and the token passing methods used in Token Ring, FDDI and MAP. The MAC layer is synonymous with the data link layer in the OSI model. For a diagram, see "LANs" under *data link protocol*.

MacLink Plus

A Macintosh file transfer program from DataViz Corporation, Trumbull, CT, that provides document conversion for a wide variety of Mac and PC formats. Versions are also available for Sun, NeXT and Wang systems.

Mac OS

(MACintosh Operating System) In late 1994, Apple formally renamed its System 7 operating system Mac OS and introduced the Mac OS logo. However, the term has been used for years to refer to the current version of the operating system running in the Macintosh.

MacPaint II

A full-featured Macintosh paint program from Claris that was originally developed by Apple and bundled with every Mac up until the Mac Plus. MacPaint's PICT file format is used for printing the screen. By pressing Command-shift-3, the current screen is stored in a PICT file for printing either in MacPaint or other program.

macro

(1) A series of menu selections, keystrokes and/or commands that have been recorded and assigned a name or key combination. When the macro name is called or the macro key combination is pressed, the steps in the macro are executed from beginning to end.

Macros are used to shorten long menu sequences as well as to create miniature programs within an application. Macro languages often include programming controls (IF THEN, GOTO, WHILE, etc.) that automate sequences like any programming language. See *macro recorder*, *batch file* and *shell script*.

(2) In assembly language, a prewritten subroutine that is called for throughout the program. At assembly time, the macro calls are substituted with the actual subroutine or instructions that branch to it. The high-level language equivalent is a

function.

(3) In dBASE programming, a variable which references another variable that actually contains the data. At runtime, the macro variable is substituted with the data variable.

macro assembler

An assembly language that allows macros to be defined and used.

macro call

Same as *macro instruction*.

macro generator

See *macro recorder*.

macro instruction

An instruction that defines a macro. In assembly language, MACRO and ENDM are examples that define the beginning and end of a macro. In C, the #DEFINE statement is used.

macro language

(1) Commands used by a macro processor. Same as *script*.
(2) An assembly language that uses macros.

Macromedia

(Macromedia, Inc., San Francisco, CA) A software company specializing in multimedia authoring tools. It was founded in 1992 by the merger of Aurhorware, Inc., which was founded in 1984, and MacroMind-Paracomp. Macromind was founded in 1984 and merged with Paracomp in 1991. Its primary products are Aurthorware Professional and Macromedia Director, both for Macintosh and Windows.

Macromedia Freehand

A full-featured drawing program for Windows and Macintosh from Macromedia. It combines a wide range of drawing tools with special effects. FreeHand was first available on the Mac and was originally Aldus Freehand from Aldus Corporation.

MacroMind

See *Macromedia*.

macro processor

(1) Software that creates and executes macros from the keyboard.
(2) The part of an assembler that substitutes the macro subroutines for the macro calls.

macro recorder

A program routine that converts menu selections and keystrokes into a macro. A user turns on the recorder, calls up a menu, selects a variety of options, turns the recorder off and assigns a key command to the macro. When the key command is pressed, the selections are executed.

MacTerminal

Macintosh terminal emulation software from Apple that allows a Mac to function as an IBM 3278 Model 2 (when used with an AppleLine Protocol Converter) or Digital VT 52 or VT 100 terminal.

Mac to midrange

Using the Macintosh as the terminal to IBM S/3x and AS/400 computers. Apple and third party connectivity products add local processing and a friendly interface to IBM midrange computers.

MacTwin

Mac to IBM midrange connectivity from Andrew/KMW, which includes a card for the Mac that connects to the twinax cabling from the S/3x or AS/400. Software for the Mac provides 5250, 3196 and 3197 emulation.

MacWrite II

A full-featured Macintosh word processing program from Claris Corporation, that was originally packaged with every Mac 128 and 512.

mag

Abbreviation for "magnetic."

magazine style columns

Text that is displayed in side-by-side columns. The text flows from the bottom of one column to the top of the next column on the same page.

Magazine Columns

Magellan

The PC disk management utility from Lotus that popularized the file viewer. A file viewer lets you look into various data files as if you were using the applications that created them.

Magic Cap

(Magic Communicating Applications Platform) An object-oriented control program from General Magic for personal intelligent communicating devices (PDAs, hand-held units, etc.) that includes the Telescript language. See *Telescript* and *PersonaLink*.

Magic Link

A PDA from Sony that uses the Magic Cap operating system and includes an infrared port, fax/modem and PCMCIA slot. It has a built-in PIM and direct connection to AT&T's PersonaLink service, which requires a phone jack for communication.

magnetic card

(1) See *magnetic stripe*.
(2) Magnetic tape strips used in early data storage devices and word processors. See *CRAM, RACE* and *Data Cell*.

magnetic coercivity

The amount of energy required to alter the state of a magnet. The higher a magnetic disk's coercivity index, the more data it can store.

magnetic disk

The primary computer storage device. Like tape, it is magnetically recorded and can be re-recorded over and over. Disks are rotating platters with a mechanical arm that moves a read/write head between the outer and inner edges of the platter's surface. It can take as long as one second to find a location on a floppy disk to as short as one millisecond on an ultra-fast hard disk. See *floppy disk* and *hard disk*.

Tracks and Sectors

The disk surface is divided into concentric tracks (circles within circles). The thinner the tracks, the more storage. The data bits are recorded as tiny spots on the tracks. The tinier the spot, the more bits per inch and the greater the storage. Most disks hold the same number of bits on each track, even though the outer tracks are physically longer than the inner ones. Some disks pack the bits as tightly as possible within each track.

Tracks are further divided into sectors, which hold the least amount of data that can be read or written at one time; for example, READ TRACK 7 SECTOR 24. In order to update the disk, one or more sectors are read into the computer, changed and written back to disk. The operating system figures out how to fit data into these fixed spaces. See *hard disk, floppy disk* and *storage technologies*.

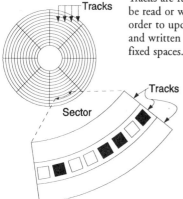

Sectors on a Disk

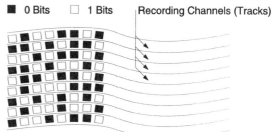

Recorded Bits on Magnetic Tape

magnetic disk & tape

The primary computer storage media. The choice depends on accessing requirements. Disk is direct access; tape is sequential access. Locating a program or data on disk can take a fraction of a second. On tape, it can take seconds or minutes.

On minis and mainframes, disks are used for daily transaction processing, and tapes are used for backup and history. Tapes have traditionally been more economical for archival storage and easier to transport than disk packs.

For personal computers, hard disks are used for all interactive processing, and both floppy disks and tapes are used for backup. Bernoulli disks and removable hard disks are increasingly becoming backup alternatives.

In time, magnetic disks may be as obsolete as punched cards. Optical disks are getting faster and cheaper, and optical technologies that employ no moving parts may supersede them all. Compared to the magical technology within the chip, whirling chunks of metal around is rather old fashioned, don't you think? See *holographic storage* and *storage technologies*.

magnetic drum

An early high-speed, direct access storage device that used a magnetic-coated cylinder with tracks around its circumference. Each track had its own read/write head.

magnetic field

An invisible energy emitted by a magnet. Same as *flux*.

magnetic ink

A magnetically detectable ink used to print the MICR characters that encode account numbers on bank checks.

magnetic oxide

See *ferric oxide*.

magnetic recording

With regard to computers, the technique used to record, or write, digital data in the form of tiny spots (bits) of negative or positive polarity on tapes and disks. A read/write head discharges electrical impulses onto the moving ferromagnetic surface. Reading is accomplished by sensing the polarity of the bit with the read/write head.

magnetic stripe

A small length of magnetic tape adhered to ledger cards, badges and credit cards. It is read by specialized readers that may be incorporated into accounting machines and terminals. Due to heavy wear, the data on the stripe is in a low-density format that may be duplicated several times.

magnetic tape

Tape Drive
The 1/2" reel-to-reel tape goes back to the early days and is still used.

A sequential storage medium used for data collection, backup and historical purposes. Like videotape, computer tape is made of flexible plastic with one side coated with a ferromagnetic material. Tapes come in reels, cartridges and cassettes of many sizes and shapes. Although still used, the 1/2" open-reel tape from the earliest days of computers has been mostly superseded by cartridges with enhanced storage capacities.

Locating a specific item on tape requires reading everything in front of it. There is no fast forward. In order to add and delete records, the current tape is input to the computer and a blank tape is used for output. If data on tape is only changed and the byte count is not altered, some tape drives can update in place by reading a block of data and writing back over the same area.

Except for QIC and DAT tape cartridges, which use serpentine and helical scan methods, data bits are recorded on parallel tracks that run the length of the tape. For example, 9-track tape holds one byte of data across the tape's width (8 bits plus parity). Mainframe tape cartridges use 18- and 36-track tape, placing two and four bytes across the width. Data is recorded in blocks of contiguous bytes, separated by a space called an interrecord or interblock gap.

Tape is more economical than disks for archival data. However, if tapes are stored for the duration, they must be periodically recopied or the tightly coiled magnetic surfaces may contaminate each other.

Storage capacity is measured in bits per inch (bpi). The once-widely-used 1/2" reel-to-reel tape formats store one byte from top to bottom on nine parallel tracks at 200, 556, 800, 1650 and 6250 bpi. IBM's 3480 and 3490 tape cartridges store two to four bytes on 18 or 36 parallel tracks at 38000 bpi.

Tape drive speed is measured in inches per second (ips), thus, transfer rate = ips X bpi. See *tape backup* and *storage technologies*.

magnetographic

A non-impact printer technology from Groupe Bull that prints up to 90 ppm. A magnetic image is created by a set of recording heads across a magnetic drum. Monocomponent toner is applied to the drum to develop the image, which is transferred to paper by light pressure and an electrostatic field. The toner is then fused by heat. The print quality is not as good as a laser printer, but the machines require less maintenance.

magneto-optic

A high-density, rewritable recording method that uses a combination of magnetic

3.5" Magneto-optic Cartridge

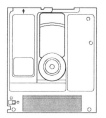

5.2c5" Magneto-optic Cartridge

disk and optical methods. Data is written by the use of a laser and a magnet. The recording material is initially magnetized in one direction. The laser focuses on one bit and heats the material to the Curie point, which is the temperature that allows the molecules to be realigned when subjected to a magnetic field. The magnet changes the polarity for that bit.

Reading is accomplished with a lower-power laser that reflects light from the bits. The light is rotated slightly depending on the polarity of the bit, and the difference in rotation is sensed. Writing takes two passes. The existing bits are set to zero in one pass, and data is written on the second pass. A newer direct overwrite method erases and writes in one rotation. See *Curie point, Kerr effect* and *optical disk*.

magnetoresistive

A technology used for the read element of a read/write head on a high-density magnetic disk. Such drives use a magnetoresistive read sensor for reading and an inductive element for writing. As storage capacity increases and the bit gets smaller, the magnetic field of the bit becomes weaker. The magnetoresistive head is more sensitive to magnetic fields than inductive read heads.

Magnetoresistance means that the resistance to electricity changes in a material when brought in contact with a magnetic field, in this case, the read element material and the magnetic bit.

Although this technology was used earlier in analog tape recorders, in 1991, IBM was the first manufacturer to use it as the read elements in computer disk drives. IBM is also involved in giant magnetoresistive (GMR) technology, which uses various thin film layers to produce a greater change in resistance and is even more sensistive than magnetoresistive (MR).

mail API

See *messaging API* and *MAPI*.

mailbox

A simulated mailbox on disk that holds incoming electronic mail.

mail enabled

Refers to an application that has built-in, although typically very limited, mail capabilities. For example, it can send or send and receive a file that it has created over one or more messaging systems. See *messaging API*.

mail merge

Printing customized form letters. A common feature of a word processor, it uses a letter and a name and address list. In the letter, Dear A: Thank you for ordering B from our C store..., A, B and C are merge points into which data is inserted from the list. See *field squeeze* and *line squeeze*.

mail protocol

See *messaging protocol* and *messaging system*.

mail system

See *electronic mail* and *messaging system*.

mainframe

A large computer. In the "ancient" mid 1960s, all computers were called mainframes, since the term referred to the main CPU cabinet. Today, it refers to a large computer system.

There are small, medium and large-scale mainframes, handling from a handful to several thousand online terminals. Large-scale mainframes can have hundreds of megabytes of main memory and terabytes of disk storage. Large mainframes use smaller computers as front end processors that connect to the communications networks.

Mainframe

A mainframe is a large-scale computer that can serve from hundreds to several thousands of users. IBM is the major vendor with its System/390 family and SNA networking architecture. An IBM mainframe was designed as a hierarchical system, in which the central machine has complete control. Over the years, extensions to SNA have allowed mainframes to participate in peer-to-peer and client/server environments.

In the SNA world, the primary input/output device is the 3270 terminal. 3270s can be replaced with PCs using 3270 emulation (hardware and software), which can conduct a session with the mainframe while running other DOS and Windows applications.

There is such a large investment in mainframe applications that the mainframe still plays a major role in enterprise computing. Although its demise is often predicted, chances are it will never go away. In fact, it may even play a larger role in time.

Whether dollar for dollar, they yield the greatest value, they still provide the fastest transaction processing performance into a single database than minicomputers.

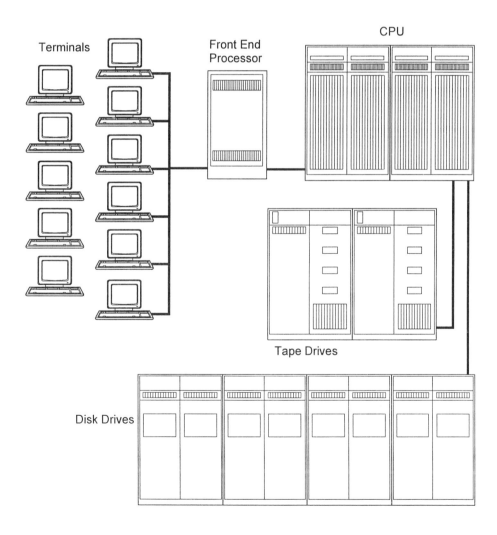

There Was a Time
There was a time when mainframes meant "complicated" and required the most expertise in programming and operations. That is no longer the case. PCs and PC networks make mainframes look easy. Nothing is more complicated than the PC/DOS/Windows environment. Add NetWare, Windows NT and other network operating systems, throw in a little UNIX for good measure, and you have enterprise computing at its most complex since the beginning of written history.

main line, main loop

The primary logic in a program. It contains the instructions that are repeated after each event or transaction has been processed. See *loop*.

main memory, main storage

Same as *memory*.

maintenance

(1) Hardware maintenance is the testing and cleaning of equipment.
(2) Information system maintenance is the routine updating of master files, such as adding and deleting employees and customers and changing credit limits and product prices.
(3) Software, or program, maintenance is the updating of application programs in order to meet changing information requirements, such as adding new functions and changing data formats. It also includes fixing bugs and adapting the software to new hardware devices.
(4) Disk or file maintenance is the periodic reorganizing of disk files that have become fragmented due to continuous updating.

maintenance credits

Monetary credits issued to a customer by the vendor for qualified periods during which the vendor's products are not functioning properly.

maintenance service

A service provided to keep a product in good operating condition.

major key

The primary key used to identify a record, such as account number or name.

make

To compile a multi-module program. The make utility recompiles only those modules that have been updated since the last compilation.

male connector

A plug that is designed to fit into a particular socket.

Maltron keyboard

A keyboard that uses independent left- and right-hand modules shaped to conform to the natural position of the hands, designed to prevent strain (RSI).

MAN

(Metropolitan Area Network) A communications network that covers a geographic area such as a city or suburb. See *LAN* and *WAN*.

management console

A terminal or workstation used to monitor and control a network.

management information system
See *MIS*.

management science
The study of statistical methods, such as linear programming and simulation, in order to analyze and solve organizational problems. Same as *operations research*.

management support
See *DSS* and *EIS*.

management system
The leadership and control within an organization. It is made up of people interacting with other people and machines that, together, set the goals and objectives, outline the strategies and tactics, and develop the plans, schedules and necessary controls to run an organization.

Manchester Code
A self-clocking data encoding method that divides the time required to define the bit into two cycles. The first cycle is the data value (0 or 1) and the second cylce provides the timing by shifting to the opposite state.

man machine interface
Same as *user interface*.

MANTIS
An application development language from Cincom Systems, Inc., Cincinnati, OH, that runs on IBM mainframes, VAXs and other mainframes. It provides procedural and non-procedural languages for developing prototypes and applications and works with Cincom's SUPRA database, DB2 and IMS.

mantissa
The numeric value in a floating point number. See *floating point*.

MAP
(Manufacturing Automation Protocol) A communications protocol introduced by General Motors in 1982. MAP provides common standards for interconnecting computers and programmable machine tools used in factory automation. At the lowest physical level, it uses the IEEE 802.4 token bus protocol.

MAP is often used in conjunction with *TOP*, an office protocol developed by Boeing Computer Services. TOP is used in the front office and MAP is used on the factory floor.

map
(1) A set of data that has a corresponding relationship to another set of data.
(2) A list of data or objects as they are currently stored in memory or disk.
(3) To transfer a set of objects from one place to another. For example, program modules on disk are mapped into memory. A graphic image in memory is mapped onto the video screen. An address is mapped to another address.
(4) To relate one set of objects with another. For example, a logical database structure is mapped to the physical database. A vendor's protocol stack is mapped to the OSI model.

MAPI
(Mail API) A programming interface that enables an application to send and receive mail over the Microsoft Mail messaging system. Simple MAPI is a subset of MAPI that includes a dozen functions for sending and retrieving mail.

MAPPER

(MAintaining, Preparing and Processing Executive Reports) A Unisys mainframe fourth-generation language. In 1980, it was introduced as a high-level report writer and was later turned into a full-featured development system used successfully by non-technical users.

mapping

See *map* and *digital mapping.*

marginal test

A system test that introduces values far above and far below the expected values.

mark

(1) A small blip printed on or notched into various storage media used for timing or counting purposes.

(2) To identify a block of text in order to perform some task on it such as deletion, copying and moving.

(3) To identify an item for future reference.

(4) In digital electronics, a 1 bit. Contrast with *space.*

(5) On magnetic disk, a recorded character used to identify the beginning of a track.

(6) In optical recognition and mark sensing, a pencil line in a preprinted box.

(7) On magnetic tape, a *tape mark* is a special character that is recorded after the last character of data.

Mark I

An electromechanical calculator designed by professor Howard Aiken, built by IBM and installed at Harvard in 1944. It strung 78 adding machines together to perform three calculations per second. It was 51 feet long, weighed five tons and used punched cards and typewriters for I/O. Made of 765,000 parts, it sounded like a thousand knitting needles according to Admiral Grace Hopper. The experience helped IBM develop its own computers a few years later.

Mark I
Five tons of gears to perform three calculations per second! *(Photo courtesy of Smithsonian Institution.)*

marking engine

See *printer engine.*

MARK IV

See *Crosstalk* and *MARK IX*.

MARK IX

An application generator from Sterling Software's Answer Systems Division, Woodland Hills, CA, that runs on IBM mainframes and personal computers. It stems from MARK IV, the first report writer to use fill-in-the-blanks forms. MARK V was a subsequent online version.

mark sensing

Detecting pencil lines in predefined boxes on paper forms. The form is designed with boundaries for each pencil stroke that represents a yes, no, single digit or letter, providing all possible answers to each question. A mark sense reader detects the marks and converts them into digital code.

markup language

See *SGML* and *HTML*.

MAS

(1) (Multiple Address System) A radio service in the 932-932.5 and 941-941.5Mhz frequency that covers a 25-mile radius from the antenna. It is used for sensor-based and transaction systems (ATMs, reservations, alarms, traffic control, etc.).

(2) (Multiple Award Schedule) A list of approved products available for purchase by U.S. government agencies.

(3) (Macintosh Application System) Software that allows a Macintosh 680x0 application to run in a PowerPC. It includes a 680x0 emulator and the Macintosh Toolbox, which contains the Mac's graphical functions. The Macintosh graphical user interface runs native in the PowerPC while only the Motorola 680x0 instructions are emulated.

mask

(1) A pattern used to transfer a design onto an object. See *photomask*.

(2) A pattern of bits used to accept or reject bit patterns in another set of data. For example, the Boolean AND operation can be used to match a mask of 0s and 1s with a string of data bits. When a 1 occurs in both the mask and the data, the resulting bit will contain a 1 in that position.

Hardware interrupts are often enabled and disabled in this manner with each interrupt assigned a bit position in a mask register.

maskable interrupts

Hardware interrupts that can be enabled and disabled by software.

mask bit

A 1 bit in a mask used to control the corresponding bit found in data.

masked

A state of being disabled or cut off.

MASM

See *macro assembler*.

massage

To process data.

massively parallel processor

See *MPP*.

mass storage

A high-capacity, external storage such as disk or tape.

master

Primary, controlling. See *master-slave communications* and *master file*.

master card

A master record in punched card format.

master clock

A clock that provides the primary source of internal timing for a processor or stand-alone control unit.

master console

The main terminal used by the computer operator or systems programmer to command the computer.

master control program

See *operating system*.

master file

A collection of records pertaining to one of the main subjects of an information system, such as customers, employees, products and vendors. Master files contain descriptive data, such as name and address, as well as summary information, such as amount due and year-to-date sales. Contrast with *transaction file*.

Following are the kinds of fields that make up a typical master record in a business information system. There can be many more fields depending on the organization. The "key" fields below are the ones that are generally indexed for matching against the transaction records as well as fast retrieval for queries. The account number is usually the primary key, but name may also be primary. There can be secondary indexes; for example, in an inverted file structure, almost all the fields could be indexed. See *transaction file* for examples of typical transaction records.

Sample Master Records (subjects)

Key Field		Fields					
Employee Number	Name	Address	Date of hire	Date of birth	Title	Job Class	Pay Rate
Customer Number	Name	Bill to	Ship to	Credit Limit	Date 1st Order	Sales to date	YTD Sales
Vendor Number	Name	Address	Terms	Quality Rating	Shipping History		
Product Number	Description	Quantity On hand	Location	Primary Vendor	Secondary Vendor		

Records

master record

A set of data for an individual subject, such as a customer, employee or vendor. See *master file*.

master-slave communications

Communications in which one side, called the master, initiates and controls the session. The other side (slave) responds to the master's commands.

match print

A high-quality sample of printed output. Samples of ads or artwork are called *comps* in the graphics arts industry. The match print comp is made by exposing the four negatives used to make the printing plates onto acetates of four different colors. The acetates are then sandwiched together.

A high quality comp can also be made with an Iris Graphics ink jet printer, which can produce output up to 1800 dpi.

Mathcad

Mathematical software from Mathsoft, Inc., Cambridge, MA, for PCs and Macs. It allows complicated mathematical equations to be expressed, performed and displayed.

math coprocessor

A mathematical circuit that performs high-speed floating point operations. It may be built into the CPU chip, as in the 486DX, or it may be a separate chip, such as the 387 and 487, which work with the 386 and 486SX respectively.

The math coprocessor is used primarily in CAD and spreadsheet applications to improve performance. It is of such importance to computation-intensive CAD work, that some CAD programs will not operate without a coprocessor. Spreadsheet programs may test for its existence and then use it, but it is not mandatory. See *array processor* and *vector processor*.

Math Coprocessor
In a PC, the coprocessor is a chip.

Mathematica

Mathematical software for the Macintosh, DOS, Windows, OS/2 and various UNIX platforms from Wolfram Research, Inc., Champaign, IL. It includes numerical, graphical and symbolic computation capabilities, all linked to the Mathematica programming language. Its use requires a math coprocessor.

mathematical expression

A group of characters or symbols representing a quantity or an operation. See *arithmetic expression*.

mathematical function

A rule for creating a set of new values from an existing set; for example, the function $f(x) = 2x$ creates a set of even numbers (if x is a whole number).

matrix

An array of elements in row and column form. See *x-y matrix*.

matrix printer

See *dot matrix* and *printer*.

MAU

(Multi-station Access Unit) A central hub in a Token Ring local area network. See *hub*.

maximize

In a graphical environment, to enlarge a window to full size. Contrast with *minimize*.

MB, Mb

(1) (M "upper case B") (MegaByte or MotherBoard) MB mostly stands for megabyte, but on ads for raw components, it may refer to motherboard.
(2) (M "lower case b") (MegaBit) Mb should stand for megabit, but adherence to lower case "b" for bit is not always followed. Mb often refers to megabyte. See *space/time* for common usage.

Mbit

See *megabit*.

Mbits/sec

(MegaBITS per SECond) One million bits per second. See *space/time*.

Mbone

(Multicast backBONE) A collection of sites on the Internet that support the IP multicasting protocol (one-to-many) and allow for live audio and videoconferencing.

MBps, Mbps

(MegaBytes Per Second, MegaBits Per Second) One million bytes per second, one million bits per second. Adherence to "b" for bit and "B" for byte is not always followed. However, since the ps stands for "per second," and transmission rates are given in bits per second, it is often likely that MBps may erroneously refer to megabits per second. See *space/time* for common usage.

M-byte

See *megabyte*.

Mbytes/sec

(MegaBYTES per SECond) One million bytes per second. See *space/time*.

MCA

See *Micro Channel*.

MCGA

(Multi Color Graphics Array) An IBM video display standard built into low-end PS/2 models. It is not well supported by software vendors. See *PC display modes*.

MCI

(Media Control Interface) A high-level programming interface from IBM/Microsoft for controlling multimedia devices. It includes text commands such as open, play and close for languages such as Visual Basic, as well as functions for languages such as C. See *RIFF* and *AVI*.

MCI decision

An FCC decree in 1969 that granted MCI the right to compete with the Bell System by providing private, intercity telecommunications services.

MCM

(MultiChip Module or MicroChip Module) A chip housing that uses a ceramic base and contains two or more raw chips closely connected with high-density lines. This packaging method saves space and speeds processing due to short leads between chips.
MCMs were originally called microcircuits or hybrid microcircuits, since this technique is well suited for mixing analog and digital components together.
MCMs are a more workable solution to wafer scale integration, in essence, building the "superchip," which has been very difficult to implement.

MCS

(1) (Microsoft Consulting Services) The consulting arm of Microsoft which offers support for installation and maintenance of Microsoft applications and operating systems.
(2) (Multivendor Customer Service) The consulting arm of Digital Equipment that was founded in 1993. It provides hardware, software and network services for a variety of platforms.

(3) (Multimedia Conference Server) A family of videoconferencing servers from VideoServer, Inc., Lexington, MA. The MCS was the first multipoint control unit to comply with H.320.

(4) A family of microcontroller units (MCUs) from Intel. In 1995, Intel introduced its 8-bit MCS 251 chips which are binary compatible with its older MCS 51 series.

MCU

(1) (MicroController Unit) A control unit on a single chip.

(2) (Multipoint Control Unit) A device that connects multiple sites or stations for videoconferencing. The MCU joins the lines and switches the video depending on who is speaking or under the direction of one user who acts as moderator.

MD

See *minidisc.*

MDA

(Monochrome Display Adapter) The first IBM PC monochrome video display standard for text only. Due to its lack of graphics, MDA cards were often replaced with Hercules cards, which provided both text and graphics. See *PC display modes.*

MDBS IV

A DBMS from Micro Data Base Systems, Inc., Lafayette, IN, that runs on DOS, OS/2, UNIX, MPE and VMS servers. Noted for its performance and maturity (in 1984, MDBS III was the first client/server DBMS), it provides a superset of hierarchical, network and relational storage concepts. M/4 for Windows is a single-user Windows version.

MD DATA

The data storage counterpart of Sony's MiniDisc drive. See *MiniDisc.*

MDF

(Main Distribution Frame) A connecting unit between external and internal lines. It allows for public or private lines coming into the building to connect to internal networks. See *CDF.*

MDI

(1) (Multiple Document Interface) A Windows function that allows an application to display and lets the user work with more than one document at the same time. If the application is not programmed for MDI and you want to work with multiple documents of the same type concurrently, you must load the application again for each subsequent document. Contrast with *SDI.*

(2) (Medium Dependent Interface) Refers to an Ethernet port connection. The MDI-X port on an Ethernet hub is used to connect to a workstation (the X stands for crossing the transmit and recieve lines). An MDI port (not crossed) is used to connect to the MDI-X port of another hub.

mechanical mouse

A mouse that uses a rubber ball that rolls against wheels inside the unit. Contrast with *optical mouse.*

media

A material that stores or transmits data, for example, floppy disks, magnetic tape, coaxial cable and twisted pair.

media access method

See "LANs" under *data link protocol.*

media control
Also called *media processing,* in computer telephony it refers to some processing or altering of the call; for example, digitizing the content. Contrast with *call control.*

media conversion
Converting data from one storage medium to another, such as from disk to tape or from one type of disk pack to another.

media failure
A condition of not being able to read from or write to a storage device, such as a disk or tape, due to a defect in the recording surface.

MediaMap
(MediaMap, Cambridge, MA) A public relations information source for the high-tech industry that maintains editorial lists and schedules for every major computer media organization, including trade and national press, TV and radio, user groups and syndicated columns. Its MediaManager software for PCs and Macs provides a complete media contact management system and allows searches based on editorial niche and scheduled story opportunities.

Media Player
A Windows multimedia utility that is used to play sound and video files.

Media Vision
(Media Vision Technology, Inc., Fremont, CA) A manufacturer of Sound Blaster-compatible products for PCs founded in 1990. Media Vision was the first to introduce a 16-bit sound card (Pro Audio line) and multimedia upgrade kit.

medium frequency
An electromagnetic wave that oscillates in the range from 300,000 to 3,000,000 Hz. See *electromagnetic spectrum.*

Medline
The online database of the U.S. National Library of Medicine (NLM). The data is available for a fee on the Internet, CompuServe and directly from the NLM. Medline contains millions of articles from thousands of medical publications.

meg, mega
(1) Million. Abreviated "M." It often refers to the precise value 1,048,576 since computer specifications are usually binary numbers. See *binary values* and *space/time.*
(2) (MEGA) A personal computer series from Atari that is Motorola 68000 based, runs under GEM and the TOS operating system and includes a MIDI interface. It is ST compatible.

megabit
One million bits. Also Mb, Mbit and M-bit. See *mega* and *space/time.*

megabyte
One million bytes. Also MB, Mbyte and M-byte. See *mega* and *space/time.*

megaflops
(mega FLoating point OPerations per Second) One million floating point operations per second.

megahertz
One million cycles per second. See *MHz*.

megapel display
In computer graphics, a display system that handles a million or more pixels. A resolution of 1,000 lines by 1,000 dots requires a million pixels for the full screen image.

membrane keyboard
A dust and dirtproof keyboard constructed of two thin plastic sheets (membranes) that contain flexible printed circuits made of electrically conductive ink. The top membrane is the printed keyboard and a spacer sheet with holes is in the middle. When a user presses a simulated key, the top membrane is pushed through the spacer hole and makes contact with the bottom membrane, completing the circuit.

Membrane Keyboard
This type of keyboard is used with an overlay for many different kinds of applications.
(Photo courtesy of Polytel Computer Products Corporation.)

memo field
A data field that holds a variable amount of text. The text may be stored in a companion file, but it is treated as if it were part of the data record. For example, in the dBASE command **list name, biography**, name is in the data file (DBF file) and biography could be a memo field in the text file (DBT file).

memory
The computer's workspace (physically, a collection of RAM chips). It is an important resource, since it determines the size and number of programs that can be run at the same time, as well as the amount of data that can be processed instantly. All program execution and data processing takes place in memory. The program's instructions are copied into memory from disk or tape and then extracted from memory into the control unit circuit for analysis and execution. The instructions direct the computer to input data into memory from a keyboard, disk, tape or communications channel.

As data is entered into memory, the previous contents of that space are lost. Once the data is in memory, it can be processed (calculated, compared and copied). The results are sent to a screen, printer, disk, tape or communications channel.

Memory is like an electronic checkerboard, with each square holding one byte of data or instruction. Each square has a separate address like a post office box and can be manipulated independently. As a result, the computer can break apart programs into instructions for execution and data records into fields for processing.

Memory Doesn't Usually Remember
Oddly enough, the computer's memory doesn't remember anything when the power is turned off. That's why you have to save your files before you quit your program. Although there are memory chips that do hold their content permanently (ROMs,

PROMs, EPROMs, etc.), they're used for internal control purposes and not for the user's data.

"Remembering" memory in a computer system is its disks and tapes, and although they are also called memory devices, many prefer to call them storage devices (as we do) in order to differentiate them from internal memory. Perhaps in time, memory will refer to disks exclusively and RAM will refer to working memory. Until then, its usage for both RAM and disk only adds confusion to the most confusing industry on earth.

Memory Can Get Clobbered!
Memory is such an important resource that it cannot be wasted. It must be allocated by the operating system as well as applications and then released when not needed. Errant programs can grab memory and not let go of it even when they are closed, which results in less and less memory available as you load and use more programs.

In addition, if the operating system is not advanced, a malfunctioning application can write into memory used by another program, causing all kinds of unspecified behavior. You discover it when the system freezes or something wierd happens all of a sudden. If you were to really look into memory and watch how much and how fast data and instructions are written into and out of it in the course of a day, it's truly a miracle that it works.

Other terms for memory are *RAM, main memory, main storage, primary storage, read/write memory, core* and *core storage*. See also *SIMM*.

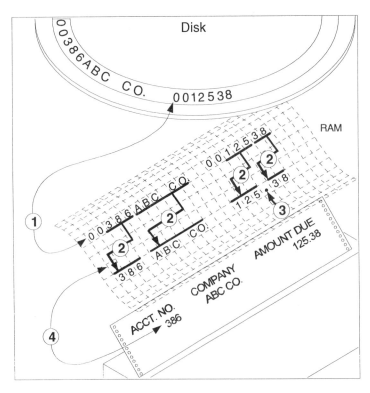

Memory Lets Data Be Broken Apart
(1) A complete data record is read from the disk and written into memory.
(2) The individual characters are copied from the input buffer to the output buffer. A format instruction strips preceding zeros out of the numeric field.
(3) The decimal point also comes from the format instruction.
(4) The formatted line is read from memory and transmitted to the printer.

memory allocation

Reserving memory for specific purposes. Operating systems generally reserve all the memory they need at startup. Application programs use memory when loaded and may allocate more after being loaded. If there is not enough free memory, they cannot run.

On a personal computer, memory can be allocated for a disk cache, which retains large chunks of data from the disk in faster RAM. However, a large disk cache that speeds up one application may slow down another because there is less normal memory available.

Memory can be allocated for a RAM disk, which simulates a disk drive in memory. Disk files are copied to the RAM disk and all accesses take place in faster memory. RAM disks may dramatically speed up one program and have little effect on others. Like the disk cache, it takes away from the total available memory.

On DOS PCs before DOS 6, users were expected to allocate the right mix of EMS and extended memory, causing third-party memory managers such as QEMM and 386MAX to become popular because they did it automatically. DOS 6 provides automatic allocation, and Windows 95 includes even more dynamic memory allocations. Users should never have to make such technical decisions. After all, that's what a computer is supposed to do. See *DOS memory manager*.

memory bank

(1) A physical section of memory. See *memory interleaving*.
(2) Refers generically to a computer system that holds data.

memory based

Programs that hold all data in memory for processing. Almost all spreadsheets are memory based so that a change in data at one end of the spreadsheet can be instantly reflected at the other end.

memory cache

See *cache*.

memory card

A credit-card-sized memory module used as an additional disk or disk alternative in laptops and palmtops. Called IC cards, ROM cards and RAM cards, they use a variety of chip types, including RAM, ROM, EEPROM and flash memory. RAM cards used in this manner contain a battery to keep the cells charged.

Note that when you add more memory in a laptop, the plug-in cards may also be called memory cards or RAM cards, but these are not substitutes for disk. They extend the computer's normal RAM memory and are typically contained on proprietary plug-in cards or modules. The memory card that functions as a disk typically uses the PCMCIA architecture and requires special software that accompanies the computer. See *solid state disk* and *flash memory*.

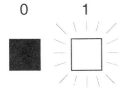

0   1

memory cell

One bit of memory. In dynamic RAM memory, a cell is made up of one transistor and one capacitor. In static RAM memory, a cell is made up of about five transistors.

memory chip

A chip that holds programs and data either temporarily (RAM), permanently (ROM, PROM) or permanently until changed (EPROM, EEPROM).

memory cycle

A series of operations that take place to read or write a byte of memory. For destructive memories, it includes the regeneration of the bits.

**Here Today
Gone Tomorrow**
Memory is like a post office box. Each byte retains the information stored in it until the next set of data or program is written into it.

memory cycle time

The time it takes to perform one memory cycle.

memory dump

A display or printout of the contents of memory. When a program abends, a memory dump can be taken in order to examine the status of the program at the time of the crash. The programmer looks into the buffers to see which data items were being worked on when it failed. Counters, variables, switches and flags are also inspected.

memory effect

See *nickel cadmium* and *nickel hydride*.

memory interleaving

A category of techniques for increasing memory speed. For example, with separate memory banks for odd and even addresses, the next byte of memory can be accessed while the current byte is being refreshed.<TERM>memory leak
A reserved section of memory that has not been freed up and turned back into the general memory pool. When an application allocates memory, it is either supposed to deallocate it when it no longer needs it. In some environments, the operating system can determine what is in memory that is no longer used and deallocate it. See *garbage collection*.

memory management

Refers to a variety of methods used to store data and programs in memory, keep track of them and reclaim the memory space when they are no longer needed. In traditional minicomputers and mainframes, it comprises virtual memory, bank switching and memory protection techniques. See *virtual memory, memory protection* and *garbage collection*.

Memory management has become a major issue with PCs, because the PC has more different types of memory regions than any computer in history. In a PC, it refers to managing conventional memory, the upper memory area (UMA), the high memory area (HMA), extended memory and expanded memory.

By reserving fixed areas in upper memory (UMA) for use by the operating system, expanding the PC has been a memory management nightmare. Countless books have been written on a problem that never should have existed in the first place. There are even two-day courses on the subject.

memory manager

Software that manages memory in a computer. See *memory management*.

memory map

The location of instructions and data in memory. See *PC memory map* for a digaram of the PC's upper memory area.

memory mapped I/O

A peripheral device that assigns specific memory locations to input and output. For example, in a memory mapped display, each pixel or text character derives its data from a specific memory byte or bytes. The instant this memory is updated by software, the screen is displaying the new data.

memory protection

A technique that prohibits one program from accidentally clobbering another active program. Using various different techniques, a protective boundary is created around the program, and instructions within the program are prohibited from referencing data outside of that boundary.

memory resident

A program that remains in memory at all times. See *TSR.*

memory sniffing

Coined by Data General, a diagnostic routine that tests memory during normal processing. The processor uses cycle stealing techniques that allow it to test memory during unused machine cycles. A memory bank can be "sniffed" every few minutes.

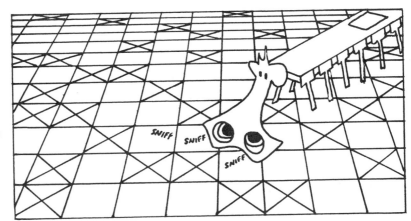

Memory Sniffing

memory typewriter

A typewriter that holds a few pages of text in its memory and provides limited word processing functions. With a display screen of only one or two lines, editing is tedious.

menu

An on-screen list of available functions, or operations, that can be performed currently. Depending on the type of menu, selection is accomplished by (1) highlighting the menu option with a mouse and releasing the mouse, (2) pointing to the option name with the mouse and clicking on it, (3) highlighting the option with the cursor keys and pressing Enter, or (4) pressing the first letter of the option name or some designated letter within the name.

menu bar

A row of on-screen menu options.

menu-driven

Using menus to command the computer. Contrast with *command-driven.*

menuing software

Software that provides a menu for launching applications and running operating system commands.

merge

See *mail merge* and *concatenate.*

merge purge

To merge two or more lists together and eliminate unwanted items. For example, a new name and address list can be added to an old list while deleting duplicate names or names that meet certain criteria.

mesa

A semiconductor process used in the 1960s for creating the sublayers in a transistor. Its deep etching gave way to the planar process.

mesh network

A net-like communications network in which there are at least two pathways to each node. Since the term network means net-like as well as communications network, the term mesh is used to avoid saying network communications network.

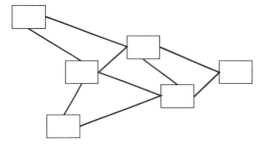

message

(1) In communications, a set of data that is transmitted over a communications line. Just as a program becomes a job when it's running in the computer, data becomes a message when it's transmitted over a network.
(2) In object-oriented programming, communicating between objects, similar to a function call in traditional programming.

message based

An interface that is based on a set of commands. A message-based system is a type of client/server relationship, in which requests are made by a client component, and the results are provided by a server component. It implies greater flexibility and interoperability in contrast with a hard coded operation, which would have to be modified by reprogramming the source code.

message handling

(1) An electronic mail system. See *messaging system.*
(2) In communications, the lower level protocols that transfer data over a network, which assemble and disassemble the data into the appropriate codes for transmission.

Message Handling Service

See *MHS.*

message handling system

Same as *messaging system.*

MessagePad

The first PDA from Apple to use the Newton technology. Introduced in the summer of 1993, it is a hand-held personal organizer that recognizes hand printing. It can add an appointment to a calendar and dial a phone or send a fax.

message queue

A storage space in memory or on disk that holds incoming transmissions until the computer can process them.

message switch

A computer system used to switch data between various points. Computers have always been ideal switches due to their input/output and compare capabilities. It inputs the data, compares its destination with a set of stored destinations and routes it accordingly. Note: A message switch is a generic term for a data routing device, but a messaging switch converts mail and messaging protocols.

message transfer agent

The store and forward capability in a messaging system. See *messaging system*.

messaging API

A programming interface that enables an application to send and receive messages and attached files over a messaging system. VIM, MAPI and CMC are examples. Novell's SMF-71, although also called an API, is actually the message format that mail must be placed into for submission to Novell's MHS. There are no functions associated with it.

messaging gateway

A computer system that converts one messaging protocol to another. It provides an interface between two store and forward nodes, or message transfer agents (MTAs).

messaging protocol

The rules, formats and functions for exchanging messages between the components of a messaging system. The major industry messaging protocols are the international X.400, SMTP (Internet), IBM's SNADS and Novell's MHS. Widely-used messaging products such as cc:Mail and Microsoft Mail use proprietary messaging protocols.

messaging switch

A messaging hub that provides protocol conversion between several messaging systems. Examples of switches include Soft-Switch's EMX, HP's OpenMail and Digital's MAILbus. A messaging switch differs from a messaging gateway in that it supports more than two protocols and connections as well as providing management and directory integration.

messaging system

Software that provides an electronic mail delivery system. It is comprised of three functional areas, which are either packaged together or are modularized as independent components. (1) The user agent, or UA, submits and receives the message. (2) The message transfer agent, or MTA, stores and forwards the message. (3) The message store, or MS, holds the mail and allows it to be selectively retrieved and deleted. It also provides a list of its contents.
Messaging products such as cc:Mail, Microsoft Mail, PROFS, DISOSS and ALL-IN-1 implement the entire messaging system. Other products must use components of other systems; for example, DaVinci Mail uses Novell's MHS.

metadata

Data that describes other data. See *data dictionary* and *repository*.

metafile

A file that contains other files. It generally refers to graphics files that can hold vector drawings and bitmaps. For example, a Windows Metafile (WMF) can store pictures in vector graphics and raster graphics formats as well as text. A Computer Graphics Metafile (CGM) also stores both types of graphics.

metalanguage

A language used to describe another language.

metal oxide semiconductor
See *MOS.*

metal oxide varistor
See *MOV.*

metamail
A public-domain UNIX utility that composes and decomposes a MIME message on the Internet.

metamerism
The quality of some colors that causes them to appear differently under different light sources. For example, two color samples might appear the same in natural light, but not in artifical light.

metaphor
The derivation of metaphor means "to carry over." Thus the "desktop metaphor" as so often described means that the office desktop has been brought over and simulated on computers.

meter
The basic unit of the metric system (39.37 inches). A yard is about 9/10ths of a meter (0.9144 meter).

method
In object-oriented programming, a method is the processing that an object performs. When a message is sent to an object, the method is implemented.

methodology
The specific way of performing an operation that implies precise deliverables at the end of each stage.

metric
Measurement. Although metric generally refers to the decimal-based metric system of weights and measures, software engineers often use the term as simply "measurement." For example, "is there a metric for this process?" See *software metrics.*

metropolitan area network
See *MAN.*

MFC
See *Microsoft C* and *Visual C++.*

Mflops
See *megaflops.*

MFM
(Modified Frequency Modulation) A magnetic disk encoding method used on most floppy disks and most hard disks under 40MB. It has twice the capacity of the earlier FM method, transfers data at 625 Kbytes per second and uses the ST506 interface. See *hard disk.*

MGA
(Monochrome Graphics Adapter) A display adapter that employs Hercules Graphics, combining graphics and text on a monochrome monitor.

MGP

(Monochrome Graphics Printer port) A display adapter that employs Hercules Graphics and a parallel printer port on the same expansion board.

MHS

(1) (Message Handling Service) A messaging system from Novell that supports multiple operating systems and other messaging protocols. Optional modules support SMTP, SNADS and X.400. It uses the SMF-71 messaging format. Standard MHS runs on a DOS machine attached to the server. Global MHS runs as a NetWare NLM. Under NetWare, MHS runs on top of IPX.

(2) See *messaging system*.

MHz

(MegaHertZ) One million cycles per second. It is used to measure the transmission speed of electronic devices, including channels, buses and the computer's internal clock. Megahertz is generally equivalent to one million bits per second or to one million times some number of bits per second.

When it refers to the computer's clock, it is used to measure the speed of the CPU. For example, a 50MHz 486 computer processes data internally (calculates, compares, copies) twice as fast as a 25MHz 486. However, this does not mean twice as much finished work in the same time frame, because cache design, disk speed and software design all contribute to the computer's actual performance, or throughput. See *MIPS*.

MHz Is the Heartbeat

When referencing CPU speed, the megahertz rating is really the heartbeat of the computer, providing the raw, steady pulses that energize the circuits. If you know a little of the German language, it's easy to remember this. The word "Herz," pronounced "hayrtz," means heart.

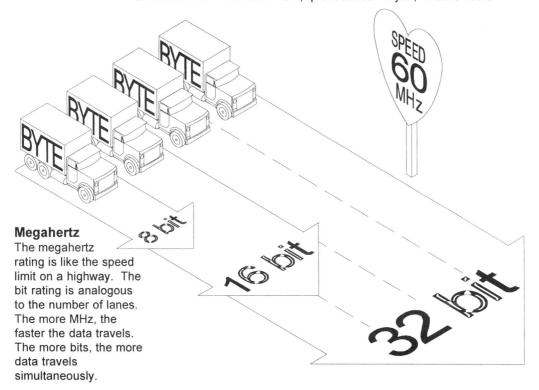

Megahertz
The megahertz rating is like the speed limit on a highway. The bit rating is analogous to the number of lanes. The more MHz, the faster the data travels. The more bits, the more data travels simultaneously.

MIB

(Management Information Base) An SNMP structure that describes the particular device being monitored. See *SNMP*.

MIC connector

(Medium Interface Connector) A fiber-optic cable connector that handles a pair of cables. The design of the plug and socket ensures that the polarity is maintained (transmit and receive cables are in correct order). It is used in FDDI and a variety of LANs and wiring hubs. See *fiber-optic connectors*.

mickey

A unit of mouse movement typically set at 1/200th of an inch.

MICR Characters

MICR

(Magnetic Ink Character Recognition) The machine recognition of magnetically-charged characters typically found on bank checks and deposit slips. MICR readers detect the characters and convert them into digital data.

micro

(1) A microcomputer or personal computer.
(2) One millionth or 10 to the -6th power. See *space/time*.
(3) Microscopic or tiny.

Micro Channel

Also known as MCA (Micro Channel Architecture), it is an IBM 32-bit bus used in most PS/2s, the RS/6000 series and certain ES/9370 models. MCA boards are not interchangeable with ISA and EISA boards.

Micro Channel provides auto configuration, which means that a unique identification is built into each expansion board, allowing it to be configured by software rather than by setting jumpers or DIP switches on the board itself. This system identifies conflicts ahead of time and assists users in configuring their systems when a new peripheral is added.

Micro Channel transfers data at 20MBytes/sec and has modes for increasing speeds to 40 and 80MB. It also has specifications for 64 bits and 160MB transfer. Micro Channel supports up to 15 levels of bus mastering.

ISA

EISA

PCI

VL-bus

Micro Channel

microchip

Same as *chip*.

microchip module

See *MCM*.

microcircuit

A miniaturized, electronic circuit, such as is found on an integrated circuit. See *chip* and *MCM*.

microcode

A permanent memory that holds the elementary circuit operations a computer must perform for each instruction in its instruction set. It acts as a translation layer between the instruction and the electronic level of the computer and enables the computer architect to more easily add new types of machine instructions without having to design electronic circuits. Microcode is used in CISC architecture. See *microprogramming*.

Microcom Protocol

See *MNP*.

Microcomputer

A microcomputer is a single-user computer generally classified as either a personal computer or a workstation. PCs and Macs make up the two major categories of personal computers. PCs generally run under DOS and Windows and Macs run under the Mac OS, which is called *System 7*. Workstations come from Sun, HP, DEC and several other vendors. They are UNIX-based systems used mostly for graphics and scientific work.

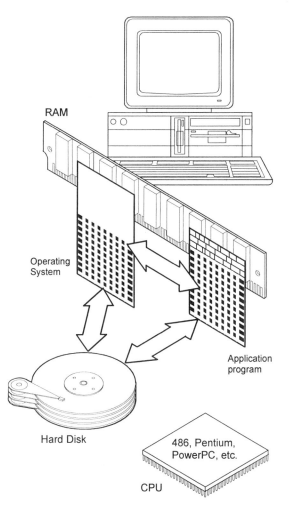

RAM

Operating System

Hard Disk

Application program

CPU

486, Pentium, PowerPC, etc.

As personal computers get faster, they increasingly compete in the workstation market. However, simulations require immense horsepower to move their high-resolution images smoothly and quickly on screen, and, thus far, the highest-end workstations are still faster than a personal computer.

Unlike a computer on a chip, which uses memory (RAM) only for proc-essing data, a microcomputer uses memory to temporarily hold the programs that are running as well. After loading (copying) the operating system into memory from the disk at startup, the applications are then loaded into memory.

When the application program is no longer needed, instructions from another program can use that same memory space. If there is not enough memory to run all the desired app-lications, the operating system swaps out some of the instructions to disk and brings them back in when required.

Unlike a computer on a chip, in a microcomputer, the clock is a separate chip, and the I/O control unit is contained on an expansion card that plugs into the computer's bus.

Microcomputer Industry Association
See *CompTIA*.

microcontroller
See *MCU*.

microelectronic
The miniaturization of electronic circuits. See *chip*.

microfiche
Pronounced "micro-feesh." A 4x6" sheet of film that holds several hundred miniaturized document pages. See *micrographics*.

microfilm
A continuous film strip that holds several thousand miniaturized document pages. See *micrographics*.

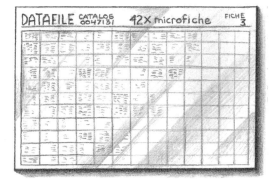

Microfiche and Microfilm

microfloppy disk
The formal name for the 3.5" floppy disk. It was developed by Sony.

Micro Focus
(Micro Focus Inc., Palo Alto, CA) A software company founded in 1976 that specializes in COBOL application development for a variety of platforms. It is known for its COBOL Workbench programming tools. Micro Focus products are used to develop applications on personal computers and workstations that are intended for execution on mainframes, as well as to move COBOL, CICS and IMS applications from the mainframe to client/server environments.

microform
In micrographics, a medium that contains microminiaturized images such as microfiche and microfilm.

micrographics
The production, handling and use of microfilm and microfiche. Images are created by cameras or by COM units that accept computer output directly. The documents are magnified for human viewing by readers, some of which can automatically locate a page using indexing techniques.
Microfiche and microfilm have always been an economical alternative for high-

volume data and picture storage. However, optical disks are competing with film-based systems and may become the preferred storage medium.

microimage
In micrographics, any photographic image of information that is too small to be read without magnification.

microinstruction
A microcode instruction. It is the most elementary computer operation that can take place; for example, moving a bit from one register to another. It takes several microinstructions to carry out one machine instruction.

microjacket
In micrographics, two sheets of transparent plastic that are bonded together to create channels into which strips of microfilm are inserted and stored.

microkernel
The hardware-dependent component of an operating system that is designed to be more easily portable to multiple platforms. The rest of the operating system interacts with the microkernel in a message-based relationship and does not have to be rewritten. Only the microkernel has to be reprogrammed to the architecture of the new hardware. See *kernel*.

microlithography
Using x rays instead of light rays to form the patterns of elements on a chip. This technology is expected to emerge by the 21st century. AT&T Bell Labs has speculated that by the year 2001, a dynamic RAM chip with one billion bits (1 gigabit) will be built using .18 micron microlithography.

micromainframe
A personal computer with mainframe or near mainframe speed.

micro manager
A person who manages personal computer operations within an organization and is responsible for the analysis, selection, installation, training and maintenance of personal computer hardware and software. See *information center* and *MMA*.

micromechanics
The microminiaturization of mechanical devices (gears, motors, rotors, etc.) using similar photomasking techniques as in chip making.

micromini
A personal computer with minicomputer or near minicomputer speed.

micron
One millionth of a meter. Approximately 1/25,000 of an inch. The tiny elements that make up a transistor on a chip are measured in microns. For example, the 486 uses 1.0 micron technology, the Pentium .8 micron.

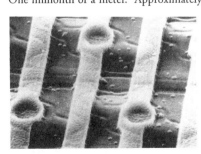

Microscopic View of a Chip
The tiny elements of a chip are measured in microns. *(Photo courtesy of AT&T.)*

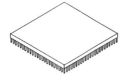

Micro PDP-11

The microcomputer version of the PDP-11 from Digital introduced in 1975. Uses the Q-bus and serves as a stand-alone computer or is built into other equipment.

microprocessor

A CPU on a single chip. In order to function as a computer, it requires a power supply, clock and memory. First-generation microprocessors were Intel's 8080, Zilog's Z80, Motorola's 6800 and Rockwell's 6502. The first microprocessor was created by Intel.

microprogram

Same as *microcode*.

microprogramming

Programming microcode.

micropublishing

In micrographics, the issuing of new or reformatted information on microfilm for sale or distribution.

microrepublishing

In micrographics, the issuing of microfilm that has been previously or is simultaneously published in hardcopy for sale or distribution.

microsecond

One millionth of a second. See *space/time*.

microsegmentation

In networking, the ability to manage a smaller number of nodes as a single segment or domain. Total microsegmentation is accomplished with a switch, which treats each node as a segment.

Microsoft

(Microsoft Corporation, Redmond, WA) The world's largest software company. Microsoft was founded in 1975 by Paul Allen and Bill Gates, two college students who wrote the first BASIC interpreter for the Intel 8080 microprocessor. Allen now runs Asymetrix Corporation.

MBASIC was licensed to Micro Instrumentation and Telemetry Systems to accompany its Altair 8800 kit. By the end of 1976, more than 10,000 Altairs were sold with MBASIC. Versions were licensed to Radio Shack, Apple and many other vendors. Later, a version called *GW-BASIC* (Gee Whiz BASIC) was developed for 16-bit personal computers.

Although Microsoft became a leader in microcomputer programming languages, its outstanding success was achieved by fitting PCs with DOS and Windows. Windows has become the clear winner on desktops, and Windows NT is making significant inroads in the server market. Microsoft has also become the leader in the applications market with its Microsoft Office suite of products that include Excel, Word, PowerPoint and Access.

Microsoft's position as the supplier of the major operating systems and applications to the world's largest computer base gives it considerable advantage.

William H. Gates, III
(Photo courtesy of Microsoft Corporation.)

Paul G. Allen
(Photo courtesy of Asymetrix Corporation.)

Microsoft Access

A database program for Windows from Microsoft that reads Paradox, dBASE and Btrieve files. Using ODBC, it reads Microsoft SQL Server, SYBASE SQL Server and Oracle data. Access BASIC is its programming language, and "Wizards" ask you questions to create forms, reports and graphs.

Microsoft BackOffice

See *BackOffice*.

Microsoft Bob

A user interface for Windows from Microsoft that is designed for novices. It provides what Microsoft has coined a "social interface," which lets you design and decorate your own rooms that contain familiar objects. A user-selectable series of animated, cartoon-like guides, including household pets such as "Rover the dog," provide online help and advice.

Bob includes programs for personal use, such a word processor for basic letter writing, a calendar, checkbook, household manager, address book and e-mail facility. It also includes financial guide programs as well as a GeoSafari quiz game. Bob is used to launch Windows and DOS programs.

Microsoft C

A C compiler and development system for DOS and Windows applications from Microsoft. Windows programming requires the Windows Software Development Kit (SDK), which is included.

Version 7.0 includes C++ capability and Version 1.0 of the Microsoft Foundation Class Library (MFC), which provide a base framework of object-oriented code to build an application upon. See *Visual C++*.

Microsoft Certified Professional

A training program that provides certification of competency in Microsoft products. Administered throughout the world at Microsoft centers as well as colleges and universities, it provides the following certification levels. The Certified Product Specialist (CPS) is for the user and reseller who supports Windows-based PCs. The Certified Systems Engineer (CSE) is for the technical specialist involved with Windows NT and other advanced Microsoft products. The Certified Trainer (CT) is for people that will train others. For more information about the program, call 800/426-9400.

Microsoft Consulting Services

The consulting arm of Microsoft which offers support for installation and maintenance of Microsoft applications and operating systems.

Microsoft Exchange

An enterprise-wide messaging and mail system from Microsoft that runs under Windows. Exchange Server is the messaging system that runs under the Windows NT Server operating system. Exchange Server includes a Visual Basic environment for developing groupware applications.

The Exchange client provides a universal mail front end and in-box for messages from online services. A more limited version of the Exchange client comes with Windows 95.

Microsoft Mail

A messaging system from Microsoft that runs on PC and AppleTalk networks. Gateways are available to a variety of mail systems including X.400, PROFS, Novell's MHS and MCI Mail. Microsoft Mail-enabled applications are written to the MAPI programming interface. See *Microsoft Exchange*.

Microsoft Network

An online service from Microsoft that was launched with Windows 95 in August 1995. It is designed as a general-purpose service with Internet capability similar to CompuServe and America Online. The built-in online registration to the service within Windows 95 was the source of much concern by the online industry, believing Microsoft was taking unfair advantage of its position in the market. See also *Windows network*.

Microsoft Office

A suite of applications for Windows, Macs and PowerMacs from Microsoft that include Microsoft's primary productivity applications: Word, Excel, Access, PowerPoint and Microsoft Mail. The applications are designed for tighter integration with sharing of common functions such as spell checking and graphing. Objects can be dragged and dropped between applications.

Microsoft SQL Server

A relational DBMS from Microsoft that runs on Windows NT servers. It is Microsoft's high-end client/server database and a key component in its BackOffice suite of server products. SQL Server was originally developed by Sybase and also sold by Microsoft for OS/2 and NT. In 1992, Microsoft began development of its own version. Today, Microsoft SQL Server and Sybase SQL Server are independent products with some compatibility.

Microsoft TechNet

A CD-ROM subscription service from Microsoft that contains technical documentation, drivers and patches for all of Microsoft's products. It includes two updated CD-ROMs every month and contains the Microsoft Knowledge Base with more than 30,000 questions and answers.

Microsoft Windows

See *Windows*.

Microsoft Windows network

See *Windows network*.

Microsoft Word

A full-featured word processing programs for DOS, Windows and Mac from Microsoft. The Windows version, Word for Windows, or WinWord, is a sophisticated program with rudimentary desktop publishing capabilities. It has become the leading word processor on PCs. The earlier DOS version provides both graphics-based and text-based interfaces for working with a document.

Microsoft Works

An integrated software package for PCs and the Macintosh from Microsoft. It provides file management with relational-like capabilities, word processing, spreadsheet, business graphics and communications capabilities in one package.

microspacing

Positioning characters for printing by making very small horizontal and vertical movements. Many dot matrix printers and all laser printers have this ability.

MicroStation

A full-featured 2-D and 3-D CADD program from Intergraph Corporation, Huntsville, AL, for PCs, Macs and Intergraph, Sun and HP workstations.

micro to mainframe

An interconnection of personal computers to mainframes. See *3270 emulator*.

MicroVAX

A series of entry-level VAXs introduced in 1983 that run under VMS or ULTRIX. Some models use the Q-bus architecture.

microwave

An electromagnetic wave that vibrates at 1GHz and above. Microwaves are the transmission frequencies used in communications satellites as well as in line-of-sight systems on earth.

Microwave Tower
This early microwave radio relay station was installed in 1968 at Boulder Junction Colorado.
(Photo courtesy of AT&T.)

middleware

Software that functions as a conversion or translation layer. The term is used to describe a diverse group of products. It may refer to software that sits between an application and a control program (operating system, network control program, DBMS, etc.) that provides a single programming interface for the applications to be written to. The application will run in as many different computer environments as the middleware runs in.

TP monitors are called middleware, because they reside between the client applications and the servers. Information Builder's EDA/SQL is called middleware, because it translates various query languages to different database programs. Microsoft's ODBC interface is also called middleware, because it provides a common API to many different databases.

MID file

See *MIDI file*.

MIDI

(Musical Instrument Digital Interface) A standard protocol for the interchange of musical information between musical instruments, synthesizers and computers. It defines the codes for a musical event, which includes the start of a note, its pitch, length, volume and musical attributes, such as vibrato. It also defines codes for various button, dial and pedal adjustments used on synthesizers.

MIDI is commonly used to synchronize notes produced on several synthesizers. Its control messages can orchestrate a series of synthesizers, each playing a part of the musical score.

A computer with a MIDI interface can be used to record a musical session, but instead of recording the analog sound waves as in a tape recorder, the computer stores the music as keystroke and control codes. The recording can be edited in an entirely different manner than with conventional recording; for example, the rhythm can be changed by editing the timing codes in the MIDI messages. In addition, the computer can easily transpose a performance from B major into D major. MIDI files also take up much less disk space than sound files that contain the actual digitized music.

The objective of MIDI was to allow the keyboard of one synthesizer to play notes generated by another. However, since Version 1.0 in 1983, MIDI has brought electronic control of music to virtually everybody, benefiting musicians and teachers alike.

MIDI makes an ideal system for storing music on digital media due to its small storage requirement compared with digitizing actual music. Since the advent of General MIDI, a standard for defining MIDI instruments, MIDI will become more widely used for musical backgrounds in multimedia applications.

See *General MIDI, MIDI sequencer, MIDI patch, MIDI voices, MPU-401, wave table synthesis, FM synthesis* and *sound card.*

midicomputer

A computer with performance and capacity between a minicomputer and a mainframe.

MIDI file

A MIDI sound file that contains MIDI messages. MIDI files used in DOS and Windows have a .MID extension. A variation of this format is the RIFF MIDI file, which uses the .RMI extension.

The format for MIDI files, or Standard MIDI File (SMF), contains a header "chunk" at the beginning of the file, which defines the format type, followed by one or more track chunks. Type 0 files store all tracks in one track chunk. Type 1 files use a separate chunk for each track, with the first chunk storing the tempo.

Type 0 files use less memory and run faster than type 1. Thus, original MIDI music is maintained in type 1 format and frequently distributed in type 0. MIDI files distributed for editing are usually in type 1 format, since it is difficult to convert from type 0 to type 1 using a MIDI sequencer.

A less-widely used type 2 file can contain several type 0 files.

MIDI Mapper

A Windows application that converts MIDI sound sequences (MIDI messages) to conform to a particular MIDI sound card or module. The keyboard map is used to assign values to non-standard keyboard keys. The patch map assigns sounds to an instrument number (see *MIDI patch*). The channel map assigns input channels to output channels.

MIDI messages

A series of MIDI notes for a musical sequence. Since MIDI data is a set of musical note definitions rather than the actual sound of the music, the contents of a MIDI file are called MIDI messages.

MIDI patch

One of 16 channels in a MIDI device. Many keyboard synthesizers and MIDI sound modules can handle several waveforms per patch, mixing different instruments together to create synthetic sounds. Each waveform counts as a MIDI voice. Some sound cards can support two or more waveforms per patch.

Before General MIDI, which standardized patches, MIDI vendors assigned patch numbers to their synthesizer products in an arbitrary manner. See *MIDI voices.*

MIDI sequencer

A hardware device or software application that allows for the composition, editing and playback of MIDI sound sequences. Media player applications can play MIDI sound files, but creating and modifying MIDI files requires a sequencer.

MIDI sound module

A stand-alone device that generates MIDI sound. Other MIDI sound-generating devices are synthesizers with keyboards and sound cards for personal computers.

MIDI voices

The number of musical notes that can be played back simultaneously in a MIDI sound device. MIDI provides up to 16 channels of simultaneous playback. The number of voices is the total number of notes from all the instruments played back through all the channels.

For example, if one of the channels (patches) is a piano, up to 10 fingers could strike the keyboard at the same time, generating 10 notes, assuming that particular piano patch triggers only one waveform (see *MIDI patch*). Typically, a MIDI sound card will support from 24 to 32 voices. Keyboard synthesizers and sound modules can handle up to 64.

midrange computer

Same as *minicomputer*, but excludes single-user minicomputer workstations. For example, an IBM AS/400 would be typically called a midrange computer, but a Sun SPARCstation would not.

MIF

(1) (Maker Interchange Format) An alternate file format for a FrameMaker document. A MIF file is ASCII text, which can be created in another program and imported into FrameMaker.

(2) (Managment Information File) A DMI file format that describes a hardware or software component used in a PC. It can contain data, code or both. See *DMI*.

mil

An Internet address domain name for a military agency. See *Internet address*.

mill

A very old term for processor (number crunching!).

milli

One thousandth or 10 to the -3rd power.

millimeter

One thousandth of a meter, or 1/25th of an inch.

million

One thousand times one thousand or 10 to the 6th power. See *mega* and *microsecond*.

millisecond

One thousandth of a second. See *space/time*.

MIL STD

(MILitary STandarD) A detailed technical specification for a product that is purchased by a U.S. military agency.

MIMD

(Multiple Instruction stream Multiple Data stream) A computer architecture that uses multiple processors, each processing its own set of instructions simultaneously and independently of the others. Contrast with *SIMD*.

MIME

(Multipurpose Internet Mail Extensions) Extensions to the SMTP format that allow it to carry multiple types of data (binary, audio, video, etc.).

mini

See *minicomputer*.

minicartridge

See *QIC*.

minicomputer

A medium-scale computer that functions as a single workstation, or as a multiuser system with up to several hundred terminals. A minicomputer system costs roughly from $20,000 to $250,000.

In 1959, Digital launched the minicomputer industry with its PDP-1. Soon after, Data General and HP introduced minis, and eventually Wang, Tandem, Datapoint and Prime joined them. IBM has introduced several minicomputer series (see *IBM minicomputers*).

Today, the term "midrange" has become popular for medium-sized computer. High-end microcomputers and low-end mainframes overlap in minicomputer price and performance.

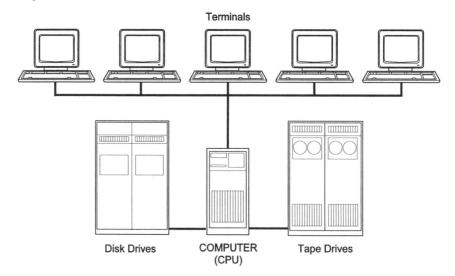

Terminals

Disk Drives   COMPUTER (CPU)   Tape Drives

MiniDisc

A compact digital audio disk drive from Sony. Introduced in late 1993, it uses a 2.5" removable, rewritable optical disk cartridge that holds up to 74 minutes of CD-quality music. Within a year, more than 1,200 prerecorded music titles were available for it.

The MiniDisc has a data storage counterpart, called the MD DATA drive, which uses 140MB cartridges that are similar to MiniDiscs, but an ID in the disk prevents them from being used in a MiniDisc drive. MD DATA drives can also play recorded and premastered MiniDiscs just as CD-ROM drives can play audio CDs.

minifloppy

The formal name for the once-ubiquitous, black floppy disk encased in a 5.25"-wide plastic jacket. Introduced by Shugart in 1978, it superseded IBM's 8" floppy. Although used extensively, the 5.25" minifloppy has finally given way to the 3.5" microfloppy, originally created by Sony.

minimize

In graphical environments, to reduce a window to an icon.

mining

See *data mining*.

mini-supercomputer

A computer that is 25% to 100% as fast as a supercomputer, but costs less. Note: A mini-supercomputer is not the same as a supermini.

MINIX

A version of UNIX for the PC, Mac, Amiga and Atari ST developed by Andrew Tannenbaum and published by Prentice-Hall. It comes with complete source code.

minor key

A secondary key used to identify a record. For example, if transactions are sorted by account number and date, account number is the major key and date is the minor key.

MIPS

(Million Instructions Per Second) The execution speed of a computer. For example, .5 MIPS is 500,000 instructions per second. High-speed personal computers and workstations perform at 100 MIPS and higher. Digital's Alpha chip has a peak rate of over 1,200 MIPS (that's 1.2 BIPS!). Inexpensive microprocessors used in toys and games may be in the .05-.1 MIPS range.

MIPS rates are not uniform. Some are best-case mixes while others are averages. In addition, it takes more instructions in one machine to do the same thing as another (RISC vs CISC, mainframe vs micro). As a result, MIPS has been called "MisInformation to Promote Sales" as well as "Meaningless Interpretation of Processor Speed."

MIPS rate is just one factor in overall performance. Bus and channel speed and bandwidth, memory speed, memory management techniques and system software also determine total throughput. See also *MIPS Computer*.

MIPS and MHz

There is a mathematical relationship between MIPS and MHz. You can derive MIPS from MHz if you know how many machine cycles it takes to execute an instruction in the CPU. For example, a 486 takes 1.9 cycles on average. To obtain MIPS on a 50MHz 486, you would divide 50 by 1.9, yielding 26 MIPS.

MIPS Computer

(MIPS Computer Systems, Inc., Sunnyvale, CA.) A microcomputer and minicomputer manufacturer that was acquired by Silicon Graphics (SGI). MIPS RISC-based R3000 and R4000 families of 32- and 64-bit microprocessors are widely used in the industry. They are designed by MIPS and made under license by NEC and other companies. Silicon Graphics workstations are powered by MIPS chips as well as computer systems from companies such as Pyramid, Tandem, NEC and Siemens/Nixdorf.

Mirror III

A DOS communications program from Softklone Distributing Corporation, Tallahassee, FL, that supports a variety of terminals and protocols and provides a learn mode for recording common sequences. Its scripting language is called PRISM.

mirroring

See *disk mirroring*.

Mirrors

Software from Micrografx, Inc., Richardson, TX, that allows Windows programs to be converted to OS/2 with minimal modification.

MIS

(1) (Management Information System) An information system that integrates data from all the departments it serves and provides operations and management with the information they require.

It was "the" buzzword of the mid to late 1970s, when online systems were implemented in all large organizations. See *DSS*.

(2) (Management Information Services) See *Information Systems*.

mission critical

Vital to the operation of an organization. In the past, mission critical information systems were implemented on mainframes and minicomputers. Increasingly, they are being designed for and installed on personal computer networks. See *client/server*.

mixed object

Same as *compound document*.

M-JPEG

See *MPEG*.

MKS

(Mortice Kern Systems Inc., Waterloo, Ontario) A software company that specializes in programming tools and utilities for a variety of platforms. For example, its RCS system for Windows, OS/2 and UNIX is a version control software package.

ML

A symbolic programming language developed in the 1970s at the University of Edinburgh, Scotland. Although similar to LISP, its commands and structures are like Pascal.

MM

(1) See *Multiple Master*.
(2) (mm) (MilliMeter) One thousandth of a meter.

MMA

(Microcomputer Manager's Association, Inc., P.O.Box 4615, Warren, NJ, 908/580-9091) A membership organization with chapters throughout the U.S. devoted to educating personnel responsible for personal computers. Provides seminars, conferences, trade show events, job bank and newsletters.

MMU

(Memory Management Unit) A virtual memory circuit that translates logical addresses into physical addresses.

mnemonic

Pronounced "nuh-monic." Means memory aid. A name assigned to a machine function. For example, in DOS, COM1 is the mnemonic assigned to serial port #1. Programming languages are almost entirely mnemonics.

MNP

(Microcom Networking Protocol) A family of communications protocols from Microcom, Inc., Norwood, MA, that have become de facto standards for error correction (classes 2 though 4) and data compression (class 5).

Class	Features
1	Half-duplex asynchronous transmission. (Early mode, no longer used.)
2	Full-duplex asynchronous transmission.
3	Full-duplex synchronous transmission using HDLC framing techniques using 64-byte blocks. Start/stop bits stripped.
4	Increased throughput. Shorter headers, frames up to 256 bytes. Some vendors adjust frame size based on line quality.
5	Compresses data up to two times.
6	Starts at V.22bis modulation and switches to turnaround of V.29 transmission.
7	Compresses data up to three times.
8	Not in use.
9	Adds Piggy-back Acknowledgement** and selective retransmission for more efficient transport of data. Provides better performance over variety of links.
10	Adds Adverse Channel Enhancements** for efficient operation on noisy lines (rural, cellular, international, etc.).

** Proprietary Microcom techniques.

MO, M-O

See *magneto-optic*.

Mobitex

A packet radio service from RAM Mobile Data (joint venture of RAM Broadcasting and BellSouth). Base stations serve major cities throughout the U.S.

mod

See *modulo*.

modal

Mode oriented. A modal operation switches from one mode to another. Contrast with *non-modal*.

modal bandwidth

The capacity of an optical fiber measured in MHz-km (megahertz over one kilometer). One MHz-km equals approximately .7 to .8 Mbps. Thus, a 100 MHz-km fiber can carry about 70 to 80 Mbps of data.

modal dispersion

A signal distortion in an optical fiber in which the light pulses spread out, and the receiving device cannot detect the beginnings and ends of pulses.

MO:DCA

(Mixed Object:Document Content Architecure) An IBM compound document format for text and graphics elements in a document. It supports Revisable Documents, which are editable like revisable-form DCA, Presentation Documents, which provide specific output formatting similar to DCA final-form, and Resource Documents, which hold control information such as fonts.

Formats for specific objects are specified in OCAs (Object Content Architectures): PTOCA for Presentation and Text that has been formatted for output, GOCA for vector Graphics objects, IOCA for bitmapped Images and FOCA for Fonts.

mode

An operational state that a system has been switched to. It implies at least two possible conditions. There are countless modes for hardware and software. See *Real Mode, Protected Mode, burst mode, insert mode, supervisor state* and *program state.*

model

(1) A style or type of hardware device.

(2) A mathematical representation of a device or process used for analysis and planning. See *data model, data administration, financial planning system* and *scientific applications.*

model-based expert system

An expert system based on fundamental knowledge of the design and function of an object. Such systems are used to diagnose equipment problems, for example. Contrast with *rule-based expert system.*

modeling

Simulating a condition or activity by performing a set of equations on a set of data. See *data model, data administration, financial planning system* and *scientific applications.*

modem

(MOdulator-DEModulator) A device that adapts a terminal or computer to a telephone line. It converts the computer's digital pulses into audio frequencies (analog) for the telephone system and converts the frequencies back into pulses at the receiving side. The modem also dials the line, answers the call and controls transmission speed, which ranges from 300 to 14,400 bps and higher.

Other kinds of modems are made for a variety of modulation requirements; for example, broadband modems connect lines to high-speed broadband channels.

For hookup to a personal computer, an internal modem needs a free expansion slot, while an external modem in its own case requires a free serial port. A communications program drives the modem. It turns the personal computer into an interactive terminal and file transfer program that controls the modem and transmission. The term modem is also used as a verb; for example, "I'll modem you later." See *communications program.*

The recent migration from 2,400 bps modems to 9,600 and 14,400 bps makes it simpler to transfer large files. The number of characters transmitted is about 10% of the bit rate; thus, 9,600 bps is equivalent to sending 960 bytes of text in one second. At 9,600 bps, it takes a little more than two seconds to display a full screen of text, but considerably more for graphics. Remote control software, which lets you take complete control of another machine via modem, constantly refreshes the remote screen with changes and requires the fastest modem.

New modems have built-in error correction (V.42) and data compression (V.42bis, MNP 5), which means faster transmission if both sides have the same capability. They also have automatic feature negotiation, which adjusts to the other modem's speed and hardware protocols.

Most personal computer modems use the Hayes AT command set, which is the series of machine instructions that control the modem. See *AT command set* and *Hayes Smartmodem.*

Modem Status Signals

The following acronyms are used with the display lights on the modem to identify the unit's current status. There are several acronyms used for certain operations.

Acronym	Meaning	Acronym	Meaning
AA	Auto answer mode	PW	RPower on
CA	Compression active	RI	Ringing
CD	Carrier detect	RNG	Ringing
CTR	Clear to send	RTS	Request to send
DTR	Terminal ready	RXD	Receiving data
EC	Error control active	RD	Receiving data
HS	High speed	SD	Transmitting (send) data
LB	Low battery	TM	Test mode
MR	Modem ready	TD	Transmitting (send) data
OH	Off hook	TR	Terminal ready
		TXD	Transmitting (send) data

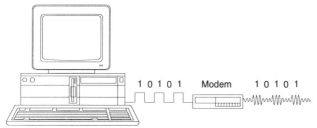

modem eliminator

A device that allows two close computers to be connected without modems. For personal computers, it is the same as a null modem cable. In synchronous systems, it provides active intelligence for synchronization.

modem lights

See "Modem Status Signals" under *modem*.

modem server

See *communications server*.

modify structure

A database command that changes a file's structure. Field lengths and field names can be changed, and fields can be added or deleted. It may convert the old data file into the new structure without data loss, unless fields have been truncated or deleted.

Modula-2

(MODUlar LAnguage-2) An enhanced version of Pascal introduced in 1979 by Swiss professor Nicklaus Wirth, creator of Pascal. It supports separate compilation of modules. The following example changes Fahrenheit to Celsius:

```
      MODULE FahrToCent;
  FROM InOut IMPORT ReadReal,WriteReal,
  WriteString,WriteLn;
  VAR Fahr:REAL;
  BEGIN
  WriteString("Enter Fahrenheit ");
  ReadReal(Fahr);
  WriteLn;
  WriteString("Celsius is ");
  WriteReal((Fahr - 32) * 5 / 9);
      END   FahrToCent
```

**Main
Loop**

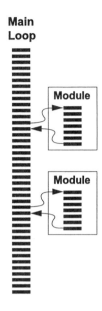

Module

Module

modularity

The characteristic of a system that has been divided into smaller subsystems which interact with each other.

modular programming

Breaking down the design of a program into individual components (modules) that can be programmed and tested independently. It is a requirement for effective development and maintenance of large programs and projects.

Modular programming has evolved into object-oriented programming, which provides formal rules for developing self-contained software modules. See *object-oriented programming*.

Modular Windows

A subset of Windows for TV-based consumer electronics. It does not use Program Manager, scroll bars and overlapping windows. The application is the window.

modulate

To vary a carrier wave. Modulation blends a data signal (text, voice, etc.) into a carrier for transmission over a network. Major methods are AM (amplitude modulation) - modulate the height of the carrier wave, FM (frequency modulation) - modulate the frequency of the wave, and PM (phase modulation) - modulate the polarity of the wave. Contrast with *demodulate*. See *carrier*.

module

A self-contained hardware or software component that interacts with a larger system. Hardware modules are often made to plug into a main system. Program modules are designed to handle a specific task within a larger program.

modulo

A mathematical operation (modulus arithmetic) in which the result is the remainder of the division. For example, 20 MOD 3 results in 2 (20/3 = 6 with remainder of 2.

moire

Pronounced "mor-ray." In computer graphics, a visible distortion. It results from a variety of conditions; for example, when scanning halftones at a resolution not consistent with the printed resolution or when superimposing curved patterns on one another. Internal monitor misalignment can also be a cause.

molecular beam epitaxy

A technique that "grows" atomic-sized layers on a chip rather than creating layers by diffusion.

monadic

One. A single item or operation that deals with one item or operand.

Monarch

A data capture program from Personics, Wilmington, MA, that is used to transfer data from mainframe and minicomputer reports to the PC. It uses report files that contain data ready to print. Users identify the data directly from the report format on screen, and the program copies the data into the fields of various database or spreadsheet formats for the PC.

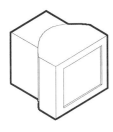

monitor

(1) A display screen used to present output from a computer, camera, VCR or other video generator. A monitor's clarity is based on video bandwidth, dot pitch, refresh rate and convergence. See *VGA, analog monitor, digital monitor* and *how to select a PC display system.*

(2) Software that provides utility and control functions such as setting communications parameters. It typically resides in a ROM chip and contains startup and diagnostic routines.

(3) Software that monitors the progress of activities within a computer system.

(4) A device that gathers performance statistics of a running system via direct attachment to the CPU's circuit boards.

monitor calibrator

A hand-held device that is placed over the screen of a monitor and "reads" the colors.

monitor profile

A file of attributes about a specific monitor, which includes information about its gamma, white point and phosphors. It is used to produce accurate color conversion from the display to some other destination such as a printer.

monochrome

Also called "mono." The display of one foreground color and one background color; for example, black on white, white on black and green on black.

Non-color laptop PCs commonly use "monochrome VGA" screens, which are actually gray-scale screens. This is like black and white TV and is not the same as the monochrome screens widely used over the years on mini and mainframe terminals and PCs using the MDA adapter, which display a solid color and no shades in between.

monolithic integrated circuit

The common form of chip design, in which the base material (substrate) contains the pathways as well as the active elements that take part in its operation.

monophonic

Sound reproduction using a single channel. Contrast with *stereophonic.*

monospaced font

A font in which each character is the same width. The "i" takes up the same horizontal space as an "m." Courier is a common monospaced font. Contrast with *proportional spacing.*

Monte Carlo method

A technique that provides approximate solutions to problems expressed mathematically. Using random numbers and trial and error, it repeatedly calculates the equations to arrive at a solution.

Moore's law

A statement made years ago by Intel co-founder Gordon Moore regarding the pace of semiconductor technology, which has proven fairly accurate. He said that the number of transistors on a chip will double every 18 months. More recently, he said that the cost of a semiconductor manufacturing plant doubles with each generation of microprocessor.

MORE II

A Macintosh desktop presentation program and outline processor from Symantec Corporation, Cupertino, CA, that includes writing, spell checking, presentation-quality text and graphics and 35mm slide output.

morphing

Transforming one image into another; for example, a car into a tiger or a lady into a cat, as in the following example. The term comes from metamorphosis. Morphing programs work by marking the prominent points, such as tips and corners, on the before and after images. The points are used to mathematically compute the movements from one object into another. See *tweening*.

Morphing
This morphing sequence was created in VideoCraft from Andover Advanced Technologies.

morray

See *moire*.

Morse code

A character code represented by dots and dashes, developed by Samuel Morse in the mid-19th century. A dot can be a voltage, carrier wave or light beam of one duration, while a dash is a longer duration. It was used to send telegraph messages before the telephone and was used in World War II for signalling by light.

MOS

(Metal Oxide Semiconductor) Pronounced "moss." One of two major categories of chip design (the other is bipolar). It derives its name from its use of metal, oxide and semiconductor layers. There are several varieties of MOS technologies, including PMOS, NMOS and CMOS.

Mosaic

A Web browser created by the University of Illinois National Center for Supercomputing Applications (NCSA) and released on the Internet in early 1993. Mosaic was "the" application that caused interest in the World Wide Web to explode. Originally developed for UNIX, it was soon ported to Windows. An enhanced version of NCSA Mosaic is offered by Spyglass, Inc., Naperville, IL. See *NetScape*.

MOSFET

(Metal Oxide Semiconductor Field Effect Transistor) A common type of transistor fabricated as a discrete component or into MOS integrated circuits.

most significant digit

The leftmost, non-zero digit in a number. It is the digit with the greatest value in the number.

motherboard

The main printed circuit board in an electronic device, which contains sockets that accept additional boards. In a personal computer, the motherboard contains the bus, CPU and coprocessor sockets, memory sockets, keyboard controller and supporting chips.

Chips that control the video display, serial and parallel ports, mouse and disk drives may or may not be present on the motherboard. If not, they are independent controllers that are plugged into an expansion slot on the motherboard.

Motif

The graphical user interface (GUI) endorsed by the Open Software Foundation. It has become the standard graphical interface for UNIX. Motif, Windows and Mac are the three major GUIs. See *OSF*.

Motion JPEG

See *MPEG*.

motion path

In computer graphics, the path to be followed by an animated object.

motion video

Refers to moving video images, but does not imply a frame rate. Full-motion video refers to fluid, TV-like images displayed at a rate of 24 to 30 frames per second.

Motorola

(Motorola, Inc., Schaumburg, IL) A leading manufacturer of semiconductor devices founded in Chicago in 1928 by Paul V. Galvin as the Galvin Manufacturing Corporation. Its first product allowed radios to operate from household current instead of batteries. In the 1930s, the company commercialized car radios under the Motorola brand suggesting "sound in motion," and in 1947, changed the company name.

By the 1960s, it was a leader in communications and consumer electronics and had built its first semiconductor facility. It eventually moved from the consumer side, selling its color TV business in the mid-1970s.

Although Motorola is known in computers for its 68000 microprocessor family, and now the PowerPC line, it is also involved in radio and data communications systems and automotive and industrial products, among others.

mount

To cause a file on a remote workstation or server to be available for access locally. For example, in NFS (Network File System), a server maintains a list of its directories that are available to clients. When a client mounts a directory on the server, that directory and its subdirectories become part of the client's directory hierarchy. See *automounting*.

mouse

A popular pointing device that is used to move the cursor on screen. Mouse movement is relative. The screen cursor moves from its existing location. The mouse could be moved across your arm, and the screen cursor would move as well. The mouse on a tablet, which is correctly called the *tablet cursor* is not relative. The tablet cursor makes contact with the tablet with absolute reference. Placing it on the upper left part of the tablet moves the screen cursor to that same location on screen. See *mechanical mouse, optical mouse, serial mouse, bus mouse, mickey, trackball, pointing stick* and *touchpad.*

mouse pad

A fabric-covered rubber pad roughly 9" square that provides a smooth surface for rolling a mouse.

mouse port

A socket in the computer into which a mouse is plugged.

Serial DB9   Bus Connector

mouse trails

The creation of repeating, trailing images of the pointer when it moves across the screen in order to make it more visible on passive matrix screens. See *submarining*.

MOV

(1) (Metal Oxide Varistor) A discrete electronic component used in surge suppresssors that diverts excessive voltage to the ground and/or neutral lines.
(2) An assembly language instruction that moves (copies) data from one location to another.

move

(1) In programming, to copy data from one place in memory to another. At the end of the move, source and destination data are identical.
(2) In word processing and graphics, to relocate text and images to another part of the document or drawing.

movie file

A file that contains full-motion, digital video, such as an AVI file.

Mozart

A screen scraper from Mozart Systems Corporation, Burlingame, CA, that is used to turn a character-based mainframe screen into a Windows or DOS front end via 3270 emulation. It is noted for being able to easily combine multiple terminal screens into one. Mozart was originally named Enter 3270.

MP

See *multiprocessing*.

MPC

(Multimedia PC) Requirements for a multimedia PC as specified by the Multimedia PC Marketing Council, a subsidiary of the Software Publishers Association, 1730 M St., N.W., Washington, DC 20036, 202/331-0494.
Vendors certified by the Multimedia PC Marketing Council may display the MPC2 and MPC3 insignias on their products.
The first MPC specification was published in 1990. Level 2 of the specification was published in 1993, and Level 3 in 1995. Level 3 reflects the demands made by the latest multimedia software. Level 1, which required only a 386SX with 3MB of RAM is not listed and not recommended.

Minimum Requirements	Level 2	Level 3
RAM	4MB	8MB
Processor	25MHz 486SX	75MHz Pentium
Input	2-button mouse	2-button mouse
	101 key keyboard	101 key keyboard
Hard disk	160MB	540MB
CD-ROM	300KB transfer rate, 400 ms access time	600KB transfer rate, 250 ms access time
	CD-ROM XA multisession	CD-ROM XA multisession
Sound	16-bit, 8 voice synthesizer	16-bit, wavetable, MIDI playback
	MIDI playback	
Ports	MIDI, joystick	MIDI, joystick
Graphics performance	1.2 megapixels/sec @ 40% CPU	color space conversion & scaling, direct access to frame buffer
Video playback	n/a	OM1-compliant MPEG1 (hardware or software)

MPC601

See *PowerPC*.

MPEG

(Moving Pictures Experts Group) An ISO/ITU standard for compressing video. MPEG-1, which is used in CD-ROMs and Video CDs, provides a resolution of 352x240 at 30 fps with 24-bit color and CD-quality sound. Some MPEG boards can also magnify the image to full screen. MPEG-2 is a full-screen video standard used in upcoming DVD media that hold significantly more data than current-day CDs. MPEG is a lossy method.

MPEG uses the same intraframe coding as JPEG for individual frames, but also uses interframe coding, which further compresses the video data by encoding only the differences between periodic key frames, known as I-frames.

A variation of MPEG, known as Motion JPEG, or M-JPEG, does not use interframe coding and is thus easier to edit in a nonlinear editing system than full MPEG.

For effective playback, MPEG-encoded material requires either a fast computer (Pentium, PowerPC, etc.) or a plug-in MPEG board such as Sigma Designs' RealMagic. It is expected that MPEG circuits will be built into future computers. See *JPEG*.

MPE/iX

(MultiProgramming Executive/POSIX) A POSIX-compliant multitasking operating system that runs on the HP 3000 series. The earlier non-POSIX version was called MPE.

MPP

(Massively Parallel Processor) A parallel processing architecture that uses hundreds or thousands of processors. Some might contend that a computer system with 64 or more CPUs is a massively parallel processor. However, the number of CPUs is not so much the issue as the architecture. MPP systems use a different programming paradigm than the more common symmetric multiprocessing (SMP) systems used as servers.

In an MPP, each CPU contains its own memory and copy of the operating system and application. As a result, an information processing problem must be breakable into pieces that can be all solved simultaneously. In scientific environments, simulations and various mathematical problems can be split apart and processed at the same time. In the business world, database searches lend themselves to this. For example, a parallel data query (PDQ) breaks a query into multiple searches so that several parts of the database can be searched concurrently. See *SMP*.

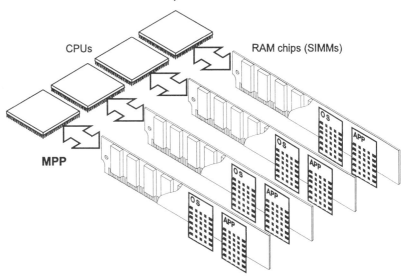

MPR

(MultiProtocol Router) Software from Novell that provides router capabilities for its NetWare servers. It supports IPX, IP, AppleTalk and OSI protocols as well as all the major LANs and WANs.

MPR II

The Swedish government standard for maximum video terminal radiation. The earlier MPR I is less stringent. See *TCO*.

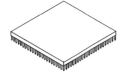

MPU

(MicroProcessor Unit) Same as *microprocessor*.

MPU-401

A MIDI standard from Roland Corporation that has become the de facto interface for connecting a personal computer to a MIDI device.

MR, M-R

See *magnetoresistive*.

MRCI

(Microsoft Realtime Compression Interface) The programming interface for Microsoft's DoubleSpace technology used in DOS 6.

ms

(1) (MilliSecond) See *space/time*.
(2) (MS) See *Microsoft*.

MSa/s

(MegaSAmples per Second) A measurement of sampling rate in millions of samples per second.

MSCDEX

(MicroSoft CD-ROM EXtensions) See *CD-ROM Extensions*.

MSD

(MicroSoft Diagnostics) A utility that accompanies Windows 3.1 and DOS 6 that reports on the internal configuration of the PC. A variety of information on disks, video, drivers, IRQs and port addresses is provided.

MS-DOS

(MicroSoft-Disk Operating System) A single user operating system for PCs from Microsoft. It is functionaly identical to IBM's PC-DOS version, except that starting with DOS 6, MS-DOS and PC-DOS each provide different sets of auxiliary utility programs. Both MS-DOS and PC-DOS are called DOS. See *DOS*.

MSDOS.SYS

One of two hidden system files that make up Microsoft's MS-DOS. The other is IO.SYS. These two system files are loaded into memory when the computer is booted. They process the instructions in CONFIG.SYS, then load COMMAND.COM and finally process the instructions in AUTOEXEC.BAT. The PC-DOS counterparts of these system files are IBMBIO.COM and IBMDOS.COM.

In Windows 95, MSDOS.SYS is a text configuration file rather than an executable program. It determines among other things whether the computer boots into DOS or into Windows 95. IO.SYS is still a binary executable that is loaded when the computer is booted.

MSI

(Medium Scale Integration) Between 100 and 3,000 transistors on a chip. See *SSI, LSI, VLSI* and *ULSI*.

MSN

See *Microsoft Network*.

MS-Net

(MicroSoft Network) Microsoft's version of PC-Network introduced in 1985.

MSP

(1) A Microsoft Paint graphics file format.
(2) (Microsoft Solution Provider) A Microsoft certification for qualifying resellers that sell and provide training and support on Microsoft products. A certain number of employees must be Microsoft Certified Professionals.
(3) (Multi-Tech Supervisory Protocol) A simultaneous voice and data (SVD) protocol from Multi-Tech Systems, Inc., Mounds View, MN. When a telephone handset is picked up, the modem switches to packet mode, digitizes the voice and interleaves the voice packets with the data packets. See *SVD*.
(4) (Media Suite Pro) A popular Macintosh-based nonlinear video editing system from Avid Technologies, Tewksbury, MA.
(5) An operating system used in Fujitsu IBM-compatible mainframes.
(6) (Multiprocessing Server Pack) A utility that enables LAN Manager to utilize a computer's multiprocessing capabilities.

MS-Windows, MS-Works

See *Windows* and *Microsoft Works*.

MTA

(Message Transfer Agent) The store and forward part of a messaging system. See *messaging system*.

MTBF

(Mean Time Between Failure) The average time a component works without failure. It is the number of failures divided by the hours under observation.

M Technology Association

See *MUMPS*.

MTS

(Modular TV System) The stereo channel added to the NTSC standard, which includes the SAP audio channel for special use.

MTTR

(Mean Time To Repair) The average time it takes to repair a failed component.

MUD

(MultiUser Dungeons) Games that are played by multiple users on the Internet, using the Internet Relay Chat (IRC). MUD also stands for multiuser dialogues. A companion to MUDs are MUSEs, which stand for multiuser simulation environments or multiuser shared environments.

MUG

(Macintosh User Group) There are many Mac user groups throughout the world. One organization that disseminates press releases and product ads to over 1,300

MUGs is Pawtuckaway Graphics, 53 Lakeview Dr., Raymond, NH 03077, 603/895-6227.

MULTIBUS

An advanced bus architecture from Intel used in industrial, military and aerospace applications. It includes message passing, auto configuration and software interrupts. MULTIBUS I is 16-bits; MULTIBUS II is 32-bits.

multicast

To transmit a message to multiple recipents at the same time. Multicasting is used in teleconferencing and data communications networks. Multicast is a one-to-many transmission that implies sending to several designated recipients, whereas broadcast implies sending to everyone connected to the network. Contrast with *unicast*.

multicast backbone

See *Mbone*.

multichip module

See *MCM*.

multicomputer

A computer made up of several computers. The term generally refers to an architecture in which each processor has its own memory rather than multiple processors with a shared memory. See *parallel computing*.

multi-config

A multiple configuration. It often refers to the multiple startup options in DOS starting with DOS 6.

MULTICS

(MULTiplexed Information and Computing Service) Developed at MIT and Bell Labs in the mid 1960s, MULTICS was the first timesharing operating system. It was used on GE's mainframes, which were absorbed into the Honeywell product line, later acquired by Bull.

multidimensional database

See *OLAP database*.

multidimensional query

Asking for a multidimensional view of data.

multidimensional spreadsheet

See *spreadsheet*.

multidimensional views

Looking at data in several dimensions; for example, sales by region, sales by sales rep, sales by product category, sales by month, etc. See *OLAP database*.

multidrop line

See *multipoint line*.

MultiFinder

See *Finder*.

multifrequency monitor

A monitor that adjusts to all frequencies within a range (multiscan) or to a set of specific frequencies, such as VGA and Super VGA.

multifunction drive

A storage drive that reads and writes more than one type of storage medium. For example, a magneto-optic disk drive can be used for rewritable disks as well as write once disks. A Floptical drive can read and write floppy and Floptical disks.

multilaunch

To open the same application that is stored in a server simultaneously in two or more clients.

multilayer, multilevel optical disk

An optical disk technology that uses multiple platters sandwiched together with a tiny spacer between them. The different layers are accessed by moving the lens up and down and focusing on one of the disk surfaces. IBM demonstrated this technology in 1994 at its Almaden Research Center in San Jose, CA, and showed its feasibility with various optical technologies. It is expected that, in time, all optical disks, including audio CDs and CD-ROMs, will employ multilevel technology to increase storage capacity.

multiline

A cable, channel or bus that contains two or more transmission paths (wires or optical fibers).

multimastering

See *bus mastering*.

MultiMate

A PC word processing program from Ashton-Tate that was originally noted for its similarity to the Wang word processors of the 1970s. Version 4.0 (1989) introduced a number of advanced features.

multimedia

Disseminating information in more than one form. It includes the use of text, audio, graphics, animated graphics and full-motion video. Multimedia programs are typically games, encyclopedias and training courses on CD-ROM. However, any application with sound and/or video can be called a multimedia program. See *hot topics* and *MPC*.

multimedia conferencing

See *videoconferencing* and *data conferencing*.

Multimedia Extensions

Windows routines that support audio recording and playback, animation playback, joysticks, MIDI, the MCI interface for CD-ROM, videodiscs, videotapes, etc., and the RIFF file format. See *MPC*.

multimedia monitor

A monitor that contains built-in speakers. In time, multimedia monitors are expected to contain a built-in camera for videoconferencing.

multimedia PC

A PC that includes stereo sound and a CD-ROM drive. PCs that are sold with the MPC label meet the technical requirements of the Multimedia PC Marketing Council, but the requirements are easily met today with new 486 PCs and double-speed CD-ROM drives.

To upgrade an older system to multimedia requires installing a CD-ROM drive, a sound card and shielded speakers, which can be purchased separately or together in a multimedia upgrade kit. See *MPC* and *multimedia upgrade kit*.

multimedia upgrade kit

The hardware and software necessary to turn a standard PC into a multimedia PC (MPC). The package includes a CD-ROM drive, sound card and speakers. Some combination of bundled software and/or CD-ROMs may also be included. The advantage of the kit is that the CD-ROM controller card and sound card have been preset to avoid potential conflicts with each other, and the correct cables are included. See *CD-ROM audio cable*.

multimode fiber

An optical fiber with a core diameter of from 50 to 100 microns. It is the most commonly used optical fiber. Light can enter the core at different angles, making it easier to connect the light source. However, light rays bounce around within the core causing some distortion and providing less bandwidth than single-mode fiber. Contrast with *single-mode fiber*.

MultiPlan

An early spreadsheet for CP/M machines and PCs from Microsoft. It was one of the first spreadsheets.

Multiple Master

A font technology from Adobe Systems, Mountain View, CA, that allows a typeface to be generated in different styles, from condensed to expanded and from light to heavy. Multiple Master can generate fonts that are more optically correct at both extremes in size from very small to very large than standard Type 1 fonts.

multiplexing

Transmitting multiple signals over a single communications line or computer channel. The two common multiplexing techniques are FDM, which separates signals by modulating the data onto different carrier frequencies, and TDM, which separates signals by interleaving bits one after the other.

multiplexor

In communications, a device that merges several low-speed transmissions into one high-speed transmission and vice versa. Contrast with *inverse multiplexor*.

multiplexor channel

A computer channel that transfers data between the CPU and several low-speed peripherals (terminals, printers, etc.) simultaneously. It may have an optional burst mode that allows a high-speed transfer to only one peripheral at a time.

multiple zone recording

See *ZBR*.

multiplier-accumulator

A general-purpose floating point processor that multiplies and accumulates the results of the multiplication. Newer versions also perform division and square roots.

multipoint control unit

See *MCU*.

multipoint line

In communications, a single line that interconnects three or more devices.

multiported memory

A type of memory that provides more than one access path to its contents. It allows the same bank of memory to be read and written simultaneously. See *video RAM*.

multiport repeater

A hub in a 10BaseT network is often known as a multiport repeater, because it sends any input signal to all outputs. See *10BaseT*.

multiprocessing

Simultaneous processing with two or more processors in one computer, or two or more computers processing together. When two or more computers are used, they are tied together with a high-speed channel and share the general workload between them. If one fails, the other takes over.

It is also accomplished in special-purpose computers, such as array processors, which provide concurrent processing on sets of data. Although computers are built with various overlapping features, such as executing instructions while inputting and outputting data, multiprocessing refers specifically to concurrent instruction executions. See *parallel processing, SMP, MPP, bus mastering* and *fault tolerant*.

multiprogramming

Same as *multitasking*.

multiprotocol router

A router that supports two or more communications protocols, such as IPX, TCP/IP and DECnet. It is used to switch network traffic between different LANs located throughout the enterprise as well as to switch LAN traffic to WANs.

multiscan monitor

A monitor that adjusts to all frequencies within a range. See *multifrequency monitor*.

multisession

See *Photo CD*.

MultiSync monitor

A family of multiscan monitors from NEC Technologies, Inc. NEC popularized the multiscan monitor.

multitasking

The running of two or more programs in one computer at the same time. The number of programs that can be effectively multitasked depends on the type of multitasking performed (preemtive vs cooperative), CPU speed and memory and disk capacity.

Programs can be run simultaneously in the computer because of the differences between I/O and processing speed. While one program is waiting for input, instructions in another can be executed. During the milliseconds one program waits for data to be read from a disk, millions of instructions in another program can be executed. In interactive programs, thousands of instructions can be executed between each keystroke on the keyboard.

In large computers, multiple I/O channels also allow for simultaneous I/O operations to take place. Multiple streams of data are being read and written at the exact same time.

In the days of mainframes only, multitasking was called *multiprogramming*, and multitasking meant *multithreading*.

multithreading

Multitasking within a single program. It allows multiple streams of execution to take place concurrently within the same program, each stream processing a different transaction or message. Multithreading generally uses reentrant code, which cannot be modified when executing, so that the same code can be shared by multiple programs.

In a symmetric multiprocessing (SMP) operating system, multithreading allows multiple CPUs to be controlled at the same time. It is also used to create synchronized audio and video applications.

multi-timbral

The ability to play multiple instrument sounds (patches) simultaneously. See *MIDI patch* and *timbre*.

multiuser

A computer shared by two or more users.

multiuser DOS

(1) A DOS-compatible operating system that runs multiple terminals from a single PC.

(2) (Multiuser DOS) A multiuser DOS-compatible operating system from Novell that runs multiple terminals from a single 386 or higher PC. Supersedes Concurrent DOS.

multivariate

The use of multiple variables in a forecasting model.

MUMPS

An advanced, high-level programming language and integrated database used for business applications. It has extensive string handling making it suitable for databases with vast amounts of free text.

MUMPS has unique features including the ability to store both data and program statements in its database. In addition, formulas written in a program can be stored and used by other programs. Developed in 1966 at Massachusetts General Hospital (Mass. Utility MultiProgramming System), it has been used extensively in health-care.

The following example converts Fahrenheit to Celsius:

```
READ "Enter Fahrenheit ",FAHR
SET CENT=(FAHR-32)*5/9
WRITE "Celsius is", CENT
```

The M Technology Association (formerly MUMPS Users Group) is an organization that supports the MUMPS community through training, meetings and distribution of publications and software. Address: 1738 Elton Rd., Suite 205, Silver Spring, MD 20903, 301/431-4070.

MUSE

See *MUD*.

music CD

Generally refers to an audio CD, otherwise known as "Red Book audio." However, the term could refer to a CD-ROM that contains sound files, such as WAV and MID files.

MUX

(MUltipleXor) See *multiplexor*.

MVGA

(Monochrome VGA) The type of display often found on a non-color laptop. It should more accurately be called "gray scale VGA," since monochrome means two colors; for example, black and white and no shades in between.

MVIP

(MultiVendor Integration Protocol) A voice bus and switching protocol for PCs originated by a number of companies, including Natural Microsystems of Natick, MA, its major supporter. It provides a second communications bus within the PC that is used to multiplex up to 256 full-duplex voice channels from one voice card to another.

Digital voice, fax, video (any digital data) is bussed over a ribbon cable connected at the top of each ISA, EISA or Micro Channel card. For example, several fax boards could be cabled to a board that multiplexes their lines onto a T1 channel. Using the high bandwidth of this second bus, video conferencing systems are built around MVIP.

MVIP products can make the PC perform like a small-scale PBX. For example, an interactive voice response system on one card could pass incoming voice conversations to a card that switches the lines to live agents in a call center.

The ability to plug a card into a standard AT bus and perform voice and video processing is opening up a whole new world to vendors. It allows far more flexible and affordable systems to be built, and it helps solve worldwide interface problems. A variety of interface cards from different countries can be plugged in, allowing MVIP products to connect to telephone systems all around the world.

MVP

(Multimedia Video Processor) A high-speed DSP chip from TI introduced in 1994. Formally the TMS320C80, it combines RISC technology with the functionality of four DSPs on one chip.

MVS

(Multiple Virtual Storage) Introduced in 1974, the primary operating system used on IBM mainframes (the others are VM and DOS/VSE). MVS is a batch processing-oriented operating system that manages large amounts of memory and disk space. Online operations are provided with CICS, TSO and other system software.

MVS/XA (MVS/eXtended Architecture) manages the enhancements, including 2GB of virtual memory, introduced in 1981 with IBM's 370/XA architecture.

MVS/ESA (MVS/Enterprise Systems Architecture) manages the enhancements made to large scale mainframes, including 16TB of virtual memory, introduced in 1988 with IBM's ESA/370 architecture. MVS/ESA runs on all models of the System/390 ES/9000 product line introduced in 1990.

MVS/ESA

See *MVS*.

MVS/XA

See *MVS*.

MYOB

Digispeak for "mind your own business."

N

NACCB

(National Association of Computer Consultant Businesses, 1250 Connecticut Ave. N.W., Suite 700, Washington, DC 20036, 202/637-9134) An organization representing companies that provide professional help in information and engineering fields. Founded in 1987, it is concerned with legislation that affects computer consultants.

NACOMEX

(NAtional COMputer EXchange) See *computer exchange*.

NAEC

See *NetWare certification*.

nag screen

An advertisement in a shareware program that asks the user to register and pay for the software. Although it generally pops up at the beginning or end of the program, it can appear at certain intervals as it is being used.

NAK

(Negative AcKnowledgement) A communications code used to indicate that a message was not received, or that a terminal does not wish to transmit. Contrast with *ACK*.

Named Pipes

An IPC facility in LAN Manager that allows data to be exchanged from one application to another either over a network or running within the same computer. The use of the term pipes for interprocess communication was coined in UNIX.

name service, naming service

Software that converts a name into a physical address on a network, providing logical to physical conversion. Names can be user names, computers, printers, services or files. The transmitting station sends a name to the server containing the naming service software, which sends back the actual address of the user or resource. It serves as a Yellow Pages for the network, which is precisely what Sun's NIS system was originally called. Novell's naming service for NetWare 4.0 is called NDS (NetWare Directory Service). In AppleTalk, the naming service is embedded within the protocol. See *directory service*.

NAND

(Not AND) A Boolean logic operation that is true if any single input is false. Two-input NAND gates are often used as the sole logic element on gate array chips, because all Boolean operations can be created from NAND gates.

Inputs		Output
0	0	1
0	1	1
1	0	1
1	1	0

nano

One billionth or 10 to the -9th power.

nanometer

One billionth of a meter. One nanometer is equal to 10 angstroms. Nanometers are used to measure the wavelengths of light.

nanosecond

One billionth of a second. Used to measure the speed of logic and memory chips, a nanosecond can be visualized by converting it to distance. In one nanosecond, electricity travels about six inches in a wire.

Even at 186,000 miles per second, electricity is never fast enough for the hardware designer who worries over a few inches of circuit path. The slightest delay is multiplied millions of times, since millions of pulses are sent through a wire in a single second. See *space/time*.

nanotechnology

A future science that builds devices at the atomic and molecular level. For example, a bit might be represented by only one atom some time in the future. Nanotechnology could be used to build anything, not just computers and communications devices.

NAPLPS

(North American Presentation-Level Protocol Syntax) An ANSI-standard protocol for videotex and teletext. It compresses data for transmission over narrow-bandwidth lines and requires decompression on the receiving end. PRODIGY uses this format for transmitting and displaying some of its graphics.

narrowband

In communications, transmission rates from 50 bps to 64 Kbps. Earlier uses of the term referred to 2,400 bps or less or to sub-voice grade transmission from 50 to 150 bps. Contrast with *wideband* and *broadband*.

NAS

(Network Application Support) Digital's implementation of open systems, which provides standards-based software that allows a variety of workstations (VMS, ULTRIX, Sun, DOS, Windows, OS/2, Mac, etc.) to interface via VAX and ULTRIX servers.

NASI

(1) (NetWare Asynchronous Service Interface) A protocol from Novell for connecting to modems in a communications server. It was derived from the NCSI protocol. NASI provides more advanced features than the common int 14 (interrupt 14) method. It allows a specific modem or line to be chosen. It frees the call more quickly, and it transfers data more efficiently.

(2) (National Association of Systems Integrators, 412 High Plain Street, Unit #1, Walpole, MA 02081, 508/668-8900) An organization of more than 5,000 members founded in 1991, dedicated to exchanging up-to-date information on members' products and services. Its annual Computer Suppliers & Services Directory, in print and on disk, is organized by zipcode.

National Computer Exchange

See *computer exchange*.

National Cristina Foundation

(591 W. Putnam Ave., Greenwich, CT 06830, 800/274-7846) A not-for-profit organization, founded by Bruce McMahan and Yvette Marrin and named in honor of McMahan's daughter who has cerebral palsy. It channels used and surplus computers and software to NCF network partner organizations that train people with disabilities, at risk students and the disadvantaged in the U.S. and abroad.

native language

Same as *machine language*. See *native mode*.

native mode

(1) The normal running mode of a computer, executing programs from its built-in instruction set. Contrast with *emulation mode*.

(2) The highest performance state of a computer, such as a 486 or Pentium running in Protected Mode.

NATURAL

A fourth-generation language from Software AG, Reston, VA, that runs on a variety of computers from micro to mainframe.

natural language

English, Spanish, French, German, Japanese, Russian, etc.

natural language query

A query expressed by typing English, French or any other spoken language in a normal manner. For example, "how many sales reps sold more than a million dollars in any eastern state in January?" In order to allow for spoken queries, both a voice recognition system and natural language query software are required.

natural language recognition

Same as *voice recognition*.

NAU

(1) (Network Access Unit) An interface card that adapts a computer to a local area network.

(2) (Network Addressable Unit) An SNA component that can be referenced by name and address, which includes the SSCP, LU and PU.

Naviken

A format used for geographic databases that originated in Japan. Naviken CD-ROMs have become a de facto standard for car navigation maps. See *GPS*.

NB card

(NuBus card) See *NuBus*.

NC

See *numerical control*.

NCB

(Network Control Block) A packet structure used by the NetBIOS communications protocol.

NCF

See *National Cristina Foundation*.

NCF file

(NetWare Command File) A file of NetWare commands that are executed one at a time, similar to a DOS batch (.BAT) file. The NetWare AUTOEXEC.NCF file is executed in the server at startup, just like the DOS AUTOEXEC.BAT file.

NCGA

(National Computer Graphics Association, 2722 Merrilee Dr., Suite 200, Fairfax, VA 22031, 800/225-NCGA) An organization dedicated to developing and promoting the computer graphics industry. It maintains a clearinghouse for industry information and strives to encourage communication among computer graphics users, consultants, educators and vendors.

NCP

(1) (Network Control Program) See *SNA* and ***network control program.***
(2) (NetWare Core Protocol) Application layer protocols in the NetWare network operating system. It is the internal NetWare language used to communicate between client and server and provides functions such as opening, closing, reading and writing files and obtaining access to the NetWare bindery and NDS naming service databases.
(3) (Not Copy Protected) Software that can be easily copied.

NCR

See *AT&T GIS.*

NCR paper

(No Carbon Required paper) A multiple-part paper form that does not use carbon paper. The ink is adhered to the reverse side of the previous sheet.

NCSA

(1) (National Center for Supercomputer Applications) A high-performance computing facility located at the University of Illinois at Urbana-Champaign. Founded in 1985 by a National Science Foundation grant, the NCSA provides supercomputer resources to hundreds of universities and organizations engaged in scientific research. It is also a major World Wide Web site.
(2) (National Computer Security Association, 10 S. Courthouse Ave., Carlisle, PA 17013, 717/258-1816) A membership organization founded in 1989 with the purpose of education, creating an awareness of and providing a clearing house for computer security issues. NCSA sells all the major books written on the subject. An annual conference is hosted in Washington, DC.

NCSC

(National Computer Security Center) The arm of the U.S. National Security Agency that defines criteria for trusted computer products. Following are the Trusted Computer Systems Evaluation Criteria (TCSEC), DOD Standard 5200.28, also known as the Orange Book, and the European equivalent. The Red Book is the Orange Book counterpart for networks. Level D is a non-secure system.

Level C provides discretionary access control (DAC). The owner of the data can determine who has access to it.

C1 Requires user log-on, but allows group ID.

C2 Requires individual user log-on with password and an audit mechanism.

Levels B and A provide mandatory access control (MAC). Access is based on standard DOD clearances. Each data structure contains a sensitivity level, such as top secret, secret and unclassified, and is available only to users with that level of clearance.

B1 DOD clearance levels.

B2 Guarantees path between user and the security system. Provides assurances that system can be tested and clearances cannot be downgraded.

B3 System is characterized by a mathematical model that must be viable.

A1 System is characterized by a mathematical model that can be proven. Highest security. Used in military computers.

European Ratings

The European Information Technology Security Evaluation Criteria (ITSEC) is similar to TCSEC, but rates functionality (F) and effectiveness (E) separately.

Orange Book TCSEC	ITSEC
D	E0
C1	F-C1, E1
C2	F-C2, E2
B1	F-B1, E3
B2	F-B2, E4
B3	F-B3, E5
A1	F-B3, E6

NCSI

(Network Communications Services Interface) Also called "nixie," it is a protocol used to handle serial port communications on a network. NCSI applications talk to the NCSI driver rather than directly to the COM port, which allows redirection of the data to a communications server on the network. See *NASI*.

n-dimensional

Some number of dimensions.

NDIS

(Network Driver Interface Specification) A network driver interface from Microsoft. See *network driver interface*.

NDS

See *NetWare Directory Service*.

NE

(Not Equal to) See *relational operator*.

NE1000

An 8-bit Ethernet network adapter from Novell that became a de facto standard. Many earlier Ethernet adapters were NE1000 compatible.

NE2000

A 16-bit Ethernet network adapter from Novell that became a de facto standard. Many Ethernet adapters are NE2000 compatible.

nearline, near online

Available almost immediately. Libraries of tape cartridges and optical disk jukeboxes are called near online, or nearline, devices because they are not as fast as online disks. They take several seconds to retrieve the appropriate storage module before it can be read.

near pointer

In an x86 segmented address, a memory address within a single segment (the offset). Contrast with *far pointer*.

negative logic

The use of high voltage for a 0 bit and low voltage for a 1 bit. Contrast with *positive logic*.

nematic

The stage between a crystal and a liquid that has a threadlike nature; for example, a liquid crystal.

nemonic

See *mnemonic*.

neper

The unit of measurement based on Napierian logarithms that represents the ratio between two values, such as current or voltage.

nerd

A person typically thought of as dull socially. Nerds often like technical work and are generally introspective. Contrast with *hacker*, a technical person that may or may not be a nerd.

NEST

(Novell Embedded Systems Technology) Extensions to NetWare 4.x that provide networking connectivity to business machines and consumer products. NEST can link copy machines, fax machines, VCRs, TVs, virtually any appliance that might be controlled by a centralized network. It is expected that this technology will expand in the 1996-1997 timeframe.

nesting

In programming, the positioning of a loop within a loop. The number of loops that can be nested may be limited by the programming language. See *loop*.

net

Abbreviation of network. "The Net" often refers to the Internet.

NetBEUI

(NetBIOS Extended User Interface) Pronounced "net-booey," it is an enhanced version of the NetBIOS protocol used by network operating systems such as LAN Manager, LAN Server, Windows for Workgroups and Windows NT. It formalizes the transport frame that was never standardized in NetBIOS and adds additional functions.

NetBIOS

A commonly-used network protocol for PC local area networks. NetBIOS provides session and transport services (layers 4 and 5 of the OSI model). NetBIOS did not provide a standard frame format for transmission over the network, causing various different implementations of NetBIOS to be created. For example, Artisoft's LANtastic uses a proprietary version of NetBIOS for transmission between client and server. The frame format was later formalized in NetBEUI.

There are two NetBIOS modes. The Datagram mode is the fastest mode, but does not guarantee delivery. It uses a self-contained packet with send and receive name, usually limited to 512 bytes. If the recipient device is not listening for messages, the datagram is lost. The Session mode establishes a connection until broken. It guarantees delivery of messages up to 64KB long.

There is no routing layer in NetBIOS or NetBEUI, thus there is no internetworking capability. Other protocols, such as IPX and IP, must be used for internetworking, although NetBIOS is often used to establish the connection as in the NetWare example below. See *NetBEUI*.

OSI Layer	Netware Emulation Of NetBIOS
5	NetBIOS Session Layer
4	NetwareTransport Protocol PEP (Packet Exchange Protocol)
3	Netware Networking Protocal IPX (Internet Packet Exchange)
2	Data Link Layer (Ethernet, Token Ring)

netbooey

See *NetBEUI.*

netiquette

(NETwork etIQUETTE) Proper manners when using an online service or BBS. Emily Post may not have told you to curtail your cussing via modem, but netiquette has been established to remind you that profanity is not in good form over the network.

Using UPPER CASE TO MAKE A POINT all the time and interjecting emoticons throughout a message is also not good netiquette. See *flame.*

NetNews

See *Usenet.*

NETROOM

A DOS memory manager from Helix Software Company, Long Island City, NY. NETROOM3's "cloaking" runs the system and video BIOS in extended memory freeing upper memory blocks for other purposes. New BIOSs are included which provide an automatic BIOS upgrade for the PC. Also included are cloaked utilities (disk cache, RAM drive, screen saver, etc.) that run mostly in extended memory.

NetScape Navigator

A Web browser for Windows, Macintosh and X Windows from NetScape Communications Corporation (formerly Mosaic Communications). It provides secure transmission over the Internet, and NetScape server software provides encryption based on the RSA method. Navigator has become the most popular Web browser, and Navigator 2.0 supports Adobe Acrobat documents and Java applications.

NetView

IBM SNA network management software that provides centralized monitoring and control for SNA, non-SNA and non-IBM devices. NetView/PC interconnects NetView with Token Ring LANs, Rolm CBXs and non-IBM modems, while maintaining control in the host.

netViz

A network diagramming program for Windows from Quyen Systems, Inc., Rockville, MD. It keeps the lines connected to the objects when they are moved and also allows a database to be linked to diagram objects for equipment and network documentation. More than 400 predefined symbols are included.

NetWare

A family of network operating systems from Novell that support DOS, OS/2, Mac and UNIX clients and various LAN access methods including Ethernet, Token Ring

and ARCNET. NetWare is the most widely-used LAN control program.
Personal NetWare is a peer-to-peer network operating system, which allows any client workstation to be a server. It supersedes earlier peer-to-peer versions known as NetWare Lite and NetWare ELS (Entry Level System). Personal NetWare is also included with Novell's DOS operating system.

NetWare 2.x (originally Advanced NetWare 286) runs in a dedicated file server (286 and up) and supports up to 100 concurrent users per server. This version is no longer being updated.

NetWare 3.x (originally NetWare 386), which supports up to 250 concurrent users, runs on 386 servers and up and takes advantage of the 32-bit architecture.

NetWare 4.0, introduced in 1993, is backward compatible with NetWare 2.x and 3.x and includes the NetWare Directory Service (NDS), which provides X.500 compatibility (see *NDS*). A NetWare 4.x server supports up to 1,000 concurrent users and also includes realtime disk compression for the server. Currently NetWare 4.x runs on Intel-based computers; however, versions for the PowerPC, Alpha, HP PA-RISC, SPARC and Pentium (exploiting the Pentium architecture) are expected. Except for Personal NetWare, NetWare is a stand-alone operating system that runs in the server. It does not use DOS or any other operating system. The hard disks in a NetWare server are formatted with a Novell format, not a DOS format.

SFT NetWare (System Fault Tolerant) provides automatic recovery from network malfunctions. NetWare for VMS provides NetWare connectivity to VAX networks. Portable NetWare provides NetWare source code for conversion to other platforms. See *IPX, SPX* and *MHS*.

NetWare certification

Novell provides certification for technical competence with self-study tests and courses given at National Authorized Education Centers (NAECs). Certificates include CNA (Certified NetWare Administrator), CNE (Certified NetWare Engineer), ECNE (Enterprise CNE, which includes WAN expertise) and CNI (Certified NetWare Instructor).

NetWare Core Protocol

Application layer protocols in the NetWare network operating system. It is the internal NetWare language used to communicate between client and server and provides functions such as opening, closing, reading and writing files and obtaining access to the naming service databases (bindery and NDS).

NetWare Directory Service

Also known as *NDS*, it is a global naming service in NetWare 4.0 based on X.500 for compatibility with other public directories. The NDS Directory maintains information about all the resources in the network, including users, groups, servers, volumes and printers. NDS replaces the bindery file used in previous versions of NetWare and is backward compatible with it.

Compared to the bindery's single server orientation, NDS is designed to manage all servers in the network and allows its database to be replicated to support this capability. With NDS, users log into the network, not into a specific server.

In NDS, every network resouce, such as a user, server, server volume, printer and print queue is called an object. Each object contains properties (fields); for example, a user object would contain login ID, password, name, address, telephone and node address. An NDS database is a hierarchical structure that can store the resources of not only multiple networks but the internetworking of an entire multinational enterprise.

Novell is licensing NDS to a number of UNIX vendors. In a mixed UNIX/NetWare shop, such implementations provide network administrators with a single point of management of user accounts.

NetWare Global Messaging

E-mail software from Novell for NetWare 3.x that includes directory synchronization across distributed servers and provides optional interfaces to X.400, SMTP and SNADS. See *SMF*.

NetWare Loadable Module

Known as an *NLM*, it is software that enhances or provides additional functions in a NetWare 3.x or higher server. Support for database engines, workstations, network protocols, fax and print servers are examples. The NetWare 2.x counterpart is a VAP.

NetWare Management System

Also known as *NMS*, it is an SNMP-based network management software from Novell for monitoring and controlling NetWare networks.

NetWare NFS

Software from Novell that implements the NFS distributed file system on NetWare 3.11 servers. It allows UNIX and other NFS client machines to access files on the NetWare server. See *LAN Workplace* and *UnixWare*.

NetWare Users International

A voluntary organization of more than 250 NetWare user groups worldwide. For information, call 800/228-4NUI within the U.S. or 801/429-7000 outside the U.S.

NetWire

Novell's BBS on CompuServe, which provides technical support for its NetWare products.

network

(1) An arrangement of objects that are interconnected. See *LAN* and *network database*.
(2) In communications, the transmission channels interconnecting all client and server stations as well as all supporting hardware and software.

network accounting

The reporting of network usage. It gathers details about user activity including the number of logons and resources used (disk accesses and space used, CPU time, etc.).

network adapter

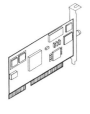

A printed circuit board that plugs into both the clients (personal computers or workstations) and servers and controls the exchange of data between them. The network adapter provides services at the data link level of the network, which is also known as the *access method* (OSI layers 1 and 2).
The most common network adapters are Ethernet and Token Ring. Sometimes, the Ethernet adapter is built into the motherboard. LocalTalk, which provides the data link services of Apple's AppleTalk network, is built into all Macintoshes.
A transmission medium, such as twisted pair, coax or fiber optic, interconnects all the adapters in the network. A network adapter is also called a *NIC*, or network interface card.

network administrator

A person who manages a communications network within an organization. Responsibilities include network security, installing new applications, distributing software upgrades, monitoring daily activity, enforcing licensing agreements, developing a storage management program and providing for routine backups.

network analyzer

Software only or a combination of hardware and software that monitors traffic on a network. It can also read unencrypted text transmitted over the network.

network architecture

(1) The design of a communications system, which includes the hardware, software, access methods and protocols used. It also defines the method of control: whether computers can act independently or are controlled by other computers monitoring the network. It determines future flexibility and connectability to foreign networks. (2) The access method in a LAN, such as Ethernet, Token Ring and LocalTalk.

network card

See *network adapter*.

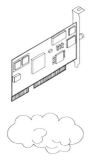

network cloud

A cloud-like symbol in a network diagram used to reduce an entire communications network into points of entry and exit. It infers that although there may be any number of switches, routers, trunks, and other network devices within the cloud, the point of interconnection to the cloud (network) is the only technical issue in the diagram. Clouds are often used to depict a WAN (wide area network).

network control program

Software that manages the traffic between terminals and the host mini or mainframe. It resides in the communications controller or front end processor. In a personal computer LAN, it is called a *network operating system* and resides in the server and manages requests from the workstations. IBM's SNA network control program is called *NCP*.

network database

(1) A database that runs in a network. It implies that the DBMS was designed with a client/server architecture.
(2) A database that holds addresses of other users in the network.
(3) A database organization method that allows for data relationships in a net-like form. A single data element can point to multiple data elements and can itself be pointed to by other data elements. Contrast with *relational database*.

network drive

A disk or tape drive connected to a server in the network that is shared by multiple users. Contrast with *local drive*.

network driver

Software that activates the actual transmission and receipt of data over the network. It provides the data link protocol (Ethernet, Token Ring, etc.) that controls the specific brand of network adapter installed in the computer.

network driver interface

A software interface between the transport protocol and the data link protocol (network driver). The interface provides a protocol manager that accepts requests from the transport layer and activates the network adapter. Network adapters with compliant network drivers can be freely interchanged.
This method allows multiple protocol stacks to run over one network adapter. For example, a PC can connect to a NetWare network running SPX/IPX and a UNIX network running TCP/IP. It also allows one transport protocol to run over different network adapters; for example, SPX/IPX over Ethernet and Token Ring.
In PC LANs, the two primary network driver interfaces are Novell's ODI and Microsoft's NDIS. Novell provides an ODI interface utility that allows NDIS and ODI protocols to work in the same computer.

network layer

Internetworking services provided by the network as defined by layer 3 of the OSI model. See *OSI.*.

network management

Monitoring an active communications network in order to diagnose problems and gather statistics for administration and fine tuning. Examples of network management products are IBM's NetView, HP's OpenView, Sun's SunNet Manager and Novell's NMS. Almost all network management software supports the SNMP network management protocol. Other management protocols are CMIP and DME. See *systems management* and *configuration management*.

network management console

The client component of network management software that provides the user interface and "control room" view of the network.

network manager

See *network administrator*.

network modem

A modem shared by all users in a network. See *ACS*.

network operating system

Also called a *NOS*, it is an operating system that manages network resources. It manages multiple requests (inputs) concurrently and provides the security necessary in a multiuser environment. It may be a completely self-contained operating system, such as NetWare, or it may require an existing operating system in order to function (LAN Manager requires OS/2; LANtastic requires DOS, etc.).
One piece of the network operating system resides in each client machine and another resides in each server. It allows the remote drives on the server to be accessed as if they were local drives on the client machine. It allows the server to handle requests from the client to share files and applications as well as network devices such as printers, faxes and modems.
In a peer-to-peer network, the network operating system allows each station to be both client and server. In a non-peer-to-peer network, dedicated servers are used, and files on a client machine cannot be retrieved by other users.
In networks of PCs, NetWare is the most widely used network operating system. LAN Server, LAN Manager, VINES, Windows NT, Windows for Workgroups, Windows 95 and LANtastic are also examples.
UNIX, combined with TCP/IP and NFS, VMS combined with DECnet, the Mac OS combined with AppleTalk, and SNA, combined with VTAM and NCP, also provide network operating system services.
Along with file and print services, a network operating system may also include directory services and a messaging system as well as network management and multiprotocol routing capabilities.

network protocol

A communications protocol used by the network. There are many layers of network protocols. See *OSI model*.

network ready

Software designed to run in a network. It implies that multiple users can share databases without conflict.

network security

The authorization of access to files and directories in a network. Users are assigned ID numbers and passwords that allow them access to information and programs.

neural network

A modeling technique based on the observed behavior of biological neurons and used to mimic the performance of a system. It consists of a set of elements that start out connected in a random pattern, and, based upon operational feedback, are molded into the pattern required to generate the required results. It is used in applications such as robotics, diagnosing, forecasting, image processing and pattern recognition.

newbie

The first-time user of computers or of a particular environment, such as Windows or UNIX. The term is often used for newcomers to the Internet.

New Era

See *INFORMIX.*

newline

End of line code. See *CR/LF.*

NeWS

(Network Extensible Windowing Support) A networked windowing system (similar to X Windows) from SunSoft that renders PostScript fonts on screen the way they print on a PostScript printer.

newsgroup

A collection of messages about a particular subject on the Internet. See *Usenet.*

newsreader

An Internet utility, such as nn, rn or tin, that is used to read the messages in a newsgroup.

Newton

An artificial intelligence technology from Apple for use in PDAs and other hand-held and desktop appliances. See *MessagePad.*

NewWave

An object-oriented Windows shell from HP that integrates data and activates tasks within the system. It allows data from different applications to be merged to create a compound document. Hot links automatically update the document if data in one of the source files is updated.

NewWave allows for the creation of agents, which are automatic procedures that can be activated based on time or events. For example, at month end, an agent could extract data from the corporate mainframe and prepare a report using several application programs. Programs must be modified to run under NewWave.

NeXT

(NeXT, Inc., Redwood City, CA) Founded in 1985 by Steven Jobs, co-founder of Apple, NeXT created a family of high-resolution, UNIX-based workstations running its NEXTSTEP environment. The first machine was introduced in 1988. Manufacturing of the hardware ceased in early 1993, but NeXT is continuing with its NEXTSTEP software for the Intel x86 platform.

NEXTSTEP

A UNIX-based, object-oriented development environment from NeXT Computer, Redwood City, CA. It runs on NeXT computers, x86s (386 and up) and Sun and HP workstations, providing an advanced, integrated environment for creating applications. Insiginia Solution's SoftPC allows DOS and Windows applications to run on a NEXTSTEP/x86 machine. See *OpenStep.*

NFS

(Network File System) A distributed file system from SunSoft that allows data to be shared across a network regardless of machine, operating system, network architecture or protocol. This de facto UNIX standard lets remote files appear as if they were local on a user's machine. The combination of TCP/IP, NFS and NIS comprise the primary networking components of UNIX.

NGM

See *NetWare Global Messaging*.

NI

See *non-interlaced*.

nibble

Half a byte (four bits).

nibble mode memory

A type of dynamic RAM that outputs four consecutive bits (nibble) at one time.

NIC

(Network Interface Card) Same as *network adapter*. See also *InterNIC*.

NICAD

A trademark of SAFT America Inc., Valdosta, GA, for nickel cadmium products. See *nickel cadmium*.

nickel cadmium

(NiCd) A rechargeable battery technology that has been widely used in portable applications, including portable computers. It provides more charge per pound than lead acid batteries, but less than nickel hydride or zinc air. Its major problem is a so-called "memory effect," in which the battery seems to remember how full it was when you last charged it, and it doesn't go past that point the next time. Nickel cadmium batteries should be completely drained periodically to maintain the longest charge. It uses a nickel and cadmium plate and potassium hydroxide as the electrolyte. See *lead acid, nickel hydride* and *zinc air*.

nickel hydride

A rechargeable battery technology that provides more charge per pound than lead acid and nickel cadmium, but less than zinc air. It does not suffer from the nickel cadmium memory effect. It uses nickel and metal hydride plates with potassium hydroxide as the electrolyte. See *lead acid, nickel cadmium* and *zinc air*.

NIS

(Network Information Services) A naming service from SunSoft that allows resources to be easily added, deleted or relocated. Formerly called Yellow Pages, NIS is a de facto UNIX standard. NIS+ is a redesigned NIS for Solaris 2.0 products. The combination of TCP/IP, NFS and NIS comprise the primary networking components of UNIX.

NIST

(National Institute of Standards & Technology) The standards-defining agency of the U.S. government, formerly called the National Bureau of Standards.

NJE

(Network Job Entry) An IBM mainframe protocol that allows two JES devices to communicate with each other.

N-key rollover

A keyboard circuit built into most keyboards and vital for fast typing. To test this capability, press four adjacent keys in sequence without removing any finger from any of the keys. If all four letters appear on screen, it has this feature.

NLM

See *NetWare Loadable Module.*

NLQ

(Near Letter Quality) The print quality that is almost as sharp as an electric typewriter. The slowest speed of a dot matrix printer often provides NLQ.

NMI

(NonMaskable Interrupt) A high-priority interrupt that cannot be disabled by another interrupt. It is used to report malfunctions such as parity, bus and math coprocessor errors.

NMOS

(N-Channel MOS) Pronounced "N moss." A type of microelectronic circuit used for logic and memory chips. NMOS transistors are faster than their PMOS counterpart and more of them can be put on a single chip. It is also used in CMOS design.

NMS

See *NetWare Management System.*

nn

(NetNews) A newsreader for reading the messages in a newsgroup on the Internet. See *Usenet.*

NNI

(Network-to-Network Interface) An interface between networks. See *UNI.*

NNTP

(Network News Transfer Protocol) The protocol used to connect to Usenet groups on the Internet. Usenet newsreaders support the NNTP protocol.

node

(1) In communications, a node is a network junction or connection point. For example, a personal computer in a LAN is a node. A terminal connected to a minicomputer or mainframe is a node.
(2) In database management, a node is an item of data that can be accessed by two or more routes.
(3) In computer graphics, a node is an endpoint of a graphical element.
(4) In massively parallel computers, a node is a single processor. In symmetric multiprocessing (SMP), a node is a complete processing unit, which includes includes shared memory, I/O and all the processors attached to it.

noise

An extraneous signal that invades an electrical transmission. It can come from strong electrical or magnetic signals in nearby lines, from poorly fitting electrical contacts, and from power line spikes.

NOMAD

A relational DBMS from Thomson Software Products, Norwalk, CT, that runs on

IBM mainframes, PCs and VAXs. Introduced in the mid 1970s, it was one of the first database systems to provide a non-procedural language for data manipulation. NOMAD can also access data on Oracle, Sybase, DB2 and other databases.

NOMDA
(National Office Machine Dealers Association) An association that merged with LANDA to become the Business Technology Association. See *BTA*.

non-blocking
The ability of a signal to reach its destination without interference or delay.

non-breaking space
See *hard space*.

non-document mode
A word processing mode used for creating source language programs, batch files and other text files that contain only text and no proprietary headers and format codes. All text editors, as well as XyWrite word processors, automatically output this format.

non-impact printer
A printer that prints without banging a ribbon onto paper, such as a thermal or ink jet printer. See *printer*.

non-interlaced
Illuminating a CRT by displaying lines sequentially from top to bottom. Non-interlaced monitors eliminate annoying flicker found in interlaced monitors, which illuminate half the lines in the screen in the first cycle and the remaining half in the second cycle. Contrast with and see *interlaced* for a diagram.

nonlinear
A system in which the output is not a uniform relationship to the input.

nonlinear video editing
Storing video in the computer for editing. It is much easier to edit video in the computer than with earlier analog editing systems. Today's digital nonlinear editing systems provide high-quality post-production editing on a personal computer. However, lossy compression is used to store digital images, and some detail will be lost.

Depending on the purpose for the video presentation, output is either the final video turned back into analog or an edit decision list (EDL) that describes frame sources and time codes in order to quickly convert the original material into the final video in an editing room. For commercial production, the latter allows editing to be done offline rather than in a studio that costs several hundred dollars per hour.

Prior to digital, a system using several analog tape decks was considered a nonlinear video editing system. Contrast with *linear video editing*.

nonmaskable interrupt
See *NMI*.

non-modal
Not mode oriented. A non-modal operation moves from one situation to another without apparent mode switching.

non-numeric programming

Programming that deals with objects, such as words, board game pieces and people, rather than numbers. Same as *list processing*.

non-preemptive multitasking

A multitasking environment in which an application is able to give up control of the CPU to another application only at certain points, such as when it is ready to accept input from the keyboard. Under this method, one program performing a large number of calculations for example, can dominate the machine and cause other applications to have limited access to the CPU.

Non-preemtive multitasking is also called *cooperative multitasking*, because programs must be designed to cooperate with each other in order to work together effectively in this environment.

A non-preemtive multitasking operating system cannot guarantee service to a communications program running in the background. If another application has usurped the CPU, the CPU cannot process the interrupts from the communications program quickly enough to capture the incoming data, and data can be lost.

Contrast with *preemptive multitasking*.

non-procedural language

A computer language that does not require traditional programming logic to be stated. For example, a command, such as LIST, might display all the records in a file on screen, separating fields with a blank space. In a procedural language, such as COBOL, all the logic for inputting each record, testing for end of file and formatting the screen has to be explicitly programmed.

Query languages, report writers, interactive database programs, spreadsheets and application generators provide non-procedural languages for user operation. Contrast with and see *procedural language* for an example.

non-routable protocol

A communications protocol that contains only a device address and not a network address. It does not incorporate an addressing scheme for sending data from one network to another. Examples of non-routable protocols are NetBIOS and DEC's LAT protocols. Contrast with *routable protocol*.

Non-system disk error or disk error

A DOS error message. The full message is

Non-system disk or disk error
Replace and press any key when ready

This usually means there's a non-bootable floppy in drive A. The computer looks for DOS on a floppy before it looks for DOS on the hard disk. If an ordinary floppy is in drive A at startup, it causes this error. Remove the disk and press any key.

non trivial

A favorite word used among programmers for any task that isn't simple.

non-volatile memory

Memory that holds its content without power. Firmware chips (ROMs, PROMs, EPROMs, etc.) are examples. Disks and tapes may be called non-volatile memory, but they are usually considered storage devices.

Sometimes the term refers to memory that is inherently volatile, but maintains its content because it is connected to a battery at all times.

NOR

(Not **OR**) A Boolean logical operation that is true if all inputs are false, and false if any input is true. An exclusive NOR is true if both inputs are the same.

NOR		EXCLUSIVE NOR	
Inputs	Output	Inputs	Output
0 0	1	0 0	1
0 1	0	0 1	0
1 0	0	1 0	0
1 1	0	1 1	1

normalization

In relational database management, a process which breaks down data into record groups for efficient processing. There are six stages. By the third stage (third normal form), data is identified only by the key field in the record. For example, ordering information is identified by order number, customer information, by customer number.

normal wear

Deterioration due to natural forces that act upon a product under average, everyday use.

Northgate

(Northgate Computer Systems, Inc., Eden Prarie, MN) A PC manufacturer founded in 1987 by Arthur Lazere that is known for its high-end systems and keyboards. Its PCs are sold mostly through direct marketing, but its highly-praised line of OmniKey keyboards is also sold through dealers. In 1995, Northgate was acquired by PAJ Electronics, Van Nuys, CA.

Norton Desktop

Popular shells for DOS and Windows from Symantec. They include a comprehensive package of utilities and provide a large amount of customizability.

Norton Navigator

A Windows 95 shell from Symantec. It is the sucessor to Norton Desktop for Windows 3.x and provides multiple desktops and enhanced file manipulation.

Norton Utilities

Widely-used utility programs for the PC and Macintosh from Symantec Corporation, Cupertino, CA. It includes programs to search, edit and undelete files, to restore damaged files and to defragment the disk, plus more. Originally from Peter Norton Computing, these programs were among the first to popularize disk utilities for the PC.

NOS

See *network operating system.*

NOS/VE

(Network Operating System/Virtual Environment) A multitasking, virtual memory operating system from Control Data that runs on its mainframes.

NOT

A Boolean logic operation that reverses the input. If a 0 is input, a 1 is output, and vice versa. See *AND, OR & NOT.*

notation

How a system of numbers, phrases, words or quantities is written or expressed. Positional notation is the location and value of digits in a numbering system, such as the decimal or binary system.

notebook computer

A laptop computer that weighs from approximately five to seven pounds. A notebook that weighs under five pounds is usually called a *subnotebook*. For features of a portable computer, see *laptop computer*.

Notes

See *Lotus Notes*.

Notes ViP

See *Lotus Notes Visual Programmer*.

Not ready error reading drive x

A DOS error message. The full message is

> Not ready reading drive x
> Abort, Retry, Fail?

This means the drive door is left open, or the floppy disk is not in the drive. Either put the appropriate floppy disk in the drive or close the drive door (turn lever) and press R.
To switch to another drive, press F, and type in the drive letter you want to go back to when you get the "Current drive is no longer valid>" message. In DOS versions prior to 4.0, type I for Ignore rather than F for Fail.

Not ready writing device PRN

A DOS error message. The full message is

> Not ready writing device PRN
> Abort, Retry, Fail?

This means the printer is turned off or unavailable. Press A to cancel, or turn the printer on and press R. You might also check the cable connection to the printer.

Nova

A minicomputer series from Data General. When introduced in 1969, it was the first 16-bit mini to use four CPU accumulators, quite advanced for its time. Novas and its RDOS operating system were used extensively in the OEM marketplace.

NovaNET

A satellite-based network for educational services created by the Education Research Lab of the University of Illinois. It includes over 10,000 hours of lesson material from third grade to post graduate work in over a hundred subject areas.

Novell

(Novell Inc., Provo, UT) Novell was founded as Novell Data Systems in 1981 by Jack Davis and George Canova. It initially manufactured terminals for IBM mainframes. In 1983, Ray Noorda became CEO and president of a restructured Novell, Inc., which would concentrate on the development of its NetWare operating system. NetWare has grown into the most widely used network operating system in the world.
With the acquisition of AT&T's UNIX in 1993 and WordPerfect and Quattro Pro

in 1994, Novell extended its system software products and also branched out into applications. It planned to integrate UnixWare and NetWare into a "super" network operating system, but instead sold UNIX to the Santa Cruz Operation (SCO) in 1995. As of late 1995, Novell announced its intention to sell its applications divisions and is expected to concentrate solely on NetWare once again.

Novell DOS

A DOS-compatible operating system from Novell that has been discontinued. Originally DR DOS from Digital Research, Novell acquired the company in late 1991, enhanced the product and released it as Novell DOS 7 in 1994. It includes new utilities, built-in NetWare client support, peer-to-peer networking, preemptive multitasking and the ability to store drivers in extended memory.

Over the years, DR DOS was always noted for its advanced features, which inspired Microsoft to improve subsequent versions of MS-DOS.

Novell network

A LAN controlled by one of Novell's NetWare operating systems. See *NetWare*.

no wait state memory

Memory fast enough to meet the demands of the CPU. Idle wait states do not have to be introduced.

nroff

(Nontypesetting RunOFF) A UNIX utility that formats documents for terminals and dot matrix printers. Using a text editor, troff codes are embedded into the text and the nroff command converts the document into the required output. Complex troff codes are ignored. See *troff*.

NRZ

(Non-Return-To-Zero) A signalling method used in magnetic recording and communications that does not automatically return to a neutral state after each bit is transmitted.

ns

(NanoSecond) See *nanosecond*.

NSP

(Native Signal Processing) A series of enhancements to Pentium and subsequent CPUs that enable software to do what has been previously done in hardware. Large caches and additional instructions that support multimedia allow the equivalent of graphics accelerators, video accelerators, modems and sound cards to be delivered via software using the system CPU rather than by separate DSP and CPU chips on the peripheral controller cards.

NSTL

(National Software Testing Lab, Philadelphia) An independent organization that evaluates computer hardware and software. It adheres to controlled testing methods to ensure objective results and publishes its findings in Software Digest Ratings Report and PC Digest.

NT

See *Windows NT*.

NT1

(Network Terminator 1) A device that terminates an ISDN line at the customer's premises. See *ISDN*.

NTAS

(NTAdvanced Server) The server version of Windows NT. See *Windows NT*.

NTFS

(NTFile System) A file system used in Windows NT which uses the Unicode character set and allows file names up to 255 characters in length. The NTFS is designed to recover on the fly from hard disk crashes. Windows NT supports multiple file systems. It can run with a DOS FAT, an OS/2 HPFS and a native NTFS, each in a different partition on the hard disk. NT's security features require that the NTFS be used.

NTSC

(National TV Standards Committee) The U.S. colored TV standard administered by the FCC. It currently broadcasts at 525 lines of resolution that are transmitted as 30 interlaced frames per second (60 half frames per second, or 60 "fields" per second in TV jargon). It is a composite of red, green and blue signals for color and includes an FM frequency for audio and an MTS signal for stereo.

The NTSC will reconvene in order to change TV standards. See *HDTV*. Contrast with the European PAL color TV standard at 625 lines of resolution and SECAM at 819 lines.

NuBus

A bus architecture (32-bits) originally developed at MIT and defined as a Eurocard (9U). Apple has changed its electrical and physical specs for its Macintosh series. Many Macs have one or more NuBus slots for peripheral expansion.

NuBus Card
NuBus uses a 96-pin plug and socket.

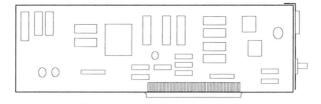

NUI

(1) (Notebook User Interface) A term coined by Go Corporation for its PenPoint pen-based interface.

(2) (NetWare Users International) A voluntary organization of more than 250 NetWare user groups worldwide. For information, call 800/228-4NUI within the U.S. or 801/429-7000 outside the U.S. and ask for NUI.

(3) (Network User Identifier) A code used to gain access into local European packed-switched networks.

null

The first character in ASCII and EBCDIC. In hex, it prints as 00; in decimal, it prints as a blank. It is naturally found in binary numbers when a byte contains no 1 bits. It is also used to pad fields and act as a delimiter; for example, in C, it specifies the end of a character string.

null modem cable

An RS-232 cable used to connect two personal computers in close proximity. It connects to both serial ports and crosses the sending wire on one end to the receiving wire on the other.

null pointer

In programming, a reference to zero. May be the response of an unsuccessful search function.

null string

In programming, a character string that contains no data.

number crunching

Refers to computers running mathematical, scientific or CAD applications, which perform large amounts of calculations.

Number Nine

(Number Nine Visual Technology Corporation, Lexington, MA) A manufacturer of PC display adapters founded in 1982 as Number Nine Computer Corporation by Andrew Najda and Stan Bialek. Over the years, Number Nine display adapters have been highly praised for advancing the state of the art. Products often begin with a #9, such as #9GXe and #9FX.

numbers

In a computer, numbers can be stored in several forms. Although they are all coded as binary digits (bits), BCD and packed decimal numbers retain the decimal relationship of a number, whereas fixed and floating point do not.

Binary Coded Decimal (BCD)

BCD encodes each decimal digit in a single byte. The number 6508 would take four bytes. A variation, called *packed decimal*, encodes two digits in one byte. 6508 would take two bytes.

Decimal	Packed Decimal
6 5 0 8	65 08

6508	6508 00

Fixed Point   Floating Point

Binary Fixed Point

This method converts the entire decimal number into a binary number, placing it in a fixed unit of storage. The number 6508 would require at least two bytes. Binary numbers are calculated faster than decimal (BCD) numbers.

Bytes	Bits	Values
1	8	0 to 255
2	16	0 to 65,535
4	32	0 to 4,294,967,295

Binary Floating Point

Floating point allows very small fractions and very large numbers to be maintained and calculated quickly. Both the mantissa (significant digits) and the exponent (power to which the base is raised) are converted into binary numbers. See *floating point*.

numerical aperture

The amount of light that can be coupled to an optical fiber. The greater the aperture, the easier it is to connect the light source to the fiber.

numerical control

A category of automated machine tools, such as drills and lathes, that operate from instructions in a program. Numerical control (NC) machines are used in manufacturing tasks, such as milling, turning, punching and drilling. First-generation machines were hardwired to perform specific tasks or programmed in a very low-level machine language. Today, they are controlled by their own microcomputers and programmed in high-level languages, such as APT and COMPACT II, which automatically generate the tool path (physical motions required to perform the operation).

The term was coined in the 1950s when the instructions to the tool were numeric codes. Just like the computer industry, symbolic languages were soon developed, but the original term remained.

numeric data

Refers to quantities and money amounts used in calculations. Contrast with *string* or *character data*.

numeric field

A data field that holds only numbers to be calculated. Contrast with *character field*.

numeric keypad

A four-row keyboard.

Calculator	Telephone
789	123
456	456
123	789
0	0

Num Lock

(NUMeric Lock) A keyboard key used to toggle a combination number/cursor keypad between number keys and cursor keys.

NVRAM

(Non-Volatile RAM) See *non-volatile memory*.

Nx586

A family of Pentium-class CPUs from NexGen, Inc., Milpitas, CA. The P100, P90, P80 and P75 chips provide 93MHz, 84MHz, 75MHz and 70MHz speeds respectively. Nx586 chips are designed with two internal 16KB caches. The math coprocessor is an external option.

NxN switch

See *crosspoint switch*.

NZ

(Non Zero) A value greater or less than 0.

O

OA
See *office automation*.

OADG
(Open Architecture Development Group) An organization founded by IBM Japan in 1991 to promote PC standards in Japan. See *DOS/V*.

OAI
(Open Application Interface) A computer to telephone interface that lets a computer control and customize PBX and ACD operations.

object
(1) In object-oriented programming, a self-contained module of data and its associated processing. Objects are the software building blocks of object technology. See *object technology* and *object-oriented programming*.
(2) In a compound document, an independent block of data, text or graphics that was created by a separate application.

object code
Same as *machine language*. This is an early term that has no relationship to object technology.

object computer
Same as *target computer*. This is an early term that has no relationship to object technology.

object database
See *object-oriented database*.

Object Database Management Group
An organization founded in 1991 to promote standards for object databases. The ODMG standard adds programming extensions to C++ and Smalltalk for accessing an object-oriented database. It also includes a superset of SQL 92 Entry Level, the most widely supported version of SQL.
The Object Database Management Group (ODMG) defines an interface to the database, whereas the Object Management Group (OMG) defines an interface for using objects in a distributed environment. The ODMG object model complies with the core model of the Object Management Architecture (OMA) of the OMG. See *OMA* and *CORBA*.

Objective-C
An object-oriented C programming language from The Stepstone Corporation that runs on PCs and popular workstations. It was the first commercial object-oriented extension of the C language.

object language
(1) A language defined by a metalanguage.
(2) An object-oriented programming language.
(3) Same as *machine language* or *target language*.

Object Linking and Embedding
See *OLE*.

Object Management Architecture
A definition of a standard object model from the Object Management Group. It defines the behavior of objects in a distributed environment. The communications

component of the Object Management Architecture, or OMA, is the Common Object Request Broker, or CORBA. CORBA is often referenced more than OMA, but it is part of OMA and thus implies OMA. See *CORBA*.

Object Management Group

An international organization founded in 1989 to endorse technologies as open standards for object-oriented applications. The OMG specifies the Object Management Architecture (OMA), a definition of a standard object model for distributed environments. Address: 492 Old Connecticut Path, Framingham, MA 01701, 508/820-4300. Also see *Object Database Management Group*.

object model

(1) A description of an object architecture, including the details of the object structure, interfaces between objects and other object-oriented features and functions.

(2) An object-oriented description of an application.

object module

The output of an assembler or compiler, which must be linked with other modules before it can be executed. This is an early term that has no relationship to object technology.

object oriented

See *object technology* and *object-oriented programming*.

object-oriented analysis

The examination of a problem by modeling it as a group of interacting objects. An object is defined by its class, data elements and behavior. For example; in an order processing system, an invoice is a class, and printing, viewing and totalling are examples of its behavior. Objects (individual invoices) inherit this behavior and combine it with their own data elements.

object-oriented database

A database that holds abstract data types (objects) and is managed by an object-oriented database management system (DBMS). See *object-oriented DBMS*.

object-oriented DBMS

A database management system (DBMS) that manages objects, which are abstract data types. An object-oriented DBMS, or ODBMS, is suited for multimedia applications as well as data with complex relationships that are difficult to model and process in a relational DBMS. In addition, ordinary business applications are increasingly being designed as object-oriented models.

Since the rules for processing the data are part of an object, any type of data can be stored. An ODBMS allows for fully integrated databases that hold data, text, pictures, voice and video. Objects can point to actual data physically located outside of the object database as independent files, such as graphics and video files on a hard disk or CD-ROM for example. This inherent object flexibility lets an ODBMS function as a master repository of information about the information in an enterprise.

Relational DBMSs are primarily designed to handle numbers, alphanumeric text and dates. They may also support a BLOB field, which holds any binary data (image, sound or video clip) or holds a name to that file, but the routine to handle that BLOB must be written into or called for by the application that accesses the database.

In an object database, a picture or video clip may take the form of an object that literally says "go get that picture file and go run this routine to display it." The application is not responsible for each new type of format and its associated

Object Modeling versus Relational Modeling

Object-oriented information systems provide more flexibility than systems designed for relational databases. While relational databases easily provide one-to-many and many-to-one relationships, object databases allow for many to many. Information systems that require complex relationships can be easily modeled with object technology, but are often "shoehorned" into the row and column format of relational tables.

Tables

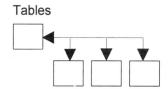

Objects

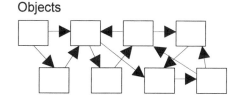

Another advantage to objects is that they can contain anything. Relational structures are always rows and columns, but objects can hold alphanumeric data, arrays, images and video, virtually anything.

Relational format: rows and columns

Object format: any structure

Rows and colums

Arrays

n, n, n, n, n, n, n, n, n, n, n, n

Images

Video

When information systems are modeled as objects, they can employ the powerful inheritance capability. Instead of building a table of employees with department and job information in separate tables, the type of employee is modeled. The employee class contains the data and the processing for all employees. Each subclass (manager, secretary, etc.) contains the data and processing unique to that person's job. Changes can be made globally or individually by modifying the class in question.

Relational modeling

| Employee Table | Department Table | Job Table |

Object modeling

Employee Class

Manager Class | Secretary Class | Clerk Class

processing. The methods, or processing, in the object dynamically invoke the necessary procedures to handle that type of data. This provides flexibility in an ever-changing world of formats and interfaces.

Some ODBMSs are purely object oriented and are accessed from an application program written in an object-oriented programming language. Many allow access via an SQL-like language or derivative, while others combine relational and object orientation in a unified product. See *ODMG*.

Examples of ODBMSs are Servio Corporation's Gemstone, Object Design's Object Store, Ontos' ONTOS DB, HP's Open ODB and UniSQL's UniSQL/X.

object-oriented design

Transforming an object-oriented model into the specifications required to create the system. Moving from object-oriented analysis to object-oriented design is accomplished by expanding the model into more and more detail.

object-oriented graphics

Same as *vector graphics*.

object-oriented interface

A graphical interface that uses icons and a mouse, such as Mac, Windows and Motif.

object-oriented operating system

An operating system that is based on objects.

object-oriented programming

Abbreviated "OOP," programming that supports object technology. It is an evolutionary form of modular programming with more formal rules that allow pieces of software to be reused and interchanged between programs. Major concepts are (1) encapsulation, (2) inheritance, and (3) polymorphism.

Encapsulation is the creation of self-sufficient modules that contain the data and the processing (data structure and functions that manipulate that data). These user-defined, or abstract, data types are called classes. One instance of a class is called an object. For example, in a payroll system, a class could be defined as Manager, and Pat and Jan, the actual objects, are instances of that class.

Classes are created in hierarchies, and **inheritance** allows the knowledge in one class to be passed down the hierarchy. New objects can be created by inheriting characteristics from existing classes. For example, the object MACINTOSH could be one instance of the class PERSONAL COMPUTER, which could inherit properties from the class COMPUTER SYSTEMS. Adding a new computer requires entering only what makes it different from other computers, while the general characteristics of personal computers can be inherited.

Object-oriented programming allows procedures about objects to be created whose exact type is not known until runtime. For example, a screen cursor may change its shape from an arrow to a line depending on the program mode. The routine to move the cursor on screen in response to mouse movement would be written for "cursor," and **polymorphism** would allow that cursor to be whatever shape is required at runtime. It would also allow a new shape to be easily integrated into the program.

The SIMULA simulation language was the original object-oriented language. It was used to model the behavior of complex systems. Xerox's Smalltalk was the first object-oriented programming language and was used to create the graphical user interface whose derivations are so popular today. C++ has become the major commercial OOP language, because it combines traditional C programming with object-oriented capabilities. ACTOR and Eiffel are also meaningful OOP languages. The following list compares some fundamental object-oriented programming terms with traditional programming terms and concepts. See *object technology*.

Object-oriented programming	Traditional programming
class	data type + characteristics
instance	variable
instantiate	declare a variable
method	processing code
message	call
object	data type + processing

Object Packager

A Windows utility that embeds a document as an icon inside another document. It is part of Windows' OLE (object linking and embedding). It also allows objects created by non-OLE-compliant applications to be embedded. When the icon is double clicked, the application that created it is opened to view and edit it. See *OLE*.

ObjectPro

An object-oriented client/server development system from Trinzic Corporation, Palo Alto, CA. It includes its own programming language and generates executable programs for Windows, RS/6000 and Sun clients. It supports the major databases and also provides an interpreted mode for development.

object program

A machine language program ready to run in a particular operating environment. It has been assembled, or compiled, and link edited. This is an early term that has no relationship to object technology.

object references

To learn about object technology, two excellent easy-to-read books on the subject are David Taylor's "Object-Oriented Technology: A Manager's Guide" (Addison-Wesley ISBN 0-201-56358-4) and "Business Engineering with Object Technology" (Wiley ISBN 0-471-04521-7). These are excellent starter books.

For more in-depth analysis, also read "Object-Oriented Analysis and Design" by Grady Booch (Benjamin Cummings ISBN 0-8053-5340-2) and "Object-Oriented Modeling and Design" by James Rumbaugh, et al (Prentice-Hall, ISBN 0-13-629841-0).

Object Request Broker

See *ORB*.

Object Studio

An object-oriented client/server development system from Easel Corporation, Burlington, MA, that supports Windows, OS/2 and various UNIX clients and the major server databases. Its Synchronicity module is used to graphically design the business object model (data and business logic) and generate Enfin Smalltalk code. A visual programming tool is used to create the user interfaces.

object technology

The use of objects as the building blocks for applications. Objects are software routines designed according to a set of rules that allows them to function as independent building blocks that interact with each other.

Just as hardware components are routinely designed as modules to plug into and work with each other, objects are software components designed to work together. The ultimate goal of objects is that it should not matter which source language they were programmed in or in which computer on the network they are running in.

They are designed to interoperate strictly through the messages passed between them.

Objects as building blocks are an evolutionary architecture, being a more formalized approach to modular programming, which has been around for years. What is revolutionary about objects is that they provide a new way of modeling applications, and this is expected to have a significant impact on application development. With objects, a system can be designed as familiar business functions, and the design can be carried all the way down to the programming level. In traditional systems analysis, the programs are decomposed into procedures that are more alien to the business model. Thus, object technology assists business process reengineering (BPR) by providing an implementation method that more closely supports the business processes being designed.

However, in order to design object-oriented applications, programmers, and especially systems designers, must undergo a major paradigm shift. It has often been said that object technology is easier to comprehend by non-computer professionals that have not been steeped in procedural logic. See *object references* and *object-oriented programming*.

ObjectView

A Windows-based client/server application development software from Sterling Software, Atlanta, GA (formerly KnowledgeWare). ObjectView applications can access multiple databases of varying types, including Oracle and Sybase. Business graphics and spreadsheet capabilities can be included.

ObjectVision

Application development software from Borland for creating Windows and OS/2 2.0 applications. Uses visual techniques for user interface design as well as for programming logic. It also provides links to spreadsheets and databases.

ObjectWindows

See *OWL*.

Obsydian

See *Synon/2E*.

OC-1, 3, etc.

See *SONET*.

occam

A parallel processing language designed to handle concurrent operations. The INMOS Transputer executes occam almost directly. In the following statements, two items of data are read and incremented at the same time. PAR specifies that following statements are to be executed concurrently, and SEQ indicates that the following statements are executed sequentially.

```
PAR
 SEQ
   chan1 ? item1
   item1 := item1 + 1
 SEQ
   chan2 ? item2
   item2 := item2 + 1
```

OCR

(Optical Character Recognition) Machine recognition of printed characters. OCR systems can recognize many different OCR fonts, as well as typewriter and computer-printed characters. Advanced OCR systems can recognize hand printing.

Sample OCR Fonts

(Sample fonts courtesy of Recognition Equipment Corporation.)

OCR-A (FULL ALPHA)
NUMERIC   0123456789
ALPHA   ABCDEFGHIJKLMNOPQRSTUVWXYZ
SYMBOLS   >$/-+-#"

OCR-A (NRMA/EURO BANKING)	OCR-B(SUBSET 1, ECMA 11 and ANSI X3.49-1975)
NUMERIC 0123456789	NUMERIC 00123456789
ALPHA ACDMNPRUXY	ALPHA ACENPSTVX
SYMBOLS >$/+#"♪¥⊣	SYMBOLS <+>-¥

OCR MULTIFONT
OCR-B   ¥00123456789><++#
12L/12F   ¥0123456789+#
1403-OCR   00123456789><+#
407-1   0123456789

octal

A numbering system that uses eight digits. It is used as a shorthand method for representing binary characters that use six-bits. Each three bits (half a character) is converted into a single octal digit. Okta is Greek for 8.

Decimal	Binary	Octal
0	000	0
1	001	1
2	010	2
3	011	3
4	100	4
5	101	5
6	110	6
7	111	7

octet

An eight-bit storage unit. In the international community, octet is often used instead of byte.

OCX

(OLE Custom control) An object-oriented custom control that is developed under OLE. OCXs are created as separate executable modules and are dynamically linked to the application at runtime. An OCX object allows the application more control and customization of the object's functions than does a standard OLE object. OCXs come in 16-bit and 32-bit versions and are the successor to the 16-bit VBX controls. See *custom control* and *VBX.*

ODAPI

(Open Data API) A database programming interface from Borland that was rewritten and turned into the IDAPI interface. See *Borland Database Engine.*

ODBC

(Open DataBase Connectivity) A database programming interface from Microsoft that provides a common language for Windows applications to access databases on a network. It is part of Microsoft's WOSA strategy. ODBC is a superset of the SQL Access Group's Call Level Interface (CLI).

ODBMS

See *object-oriented DBMS*.

odd parity

See *parity checking*.

ODI

(Open Data-Link Interface) A network driver interface from Novell. ODI is based on the LSL interface developed by AT&T for its UNIX System V operating system. See *network driver interface* and *LSL*.

ODMG

See *Object Database Management Group*.

Oe

See *Oersted*.

OEM

(Original Equipment Manufacturer) A manufacturer that sells equipment to a reseller. Also refers to the reseller itself. OEM customers either add value to the product before reselling it, private label it, or bundle it with their own products. See *VAR*.

OEM font

A font that uses the extended ASCII characters as defined by IBM for the original PC. The OEM, or DOS/OEM character set contains line draw and other symbols commonly used by DOS programs to create charts and simple graphics. Also known as the PC-8 symbol set as well as Code Page 437, the OEM character set is built into every display adapter. It is also the character set in several fonts used by Windows in order to display DOS applications properly. See *ASCII chart* for the actual characters.

Oersted

Pronounced "ers-ted," the measurement of magnetic resistance. The higher the "Oe," the more current required to magnetize it.

off-hook

The state of a telephone line that allows dialing and transmission but prohibits incoming calls from being answered. The term stems from the days when a telephone handset was lifted off of a hook. Contrast with *on-hook*.

office automation

The integration of office information functions, including word processing, data processing, graphics, desktop publishing and e-mail.

The backbone of office automation is a LAN, which allows users to transmit data, mail and even voice across the network. All office functions, including dictation, typing, filing, copying, fax, Telex, microfilm and records management, telephone and telephone switchboard operations, are candidates for integration.

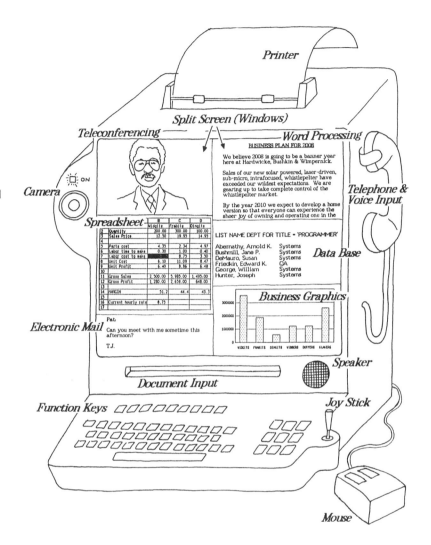

Office Automation

This drawing was created by the author in 1981 and embodies the functions that are finally being fully integrated on a desktop machine.

OfficeJet

A combination ink jet printer, copier and fax machine from Hewlett-Packard Company. Introduced in 1994, this first combo unit from HP is two separate devices in one box: a computer printer and fax machine. There is no way to fax from or to the computer. Its copy facility allows for reductions of up to 70%.

Office Vision

Integrated office automation applications from IBM that run in all IBM computer families. It was the first major implementation of SAA and incorporates the Presentation Manager interface across OS/2 networks, AS/400s and mainframes. Introduced in 1989, it includes e-mail, scheduling, document creation and distribution as well as decision support and graphics capabilities among all users.

offline

Not connected to or not installed in the computer. If a terminal, printer or other device is physically connected to the computer, but is not turned on or in ready mode, it is still considered offline.

Disks and tapes that have been demounted and stored in the data library are considered offline. Contrast with *online*.

offline browser

See *offline reader*.

offline navigator

See *offline reader*.

offline reader

Software that downloads e-mail and selected data from an online service, allowing the user to browse the captured material after disconnecting. It automates retrieving routine data and saves online fees by shortening the connect time.

offline storage

Disks and tapes that are kept in a data library.

offload

To remove work from one computer and do it on another. See *cooperative processing*.

offset

(1) The distance from a starting point, either the start of a file or the start of a memory address. Its value is added to a base value to derive the actual value. An offset into a file is simply the character location within that file, usually starting with 0; thus "offset 240" is actually the 241st byte of the file. See *relative address*.

(2) In word processing, the amount of space a document is printed from the left margin.

off-the-shelf

Refers to products that are packaged and available for sale.

OH

See *off-hook* and *modem*.

ohm

A unit of measurement for electrical resistance. One ohm is the resistance in a circuit when one volt maintains a current of one amp.

OLAP database

(OnLine Analytical Processing database) A database designed for fast access to summarized data. Using specialized indexing techniques, it processes queries that pertain to large amounts of data and multidimensional views of data much faster than traditional relational databases. See *EIS* and *star schema*.

olay

See *OLE*.

OLCP

(OnLine Complex Processing) Processing complex queries, long transactions and simultaneous reads and writes to the same record. Contrast with *OLTP*, in which records are updated in a more predictable manner.

OLE

Microsoft's object-oriented technology for Windows, which is based on its Common Object Model (COM). OLE started out as a compound document protocol (Object Linking and Embedding), allowing one document to be linked or embedded within another. As of Version 2.0, OLE is evolving into a full-blown object technology that is expected to provide the same services as the industry-standard CORBA.

As a compound document protocol, OLE allows an object such as a spreadsheet or video clip to be embedded into a document, called the *client application* or *OLE container*. When the object is double clicked, the application that created it, known as the *OLE server*, is launched in order to edit it. The server application appears to run within the container application.

An object can be linked instead of embedded, in which case the OLE container does not physically hold the object, but provides a pointer to it. If a change is made to a linked object, all the documents that contain that same link are automatically updated the next time you open them. An application can be both client and server. See *Object Packager*.

As of Version 2.0, OLE also provides for object automation, which allows an application to invoke and run external objects, initially within the same computer, and eventually distributed throughout the network. As of late 1995, OLE does not provide distributed operation, but IONA Technology's Orbix, which is a CORBA-compliant object system, provides OLE to CORBA conversion and allows OLE objects to be executed within a heterogeneous, distributed environment.

(See illustration on following page)

OLE container

An OLE application that contains the linked or embedded object. See *OLE*.

OLR

See *offline reader*.

OLTP

(OnLine Transaction Processing) See *transaction processing* and *OLCP*.

OM1

(Open MPEG-1) A programming interface developed by the Open PC MPEG Consortium for interactive MPEG-1 titles. It provides a common set of commands for programming interactive games that are compressed under MPEG. OM1 is based on Sigma Design's RealMagic MPEG-1 board and has become a de facto standard.

OMA

See *Object Management Architecture*.

OME

(Open Messaging Environment) An open messaging system from Novell. It is based on Microsoft's MAPI and is a superset of Novell's MHS and WordPerfect Office's messaging systems.

OMG

See *Object Management Group*.

OLE

OLE stands for Object Linking and Embedding. It was originally developed as a compound document protocol, which allows one document to be embedded within or linked to another. Microsoft is extending OLE into a complete object-oriented distributed processing system. It allows programs to execute independent software components no matter where they reside in the network similar to the Object Management Group's CORBA and OSF's DCE systems.

Object Linking

If an object is linked rather then embedded, it references an original file outside of the document. Thus, if you make a change to a linked object, all the documents that contain that link are automatically updated!

Embedding

When an object (document, drawing, sound, etc.) that is embedded is clicked, the application that created it is loaded so that you can edit it. Changes made to the embedded object affect *only* the document that contains it.

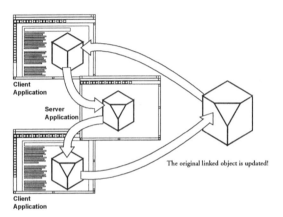

The original linked object is updated!

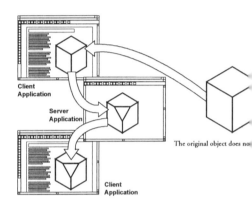

The original object does no|

Network OLE

Network OLE, expected in the 1996-1997 timeframe, extends OLE into an object-oriented distributed processing system. Client applications, called *OLE automation controllers*, can execute software components throughout the enterprise regardless of where they are located. These components, which are called *OLE automation servers*, can reside on independent component servers, regular network servers or within various clients themselves. Network OLE competes with the Object Management Group's CORBA system for distributing objects throughout an enterprise. It is expected that both OLE and CORBA will coexist and that standards for OLE/CORBA interoperability will be implemented.

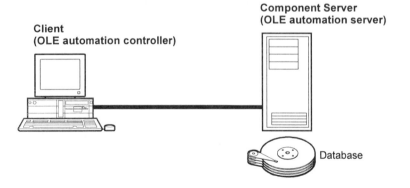

OMI

(Open Messaging Interface) A messaging protocol developed by Lotus, now included in VIM.

omnidirectional

In all directions. For example, an omnidirectional antenna can pick up signals in all directions.

OmniPage

Character recognition software for PCs and the Macintosh from Caere Corporation, Los Gatos, CA. It was the first personal computer software that could distinguish text from graphics and convert a wide variety of fonts into text.

OMNIS 7

A client/server development system for creating Windows, Mac and PowerMac applications from Blyth Software, Foster City, CA. It includes its own database manager for local and laptop use and supports a wide variety of databases. OMNIS includes visual programming tools and a 4GL for application development. Client support for NT, OS/2, Solaris, AIX and HP-UX is expected.

OMT

(Object Modeling Technique) An object-oriented analysis and design method developed by James Rumbaugh. See *object references*.

ONA

(Open Network Architecture) An FCC plan that allows users and competing enhanced service providers (ESPs) equal access to unbundled, basic telephone services. The Open Network Provision (ONP) is the European counterpart.

ONC

(Open Network Computing) A family of networking products from SunSoft for implementing distributed computing in a multivendor environment. Includes TCP/IP and OSI protocols, NFS distributed file system, NIS naming service and TI-RPC remote procedure call library. ONC+ adds Federated Services, which is an interface for third-parties to connect network services into the Solaris environment.

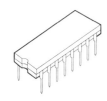

one-chip computer

See *computer on a chip*.

one-off

One at a time. CD-ROM recorders (CD-R drives) are commonly called one-off machines because they write one CD-ROM at a time.

on-hook

The state of a telephone line that can receive an incoming call. Contrast with *off-hook*.

onion diagram

A graphical representation of a system that is made up of concentric circles. The innermost circle is the core, and all outer layers are dependent on the core.

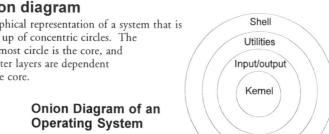

**Onion Diagram of an
Operating System**

online

Available for immediate use. If your data is on disk attached to your computer, the data is online. If it is on a disk in your desk drawer, it is offline. If you use an online service, such as CompuServe or PRODIGY, you are online when you have made the connection via modem and logged on with your account number. When you log off, you are offline.

A peripheral device (terminal, printer, etc.) that is turned on and connected to the computer is said to be online. However, a printer can be taken offline by simply pressing the ONLINE or SEL button. It is still attached and connected, but is internally cut off from receiving data from the computer. Pressing the ONLINE or SEL button will turn it back online.

In the 1960s and 70s, the ancient days of computers, systems were designed as either online or batch. Online meant terminals were connected to a central computer, and batch meant entering batches of transactions (from punched cards or tape) on a second or third shift. Other terms, such as *realtime* and *transaction processing* evolved from online processing. See also *near online*.

Want to Impress Your friends?
Although complete overkill, it is not incorrect to say that one has an online, realtime, interactive, transaction processing system. However, don't say this to an experienced systems analyst!

on-line means happiness!

that is immediately available.

online industry

The collection of service organizations that provide dial-up access to databases, shopping, news, weather, sports, e-mail, etc. See *online services*.

online complex processing

See *OLCP*.

online help

On-screen instruction

online services

Following are major online information service organizations, including the types of databases provided. "Wide variety" generally includes news, weather and shopping as well as information on a host of topics. Most services provide e-mail and many provide access to e-mail and news groups on the Internet. Full Internet access is expected on many services in the future.

America Online, Inc.
Databases: wide variety, personal computer technical
8619 Westwood Center Dr.
Vienna, VA 22182
800/827-6364
703/448-8700

BIX
Databases: personal computer technical
Byte Information Exchange
900 Chelmsford St.
Lowell, MA 01851
800/695-4775
617/492-8300

CompuServe Information Service, Inc.
Databases: wide variety, personal computer technical
P.O. Box 20212
Columbus, OH 43220
800/848-8990
614/457-8650

DataTimes Corporation
Databases: newspapers, magazines, financial
14000 Quail Springs Pkwy., Suite 450
Oklahoma City, OK 73134
800/642-2525
405/751-6400

Delphi Internet Services
Databases: wide variety, access to Knight-Ridder, full Internet access
News Corporation
1030 Massachusetts Ave.
Cambridge, MA 02138
800/695-4005

Dow Jones News/Retrieval Service
Databases: financial plus shopping airline reservations, etc.
P.O. Box 300
Princeton, NJ 08543
800/522-3567
609/520-4000

EasyLink
Services: e-mail, Telex, EDI
Databases: access to major providers (Knight-Ridder, CompuServe, etc.)
AT&T EasyLink Services
400 Interpace Pkwy.
Parsippany, NJ 07054
800/242-6005
201/331-4000

eWorld
Databases: consumer, family oriented
One Infinite Loop
Cupertino, CA 95014
800/775-4556

GEnie
Databases: wide variety
General Electric Information Services Co.
401 N. Washington St.
Rockville, MD 20850
800/638-9636
301/340-4000

Knight-Ridder Information Inc.
Databases: over 400 (largest)
2440 El Camino Real
Mountain View, CA 94040
800/334-2564
415/254-7000

Mead Data Central
Databases: news (NEXIS), legal (LEXIS)
P.O. Box 933
Dayton, OH 45401
800/227-4908
513/865-6800

Questel Orbit Inc.
Databases: medical (BRS), patent, trademark (ORBIT)
8000 Westpark Dr.
McClean, VA 22102
ORBIT 800/456-7248
BRS 800/289-4277

MEDLARS
Databases: medical
National Library of Medicine
8600 Rockville Pike
Bethesda, MD 20894
800/638-8480
301/496-6193

MCI Mail
Services: e-mail, Telex, fax
Databases: access to Dow Jones
1133 19th St., NW
Washington, DC 20036

800/444-6245
202/833-8484

Microsoft Network
Databases: wide variety, PC oriented
1022 MCI Drive
Pinellas Park, FL 34666
800/386-5550

NewsNet, Inc.
Databases: newsletters
945 Haverford Rd.
Bryn Mawr, PA 19010
800/952-0122
610/527-8030

PRODIGY
Databases: wide variety, shopping
445 Hamilton Ave.
White Plains, NY 10601
800/776-3449
914/448-8000

VU/TEXT Information Services, Inc.
Databases: newspapers
2005 Market St., Suite 1010
1 Commercial Place
Philadelphia, PA 19103
800/334-2564
215/587-4400

WESTLAW
Databases: legal (plus access to
Knight-Ridder and Dow Jones)
West Publishing Co.
620 Opperman Dr.
Eagan, MN 55123
800/WESTLAW
612/687-7000

online transaction processing
See *transaction processing* and *OLCP*.

on the fly
As needed. It implies little or no degradation in performance to accomplish the task. See *realtime* and *realtime compression*.

OO
Object oriented.

OOA
See *object-oriented analysis*.

OOAD
(Object-Oriented Analysis & Design) See *object-oriented analysis* and *object-oriented design*.

OOBE
(Out Of Box Experience) The experience of setting up and using a new computer or software package.

oobie
See *OOBE*.

OOD
See *object-oriented design*.

OODB
See *object-oriented database*.

OODBMS
See *object-oriented DBMS*.

OOOS
See *object-oriented operating system*.

OOP, OOPS

See *object-oriented programming*.

OOPL

(OOP Language) An object-oriented programming language.

OORDBMS

(Object-Oriented Relational DBMS) A relational database management system that has object-oriented capabilities.

OOT

(Object-Oriented Technology) See *objects* and *object-oriented programming*.

op amp

(Operational Amplifier) A device that amplifies analog signals. It uses two inputs; one for power and one for data. It is used in myriads of applications from communications to stereo.

op code

See *operation code*.

open

(1) To identify a disk or tape file for reading and writing. The open procedure "locks on" to an existing file or creates a new one.
(2) With regard to a switch, open is "off."
(3) Made to operate with other products. See *open architecture* and *open systems*.

open architecture

A system in which the specifications are made public in order to encourage third-party vendors to develop add-on products. Much of Apple's early success was due to the Apple II's open architecture. The PC is open architecture.

open computing

See *open systems*.

OpenDoc

An object-oriented architecture that allows compound documents (text, graphics, sound, etc.) to be created by interchangeable software components. OpenDoc is managed by Component Integration Labs, a vendor consortium in Sunnyvale, CA. Like Microsoft's OLE, documents and images can be embedded within or linked to documents that are set up as the container. OpenDoc is a superset of OLE, and OLE objects can be placed into OpenDoc documents and behave like OLE objects. OpenDoc refers to the data components in a document as parts, whereas OLE calls them objects.

OpenDoc supports small software modules, called "part handlers" in addition to linking to full applications. For example, rather than requiring the full application that created the text, a part handler can be used to edit text in all documents no matter how they were created. The menus change automatically as the cursor is moved onto different parts of the document, activating the tools required to edit it. OpenDoc software modules are SOM objects, which are CORBA compliant. CORBA is the industry standard architecture for distributing objects in a heterogeneous environment, which means that if a particular processing function is not available on the local machine, a remote process (object) can be called via SOM or some other CORBA-compliant ORB.

open file

A file, typically a disk file, that has been made available to the application by the operating system for reading and/or writing. All files must be "opened" before they can be accessed and "closed" when no longer required.

OpenGL

(**OPEN** Graphics Language) A 3-D graphics language developed by Silicon Graphics and endorsed by a variety of vendors. Windows NT Version 3.5 supports OpenGL.

OPEN LOOK

An X Window-based graphical user interface for UNIX developed by Sun. It has been widely used by Sun and was defined and distributed by AT&T when it was still involved with UNIX. OPEN LOOK is giving way to Motif, which has become the standard user interface in the UNIX world.

OpenMail

An electronic mail system from HP that runs on UNIX servers. It complies with the X.400 messaging and X.500 directory standards and supports all major mail programs that run on the client.

OpenPIC

(**OPEN** Programmable Interrupt Controller) An SMP chip architecture endorsed by AMD and Cyrix Corporation that provides symmetric multiprocessing (SMP) for x86 and PowerPC systems It can support up to 32 processors. See *APIC*.

open pipe

A continuous path from sender to receiver, such as found in a circuit-switching network or leased line. Transmitted data is not broken up into packets.

open shop

A computing environment that allows users to program and run their own programs. Contrast with *closed shop*.

OpenStep

An operating system-independent object standard that is based on NeXT's NEXTSTEP object-oriented software. It comprises the object layer within NEXTSTEP that is separate and apart from the kernel. In 1995, OpenStep is expected to be released in new versions of Sun, Digital and HP operating systems. The goal of OpenStep is to create an open, portable standard for object-oriented computing that allows objects to be easily used in a distributed, heterogeneous environment.

open system

A vendor-independent system that is designed to interconnect with a variety of products. It implies that standards are determined from a consensus of interested parties rather than one or two vendors.
Sometimes, the PC is called an open system, but it is more an open architecture than an open system, because Intel and Microsoft have strong control over the hardware and system software. Contrast with *closed system*. See *open systems, OSI, OSF* and *X/Open*.

open systems

For years, open systems and UNIX-based computing have been synonymous, because UNIX runs on more different kinds of computers than any other operating system. The goal of open systems is interoperability between hardware and software that is defined by the industry at large and not one or two vendors.

Open systems includes database management systems (DBMSs) that run on many different platforms as well and any other tools that are used cross platforms. While this provides a certain freedom for future changes, it is by no means a problem free environment and never will be. Whenever several hardware platforms are used, a version of each software product must be available for that platform.

For example, in order to migrate an application from one UNIX system to another, all the system software components (DBMSs, TP monitors, compilers, etc.) that are currently linked to that application must also be available for the new system. Otherwise, custom conversion programs must be developed and more conversion effort is required.

The goal of open systems is a beautiful one, very much akin to world peace. Everyone pledges allegiance to it, but getting there seems to take forever.

OpenView

Network management software from HP. It supports SNMP and CMIP protocols, and third-party products that run under OpenView support SNA and DECnet network management protocols. OpenView is an enterprise-wide network management solution.

OpenVMS

A version of the VMS operating system from Digital that is POSIX and XPG3-compliant and runs on VAX and Alpha systems.

operand

The part of a machine instruction that references data or a peripheral device. In the instruction, **ADD A to B**, A and B are the operands (nouns), and ADD is the operation code (verb). In the instruction **READ TRACK 9, SECTOR 32**, track and sector are the operands.

operating system

The master control program that runs the computer. It is the first program loaded when the computer is turned on, and its main part, called the kernel, resides in memory at all times. It may be developed by the vendor of the computer it's running in or by a third party.

It is an important component of the computer system, because it sets the standards for the application programs that run in it. All programs must "talk to" the operating system.

The main difference between an operating system and a network operating system is its multiuser capability. Operating systems, such as Macintosh System 7, DOS and Windows, are single user, designed for one person at a desktop computer. Windows NT and UNIX on the other hand are network operating systems, because they are designed to manage multiple user requests at the same time.

An operating system is also called an *executive* or *supervisor*. Operating systems perform the following functions.

User Interface   The user interface, or shell, provides the interaction between the user and the operating system. Operating systems may allow for different shells; for example, DOS and UNIX provide command-driven interfaces but can host other shells that provide a menu-driven or graphical interface. Even Windows, which is graphics based to begin with, allows other shells to provide an interface to the user.

Job Management   Job management controls the running of programs. Which one gets executed first, then next. In small computers, the operating system responds to interactive commands from the user and loads the requested application program into memory for execution. Larger computers are more oriented to accepting a batch of instructions. For example, job control language (JCL) may describe the programs that must be run for an entire shift. In some cases, the output of one program may then be input into another and so on.

Task Management

Task management controls the simultaneous execution of programs. In single tasking computers, the operating system has virtually no task management to do, but in multitasking computers, it is responsible for the concurrent operation of one or more programs (jobs). Advanced operating systems have the ability to prioritize programs so that one job gets done before the other.

In order to provide users at terminals with the fastest response time, batch programs can be put on lowest priority and interactive programs can be given highest priority. Advanced operating systems can be fine tuned by the computer operator so that a specific job can be speeded up or slowed down.

Multitasking is accomplished by executing instructions for one function while data is coming into or going out of the computer for another. Large computers are designed to overlap these operations, and data can move simultaneously in and out of the computer through separate channels with the operating system governing these actions.

In small computers, the operating system can monitor idle time when a user is interactively working with a program to execute another program in the background. Even the milliseconds between keystrokes can be used for something else. A user, pausing at the keyboard for just a couple of seconds, is light years to the computer, which can use that time to execute hundreds of thousands of instructions.

Data Management

Data management keeps track of data on the disk; hence the term DOS, or disk operating system. The application program does not know where the data is actually stored or how to get it. That knowledge is contained in the operating system's access method, or device driver, routines. When a program is ready to accept data, it signals the operating system with a message. The operating system finds the data and delivers it to the program. Conversely, when the program is ready to output, the operating system transfers the data from the program onto the available space on disk.

Device Management

Device management controls the input and output of data to and from the peripheral devices. In theory, the operating system is supposed to manage all devices, not just disk drives. It is supposed to handle the input and output to the display screen as well as the printer. By keeping the details of the peripheral device within the operating system, a device can be replaced with a newer model, and only the routine in the operating system that deals with that device needs to be replaced.

In the DOS world, software developers often bypassed the operating system, because DOS either did not support the device or added too much performance overhead. Developers of graphics, word processing and desktop publishing applications were made responsible for providing drivers (routines) for all the popular displays and printers, adding an enormous burden to their development efforts.

This is a major reason why Windows, which provides device management for all peripherals, became so popular.

Security

Multiuser operating systems maintain a list of authorized users and provide password protection to unauthorized users who may try to gain access to the system. Large operating systems also maintain activity logs and accounting of the user's time for billing purposes. They also provide backup and recovery routines to start over again in the event of a system failure.

History

The earliest operating systems were developed in the late 1950s to manage tape storage, but programmers mostly wrote their own I/O routines. In the mid 1960s, operating systems became essential to manage disks, complex timesharing and multitasking systems.

Today, all multi-purpose computers from micro to mainframe use an operating system. Special-purpose devices (appliances, games, toys, etc.) generally do not. They usually employ a single program that performs all the required I/O and processing tasks.

Common Operating Systems

PCs use DOS, Windows, OS/2, SCO XENIX and AIX. Windows is the most popular operating environment for PCs, although it is technically not a complete operating system since it requires and interacts with DOS. Windows NT and Windows 95 are complete operating systems.

The old Apple II's used the ProDOS operating system. The Macintoshes use System 7 as well as A/UX, Apple's UNIX version. Digital's VAX series uses VMS and ULTRIX (UNIX). IBM mainframes use MVS, VM and VSE.

In the past, when a vendor introduced a new operating system, users had little understanding of this behind-the-glass-enclosed-datacenter phenomenon. Today, it is squarely in their hands.

Perhaps the Japanese have the right idea with their TRON operating system. It is intended to be a common interface across all applications from a microwave oven to the largest supercomputer!

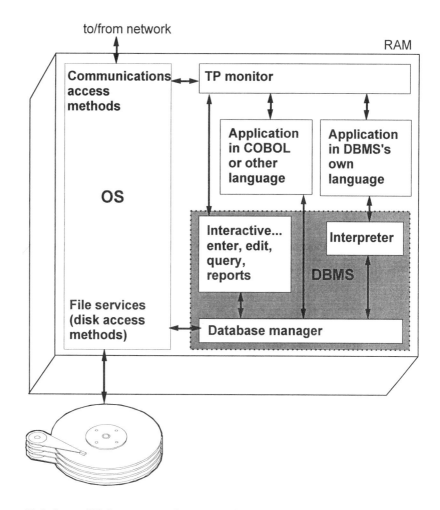

Mainframe/Minicomputer Operating System
This diagram shows the interaction between the operating system and other software components in a mainframe or minicomputer. On the following page, the illustration depicts interaction in a desktop computer.

Operating System and Application Interaction

The following illustration depicts the interaction between the operating system and the applications. The operating system is the master control program, which is automatically loaded at startup. It allows the applications to be launched and keeps track of them. All applications must "talk to" the operating system as well as the machine language of the hardware platform they are running on.

The GUI ("gooey") part of the operating system provides the graphical interface and windowing environment that has become so popular (Mac, Windows, Motif). The operating system launches applications (jobs) and runs them simultaneously (multitasking). It also provides the spooling and print services required by applications as well as the file services for storing and retrieving the data on the disk.

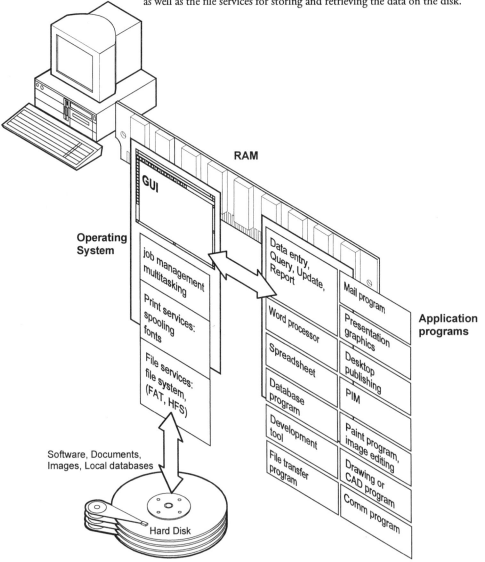

RAM

GUI

Operating System

job management multitasking

Print services: spooling fonts

File services: file system, (FAT, HFS)

Data entry, Query, Update, Report

Mail program

Word processor

Presentation graphics

Spreadsheet

Desktop publishing

Database program

PIM

Development tool

Paint program, image editing

File transfer program

Drawing or CAD program

Comm program

Application programs

Software, Documents, Images, Local databases

Hard Disk

operation code

The part of a machine instruction that tells the computer what to do, such as input, add or branch. The operation code is the verb; the operands are the nouns.

operations research

See *management science.*

operator

(1) A person who operates the computer and performs such activities as commanding the operating system, mounting disks and tapes and placing paper in the printer. Operators may also write the job control language (JCL), which schedules the daily work for the computer.
(2) In programming and logic, a symbol used to perform an operation on some value. See *arithmetic operator* and *Boolean operator.*

operator overloading

In programming, the ability to use the same operator to perform different operations. For example, arithmetic operators such as +, -, * and / could be defined to perform differently on certain kinds of data.

OPI

(Open Prepress Interface) An extension to PostScript by Aldus Corporation (now Adobe Systems) to provide a format for color separations.

optical character recognition

See *OCR.*

optical disk

3.5" Magneto-optic disk

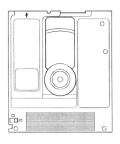

5.25" Magneto-optic disk

A direct access disk written and read by light. CDs, CD-ROMs and videodiscs are optical disks that are recorded at the time of manufacture and cannot be erased. WORM (Write Once Read Many) disks and CD-R disks are recorded in the user's environment, but cannot be erased.

Erasable, or rewritable, optical disks function like magnetic disks and can be rewritten over and over. In the late 1980s, a variety of vendors began to manufacture optical disks that primarily use the magneto-optic (MO) recording technology.

Erasable optical disks use removable cartridges that come in two sizes. The 3.5" disks are single sided and hold 128MB and 230MB. The 5.25" disks are double sided and hold a total of 650MB and 1.3GB, but must be manually flipped over for each side. Capacities will increase to 650MB and 2.6GB respectively in the 1995-1996 timeframe.

In August 1995, Pinnacle Micro, Irvine, CA, announced its Apex erasable optical drive that reads and write proprietary 4.6GB cartridges as well industry standard 2.6GB cartridges.

The term optical disk may refer to all the above-mentioned devices, but typically refers to erasable and write once disks (WORM, CD-R), not the read-only audio CD, CD-ROM and videodisc formats.

It is very likely that erasable optical disks will replace magnetic disks some time in the future. Although some argue this will not happen, there are significant advantages to optical disks. They have greater storage capacities and they are approaching magnetic disk speeds. In addition, optical disks are not subject to head crashes or corruption from stray magnetic fields. They have a 30-year life and are less vulnerable to extremes of hot and cold than magnetic disks.

Even more interesting optical technologies are on the horizon. The lasers that read the tracks on spinning optical disks can also be moved across banks of stationary optical material. After the turn of the century, holographic storage devices will provide staggering storage capacities in the form of holograms. See *ISO 13346, multilevel optical disk, holographic storage* and *legality of optical storage.*

optical disk library

Also called an *optical jukebox*, it is an optical disk storage system that houses multiple disk platters. It is similar to a music jukebox, except that instead of "playing one tune," more than one drive can be used to read and write several disks simultaneously. Such devices are made for rewritable optical disks, write once disks and CD-ROMs, and can hold from a handful to several thousand disks or cartridges.

optical fiber

A thin glass wire designed for light transmission, capable of transmitting billions of bits per second. Unlike electrical pulses, light pulses are not affected by random radiation in the environment.

An optical fiber is constructed of a transparent core made of pure silicon dioxide (SiO2), through which the light travels. This core is so transparent that you could see through a three-mile thick window made out of it. The core is surrounded by a cladding layer that reflects light, keeping it in the core. The cladding is surrounded by a plastic layer, a layer of kevlar fibers for strength and an outer sheath of plastic or Teflon.

Multimode fiber is the most commonly used, which has a core diameter of from 50 to 100 microns. For intercity cabling and highest speed, single-mode fiber with a core diameter of less than 10 microns is used. See *FDDI* and *cable categories*.

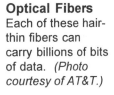

Optical Fibers
Each of these hair-thin fibers can carry billions of bits of data. *(Photo courtesy of AT&T.)*

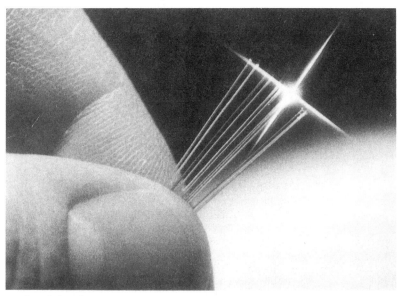

optical isolator

A device used with current loop transmission that uses an LED and photoresistor to detect current in the line.

optical library

See *optical disk library*.

optical mouse

A mouse that uses light to get its bearings. It is rolled over a small desktop pad that contains a reflective grid. The mouse emits a light and senses its reflection as it is moved. Contrast with *mechanical mouse*.

optical reader

An input device that recognizes typewritten or printed characters and bar codes and converts them into their corresponding digital codes.

optical recognition

See *OCR.*

optimizer

Hardware or software that improves performance. See *defragger* and *disk management.*

optoelectronics

Merging light and electronics technologies, such as in optical fiber communications systems.

OR

A Boolean logic operation that is true if any of the inputs is true. An exclusive OR is true if only one of the inputs is true, but not both.

OR		EXCLUSIVE OR	
Inputs	Output	Inputs	Output
0 0	0	0 0	0
0 1	1	0 1	1
1 0	1	1 0	1
1 1	1	1 1	0

Oracle

(1) A relational database management system (DBMS) from Oracle Corporation, Redwood Shores, CA, that runs on a wide variety of computer platforms from micro to mainframe. Oracle was the first DBMS to incorporate the SQL language and to run on a wide variety of platforms. As a result, it has been very successful. Applications can be developed with Oracle's Cooperative Development Environment (CDE), which includes a variety of tools for client/server development. See *CDE.*
(2)A European broadcast television text-message service.<TERM>Oracle Browser, Data Query, Forms, Reports
See *Developer/2000.*

Oracle Documents

An earlier name for a variety of Oracle software products, including a messaging system, text database and document management system. Each of the products was later offered separately.

Oracle Media Server

An multimedia system for interactive TV delivery from Oracle Corporation that runs on nCUBE, HP and other hardware platforms. The client software runs on Macs, PCs and set-top boxes. It is designed to store and disseminate multiple streams of text (news), images, audio and video on demand.

Oracle Parallel Server

A version of the Oracle database system designed for massively parallel processors (MPPs). It allows multiple CPUs to access a single database.

Orange Book

See *NCSC* and *CD.*

ORB

(Object Request Broker) Software that handles the communication of messages from the requesting program (client) to the object as well as any return values from the object back to the calling program. See *CORBA*.

ORB gateway

Software that translates messages between two different ORBs.

Orbix

A CORBA-compliant ORB from IONA Technologies Inc., Dublin, Ireland (U.S. office, Marlboro, MA). Founded in 1991, IONA is a leading member of the OMG, and Orbix has become the most popular CORBA-based system due to its multi-platform support and OLE integration. Orbix provides OLE to CORBA conversion, making it the only distributed solution for OLE automation at the present time.

ordinal number

The number that identifies the sequence of an item, for example, record #34. Contrast with *cardinal number*.

org

An Internet address domain name for a non-profit organization. See *Internet address*.

orientation

In typography, the direction of print across a page. See *portrait*.

original equipment manufacturer

See *OEM*.

orphan

See *widow & orphan*.

OS

See *operating system*.

OS/2

A single user, multitasking operating system for PCs from IBM that runs OS/2, DOS and Windows applications. It provides both a graphical user interface as well as a command line interface similar to DOS. Many OS/2 and DOS commands are the same.

The first versions of OS/2 were written for 286s and were developed jointly by IBM and Microsoft. Subsequent releases, starting with Version 2.0, were written for 32-bit 386s and up and are solely the product of IBM. OS/2 is highly regarded as a robust operating system, which prevents an errant application from freezing the computer.

OS/2's graphical user interface, called *Presentation Manager* (PM) in Versions 1.x and *Workplace Shell*, starting with Version 2.0, is similar to Windows and the Macintosh. The term Presentation Manager however still refers to the programming interface used to write OS/2 graphical applications.

OS/2 provides a dual boot feature. When you turn the computer on, you can boot either OS/2 or DOS. Included with OS/2 is Adobe Type Manager for rendering Type 1 fonts on screen and providing PostScript output on non-PostScript printers.

OS/2 16-bit Version 1.x

The first versions (1.0, 1.1, etc.) were written for the 16-bit 286. DOS compatibility was limited to about 500K. Version 1.3 (OS/2 Lite) required 2MB

RAM instead of 4MB and included Adobe Type Manager. IBM's Extended Edition version included Communications Manager and Database Manager.

OS/2 32-bit Version 2.x - IBM

Introduced in April 1992, this 32-bit version for 386s and up from IBM multitasks DOS, Windows and OS/2 applications. Data can be shared between applications using the clipboard and between Windows and PM apps using the DDE protocol. Version 2.x provides each application with a 512MB virtual address space, which allows huge tasks to be easily managed.

Version 2.1 supports Windows' Enhanced Mode and applications that take full advantage of Windows 3.1. It also provides support for more video standards and CD-ROM drives than Version 2.0.

Communications and database management for OS/2 are provided by Communications Manager/2 (CM/2) and Database Manager/2 (DB2/2). CM/2 replaces Communications Manager, which was part of OS/2 2.0's Extended Services option.

OS/2 32-bit Version 3 - IBM

In late 1994, IBM introduced Version 3 of OS/2, known as OS/2 Warp. It runs in only 4MB of memory and includes a variety of full applications, including Internet access. See *OS/2 Warp*.

Windows NT - Microsoft

Originally to be named OS/2 Version 3.0, this 32-bit version from Microsoft was renamed *Windows NT* and introduced in 1993. Windows NT can run character-based OS/2 applications; however, almost all OS/2 applications use the graphical Presentation Manager interface.

See *Windows NT*.

OS/2 for Windows

A special edition of OS/2 Version 2.1 for PCs that already have DOS and Windows 3.1 installed. It is less expensive than the full OS/2, because it does not include the Windows code. This was superseded by OS/2 Warp.

OS/2 PM

(OS/2 Presentation Manager) The graphical user interface in OS/2 Version 1.x. It is now called *Workplace Shell* in Versions 2.x. See *OS/2*.

OS/2 Warp

Introduced in late 1994 and officially known as OS/2 Warp, Version 3, it is the successor to OS/2 for Windows and OS/2 Version 2.1. It is an enhanced version that can run in 4MB of memory, but 8MB is a more realistic minimum. It includes a simpler installation, improved multimedia support, Internet utilities with access via IBM's Global Network and a variety of bundled applications. The applications include IBM Works, a productivity suite, a fax program, PIM, comm program and others.

There are two versions of OS/2 Warp. One requires Windows 3.1 to be installed, the other includes a modified version of Windows 3.1. For the history of OS/2, see *OS/2*. See also *Warp Server*.

OS/2 Warp Connect

The networking version of OS/2 Warp. It includes peer-to-peer networking to OS/2 and Windows for Workgroup machines as well as to Windows NT servers. See *Warp Server*.

OS/400

The operating system designed for the AS/400 minicomputer from IBM.

OS/8

A single user, multitasking operating system from Digital for its PDP-8 computers. Variants run on DECstation and DECmate systems.

OS/9

A UNIX-like, realtime operating system from Microware Systems Corporation for Motorola 68000 CPUs. Originally developed for the 6809 chip, a version of OS/9 was created for CD-I players.

OS/9000

A portable version of OS/9, written in C, which runs on 386s and up and 68020s and up.

oscillate

To swing back and forth between the minimum and maximum values. An oscillation is one cycle, typically one complete wave in an alternating frequency.

oscillator

An electronic circuit used to generate high-frequency pulses. See *clock*.

oscilloscope

Test instrument that displays electronic signals (waves and pulses) on a screen. It creates its own time base against which signals can be measured, and display frames can be frozen for visual inspection.

OSF

(Open Software Foundation, 11 Cambridge Center, Cambridge, MA 02142, 617/621-8700) A non-profit organization dedicated to delivering an open computing environment based on standards. Formed in 1988, it solicits technologies from industry, invites member participation to set technical direction and licenses software to members.
The OSF licenses source code, which is compiled into machine code for various platforms by its members. The source code, originally developed inhouse, is currently outsourced. Following are OSF's major products.

OSF/1
OSF/1 is the operating system that uses Carnegie Mellon's Mach kernel. It is a B1-secure, symmetric multiprocessing operating system that can run on multiple processors within the same machine. Compliant with POSIX, XPG4 and SVID base and kernel extensions. IBM, HP, DEC and Hitachi are major users of OSF/1 in full or in part.

Motif
Motif is a graphical user interface (GUI) for applications running on any system with X Window Version 11. Compliant with POSIX, ANSI C and XPG, Motif is the de facto standard graphical interface for UNIX.

DCE
The Distributed Computing Environment is a set of integrated programs that provides an environment for developing and maintaining client/server applications across heterogeneous platforms in a network. DCE includes security, directory naming, time synchronization, file sharing, RPCs and multithreading services. Increasingly, database vendors are adding support for DCE. Thus, enterprise adoption of DCE will let users access databases by name no matter where they reside in the network. See *application partitioning*.

DME
The Distributed Management Environment is a set of integrated programs that provides coherent management of systems and networks. DME provides services for software distribution and licensing and supports X/Open's XMP high-level management protocol.

ANDF
The Architecture Neutral Distribution Format supports developing portable applications. The developer generates an intermediate ANDF language that can be

shrink-wrapped. Each target machine would then have an ANDF compiler that compiles the intermediate language into machine language when it is installed. **In order for ANDF to provide universal, shrink-wrapped UNIX software, every hardware vendor would have to support it. Because UNIX runs on so many different computers, shrink-wrapped UNIX may always be a dream, unless the hardware world were to consolidate into two or three platforms some day. See** *PowerOpen.*

OSF/Motif

See *Motif* and *OSF.*

OSI

(Open System Interconnection) An ISO standard for worldwide communications that defines a framework for implementing protocols in seven layers.
Control is passed from one layer to the next, starting at the application layer in one station, proceeding to the bottom layer, over the channel to the next station and back up the hierarchy. Most of this functionality exists in all communications networks; however, non-OSI systems often incorporate two or three layers into one. Vendors have agreed to support OSI in one form or another; however OSI serves more as a model than a universal standard. Many OSI components are too loosely defined, and proprietary standards are entrenched. One exception is the OSI-compliant X.400 e-mail protocol that is widely implemented. Learning the OSI layers and functions is essential for understanding communications networks.

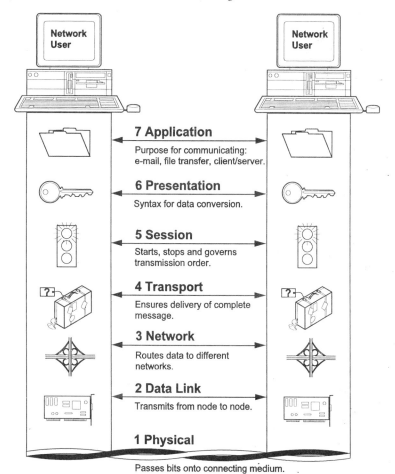

Network User   **Network User**

7 Application
Purpose for communicating: e-mail, file transfer, client/server.

6 Presentation
Syntax for data conversion.

5 Session
Starts, stops and governs transmission order.

4 Transport
Ensures delivery of complete message.

3 Network
Routes data to different networks.

2 Data Link
Transmits from node to node.

1 Physical
Passes bits onto connecting medium.

Application: Layer 7

The top layer defines the language and syntax that programs use to communicate with other programs. The application layer represents the purpose of communicating in the first place. For example, a program in a client workstation uses commands to request data from a program in the server. Common functions at this layer are opening, closing, reading and writing files, transferring files and e-mail messages, executing remote jobs and obtaining directory information about network resouces.

Presentation: Layer 6

When data is transmitted between different types of computer systems, the presentation layer negotiates and manages the way data is represented and encoded. For example, it provides a common denominator between ASCII and EBCDIC machines as well as between different floating point and binary formats. Sun's XDR and OSI's ASN.1 are two protocols used for this purpose. This layer is also used for encryption and decryption.

Session: Layer 5

Provides coordination of the communications in an orderly manner. It determines one-way or two-way communications and manages the dialogue between both parties; for example, making sure that the previous request has been fulfilled before the next one is sent. It also marks significant parts of the transmitted data with checkpoints to allow for fast recovery in the event of a connection failure.
In practice, this layer is often not used or services within this layer are sometimes incorporated into the transport layer.

Transport: Layer 4

The transport layer is responsible for overall end to end validity and integrity of the transmission. The lower data link layer (layer 2) is only responsible for delivering packets from one node to another. Thus, if a packet gets lost in a router somewhere in the enterprise internet, the transport layer will detect that. It ensures that if a 12MB file is sent, the full 12MB is received.
"OSI transport services" include layers 1 through 4, collectively responsible for delivering a complete message or file from sending to receiving station without error.

Network: Layer 3

The network layer establishes the route between the sending and receiving stations. The node to node function of the data link layer (layer 2) is extended across the entire internetwork, because a routable protocol contains a network address in addition to a station addresses.
This layer is the switching function of the dial-up telephone system as well as the functions performed by routable protocols such as IP, IPX, SNA and AppleTalk. If all stations are contained within a single network segment, then the routing capability in this layer is not required.

Data Link: Layer 2

The data link is responsible for node to node validity and integrity of the transmission. The transmitted bits are divided into frames; for example, an Ethernet or Token Ring frame for local area networks (LANs). Layers 1 and 2 are required for every type of communications. For more on this layer, see *data link protocol.*

Physical: Layer 1

The physical layer is responsible for passing bits onto and receiving them from the connecting medium. This layer has no understanding of the meaning of the bits, but deals with the electrical and mechanical characteristics of the signals and signalling methods. For example, it comprises the RTS and CTS signals in an RS-232 environment, as well as TDM and FDM techniques for multiplexing data on a line.

OSPF

(Open Shortest Path First) A router protocol that determines the least expensive path for routing a message. OSPF was originally developed to replace the RIP protocol.

OSTA

(Optical Storage Technology Association, 311 E. Carillo St., Santa Barbara, CA 93101, 805/963-3853) A membership organization composed of major optical drive manufacturers. Its purpose is to endorse standards and promote the use of optical media in computing.

OT

(Object Technology) The use of objects.

OTOH

Digispeak for "on the other hand."

OTPROM

(One Time PROM) A PROM chip that can be programmed only once.

outdent

Same as *hanging indent* and *hanging paragraph*.

outline font

A type of font made from basic outlines of each character. The outlines are scaled into actual characters (bitmaps) before printing. See *scalable font*.

outline processor

Software that allows the user to type in thoughts and organize them into an outline form.

out of band

Outside the primary frequency or system. See *signaling in/out of band*.

output

(1) Any computer-generated information displayed on screen, printed on paper or in machine readable form, such as disk and tape.
(2) To transfer or transmit from the computer to a peripheral device or communications line.

output area

A reserved segment of memory used to collect data to be transferred out of the computer. Same as *buffer*.

output bound

Excessive slowness due to output functions, typically slow-speed communications lines or printers. See *print buffer*.

output device

Any peripheral that presents output from the computer, such as a screen or printer. Although disks and tapes receive output, they are called storage devices.

outsourcing

Contracting with outside consultants, software houses or service bureaus to perform systems analysis, programming and datacenter operations. See *facilities management*.

Overall Viewer

Presentation software for Windows from Software Garden, Inc., Newton Highlands, MA, that provides magnified details of a large image without losing sight of the overall image. Each window shows a higher magnification of the previous window. It is used to display maps and large images as well as catalogs and other hierarchical databases that incorporate images.

OverDrive CPU

A family of CPUs from Intel for upgrading slower 486s and Pentiums. For the 486, there are 486 and Pentium OverDrive chips. Depending on the motherboard, the old chip is either replaced or the new one is installed in the upgrade socket, leaving the old chip intact or removing it.

Pentium Overdrive chips for older Pentiums will be installed in the original socket, replacing the old one.

overflow error

An error that occurs when calculated data cannot fit within the designated field. The result field is usually left blank or is filled with some symbol to flag the error condition.

overhead

(1) The amount of processing time used by system software, such as the operating system, TP monitor or database manager.

(2) In communications, the additional codes transmitted for control and error checking, which take more time to process.

overlay

(1) A preprinted, precut form placed over a screen, key or tablet for indentification purposes. See *keyboard template*.

(2) A program segment called into memory when required. When a program is larger than the memory capacity of the machine, the parts of the program that are not in constant use can be set up as overlays. When called in, the contents of the previous overlay is lost. Virtual memory is a system of automatic overlays.

overlay card

A controller that digitizes NTSC signals from a video source for display in the computer.

overloading

In programming, the ability to use the same name for more than one variable or procedure, requiring the compiler to differentiate them based on context.

oversampling

Creating a more accurate digital representation of an analog signal. In order to work with real-world signals in the computer, analog signals are sampled some number of times per second (frequency) and converted into digital code. Using averaging and different algorithms, samples can be generated between existing samples, creating more digital information for complex signals, "smoothing out the curve" so to speak. Sampling requires at least twice the bandwidth of the frequency being sampled. For example, with regard to sound, 20KHz is the highest frequency perceptible to the human ear, and sampling is done at 44.1KHz for high quality audio playback. A 2x oversampling means that the CD player runs at twice the rate, or 88.2KHz, and inserts a made-up sample in between each real sample on the disc. An 8x oversampling runs eight times faster and so on. See *sampling rate*.

overscan

Outside of the normal rectangular viewing area on a display screen. Contrast with *underscan*.

overstrike

(1) To type over an existing character.
(2) A character with a line through it, ~~such as this.~~

overwrite

(1) A data entry mode that writes over existing characters on screen when new characters are typed in. Contrast with *insert mode*.
(2) To record new data on top of existing data such as when a disk record or file is updated.

OWL

(ObjectWindows Library) A class library of Windows objects from Borland that serves as application frameworks for developing Windows applications in C++. It is the Borland counterpart of the Microsoft Foundation Class Library (MFC).

P

P1394

See *FireWire*.

P24T

See *Pentium*.

P5, P6

The Intel code names for the Pentium and Pentium Pro.

P68

The Intel code name for the successor to the Pentium Pro. It is expected to be an x86-only CPU rather than have x86 and HP PA-RISC capability as with the P7.

P7

The code name from Intel for the successor to the Pentium Pro and P68. It is expected in the 1996-1997 time frame with as many as 25 million transistors. Both Intel and HP are working on the chip, which is expected to be able to run x86 and PA-RISC applications simultaneously.

P75, P90, P100, etc.

Generally refers to Pentium CPUs or Pentium systems running at 75, 90, 100MHz, etc.

PABX

(Private Automatic Branch eXchange) Same as *PBX*.

PACBASE

Integrated CASE software for IBM, Bull HN and Unisys mainframes from CGI Systems, Pearl River, NY. It supports a wide variety of databases including DB2 and Oracle. PACLAN is the version for PCs running on LANs.

pack

(1) To compress data in order to save space. Unpack refers to decompressing data. See *data compression*.
(2) An instruction that converts a decimal number into a packed decimal format. Unpack converts a packed decimal number into decimal.
(3) In database programs, a command that removes records that have been marked for deletion.

packaged software

See *software package*.

Packard Bell

(Packard Bell Electronics, Inc., Westlake Village, CA) A major PC manufacturer that pioneered sales into the mass-market retail chains in the late 1980s. As of 1994, it was the leading vendor in that market. Packard Bell is a privately-held company that distributes PCs to more than 11,000 retail outlets in the U.S. and 13,000 worldwide. It was also the first to offer toll-free support to retail end users.
The original Packard Bell was founded in 1926 as a consumer radio manufacturer and later entered the defense electronics industry. It was acquired by Teledyne in 1968. In 1986, Beny Alagem and a group of partners acquired the Packard Bell name from Teledyne and formed the company that exists today.

packed decimal

A storage mode that places two decimal digits into one byte, each digit occupying four bits. The sign occupies four bits in the least significant byte.

packet

A block of data (a frame) used for transmission in LANs and packet switching systems.

packet cellular

The transmission of data over the cellular network. Data is divided into packets, or frames, for error checking. Contrast with *circuit cellular*. See *CDPD* and *wireless*.

packetized voice

The transmission of realtime voice in a packet switching network.

packet overhead

Refers to the time it takes to transmit data on a packet-switched network. Each packet requires extra bytes of format information, which, combined with the assembly and dissassembly of packets, reduces the overall transmission speed of the raw data.

packet radio

The wireless transmission of data, which is divided into packets, or frames, for error checking. See *Ardis* and *Mobitex*.

packet switching

A networking technology used in wide area networks (WANs) that breaks up a message into smaller packets for transmission and switches them to their required destination. Unlike circuit switching, which requires a constant point-to-point circuit to be established, each packet in a packet switched network contains a destination address. Thus all packets in a single message do not have to travel the same path. They can be dynamically routed over the network as circuits become available or unavailable. The destination computer reassembles the packets back into their proper sequence.

Packet switching efficiently handles messages of different lengths and priorities. By accounting for packets sent, a public network can charge customers for only the data they transmit. Packet switching is suitable for data, but not realtime voice and video.

The international standard for wide area packet switching networks is X.25, which was defined when all circuits were analog and very susceptible to interference. Newer technologies, such as frame relay and SMDS are designed for today's almost-error-free digital lines.

ATM uses a cell-switching technology that provides the bandwidth-sharing efficiency of packet switching with the guaranteed bandwith of circuit switching. Public packet switching networks may provide value added services, such as protocol conversion and electronic mail. Contrast with *circuit switching*.

packing density

The number of bits or tracks per inch of recording surface. Also refers to the number of memory bits or other electronic components on a chip.

pad

(1) To fill a data structure with padding characters.

(2) (PAD) (Packet Assembler/Disassembler) A communications device that formats outgoing data into packets of the required length for transmission in an X.25 packet switching network. It also strips the data out of incoming packets.

padding

Characters used to fill up unused portions of a data structure, such as a field or communications message. A field may be padded with blanks, zeros or nulls.

paddle

An input device that moves the screen cursor in a back-and-forth motion. It has a dial and one or more buttons and is typically used in games to hit balls and steer objects. See *joy stick*.

page

(1) In virtual memory systems, a segment of the program that is transferred into memory.

(2) In videotex systems, a transmitted frame.

(3) In word processing, a printed page.

page break

In printing, a code that marks the end of a page. A "hard" page break, inserted by the user, breaks the page at that location. "Soft" page breaks are created by word processing and report programs based on the current page length setting.

page description language

A device-independent, high-level language for defining printer output. If an application generates output in a page description language, such as PostScript, the output can be printed on any printer that supports it.

Much of the character and graphics shaping is done within the printer rather than in the user's computer. Instead of downloading an entire font from the computer to the printer, which includes the design of each character, a command to build a particular font is sent, and the printer creates the characters from font outlines. Likewise, a command to draw a circle is sent to the printer rather than sending the actual bits of the circle image.

page fault

A virtual memory interrupt that signals that the next instruction or item of data is not in physical memory and must be swapped back in from the disk. If the required page on disk cannot be found, then a page fault error occurs, which means that either the operating system or an application has corrupted the virtual memory. If such an error occurs, the user has to reload the application.

page frame

See *EMS*.

page header

Common text that is printed at the top of every page. It generally includes the page number and headings above each column.

PageMaker

A full-featured desktop publishing program for the PC and Macintosh from Adobe Systems, Inc., Mountain View, CA. Originally introduced for the Mac in 1985 by Aldus Corporation, it set the standard for desktop publishing. In fact, Paul Brainerd, president of Aldus, coined the term desktop publishing. The PC version was introduced in 1987.

page makeup

Formatting a printed page, which includes the layout of headers, footers, columns, page numbers, graphics, rules and borders.

page mode memory

The common dynamic RAM chip design. Memory bits are accessed by row and column coordinates. Without page mode, each bit is accessed by pulsing the row and column select lines. With page mode, the row (page) is selected only once for all bits (columns) within the row, resulting in faster access.

page printer

A type of printer that prints a page at a time. See *laser printer* and *ion deposition.*

**High-Speed
Page Printer**
This is the type of
machine used to
print thousands of
customized letters
per day.

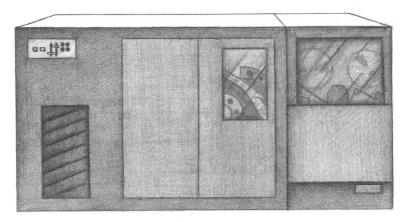

page recognition

Software that recognizes the content of a printed page which has been scanned into the computer. It uses OCR to convert the printed words into computer text and should be able to differentiate text from other elements on the page, such as pictures and captions.

pagination

(1)Page numbering.
(2)Laying out printed pages, which includes setting up and printing columns, rules and borders. Although pagination is used synonymously with *page makeup*, the term often refers to the printing of long manuscripts rather than ads and brochures.

paging

(1) In a virtual memory computer, paging is the transfer of program segments (pages) into and out of memory. Although paging is the primary mechanism for virtual memory, excessive paging is not desired. See *thrashing*.
(2) A communications service that is evolving from a one-way beeper service to a one-way text service, and eventually, to a two-way text and voice service. It is expected that the paging industry will undergo several changes as new hand-held devices and wireless services mature. See *PCS*.

paint

(1) In computer graphics, to "paint" the screen using a tablet stylus or mouse to simulate a paintbrush.
(2)To transfer a dot matrix image as in the phrase "the laser printer paints the image onto a photosensitive drum."
(3) To create a screen form by typing anywhere on screen. To "paint" the screen with text.

Painter

A full-featured paint program for Macintosh and Windows from Fractal Design Corporation, Aptos, CA. Painter is noted for its sophisticated image editing capabilities as well as its ability to simulate natural painting styles, such as oil, watercolor and charcoal, on almost every kind of paper texture. The disks and manuals come appropriately packaged... in a paint can!

paint program

A graphics program that allows the user to simulate painting on screen with the use of a mouse or graphics tablet. The images that are generated in a paint program, which are made up of dots, are called *bitmaps*, or *raster graphics* images. Full-featured paint programs are called *image editors*. They include a variety of image editing capabilities for enhancing scanned images, which are also created as bitmaps. Unlike drawing programs, which generate vector graphics images, the picture objects created in a paint program cannot be easily isolated and scaled independently. Raster graphics files are much like a painted canvas: objects are "painted" together. However, colors can be changed and parts or all of an image can be run through image filters to create a wide variety of special effects. See *image editor*.

Paint Program
A paint program turns brush strokes into dots, which is known as a raster graphics format.

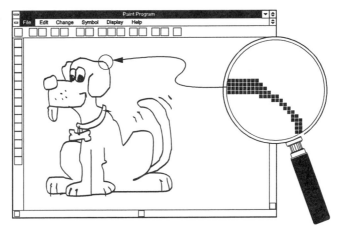

See the Difference
See page 256 for a diagram illustrating the difference between a paint program and a drawing program.

PAL

(1) (Paradox Application Language)   Paradox's programming language.
(2) (Programmable Array Logic)   A programmable logic chip (PLD) technology from Advanced Micro Devices.
(3)(Phase Alternating Line)   A European color TV standard that broadcasts an analog signal at 625 lines of resolution 25 interlaced frames per second (50 half frames per second).   PAL's color transmission is accurate, requiring no hue control on a PAL TV.   Contrast with *NTSC* and *SECAM*.

palette

(1) In computer graphics, the total range of colors that can be used for display, although typically only a subset of them can be used at one time.   May also refer to the collection of painting tools available to the user.
(2) A set of functions or modes.

palmtop

A computer small enough to hold in one hand and operate with the other.   Palmtops may have specialized keyboards or keypads for data entry applications or have small qwerty keyboards.

pan

(1) In computer graphics, to move (while viewing) to a different part of an image without changing magnification.
(2) To move (while viewing) horizontally across a text record.

Panda Project
See *Archistrat computer*.

Pantone Matching System
See *PMS*.

Panvalet
See *CA-Panvalet*.

paperless office
Long predicted, the paperless office is still a myth. Although paper usage has been reduced in some organizations, it has increased in others. Today's PCs make it easy to churn out documents.

In time, laptop computers with immense storage and high-resolution screens will serve to replace paper when travelling. Optical fiber networks will make it easy to send data, pictures, voice and video quickly.

As color laser printers become commonplace, it will be easy to reproduce any document, no matter how complex. People will eventually get used to the idea that a paper document is no better proof of a transaction than its electronic form. When this occurs, the paperless office will arrive.

paper tape
(1)A slow, low-capacity, sequential storage medium used in the first half of the 20th century to hold data as patterns of punched holes.
(2)A paper roll printed by a calculator or cash register.

Paper Tape
Once widely used, paper tape has gone the way of the punched card.

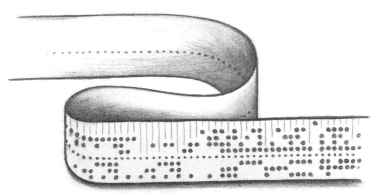

paradigm
Pronounced "para-dime." A model, example or pattern.

Paradise
A family of display adapters for PCs from the Paradise subsidiary of Western Digital Corporation, Irvine, CA.

Paradox
A relational database management (DBMS) and application development system for DOS and Windows from Borland. Paradox is known for its ease of use and query by example method for asking questions. Its PAL programming language is unique. Many PAL statements are interactive Paradox commands, so that a Paradox user can adjust to programming more easily. Version 4.0 supports memo fields and BLOBs. The Paradox engine (available separately) lets C applications access Paradox databases.

Paradox for Windows comes with the Borland Database Engine, which turns Paradox into a client/server development system that can access remote database servers (see *Borland Database Engine*).

paragraph

In DOS programming, a 16 byte block. Memory addresses are generated as "segment:offset," where the segment is expressed in paragraphs. To compute an address, the segment register is shifted left four bits (multiplying it by 16). For example, the address A000:0100 = 655,616:

```
Segment   A000      655,360   (40,960 X 16)
Offset    0100          256
Result    A0100     655,616
```

This means there are 4,096 possibilities for expressing each memory byte, a situation that has helped generate confusion.

paragraph tag

In desktop publishing, a style sheet assigned to a text paragraph. It defines font, tab, spacing and other settings.

parallel computing

Solving a problem with multiple computers or computers made up of multiple processors. It is an umbrella term for a variety of architectures, including symmetric multiprocessing (SMP) and massively parallel processors (MPPs). See *SMP, MPP, pipeline processing, array processor, vector processor* and *hypercube.*

parallel data query

See *PDQ.*

Parallel Enterprise Server

A family of S/390 mainframes from IBM that are air cooled and use microprocessor-based CMOS technology. Using symmetric multiprocessing (SMP), one Server can hold up to 10 CPUs, and up to 32 Servers can be tied together. The first models of this type were introduced in 1994. Parallel Enterprise Servers are increasingly replacing older air-cooled and low-end water-cooled bipolar-based mainframes.

parallel interface

A multiline channel that transfers one or more bytes simultaneously. Personal computers generally connect printers via a Centronics 36-wire parallel interface, which transfers one byte at a time over eight wires, the remaining ones being used for control signals. Large computer parallel interfaces transfer more than one byte at a time. It is faster than a serial interface, because it transfers several bits concurrently. Contrast with *serial interface*. See *Centronics.*

parallelism

An overlapping of processing, input/output (I/O) or both.

parallelizing

To generate instructions for a parallel processing computer.

parallel port

A socket on a computer used to connect a printer or other peripheral device. It may also be used to attach a portable hard disk, tape backup or CD-ROM. Transferring files between two PCs can be accomplished by cabling the parallel ports of both machines together and using a file transfer program such as LapLink.

Parallel Port
This is the parallel port on the back of a PC.

On the back of a PC, the parallel port is a 25-pin female DB-25 connector. In a PC, the parallel port circuit is contained on a small expansion card that plugs into an expansion slot. Typically two serial ports, one parallel port and one game port are on the card. These ports are often also included on an IDE host adapter card, which takes up only one expansion slot and provides hard and floppy disk control as well as I/O.

The Enhanced Parallel Port, or EPP, is a higher-speed parallel port standard that has been sanctioned by the IEEE. The EPP is expected to become widely used on PCs. See *IEEE 1284*.

parallel processing

(1)An architecture within a single computer that performs more than one operation at the same time. See *pipeline processing, array processor* and *vector processor*.
(2)An architecture using mulitiple computers. See *parallel computing*.

parallel server

A computer system used as a server that provides various degrees of simultaneous processing. See *SMP, massively parallel* and *multiprocessing*.

parallel transmission

Transmitting one or more bytes at a time using a cable with multiple lines dedicated to data (8, 16, 32 lines, etc.). Contrast with *serial transmission*.

parameter

(1) Any value passed to a program by the user or by another program in order to customize the program for a particular purpose. A parameter may be anything; for example, a file name, a coordinate, a range of values, a money amount or a code of some kind. Parameters may be required as in parameter-driven software (see below) or they may be optional. Parameters are often entered as a series of values following the program name when the program is loaded.

A DOS switch is a parameter. For example, in the DOS Dir command   **dir /p** the DOS switch **/p** (pause after every screenful) is a parameter.

(2) In programming, a value passed to a subroutine or function for processing. Programming today's graphical applications with languages such as C, C++ and Pascal requires knowledge of hundreds, if not thousands, of parameters.

In the following C function, which creates the text window for the Windows version of this database, there are 11 parameters passed to the CreateWindow routine. Some of them call yet other functions for necessary information. In order to call this routine in a program, the programmer must decide what the values are for every parameter.

```
hWndText = CreateWindow    (
    "TextWClass",
    NULL,
    WS_CHILD|WS_BORDER|WS_VSCROLL|WS_TABSTOP,
    xChar*23+GetSystemMetrics(SM_CXVSCROLL)+8,
    yChar*4,
    Rect.right-Rect.left+1-xChar*23
       -2*GetSystemMetrics(SM_CXVSCROLL)+5,
    yChar*(Lines+1)+2,
    hWnd,
    IDC_TEXTLIST,
    (HANDLE)hInstance,
    NULL                   )  ;
```

parameter-driven

Software that requires external values expressed at runtime. A parameter-driven program solves a problem that is partially or entirely described by the values (parameters) that are entered at the time the program is loaded. For example, typing **bio 6-20-36** might load a program that calculates biorhythms for someone born on June 20, 1936. In this case, the date is a required parameter. The more user-friendly approach is a menu-driven program that would have you select a menu option and present you with a data entry box to type in date of birth. Parameter-driven software is widely used when a program is called for and loaded by another program rather than by the user. Since the parameters are generated by one program and used by another, any number of parameters can be passed no matter how obscure the codes.

parameter RAM

See *PRAM*.

PARC

(Palo Alto Research Center) Xerox's research and development center where the Smalltalk programming language and GUI interface were developed. Established in 1970, it is located in the Stanford University Industrial Park, Palo Alto, CA.

parent-child

In database management, a relationship between two files. The parent file contains required data about a subject, such as employees and customers. The child is the offspring; for example, the child of a customer file may be the order file.

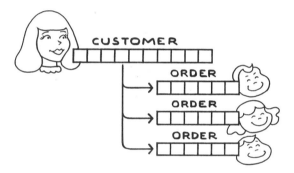

parent program

The main, or primary, program or first program loaded into memory. See *child program*.

PA-RISC

See *HP PA-RISC*.

parity bit

An extra bit attached to the byte, character or word used to detect errors in transmission.

parity checking

An error detection technique that tests the integrity of digital data within the computer system or over a network. Parity checking uses an extra ninth bit that holds a 0 or 1 depending on the data content of the byte. Each time a byte is transferred or transmitted, the parity bit is tested.
Even parity systems make the parity bit 1 when there is an even number of 1 bits in the byte. Odd parity systems make it 1 when there is an odd number of 1 bits.

parity drive

A separate disk drive that holds parity bits in a disk array. See *RAID*.

parity error

An error condition that occurs when the parity bit of a character is found to be incorrect.

park

To retract the read/write head on a hard disk to its home location before the unit is physically moved in order to prevent damage. Most modern drives park themselves when the power is turned off.

parse

To analyze a sentence or language statement. Parsing breaks down words into functional units that can be converted into machine language. For example, to parse the dBASE expression

```
sum salary for title = "MANAGER"
```

SUM must be identified as the primary command, FOR as a conditional search, TITLE as a field name and MANAGER as the data to be searched.

Parsing breaks down a natural language request, such as "**What's the total of all the managers' salaries**" into the commands required by a high-level language, such as in the example above.

parser

A routine that performs parsing operations on a computer or natural language.

partition

A reserved part of disk or memory that is set aside for some purpose.

partitioning

To divide a resource or application into smaller pieces. See *partition, application partitioning* and *PDQ*.

Pascal

A high-level programming language developed by Swiss professor Niklaus Wirth in the early 1970s and named after the French mathematician, Blaise Pascal. It is noted for its structured programming, which caused it to achieve popularity initially in academic circles. Pascal has had strong influence on subsequent languages, such as Ada, dBASE and PAL. See *Turbo Pascal*.

Pascal is available in both interpreter and compiler form and has unique ways of defining variables. For example, a set of values can be stated for a variable, and if any other value is stored in it, the program generates an error at runtime. A Pascal set is an array-like structure that can hold a varying number of predefined values. Sets can be matched and manipulated providing powerful non-numeric programming capabilities.

The following Turbo Pascal example converts Fahrenheit to Celsius:

```
program convert;
var
fahr, cent : integer;
begin
 write('Enter Fahrenheit ');
 readln(fahr);
 cent := (fahr - 32) * 5 / 9;
 writeln('Celsius is ',cent)
end.
```

Pascaline

A calculating machine developed in 1642 by French mathematician Blaise Pascal. It could only add and subtract, but gained attention because 50 units were placed in prominent locations throughout Europe. Accountants expressed grave concern that they might be replaced by technology!

The Pascaline
We worried three centuries ago about losing our jobs. We worry today about losing jobs. No matter how much technology we develop on this planet, we still worry! *(Photo courtesy of Pascal Institute.)*

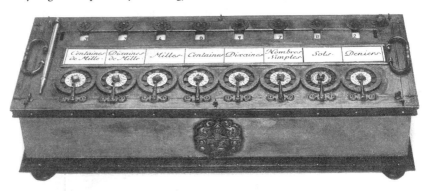

passive hub

A central connecting device in a network that joins wires from several stations in a star configuration. It does not provide any processing or regeneration of signals. Contrast with *active hub* and *intelligent hub*. See *hub*.

passive matrix

A common LCD technology used in laptops. See *LCD*.

passive star

See *passive hub*.

Passport

An object-oriented client/server development system from InSync Software, Ronkonkoma, NY, that supports Windows, OS/2 and Motif clients, VAXes and a wide variety of UNIX servers as well as all the major SQL databases. It includes visual programming utilities and fully supports event-driven systems that respond to realtime interrupts. Originally developed for the VAX/VMS world in the mid 1980s, Passport generates C source code and is designed to easily integrate with other third-party GUIs and software.

passthrough SQL

See *embedded SQL*.

password

A word or code used to serve as a security measure against unauthorized access to data. It is normally managed by the operating system or DBMS. However, the computer can only verify the legitimacy of the password, not the legitimacy of the user. See *NCSC*.

Password Tips from the Office of Standards and Product Evaluation National Computer Security Center:

CHANGE PASSWORD FREQUENTLY—The longer you use a password, the higher the risk of losing it.

USE GOOD PASSWORDS—Don't use persons, places or things that can be identified with you.

DON'T DISCLOSE YOUR PASSWORD—Your password is as valuable as the information it protects.

INSPECT YOUR DATA—If you suspect someone has tampered with your files, report it immediately.

NEVER LEAVE AN ACTIVE TERMINAL UNATTENDED—Always log off or lock your terminal before leaving it.

REPORT SUSPECTED COMPUTER ABUSE—Whether directed against you or not, abuse or misuse of your computer resources only hinders the timely completion of your tasks.

paste

See *cut & paste*.

patch

A temporary or quick fix to a program. Too many patches in a program make it difficult to maintain. It may also refer to changing the actual machine code when it is inconvenient to recompile the source program. See *MIDI patch*.

patch panel

A group of sockets that function as a manual switching center between incoming and outgoing lines in a communications or other electronic or electrical system.

path

(1) In communications, the route between any two nodes. Same as line, channel, link or circuit.
(2) In database management, the route from one set of data to another, for example, from customers to orders.
(3) The route to a file on a disk. In DOS, Windows and OS/2, the path for file MYLIFE located in subdirectory STORIES within directory JOE on drive C: looks like:

```
c:\joe\stories\mylife
```

The equivalent UNIX path follows. UNIX knows which drive is used:

```
/joe/stories/mylife
```

The Macintosh also uses a path in certain command sequences; for example, with "hard disk" as the drive, the same path is:

```
hard disk:joe:stories:mylife
```

Path not found

A DOS error message that means you entered an invalid path name.

PATHWORKS

A network operating system from Digital that lets a VAX minicomputer function as a server for DOS, Windows, Windows NT, OS/2 and Macintosh clients. DECnet, TCP/IP, AppleTalk and NetWare protocols are supported.

PAX

(1) (Private Automatic Exchange) An inhouse intercom system.
(2) (Parallel Architecture Extended) A parallel processing environment standard based on Intel's i860 RISC chip, UNIX System V and Alliant Computer's parallel and 3-D graphics technologies.

PAX-1

Software from VXM Technologies, Boston, MA, that allows a network of computers to function as a single parallel processing system. It runs in an Ethernet network under TCP/IP and supports personal computers, minis and mainframes.

payware

Software distributed for money. Contrast with *freeware*.

PB

See *PowerBuilder*.

PBX

(Private Branch eXchange) An inhouse telephone switching system that interconnects telephone extensions to each other, as well as to the outside telephone network. It may include functions such as least cost routing for outside calls, call forwarding, conference calling and call accounting.
Modern PBXs use all-digital methods for switching and can often handle digital terminals and telephones along with analog telephones.

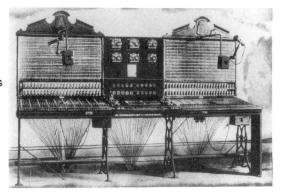

PBX

Not exactly an example of today's PBXs, this PBX was installed in Bangor, Maine in 1883. *(Photo courtesy of AT&T.)*

PC

(1) Also see *printed circuit board*.
(2) (Personal Computer) Although the term PC is sometimes used to refer to any kind of personal computer (Mac, Amiga, etc.), in this book and in general, PC refers to computers that conform to the PC standard originally developed by IBM.
Today the PC industry is governed by Intel, Microsoft and major PC vendors collectively. The PC is the world's largest computer base; 1995 estimates are between 150 and 200 million installed units. A rather wide range, one wonders who's keeping count.
PCs are used as stand-alone personal computers or as workstations and file servers in a local area network. They predominantly run under DOS and Windows; however, they are occasionally used as a central computer in a multiuser environment under UNIX and other operating systems.
IBM's first PC models had names: XT, AT, Convertible, etc. Models of the second-generation PS/2 series use numbers: Model 30, 55, 80, etc. (see *IBM PC*).
Compatibles often use the CPU designation in the name, such as "486 Turbo."

Although there are literally thousands of PC vendors, from mom and pop shops to large mail order houses (Dell, Gateway, etc.) to the major computer companies (Compaq, HP, Digital, etc.), and of course IBM, still one of the world's largest PC makers, all PCs use an Intel x86 or compatible CPU. See *PC CPU models*.

First attempts at cloning the IBM PC were not all successful. From 1982 to 1985, there were a lot of "almost compatible" PCs. However, as soon as the part of the operating system known as the BIOS was successfully cloned and made commercially available, true compatibles appeared in abundance.

Today, you can replace floppies, hard disks and video displays, as well as add a scanner, CD-ROM or other device without too much difficulty. In general, PC components are interchangeable. Expansion cards are easily plugged in and out, and an entire motherboard can be replaced with one (from a different vendor) in about a half hour.

The problems come when you add a second or third device and run into a conflict with an existing one. In addition, having to modify DOS's infamous AUTOEXEC.BAT and CONFIG.SYS configuration files causes every novice to flinch in the beginning.

Conflicts aside, the PC has become a commodity item, winding its way onto the shelves of a wide variety of retail outlets. This is a testimonial to the power of a computer standard, even one fraught with as many loopholes and inconsistencies as this one. With built-in Plug and Play, the Windows 95 operating system is the first attempt to solve these problems. In time, it is expected that when all hardware devices conform to the Plug and Play standard, the PC will be as easy to configure as the Macintosh, which has always been a plug and play machine.

Today, most PCs run most software and work with most plug-in boards, but there are always exceptions. With the myriads of adapters and applications available for the PC, one device, application, TSR or utility can always conflict with another.

The way to guarantee that something works is to try it. This has been true since day one in the computer business.

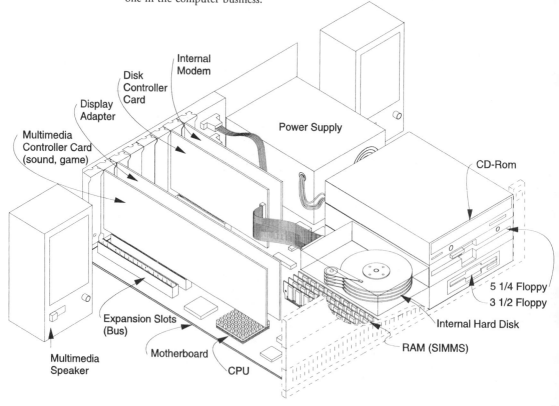

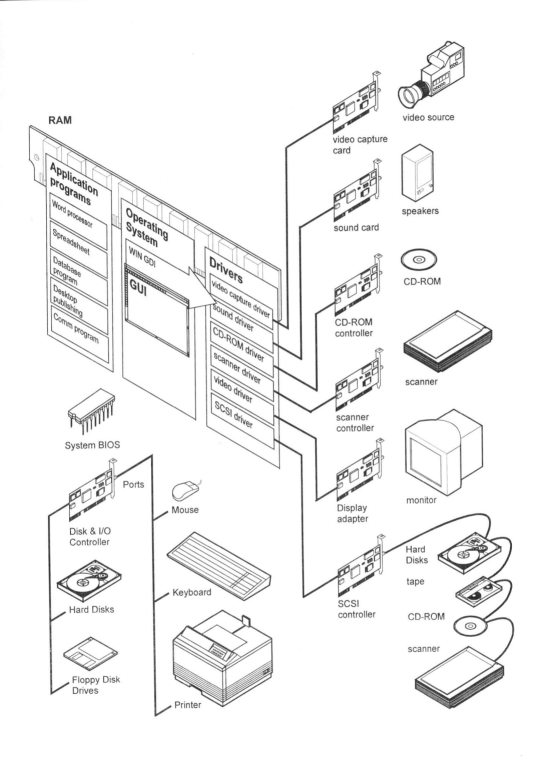

RAM

Application programs

Word processor

Spreadsheet

Database program

Desktop publishing

Comm program

Operating System

WIN GDI

GUI

Drivers

video capture driver

sound driver

CD-ROM driver

scanner driver

video driver

SCSI driver

System BIOS

Ports

Mouse

Disk & I/O Controller

Hard Disks

Keyboard

Floppy Disk Drives

Printer

video capture card

video source

sound card

speakers

CD-ROM controller

CD-ROM

scanner controller

scanner

Display adapter

monitor

SCSI controller

Hard Disks

tape

CD-ROM

scanner

PC-8

A symbol set that contains the extended ASCII characters of the IBM PC.

PC-98

A personal computer series from NEC. It is the most popular PC in Japan.

PC/104

A PC bus architecture that uses 3.5" square modules that snap together. This "stack through" bus provides a modular, compact and rugged design for building process control and embedded systems.

PCB, PC board

See *printed circuit board.*

PC bus

The bus architecture used in first-generation IBM PCs and XTs. It refers to the original 8-bit bus, which accepted only 8-bit expansion boards. In 286s and up, it was superseded by the 16-bit AT bus, later known as the ISA bus. Contrast with *ISA, EISA* and *Micro Channel.*

PC Card

(1)A credit-card sized, removable module that contains memory, I/O or a hard disk. The term may refer to a variety of proprietary card-sized products; however, the term "PC Card" is PCMCIA's trademark for its PC card standard. See *PCMCIA.*
(2) The term PC card (lower case "c") might refer to any expansion board for a PC.

PC color codes

Following are the color numbers for the 16 foreground and eight background colors in text mode. Foreground and background numbers are added together; for example, white text on a red background is 79. To blink the text, add 128.

Background Number	Color	Foreground Number	Foreground Number	Color
0	Black	0	8	Dark gray
16	Blue	1	9	Light blue
32	Green	2	10	Light green
48	Cyan	3	11	Light cyan
64	Red	4	12	Light red
80	Magenta	5	13	Light magenta
96	Brown	6	14	Yellow
112	Light gray	7	15	White
			128	Blinking

PC CPU models

The brains of the PC is a CPU, or processor, from the Intel 8086 family (x86) of microprocessors or from a company that makes x86-compatible CPUs, such as AMD (Advanced Micro Devices) and Cyrix Corporation. IBM also makes its own x86-compatible chips. Following are the major classes of PCs.

XT Class - 8086, 8088

The original PC launched by IBM in 1981 used the 16-bit 8088 CPU. This chip family was designed so that the major installed base of CP/M applications could be easily ported to the new architecture.
Unfortunately, it was limited to one megabyte of memory and was designed without much flexibility. Who knew this would become the world's greatest hardware

standard. Although more advanced CPUs (386, 486, etc.) came later, they had to build in 16-bit operating modes to conform to the original standard and run all the DOS and Windows 3.x applications on the market.

These first PCs, known as XT-class machines, survive in a second-hand market, but are best used with older software that does not place much demand on the computer. XTs are too slow for almost all of today's applications.

AT Class - 286

First used in the IBM AT in 1984, the 286's 16-bit CPU can address up to 16 megabytes of memory. ATs were just faster XTs, and memory above one megabyte was rarely used for applications until Windows 3.0 became popular. By then, 386s and 486s were widely used.

AT-class machines are fast enough for most DOS applications, but are extremely sluggish under Windows. However, they can run Windows 3.0 and 3.1, but not Windows 95.

386, 486, Pentium

First used by Compaq in 1986, the 386, or 386DX, is a 32-bit machine that runs faster than the 286 and can address an unbelievable four gigabytes of memory, although motherboards generally only have slots for up to 64 or 128 megabytes. Its flexible architecture allows both extended and expanded (EMS) memory to be allocated on demand (see *memory allocation*). 386s will also run OS/2 2.0, Windows NT, Windows 95 and other 32-bit operating systems and applications. The advances in the 386 are carried forth in the 486 and Pentium CPUs.

With initial models introduced in late 1989, the 486, or 486DX, is two to five times as fast as a 386, depending on clock rates, and has a built-in math coprocessor, required by CAD programs. The 486 is better suited for today's demanding applications than the 386 and has become the entry-level CPU in the Intel x86 line. The 486SX runs at slower speeds than the 486DX and makes the coprocessor an optional item.

Introduced in 1993, the Pentium is the successor to the 486 and has become widely used as the CPU in desktop and laptop PCs. The Pentium Pro was introduced in 1995, but initially seems suited for servers or workstations that run 32-bit operating systems, such as Windows 95, Windows NT and UNIX. See *PC operating environments.*

PC Memory

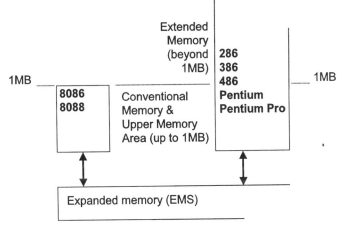

PC data buses

The bus in a PC is the common pathway between the CPU and the peripheral devices. Controller boards for the video, disks and other devices plug directly into slots in the bus.

ISA

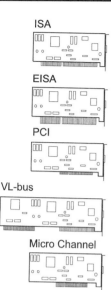

EISA

PCI

VL-bus

Micro Channel

ISA

The original PC used an 8-bit bus (transfers 8 bits simultaneously) known as the PC or XT bus. With the 286-based AT model, the bus was extended to 16-bits. Machines come with a mix of 8-bit and 16-bit expansion slots. 8-bit expansion cards fit in both slots, but 16-bit cards require 16-bit slots. The 16-bit bus has becomn known as the ISA ("i-suh") bus, or Industry Standard Architecture bus.

Micro Channel

When IBM introduced the PS/2 line, it switched from the ISA bus to the high-speed 32-bit Micro Channel (MCA) bus. The MCA also provides bus mastering, which has yet to be exploited. Later, IBM introduced ISA PS/2 models for greater compatibility. ISA and MCA expansion boards are not interchangeable.

EISA

To counter the Micro Channel and extend the ISA bus from 16 bits to 32 bits, EISA ("e-suh") was conceived by the compatible vendors in 1988. The EISA bus accepts both EISA and ISA boards, but still runs at the same clock speeds as the ISA bus in order to accomodate ISA boards.

Local Bus

VESA's VL-bus and Intel's PCI bus are buses that improve performance by providing a high-speed channel directly to the CPU that bypasses the slower ISA and EISA buses.
See *ISA, EISA, Micro Channel, VL-bus* and *PCI*.

PCD file
See *Photo CD*.

PC display modes

The screen resolution on a PC is determined by an expansion board, called a *display adapter* or *graphics adapter*, which is plugged into one of the computer's expansion slots. The monitor must also be able to adjust to the resolutions of the display adapter. The common display adapter today is the VGA adapter, which supports a number of resolutions that have been standardized by VESA. See *VESA BIOS Extension.*

When the computer boots up in DOS, the display is in text mode with an on-screen resolution of 720x400 pixels with a maximum of 16 colors. When the PC is switched to graphics, either for Windows or a graphics-based DOS application, the resolution and colors can change depending on the capabilities of the display adapter, monitor and application.

All display adapters come with their own software drivers for Windows. The driver is installed after the adapter is plugged in. The driver lets Windows display its output at all the resolutions and colors the display adapter is capable of. Users switch resolutions by activating a software control panel that manages the driver. The display adapter may also come with drivers for major DOS applications such as AutoCAD and WordPerfect. These drivers have no effect on Windows or other DOS applications.

VESA supports four screen resolutions: 640x480, 800x600, 1024x768 and 1280x1024. On monitors smaller than 15", the lower 640x480 graphics resolution is usually preferred. On 17" monitors, either 800x600 or 1024x768 is commonly used. On 20 and 21" monitors, 1024x768 and 1280x1024 resolutions are used. For desktop publishing applications that require two visible pages on screen, non-VESA resolutions of 1600x1200 and 1600x1280 are also used. These resolutions are expected to be supported by VESA some time in the future.

There are also display adapters and monitors that provide even higher resolutions, such as 2016x1660 and 2048x1536. Often monochrome only, these systems are used for document imaging where on-screen text must be as readable as possible.

Summary of PC Display Standards

VESA Standards - Super VGA

640x480	text & graphics (256-16M colors)
800x600	text & graphics (16-16M colors)
1024x768	text & graphics (16-16M colors)
1280x1024	text & graphics (16-16M colors)

IBM Standards

MDA	720x350 text only, monochrome
CGA	320x200 text & graphics (4 colors)
EGA	640x350 text & graphics (16 colors)
MCGA	640x400 text; 320x200 graphics (256 cols)
VGA	720x400 text; 640x480 graphics (16 colors)
8514	1024x768 text & graphics (256 colors)
XGA	1024x768 text & graphics (256 colors)

Hercules Standard

720x348 text & graphics (monochrome)

PC-DOS

The DOS operating system from Microsoft supplied by IBM with its PCs. Up until DOS 6, PC-DOS was almost identical to Microsoft's MS-DOS for non-IBM PCs, and both versions are called *DOS*. See "IBM's DOS 6" under *DOS 6*.

PC EXPO

A trade show for resellers and corporate PC buyers held in the summer (New York) and fall (Chicago). It started in New York in 1983 with 120 exhibitors and 9,600 attendees. In 1995, more than 800 exhibitors drew 130,000 attendees. PC EXPO is sponsored by the Blenheim Group PLC, One Executive Drive, Fort Lee, NJ 07024, 800/829-3976. See also *Blenheim shows*.

PC floppy disks

Until late 1994, there were two kinds of floppy disks routinely used in a PC: the 5.25" disk, which is housed in a square, flexible envelope, and the 3.5" disk, housed in a rigid plastic case. Today, the 5.25" format is obsolete, and a 3.5" floppy drive is all that is necessary unless you have to work with older disks.

The low-density 360KB, 5.25" disk, introduced soon after the first PC, was widely used for retail software, because it provided a common distribution medium. Even after the high-density 5.25" was introduced on IBM's AT in 1984, which holds 1.2 megabytes, the 360KB disks were still often used. The 1.2MB drives can read and write the 360KB disks.

If there is no manufacturer's label on a 5.25" diskette, you cannot tell by looking at it whether it is a 360KB or 1.2MB disk. If the disk is used, you can get a byte count by viewing its file contents in Windows or DOS.

The 3.5" diskettes were first introduced in a low-density 720KB version on IBM's Convertible laptop. Capacity was doubled to 1.44MB with the PS/2 line. Due to their greater storage and convenience, 3.5" drives have been retrofitted to many machines and the 3.5" diskette has become the standard. 1.44MB drives can read, write and format 720KB disks.

You can tell the difference between the 720KB and 1.44MB disks. Looking at it from the label side with the aluminum slider at the bottom, the 1.44MB disk has a hole in the upper left corner, while the 720KB disk does not.

Some IBM models include the extra-high density 2.88MB floppy drives, which are compatible with the 1.44MB disks. This format has not caught on universally, and even IBM uses it selectively.

Floppy Disk Formats:

720KB   3.5"   DS/DD   Low density (Double Density)
1.44MB   3.5"   DS/HD   High density
2.88MB   3.5"   DS/ED   Extra-high density

360KB   5.25"   DS/DD   Low density (Double Density)
1.2MB   5.25"   DS/HD   High density

The DS stands for double sided.

PC hard disks

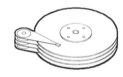

The primary storage medium in a PC is a non-removable hard disk. Hard disks are available with storage capacities from 100MB to 2GB and above. Buying a system with less than a 500MB hard disk may be shortsighted, considering the lower cost of today's drives. Applications are getting larger and are using more and more of the hard disk all the time.

There have been several hard disk interface standards used for PCs, including MFM, RLL, ESDI, IDE and SCSI (see *hard disk*). Today, most hard drives sold with PCs are IDE and SCSI. It depends on the controller (expansion board) whether or not another hard disk interface type can co-exist in the PC. In some cases, IDE and SCSI drives can co-exist, in others they cannot.

The IDE host adapter (expansion board) that plugs into a PC can generally control two IDE hard disks. Installing the second IDE hard disk on a reasonably-new PC is not complicated (see *IDE*).

Since most hard disks are not removable, the low-level physical format of one drive has no bearing on that of another in a different machine. For example, two computers can be cabled together and files can be transferred from the IDE hard disk of one PC to the SCSI disk of another. The hard disk controllers are reading and writing their disks according to their own technology.

Removable disk drives and Bernoulli disks provide the convenience of transportability and unlimited amounts of storage, although each drive holds only one disk module at a time. Cartridges come in 40MB and higher capacities, and optical disks hold up to 600MB and more. Each cartridge is of a proprietary design and can be inserted only into the drive it is designed for.

As storage capacity grows, so does performance. Disk access times run from 9 milliseconds (fast) to 100 ms (slow). See *hard disk*.

PCI

(Peripheral Component Interconnect) A local bus for personal computers that provides a high-speed data path between the CPU and peripheral devices (video, disk, network, etc.). There are typically three or four PCI slots on the motherboard. There may also be one or two built-in PCI controllers (IDE, SCSI, network, etc.) on the motherboard.

In a PC, the PCI bus coexists with the ISA or EISA bus. ISA and EISA boards still plug into an ISA or EISA slot, while high-speed PCI boards plug into a PCI slot. PCI provides "plug and play" capability, automatically configuring the PCI cards at startup. When PCI is used with the ISA bus, the only thing that is generally required is to indicate in the CMOS RAM which IRQs are already in use by ISA cards. PCI takes care of the rest.

PCI runs at 33MHz, supports 32- and 64-bit data paths and bus mastering. The first PCs with PCI buses became available in late 1993. PCI is processor independent and is available for PCs, PowerPCs and other CPUs. This architecture is sanctioned by the PCI special interest group (SIG), supported by over 100 manufacturers. Its chief designer and promoter is Intel.

The number of peripheral devices the bus can handle is based on loads, which have to do with inductance, capacitance and other electrical characteristics. Normally

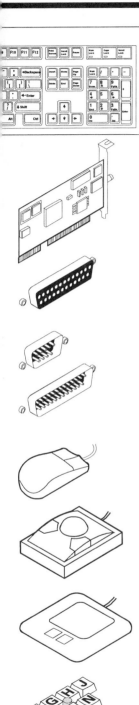

there are 10 loads per bus. The basic PCI chipset uses three, leaving seven for peripherals. Controllers built onto the motherboard use one load, whereas controllers that plug into an expansion slot use 1.5 loads.

PC input/output

There are three ways of getting data into and out of the PC. The first is via the keyboard, which plugs into a keyboard connector always built onto the motherboard. The keyboard plugs directly into the 5-pin DIN receptacle. The PS/2 uses a 6-pin mini-DIN connector.

The second is via the data bus, or expansion bus, which is a set of slots on the motherboard. Expansion boards, or cards, are plugged into the slots and contain cables to their respective devices. These cards are control circuits for disk drives, the video display, CD-ROM reader and network adapter for example.

The third way is through serial and parallel ports which are input/output pathways built into the motherboard or contained on a separate expansion board. On the back of the PC, there are typically two serial ports (one 9-pin male and one 25-pin male). In DOS, the first port is named COM1, and the second is COM2. Both ports provide the same capability. The parallel port (LPT1) uses a 25-pin female connector on the PC.

The serial ports are typically used for modems, mice, scanners and digitizer tablets, and the parallel port is used for the printer, although some printers use a serial port. Both serial and parallel ports can be used for file transfer between two computers cabled together.

Mice can be purchased for either the serial port (serial mouse) or for connection via an expansion board (bus mouse). Some scanners and printers require an expansion board, which accompanies the product when you buy it and must be plugged into the PC.

PC I/O addressing

This is a method for passing signals from the CPU to the controller boards of peripheral devices on x86 machines. I/O addresses, also called port addresses, reference a separate memory space on peripheral boards. This is often confused with memory-mapped peripherals, such as video cards, which use a block of upper memory (UMB) in the upper memory area (UMA). Peripheral devices often use both methods: an I/O address for passing control signals and an upper memory block (UMB) for transferring and buffering data to and from the CPU.

There is a 64K address space for I/O addresses, although typically less than 1K is used. Each board that uses an I/O address contains a few bytes of memory (16, 32, etc.) set to a default address range. One or more alternate addresses is also provided to resolve conflicts with other boards. These I/O spaces are a bunch of tiny memory banks scattered over different devices. As long as each one is set to a different address, the CPU can transmit signals to the appropriate boards without conflict.

An I/O address operation takes place as follows. If a program needs to send a byte to the serial port, it issues an OUT instruction to the CPU with the address of that serial port. The CPU notifies the address bus to activate the I/O space, not regular memory, and the address bus signals the appropriate byte location on the board. The CPU then sends the data character over the data bus to that memory location.

PCjr

(PC junior) IBM's first home computer introduced in 1983. Its original keyboard was unsuitable for typing, but adequate keyboards were later added. It was discontinued in 1985.

PC keyboard

(1) The keyboard introduced with the IBM PC that provides a dual-function keypad for numeric entry and cursor movement. It was severely criticized for its non-

standard shift key placement, which was corrected with the AT keyboard. Regardless of key placement, users love the feel of IBM keyboards.
(2) Any keyboard made for the PC, including the PC keyboard, AT keyboard and Enhanced keyboard.

PC keyboards

IBM has had three generations of keyboards since the introduction of the original PC, all of which have been an annoyance for the touch typist. The original "PC keyboard" used an awkward return and left shift key placement. Finally corrected on the "AT keyboard," the backspace key was made harder to reach. The "Enhanced keyboard" relocated a host of keys, including the function keys, making it impossible to assign them intelligently. What was easy on one keyboard is hard to reach on the other.

Keyboard manufacturers make both the AT keyboard and the Enhanced keyboard with the same key placement. Only a few dare to be different and incorporate the best features of both.

One advantage of PC keyboards is that they usually work on all PCs, including laptops and even XTs, in which case there is a switch on the bottom of the keyboard marked XT and AT. Switch it to XT for XTs and AT for all others. PC keyboards use a 5-pin DIN connector that plugs into a socket on the motherboard. With an adapter, the larger 5-pin DIN plug can be connected to the smaller 6-pin mini DIN socket used on laptops and PS/2s.

Key placement on some PC laptops is dreadful, placing often-used Ctrl and Alt keys in hard to reach locations and forcing users to press the Fn key for commonly-used functions. Touch typists beware!

PCL

(Printer Control Language) The command language for the HP LaserJet printers. It has become a de facto standard used in many printers and typesetters. PCL Level 5, introduced with the LaserJet III in 1990, also supports Compugraphic's Intellifont scalable fonts.

PC LAN

(1) A network of IBM or IBM-compatible PCs.
(2) A network of any variety of personal computers.

PCM

(1) (Pulse Code Modulation) A technique for digitizing speech by sampling the sound waves and converting each sample into a binary number. It uses waveform coding that samples a 4KHz bandwidth 8,000 times a second. Each sample is an 8 bit number, resulting in 64K bits of data per second. See *ADPCM*.
(2) (Plug Compatible Manufacturer) An organization that makes a computer or electronic device that is compatible with an existing machine.

PCMCIA

(Personal Computer Memory Card International Association, 1030G East Duane Ave., Sunnyvale, CA 94086, 408/720-0107) A non-profit trade association founded in 1989 to standardize a method for connecting peripherals to portable computers. PCMCIA created a 16-bit socket, and the formal name for the credit card-sized cards that plug into it is the "PC Card," although "PCMCIA Card" has become the more widely used term.

PCMCIA cards are used to attach modems, network adapters, sound cards, radio transceivers, solid state disks and hard disks to a portable computer. The PCMCIA card is a "plug and play" device, which is configured automatically by the PCMCIA Card Services software (see below).

All PCMCIA cards are 85.6 mm long by 54 mm wide (3.37" x 2.126") and use a

68-pin connector. The original Type I card is 3.3 mm thick and is now used for memory in palmtops and other light-weight applications.

The Type II card, which is 5.0 mm thick, is commonly used for memory, modems and LAN adapters in laptops. The Type III card is 10.5 mm thick and is used to hold a hard disk, wireless transceiver or other peripheral that needs more space. One Type III slot can hold one Type III or two Type II cards.

Toshiba introduced a 16 mm Type IV card, but this has not been officially adopted by the PCMCIA. Smaller cards will work in a Type IV slot.

Card and Socket Services

In order to use a PCMCIA slot in the computer, PCMCIA Card and Socket services must be loaded, typically at system startup. Card and Socket Services software is generally included with laptops that have PCMCIA slots. It also comes packaged with PCMCIA cards.

Card Services manage system resources required by the PCMCIA card, and, on PCs, determines which IRQs and memory and I/O addresses are assigned. They also manage hot swapping and pass changes in events to higher-level drivers written for specific PCMCIA cards.

Card Services talk to Socket Services, which is the lowest level of software that communicates directly with the PCMCIA controller chips. Socket Services can be built into the system BIOS or added via software.

PC Card-16 and CardBus

In early 1995, PCMCIA issued Release 2.1 of its standard, which incorporates the second generation of the PC Card, known as the CardBus (PC Cards will be henceforth called PC Card-16 cards). Although electrically different, the CardBus is architecturally identical to the PCI bus.

The CardBus supports bus mastering and accomodates cards operating at different voltages. Its advanced power managment features allows the computer to take advantage of CardBus cards designed to idle or turn off in order to increase battery life. The CardBus specification allows data transfer up to 132 Mbytes/sec over a 33MHz, 32-bit data path.

PC Card

PC memory

The original PC design was constrained to one megabyte of memory. In addition, certain parts of the operating system were placed into fixed locations in the upper part of memory without any method for cooperatively storing additional drivers and programs. This design gave rise to the most confusing platform in history.

Following are the different types of memory in a PC. In other computers, there is just plain memory. In mainframes and supercomputers, there are also large, auxiliary memory banks that function as caches between disk and RAM.

Conventional Memory	First 640K
UMA (Upper Memory Area)	Next 384K
HMA (High Memory Area)	Next 64K
Extended Memory	From 1MB up
EMS (Expanded Memory)	Additional memory beyond 1MB bank switched into the UMA

PC Memory Map

This chart shows how the first megabyte of memory is used in a PC.

Address			
			Extended memory
11000:0000 1088K			
	High Memory Area (HMA)		
10000:0000 1024K			
	PC ROM BIOS	PS/2 ROM BIOS & VGA ROM	
F000:0000 960K			
			Top 384K of the first megabyte of RAM is called the Upper Memory Area (UMA), comprised of Upper Memory Blocks (UMBs)
E000:0000 896K			
	Available for drivers and EMS page frame		
D000:0000 832K			
C800:0000 800K			
	EGA, VGA ROM BIOS		
C000:0000 768K			
	Free		
BC00:0000 752K			
	CGA graphics, CGA, EGA, VGA text	Hercules graphics	
B800:0000 736K			
	Free		
B400:0000 720K			
	MDA RAM		
B000:0000 704K			
	EGA, VGA graphics RAM		
A000:0000 640K			
			Lower 640K is used by DOS and user programs
	User programs		
	DOS and COMMAND.COM Interrupt vectors		
0K			

PC-MOS/386

A multiuser PC operating system from The Software Link, Inc., Norcross, GA. It runs most standard DOS applications as well as applications written for the 386's Protected Mode.

PC network

(1) A network of IBM and/or IBM-compatible PCs.
(2) A network of any variety of personal computers.
(3) (PC Network) The first PC LAN from IBM introduced in 1984. It inaugurated the NetBIOS interface and uses the CSMA/CD access method. Token Ring support was added later. See *MS-Net*.

p-code

See *pseudo language* and *UCSD p-System*.

PC operating environments

Almost all PCs use the DOS operating system, which was developed for the 8088 CPU with its maximum of one megabyte of RAM. The PC was also designed so that the first 640K of the one megabyte is used for applications, while the next 384K, or UMA (upper memory area), is used by the operating system to control peripheral devices. Since some of the 640K is also used by DOS, only about 570K to 600K is available to user programs.

As users became comfortable with PCs, they wanted more than one application open and active at the same time. In order to get around DOS' single task nature and the PC's 640K limit, a variety of add-ons, techniques and remedies have been created to solve this dilemma. Following is a synopsis.

TSRs

In 1984, Borland introduced Sidekick and popularized the TSR, or popup, program. Sidekick stayed in memory but swapped in and out of view by pressing a hotkey, and users could instantly switch to a handy phone directory or notepad. However, keeping many TSRs in memory may not leave room for important, big applications, and TSRs are known to cause conflicts.

Expanded Memory

In 1984, expanded memory (EMS) was created to break the one megabyte barrier. An EMS board with multiple megabytes of RAM could be plugged in, and its memory used directly by EMS applications.

Lotus 1-2-3 quickly took advantage of it and hundreds of other applications have been written to use it. EMS can be installed in all PCs from XTs on up, a major advantage when XTs were purchased widely. See *EMS* for details.

Task Switchers & Multitaskers

Programs such as Software Carousel extend DOS's capabilities by allowing the user to keep a variety of programs open at the same time and switch back and forth between them. These "task switchers" use EMS memory, extended memory and/or the hard disk to swap applications in and out of conventional memory.

Combining multitasking with task switching, Quarterdeck's popular DESQview was the first control program to use expanded (EMS) memory to allow programs to run in, not just reside in, the background.

Memory Managers

Memory managers were developed to store TSRs and other memory-resident software (drivers) in the 384K UMA (upper memory area), thus freeing more precious "conventional memory" in the 640K region.

Memory managers manage both extended and EMS memory, and products, such as QEMM-386, 386MAX and DOS 6's EMM386.EXE, can allocate both types on demand on 386s and up. See *DOS memory manager* and *memory allocation*.

Extended Memory and Windows 3.x

By the late 1980s, the DOS extender was introduced, which is software that allows DOS applications to run in, not just reside in, extended memory in 286s and up. Paradox 386 and Lotus 1-2-3 Version 3.0 were some of the first programs to use it. Windows uses its own DOS extender to manage up to 16MB of memory in Windows 3.0 and up to 256MB in Windows 3.1. It lets users launch, keep active and switch between several Windows and DOS applications. Windows' ability to finally use large amounts of memory in the PC contributed to its success.

DOS 5 & 6

DOS 5 added a task switching capability that runs multiple DOS applications and swaps inactive ones to disk. It improved memory management, freeing up more conventional memory by loading operating system components into upper memory areas (HMA and UMA).

DOS 6 improved memory management and added realtime compression. It can allocate extended memory and EMS memory on demand, making it more flexible for running a mix of old DOS and new Windows programs. Its DoubleSpace or DriveSpace compression can double the capacity of a hard disk. In DOS 6, for the first time, a variety of stand-alone utility programs have been included.

DR DOS

DR DOS is a DOS-compatible operating system with advanced memory management and other features that always inspired Microsoft to include similar functionality in its subsequent DOS releases. Novell acquired DR DOS and added NetWare functionality to it, but has not continued to market it.

Advanced Operating Systems

The OS/2 operating system from IBM is highly regarded. Its Workplace Shell interface is similar to Windows, and it can also run DOS and Windows applications. OS/2 requires a 386 or higher machine.

Microsoft turned its development of OS/2 into Windows NT, a redesigned operating system for 386s and up. NT is a stand-alone operating system that doesn't use DOS, although it runs existing DOS and Windows applications. NT is more geared more for the network server than the desktop, but versions are available for both client and server. Windows 95 is also a stand-alone operating system that runs earlier DOS and Windows applications.

The Bad News

The legacy of TSRs, memory managers and task switchers combined with the various versions of DOS and Windows make quite a nightmare for the micro manager responsible for personal computers in a large enterprise.

The Good News

If somebody already set up your PC, you may not have to deal with any of the bad news!

In addition, Windows has become "the" desktop operating system. Although Windows is a complicated environment to develop for, and it is not as easy to use as was intended, it offers much more consistency, integration and standardization than the DOS world ever did. It is the clear winner. Windows 95 has improved stability over Windows 3.1, but still has to deal with DOS and Windows 3.1 applications until they dissapear forever.

You should be able to buy Windows software packages for years to come. You should also be able to run your DOS programs for a long time. All future operating systems for the desktop must be able to run DOS and Windows programs.

The PowerPC: The Next Generation

The alliance of IBM, Apple and Motorola launched the PowerPC chip in 1993. The Power Macintoshes, the first machines to use the PowerPC, provide extraordinary performance using the Macintosh operating system. The PowerMacs can also run DOS and Windows applications under emulation. IBM has introduced PowerPC-based PCs in 1995 with new operating systems that also run DOS and Windows applications.

When IBM releases its PowerPC 615-based machines in 1996, PowerPCs will be able to run DOS and Windows applications without emulation. The 615 executes x86 and PowerPC instructions natively on the chip. It's a whole new ballgame!

PC Paintbrush

A PC paint program from ZSoft Corporation, Marietta, GA, that is widely used and has set an industry standard graphics format. Its PCX raster graphics format is generated and accepted by many graphics, word processing and desktop publishing programs.

PC printers

There are hundreds of printer models that work with PCs from dot matrix to ink jet to laser printers and most of them plug into the PC's parallel port. Printing text files directly from DOS works with all printers, but in order to select fonts, boldface, underline and other print attributes, the application must support the printer.

Word processing, desktop publishing, CAD and any other DOS package that offers full-featured printing, provides drivers for the popular printers. These drivers are selected by the user when installing the program, and fonts installed for one application are often not sharable by another.

One of the significant advantages of Windows is that once the printer installation has been performed for Windows, every Windows application can use all the installed fonts. All Windows applications use the print services in Windows to do their printing. Once products such as LaserMaster's WinJet system, which extends Windows' printing capabilities, is hooked into Windows, then all applications use it. In either case, Windows provides a single, central facility for managing all the installed fonts and doing the printing.

PCradio

An IBM laptop designed for mobile use. It is a ruggedized machine that provides cellular, wireless data radio (Ardis) and modem communications.

PCS

(1) (Personal Communications Services) Refers to a variety of wireless services emerging after the U.S. Government auctioned commercial licenses in late 1994 and early 1995. This two gigahertz radio spectrum will be used for digital transmission that will compete with cellular and other wireless services.

(2) (Personal Conferencing Specification) A videoconferencing technology that uses Intel's Indeo compression method. It is endorsed by the Intel-backed Personal Conferencing Working Group (PCWG). Initially competing against H.320, Intel subsequently announced its videoconferencing products will also be H.320 compliant.

PCTE

(Portable Common Tool Environment) An ECMA standard for exchanging data between CASE tools. See *CDIF*.

PC Tools

A popular and comprehensive packages of utilities for DOS and Windows from Symantec (originally Central Point Software). They include a DOS or Windows shell as well as antivirus, file management, caching, backup, compression and data recovery utilities.

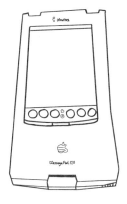

PDA
Apple's Newton ushered in the era of the personal digital assistant.

PCX

A widely-used raster graphics file format developed by Zsoft Corporation, Marietta, GA, that handles monochrome, 2-bit, 4-bit, 8-bit and 24-bit color and uses RLE to achieve compression ratios of approximately 1.1:1 to 1.5:1. Images with large blocks of solid colors compress best under the RLE method.

PDA

(Personal Digital Assistant) A handheld computer that serves an an organizer, electronic book or note taker and includes features such as pen-based entry and wireless transmission to a cellular service or desktop system.

PDES

(Product Data Exchange Specification) A standard format for exchanging data between advanced CAD and CAM programs. It describes a complete product, including the geometric aspects of the images as well as manufacturing features, tolerance specifications, material properties and finish specifications. See *IGES*.

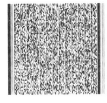

PDF417 Bar Code
This PDF417 image contains the entire Gettysburg address. *(Photo courtesy of Symbol Technology, Inc.)*

PDF417

A two-dimensional bar code developed by Symbol Technology, Inc., Bohemia, NY. The bar code is read horizontally and vertically and can hold 1,800 characters in the area the size of a postage stamp. Symbol Technologies and other companies make PDF417 readers.

PDF file

(Portable Document Format file) The file format used by the Acrobat document exchange system. See *Acrobat*.

PDIAL

(Public Dialup Internet Access List) A list of Internet providers maintained by Peter Kaminsky. To obtain PDIAL, send an e-mail message with the appropriate phrase (see below) to the Internet address:

```
info-deli-server@netcom.com.
```

If you are on CompuServe, send the message to

```
>internet:info-deli-server@netcom.com
```

Phrase	To obtain
Send PDIAL	Latest edition
Subscribe PDIAL	Future editions
Subscribe Info-Deli-News	News about PDIAL

PDIP

(Plastic **DIP**) A common type of DIP made of plastic.

PDL

See *page description language*.

PDP

(Programmed Data Processor) A minicomputer family from Digital that started with the 18-bit PDP-1 in 1959. Its $120,000 price was much less than the million dollar machines of the time and 50 units were built. In 1965, Digital legitimized the minicomputer industry with the PDP-8, which sold for about $20,000. By the late 1970s, the PDP-8 processor was put on a single chip and used in DECmate workstations. Other PDPs were built, including 12-, 18- and 36-bit machines, the larger ones evolving into DECsystem models. In 1970, Digital introduced the 16-bit PDP-11, which became

PDP-8
In 1965, this $20,000 computer legitimized the minicomputer industry. *(Photo courtesy of Digital Equipment Corporation.)*

the most widely used minicomputer with over 50,000 systems sold. The PDP series was followed by the VAX series in 1977; however, PDP-11s are still made.

PDQ

(Parallel Data Query) A query optimized for massively parallel processors (MPPs). The software breaks down the query into pieces so that several parts of the database can be searched simultaneously. See *SMP*.

PDS

(1) (Processor Direct Slot) In the Macintosh, an expansion socket used to connect high-speed peripherals as well as additional CPUs. It is equivalent to the local bus in the PC. There are different types of PDSs for various Macintosh models and types. Some Macs do not have a PDS, others have both PDS and NuBus slots.
(2) (Premises Distribution System) The cabling, racks and adapters that connect telephone wires within a building or group of buildings to each other and to external lines of the telephone company.

PD software

See *public domain software*.

PE

(1) (Phase Encoding) An early magnetic encoding method used on 1600bpi tapes in which a 1 is an up transition and a 0 is a down transition in the center of the bit cell.
(2) (Processing Element) One of multiple CPUs in a parallel processing system.
(3) (Professional Engineer) An engineering degree.

peek/poke

Instructions that view and alter a byte of memory by referencing a specific memory address. Peek displays the contents; poke changes it.

peer

In communications, a functional unit that is on the same protocol layer as another.

peer-to-peer communications

Communications in which both sides have equal responsibility for initiating, maintaining and terminating the session. Contrast with *master-slave communications*, in which the host determines which users can initiate which sessions. If the host were programmed to allow all users to initiate all sessions, it would look like a peer-to-peer system to the user.

peer-to-peer network

A communications network that allows all workstations and computers in the network to act as servers to all other users on the network. Dedicated file servers may be used, but are not required as in a *client/server network*.
Do not confuse this term with "peer-to-peer communications." A peer-to-peer network implies peer-to-peer communications, but peer-to-peer communications does not imply a peer-to-peer network. Don't you love the extensive thought and analysis that goes into naming things in this business in order to make the terms perfectly clear and understandable!

PE format

(Portable Executable format) A Win32 file format for executable programs (EXEs and DLLs) supported under Windows 3.1 Enhanced Mode (Win32s) and Windows NT.

pel

Same as *pixel*.

pen-based computing

Using a stylus to enter hand writing and marks into a computer. See *gesture recognition*.

pen plotter

See *plotter*.

PenPoint

An operating system from Go Corporation, Foster City, CA, that provides a stylus (pen) interface for hand-written input. It uses a DOS-compatible file system, but does not run DOS applications. The direction, speed and order of the user's pen strokes is analyzed for recognition. See *NUI*.

Pentium

Introduced in 1993, the Pentium is the sucessor to the 486. Pentium refers to the Pentium CPU chip or the PC that uses it. The Pentium was originally thought to be named the 586. Depending on the clock speed, the Pentium runs up to four times as fast as a 50MHz 486, Although its integer performance rivals major RISC-based CPUs (Alpha, HP-PA, MIPS, SPARC, etc.), its floating point performance is generally slower.

Pentium PCs have become widely used in both desktops and laptops. The P24T is the code name for a scaled-down Pentium used to upgrade a 486 on motherboards that have the required socket (see *OverDrive CPU*).

Pentium CPU Technical Specs

It is a 32-bit multitasking microprocessor in a 273-pin PGA package. Same registers and operational modes as the 386. Uses RISC design techniques and obtains its speed by using two internal 8K caches (one for code, the other for data) and a "superscaler" dual pipeline architecture, which executes two instructions in the same clock cycle when it determines that the next instruction is not dependent on the outcome of the current one.

The Pentium uses a 64-bit internal bus compared to 32-bits on the 486. PC makers use a variety of high-speed bus and cache controllers to enhance performance; for example, a 128-bit memory bus can be used to extract data 128 bits at a time into the external cache, which feeds it to the CPU 64 bits at a time.

The first Pentium models had internal and local bus speeds of 60 and 66MHz. The 75, 90 and 100MHz models are faster and run cooler, using only 3.3 volts instead of 5 volts. In 1995, 120MHz and 133MHz chips were introduced, and faster chips are expected shortly.

The Pentium chip contains 3.1 million transistors and uses .8 micron technology (transistor elements are as small as .8 micron).

The following list contains the bus speeds of most Pentium chips.

Pentium Model	Local bus (system bus)
60MHz	60Mhz
66MHz	66Mhz
75MHz	50Mhz
90MHz	60Mhz
100MHz	66Mhz
120MHz	60Mhz
133MHz	66Mhz

Pentium Pro

Currently, the fastest CPU in the Intel x86 line. Pentium Pro refers to the Pentium Pro CPU chip or the PC that uses it. Introduced in 1995, initial models run at 150MHz and 166MHz, and faster chips up to 300MHz are planned. Initial tests of the Pentium Pro indicate that the chip is better suited to running 32-bit operating systems and applications, and performance is degraded when running 16-bit applications.

It is expected that the Pentium will become the entry-level desktop CPU chip, and the Pentium Pro will be used in servers and high-end workstations, many of which will employ a symmetric multiprocessing (SMP) architecture where two or more CPU chips are used to increase performance.

Pentium upgradable

The ability to be upgraded to a Pentium CPU. 486 motherboards designed for Pentium upgrades contain a ZIF socket to make chip changing easy and are, in theory, designed to support the higher speeds of the Pentium chip.

Pen Windows

An extension to Windows that allows pen-based computing.

PeopleSoft

(PeopleSoft, Walnut Creek, CA) A software company that specializes in human resource and accounting packages for client/server environments. All major databases are supported. The products are known for their ease of modification and custom development using the PeopleTools development system.

PEP

(1) (Packet Exchange Protocol) A Xerox protocol used internally by NetWare to transport internal Netware NCP commands (NetWare Core Protocols). It uses PEP and IPX for this purpose. Application programs use SPX and IPX.

(2) A high-speed modem protocol from Telebit Corporation, Sunnyvale, CA, suited for cellular phone use.

PEPPER board

An earlier family of high-resolution graphics display boards for PCs from Number Nine Visual Technology Corporation, Lexington, MA.

PerfectOffice

A suite of applications for Windows from Novell that includes WordPerfect, Quattro Pro, Presentations (presentation graphics), InfoCentral PIM, Envoy document exchange software and GroupWise e-mail and calendar. PerfectOffice Professional also includes Paradox and AppWare.

performance ratings

See *DOSmark, Winmark, SPECmark, Landmark rating, Dhrystones, Whetstones, iCOMP, PLB* and *MIPS*.

peripheral

Any hardware device connected to a computer, such as a monitor, keyboard, printer, plotter, disk or tape drive, graphics tablet, scanner, joy stick, paddle and mouse.

peripheral controller

See *control unit.*

Perl

(Practical Extraction Report Language) A UNIX programming language written by Larry Wall that combines syntax from several UNIX utilities and languages. Perl is designed to handle a variety of system administrator functions.

permanent font

(1) A soft font that is kept in the printer's memory until the printer is turned off.
(2) Same as *internal font*.

permanent memory

Same as *non-volatile memory*.

permutation

One possible combination of items out of a larger set of items. For example, with the set of numbers 1, 2 and 3, there are six possible permutations: 12, 21, 13, 31, 23 and 32.

perpendicular recording

See *vertical recording*.

per seat

Per workstation. Software licensed on a per seat basis is priced according to the number of personal computers or workstations that it will be used in.

persistence

(1) In a CRT, the time a phosphor dot remains illuminated after being energized. Long-persistence phosphors reduce flicker, but generate ghost-like images that linger on screen for a fraction of a second.
(2) In object technology, an object that exists after the program that created it. See *persistent object*.

Per Seat

persistent data

Data that exists from session to session. Persistent data is stored in a database on disk or tape. Contrast with *transient data*.

persistent link

See *hot link*.

persistent object

An object that continues to exist after the program that created it has been unloaded. An object's class and current state must be saved for use in subsequent sessions.

personal communicator

See *PDA*.

personal computer

Synonymous with microcomputer, a computer that serves one user. It is used at home and in the office for almost all applications traditionally performed on larger computers.

With the addition of a modem, it becomes a terminal, capable of retrieving information from other computers and online services worldwide.

There are a variety of personal computers on the market, priced from $300 to over $10,000. Size is based on its memory and disk capacity. Speed is based on the CPU that runs it, and output quality is based on the resolution of its display screen and printer.

Major suppliers of personal computers The personal computer world is overwhelmingly dominated by IBM PCs and IBM-compatible PCs. There are hundreds of vendors and thousands of models, although all models fall into a handful of categories (see *PC*).

The next largest supplier is Apple Computer, with its Macintosh family and Apple IIe. The Apple II has been widely used in schools, but is rapidly giving way to the Macs. Macintoshes are popular with individuals and are increasingly being purchased by large corporations.

Both Atari and Commodore continue to carve out a niche and are popular as home and small business computers. Each of them has support from software vendors providing a rounded supply of applications.

The history of personal computers

The industry began in 1977, when Apple, Radio Shack and Commodore introduced the first off-the-shelf computers as consumer products.

The first machines used an 8-bit microprocessor with a maximum of 64K of memory and floppy disks for storage. The Apple II, Atari 500, and Commodore 64 became popular home computers, and Apple was successful in companies after the VisiCalc spreadsheet was introduced. However, the business world was soon dominated by the Z80 processor and CP/M operating system, used by countless vendors in the early 1980s, such as Vector Graphic, NorthStar, Osborne and Kaypro. By 1983, hard disks began to show up on these machines, but CP/M was soon to be history. In 1981, IBM introduced the PC, an Intel 8088-based machine, slightly faster than the genre, but with 10 times the memory. It was floppy-based, and its DOS operating system from Microsoft was also available for the clone makers (MS-DOS). The 8088 was cleverly chosen so that CP/M software vendors could convert to it easily. They did!

dBASE II was introduced in 1981 bringing mainframe database functions to the personal computer level and launching an entire industry of compatible products and add-ons. Lotus 1-2-3 was introduced in 1982, and its refined interface and combined graphics helped spur sales of the new standard. The IBM PC was successfully cloned by Compaq and unsuccessfully by others. However, by the time IBM announced the AT in 1984, vendors were effectively cloning the PC and, as a group, eventually grabbed the majority of the PC market.

In 1983, Apple introduced the Lisa, a graphics-based machine that simulated the user's desktop. Although ahead of its time, Lisa was abandoned for the Macintosh in 1984. The graphics-based desktop environment caught on with the Mac, especially in desktop publishing, and the graphical interface, or "gooey," (GUI) worked its way to the PC world with Microsoft Windows, and, eventually Ventura Publisher with its GEM interface.

In 1986, the Compaq 386 ushered in the first Intel 386-based machine. In 1987, IBM introduced the PS/2, its next generation of personal computers, which added improved graphics, 3.5" floppy disks and an incompatible bus to help fend off the cloners. OS/2, jointly developed by IBM and Microsoft, was also introduced to handle the new machines, but the early versions didn't catch on. In the same year, more powerful Macintoshes were introduced, including the Mac SE and Mac II, which opened new doors for Apple. In 1989, the PC makers introduced 486-based computers, and Apple gave us faster Macs, which it has continued to do each year since.

In 1990, Microsoft's introduced Windows 3.0, which is rapidly becoming the most widely-used graphical environment. Software publishers are developing Windows versions of all their products. In 1991, Microsoft and IBM decided to go it alone each working on their own version of the future PC operating system (IBM's OS/2 2.0 and Microsoft's Windows NT). OS/2 2.0 has been moderately successful, and Windows NT is expected to gain market share.

1992 was the year of PC price cuts with all major suppliers slashing prices to keep in line with mail-order vendors, such as Gateway 2000. Gateway, along with others, drove down the cost of high-end systems by mail. Prices keep getting lower, machines keep getting faster. In 1993, Intel introduced its Pentium CPU, successor to the 486. It contains 3,100,000 transistors and is 300 times faster than the original PC. As a result, the 486 has become the entry level PC.

Inspired by Radio Shack's Model 100 in 1984 and ignited by Toshiba and Zenith, the laptop market provides a fascinating growth area in personal computing. More circuits are being stuffed into less space, providing computing power on the go that few would have imagined back in 1977.

Just as the IBM and compatible PC world matures, the joint venture of IBM, Apple and Motorola arrives to challenge the personal computer industry once again. In 1993, IBM and Motorola introduced their first PowerPC chips, an entirely new desktop architecture that can be used to run almost all existing applications while providing an advanced platform for the future. As of the beginning of 1995, over a million PowerPC chips have been shipped as the CPUs in Apple PowerMacs and various IBM RS/6000 workstations.

The Future

The personal computer industry sprang up without any planning. All of a sudden, it was there. Machines were bought to solve individual problems, such as automating a budget or typing a letter.

However, in large organizations, the real data exists in the mainframe, and it doesn't make sense to have an employee retype the mainframe reports into the micro in order to analyze and manipulate it. Personal computers can serve as invaluable tools for the user when they are designed into the fabric of the organization. The major issue of the 1990s is to tie them together in LANs and interconnect them with the company's minis and mainframes.

Fast personal computers are changing the marketplace. Not only do they compete with minicomputer workstations, but, networks of these machines are rapidly replacing traditional minicomputer and mainframe systems.

High-powered desktop computers will encourage the development of more artificial intelligence applications that are the backbone of the next computing generation. By the turn of the century, you should be able to talk to your computer as easily as typing on it.

As stand-alone machines, personal computers have placed creative capacity into the hands of an individual that would have cost millions of dollars less than 25 years ago. It slowly but surely is shifting the balance of power from the large company to the small, from the elite to the masses, from the wealthy to individuals of modest means. The personal computer has revolutionized the computer industry and the world.

The First Personal Computer

In the mid 1970s, Xerox developed the Alto, which was the forerunner of its Star workstation and inspiration for Apple's Lisa an Macintosh.

PersonaLink

An online service from AT&T designed for mobile travellers with PDAs and laptops. It supports General Magic's Telescript system of intelligent agents. PersonaLink's initial offerings are brief news, weather and an e-mail, but as shopping and other services are added, Telescript agents can be programmed to search for specific information or alert the user if a certain event occurs (price goes up, down, etc.). Much is expected from services such as this, so stay tuned!

PET computer

(Personal Electronic Transaction computer) A CP/M and floppy disk-based personal computer introduced in 1977 by Commodore. It was one of the three first personal computers.

PEX

(PHIGS Extensions to X) A set of 3-D extensions to the X Window System. See *PHIGS* and *X Window*.

PFA file

(Printer Font ASCII file) A Type 1 font file that contains the mathematical outlines of each character in the font. The codes in this file are in ASCII (raw text). See *PFB file* and *PostScript*.

PFB file

(Printer Font Binary file) A Type 1 font file that contains the mathematical outlines of each character in the font. It is an encrypted version of the PFA file. See *PFA file*, *PFM file* and *PostScript*.

PFM file

(Printer Font Metrics file) A Type 1 font file that contains the measurements of each character in the font. In a PC, both PFM and PFB files are required. The PFB files are located in the \WINDOWS\PSFONTS directory, and the PFM files are in \WINDOWS\PSFONTS\PFM. See *PFB file* and *PostScript*.

PFS:First Choice

An integrated software package for PCs from SoftKey International, Inc., Cambridge, MA, that provides word processing, database, spreadsheet, graphics and communications capabilities.

PFS:Write

See *Professional Write*.

PGA

(1) (Pin Grid Array) A chip housing with high density of pins (200 pins can fit in 1.5" square). Used for large amounts of I/O, its underside looks like a "bed of nails." (2) (Programmable Gate Array) A type of gate array that is programmed by the customer. (3) (Professional Graphics Adapter) An early IBM display standard for PCs (640x480x256) with 3-D processing. It was not widely used.

PGP

(Pretty Good Privacy) An encryption program developed by Phil Zimmermann that is based on RSA public-key cryptography. A version for personal, non-business use is available on various BBSs and Internet hosts. A commercial version of PGP is available for UNIX, DOS, Windows and Mac platforms from Viacrypt, Phoenix, AZ. See *encryption* for an explanation of public-key cryptography.

PgUp/PgDn keys

The Page Up and Page Down keys are typically used to move text up and down one screenful, but they can be programmed to do anything.

phase change printer

See *solid ink printer*.

phase change recording

An optical recording technique that uses a short, high-intensity laser pulse to create a bit by altering the crystalline structure of the material. The bit either reflects or absorbs light when read. A medium-intensity pulse is used to restore the crystalline structure.

phase encoding

See *PE*.

phase locked

A technique for maintaining synchronization in an electronic circuit. The circuit receives its timing from input signals, but also provides a feedback circuit for synchronization.

phase modulation

A transmission technique that blends a data signal into a carrier by varying (modulating) the phase of the carrier. See *modulate*.

phase-shift keying

See *DPSK*.

PHIGS

(Programmer's Hierarchical Interactive Graphics Standard) A graphics system and language used to create 2-D and 3-D images. Like the GKS standard, PHIGS is a device independent interface between the application program and the graphics subsystem.

It manages graphics objects in a hierarchical manner so that a complete assembly can be specified with all of its subassemblies. It is a very comprehensive standard requiring high-performance workstations and host processing.

Phoenix BIOS

A PC-compatible BIOS from Phoenix Technolgies, Ltd., Norwood, MA. Phoenix was the first company to successfully mass produce the ROM BIOS for the PC.

phone connector

(1) A plug and socket for a two or three-wire coaxial cable used to plug microphones and headphones into amplifiers. The plug is a single prong a quarter inch in diameter and 1.25" in length. See *phono connector*.
(2) A plug and socket for a telephone line, typically the RJ-11 modular connector.

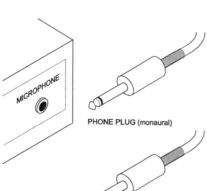

PHONE PLUG (monaural)

PHONE PLUG (stereo)

phone hawk

A person who calls up a computer via modem and either copies or destroys data.

phoneme

A speech utterance, such as "k," "ch," and "sh," that is used in synthetic speech systems to compose words for audio output.

PhoneNET

Communications products from Farallon Computing, Inc., Emeryville, CA, that extend LocalTalk distances to 3,000 feet and use unshielded twisted phone lines instead of shielded twisted pair. Configurations include daisy chain, passive star as well as active star topologies for both EtherTalk and LocalTalk. Optional Traffic Watch software provides network management and administration.

Phone Notes

See *Lotus Notes*.

Phong shading

In computer graphics, a technique developed by Phong Bui Tuong that computes a shaded surface based on the color and illumination at each pixel. It is more accurate than Gouraud shading, but requires much more extensive computation.

phono connector

Also called an RCA connector, a plug and socket for a two-wire coaxial cable used to connect audio and video components. The Apple II has a video out phono connector for a TV. The plug is a 1/8" thick prong that sticks out 5/16" from the middle of a cylinder. See *phone connector*.

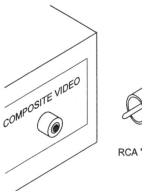

RCA "PHONO" CONNECTOR

phosphor

A rare earth material used to coat the inside face of a CRT. When struck by an electron beam, the phosphor emits a visible light for a few milliseconds. In color displays, red, green and blue phosphor dots are grouped as a cluster.

Photo CD

A CD imaging system from Kodak that digitizes 35mm slides or negatives onto a CD-ROM disc. The Photo CD is created by photo finishers that have a Kodak Picture Imaging Workstation. It takes about a half hour to put 100 photos (the maximum per disc) onto the CD. Each photographic-quality image (2048x3072x24) compresses into six megabytes. A replica of each image in the form of contact prints is also included.

The minimum RAM required is 4MB, but 10MB is needed in order to display an image in full resolution. Hardware requirements for Photo CDs are a CD-ROM drive that conforms to the CD-ROM XA standard.

Earlier CD-ROM drives are single session drives, which can only read the original set of images recorded on the disc. A multisession drive is required to read Photo

CD images that were added after the original set. Most new CD-ROM drives provide multisession capability.

Other formats include the Photo CD Portfolio, which holds up to 800 TV-quality images (512x768), the Pro Photo CD, which stores images from professional format film (120, 4x5, etc.), the Photo CD Catalog, which holds thousands of pictures and the Photo CD Medical disk for storing film-based images.

There are a variety of software packages that access Photo CD images, and increasingly, paint, drawing and image enhancement programs are importing the Photo CD format (PCD file).

A Kodak Photo CD player is available that lets you view the Photo CDs on your TV and also play audio CDs.

photocomposition

Laying out a printed page using electrophotographic machines, such as imagesetters and laser printers. See *page makeup* and *pagination*.

photoconductor

The type of material typically used in a photodetector. It increases its electrical conductivity when exposed to light.

photodetector

A device that senses the light pulses in an optical fiber and converts them into electrical pulses. It uses the principle of photoconductivity, which is exhibited in certain materials that change their electrical conductivity when exposed to light.

photo editing, photo illustration program

See *image editing* and *image editor*.

photolithography

A lithographic technique used to transfer the design of the circuit paths and electronic elements on a chip onto a wafer's surface. A photomask is created with the design for each layer of the chip. The wafer is coated with a light-sensitive film (photoresist) that is hardened when exposed to light shining through the photomask. The wafer is then exposed to an acid bath (wet processing) or hot ions (dry processing), and the unhardened areas are etched away.

photomask

An opaque image on a transluscent plate that is used as a light filter to transfer an image from one device to another. See *chip*.

photomicrography

Photographing microscopic images.

photon

A unit of energy. Elementary particle of electromagnetic radiation (light, radio waves, X-rays, etc.).

photonics

The science of building machine circuits that use light instead of electricity.

photooptic memory

A storage device that uses a laser beam to record data onto a photosensitive film.

photorealistic

Having the image quality of a photograph.

photorealistic image synthesis

In computer graphics, a format for describing a picture that depicts the realism of the actual image. It includes such attributes as surface texture, light sources, motion blur and reflectivity.

photoresist

A film used in photolithography that temporarily holds the pattern of a circuit path or microscopic element of a chip. When exposed to light, it hardens and is resistant to the acid bath that washes away the unexposed areas.

photosensitive

A material that changes when exposed to light.

photosensor

A light-sensitive device that is used in optical scanning machinery.

Photoshop

See *Adobe Photoshop*.

phototypesetter

See *imagesetter*.

physical

Refers to devices at the electronic, or machine, level. Contrast with *logical*. See *logical vs physical*.

physical address

The actual, machine address of an item or device.

physical format

See *record layout* and *low-level format*.

physical link

(1) An electronic connection between two devices.
(2) In data management, a pointer in an index or record that refers to the physical location of data in another file.

physical lock

A device that prevents access to data, such as a key lock switch on a computer or a file protection mechanism on a floppy disk. Contrast with *logical lock*.

Physical Unit

See *PU*.

PIC

(1) (PICture) A file extension used for graphics formats. Lotus PIC is a vector format for 1-2-3 charts and graphs. Videoshow PIC is a vector format that is a subset of the NAPLPS standard.
(2) (Personal Intelligent Communicator) A hand-held computer from General Magic that uses 3" CD-ROMs and has a HyperCard-like interface. Cellular phone and wireless communications for networks, radio and TV are planned.
(3) (Programmable Interrupt Controller) An Intel 8259A chip that controls interrupts. Starting with the 286-based AT, there are two PICs in a PC, providing a total of 15 usable IRQs. The PIC has been superseded by an Advanced Programmable Interrupt Controller, or 82489DX chip, that is enhanced for multiprocessing. See *IRQ*.

pica

(1) In word processing, a monospaced font that prints 10 characters per inch.

(2) In typography, about 1/6th of an inch (0.166") or 12 points.

Pick System

A multiuser operating environment and database management system (DBMS) from Pick Systems, Inc., Irvine, CA, that runs on a variety of platforms, including x86, 680x0 and RS/6000. It is highly praised for its ease of use and flexibility. Most customers use only the DBMS portion of the Pick System today.

It was originally developed by Richard Pick, who created a system for the U.S. Army while working at TRW Corporation. He later transformed it into the Reality operating system for Microdata and then obtained the right to license it to other vendors.

pico

One trillionth or 10 to the -12th power.

picosecond

One trillionth of a second. Pronounced "pee-co-second."

PICT

(PICTure) A Macintosh graphics file format that stores images in the QuickDraw vector format. The PICT2 format can also include gray-scale bitmapped images. When PICT files are converted to the PC, they use the .PCT file extension.

The raw data of this telephone number:

2152978082

is filtered through this picture ↓

(999) 999-9999

and is converted into this ↓

(215) 297-8082

picture

In programming, a pattern that describes the type of data allowed in a field or how it will print. The pattern is made up of a character code for each character in the field; for example, 9999 is a picture for four numeric digits. A picture for a telephone number could be (999) 999-9999. XXX999 represents three alphanumerics followed by three numerics. Pictures are similar but not identical in all programming languages.

picture element

See *pixel*.

Picture Publisher

A full-featured image editing program for Windows from Micrografx. It includes a customizable user interface and provides layers for building composite pictures. In Version 5.0, every user action is recorded in a command list that can be edited and used as a macro.

PID

(1) (Process IDentifier) A temporary number assigned by the operating system to a process or service.

(2) (Proportional Integral Derivative) A controller used to regulate a continuous process such as grinding or cooking.

pie chart

A graphical representation of information in which each unit of data is represented as a pie-shaped piece of a circle. See *business graphics*.

piezoelectric

The property of certain crystals that oscillate when subjected to electrical pressure (voltage).

PIF

(Program Information File) A Windows data file used to hold requirements for DOS applications running under Windows. Windows comes with a variety of PIFs, but users can edit them and new ones can be created with the PIF editor if a DOS application doesn't work properly. An application can be launched by clicking on its PIF.

piggyback board

A small printed circuit board that plugs into another circuit board in order to enhance its capabilities. It does not plug into the motherboard, but would plug into the boards that plug into the motherboard.

PIL

(Publishing Interchange Language) A standard for document interchange that defines the placement of text and graphics objects on the page. It does not address the content of the objects.

PILOT

(Programmed Inquiry Learning Or Teaching) A high-level programming language used to generate question-and-answer courseware. A version that incorporates turtle graphics runs on Atari personal computers.

PIM

(Personal Information Manager) Software that organizes random information for fast retrieval. It provides a combination of features such as a telephone list with automatic dialing, calendar, scheduler and tickler. A PIM lets you jot down text for any purpose and retrieve it based on any of the words you typed in. PIMs vary widely, but all of them attempt to provide methods for managing information the way you use it on a daily basis.

pin

(1) The male lead on a connecting plug (serial port, monitor cable, keyboard connector, etc.) or the spiderlike foot on a chip. Each pin is plugged into a socket to complete the circuit.
(2) (PIN) (Personal Identification Number) A personal password used for identification purposes.
(3) (PIN) (Processor Independent NetWare) A version of NetWare designed for portability to multiple platforms starting at the feature level of NetWare 4.1. A PIN version of NetWare is expected to be released in late 1995 for the PowerPC.

pinch roller

A small, freely-turning wheel in a tape drive that pushes the tape against a motor-driven wheel in order to move it.

pin compatible

Refers to a chip or other electronic module that can be plugged into the same socket as the chip or module it is replacing.

pincushioning

A screen distortion in which the sides bow in. Contrast with *barrel distortion*.

pin feed

A method for moving continuous paper forms. Pins at both ends of a rotating platen or tractor engage the forms through pre-punched holes at both sides.

PING

(Packet INternet Groper) An Internet utility used to determine whether a particular IP address is online. It is used to test and debug a network by sending out a packet and waiting for a response.

ping pong

(1) A half-duplex communications method in which data is transmitted in one direction and acknowledgement is returned at the same speed in the other. The line is alternately switched from transmit to receive in each direction. Contrast with *asymmetric modem*.
(2) To go in one direction and then in the other.

ping-pong buffer

See *double buffering*.

pin grid array

See *PGA*.

Pink

(1) The code name for Taligent's object-oriented operating system. See *Taligent*.
(2) A postprocessing program for creating Video CDs from Philips that multiplexes audio and video streams together.

pinouts

The description and purpose of each pin in a multiline connector.

PIO

(Programmed I/O) Transferring data between the CPU and peripheral devices via the CPU's registers. Contrast with *DMA*.

PIP

(Peripheral Interchange Program) A CP/M utility program used to copy files.

pipe

A shared space that accepts the output of one program for input into another. In DOS, OS/2 and UNIX, the pipe command is a vertical line (|). For example, in DOS and OS/2, the statement, **dir | sort** directs the output of the directory list to the sort utility.

pipeline processing

A category of techniques that provide simultaneous, or parallel, processing within the computer It refers to overlapping operations by moving data or instructions into a conceptual pipe with all stages of the pipe processing simultaneously. For example, while one instruction is being executed, the computer is decoding the next instruction. In vector processors, several steps in a floating point operation can be processed simultaneously.

piracy

The illegal copying of software for personal or commercial use.

pitch

The number of printed characters per inch. With proportionally spaced characters, the pitch is variable and must be measured as an average. See *dot pitch*.

pixel

(PIX [picture] ELement) The smallest element on a video display screen. A screen is broken up into thousands of tiny dots, and a pixel is one or more dots that are treated as a unit. A pixel can be one dot on a monochrome screen, three dots (red, green and blue) on color screens, or clusters of these dots.

For monochrome screens, the pixel, normally dark, is energized to different light intensities, creating a range from dark to light. For color, each red, green and blue dot is energized to different intensities, creating a range of colors perceived as the mixture of these dots. Black is all three dots off, white is all three dots on, and grays are even intensities of each color.

The number of bits assigned to each pixel in its associated digital memory determines the number of shades and colors that can be represented. The most economical system is monochrome in which one bit is used per pixel (on or off). In the most elaborate color displays, which use up to four full bytes for each of the red, green and blue dots, each pixel can display billions of different shades. Considering that a high-resolution screen may use a million pixels, many megabytes of memory would have to be reserved to hold such an image.

pixelated

The appearance of pixels in a bitmapped image. For example, when an image is displayed or printed too large, the individual, square pixels are discernible to the naked eye where one color or shade of gray blends into another. Sometimes, images are pixelated purposefully for special effects.

pixel depth

Same as *bit depth*.

pixel graphics

Same as *raster graphics*.

PixelPaint

A Macintosh drawing program from SuperMac Technology, Sunnyvale, CA, that is known for its extensive paint palette and color mixing schemes.

PK software

Popular PC shareware compression programs from PKWARE Inc., Brown Deer, WI(PK stands for Phil Katz). PKZIP compresses files into a ZIP file and PKUNZIP decompresses them. PKSFX compresses files into a self-extracting EXE file that decompresses when loaded and doesn't require the PKUNZIP program. ZIP2EXE creates the self-extracting file from an existing ZIP file.

PKLITE is a program that compresses only EXE and COM program files. Unlike ZIP'd files, which are compressed for archiving or distribution and decompressed upon installation, PKLITE'd files stay compressed all the time and decompress automatically when loaded.

PKWARE also provides its data compression library (DCL) to developers that want to include realtime compression and decompression of data in their applications. The Pkzip programs are also available on other platforms from a third party. See *Pkzip cross platform*.

PKARC and PKXARC were previous compression programs that are no longer supported.

Pkunzip, PKzip

See *PK software*.

Pkzip cross platform

Pkzip, Pkunzip and PKWARE's Data Compression Library (DCL) are available on MVS, AS/400 and various UNIX platforms, including HP 9000, ICL, MIPS, RS/6000, SPARC and VAX. This allows files, for example, that are Zip'd in DOS to be Unzip'd on a UNIX machine. For information, contact Ascent Solutions, Inc.,

10460 Miamisburg-Springboro Pike, Dayton OH 45342, 513/885-2031.

PLA

(Programmable Logic Array) A programmable logic chip (PLD) technology from Philips/Signetics.

plaintext

Normal text that has not been encrypted and is readable by text editors and word processors. Contrast with *ciphertext.*

planar

A technique developed by Fairchild Instruments that creates transistor sublayers by forcing chemicals under pressure into exposed areas. Planar superseded the mesa process and was a major step toward creating the chip.

planar area

In computer graphics, an object that has boundaries, such as a square or polygon.

planning system

See *spreadsheet* and *financial planning system.*

plasma display

Also called *gas discharge,* a flat-screen technology that contains an inert ionized gas sandwiched between x- and y-axis panels. A pixel is selected by charging one x- and one y-wire, causing the gas in that vicinity to glow a bright orange.

platen

A long, thin cylinder in a typewriter or printer that guides the paper through it and serves as a backstop for the printing mechanism to bang into.

platform

The hardware architecture of a particular CPU model or computer family. For example, the x86, or PC, is the world's largest hardware platform. VAX, AS/400 and SPARC are other examples (see *hardware platforms* for a complete list).

The term is also used to refer to the operating system, such as DOS, Windows or UNIX. In such cases, the hardware is implied, because programs presented to the computer for execution must talk to the both the operating system and the computer's machine language.

When a program is said to be "for Windows," or "it supports Windows," it means it runs on a PC. However, if Windows were to become widely used on other platforms, then "Windows for x86" and "Windows for PowerPC" are the designations that would have to be used to make it clear what a program actually runs on.

The phrase "runs on the UNIX platform" is even more ambiguous, since some variation of UNIX runs on everything. Such a phrase would imply the major UNIXs. However, if you need to know what runs on what, you need more details. Which hardware platforms? Which version of UNIX?

The terms platform and environment are used interchangeably. See *environment.*

PLATO

(Programmed Logic for Automatic Teaching Operations) Developed by Donald Bitzer and originally marketed by CDC, it was the first CBT system to combine graphics and touch-sensitive screens for interactive training.

platter

One of the disks in a disk pack or hard disk drive. Each platter provides a top and bottom recording surface. See *magnetic disk.*

PLB

(Picture Level Benchmark) The Graphics Performance Characterization (GPC) committee's benchmark, available through NCGA, for measuring graphics workstation performance. The Benchmark Interface Format (BIF) defines the PLB format, the Benchmark Timing Methodology (BTM) performs the test and the Benchmark Reporting Format (BRF) generates results in GPCmarks. Image quality is not rated.

PLC

(Programmable Logic Controller) A computer used in process control applications. PLC microprocessors are typically RISC-based and are designed for high-speed, realtime and rugged industrial environments.

PLCC

(Plastic LCC) A widely-used type of leaded chip carrier. See *LCC.*

PLD

(Programmable Logic Device) A logic chip that is programmed at the customer's site. There are a wide variety of PLD techniques; however, most PLDs are compatible with the PAL method from Advanced Micro Devices.
The PLD is not a storage chip like a PROM or EPROM, although fuse-blowing techniques are used. It contains different configurations of AND, OR and NOR gates that are "blown" together. Contrast with *gate array*, which requires a manufacturing process to complete the programming.

PL/I

(Programming Language 1) A high-level IBM programming language introduced in 1964 with the System/360 series. It was designed to combine features of and eventually supplant COBOL and FORTRAN, which never happened. A PL/I program is made up of procedures (modules) that can be compiled independently. There is always a main procedure and zero or more additional ones. Functions, which pass arguments back and forth, are also provided.

PL/M

(Programming Language for Microprocessors) A dialect of PL/I developed by Intel as a high-level language for its microprocessors. PL/M+ is an extended version of PL/M, developed by National Semiconductor for its microprocessors.

plot

To create an image by drawing a series of lines. In programming, a plot statement creates a single vector (line) or a complete circle or box that is made up of several vectors.

plotter

A graphics printer that draws images with ink pens. It requires data in vector graphics format, which makes up an image as a series of point-to-point lines. See *flatbed plotter* and *drum plotter.*

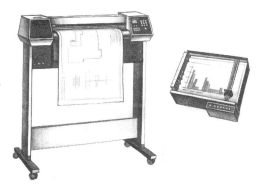

Plotters
The unit on the left is a drum plotter. The one on the right is a flatbed plotter.

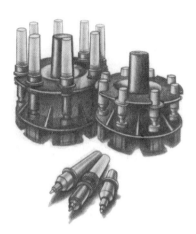

Drawing Pens
A different pen is used for each color on a plotter.

Plotter in a Cartridge
HPGL emulation in a cartridge for laser printers from Pacific Data Products, San Diego, CA.

PLP
(Presentation Level Protocol) A North American standard protocol for videotex.

plug and hope
Refers to the frustration of installing additional peripheral devices on a PC. See *plug and tell, plug and play* and *how to install a PC peripheral.*

plug and play
(1) The ability to add a new component and have it work without having to perform any technical analysis or procedure.
(2) (Plug and Play) Also known as *PnP*, it is an Intel standard for the design of PC expansion boards. Plug and Play is supported directly in Windows 95. It eliminates the frustration of configuring the system when adding new peripherals. IRQ and DMA settings and I/O and memory addresses self configure on startup.
Implementing Plug and Play requires a system BIOS on the motherboard that supports Plug and Play as well as Plug and Play expansion cards. Plug and Play can also be retrofitted to older systems by installing the DWCFGMG.SYS driver and using new Plug and Play cards.
A Plug and Play system will also assist with older non-Plug and Play cards. When a non-Plug and Play card is installed, the ISA Configuration Utility, or ICU, will check its list of known card requirements and recommend the appropriate settings. If the card is not in the list, it will also help the user determine the correct settings, providing a "plug and tell" capability.
In time, when all systems and cards are Plug and Play, we can forget the "plug and hope" days of installing PC peripherals. See *how to install a PC peripheral.*

plug and tell
Refers to installing new peripheral devices in a PC and using a utility program that helps to configure the device properly. Micro Channel and EISA bus installations, as well as installing a non-Plug and Play card in a Plug and Play machine, are plug and tell because they analyze the system and recommend which settings should be made. Plug and tell is between the "plug and hope" of installing a legacy ISA card in a PC and the "plug and play" of installing an ISA Plug and Play card in a Plug and Play machine.

plugboard

A board containing a matrix of sockets used to program early tabulating machines and computers. Each wire directs a column of data from source to destination, or it functions as a switch by closing a circuit. Complicated programs looked like "mounds of spaghetti."

The Author Hard at Work

In 1962, Alan Freedman was a "Tabulating Technician" for the Pennsylvania Department of Revenue. Programming punched card accounting machines was akin to setting up electronic circuits.

plug compatible

Hardware that is designed to perform exactly like another vendor's product. A plug compatible CPU runs the same software as the machine it's compatible with. A plug compatible peripheral works the same as the device it's replacing.

plugs & sockets

The physical connectors used to link together all variety of electronic devices. See illustrations on the following page.

PM

See *preventive maintenance, Presentation Manager, Program Manager* and *phase modulation.*

PMMU

(Paged Memory Management Unit) A virtual memory chip for the 68020 processor (it is built in on the 68030), which is required to run A/UX on the Mac or any 68020 platform running hardware virtual memory.

PMOS

(Positive channel MOS) Pronounced "P moss." A type of microelectronic circuit in which the base material is positively charged. PMOS transistors were used in the first microprocessors and are still used in CMOS. They are also used in low-cost products (calculators, watches, etc.).

PMS

(Pantone Matching System) A color matching system that has a number assigned to over 500 different colors and shades. This standard for the printing industry has been built into many graphics and desktop publishing programs to ensure color accuracy.

Plugs and sockets

DB9
Serial port (mouse,
449 secondary, etc.)

High Density DB15
VGA port

DB15
Ethernet AUI, game port

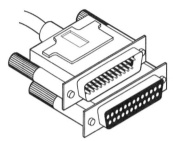

DB25 (4, 12, or 24 pin)
RS-232 (modem, scanner, etc.)
Parallel port, RS-530

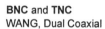

BNC
Coaxial

BNC and TNC
WANG, Dual Coaxial

Twinaxial
IBM Systems 34, 36, 38, 5520
and others

---

36 pin
Parallel printers: Centronics,
EPSON, and Gemini

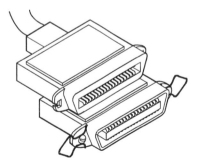

Telco
Telephone

IEEE-488
GPIB, HPIB

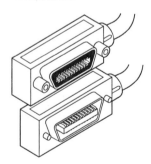

DB37
RS-449, 442, 423, Bernoulli

DB50
Dataproducts, Datapoint,
UNIVAC and others

Keyboard
5 Pin Din

PS/2 Connector

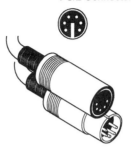

Mouse
Serial DB9   Bus Connector

PS/2 Connector

M/34
V.35

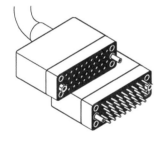

M/50
Dataproducts, UNIVAC, DEC
and others

Mate-N-Lock
Current Loop, Telephone

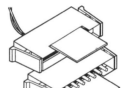

RJ-11
Voice Telephone

RJ-45
Data Telephone

Barrier Block
Utility current loop, and other
2- or 4-wires

DB to DB Adapter

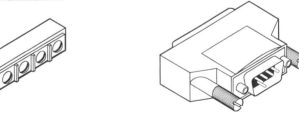

PnP
See *Plug and Play.*

POA
See *PowerOpen Association.*

pocket computer
A hand-held, calculator-sized computer that runs on batteries. It can be plugged into a personal computer for data transfer.

POE
See *PowerOpen.*

point
(1)To move the cursor onto a line or image on screen by rolling a mouse across the desk or by pressing the arrow keys.
(2) In typography, a unit equal to 1/72nd of an inch, used to measure the vertical height of a printed character.

point and shoot
To select a menu option or activate a function by moving the cursor onto a line or object and pressing the return key or mouse button.

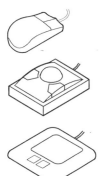

pointer
(1) In database management, an address embedded within the data that specifies the location of data in another record or file.
(2) In programming, a variable that is used as a reference to the current item in a table (array) or to some other object, such as the current row or column on screen.
(3) An on-screen symbol used to identify menu selections or the current screen location. It is moved by a mouse or other pointing device.

pointing device
An input device used to move the screen pointer (cursor) on screen. The major pointing devices are the mouse, trackball, pointing stick and touchpad.

pointing stick
A pointing device that looks like a pencil eraser between the G, H and B keys. It is moved with the forefinger, while the thumb is used to press related keys located in front of the space bar. IBM popularized this device by introducing the TrackPoint on its ThinkPad notebooks. See *mouse, trackball* and *touchpad.*

Pointing Devices
From top to bottom, the mouse, trackball, touchpad and pointing stick.

point of presence
See *POP.*

point of sale
Capturing data at the time and place of sale. Point of sale systems use personal computers or specialized terminals that are combined with cash registers, optical scanners for reading product tags, and/or magnetic stripe readers for reading credit cards.
Point of sale systems may be online to a central computer for credit

BAR CODE

checking and inventory updating, or they may be stand-alone machines that store the daily transactions until they can be delivered or transmitted to the main computer for processing.

point-to-multipoint
A communications network that provides a path from one location to multiple locations (from one to many).

point-to-point
A communications network that provides a path from one location to another (point A to point B).

Point-to-Point Protocol
See *PPP*.

Poisson distribution
A statistical method developed by the 18th century French mathematician S. D. Poisson, which is used for predicting the probable distribution of a series of events. For example, when the average transaction volume in a communications system can be estimated, Poisson distribution is used to determine the probable minimum and maximum number of transactions that can occur within a given time period.

poke
See *peek/poke*.

polarity
(1)The direction of charged particles, which may determine the binary status of a bit.
(2) In micrographics, the change in the light to dark relationship of an image when copies are made. Positive polarity is dark characters on a light background; negative polarity is light characters on a dark background.

polarized
A one-way direction of a signal or the molecules within a material pointing in one direction.

Polish notation
A method for expressing a sequence of calculations developed by the Polish logician Jan Lukasiewicz in 1929. For example, A(B+C) would be expressed as
* A + B C. In reverse Polish notation, it would be A B C + *.

polling
A communications technique that determines when a terminal is ready to send data. The computer continually interrogates its connected terminals in a round robin sequence. If a terminal has data to send, it sends back an acknowledgement and the transmission begins. Contrast with *interrupt-driven*, in which the terminal generates a signal when it has data to send.

polling cycle
One round in which each and every terminal connected to the computer or controller has been polled once.

polygon
In computer graphics, a multi-sided object that can be filled with color or moved around as a single entity.

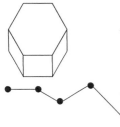

polyhedron

An object with more than six surfaces. A group of connected polygons.

polyline

In computer graphics, a single entity that is made up of a series of connected lines.

polymorphic tweening

See *tweening*.

polymorphic virus

A virus that changes its binary pattern each time it infects a new file to keep it from being identified. See *stealth virus*.

polymorphism

Meaning many shapes. In object-oriented programming, the ability of a generalized request (message) to produce different results based on the object that it is sent to.

polyphonic

The ability to play back some number of musical notes simultaneously. For example, 16-voice polyphony means a total of 16 notes, or waveforms, can be played concurrently.

Polyvision

A flat panel display from Alpine Polyvision Inc. that uses a plastic film of metal ions sandwiched between horizontal and vertical electrodes. Where current intersects, the metal ions turn black.

pop

(1) See *push/pop*.
(2) (Point of Presence) The place where a line from a long distance carrier (IXC) connects to the line of the local telephone company or to the user if the local company is not involved.
(3) (Post Office Protocol) A protocol commonly used by an electronic mail program to download messages from a mail server on the Internet.

POP-11

(Package for Online Programming) A general-purpose programming language with list processing and compiler writing functionality from SD-Scicon PLC.

pop-down menu

See *pull-down menu*.

populate

To plug in chips or components into a printed circuit board. A fully populated board is one that contains all the devices it can hold.

popup

(1) A type of menu called for and displayed on top of the existing text or image. When the item is selected, the menu disappears and the screen is restored.
(2) Same as *TSR*.

port

(1) A pathway into and out of the computer. The serial and parallel ports on a personal computer are external sockets for plugging in communications lines, modems and printers. On a front end processor, serial ports connect to communications lines and modems.

(2)To convert software to run in a different computer environment.

portable

Refers to software that can be easily moved from one type of machine to another. It implies a product that has a version for several hardware platforms or has built-in capabilities for switching between them. However, a program that can be easily converted from one machine type to another is also considered portable.

portable computer

A personal computer that can be easily transported. Compared to desktop models, it has limited expansion slots and disk capacity.

The first portable was the Osborne I, a CP/M machine that was soon followed by many others, such as the Kaypro and Otrona's Attache. In late 1982, Compaq introduced the first MS-DOS portable. See *laptop computer, notebook computer* and *pocket computer*.

Portable NetWare

An OEM version (C source code) of Novell's NetWare operating system that can be compiled for a specific vendor's machine.

port address

A physical identification of an I/O port. See *I/O address*.

port expander

A device that connects several lines to one port in the computer. The port may be one interface type that is expanded into several by this device (see *port multiplier*), or it may contain multiple interfaces. For example, a port expander may provide additional serial and parallel ports on a laptop.

port multiplier

Also called a *fan-out*, it is a device that expands one port into several. For example, an Ethernet port multiplier allows multiple stations to be connected to a 10Base5 cable via one transceiver tap. Otherwise, each station requires its own transceiver.

portrait

An orientation in which the data is printed across the narrow side of the form.

port replicator

A device used to connect peripherals to a laptop. All the desktop devices are permanently plugged into the port replicator, which quickly connects to the laptop. It is like a docking station without expansion slots.

POS

See *point of sale*.

128 shades

8 shades

4 shades

Posterization
The examples above show the posterization effect when the number of colors or shades is dramatically reduced.

POSIT
(Profiles for Open Systems Internetworking Technolgoies) A set of voluntary standards published by the National Institute of Standards and Technology (NIST) for network equipment purchased by the U.S. government. It is the successor to GOSIP.

positive logic
The use of low voltage for a 0 bit and high voltage for a 1 bit. Contrast with *negative logic.*

POSIX
(Portable Operating System Interface for UNIX) An IEEE 1003.1 standard that defines the language interface between application programs and the UNIX operating system. Adherence to the standard ensures compatibility when programs are moved from one UNIX computer to another. POSIX is primarily composed of features from UNIX System V and BSD UNIX.

POST
(Power On Self Test) A series of built-in diagnostics that are performed when the computer is first started. Proprietary codes are generated (POST codes) that indicate test results. See *diagnostic board.*

posterization
The effect produced when a photographic image is displayed or printed with a small number of colors or shades of gray. For example, displaying color photographs or video with 16 colors produces a visible posterization, but the images are discernible. At 256 colors, the flesh tones on color images are still somewhat posterized. For realistic flesh tones, it takes 65K colors. For absolute realism, it requires 16M colors.

postfix notation
See *reverse Polish notation.*

Post Office Protocol
See *POP.*

postprocessor
Software that provides some final processing to data, such as formatting it for display or printing.

PostScript
A page description language from Adobe Systems, Inc., Mountain View, CA, that is used extensively on Macs and PCs as well as workstations, minis and mainframes. It is the de facto standard in commercial typesetting and printing houses. Most all accept and may even require PostScript files as electronic input.

PostScript commands do not drive the printer directly. They are language statements in ASCII text that are translated into the printer's machine language by a PostScript interpreter built into the printer. Fonts are scaled to size by the interpreter, thus eliminating the need to store a variety of font sizes on disk. PostScript Level 2, downward compatible with original PostScript, adds data compression and enhancements, especially for color printing.

PostScript fonts come in Type 1 and Type 3 formats, and Adobe makes only Type 1. Type 1 fonts are widely used and are made by other companies as Adobe later made the format public.

Type 1 fonts are encrypted and compressed and also allow for hints, which improve the appearance of text at 300 dpi and lower resolutions. Type 1 fonts use a simpler, more efficient command language than Type 3. With Adobe Type Manager, Type 1

fonts can also be used on non-PostScript printers. See *Adobe Type Manager.*
Type 3 fonts do not use encryption or hints, but can use the entire PostScript
language to create complex designs. They can also be bitmaps. Type 3 fonts are not
widely used; however, in order to speed up printing small fonts on PostScript
printers, Windows 3.1 creates Type 3 bitmaps from its TrueType outlines.

Type 1 Font Files

Type 1 fonts are distributed by Adobe as two files. One contains the
outlines, and the other contains the font metrics, which includes character
widths and heights and kerning values.

Type 1 font distribution disks for Windows contain PFB, AFM and INF
files. The PFB (Printer Font Binary) outline files are copied to the hard
disk, and the AFM (Adobe Font Metric) files are converted into PFM
(Printer Font Metric) files on the hard disk. INF files contain information
that the font installer requires.

A font generator, called **Font Foundry,** is available from Adobe that
converts Type 1 outlines into bitmaps for HP printers (.SFP and .SFL files)
and screen fonts for DOS applications, such as WordPerfect and the GEM
version of Ventura Publisher.

Type 1 font distribution disks for the Mac contain outline and metric files
that are copied onto the hard disk. For example, a Helvetica font would
have an outline file named "Helve" and a font metrics file named
"Helvetica." The icon for the font metrics file looks like a suitcase, and is
often called the "suitcase file." A Helve.AFM file may also be included on
the distribution disk.

PostScript font distribution disks for UNIX contain both AFM and PFA
(Printer Font ASCII) files. The PFA files contain the PostScript ASCII
code of the outline.

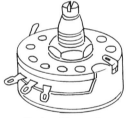

Potentiometer

pot, potentiometer

A device that controls the amount of current that flows through a circuit, such as a
volume switch on a radio.

POTS

(Plain Old Telephone Service) The traditional analog telephone network. See
AMPS.

power

(1) See *computer power.*
(2) (POWER) (Performance Optimization With Enhanced RISC) A RISC-based
CPU architecture from IBM used in its RS/6000 workstation and parallel computer
line. The PowerPC, enhanced by Motorola and Apple, is a single-chip version of the
POWER architecture.

PowerBook

power adapter

A transformer that converts AC power from a wall outlet into the DC power
required by an electronic device.

PowerBook

A family of Macintosh portable computers from Apple that include a trackball
centered in a wrist rest. PowerBooks are very popular. See *Macintosh* for
specifications.

PowerBuilder

A popular application development system for Windows client/server environments
from Powersoft Corporation, Concord, MA. It supports various databases, including
DB2 and Oracle, and is also packaged with the Watcom SQL database.

PowerBuilder provides visual programming tools as well as a BASIC-like programming language called PowerScript. Macintosh, Windows NT and UNIX support is also provided.

PowerMaker is a subset of PowerBuilder with a simplified interface for non-programmers and departmental use. PowerViewer is the query, reporting and business graphics generator for both products.

PowerCD

A consumer-oriented CD-ROM player from Apple that connects to a TV for Photo CD use, to a Macintosh for data, audio and Photo CD or to a stereo for audio CDs.

power down

To turn off the computer in an orderly manner by making sure all applications have been closed normally and then shutting the power.

power good

A signal transmitted from the power supply to the circuit board indicating that the power is stable. For various power supply definitions, see *power supply*.

PowerHouse

A fourth-generation language from Cognos that was introduced in the late 1970s for midrange computers. It supports both character-oriented, terminal-based applications as well as Windows clients. Applications developed under PowerHouse can be imported into Cognos' Axiant client/server environment.

Power Macintosh, PowerMac

A PowerPC-based Macintosh. With the first models introduced in March 1994, Apple plans to eventually migrate all Macintoshes from the Motorola 680x0 family of CPUs to the PowerPC RISC chip. PowerMacs run the PowerPC version of the Mac System 7 operating system and also run DOS and Windows applications by way of Insignia Solutions' SoftWindows, which is an optional feature.

Traditional 680x0 applications generally run as fast or faster on the PowerMacs, depending on how graphics intensive the application. Although 680x0 applications are emulated on the PowerMacs, they can pick up speed, because Apple's QuickDraw graphics engine is running in native PowerPC code.

Native PowerMac applications run much faster on the PowerMacs. By the summer of 1994, over 100 Mac applications had been ported to the new architecture. It is expected that all Mac applications will eventually run native on the PowerMacs. In order to accomodate this dual platform, Apple has created a "fat binary" disk format that allows software to be distributed in both 680x0 and PowerPC executable form. Windows applications generally run at the speed of a 486/25 on the PowerMac, which is reasonable, considering the application is emulated. This rather acceptable performance is achieved because SoftWindows uses native Windows code from Microsoft, ported to PowerPC machine language. The Windows application itself is emulated from x86 to PowerPC, but when a call is made to Windows, Windows is running native on the PowerPC. Since there are countless calls to Windows from the application, much Windows execution is native PowerPC.

The first PowerMac models use the 601 CPU chip. When models using the 604 and 620 chips are available, performance will increase dramatically, and DOS and Windows applications are expected to run extremely fast, especially on the 620. Initial PowerMacs came in 60MHz, 66MHz and 80MHz versions, known as the 6100/60, 7100/66 and 8100/80, with 8MB of RAM, expandable to 72, 136 and 264MB respectively. Internal hard disks range from 160MB to 1GB. All models are available in an AV configuration, a suite of communications technologies that let you send and receive faxes, play high-quality sound and import and export video.

power management

Maximizing battery power by using low-voltage CPUs and slowing down
components when they are inactive. See *SMM*.

PowerOpen

A standard for a UNIX-based operating system running on the PowerPC platform.
An application certified as PowerOpen compliant will run on a PowerPC under any
PowerOpen-compliant operating system. This is officially known as the PowerOpen
Environment (POE).

Apple's Macintosh Application System (MAS) is expected to allow PowerOpen
operating system vendors to run Mac applications. It includes an emulator and the
Macintosh Toolbox, which allows the Mac interface to run native while emulating
680x0 instructions in the application. DOS and Windows emulation are also
expected, most likely from Insignia Solutions.

The POE is an application binary interface (ABI) specification, which differs from
an application program interface (API). An API deals with the linkage between the
application and the operating system. An ABI takes it a step further, defining API
and machine language compatibility for the hardware platform, in this case, the
PowerPC. The goal is to create a market for shrink-wrapped PowerPC applications
just as there is for DOS, Windows and the Mac.

What has kept UNIX from this very desirable position all these years are all the
different varieties of UNIX and the platforms they run on. If the PowerPC chip
continues to be the leading RISC-based hardware platform (it's already the leader in
units shipped after one year), wider adoption of the chip could promote more
support for PowerOpen compatibility.

Both operating system and application developers will seek POE certification,
ensuring that their products are interoperable on this platform. However, it's always
a chicken-egg proposition with this business, so stay tuned!

PowerOpen Association

(10050 N. Wolf Road, Cupertino, CA 95014, 408/366-0460) An independent
membership organization founded in 1993 by Apple, IBM, Motorola, Bull, Harris,
Thompson-CSF and Tadpole Technologies. It is dedicated to the broad acceptance
of an open systems standard based on the PowerOpen Environment (POE).
Certification ensures that the products are X/Open and Spec 1170 compliant and
that they run on the PowerPC. See *PowerOpen*.

PowerPC

A family of CPU chips designed by Apple, IBM and Motorola, introduced in 1993.
Both IBM and Motorola offer the chips for sale to PowerPC resellers, but IBM owns
the architecture, and Motorola is a licensee of it. The PowerPC is designed to span a
range of computing devices from hand-held machines to supercomputers.

PowerPC chips are the CPUs in the PowerMacs, Apple's latest line of Macintoshes,
which run a version of System 7 that supports Mac/680x0 and Mac/PowerPC
applications. IBM is using the PowerPC chips in certain RS/6000 models and is
offering PowerPC systems that run AIX and Windows NT. OS/2 Warp for the
PowerPC is expected in late 1995.

Other operating systems, including Sun's Solaris, Taligent's object-oriented OS and
various pen-based systems are expected for the PowerPC. All PC manufacturers can
purchase PowerPC chips from IBM and Motorola and license operating systems
from IBM, Apple and others.

The PowerPC is the latest architecture for the desktop that provides a platform for
advanced applications while supporting existing applications via emulation and
native graphical interface support for Macintosh and Windows.

Off to a Running Start	More than a million PowerPC systems were shipped within its first year, making it the market leader in RISC-based systems by annual units sold. With all the forces in place to promote the PowerPC, (Apple-IBM-Motorola, PowerOpen Association, Windows NT, etc.), the PowerPC market is expected to grow well into the future.
PowerPC CPU Technical Specs	The PowerPC is a refined version of IBM's RS/6000 single-chip CPU. It is a RISC-based 32-bit multitasking microprocessor that has an internal 64-bit data path to memory similar to the Pentium. The first PowerPC chip, the 601 (MPC601), runs at 50 and 66MHz and is as fast or faster than a Pentium, but is half the size and uses half the electricity. A low-power 603 is designed for notebooks and runs at 75MHz. The 603e raises the speed to 100MHz and doubles the internal cache to 32KB. An ultra-low power 602 has been designed for consumer products. The 604 is approximately 50 to 100% faster than the 601 depending on clock speed, and the upcoming 620 is expected to be at least twice as fast as the 601. See *CHRP*.

power platform

Refers to a mature, high-speed computer system.

PowerPlay

A decision support system from Cognos that summarizes information for management. It combines EIS and DSS features in an integrated environment, and its Transformer creates multidimensional views of information. It runs on Windows clients and VMS and UNIX servers.

PowerPoint

A presentation graphics program from Microsoft for Macintosh and Windows. It was the first desktop presentation program for the Mac.

PowerSCSI!

Software from Future Domain Corporation that accompanies its SCSI host adapters for PCs allowing them to control all SCSI peripherals. It translates the popular methods for accessing SCSI devices, including DOS' int 13, Windows FastDisk, ASPI and various CD-ROM methods into industry standard CAM, supported on its host adapter. See *CorelSCSI*.

PowerShare

Software from Apple that resides in a Macintosh server and provides messaging store and forward, authentication of network users, encryption of messages and other workgroup/enterprise services.

Powersoft

(Powersoft Corporation, Concord, MA) Powersoft is the developer of the popular PowerBuilder application development system. In November 1994, Sybase, Inc. and Powersoft announced their agreement to merge, making Powersoft an independent subsidiary of Sybase. This creates a software company with 4,400 employees and revenues exceeding $700 million.

power supply

An electrical system that converts AC current from the wall outlet into the DC currents required by the computer circuitry. In a personal computer, +5, -5, +12 and -12 voltages are generated. The 5 volts are used for the electronic circuitry, and the 12 volts are required for the drives.

The following power supply definitions are reprinted with permission from PC Power & Cooling, Inc., Carlsbad, CA 92008, a manufacturer of exceptionally high-quality power supplies.

These terms are reprinted with permission of PC Power & Cooling, Inc.

agency approval

UL, CSA and TUV are safety agencies that test specifications such as component spacing, hi-pot isolation, leakage currents, circuit board flammability and temperature rating. Hi-pot (high-potential) isolation is the ability to accept voltage surges with safety.

efficiency

Ratio of output power to input power expresses as a percentage.

EMI

(ElectroMagnetic Interference) Noise generated by the switching action of the power supply and other system components. Conducted EMI is radiation reflected back into the power line, which is normally controlled with a line filter. Radiated EMI is that portion that would radiate into free space, but is suppressed by enclosing a power supply's circuitry in a metal case. The FCC governs conducted and radiated emission levels in the U.S.

fan rating

Airflow rated in cubic feet per minute. A 100% increase in airflow will reduce system operating temperatures by 50% relative to ambient temperature. For each 18 degrees (Fahrenheit) of reduction, the life of the system is doubled (Arrhenius equation).

hold-up time

Time period that a power supply's output will remain within specified limits, following power disturbances or a loss of input power. Adequate hold-up time keeps the computer running until a standby UPS takes over within a few milliseconds.

load regulation

Change in output voltage due to a varying load. Expressed as a percent of the normal output voltage, a power supply with tight load regulationdelivers optimum voltages regardless of system configuration. This is tested by measuring the difference in output voltage when applying a light load and a heavy load.

line regulation

Change in output voltage due to varying input voltage. Expressed as a percent of the normal ouput voltage, a power supply with tight line regulation delivers optimum voltages throughout the operating range. This is tested by measuring the difference in output voltages while varying the input voltage from minimum to maximum, i.e., from 85 to 135 volts.

MTBF

(Mean Time Between Failure) Measurement of the relative reliability of a power supply based upon actual operating data or calculated according to MIL-HDBK-217.

noise (loudness)

Issues include fan blade pitch and speed, hub size, venturi depth, bearing quality and layout of power supply components. Acoustical noise is measured logarithmically; each 3 db reduction represents 50% less noise.

operating range

Minimum and maximum input voltage limits within which a power supply will operate to specifications. A power supply with a wide input range is recommended when the line voltage is subject to brownouts and surges.

operating temperature

Range of ambient temperatures within which a power supply can be safely operated.

These terms are reprinted with permission of PC Power & Cooling, Inc.

output current
Maximum current that can be continuously drawn from the output of a power supply. PC motherboards and expansion cards draw 5 volt current. Drive motors draw 12 volts.

overcurrent protection
Circuit that shuts down the power supply from excessive current, inluding short circuits.

overvoltage protection
Circuit that shuts down the power supply if the output voltage exceeds a specified limit.

power good signal
Signal used to prevent the computer from starting until the power has stabilized. The power good line switches from 0 to +5 volts within one tenth to one half second after the power supply reaches normal voltage levels. Whenever low input voltage causes the output voltage to fall below operating levels, the power good signal goes back to zero.

ripple
AC voltage superimposed onto the DC output, expressed as a percent of the normal output voltage or as peak to peak volts. A power supply with clean DC output is essential for computers with high-speed CPUs and memory.

transient response
Time required for the output voltage to return within the regulation envelope following a 50% load change. A power supply with quick transient response will reduce the risk of read/write errors.

power surge
An oversupply of voltage from the power company that can last up to several seconds. Power surges are the most common cause of loss to computers and electronic equipment. See *spike* and *sag*.

PowerTalk
Secure messaging software from Apple that is included in the System 7 operating system (starting with Mac System 7 Pro). PowerTalk provides a unified mail box that holds different types of communications, including e-mail, fax, voice mail and pager. It provides for RSA digital signatures, which guarantees the authenticity of documents electronically signed by other users.
PowerTalk uses the AppleTalk transport protocol for network transmission.
PowerTalk runs on individual Macs, while PowerShare runs on Mac servers.

power up
To turn the computer on in an orderly manner.

power user
A person who is very proficient with personal computers. It implies knowledge of a variety of software packages.

PPC
See *PowerPC.*

PPD file
(PostScript Printer Description file) A file that contains detailed information about a particular printer. Although PostScript is a device-independent language, the

PostScript driver uses information in the PPD file to take advantage of special features in the target printer or imagesetter. The PPD file is an ASCII file that can be transferred between PCs and Macs.

pph

(Pages Per Hour) Measures printing speed.

ppi

(1) (Pixels Per Inch) The measurement of the display or print elements.
(2) (Points Per Inch, Pulses Per Inch) The measurement of mouse movement.

ppm

(Pages Per Minute) The measurement of printer speed. See *gppm*.

PPP

(Point-to-Point Protocol) A data link protocol that provides dial-up access over serial lines. It can run on any full-duplex link from POTS to ISDN to high-speed lines (T1, T3, etc.). Developed by the Internet Engineering Task Force in 1991, it has become popular for Internet access as well as a method for carrying higher level protocols.

PPP encapsulates protocols in specialized Network Control Protocol packets; for example, IPCP (IP over PPP) and IPXCP (IPX over PPP). It can be used to replace a network adapter driver, allowing remote users to log on to the network as if they were inhouse. PPP can hang up and redial on a low-quality call.

PPP also provides password protection using the Password Authentication Protocol (PAP) and the more rigorous Challenge Handshake Authentication Protocol (CHAP). See *SLIP*.

pps

(Packets Per Second) The measurement of LAN transmission speed.

PQFP

(Plastic Quad Flat Package) A surface mount chip housing with flat leads on all four sides. The PQFP is widely used.

PRAM

(Parameter RAM) Pronounced "P RAM." A battery-backed part of the Macintosh's memory that holds Control Panel settings and the settings for the hidden desktop file. If the command and option keys are held down at startup, the desktop settings are cleared and a dialog to rebuild the desktop is initiated.

precedence

The order in which an expression is processed. Mathematical precedence is normally:
1. unary + and - signs
2. exponentiation
3. multiplication and division
4. addition and subtraction

In order to properly compute the formula that converts Fahrenheit to Celsius, which is **fahrenheit-32*5/9**, the expression

```
(fahrenheit-32)*5/9
```

must be used with parentheses separating the fahrenheit-32 from the multiplication. Since multiplication is evaluated before subtraction, 32 would be multiplied by 5 first, which is not what is wanted.

Logical precedence is normally

1. NOT
2. AND
3. OR

In the dBASE query:

```
list for item = "TIE" .and. color = "GRAY" .or. color = "RED"
```

all gray ties and anything red will be selected, since ANDs are evaluated before ORs. Grouping the colors in parentheses as in the example below yields only gray and red ties.

```
(color="GRAY" .or. color="RED")
```

precision
The number of digits used to express the fractional part of a number. The more digits, the more precision. See *single precision* and *double precision*.

predicate
In programming, a statement that evaluates an expression and provides a true or false answer based on the condition of the data.

preemptive multitasking
A multitasking method that shares processing time with all running programs. Preemtive multitasking creates a true timesharing environment in which all running programs get a recurring slice of time from the CPU. Depending on the operating system, the time slice may be the same for all programs or it may be adjustable to meet the current mix of programs and users. For example, background programs can be given more CPU time no matter how heavy the foreground load and vice versa. Preemptive multitasking is vital in a mainframe, but is also useful in a desktop operating system. For example, it ensures that data will not be lost if a transmission is taking place in the background. The OS is able to grab the machine cycles that the modem or network program needs to keep processing the incoming data stream. Contrast with *non-preemtive multitasking*.

prefix notation
See *Polish notation*.

PReP
(PowerPC REference Platform) A common specification for PowerPCs from IBM and Apple that allows them to run a variety of operating systems. PReP has been superseded by CHRP.

prepress
In typography and printing, the preparation of camera-ready materials up to the actual printing stage, which includes typesetting and page makeup.

preprocessor
Software that performs some preliminary processing on the input before it is processed by the main program.

presentation graphics
Presentation materials for overheads, 35mm slide shows and computer-driven slide shows (screen shows). Presentation graphics programs provide a wide selection of predefined backgrounds and page layouts as well as the ability to create various types

of business graphics for charting numerical data. They include drawing and painting tools and the ability to select from stock graphical elements to illustrate a page. For computer-driven slide shows, the application provides a variety of special effects that can be used to fade and wipe one frame into another such as commonly found in the video world. Sound and video can also be merged into the presentation. Examples of Windows presentation graphics programs are Harvard Graphics, Freelance Graphics, PowerPoint and Charisma.

Presentation Manager

A graphical user interface (GUI) library used to develop OS/2 applications. Character-based OS/2 applications can be developed similar to DOS applications, but OS/2 PM applications are graphics based like Macintosh, Windows and Motif applications. The term used to be the name of the interface itself, which is now called *Workplace Shell*.

Prestel

A commercial videotex service of British Telecom (formerly part of the British Post Office).

preventive maintenance

The routine checking of hardware that is performed by a field engineer on a regularly scheduled basis. See *remedial maintenance*.

primary index

The index that controls the current processing order of a file. It maintains an index on the primary key. See *secondary index*.

primary key

An indexed field that maintains the primary sequence of the file/table.

primary storage

The computer's internal memory (RAM). Contrast with *secondary storage*.

primitive

(1) In computer graphics, a graphics element that is used as a building block for creating images, such as a point, line, arc, cone or sphere.
(2) In programming, a fundamental instruction, statement or operation.
(3) In microprogramming, a microinstruction, or elementary machine operation.

print column

A column of data on a printed report that may be subtotalled or totalled. Print columns are the heart of a report writer's description.

printed circuit board

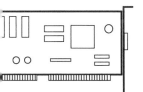

A flat board that holds chips and other electronic components. The board is made of reinforced fiberglass or plastic and interconnects components via copper pathways. The main printed circuit board in a system is called a system board or motherboard, while smaller ones that plug into the slots in the main board are called *boards* or *cards*.

The printed circuit board of the 1960s connected discrete components together. The circuit board of the 1990s interconnects chips, each containing hundreds of thousands and millions of elementary components.

The "printed" circuit is really an etched circuit. A copper foil is placed over the glass or plastic base and covered with a photoresist. Light is shined through a negative image of the circuit paths onto the photoresist, hardening the areas that will remain after etching. When passed through an acid bath, the unhardened areas are washed away. A similar process creates the microminiaturized circuits on a chip (see *chip*).

printer

A device that converts computer output into printed images. Following is an overview of printer types.

Serial Printers

Serial printers print a character at a time from approximately 10 to 400 cps (about 6 to 240 lpm). Serial printers use dot matrix and character printer technologies. Serial printers are referred to as character printers regardless of the printing technology employed.

Line Printers

Line printers print a line at a time from approximately 100 to 5,000 lpm and are the standard impact printers found in datacenters. They employ drum, chain, train, band, dot matrix and dot band technologies.

Page Printers

Page printers, also called *laser printers*, print a page at time from approximately 4 to 215 ppm (400 to 14,000 lpm), and generally use the copy machine electrophotographic technique. High-speed page printers are used in large datacenters, and desktop laser printers are now commonplace for personal computers.

Graphics Printers

Graphics printers use impact serial dot matrix, impact line dot matrix, impact line dot band and all non-impact technologies.

Color Printers

Color printers use impact dot matrix with multiple color ribbons, electrophotographic with multiple color toners, electrostatic plotters with multiple color toners, printers using Cycolor technology, ink jet with multiple color inks and thermal-transfer with multiple colors.

Impact Printers

Band, Chain & Train Printers

A continuous loop of several character sets connected together spins horizontally around a set of hammers. When the desired character is in front of the selected print location, that particular hammer hits the paper forcing the shaped character image on the band, chain, or train into the ribbon and onto the paper.
Since the chain, band, or train moves so fast, it appears to print a line at a time. A band is a solid loop, while the chain is individual character images (type slugs) chained together. The train is individual character images (type slugs) revolving in a track, one pushing the other. See *band printer* and *chain printer*.

Drum Printer

A rotating drum (cylinder) contains the character set carved around it for each print location, like an odometer. When the desired character for the selected print location has rotated around to the hammer line, the appropriate hammer hits the paper from behind, forcing it against the ribbon that is between the paper and the drum. Since the drum rotates so fast, it appears to print a line at a time. See *drum printer*.

Character Printers

Character printers are similar to Selectric typewriters, printing one character at a time. A daisy wheel or similar mechanism is moved serially across the paper. At the selected print location, a hammer hits the shaped character image on the wheel into the ribbon and onto the paper.

Serial Dot Matrix

A vertical set of printing wires moves serially across the paper, formulating characters by impacting a ribbon and transferring dots of ink onto the paper. The clarity of the character is determined by how close the dots print together.

Line Dot Matrix
A stationary or oscillating line of printing wires generates images by impacting a ribbon and transferring dots of ink onto the paper a line at a time.

Dot Band Matrix
A combination band and dot matrix configuration. A steel band is etched to create fingers (petals). At the tip of each finger is an anvil with a steel dot attached. Print hammers impact the anvils, which are larger than the dots, allowing the dots to be printed in areas between the hammer faces. Different size dots may be used on different bands to change the speed of printing and the print resolution.

Non-Impact Printers

Electrophotographic
A drum is charged with a high voltage and an image source paints a negative light copy of the image to be printed onto the drum. Where the light falls onto the drum, the drum is discharged. A toner (ink) is allowed to adhere to the charged portion of the drum. The drum then fuses the image onto the paper by pressure and heat. See *electrophotographic*.

Electrosensitive
Dots are charged onto specially coated silver-colored paper, usually in a serial fashion. The charge removes the aluminum coating, leaving a black image.

Electrostatic
Dots are charged onto specially coated paper, usually a line at a time. An ink adheres to the charges that become embedded into the paper by pressure or by heat.

Ink Jet
Continuous streams of ink are sprayed onto paper, or droplets of ink generate a dot matrix image, usually in a serial fashion. Another technique uses ink in a solid form, which is melted just before it is ejected.

Ionographic
A technology that uses ion deposition and is similar to direct electrostatic, except that in this type of indirect electrostatic, the image is formed on a dielectric surface and then transferred to plain paper.

Magnetographic
A magnetic image is created by a set of recording heads across a magnetic drum. Monocomponent toner is applied to the drum to develop the image. It is transferred to paper by light pressure and an electrostatic field. The toner is then fused by heat.

Thermal
Dots are burned onto specially coated paper that turns black or blue when heat is applied to it. A line of heat elements forms a dot matrix image as the paper is passed across it, or a serial head with heating elements is passed across the paper.

Thermal Wax Transfer
Dots of ink are transferred from a mylar ribbon onto paper by passing the ribbon and the paper across a line of heat elements, or by passing a serial head with heating element across the paper. See *thermal wax transfer*.

Thermal Dye Transfer
Also called dye sublimation and thermal dye diffusion, this technique is similar to thermal wax transfer. However, instead of an ink, dyes are used, which are vaporized onto a special coated paper creating continuous tone color for photorealistic quality. See *thermal dye transfer*.

printer buffer

A memory device that accepts printer output from one or more computers and transmits it to the printer. It lets the computer dispose of its printer output at full speed without waiting for each page to print. Printer buffers with automatic switching are connected to two or more computers and accept their output on a first-come, first-served basis.

printer cable

A wire that connects a printer to a computer. On a PC, the cable has a 25-pin DB-25 male connector for the computer and a 36-pin Centronics male connector for the printer.

PC Printer Cable
The left side of this cable connects to the PC, and the right side connects to the printer.

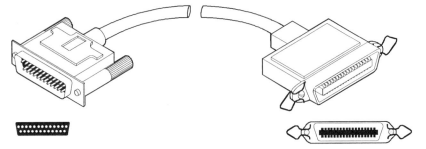

printer description file

A configuration file that contains information about a specific printer. See *PPD file*.

printer driver

Software routine that converts an application program's printing request into the language the printer understands.

printer engine

The unit within a printer that does the actual printing. In a laser printer, it includes the laser and mechanism to transfer the toner onto the paper. A printer engine is specified by its resolution and speed. See *electrophotographic*.

printer file

(1) A document in print image format ready to be printed. See *print to disk*.
(2) Same as *printer driver*.

printer font

A font used for printing. Printer and screen resolutions are not the same, thus fonts generated for the printer will not display accurately on screen. Contrast with *screen font*.

print head

A mechanism that deposits ink onto paper in a character printer.

print image

A text or graphics document that has been prepared for the printer. Format codes for the required printer have been embedded in the document at the appropriate places. With text files, headers, footers and page numbers have been created and inserted in every page.

print image format
See *print image*.

Print Manager
In Windows 3.x, the software that prints documents in the background. It is also used if the computer is connected to a network and the printer is shared with other users. Print Manager is the Windows print spooler, which accepts the incoming print jobs, stores them and prints them in the background.

printout
(PRINTer OUTput) Same as *hard copy*.

print queue
Disk space that holds output designated for the printer until the printer can receive it.

print screen
The ability to print the current on-screen image. See *screen dump*.

print server
A computer in a network that controls one or more printers. It stores the print-image output from all users of the system and feeds it to the printer one job at a time. This function may be part of the network operating system or an add-on utility.

print spooler
Software that manages printing in the computer. When an application is requested to print a document, it quickly generates the output on disk and sends it to the print spooler, which feeds the print images to the printer at slower printing speeds. The printing is then done in the background while the user interacts with other applications in the foreground. See *spooling* and *Print Manager*.

print to disk
To redirect output from the printer to the disk. The resulting file contains text and graphics with all the codes required to direct the printer to print it. The file can be printed later or at a remote location without requiring the word processor, DTP or drawing program that was originally used to create it. This is actually the first stage of a print spooling operation. See *print spooler*.

PRISM
(1) (Photorefractive Information Storage Materials Consortium) A collaboration of IBM, Stanford University, GTE, Hughes Research Labs, Optitek, SRI International and Rockwell Science Center that is funded by the U.S. Government's Advanced Research Projects Agency for the purpose of researching holographic storage.
(2) (PRogrammable Integrated Scripts for Mirror) The programming language for the Mirror communications programs.

privacy
The authorized distribution of information (who has a right to know?). Contrast with *security*, which deals with unauthorized access to data.

Private Eye
A headband-mounted LED display system from Reflection Technology, Waltham, MA, that plugs into a PC. Its 1x1" screen gives the appearance of a 12" monitor floating in space in front of the viewer.

private file

A file made available only to the user that created it. Contrast with *public file*.

private key

See *encryption*.

private line

(1) A dedicated line leased from a common carrier.
(2) A line owned and installed by the user.

PRMD

(PRivate Management Domain) An inhouse e-mail service. See *X.400*.

PRML

(Partial Response Maximum Likelihood) A technique used to differentiate a valid signal from noise by measuring the rate of change at various intervals of the rising waveform. Bits generated by a modem or hard disk platter have uniform characteristics, whereas random noise does not.

On magnetic disks, PRML increases the number of bits that can be recorded over earlier methods. It uses an RLL encoding sequence of 0,4,4 and provides an 8:9 ratio of user data to recorded data. See *RLL*.

PRN

(PRiNter) The DOS name for the first connected parallel port.

problem-oriented language

A computer language designed to handle a particular class of problem. For example, COBOL was designed for business, FORTRAN for scientific and GPSS for simulation.

procedural language

A programming language that requires programming discipline, such as COBOL, FORTRAN, BASIC, C, Pascal and dBASE. Programmers writing in such languages must develop a proper order of actions in order to solve the problem, based on a knowledge of data processing and programming. Contrast with *non-procedural language*.

The following dBASE examples show procedural and non-procedural ways to list a file. Procedural and non-procedural languages are also considered third and fourth-generation languages.

```
Procedural (3GL)            Non-procedural (4GL)
  USE FILEX                   USE FILEX
  DO WHILE .NOT. EOF          LIST NAME, AMOUNTDUE
   ? NAME, AMOUNTDUE
   SKIP
  ENDDO
```

procedure

(1) Manual *procedures* are human tasks.
(2) Machine *procedures* are lists of routines or programs to be executed, such as described by the job control language (JCL) in a mini or mainframe, or the batch processing language in a personal computer.
(3) In programming, another term for a subroutine or function.

procedure oriented

An application that forces the user to follow a predefined path from step A to step B. Data entry programs are typical examples. Contrast with *event driven*.

process

To manipulate data in the computer. The computer is said to be processing no matter what action is taken upon the data. It may be updated or simply displayed on screen.

In order to evaluate a computer system's performance, the time it takes to process data internally is analyzed separately from the time it takes to get it in and out of the computer. I/O is usually more time consuming than processing. See *computer (The 3 C's)*.

process bound

An excessive amount of processing in the CPU that causes an imbalance between I/O and processing. In a multitasking system, process-bound applications may slow down other applications and other users depending on how the operating system slices time (see *preemtive multitasking*). A personal computer can become process bound when it is recalculating a spreadsheet, for example.

Process Charter

A flowcharting and simulation program for Windows from Scitor Corporation, Foster City, CA. It provides the ability to model and simulate a process based on the resources required for each step.

process color

A color printed from four separate printing plates. Four-color process printing uses cyan, magenta, yellow and black (CMYK) inks to produce full color reproduction. Contrast with *spot color*.

process control

The automated control of a process, such as a manufacturing process or assembly line. It is used extensively in industrial operations, such as oil refining, chemical processing and electrical generation. It uses analog devices to monitor real-world signals and digital computers to do the analysis and controlling. It makes extensive use of analog/digital, digital/analog conversion.

process identifier

See *PID*.

processing

Manipulating data within the computer. The term is used to define a variety of computer functions and methods. See *centralized processing, distributed processing, batch processing, transaction processing, multiprocessing* and *computer (The 3 C's)*.

processor

(1) Same as *CPU*.
(2) May refer to software. See *language processor* and *word processor*.

Procomm

A popular PC shareware communications program from Datastorm Technologies, Inc., Columbia, MO, that supports a wide number of protocols and terminals. Procomm Plus is the commercial version with more features.

PRODIGY

An online information service (partnership of IBM and Sears) that includes weather and stock market reports, airline scheduling and at-home shopping. Users receive a communications program that must be installed in their personal computer, which provides full-screen displays and simplifies the logon. In early 1995, PRODIGY was the first major online service to provide a World Wide Web browser for the Internet. See *online services*.

ProDOS

(PROfessional Disk Operating System) An operating system for the Apple II family that superseded Apple's DOS 3.3. It provides a hierarchical file system with file names up to 15 characters in length.

production database

A central database containing an organization's master files and daily transaction files.

production system

A computer system used to process an organization's daily work. Contrast with a system used only for development and testing or for ad hoc inquiries and analysis.

productivity software

Refers to word processors, spreadsheets, database management systems, PIMs, schedulers and other software packages that are designed for individual use. Contrast with custom-designed, multiuser information systems which provide the primary data processing in an organization.

productivity suite

A suite of applications that generally includes a word processor, spreadsheet, database program, comm program and perhaps a presentation graphics or charting program.

Professional Write

A word processing program for DOS and Windows from SoftKey International, Inc., Cambridge, MA. It is easy to use and meets the needs of many who write uncomplicated letters and memos. Originally called PFS:Write, it was one of the earliest PC word processors.

Professional YAM

(Professional Yet Another Modem) A PC communications program from Omen Technology, Inc., Portland, OR, for the serious communications user. It is a flexible, full-featured program that supports a wide variety of terminals and protocols.

PROFS

(PRofessional OFfice System) IBM office automation software for the VM mainframe environment. It provides an e-mail facility for text and graphics, a library service for centrally storing text, electronic calendars and appointment scheduling, and it allows document interchange with DISOSS users. PROFS uses IBM's proprietary ZIP messaging protocol.

PROGMAN.INI

A Windows configuration file that describes the current state of the Program Manager layout. For example, the [Settings] section describes the on-screen location of the Program Manager window. The [Group] section identifies the group window files. Like WIN.INI and SYSTEM.INI, Windows' major configuration files, PROGMAN.INI can also be edited by the user if required. It usually isn't.

program

A collection of instructions that tell the computer what to do. A program is called *software*; hence, program, software and instructions are synonymous. A program is written in a programming language and is converted into the computer's machine language by software called assemblers, compilers and interpreters.

A program is made up of

> machine instructions
> buffers
> constants and counters

Instructions are the directions that the computer follows (program logic). Buffers are reserved space, or input/output areas, that accept and hold the data while it's being processed. They can receive any kind of information required by the program. Constants are fixed values used to compare the data against, such as minimums and maximums and dates. Menu titles and error messages are another example of constants.

Counters, also called *variables*, are reserved space for summing money amounts, quantities, virtually any calculations, including those necessary to keep track of internal operations, such as how many times a function should be repeated.

The program calls for data in an input-process-output sequence. After data has been input into one of the program's buffers from a peripheral device (keyboard, disk, etc.), it is processed. The results are then output to a peripheral device (screen, printer, etc.). If data has been updated, it is output back onto the disk.

The application program, which does the actual data processing, does not instruct the computer to do everything. When it is ready for input or needs to output data, it sends a request to the operating system, which performs those services and then turns control back to the application program.

Following is a conceptual illustration of a program residing in memory. In the physical reality of memory, everything below would be in binary coded form (0s and 1s).

Although represented as small blocks below, machine instructions can be variable in length and they are in some kind of logical sequence. Some of the instructions would be GOTO instructions that point back to the beginning of a routine or to other parts of the program, for example.

For an understanding of what the computer does to process data, look up *computer* and read about The 3 C's (calculate, compare and copy).

Anatomy of a Program

The Data

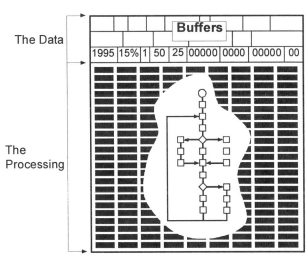

The
Processing

program counter

A register or variable used to keep track of the address of the current or next instruction. See *address register* and *instruction register*.

program development

See *system development cycle*.

program generator

See *application generator*.

program logic

A sequence of instructions in a program. There are many logical solutions to a problem. If you give a specification to ten programmers, each one may create program logic that is slightly different than all the rest, but the results can be the same. The solution that runs the fastest is usually the most desired, however. Program logic is written using three classes of instructions: sequential processing, selection and iteration.

1. Sequential processing is the series of steps that do the actual data processing. Input, output, calculate and move (copy) instructions are used in sequential processing.

2. Selection is the decision making within the program and is performed by comparing two sets of data and branching to a different part of the program based on the results. In assembly languages, the compare and branch instructions are used. In high-level languages, IF THEN ELSE and CASE statements are used.

3. Iteration is the repetition of a series of steps and is accomplished with DO LOOPS and FOR LOOPS in high-level languages and GOTOs in assembly languages. See *loop*.

Program Logic
INPUT, PROCESS, OUTPUT and GO TO operations are the primary instructions built into every computer. Although program logic becomes quite complicated in actual practice, it is all based on inputting data into the computer, processing it and outputting the results. The main loop of many data processing programs performs this sequence over and over again.

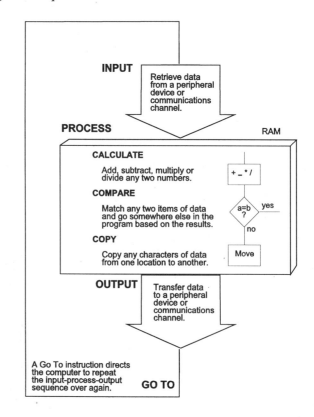

INPUT — Retrieve data from a peripheral device or communications channel.

PROCESS — RAM

CALCULATE — Add, subtract, multiply or divide any two numbers. + _ * /

COMPARE — Match any two items of data and go somewhere else in the program based on the results. a=b? yes no

COPY — Copy any characters of data from one location to another. Move

OUTPUT — Transfer data to a peripheral device or communications channel.

A Go To instruction directs the computer to repeat the input-process-output sequence over again. GO TO

programmable

Capable of following instructions. What sets the computer apart from all other electronic devices is its programmability.

programmable calculator

A limited-function computer capable of working with only numbers and not alphanumeric data.

program maintenance

Updating programs to reflect changes in the organization's business or to adapt to new operating environments. Although maintaining old programs written by ex-employees is often much more difficult than writing new ones, the task is usually given to junior programmers, because the most talented professionals don't want the job.

Program Manager

The control center for Windows 3.x operation. It provides the means to launch applications and manage the desktop. Program Manager may be replaced with another shell, such as Norton's Desktop for Windows, HP's Dashboard or Quarterdeck's SideBar, all of which provide similar functionality with a different user interface.

programmer

A person who designs the logic for and writes the lines of codes of a computer program. See *application programmer* and *systems programmer*.

Programmer's Switch

The physical buttons included with the Macintosh (fkey on the LC) that include a System Reset button and a Debugging button that will invoke MacsBug if present or switch to the built in monitor in ROM.

programmer analyst

A person who analyzes and designs information systems and designs and writes the application programs for the system. In theory, a programmer analyst is both systems analyst and applications programmer. In practice, the title is sometimes simply a reward to a programmer for tenure. Which skill is really dominant is of concern when recruiting people with such titles.

programming

Creating a computer program. The steps are:
1. Developing the program logic to solve the particular problem.
2. Writing the program logic in a specific programming language (coding the program).
3. Assembling or compiling the program to turnit into machine language.
4. Testing and debugging the program.
5. Preparing the necessary documentation.

The logic is the most difficult part of programming. Writing the language statements is comparatively easy once the solution has been developed. However, regardless of how difficult the program may be, documenting it is considered the most annoying activity by most programmers.

Programming

Creating a computer program (See *Machine Language*). The logic is the most difficult part of programming. Writing the language statement is comparatively easy once the solution has been developed. However, regardless of how difficult the program may be, documenting it is considered the most annoying activity by most programmers. The steps are:

INPUT INTO MEMORY
CALCULATE
COMPARE
COPY
OUTPUT
GO TO

1. Develop the program logic to solve the particular problem. (See *Boolean Logic*).
2. Using a text editor or word processor, the programmer writes the program language in a specific programming language (coding the program).

3. The Assembler or Compiler translates the source language into machine language.

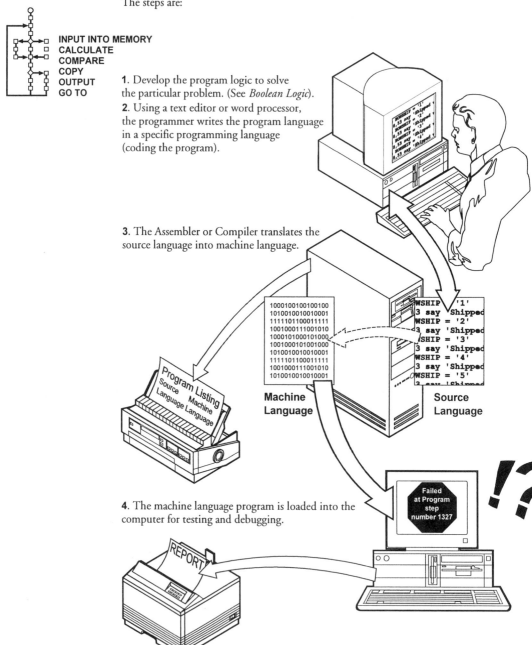

Program Listing
Source   Machine
Language Language

Machine Language

Source Language

```
1000100100100100
1010010010010001
1111101100011111
1001000111001010
1000010100101000
1001000101001000
1010010010010001
1111101100011111
1001000111001010
1010010010010001
```

```
WSHIP    '1'
3 say 'Shipped
WSHIP = '2'
3 say 'Shipped
SHIP = '3'
3 say 'Shipped
WSHIP = '4'
3 say 'Shipped
WSHIP = '5'
```

Failed at Program step number 1327

4. The machine language program is loaded into the computer for testing and debugging.

REPORT

5. The results of testing and debugging are output to the necessary documentation.

programming interface

See *API.*

programming language

A language used to write instructions for the computer. It lets the programmer express data processing in a symbolic manner without regard to machine-specific details.

The statements that are written by the programmer are called *source language*, and they are translated into the computer's *machine language* by programs called *assemblers, compilers* and *interpreters*. For example, when a programmer writes MULTIPLY HOURS TIMES RATE, MULTIPLY must be turned into a code that means multiply, and HOURS and RATE must be turned into memory locations where those items of data are actually located.

Like human languages, each programming language has its own grammar and syntax. There are many dialects of the same language, and each dialect requires its own translating system. Standards have been set by ANSI for many programming languages, and ANSI-standard languages are dialect free. However, it can take years for new features to be included in ANSI standards, and new dialects inevitably spring up as a result.

Programming languages fall into two categories: low-level assembly languages and high-level languages. Assembly languages are available for each CPU family, and each assembly instruction is translated into one machine instruction by the assembler program. With high-level languages, a programming statement may be translated into one or several machine instructions by the compiler.

Following is a synopsis of the major high-level languages. Look up each one for more details.

Ada

Comprehensive, Pascal-based language used by the Department of Defense.

ALGOL

International language for expressing algorithms.

APL

Used for statistics and mathematical matrices. Requires special keyboard symbols.

BASIC

Developed as a timesharing language in the 1960s. It has been widely used in microcomputer programming in the past, and various dialects of BASIC have been incorporated into many different applications.

C

Developed in the 1980s at AT&T. Widely used to develop commercial applications. UNIX is written in C.

C++

Object-oriented version of C that is popular because it combines object-oriented capability with traditional C programming syntax.

COBOL

Developed in the 1960s. Widely used for mini and mainframe programming. Also available for personal computers.

dBASE

Widely used in business applications. Offshoots of dBASE ("Xbase" languages) are Clipper, Quicksilver, FoxBase and FoxPro.

FORTH
Developed in the 1960s, FORTH is used in process control and game applications.

FORTRAN
Developed in 1954 by IBM, it was the first major scientific programming language. Some commercial applications have been developed in it, and it continues to be widely used.

LISP
Developed in 1960. Used for AI applications. Its syntax is very different than other languages.

Logo
Developed in the 1960s, it is noted for its ease of use and "turtle graphics" drawing functions.

Modula-2
Enhanced version of Pascal introduced in 1979.

MUMPS
Originally Massachusetts Utility MultiProgramming System, it includes its own database. It is widely used in medical applications.

Pascal
Originally an academic language developed in the 1970s. Borland commercialized it with its Turbo Pascal.

Prolog
Developed in France in 1973. Used throughout Europe and Japan for AI applications.

REXX
Runs on IBM mainframes. Used as a general purpose macro language.

Visual Basic
Version of BASIC for Windows programming from Microsoft that is very popular.

program state
An operating mode of the computer that executes instructions in the application program. Contrast with *supervisor state*.

program statement
A phrase in a high-level programming language. One program statement may result in several machine instructions when the program is compiled.

program step
An elementary instruction, such as a machine language instruction or an assembly language instruction. Contrast with *program statement*.

program-to-program communications
Communications between two programs. Often confused with peer-to-peer communications, it is a set of protocols a program uses to interact with another program. Peer-to-peer establishment is the network's responsibility. You can have program-to-program communications in a master-slave environment without peer-to-peer capability.

Progress

An application development system for client/server environments from Progress Software, Corporation, Bedford, MA. It supports a variety of clients, including DOS, Windows, OS/2, AIX, HP-UX and Sun. It includes its own relational DBMS, but interfaces to Oracle, Sybase and others. The majority of Progress systems are created by third-party developers. The company was founded in 1984.

progressive scan

Same as *non-interlaced*.

projection panel

See *LCD panel*.

project life cycle

See *full project life cycle* and *system life cycle*.

project manager

Software used to monitor the time and materials on a project. All tasks to complete the project are entered into the database, and the program computes the critical path, the series of tasks with the least amount of slack time. Any change in the critical path slows down the entire project.

Prokey

A keyboard macro processor for DOS and Windows from CE Software, Inc., West Des Moines, IA, that allows users to eliminate repetitive typing by setting up an occurrence of text or a series of commands as a macro.

Prolog

(PROgramming in LOGic) A programming language used for developing AI applications (natural language translation, expert systems, abstract problem solving, etc.). Developed in France in 1973, it is used throughout Europe and Japan and is gaining popularity in the U.S.

Similar to LISP, it deals with symbolic representations of objects. The following example, written in University of Edinburgh Prolog, converts Fahrenheit to Celsius:

```
convert:- write('Enter Fahrenheit'),
read(Fahr),
write('Celsius is '),
Cent is (5 * (Fahr - 32)) / 9,
write(Cent),nl.
```

PROM

(Programmable Read Only Memory) A permanent memory chip that is programmed, or filled, by the customer rather than by the chip manufacturer. It differs from a ROM, which is programmed at the time of manufacture. PROMs have been mostly superseded by EPROMs, which can be reprogrammed. See *PROM programmer*.

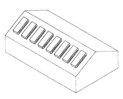

PROM blower, PROM programmer

A device that writes instructions and data into PROM chips. The bits in a new PROM are all 1s (continuous lines). The PROM programmer only creates 0s, by "blowing" the middle out of the 1s. Some earlier units were capable of programming both PROMs and EPROMs.

prompt

A software message that requests action by the user; for example, "Enter employee name." Command-driven systems issue a cryptic symbol when ready to accept a command; for example, the dot (.) in dBASE, the $ or % in UNIX, and the venerable C:\> in DOS. See *DOS prompt*.

propagation

The transmission (spreading) from one place to another.

propagation delay

The time it takes to transmit a signal from one place to another.

property list

In a list processing language, an object that is assigned a descriptive attribute (property) and a value. For example, in Logo, **PUTPROP "KAREN "LANGUAGE "PARADOX** assigns the value PARADOX to the property LANGUAGE for the person named KAREN. To find out what language Karen speaks, the Logo statement **PRINT GETPROP "KAREN "LANGUAGE** will generate PARADOX as the answer.

proportional spacing

Character spacing based on the width of each character. For example, an I takes up less space than an M. In monospacing (fixed), the I and M each take up the same space. See *kerning*.

proprietary software

Software owned by an organization or individual. Contrast with *public domain software*.

Protected Mode

In PCs, starting with the 286, an operational state that allows the computer to address all of its memory. It also prevents an errant program from entering into the memory boundary of another. In a 386 and higher machine, it provides access to 32-bit instructions and sophisticated memory management modes.
For example, Windows 95 and OS/2 are 32-bit operating systems and their operations are performed in Protected Mode in contrast to the 16-bit Real Mode of DOS and Windows 3.1. See *32-bit processing, Real Mode, Virtual 8086 Mode* and *memory protection*.

Protected Mode driver

A PC driver that is written to the original 32-bit 386 architecture, which allows access to 32-bit instructions and four gigabytes of memory. Protected Mode drivers run in extended memory (above one megabyte).
Windows 95 provides Protected Mode, 32-bit drivers for all the popular peripheral devices. If it does not include a driver for a particular device, it loads the 16-bit driver that was used under DOS/Windows 3.x.

protocol

Rules governing transmitting and receiving of data. See *communications protocol* and *OSI*.

protocol analyzer

See *network analyzer*.

protocol stack

The hierarchy of protocols used in a communications network. Network architectures designed in layers, such as TCP/IP, OSI and SNA, are referred to as stacks. See *OSI model*.

protocol suite

Same as *protocol stack*.

prototyping

(1) Creating a demo of a new system. Prototyping is essential for clarifying information requirements. The design of a system (functional specs) must be finalized before the system can be built. While analytically-oriented people may have a clear picture of requirements, others may not.

Using fourth-generation languages, systems analysts and users can develop the new system together. Databases can be created and manipulated while the user monitors the progress.

Once users see tangible output on screen or on paper, they can figure out what's missing or what the next question might be if this were a production system. If prototyping is carefully done, the end result can be a working system.

Even if the final system must be reprogrammed in other languages for standardization or machine efficiency, prototyping has served to provide specifications for a working system rather than a theoretical one.

(2) See *function prototyping*.

PR/SM

(Processor Resource/Systems Manager) An IBM mainframe feature that allows the CPU to run as multiple logical processors, each capable of running a different operating system and set of applications. Standard on ES/9000 models, it is an upgrade to 3090 processors.

Prt Sc

See *print screen*.

PS

(Personal Services) IBM office automation software for PCs, minis and mainframes, which includes word processing, electronic mail and library services.

PS/1

An IBM home computer series introduced in 1990. The original models featured an integrated monitor and easy-to-open case. The first PS/1 was a 286 with an ISA-bus. See *PC*.

PS/2

An IBM personal computer series introduced in 1987, superseding the original PC line. It introduced the 3.5" floppy disk, VGA graphics and Micro Channel bus. The 3.5" disks and VGA are now common in all PCs, but the Micro Channel is used primarily by IBM. Smaller PS/2 models use the ISA bus. See *PC*.

PS/2 bus

Same as *Micro Channel*.

PS/2 connector

A 6-pin mini DIN plug and socket used to connect a keyboard and mouse to an IBM PS/2 computer as well as to all types of laptops. The socket is on the computer. The plug is on the mouse and keyboard cable. See *PS/2 port* and *bus mouse*.

PS/2 keyboard

A keyboard that uses a PS/2 connector to plug into the computer. If the PC does not have a PS/2 socket, a PS/2 keyboard can be plugged into the standard keyboard socket using a PS/2 to PC keyboard adapter.

PS/2 mouse

A mouse that uses a PS/2 plug to connect to the computer. If the PC does not have a PS/2 socket, a PS/2 mouse can be plugged into the PC's serial port using a PS/2 to serial port adapter. The connectors on a PS/2 mouse and a bus mouse are similar. See *bus mouse.*

PS/2 port

A hardware interface that uses the PS/2 connector plug and socket. PS/2 ports are used for the serial port to connect a mouse and the keyboard port to connect the keyboard. In order to conserve space on some laptops, one PS/2 port is used for both mouse and keyboard and is switchable between them. See *PS/2 connector.*

pseudo compiler

A compiler that generates a pseudo language, or intermediate language, which must be further compiled or interpreted for execution.

pseudo-duplexing

A communications technique that simulates full-duplex transmission in a half-duplex line by turning the line around very quickly.

pseudo language

An intermediate language generated from a source language, but not directly executable by a CPU. It must be interpreted or compiled into machine language for execution. It facilitates the use of one source language for different types of computers. See "ANDF" in *OSF* definition.

PSN

(Packet-Switched Network) A communications network that uses packet switching technology.

PSS

See *EPSS.*

PSTN

(Public Switched Telephone Network) The worldwide voice telephone network.

PSW

(Program Status Word) A hardware register that maintains the status of the program being executed.

p-System

See *UCSD p-System.*

PTT

(Postal, Telegraph & Telephone) The governmental agency responsible for combined postal, telegraph and telephone services in many European countries.

PU

(Physical Unit) In SNA, software responsible for managing the resources of a node, such as data links. A PU supports a connection to the host (SSCP) for gathering network management statistics.

PU 2.1

(Physical Unit 2.1) In SNA, the original term for Node Type 2.1, which is software that provides peer-to-peer communications between intelligent devices (PCs, workstations, minicomputers). Only LU 6.2 sessions are supported between Type 2.1 nodes (PU 2.1).

public domain software

Software in which ownership has been relinquished to the public at large. See *freeware* and *shareware*.

public file

A file made available to all other users connected to the system or network. Contrast with *private file*.

public key

See *encryption*.

Publish and Subscribe

A Macintosh System 7 capability that provides hot links between files. All or part of a file can be published into an "edition file," which is imported into a subscriber file. When any of the published files are updated, the subscriber file is also updated.

puck

The mouse-like object used to draw on a digitizer tablet.

pull-down menu

Also called a pop-down menu, a menu that is displayed from the top of the screen downward when its title is selected. The menu remains displayed while the mouse button is depressed. To select a menu option, the highlight bar is moved (with the mouse) to the appropriate line and the mouse button is let go.

The drop-down menu is a variation that keeps the menu open after its title is selected. To select a menu option, the highlight bar is moved to the line and the mouse button is clicked. Key commands may also activate drop-down menus.

pulse code modulation

See *PCM*.

pulse level device

A disk drive or other device that inputs and outputs raw voltages. Data coding/decoding is in the controller the device. Contrast with *bit level device*.

PUMA

(Programmable Universal Micro Accelerator) A Chips and Technolgies' chipset that accelerates graphics operations for the screen and printer.

punch block

Also called a quick-connect block, a device that interconnects telephone lines from remote points. The wires are pushed, or punched, down into metal teeth that strip the insulation and make a tight connection.

punched card

An early storage medium made of thin cardboard stock that holds data as patterns of punched holes. Each of the 80 or 96 columns holds one character. The holes are punched by a keypunch machine or card punch peripheral and are fed into the computer by a card reader.

Although still used as turnaround documents, punched cards are practically obsolete.

However, from 1890 until the 1970s, they were synonymous with data processing. Concepts were simple: the database was the file cabinet; a record was a card. Processing was performed on separate machines called sorters, collators, reproducers, calculators and accounting machines.

Punched Card

The 80-column punched card was the precursor to magnetic tape and disk. Millions of customer, vendor and payroll accounts were kept on punched cards, which were sorted, collated and summarized on tabulating machines.

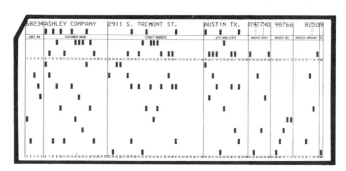

push/pop

Instructions that store and retrieve an item on a stack. Push enters an item on the stack, and pop retrieves an item, moving the rest of the items in the stack up one level. See *stack*.

put

In programming, a request to store the current record in an output file. Contrast with *get*.

PVC

(Permanent Virtual Circuit) A point-to-point connection that is established ahead of time. All PVCs defined at the time of subscription to a particular service are known as a VPN (virtual private network). Contrast with *SVC*.

PVCS

A system of version control and configuration management from Intersolv, Inc., Rockville, MD, that runs on DOS, Windows, OS/2 and various UNIX platforms. In 1994, it was the most widely used SCM system on PC LANs.

Px64

An ITU standard for transmitting audio and video in 64 Kbits/sec ISDN channels (P represents number of channels used). Although video conferencing can be done in only one or two channels, more channels are required for smooth motion. Px64 uses two screen formats. The CIF (Common Intermediate Format) generates a 352x288 resolution, while QCIF (Quarter CIF) is 176x144. CIF transmits at 36.45 Mbits/sec; QCIF is 9.115 Mbits/sec. See *H.261*.

Pyramid

(Pyramid Technology Corporation, San Jose, CA) A computer company founded in 1981 that specializes in multiprocessing open systems. It originally adapted UNIX to symmetric multiprocessing (SMP) for its proprietary MIServer architecture that was also licensed to other vendors. Its current line is the R4400-based Nile Series that provides scalable processing up to 16 CPUs. Pyramid helped pioneer SMP on open systems, and its DC/OSx operating system is the SMP implementation of UNIX System V Release 4.

Q

Q&A

An integrated file manager and word processor for DOS and Windows from Symantec Corporation, Cupertino, CA, that includes mail merge capability as well as a programming language for customizing data entry forms and reports. Its Intelligent Assistant feature provides a query language that can learn new words from the user.

QAM

(1) (Quadrature Amplitude Modulation) A modulation technique that generates four bits out of one baud. For example, a 600 baud line (600 shifts in the signal per second) can effectively transmit 2,400 bps using this method. Both phase and amplitude are shaped with each baud, resulting in four possible patterns.
(2) (Quality Assessment Measurement) A system used to measure and analyze voice transmission.

QBasic

A BASIC interpreter from Microsoft that comes with DOS starting with DOS 5. It supersedes Microsoft's GW-BASIC and includes REMLINE.BAS, a program that helps convert GW-BASIC programs to QBasic.

QBE

See *query by example*.

Q-bus

A bus architecture used in Digital's PDP-11 and MicroVAX series.

QCIF

(Quarter **CIF**) A video format that transmits 9.115 Mbits/sec at 30 frames/sec, one quarter the speed of CIF. See *H.261*.

QEMM

(Quarterdeck **EMM**) A popular DOS and Windows memory manager for 386s and up from Quarterdeck Office Systems, Santa Monica, CA. QEMM was widely used in the DOS-only days and continues to be used under Windows to efficiently manage the first megabyte of memory.

QIC

(Quarter Inch Cartridge) A magnetic tape commonly used for backing up data. The tape is 1/4" wide (6.35mm) and is recorded using the serpentine method. Cartridge capacities range from 40MB to 13GB.

QIC tapes come in 3.5" minicartridges and 5.25" data cartridges. Minicartridges and data cartridges are also known as DC2000 and DC6000 cartridges.

The most common QIC tape is the 3.5" QIC-80 drive, which uses the DC2120 Minicartridge with a raw capacity of 120MB. These drives are often rated at 250MB, because backup software uses data compression to double capacity. Using the 170MB extended-length DC2120XL (QIC-160) Minicartridge, capacity is increased up to 350MB compressed. For backing up larger hard disks, the QIC-3010 and QIC-3020 drives, also in the same 3.5" form factor, provide 340MB and 680MB of raw storage and generally double that with compression.

Minicartridge Drives (3.5")

Recording Format	Media Type	Storage (MB)	Interfaces:		
			Read Compatibility	Basic	Intelligent
QIC-40-MC	DC2000	40		QIC-107 QIC-115 QIC-117	
QIC-80-MC	DC2120 DC2080 QIC-159 QIC-160	120 80 208 170	40	QIC-107 QIC-115 QIC-117	
QIC-100-MC	DC2000	20/40		QIC-103	SCSI
QIC-128-MC	DC2110 DC2165	86 128	100	QIC-103	SCSI
QIC-3010-MC	QIC-143 QIC-148	340 425	40/80	QIC-107 QIC-115 QIC-117	Floppy or IDE
QIC-3020-MC	QIC-143 QIC-148	680 833	40/80 3010	QIC-107 QIC-115 QIC-117	Floppy or IDE
QIC-3030-MC	QIC-143	580			SCSI-2
QIC-3040-MC	QIC-143 QIC-148	840 1GB			SCSI-2 SCSI-2
QIC-3050-MC	QIC-143	1GB			SCSI-2
QIC-3070-MC	QIC-138	4GB	3030		SCSI-2
QIC-3080-MC	QIC-152 QIC-156	1.6GB			SCSI-2
QIC-3110-MC	QIC-153	2GB			SCSI-2

Data Cartridge Drives (5.25")

Recording Format	Media Type	Storage (MB)	Interfaces:		
			Read Compatibility	Basic	Intelligent
QIC-24-DC	DC600A	60		QIC-38	SCSI
QIC-120-DC	DC6150	125	24		SCSI
QIC-150-DC	DC6250 DC6150	250 150	24/120		SCSI
QIC-525-DC	DC6525 DC6320	525 320	120/150		SCSI SCSI-2
QIC-1000-DC	QIC-136	1.2GB	120/150/525		SCSI SCSI-2
QIC-1350-DC	QIC-137	1.6GB	525/1000		SCSI-2
QIC-2GB-DC	QIC-136	2.5GB	120/150/525/1000		SCSI-2
QIC-2100-DC	QIC-137	2.6GB	525/1000/1350		SCSI-2
QIC-5GB-DC	QIC-137	5GB	24/120/150/525 1000/1350/2GB/2100		SCSI-2
QIC-5010-DC	QIC-139	13GB	150/525/1000 1350/2100		SCSI-2

QIC-157

A QIC specification for increased transfer rates under the ATAPI interface. ATAPI is the interface under Enhanced IDE that supports CD-ROMs and tape drives. See *Enhanced IDE* and *ATA*.

QIC-WIDE

(Quarter Inch Cartridge-WIDE) An extension to the QIC tape from Sony that provides more storage capacity than quarter inch tape. It uses .315" wide tape rather than .25", a thin base film that increases length from 300 to 400 feet and a higher recording density. It uses the standard QIC minicartridge with a redesigned housing. QIC-WIDE drives support both QIC-WIDE and QIC formats.

QMF

(Query Management Facility) An IBM fourth-generation language for end-user interaction with DB2.

Qmodem Pro

Communications programs for DOS and Windows from Mustang Software, Inc., Bakersfield, CA. The programs support a wide variety of modems as well as all the major file transfer protocols and terminal emulations. The Windows version is noted for its integrated fax facilities allowing the user to fax directly from within any Windows word processor. Mustang Software is also the publisher of the popular WILDCAT! BBS software.

QMS

(1) (QMS, Inc., Mobile, AL) A manufacturer of laser printers founded in 1977 by Jim Busby. Initially involved with controllers for printing bar codes and labels, it got into the laser printer business in the mid 1980s. QMS, concurrent with Apple, pioneered the PostScript printer. It also introduced the first auto switching printer and the first Kanji color laser printer.

(2) (Quality Management System) A system that ensures that a manufacturing process or service is performed at a quality level. See *TQM* and *ISO 9000*.

QNX

A multiuser, multitasking, realtime operating system for PCs from QNX Software Systems, Ltd., Kanata, Ontario, noted for its low-memory requirement and rapid response. Similar to UNIX, it has been in use since the early 1980s.

quadbit

A group of four bits used in QAM modulation.

quadrillion

One thousand times one trillion or 10 to the 15th power. See *femtosecond*.

quantize

To assign a number to a sample. The larger the number the more the digital sample represents the analog signal. See *sampling*.

quantum computing

A future technology for designing computers based on quantum mechanics, the energy levels in the atom. If this is ever realized, it means speeds a thousand times greater than today's technologies.

QuarkXpress

A desktop publishing program for the Macintosh and Windows from Quark, Inc.,

Denver, CO. Originally developed for the Mac, it is noted for its precise typographic control and advanced text and graphics manipulation.

quartz crystal

A slice of quartz ground to a prescribed thickness that vibrates at a steady frequency when stimulated by electricity. The tiny crystal, about 1/20th by 1/5th of an inch, creates the computer's heartbeat.

Quattro Pro

A PC spreadsheet from Novell that provides advanced graphics and presentation capabilities. It has an optional interface that is keystroke, macro and file compatible with Lotus 1-2-3. Version 2.0 adds goal seeking, 3-D graphing and the ability to create multi-layered slide shows. Quattro Pro was originally developed by Borland and was purchased by Novell in 1994.

query

To interrogate a database (count, sum and list selected records). Contrast with *report*, which is usually a more elaborate printout with headings and page numbers. The report may also be a selective list of items; hence, the two terms may refer to programs that produce the same results.

Defining a query for a relational database can be extremely simple or very complex. If the query is based on one matching condition, such as "retrieve all customers who owe us more than $10,000," it is usually pretty easy to define in a query language or program. However, "retrieve all customers who owe us more than $10,000 from purchasing toasters" is not easy. It requires several steps to determine how many toaster orders make up the balance. In fact, this is actually very complicated to program if it is absolutely necessary that the $10,000 be for toaster orders and nothing else.

In addition, relational databases are designed to eliminate redundancy. The idea is to store a data item in one table and not have it duplicated in others. For example, an order record will contain the product number ordered, but often not its description. The description is stored in a product table. Thus, any printout of products ordered and their descriptions requires that the order table be linked to the product table for that query or report. Linking customer, order and product tables is a common example of relating tables to satisfy a query.

Most queries require at least the following conditions to be stated. First, which table or tables is the data coming from. If from two or more tables, what is the link between (typically account number or name). Next, define the selection criteria, which is the matching condition or filter. Lastly, define which fields in the tables are to be displayed or printed in the result.

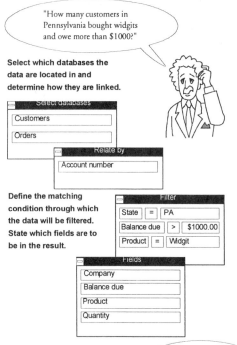

"How many customers in Pennsylvania bought widgits and owe more than $1000?"

Select which databases the data are located in and determine how they are linked.

Select databases
- Customers
- Orders

Relate by
- Account number

Define the matching condition through which the data will be filtered. State which fields are to be in the result.

Filter
State	=	PA
Balance due	>	$1000.00
Product	=	Widgit

Fields
- Company
- Balance due
- Product
- Quantity

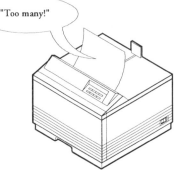

"Too many!"

The Query Statement
This diagram depicts the typical conditions that have to be stated when querying a relational database.

query by example

A method for describing a query originally developed by IBM for mainframes. A replica of an empty record is displayed and the search conditions are typed in under their respective columns. For example, to select all California customers, an empty customer record is displayed on screen, and the user types in the letters "CA" under the STATE column.

This visual approach has been adopted by nearly every modern query program. Although there are differences from one to another with regard to expressing complicated queries, everything is selected from a menu by the user. The program turns the visual query into the command language, such as SQL, necessary to interrogate the database.

query language

**Query
Programs
Are Tough**
A good query
program allows you
to interrogate your
database and get
the answers you
require.

A generalized language that allows a user to select records from a database. It uses a command language, menu-driven method or a query by example (QBE) format for expressing the matching condition.

Query languages are usually included in DBMSs, and stand-alone packages are available for interrogating files in non-DBMS applications. See *query program*.

query program

Software that counts, sums and retrieves selected records from a database. It may be part of a large application and be limited to one or two kinds of retrieval, such as pulling up a customer account on screen, or it may refer to a query language that allows any condition to be searched and selected.

queue

Pronounced "Q." A temporary holding place for data. See *message queue* and *print queue*.

QuickApp

A software tool from Attachmate Corporation, Bellevue, WA, that adds screen scraping capability to client/server development systems. QuickApp scans and records the mainframe terminal screens that are displayed on the PC via a 3270 emulator. QuickApp navigation engines that work within languages, such as PowerBuilder, Visual Basic, SQLWindows, ObjectView and Visual C++, allow developers point and click access to on-screen fields.

Quick B

CompuServe's communications protocol for downloading files.

QuickBASIC

A popular BASIC compiler from Microsoft that adds advanced features to the BASIC language.

QuickBooks

A small business accounting system for Windows from Intuit, Inc., Menlo Park, CA. It works like the popular Quicken program, but is designed to track a whole business.

QuickC

A C compiler and development system from Microsoft that is compatible with Microsoft C and used by the beginner or occasional programmer. QuickC for Windows is a version that provides a Windows-based environment for developing Windows applications. See *Visual C++*.

QuickDB

An ODBC driver from Attachmate Corporation, Bellevue, WA, that provides an
APPC connection directly from the client to communicate with IBM's DRDA
interface.

QuickDraw

The graphics display system built into the Macintosh. It accepts commands from
the application and draws the corresponding objects on the screen. It provides a
consistent interface that software developers can work with.
QuickDraw GX adds capabilities to QuickDraw, including special graphics effects,
more sophisticated font kerning and ligature handling and enhanced printer
management. Applications must be programmed for GX in order to take advantage
of most of its capabilities.

Quicken

A popular financial management program for PCs and Macs from Intuit, Inc.,
Menlo Park, CA. It is used to write checks, organize investments and produce a
variety of reports for personal finance and small business.

QuickPascal

A pascal compiler from Microsoft that is compatible with Turbo Pascal and provides
object oriented capabilities.

QuickPeer

A software tool from Attachmate Corporation, Bellevue, WA, that generates the
communications code for developing three-tier client/server systems. It works with
languages such as PowerBuilder, Visual Basic, SQLWindows, ObjectView and Visual
C++. It eliminates writing highly technical code in languages such as C to support
the communications protocols.

Quicksilver

A family of dBASE III PLUS compilers originally developed by WordTech Systems,
Inc. In 1992, the technology was acquired by Borland. See *Arago*.

QuickTime

Multimedia extensions to Macintosh's System 7 that add sound and video
capabilities. A QuickTime file can contain up to 32 tracks of audio, video, MIDI or
other time-based control information. Most major Macintosh DBMSs (database
management systems) support QuickTime. Apple also provides a QuickTime for
Windows version for Windows-based PCs.

Quicktime VR

The virtual reality version of QuickTime. It allows subjects to be viewed on screen
in 3-D space. Scenes are compiled from renderings or from multiple still shots taken
of all sides.

quit

To exit the current program. It's a good habit to quit a program before turning the
computer off. Some programs don't close all files properly until quit is activated.

qwerty keyboard

The standard English language typewriter keyboard.
Q, w, e, r, t and y are the letters on the top left, alphabetic row. It was originally
designed to slow typing to prevent the keys from jamming. See *Dvorak keyboard*.

R

R/2, R/3

An integrated suite of client/server applications from SAP America, Inc. It is the client/server versions of SAP's R/2 mainframe applications. R/3 includes information systems for manufacturing, distribution, order processing, accounting and human resources. It includes the ABAP/4 Development Workbench.

R3000, R4000, R4400

See *MIPS Computer.*

RACE

(Random Access Card Equipment) An early RCA mass storage device. Magnetic cards were released from a cartridge, passed down a raceway and wrapped around a read/write head. It often jammed!

RACF

(Resource Access Control Facility) IBM mainframe security software introduced in 1976 that verifies user ID and password and controls access to authorized files and resources.

rack

A frame or cabinet into which components are mounted.

rack mounted

Components that are built to fit in a metal frame. Electronic devices, such as testing equipment and tape drives, are often rack mounted units.

RAD

(Rapid Application Development) Developing systems incrementally and delivering working pieces every three to four months, rather than waiting until the entire project is programmed before implementing it. Over the years, many information projects have failed, because, by the time the implemention took place, the business had changed.

RAD employs a variety of automated design and development tools, including CASE, 4GLs, visual programming and GUI builders, that get prototypes up and running quickly.

RAD was coined years ago by industry guru, James Martin, and focuses on personnel management and user involvement as much as on technology. Joint application development (JAD) is another RAD concept.

radio

The transmission of electromagnetic energy (radiation) over the air or through a hollow tube called a waveguide. Although radio is often thought of as only AM or FM, all airborne transmission is radio, including satellite and line-of-sight microwave.

radio buttons

A series of on-screen buttons that allow only one selection. If a button is currently selected, it will de-select when another button is selected.

Radio Shack

See *Tandy.*

radix

The base value in a numbering system. For example, in the decimal numbering system, the radix is 10.

radix point

The location in a number that separates the integral part from the fractional part. For example, in the decimal system, it is the decimal point.

RAD tool

Any program or utility that speeds up the development and programming of an application. Visual programming tools are widely used to quickly develop graphical front ends.

ragged right

In typography, non-uniform text at the right margin, such as the text you're reading.

RAID

(Redundant Array of Independent Disks) A category of disk arrays (two or more drives working together) that provide increased performance and various levels of error recovery and fault tolerance. The disk controller is designed to perform these techniques. RAID can also be implemented in software using standard controllers. The term used to mean Redundant Arrays of "Inexpensive" Disks, which was the title of a paper written in 1988 by the University of California at Berkeley. RAIDs were contrasted with SLEDs (Single Large Expensive Disks), which were still popular on large computers. Today, all hard disks are inexpensive by comparison, and The RAID Advisory Board, St. Peter, MN, sanctions RAID terminology and architecture.

Level	Configuration
0	Disk striping only. Offers high data transfer rates but no data reliability. It is essentially non-RAID, but is documented specifications.
1	Uses disk mirroring to provide 100% duplication of data. Offers highest cost of storage.
2	High performance. Uses Hamming code for error detection and correction. Interleaves data by bit or block. Rarely used.
3	High performance. Popular. Uses parity checking but cannot guarantee on-the-fly recovery. Interleaves data by bit or block.
4	Uses dedicated parity drive. Can be used with only two drives. Interleaves data by sector. Handles multiple I/Os from sophisticated operating systems. Not widely used.
5	Most popular RAID method. Works with two or more drives. Parity is spread across several drives. Can be made fault tolerant.
6	More reliable extension to Level 5. Parity is computed twice either with same or different algorithms.
53	Uses combination of disk striping (Level 0) and Level 3 methods to provide performance and reliability.

RAM

(Random Access Memory) The computer's primary workspace. The "random" means that the contents of each byte can be directly accessed without regard to the bytes before or after it. This is also true of other types of memory chips, including ROMs and PROMs. However, unlike ROMs and PROMs, RAM chips require power to maintain their content, which is why you must save your data onto disk before you turn the computer off. Any running programs and all the data they currently reference, such as the spreadsheet or word processing document you are working on, are lost without power. See *dynamic RAM, static RAM, memory* and *SIMM.*

RAMAC

(Random Access Method of Accounting and Control) The first hard disk computer which was introduced by IBM in 1956. All 50 of its 24" platters held a total of five million characters! It was half computer, half tabulator. It had a drum memory for program storage, but its I/O was wired by plugboard.

After 38 years, IBM resurrected the RAMAC name with the introduction of a high-capacity disk storage system in 1994. The differences between the 1956 and 1994 RAMACs are rather dramatic. Areal density rose from 2000 bits per square inch to 260 million increasing total storage capacity from 5MB to 90GB. Access times changed from 600 ms to 9.5 ms.

The First RAMAC

Each of the two-foot-diameter platters held 100 thousand bytes, or characters, as they were called in those days. That much recording surface today can hold 50 billion bytes! *(Photos courtesy of International Business Machines Corporation.)*

RAM card

(1) A printed circuit board containing memory chips that is plugged into a socket within the computer.

(2) A credit-card-sized module that contains memory chips and battery. See *memory card.*

RAM chip

(Random Access Memory chip) A memory chip. See *dynamic RAM, static RAM, RAM* and *memory.*

RAM cram

Insufficient memory to run applications, especially in DOS PCs with its 1MB memory limit.

RAMDAC

(Random Access Memory Digital to Analog Converter) The VGA controller chip that maintains the color palette and converts data from memory into analog signals for the monitor.

RAM disk

A disk drive simulated in memory. To use it, files are copied from magnetic disk into the RAM disk. Processing is faster, because there's no mechanical disk action, only memory transfers. Updated data files must be copied back to disk before the power is turned off, otherwise the updates are lost. Same as *E-disk* and *virtual disk*.

Ramdrive

A RAM disk driver that comes with DOS, starting with DOS 4.0.

RAMIS

See *CA-RAMIS*.

RAM network

See *Mobitex*.

RAM refresh

Recharging dynamic RAM chips many times per second in order to keep the bit patterns valid.

RAM resident

Refers to programs that remain in memory in order to interact with other programs or to be instantly popped up when required by the user. See *TSR*.

random access

Same as *direct access*.

random access memory

See *RAM*.

random noise

Same as *Gaussian noise*.

random number generator

A program routine that produces a random number. Random numbers are created easily in a computer, since there are many random events that take place; for example, the duration between keystrokes. Only a few milliseconds' difference is enough to seed a random number generation routine with a different number each time. Once seeded, an algorithm computes different numbers throughout the session.

range

(1) In data entry validation, a group of values from a minimum to a maximum.

(2) In spreadsheets, a series of cells that are worked on as a group. It may refer to a row, column or rectangular block defined by one corner and its diagonally opposite corner.

ransom note typography

Using too many fonts in a document. The term comes from the text in a ransom note that is pasted together from words cut out of different magazines and newspapers.

The ease with which fonts can be selected in a word processor has led many inexperienced people to use too many fonts in a document or newsletter. Typographers and graphics artists know that only two or three fonts are necessary for the most professional appearance.

RapidCAD

An earlier chipset from Intel that replaced the 386DX CPU and provided improved performance for CAD applications.

RARP

See *ARP*.

RAS

(1) (Remote Access Server) A network server that provides access to remote computer users via modem.

(2) (Remote Access Service) Software in Windows for Workgroups and Windows NT that provides access to remote computer users via modem. Windows for Workgroups provides client access to a Windows NT 3.5 server. Windows 95 provides connectivity to Windows, NetWare and UNIX servers that support the PPP protocol. Windows 95 also includes server support so users can dial into their own local machines and gain access to the network.

(3)(Reliability Availability Serviceability) Originally an IBM term, it refers to a computer system's overall reliability, its ability to respond to a failure and its ability to undergo maintenance without shutting it down entirely.

raster display

A display terminal that generates dots line by line on the screen. TVs and almost all computer screens use the raster method. Contrast with *vector display*.

raster graphics

In computer graphics, a technique for representing a picture image as a matrix of dots. It is the digital counterpart of the analog method used in TV. However, unlike TV, which uses one standard, there are many raster graphics standards. See *graphics*. Contrast with *vector graphics*.

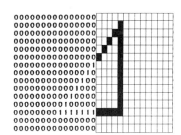

Raster graphics

rasterize

To perform the conversion of vector graphics images, vector fonts or outline fonts into bitmaps for display or printing. Unless output is printed on a plotter, which uses vectors directly, all non-bitmapped images must be rasterized into bitmaps for display or printing. See *font scaler*.

raster scan

Displaying or recording a video image line by line.

Rational Apex

A comprehensive Ada development environment for UNIX systems from Rational Software Corporation, Santa Clara, CA. It evolved from the original, proprietary hardware-based Ada environment that the company was founded on in 1980. The tools in this environment are being extended to C and C++.

Rational Rose

An object-oriented analysis and design tool that runs on Windows and UNIX platforms from Rational Software Corporation, Santa Clara, CA. It uses the Booch modeling method and is being extended to Rumbaugh's Object Modeling Technique (OMT). Rational is also unifying both approaches.

The base product is used for modeling applications, but versions of Rose are available that generate C++, Smalltalk, Ada, SQLWindows and ObjectPro code.

raw data

Data that has not been processed.

ray tracing

In computer graphics, the creation of reflections, refractions and shadows on a graphics image. It follows a series of rays from a specific light source and computes each pixel in the image to determine the effect of the light. It is a very process-intensive operation.

Ray Tracing
The shadows in this picture were created by the alogrithms in the software that simulate a hypothetical beam of light from a designated source. *(Photo courtesy of Computer Sciences Department, University of Utah.)*

R:BASE

A relational DBMS for PCs from Microrim, Inc., Bellevue, WA, that provides interactive data processing, a complete programming language and an application generator. It was the first DBMS to compete with dBASE II in the early 1980s.

RBOC

(Regional Bell Operating Company) One of seven regional telephone companies created by divestiture: Nynex, Bell Atlantic, BellSouth, Southwestern Bell, US West, Pacific Telesis and Ameritech.

RCA connector

Same as *phono connector.*

RCDD

See *BICSI.*

RCS

(1) (Remote Computer Service) A remote timesharing service.
(2) (Revision Control System) A UNIX utility that provides version control.

Rdb

(Relational DataBase/VMS) A relational DBMS from Digital widely used on its VAX series.

RDBMS

(Relational DataBase Management System) See *relational database*.

RDRAM

(Rambus **DRAM**) A dynamic RAM chip from Rambus, Inc., that transfers data at 500MBytes/sec (3-10 times faster than DRAM and VRAM chips). It requires modified motherboards, but eliminates the need for memory caches.

read

To input into the computer from a peripheral device (disk, tape, etc.). Like reading a book or playing an audio tape, reading does not destroy what is read.

A read is both an input and an output (I/O), since data is being output from the peripheral device and input into the computer. Memory is also said to be read when it is accessed to transfer data out to a peripheral device or to somewhere else in memory. Every peripheral or internal transfer of data is a read from somewhere and a write to somewhere else.

read channel

A circuit in a disk drive that encodes the data bits into flux changes for recording and decodes the magnetic flux changes into bits for reading.

read cycle

The operation of reading data from a memory or storage device.

reader

A machine that captures data for the computer, such as an optical character reader, magnetic card reader and punched card reader. A microfiche or microfilm reader is a self-contained machine that reads film and displays its contents.

read error

A failure to read the data on a storage or memory device. Although it is not a routine phenomenon, magnetic and optical recording surfaces can become contaminated with dust or dirt or be physically damaged, and cells in memory chips can malfunction.

When a read error occurs, the program will allow you to bypass it and move on to the next set of data, or it will end, depending on the operating system. However, if the damaged part of a disk contains control information, the rest of the file may be unreadable. In such cases, a recovery program must be used to retrieve the remaining data if there is no backup.

readme file

A text file copied onto software distribution disks that contains last-minute updates or errata that have not been printed in the documentation manual.

read only

(1) Refers to storage media that permanently hold their content; for example, ROM and CD-ROM.
(2) A file which can be read, but not updated or erased. See *file attribute*.

read-only attribute

A file attribute that, when turned on, indicates that a file can only be read, but not updated or erased.

readout

(1) A small display device that typically shows only a few digits or a couple of lines of data.

(2) Any display screen or panel.

read/write

(1) Refers to a device that can both input and output or transmit and receive.

(2) Refers to a file that can be updated and erased.

read/write channel

Same as *I/O channel*.

read/write head

A device that reads (senses) and writes (records) data on a magnetic disk or tape. For writing, the surface of the disk or tape is moved past the read/write head. By discharging electrical impulses at the appropriate times, bits are recorded as tiny, magnetized spots of positive or negative polarity.

For reading, the surface is moved past the read/write head, and the bits that are present induce an electrical current across the gap.

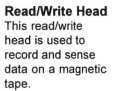

Read/Write Head
This read/write head is used to record and sense data on a magnetic tape.

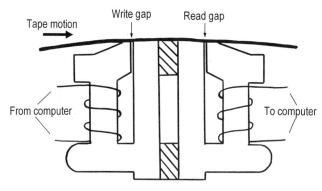

real address

Same as *absolute address*.

Realizer

See *CA-Realizer*.

RealMagic

An MPEG-1 playback board for PCs from Sigma Designs, Inc., Fremont, CA. Originally called ReelMagic, it also defined a programming interface that was the basis for OM1, now a de facto standard for interactive games.

Real Mode

An operational state in Intel 286s and up in which the computer functions as an 8086/8088. It is limited to one megabyte of memory. See *Protected Mode* and *Virtual 86 Mode*.

Real Mode driver

A PC driver that is written to the original 16-bit 8086/8088 architecture, which is limited to one megabyte of memory. Real Mode drivers must run within the first megabyte.

real storage

Real physical memory in a virtual memory system.

realtime

An immediate response. It refers to process control and embedded systems; for example, space flight computers must respond instantly to changing conditions. It also refers to fast transaction processing systems as well as any electronic operation fast enough to keep up with its real-world counterpart (animating complex images, transmitting live video, etc.).

realtime clock

An electronic circuit that maintains the time of day. It may also provide timing signals for timesharing operations.

realtime compression

The ability to compress and decompress data without any noticeable loss in speed compared to non-compressed data. PC products such as Stacker and SuperStor let you create a separate compressed drive on your hard disk. All data written to that drive is compressed and decompressed when read back. Realtime compression is included in DOS starting with DOS 6. See *JPEG*.

realtime conferencing

See *teleconferencing*.

realtime image

A graphics image that can be animated on screen at the same speed as the real-world object.

realtime information system

A computer system that responds to transactions by immediately updating the appropriate master files and/or generating a response in a time frame fast enough to keep an operation moving at its required speed. See *transaction processing*.

realtime operating system

A master control program that can provide immediate response to input signals and transactions.

realtime system

A computer system that responds to input signals fast enough to keep an operation moving at its required speed.

realtime video

The ability to transmit video live without missing any frames. It requires very high transmission capacity. See *ATM*.

reasonable test

A type of test that determines if a value falls within a range considered normal or logical. It can be made on electronic signals to detect extraneous noise as well as on data to determine possible input errors.

reboot

To reload the operating system and restart the computer. See *boot*.

receiver

A device that accepts signals. Contrast with *transmitter*.

record

(1) A group of related fields that store data about a subject (master record) or activity (transaction record). A collection of records make up a file.

Master records contain permanent data, such as account number, and variable data, such as balance due. Transaction records contain only permanent data, such as quantity and product code. See *master file* and *transaction file* for examples of record contents.

(2) In certain disk organization methods, a record is a block of data read and written at one time without any relationship to records in a file.

record format

Same as *record layout*.

record head

A device that writes a signal on tape. Some tape drives and all disk drives use a combination read/write head.

record layout

The format of a data record, which includes the name, type and size of each field in the record.

Name	Address	City	State	ZIP
Conrad, James R.	809 Garibaldi Lane	Benton Falls	TN	37255-0265

record locking

See *file and record locking*.

record mark

A symbol used to identify the end of a record.

record number

The sequential number assigned to each physical record in a file. Record numbers change when the file is sorted or records are added and deleted.

records management

The creation, retention and scheduled destruction of an organization's paper and film documents. Computer-generated reports and documents fall into the records management domain, but traditional data processing files do not.

recovery

See *backup & recovery, checkpoint/restart* and *tape backup*.

rectifier

An electrical circuit that converts AC into DC current with the use of diodes that act as one-way valves. Contrast with *inverter*.

recursion

In programming, the ability of a subroutine or program module to call itself. It is helpful for writing routines that solve problems by repeatedly processing the output of the same process.

recycle bin

In Windows 95, an icon of a waste can used for deleting files. The icon of a file or folder is dragged to the trash can and released. See *trash can*.

redaction

The editing done to sensitive documents before release to the public.

Red Book

(1) The documentation of the U.S. National Security Agency that defines criteria for secure networks. The volumes are "Trusted Network Interpretation of the Trusted Computer System Evaluation Criteria" (NCSC-TG-005) and "Trusted Network Interpetation Environments Guideline: Guidance for Applying the Trusted Network Interpretation" (NCSC-TG-011). It is the network counterpart of the Orange Book for computers. See *NCSC*.

(2) The documentation for the technical specification of audio CDs (CD-DA), which includes such details as sampling and transfer rates. "Red Book audio" refers to digital sound that conforms to the common standard used in music compact discs. See *CD*.

redirection

Diverting data from its normal destination to another; for example, to a disk file instead of the printer, or to a server's disk instead of the local disk. See *redirector*.

redirector

In a LAN, software that routes workstation (client) requests for data to the server.

redundancy check

In communications, a method for detecting transmission errors by appending a calculated number onto the end of each segment of data. See *CRC*.

reengineering

Using information technology to improve performance and cut costs. Its main premise, as popularized by the book "Reengineering the Corporation" by Michael Hammer and James Champy, is to examine the goals of an organization and to redesign work and business processes from the ground up rather than simply automate existing tasks and functions.

According to the authors, reengineering is driven by open markets and competition. No longer, can we enjoy the protection of our own country's borders as we could in the past. Today, we are in a global economy, and worldwide customers are more sophisticated and demanding.

In addition, modern industrialization was based on theories of fragmentation and specialization, which have led to the "left eye" specialist with millions of workers doing dreary, monotonous jobs as well as the creations of departments, functions and business units governed by multiple layers of management. Management has been the necessary glue to control the fragmented workplace.

In order to be successful in the future, the organization will have fewer layers of management and fewer, but more highly-skilled workers that do more complex tasks. Information technology, used for the past 50 years to automate manual tasks, will be used to enable new work models. The successful organization will not be "technology driven," rather it will be "technology enabled."

Although reengineering may, in fact, reduce a department of 200 employees down to 50, it is not just about eliminating jobs. It's goals are customer oriented; for example, it's about processing a contract in 24 hours instead of two weeks or performing a telecommunications service in one day instead of 30. It's about reducing the time it takes to get a drug to market from eight years to four years or reducing the number of suppliers from 200,000 to 700.

Reengineering is about radical improvement, not incremental changes.

reentrant code

A programming routine that can be used by multiple programs simultaneously. It is used in operating systems and other system software as well as in multithreading, where concurrent events are taking place. It is written so that none of its code is modifiable (no values are changed) and it does not keep track of anything. The calling programs keep track of their own progress (variables, flags, etc.), thus one copy of the reentrant routine can be shared by an any number of users or processes. Conceptually, it is as if several people were each baking a cake from a single copy of a recipe on the wall. Everyone looks at the master recipe, but keeps track of their own progress by jotting down the step they are at on their own scratchpad so they can pick up where they left off. The master recipe is never disturbed.

referential integrity

A database management safeguard that ensures every foreign key matches a primary key. For example, customer numbers in a customer file are the primary keys, and customer numbers in the order file are the foreign keys. If a customer record is deleted, the order records must also be deleted otherwise they are left without a primary reference. If the DBMS doesn't test for this, it must be programmed into the applications.

reflection mapping

In computer graphics, a technique for simulating reflections on an object.

Reflective Memory

A memory bus technology from Encore Computer that allows simultaneous reads and writes to multiple memories. It is used in Encore's SMP computer systems, in which memory is shared among multiple CPUs.

reflective spot

A metallic foil placed on each end of a magnetic tape. It reflects light to a photosensor to signal the end of tape.

reflective VGA

An LCD screen that needs bright ambient light for viewing. Backlit and sidelit screens are much easier to see.

reformat

(1)To change the record layout of a file or database.
(2)To initialize a disk over again.

refraction

The bending of electromagnetic waves as they pass at an angle between materials with different refractive indices. Refraction is an important characteristic in optical systems, which deal with light travelling through optical fibers and lenses. See *refractive index.*

refractive index

A measurement of how light bends in an optical medium such as an optical fiber or lens. The measurement is the ratio of the speed of light in a vacuum compared to the speed of light through the medium. See *refraction.*

refresh

To continuously charge a device that cannot hold its content. CRTs must be refreshed, because the phosphors hold their glow for only a few milliseconds. Dynamic RAM chips require refreshing to maintain their charged bit patterns.

refresh rate

(1) The number of times per second that a device is re-energized, such as a CRT or dynamic RAM chip. See *vertical scan frequency*.

(2) In computer graphics, the time it takes to redraw or redisplay an image on screen.

REGEDIT.EXE

The Registration editor in Windows 95 that allows updating of the Registry. See *Registry*.

regenerator

(1) In communications, the same as a *repeater*.

(2) In electronics, a circuit that repeatedly supplies current to a memory or display device that continuously loses its charges or content.

ReGIS

(REmote Graphics InStruction) A graphics language from Digital used on graphics terminals and first introduced on the PDP-11.

register

A small, high-speed computer circuit that holds values of internal operations, such as the address of the instruction being executed and the data being processed. When a program is debugged, register contents may be analyzed to determine the computer's status at the time of failure.

In microcomputer assembly language programming, programmers reference registers routinely. Assembly languages in larger computers are often at a higher level.

register level compatibility

A hardware component that is 100% compatible with another device. It implies that the same type, size and names of registers are used.

Registry

A Windows 95 database that holds configuration data about the hardware and environment of the PC it has been installed in. It is made up of the SYSTEM.DAT and USER.DAT files. Many settings that were previously stored in WIN.INI and SYSTEM.INI in Windows 3.1 are in the Registry.

The Registry can be edited directly with the Registry editor (REGEDIT.EXE), but that is usually only done for very technical enhancements or as a last resort. Routine access is done via the Control Panels in My Computer and the Properties menu option, which is on the File menu. In addition, right clicking on almost every icon brings the option of selecting Properties.

regression analysis

In statistics, a mathematical method of modeling the relationships among three or more variables. It is used to predict the value of one variable given the values of the others. For example, a model might estimate sales based on age and gender. A regression analysis yields an equation that expresses the relationship. See *correlation*.

regression testing

In software development, testing a program that has been modified in order to ensure that additional bugs have not been introduced. When a program is enhanced, testing is often done only on the new features. However, adding source code to a program often introduces errors in other routines, and many of the old and stable functions must be retested along with the new ones.

reinstall

To go through the installation process once again, because files have become corrupted. See *reload*.

related files

Two or more data files that can be matched on some common condition, such as account number or name.

relational algebra

(1) The branch of mathematics that deals with relations; for example, AND, OR, NOT, IS and CONTAINS.
(2) In relational database, a collection of rules for dealing with tables; for example, JOIN, UNION and INTERSECT.

relational calculus

The rules for combining and manipulating relations; for example De Morgan's law, "the complement of a union is equal to the union of the complements."

relational database

A database organization method that links files together as required. In non-relational systems (hierarchical, network), records in one file contain embedded pointers to the locations of records in another, such as customers to orders and vendors to purchases. These are fixed links set up ahead of time to speed up daily processing.

In a relational database, relationships between files are created by comparing data, such as account numbers and names. A relational system has the flexibility to take any two or more files and generate a new file from the records that meet the matching criteria (see *join*).

Routine queries often involve more than one data file. For example, a customer file and an order file can be linked in order to ask a question that relates to information in both files, such as the names of the customers that purchased a particular product. In practice, a pure relational query can be very slow. In order to speed up the process, indexes are built and maintained on the key fields used for matching. Sometimes, indexes are created "on the fly" when the data is requested.

The term was coined in 1970 by Edgar Codd, whose objective was to easily accomodate a user's ad hoc request for selected data.

Relational terms	Common terms
table or relation	file
tuple	record
attribute	field

relational DBMS

See *relational database* and *DBMS*.

relational operator

A symbol that specifies a comparison between two values.

Relational Operator		Symbol
EQ	Equal to	=
NE	Not equal to	<> or # or !=
GT	Greater than	>
GE	Greater than or equal to	>=
LT	Less than	<
LE	Less than or equal to	<=

relational query

A question asked about data contained in two or more tables in a relational database. The relational query must specify the tables required and what the condition is that links them; for example, matching account numbers. Relational queries are tricky to specify. Both the knowledge of the query language and the database structure is necessary. Even with graphical interfaces that let you drag a line from one field to another, you still need to know how the tables were designed to be related.

A Relational Query in Paradox

In the mid 1980s, Paradox was the first DBMS on a PC that made linking tables easier. Although not as sophisticated as some of today's query methods, the ability to associate relationships by typing in a sample word was a breakthrough. The Customer No. and Part No. fields are related by typing in the common words "ABC" and "XYZ." Any words would suffice as long as they are the same. The word is typed in after pressing a key stating that a relationship would be entered.

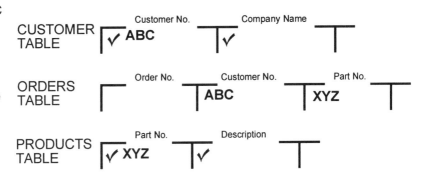

✓ The checkmark is a special symbol inserted to include this field in the result.

relative address

A memory address that represents some distance from a starting point (base address), such as the first byte of a program or table. The absolute address is derived by adding it to the base address.

relative path

An implied path. When a command is expressed that references files, the current working directory is the implied, or relative, path if the full path is not explicitly stated. Contrast with *full path*.

relative vector

In computer graphics, a vector with end points designated in coordinates relative to a base address. Contrast with *absolute vector*.

relay

An electrical switch that allows a low power to control a higher one. A small current energizes the relay, which closes a gate, allowing a large current to flow through.

Relay Gold

A PC communications program from Microcom, Inc., Norwood, MA, that provides standard asynchronous transmission as well as mainframe file transfer and LAN support.

reload

To load a program from disk into memory once again in order to run it. Reload is entirely different than reinstall. Reinstall means that you have to run the install program from a floppy disk or CD-ROM and perform the installation procedure all over again.

Reloading is common when the program crashes. Reinstalling is much less common, but necessary if program files have become unreadable due to damaged sectors on the disk or because files were accidentally erased. This can also happen due to program error, in which the program erroneously writes incorrect data to some of its own configuration and status files.

relocatable code

Machine language that can be run from any memory location. All modern computers run relocatable code. See *base/displacement*.

Rem

(REMarks) A programming language statement used for documentation. Rem statements are not executed by the compiler. They are created for people to read. Rem is also used in DOS batch files for comments as well as for disabling instructions. For example, inserting the word **rem** at the beginning of a line in AUTOEXEC.BAT or CONFIG.SYS prevents the executable function on that line from taking place. The line is said to be "rem'd out."

remedial maintenance

A repair service that is required due to a malfunction of the product. Contrast with *preventive maintenance*.

remote access server

A computer in a LAN that provides remote access to portable computers. It supports a number of modems and/or ISDN adapters and allows remote users dial-up access to the network. It may be employed as remote access software in a server or it may be a proprietary system such as Shiva's LANRover. See *RAS* and *communications server*.

remote access software

See *remote control software*.

remote batch

See *RJE*.

remote communications

(1) Communicating via long distances.
(2) See *remote control software*.

remote console

A terminal or workstation in a remote location that is used to monitor and control a local computer.

remote control software

Software, installed in both machines, that allows a user at a local computer to have control of a remote computer via modem. Both users run the remote computer and see the same screen. Remote control operation is used to take control of an unattended desktop personal computer from a remote location as well as to provide instruction and technical support to remote users.

Remote control is different than a remote node operation. In remote control, only keystrokes are transmitted from and screen updates are transmitted to the remote machine as all processing takes place in the local computer. All file transfers are done locally or over a high-speed LAN. In a remote node setup, the user is logged onto the network using the phone line as an extension to the network. Thus, all traffic has to flow over a low-speed telephone line.

When working with large files, remote control is faster than remote node, and it gives users the flexibility to do whatever they want on the local machine. However, remote control sessions move screen changes constantly to the remote machine and graphics applications are slow. Remote control usually requires more network ports than remote node for the same number of users. In addition, in remote control, you don't do any local processing in the remote machine so online sessions are often longer than with remote node. See *application sharing*.

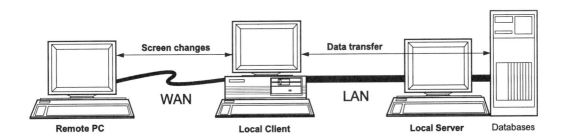

Screen changes   Data transfer

WAN   LAN

Remote PC   **Local Client**   **Local Server**   Databases

Remote Control

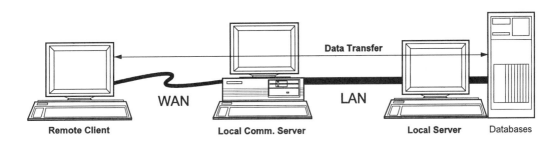

Data Transfer

WAN   LAN

Remote Client   **Local Comm. Server**   **Local Server**   Databases

Remote Node

remote node
See *remote control software*.

remote-office router
A router specialized to route data to its counterpart in a remote site. Configuring the router is done at the central site, thus network administration is simplified. 3Com pioneered the concept with its Boundary Routing.

remote resource
A peripheral device, such as a disk, modem or printer, that is available for shared use in the network. Contrast with *local resource*.

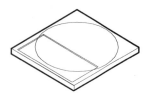

removable disk

A disk unit that is inserted into a disk drive for reading and writing and removed when not required; for example, floppy disks, disk cartridges and disk packs. Other than floppies, the leading removable disk drives on desktop computers are SyQuest's 3.5" and 5.25" magnetic disks and 3.5" and 5.25" optical disks from a variety of manufacturers.

render

To draw a real-world object as it actually appears.

rendering

In computer graphics, creating a 3-D image that incorporates the simulation of lighting effects, such as shadows and reflection.

Renderman interface

A graphics format from Pixar, Point Richmond, CA, that uses photorealistic image synthesis. Developer's Renderman (PCs and UNIX) and Mac Renderman (Macintosh) are Pixar programs that apply photorealistic looks and surfaces to 3-D objects.

Renovator

See *ESL Renovator*.

repeater

(1) A communications device that amplifies or regenerates the data signal in order to extend the transmission distance. Available for both analog and digital signals, it is used extensively in long distance transmission. It is also used to tie two LANs of the same type together. Repeaters work at layer 1 of the OSI model. See *bridge* and *router*.

(2) The term may also refer to a multiport repeater, which is a hub in a 10BaseT network.

Replica

Document exchange software from Farallon Computing, Inc., Alameda, CA, that converts a Windows or Macintosh document into a proprietary file format for viewing on other machines. The Replica viewer can be distributed to the target machines or embedded within the Replica document file itself, turning it into a single-document viewer.

replication

In database management, the ability to keep distributed databases synchronized by routinely copying the entire database or subsets of the database to other servers in the network.

There are various replication methods. Primary site replication maintains the master copy of the data in one site and sends read-only copies to the other sites. In a workflow environment, the master copy can move from one site to another. This is called shared replication or transferred ownership, replication. In symmetric replication, also known as update-anywhere or peer-to-peer replication, each site can receive updates, and all other sites are updated. Failover replication, or hot backup, maintains an up-to-date copy of the data at a different site for backup. See *distributed database*.

report

A printed or microfilmed collection of facts and figures with page numbers and page headings. See *report writer* and *query*.

report file
A file that describes how a report is printed.

report format
The layout of a report showing page and column headers, page numbers and totals.

report generator
Same as *report writer*.

Report Program Generator
See *RPG*.

report writer
Software that prints a report based on a description of its layout. As a stand-alone program or part of a DBMS or file manager, it can sort selected records into a new sequence for printing. It may also print standard mailing labels.

A report is described by entering text for the page header and stating the position of the print columns (data fields) and which ones are totalled or subtotalled. Once created, the description is stored in a report file for future use.

Developed in the early 1970s, report writers (report generators) were the precursor to query languages and were the first programs to generate computer output without having to be programmed.

repository
A database of information about applications software that includes author, data, elements, inputs, processes, outputs and interrelationships. A repository is used in a CASE or application development system in order to identify objects and business rules for reuse. It may also be designed to integrate third-party CASE products.

reproducer
An early tabulating machine that duplicated punched cards.

reprographics
Duplicating printed materials using various kinds of printing presses and high-speed copiers.

ResEdit
(Resource Editor) A Macintosh system utility used to edit the resource fork.

reserved word
A verb or noun in a programming or command language that is part of the native language.

reset button
A computer button or key that reboots the computer. All current activities are stopped cold, and any data in memory is lost. On a printer, the reset button clears the printer's memory and readies it to accept new data.

resident module
The part of a program that must remain in memory at all times. Instructions and data that stay in memory can be accessed instantly.

resident program
A program that remains in memory at all times. See *TSR*.

resistor

An electronic component that resists the flow of current in an electronic circuit.

Resistors

Resistors come in a variety of sizes and configurations. They are also built into the chip along with other tiny electronic components by the tens and hundreds of thousands.

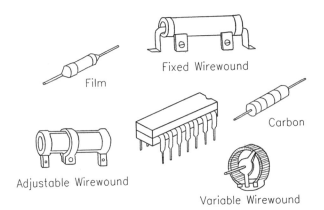

Film

Fixed Wirewound

Carbon

Adjustable Wirewound

Variable Wirewound

resolution

(1) The degree of sharpness of a displayed or printed character or image. On screen, resolution is expressed as a matrix of dots. VGA resolution of 640x480 means 640 dots across each of 480 lines. Sometimes the number of colors are added to the spec; for example, 640x480x16 or 640x480x256. The same resolution looks sharper on a small screen than a large one. See *how to select a PC display system*.

For printers, resolution is expressed as the number of dots per linear inch. 300 dpi means 90,000 dots per square inch (300x300). Laser printers and plotters have resolutions from 300 to 1000 dpi and more, whereas most display screens provide less than 100 dpi. That means jagged lines on screen may smooth out when they print.

(2) The number of bits used to record the value of a sample in a digitized signal. See *sampling rate*.

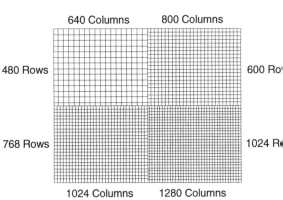

640 Columns   800 Columns

480 Rows   600 Ro

768 Rows   1024 R

1024 Columns   1280 Columns

resolve

To change, transform or solve a problem. The phrase "external references are resolved" refers to determining the addresses that link modules together; that is, solving the unknown links.

resource compiler

In a graphical interface (GUI), software that converts and links a resource (menu, dialog box, icon, font, etc.) into the executable program.

resource fork

The resource part of a Macintosh file. For example, in a text document, it contains format codes with offsets into the text in the data fork. In a program, it contains executable code, menus, windows, dialog boxes, buttons, fonts and icons.

resource requirements
The components of a system that are required by software or hardware. It refers to resources that have finite limits such as memory and disk. In a PC, it may refer to the resources required to install a new peripheral, namely IRQs, DMA channels, I/O addresses and memory addresses. All of these are finite resources within the computer. See *how to install a PC peripheral.*

response time
The time it takes for the computer to comply with a user's request, such as looking up a customer record.

responsibility
In object technology, a processing step that an object can perform.

restart
To resume computer opertion after a planned or unplanned termination. See *boot, warm boot* and *checkpoint/restart.*

restricted function
A computer or operating system function that cannot be used by an application program.

retrieve
To call up data that has been stored in a computer system. When a user queries a database, the data is retrieved into the computer first and then transmitted to the screen.

return key
Also called the *enter key*, the keyboard key used to signal the end of a line of data or the end of a command. In word processing, return is pressed at the end of a paragraph, and a return code is inserted into the text at that point. See *CR.*

reusability
The ability to use all or the greater part of the same programming code or system design in another application.

reverse engineer
To isolate the components of a completed system. When a chip is reverse engineered, all the individual circuits that make up the chip are identified. Source code can be reverse engineered into design models or specifications. Machine language can be reversed into assembly langauge (see *disassembler*).

reverse polish notation
A mathematical expression in which the numbers precede the operation. For example, 2 + 2 would be expressed as 2 2 +, and 10 - 3 * 4 would be 10 3 4 * -. See *FORTH.*

reverse video
A display mode used to highlight characters on screen. For example, if the normal display mode is black on white, reverse video would be white on black.

revision level
See *version number.*

rewritable

Refers to storage media that can be written, erased and rewritten many times. Magnetic disks and tapes and magneto-optic disks are examples. See *write once.*

REXX

(REstructured EXtended eXecutor) An IBM mainframe structured programming language that runs under VM/CMS and MVS/TSO. It can be used as a general-purpose macro language that sends commands to application programs and to the operating systems. REXX is also included in OS/2 Version 2.0.

The following REXX example converts Fahrenheit to Celsius:

```
Say "Enter Fahrenheit "
Pull FAHR
Say "Celsius is " (FAHR - 32) * (5 / 9)
```

RF

(Radio Frequency) The range of electromagnetic frequencies above the audio range and below visible light. All broadcast transmission, from AM radio to satellites, falls into this range, which is between 30KHz and 300GHz. See *RF modulation.*

RFI

(Radio Frequency Interference) High-frequency electromagnetic waves that eminate from electronic devices such as chips.

RF/ID

(Radio Frequency/IDentification) An identification system that uses tags that transmit a wireless message. The tag gets its power from a hand-held gun/reading unit.

RF modulation

The transmission of a signal through a carrier frequency. In order to connect to a TV's antenna input, some home computers and all VCRs provide RF modulation of a TV channel, usually Channel 3 or 4. See *FCC class.*

RFP

(Request For Proposal) A document that invites a vendor to submit a bid for hardware, software and/or services. It may provide a general or very detailed specification of the system.

RFS

(Remote File System) A distributed file system for UNIX computers introduced by AT&T in 1986 with UNIX System V Release 3.0. It is similar to Sun's NFS, but only for UNIX systems.

RF shielding

A material that prohibits electromagnetic radiation from penetrating it. Personal computers and electronic devices used in the home must meet U.S. government standards for electromagnetic interference.

RFT

See *DCA.*

RGB

(Red Green Blue) The color model used for generating video on a monitor. It displays colors as varying intensities of red, green and blue dots. When all three are turned on high, white is produced. As intensities are equally lowered, shades of gray are derived. The base color of the screen appears when all dots are off. See *colors.*

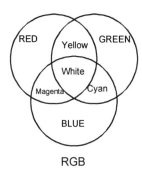
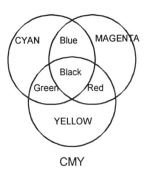

DISPLAY SCREENS
(Additive)

RED · Yellow · GREEN · White · Magenta · Cyan · BLUE

RGB

PRINTERS
(Subtractive)

CYAN · Blue · MAGENTA · Black · Green · Red · YELLOW

CMY

RGB monitor

(1) A video display screen that requires separate red, green and blue signals from the computer. It generates a better image than composite signals (TV) which merge the three colors together. It comes in both analog and digital varieties.

(2) Sometimes refers to a CGA monitor that accepts digital RGB signals.

ribbon cable

A thin, flat, multiconductor cable that is widely used in electronic systems; for example, to interconnect peripheral devices to the computer internally.

Ribbon Cable

rich e-mail

E-mail annotated with voice messages.

rich text

(1) Text that includes formatting commands for bold, italic, etc. It may also refer to the mixing of graphics with text.

(2) Text in Microsoft's RTF format. See *RTF*.

RIFF

(1) (Resource Interchange File Format) A multimedia data format jointly introduced by IBM and Microsoft. See *MCI*.

(2) An earlier raster graphics format developed for Letraset's ImageStudio and Ready, Set, Go programs for the Macintosh.

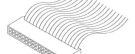

right click

To press the right button on the mouse.

right justify

Same as *flush right*.

rightsizing

Selecting a computer system, whether micro, mini or mainframe, that best meets the needs of the application.

rigid disk

Same as *hard disk*.

ring

One stage or level in a set of prioritized stages or levels, typically involved with security and password protection.

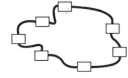

ring network

A communications network that connects terminals and computers in a continuous loop.

RIP

(1) (Raster Image Processor) In computer graphics, the hardware, software (or both) that prepares data for the screen or printer, which is a raster output device. RIPs are designed to rasterize a specific type of data, such as PostScript or vector graphics images, as well as different kinds of raster data.

As desktop computers become more powerful, software RIPs become more appealing than hardware RIPs. Software can be upgraded much more easily than hardware, and the operation can be speeded up by installing the RIP in a faster CPU.

(2) (Routing Information Protocol) A routing protocol in TCP/IP and NetWare used to identify all attached networks as well as the number of router hops required to reach them. The responses are used to update a router's routing table.

(3) (Remote Imaging Protocol) A graphics format from TeleGrafix Communications, Inc., designed for transmitting graphics over low-speed lines. Using a communications program that supports RIP enables graphical interfaces to be used on a BBS with respectable performance via modem.

RISC

(Reduced Instruction Set Computer) A computer architecture that reduces chip complexity by using simpler instructions. RISC compilers have to generate software routines to perform complex instructions that were previously done in hardware by CISC computers. In RISC, the microcode layer and associated overhead is eliminated.

RISC keeps instruction size constant, bans the indirect addressing mode and retains only those instructions that can be overlapped and made to execute in one machine cycle or less. The RISC chip is faster than its CISC counterpart and is designed and built more economically.

RISC System/6000

See *RS/6000*.

RJ-11

A four or six-wire telephone connector. The four-wire plug and socket is the common connector between the handset and the telephone and for plugging telephones and modems into wall outlets.

RJ-45

An eight-wire telephone connector.

RJE

(Remote Job Entry) Transmitting batches of transactions from a remote terminal or computer. The receiving computer processes the data and may transmit the results back to the RJE site for printing. RJE hardware at remote sites can employ teleprinters with disk or tape storage or complete computer systems.

RLE

(Run Length Encoding) A simple data compression method that converts a run of identical characters into a code. A rough example might be []36* where [] is a code and 36* means 36 *'s follow. Microsoft includes an RLE codec in Video for Windows; however, other compression methods are far superior for full-motion video.

RLL

(Run Length Limited) An encoding method commonly used on magnetic disks, including RLL, IDE, SCSI, ESDI, SMD and IPI interfaces. The actual number of bits recorded on the disk is greater than the data bits. Earlier drives inserted extra bits into the data stream so there was more space between signals when reading the data back. As electronics improve, fewer extra bits are inserted, and the ratio of data bits to recorded bits becomes greater.

The "run length" is the number of consecutive 0s before a 1 bit is recorded. For example, RLL 1,7 means there must be at least one 0 between every 1, and the 7 means a maximum of eight time periods between flux transitions. See *hard disk*.

RLL interface

See *ST506 RLL*.

rlogin

(Remote **LOGIN**) A UNIX command that allows a user to remotely log into a server on the network as if it were a terminal directly connected to that computer. After logging in, the user can use the services on that server. Rlogin is similar to the Telnet command, except that rlogin also passes information to the server about the type of client machine, or terminal, used. See *rsh*.

RMON

See *SNMP*.

RMS

(1) (Record Management Services) A file management system used in VAXs.
(2) (Root Mean Square) A method used to measure electrical output in volts and watts.

rn

(ReadNews) A newsreader for reading the messages in a newsgroup on the Internet. See *Usenet*.

RoboCAD

A PC CAD program from Robo Systems International, Inc., Newtown, PA, that includes a wide variety of features and text functions. It provides up to 256 colors and layers, has two drawing pages and a scratch pad, and can transfer data to its solid modeling program.

robot

A stand-alone hybrid computer system that performs physical and computational activities. It is a multiple-motion device with one or more arms and joints that is capable of performing many different tasks like a human. It can be designed similar to human form, although most industrial robots don't resemble people at all.

It is used extensively in manufacturing for welding, riveting, scraping and painting. Office and consumer applications are also being developed. Robots, designed with AI, can respond to unstructured situations. For example, specialized robots can identify objects in a pile, select the objects in the appropriate sequence and assemble them into a unit.

Robots use analog sensors for recognizing real-world objects and digital computers for their direction. Analog to digital converters convert temperature, motion, pressure, sound and images into binary code for the robot's computer. The computer directs the physical actions of the arms and joints by pulsing their motors.

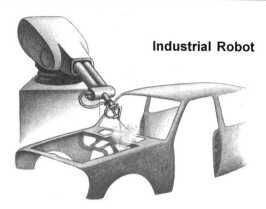

Industrial Robot

robotics

The art and science of the creation and use of robots.

robust

Refers to software without bugs that handles abnormal conditions well. It is often said that there is no software package totally bug free. Any program can exhibit odd behavior under certain conditions, but a robust program will not lock up the computer, cause damage to data or send the user through an endless chain of dialog boxes without purpose. Whether or not a program can be totally bug free will be debated forever. See *industrial strength*.

ROFL

Digispeak for "rolling on the floor laughing."

rollback

A database management system feature that reverses the current transaction out of the database, returning the database to its former state. This is done when some failure interrupts a half-completed transaction.

roll in/roll out

A swapping technique for freeing up memory temporarily in order to perform another task. The current program or program segment is stored (rolled out) on disk, and another program is brought into (rolled in) that memory space.

rollover

See *n-key rollover*.

ROM

(Read Only Memory) A memory chip that permanently stores instructions and data. Its contents are created at the time of manufacture and cannot be altered. ROM chips are used to store control routines in personal computers (ROM BIOS), peripheral controllers and other electronic equipment. They are also often the sole component of a cartridge that plugs into printers, video games and other systems. When computers are used in hand-held instruments, appliances, automobiles and any other such devices, the instructions for their routines are generally stored in ROM chips or some other non-volatile chip such as a PROM or EPROM. Instructions may also be stored in a ROM section within a general-purpose computer on a chip. See *PROM, EPROM* and *EEPROM*. Contrast with *RAM*.

ROMable

Machine language capable of being programmed into a ROM chip. Being "read only" the chip cannot be updated and ROMable programs must use RAM or disk for holding changing data.

ROM BIOS

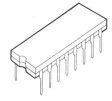

(ROM Basic Input Output System) In a PC, a basic part of the operating system permanently stored in a ROM chip. PCs have been traditionally built with the BIOS in ROM. Increasingly however, the BIOS is stored in a flash memory chip so that it can be updated in place rather than requiring a physical replacement. See *BIOS.*

ROM BIOS swapping

Alternating areas in the UMA (640K-1M) between ROM BIOSs and applications as needed.

ROM card

A credit-card-sized module that contains permanent software or data. See *memory card.*

ROM emulator

A circuit that helps debug a ROM chip by simulating the ROM with RAM. The RAM circuit plugs into the ROM socket. Since RAM can be written over, whereas ROM cannot, programming changes can be made easily.

root directory

In hierarchical file systems, the starting point in the hierarchy. When the computer is first started, the root directory is the current directory. Access to directories in the hierarchy requires naming the directories that are in its path.
In DOS, the command line symbol for the root directory is a backslash (\). In UNIX, it is a slash (/).

ROP

(1) (Raster Operation) An instruction that manipulates the bits of a raster graphics image in some manner.
(2) (RISC Operation) An instruction in a RISC processor.

rotational delay

The amount of time it takes for the disk to rotate until the required location on the disk reaches the read/write head.

RO terminal

(Receive Only terminal) A printing device only (no keyboard).

round robin

Continuously repeating sequence, such as the polling of a series of terminals, one after the other, over and over again.

routable protocol

A communications protocol that contains a network address as well as a device address, allowing data to be routed from one network to another. Examples of routable protocols are SNA, OSI, TCP/IP, XNS, IPX, AppleTalk and DECnet. Contrast with *non-routable protocol.*

router

A computer system that stores and forwards data packets from one local area network

(LAN) or wide area network (WAN) to another. Routers see the network as network addresses and all the possible paths between them. They read the network address in a transmitted message and can make a decision on how to send it based on the most expedient route (traffic load, line costs, speed, bad lines, etc.). Routers work at the network layer (layer 3 of the OSI model), whereas bridges work at the data link layer (layer 2).

Routers with high-speed buses in the gigabit range can serve as an internet backbone, interconnecting all networks in the enterprise.

Routers can only route a message that is transmitted by a routable protocol such as IPX and IP. Messages in non-routable protocols, such as NetBIOS and LAT, cannot be routed, but they can be transferred from LAN to LAN via a bridge. Because routers have to inspect the network address in the protocol, they do more processing than a bridge and add overhead to the network.

In Novell terminology, a router is a network-layer bridge.

The major router vendors are Cisco Systems and Bay Networks. See *bridge, brouter, gateway, hub* and *intermediate node routing*.

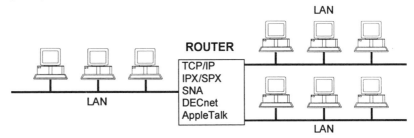

router protocol

A protocol used by routers to report their status to other routers in the network and keep their internal tables up-to-date. See *RIP* and *OSPF*.

routine

A set of instructions that perform a task. Same as *subroutine, module, procedure* and *function*.

routing

See *intermediate node routing* and *router*.

routing protocol

A communications protocol used to update the routing table in a router.

row

A horizontal set of data or components. In a graph, it is called the x-axis. Contrast with *column*.

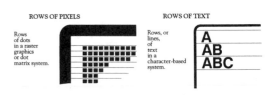

ROWS OF PIXELS

Rows of dots in a raster graphics or dot matrix system.

ROWS OF TEXT

Rows, or lines, of text in a character-based system.

A
AB
ABC

ROWS OF DATA

	NAME	STREET	BALANCE
Rows, lines or records in a spreadsheet, text or database file.	Jones, Jennifer A.	10 West Main Ave.	0000208.49
	Russo, George C.	23 East Benton St.	0000107.49
	Morrison, Emil T.	1240 Parkway East	0001005.77
	Fernandez, Joseph R.	39 Gate Drive	0003484.49

RPC

(Remote Procedure Call) A type of interface that allows one program to call another in a remote location. Using a standard RPC allows an application to be used in a variety of networks without change.

RPG

(Report Program Generator) One of the first program generators designed for business reports, introduced in 1964 by IBM. In 1970, RPG II added enhancements that made it a mainstay programming language for business applications on IBM's System/3x midrange computers. RPG III, which added more programming structures, is widely used on the AS/400. RPG statements are written in columnar format.

The following RPG III System/38-AS/400 example changes Fahrenheit to Celsius. The A lines are Data Description Specs (DDS) code. They define a display file and are compiled separately. The F line links RPG code (C lines) to the A lines:

```
A         R FHEITR
A                              6 18'Enter Fahrenheit: '
A         FRHEIT     3Y   0B   6 42DSPATR(PC)
A                                EDTCDE(J)
A                              9 18'Celsius is '
A         CGRADE     3Y   0B   9 42DSPATR(PC)
A                                EDTCDE(J)
FFHEITD   CF     E        WORKSTN
C                    EXFMTFHEITR
C                    Z-ADDO          CGRADE
C         FRHEIT     SUB    32       CGRADE
C         CGRADE     MULT   5        CGRADE
C         CGRADE     DIV    9        CGRADE     H
C                    EXFMTFHEITR
```

rpm

(Revolutions Per Minute) The measurement of the rotational speed of a disk drive. Floppy disks rotate at 300 rpm, while hard disks rotate from 2,400 to 3,600 rpm and more.

RPQ

(Request for Price Quotation) A document that requests a price for hardware, software or services to solve a specific problem. It is created by the customer and delivered to the vendor.

RS-170

An NTSC standard for composite video signals.

RS-232

(Recommended Standard-232) A TIA/EIA standard for serial transmission between computers and peripheral devices (modem, mouse, etc.). It uses a 25-pin DB-25 or 9-pin DB-9 connector. Its normal cable limitation of 50 feet can be extended to several hundred feet with high-quality cable.

RS-232 defines the purpose and signal timing for each of the 25 lines; however, many applications use less than a dozen. RS-232 transmits positive voltage for a 0 bit, negative voltage for a 1.

In 1984, this interface was officially renamed TIA/EIA-232-E standard (E is the current revision, 1991), although most people still call it RS-232.

Common RS-232
Pin Configurations

RS-232 Pin Signals

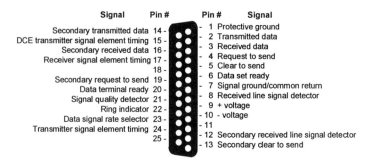

Signal	Pin #	Pin #	Signal
Secondary transmitted data	14	1	Protective ground
DCE transmitter signal element timing	15	2	Transmitted data
Secondary received data	16	3	Received data
Receiver signal element timing	17	4	Request to send
	18	5	Clear to send
Secondary request to send	19	6	Data set ready
Data terminal ready	20	7	Signal ground/common return
Signal quality detector	21	8	Received line signal detector
Ring indicator	22	9	+ voltage
Data signal rate selector	23	10	- voltage
Transmitter signal element timing	24	11	
	25	12	Secondary received line signal detector
		13	Secondary clear to send

RS-422, 423

A TIA/EIA standards for serial interfaces that extend distances and speeds beyond RS-232. RS-422 is a balanced system requiring more wire pairs than RS-423 and is intended for use in multipoint lines. They use either a 37-pin connector defined by RS-449 or a 25-pin connector defined by RS-530.

RS-449 and RS-530 specify the pin definitions for RS-422 and RS-423. RS-422/423 specify electrical and timing characteristics.

RS-449

Defines a 37-pin connector for RS-422 and RS-423 circuits.

RS-485

A TIA/EIA standard for multipoint communications lines. It can be implemented with as little as a wire block with four screws or with DB-9 or DB-37 connectors. By using lower-impedance drivers and receivers, RS-485 allows more nodes per line than RS-422.

RS-530

Defines a 25-pin connector for RS-422 and RS-423 circuits. It allows for higher speed transmission up to 2Mbits/sec over the same DB-25 connector used in RS-232, but is not compatible with it.

RS/6000

(RISC System/6000) IBM family of RISC-based computer systems introduced in 1990. It comes in workstation (POWERstation) and server (POWERserver) models and uses the Micro Channel bus. It introduced Version 3 of AIX and two graphical user interfaces: AIXwindows Environment/6000 (enhanced X Window system) and AIX NeXTStep Environment/6000 from NeXT Computer.

RS/6000s started out using IBM's RISC chip, called POWER. Starting in 1993, certain models began using the PowerPC chip, a single-chip version of the POWER architecture, which was enhanced by Motorola and Apple. Software is compatible on both platforms, unless it uses PowerPC-only instructions. New models of the RS/6000s will use the PowerPC chip.

RSA

(Rivest-Shamir-Adleman) A highly-secure encryption method by RSA Data Security, Inc., Redwood City, CA, that uses a two-part key. The private key is kept by the owner; the public key is published.

Data is encrypted by using the recipient's public key, which can only be decrypted by the recipient's private key. RSA is very computation intensive, thus it is often used to create an "RSA digital envelope," which holds an RSA-encrypted DES key and DES-encrypted data.

RSA is also used for authentication. You can verify who you are with a digital signature by encrypting with your private key and letting others decrypt your message with your public key. This requires the sender to compute a hash value of the message being sent, which is encrypted along with the message. The recipient decrypts the hash value and computes the hash value from the message using the same algorithm. If they match, the signature is authenticated.

The RSA algorithm is also implemented in hardware. As RSA chips get faster, RSA encoding and decoding add less overhead to the operation. For more on public keys, see *encryption*.

RSCS

(Remote Spooling Communications Subsystem) Software that provides batch communications for IBM's VM operating system. It accepts data from remote batch terminals, executes them on a priority basis and transmits the results back to the terminals. The RSCS counterpart in MVS is called JES. Contrast with *CMS*, which provides interactive communications for VM.

rsh

(Remote SHell) A UNIX command that enables a user to remotely log into a server on the network and pass commands to it. It is similar to the rlogin command, but provides passing of command line arguments to the command interpreter on the server at the same time. Rsh can be used within programs as well as from the keyboard.

RSI

(Repetitive Strain Injury) Ailments of the hands, neck, back and eyes due to computer use. The remedy for RSI is frequent breaks which should include stretching or yoga postures. See *carpal tunnel syndrome*.

RSTS/E

A PDP-11 operating system from Digital.

RSX-11

(Resource Sharing eXtension-PDP 11) A multiuser, multitasking operating system from Digital that runs on its PDP-11 series.

RT

A RISC-based workstation from IBM introduced in 1986 that was superseded by the RS/6000 family.

RT-11

A single user, multitasking operating system from Digital that runs on its PDP-11 series.

RTF

(Rich Text Format) A Microsoft standard for encoding formatted text and graphics. It was adapted from IBM's DCA format and supports ANSI, IBM PC and Macintosh character sets.

RTFM

(Read The Flaming Manual) The last resort when having a hardware or software problem! The definition of this acronym is rated G. You can figure out what it really means.

This is, of course, a sad but true state of affairs. Most people do not like to read documentation, because too many manuals that come with software are difficult, if not downright impossible, to understand. The online help isn't much better. Technical documentation is often a last minute rush job with programmers trying to communicate to writers. At times, programmers write the documentation themselves, which is typically a disaster.

Some day perhaps, the great minds in the software publishing industry will realize that if they put more time, energy and skilled writers into the documentation, they wouldn't be drowning in technical support. Of course, if software were designed better from the start, you wouldn't have the problems in the first place.

Until that day arrives, you have several choices for problem resolution if the manual and online help don't help. You can call tech support and wait on hold, or you can fax or e-mail your vendor an explanation of the problem and wait a day or two for a reply, or you can look it up in one or more good books on the subject.

RTOS

(RealTime Operating System) An operating system designed for use in a realtime computer system. See *realtime system, embedded system, process control* and *OS/9*.

RTS

(Request To Send) An RS-232 signal sent from the transmitting station to the receiving station requesting permission to transmit. Contrast with *CTS*.

RTTI

(RunTime Type Information) A facility that allows an object to be queried at runtime to determine its type. One of the fundamental principles of object technology is polymorphism, which is the ability of an object to dynamically change at runtime.

rubber banding

In computer graphics, the moving of a line or object where one end stays fixed in position.

rubout key

A keyboard key on a terminal that deletes the last character that was entered.

rule-based expert system

An expert system based on a set of rules that a human expert would follow in diagnosing a problem. Contrast with *model-based expert system*.

ruler line

A graphic representation of a ruler on screen that is used for laying out text and graphics.

rules

(1)A set of conditions or standards which have been agreed upon.
(2) In printing, horizontal and vertical lines between columns or at the top and bottom of a page in order to enhance the appearance of the page.

RUMBA

A family of PC-to-host connectivity software from Wall Data Inc., Kirkland, WA. RUMBA provides Windows, Windows NT Workstation and OS/2 front ends to IBM mainframes, AS/400s and VAXes through a wide variety of network configurations. RUMBA coax adapters (3270 emulators) are also available.

Rumbaugh

See *OMT*.

run

(1)To execute a program.
(2) A single program or set of programs scheduled for execution.

run around

In desktop publishing, the flowing of text around a graphic image.

run native

To "run native" is to execute software written for the native mode of the computer. Contrast with running a program under some type of emulation or simulation. Running native has traditionally been the fastest way to execute instructions on a computer. However, if as expected in the future, machines are so fast they can run emulated programs without any noticeable delay to the user, this will no longer be the important issue it is today.

run on top of

To run as the control program to some other program, which is subordinate to it. Contrast with *run under*.

runtime

Refers to the actual execution of a program.

runtime version

Software that enables another program to execute on its own or with enhanced capabilities. For example, a full-featured database management system (DBMS) includes a programming language for developing applications. The language is generally an interpreted one, which means that the DBMS software must be loaded into the computer in order to run the programs (see *interpreter*). A runtime version of the DBMS would allow the developer to create the application in that language and to package it for customers that have not purchased the DBMS. The runtime version "runs" the application, but does not allow the user access to all the bells and whistles that the owner of the full DBMS has.

In the book "Dvorak Predicts," published by Osborne McGraw-Hill, the well-known computer columnist, John Dvorak, proposes an interesting runtime version. He says that Apple should create a "runtime Mac." As an example, he uses an automobile tune-up kit, suggesting that its probes to the spark plugs, exhaust pipe, etc., be controlled by a computer using the Mac interface for that application only. He claims that the advantages are lower hardware costs if a full-blown Mac isn't required and that the Mac's interface would become widely known if runtime Macs were used for many specialized jobs.

run under

To run within the control of a higher-level program. Contrast with *run on top of.*

RXD

(Receiving Data) See *modem*.

S

S-100 bus

An IEEE 696, 100-pin bus standard used extensively in first-generation personal computers (8080, Z80, 6800, etc.). It is still used in various systems.

S3 chip

Refers to one of the graphics accelerator chips (86C911, 86C928, etc.) from S3, Inc., San Jose, CA, used in a variety of display adapters.

S/3x, S/360, S/370, S/390

See *System/3x, System/360, System/370* and *System/390*.

SAA

(System Application Architecture) Introduced in 1987, SAA is a set of standards from IBM that provide consistency across all IBM platforms. It governs user interfaces, programming interfaces and communications protocols. Categories are Common User Access (CUA), Common Programming Interface for Communications (CPI-C) and Common Communications Support (CCS). See *CUA, CPI-C* and *CCS*.

sabermetrician

Nickname for a statistician who uses computers to predict future performance of sports teams and players.

sag

(1) A momentary drop in voltage from the power source. Contrast with *spike*.
(2) (SAG) (SQL Access Group) See *CLI*.

salary survey

Following is the 1995 Source Edp salary survey of computer professionals, reprinted with permission from Source Services, Irving, TX. The following salaries are based on an analysis of the current salaries of more than 75,000 computer professionals nationwide. See *Source Edp*.

The following information contains three parts. The first is the salaries, expressed in thousands of 1994 U.S. dollars. The second is a sample of three job titles based on region. The third is a description of the job titles.

What They Earn

PROGRAMMING	20%	Median	80%
MAINFRAME			
Jr. programmer	32	34	39
Programmer analyst	33	40	45
Sr. prog. analyst	36	43	52
MIDRANGE			
Jr. programmer	28	33	39
Programmer analyst	33	40	45
Sr. prog. analyst	35	42	53
MICROCOMPUTER			
Jr. programmer	30	37	43
Programmer analyst	35	42	50
Sr. prog. analyst	38	47	58
SOFTWARE ENGINEER			
Jr. software eng.	30	35	45
Software engineer	35	45	50
Sr. software eng.	28	48	60
SYSTEMS ANALYSIS			
Systems analyst	40	49	60
Consultant	40	50	70
EIS analyst	35	40	50
SPECIALISTS			
Database analyst	42	51	59
Database admin.	40	45	53
LAN admin.	33	40	50
PC support	29	35	45
PC analyst	32	42	52
System admin./mgr.	35	42	52
Telecom analyst	35	44	55
Data comm analyst	38	45	57
System programmer	40	49	58

EDP auditor	33	38	44
Sr. EDP auditor	38	48	58
Technical writer	26	33	40
Technical editor	30	40	48
Systems integrator	35	42	52

MANAGEMENT
MIS DIRECTOR/CIO

Small/medium shop	48	60	75
Large shop	60	75	96
Applications dev.	55	65	80
Technical services	50	60	75
Project manager	50	61	75
Project leader	40	49	60

SALES

Account rep.	40	55	75
Pre/post sales support	32	39	48
Management	51	75	100

DATACENTER

Datacenter manager	35	46	59
Operator	19	23	26
Sr. operator	22	26	34
Technician	25	32	39
Sr. technician	28	35	45
Comm/network operator	25	34	40
Sr. comm/network oper.	30	40	52

Where They Earn It

The salaries of microcomputer programmer/analyst, systems analyst and account representative are detailed by region.

(1) Microcomputer programmer analyst
(2) Systems analyst
(3) Account representative

NEW ENGLAND

	(1)	(2)	(3)
New Hampshire	42	45	66
Boston	44	48	67
Hartford	42	46	57
Upper Fairfield, CT	45	46	59

MIDDLE ATLANTIC

	(1)	(2)	(3)
Westchester, NY & Lower Fairfield, CT	46	47	76
New York City	46	53	75
Central, Northern New Jersey	45	49	56
Long Island	43	46	53
Philadelphia & Southern New Jersey	38	48	53
Baltimore	37	43	62
Washington, DC	40	47	67
Upstate New York	36	37	53

EAST NORTH CENTRAL

Western Michigan	31	43	56
Detroit	40	47	70
Cleveland/Akron	36	46	53
Pittsburgh	32	42	60
Indianapolis/Ft. Wayne	35	44	54
Cincinnati/Dayton	38	44	67
Columbus	33	46	68
Louisville	38	45	57

(1) Microcomputer programmer analyst
(2) Systems analyst
(3) Account representative

WEST NORTH CENTRAL

	(1)	(2)	(3)
Minneapolis/St. Paul	42	47	63
Green Bay/Fox Valley	35	43	57
Milwaukee	40	46	65
Chicago	43	49	64
Omaha/Des Moines	32	44	66
St. Louis	35	46	70
Kansas City	36	46	68
Wichita/Topeka	30	45	63

SOUTH ATLANTIC

Atlanta	44	53	74
Charlotte	38	41	68
Raleigh/Durham	41	44	65
Tampa/Orlando	37	39	64
Miami	38	46	63

SOUTH CENTRAL

Tulsa/Oklahoma City	31	46	64
Memphis/Nashville	37	46	56
Dallas/Ft. Worth	40	53	81
San Antonio/Austin	36	46	72
Houston	41	51	72

MOUNTAIN

Denver	43	48	55
Phoenix	38	48	56
Albuquerque	35	46	52

PACIFIC

Seattle	46	47	69
Portland	45	48	67
San Francisco/San Jose	46	55	83
Los Angeles	47	60	85
Orange County	46	59	85
San Diego	42	50	63

CANADA

Toronto	41	47	74

What They Do   Following are the descriptions of the jobs surveyed.

Mainframe Programmer
Codes and maintains business application programs from user instructions or formal functional specifications. Develops and supports large-scale batch or high-volume transaction environments that require mainframe processing power. Programs in business-oriented languages such as COBOL, PL/I or 4GLs.

Midrange Programmer
Develops and supports enterprise-oriented applications for large companies or general business applications for medium companies. Programs in business-oriented languages such as COBOL and RPG/400, system-oriented languages such as C and Pascal, object-oriented languages such as C++ and Smalltalk or 4GLs.

Microcomputer Programmer
Develops and supports small-scale user interface and database-oriented applications. Programs in business-oriented languages such as COBOL, 4GLs such as SQL, PAL, PowerBuilder, Visual Basic and Xbase, or systems-oriented languages such as C or Pascal.

Software Engineer
Designs and develops systems-level software such as operating systems, network management, database management software, languages and GUIs. Als designs and develops genreal applications software such as spreadsheets, word processors, graphics packages and communications packages. Programs in system and object-oriented languages such as C, C++, Assembly, Smalltalk or PL/I.

Systems Analyst
Works directly with management and users to analyze, specify and design business applications. Develops detailed functional specs, system specs and program specs using structured design methodologies and CASE tools.

Consultant
Gives detailed technical and analytical advice during the development of a major application. Often compensated at an hourly rate or employed by outside companies and provides both analytical and programming services on a per project basis.

EIS Analyst
Works directly with senior business managment to develop business models and executive-level analytical tools using 4GLs and modeling software such as Comshare's System W, Pilot's Lightship and SAS.

Database Analyst
Uses data modeling techniques to analyze and specify data usage within an application area. Defines both logical views and physical data structures.

Database Administrator
Administers and controls an organization's data resources. Uses data dictionary software packages to ensure data integrity and security, recover corrupted data and eliminate data redundancy and tuning tools to improve database performance.

System Administrator/Manager
Installs minicomputer operating systems software, database management systems software, compilers and utilities. Monitors and tunes systems software, peripherals and networks. Installs new users, creates batch administration scripts and runs systems backups. Resolves systems problems.

LAN Administrator
Installas and maintains LAN hardware and sotare. Troubleshoots network usage and computer peripherals. Installs new user. Performs system backups and data recovery. Resolves LAN communications problems.

PC Support/PC Analyst
Works with microcomputer applications including word processors, spreadsheets, presentation graphics, database management systems, electronic mail and communications. Also evaluates, installs and supports PCs, Macs and associated peripherals.

Telecomm Analyst
Evaluates, selects, installs and minatains data and voice communicatoins software, hardware and network. Evaluates tariffs. Serves as liaison to common carriers and vendors.

System Programmer
Installs and maintains mainframe operating systems, communications software, database management software, compilers and utility programs. Provides technical support to applications programmers, hardware/software evaluation and planning. Creates and modifies special-purpose utility programs. Ensures systems efficiency and integrity.

EDP Auditor
Analyzes the system function and operations to determine adquate security and controls. Evaluates systems and operational procedures and reports findings to senior management. Writes ad hoc report programs using 4GLs and uses specialized audit software.

Technical Writer/Editor
Works directly with systems analysts and programmers to write and edit program and system documentation, user manuals, training courses and procedures. Also prepares proposals and technical reports.

Systems Integrator
Combines knowledge of multiple platforms, applications development, LANs and packaged software to create quick, low-cost solutions to specific business requirements. Assists the organization in establishing operational procedures, redefining work flows and overseeing application implementation.

MIS Director/CIO
Determines the overall strategic direction and business contribution of the information systems function.

Applications Development Manager/Director
Plans and oversees multiple projects and project managers. Works with CIO and senior management to determine systems development strategy and standards. Adminsters department budget and reviews project managers.

Technical Services Director
Plans and oversees the research, evaluation and integration of new technology, systems development methodologies, data administration, capacity planning, training and technical support.

Project Manager
Plans and oversees the development and support of a specific application or functional area. Administers performance appraisals, salaries, hiring and budgets.

Project Leader

Coordinates resources, schedules and communications for application development projects. Develops project schedules and assigns tasks. Performs both systems analysis and programming. Serves as contact with user groups and systems management.

Account Representative

Identifies new customers, analyzes customer needs, proposes business solutions, negotiates and oversees the implementation of new projects.

Pre/Post Sales Support Rep

Supports the sales effort by analyzing customer requirements, proposing and demonstrating technical solutions, ensuring acceptable product installations, training users and providing technical support and problem resolution.

Datacenter Manager

Plans and directs all computer and peripheral machines operations, data entry, data control scheduling and quality control.

Computer Operator

Operates, monitors and supports computer processing. Performs systems backups and data recovery. Mounts tapes and removable storage media. Distributes output and schedules machine utilization.

Operations Support Technician

Analyzes and supports computer operations by controlling production applications, monitoring system resources and response time and providing first-line support for operational problems.

Communications/Network Operator

Monitors and maintains communications network operations. Troubleshoots hardware, software and transmission problems.

SAM

(1) (Symantec AntiVirus for Macintosh) A popular Macintosh antivirus program from Symantec Corporation, Cupertino, CA.
(2) See *sequential access method*.

Samna

One of the first full-featured word processors for PCs (1983) from Samna Corporation, which was acquired by Lotus.

sampling

(1) In statistics, the analysis of a group by determining the characteristics of a significant percentage of its members chosen at random.
(2) In digitizing operations, the conversion of real-world signals or movements at regular intervals into digital code. See *sampling rate* and *oversampling*.

sampling rate

In digitizing operations, the frequency with which samples are taken and converted into digital form. The sampling frequency must be at least twice that of the analog frequency being captured. For example, the sampling rate for hi-fi playback is 44.1KHz, slightly more than double the 20KHz frequency a person can hear. The higher the sampling rate, the closer real-world objects are represented in digital form.
Another attribute of sampling is quantizing, which creates a number for the sample. The larger the maximum number, also called resolution or precision, the more

granularity of the scale and the more accurate the digital sampling. See *oversampling.*

a

sans-serif

a

serif

sans-serif

A typeface style without serifs, which are the short horizontal lines added at the tops and bottoms of the vertical member of the letter. Helvetica is a common sans-serif font.

Santa Cruz Operation

See *SCO.*

SAP

(1) (Service Advertising Protocol) A NetWare protocol used to identify the services and addresses of servers attached to the network. The responses are used to update a table in the router known as the Server Information Table.

(2) (Secondary Audio Program) An NTSC audio channel used for auxiliary transmission, such as foreign language broadcasting or teletext.

(3) (SAP America, Inc., Lester, PA) The U.S. branch of the German software company, SAP AG. SAP's R/3 integrated suite of applications and its ABAP/4 Development Workbench became popular starting around 1993. See *R/3.*

SASI

(Shugart Associates Systems Interface) A peripheral interface developed by Shugart and NCR in 1981 that evolved into the ANSI SCSI standard in 1986.

SAS System

(1) Originally called the "Statistical Analysis System," SAS is an integrated set of data management tools from SAS Institute Inc., Cary, NC, that runs on PCs to mainframes. It includes a complete programming language as well as modules for spreadsheets, CBT, presentation graphics, project management, operations research, scheduling, linear programming, statistical quality control, econometric and time series analysis and mathematical, engineering and statistical applications.

(2) See *FDDI.*

SATAN

(Security Analysis Tool for Auditing Networks) A utility that analyzes security vulnerabilities on the Internet. In April 1995, it was placed onto the Net as freeware by computer security specialist Dan Farmer.

satellite

See *communications satellite.*

satellite channel

A carrier frequency used for satellite transmission.

satellite computer

A computer located remotely from the host computer or under the control of the host. It can function as a slave to the master computer or perform offline tasks.

satellite link

A signal that travels from the earth to a communications satellite and back down again. Contrast with *terrestrial link.*

saturation

(1) On magnetic media, a condition in which the magnetizable particles are completely aligned and a more powerful writing signal will not improve the reading back.

(2) In a bipolar transistor, a condition in which the current on the gate (the trigger) is equal to or greater than what is necessary to close the switch.

(3) In a diode, a condition in which the diode is fully conducting.

save

To copy the document, record or image being worked on onto a storage medium. Saving updates the file by writing the data that currently resides in memory (RAM) onto disk or tape. Most applications prompt the user to save data upon exiting. All processing is done in memory (RAM). When the processing is completed, the data must be placed onto a permanent storage medium such as disk or tape.

save as

To copy the document or image being worked on onto a storage medium as a new file. "Save as" provides an easy way to make multiple copies of a document or image. With your document or image on screen, select "Save as" from the File menu. You will be prompted for a new file name.

Sbus

Originally a proprietary bus from Sun, the Sbus has been released into the public domain. The IEEE standardized a 64-bit version in 1993.

SCAI

(Switch-to-Computer Applications Interface) A standard for integrating computers to a PBX. See *switch-to-computer*.

scalability

The ability to expand. Implies minimal change in current procedures in order to accomodate growth.

scalable

Capable of being changed in size and configuration.

scalable font

A font that is created in the required point size as needed to display or print a document. The dot patterns (bitmaps) are generated from a set of outline fonts, or base fonts, which contain a mathematical representation of the typeface. Although a bitmapped font designed from scratch for a particular font size will always look the best, scalable fonts eliminate storing dozens of different font sizes on disk. Contrast with *bitmapped font*.

The two major scalable fonts are Adobe's Type 1 PostScript and Apple/Microsoft's TrueType. There are more Type 1 fonts available, although TrueType fonts are rapidly becoming as abundant. Agfa's Intellifont and Bitstream's Speedo fonts are also used.

scalar

A single item or value. Contrast with *vector* and *array*, which are made up of multiple values.

scalar processor

A computer that performs arithmetic computations on one number at a time. Contrast with *vector processor*.

scalar variable

In programming, a variable that contains only one value.

scale

(1) To resize a device, object or system, making it larger or smaller.

(2) To change the representation of a quantity in order to bring it into prescribed limits of another range. For example, values such as 1249, 876, 523, -101 and -234 might need to be scaled into a range from -5 to +5.

(3) To designate the position of the decimal point in a fixed or floating point number.

SCAM

(SCSI Configuration AutoMatically) A subset of Plug and Play that allows SCSI IDs and termination to be handled by software. SCAM eliminates the need to install terminators and manually set different ID numbers on SCSI devices.

scan

(1) In optical technologies, to view a printed form a line at a time in order to convert images into bitmapped representations, or to convert characters into ASCII text or some other data code.

(2) In video, to move across a picture frame a line at a time, either to detect the image in an analog or digital camera, or to refresh a CRT display.

(3) To sequentially search a file.

ScanDisk

Starting with MS-DOS 6.2, ScanDisk is an external command that detects and repairs errors on disk. It is easier to use and more thorough than the Chkdsk command. If ScanDisk finds any areas on the disk unreadable, it will try to recover the data stored there by moving it to other clusters. It will then mark the clusters as "bad" so they cannot be used again.

scan head

An optical sensing device in an scanner or fax machine that is moved across the image to be scanned.

ScanJet

A family of popular desktop scanners from HP. Monochrome and color models are available.

scan line

One of many horizontal lines in a graphics frame.

scanner

A device that reads text, images and bar codes. Text and bar code scanners recognize printed fonts and bar codes and convert them into a digital code (ASCII or EBCDIC). Graphics scanners convert a printed image into a video image (raster graphics) without recognizing the actual content of the text or pictures. See *flatbed scanner, sheet-fed scanner, hand-held scanner* and *drum scanner*.

Flatbed Scanner
Scanners turn everything they scan into a bitmapped image made up of dots.

scan rate

The number of times per second a scanning device samples its field of vision. See *horizontal scan frequency*.

scatter diagram, scatter plot

A graph plotted with dots or some other symbol at each data point. Also called a scatter plot or dot chart.

scatter read

The capability that allows data to be input into two or more noncontiguous locations of memory with one read operation. See *gather write*.

SCbus

See *SCSA*.

SC connector

A fiber-optic cable connector that uses a push-pull latching mechanism. It is used in FDDI, Fiber Channel and B/ISDN applications. See *fiber-optic connectors*.

SCERT II

(Systems and Computers Evaluation and Review Technique) Pronounced "skirt." Software from Pinnacle Software Corporation, Washington, DC, that measures the performance of a system by modeling the computer environment and applications.

scheduler

The part of the operating system that initiates and terminates jobs (programs) in the computer. Also called a dispatcher, it maintains a list of jobs to be run and allocates computer resources as required.

scheduling algorithm

A method used to schedule jobs for execution. Priority, length of time in the job queue and available resources are examples of criteria used.

schema

Pronounced "skeema." The definition of an entire database. Schemas are often designed with visual modeling tools, which automatically create the SQL code necessary to define the table structures. A subschema is an individual user's view of the database. See *data model*.

Scheme

A LISP dialect developed at MIT and Indiana University. TI has a personal computer version of Scheme called PC Scheme.

Schottky

A category of bipolar transistor known for its fast switching speeds in the three-nanosecond range. Schottky II devices have switching speeds in the range of a single nanosecond.

SCI

(Scalable Coherent Interface) An IEEE standard for a high-speed bus that uses wire or fiber optic cable. It can transfer data up to 1GBytes/sec.

scientific application

An application that simulates real-world activities using mathematics. Real-world objects are turned into mathematical models and their actions are simulated by executing the formulas.

For example, some of an airplane's flight characteristics can be simulated in the computer. Rivers, lakes and mountains can be simulated. Virtually any objects with known characteristics can be modeled and simulated.

Simulations use enormous calculations and often require supercomputer speed. As personal computers become more powerful, more laboratory experiments will be converted into computer models that can be interactively examined by students without the risk and cost of the actual experiments.

scientific computer

A computer specialized for high-speed mathematic processing. See *array processor* and *floating point processor*.

scientific language

A programming language designed for mathematical formulas and matrices, such as ALGOL, FORTRAN and APL. Although all programming languages allow for this kind of processing, statements in a scientific language make it easier to express these actions.

scientific notation

The display of numbers in floating point form. The number (mantissa) is always equal to or greater than one and less than 10, and the base is 10. For example, 2.345E6 is equivalent to 2,345,000. The number following E (exponent) represents the power to which the base should be raised (number of zeros following the decimal point).

scissoring

In computer graphics, the deleting of any parts of an image which fall outside of a window that has been sized and laid over the original image. Also called clipping.

SCL

(1) (Switch-to-Computer Link) Refers to applications that integrate the computer through the PBX. See *switch-to-computer*.

(2) A file extension used for ColoRIX raster graphics file format (640x400 256 colors).

SCM

(1) (Software Configuration Management) See *configuration management*.

(2) (Service Control Manager) The part of Windows NT that launches background tasks. Developers can write executable programs that run under the control of the SCM.

(3) (Single Chip Module) A chip package that contains one chip. Contrast with *MCM*.

SCM file

(ScreenCam Movie file) A file created by Lotus' ScreenCam recorder program.

SCMS

(Serial Copy Management System) A copy protection method used for recordable audio CDs that allows one copy of the original to be made.

SCO

(The Santa Cruz Operation, Inc., Santa Cruz, CA) A system software company that specializes in UNIX operating systems. Founded in 1979 initially as a custom programming house, its first operating system product was SCO XENIX in 1984. It ran on the Apple Lisa, IBM PC XT and the DEC Pro 350. Subsequently, all SCO products were developed for Intel's x86 machines. As of 1995, with more than a million installed nodes, SCO is the leader in UNIX operating systems for the Intel platform.

In late 1995, SCO purchased UnixWare from Novell and is expected to combine UnixWare 2.0 (UNIX System V Release 4) with its own UNIX-based Open Server and release a merged product in 1997. SCO also plans on licensing Novell's directory services (NDS) and other technologies into future versions of its products.

SCO Merge

Software from SCO that adds DOS compatibility to SCO UNIX. It includes a licensed copy of DOS 6 and can run DOS applications and Windows applications in Standard Mode.

SCO MPX

(SCO MultiProcessor EXtension) See *SCO SMP*.

SCO Open Desktop, Open Server

A family of client and server operating systems from SCO based on SCO UNIX. It includes the Motif and X Window user interfaces and standard UNIX networking (TCP/IP, NFS and NIS). SCO Open Server Release 5 Desktop (formerly SCO Open Desktop) is the single-user client version, and SCO Open Server Release 5 Enterprise is the current server version.

scope

(1)A CRT screen, such as used on an oscilloscope or common display terminal.
(2) In programming, the visibility of variables within a program; for example, whether one function can use a variable created in another function.
(3) In dBASE, a range of records, such as the "next 50" or "current record to end of file."<TERM>SCO SMP
Software that adds SMP capability to SCO Open Server operating systems. SCO SMP was originally called SCO MPX (SCO MultiProcessor Extension).

SCO UNIX

An enhanced version of UNIX System V Release 3.2 for 386s and up from SCO. SCO UNIX has more security, networking and standards conformance than SCO XENIX and is the foundation of SCO's Open Server products. SCO UNIX servers are used to support dumb terminals as well as Windows, X terminal and SCO Open Server clients.

SCO VP/ix

Software from SCO that adds DOS capability to machines running SCO XENIX. It includes a licensed copy of DOS 3.0.

SCO Wabi

Software from SCO that adds Wabi capability to SCO Open Server products. Wabi provides Windows 3.1 compatibility.

SCO XENIX

A version of UNIX System V for 286 PCs and up from SCO. Developed by Microsoft, it was the original UNIX system for personal computers. SCO XENIX is a fast multiuser operating system that takes less memory than SCO UNIX and is used in a variety of vertical market applications for small workgroups.

scrambler

A device or software program that encodes data for encryption.

scrambling

Encoding data to make it indecipherable. See *encryption*, *DES* and *RSA*.

Scrapbook

A Macintosh disk file that holds frequently-used text and graphics objects, such as a company letterhead. Contrast with *Clipboard*, which holds data only for the current session.

scratchpad

A register or reserved section of memory or disk used for temporary storage.

scratch tape

A magnetic tape that can be erased and reused.

screen

The display area of a video terminal or monitor. It is either a CRT or one of the flat panel technologies.

screen angle

The angle at which a halftone screen is placed over an image. Generally, 45 degrees produces the best results. In a digital system, the screen angle is simulated by the placement of the dots within the halftone cells. See *halftone*.

ScreenCam

Screen recording software from Lotus that is used to make "movies" of software actions for demos and training purposes. Voice annotations can be added with a microphone and sound card. A runtime player, which can be freely distributed, plays the .SCM files. The player can also be combined with the file, providing a self-running ScreenCam movie.

screen capture

Transfering the current on-screen image to a text or graphics file.

screen dump

Printing the current on-screen image. In PCs, pressing Shift-PrtSc prints the screen. If the screen contains graphics, the DOS Graphics utility must be loaded. Third party screen capture programs also dump graphic screens to the printer or to disk. In the Macintosh, pressing Command-shift-3 creates a MacPaint file of the current screen.
In Windows 3.1 and 95, pressing PrintScreen places a copy of the current screen into the Clipboard. Pressing Alt-PrintScreen copies just the current window.

screen font

A font used for on-screen display. For true WYSIWYG systems, screen fonts must be matched as close as possible to the printer fonts. Contrast with *printer font*.

screen frequency

The resolution of a halftone. It is the density of dots (how far they're spaced apart from each other) measured in lines per inch. In a digital system, the screen frequency is simulated by the placement of the dots within the halftone cells. See *halftone*.

screen grabber

A program that saves the current screen image and other screen status information in order for the screen to be restored at a later time. In Windows, grabber programs capture DOS screens, and there is a grabber for Standard Mode and one for 386 Enhanced Mode.

screen overlay

(1) A clear, fine-mesh screen that reduces the glare on a video screen.
(2) A clear touch panel that allows the user to command the computer by touching displayed buttons on screen.
(3) A temporary data window displayed on screen. The part of the screen that was overlaid is saved and restored when the screen overlay is removed.

screen saver

A utility that prevents a CRT from being etched by an unchanging image. After a specified duration without keyboard or mouse input, it blanks the screen or displays moving objects. Pressing a key or moving the mouse restores the screen.
It would actually take many hours to burn in an image on today's color monitors. However, the entertainment provided by these utilities (swimming fish, flying toasters, etc.) has made them very popular.

screen scraper

Also called *frontware*, it is software that adds a graphical user interface to character-based mainframe and minicomputer applications. The screen scraper application runs in the personal computer which is used as a terminal to the mainframe or mini via 3270 or 5250 emulation.
Popular screen scrapers are Knowledgeware's Flashpoint, Mozart Systems Corporation's Mozart and Easel's ESL Renovator. Attachmate's QuickApp adds screen scraper capability to development systems such as PowerBuilder, Visual Basic and SQLWindows.

script

(1)A typeface that looks like handwriting or calligraphy.
(2) A program written in a special-purpose programming language such as used in a communications program or word processor. Same as *macro*.

ScriptX

A multimedia technology from Kaleida Labs, Inc. that includes data formats, a scripting language and a runtime environment. It is designed for creating applications that can be played on a variety of personal computers and consumer electronic devices.

scroll

To continuously move forward, backward or sideways through the images on screen or within a window. Scrolling implies continuous and smooth movement, a line, character or pixel at a time, as if the data were on a paper scroll being rolled behind the screen.

Scroll
Arrow

Thumb

Scroll
Bar

scrollable

See *scroll.*

scrollable field

A short line on screen that can be scrolled to allow editing or display of larger amounts of data in a small display space.

scrollable window

A window that contains more data than is visible at one time. Its contents can be scrolled (moved up, down, sideways within the window) in order to view the entire document, image or list of items.

scroll arrow

On-screen arrow that is clicked in order to scroll the screen in the corresponding direction. The screen moves one line, or increment, with each mouse click.

scroll back buffer

Reserved memory that holds a block of transmitted data, allowing the user to browse back through it.

scroll bar

A horizontal or vertical bar that contains a box that looks like an elevator in a shaft. The bar is clicked to scroll the screen in the corresponding direction, or the box (elevator, thumb) is clicked and then dragged to the desired direction.

Scroll Lock

On PC keyboards, a key used to toggle between a scrolling and non-scrolling mode. When on, the arrow keys scroll the screen regardless of the current cursor location. This key is rarely used for its intended purpose and may be used for just about anything. Most applications do not use it a all.

SCSA

(Signal Computing System Architecture) An open architecture from Dialogic Corporation for transmitting signals, voice and video. Its backbone is the SCbus, a 131Mbps data path that provides up to 2048 time slots, the equivalent of 1,024 two-way voice conversations at 64Kbps.

SCSI

(Small Computer System Interface) Pronounced "scuzzy." SCSI is a hardware interface that allows for the connection of up to seven or 15 peripheral devices (hard disk, CD-ROM, scanner, etc.) to a single expansion board in the computer. The expansion board is called a *SCSI host adapter* or *SCSI controller.*

SCSI is widely used as a hardware interface in all types and sizes of computers from micro to mainframe. In personal computers, SCSI has been directly supported by the Macintosh operating system, which has made the Mac a plug and play computer for years. Although Windows 95 supports SCSI, DOS and Windows 3.x do not. Attaching SCSI devices to a DOS or Windows 3.x system requires adding the appropriate SCSI driver.

The initial lack of support for SCSI in the PC world gave rise to different implementations. Before Adaptec's ASPI and ANSI's CAM were developed, there was no guarantee that a SCSI device would work with a SCSI host adapter in a PC. Quite often, hooking up two SCSI devices meant plugging in two different SCSI host adapters, negating SCSI's primary advantage of connecting multiple peripherals. ASPI and CAM provide common interfaces between the drivers and the host adapters and have mostly resolved SCSI incompatibilities in PCs. Windows 95 supports popular SCSI host adapters directly. It also supports ASPI and CAM so that older applications and drivers will run under Windows 95 if Win 95 does not support that peripheral with a native driver.

SCSI Is Like a LAN

SCSI is a bus structure itself and functions like a mini-LAN connecting eight or 16 devices. The host adapter counts as one device, thus up to seven or 15 peripherals can be attached depending on the SCSI type. SCSI allows any two devices to communicate at one time (host to peripheral, peripheral to peripheral). Each SCSI device can be further broken up into eight logical units, identified by logical unit numbers (LUNs) 0 to 7. Although most SCSI devices contain only one media unit and are addressed as LUN 0, CD-ROM and optical disk jukeboxes contain multiple units of storage. Each disk in these devices can be addressed independently via LUN numbers; for example, a four-disk jukebox could be assigned LUN 0 to 3.

SCSI Specifications

Type	Bus Width (bits)	Pins	Cable Max Length (ft)	Transfer Rate MB/ Sec	Maximum Devices
SCSI-1	8	25	19.7	5	8
SCSI-2	8	50	19.7	5	8
Fast SCSI-2	8	50	9.8	10	8
Wide SCSI-2 or					
Fast Wide SCSI-2	16	68	9.8	10-20	16
8-bit Ultra SCSI-3	8	50	**	20	8
16-bit Ultra SCSI-3	16	68	**	20-40	16

** 9.8 ft - up to four devices
   4.9 ft - five or more devices

Version Compatibility

The different SCSI types provide backward and forward compatibility. If a new SCSI host adapter is used with an older SCSI drive, the drive will run at its maximum speed. If an older SCSI host adapter is used with a newer drive, the drive will run at the host adapter's maximum speed.

SCSI and IDE Drives

You can install SCSI hard disk drives in a PC that already contains one or two IDE disk drives. The IDE drive will still be the boot drive, and the SCSI drives will provide additional storage. Follow the instructions in your SCSI host adapter manual carefully to make the correct settings. SCSI host adapters usually provide floppy disk control, which can be disabled since the IDE controller is already handling it.

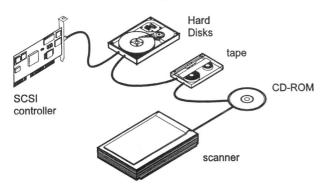

Hard Disks

tape

CD-ROM

SCSI controller

scanner

IDs and Termination

SCSI devices are daisy chained together. Each device has two ports, one for the incoming cable and another for the outgoing cable to the next device. Each device must be set to a unique ID number, which is normally done by manually flipping a rotary switch on the device itself. The highest number has the highest priority. Thus, the host adapter usually defaults to ID 7 in the case of an 8-device SCSI system.
(continued on page 761)

SCSI-1

Host Adapter to Peripheral

DB25 pin male

Telco 50 pin male

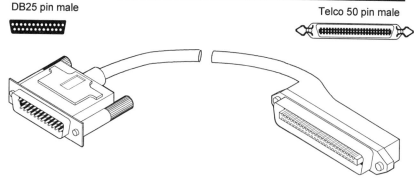

Peripheral to Peripheral

Telco 50 pin male

Telco 50 pin male

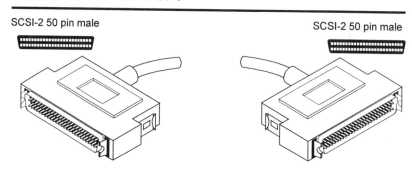

SCSI-2 and 8-bit SCSI-3

Host Adapter to Peripheral

SCSI-2 50 pin male

SCSI-2 50 pin male

Peripheral to Peripheral

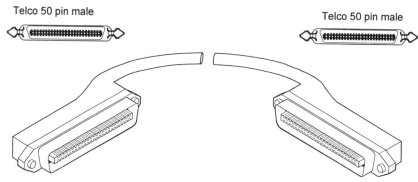

Wide SCSI-2 and 16-bit SCSI-3

Host Adapter to Peripheral

SCSI-3 68 pin male

SCSI-3 68 pin male

Peripheral to Peripheral

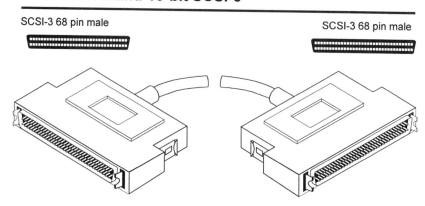

A subset of the Plug and Play standard, called *SCAM* (SCSI Configuration AutoMatically), allows termination to be performed and IDs to be set by software rather than manually.

Parallel to SCSI
There are adapters that allow SCSI peripherals to be connected via the parallel port. Although the parallel port's transfer rate is considerably less than the SCSI host adapter, it does provide a means to hook up SCSI devices that might be otherwise impossible, such as to a laptop with no built-in SCSI port or PC Card slots.

Single Ended vs Differential
There are two types of SCSI signalling. Single-ended SCSI allows devices to be attached in a total cable length of 19.7 feet or 9.8 feet for Fast SCSI. Most SCSI devices to date are single ended.
Differential SCSI is used when devices are spread out across a room, because the total cable length is incrased to about 80 feet. Differential devices cost more than single-ended ones.
Single-ended SCSI uses a data line and ground. Differential SCSI uses data low and data high lines to increase transmission distance.

scuzzy
See *SCSI*.

SDBN
(Software-Defined Broadband Network) A future high-bandwidth service from AT&T for data, voice and video. It uses ATM cell relay technology with speeds up to 600 Mbits/sec.

SDF
(Standard Data Format) A simple file format that uses fixed length fields. It is commonly used to transfer data between different programs.

SDF

```
Pat Smith      5 E. 12 St.      Rye        NY
Robert Jones   200 W. Main St.  Palo Alto  CA
```

Comma delimited

```
"Pat Smith","5 E. 12 St.","Rye","NY"
"Robert Jones","200 W. Main St.","Palo Alto","CA"
```

SDH
(Synchronous Digital Hierarchy) The European counterpart to SONET. Speeds supported include 155 and 622 Mbits/sec and 2.5 GBits/sec.

SDI
(1) (Switched Digital International) An AT&T dial-up service providing 56 and 64 Kbits/sec digital transmission to international locations.
(2) (Single Document Interface) A Windows function that allows an application to display and lets the user work with only one document at a time. SDI applications require that the user load the application again for the second and each subsequent document to be worked on concurrently. Contrast with *MDI*.
(3) (Standard Drive Interface) A hard disk interface for VAXs.
(4) (Serial Data Interface) See *serial interface*.
(5) (Strategic Defense Initiative) A high-tech defense system for the U.S. proposed during the Reagan administration.

SDK

(Software Developer's Kit) See *developer's toolkit* and *Windows SDK*.

SDLC

(Synchronous Data Link Control) The primary data link protocol used in IBM's SNA networks. It is a bit-oriented synchronous protocol that is a subset of the HDLC protocol.

SDP

(Streaming Data Procedure) A Micro Channel mode that increases data transfer from 20MB per second to 40MB per second.

SDRAM

(Synchronous **DRAM**) A high-speed DRAM memory that can transfer bursts of non-contiguous data at 100MBytes/sec. JEDEC is also specifying a SDRAM standard.

SE

See *systems engineer* and *Macintosh*.

Seagate

(Seagate Technology, Inc., Scotts Valley, CA) The largest independent manufacturer of disk drives. Founded in 1979 by Alan Shugart, Tom Mitchell and Doug Mahon, it was the first to offer a 5MByte drive using 5.25" platters making it ideal for the burgeoning desktop computer industry. Seagate became the first company to ship 10 million drives. In 1989, it aquired Imprimis Technology, a CDC subsidiary making workstation and mainframe drives, nearly doubling Seagate's revenue to $2.5 billion. Seagate's 1994 revenues were 3.5 billion.

SEAlink

A version of Xmodem that uses a sliding window protocol, transmits file name, date and size and provides batch file transfer. Good for delay-introduced transmissions (packet switching, satellites).

seamless integration

An addition of a new application, routine or device that works smoothly with the existing system. It implies that the new feature can be activated and used without problems. Contrast with *transparent*, which implies that there is no discernible change after installation.

search and replace

To look for an occurrence of data or text and replace it with another set of data or text.

search key

In a search routine, the data entered and used to match other data in the database.

search path

The route to a particular file. See *path*.

seashell

The "C" shell in UNIX. See *UNIX*.

seat

See *per seat*.

SECAM

(Systeme Electronique Couleur Avec Memoire) A French and Eastern European color TV standard that broadcasts an analog signal at 819 lines of resolution 25 interlaced frames per second (50 half frames per second). Mostly used in France, it is slowly being switched over to the European PAL standard. Contrast with *NTSC* and *PAL*.

secondary channel

In communications, a subchannel that is derived from the main channel. It is used for diagnostic or supervisory purposes, but does not carry data messages.

secondary index

An index that is maintained for a data file, but not used to control the current processing order of the file. For example, a secondary index could be maintained for customer name, while the primary index is set up for customer account number. See *primary index*.

secondary storage

External storage, such as disk and tape.

second-generation computer

A computer made of discrete electronic components. In the early 1960s, the IBM 1401 and Honeywell 400 were examples.

second source

An alternative supplier of an identical or compatible product. A second source manufacturer is one that holds a license to produce a copy of the original product from another manufacturer.

secret key

See *encryption*.

sector

The smallest unit of storage read or written on a disk. See *magnetic disk*.

sector interleave

Sector numbering on a hard disk. A one to one interleave (1:1) is sequential: 0,1,2,3, etc. A 2:1 interleave staggers sectors every other one: 0,4,1,5,2,6,3,7. In 1:1, after data in sector 1 is read, the disk controller must be fast enough to read sector 2, otherwise the beginning of sector 2 will pass the read/write head and must rotate around to come under the head again. If it isn't fast enough, a 2:1 or 3:1 interleave gives it time to read all sectors in a single rotation, eliminating wasted rotations.

The best interleave depends on the disk and disk controller. It can be changed with a low-level format program.

sector map

See *sector interleave*.

sector sparing

Maintaining a spare sector per track to be used if another sector becomes defective.

SecurID card

An authentication token from Security Dynamics, Inc., Cambridge, MA, that uses a smart card that authorized users keep in their possession. The card's microprocessor and the host computer are synchronized by a unique number and the time of day.

Secur ID Card
(Photo courtesy of Security Dynamics, Inc.)

When users log onto a SecurID-enabled host, they type in the number displayed on their cards at that moment as an additional passcode. If the number matches the number that the host computes, the user is presumed to be the valid holder of the card.

security

The protection of data against unauthorized access. Programs and data can be secured by issuing identification numbers and passwords to authorized users of a computer. However, systems programmers, or other technically competent individuals, will ultimately have access to these codes.

Passwords can be checked by the operating system to prevent users from logging onto the system in the first place, or they can be checked in software, such as DBMSs, where each user can be assigned an individual view (subschema) of the database. Any application program running in the computer can also be designed to check for passwords.

Data transmitted over communications networks can be secured by encryption to prevent eavesdropping.

Although precautions can be taken to detect an unauthorized user, it is extremely difficult to determine if a valid user is performing unauthorized tasks. Effective security measures are a balance of technology and personnel management. See *NCSC, NCSA* and *Computer Security Act*.

security kernel

The part of the operating system that grants access to users of the computer system.

security levels

See *NCSC*.

sed

(Stream EDitor) A UNIX editing command that makes changes a line at a time and is used to edit large files that exceed buffer limitations of other editors.

seed

(1) The starting value used by a random number generation routine to create random numbers.
(2) (SEED) (Self-Electro-optic-Effect Device) An optical transistor developed by David Miller at Bell Labs in 1986.

seek

(1)To move the access arm to the requested track on a disk.
(2)An assembly language instruction that activates a seek operation on disk.
(3)A high-level programming language command used to select a record by key field.

seek time

The time it takes to move the read/write head to a particular track on a disk.

segment

(1)Any partition, reserved area, partial component or piece of a larger structure. See *overlay*.
(2) One of the bars that make up a single character in an LED or LCD display.
(3) For DOS segment addressing, see *paragraph*.

segmented address space

Memory addressing in which each byte is referenced by a segment, or base, number and an offset that is added to it. Contrast with *flat address space*.

SEI

(Software Engineering Institute, Pittsburg, PA) An organization associated with Carnegie Mellon University that is devoted to the advancement of software engineering. Its Capability Maturity Model (CMM) is used to assess an organization's ability to manage its software development. The results are stated as adhering to one of five levels: Initial, Repeatable, Defined, Managed and Optimizing. The more an organization depends on formal rules to keep projects on schedule and relies less on individual performers, the higher the ranking.

Sel

(SELect) A toggle switch on a printer that takes the printer alternately between online and offline.

selection sort

A search for specific data starting at the beginning of a file or list. It copies each matching item to a new file so that the selected items are in the same sequence as the original data.

selective calling

In communications, the ability of the transmitting station to indicate which station in the network is to receive the message.

selector channel

A high-speed computer channel that connects a peripheral device (disk, tape, etc.) to the computer's memory.

selector pen

Same as *light pen*.

Selectric typewriter

Introduced in 1961 by IBM, the first typewriter to use a golf-ball-like print head that moved across the paper, rather than moving the paper carriage across the print mechanism. It rapidly became one of the world's most popular typewriters. IBM has always excelled in electromechanical devices. In 1991, IBM's typewriter division was spun off into Lexmark International.

self-booting

Refers to automatically loading the operating system upon startup.

self-checking digit

See *check digit*.

self-clocking

Recording of digital data on a magnetic medium such that the clock pulses are intrinsically part of the recorded signal. A separate timer clock is not required. Phase encoding is a commonly-used self-clocking recording technique.

self-documenting code

Programming statements that can be easily understood by the author or another programmer. COBOL provides more self-documenting code than does C, for example.

self-extracting file

One or more compressed files that have been converted into an executable program which decompresses its contents when run.

semantic error

In programming, writing a valid programming structure with invalid logic. The compiler will generate instructions that the computer will execute, because it understands the syntax of the programming statements, but the output will not be correct.

semantic gap

The difference between a data or language structure and the real world. For example, in order processing, a company can be both customer and supplier. Since there is no way to model this in a hierarchical database, the semantic gap is said to be large. A network database could handle this condition, resulting in a smaller semantic gap.

semantics

The study of the meaning of words. Contrast with *syntax*, which governs the structure of a language.

semaphore

(1) A hardware or software flag used to indicate the status of some activity.
(2) A shared space for interprocess communications (IPC) controlled by "wake up" and "sleep" commands. The source process fills a queue and goes to sleep until the destination process uses the data and tells the source process to wake up.

semiconductor

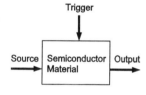

A solid state substance that can be electrically altered. Certain elements in nature, such as silicon, perform like semiconductors when chemically combined with other elements. A semiconductor is halfway between a conductor and an insulator. When charged with electricity or light, semiconductors change their state from nonconductive to conductive or vice versa.
The most significant semiconductor is the transistor, which is simply an on/off switch.

semiconductor device

An elementary component, such as a transistor, or a larger unit of electronic equipment comprised of chips.

sensor

A device that measures or detects a real world condition, such as motion, heat or light and converts the condition into an analog or digital representation. An optical sensor detects the intensity or brightness of light, or the intensity of red, green and blue for color systems.

sequel

See *SQL*.

sequence check

Testing a list of items or file of records for correct ascending or descending sequence based on the item or key fields in the records.

Sequent

(Sequent Computer Systems, Inc., Beaverton, OR)
A computer company founded in 1983 by 17 ex-employees of Intel that specializes in multiprocessing systems for the client/server environment. Sequent pioneered adapting SMP to UNIX and, according to InfoCorp research for 1992 and 1993, is the worldwide market share leader for large UNIX systems over $700,000.
Sequent's SMP machines are all Intel based and are scalable up to 30 Pentium

processors. Its Symmetry series runs the UNIX-based DYNIX/ptx operating system, and the WinServer series runs Windows NT.

sequential
One after the other in some consecutive order such as by name or number.

sequential access method
Organizing data in a prescribed ascending or descending sequence. Searching sequential data requires reading and comparing each record, starting from the top or bottom of file.

sequential scan
Same as *non-interlaced.*

serial
One after the other.

serial bus
A type of bus that transmits data serially. Ethernet is an example of a serial bus on a network. Serial buses are also expected to become popular for attaching multiple peripherals to computers.
Although both use serial transmission, a serial bus differs from a serial port. The serial port connects the computer to one peripheral device. A serial bus allows for the connection of multiple devices.

serial computer
A single-processor computer that executes one instruction after the other. Contrast with *parallel computer.*

Serial Infrared
See *SIR.*

serial interface
A data channel that transfers digital data in a serial fashion: one bit after the other. Telephone lines use serial transmission for digital data, thus modems are connected to the computer via a serial port. So are mice and scanners. Serial interfaces have multiple lines, but only one is used for data.
For the difference between the serial and parallel ports, see *serial port.* Contrast with *parallel interface.* See *RS-232*

serialize
To convert a parallel signal made up of one or more bytes into a serial signal that transmits one bit after the other.

serial mouse
A mouse that plugs into the serial port on a PC. Serial mice are the most common type. Contrast with *bus mouse.*

serial number
A unique number assigned by the vendor to each unit of hardware or software. See *signature.*

serial port
A socket on a computer used to connect a modem, mouse, scanner or other serial interface device to the computer. The Macintosh uses the serial port to attach a printer, whereas the PC uses the parallel port. Transferring files between two

personal computers can be accomplished by cabling the serial ports of both machines together and using a file transfer program.

The serial port uses DB-9 and DB-25 connectors. On the back of most newer PCs is one 9-pin male connector for serial port #1, named COM1 and typically used for the mouse, as well as one 25-pin male connector for serial port #2, named COM2 and typically used for a modem.

In a PC, serial port circuits are contained on a small expansion card that plugs into an expansion slot. Typically two serial ports, one parallel port and one game port are on the card. These ports are often also included on an IDE host adapter card, which takes up only one expansion slot and provides hard and floppy disk control as well as I/O. Contrast with *parallel port.* See *serial interface* and *RS-232.*

Why Serial and Parallel Ports?

The serial port is designed primarily to accomodate modems, which require a serial connection to the telephone system. Data bits are passed one after the other (serially) over the single line provided by the telephone wiring.

Serial Ports on a PC

These are the typical serial port sockets on a PC. COM1 is a 9-pin socket typically used for the mouse, and COM2 is a 25-pin socket typically used for a modem.

On the other hand, local devices such as a printer are not restricted to single-channel transmission. The parallel port, which contains eight lines for transmitting an entire byte (eight bits) simultaneously, provides a higher-speed pathway between the computer and a peripheral device.

All other interfaces used in a computer, such as SCSI and IDE as well as the ISA, EISA and Micro Channel buses, are also parallel in design. They provide 8, 16 or 32 wires for simultaneous transfer of data bits.

serial printer

A type of printer that prints one character at a time, in contrast to a line or page at a time. In this context, serial has no relationship to a serial or parallel interface that is used to attach the printer to the computer. See *printer.*

serial transmission

Transmitting data one bit at a time. Contrast with *parallel transmission.*

Series/1

An IBM minicomputer series introduced in 1976. It was used primarily as a communications processor and for data collection in process control.

serif

Short horizontal lines added to the tops and bottoms of traditional typefaces, such as Times Roman. Contrast with *sans-serif.*

serpentine recording

Tape recording format of parallel tracks in which the data "snakes" back and forth from the end of one track to the beginning of the next track.

server

A computer in a network shared by multiple users. See *file server* and *print server.*

server application

(1) An application designed to run in a server. See *client/server.*
(2) Any program that is run in the server, whether designed as a client/server application or not.
(3) See *OLE.*

service

Functionality derived from a particular software program. For example, network services may refer to programs that transmit data or provide conversion of data in a

Server Platforms (CPU & NOS)

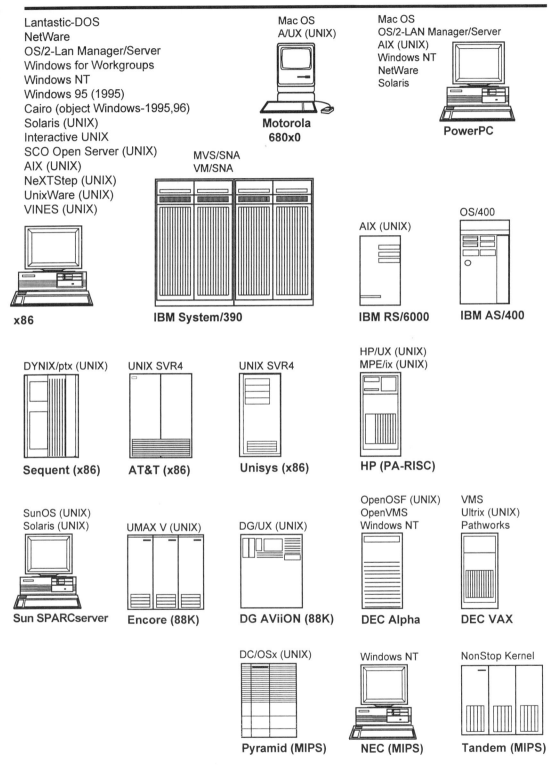

Lantastic-DOS
NetWare
OS/2-Lan Manager/Server
Windows for Workgroups
Windows NT
Windows 95 (1995)
Cairo (object Windows-1995,96)
Solaris (UNIX)
Interactive UNIX
SCO Open Server (UNIX)
AIX (UNIX)
NeXTStep (UNIX)
UnixWare (UNIX)
VINES (UNIX)

x86

Mac OS
A/UX (UNIX)

Motorola 680x0

Mac OS
OS/2-LAN Manager/Server
AIX (UNIX)
Windows NT
NetWare
Solaris

PowerPC

MVS/SNA
VM/SNA

IBM System/390

AIX (UNIX)

IBM RS/6000

OS/400

IBM AS/400

DYNIX/ptx (UNIX)

Sequent (x86)

UNIX SVR4

AT&T (x86)

UNIX SVR4

Unisys (x86)

HP/UX (UNIX)
MPE/ix (UNIX)

HP (PA-RISC)

SunOS (UNIX)
Solaris (UNIX)

Sun SPARCserver

UMAX V (UNIX)

Encore (88K)

DG/UX (UNIX)

DG AViiON (88K)

OpenOSF (UNIX)
OpenVMS
Windows NT

DEC Alpha

VMS
Ultrix (UNIX)
Pathworks

DEC VAX

DC/OSx (UNIX)

Pyramid (MIPS)

Windows NT

NEC (MIPS)

NonStop Kernel

Tandem (MIPS)

network. Database services provides for the storage and retrieval of data in a database.

service bureau

An organization that provides data processing and timesharing services. It may offer a variety of software packages, batch processing services (data entry, COM, etc.) as well as custom programming.

Customers pay for storage of data on the system and processing time used. Connection is made to a service bureau through dial-up terminals, private lines, or other networks, such as Telenet or Tymnet.

Service bureaus also exist that support desktop publishing and presentations and provide imagesetting, color proofing, slide creation and other related services on an hourly or per item basis.

servo

An electromechanical device that uses feedback to provide precise starts and stops for such functions as the motors on a tape drive or the moving of an access arm on a disk.

session

(1) In communications, the active connection between a user and a computer or between two computers.

(2) Using an application program (period between starting up and quitting).

set theory

The branch of mathematics or logic that is concerned with sets of objects and rules for their manipulation. UNION, INTERSECT and COMPLEMENT are its three primary operations and they are used in relational databases as follows.

Given a file of Americans and a file of Barbers, UNION would create a file of all Americans and Barbers. INTERSECT would create a file of American Barbers, and COMPLEMENT would create a file of Barbers who are not Americans, or of Americans who are not Barbers. See *fuzzy logic*.

set-top box

The cable TV box that "sits on top" of the TV set. A variety of new set-top boxes are expected for emerging video-on-demand and other interactive cable services.

SETUP.INF

A file that contains information Windows needs to install itself into the PC. See *INF file*.

setup program

(1) Same as *install program*.

(2) In a PC, a built-in configuration program that uses parameters in the CMOS RAM. See *CMOS RAM*.

setup string

A group of commands that initialize a device, such as a printer. See *escape character*.

seven dwarfs

IBM's early competitors in the mainframe business: Burroughs, CDC, GE, Honeywell, NCR, RCA and Univac.

seven-segment display

A common display found on digital watches and readouts that looks like a series of 8s. Each digit or letter is formed by selective illumination of up to seven separately addressable bars.

sex changer

See *gender changer*.

SGI

(Silicon Graphics, Inc., Mountain View, CA) A manufacturer of very high-end graphics workstations, founded in 1982 by Jim Clark. Its UNIX-based operating system is IRIX. SGI had been using MIPS processors for a number of years and acquired MIPS Computer Systems in 1992. Its current line is based on the MIPS R4000 64-bit CPUs (see *MIPS Computer*).

No matter how much better the graphics get on personal computers, the graphics are always superior on SGI workstations. Running a flight simulator on an SGI machine is considerably more realistic than on a PC; however, SGI workstations can cost from 20 to 50 times as much. They are naturally used in commercial graphics applications, where the state of the art is always being pushed.

SGML

(Standard Generalized Markup Language) An ISO standard for defining the formatting in a text document. It is a comprehensive language that can even define hypertext links. In order to decipher format commands in an SGML document, SGML uses format definitions in a separately-created DTD (Document Type Definition) file. As a result, SGML is often called a metalanguage, because it describes another language; in this case, the actual formatting commands that are embedded in the text.

SGML has become popular due to the tremendous increase in electronic publishing over the last decade. Increasingly, word processors and publishing systems are built to import and export SGML files. The industry needed a non-proprietary document format that would support all kinds of page layouts. In addition, HTML, a subset of SGML, is the foundation document format for the World Wide Web. See *HTML*.

sh

(SHell) A UNIX command that invokes a different shell. It can be used like a batch file to execute a series of commands saved as a shell.

shadow batch

A data collection system that simulates a transaction processing environment. Instead of updating master files (customers, inventory, etc.) when orders or shipments are initiated, the transactions are stored in the computer. When a user makes a query, the master record from the previous update cycle is retrieved; but before it's displayed, it's updated in memory with any transactions that may affect it. The up-to-date master record is then displayed for the user. At the end of the day or period, the transactions are then actually batch processed against the master file.

shadow mask

A thin screen full of holes that adheres to the back of a color CRT's viewing glass. The electron beam is aimed through the holes onto the phosphor dots.

shadow RAM

A RAM copy of a PC's ROM BIOS. In order to improve performance, the BIOS, which is stored in a ROM chip, is copied to and executed from RAM. RAM chips are accessed faster than ROMs.

shared DASD

A disk system accessed by two or more computers within a single datacenter. Disks shared in personal computer networks are called file servers or database servers.

shared logic

Using a single computer to provide processing for two or more terminals. Contrast with *shared resource*.

shared media LAN

A local area network that shares a common path (line, cable, etc.) between all nodes. The bandwidth of the line is the total transmission capacity of all transmitting stations at any given time. Contrast with a LAN that uses a *switching hub*, in which any two stations have the full bandwidth of the line.

shared resource

Sharing a peripheral device (disk, printer, etc.) among several users. For example, a file server and laser printer in a LAN are shared resources. Contrast with *shared logic*.

SHARE.EXE

An external DOS command that provides file sharing and file locking in a network environment. It manages files that are used by multiple applications at the same time. Some applications automatically install the SHARE.EXE utility, others alert you that it is required. SHARE.EXE is generally loaded from AUTOEXEC.BAT, but starting with DOS 5, can be loaded in the CONFIG.SYS file with the Install command.

Share is required for Windows programs that support OLE Version 2 even on stand-alone machines. Windows for Workgroups automatically installs Vshare, the Windows version of DOS Share. In this case, SHARE.EXE is not required unless one or more DOS applications need it.

The Windows for Workgroups VSHARE.386 driver cannot be used in Windows 3.1. However, a Windows 3.1-compatible version of VSHARE.386 is available from Microsoft.

shareware

Software distributed on a trial basis through BBS's, online services, mail-order vendors and user groups. Shareware is software on the honor system. If you use it regularly, you're required to register and pay for it, for which you will receive technical support and perhaps additional documentation or the next upgrade. Paid licenses are required for commercial distribution.

There are tens of thousands of shareware programs, some fantastic, some awful. Shareware vendors compile catalogs with hundreds and thousands of products and sell them by mail or at shows for a small fee. That fee is not the registration fee, but the fee for distributing the shareware to you. See *freeware, public domain software, ASP* and *ZD Net*.

sheet-fed scanner

A scanner that allows only paper to be scanned rather than books or other thick objects. It moves the paper across a stationary scan head. Contrast with *flatbed scanner, hand-held scanner* and *drum scanner*.

sheet feeder

A mechanical device that feeds stacks of cut forms (letterheads, legal paper, etc.) into a printer.

shelfware

Products that remain unsold on a dealer's shelf or unused by the customer.

shell

An outer layer of a program that provides the user interface, or way of commanding the computer. Shells are typically add-on programs created for command-driven operating systems, such as UNIX and DOS. It provides a menu-driven or graphical icon-oriented interface to the system in order to make it easier to use. Starting with DOS 4.0, DOS comes with its own optional shell called *DOSshell.*

shell account

See *UNIX shell account.*

shell out

To temporarily exit an application, go back to the operating system, perform a function and then return to the application.

shell script

A file of executable UNIX commands created by a text editor and made executable with the Chmod command. It is the UNIX counterpart to a DOS batch file.

shielded twisted pair

See *twisted pair.*

shift register

A high-speed circuit that holds some number of bits for the purpose of shifting them left or right. It is used internally within the processor for multiplication and division, serial/parallel conversion and various timing considerations.

Shiva

(Shiva Corporation, Burlington, MA) The leading remote access server manufacturer founded in 1985. Shiva's first products were its NetModem network modems for the Macintosh and later for PCs. Its LANRover is a proprietary remote access server, providing remote users access to LANs via modem. Shiva has also developed the remote access software in Windows 95.

Shlaer-Mellor

An object-oriented analysis and design method developed by Sally Shlaer and Stephen Mellor. The method is applied by partitioning the system into domains. Each domain is analyzed, and the analysis is verified by simulation. A translation method is specified, and the domain models are translated into the object-oriented architecture of the target system.

SHL TRANSFORM

A software environment from SHL Systemhouse, Chicago, IL, that provides business and software engineering methodologies for transition to client/server. It runs on Windows clients and a variety of servers and includes support tools and context-based training for implementing the methodologies, which are contained in a knowledge base of more than 10,000 objects. The material is delivered through full-motion and still-frame video, audio, hypertext, hypergraphics and full-text searching.

short

In programming, an integer variable. In C, a long is two bytes and can be signed (-32K to +32K) or unsigned (64K). Contrast with *long.*

short card

In a PC, a plug-in printed circuit board that is half the length of a full-size board. Contrast with *long card.*

short-haul modem

In communications, a device that transmits signals up to about a mile. Similar to a line driver that can transmit up to several miles.

shrink-wrapped software

Refers to store-bought software, implying a standard platform that is widely supported.

SI

See *systems integration.*

sideband

In communications, the upper or lower half of a wave. Since both sidebands are normally mirror images of each other, one of the halves can be used for a second channel to increase the data-carrying capacity of the line or for diagnostic or control purposes.

SideBar

A Windows shell from Quarterdeck Office Systems that streamlines the Windows desktop. It can replace Program Manager and File Manager or stay synchronized with them. SideBar was originally developed by Mike McCue of Paper Software.

Sidekick

A personal information manager (PIM) for Windows from Starfish Software, Scotts Valley, CA. Introduced by Borland in 1984, it was the first popular popup (TSR) program for DOS PCs. It included a calculator, notepad, appointment calendar, phone dialer and ASCII table. Later versions added more notepad commands, calendar alarms, scientific and programming calculators, limited file management and an outliner.

SIDF

(System Independent Data Format) A tape format designed as a standard for tape backup systems. If widely used, tapes created by one backup software vendor on one platform would be readable by another vendor's software on another platform. Using a Field Identifier (FID) that identifies the operating system the data was created on, the SIDF format can be extended to support future file systems. Originating from Novell's Storage Management Services (SMS) and governed by the SIDF Association based in Arlington Heights, IL, SIDF is expected to become an international standard.

Siemens

See *SNI.*

Sieve of Eratosthenes

A benchmark program used to test the mathematical speed of a computer. The program calculates prime numbers based on Eratosthenes's algorithm.

SIG

(Special Interest Group) A group of people that meets and shares information about a particular topic of interest. It is usally a part of a larger group or association.

SIGCAT Foundation

(Special Interest Group on CD-ROM Applications and Technology, 11343 Sunset Hills Road, Reston, VA 22090, 703/435-5200) A non-profit user group founded by Jerry McFaul in 1986. With more than 8,000 members in over 50 countries, it is made up of several working groups devoted to the advancement of CD-ROM technology. It provides catalogs, publications and hosts regular meetings and an annual conference. A free membership includes a publication of events and resources.

SIGGRAPH

A special interest group on computer graphics that is part of the ACM.

sign

A symbol that identifies a positive or negative number. In digital code, it is either a separate character or part of the byte. In ASCII, the sign is kept in a separate character typically transmitted in front of the number it represents (+ and - is 2B and 2D in hex).

In EBCDIC, the minus sign can be stored as a separate byte (hex 60), or, more commonly, as half a byte (+ and - is C and D in hex), which is stored in the high-order bits of the least significant byte. For packed decimal, it is in the low-order bits of the least significant byte.

signal

Any electrical or light pulse or frequency.

signal converter

A device that changes the electrical or light characteristics of a signal.

signaling in/out of band

In communications, signaling "in band" refers to sending control signals within the same frequency range as the data signal. For example, a Switched 56 service transmits over a 64 Kbps channel, but uses one out of every eight bits for signaling. Signaling "out of band" refers to sending control signals outside of the data signal. For example, Basic Rate ISDN (BRI) uses two 64 Kbps channels for data and a separate 16 Kbps channel for signaling.

signal processing

See *DSP*.

signal to noise ratio

The ratio of the amplitude (power, volume) of a data signal to the amount of noise (interference) in the line. Usually measured in decibels, it measures the clarity or quality of a transmission channel, audio signal or electronic device.

signature

(1) A unique number built into hardware or software for identification.
(2) (Signature) The successor to the XyWrite III Plus word processor. See *XyWrite III Plus*.

significant digits

Those digits in a number that add value to the number. For example, in the number 00006508, 6508 are the significant digits.

sign on/sign off

Same as *log-on/log-off*. See also *Synon/2E*.

silica

Same as *silicon dioxide*.

silica gel

A highly absorbent form of silicon dioxide often wrapped in small bags and packed with equipment to absorb moisture during shipping and storage.

silicon

(Si) The base material used in chips. Next to oxygen, it is the most abundant element in nature and is found in a natural state in rocks and sand. Its atomic structure and abundance make it an ideal semiconductor material. In chip making, it is mined from rocks and put through a chemical process at high temperatures to purify it. To alter its electrical properties, it is mixed (doped) with other chemicals in a molten state.

silicon compiler

Software that translates the electronic design of a chip into the actual layout of the components.

silicon dioxide

(SiO^2) A hard, glassy mineral found in such materials as rock, quartz, sand and opal. In MOS chip fabrication, it is used to create the insulation layer between the metal gates of the top layer and the silicon elements below.

silicon disk

A disk drive that is permanently simulated in memory. Typically used in laptops for weight reduction, it requires constant power from a battery to maintain its contents.

silicon foundry

See *foundry*.

Silicon Graphics

See *SGI*.

silicon nitride

(Si^3N^4) A silicon compound capable of holding a static electric charge and used as a gate element on some MOS transistors.

Silicon Valley

The area around San Jose (south of San Francisco) noted for its large number of high-tech companies.

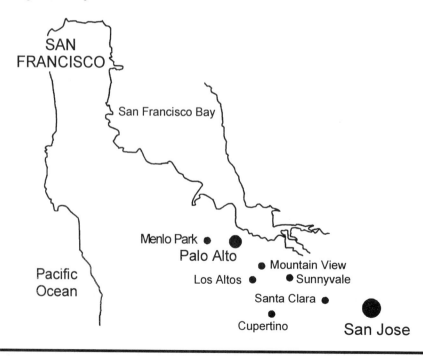

SIM

(Society for Information Management) An organization of MIS professionals founded as the Society for MIS in 1968. It is an exchange for technical information and offers educational and research programs, competitions and awards to its members. Address: 111 East Wacker Dr., Suite 600, Chicago, IL 60601.

SimCity 2000

A popular educational game for kids and adults for DOS and Macintosh from Maxis, Orinda, CA. The purpose is to create a city that literally expands itself if the infrastructure is well designed. After installing a power plant, electric lines, highways and setting up residential and commercial zones, the people come and build up the city. You can influence the politics, taxation, even determine how much natural disaster befalls the citizens. It's quite amazing!

SIMD

(Single Instruction stream Multiple Data stream) A computer architecture that performs one operation on multiple sets of data, for example, an array processor. One computer or processor is used for the control logic and the remaining processors are used as slaves, each executing the same instruction. Contrast with *MIMD*.

SIMM

(Single In-line Memory Module) A narrow printed circuit board that holds memory chips. It plugs into a SIMM socket on the motherboard or memory board. The first SIMM format that became popular on personal computers is 3.5" long and uses a 30-pin connector. A larger format that is 4.25" long uses 72-pins and contains from one to 64 megabytes of RAM.

PCs use either nine-bit memory (eight bits and a parity bit) or eight-bit memory without parity. Macintoshes use eight-bit memory without parity.

30-pin SIMMs

Configuration	Capacity	Chip layout
1x3	1MB	Two 4Mb chips, one 1Mb chip
1x9	1MB	Nine 1Mb chips
2x9	2MB	Nine 2Mb chips
4x9	4MB	Nine 4Mb chips
16x9	16MB	Nine 16Mb chips
1x2	1MB	Two 4Mb chips (no parity)
1x8	1MB	Eight 1Mb chips (no parity)
2x8	2MB	Eight 2Mb chips (no parity)
4x8	4MB	Eight 4Mb chips (no parity)
16x8	16MB	Eight 8Mb chips (no parity)

72-pin SIMMs

Configuration	Capacity	Chip layout
256x36	1MB	The number of chips on a 72-pin SIMM is not
512x36	2MB	expressed in its designation. For example, 8x36
1x36	4MB	means only that 8 million 36-bit words are available
2x36	8MB	to the motherboard.
4x36	16MB	
8x36	32MB	
16x36	64MB	
1x32	4MB	(no parity)
2x32	8MB	(no parity)
4x32	16MB	(no parity)
8x32	32MB	(no parity)
16x32	64MB	(no parity)

The Speed of the Chip
A number, typically from 50 to 80, following the above designation is chip speed; for example, 1x9-60 means 60 nanosecond 1MB SIMMs.

Multiple SIMMs May Be Required
On PCs, SIMMs are installed in multiples of two on 286s and 386SXs, and multiples of four on 386DXs and up. On 486s and up, the number that must be installed at one time depends on the motherboard.

SIMM Modules
The unit on the left is a 30-pin SIMM. On the right, a 72-pin SIMM.

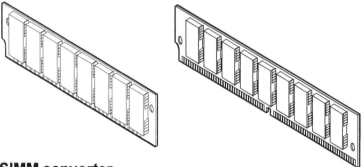

SIMM converter
A printed circuit board that allows older 30-pin SIMMs to be plugged into the newer 72-pin socket. The board contains a 72-pin plug and a number of 30-pin sockets. SIMM converters are also used to expand a single 30-pin or 72-pin socket to multiple SIMM modules.

simplex
One way transmission. Contrast with *half-duplex* and *full-duplex*.

SIMSCRIPT
A programming language used for discrete simulations.

SIMULA
A simulation language originating in the late 1960s that was used to model the behavior of complex systems. SIMULA was the original object-oriented language.

simulation
(1)The mathematical representation of the interaction of real-world objects. See *scientific application*.
(2)The execution of a machine language program designed to run in a foreign computer.

simultaneous voice and data
See *SVD*.

sine
In a right triangle, the ratio of the side opposite an acute angle (less than 90 degrees) and the hypotenuse. The cosine is the ratio between the adjacent side and the hypotenuse. These angular functions are used to compute circular movements.

sine wave
A uniform wave that is generated by a single frequency.

Sine Wave

single board computer

A printed circuit board that contains a complete computer, including processor, memory, I/O and clock.

single density disk

The first-generation floppy disk.

single-ended configuration

Electrical signal paths that use a common ground, which are more susceptible to noise than *differential configuration*.

single-mode fiber

An optical fiber with a core diameter of less than 10 microns, used for high-speed transmission and long distances. It provides greater bandwidth than multimode fiber, but its smaller core makes it more difficult to couple the light source. Contrast with *multimode fiber*.

single precision

The use of one computer word to hold a numeric value for calculation. Contrast with *double precision*.

single session

See *Photo CD*.

single sided disk

A floppy disk that stores data on only one side.

single-system image

An operational view of multiple networks, distributed databases or multiple computer systems as if they were one system.

single threading

Processing one transaction to completion before starting the next.

sink

A device or place that accepts something. See *heat sink* and *data sink*.

SIP

(1) (Single In-line Package) A type of chip module that is similar to a SIMM, but uses pins rather than edge connectors. SIPs are sometimes called SIPPs (Single In-Line Pin Package).

(2) (SMDS Interface Protocol) The protocol used to support SMDS service. It is composed of the Level 3 Protocol Data Unit (L3_PDU), which contains source and destination addresses and an information field up to 9188 bytes long. See *SMDS*.

(3) (Software Integration Platform) A specification that provides a common format and interface for storing and retrieving geographic data for the petroleum industry.

SIR

(Serial InfraRed) An infrared (IR) technology from HP that allows wireless data transmission between two devices up to one meter apart. Both devices must be lined up to each other. Future enhancements will allow greater distances and wider angles. It is expected that SIR ports will be come popular, if not standard, on laptops.

SISD

(Single Instruction stream Single Data stream) The architecture of a serial computer. Contrast with *SIMD* and *MIMD*.

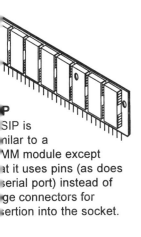

P

SIP is
nilar to a
MM module except
it it uses pins (as does
serial port) instead of
ge connectors for
sertion into the socket.

site license

A license to use software within a facility. It provides authorization to make copies and distribute them within a specific jurisdiction.

SIXEL

A graphics language from Digital that supersedes ReGIS. ReGIS to SIXEL conversion programs are available.

skew

(1)The misalignment of a document or punched card in the feed tray or hopper that prohibits it from being scanned or read properly.
(2) In facsimile, the difference in rectangularity between the received and transmitted page.
(3) In communications, a change of timing or phases in a transmission signal.
(4) See *cylinder skew* and *head skew*.

SkyTel

(SkyTel Corporation, Washington, DC) A paging service provider. In 1987, it was the first to provide nationwide paging. The SkyPager service transmits a 12-digit number. SkyTalk beeps the pager, and the user dials in to listen to voice messages. SkyWord transmits text to the recipient's paging device.

sky wave

A radio signal transmitted into the sky and reflected back down to earth from the ionosphere.

SL

See *SL Enhanced.*

slave

A computer or peripheral device controlled by another computer. For example, a terminal or printer in a remote location that only receives data is a slave. When two personal computers are hooked up via their serial or parallel ports for file exchange, the file transfer program may make one computer the master and the other the slave.

slave tube

A display monitor connected to another monitor in order to provide an additional viewing station.

SLC

See *386SLC.*

SLED

(Single Large Expensive Disk) The traditional hard disk drive used in minicomputers and mainframes. Such drives were widely used starting in the mid 1960s through the late 1980s. Today, all hard disks are small and inexpensive by comparison. See *RAID.*

sleep

(1) In programming, an inactive state due to an endless loop or programmed delay. A sleep statement in a programming language creates a delay for some specified amount of time.
(2)The inactive status of a terminal, device or program that is awakened by sending a code to it.

SL Enhanced

The designation for Intel's power-saving features in its CPU chips. SL Enhanced chips use 3.3 volts instead of 5 and can go into a sleep, or idle, state that uses less than one watt of power. Its System Management Mode can shut down peripherals in portable PCs to save energy.

slew rate

(1) How fast paper moves through a printer (ips).
(2) The speed of changing voltage.

sliding window

(1) A communications protocol that transmits multiple packets before acknowledgement. Both ends keep track of packets sent and acknowledged (left of window), those which have been sent and not acknowledged (in window) and those not yet sent (right of window).
(2) A view of memory that can be instantly shifted to another location.

slime

A dweeb's term for a sales person. See *dweeb*.

SLIP

(Serial Line IP) A data link protocol that is commonly used for dial-up access to networks that support TCP/IP. It is commonly used to gain access to the Internet as well as to provide dial-up access between two LANs. SLIP transmits IP packets over any serial link (dial up or private lines). See *CSLIP* and *PPP*.

slipstream

To fix a bug or add enhancements to software without identifying such inclusions by creating a new version number.

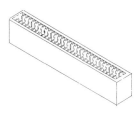

slot

(1) A receptacle for additional printed circuit boards.
(2) A receptacle for inserting and removing a disk or tape cartridge.
(3) In communications, a narrow band of frequencies. See *time slot*.
(4) May refer to reserved space for temporary or permanent storage of instructions, data or codes.

slot mask

The Sony Trinitron counterpart to the shadow mask. It uses vertical rectangular slots instead of holes.

slow scan TV

The transmission of still video frames over telephone lines. Not realtime transmission, it takes several seconds to transmit one frame. Also called electronic still photography (ESP).

slug

A metal bar containing the carved image of a letter or digit that is used in a printing mechanism.

SMA

(1) (Software Maintenance Association) A non-profit professional organization founded in 1985 and dedicated to enhance understanding of software maintenance and to advance those concerned with it. Active chapters are in major cities worldwide. Annual conference is held in the spring. Address: Ms. Robin Gross, Box 12004, Vallejo, CA 94590, 707/643-4423.

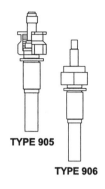

TYPE 905

TYPE 906

**SMA
Connectors**

(2) (Systems Management Architecture) An IBM network management repository.
(3) (Spectrum Manufacturers Association) A DBMS standard for application
compatibility.

SMA connector

A fiber-optic cable connector that uses a plug which is screwed into a threaded
socket. It was the first connector for optical fibers to be standardized. Two SMA
connectors are used for each pair of cables. See *fiber-optic connectors*.

Smalltalk

An operating system and object-oriented programming language that was developed
at Xerox Corporation's Palo Alto Research Center. As an integrated environment, it
eliminates the distinction between programming language and operating system. It
also allows the programmer to customize the user interface and behavior of the
system.
Smalltalk was the first object-oriented programming language and was used on
Xerox's Alto computer, which was designed for it. It was originally used to create
prototypes of simpler programming languages and the graphical interfaces that are so
popular today.

Smalltalk V

A version of Smalltalk for PCs from Digitalk, Inc., Los Angeles. Versions for DOS,
OS/2, Windows and the Mac are also available.

smart cable

A cable with a built-in microprocessor used to connect two devices. It analyzes
incoming signals and converts them from one protocol to another.

smart card

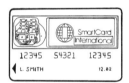

A credit card with a built-in microprocessor and memory used for identification or
financial transactions. When inserted into a reader, it transfers data to and from a
central computer. It is more secure than a magnetic stripe card and can be
programmed to self-destruct if the wrong password is entered too many times. As a
financial transaction card, it can store transactions and maintain a bank balance.

Smartcom

A family of communications programs for PCs and Macs from Hayes
Microcomputer Products, Inc., Atlanta, GA. Versions emulate a several terminals
and support a variety of protocols, including the Hayes V-series. Smartcom EZ is
for the novice.

Smartdrive

A disk cache program that comes with DOS and Windows. In DOS 4.0 and
Windows 3.0, the name of the driver file is SMARTDRV.SYS. Starting with DOS
5 and Windows 3.1, the name of the driver is SMARTDRV.EXE.

smart hub

See *intelligent hub*.

smart install program

An install program that configures itself automatically based on the hardware
environment.

SmartKey

A PC keyboard macro processor from No Brainer Software, Midvale, UT. It was one
of the first macro processors that let users eliminate repetitive typing by creating a
macro for an occurrence of text or a series of commands.

SmartSuite

A suite of applications for Windows and OS/2 from Lotus that includes the 1-2-3 spreadsheet, Ami Pro word processor, Freelance Graphics, Approach database, Organizer PIM and Adobe Type Manager. Also included is a common toolbar for launching the applications and selecting predefined macros that provide tighter integration between the applications.

smart terminal

A video terminal with built-in display characteristics (blinking, reverse video, underlines, etc.). It may also contain a communications protocol. The term is often used synonymously with intelligent terminal. See *intelligent terminal* and *dumb terminal.*

SmartWare

An integrated software package for PCs and various UNIX-based systems from Informix Software, Inc., Menlo Park, CA, that includes a programming language.

SMB

(Server Message Block) A message format derived from the Microsoft/3Com file sharing protocol. It provides services at the application layer (layer 7 of the OSI model) and is used with NetBIOS and NetBEUI protocols in networks such as LAN Manager, LAN Server and Windows NT. It is used to transfer file requests (open, close, read, write, etc.) between clients and servers as well as within the server for internal operations. For network transfer, SMBs are carried within the NetBIOS network control block (NCB) packet.

SMD

(1) (Storage Module Device) A high-performance hard disk interface used with minis and mainframes that transfers data in the 1-4 MBytes/sec range (SMD-E provides highest rate). See *hard disk.*
(2) (Surface Mount Device) A surface mounted chip.

SMDS

(Switched Multimegabit Data Service) A high-speed, switched data communications service offered by the local telephone companies for interconnecting LANs in different geographic locations. It was introduced in 1992 and became generally available nationwide by 1995.

Connection to an SMDS service can be made from a variety of devices, including bridges, routers, CSU/DSUs as well as via frame relay and ATM networks. SMDS can employ various networking technologies. Early implementations use the IEEE 802.6 DQDB MAN technology at rates up to 45 Mbps.

Data is framed for transmission using the SMDS Interface Protocol (SIP), which packages data as Level 3 Protocol Data Units (L3_PDU). The L3_PDU contains source and destination addresses and a data field that holds up to 9188 bytes.

SMF

(1) (Standard Messaging Format) An electronic mail format for Novell's MHS messaging system. The application puts the data into this format in order to send an e-mail message. NGM (NetWare Global Messaging) is based on SMF-71, which supports long addresses and synchronized directories.
(2) (Standard MIDI file) See *MIDI file.*
(3) See *single-mode fiber.*

SMI

(1) (Simple Mail Interface) A subset of functions within the VIM messaging protocol used by applications to send e-mail and attachments. Future versions of VIM will use the CMC API rather than SMI.

(2) (Structure of Management Information) A definition for creating MIBs in the SNMP protocol.

(3) (System Management Interrupt) A hardware interrupt in Intel SL Enhanced 486 and Pentium CPUs used for power management. This interrupt is also used for virus checking.

smiley

See *emoticon.*

SMM

(System Management Mode) An energy conservation mode built into Intel SL Enhanced 486 and Pentium CPUs. During inactive periods, SMM initiates a sleep mode that turns off peripherals or the entire system. It retains the computer's status in a protected area of memory called the SMRAM (System Management RAM).

smoke test

A test of new or repaired equipment by turning it on. If there's smoke, it doesn't work!

smoothed data

Statistical data that has been averaged or otherwise manipulated so that the curves on its graph are smooth and free of irregularities.

smoothing circuit

An electronic filtering circuit in a DC power supply that removes the ripples from AC power.

SMP

(Symmetric MultiProcessing) A multiprocessing computer system in which multiple CPUs, residing in one cabinet, share the same memory. SMP systems provide scalability. As business increases, additional CPUs can be added to absorb the increased transaction volume.

SMP systems range from two to as many as 32 or more processors. However, if one CPU fails, the entire SMP system, or node, is down. Clusters of two or more SMP nodes can be used to provide high availability, or fault resilience, in case of failure. The other nodes continue to operate in the event that one fails.

A single CPU generally boots the system and loads the SMP operating system, which brings the other CPUs online. There is only one instance of the operating system and one instance of the application in memory. The operating system uses the CPUs as a pool of processing resources, all executing simultaneously, either processing data or in an idle loop waiting to do something. The operating system's multithreading capability allows it to control multiple CPUs.

SMP speeds up whatever processes can be overlapped. For example, in a desktop computer, it would speed up the running of multiple applications simultaneously. Switching between applications would also be faster, but if the application is not designed for SMP use, there will be little or no performance improvement within the application itself.

Clusters of SMP nodes are also used to increase processing capability. However, when SMP is used in this manner, it functions as a massively parallel processor (MPP). MPP systems use different programming paradigms than SMP systems, because there are not only multiple CPUs, but multiple memories each with a copy of the operating system and application. It requires a problem to be split into smaller pieces that can be solved simultaneously.

For example, in the commercial world, a parallel data query (PDQ) breaks down a query into multiple searches so that several parts of the database can be searched simultaneously. The Oracle Parallel Server software was the first DBMS designed for

MPP use, allowing multiple instances of itself, each in a different CPU, to access a common database.

Sequent, Pyramid and Encore pioneered SMP on UNIX platforms. SMP servers are also available from IBM, HP, AT&T GIS, Unisys and others. Many versions of UNIX as well as proprietary operating systems, such as Windows NT, OS/2 and NetWare, have been designed for or are being revamped for SMP. SMP usage is expected to grow rapidly, and applications are increasingly being designed to take advantage of the SMP architecture.

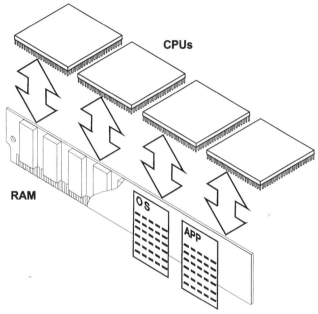

SMPTE

(Society for Motion Picture and TV Engineers, 595 W. Hartsdale Ave., White Plains, NY 10607, 914/761-1100) An organization that prepares standards and documentation for TV production. SMPTE time code records hours, minutes, seconds and frames on audio or videotape for synchronization purposes.

SMR

(Specialized Mobile Radio) Communications services used by taxicabs, trucks and other mobile businesses. Throughout the U.S., approximately 3,000 independent operators are licensed by the FCC to provide this service.

SMRAM

See *SMM*.

SMS

(1) (Storage Management System) Software used to routinely back up and archive files. See SMS definition below and *HSM*.

(2) (Storage Management Services) Software from Novell that allows data to be stored and retrieved on NetWare servers independent of the file system the data is maintained in (DOS, OS/2, Mac, etc.). It is used to back up data from heterogeneous clients on the network. Various third-party backup products are SMS compliant. See *SIDF*.

(3) (Systems Management Server) Systems management software from Microsoft that runs on Windows NT Server 3.5. It requires a Microsoft SQL Server database and is used to distribute software, monitor and analyze network usage and perform various network administration tasks.

SMT

(1) See *surface mount*.
(2) (Station ManagemenT) An FDDI network management protocol that provides direct management. Only one node requires the software.

SMTP

(Simple Mail Transfer Protocol) A messaging protocol used in TCP/IP networks. See also *SNMP*.

SNA

(Systems Network Architecture) IBM's mainframe network standards introduced in 1974. Originally a centralized architecture with a host computer controlling many terminals, enhancements, such as APPN and APPC (LU 6.2), have adapted SNA to today's peer-to-peer communications and distributed computing environment. Following are some of SNA's basic concepts.

Nodes and Data Links

In SNA, nodes are end points or junctions, and data links are the pathways between them. Nodes are defined as Type 5 (hosts), Type 4 (communications controllers) and Type 2 (peripheral; terminals, PCs and midrange computers).
Type 2.0 nodes can communicate only with the host, and Type 2.1 nodes can communicate with other 2.1 nodes (peer-to-peer) without going to the host. Data links include high-speed local channels, the SDLC data link protocol and Token Ring.

SSCPs, PUs and LUs

The heart of a mainframe-based SNA network is the SSCP (System Services Control Point) software that resides in the host. It manages all resources in its domain. Within all nodes of an SNA network, except for Type 2.1, there is PU (Physical Unit) software that manages node resources, such as data links, and controls the transmission of network management information. In Node Type 2.1, Control Point software performs these functions.
In order to communicate user data, a session path is created between two end points, or LUs (Logical Units). When a session takes place, an LU-LU session is established between an LU in the host (CICS, TSO, user appliction, etc.) and an LU in the terminal controller or PC. An LU 6.2 session provides peer-to-peer communication and lets either side initiate the session.

VTAM and NCP

VTAM (Virtual Telecommunications Access Method) resides in the host and contains the SSCP, the PU for the host, and establishes the LU sessions within the host. NCP (Network Control Program) resides in the communications controller (front end processor) and manages the routing and data link protocols, such as SDLC and Token Ring.

SNA-A

See *SNA Over Async*.

SNADS

(SNADistribution Services) An IBM messaging protocol used by IBM office automation products such as DISOSS and AS/400 Office. Various messaging gateways and messaging switches support SNADS.

SNA Over Async

Software that allows SNA applications to hook into an SNA network via modem. With the SNA Over Async (SNA-A) program in a remote computer and the connecting network node, applications that normally run on a LAN or through 3270 emulation can connect over a telephone line without modification.

The SNA Protocol Stack

The SNA architecture is implemented in functional layers with each layer passing control to the next layer. This layering is called a protocol stack. SNA has had major influence on the development of the OSI model, but OSI does not implement every layer exactly the same.

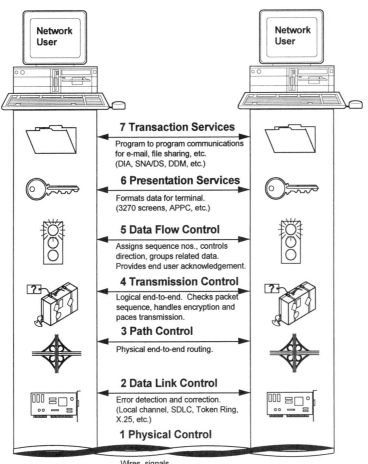

7 Transaction Services
Program to program communications for e-mail, file sharing, etc. (DIA, SNA/DS, DDM, etc.)

6 Presentation Services
Formats data for terminal. (3270 screens, APPC, etc.)

5 Data Flow Control
Assigns sequence nos., controls direction, groups related data. Provides end user acknowledgement.

4 Transmission Control
Logical end-to-end. Checks packet sequence, handles encryption and paces transmission.

3 Path Control
Physical end-to-end routing.

2 Data Link Control
Error detection and correction. (Local channel, SDLC, Token Ring, X.25, etc.)

1 Physical Control
Wires, signals. (RS-232, 802.5, etc.)

SNA	OSI
Transaction	Application
Presentation	Presentation
Data Flow	Session
Transmission	Transport
Path Control	Network
Data Link	Data Link
Physical	Physical

snapshot

The saved current state of memory including the contents of all memory bytes, hardware registers and status indicators. It is periodically taken in order to restore the system in the event of failure.

snapshot dump

A memory dump of selected portions of memory.

snapshot program

A trace program that provides selected dumps of memory when specific instructions are executed or when certain conditions are met.

snap to

A feature in a drawing program that moves a text or graphic element to the closest grid line.

snd

(SouND resource) A Macintosh resource fork that contains sound information, including compression ratios if used and sampling rate.

sneakernet

Carrying floppy disks from one machine to another to exchange information, when you don't have a network.

SNI

(1) (Subscriber Network Interface) The point of interface between the customer's equipment (CPE) and a communications service from a common carrier.

(2) (SNA Network Interconnection) Using a mainframe as a gateway between two independent SNA networks.

(3) (Siemens Nixdorf Information Systems - Siemens Nixdorf Informationssysteme AG) The new name of this German computer company after the 1990 merger of Nixdorf AG and Siemens AG. AG is the German acronymn for corporation (AktienGesellshaft).

sniffer

Software and/or hardware that analyzes traffic and detects bottlenecks and problems in a network.

SNMP

(Simple Network Management Protocol) A widely-used network monitoring and control protocol. Data is passed from SNMP agents, which are hardware and/or software processes reporting activity in each network device (hub, router, bridge, etc.) to the workstation console used to oversee the network. The agents return information contained in a MIB (Management Information Base), which is a data structure that defines what is obtainable from the device and what can be controlled (turned off, on, etc.).

SNMP 2 provides enhancements including security and an RMON (Remote Monitoring MIB), which provides continuous feedback without having to be queried by the SNMP console. Originating in the UNIX community, SNMP has spread to VMS, DOS and other environments. See also *SMTP*.

SNOBOL

(StriNg Oriented symBOlic Language) One of the first list processing languages (Bell Labs; early 1960s). It was used for text processing and compiler development.

snow

The flickering snow-like spots on a video screen caused by display electronics that are too slow to respond to changing data.

SNR

See *signal to noise ratio.*

socket

(1) A receptacle which receives a plug.
(2) See *UNIX socket.*

socket services

Low-level software that manages a PCMCIA controller. See *PCMCIA.*

soft

Flexible and changeable. Software can be reprogrammed for different results. The computer's soft nature is its greatest virtue; however, the reason it takes so long to get new systems developed has little to do with the concept. It is based on how systems are developed (file systems vs database management), the programming languages used (assembly vs high-level), combined with the skill level of the technical staff, compounded by the organization's bureaucracy.

SOFTBANK COMDEX

See *COMDEX.*

soft boot

Same as *warm boot.*

soft copy

Refers to data displayed on a video screen. Contrast with *hard copy.*

soft error

A recoverable error, such as a garbled message that can be retransmitted. Contrast with *hard error.*

soft font

A set of characters for a particular typeface that is stored on the computer's hard disk, or in some cases the printer's hard disk, and downloaded to the printer before printing. Contrast with *internal font* and *font cartridge.*

soft hyphen

A hyphen that prints if it winds up at the end of the line, but does not print otherwise. Contrast with *hard hyphen.* See *discretionary hyphen.*

soft key

A keyboard key that is simulated by an icon on screen.

SoftKey

(SoftKey International, Inc., Cambridge, MA) A software company that was originally founded in 1984 in Toronto. In 1994, it came to the U.S. with a merger of Spinnaker Software and Wordstar International.

soft patch

A quick fix to machine language currently in memory that only lasts for the current session.

SoftPC

A family of PC emulation programs from Insignia Solutions, Inc., Andover, MA, that allow DOS and Windows programs to run on Macintosh, UNIX workstations and the PowerPC.

soft return

A code inserted by the software into a text document to mark the end of the line. When the document is printed, the soft return is converted into the end-of-line code required by the printer. Soft returns are determined by the right margin and change when the margins are changed.

In graphics-based environments, such as in the Macintosh, soft returns are not used as the text must be free to change within movable windows.

With PCs, soft return codes differ; for example, WordPerfect uses a return (ASCII 13) and WordStar uses a line feed (ASCII 10).

Contrast with *hard return*.

soft sectored

A common method of identifying sectors on a disk by initially recording sector information on every track with a format program. Contrast with *hard sectored*.

Soft-Switch

E-mail switching software and hardware from Soft-Switch, Inc., Wayne, PA, that provides an e-mail backbone for organizations with diverse e-mail systems. It directly supports X.400, SNADS and SMTP and provides gateways to other e-mail systems. Soft-Switch Central is software for IBM MVS and VM mainframes, and its EMX 88000-based e-mail server connects to Token Ring, Ethernet, X.25 and SDLC.

software

Instructions for the computer. A series of instructions that performs a particular task is called a program. The two major categories are *system software* and *application software*. System software is made up of control programs, including the operating system, communications software and database manager.

Application software is any program that processes data for the user (inventory, payroll, spreadsheet, word processor, etc.). A common misconception is that software is also data. It is not. Software tells the hardware how to process the data.

Software is "run."
Data is "processed."

**Software Is a
Recipe for the
Computer**

software architecture

The design of application or system software that incorporates protocols and interfaces for interacting with other programs and for future flexibility and expandability. A self-contained, stand-alone program would have program logic, but not a software architecture.

software bug

A problem that causes a program to abend (crash) or produce invalid output. Problems that cause a program to abend are invalid data, such as trying to divide by zero, or invalid instructions, which are caused by bad logic that misdirects the computer to the wrong place in the program.

A program with erroneous logic may produce bad output without crashing, which is the reason extensive testing is required for new programs. For example, if the program is supposed to add an amount, but instead, it subtracts it, bad output results. As long as the program performs valid machine instructions on data it knows how to deal with, the computer will run.

Software Carousel
A DOS task switching program from SoftLogic Solutions, Inc., Manchester, NH, that allows the user to have up to a dozen applications open at the same time and switch back and forth between them.

software codec
A compression/decompression routine that is implemented in software only without requiring specialized DSP hardware. See *codec*.

software engineering
The design, development and documentation of software. See *CASE, systems analysis & design, programming, object-oriented programming, software metrics* and *Systemantics*.

software failure
The inability of a program to continue processing due to erroneous logic. Same as *crash, bomb* and *abend*.

software house
An organization that develops customized software for a customer. Contrast with *software publisher*, which develops and markets software packages.

software IC
An object-oriented programming class packaged for sale. The term was coined by The Stepstone Corporation.

software interface
Same as *API*.

software interrupt
An interrupt caused by an instruction in the program. See *interrupt*.

software metrics
Software measurements. Using numerical ratings to measure the complexity and reliability of source code, the length and quality of the development process and the performance of the application when completed.

software package
An application program developed for sale to the general public.

software program
A computer program (computer application). All computer programs are software. Usage of the two words together is redundant, but common.

software programmer
Same as *systems programmer*.

software protection
See *copy protection*.

software publisher
An organization that develops and markets software. It does market research,

production and distribution of software. It may develop its own software, contract for outside development or obtain software that has already been written.

software stack

A stack that is implemented in memory. See *stack*.

software tool

A program used to develop other software. Any program or utility that helps a programmer design, code, compile or debug sofware can be called a tool.

software vendors

Following is Software Magazine's ranking of the Top 100 Independent Software Vendors for calendar 1994. The total revenues of 24 billion dollars from all the companies in the list come from packaged software sales worldwide. Consulting, custom services and programming revenues are excluded. The following companies collectively employ nearly 140,000 people.
See also *hardware vendors* and *vendors*.

Top 100 Independent Software Vendors
Ranked by Software Package Revenues Worldwide

Reprinted with the permission of Software Magazine, July 1995, Sentry Publishing Company, Inc., One Research Drive, Westborough, MA 01581.

(* = privately held)

1994 packaged software revenues Number
COMPANY NAME   ($ millions) employees
HQ city (date founded)

1 MICROSOFT CORP.
Redmond, WA (1975)   5044   16300
2 COMPUTER ASSOCIATES INT'L., INC.
Islandia, NY (1976)   2455   8000
3 NOVELL, INC.
Provo, UT (1983)   1918   7900
4 ORACLE CORP.
Redwood Shores, CA (1977) 1736   14830

5 LOTUS DEVELOPMENT CORP.
Cambridge, MA (1982)   971   5519
6 SAP AG (SAP AMERICA)
Lester, PA (1972)   807   5044
7 SYBASE, INC.
Emeryville, CA (1984)   615   4016
8 ADOBE SYSTEMS INC.
Mountain View, CA (1982) 598   1584

9 SAS INSTITUTE, INC.*
Cary, NC (1976)   472   3260
10 LEGENT CORP.
Vienna, VA (1989)   471   2700
11 SOFTWARE AG*
Reston, VA (1969)   364   4600
12 INFORMIX SOFTWARE INC.
Menlo Park, CA (1980)   364   2212

13 COMPUWARE CORP.
Farmington Hills, MI (1973) 353   3940
14 BMC SOFTWARE, INC.
Houston, TX (1980)   329   1142
15 SYMANTEC CORP.
Cupertino, CA (1982)   323   1404
16 AMERICAN MANAGEMENT SYSTEMS
Arlington, VA (1970)   321   4500

17 ATTACHMATE CORP.*
Bellevue, WA (1984)   312   2000
18 DUN & BRADSTREET SOFTWARE
Atlanta, GA (1990)   304   2500
19 STERLING SOFTWARE, INC.
Dallas, TX (1981)   299   3600
20 BORLAND INT'L. INC.
Scotts Valley, CA (1983) 250   1138

21 SYSTEM SOFTWARE ASSOCIATES INC.
Chicago, IL (1981)   240   1800
22 CANDLE CORP.*
Santa Monica, CA (1977)   213   1090
23 INFORMATION BUILDERS INC.*
New York, NY (1975)   204   1725
24 J.D. EDWARDS & CO.*
Denver, CO (1977)   190   1614

25 THE SANTA CRUZ OPERATION*
Santa Cruz, CA (1979)   170   1320
26 CLARIS CORP.

Santa Clara, CA (1987)   157   700
27 CINCOM SYSTEMS, INC.*
Cincinnati, OH (1968)   151   951
28 BOOLE & BABBAGE, INC.
Sunnyvale, CA (1967)   135   749

29 BANYAN SYSTEMS, INC.
Westborough, MA (1983)131   850
30 MICRO FOCUS INC.
Palo Alto, CA (1976)   131   762
31 DELRINA CORP.
San Jose, CA (1988)   128   550
32 PROGRESS SOFTWARE CORP.
Bedford, MA (1981)   124   1008

33 COGNOS, INC.
Ottawa, Ontario (1969)   114   1000
34 PEOPLESOFT, INC.
Walnut Creek, CA (1987)   108   651
35 INTERSOLV, INC.
Rockville, MD (1991)   107   615
36 POWERSOFT CORP.
Burlington, MA (1974)   106   850

37 CHEYENNE SOFTWARE, INC.
Roslyn Heights, NY (1983) 104   500
38 WALL DATA, INC.
Redmond, WA (1982)   101   654
39 COMSHARE, INC.
Ann Arbor, MI (1966)   100   670
40 IRI SOFTWARE
Waltham, MA (1982)   97   950

41 MARCAM CORP.
Newton, MA (1980)   92   1200
42 PLATINUM TECHNOLOGY, INC.
Oakbrook Terrace, IL ('87)   90   613
43 WRQ INC.*
Seattle, WA (1981)   89   392
44 SOFTWARE ENGINEERING OF AMERICA, INC.*
Lake Success, NY (1982)   88   327

45 HYPERION SOFTWARE CORP.
Stamford, CT (1981)   87   700
46 FTP SOFTWARE INC.
North Andover, MA (1986) 86   491
47 FILENET CORP.
Costa Mesa, CA (1981)   86   937
48 ROSS SYSTEMS INC.
Redwood City, CA (1972)   74   540

49 JBA HOLDINGS PLC.
Rolling Meadows, IL (1981)74   1200
50 INTERLEAF, INC.
Waltham, MA (1981)   72   779
51 SOFTLAB, INC.*
Atlanta, GA (1971)   71   800

52 BAAN CO.
Menlo Park, MI (1978)   71   943

53 FRAME TECHNOLOGY CORP.
San Jose, CA (1986)   65   440
54 GUPTA CORP.
Menlo Park, CA (1984)   63   400
55 NETMANAGE INC.
Cupertino, CA (1990)   62   355
56 LAWSON SOFTWARE*
Minneapolis, MN (1975)   59   580

57 RATIONAL*
Santa Clara, CA (1980)   57   415
58 SEER TECHNOLOGIES*
Cary, NC (1990)   53   734
59 SOFTWARE PUBLISHING CORP.
Mountain View, CA (1980) 51   230
60 TEKNEKRON SOFTWARE SYSTEMS. INC.
Palo Alto, CA (1985)   50   300

61 CAERE CORP.
Los Gatos, CA (1973)   50   304
62 SPSS, INC.*
Chicago, IL (1975)   46   410
63 LANDMARK SYSTEMS CORP.*
Vienna, VA (1982)   45   209
64 LUCAS INDUSTRIES PLC.
Fairfax, VA (1976)   45   465

65 DATASTORM TECHNOLOGIES, INC.*
Columbia, MO (1985)   44   244
66 SYNON CORP.*
Larkspur, CA (1986)   44   438
67 NEXT COMPUTER INC.*
Redwood City, CA (1985)   43   275
68 AMERICAN SOFTWARE INC.
Atlanta, GA (1970)   43   620

69 SOFTWARE 2000, INC.*
Hyannis, MA (1981)   42   443
70 WALKER INTERACTIVE SYSTEMS, INC.
San Francisco, CA (1969)   42   428
71 VMARK SOFTWARE INC.
Westborough, MA (1984)   42   255
72 MACROMEDIA INC.
San Francisco, CA (1992)   41   175

73 CADRE TECHNOLOGIES, INC.*
Providence, RI (1982)   41   281
74 INTEGRATED SYSTEMS, INC.
Santa Clara, CA (1980)   40   300
75 MACRO 4, PLC.
Parsippany, NJ (1968)   39   227
76 APERTUS TECHNOLOGIES, INC.
Eden Prarie, MN (1979)   39   300

77 TRINZIC CORP.
Redwood City, CA (1992)   38   280
78 RAXCO, INC.*
Rockville, MD (1977)   36   270
79 VISUAL EDGE SOFTWARE, LTD.*
Cupertino, CA (1985)   35   50
80 BGS SYSTEMS, INC.
Waltham, MA (1975)   34   209

81 INTERSYSTEMS CORP.*
Cambridge, MA (1978)   34   142
82 GROUP 1 SOFTWARE, INC.
Lanham, MD (1981)   33   197
83 MCAFEE ASSOCIATES, INC.
Santa Clara, CA (1989)   33   128
84 SYSTEMS UNION GROUP, LTD.*
White Plains, NY (1981)   33   275

85 COMPUTRON TECHNOLOGIES CORP.*
Rutherford, NJ (1982)   32   335
86 PLATINUM SOFTWARE CORP.
Irvine, CA (1984)   32   474
87 MANUGISTICS GROUP INC.
Rockville, MD (1969)   32   400
88 CYBORG SYSTEMS, INC.*
Chicago, IL (1974)   32   300

89 VISUAL NUMERICS INC.*
Houston, TX (1992)   32   186
90 PRAXIS INTERNATIONAL, INC.*
Cambridge, MA (1965)   31   263
91 MAPINFO CORP.
Troy, NY (1986)   30   228
92 WIND RIVER SYSTEMS*
Alameda, CA (1983)   29   152

93 4TH DIMENSION SOFTWARE
Irvine, CA (1983)   28   299
94 QUARTERDECK OFFICE SYSTEMS
Santa Monica, CA (1982)   28   210
95 PROJECT SOFTWARE & DEVELOPMENT, INC.
Cambridge, MA (1968)   28   230
96 HUMMINGBIRD COMMUNICATIONS, LTD.
Mountain View, CA (1984) 28   121

97 BUSINESS OBJECTS, S.A.
Cupertino, CA (1990)   28   214
98 THE CODA GROUP, PLC.
Manchester, NH (1979)   27   350
99 OPENCONNECT SYSTEMS, INC.*
Dallas, TX   27   193
100 UNIFY CORP.*
Sacramento, CA (1980)   27   195

SoftWindows

Windows emulation software for the PowerPC and various UNIX platforms from Insignia Solutions. It allows Windows applications to run on these non-Windows platforms. The first versions of SoftWindows provided support for Windows Standard Mode applications, which can run in a 286. Many applications require Windows 386 Enhanced Mode, which requires a 386 or above (486, Pentium, etc.). SoftWindows 2.0 adds support for 386 Enhanced Mode and can thus run many more Windows applications. See *PowerMac*.

SOG

(Small Outline Gullwing) Same as *SOIC*.

SOHO

(Small Office/Home Office) Refers to the small business or business-at-home user. This market segment demands as much or more than the large corporation. The small business entrepreneur generally wants the latest, greatest and fastest equipment, and this market has always benefited from high technology, allowing it to compete on a level playing ground with the bigger companies.

SOIC

(Small Outline IC) A small-dimension, surface mount DIP that uses gullwing-shaped pins extending outward.

SOJ

(Small Outline J lead) A small-dimension, surface mount DIP that uses J-shaped pins extending inward.

Solaris

A multitasking, multiprocessing distributed computing environment from SunSoft for SPARC computers, 386s and up and the PowerPC. Solaris provides an enterprise-wide networking environment that can manage up to 40,000 nodes from one central station.

Solaris, originally introduced for Sun's own SPARC systems, combined many of Sun's UNIX components into one package, including the SunOS operating system based on UNIX SVR4, ONC networking products (NFS, NIS, etc.) and OpenWindows (Sun's version of X Windows). Also included are the Open Look and Motif graphical interfaces.

As of Solaris 2.1, an x86 version of Solaris was introduced, which runs applications written for Solaris and Sun's INTERACTIVE UNIX for x86 machines.

Solaris optionally includes Sun's Wabi emulator, which runs Windows applications by turning Windows calls into X Window calls. DOS emulation is provided by Merge, a third-party product from Locus Computing. As of Solaris 2.5, a version for the PowerPC is expected.

Solaris is very popular as a server operating system, providing the robustness and scalability expected from UNIX-based SMP systems.

solder mask

An insulating pattern applied to a printed circuit board that exposes only the areas to be soldered.

solenoid

A magnetic switch that closes a circuit, often used as a relay.

solid ink printer

A printer that uses solid wax inks that are melted and sprayed onto a drum or belt. The ink is then transferred onto the paper without a fusing step.

solid logic

Same as *solid state*.

solid modeling

A mathematical technique for representing solid objects. It is the least abstract form of CAD. Unlike wireframe and surface modeling, solid modeling systems ensure that all surfaces meet properly and that the object is geometrically correct. A solid model can also be sectioned (cut open) to reveal its internal features. Solids allow interference checking, which tests to see if two or more objects occupy the same space.

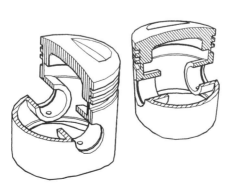

Solid Modeling
When objects are modeled as solids, they can be sliced in half just like the real object. *(Photo courtesy of Robo Systems Corporation.)*

solid state

An electronic component or circuit made of solid materials, such as transistors, chips and bubble memory. There is no mechanical action in a solid state device, although an unbelievable amount of electromagnetic action takes place within.

For data storage, solid state devices are much faster and more reliable than mechanical disks and tapes, but are more expensive. Although solid state costs continually drop, disks, tapes and optical disks also continue to improve their cost/performance ratio.

The first solid state device was the "cat's whisker" of the 1930s. A whisker-like wire was moved around on a solid crystal in order to detect a radio signal.

solid state disk

A disk drive made of memory chips used for high-speed data access or in hostile environments. Solid state disks are used in battery-powered, hand-held devices as well as in desktop units with hundreds of megabytes of storage that contain their own UPS systems.

Different types of storage chips are used for solid state disks, both volatile and non-volatile. However a solid state disk looks like a standard disk drive to the operating system, not a proprietary one that requires additional drivers. See *flash disk*.

solid state memory

Any transistorized, semiconductor or thin film memory that contains no mechanical parts.

solid state relay

A relay that contains no mechanical parts. All switching mechanisms are semiconductor or thin film components.

solver

Mathematical mechanisms that allow spreadsheets to perform goal seeking.

SOM

(1) (System Object Model) An object architecture from IBM that provides a full implementation of the CORBA standard. SOM is language independent and is supported by a variety of large compiler and application development vendors.
It is expected that IBM will promote SOM heavily because its future operating systems are built around objects. DSOM, for distributed SOM, allows objects to be used across the network.
(2) (Self Organizing Map) A two-dimensional map that shows relationships in a neural network.

SONET

(Synchronous Optical NETwork) A fiber optic transmission system for high-speed digital traffic. Employed by telephone companies and common carriers, SONET speeds range from 51 megabits to multiple gigabits per second. SONET is an intelligent system that provides advanced network management, a standard optical interface and more flexibility than the T1 and T3 lines now in common use. Although it is expected to eventually obsolete T-carrier lines, SONET can be used to carry existing T-carrier traffic in the meantime.
SONET is specified in the Broadband ISDN (BISDN) standard. The European counterpart is SDH. Following are the levels of service. The STS (Synchronous Transport Signal) designation refers to the electrical signal, and OC (Optical Carrier) refers to the optical signal, which is identical because it is a one-to-one conversion.

Sonet Circuits

Service	Speed	(Mbps)
STS-1	OC-1	51.84 (28 DS1s or 1 DS3)
STS-3	OC-3	155.52 (3 STS-1s)
STS-3c	OC-3c	155.52 (concatenated)
STS-12	OC-12	622.08 (12 STS-1s, 4 STS-3s)
STS-12c	OC-12c	622.08 (12 STS-1s, 4 STS-3c's)
STS-48	OC-48	2488.32 (48 STS-1s, 16 STS-3s)
STS-192	OC-192	9953.28 (192 STS-1s, 64 STS-3s)

sort

To reorder data into a new sequence. The operating system can typically sort file names and text lists. Word processors typically allow lines of text to be reordered, and database programs sort records by one or more fields, often generating a new file.

A Sort
Sorting orders data into a prescribed sequence.

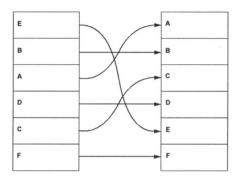

sort algorithm

A formula used to reorder data into a new sequence. Like all complicated problems, there are many solutions that can achieve the same results. One sort algorithm can resequence data faster than another. In the early 1960s, when tape was "the" storage medium, the sale of a computer system may have hinged on the sort algorithm, since without direct access capability, every transaction had to be sorted into the sequence of the master file.

sorter

(1) A sort program.
(2) A person who manually puts data into a specific sequence.
(3) An early tabulating machine that routed punched cards into separate stackers based on the content of a card column. The complete operation required passing the cards through the machine once for each column sorted.

sort key

A field or fields in a record that dictate the sequence of the file. For example, the sort keys STATE and NAME arrange the file alphabetically by name within state. STATE is the major sort key, and NAME is the minor key.

SOS

(1) (Silicon On Sapphire) An MOS chip-fabrication method that places a thin layer of silicon over a sapphire substrate (base).
(2) (Sophisticated Operating System) The operating system used on the Apple III.

sound bandwidth

A range of sound frequencies. The human ear can perceive approximately from 20 to 20,000Hz, but human voice is confined to within 3,000Hz.

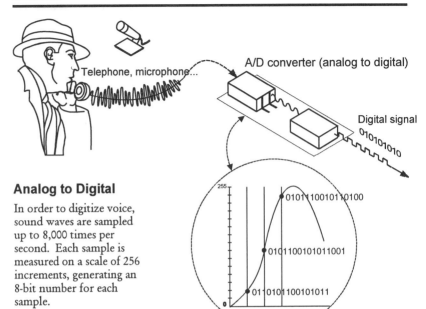

Telephone, microphone...

A/D converter (analog to digital)

Digital signal
010101010

Analog to Digital

In order to digitize voice, sound waves are sampled up to 8,000 times per second. Each sample is measured on a scale of 256 increments, generating an 8-bit number for each sample.

255

0101 1100101 10100

0101100101011001

01 0101 100101011

0

Music is sampled 44,000 times per second on a scale of 65,536 increments, which requires a 16-bit number for each sample. Hi-fi stereo sound uses up more than 1,400,000 bits per second.

Digital to Analog

Today's audio CDs can hold almost seven billion bits of music, equivalent to 460 high-density 3.5" floppy disks. The bits are packed 46 million to a square centimeter!

The laser in a CD player reads the digital samples and recreates the original sound vibrations that are sent to the amplifier, which is still analog. If the original recording was made on a digital tape recorder, there is no background noise or hiss, which is generated by analog recording methods.

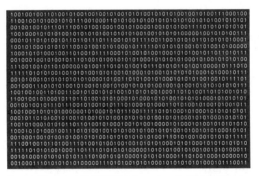

One millisecond (1/1000th of a second) of hi-fi stereo sound generates this many bits.

Sound Blaster

A family of sound cards from Creative Labs, Inc., Milpitas, CA. The Sound Blaster protocol has become a de facto audio standard for PCs.

sound board, sound card

Also called *audio adapter*, it is a personal computer expansion board that records and plays back sound, providing outputs directly to speakers or an external amplifier. Many sound cards also include MIDI capability.

Standards

The three major standards in the PC world for sound are SoundBlaster, Ad Lib and Windows. Some cards support all three, which is more desirable if you have a mix of DOS and Windows multimedia applications.

Sampling Rates and Sampling Sizes

Sampling rates of 11.025, 22.05 and 44.1KHz define the number of times per second analog sound is turned into a number. Sampling sizes of 8-bit and 16-bit define the granularity, or fineness, of the sample. An 8-bit size means each sample is measured on a scale of 256 increments; a 16-bit sample is 65,536 increments. The larger the number in both cases, the more precise the sample and the more realistically musical passages can be captured.

The MPC Level 1 specification requires the card to be able to record sound at 8-bits and 11.025KHz. It must be able to play back at 11.025 and 22.05KHz. See *MPC*. The MPC Level 2 specification requires the card to be able to record and play back at 16 bits at all three sampling rates.

SND, WAV and MIDI Files

Sound files, (.SND extension) and Windows wave files (.WAV extension) are digital sound files. Analog sound has been converted into digital form, and these files take up a lot of disk space. Without compression, ten seconds of high-fidelity sound (16-bit stereo at 44.1KHz) can take more than 5MB.

MIDI files (.MID extendion) contain a coded representation of the musical notes as played on an instrument; for example, middle C on a piano. MIDI files take up considerably less space than SND and WAV files, but require a MIDI synthesizer on the sound card. MPC requires MIDI on the board.

There are two kinds of MIDI sound reproduction methods used in sound cards. FM synthesis simulates musical notes. Wave table synthesis (or waveform synthesis) actually holds digitized samples of the notes and produces richer sound.

Another MIDI feature is the number of voices, or notes, that can be played back simultaneously. MPC requires an 8-voice synthesizer, but high-quality sound cards can have up to 32 MIDI voices.

Compression Standards

Compression for wave files helps reduce disk space, but can cause some loss in fidelity. Some sound cards provide built-in compression, but there are various methods that are used. The MPC Council recommends the ADCPM compression method adopted by the Interactive Multimedia Association (IMA).

Multimedia Speakers

Speakers placed in close proximity to CRT screens must be shielded, or you will see visible interference on the screen. All speakers designed for personal computer use are shielded.

source

(1) One side of a field effect transistor. See *drain*.
(2) (The Source) An online information service in McLean, VA, launched in 1979 and purchased by CompuServe in 1989.

source code

A program in its original form as written by the programmer. It is not executable by the computer directly. It must be converted into machine language by compilers, assemblers and interpreters.

In some cases, source code can be converted into another dialect or a different language by a conversion program.

source code compatible

Able to run a program on a different platform by recompiling its source code into that machine code.

source computer

The computer in which a program is being assembled or compiled. Contrast with *object computer*.

source data

The original data that is handwritten or printed on a source document or typed into the computer system from a keyboard or terminal.

source data acquisition

Same as *source data capture*.

source data capture

Capturing data electronically when a transaction occurs; for example, at the time of sale.

source directory

The directory from which data is obtained.

source disk

The disk from which data is obtained. Contrast with *target disk*.

source document

The paper form onto which data is written. Order forms and employment applications are examples.

source drive

The disk or tape drive from which data is obtained. Contrast with *target drive*.

Source Edp

A recruiting firm founded by computer people in 1962. It continues to maintain the policy that former computer professionals can better evaluate the career needs of individuals within the profession. Source Edp headquarters are in Irving, TX, with offices located throughout the U.S. and in North York, Ontario. See *salary survey*.

source language

The language used in a source program. Contrast with *target language* and *machine language*. See *source code*.

source program

A program in its original form, as written by the programmer. See *source code*.

source route bridging

A communications protocol in which host stations are aware of the bridges in the network and provide the information necessary to route messages via the bridges. It requires that the source frames contain the route to the destination station. Token Ring uses this method. Contrast with *transparent bridge*. See *SRT*.

source statement

An instructional phrase in a programming language (source language).

SP2

A massively parallel computer system from IBM that supports from two to 512 RS/ 6000 processors. It runs AIX and uses IBM's POWERparallel architecture, which includes a communications system between processors called the High-Performance Switch. In 1994, the University of New Mexico's Maui High Performance Computing Center installed an SP2 with 400 CPUs, which provides 100 gigaflops of computational power.

SPA

(Software Publishers Association, 1730 M St., N.W., Washington, DC 20036, 202/ 452-1600) A trade organization of the personal computer software industry that supports legislation for copyright enforcement. It conducts raids on organizations suspected of illegal copying and files lawsuits against violators.

To blow the whistle on a company that has a policy of making illegal copies, call 800/388-PIR8.

space

In digital electronics, a 0 bit. Contrast with *mark*.

space/time

The following units of measure are used to define storage and transmission capacities.

Bits, bytes and cycles		Fractions of a second	
Kilo (K) Thousand	1,024	ms (millisecond) thousandth	1/1,000
Mega (M) Million	1,048,576	µs (microsecond) millionth	1/1,000,000
Giga (G) Billion	1,073,741,824	ns (nanosecond) billionth	1/1,000,000,000
Tera (T) Trillion	1,099,511,627,776	ps (picosecond) trillionth	1/1,000,000,000,000
Peta (P) Quadrillion	1,125,899,906,842,624	fs (femtosecond) quadrillionth	1/1,000,000,000,000,000

How Components Are Measured

Storage/channel	capacity	Transmission speed	
CPU word size	Bits	CPU clock speed	MHz
Bus size	Bits	Bus speed	MHz
Disk, tape	Bytes	Network line/channel	bits per sec
MEMORY		Disk transfer rate	bits or bytes per sec
Overall capacity	Bytes	Disk acess time	ms
SIMM or SIP module	Bytes	Memory access time	ns
Individual chip	Bits	Machine cycle	µs and ns
		Instruction execution	µs and ns
		Transistor switching	ns, ps and fs

spaghetti code

Program code written without a coherent structure. The logic moves from routine to routine without returning to a base point, making it hard to follow. It implies excessive use of the GOTO instruction, which directs the computer to branch to another part of the program without a guarantee of returning.

In structured programming, functions are used, which are subroutines that guarantee a return to the instruction following the one that called it.

Spaghetti Code
Tracing the logic of spaghetti code means running around the program.

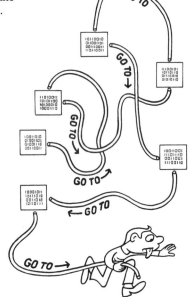

spamming
Sending copies of the same message to large numbers of newsgroups on the Internet.

spanning tree algorithm
An algorithm used in transparent bridges that dynamically determines the best path from source to destination. It avoids bridge loops (two or more paths linking one segment to another), which can cause the bridges to misinterpret results.

SPARC
(Scalable Performance ARChitecture) A 32-bit RISC CPU developed by Sun and licensed by SPARC International, Menlo Park, CA.

spatial data
Data that is represented as 2-D or 3-D images.

spawn
To launch another program from the current program. The DOS TSR version of this database is called POPCDE.EXE. It resides in RAM and "spawns" CDEDOS.EXE when the hotkey is pressed.

spec
See *specs* and *specification.*

Spec 1170
See *X/Open.*

SPECfp
See *SPECmark.*

special character
Non-alphabetic or non-numeric character, such as @, #, $, %, &, * and +.

special-purpose computer
A computer designed from scratch to perform a specific function. Contrast with *general-purpose computer.*

special-purpose language

A programming language designed to solve a specific problem or class of problems. For example, LISP and Prolog are designed for and used extensively in AI applications. Even more specific are languages such as COGO, for civil engineering problems, and APT for directing machine tools. Contrast with *general-purpose language*.

specification

A definition (layout, blueprint, design) of hardware or software. See *specs* and *functional specification*.

SPECint

See *SPECmark*.

SPECmark

(Standard Performance Evaluation Corporation **MARK**) A suite of 10 benchmarks distributed by SPEC that test integer (SPECint) and floating point (SPECfp) performance of a computer. SPEC reporting requires all 10 numbers as users may only need subsets.
A VAX-11/780 is a one-SPECmark machine. SPECmark benchmarks closely track VUPs ratings from Digital's internal benchmarks.

specs

(SPECificationS) The details of the components built into a device. See *specification*.

spec sheet

A detail listing of the components of a system.

spectral color

In computer graphics, the color of a single wavelength of light, starting with violet at the low end and proceeding through indigo, blue, green, yellow and orange and ending with red.

spectral response

The variable output of a light-sensitive device that is based on the color of the light it perceives.

spectrum

A range of electromagnetic frequencies. See *electromagnetic spectrum* and *radio*.

speech recognition

Same as *voice recognition*.

speech synthesis

Generating machine voice by arranging phonemes (k, ch, sh, etc.) into words. It is used to turn text input into spoken words for the blind. Speech synthesis performs realtime conversion without a pre-defined vocabulary, but does not create human-sounding speech. Although individual spoken words can be digitized into the computer, digitized voice takes a lot of storage, and resulting phrases still lack inflection.

speed buffering

A technique that compensates for speed differences between input and output. Data is accepted into the buffer at high speed and transferred out at low speed, or vice versa.

Speed Doubler
The name of Intel's clock-doubled DX2 chips.

Speedo
A scalable font technology from Bitstream Inc., Cambridge, MA. See *FaceLift*.

speed of electricity/light
Electricity and light travel at approximately 186,000 miles per second, which is seven times around the equator per second. This inherent speed of Mother Nature is why computers are so fast. Within the tiny chip, electricity has to flow only a couple of millimeters, and, within an entire computer, only a few feet.

As fast as that is, it's never fast enough. There is resistance in the lines, and even though transistors switch in billionths of a second, CAD, image processing and scientific applications are always exhausting the fastest computers.

Speedware
A development system from Speedware Corporation, Toronto, Ontario, that creates programs for the HP 3000, RS/6000 and AS/400. Applications can also be ported to run on DOS and Windows machines with runtime versions of Speedware for those platforms.

spelling checker
A separate program or word processing function that tests for correctly-spelled words. It can test the spelling of a marked block, an entire document or group of documents. Advanced systems check for spelling as the user types and can correct common typos and misspellings on the fly.

Spelling checkers simply compare words to a dictionary of words, and the wrong use of a correctly-spelled word cannot be detected. See *grammar checker*.

spherization
In computer graphics, turning an image into a sphere.

SPI
(Service Provider Interface) The programming interface for developing Windows drivers under WOSA. In order to provide common access to services, the application (query, word processor, e-mail program, etc.) is written to a particular WOSA-supported interface, such as ODBC or MAPI, and the developer of the service software (database manager, document manager, print spooler, etc.) writes to the SPI for that class of service.

SPID
(Service Profile IDentifier) A number assigned to an ISDN line by the ISDN service provider that identifies certain characteristics of the line.

spike
Also called a transient, a spike is a burst of extra voltage in a power line that lasts only a fraction of a second. Contrast with *sag*. See *power surge*.

spindle
A rotating shaft in a disk drive. In a fixed disk, the platters are attached to the spindle. In a removable disk, the spindle remains in the drive.

SpinRite
A low-level formatting program for PCs from Gibson Research, Aliso Viejo, CA, that reformats without erasing data. It rewrites only sector ID, which may have drifted over time. Version 3.0 can low-level format IDE drives, which have typically required proprietary format programs.

SPL

(1) (Systems Programming Language) The assembly language for the HP 3000 series. See *assembly language* for an SPL program example.
(2) (Structured Programming Language) See *structured programming*.

spline

In computer graphics, a smooth curve that runs through a series of given points. The term is often used to refer to any curve. See *Bezier* and *B-spline*.

split screen

The display of two or more sets of data on screen at the same time. It implies that one set of data can be manipulated independently of the other. Split screens, or windows, are usually created by the operating system or application software, rather than the hardware.

spooler

See *print spooler* and *spooling*.

spooling

(Simultaneous Peripheral Operations OnLine) The overlapping of low-speed operations with normal processing. It originated with mainframes in order to optimize slow operations such as reading cards and printing. Card input was read onto disk and printer output was stored on disk. In that way, the actual business data processing was done at high speed, since all I/O was on disk.
Today, spooling is used to buffer data for the printer as well as remote batch terminals. See *print spooler*.

spot color

A color that is printed from one printing plate which contains that particular ink. Contrast with *process color*.

SPP

(1) (Scalable Parallel Processor) A multiprocessing computer that can be upgraded by adding more CPUs.
(2) (Standard Parallel Port) The parallel port that has been used on PCs since their inception. Contrast with the higher-speed EPP and ECP ports. See *IEEE 1284*.

spreadsheet

Software that simulates a paper spreadsheet, or worksheet, in which columns of numbers are summed for budgets and plans. It appears on screen as a matrix of rows and columns, the intersections of which are identified as cells. Spreadsheets can have thousands of cells and can be scrolled horizontally and vertically in order to view them. The cells are filled with:

1. labels
2. numeric values
3. formulas

The labels, can be any descriptive text, for example, RENT, PHONE or GROSS SALES.
The values are the actual numeric data used in the budget or plan, and the formulas command the spreadsheet to do the calculations; for example, SUM CELLS A5 TO A10.
Formulas are easy to create, since spreadsheets allow the user to point to each cell and type in the arithmetic operation that affects it. Roughly speaking, a formula is created by saying "this cell PLUS that cell TIMES that cell."
The formulas are the spreadsheet's magic. After numbers are added or changed, the

formulas will recalculate the data either automatically or with the press of a key. Since the contents of any cell can be calculated with or copied to any other cell, a total of one column can be used as a detail item in another column. For example, the total from a column of expense items can be carried over to a summary column showing all expenses. If data in the detail column changes, its column total changes, which is then copied to the summary column, and the summary total changes. Done manually, each change would require recalculating, erasing and changing the totals of each column. The automatic ripple effect allows users to create a plan, plug in different assumptions and immediately see the impact on the bottom line. This "what if?" capability makes the spreadsheet indispensable for budgets, plans and other equation-based tasks.

The spreadsheet originated with VisiCalc in 1978 for the Apple II, and was followed by SuperCalc, Multiplan, Lotus 1-2-3 and a host of others.

Classes of Spreadsheets

2-D

Every spreadsheet can create a two-dimensional matrix of rows and columns. In order to summarize data, totals from various parts of the spreadsheet can be summed to another part of the spreadsheet.

3-D

Each cell in the spreadsheet has an X, Y and Z reference. For example, a spreadsheet of expense items by month uses two dimensions, but expense items by month by department requires three.

While this method is superior for consolidating and summarizing data, it lacks some of the flexibility required by sophisticated applications. In addition, all data typically resides in one file as with a standard 2-D spreadsheet.

Multidimensional

Multidimensional spreadsheets support more than three axes and allow the data and the relationships to be viewed from different perspectives. Data is not stored by cell references (A1, B2, etc.), but by name. Formulas are not placed into cells as in a traditional spreadsheet, but are defined separately as in a modeling language; for example, "gross profit=gross sales-cost of goods."

With name references, data can be used in multiple spreadsheets with greater accuracy, and new spreadsheets can be created more easily. However, since data isn't tied to cell references, this method lacks the flexibility and ease of use that caused the traditional 2-D spreadsheet to revolutionize the computer industry.

Analytical Databases

The need for multidimensional views of large amounts of data has given rise to a variety of methods over the years. All sorts of modeling programs have been created, but none have been as easy to use as the spreadsheet. Some combine spreadsheets with traditional database management. For example, TM/1 was one of the first programs to provide multiple dimensions and isolate the data from the spreadsheet. This method provides database consistency (the data is not replicated in every spreadsheet) with the ease of use of the spreadsheet for creating the viewing models. Organizations that analyze large amounts of sales history and other data are increasingly using OLAP (OnLine Analytical Processing) databases. OLAP databases use proprietary algorithms for summarizing data so that multidimensional views can be quickly queried. See *OLAP database*.

spreadsheet compiler

Software that translates spreadsheets into stand-alone programs that can be run without the spreadsheet package that created them.

spread spectrum

A radio transmission that continuously changes carrier frequency according to a unique pattern in both sending and receiving devices. It is used for security as well as to allow multiple wireless transmissions in the same space.

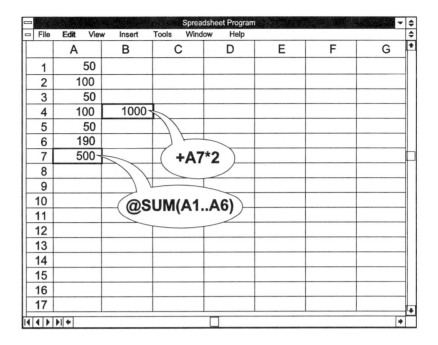

spreadsheet

sprite

An independent graphic object controlled by its own bit plane (area of memory). Commonly used in video games, sprites move freely across the screen, passing by, through and colliding with each other with much less programming.

sprocket feed

Same as *pin feed*.

SPS

(Standby Power System) A UPS system that switches to battery backup upon detection of power failure.

SPSS

A statistical package from SPSS, Inc., Chicago, that runs on PCs, most mainframes and minis and is used extensively in marketing research. It provides over 50 statistical processes, including regression analysis, correlation and analysis of variance. Originally named Statistical Package for the Social Sciences, it was written by Norman Nie, a professor at Stanford. In 1976, he formed SPSS, Inc.

spt

(Sectors Per Track) The number of sectors in one track.

SPX

(Sequenced Packet EXchange) The NetWare communications protocol used to control the transport of messages across a network. SPX ensures that an entire message arrives intact and uses NetWare's IPX protocol as its delivery mechanism. Application programs use SPX to provide client/server and peer-to-peer interaction between network nodes. SPX provides services at layer 4 of the OSI model.

SQL

(Structured Query Language) Pronounced "SQL" or "see qwill," a language used to interrogate and process data in a relational database. Originally developed by IBM for its mainframes, all database systems designed for client/sever environments support SQL. SQL commands can be used to interactively work with a database or can be embedded within a programming language to interface to a database. Programming extensions to SQL have turned it into a full-blown database programming language. Some of the major database management systems (DBMSs) that support SQL are DB2, SQL/DS, Oracle, Sybase, SQLbase, INFORMIX and CA-OpenIngres (Ingres).

The following SQL query selects customers with credit limits of at least $5,000 and puts them into sequence from highest credit limit to lowest. The bold words are SQL verbs.

```
SELECT NAME, CITY, STATE, ZIPCODE
FROM CUSTOMER
WHERE CREDITLIMIT > 4999
ORDER BY CREDITLIMIT DESC
```

SQL - A Standard?

The American National Standards Institute (ANSI) has standardized the SQL language, but it does not cover all the bases. Each database management system (DBMS) has its own enhancements, quirks and tricks that, for all intents and purposes, makes SQL non standard. Moving an application from one SQL database to another generally requires hand tailoring to convert some of the SQL statements. So what's new? See *CLI, ODBC* and *IDAPI.*

SQLBase

Officially known as Gupta SQLBase Server, it is a relational DBMS for DOS, OS/2, NetWare, NT and Sun servers from Gupta Corporation, Menlo Park, CA. It is one of the leading database programs on servers running OS/2 and NetWare. SQLBase has been Gupta's flagship product since the company was founded in 1984. See *SQLWindows.*

SQL/DS

(SQL/Data System) A full-featured relational DBMS from IBM for VSE and VM environments that has integrated query and report writing facilities.

SQL engine

A program that accepts SQL commands and accesses the database to obtain the requested data. Users' requests in a query language or database language must be translated into an SQL request before the SQL engine can process it.

SQL Forms

An earlier version of Oracle Forms, an application development tool for client/server systems. See Developer/2000.

SQL precompiler

Software that turns SQL commands written within a source program into the appropriate function calls for the database management system (DBMS) being used. After the SQL precompiler stage, the resulting program is translated into machine language by the COBOL compiler or the compiler of whatever language the program is written in. See *embedded SQL.*

SQL Server

A relational DBMS from Sybase, Inc., Emeryville, CA, that runs on OS/2 and Windows NT PCs, NetWare servers, VAXs and UNIX servers. It is designed for client/server use and is accessed by applications using SQL or via Sybase's own QBE and decision support utilities.

SQL Server was also available through Microsoft as Microsoft SQL Server for OS/2 and Microsoft SQL Server for Windows NT. In 1992, Microsoft started to modify the program and eventually rewrote its own version that it sells independently.

SQLWindows

Officially known as Gupta SQLWindows, it is a high-level application development system for Windows from Gupta Corporation, Menlo Park, CA. It is used to write Windows applications that access SQL databases in a client/server environment. SQLWindows Solo is a demonstration version that provides all of the functionality of SQLWindows, but works only on a single machine. See *SQLBase*.

square wave

A graphic image of a digital pulse as visualized on an oscilloscope. It appears square because it rises quickly to a particular amplitude, stays constant for the duration of the pulse and drops fast at the end of it.

Square Wave

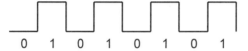

```
0   1   0   1   0   1   0   1
```

SQUID

(Superconducting Quantum Interference Device) An electronic detection system that uses Josephson junctions circuits. It is capable of detecting extremely weak signals.

S-RAM, SRAM

See *static RAM*.

SRB

See *source route bridging*.

SRPI

(Server Requester Programming Interface) An IBM programming interface that allows a PC to interact with a mainframe. See *ECF*.

SRT

(1) (Source Routing Transparent) An IEEE-standard that provides bridging between Ethernet and Token Ring networks. Ethernet LANs use transparent bridging, and Token Ring LANs use source route bridging (SRB). The SRT method sends Ethernet packets via transparent bridging and Token Ring packets via SRB.
(2) (Speech Recognition Technology) See *voice recognition*.

SSA

(Serial Storage Architecture) A peripheral interface from IBM that transfers data at 20MBytes/sec in one direction, but can operate full-duplex. SSA's ring configuration allows remaining devices to function if one fails. SCSI software can be mapped over SSA allowing existing SCSI devices to be used. SSA is expected to gain momentum in the 1995-1996 timeframe.

SSCP

(System Services Control Point) A controlling program in an SNA domain. It resides in the host and is a component within VTAM.

SSD

See *solid state disk*.

SS/DD

(Single Sided/Double Density) Refers to earlier floppy disk formats that store data on only one side of the disk.

SSI

(Small Scale Integration) Up to 100 transistors on a chip. See *MSI, LSI, VLSI* and *ULSI*.

SSP

(System Support Program) A multiuser, multitasking operating system from IBM that is the primary control program for System/34 and System/36.

ST

A personal computer series from Atari that uses a Motorola 68000 CPU and includes the GEM interface, ROM-based TOS operating system, a MIDI interface and a three-voice sound chip. The 520ST has 512K RAM; the 1040ST has 1MB. Display is 640x200, 16 colors. The current model is the 1040STE.

ST412

An enhancement to the ST506 standard that buffers track-to-track commands for a continuous seek to the required track. All new ST506 drives/controllers incorporate this, thus ST412, ST506/412 and current ST506 units are the same.

ST506

A hard disk interface commonly used in drives of 40MB and less. It transfers data at 625 KBytes/sec and uses the MFM encoding method. See *ST412* and *hard disk*.

ST506 RLL

(ST506 Run-Length Limited) A hard disk interface (also called RLL interface) that increases capacity and speed by 50% over ST506 MFM drives and transfers data at 937 KBytes/sec. With MFM drives certified for increased capacity, the ST506 MFM controller can be replaced with an ST506 RLL controller and the drive can be reformatted. See *hard disk*.

stack

(1) A set of hardware registers or a reserved amount of memory used for arithmetic calculations or to keep track of internal operations. Stacks keep track of the sequence of routines called in a program. For example, one routine calls another, which calls another and so on. As each routine is completed, the computer returns control to the calling routine all the way back to the first one that started the sequence. Stacks used in this way are LIFO based: the last item, or address, placed (pushed) onto the stack is the first item removed (popped) from the stack.
Stacks are also used to hold interrupts until they can be serviced. Used in this manner, they are FIFO stacks, in which the first item onto the stack is the first one out of the stack.
An "internal stack failure" is a fatal error which means that the operating system has lost track of its next operation. Restarting the computer usually corrects this, otherwise the operating system may have to be re-installed.
(2) See *protocol stack* and *HyperCard*.

stackable hub

A type of 10BaseT Ethernet hub that can be expanded by daisy chaining additional hubs together. Such units are designed to stack vertically.

stacker

(1) An output bin in a document feeding or punched card machine. Contrast with *hopper*.

(2) (Stacker) A realtime compression program from Stac Electronics, Carlsbad, CA, that doubles the disk capacity of a PC. A coprocessor board is optionally available.

stack overflow

An error condition that occurs when there is no room in the stack for a new item. Contrast with *stack underflow*.

In DOS, a Stack overflow error message means that there is not enough room on the stack to handle hardware interrupts. Increase the number of stacks in the STACKS= command in the CONFIG.SYS file.

You can also get this message when other things go haywire; for example, a bad expansion board or one that isn't seated properly in the slot can cause erratic signals eventually leading to this message.

stack pointer

An address that identifies the location of the most recent item placed on the stack.

stack underflow

An error condition that occurs when an item is called for from the stack, but the stack is empty. Contrast with *stack overflow*.

stackware

A HyperCard application that is made up of a HyperCard stack (data) and HyperTalk programming.

STAIRS

(STorage And Information Retrieval System) An IBM text document management system for mainframes. It allows users to search for documents based on key words or word combinations.

standard

A specification for hardware or software that is either widely used and accepted (de facto) or is sanctioned by a standards organization (de jure). See *standards & compatibility*.

standard cell

The finished design of an electronic function ready for chip fabrication. It can be as small as a clock circuit or as large as a microprocessor. It is used to make custom-designed chips.

standard deviation

In statistics, the average amount a number varies from the average number in a series of numbers.

Standard Mode

Windows operation mode. See *Windows*.

standards & compatibility

Standards is the most important issue in the computer field. As an unregulated industry, we have wound up with thousands of data formats and languages, but very few standards that are universally used. This subject is as heated as politics and religion to vendors and industry planners.

No matter how much the industry talks about compatibility, new formats and languages appear routinely. The standards makers are always trying to cast a standard in concrete, while the innovators are trying to create a new one. Even when standards are created, they are violated as soon as a new feature is added by the vendor.

If a format or language is used extensively and others copy it, it becomes a de facto standard and may become as widely used as official standards from ANSI and IEEE. When de facto standards are sanctioned by these organizations, they become stable, at least, for a while.

In order to truly understand this industry, it is essential to understand the categories for which standards are created.

Machine Languages

Machine language is the fundamental standard for hardware compatibility. It is the language the CPU understands. All programs that are presented to the computer for execution must be in the machine language of that particular CPU family.

Vendors may produce systems with different machine languages. IBM's mainframe family differs from its AS/400 midrange series, which is also different than its RS/6000 series. Digital's newer Alpha line of computers does not understand the machine language of the many earlier VAX computers that have been installed. For all the major hardware platforms, see *hardware platforms*.

After a program is written, it must be translated (assembled, compiled or interpreted) into the machine language the computer understands. In order to run in a different machine, the program must be reassembled or recompiled into a different machine language.

Since the late 1960s, companies seeking a chunk of the IBM market have designed computers that run the same machine language as the IBM mainframes. RCA's Spectra 70 was the first IBM-compatible mainframe, and companies, such as Amdahl, Itel, National Advanced Systems, Hitachi and Fujitsu have introduced IBM-compatible mainframes at one time or another.

IBM PC machine language compatibility is achieved by using a processor from Intel's x86 family of microprocessors or one of the Intel clone chips.

Machine language compatibility can also be achieved by emulation. An emulator is software (or hardware or both) that executes the machine language of another computer directly. With DOS and Windows emulation in a UNIX workstation or a PowerMac, users can run non-native programs in their computer.

Emulation goes back to the 1950s and 1960s when IBM built a 1401 emulator in its System/360 to ease migration from the very popular 1401s to the new 360s. The terms simulator and emulator are used interchangeably.

Data Codes/ characters Codes

The data code built into the computer determines how each letter, digit or special character ($, %, #, etc.) is represented in binary code. Fortunately, there are only two methods in wide use: EBCDIC and ASCII. IBM minis and mainframes use EBCDIC. ASCII is used for most everything else, including all PCs and Macs. ASCII is a 7-bit code placed into an 8-bit storage unit. The seven bits provide the basic set of 128 ASCII characters. The 8th bit adds storage for another 128 symbols, and these symbols vary from font to font and system to system. For example, the DOS character set contains line drawing and foreign language characters. The ANSI character set places the foreign language characters in different locations. In the Mac, the upper 128 characters can be custom drawn.

When systems are moved from one computer to another, converting between ASCII and EBCDIC is just a small part of the data conversion process. It is done in conjunction with converting file formats from the old to the new systems.

The following is a sample of ASCII and EBCDIC code. See *ASCII chart, hex chart* and *EBCDIC chart*.

Character	ASCII	EBCDIC
space	01000000	00100000
period	01001011	00101110
< sign	01001100	00111100
+ sign	01001110	00101011
$ sign	01011011	00100100
A	11000001	01000001
B	11000010	01000010

Hardware Interfaces

The hardware interface specifies the plugs, sockets, cables and electrical signals that pass through each line between the CPU and a peripheral device or communications network.

Common hardware interfaces for personal computers are the Centronics parallel interface used for printers and the RS-232 interface, typically used for modems, graphics tablets, mice and printers. In addition, the IDE and SCSI interfaces are commonly used for disks and tapes, and the GPIB IEEE 488 standard is used for process control instruments.

The bus in a computer's motherboard, into which additional printed circuit boards are inserted, is a hardware interface. For example, the Micro Channel in IBM's PS/2 series accepts a physically different board than the original PC bus. The PCI bus and the VL-bus also have different pin configurations and are not interchangeable. LANs, such as Ethernet and Token Ring, dictate the hardware interface as part of their specifications. An Ethernet cable cannot connect to a Token Ring board, and vice versa.

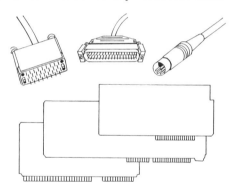

Storage Media

There are many varieties of disk cartridges, floppy disks, reel-to-reel tapes, tape cartridges and tape cassettes. Each one has its own unique shape and size and can be used only in drives designed to accommodate them. With removable media, the physical standard is half the compatibility issue. The other half is the recording pattern, which is invisible to the human eye. Magnetic tapes and disks fresh out of the box are blank. The

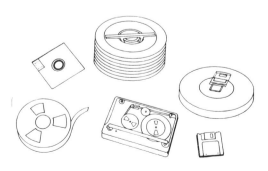

recording tracks are placed onto the surface by the read/write head of the storage drive. Thus, the same floppy disk that stores 720K bytes in one disk drive, can hold 800K if formatted for another. If the computer reads an incompatible tape or reads and writes and incompatible disk, it will signal a read/write error.

For minicomputers and mainframes, half-inch magnetic tape reels and cartridges are the common interchangeable medium. For personal computers, the 3.5" floppy disk is the standard.

Operating Systems

An operating system is a master control program that manages the running of the computer system. In all environments, except for specialized scientific and process control applications, the operating system interacts with the application programs. The application programs must "talk" to the operating system.

If application programs are moved to a different computing environment, they have to be converted to interface with a different operating system. If a new operating system is installed that is not compatible with the old one, the application programs have to be converted to the new operating system.

Communications & Networking

Transmitting between two personal computers is relatively simple. All that's required is a modem and communications program in each computer that uses the same file transfer protocol. Most comm programs support several protocols and are widely used to upload and download files and gain access to a BBS or online service. Connecting to a major online service, such as America Online or CompuServe, is even more straightforward when you use the service's front-end software.

Communications within the enterprise is far more complex. Over the years, organizations have developed islands of computer systems, each with their own networking protocols and access methods. The enterprise is faced with tying mainframes, minis and PCs together for file sharing, electronic mail and routine data processing.

It is a duanting task connecting client machines running DOS, Windows, Mac and Motif with servers that run DOS, Windows, Mac, VMS, MVS and UNIX via protocols such as TCP/IP, IPX and NetBIOS over topologies such as Ethernet, Fast Ethernet, Switched Ethernet, Token Ring, FDDI and ATM using devices such as bridges, routers, hubs, switches and gateways, and there you have it. Oh, add interfacing between multiple mail and messaging systems and managing the entire process from one management console.

To understand the layers of protocols required to transmit a message from one machine to another, review the layers of the OSI model. OSI is a seven-layer reference model for worldwide communications defined by the International Standards Organization (ISO). Originally thought to be the future standard for communications, it was never widely supported. However, it does serve as a teaching model to line up other protocols against. See *enterprise networking, client/server* and *OSI model.*

Programming Languages

Every software program is written in a programming language, and there is at least one programming language for every major CPU series. There is typically an assembly language and a number of high-level languages for each family. Assembly languages are machine specific, and the machine language they generate runs on only one CPU family. Unless the machine languages are very similar, it is difficult to translate an assembly language program from one CPU series into another.

The high-level programming language was created to eliminate this machine dependency. Programming languages, such as COBOL, FORTRAN and BASIC are designed to run on many different computers. However, due to dialects of each language, compatibility is always an issue. Each compiler vendor keeps adding new features to its language thereby making it incompatible with previous or other versions.

By the time a new feature becomes a standard, a dozen new features have been already implemented. For example, dBASE became a de facto standard business programming language. Since 1981, dBASE spawned competitive products, such as Clipper, QuickSilver, Force III, dbXL and Foxbase, all of which are incomplete versions of dBASE. None of them provides every command in dBASE, and they all provide features not found in dBASE.

There's no rule of thumb for translating one dialect of a programming language into another. The job may be difficult or easy. At times, software is written to translate one dialect into another, as well as one programming language into another. If the translation program cannot translate the program entirely, then manual tailoring is necessary. In these cases, it is often easier to rewrite the program from scratch.

Compatibility can be achieved when a programming language conforms to the ANSI (American National Standards Institute) standard for that language. If the same version of an ANSI COBOL compiler is available for two different CPUs, a program written in ANSI COBOL will run on both machines. Beyond traditional programming languages such as COBOL and C, known as third-generation languages, or 3GLs, there are more than a hundred software environments used to develop client/server applications on LANs (see *client/ server development system*). Each of them attempts to provide less programming-like and more English-like syntax, which is considered a *fourth-generation language*, or 4GL.

They also provide visual development tools to build the graphical user interface by "drawing" the screen and dragging and dropping symbols on it. They may provide the ability to point and click and drag and drop symbols to link objects together rather than by writing programming code. These software-building tools are proliferating and producing even more standards to be dealt with. The programming pools are becoming increasingly fragmented. It's no longer just COBOL or dBASE or C. Now it's PowerBuilder, SQLWindows, ObjectView, DYNASTY, OMNIS and JAM, etc. etc.

File Management Systems

In its simplest form, a data file uses fields of the same length for each item of data, for example, a plain EBCDIC or ASCII file would look like:

```
Chris Smith    34 Main St.     Bangor     ME18567
Pat Jones      10 W. 45 St.    New York   NY10002
```

A common format created by BASIC programming languages is an ASCII comma delimited file; for example, the data above would look as follows:

```
"Chris Smith","34 Main St.","Bangor","ME","18567"
"Pat Jones","10 W. 45 St.","New York","NY","10002"
```

Both file formats above are simple, contain only data (except for quotes and commas) and can be easily manipulated by a word processor. However, data files may also contain special codes that identify the way the data is structured within the file. For example, variable length records require a code in each field indicating the size of the field.

Whether fixed or variable length fields, the data in non-DBMS systems is linked directly to the processing. The program must know the layout of the fields in each record that it processes, and it cannot accept records in a different format. In order to process a different file format, the program must be changed.

Incompatible file formats often exist within the same organization because they were developed separately. The following fixed-length records are incompatible even though they contain the same data. As long as a file management system is used rather than a database management system (DBMS), the program that processes the first file structure would have to be changed to process the second.

Name	Address	City	St	Zip

Name	Address	City	St	Zip

Record Formats

These two fixed-length record layouts are incompatible even though they contain the same kinds of data. The same program cannot process them unless it's designed to input both record formats. In order to process a different file, the program has to be changed or the file structure (record layout) has to be changed.

DBMSs (Database Management Systems)

DBMSs have their own proprietary formats for storing data. For example, a header record with a unique format that contains identification data is typically placed at the beginning of each file. Codes may also be embedded in each record.

Most DBMSs have an import and export capability that converts popular database formats into their proprietary format. If not, the program usually can import and export a plain EBCDIC or ASCII file, which is stripped of all proprietary codes and can be used as a common denominator between both systems. If conversion facilities cannot be found, a custom program can be written to convert one database format into another if documentation describing the old format is available.

The application program interface (API), or language used by the application program to

"talk" to the database, is typically a proprietary language in every DBMS. However, SQL has become the de facto standard database language for client/server environments. In theory, that means any application program requesting data in the SQL language would work with any DBMS that supports SQL. Like everything else however, there are dialects of SQL, and only fundamental expressions can be guaranteed compatible. Whatever special features exist within the DBMS, proprietary syntax is needed to activate them, thus automatically making one DBMS incompatible with another.

Text Systems

Although the basic structure of an English-language text file is standard throughout the world: word, sentence, paragraph, page; every word processing, desktop publishing and typesetting program uses its own codes to set up the layout within a document. For example, the code that turns on boldface in WordPerfect Version 5.0 is [**BOLD**]; in WordStar, it's **^PB**.

The codes that define a header, footer, footnote, page number, margin, tab setting, indent and font change are unique to the word processing program in which the document was created or the desktop publishing program into which the text file is converted. Even the codes to end a line and paragraph are not the same.

Document conversion is accomplished with special conversion programs or black boxes. Although every word processing program has a search and replace capability, it may not be effective for converting embedded layout codes from one format to another. In some programs, the search & replace simply does not handle layout codes. In addition, while some systems use one code to turn a function on and another code to turn it off, other systems use the same code for on and off, requiring manual verification and tailoring when using the search & replace function.

Graphic Systems

There are many formats for storing a picture in a computer; but, unlike text and data files, which are primarily made up of alphanumeric characters, graphics formats are more complex. To begin with, there are the two major categories of graphics: vector graphics (objects made up of lines) and raster graphics (TV-like dots). Images stored in vector format can be moved to another vector system typically without loss of resolution. There are 2-D vector formats as well as 3-D vector formats. In transferring raster images among different devices, resolution is a major concern. Such transfers can occur without loss of resolution as long as the new format has the same or higher resolution as the older one. Standard graphics formats allow graphics data to be moved from

machine to machine, while standard graphics languages let graphics programs be moved from machine to machine. For example, GKS and PHIGS are major graphics languages that have been adopted by high-performance workstation and CAD vendors. Apple's consistent use of its QuickDraw language helped the Macintosh become popular in graphics-oriented applications.

High-resolution graphics has typically been expensive to implement due to its large storage and fast processing requirements. However, as personal computers become more powerful, graphics are becoming widely used in business applications. The ability to see a person's face or a product's appearance on screen is now as commonplace as text and data.

The Future

After 30 some years of computing, we've managed to create more than 3,000 languages, formats and programming interfaces in the computer business. While some of them become bona fide standards endorsed by recognized standards organizations, some of the most widely used are de facto standards. The PC is the perfect example.

The problem of standards is a never-ending dilemma. How do you forge ahead with new standards if they have to cling to the old designs for compatibility? At some point, the new has to be a break from the past, because the previous infrastructure is not usable. It seems to be the way of things.

Star

The Xerox workstation that formally introduced the graphical user interface and desktop metaphor in 1981. Although unsuccessful, it was inspiration for Xerox's subsequent computers and for Apple's Lisa and Macintosh. See *Alto*.

The First Commercial GUI
The Xerox Star was the first commercial implementation of a graphical user interface. This was the inspiration for the Macintosh and Windows. *(Photo courtesy of Xerox Corporation.)*

star design

See *star network* and *star schema*.

Starlan

A local area network from AT&T that uses twisted pair wire, the CSMA/CD access method, transmits at 1 Mbps and uses a star or bus topology. In 1988, Starlan was renamed Starlan 1, and Starlan 10 was introduced, a 10 Mbps Ethernet version that uses twisted pair or optical fibers.

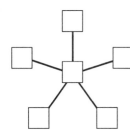

star network

A communications network in which all terminals are connected to a central computer or central hub. PBXs are prime examples as well as IBM's Token Ring and AT&T's Starlan LANs.

star query, star schema

A data warehouse design that enhances the performance of multidimensional queries on traditional relational databases. One fact table is surrounded by a series of related tables. Data is joined from one of the points to the center, providing a so called "star query." See *OLAP database*.

start bit

In asynchronous communications, the bit transmitted before each character.

start/stop transmission

Same as *asynchronous transmission*.

STARTUP.CMD

(STARTUP.CoMmanD) An OS/2 file that is executed immediately upon startup. It contains instructions that can initialize operating system settings and call in a specific application program. The DOS counterpart is AUTOEXEC.BAT.

startup routine

A routine that is executed when the computer is booted or when an application is loaded. It is used to customize the environment for its associated software.

state

In object technology, the current condition, or status, of an object. The state is the combination of the original values in the object, plus any modifications made to them.<TERM>state machine
Also called a *finite state machine*, it is a computing device designed with the operational states required to solve a specific problem. The circuits are minimized, specialized and optimized for the application. For example, chips in audio, video and imaging controllers are often designed as state machines, because they can provide faster performance at lower cost than a general-purpose CPU.

statement

In a high-level programming language, a descriptive phrase that generates one or more machine language instructions in the computer. In a low-level assembly language, programmers write instructions rather than statements, since each source language instruction is translated into one machine language instruction.

static binding

Same as *early binding*.

static column memory

A type of page mode memory that requires less electronic pulsing in order to access the memory bits.

static electricity

A stationary electrical charge that is the result of intentional charging or of friction in low-humidity environments.

static RAM

A memory chip that requires power to hold its content. Static RAM chips have access times in the 10 to 30-nanosecond range. Dynamic RAMs are usually above 30, and Bipolar and ECL memories are under 10.

A static RAM bit is made up of a pretzel-like flip-flop circuit that lets current flow through one side or the other based on which one of two transistors is activated. Static RAMs do not require refresh circuitry as do dynamic RAMs, but they take up more space and use more power.

static SQL

See *embedded SQL.*

station

A computer, workstation or terminal in a network. Same as *node.*

statistical multiplexor

In communications, a device that merges several low-speed channels into a single high-speed channel and vice versa. A standard multiplexor is set up for a fixed number of incoming channels regardless of whether every one is transmitting or not. A statistical multiplexor analyzes the traffic and dynamically changes its pattern of interleaving to use all the available capacity of the outgoing channel.

stat mux

(STATistical MUltipleXor) See *statistical multiplexor.*

status line

An information line displayed on screen that shows current activity.

ST connector

A fiber-optic cable connector that uses a bayonet plug and socket. It was the first de facto standard connector for most commercial wiring. Two ST connectors are used for each pair of cables. See *fiber-optic connectors.*

STD bus

A bus architecture used in medical and industrial equipment due to its small size and rugged design. Originally an 8-bit bus, extensions have increased it to 16 and 32 bits.

stealth virus

A virus that is able to keep itself from being detected. See *polymorphic virus.*

step frame

To capture video images one frame at a time. If a computer is not fast enough to capture analog video in realtime, the video can be forwarded and processed one frame at a time.

stepper motor

A motor that rotates in small, fixed increments and is used to control the movement of the access arm on a disk drive. Contrast with *voice coil.*

stereophonic

Sound reproduction that uses two or more channels. Contrast with *monophonic.*

stick font

Same as *vector font.*

stick model

A picture made of lines, or vectors. For example, in biomedical applications, the limbs of a person or animal are converted into lines so that the motion can be visually observed and graphically plotted and analyzed.

stiction

(STatic frICTION) A type of hard disk failure in which the read/write heads stick to the platters. The lubricant used on certain drives heats up and liquifies. When the disk is turned off, it cools down and can become like a glue.

STN

(SuperTwisted Nematic) An enhancement to the twisted nematic (TN) technology for LCD displays that twists the molecules greater than 90 degrees (from 180 to 270 degrees) for better contrast. See *TN* and *LCD.*

stop bit

In asynchronous communications, a bit transmitted after each character.

storage device

A hardware unit that holds data. In this database, the term refers only to external peripheral equipment, such as disk and tape, in contrast with memory (RAM). See *Freeman Reports.*

storage hierarchy

The range of memory and storage devices within the computer system. The following list runs from lowest to highest speed. See *holographic storage.*

> Punched cards **
> Punched paper tape **
> Removable cartridge mass storage devices (non-disk) **
> Magnetic tape
> Floppy disks
> CD-ROM and optical disks
> Magnetic disks (movable heads)
> Magnetic disks (fixed heads) **
> Bubble memory
> Low-speed bulk memory
> Main memory
> Cache memory
> Microcode
> Registers
>
> ** obsolete technologies

storage management

Administration of a backup and archival program that moves less-timely information to more economical storage media; for example, from magnetic disk to optical disk to magnetic tape. See *SMS* and *HSM.*

storage media

Disks and tapes.

Storage

Storage devices have always and will continue to play an ever increasing role in computer systems. In time, technologies such as holographic storage, may obsolete a of today's storage devices including magnetic tape, disk and even optical disk.

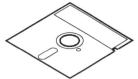

5 1/4" Floppy Disk

Although widely used for 17 years, the 5.25" floppy finally bit the dust in 1994.

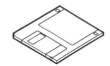

3 1/2" Floppy disk

The most ubiquitous removable storage medium. At 1.44MB, it is entirely too small for today's multimedia files. Products such as Iomega's Zip disk and the resurgence of the Floptical may supersede the 3.5" floppy.

Internal Hard Disk

Hard disk capacities have soared with prices as low as 25 cents per MB in 1995. Hard disks will remain the primary storage for a number of years, but magnetic media will someday be history. It's just a matter of time.

SyQuest Hard Disks

The Syquest cartridges are the de facto standard, transportable storage medium for service bureaus.

Bernoulli Disks

Iomega's Bernoulli cartridges were the first popular transportable storage medium. Iomega's new Jaz disk, which provides a gigabyte of removable hard disk storage is likely to become very popular.

Optical Disk

Optical disks come in 3.5" and 5 cartridges. They are removable m that are becoming as fast as magn disks. Optical disks do not "crash and they are not subject to rando electromagnetic interference.

DAT Tape Cartridge

DAT tapes provide increasing sto capacity for backup. Although m tapes were the first high-capacity medium, they will likely survive f time due to their huge amounts o surface compared with other med

CD-ROM

The CD-ROM's 650MB capacit be eclipsed with 9GB CD-ROMs expected in 1996 or 1997. Erasal ROMs, also expected in the same timeframe, may revolutionize the business. Such devices are also ex to obsolete VHS tape in the futur

The Future

Even with optical storage and removable devices char rapidly, there are technologies on the horizon that wi eventually bring storage devices up to parity with the The washing machine and jackhammer actions of the are crude by comparison to the magic that goes on wi the layers of the chip. Look up *holographic storage*.

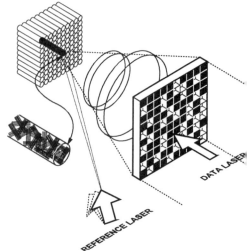

storage technologies
See *hard disk, floppy disk, optical disk, Bernoulli Box, Floptical, MiniDisc, Zip disk, CD-R, SyQuest disk, magnetic tape* and *holographic storage.*

store and forward
The temporary storage of a message for transmission to its destination at a later time. Store and forward techniques allow for routing over networks that are not accessible at all times. For example, messages crossing time zones can be forwarded during daytime at the receiving side, or messages can be forwarded at night in order to obtain off-peak rates. See *messaging protocol.*

store-and-forward switch
A switching device that stores a complete incoming data packet before it is sent out. Such switches are used when incoming and outgoing speeds differ. Contrast with *cut-through switch.*

stored procedure
In a database management system (DBMS), it is an SQL program that is stored in the database which is executed by calling it directly from the client or from a database trigger. When the SQL procedure is stored in the database, it does not have to be replicated in each client. This saves programming effort especially when different client user interfaces and development systems are used. Triggers and stored procedures are built into DBMSs used in client/server environments.

stored program concept
The fundamental computer architecture in which the computer acts upon (executes) internally-stored instructions. See *von Neumann architecture.*

STP
(Shielded Twisted Pair) Telephone wire that is wrapped in a metal sheath to eliminate external interference. See *twisted pair.*

Strand88
A parallel processing programming language developed by AI Ltd., England.

Stratus
(Stratus Computer, Inc., Marlboro, MA) A manufacturer of fault-tolerant computers founded in 1980. It supports both the VOS and FTX UNIX operating systems on its XA/R line of i860-based systems. Its earlier XA/2000 line was Motorola 680x0 based. Future systems will use HP's PA-RISC architecture.

stream
(1) A contiguous group of data.
(2) The I/O management in the C programming language. A stream is a channel through which data flows to/from a disk, keyboard, printer, etc.

streaming data
Data that is structured and processed in a continous flow, such as digital audio and video.

streaming tape
A high-speed magnetic tape drive that is frequently used to make a backup copy of an entire hard disk.

Streamline
A Macintosh tracing program from Adobe Systems Inc., Mountain View, CA. It

converts scanned or MacPaint images into PostScript files, which can be modified in Illustrator 88.

stream-oriented file

A type of file, such as a text document or digital voice file, that is more openly structured than a database file. Text and voice files contain continuous streams of characters, whereas database files contain many small repeating structures (records).

STREAMS

A feature of UNIX System V that provides a standard way of dynamically building and passing messages up and down a protocol stack. NetWare 3.x and Windows NT also support the STREAMS interface. STREAMS passes messages from the application "downstream" through the STREAMS modules to the network driver at the end of the stack. Messages are passed "upstream" from the driver to the application. A STREAMS module would be a transport layer protocol such as TCP and SPX or a network layer protocol such as IP and IPX.

STREAMS modules can be dynamically changed (pushed and popped) at runtime, allowing the stack to be used for multiple protocols. Two important STREAMS components are the TLI and LSL interfaces, which provide common languages to the transport and data link layers. See *TLI, LSL, ODI* and *OSI.*

Streettalk

A directory service in the VINES network operating system.

STRETCH

The code name for IBM's first "supercomputer," the 7030, which was started in 1955 and completed in 1961. The first of eight units was delivered to the Los Alamos Scientific Laboratory and was in use for 10 years. STRETCH was IBM's first attempt at building transistorized computers and was designed to "stretch" the speed of its current vacuum tube models by a factor of 100.

The machine was very sophisticated for its time, providing simultaneous execution of business instructions with floating point arithmetic. It was estimated that IBM lost 40 million dollars in developing STRETCH, but that the knowledge gained led to huge profits with its subsequent computers.

Stretch Computer
The computers of the 1950s were very impressive with hundreds of blinking lights and switches on their main control panel. *(Photo courtesy of Charles Babbage Institute, University of Minnesota.)*

stretch blt

An enhanced type of bitblt used for resizing video images. The function expands or contracts the number of bits while moving them from main memory to the display memory. See *bitblt.*

stretching

See *hardware scaling.*

string

(1) In programming, a contiguous set of alphanumeric characters that does not contain numbers used for calculations. Names, addresses, words and sentences are strings. Contrast with *numeric* data.

(2) Any connected set of structures, such as a string of bits, fields or records.

string handling

The abilty to manipulate alphanumeric data (names, addresses, text, etc.). Typical functions include the ability to handle arrays of strings, to left and right align and center strings and to search for an occurrence of text within a string.

Stringy Floppy

A tape drive for the Radio Shack TRS-80 personal computer that used a continuous loop cartridge of 1/16" tape from a company called Exatron in Sunnyvale, CA. It was faster than the audio cassettes used for data storage in the early days of personal computing. The company claimed it sold a few thousand of these "tape wafers." However, soon after, the floppy disk became the norm.

Why not have some fun with such a unique name. Ask your systems people if they've seen the new "Stringy Floppy" on the market, and watch the puzzled expression. Keep a straight face now!

striping

Interleaving or multiplexing data to increase speed. See *disk striping*.

stroke

(1) In printing, the weight, or thickness, of a character. For example, in the LaserJet, one of the specifications of the font description is the stroke weight from -3 to +3.

(2) In computer graphics, a pen or brush stroke or to a vector in a vector graphics image.

stroke font

Same as *vector font*.

stroke weight

The thickness of lines in a font character. The HP LaserJet III manual defines stroke weights from Ultra Thin (-7) to Ultra Black (+7), with Medium, or Text, as normal (0).

stroke writer

Same as *vector display*.

strong typing

A programming language characteristic that provides strict adherence to the rules of typing. Data of one type (integer, string, etc.) cannot be passed to a variable expecting data of a different type. Contrast with *weak typing*.

structured analysis

Techniques developed in the late 1970s by Yourdon, DeMarco, Gane and Sarson for applying a systematic approach to systems analysis. It included the use of data flow diagrams and data modeling and fostered the use of implementation-independent graphical notation for documentation.

structured design

A systematic approach to program design developed in the mid 1970s by Constantine, Yourdon, et al, that included the use of graphical notation for effective documentation and communication, design guidelines and recipes to help programmers get started.

structured programming

Techniques that impose a logical structure on the writing of a program. Large routines are broken down into smaller, modular routines. The use of the GOTO statement is discouraged (see *spaghetti code*).

Certain programming statements are indented in order to make loops and other program logic easier to follow. Structured walkthroughs, which invite criticism from peer programmers, are also used.

Structured languages, such as Pascal, Ada and dBASE, force the programmer to write a structured program. However, unstructured languages such as FORTRAN, COBOL and BASIC require discipline on the part of the programmer.

stub

A small software routine placed into a program that provides a common function. Stubs are used for a variety of purposes. For example, a stub might be installed in a client machine, and a counterpart installed in a server, where both are required to resolve some protocol, remote procedure call (RPC) or other interoperability requirement.

Stuffit

A Macintosh shareware program from Aladdin Systems, Aptos, CA, that compresses files onto multiple floppies. A commercial version adds a scripting language, file viewing and supports multiple compression techniques. It was originally developed by Raymond Lau at age 16.

style sheet

In word processing and desktop publishing, a file that contains layout settings for a particular category of document. Style sheets include such settings as margins, tabs, headers and footers, columns and fonts.

stylus

A pen-shaped instrument that is used to "draw" images or point to menus. See *light pen* and *digitizer tablet*.

subarea node

In an SNA network, a system that contains network controlling functions. It refers to a host computer or a communications controller and its associated terminals.

subdirectory

A disk directory that is subordinate to (below) another directory. In order to gain access to a subdirectory, the path must include all directories above it. See *subfolder*.

subfolder

A folder that is placed within another folder. See *subdirectory*.

submarining

The temporary visual loss of the screen pointer on a passive matrix display screen. See *mouse trails* and *active matrix*.

submenu

An additional list of options within a menu selection. There can many levels of submenus.

subnetwork

A division of a network into an interconnected, but independent, subgroup, or domain, in order to improve performance and security.

subnotebook

A laptop computer that weighs less than four pounds. Subnotebooks may use an external floppy disk to reduce weight. If you need to exchange data via diskettes in remote locations, this may be inconvenient. For features of a portable computer, see *laptop computer*.

subroutine

A group of instructions that perform a specific task. A large subroutine is usually called a module or procedure; a small one, a function or macro, but all terms are used interchangeably.

subschema

Pronounced "sub-skeema." In database management, an individual user's partial view of the database. The schema is the entire database.

subscript

(1) In word processing and mathematical notation, a digit or symbol that appears below the line. Contrast with *superscript*.
(2) In programming, a method for referencing data in a table. For example, in the table **PRICETABLE**, the statement to reference a specific price in the table might be **PRICETABLE (ITEM)**, ITEM being the subscript variable. In a two-dimensional table that includes price and discount, the statement **PRICETABLE (ITEM,DISCOUNT)** could reference a discounted price. The relative locations of the current ITEM and DISCOUNT are kept in two index registers.

subset

A group of commands or functions that do not include all the capabilities of the original specification. Software or hardware components designed for the subset will also work with the original. However, any component designed for the full original specification will not operate with the subset product. Contrast with *superset*.

substrate

The base material upon which integrated circuits are built. Silicon is the most widely used substrate for chips.

substring

A subset of an alphanumeric field or variable. The substring function in a programming language is used to extract the subset; for example, the programming expression **substr(prodcode,4,3)** extracts characters 4, 5 and 6 out of a product code field or variable.

subtract

In relational database, an operation that generates a third file from all the records in one file that are not in a second file.

subwoofer

A speaker that reproduces the lower end of the audio spectrum. A subwoofer system may include a crossover circuit which switches frequencies approximately 100Hz and under to the subwoofer, while passing the rest of the signal to the main speakers.

suite of applications

See *application suite*.

SUM II

(Symantec Utilities for Macintosh) A set of Macintosh utilities from Symantec Corporation, Cupertino, CA, that provides hard disk optimization, analysis and repair and security capabilities.

Summit

The code name for IBM's ES/9000 models. Since water cooled models below the 820 are re-architected 3090 J models, the term may stay in usage to refer to the top-end models (820, 860, 900).

Sun

(Sun Microsystems, Inc., Mountain View, CA) A manufacturer of network-based, high-performance workstations founded in 1982. Product lines include stand-alone and networked systems, diskless workstations and file servers that feature its SPARC microprocessor architecture.

Sun supports an open systems model of computing throughout its product line that allows it to interact in networks of computer systems from other vendors. Its ONC (Open Network Computing) software is supported by over 300 vendors, and its NFS (Network File System) software, which allows data sharing across the network, has become an industry standard.

In 1991, Sun split its business into the following wholly-owned subsidiaries:

> **Sun Microsystems** - Systems
> **SunSoft** - System software
> **SunPro** - Programmer productivity tools
> **SunPics** - Printing and imaging
> **SunConnect** - Network integration
> **SunExpress** - Distribution

Superbase

A relational database management (DBMS) and client/server application development system for Windows from Superbase, Inc., Bohemia, NY. It includes a database that supports a wide variety of image and multimedia types, an object-based Super Basic Language similar to Visual Basic and a suite of visual programming tools. It supports the major SQL databases as well as ODBC-compliant databases. Superbase was originally created in 1984 by Precision Software for the Commodore computer and was ported to Windows in 1989.

SuperCalc

A PC spreadsheet from Computer Associates. It was one of the first spreadsheets following in VisiCalc's footsteps in the early 1980s. SuperCalc5 (1988) provides 3-D capability, enhanced graphics and can link up to 256 spreadsheets.

superclass

In object technology, a high-level class that passes attributes and methods (data and processing) down the hierarchy to subclasses, the classes below it. Abstract superclasses are used as master structures and no objects are created for it. Concrete superclasses are used to create objects.

supercomputer

The fastest computer available. It is typically used for simulations in petroleum exploration and production, structural analysis, computational fluid dynamics, physics and chemistry, electronic design, nuclear energy research and meteorology. It is also used for realtime animated graphics.

Cray Y-MP/832
In the 1980s, certain models of Cray Research supercomputers were built in a unique semicircular cabinet with a sitting bench around it. Their silhouettes were synonymous with the fastest computers of the time.

superconductor

A material that has little resistance to the flow of electricity. Traditional superconductors operate at -459 Fahrenheit (absolute zero).

Thus far, the major use for superconductors, made of alloys of niobium, is for high-powered magnets in medical imaging machines that use magnetic fields instead of x-rays.

Using experimental materials, such as copper oxides, barium, lanthanum and yttrium, IBM's Zurich research lab in 1986 and the University of Houston in 1987 raised the temperature of superconductivity to -59 degrees Fahrenheit. If superconductors can work at reasonable temperatures, they will have a dramatic impact on the future of computing. See *Josephson junction*.

SuperDrive

The floppy disk drive used in the Macintosh. It stores 1.44MB of data in its high-density format. It also reads and writes earlier Mac 400 and 800KB disks, as well as Apple II ProDOS, MS-DOS and OS/2 formats.

super floppy

(1) A PC 3.5" floppy disk that holds 2.88MB and is compatible with the 1.44MB and 720KB formats.

(2) A very-high-capacity floppy disk in the 20MB range. See *Floptical*.

(3) (SuperFloppy) A Superdrive-compatible floppy disk for older Macintoshes from Peripheral Land, Inc., Fremont, CA.

superframe

A T1 transmission format made up of 12 T1 frames (superframe) and 24 frames (extended superframe). See *D4*.

SuperKey

A PC keyboard macro processor from Borland that lets users create keyboard macros, rearrange the keyboard and encrypt data and programs.

supermini

A large-scale minicomputer. Note: Supermini is not the same as mini-supercomputer.

SuperNOS

An advanced network operating system. Novell popularized this term for a future product intended to combine NetWare and UnixWare. However, in late 1995, Novell sold UnixWare to The Santa Cruz Operation (SCO), thus abandoning the SuperNOS project.

superscaler

A CPU architecture that allows more than one instruction to be executed in one clock cycle.

superscript

Any letter, digit or symbol that appears above the line. Contrast with *subscript*.

superserver

A high-speed network server with very large RAM and disk capacity. Superservers typically support multiprocessing.

superset

A group of commands or functions that exceed the capabilities of the original specification. Software or hardware components designed for the original specification will also operate with the superset product. However, components designed for the superset will not work with the original. Contrast with *subset*.

supertwist

An LCD technology that twists liquid molecules greater than 90 degrees in order to improve contrast and viewing angle. See *LCD*.

Super VGA

See *VGA* and *PC display modes*.

supervisor

Same as *operating system*.

supervisor call

The instruction in an application program that switches the computer to supervisor state.

supervisor control program

The part of the operation system that always resides in memory. Same as *kernel*.

supervisor state

Typically associated with mainframes, it is a hardware mode in which the operating system executes instructions unavailable to an application program; for example, I/O instructions. Contrast with *program state*.

suppliers

See *hardware vendors, software vendors, vendors,* and *online services*.

support

(1) The assistance provided by a hardware or software vendor in installing and maintaining its product.
(2) Software or hardware designed to include or work with some other software or hardware product. For example, if a word processor "supports the LaserJet," it can activate special features of that printer. If a computer "supports multiprocessing," it can host more than one CPU internally. If a development system "supports Windows," it is used to create applications for Windows. If a system "supports the major databases," it provides interfaces to those databases.

SUPRA

A relational DBMS from Cincom Systems, Inc., Cincinnati, OH, that runs on IBM mainframes and VAXs. It includes a query language and a program that automates the database design process.

surface

In CAD, the external geometry of an object. Surfaces are generally required for NC (numerical control) modeling rather than wireframe or solids.

surface modeling

In CAD, a mathematical technique for representing solid-appearing objects. Surface modeling is a more complex method for representing objects than wireframe modeling, but not as sophisticated as solid modeling.
Although surface and solid models can appear the same on screen, they are quite different. Surface models cannot be sliced open as can solid models. In addition, in surface modeling, the object can be geometrically incorrect; whereas, in solid modeling, it must be correct.

surface mount

A circuit board packaging technique in which the leads (pins) on the chips and components are soldered on top of the board, not through it. Boards can be smaller and built faster.

surfing

Scanning online material, such as databases, news clips and forums. The term originated from "channel surfing," the rapid changing of TV channels to find something of interest.

surge

See *power surge*.

surge protector

A device that protects a computer from excessive voltage (spikes and power surges) in the power line. See *voltage regulator* and *UPS*.

surge suppressor

Same as *surge protector*.

suspend and resume

To stop an operation and restart where you left off. In portable computers, the hard disk is turned off, and the CPU is made to idle at its slowest speed. All open applications are retained in memory.

SV

(Scientific Visualization) See *visualization*.

SVC

(Switched Virtual Circuit) A Network connection from sender to recipient that is established at the time the transmission is required. This is what occurs in a switched public network. Contrast with *PVC*.

SVD

(Simultaneous Voice and Data) The concurrent transmission of voice and data by modem over a single analog telephone line. The first SVD technologies on the market are MultiTech's MSP, Radish's VoiceView, AT&T's VoiceSpan and the all-digital DSVD, endorsed by Intel, Hayes and others.

SVGA

(Super VGA) See *VGA*.

S-VHS

(Super-VHS) A video recording and playback system that uses a higher-quality VHS cassette and the S-video technology. VCRs that support S-VHS can also record and play back normal VHS tapes.

SVID

(System VInterface Definition) An AT&T specification for the UNIX System V operating system. SVID Release 3 specifies the interface for UNIX System V Release 4.

S-video

(Super-video) A video technology, also called Y/C video, that records and maintains luminance (Y) and color information (C) separately. S-VHS and Hi-8 cameras and VCRs use this method, which provide a better color image than standard VHS and

8mm formats. S-video hookups use a special 5-pin connector rather than the common RCA phono plug.

SVR4

See *System V Release 4.0*.

swap file

A disk file used to temporarily save a program or part of a program running in memory. See *Windows swap file*.

swapping

Replacing one segment of a program in memory with another and restoring it back to the original when required. In virtual memory systems, it is called paging.

switch

(1) A mechanical or electronic device that directs the flow of electrical or optical signals from one side to the other. Switches with multiple input and output ports such as a PBX are able to route traffic." See *data switch* and *transistor*.
With regard to a simple on/off switch, remember...

MECHANICAL SWITCH
(Toggle Switch)

ELECTRONIC SWITCH
(Transistor)

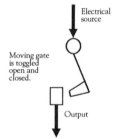

Moving gate is toggled open and closed.

Electrical source

Output

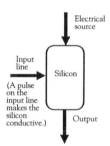

Electrical source

Input line

Silicon

(A pulse on the input line makes the silicon conductive.)

Output

Open is "off." Closed is "on."
(2) In programming, a bit or byte used to keep track of something. Sometimes refers to a branch in a program.
(3) A modifier of a command.

Switched 56

A digital service at 56 kilobits per second provided by the local telephone companies and long distance carriers. It works like the dial-up telephone system, only for digital data. You pay a monthly charge plus so much per minute of digital traffic. The rates are similar to voice calls on the analog network. For connection, a DSU/CSU is used instead of a modem.
The Switched 56 service uses a 64 Kbps channel, but reserves one out of every eight bits for in band signaling.

switched digital service

See *Switched 56*.

switched Ethernet

An Ethernet network that runs through a high-speed switch. Switched Ethernet is easily installed in an existing 10BaseT network, because the network adapters (NICs) in each machine are still used. The Ethernet hub is changed to an Ethernet switch, and the medium is no longer shared, rather there is dedicated bandwidth between any two stations. The switch, which is capable of handling hundreds of megabits per second, allows each user the full Ethernet bandwidth of 10 Mbps to another node. See *FDSE*.

switched line

In communications, a link that is established in a switched network, such as the international dial-up telephone system, a Switched 56 digital line or ISDN.

switched network

(1) The international dial-up telephone system.
(2) A network in which a temporary connection is established from one point to another for either the duration of the session (circuit switching) or for the transmission of one or more packets of data (packet switching).

switching hub

A device that acts as a central switch or PBX, connecting one line to another. In a local area network (LAN), a switching hub gives any two stations on the network the full bandwidth of the line. Contrast with *shared media LAN*, in which all stations share the bandwidth of a common transmission path. See *hub*.

switch-to-computer

To integrate voice telephone and database access. For example, in customer service applications, using telephone services, such as automatic number identification (ANI) and automatic call distribution (ACD), an incoming call can retrieve and route the customer's file to the next available human agent.

SX

See *386SX, 486SX* and *LaserJet*.

Sybase database

See *SQL Server*.

Sybase System

A family of SQL development tools from Sybase, Inc., Emeryville, CA, that includes SQL Server, SQL Toolset (design, development and control) and Client/Services Interfaces (distributed database architecture). See *SQL Server*.

SYLK file

(SYmbolic LinK file) A spreadsheet file format originating with Multiplan that is used by a number of spreadsheet programs.

Symantec

(Symantec Corporation, Cupertino, CA) A software company founded in 1982 by Dr. Gary Hendrix. It was acquired by Gordon Eubanks in 1984 and released its Q&A file manager the following year. In 1990, it merged with Peter Norton Computing, Inc., developer of the well-known Norton Utilities and Norton Desktop programs. Since then, it has acquired more than a dozen other software companies, including Central Point Software, maker of PC Tools, and Zortech, developer of of C++ compilers.

symbol

In data compression, a unit of data (byte, floating point number, spoken word, etc.) that is treated independently.

symbolic language

(1) A programming language that uses symbols, or mnemonics, for expressing operations and operands. All modern programming languages are symbolic languages.
(2) A language that manipulates symbols rather than numbers. See *list processing*.

symbol set
Same as *character set*.

symmetric multiprocessing
See *SMP*.

Symphony
An Integrated software package for PCs from Lotus that includes word processing, database management, speadsheet, business graphics, communications and a macro language.

sync character
In synchronous communications systems, a special character transmitted to synchronize timing.

sync generator
A device that supplies synchronization signals to a series of cameras to keep them all in phase.

synchronous
(1) A sequence of fixed or concurrent events. See *synchronous transmission*.
(2) Completing the current I/O operation before the next one is started.
(3) In SCSI, the transfer of data without immediate acknowledgment of each byte.
(4) Contrast with *asynchronous*.

synchronous protocol
A communications protocol that controls a synchronous transmission, such as bisync, SDLC and HDLC. Contrast with *asynchronous protocol*.

synchronous transmission
The transmission of data in which both stations are synchronized. Codes are sent from the transmitting station to the receiving station to establish the synchronization, and data is then transmitted in continuous streams.
Modems that transmit at 1200 bps and higher often convert the asynchronous signals from a computer's serial port into synchronous transmission over the transmission line. Contrast with *asynchronous transmission*.

Synon/2E
An integrated development environment for AS/400s from Synon, Inc., Larkspur, CA. Synon/2E was introduced in the same year as the AS/400 (1988) and is the leading tools product in this market. It provides an upper and lower CASE environment that generates COBOL and RPG code. Synon was founded in England in 1983 by Simon Williams. The name came from and is pronounced "sign on."
Synon's Obsydian is an object-oriented PC-based environment that is used to develop C++ code for Windows clients and RPG code for AS/400 servers.

SynOptics
See *Bay Networks*.

syntax
The rules governing the structure of a language statement. It specifies how words and symbols are put together to form a phrase.

syntax error
An error that occurs when a program cannot understand the command that has been entered. See *parse*.

synthesize

To create a whole or complete unit from parts or components.

synthesizer

A device that generates sound by creating waveforms electronically (FM synthesis) or from stored samples of musical instruments (wave table synthesis). See *MIDI* and *speech synthesis*.

SyQuest disk

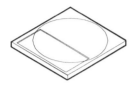

A removable hard disk drive from SyQuest Technology, Inc., Fremont, CA. Using the SCSI interface, SyQuest's 5.25" drives hold 44, 88 and 200MB cartridges. The 3.5" drives hold 105 and 270MB formats. SyQuest also introduced an 80MB PCMCIA drive in 1995.

SyQuest drives are widely used as an interchange medium in service bureaus and have become the de facto standard for removable magnetic media on the desktop. By the end of 1994, more than one million units were shipped. The company was founded in 1982 by Syed Iftikar (Sy's Quest) and originally made 3.9" drives for the military. It introduced its first 5.25" drive in 1986.

sysgen

(SYStem GENeration) The installation of a new or revised operating system. It includes selecting the appropriate utility programs and identifying the peripheral devices and storage capacities of the system the operating system will be controlling.

sysop

(SYStem OPerator) Pronounced "siss-op." A person who runs an online communications system or bulletin board. The sysop may also act as mediator for system conferences.

Sysplex

IBM's umbrella name for its System/390 multiprocessing architecture. Also known as Parallel Sysplex, it includes a variety of features that allow multiple S/390 computers to be coupled together as a single system with data sharing and workload balancing. For example, the Sysplex Timer external clock is used to synchronize time-of-day clocks in multiple processors. If failure occurs in a multiprocessor complex, precise transaction time stamps are required for accurate rollback and recovery.

SysReq key

(SYStem REQuest key) A keyboard key on a terminal keyboard that is used to get the attention of the central computer. The key exists on PC keyboards, but is rarely used by applications.

system

(1) A group of related components that interact to perform a task.
(2) A *computer system* is made up of the CPU, operating system and peripheral devices.
(3) An *information system* is made up of the database, all the data entry, update, query and report programs and manual and machine procedures.
(4)"The system" often refers to the operating system.

System/3

A batch-oriented minicomputer from IBM. Introduced in 1969, it introduced a new punched card about half the size of previous ones. With the addition of the Communications Control Program (CCP), it could handle interactive terminals.

System/3x

Refers to IBM System/34, System/36 and System/38 midrange computers.

System 7

(1) A major upgrade of the Macintosh operating system introduced in 1991. It includes virtual memory, increased memory addressing, hot links (Publish & Subscribe), multitasking (MultiFinder no longer optional), TrueType fonts and a variety of enhancements to the user interface.

System 7 Pro was a superset of 7.1, which added PowerTalk communications, the AppleScript scripting language and QuickTime for sound, movies and animation. System 7.5, the current version, is an upgrade of System 7 Pro that includes AppleGuide, an advanced online help system, and QuickDraw GX, which provides more sophisticated graphics capabilities.

(2) (System/7) A sensor-based minicomputer from IBM introduced in 1970 and used for process control. It was superseded by the Series/1.

System/32

A batch-oriented minicomputer from IBM. Introduced in 1975, it provided a single terminal for operator use. It was superseded by the System/34, which could run System/32 applications in a special mode.

System/34

A multiuser, multitasking minicomputer from IBM, introduced in 1977. The typical system had from a handful to a dozen terminals and could run System/32 programs in a special mode. Most large System/34 users migrated to the System/38, while small users migrated to the System/36.

System/36

A multiuser, multitasking minicomputer from IBM that was introduced in 1983. It superseded the System/34 and is mostly compatible with it. System/34 programs run in the System/36 after recompilation. The typical system supports from a handful to a couple of dozen terminals.

Although superseded by the AS/400, System/36 applications have to be recompiled to run on it. As a result, as of late 1994, a large number of System/36s still remain in use. With the announcement of the AS/400 Advanced System/36, which runs System/36 applications natively, it is expected that System/36s will finally begin to fade into history.

System/38

A minicomputer from IBM that includes an operating system with an integrated relational database management system. Introduced in 1978, it was an advanced departure from previous System/3x computers. The typical system handles from a dozen to several dozen terminals. It has been superseded by the AS/400.

System/88

A family of fault-tolerant midrange computers from IBM used for online transaction processing. Uses the System/88 virtual memory and System/88 FTX (Fault Tolerant UNIX) operating systems. Includes 4579 and 4576 multiprocessor series and 4593 entry-level models.

System/360

IBM's first family of computer systems introduced in 1964. It was the first time in history that a complete line of computers was announced at one time. Although considerable enhancements have been made, much of the 360 architecture is still carried over in current-day IBM mainframes. See *IBM mainframes.*

System/370

The mainframe product line introduced in 1970 by IBM (superseding System/360), which added virtual memory and other enhancements. Subsequent series include the 303x, 43xx, 308x, 309x and 9370, all 370-architecture machines. The 370 architecture was brought down to the PC level in 1983 with the PC XT/370, and then again in 1989 with the VM/SP Technical Workstation. See *IBM mainframes*.

System/390

The mainframe product line introduced in 1990 by IBM (superseding System/370) that features ESA/390 architecture and operating systems, ES/9000 hardware (18 models introduced), ESCON fiber optic channels, Sysplex multiprocessing and SystemView.

In 1994, IBM introduced its next generation of System/390 systems, the Parallel Enterprise Servers. These are SMP machines that contain single-chip CMOS CPUs and use less power and dissipate less heat than the bipolar-based ES/9000 models. In 1995, IBM introduced new models that provide up to 10-way SMP within the same machine. Up to 32 10-way systems can be hooked together providing a multiprocessing system with up to 320 CPUs.

As processing requirements increase, customers are expected to migrate from the older ES/9000s to the new more cost effective SMP machines.

System 2000

(1) A hierarchical, network and relational DBMS from the SAS Institute, Cary, NC, that runs on IBM, CDC and Unisys computers. It has been integrated into the SAS System.

(2) See *FTS 2000*.

system administrator

A person who manages a multiuser computer system. Responsibilities are similar to that of a network administrator. A system administrator would perform systems programmer activities with regard to the operating system and other network control programs.

Systemantics

An insightful book on the systems process by John Gall (1977). The following is copied with permission from Random House.

A Concise Summary of the Field of General Systemantics

Systems are seductive. They promise to do a hard job faster, better, and more easily than you could do it by yourself. But if you set up a system, you are likely to find your time and effort now being consumed in the care and feeding of the system itself. New problems are created by its very presence. Once set up, it won't go away, it grows and encroaches. It begins to do strange and wonderful things. Breaks down in ways you never thought possible. It kicks back, gets in the way, and opposes its own proper function. Your own perspective becomes distorted by being in the system. You become anxious and push on it to make it work. Eventually you come to believe that the misbegotten product it so grudgingly delivers is what you really wanted all the time. At that point encroachment has become complete...

you have become absorbed...

you are now a systems person!

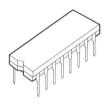

system BIOS

On a PC, a part of the operating system that is coded into a memory chip on the motherboard. The system BIOS has traditionally been stored in a ROM chip, which cannot be updated and must be replaced if new functions are required. Increasingly, the system BIOS is stored in a flash memory chip, which can be updated in place on the motherboard. It is expected that all BIOSs stored in chips will eventually be updatable in place. See *BIOS*.

system board

A printed circuit board that contains the primary CPU. In a personal computer, it is also called the *motherboard*.

system bus

The primary pathway between the CPU, memory and high-speed peripherals. Same as *local bus*.

system development cycle

The sequence of events in the development of an information system (application), which requires mutual effort on the part of user and technical staff.

> 1. SYSTEMS ANALYSIS & DESIGN
>   feasibility study
>   general design
>   prototyping
>   detail design
>   functional specifications
>
> 2. USER SIGN OFF
>
> 3. PROGRAMMING
>   design
>   coding
>   testing
>
> 4. IMPLEMENTATION
>   training
>   conversion
>   installation
>
> 5. USER ACCEPTANCE

system development methodology

The formal documentation for the phases of the system development cycle. It defines the precise objectives for each phase and the results required from a phase before the next one can begin. It may include specialized forms for preparing the documentation describing each phase.

system disk

A hard or floppy disk that contains part or all of the operating system or other control program. See *bootable disk*.

system failure

A hardware or operating system malfunction.

system file

A machine language file that is part of the operating system or other control program. It may also refer to a configuration file used by such programs.

System Development Cycle

The systems development cycle starts with the user's information requirements, which are the raw ingredients for data administration and systems analysis and design. The functional specs are the blueprint for the information system. They define the database structure, application programs (data entry, update, query and report programs) and manual and machine procedures. The application programmer writes the programs, and system programmers provide the infrastructure support. The cycle is ever moving. Changes in user requirements start the process all over again.

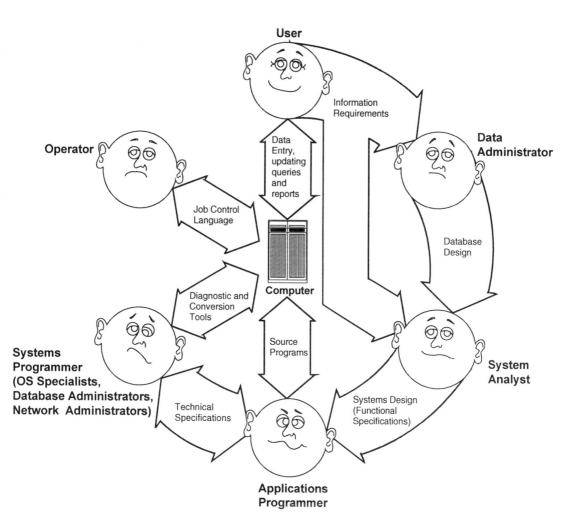

system folder

The operating system folder in the Macintosh that contains the System, Finder and MultiFinder, printer drivers, fonts, desk accessories, INITs and cdevs.

system font

The primary font used by the operating system or other control program to display messages and menus unless otherwise directed.

system image

The current contents of memory, which includes the operating system and running programs.

SYSTEM.INI

(SYStem INItialization) A Windows configuration file that describes the current state of the computer system environment. It contains hundreds of entries and is read by Windows on startup. It identifies such things as the drivers in the system, how DOS applications are handled and provides immense detail about internal Windows settings.

The information in SYSTEM.INI is updated by Windows when you change various defaults; however, in order to tweak system performance, the file can be edited with a text editor or a word processor that imports ASCII files.

Most of the time, users do not deal with SYSTEM.INI; however, on occasion, a line in the 386 Enhanced section ([386Enh]) may have to be modified. Sometimes an **EMMExclude=** statement is added or changed to exclude a section of upper memory used by a new peripheral from the general pool of memory that Windows uses. WIN.INI is another major configuration file read by Windows at startup. See *WIN.INI*.

system level

An operation that is performed by the operating system or some other control program.

system life cycle

The useful life of an information system. Its length depends on the nature and volatility of the business, as well as the software development tools used to generate the databases and applications. Eventually, an information system that is patched over and over no longer is structurally sound enough to be expanded.

Tools like DBMSs allow for changes more readily, but increased transaction volumes can negate the effectiveness of the original software later on.

system memory

The memory used by the operating system.

system program

A component of system software.

system prompt

An on-screen symbol that indicates the operating system is ready for a command. See *DOS prompt*.

systems

A general term for the department, people or work involved in systems analysis & design activities.

systems analysis & design

The examination of a problem and the creation of its solution. Systems analysis is effective when all sides of the problem are reviewed. Systems design is most effective when more than one solution can be proposed. The plans for the care and feeding of a new system are as important as the problems they solve. See *system development cycle* and *Systemantics.*

systems analyst

The person responsible for the development of an information system. They design and modify systems by turning user requirements into a set of functional specifications, which are the blueprint of the system. They design the database or help design it if data administrators are available. They develop the manual and machine procedures and the detailed processing specs for each data entry, update, query and report program in the system.

Systems analysts are the architects, as well as the project leaders, of an information system. It is their job to develop solutions to user's problems, determine the technical and operational feasibility of their solutions, as well as estimate the costs to develop and implement them.

They develop prototypes of the system along with the users, so that the final specifications are examples of screens and reports that have been carefully reviewed. Experienced analysts leave no doubt in users' minds as to what is being developed, and they insist that all responsible users review and sign off on every detail.

Systems analysts require a balanced mix of business and technical knowledge, interviewing and analytical skills, as well as a good understanding of human behavior. See *Systemantics.*

systems disk

A disk pack or disk drive reserved only for system software, which includes the operating system, assemblers, compilers and other utility and control programs.

systems engineer

Often a vendor title for persons involved in consulting and pre-sales activities related to computers. See *systems analyst, systems programmer, programmer analyst* and *application programmer.*

systems house

An organization that develops customized software and/or turnkey systems for customers. Contrast with *software house,* which develops software packages for sale to the general public. Both terms are used synonymously.

systems integration

Making diverse components work together. See *NASI.*

systems integrator

An individual or organization that builds systems from a variety of diverse components. With increasing complexity of technology, more customers want complete solutions to information problems, requiring hardware, software and networking expertise in a multivendor environment. See *OEM, VAR* and *NASI.*

systems management

(1) The management of systems development, which includes systems analysis & design, application development and implementation. See *system development cycle.*
(2) Software that manages computer systems in an enterprise, which may include any and all of the following functions: software distribution, version control, backup & recovery, printer spooling, job scheduling, virus protection and performance and capacity planning. Depending on organizational philosophy, systems management may include network management or be a part of it. See *network management* and *configuration management.*

system software

Programs used to control the computer and develop and run application programs. It includes operating systems, TP monitors, network operating systems and database managers. Contrast with *application program.*

The following diagram shows the flow between system software and application software residing in memory in a multiuser computer. The operating system (OS), TP monitor, database manager and interpreter are considered system software. The applications and interactive DBMS query and edit would be considered application software.

Following are the major categories of system software. See *application software* for a list of major application software categories.

Operating System

Manages the computer system. Provides file, task and job management. All application programs "talk to" the operating system.

DOS, Windows, OS/2, UNIX, VMS, MVS, VM and Windows NT are examples.

Database Management System (DBMS)

Manages the storage, retrieval, security and integrity of the database. A DBMS may provide interactive data entry, updating, query and reporting or rely entirely on the application program for such functions. The DBMS may reside in a mainframe or in a file server in a client/server architecture. Popular DBMSs support the SQL query language. Many DBMSs provide a complete programming language for application development.

Examples of popular mainframe and client/server DBMSs are DB2, Oracle, Sybase, Rdb, Informix, Ingres and Progress. dBASE and Paradox are used for many PC applications.

TP Monitor

Mainframe/midrange program that distributes input from multiple terminals to the appropriate application. This functions is also provided in LAN operating systems. CICS is widely used in IBM mainframes, and Tuxedo is widely used in UNIX systems.

Network Operating System

Manage traffic and security between client workstations and file servers in a network. Examples are NetWare, LAN Manager, LAN Server, VINES, NFS (UNIX), Windows NT and LANtastic.

Communications Protocol

Set of rules, formats and functions for sending data across the network. There are many protocol layers starting at the top application layer to the bottom physical layer (see *OSI model*).

Popular transport protocols are NetBIOS, NetBEUI, IPX/SPX and TCP/IP. Popular data link protocols, or access methods, used to transmit data from point to point are Ethernet, Token Ring, SDLC and RS-232.

Messaging Protocol

Set of rules, formats and functions for sending, storing and forwarding e-mail in a network. The major messaging protocols are SNADS, MHS, SMTP, X.400 and the proprietary protocols used in cc:Mail and Microsoft Mail.

Driver

Software that supports a peripheral device, such as a display adapter or CD-ROM. The driver contains the detailed machine language necessary to activate all functions in the device. The operating system commands the driver, which in turn commands the hardware device.

BIOS

(Basic Input/Output System) The part of the operating system that manages the essential peripherals such as the keyboard, monitor and disks. It also contains internal functions such as the system timer and realtime clock. See *BIOS*.

Programming Language

Translate source language into machine language using assemblers, compilers, interpreters and application generators. All system software and application software must be programmed in a programming language and turned into machine language for execution.

Examples of programming languages are assembly language, BASIC, FORTRAN, C, C++, Pascal, dBASE, Paradox, Visual Basic and COBOL.

See *application software* for a list of major application software categories.

systems programmer

(1) In the IS department of a large organization, a technical expert on some or all of the computer's system software (operating systems, networks, DBMSs, etc.). They are responsible for the efficient performance of the computer systems.

They usually don't write programs, but perform a lot of technical tasks that integrate vendors' software. They also act as technical advisors to systems analysts, application programmers and operations personnel. For example, they would know whether additional tasks could be added to the computer and would recommend conversion to a new operating or database system in order to optimize performance.

In mainframe environments, there is one systems programmer for about 10 or more application programmers, and systems programmers generally have considerably higher salaries than application programmers. In smaller environments, users rely on vendors or consultants for systems programming assistance. In fact, end users are actually performing systems programmer functions when they install new software or hardware on their own personal computers. See *system administrator*.

(2) In a computer hardware or software organization, a person who designs and writes system software. In this case, a systems programmer is a programmer in the traditional sense.

system test

Running a complete system for testing purposes. See *unit test*.

system time/date

The on-going time of day in the computer, which is maintained by a battery when the computer is turned off. It is used to time stamp all newly-created files and activate time-dependent processes.

system unit

The primary computer equipment. Housed in a desktop or floor-standing cabinet, it contains such components as the motherboard, CPU, RAM and ROM chips, hard and floppy disks and several input/output ports.

SystemView

An IBM architecture for computer systems management introduced with System/390 that provides an enterprise-wide approach for controlling multiple systems and networks. It will be implemented in stages through the 1990s. NetView is a major component.

System V Interface Definition

See *SVID*.

System V Release 4.0

A unified version of UNIX released in 1989. See *UNIX*.

systolic array

An array of processing elements (typically multiplier-accumulator chips) in a pipeline structure that is used for applications such as image and signal processing and fluid dynamics. The "systolic," coined by H. T. Kung of Carnegie-Mellon, refers to the rhythmic transfer of data through the pipeline like blood flowing through the vascular system.

SYZYGY

Pronounced "SIZE-uh-gee." PC workgroup software from Information Research Corporation, Charlottesville, VA. Used for coordinating schedules, resources and budgets for group projects and includes e-mail and a calendar with to-do and activity blists.

T

T

See *tera.*

T-1, T1

(1) A 1.544 megabit T-carrier channel that can handle 24 voice or data channels at 64 Kbits/sec. The standard T1 frame is 193 bits long, which holds 24 8-bit voice samples and one synchronization bit. 8,000 frames are transmitted per second. See *DS, D4* and *ESF.*

(2) See *Type 1 font.*

T.120

An ITU data conferencing standard for sharing data among multiple users. It defines interfaces for whiteboards, application viewing and application sharing. The ITU standard for videoconferencing is H.320.

T1 font

See *Type 1 font.*

T-2, T2

A 6.312 megabit T-carrier channel that can handle 96 voice or data channels at 64 Kbits/sec. See *DS.*

T-3, T3

A 44.736 megabit T-carrier channel that can handle 672 voice or data channels at 64 Kbits/sec. T3 requires fiber optic cable. See *DS.*

TA

(Terminal Adapter) See *ISDN terminal adapter.*

tab

(1) To move the cursor on a display screen or the print head on a printer to a specified column (tab stop). There are both horizontal and vertical tab characters in the ASCII character set. See *tab stop.*

(2) A small flap used for identification and quick access that projects out from a page of paper or file folder. Its electronic equivalent on screen can be clicked to launch a program or function or to access a record or document.

tab character

A control character in a document that represents movement to the next tab stop. In the ASCII character set, a horizontal tab is ASCII 9, and a vertical tab is ASCII 11. See *ASCII chart.*

tab delimited

A text format that uses tab characters as separators between fields. Unlike comma delimited files, alphanumeric data is not surrounded by quotes.

tab key

A keyboard key that moves the cursor to the next tab stop.

table

(1) In programming, a collection of adjacent fields. Also called an *array*, a table contains data that is either constant within the program or is called in when the program is run. See *decision table.*

(2) In a relational database, the same as a file; a collection of records.

table lookup

Searching for data in a table, commonly used in data entry validation and any operation that must match an item of data with a known set of values.

tablet

See *digitizer tablet.*

table view

A screen display of several items or records in rows and columns. Contrast with *form view.*

tab stop

A location on a horizontal line that has been defined to begin a column of text. Tab stops are necessary for multiple columns when proportional fonts are used. Pressing the space bar several times to move to the next column provides proper alignment only with monospaced characters. With proportional fonts, although the space bar moves a fixed amount, the varying widths of text in one column cause misalignment to the column on the right.

With typewriters, tab stops are mechanical gizmos that halt the movement of the carriage. In word processing, they are column numbers that are maintained by the software.

tabular form

Same as *table view* with respect to printed output.

tabulate

(1) To arrange data into a columnar format.
(2) To sum and print totals.

tabulating equipment

Punched card machines, including keypunches, sorters, collators, interpreters, reproducers, calculators and tabulators.

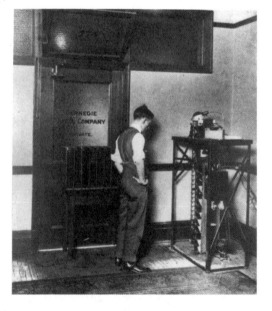

Tabulating Equipment
This picture was taken in 1918. The machine is a punched card sorter made by the Computing-Tabulating-Recording Company. In 1924, the company was renamed International Business Machines Corporation. *(Photo courtesy of International Business Machines Corporation.)*

tabulator

A punched card accounting machine that prints and calculates totals.

Tadpole

(Tadpole Technology, Inc., Austin, TX) Founded in 1988, it is a wholly-owned subsidiary of the British company, Tadpole Technology plc, which was founded in 1984. Until 1992, its focus was board level products and related software to OEM customers. In 1992, it began the introduction of workstation-class notebooks, starting with the Sun-compatible SPARCbook. Tadpole also developed IBM's RS/6000 notebook as well as its own line of Pentium notebooks. An Alpha-based notebook is expected in 1995.

tag

(1) A set of bits or characters that identifies various conditions about data in a file and is often found in the header records of such files.
(2) A name (label, mnemonic) assigned to a data structure, such as a field, file, paragraph or other object.
(3) The key field in a record.
(4) A brass pin on a terminal block that is connected to a wire by soldering or wire wrapping.

tag RAM

A specialized bank of static RAM used to hold addresses. When a stored address matches an input address, a signal is output to perform a function. It is used with hardware devices such as CPU caches to keep track of which memory addresses are stored in the cache.

tag sort

A sorting procedure in which the key fields are sorted first to create the correct order, and then the actual data records are placed into that order.

Taligent

(Taligent, Inc., Cupertino, CA) A software company initially formed by Apple and IBM to develop the next-generation operating system. The operating system (TalOS) was to be based on Apple's object-oriented operating system, code named Pink. HP has since joined the organization.
Today, the operating system is on hold, but Taligent has released its CommonPoint application system, formerly entitled the Taligent Application Environment (TalAE). CommonPoint is a set of object-oriented application frameworks for AIX, OS/2, HP-UX and the PowerMac. Also planned are development tools that support this environment, including cpConstructor, a graphical user interface builder.

talk-off

An unintentional command activation when a human voice generates the same tone as a control signal.

Tandem

(Tandem Computers Inc., Cupertino, CA) A manufacturer of fault-tolerant computers founded in 1974 by James Treybig. It was the first company to address the transaction processing (OLTP) market for online reservations and financial transfers by providing computers designed from the ground up for fault-tolerant operation.
Tandem's flagship fault-tolerant product is its MIPS-based Himalaya series which runs the NonStop Kernel operating system, compatible with Tandem's Guardian OS. The Himalaya holds the world's record for number of transactions processed per second. Tandem also offers its Integrity line of MIPS-based servers that run NonStop-UX (UNIX).

tandem processors

Two processors hooked together in a multiprocessor environment.

Tandy

(Tandy Corporation, Ft. Worth, TX) A manufacturer of PCs and electronics that started as a family leather business in 1919. In 1963, it acquired the nine Radio Shack stores in Boston. Today, it has over 7,000 company-owned stores and franchises.

In 1977, it introduced one of the first personal computers, the TRS-80 Model I. Tandy's Model 100 and 200 lightweight portables were also inspiration to the laptop generation. Its first computers were proprietary, and its initial PCs were non-standard. However, starting with the Model 1000 in 1984, Tandy offered a full line of IBM-compatible PCs.

In 1993, Tandy sold its PC manufacturing facilities to AST and began to eliminate the Tandy brand name on its machines. Radio Shack stores currently offer a variety of machines from AST, IBM and others.

tap

In communications, a connection onto the main transmission medium of a local area network. See *transceiver*.

tape

See *magnetic tape* and *paper tape*.

tape backup

The use of magnetic tape for storing duplicate copies of hard disk files. For mainframes and minis, half-inch tape cartridge drives are widely used. On the desktop, QIC is commonly used with DAT gaining ground. On LANs, DAT and 8mm usage is increasing. See *QIC*, *DAT* and *Exabyte*.

tape cartridge

See *data cartridge*.

tape cassette

See *data cassette*.

tape drive

A physical unit that holds, reads and writes the magnetic tape. See *magnetic tape*.

tape dump

A printout of tape contents without any report formatting.

tape library

A high-capacity data storage system for storing, retrieving, reading and writing multiple magnetic tape cartridges. It contains storage racks for holding the cartridges and a robotic mechanism for moving the cartridge to the drive.

Tape libraries are available for half-inch, DAT, 8mm and QIC tape cartridges. Smaller units can have several drives for simultaneous reading and writing and may hold from a handful to several hundred cartridges. Large units can have hundreds of drives and hold several thousand cartridges.

It takes several seconds to find, retrieve and load a cartridge, making it available for reading and writing.

tape mark

A control code used to indicate the end of a tape file.

tape transport

The mechanical part of a tape drive.

TAPI

(Telephony API) A programming interface from Microsoft and Intel that is part of Microsoft's WOSA architecture. It allows Windows client applications to access voice services on a server. TAPI is designed to provide interoperability between PCs and telephone equipment, including phone systems and PBXs. See *WOSA*.

tar

A UNIX utility for archiving files, often used in conjunction with "compress."

Targa

A raster graphics file format developed by Truevision, Inc., Indianapolis, IN. It uses the .TGA file extension and handles 16-, 24- and 32-bit color. It is also the trade name of a line of video graphics boards used in high-resolution imaging.

target computer

The computer into which a program is loaded and run. Contrast with *source computer*. See *cross assembler* and *cross compiler*.

target directory

The directory into which data is being sent. Contrast with *source directory*.

target disk

The disk onto which data is recorded. Contrast with *source disk*.

target drive

**Windows 95
Taskbar**
The taskbar can be positioned horizontally or vertically.

The drive containing the disk or tape onto which data is recorded. Contrast with *source drive*.

target language

The language resulting from a translation process such as assembling or compiling. Contrast with *source language*.

target machine

Same as *target computer*.

tariff

A schedule of rates for common carrier services.

task

An independent running program. See *multitasking*.

taskbar

An on-screen toolbar that displays the active applications (tasks). Windows 95 has popularized the taskbar. Clicking on a taskbar button restores the application to its previous appearance.

task management

The part of the operating system that controls the running of one or more programs (tasks) within the computer at the same time.

task swapping

Switching between two applications by copying the current running program to disk or other high-speed storage device (auxiliary memory, EMS, etc.) and loading another program into that program space.

task switching

Switching between active applications. See *context switching*.

TAXI

(Transparent Asynchronous Transmitter/Receiver Interface) A 100 Mbps/sec ATM transmission standard defined by the ATM Forum.

Tazz

Short for Tasmanian Devil, Tazz is a code name for a Windows 95 telephone application from Microsoft. It uses Microsoft's TAPI interface and a third-party speech-recognition engine. It will control new multimedia modems that handle both voice and data. Tazz is expected to be introduced after the release of Windows 95.

TB, Tb

See *terabyte* and *terabit*.

Tbits/sec

(TeraBITS per SECond) Trillion bits per second.

TBps, Tbps

(TeraBytes Per Second, TeraBits Per Second) Trillion bytes per second. Trillion bits per second.

T-byte

See *terabyte*.

Tbytes/sec

(TeraBYTES per SECond) Trillion bytes per second.

TC

See *true color*.

T-cal

See *thermal calibration*.

TCAM

(TeleCommunications Access Method) IBM communications software widely used to transfer data between mainframes and 3270 terminals. See *access method*.

T-carrier

A digital transmission service from a common carrier. Introduced by AT&T in 1983 as a voice service, its use for data has grown steadily.
T-carrier service requires multiplexors at both ends that merge the various signals together for transmission and split them at the destination. Multiplexors analyze the traffic load and vary channel speeds for optimum transmission. See *DS*.

TCM

(1) (Trellis-Coded Modulation/Viterbi Decoding) A technique that adds forward error correction to a modulation scheme by adding an additional bit to each baud. TCM is used with QAM modulation, for example.
(2) (Thermal Conduction Module) An IBM circuit packaging technique that seals chips, boards and components into a module that serves as a heat sink. TCMs are mostly water cooled, although some are air cooled.

TCO

Refers to the Swedish Confederation of Professional Employees, which has set stringent standards for devices that emit radiation. See *MPR II*.

TCP/IP

(Transmission Control Protocol/Internet Protocol) A communications protocol developed under contract from the U.S. Department of Defense to internetwork dissimilar systems. It is a de facto UNIX standard, but is now supported on almost all platforms. TCP/IP is the protocol of the Internet.

The TCP part of TCP/IP provides transport protocol functions, which ensures that the total amount of bytes sent is received correctly at the other end. The IP part of TCP/IP provides the routing mechanism. TCP/IP is a routable protocol, which means that the messages transmitted contain the address of a destination network as well as a destination station. This allows TCP/IP messages to be sent to multiple networks within an organization or around the world, hence its use in the worldwide Internet (see *Internet address*).

TCP/IP includes a file transfer capability called FTP, or File Transfer Protocol. This function allows files to be downloaded and uploaded between TCP/IP sites. SMTP, or Simple Mail Transfer Protocol, is TCP/IP's own messaging system for electronic mail, and the Telnet protocol provides terminal emulation. This allows a personal computer or workstation to emulate a variety of terminals connected to mainframes and midrange computers.

The combination of TCP/IP, NFS and NIS comprise the primary networking components of the UNIX operating system.

The following chart compares the TCP/IP layers with the Department of Defense and Open System Interconnection models.

FTP SMTP Telnet	Process	Application
		Presentation
		Session
TCP	Host to host	Transport
IP	Internet	Network
IEEE 802 X.25, etc.	Network Access	Data Link
		Physical
TCP/IP	DOD	OSI

TCP/IP stack

An implementation of the TCP/IP communications protocol. Network architectures designed in layers, such as TCP/IP, OSI and SNA, are called *stacks*.

TCSEC

See *NCSC*.

TCU

(Transmission Control Unit) A communications control unit controlled by the computer that does not execute internally stored programs. Contrast with *front end processor*, which executes its own instructions.

TDM

(Time Division Multiplexing) A technology that transmits multiple signals simultaneously over a single transmission path. Each lower-speed signal is time sliced into one high-speed transmission. For example, three incoming 1,000 bps signals (A, B and C) can be interleaved into one 3,000 bps signal (AABBCCAABBCCAABBCC). The receiving end divides the single stream back into its original signals.

TDM is the technology used in T-carrier service (DS0, DS1, etc.), which are the leased lines common in wide area networks (WANs). Contrast with *FDM*. See *baseband*.

TDMA

(Time Division Multiple Access) A satellite and cellular phone technology that interleaves multiple digital signals onto a single high-speed channel. For cellular, TDMA triples the capacity of the original analog method (FDMA). It divides each channel into three subchannels providing service to three users instead of one. See *FDMA*, *CDMA* and *CDPD*.

Team Enterprise Developer

A client/server application development system from Symantec that supports Windows clients and a variety of databases, including Access, SQL Server, Oracle and Sybase. It is a fully integrated system that is repository-driven. It also includes entity relationship diagrams and version control.

tear-off menu

An on-screen menu or palette that can be moved off of its primary position and relocated to any part of the screen.

tech support

Technical assistance from the hardware manufacturer or software publisher. Unless you have a simple, straightforward question, in order to get help from a tech support representative, place your telephone call while you are at your computer. Intermittent problems are very difficult to resolve. If you cannot recreate the problem on screen, there may be very little a tech support person can do to help you.

tech writer

A person who is responsible for writing documentation for a hardware or software product.

telco

(TELephone COmpany) A company that provides telephone services. It generally refers to the local telephone companies rather than the long-distance suppliers.

tele

("long distance") Operations performed remotely or by telephone.

telecommunications, telecom

Communicating information, including data, text, pictures, voice and video over long distance. See *communications*.

telecommunity

A society in which information can be transmitted or received freely between all members without technical incompatibilities.

telecommuting

Working at home and communicating with the office by electronic means.

teleconferencing

("long distance" conferencing) A communications session among several people that are geographically separated. See *videoconferencing, audioconferencing, computer conferencing* and *data conferencing.*

telecopying

("long distance" copying) The formal term for fax.

telefax

The european term for a fax machine.

telegraph

A low-speed communications device that transmits up to approximately 150 bps. Telegraph grade lines, stemming from the days of Morse code, can't transmit a voice conversation.

The First Almost-Digital Communications Morse code was sort of digital, because it used only two codes, the dot and dash. But it was the duration of the signal that determined the dot or dash, not a difference in voltage or presence or lack of a pulse.

telemanagement

Management of an organization's telephone systems, which includes maintaining and ordering new equipment and monitoring the expenses for all telephone calls.

telemarketing

Selling over the telephone.

telematics

The convergence of telecommunications and information processing.

telemedicine

("long distance" medicine) Using videoconferencing for medical diagnosis. With a videoconferencing link to a large medical center, rural health care facilities can perform diagnosis and treatment available only in larger metropolitan areas. A specialist can monitor the patient remotely taking cues from the general practitioner or nurse that is actually examining the patient. A patient's blood can be placed under a microscope in the remote facility and transmitted for examination.

telemetry

Transmitting data captured by instrumentation and measuring devices to a remote station where it is recorded and analyzed. For example, data from a weather satellite is telemetered to earth.

Telenet

A value-added, packet switching network that enables many varieties of terminals and computers to exchange data. It is a subsidiary of US Sprint. See also *Telnet*.

telephone

("long distance" + "sound") See *POTS*.

telephone channel

See *voice grade*.

telephone wiring

See *twisted pair*.

telephony

The science of converting sound into electrical signals, transmitting it within cables or via radio and reconverting it back into sound.

Telephony API

See *TAPI*.

Telephony Server NLM

A NetWare NLM that provides an interface between a NetWare server and a PBX. The physical connection is made by cabling the PBX to a card in the server. The NLM provides an open programming interface that allows PBX manufacturers to write drivers for their products.

The first implementation of this is AT&T's Definity PBX, which physically connects via an AT&T card in the NetWare server and allows all network users with AT&T phones to have access to the PBX through their PCs.

Telephony Services API

See *TSAPI*.

teleprinter

A typewriter-like terminal with a keyboard and built-in printer, often a portable unit. Contrast with *video terminal*.

Teleprinter

teleprocessing

("long distance" processing) An early IBM term for data communications.

teleprocessing monitor

See *TP monitor*.

Telescript

A programming language and software for communications from Genéral Magic. It embeds intelligence in e-mail and other applications allowing them to cooperate with one another and allows messages to move intelligently through diverse public and private networks. Telescript can be added to existing and future operating systems. See *Magic Cap*.

teleservices

(TELEphone SERVICES) An umbrella term for products and services that integrate telephones and computers. See *audiotex*.

Teletex

See *Telex*.

teletext

A broadcasting service that transmits text to a TV set that has a teletext decoder. It uses the vertical blanking interval of the TV signal (black line between frames when vertical hold is not adjusted) to transmit about a hundred frames. See *videotex*.

Teletype

The trade name of Teletype Corporation, which refers to a variety of teleprinters used for communications. The Teletype was one of the first communications terminals in the U.S.

teletype interface

See *teletype mode*.

teletype mode

Line-at-a-time output like a typewriter. Contrast with *full-screen mode*.

teletypewriter

A low-speed teleprinter, often abbreviated "TTY."

televaulting

Continuous transmitting of data to vaults for backup purposes. The term was coined by TeleVault Technology Inc.

Telex

An international dial-up communications service that uses teleprinters and transmits Baudot code at 50 bps (66 words/minute). In the U.S., it is administered by Western Union, which in 1971 purchased the Bell System's TWX service and connected it to the Telex network.

In the early 1980s, a new service called Teletex was initiated that provides higher speeds and upper and lowercase text to subscribers using intelligent terminals and personal computers. Group 3 fax machines quickly supplanted Telex transmission.

TeLink

An Xmodem protocol with batch file transfer designed for the Fido BBS. It sends file name, date and size in the first block.

Telnet

A terminal emulation protocol commonly used on the Internet. It allows a user to log onto and run a program from a remote terminal or computer. Telnet was originally developed for ARPAnet and is part of the TCP/IP communications protocol.

Although most computers on the Internet require users to have an established account and password, there are many that allow public access to certain programs, typically, search utilities, such as Archie or WAIS. See also *Telenet.*

Telon

See *CA-Telon.*

TEMPEST

Security against external radiation from data processing equipment. Equipment and cables that meet TEMPEST requirements have extra shielding in order to prevent data signals from escaping and being picked up by unauthorized listeners.

template

(1) A plastic or stiff paper form that is placed over the function keys on a keyboard to identify their use.
(2) The programmatic and descriptive part of a programmable application; for example, a spreadsheet that contains only descriptions and formulas or a HyperCard stack that contains only programming and backgrounds. When the template is filled with data, it becomes a working application.

temporary font

A soft font that remains in the printer's memory until the printer is reset manually or by software. Contrast with *permanent font.*

ter

Third version. See *bis.*

tera

Trillion. Abbreviated "T." It often refers to the precise value 1,099,511,627,776 since computer specifications are usually binary numbers. See *binary values* and *space/time.*

terabit

One trillion bits. Also Tb, Tbit and T-bit. See *tera* and *space/time.*

terabyte

One trillion bytes. Also TB, Tbyte and T-byte. See *tera* and *space/time.*

teraflops

(tera FLoating point OPerations per Second) One trillion floating point operations per second.

terminal

(1) An I/O device for a computer that usually has a keyboard for input and a video screen or printer for output.
(2) An input device, such as a scanner, video camera or punched card reader.
(3) An output device in a network, such as a monitor, printer or card punch.
(4) A connector used to attach a wire.

terminal emulation

Using a computer to simulate the type of terminal required to gain access to another computer. See *virtual terminal.*

terminal mode

An operating mode that causes the computer to act like a terminal; ready to transmit typed-in keystrokes and ready to receive transmitted data.

terminal server

A computer or controller used to connect multiple terminals to a network or host computer.

terminal session

The time in which a user is working at a terminal.

terminal strip

An insulated bar that contains a set of screws to which wires are attached.

terminator

(1) A character that ends a string of alphanumeric characters.
(2) A hardware component that is connected to the last peripheral device in a series or the last node in a network.

terrestrial link

A communications line that travels on, near or below ground. Contrast with *satellite link*.

test automation software

Software used to test new revisions of software by automatically entering a predefined set of commands and inputs.

test data

A set of data created for testing new or revised programs. It should be developed by the user as well as the programmer and must contain a sample of every category of valid data as well as many invalid conditions.

testing

Running new or revised programs to determine if they process all data properly. See *test data*.

For testing as it pertains to professional certification, see *CCP, NetWare certification* and *Microsoft Certified Professional*.

TeX

A typesetting language used in a variety of typesetting environments. It uses embedded codes within the text of the document to initiate changes in layout including the ability to describe elaborate scientific formulas.

Texas Instruments

See *TI*.

text

Words, sentences and paragraphs. Contrast with *data*, which are defined units, such as name and amount due. Text may also refer to alphanumeric data, such as name and address, to distinguish it from numeric data, such as quantity and dollar amounts. A page of text takes about 2,000 to 4,000 bytes. See *text field*.

text based

Also called *character based*, the display of text and graphics as a fixed set of predefined characters. For example, 25 rows of 80 columns. Contrast with *graphics based*.

text box

An on-screen rectangular frame into which you type text. Text boxes are used to add text in a drawing or paint program. The flexibility of the text box is determined by the software. Sometimes you can keep on typing and the box expands to meet your input. Other times, you have to go into a different mode to widen the frame, then go back to typing in more text.

text editing

The ability to change text by adding, deleting and rearranging letters, words, sentences and paragraphs.

text editor

Software used to create and edit files that contain only text; for example, batch files, address lists and source language programs. Text editors produce raw ASCII or EBCDIC text files, and unlike word processors, do not usually provide word wrap or formatting (underline, boldface, fonts, etc.).

Editors designed for writing source code may provide automatic indention and multiple windows into the same file. They may also display the reserved words of a particular programming language in boldface or in a different font, but they do not embed format codes in the file.

text entry

Entering alphanumeric text characters into the computer. It implies typing the characters on a keyboard. See *data entry*.

text field

A data structure that holds alphanumeric data, such as name and address. If a text field holds large, or unlimited, amounts of text, it may be called a memo field. Contrast with *numeric field*.

text file

A file that contains only text characters. See *ASCII file*. Contrast with *graphics file* and *binary file*.

text management

The creation, storage and retrieval of text. It implies flexible retrieval capabilities that can search for text based on a variety of criteria. Although a word processor manages text, it usually has limited retrieval capabilities.

text mode

(1) A screen display mode that displays only text and not graphics.
(2) A program mode that allows text to be entered and edited.

text-to-speech

Converting text into voice output using speech synthesis techniques. Although initially used by the blind to listen to written material, it is now used extensively to convey financial data and other information via telephone for everyone.

A Texture-Mapped Image
The texture of the can and the surface it sits on is simulated by the computer. *(Photo courtesy Computer Sciences Department, University of Utah.)*

texture mapping

In computer graphics, the creation of a special surface. With algorithms, all kinds of textures can be produced: the rough skin of an orange, the metallic surface of a can and the irregularity of a brick. It can also be done by electronically wrapping a secondary image around an object.

TFT

(Thin Film Transistor) See *LCD* and *thin film*.

TFT LCD

(Thin Film Transistor LCD) See *LCD*.

TFTP

(Trivial File Transfer Protocol) A version of the TCP/IP FTP protocol that has no directory or password capability.

TGA

See *Targa*.

thermal dye transfer

Also called *dye sublimation* and *thermal dye diffusion,* this is a printing process similar to thermal wax transfer except that dyes are used instead of ink. The printhead heats the ribbon causing the dye to turn from a solid to a gas and condense on special coated paper. The more heat, the denser the image. Unlike other printing techniques which simulate shades of colors by dithering, thermal dye transfer creates photographic quality color.

thermal printer

A low-cost, low- to medium-resolution non-impact printer that uses heat-sensitive paper. Where the heated pins of the print head touch the paper, the paper darkens. See *printer*.

thermal recalibration

The periodic sensing of the temperature in some hard disk drives in order to make minor adjustments to the alignment of the read/write heads. In an AV drive, this process is performed only in idle periods so that there is no interruption in reading and writing long streams of data.

thermal transfer

See *thermal dye transfer* and *thermal wax transfer*.

thermal wax transfer

A printing process that transfers a waxlike ink onto paper. For example, in a color printer, a mylar ribbon is used that contains several hundred repeating sets of full pages of black, cyan, magenta and yellow ink. A sheet of paper is pressed against each color and passed by a line of heating elements that transfers the dots, or pixels, of ink onto the paper.

the Web

See *World Wide Web*.

thick Ethernet

See *10Base5* and *Ethernet*.

thick film

A layer of magnetic, semiconductor or metallic material that is thicker than the microscopic layers of the transistors on a chip. For example, metallic thick films are silk screened onto the ceramic base of hybrid microcircuits. Contrast with *thin film*.

ThickNet, ThickWire

See *10Base5* and *Ethernet*.

Thin Client

ThinkPad
The ThinkPads lead the way with the largest active matrix LCD screens.

thimble printer
A letter quality printer similar to a daisy wheel printer. Instead of a wheel, characters are formed facing out and around the rim of a thimble-shaped cup. For example, the NEC Spinwriters are thimble printers.

thin client
A client machine in a client/server environment that performs very little data processing. The application processing is done in the server. For example, a thin client can be a PC that runs only the graphical interface or an X terminal that displays the output of other machines. The counterpart to a thin client is a fat server. Contrast with *fat client*. See *X Window*.

thin Ethernet
See *10Base2* and *Ethernet*.

thin film
A microscopically thin layer of semiconductor or magnetic material that is deposited onto a metal, ceramic or semiconductor base. For example, the layers that make up a chip and the surface coating on high-density magnetic disks are called thin films.

thin film head
A read/write head for high-density disks that is made from thin layers of a conducting film deposited onto a nickel-iron core.

ThinkPad
A family of IBM notebook computers that include large screens and a built-in TrackPoint pointing device located between the G, H and B keys on the keyboard. See *IBM PC* for ThinkPad specifications.

ThinNet, ThinWire
See *10Base2* and *Ethernet*.

third-generation computer
A computer that uses integrated circuits, disk storage and online terminals. The third generation started roughly in 1964 with the IBM System/360.

third-generation language
Also known as a *3GL*, it refers to a high-level programming language such as FORTRAN, COBOL, BASIC, Pascal and C. It is a step above assembly language and a step below fourth-generation language (4GL). For an example of the difference between a 3GL and a 4GL, see *fourth-generation language*.

third normal form
See *normalization*.

THOR
(Tandy High-intensity Optical Recorder) An erasable audio CD recorder from Tandy that was scheduled for the early 1990s, but has yet to come to fruition.

Thoroughbred Basic
See *Business Basic*.

thrashing
Excessive paging in a virtual memory computer. If programs are not written to run in a virtual memory environment, the operating system may spend excessive amounts of time swapping program pages in and out of the disk.

The goal of virtual memory is to increase internal memory capacity, not to waste time reloading program segments over and over. However, a well-designed virtual memory system tracks page usage and prevents the most-often-used modules from being swapped to disk.

thread

(1) One transaction or message in a multithreaded system. See *multithreading*.
(2) In an Internet newsgroup, a topic or theme that continues to receive postings from interested parties.

threaded connector

A plug and socket that uses a threaded mechanism to lock them together. One part is screwed into the other. F and SMA connectors are examples of threaded connectors.

threaded discussion

A running log of comments and opinions about a subject. Users periodically type their comments into the computer, and the computer maintains the list in order of arrival.

threading

See *multithreading*.

three-state logic element

An electronic component that provides three possible outputs: off, low voltage and high voltage.

three-tier client/server

A three-way interaction in a client/server environment, in which the user interface is stored in the client, the bulk of the business application logic is stored in one or more servers, and the data is stored in a database server. See *two-tier client/server*.

Three-tier client/server
Separate server does some of the business logic.

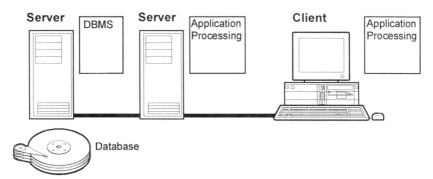

throughput

The speed with which a computer processes data. It is a combination of internal processing speed, peripheral speeds (I/O) and the efficiency of the operating system and other system software all working together.

thumb

See *elevator*.

thumbnail

A miniature representation of a page or image. A thumbnail program may be stand-alone or part of a desktop publishing or graphics program. Thumbnails take considerable time to generate, but provide a convenient way to browse through multiple images before retrieving the one you need. Programs often let you click on the thumbnail to retrieve it.

thunk

In a PC, to execute the instructions required to switch between segmented addressing of memory and flat addressing. A thunk typically occurs when a 16-bit application is running in a 32-bit address space, and its 16-bit segmented address must be converted into a full 32-bit flat address.

THz

(TeraHertZ) One trillion cycles per second.

TI

(Texas Instruments, Inc., Dallas, TX) A leading semiconductor manufacturer founded in 1930 as Geophysical Service, Inc., to provide services to the petroleum industry. During the war, GSI manufactured electronics for the Navy and later added them to its product line.

In 1951, GSI was renamed Texas Instruments and soon after entered the semiconductor business. TI was the first to commercialize the silicon transistor, pocket radio, integrated circuit, hand-held calculator, single-chip computer and the LISP chip.

In the early 1980s, TI sold a large number of its low-priced 99/4a home computers. It later introduced desktop PCs, but today offers only a line of notebook PCs.

With 1994 revenues of more than ten billion, TI's strength is integrated circuits. However, it also creates computer systems for AI applications, composite metals, electrical control products and consumer electronics, including its well-known line of calculators and educational math and reading machines.

TIA

(1) (Telecommunications Industry Association, 2001 Pennsylvania Ave., N.W., Washington, DC 20006, 202/457-4912) A membership organization founded in 1988 that sets standards for physical level interfaces (RS-232, RS-422, etc.) as well as cellular radio. It was originally an EIA working group that was spun off and merged with the USTSA (U.S. Telecommunications Suppliers Association), sponsors of the annual Supercomm conference. TIA is involved with setting telecommunications standards worldwide.

(2) Digispeak for "thanks in advance."

TIA/EIA-232

See *RS-232*.

TIA/EIA-568

Standards for wiring buildings for telecommunications.

TIA/EIA-569

Standards for telecommunications wiring and equipment spaces.

TIA/EIA-606

Standards for the administration of telecommunications wiring, equipment and grounding.

TIA/EIA-607

Standards for telecommunications grounding and bonding.

Thumbnails
The pictures above
are pages 860 and
861 of this book
in thumbnail format.

TIC

(Token Ring Interface Card) A TLA for a Token Ring NIC (network interface card).

tickler

A manual or automatic system for reminding users of scheduled events or tasks. It is used in PIMs, contact management systems and scheduling and calendar systems.

TIES

(Time-Independent Escape Sequence) A modem escape sequence that uses three pluses like the Hayes sequence, but does not require a pause before and after them. If a valid AT command code and a return follows the +++, it is considered a legitimate command. See *Hayes Smartmodem.*

TIF

A file extension used for TIFF files; for example, image1.tif. See *TIFF.*

TIFF

(Tagged Image File Format) A widely-used raster graphics file format developed by Aldus and Microsoft that handles monochrome, gray scale, 8-and 24-bit color. TIFF allows for customization, and several versions have been created, which does not guarantee compatibility between all programs.

TIFF files are compressed using several compression methods. LZW provides ratios of about 1.5:1 to 2:1. Ratios of 10:1 to 20:1 are possible for documents with lots of white space using ITU Group III & IV compression methods (fax). See *JPEG.*

TIGA

(Texas Instruments Graphics Architecture) A graphics standard from TI that provides a resolution-independent interface between a program and the graphics coprocessor. See *34010.*

Tiger

Code name for Microsoft's multimedia video-on-demand software that runs on Windows NT. It is being tested in 1995 and is expected to roll out in 1996.

tightly coupled

Refers to two or more computers linked together and dependent on each other. One computer may control the other, or both computers may monitor each other. For example, a database machine is tightly coupled to the main processor. Two computers tied together for multiprocessing are tightly coupled. Contrast with *loosely coupled,* such as personal computers in a LAN.

tile

To display objects side by side. The Tile command in a graphical interface squares up all open windows and displays them in a row and column order.

timbre

A quality of sound that distinguishes one voice or musical instrument from another. For example, MIDI synthesizers are multi-timbral, meaning that they can play multiple instruments simultaneously.

time base generator

An electronic clock that creates its own timing signals for synchronization and measurement purposes.

time-division multiplexing

See *TDM.*

timer interrupt

An interrupt generated by an internal clock. See *interrupt*.

timesharing

A multiuser computer environment that lets users initiate their own sessions and access selected databases as required, such as when using online services. A system that serves many users, but for only one application, is technically not timesharing.

Time Sharing Option

See *TSO*.

time slice

A fixed interval of time allotted to each user or program in a multitasking or timesharing system.

time slot

Continuously repeating interval of time or a time period in which two devices are able to interconnect.

timing clock

See *clock*.

timing signals

Electrical pulses generated in the processor or in external devices in order to synchronize computer operations. The main timing signal comes from the computer's clock, which provides a frequency that can be divided into many slower cycles. Other timing signals may come from a timesharing or realtime clock. In disk drives, timing signals for reading and writing are generated by holes or marks on one of the platters, or by the way the digital data is actually recorded.

tin

(Threaded Internet Newsreader) A newsreader for reading the messages in a newsgroup on the Internet. See *Usenet*.

Tiny BASIC

A subset of BASIC that has been used in first generation personal computers with limited memory.

TIRIS

(Texas Instruments Registration and Identification System) An RF/ID system from TI that uses a 3.6x29mm cylindrical tag. Reading can be done from as far as 40 inches away.

TI-RPC

(Transport-Independent-Remote Procedure Call) A set of functions from Sun for executing procedures on remote computers. It is operating system and network independent and allows the development of distributed applications in multivendor environments.

TLA

(Three Letter Acronym) The epitome of acronyms! While two-, four- and five-letter acronyms exist, there are more three-letter acronyms. Obviously, three words to describe a concept or product is the most popular.

TLI

(Transport Level Interface) A common interface for transport services (layer 4 of the

OSI model). It provides a common language to a transport protocol and allows client/server applications to be used in different networking environments. Instead of directly calling NetWare's SPX for example, the application calls the TLI library. Thus, any transport protocol that is TLI compliant (SPX, TCP, etc.) can provide transport services to that application. TLI is part of UNIX System V. It is also supported by NetWare 3.x. See *STREAMS*.

TM/1

(Tables Manager/1) A multidimensional analysis program for DOS and Windows from Sinper Corporation, Warren, NJ, that allows data to be viewed in up to eight dimensions. The data is kept in a database, and the formulas are kept in a spreadsheet, which is used as a viewer into the database. TM/1 makes it easy to display different slices of the data, and it is designed to import and cross tab large amounts of data.

TM/1 Pespectives is a spreadsheet add-in that lets Excel or 1-2-3 provide the user interface to a TM/1 database. Spreadsheet Connector is the server version.

TN

(Twisted Nematic) The first LCD technology. It twists liquid crystal molecules 90 degrees between polarizers. TN displays require bright ambient light and are still used for low-cost applications. See *STN* and *LCD*.

TNT

(1) (Transparent Network Transport) Services from the telephone companies and common carriers that provide Ethernet and Token Ring transmission over MANs and WANs.

(2) DOS extender from Phar Lap Software that allows DOS applications to use various Win32 features, including memory allocation, DLLs and threads.

(3) Code name for models of Apple's second generation PowerMacs expected in mid 1995. It includes improved video and uses the PCI bus.

(4) (Tessler's Nifty Tools, San Ramon, CA) A software company that provides a number of handy Windows utilities.

TOF

(Top Of Form) The beginning of a physical paper form. To position paper in many printers, the printer is turned offline, the forms are aligned properly and the TOF button is pressed.

toggle

To alternate back and forth between two states.

token bus network

A LAN access method that uses the token passing technology. Stations are logically connected in a ring but are physically connected by a common bus. All tokens are broadcast to every station in the network, but only the station with the destination address responds. After transmitting a maximum amount of data, the token is passed to the next logical station in the ring. The MAP factory automation protocol uses this method. See *token passing*.

token passing

A communications network access method that uses a continuously repeating frame (the token) that is transmitted onto the network by the controlling computer.

When a terminal or computer wants to send a message, it waits for an empty token. When it finds one, it fills it with the address of the destination station and some or all of its message.

Every computer and terminal on the network constantly monitors the passing tokens to determine if it is a recipient of a message, in which case it "grabs" the message and resets the token status to empty. Token passing uses bus and ring topologies. See *token bus network* and *token ring network*.

Token Ring

A local area network (LAN) developed by IBM (IEEE 802.5). It uses a token ring access method and connects up to 255 nodes in a star topology at 4 or 16 Mbps. All stations connect to a central wiring hub called the *MAU* (Multistation Access Unit) using a twisted wire cable. The central hub makes it easier to troubleshoot failures than a bus topology.

Type 1 Token Ring networks allow up to 260 stations per network and use shielded twisted pair wires with IBM style connectors. Type 3 Token Rings allow up to 72 devices per network and use unshielded twisted pair (Category 3, 4 or 5) with RJ-45 connectors.

Token Ring is a data link protocol and functions at the data link and physical levels of the OSI model (1 and 2). See *data link protocol* and *OSI model*.

Token Ring adapter

A network adapter used in a Token Ring network. See *network adapter*.

token ring network

A LAN access method that uses the token passing technology in a physical ring. Each station in the network passes the token on to the station next to it. Token Ring and FDDI LANs use the token ring access method. See *token passing*.

TokenTalk

Software for the Macintosh from Apple that accompanies its TokenTalk NB board and adapts the Mac to Token Ring Networks.

toner

An electrically charged ink used in copy machines and laser printers. It adheres to an invisible image that has been charged with the opposite polarity onto a plate or drum or onto the paper itself.

tool

(1) A program used for software development or system maintenance. Virtually any program or utility that helps programmers or users develop applications or maintain their computers can be called a tool. Visual programming products, editors, debuggers and libraries of specialized routines are examples.

In client/server development, tools are application generators, GUI builders, 4GLs, 3GLs and any supporting software.

(2) An on-screen function in an interactive program; for example, a line draw, circle draw or paintbrush option in a graphics program.

Toolbar
This toolbar is from the Windows version of this book. By clicking the various buttons, text can be captured for printing and copying, pictures, bookmarks and lookups can be retrieved and text can be searched.

toolbar

A row or column of on-screen buttons used to activate various functions of the application. The bar is typically movable so it can be placed close to the object being worked on in order to quickly switch modes and options. Toolbars can often be customized allowing buttons to be added and deleted as necessary for a user's own requirements.

Capture Pictures Next Bookmark Go To Review Review History Search

Token Ring Network

Token Ring networks, originally developed by IBM, are second to Ethernet in popularity as a local area network. Token Ring is a shared media LAN that provides up to 16Mbps of bandwidth. All stations connect to the Multistation Access Unit (MAU), which acts as a central hub. Although wired in a star topology, the token ring provides a "logical ring" within the star wiring. This means that if a line fails from one of the stations to the MAU, the logical ring continues to function. A star topology also makes it easier to troubleshoot than a bus topology, where all stations are wired in series.

Type 1 Token Ring allows up to 260 stations per network. It uses shielded twisted pair (STP) with IBM connectors. Type 3 Token Ring allows up to 72 devices per network and uses category 3, 4 or 5 unshielded twisted pair (UTP).

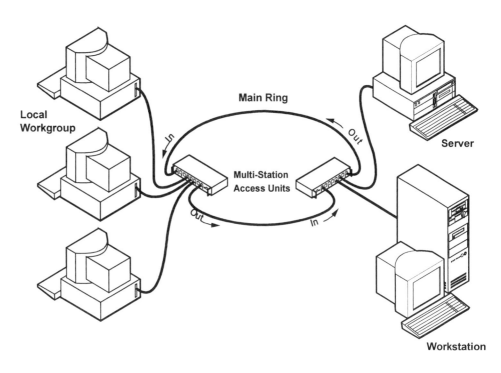

Type 1
IBM connector

The IBM connector is a combination plug and socket. Flip any Type 1 connector 180 degrees with the other and they plug together.

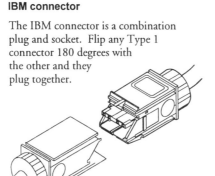

Type 3
RJ45 connector

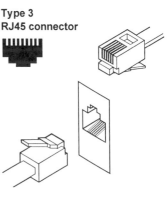

ToolBook

An application development system for Windows from Asymetrix Corporation, Bellevue, WA, that uses a "page and book" metaphor analogous to HyperCard's "card and stack." Its OpenScript language is similar to HyperTalk.

toolbox

See *toolkit* and *toolbar*.

toolkit

A set of software routines that allow a program to be written for and work in a particular environment. The routines are called by the application program to perform various functions, for example, to display a menu or draw a graphic element.

tool palette

A collection of on-screen functions, typically graphics related, that are grouped in a menu structure for interactive selection.

tools vendor

A publisher of devlopment software used by programmers, including CASE products, compilers and debuggers. See *tool*.

TOP

(Technical Office Protocol) A communications protocol for office systems from Boeing Computer Services. It uses the Ethernet access method and is often used in conjunction with *MAP*, the factory automation protocol developed by GM. TOP is used in the front office, and MAP is used on the factory floor. TOP uses the CSMA/CD access method, while MAP uses token bus.

topdown design

A design technique that starts with the highest level of an idea and works its way down to the lowest level of detail.

topdown programming

A programming design and documentation technique that imposes a hierarchical structure on the design of the program. See *structured programming*.

topics

See *industry topics* and *lessons*.

top of file

The beginning of a file. In a word processing file, it is the first character in the document. In a data file, it is either the first record in the file or the first record in the index. For example, in a dBASE file that is indexed on name, **goto top** might go to physical record #608 if record #608 is AARDVARK.

topology

(1) In a communications network, the pattern of interconnection between nodes; for example, a bus, ring or star configuration.
(2) In a parallel processing architecture, the interconnection between processors; for example, a bus, grid, hypercube or Butterfly Switch configuration.

Topologies

STAR   RING

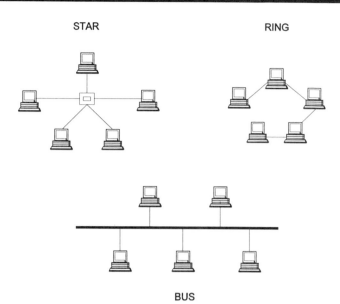

BUS

TOPS

(1) A multiuser, multitasking, timesharing, virtual memory operating system from Digital that runs on its PDP-6, DECsystem 10 and DECsystem 20 series.
(2) (Transparent OPerating System) A peer-to-peer LAN from Sitka Corporation, Alameda, CA, that uses the LocalTalk access method and connects Apple computers, PCs and Sun workstations. Its Flashcard plugs LocalTalk capability into PCs.

TOPVIEW

IBM's first windowing environment for PCs, developed in the mid 1980s. The PCs of the time were too underpowered, and the interface was too unsophisticated, so it never caught on, much like the first verisions of Windows.

TOTAL

An early network DBMS from Cincom Systems that ran on a variety of minis and mainframes.

total bypass

Bypassing local and long distance telephone lines by using satellite communications.

touchpad

A stationary pointing device that provides a small, flat surface that you slide your finger over using the same movements as you would a mouse. You can tap on the pad's surface as an alternate to pressing one of the touchpad keys. See *mouse, trackball* and *pointing stick*.

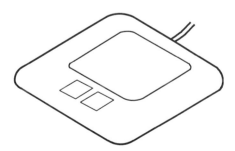

touch screen

A touch-sensitive display screen that uses a clear panel over on the screen surface. The panel is a matrix of cells that transmit pressure information to the software.

Touch Screen
This Richardson Texas firm makes touch screen overlays for PCs and Macs that are used in a wide variety of applications. *(Photo courtesy of Keytec, Inc.)*

tower

(1) A floor-standing cabinet taller than it Desktop computers can be made into towers by turning them on their side and inserting them into a floor-mounted base.
(2) (Tower) Series of UNIX-based single and multiprocessor computer systems from NCR that use the Motorola 68000 family of CPUs.

TP0-TP4

(Transport Protocol Class 0 to Class 4) The grades of OSI transport layers from least to most complete and specific. TP4 is a full connection-oriented transport protocol.

TPA

(Transient Program Area) See *transient area.*

tpi

(Tracks Per Inch) The measurement of the density of tracks recorded on a disk or drum.

TP monitor

(TeleProcessing monitor or Transaction Processing monitor) A control program that manages the transfer of data between multiple local and remote terminals and the application programs that serve them. It may also include programs that format the

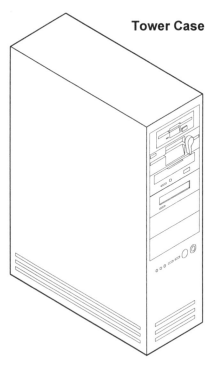

Tower Case

terminal screens and validate the data entered.

In a distributed client/server environment, a TP monitor provides integrity by ensuring that transactions do not get lost or damaged. It may be placed in a separate machine and used to balance the load between clients and various application servers and database servers. It is also used to create a high availability system by switching a failed transaction to another machine.

Examples of popular TP monitors are CICS, a veteran TP monitor used on IBM mainframes and the UNIX-based Tuxedo and Encina products.

TP-PMD

(Twisted Pair-Physical Medium Dependent) An ANSI standard for an FDDI network that uses UTP instead of optical fiber. See *CDDI*.

TPS

(1) (Transactions Per Second) The number of transactions processed within one second.

(2) (Transaction Processing System) Originally used as an acronym for such a system, it now refers to the measurement of the system (#1 above).

tpsA

A transaction per second benchmark as specified by the Transaction Processing Council. Performance is rated as the number of TPS as well as the cost of the system per single TPS; for example, 100 tpsA and $8,100 per tpsA.

TQM

(Total Quality Management) An organizational undertaking to improve the quality of manufacturing and service. It focuses on obtaining continuous feedback for making improvements and refining existing processes over the long term. See *ISO 9000*.

TR

See *Token Ring*.

trace

See *autotrace*.

track

A storage channel on disk or tape. On disks, tracks are concentric circles (hard and floppy disks) or spirals (CDs and videodiscs). On tapes, they are parallel lines. Their format is determined by the specific drive they are used in. On magnetic devices, bits are recorded as reversals of polarity in the magnetic surface. On CDs, bits are recorded as physical pits under a clear, protective layer. See *magnetic disk*.

trackball

A stationary pointing device that contains a movable ball rotated with the fingers or palm. From one to three keys are located in various positions depending on the unit. Years ago, Kensington Microware popularized the trackball with its Turbo Mouse for the Macintosh. See *mouse, pointing stick* and *touchpad.*

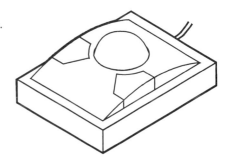

tracking

In desktop publishing, the consistent letterspacing of text. Tracking is used to expand or contract the amount of text on a page by expanding or reducing the amount of space between letters. It differs from kerning in that it is applied to an entire font or to a range of text, whereas kerning refers to certain letter pairs.

TrackPoint

The pointing stick used in IBM laptops. IBM introduced and popularized this type of pointing device on its ThinkPad laptops.

trackstick

Same as *pointing stick*.

TrackWrite

Nicknamed the "Butterfly keyboard," it is a laptop keyboard from IBM introduced in 1995 on its ThinkPad 701C. When closed, the split keyboard offsets to create a smaller footprint. When opened, it expands to full size.

tractor feed

A mechanism that provides fast movement of paper forms through a printer. It contains pins on tractors that engage the paper through perforated holes in its left and right borders. Contrast with *sheet feeder*.

Trac
feed

Tractor Feed
A tractor feed on a dot matrix printer allows for printing continuous multipart forms and mailing and diskette labels. The tractor feed contains a sprocket that grabs the perforated holes at both sides of the form and pulls it through uniformly.

Tradacoms

A European EDI standard developed by the Article Numbering Association. See *X12* and *EDIFACT*.

trademarks

With regard to trademarks in this database, it is assumed that every name of a product is a trademark of its respective organization. In fact, if a company creates a name for its product and continues to use it, it is a de facto trademark whether or not it is registered. Registration serves to formally document how long a name has been in use. To find out if a particular product is a registered trademark, contact the individual hardware or software vendor.

trade shows

See *PC EXPO, COMDEX, Blenheim shows, Computex* and *CeBIT*.

trailer

In communications, a code or set of codes that make up the last part of a transmitted message. See *trailer label*.

trailer label

The last record in a tape file. May contain number of records, hash totals and other ID.

training

(1) Teaching the details of a subject. With regard to software, training provides instruction for each command and function in an application. Contrast with *education.*

(2) In communications, the process by which two modems determine the correct protocols and transmission speeds to use.

(3) In voice recognition systems, the recording of the user's voice in order to provide samples and patterns for recognizing that voice.

train printer

A line printer mechanism similar to a chain printer, but uses unconnected type slugs that ride in a track rather than a connected chain of type. The slugs are pushed around the track by engaging with a drive gear at one end. Slugs and track come as a replaceable cartridge.

transaction

An activity or request. Orders, purchases, changes, additions and deletions are typical business transactions stored in the computer. Queries and other requests are also transactions, but are usually just acted upon and not saved. Transaction volume is a major factor in figuring computer system size and speed.

transaction file

A collection of transaction records. The data in transaction files is used to update the master files, which contain the subjects of the organization. Transaction files also serve as audit trails and are usually transferred from online disks to the data library after some period of time.

As optical disks become more economical, transaction files will remain online in the computer so that an organization's history will be immediately available for ad hoc queries. See *information system.*

On the left are the kinds of fields that make up a typical transaction record in a business information system. There can be many more fields depending on the organization. The "key" fields below are the ones that are generally indexed for fast matching against the master record. The account number is usually the primary key, but name may also be used as a primary key. See *master file* for examples of typical master records.

Sample Daily Transactions (actions)

Payroll	Employee Number	Today's Date	Hours Worked				
Order	Customer Number	Today's Date	Quantity	Product Number			
Payment	Customer Number	Today's Date	Invoice Number	Amount Paid	Check Number		
Purchase	PO Number	Today's Date	Dept.	Authorized Agent	Vendor Number	Quantity	Product Number	Due Date
Receipt	PO Number	Today's Date	Quantity	Product Number			

Maintenance (periodic transactions)

Pay Raise	Employee Number	Today's Date	Transaction Type	New rate	Management Authorization
Credit Limit Change	Customer Number	Today's Date	New limit	Management Authorization	
Product Description Change	Product Number	Today's Date	New descripton	Management Authorization	

transaction monitor

See *TP monitor.*

transaction processing

Processing transactions as they are received by the computer. Also called *online* or *realtime* systems, transaction processing means that master files are updated as soon as transactions are entered at terminals or received over communications lines.

If you save receipts in a shoebox and add them up at the end of the year for taxes, that's batch processing. However, if you buy something and immediately add the amount to a running total, that's transaction processing.

Organizations increasingly rely on computers to keep everything up-to-date all the time. A manager might need to know how many items are left on the shelf, what the latest price of a stock is or what the value of a financial portfolio is at any given moment.

Transaction processing is often called online transaction processing, or *OLTP.* The OLTP market is a demanding one. If a business depends on computers for its day-to-day operations, the computers must stay up and running during business hours. See *mission critical, industrial strength* and *fault tolerant.*

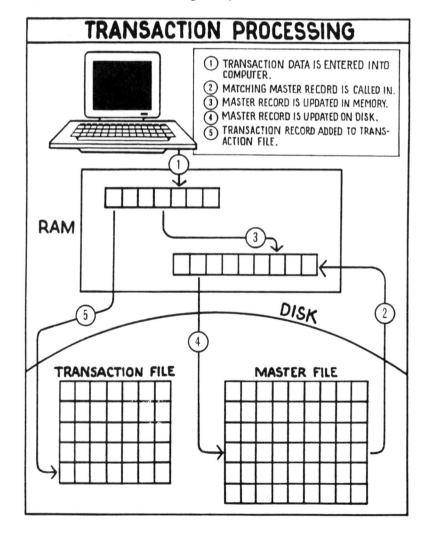

TRANSACTION PROCESSING

1. TRANSACTION DATA IS ENTERED INTO COMPUTER.
2. MATCHING MASTER RECORD IS CALLED IN.
3. MASTER RECORD IS UPDATED IN MEMORY.
4. MASTER RECORD IS UPDATED ON DISK.
5. TRANSACTION RECORD ADDED TO TRANSACTION FILE.

RAM

DISK

TRANSACTION FILE

MASTER FILE

transceiver

A transmitter and receiver of analog or digital signals. It comes in many forms; for example, a transponder or network adapter.

transcribe

To copy data from one medium to another; for example, from one source document to another, or from a source document to the computer. It often implies a change of format or codes.

transducer

A device that converts one energy into another; for example, a read/write head converts magnetic energy into electrical energy and vice versa. In process control applications, it is used to convert pressure into an electrical reading.

transfer

To send data over a computer channel or bus. "Transfer" generally applies to transmission within the computer system, and "transmit" refers to transmission outside the computer over a line or network.

Transfers are actually copies, since the data is in both locations at the end of the transfer. Input, output and move instructions activate data transfers in the computer.

transfer protocol

See *file transfer protocol.*

transfer rate

Also called data rate, the transmission speed of a communications or computer channel. Transfer rates are measured in bits or bytes per second.

transfer time

The time it takes to transmit or move data from one place to another. It is the time interval between starting the transfer and the completion of the transfer.

transformer

A device that changes AC voltage. Also called a *power adapter.* It is made of steel laminations wrapped with two coils of wire. The coil ratio derives the voltage change. For example, if the input coil has 1,000 windings, and the output has 100, 120 volts is changed to 12. In order to create direct current (DC), the output is passed through a rectifier.

transient

A malfunction that occurs at random intervals; for example, a rapid fluctuation of voltage in a power line or a memory cell that intermittently fails.

transient area

An area in memory used to hold application programs for processing. The bulk of a computer's main memory is used as a transient area.

transient data

Data that is created within an application session. At the end of the session, it is discarded or reset back to its default and not stored in a database. Contrast with *persistent data.*

transient state

The exact point at which a device changes modes, for example, from transmit to receive or from 0 to 1.

transistor

A device used to amplify a signal or open and close a circuit. In a computer, it functions as an electronic switch, or bridge. The transistor contains a semiconductor material that can change its electrical state when pulsed.

In its normal state, the semiconductor material is not conductive. When voltage is applied to it, it becomes conductive and current flows through it. The gate, or base, is the triggering line, and the source and drain or emitter and collector are the two end points.

Transistors, resistors, capacitors and diodes, make up logic gates. Logic gates make up circuits, and circuits make up electronic systems. For the history and evolution of the transistor, see *chip*.

The First Transistor
In 1947, this rather crude object was the breakthrough that caused a revolution in electronic circuits. Today, ten million transistors can fit in the same amount of space. *(Photo courtesy of AT&T.)*

translate

(1) To change one language into another; for example, assemblers, compilers and interpreters translate source language into machine language.

(2) In computer graphics, to move an image on screen without rotating it.

(3) In telecommunictions, to change the frequencies of a band of signals.

translating bridge

A type of bridge that interconnects two different types of LAN protocols, such as Ethernet and Token Ring. Translating bridges are generally very complicated devices. However, source routing transparent (SRT) bridging integrates both bridging methods of Ethernet and Token Ring to solve the problem. See *SRT*.

TransLISP PLUS

A version of LISP for PCs from Solution Systems, Inc., Wellesley, MA. It provides an interface to Microsoft C that allows a C routine to be added to the LISP library as a function.

transmission

The transfer of data over a communications channel.

transmission channel

A path between two nodes in a network. It may refer to the physical cable, the signal transmitted within the cable or to a subchannel within a carrier frequency. In radio and TV, it refers to the assigned carrier frequency.

transmission control unit

See *TCU.*

transmit
To send data over a communications line. See *transfer*.

transmitter
A device that generates signals. Contrast with *receiver*.

transmogrify
To change into something completely different.

transparent
(1) Refers to a change in hardware or software that, after installation, causes no noticeable change in operation.
(2) In computer graphics, a color that is treated as background which takes on the color of the underlying window or page.

transparent bridge
A common type of network bridge, in which the host stations are unaware of their existence in the network. A transparent bridge learns which node is connected to which port through the experience of examining which node responds to each new station address that is transmitted. Ethernet uses this type of bridge, also called an *adaptive bridge*. Contrast with *source route bridging*. See *spanning tree algorithm*.

transparent LAN service
A communications service from a local telephone company or common carrier that links remote LANs together. It is called transparent because the Ethernet, Token Ring or FDDI network is connected directly to the service at both ends regardless of the technology employed by the carrier in between. The network administrator is not responsible for dealing with a different protocol.

transponder
A receiver/transmitter on a communications satellite. It receives a microwave signal from earth (uplink), amplifies it and retransmits it back to earth at a different frequency (downlink). A satellite has several transponders.

transport layer
See *transport protocol*.

Transport Level Interface
See *TLI*.

transport protocol
A communications protocol responsible for establishing a connection and ensuring that all data has arrived safely. It is defined in layer 4 of the OSI model. Often, the term transport protocol implies transport services, which includes the lower level data link protocol that moves packets from one node to another. See *OSI model* and *transport services*.

transport services
The collective functions of layers 1 through 4 of the OSI model.

transputer
(TRANSistor comPUTER) A computer that contains a CPU, memory and communications capability on a single chip. Chips are strung together in hypercube or grid-like patterns to create large parallel processing machines, used in scientific, realtime control and AI applications.

trap

To test for a particular condition in a running program; for example, to "trap an interrupt" means to wait for a particular interrupt to occur and then execute a corresponding routine. An error trap tests for an error condition and provides a recovery routine. A debugging trap waits for the execution of a particular instruction in order to stop the program and analyze the status of the system at that moment.

trapdoor

A secret way of gaining access to a program or online service. Trapdoors are built into the software by the original programmer as a way of gaining special access to particular functions. For example, a trapdoor built into a BBS program would allow access to any BBS computer running that software.

trash can

An icon of a garbage can used for deleting files. The icon of a file is dragged to the trash can and released. In the Mac, the trash can is also used to eject a floppy by dragging the icon of the floppy disk onto it. In Windows 95, the equivalent of the trash can is the recycle bin, but it is used only for deleting files and folders, not ejecting floppies.

trashware

Software that is so poorly designed that it winds up in the garbage can.

TRAVAN

Enhanced 3.5" QIC cartridges that hold longer lengths of .315"-wide tape as used in QIC-WIDE cartridges. The common QIC-80 drive/cartridge holds 125MB of data uncompressed, while the equivalent TRAVAN tape holds 400MB. The 680MB QIC-3020 tape holds 1.6GB in TRAVAN format.

tree

A hierarchical structure. See *directory tree*.

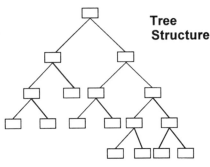

Tree Structure

Trellis-coded modulation

See *TCM*.

trends in the computer industry

See *hot topics*.

trichromatic

In computer graphics, the use of red, green and blue to create all the colors in the spectrum.

trigger

A mechanism that initiates an action when an event occurs such as reaching a certain time or date or upon receiving some type of input. A trigger generally causes a program routine to be executed.

In a database management system (DBMS), it is an SQL procedure that is executed when a record is added or deleted. It is used to maintain referential integrity in the database. A trigger may also execute a stored procedure. Triggers and stored procedures are built into DBMSs used in client/server environments. See *intelligent database.*

trillion

One thousand times one billion or 10 to the 12th power. See *tera* and *picosecond.*

Trilogy

A company founded in 1979 by Gene Amdahl to commercialize wafer scale integration and build supercomputers. It raised a quarter of a billion dollars, the largest startup funding in history, but could not create its 2.5" superchip. In 1984, it abandoned supercomputer development and later the superchip project. In 1985, Trilogy acquired Elxsi Corporation, a manufacturer of VAX-compatible systems, and eventually merged itself into Elxsi.

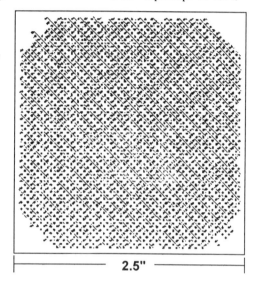

The Superchip
This is the actual size of the chip Trilogy had tried to develop using wafer scale integration. *(Diagram courtesy of Elxsi Corporation.)*

2.5"

triple precision

The use of three computer words to hold a number used for calculation, providing an enormous amount of arithmetic precision.

triple twist

A supertwist variation that twists crystals to 260 degrees for improved clarity. See *LCD.*

Triton

A family of chipsets from Intel that support the PCI bus. Triton II includes enhancements such as support for dual processors, 512MB RAM, EDO memory and memory error detection (ECC). The Triton VX chipset lets the display adapter be placed on the motherboard and share system RAM.

troff

(Typesetting RunOFF) A UNIX utility that formats documents for typesetters and laser printers. Using a text editor, troff codes are embedded into the text and the troff command converts the document into the required output. See *nroff.*

Trojan horse

A program that appears legitimate, but performs some illicit activity when it is run. It may be used to locate password information or make the system more vulnerable to future entry or simply destroy programs or data on the hard disk. A Trojan horse is similar to a virus, except that it does its damage all at once rather than replicate itself. See *virus*.

TRON

(The Realtime Operating System Nucleus) An advanced realtime computer architecture and operating system under development by Japanese universities and corporations. Its goal is a common architecture and user interface from the smallest consumer appliance to the largest supercomputer. TRON-based intelligent cars and houses are under research.

CTRON (Central TRON) is an OSI-compliant communications system for network file servers; BTRON (Business TRON) for accounting applications; ITRON (Industrial TRON) for intelligent machinery; MTRON (Macro TRON) for intelligent objects and networks (housing and urban development); -ITRON (Micro ITRON) runs on 8-bit computers for home appliances. Address: P.O.Box 23990, Tempe, AZ 85285.

TRS

(Tandy Radio Shack) An early Tandy trade name. In 1977, the TRS-80 was one of the three first personal computers. TRS-DOS was its operating system. See *personal computer*. Also see *TSR*.

TRS-80
One of the first personal computers.

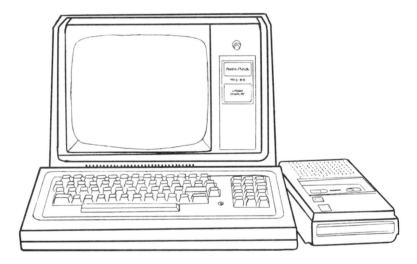

True BASIC

An ANSI-standard structured-programming version of BASIC for the PC, Mac and Amiga from True BASIC, Inc., West Lebanon, NH. Developed in 1984 by BASIC's creators, John Kemeny and Thomas Kurtz, it includes many enhancements over original BASIC. It comes in both interpreter and compiler form.

true color

(1) The ability to generate 16,777,216 colors (24-bit color). See *high color*.
(2) The ability to generate photo-realistic color images (requires 24-bit color minimum).

TrueImage

An enhanced PostScript interpreter from Microsoft that prints PostScript Type 1 and TrueType fonts.

TrueType

A scalable font technology that renders fonts for both the printer and the screen. Originally developed by Apple, it was enhanced jointly by Apple and Microsoft. TrueType fonts are used in Windows, starting with Windows 3.1, as well as in the Mac System 7 operating system.

Unlike PostScript, in which the algorithms are maintained in the rasterizing engine, each TrueType font contains its own algorithms for converting the outline into bitmaps. The lower-level language embedded within the TrueType font allows unlimited flexibility in the design. See *TrueImage*.

truncate

To cut off leading or trailing digits or characters from an item of data without regard to the accuracy of the remaining characters. Truncation occurs when data is converted into a new record with smaller field lengths than the original.

trunk

A communications channel between two points. It often refers to large-bandwidth telephone channels between major switching centers, capable of transmitting many simultaneous voice and data signals.

truth table

A chart of a logical operation's inputs and outputs. The following example is a Boolean AND truth table:

Inputs		Output
0	0	0
0	1	0
1	0	0
1	1	1

TSAPI

(Telephony Services **API**) A telephony programming interface from Novell and AT&T. Based on the international CSTA standard, TSAPI is designed to interface a telephone PBX with a NetWare server to provide interoperability between PCs and telephone equipment.

TSAT

See *VSAT*.

Tseng Labs

(Tseng Labs, Inc., Newtown, PA) A manufacturer of chipsets used in VGA graphics adapters. Since 1986, its ET3000 and ET4000 chips have been used in over 17 million video cards. Tseng's W32 family, introduced in 1993, provides graphics acceleration.

TSO

(Time Sharing Option) Software that provides interactive communications for IBM's MVS operating system. It allows a user or programmer to launch an application from a terminal and interactively work with it. The TSO counterpart in VM is called CMS. Contrast with *JES*, which provides batch communications for MVS.

TSOP

(Thin Small Outline Package) One-millimeter-thick package used to house dynamic RAM chips.

TSR

(Terminate and Stay Resident) Refers to programs that remain in memory so they can be instantly popped up over the current application by pressing a hotkey. The program is displayed either as a small window on top of the existing text or image, or it takes the full screen. When the program is exited, previous screen contents are restored.

On DOS PCs, TSRs provide quick access to a calculator, calendar or dictionary; however, conflicts may arise when multiple TSRs are loaded. Older ones may not always work with newer ones.

Task switching environments such as Windows and DESQview, provide the ability to switch back and forth between applications, thus making all programs function as a TSR.

The term refers to loading a program, terminating its action but not removing it from memory.

TSS

See *ITU*.

TTF file

(TrueType Font file) A TrueType font file in Windows that contains the mathematical outlines of each character in the font. In the Mac, the icon of a TrueType file looks like a document, dog-eared on the upper left, with three A's on it. See *FOT file*.

TTFN

Digispeak for goodbye ("ta ta for now").

TT font

See *TrueType*.

TTL

(Transistor Transistor Logic) A digital circuit in which the output is derived from two transistors. Although TTL is a specific design method, it often refers generically to digital connections in contrast with analog connections. For example, a TTL input on a monitor requires digital output from the display board rather than analog output.

TTY

(TeleTYpewriter) See *teletypewriter*.

TTY protocol

A low-speed asynchronous communications protocol with limited or no error checking.

tube

See *CRT* and *vacuum tube*.

tuner

An electronic part of a radio or TV that locks on to a selected carrier frequency (station, channel) and filters out the audio and video signals for amplification and display.

tuple

In relational database management, a record, or row. See *relational database*.

Turbo C

A C compiler from Borland used to create a wide variety of commercial products. It is known for its well-designed debugger. Borland's object-oriented versions of C are Turbo C++ and Borland C++.

The DOS version of this database is written in Turbo C. The Windows version is written in Microsoft C.

TURBOchannel

A 32-bit data bus from Digital introduced in 1990. It has a peak transfer rate of 100 MBytes/sec.

Turbo Mouse

A Macintosh trackball from Kensington Microware, Ltd., San Mateo, CA. The quicker the ball is moved, the greater the distance the pointer is moved on screen. The Turbo Mouse popularized the trackball for the Macintosh, and later models were developed for the PC.

The Turbo Mouse
In the early days of the Mac, the Turbo Mouse popularized the trackball for use with the graphical interface. *(Photo courtesy of Kensington Microware Ltd.)*

Turbo Pascal

A pascal compiler for DOS from Borland used in a wide variety of applications from accounting to complex commercial products. Turbo Pascal for Windows provides an object-oriented programming environment for Windows development. Borland is responsible for moving the Pascal language from the academic halls to the commercial world.

turnaround document

A paper document or punched card prepared for re-entry into the computer system. Paper documents are printed with OCR fonts for scanning Invoices and inventory stock cards are examples.

turnaround time

(1) In batch processing, the time it takes to receive finished reports after submission of documents or files for processing. In an online environment, turnaround time is the same as *response time*.

(2) In half-duplex transmission, the time it takes to change from transmit to receive and vice versa.

turnkey system

A complete system of hardware and software delivered to the customer ready-to-run.

turnpike effect

In communications, a lock up due to increased traffic conditions and bottlenecks in the system.

Turtle Beach

(Turtle Beach Systems, York, PA) A manufacturer of sound cards that is noted for its quality sound. Its Multisound card won many awards. Subsequent products have merged quality sound with Windows multimedia and DOS game compatibility.

turtle graphics

A method for creating graphic images in Logo. The turtle is an imaginary pen that is given drawing commands, such as go forward and turn right. On screen, the turtle is shaped like a triangle.

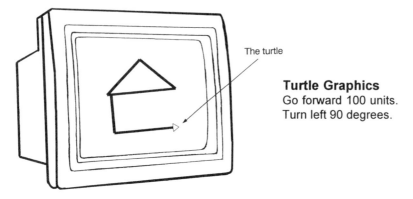

The turtle

Turtle Graphics
Go forward 100 units.
Turn left 90 degrees.

tutorial

An instructional book or program that takes the user through a prescribed sequence of steps in order to learn a product. Contrast with *documentation*, which, although instructional, tends to group features and functions by category.

TUV

(Technischer Überwachungs-Verein) Literally "Technical Watch-Over Association." A German certifying body involved with product safety for the European Community. The "TÜV Rheinland" mark is placed on tested and approved electrical and electronic devices like our UL (Underwriters Laboratory) seal.

Tuxedo

A TP monitor from Novell that runs on a variety of UNIX-based computers. Originally developed by AT&T and sold as source code, Novell has enhanced the product and is offering it as shrink-wrapped software for various UNIX servers. Tuxedo and Transarc's Encina are the major TP monitors in the UNIX client/server environment.

TV

See *NTSC*.

TV board

An expansion board in a personal computer that contains a TV tuner. It derives its source from an antenna or cable TV just like any TV set. The accompanying software is used to change the channel and create a video window that is displayed with other windows on screen. In a PC, the board is generally connected to the VGA adapter via the feature connector. The TV board may also cable directly to the computer's monitor or indirectly through the display adapter. See *feature connector* and *VESA Advanced Feature Connector*.

TV in a window
See *TV board*.

TV tuner board
See *TV board*.

TWAIN
A programming interface that lets a graphics application, such as a desktop publishing program, activate a scanner, frame grabber or other image-capturing device.

tweak
To make minor adjustments in an electronic system or in a software program in order to improve performance.

tweening
An animation technique that, based on starting and ending shapes, creates the necessary "in-between" frames. See *morphing*.

twinax
See *twinaxial*.

twinax card
An expansion board in a personal computer that emulates a 5250 terminal, the common terminal on an IBM midrange system (AS/400, System/3x).

TwinAxcess
An IBM midrange terminal emulation system for the Macintosh from Andrew/ KMW, Austin, TX. It includes a controller card and software that emulates the 5250 terminal used on System/3x and AS/400s. It allows the user to have seven concurrent sessions broadcast over LocalTalk, EtherTalk or TokenTalk networks.

twinaxial
A type of cable similar to coax, but with two inner conductors instead of one. It is used in IBM midrange (AS/400, System/3x) communications environments.

TWIP
(TWentIeth of a Point) Equal to 1/1440th of an inch.

twisted nematic
See *TN*.

twisted pair
A thin-diameter wire (22 to 26 guage) commonly used for telephone wiring. The wires are twisted around each other to minimize interference from other twisted pairs in the cable. Twisted pairs have less bandwidth than coaxial cable or optical fiber.

The two major types are unshielded twisted pair (UTP) and shielded twisted pair (STP). UTP is popular because it is very pliable and doesn't take up as much room in ductwork as does shielded twisted pair and other cables.

Shielded twisted pair is wrapped in a metal sheath for added protection against external interference. See *cable categories*.

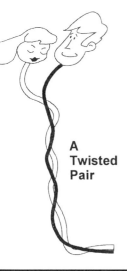

A
Twisted
Pair

two-out-of-five code

A numeric code that stores one decimal digit in five binary digits in which two of the bits are always 0 or 1 and the other three are always in the opposite state.

two-phase commit

A technique for ensuring that a transaction successfully updates all appropriate files in a distributed database environment. All DBMSs involved in the transaction first confirm that the transaction has been received and is recoverable (stored on disk). Then each DBMS is told to commit the transaction (do the actual updating).

two-tier client/server

A two-way interaction in a client/server environment, in which the user interface is stored in the client and the data is stored in the server. The application logic can be in either the client or the server. See *fat client, fat server* and *three-tier client/server*.

Two-tier client/server

Only the results of the database search are passed to the client.

Database

Server DBMS

Client Application Processing

two-wire lines

A transmission channel made up of only two wires, such as used in the common dial-up telephone network.

TWX

(TeletypeWriter eXchange Service) A U.S. and Canadian dial-up communications service that uses teleprinters and transmits 5-bit Murray code or 7-bit ASCII code at up to 150 bps. Originally part of the Bell System, it was sold to Western Union in 1971 and interconnected with Telex.

TXD

(Transmitting Data) See *modem*.

TXT file

See *ASCII file*.

Tymnet

(BTC Tymnet) A value-added, packet switching network that enables many varieties of terminals and computers to exchange data. It is a subsidiary of British Telecom Corporation.

type

(1) In data or text entry, to press the keys on the keyboard.
(2) In programming, a category of variable that is determined by the kind of data stored in it. For example, integer, floating point, string, logical, date and binary are common data types.
(3) (Type) In DOS and OS/2, a command that displays the contents of a text file.

Type 1 font, Type 3 font

A Type 1 font is a commonly-used PostScript font. A Type 3 font is a special variety that can be programmed for very complex designs, but is not widely used. See *PostScript*.

typeahead buffer

See *keyboard buffer*.

type ball

A golf ball-sized element used in typewriters and low-speed teleprinters that contains all the print characters on its outside surface. It was introduced with IBM's Selectric typewriter.

typeface

The design of a set of printed characters, such as Courier, Helvetica and Times Roman. The following chart shows common typeface measurements.

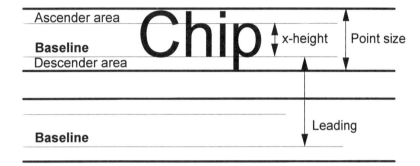

typeface family

A group of typefaces that include the normal, bold, italic and bold-italic variations of the same design.

type family

See *typeface family*.

type font

A set of print characters of a particular design (typeface), size (point size) and weight (light, medium, heavy). See *font*.

typematic

A keyboard feature that contiues to repeat a key as long as it is held down. The speed of the repeating key as well as the time interval before the repeat begins can be set by the DOS Mode command and the Macintosh Control Panel. See *DOS Mode*.

typeover mode

In word processing and data entry, a state in which each character typed on the keyboard replaces the character at the current cursor location. Contrast with *insert mode*.

type scaler

See *font scaler*.

typesetter

See *imagesetter*.

typing

(1) To input data to a typewriter or computer by pressing the keys on the keyboard.
(2) In programming, classifying variables by the kind of data they hold (string, integer, floating point, etc.). Stongly typed languages enforce strict adherance to typing and do not allow data types to be mixed in the same variable. Weakly typed languages provide minimal validation, which can result in processing errors.

U

UAE

(Uninterruptible Application Error) The Windows 3.0 error name for a program that has crashed. In Windows 3.1, it is called a General Protection Fault (GPF). See *Application Error*.

UART

(Universal Asynchronous Receiver Transmitter) An electronic circuit that transmits and receives data on the serial port. It converts bytes into serial bits for transmission, and vice versa, and generates and strips the start and stop bits appended to each character.

The older 8250A and 16450 UART chips provide a one-byte buffer for storing data. The 16550 UART provides two 16-byte buffers for incoming data and is essential for receiving at 9,600 bps and higher rates, especially under Windows or when running the communications program in the background. See *UART overrun*.

UART overrun

A condition in which a UART cannot process the byte that just came in fast enough before the next one arrives.

UCR

(Under Color Removal) A method for reducing amount of printing ink used. It substitutes black for gray color (equal amounts of cyan, magenta and yellow). Thus black ink is used instead of the three CMY inks. See *GCR* and *dot gain*.

UCSD p-System

(University of California at San Diego p-System) A software development system designed for portability. Source programs (BASIC, Pascal, etc.) are compiled into an interim "p-code," which is executed by an interpreter in the target machine.

UDP

(User Datagram Protocol) A TCP/IP protocol that allows an application to send a message to one of several applications running in the destination machine. The application is responsible for reliable delivery.

UHF

(Ultra High Frequency) The range of electromagnetic frequencies from 300MHz to 3GHz.

UI

See *user interface*.

UIMX

(User Interface Management System for X Window) Software from Visual Edge Software, Ltd., St. Laurent, Quebec, that allows a user to design and modify Open Look and Motif interfaces.

ULSI

(Ultra Large Scale Integration) More than one million transistors on a chip. See *SSI, MSI, LSI* and *VLSI*.

ultrafiche

Pronounced "ultra feesh." A microfiche that holds up to 1,000 document pages per 4x6" sheet of film. Normal microfiche stores around 270 pages.

ultraviolet

An invisible band of radiation at the high-frequency end of the light spectrum. It takes about 10 minutes of ultraviolet light to erase an EPROM chip.

ULTRIX
Digital's version of UNIX for its PDP-11 and VAX series.

UMA
(Upper Memory Area) PC memory between 640K and 1024K. See *PC memory map*.

UMB
(Upper Memory Block) Unused blocks in the UMA (640K-1M). A UMB provider, such as EMM386.EXE, is software that can load and manage drivers and TSRs in these unoccupied areas. See *PC memory map*.

unary
Meaning one; a single entity or operation or an expression with only one operand.

unbundle
To sell components in a system separately. Contrast with *bundle*.

UNC
(Universal Naming Convention) A standard for identifying servers, printers and other resources in a network, which originated in the UNIX community. A UNC path uses double slashes or backslashes to precede the name of the computer. The path (disk and directories) within the computer are separated with a single slash or backslash, as follows:

```
//servername/path      UNIX

\\servername\path      DOS/Windows
```

unconditional branch
In programming, a GOTO, BRANCH or JUMP instruction that passes control to a different part of the program. Constrast with *conditional branch*.

undelete
To restore the last delete operation that has taken place. There may be more than one level of undelete, allowing several or all previous deletions to be restored.

underflow
(1) An error condition that occurs when the result of a computation is smaller than the smallest quantity the computer can store.
(2) An error condition that occurs when an item is called from an empty stack.

underscan
Within the normal rectangular viewing area on a display screen. Contrast with *overscan*.

undo
To restore the last editing operation that has taken place. For example, if a segment of text has been deleted or changed, performing an undo will restore the original text. Programs may have several levels of undo, including being able to reconstruct the original data for all edits performed in the current session.

UNI
(User-to-Network Interface) An interface between the end user and the network. See *NNI*.

Unibus

A bus architecture from Digital that was introduced in 1970 with its PDP-11 series. Unibus peripherals can be connected to a VAX through Unibus attachments on the VAXs.

unicast

To transmit from one station to another, such as from client to server or server to server. Contrast with *multicast*.

Unicode

A superset of the ASCII character set that uses two bytes for each character rather than one. Able to handle 65,536 character combinations rather than just 256, it can house the alphabets of most of the world's languages. ISO defines a four-byte character set for world alphabets, but also uses Unicode as a subset.

unidirectional

The transfer or transmission of data in a channel in one direction only.

UNIFACE

An application development system for client/server environments from Uniface Corporation, Alameda, CA. It is a repository-driven system that imports a variety of CASE tools. It supports Windows, Mac and OS/2 clients and VMS and UNIX servers. UNIFACE is known for its scalability and deployment on large enterprise-wide applications. Uniface Corporation is part of Uniface International, which was acquired by Compuware of Farmington Hills, MI.

UniForum

(2901 Tasman Drive, Santa Clara, CA 95054, 800/255-5620) A membership association of computer professionals dedicated to advancing open systems. Membership includes the "UniForum Monthly" magazine and other technical and standards publications, discounts on products and services and eligibility to serve on committees and the Board of Directors.

UNIFY 2000

A relational DBMS for UNIX platforms from Unify Corporation, Sacramento, CA. Introduced in 1982, it was the first commercially available RDBMS for UNIX.

Unify VISION

An application development system for client/server environments from Unify Corporation, Sacramento, CA. Introduced in 1993, it provides visual programming tools and supports a variety of UNIX platforms and databases. It provides automated application partitioning for developing three-tier client/server architectures. Other Unify Corporation products are the ACCELL/SQL 4GL and UNIFY 2000 relational DBMS.

uninstall

To remove hardware or software from a computer system. In order to remove a software application from a PC, an uninstall program, also called an *uninstaller*, deletes all the files that were initially copied to the hard disk and restores the AUTOEXEC.BAT, CONFIG.SYS, WIN.INI and SYSTEM.INI files if they were modified.

Many applications come with their own uninstall utility. Otherwise, a generic uninstall program can be used to uninstall any application. It must be used when the application is first installed, because it works by monitoring and recording all changes made to the computer system.

union
In relational database, the joining of two files. See *set theory*.

UniSQL
An object-oriented DBMS from UniSQL, Austin, TX. UniSQL/X is a relational and object-oriented DBMS for UNIX servers that provides SQL and object access to the database. UniSQL/M adds object-oriented capability to SQL Server, Oracle, Ingres and other relational DBMSs.

Unisys
(Unisys Corporation, Blue Bell, PA) A computer manufacturer formed in 1986 as a merger of Burroughs and Sperry corporations. This was the largest computer merger in history.

Sperry started in 1933 in navigational guidance and control equipment. In 1955, it merged with Remington Rand, creator of the UNIVAC I, and became Sperry Rand. Sperry became known for its large-scale mainframes and for providing communications and realtime systems to the military and NASA. In 1971, it absorbed RCA's Spectra 70 computer line and supported it until it phased out.

Burroughs started as a maker of calculating machines and cash registers in 1886. It was first involved with computers by supplying memory for the ENIAC in 1952. A decade later, it introduced the B5000 computer, which was hailed for its advanced operating system. Burroughs computers became well established in the banking and finance industries.

Today, Unisys' A Series and 2200 line, ranging from desktops to high-end mainframes, are current versions of product lines originating from both companies. A full range of UNIX systems, PCs and CTOS-based machines are also available. In addition, Unisys provides integrated solutions for vertical markets as well as business consulting services.

Burroughs Adding Machine
This adding machine circa 1895 is a far cry from today's sophisticated computing machinery. Nevertheless, machines such as these helped a burgeoning nation count its growing prosperity. *(Photo courtesy of Smithsonian Institution.)*

unit record equipment
See *tabulating equipment*.

unit test
Running one component of a system for testing purposes. See *system test*.

UNIVAC I

(UNIVersal Automatic Computer) The first commercially-successful computer, introduced in 1951 by Remington Rand. Over 40 systems were sold. Its memory was made of mercury-filled acoustic delay lines that held 1,000 12-digit numbers. It used magnetic tapes that stored 1MB of data at a density of 128 cpi. In 1952, it predicted Eisenhower's victory over Stevenson, and UNIVAC became synonymous with computer (for a while). UNIVAC I's were in use up until the early 1960s.

Univac I
The circuitry that filled up the walk-in CPU of the UNIVAC I, now fits on your finger.
(Photo courtesy of Unisys Corporation.)

UniVBE

(UNIveral VESA BIOS Extension) A SciTech Software VESA driver from TR Consulting, San Jose, CA, that supports VGA adapters from more than 20 different vendors. It allows DOS applications that are written to the VESA BIOS Extension standard to work with most of the display adapters on the market.

Univel

A joint venture of Novell and USL, which created UnixWare. In 1993, Novell acquired USL and merged it and USL into Novell's Unix Systems Group.

UNIX

A multiuser, multitasking operating system originally developed by AT&T. UNIX is written in C, also developed by AT&T, which can be compiled into many different machine languages, causing UNIX to run in a wider variety of hardware than any other operating system. UNIX has thus become synonymous with "open systems." UNIX is made up of the kernel (fundamental tasks), the file system (hierarchical directory for organizing the disk) and the shell (interface that processes user commands). The major command-line interfaces are the Bourne shell, C shell and Korn shell. The UNIX vocabulary is exhaustive with over 600 commands that manipulate data and text every way conceivable. Many commands are cryptic (see comparison below), but just as Windows hides the DOS prompt, graphical user interfaces, such as Motif and Open Look, present a friendlier image to UNIX users.

Command	UNIX	DOS
List directory	ls	dir
Copy a file	cp	copy
Delete a file	rm	del
Rename a file	mv	rename
Display contents	cat	type
Print a file	lpr	print
Check disk space	df	chkdsk

The History of UNIX

UNIX was developed in 1969 by Ken Thompson at AT&T, who scaled down the sophisticated MULTICS operating system for the PDP-7. The named was coined for a single-user version (un) of MULT "ICS" (ix). More work was done by Dennis Ritchie, and, by 1974, UNIX had matured into a state-of-the-art operating system primarily on PDPs. UNIX became very popular in scientific and academic environments.

Considerable enhancements were made to UNIX at the University of California at Berkeley, and versions of UNIX with the Berkeley extensions became widely used. By the late 1970s, commercial versions of UNIX, such as IS/1 and XENIX, became available.

In the early 1980s, AT&T began to consolidate the many UNIX versions into standards which evolved into System III and eventually System V. Before divestiture (1984), AT&T licensed UNIX to universities and other organizations, but was prohibited from outright marketing of the product. After divestiture, it began to market UNIX aggressively.

Alot of Bouncing Around

In 1989, UNIX Software Operation (USO) was formed as an AT&T division. USO introduced System V Release 4.0 (SVR4), which incorporated XENIX, SunOS, Berkeley 4.3BSD and System V into one UNIX standard. The System V Interface Definition (SVID) was introduced, which defined UNIX compatibility. In 1990, USO was turned into UNIX System Laboratories, Inc. (USL), an AT&T subsidiary. In 1993, USL was acquired by Novell and merged into Novell's Unix Systems Group.

Although every major hardware vendor has a version of UNIX, X/Open and POSIX are industry associations that govern UNIX standards, commonly referred to as "open systems." The Open Software Foundation (OSF) also promotes software for universal adoption.

More attempts at unifying UNIX into one standard have been made than for any other operating system. Over the years various industry consortia have tried to make UNIX a shrink-wrapped standard like DOS, Windows and the Mac. However, since UNIX runs on so many different hardware platforms, the only way the same UNIX software package can ever run on all of them is by the use of a pseudo language, such as has been proposed by the OSF (see *ANDF* in the OSF definition). While possible in theory, this is highly unlikely in the near future.

What UNIX application developers really hope for is a single UNIX programming interface (API) so that they only have to recompile the source code for each platform, rather than maintain different versions of the source code. See *Spec 1170*.

Still Going Strong

Nevertheless, with all of its versions, UNIX has evolved into the archetype operating system for industrial-strength processing in a distributed environment. UNIX is considered by many to be the best operating system for large-scale transaction processing.

UNIX components are world class standards. The TCP/IP communications protocols are used in the Internet, the world's largest collection of networks. SMTP provides e-mail, NFS allows files to be distributed across the network, NIS provides a "Yellow Pages" directory, Kerberos provides network security, and X Window allows a user to run applications on other machines in the network simultaneously.

See *X/Open, OSF, POSIX, COSE* and *BSD UNIX*.

UNIX International

A non-profit industry association that was founded to provide direction for UNIX System V. It was disbanded at the end of 1993 after Novell purchased UNIX from AT&T.

UNIX shell account

A customer account with an Internet access provider that requires the user to enter UNIX commands to send and receive mail and files. Prior to today's graphical interfaces, Internet access was always a command line operation performed by researchers and computer buffs.

UNIX socket

A UNIX communications interface that lets an application access a network protocol by "opening a socket" and declaring a destination. Sockets are very popular because they provide a simple way to direct an application onto the network (TCP/IP protocol). NetWare 3.x also supports sockets as one of the common transport interfaces.

UnixWare

An operating system for 386s and up from The Santa Cruz Operation (SCO) based on UNIX System V Release 4.2. In late 1995, SCO purchased UnixWare 2.0 from Novell and is expected to combine it with its own UNIX (SCO Open Server Release 5) and release the merged product in 1997.

Under Novell, UnixWare Personal Edition has been a single-user version that provides client access to NetWare and runs UNIX, DOS and Windows applications. It also includes the Motif and Open Look graphical interfaces. UnixWare Application Server provides a multiuser UNIX application server in a NetWare LAN. It supports TCP/IP and X Window.

UnixWare was originally developed by Univel, a joint venture of Novell and AT&T's UNIX System Labs (USL). In 1993, Novell purchased USL and UnixWare, which is based on AT&T's UNIX System V Release 4.

unload

To remove a program from memory or take a tape or disk out of its drive.

UNMA

(Unified Network Management Architecture) A network strategy from AT&T for managing multi-vendor networks.

unmark

(1) In word processing, to deselect a block of text, which usually removes its highlight.
(2) To deselect an item that has been tagged for a particular purpose.

unpack

See *pack*.

unshielded twisted pair

See *twisted pair*.

unzip

To decompress a file with PKUNZIP. See *PK software*.

up

Refers to a device that is working.

UPC

(Universal Product Code) The standard bar code printed on retail merchandise. It contains the vendor's identification number and the product number, which is read by passing the bar code over a scanner.

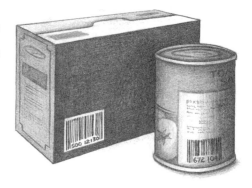

**The Ubiquitous
UPC Code**

update

To change data in a file or database. The terms update and edit are often used synonymously.

updates to this Glossary

See *Order Form*.

uplink

A communications channel from an earth station to a satellite. Contrast with *downlink*.

upload

See *download*.

upper CASE

See *front-end CASE*.

UPS

(Uninterruptible Power Supply) Backup power used when the electrical power fails or drops to an unacceptable voltage level. Small UPS systems provide battery power for a few minutes; enough to power down the computer in an orderly manner. Sophisticated systems are tied to electrical generators that can provide power for days.

A UPS system can be connected to a file server so that, in the event of a problem, all network users can be alerted to save files and shut down immediately.

An online UPS provides a constant source of electrical power from the battery, while the batteries are being recharged from AC power. An offline UPS, also known as a standby power system (SPS), switches to battery within a few milliseconds after detecting a power failure.

A surge protector filters out surges and spikes, and a voltage regulator maintains uniform voltage during a brownout, but a UPS keeps a computer running when there is no electrical power. UPS systems typically provide surge suppression and may also provide voltage regulation.

UPS - Now More Than Ever

In order to improve performance, personal computers are increasingly using write back caches, which means that updated data intended for the disk is temporarily stored in RAM. If a power failure occurs, there is more of a chance that new data will be lost, thus UPS systems are becoming important for commonplace desktop computers.

uptime

The time during which a system is working without failure. Contrast with *downtime*.

upward compatible

Also called forward compatible. Refers to hardware or software that is compatible with succeeding versions. Contrast with *downward compatible*.

URL

(Uniform Resource Locator) The Internet addressing scheme that defines the route to a file or program. For example, a home page on the World Wide Web is accessed via its URL. URLs are used as the initial address to a resource, and they are embedded within World Wide Web (HTML) documents to provide a hypertext link to another document, local or remote.

The URL defines the protocol used, the name of the server (domain name), the port address, which is often a default and the path to the particular file. For example, the following URL is the address for the directory of consultants on the World Wide Web. The home page is CONSULTANTS.HTML, which is stored in the /DIRECTORIES/ CONSULTANTS subdirectories on the WWW.COMMERCE.NET server. The HTTP defines the World Wide Web protocol.

```
http://www.commerce.net/directories/consultants/consultants.html
```

Following is a list of Internet protocols that are defined by URLs.

Prefix	To gain access to...
http://	World Wide Web server
wais://	Wide Area Information Server
ftp://	FTP server
gopher://	Gopher server
mailto://	e-mail
news://	newsgroup
telnet://	remote host - Telnet
tn3270://	remote host - 3270 emulation
rlogin://	remote host
file://	file on local system

USB

(Universal Serial Bus) A new personal computer bus endorsed by Intel and others that has a total bandwidth of 1.5MB per second. It can daisy chain up to 128 peripheral devices and is expected to become popular in the 1996 timeframe.

use-case analysis

An object-oriented method for designing information systems by breaking down requirements into user functions. Each use case is a transaction or sequence of events performed by the user. Use cases are studied to determine what objects are required to accomplish them and how they interact with other objects.

used computers

There is a thriving market in used PCs, Macintoshes and peripherals, and there are several computer exchanges throughout the U.S. that trade such equipment (see *computer exchange*).

Usenet

(USEr NETwork) A public access network on the Internet that provides user news and e-mail. It is a giant, dispersed bulletin board that is maintained by volunteers willing to provide news and mail feeds to other nodes. It began in 1979 as a bulletin board between two universities in North Carolina.

In 1995, the daily volume from all Usenet newsgroups and conferences exceeded 50MB of data. All the news that travels over the Internet is called NetNews, and a newsgroup is a running collection of messages about a particular subject. There are some 10,000 newsgroups on the Internet.

In order to read the text of a newsgroup, you need a newsreader, such as nn, rn or tin. See *NNTP*.

user

Any individual who interacts with the computer at an application level. Programmers, operators and other technical personnel are not considered users when working in a professional capacity on the computer.

user area

A reserved part of a disk or memory for user data.

User Datagram Protocol

See *UDP*.

user defined

Any format, layout, structure or language that is developed by the user.

user friendly

A system that is easy to learn and easy to use. This term has been so abused that many vendors are reluctant to use it.

user group

An organization of users of a particular hardware or software product. Members share experiences and ideas to improve their understanding and use of a particular product. User groups are often responsible for influencing vendors to change or enhance their products.

user interface

The combination of menus, screen design, keyboard commands, command language and help screens, which create the way a user interacts with a computer. Mice, touch screens and other input hardware is also included. A well-designed user interface is vital to the success of a software package. In time, interactive video, voice recognition and natural language understanding will be included.

USG

(UNIX Systems Group) The division within Novell that was responsible for UnixWare and related products. See *USL*.

USL

(UNIX System Laboratories, Inc.) An AT&T subsidiary formed in 1990, responsible for developing and marketing UNIX. In 1993, USL was acquired by Novell and merged into Novell's Unix Systems Group (USG).

USO

(UNIX Software Operation) AT&T's UNIX division before it turned into USL. See *UNIX*.

U.S. Robotics

(U.S. Robotics, Inc., Skokie, IL) A modem manufacturer highly regarded for its quality modems. The company manufactures its own chipsets (data pumps) and often leads the industry with innovations. Its HST protocol was a high-speed and reliable modem protocol before V.32bis became a standard.

USRT

(Universal Synchronous Receiver Transmitter) An electronic circuit that transmits and receives data on the serial port. It converts bytes into serial bits for transmission, and vice versa, and generates the necessary signals for synchronous transmission.

utilities

See *utility program*.

utility program

A program that supports using the computer. Utility programs, or "utilities," provide file management capabilities, such as sorting, copying, comparing, listing and searching, as well as diagnostic and measurement routines that check the health and performance of the system. Since it is easy to forget where a file has been saved, another useful utility is a "file find," which searches all directories for matching file names.

UTP

See *twisted pair*.

UTP Ethernet

(1) Same as *twisted pair Ethernet*. See *Ethernet*.
(2) May refer to pre-IEEE standard twisted pair Ethernet networks.

UTS

(Universal Timesharing System) Amdahl's version of UNIX System V. Release 4.0 is POSIX compliant.

UUCP

(UNIX to UNIX CoPy) A UNIX utility that copies a file from one computer to another. It is commonly used as a mail transfer. Unlike TCP/IP, which is a routable communications protocol, UUCP provides a point-to-point transmission where a user at one UNIX computer dials up and establishes a session with another UNIX computer.

UUencode

A UNIX utility that encodes data into 7-bit ASCII for communications over the Internet, which only supports seven bits. The UUdecode utility converts UUencoded data back into its original 8-bit format. Programs such as these are used to transmit proprietary file formats (documents, databases, spreadsheets, etc.), binary executable files as well as text files that use the full eight bits of the byte.

UUNET

(UUNET Technologies, Inc., Fairfax, VA) Founded in 1987, UUNET was the first Internet access provider. Originally offering e-mail and news, it is now a full Internet service organization providing dial-up and leased line accounts as well as archive space for files and Web pages. UUNET stands for UNIX to UNIX Network.

V

V.17

An ITU fax standard (1991) that uses TCM modulation at 12000 and 14400 bps for Group 3. It adds TCM to the V.29 standard at 7200 and 9600 bps to allow transmission over noisier lines. It also defines special functions (echo protection, turn-off sequences, etc.) for half-duplex operation. Modulation use is a half-duplex version of V.32bis.

V20, V30

An 8088- and 8086-compatible processors from NEC. Versions running at 16MHz were introduced in 1991.

V.21

An ITU standard (1964) for asynchronous 0-300 bps full-duplex modems for use on dial-up lines. It uses FSK modulation.

V.22

An ITU standard (1980) for asynchronous and synchronous 600 and 1200 bps full-duplex modems for use on dial-up lines. It uses DPSK modulation.

V.22bis

An ITU standard (1984) for asynchronous and synchronous 2400 bps full-duplex modems for use on dial-up lines and two-wire leased lines, with fallback to V.22 1200 bps operation. It uses QAM modulation.

V.23

An ITU standard (1964) for asynchronous and synchronous 0-600 and 0-1200 bps half-duplex modems for use on dial-up lines. It has an optional split-speed transmission method with a reverse channel of 0-75 bps (1200/75, 75/1200). It uses FSK modulation.

V.24

An ITU standard (1964) that defines the functions of all circuits for the RS-232 interface. It does not describe the connectors or pin assignments; those are defined in ISO 2110. In the U.S., EIA-232 incorporates the control signal definition of V.24, the electrical characteristics of V.28 and the connector and pin assignments defined in ISO 2110.

V.25

An ITU standard (1968) for automatic calling and/or answering equipment on dial-up lines. It uses parallel circuits and is similar in function to RS-366 and Bell 801 autodialers used in the U.S. The answer tone defined in V.25 is the first thing heard when calling a modem. It serves a dual function of identifying the answering equipment as being a modem and also disabling the echo suppression and echo cancellation equipment in the network so that a full-duplex modem will operate properly.

V.25bis

An ITU standard (1968) for automatic calling and/or answering equipment on dial-up lines. It has three modes: asynchronous (rarely used), character-oriented synchronous (bisync) and bit-oriented synchronous (HDLC/SDLC). Both synchronous versions are used in IBM AS/400 and other small-to-medium sized computers that do automatic dialing for remote job entry.
Due to the popularity of the Hayes AT Command Set, V.25bis is not used as widely in North America. It does not perform modem configuration functions and is limited to dialing and answering calls.

V.26

An ITU standard (1968) for synchronous 2400 bps full-duplex modems for use on four-wire leased lines. It uses DPSK modulation and includes an optional 75 bps back channel.

V.26bis

An ITU standard (1972) for synchronous 1200 and 2400 bps full-duplex modems for use on dial-up lines. It uses DPSK modulation and includes an optional 75 bps back channel.

V.26ter

An ITU standard (1984) for asynchronous and synchronous 2400 bps full-duplex modems using DPSK modulation over dial-up and two-wire leased lines. It includes a 1200 bps fallback speed and uses echo cancellation, permitting a full-duplex modem to send and receive on the same frequency.

V.27

An ITU standard (1972) for synchronous 4800 bps full-duplex modems for use on four-wire leased lines. It uses DPSK modulation.

V.27bis

An ITU standard (1976) for synchronous 2400 and 4800 bps full-duplex modems using DPSK modulation for use on four-wire leased lines. The primary difference between V.27 and V.27bis is the addition of an automatic adaptive equalizer.

V.27ter

An ITU standard (1976) for synchronous 2400 and 4800 bps half-duplex modems using DPSK modulation on dial-up lines. It includes an optional 75 bps back channel. V.27ter is used in Group 3 fax transmission without the back channel.

V.28

An ITU standard (1972) that defines the functions of all circuits for the RS-232 interface. In the U.S., EIA-232 incorporates the electrical signal definitions of V.28, the control signals of V.25 and the connector and pin assignments defined in ISO 2110.

V.29

An ITU standard (1976) for synchronous 4800, 7200 and 9600 bps full-duplex modems using QAM modulation on four-wire leased lines. It has been adapted for Group 3 fax transmission over dial-up lines at 9600 and 7200 bps.

V.32

An ITU standard (1984) for asynchronous and synchronous 4800 and 9600 bps full-duplex modems using TCM modulation over dial-up or two-wire leased lines. TCM encoding may be optionally added. V.32 uses echo cancellation to achieve full-duplex transmission.

V.32bis

An ITU standard (1991) for asynchronous and synchronous 4800, 7200, 9600, 12000 and 14400 bps full-duplex modems using TCM and echo cancellation. Supports rate renegotiation, which allows modems to change speeds as required.

V.32terbo

An AT&T standard for 19200 bps modems adopted by some modem manufacturers. See *V.34*.

V.33

An ITU standard (1988) for synchronous 12000 and 14400 bps full-duplex modems for use on four-wire leased lines using QAM modulation. It includes an optional time-division multiplexor for sharing the transmission line among multiple terminals.

V.34

An ITU standard (1994) for 28800 bps modems. Before V.34, AT&T's V.32terbo and Rockwell International's V.FC modems came on the market to provide greater speed than the V.32bis 14400 bps standard.

V.35

An ITU standard (1968) for group band modems that combine the bandwidth of several telephone circuits to achieve high data rates. V.35 has become known as a high-speed RS-232 interface rather than a type of modem. The large, rectangular V.35 connector was never specified in V.35, but has become a de facto standard for a high-speed interface.

V.42

An ITU standard (1989) for modem error checking that uses LAP-M as the primary protocol and provides MNP Classes 2 through 4 as an alternative protocol for compatibility.

V.42bis

An ITU standard (1989) for modem data compression. It uses the British Telecom Lempel Ziv technique to achieve up to a 4:1 ratio. V.42bis implies the V.42 error checking protocol.

V.54

An ITU standard (1976) for various loopback tests that can be incorporated into modems for testing the telephone circuit and isolating transmission problems. Operating modes include local and remote digital loopback and local and remote analog loopback.

V.56

An ITU standard (1972) for a method of testing modems to compare their performance. Newer procedures are currently under study.

V.110

An ITU standard (1984) that specifies how data terminal equipment (DTE) with asynchronous or synchronous serial interfaces can be supported on an ISDN network. It uses rate adaption, which involves a bit-by-bit alignment between the DTE and the ISDN B channel.

V.120

An ITU standard (1988) that specifies how DTEs with asynchronous or synchronous serial interfaces can be supported on an ISDN network using a protocol (similar to LAP-D) to encapsulate the data to be transmitted. It includes the capability of using statistical multiplexing to share a B channel connection between multiple DTEs.

VAC

(Volts Alternating Current) See *volt* and *AC.*

vacuum tube

An electronic device that controls the flow of electrons in a vacuum, used as a switch, amplifier or display screen. Used as on/off switches, they allowed the first computers to perform digital computations. Today, it is primarily the CRT in monitors and TVs.

An Early Vacuum Tube
This picture was taken in 1915 of one of the earliest vacuum tubes. *(Photo courtesy of AT&T.)*

Vacuum Tubes
Although for years vacuum tubes (right, above) have been replaced by transistors in computer circuits, they are making a comeback in stereo amplifiers. However, the cathode ray tube (CRT) on the left is as ubiquitous as ever providing the display system for every computer terminal, monitor and TV set.

VAD
(Value Added Dealer) Same as *VAR.*

VAFC
See *VESA Advanced Feature Connector.*

validity checking
Routines in a data entry program that tests the input for correct and reasonable conditions, such as numbers falling within a range and correct spelling, if possible. See *check digit.*

value
(1) The content of a field or variable. It can refer to alphabetic as well as numeric data. For example, in the expression, **state** = "PA", PA is a value.
(2) In spreadsheets, the numeric data within the cell.

value-added network
A communications network that provides services beyond normal transmission, such as automatic error detection and correction, protocol conversion and message storing and forwarding. Telenet and Tymnet are examples of value-added networks.

VAN
See *value-added network.*

VAP

(Value Added Process) Software that enhances or provides additional server functions in a NetWare 286 server. Support for different kinds of workstations, database engines, fax and print servers are examples. The NetWare 386 counterpart is the NLM.

vaporware

Software that is not completed and shipping to customers, but the announced delivery date has passed. At times, major software vendors are criticized for intentionally producing vaporware in order to keep customers from switching to competitive products that offer more features. However, today's commercial software is more difficult than ever to program, and programmers are notorious for being terrible estimators of project time. As a result, shipping dates often slip over and over again.

There is often just as large a gap between management and technical staff in software companies than there is user organizations, private or public. Dates slip because the project is not managed properly, which can be due to management's lack of understanding of the scope of the project as well as a lack of knowledge of the technical competence of the systems and programming staff.

A programming verity: as bad as programmers are at estimating the length of a project, they are equally as optimistic about their ability to meet the requirements and deadlines.

VAR

(Value Added Reseller) An organization that adds value to a system and resells it. For example, it could purchase a CPU and peripherals from different vendors, graphics software from another and package it all together as a specialized CAD system. Although VARs typically repackage products, they might also include programs they have developed themselves. The terms VAR and ISV are often used interchangeably. See *OEM, ISV* and *systems integrator*.

variable

In programming, a structure that holds data and is uniquely named by the programmer. It holds the data assigned to it until a new value is assigned or the program is finished.

Variables are used to hold control values. For example, the C statement for (x=0; x<5; x++) performs the instructions following it five times. X is a variable set to zero (x=0), incremented (x++) and tested to reach five (x<5). Variables also hold data temporarily that is being processed.

Variables are usually assigned with an equal sign; for example, **counter** = 1, places a 1 in COUNTER. Numeric data is unquoted: **counter** = 1, character data requires quotes: **product="abc4344"**. In some languages, the type of data must be declared before it is assigned; for example, in C, the statement, **int counter;** creates a variable that will only hold whole numbers.

A local variable is one that is referenced only within the subprogram, function or procedure it was defined in. A global variable can be used by the entire program.

variable length field, record

A record structure that holds fields of varying lengths. For example, PAT SMITH would take nine bytes and GEORGINA WILSON BARTHOLOMEW would take 27 plus a couple of bytes that would define the length of the field. If fixed length fields were used, at least 27 bytes would have to be reserved for both names.

There's more programming with variable length fields, because every record has to be separated into fixed length fields after it is brought into memory. Conversely, each record has to be coded into the variable length format before it is written to disk. The same storage savings can be achieved by compressing data stored on disk and decompressing it when retrieved. All blank spaces in fixed length fields would be filtered out. For acceptable performance, this method must be well integrated into the operating system. See *realtime compression*.

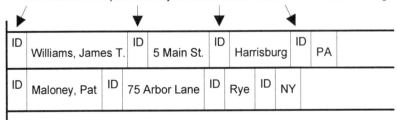

Each data field is preceded by an identification field that indicates its length

Variable Length Fields

| ID | Williams, James T. | ID | 5 Main St. | ID | Harrisburg | ID | PA |
| ID | Maloney, Pat | ID | 75 Arbor Lane | ID | Rye | ID | NY |

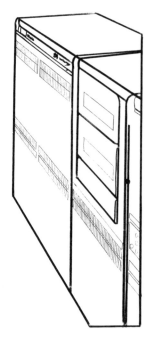

varname
(VARiable NAME) An abbreviation for specifying the name of a variable.

VAX
(Virtual Address eXtension) A family of 32-bit computers from Digital introduced in 1977 with the VAX-11/780 model. VAXes range from desktop personal computers to mainframes all running the same VMS operating system. Large models can be clustered in a multiprocessing environment to serve thousands of users. Software compatibility between models caused the VAX family to achieve outstanding success during the 1980s. VAXes also provide PDP emulation.

VAXcluster
A group of VAXs coupled together in a multiprocessing environment.

VAXELN
A realtime operating environment for VAXs from Digital. It runs under VMS and provides application development in Pascal and other languages. Resulting programs are downloaded into the target systems.

VAXmate
A partially IBM-compatible PC from Digital introduced in 1986, which has been superseded by the DECstation 200 and 300 series in 1989.

VAXstation
A single-user VAX computer that runs under VMS introduced in 1988.

VB
See *Visual Basic*.

VAX 11/780
The original VAX was the model 11/780. The VAX series was extremely successful for Digital and VAX models are still being made.

VBA
(Visual Basic for Applications) A subset of Visual Basic that provides a common macro language for Microsoft applications. VBA lets power users and programmers extend the functionality of programs such as Word, Excel and Access.

VBE, VBE/AI
See *VESA BIOS Extension* and *VESA BIOS Extension/Audio Interface*.

Vbox
(Video **box**) A hardware interface from Sony that attaches up to seven VCRs, videodiscs and camcorders to the serial port. Devices must have the Control-L (LANC) connector.

VBRUN300.DLL

(Visual Basic RUNtime 300.DLL) The Visual Basic runtime module. A Visual Basic application is made up of a series of calls to Visual Basic routines, which are contained in the DLL, and VBRUNxxx.DLL must be available to run them. The number represents the version of Visual Basic (VBRUN300, VBRUN400, etc.).

VBX

(Visual Basic custom control) An object-oriented custom control for Visual Basic applications. VBXs are created as separate executable modules and are dynamically linked to the application at runtime. VBXs have become widely used, and other languages and development systems also support them. See *custom control* and *OCX*.

Vcache

The disk cache software in Windows 95. It is a 32-bit program that dynamically allocates available free memory and replaces the Smartdrive cache in DOS/Windows 3.1.

VCPI

(Virtual Control Program Interface) A DOS extender specification for 386s and up that allows DOS extended programs to run with Real Mode programs. VCPI allows for example, Paradox 386, a DOS-extended program, to run cooperatively with DESQview, which runs multiple Real Mode programs in Virtual 8086 mode. Developed by Quarterdeck, Phar Lap Software, et al, it was the first DOS extender standard. See *DPMI*.

XMS Versus VCPI/DPMI

XMS, VCPI and DPMI all deal with extended memory. However, XMS allows data and programs to be stored in and retrieved from extended memory, whereas the VCPI and DPMI interfaces allow programs to "run" in extended memory.

VCR

(Video Cassette Recorder) A videotape recording and playback machine that comes in the following formats:
One inch tape is used for mastering video recordings. Sony Umatic 3/4" tape was widely used in commercial training. VHS 1/2" tape, first used only in the home, has mostly replaced the 3/4" tape. Sony's 1/2" Beta tape, the first home VCR format, is defunct.
Although VCRs are analog recording machines, adapters allow them to store digital data for computer backup.

VDE

(1) (Video Display Editor) A WordStar and WordPerfect-compatible shareware word processor written by Eric Meyer.
(2) (Verband Deutscher Elektrotechniker) The German counterpart of the U.S. Underwriters Lab.

Vdeck

(video deck) A frame-accurate, Super 8mm tape drive from Sony for serial-port connection to a personal computer. It contains an internal Vbox, is controlled by the ViSCA language and has no external play buttons.

VDI

(1) (Video Device Interface) An Intel standard for speeding up full-motion video performance. See *DCI*.

(2) (Virtual Device Interface) An ANSI standard format for creating device drivers. VDI has been incorporated into CGI.

Vdisk

A RAM disk driver that comes with DOS 3.0.

VDM

(Virtual DOSMachine) A DOS session created by OS/2 and Windows NT in order to emulate a DOS environment and run DOS and 16-bit Windows applications. Each application runs in a separate VDM, each one simulating an individual DOS-based PC. VDMs are multitasked along with native applications. Also see *CGM*.

VDS

(Virtual DMA Services) A programming interface that lets bus mastering devices cooperatively manage DMA channels.

VDT

(Video Display Terminal) A terminal with a keyboard and display screen.

VDT radiation

The electromagnetic radiation emitted from a computer display screen. Exhaustive testing so far seems inconclusive, but vendors recommend keeping the face at least 18 to 20 inches from the screen.

VDU

(Video Display Unit) Same as *VDT*.

vector

(1) In computer graphics, a line designated by its end points (x-y or x-y-z coordinates). When a circle is drawn, it is made up of many small vectors. See *vector graphics* and *graphics*.
(2) In matrix algebra, a one-row or one-column matrix.

vector display

A display terminal that draws vectors on the screen. Contrast with *raster display*.

vector font

A scalable font made of vectors (point-to-point line segments). It is easily scaled as are all vector-based images, but lacks the hints and mathematically-defined curves of outline fonts, such as Adobe Type 1 and TrueType.

vector graphics

In computer graphics, a technique for representing a picture as points, lines and other geometric entities. See *graphics*. Contrast with *raster graphics*.

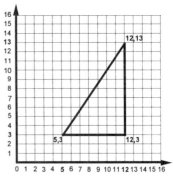

Vector graphics

vector processor

A computer with built-in instructions that perform multiple calculations on vectors (one-dimensional arrays) simultaneously. It is used to solve the same or similar problems as an array processor; however, a vector processor passes a vector to a functional unit, whereas an array processor passes each element of a vector to a different arithmetic unit. See *pipeline processing* and *array processor*.

vector to raster

See *rasterize*.

Vectra

A family of PCs from HP. Vectras are noted for their ruggedness and reliability.

veesa

See *VESA*.

Venn diagram

A graphic technique for visualizing set theory concepts using overlapping circles and shading to indicate intersection, union and complement.

Ventura Publisher

See Corel VENTURA.

verbose

Wordy; long winded. The term is often used as a switch to display the status of some operation. For example, a /v might mean "verbose mode."

verify

In data entry operations, to compare the keystrokes of a second operator with the files created by the first operator.

Veronica

A program that searches the Internet for specific resources by description, not just file name. Using Boolean searches (this AND this, this OR this, etc.), users can search Gopher servers to retrieve a selected group of menus that pertain to their area of interest. See *Gopher*.

VersaCAD

A family of CAD systems for PCs and the Macintosh from Computervision, Bedford, MA, that features 2-D geometric and construction drafting and 3-D modeling with 16 viewports. It features complete programmability and universal CAD communications. The Mac version includes CAD-oriented HyperCard stacks.

version control

The management of source code, bitmaps, documents and related files in a large software project. Version-control software provides a database that is used to keep track of the revisions made to a program by all the programmers and developers involved in it. See *configuration management*.

version number

The identification of a release of software. The difference between Version 2.2 and 2.3 can be night and day, since new releases not only add features, but often correct bugs. What's been driving you crazy may have been fixed!
Numbers, such as 3.1a or 3.11, often indicate a follow-up release only to fix a bug in the previous version, whereas 3.1 and 3.2 usually mean routine enhancements.

Version "1.0" drives terror into the hearts of experienced users. The program has just been released, and bugs are still to be uncovered.

Versit

A joint venture of Apple, AT&T, IBM and Siemens that promotes full interoperability for existing and emerging telphony, data communications and computer offerings from different vendors. Versit supports (1) Apple's GeoPort as the primary connector between the computer and the telephone, (2) an enhanced combination of CTI technologies that includes CSTA, (3) digital containers based on Apple's Bento technology, initially defining a "virtual business card" for personal data interchange, and (4) conferencing and messaging standards.

vertical bandwidth

See *vertical scan frequency.*

vertical market software

Software packages that are designed for a particular industry such as banking, insurance or manufacturing. Contrast with *horizontal market software.*

vertical recording

A magnetic recording method that records the bits vertically instead of horizontally, taking up less space and providing greater storage capacity. The vertical recording method uses a specialized material for the construction of the disk.

vertical refresh

See *vertical scan frequency.*

vertical resolution

Number of lines (rows in a matrix). Contrast with *horizontal resolution.*

vertical scaling

In multiprocessing, adding more CPUs within the same computer system. Contrast with *horizontal scaling.*

vertical scan frequency

The number of times an entire display screen is refreshed, or redrawn, per second. Measured in Hertz, display systems range from 45 to over 100Hz. For example, VGA in the U.S. is generally 56 to 60Hz; in Europe, 70Hz and above. TV is refreshed 60 half-frames/sec (interlaced) resulting in 30 full frames/sec. Contrast with *horizontal scan frequency.*

vertical software

See *vertical market software.*

VESA

(Video Electronics Standards Association) An organization of major PC vendors dedicated to improving video and multimedia standards (see VESA standards following this definition). Address: 2150 N. 1st St., San Jose, CA 95131, 408/435-0333.

VESA Advanced Feature Connector

A VESA standard point-to-point channel used to transfer video signals between two video controllers, typically between the display adapter and a video capture or TV board. The Advanced Feature Connector (VAFC) increases the original feature connector from 8 to 32 bits and from 40 to 150 Mbytes/sec. The cable is increased from 26 pins to 80. See *VGA feature connector* and *VESA Media Channel.*

VESA BIOS

A BIOS chip on a VGA display adapter that conforms to the VESA BIOS Extension standard.

VESA BIOS Extension

A VESA standard programming interface for Super VGA adapters. IBM set the original VGA standard, but many vendors created proprietary cards with higher resolutions and more colors, all under the Super VGA umbrella.

In Windows, applications call Windows to display everything. Windows then calls the display driver to draw the screen, thus, card vendors solve their incompatibilities by including their own display drivers for Windows.

In DOS, applications draw the screens directly. Since vendors of DOS games and graphics applications increasingly want to use higher resolutions and more colors, the VESA BIOS Extension (VBE) provides a standard interface to write to, including a way to query an adapter for its capabilities and to set resolution and color depth. In order to provide this capability, a software driver, commonly called a *VESA driver*, is provided by the card vendor or the game vendor. See *UniVBE*.

As of VBE Version 2.0, this standard must be implemented in the VGA card's BIOS, not as a software driver. In addition, resolutions are also selectable by pixels (640x480, 800x600, etc.), not just mode number. The VBE can be taken further. Since the card can be interrogated, it is possible to create a universal display driver that asks for and then uses the commands of the card it is driving.

Most VBE modes are outlined below. Look up *PC display modes* for the complete list.

Mode no.(hex)	Resolution	Colors	Video RAM used
101	640x480	256	300K
110	640x480	32K	600K
111	640x480	64K	600K
112	640x480	16M	900K
103	800x600	256	469K
113	800x600	32K	938K
114	800x600	64K	938K
115	800x600	16M	1406K
105	1024x768	256	768K
116	1024x768	32K	1536K
117	1024x768	64K	1536K
118	1024x768	16M	2304K
107	1280x1024	256	1280K
119	1280x1024	32K	2560K
11A	1280x1024	64K	2560K
11B	1280x1024	16M	3840K

VESA BIOS Extension/Audio Interface

A VESA standard for sound cards. Like the VBE for display adapters (see above), the purpose of the VESA BIOS Extension/Audio Interface (VBE/AI) is to provide a standard sound card interface across all platforms and environments. It also allows sound cards to be programmed using 32-bit instructions.

VESA Display Data Channel

A VESA standard communications channel between the display adapter and the monitor. The VESA Display Data Channel (DDC) requires an additional wire in the cable. The first level implementation provides a unidirectional channel that lets the monitor inform the host of its capabilities. A second bi-directional level allows the host to adjust the monitor. For example, the monitor's switch settings could be put into a software control panel.

VESA display modes
See *VESA BIOS Extension.*

VESA Display Power Management Signalling
A VESA standard for signalling the monitor to switch into energy conservation modes. VESA Display Power Management Signalling (DPMS) provides for two low energy modes: standby and suspend.

VESA driver
See *VESA BIOS Extensions.*

VESA/EISA
Refers to an EISA-bus motherboard or system that contains from one to three VL-bus slots.

VESA/ISA
Refers to an ISA-bus motherboard or system that contains from one to three VL-bus slots.

VESA local bus
See *VL-bus.*

VESA Media Channel
A VESA standard bus for transferring video signals between the display adapter and multimedia boards (TV board, audio/video capture, videoconferencing, etc.). The Media Channel (also VM Channel or VMC) was designed as a high-speed multimedia bus to accomodate realtime audio and video traffic. Up to 16 devices can be connected.
Unlike the VESA Advanced Feature Connector, which is a point-to-point channel, the VMC is a sophisticated packet-oriented, timeshared bus, which can guarantee bandwidth for realtime transmission, even more suited for audio and video than PCI. The VMC can handle up to 16 simultaneous streams of data (audio, video, etc.) and can arbitrate between 8, 16 and 32-bit connections.

VESA screen modes
See *VESA BIOS Extension* and *PC display modes.*

vesicular film
A film used to make copies of microforms. It contains its own developer and creates a pink negative or positive copy when exposed to a negative master through ultraviolet light.

Vespa
See *VSPA.*

V.Fast Class
See *V.FC.*

VFAT
(Virtual File Allocation Table) The file system used in Windows for Workgroups and Windows 95. It provides 32-bit Protected Mode access for file manipulation. VFAT is faster than, but also compatible with, the DOS 16-bit File Allocation Table (FAT).

In Windows for Workgroups, VFAT was called *32-bit file access.* In Windows 95, it supports long file names up to 255 characters.

V.FC

(V.Fast Class) A modem technology for 28800 bps from Rockwell International endorsed by many modem vendors before V.34 was finalized. V.FC is very similar to V.34, but V.FC modems require an upgraded chip for full compatibility.

VFW

See *Video for Windows.*

VGA

(Video Graphics Array) An IBM video display standard that originated with its PS/2 models. VGA has become the minimum standard for PC display. VGA supports previous CGA and EGA modes and requires an analog monitor. Its highest resolution was originally defined by IBM at 640x480 with 16 colors, but VGA vendors boosted resolution and colors to so-called "Super VGA" resolutions. VESA later standardized Super VGA modes up to 1280x1024 with 16M colors. See *VESA BIOS Extension* and *PC display modes.*

VGA adapter, VGA card

A display adapter that provides VGA resolution. Most VGA adapters are capable of 640x480, 800x600 and 1024x768 resolutions with at least 256 colors. Many go up to 1280x1024 with color depth to 16M colors (true color). Most VGA adapters build in graphics acceleration in order to provide respectable scrolling and display speed under Windows. An older VGA card without a graphics accelerator is not recommended for Windows. See *VGA, graphics accelerator* and *video accelerator.*

VGA feature connector

A point-to-point channel used to transfer video signals between two video controllers, typically between the display adapter and a video capture or TV board. Using an 8-bit data path, it provides 40 Mbytes/sec bandwidth. The port is a 26-pin male connector or a 26-pin (13 per side) edge connector at the top of the VGA board. See *VESA Advanced Feature Connector.*

VGA HC

(VGA HiColor) A VGA board that provides 32K or 64K colors using Tseng Labs' ET4000 chip or equivalent.

VGA pass through

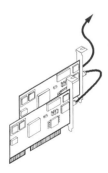

A feature of a high-resolution display adapter that is built without standard VGA capability. A standard VGA card, also installed in the computer, is cabled to the pass through circuit on the high-res adapter. When the high-resolution capability of the adapter is not used, signals from the VGA card are passed through the high-res adapter directly to the monitor. The driver that accompanies the high-res adapter turns the pass through circuit on and off.

VHD

(Very High Density) Floppy disk technologies that place 20MB and more of data on a 3.5" disk. See *Floptical.*

VHF

(Very High Frequency) The range of electromagnetic frequencies from 30MHz to 300MHz.

VHS

A VCR format introduced by JVC in 1976 to compete with Sony's Beta format.

VHS has become the standard for home and industry, and Beta is now obsolete. SVHS (Super VHS) is a subsequent format that improves resolution.

VHSIC

(Very High Speed Integrated Circuit) Pronounced "vizik." Ultra-high-speed chips employing LSI and VLSI technologies.

vi

(Visual Interface) A UNIX full-screen text editor that can be run from a terminal or the system console. It is a fast, programmer-oriented utility.

video

An audio/visual playback and recording technology used in TV. It also refers to computer screens and terminals. However, there is only one TV/video standard in the U.S., but there are dozens of computer/video display standards.

Video 1

A video compression/decompression algorithm (codec) from Microsoft that is included in Video for Windows.

Video1

A video compression/decompression algorithm from Microsoft and Media Vision that is used to compress movie files.

video accelerator

A hardware component on a display adapter that speeds up full-motion video. The primary video accelerator functions are color space conversion, which converts YUV to RGB, hardware scaling, which is used to enlarge the image to full screen and double buffering which moves the frames into the frame buffer faster.

A video accelerator card would also include graphics acceleration, which speeds routine screen displays (scrolling, images, etc.). However, the term may refer to a display adapter with only graphics acceleration and not video acceleration. Graphics card and video card are synonymous, thus graphics accelerator and video accelerator have been used synonymously.

video adapter

See *video capture board, video graphics board* and *display adapter.*

video bandwidth

The maximum display resolution of a video screen, measured in MHz, and calculated by horizontal x vertical resolution x refreshes/sec. For example, 800x600x60 = 28.8MHz. Traditional TV studio recording is limited to 5MHz, and TV broadcasting is limited to 3.58Mhz.

video board

Now that full-motion digital video is deployed on personal computers, the term "video board" can refer to either (1) a display adapter (VGA, Super VGA, etc.), or (2) a video capture board that digitizes full-motion video into the computer.

video camera

A camera that takes continuous pictures and generates a signal for display or recording. It captures images by breaking down the image into a series of lines. The U.S. and Canadian standard (NTSC) is 525 scan lines. Each line is scanned one at a time, and the continuously varying intensities of red, green and blue light across the line are filtered out and converted into a variable signal. Most video cameras are analog, but digital video cameras are also available. See *digital camera.*

Video

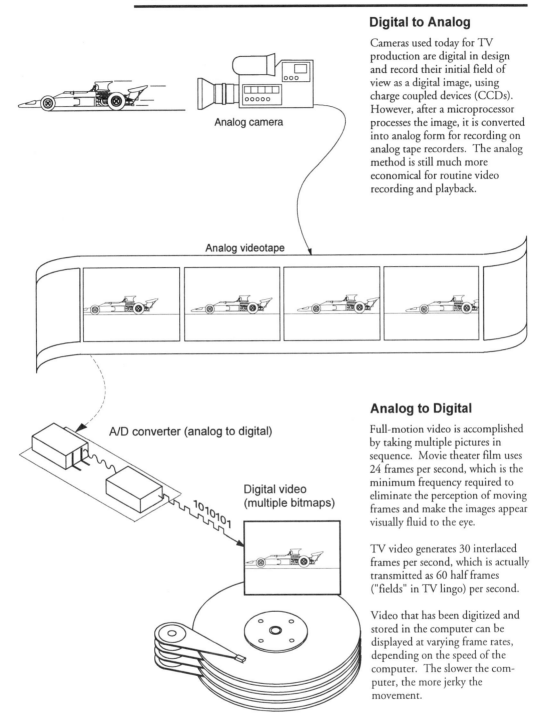

Analog camera

Analog videotape

A/D converter (analog to digital)

1010101

Digital video (multiple bitmaps)

Digital to Analog

Cameras used today for TV production are digital in design and record their initial field of view as a digital image, using charge coupled devices (CCDs). However, after a microprocessor processes the image, it is converted into analog form for recording on analog tape recorders. The analog method is still much more economical for routine video recording and playback.

Analog to Digital

Full-motion video is accomplished by taking multiple pictures in sequence. Movie theater film uses 24 frames per second, which is the minimum frequency required to eliminate the perception of moving frames and make the images appear visually fluid to the eye.

TV video generates 30 interlaced frames per second, which is actually transmitted as 60 half frames ("fields" in TV lingo) per second.

Video that has been digitized and stored in the computer can be displayed at varying frame rates, depending on the speed of the computer. The slower the computer, the more jerky the movement.

The First Video
In the late 1920s, Felix the Cat was one of the first video recording stars. These pictures depict one of the earliest video cameras and the resulting image it displayed. *(Photos courtesy of RCA Corporation.)*

video capture board

An expansion board that digitizes full-motion video from a VCR, camera or other NTSC video source. The board may also provide digital to analog conversion for recording onto a VCR.

video card

Same as *display adapter*.

Video CD

A compact disc format used to hold full-motion video. Developed by Matsushita, Philips, Sony and JVC, a Video CD holds 74 minutes of VHS-quality video and CD-quality sound. Video CD movies are compressed using the MPEG-1 method and require an MPEG decoder for playback on the computer. They can also be played on certain CD-I and 3DO players. Specifications for this format are defined in the "White Book." See *DVD*.

VideoCd

See *Video CD*.

video codec

A hardware circuit that converts NTSC video into digital code and vice versa. It incorporates a compression technique, such as MPEG, Indeo, Cinepak or Video1 to reduce the amount of digital data that is generated.
Video codec often refers to only the compression and decompression processing, which can be done in software or in hardware.

videoconferencing

A video communications session among several people that are geographically separated. This form of conferencing started with room systems where groups of people meet in a room with a wide-angle camera and large monitors and conference with other groups at remote locations. Federal, state and local governments are making major investments in group videoconferencing for distance learning and telemedicine.

Although the earliest videoconferencing was done with traditional analog TV and satellites, inhouse room systems became popular in the early 1980s after Compression Labs (CLI) pioneered digitized video systems that were highly compressed and could be transmitted over leased lines and switched digital facilities available from the telephone companies. Companies such as Compression Labs, PictureTel and VTEL produce group systems.

WAN, LAN and POTS

The standard for wide area videoconferencing is H.320, which defines the communications handshaking and the H.261 compression algorithm for reducing the digital video into a smaller bandwidth. H.320 runs over ISDN, Switched 56 and T1 lines, with ISDN rapidly becoming the de facto videoconferencing standard. Long in coming, the telephone companies are expected to provide nearly universal ISDN service by the end of 1996. Multiple ISDN lines can be coupled together providing bandwidth in multiples of 64 Kbytes/sec channels.

Desktop videoconferencing over LANs as well as over the plain old telephone system (POTS) is garnering enormous attention. By the turn of the century, video windows are expected to be commonplace on PCs. H.32Z and H.32P, standards for LANs and POTS-based systems respectively, are expected in the 1995-1996 timeframe. In the meantime, proprietary LAN and POTS systems are emerging.

Desktop videoconferencing systems come with a camera and one or two boards for video capture, video compression and ISDN hookup. Many systems are dedicated to videoconferencing, while others use third-party boards that can be used for other ISDN transmission and video purposes. Instead of ISDN adapters, LAN-based systems use network adapters, and POTS-based systems use modems.

Data Conferencing

A concomitant part of videoconferencing is data conferencing, which allows data and documents to be shared by multiple participants. The ITU's T.120 standard provides specifications for whiteboards, application sharing and application viewing (see *data conferencing*). It is expected that all data collaboration software in the future will be T.120 compliant.

The difference between conferencing systems is the number of features in their data conferencing software and the smoothness and quality of the video image, which runs at rates from a handful of frames per second over POTS to 24 and 30 frames per second on high-end systems, both LAN and WAN. Standard TV uses 30 frames per second.

Point-to-point & Multipoint

A point-to-point conference between two stations is relatively simple. A multipoint conference between three or more stations is more complex and requires a multipoint control unit, or MCU. The MCU joins the lines and switches the video depending on who is speaking or under the direction of one user who acts as moderator. Multipoint conferences can also be achieved by connecting each station to a conferencing network service such as AT&T's WorldWorx. WorldWorx and other carriers build in MCUs into their networks for such purposes.

Multipoint conferencing over LANs is expected to employ various technologies, including LAN-based MCU servers. ViewPoint Systems of Dallas, TX, is pioneering multipoint LAN conferencing entirely in software using the IP multicast feature. Companies such as Datapoint, San Antonio, TX, and Target Technologies, Wilmington, NC, provide full-motion video via servers that use an independent video network while running the data conferencing over the LAN.

This industry is expected to explode over the next several years and be fueled by personal use as well as business. Family members may be happy to justify the cost of a personal computer if they could regularly see loved ones in remote locations.

Businesses will increase productivity through telecommuting as well as savings on business trips. Consumer product manufacturers are developing POTS-based systems that hook into the TV.

video controller

(1) A device that controls some kind of video function.
(2) Same as *display adapter*.

video digitizer

Same as *frame grabber*.

videodisc

An optical disc used for full-motion video. See *DVD*, *LaserDisc* and *Video CD*.

video display board, video display card

See *display adapter* and *video graphics board*.

video display terminal/unit

Same as *video terminal*.

video editing

See *nonlinear video editing*.

video editor

A dedicated computer that controls two or more videotape machines. It keeps track of frame numbers in its own database and switches the recording machine from playback to record. The video editor reads SMPTE time codes provided on professional tape formats.

video effects

See *digital video effects*.

Video for Windows

The full-motion video software for Windows from Microsoft. It is built into Windows 95, but has to be installed into Windows 3.1. Video for Windows supports the AVI movie file format and provides the Media Player applet for playing them. The Windows 3.1 installation also includes the VidCap and VidEdit video capture and editor utilities.

In Windows 3.1, the Video 1, RLE and Indeo compression methods are included. Windows 95 adds Cinepak compression and provides MCI drivers for Sony ViSCA VCRs and LaserDisc players, which can be precisely controlled by the computer. The quality of Video for Windows playback depends on CPU speed and the resolution of the video window. At 30 frames per second, the eye perceives a smooth animated sequence. The lower the rate, the more jerky the animation. Following is a rough guide to the number of frames per second that can be achieved.

CPU	160x120	320x240	640x480
486/25	30 fps	15 fps	1 fps
486/66	30 fps	30 fps	10 fps
Pentium 90	30 fps	30 fps	20 fps

videographer

A person involved in the production of video material.

video graphics board

A video display board that generates text and graphics and accepts video from a camera or VCR. Truevision's Targa board and Vision Technologies Vision board are examples. The terms video graphics board and video display board sound alike, but video display boards are generally VGA-only display adapters and do not handle NTSC video.

However, as almost any combination of the words display, VGA and graphics, combined with the words board, controller and adapter, are used to refer to a display adapter, and, NTSC video is increasingly integrating with digital video display, it is impossible to say whether the term "video graphics board" will maintain this distinction. Video boards will eventually all be a mix of full-motion analog video and computer-generated video. Then, in time, all analog video will go by the wayside and be digital video from the start.

video on demand

The ability to deliver a movie or other video program to an individual TV set at the time requested by the customer.

video overlay

The placement of a full-motion video window on the display screen. There are various techniques used to display video on a computer's screen, depending on whether the video source has been digitized or is still in analog NTSC format. Since computer monitors are generally analog, NTSC video can be merged with signals coming from the display adapter. Increasingly, faster computer buses (PCI, VL-bus, etc.) and faster video busses (Advanced Feature Connector, VM Channel, etc.), allow for analog video to be digitized and stored with other binary data for output. Then the display adapter turns it into analog scan lines for the monitor.

videophone

(1) A telephone with built-in video capability, including a camera and screen.
(2) (VideoPhone) A line of videophones from AT&T. It uses AT&T's Global VideoPhone Standard technology, which is also licensed to other manufacturers. See *PicturePhone*.

video port

A socket on a computer used to connect a monitor. On a PC, the standard video port is a 15-pin VGA connector. See *VGA*.

video RAM

Also called *VRAM*, it is a type of memory used in a display adapter. It is designed with dual ports so that it can simultaneously refresh the screen while text and images are drawn in memory. It is faster than the common dynamic RAM (DRAM) used as main memory in the computer.

videotape

A magnetic tape used for recording full-animation video images. The most widely used videotape format is the 1/2" wide VHS cassette. VHS has all but obsoleted earlier videotape formats for home and commercial use.

video teleconferencing

See *videoconferencing*.

video terminal

A data entry device that uses a keyboard for input and a display screen for output. Although the display screen resembles a TV, it usually does not accept TV/video signals.

videotex

An interactive information technology for home shopping, banking, news, weather and e-mail. It is delivered by telephone line to a subscriber's TV through a decoder box and attached keyboard. Information is broadcast and stored in the decoder as predefined frames that are retrieved by menu. Videotex delivers simple graphics and limited animation. Used in several countries worldwide, it has yet to catch on in the U.S.

Video Toaster

A popular video production system for the Amiga computer from NewTek, Inc., Topeka, KS. The Toaster includes hardware and software that provides video functions such as digital effects, character generation and 3-D animation. The Toaster/Amiga combination has often been considered the most affordable broadcast-quality video system on the market.
In 1996, NewTek is expected to release Video Toaster for the PC. It will include plug-in boards and the software.

video window

The display of full-motion video (TV) in an independent window on a computer screen.

view

(1) To display and look at data on screen.
(2) In relational database management, a special display of data, created as needed. A view temporarily ties two or more files together so that the combined files can be displayed, printed or queried; for example, customers and orders or vendors and purchases. Fields to be included are specified by the user. The original files are not permanently linked or altered; however, if the system allows editing, the data in the original files will be changed.

Viewdata

The British term for videotex.

viewer

See *file viewer*.

viewport

(1) In the Macintosh, the entire scrollable region of data that is viewed through a window.
(2) Same as *window*.

VIM

(Vendor Independent Messaging Interface) A programming interface developed by Lotus, Novell, IBM, Apple, Borland, MCI, WordPerfect and Oracle. In order to enable an application to send and receive mail over a VIM-compliant messaging system such as cc:Mail, programmers write to the VIM interface.

VINES

(VIrtual NEtworking System) A UNIX System V-based network operating system from Banyan Systems Inc., Westboro, MA, that runs on DOS and OS/2-based servers. It provides internetworking of PCs, minis, mainframes and other computer resources providing information sharing across organizations of unlimited size. Incorporating mainframe-like security with a global directory service called Streettalk, VINES allows access to all network users and resources. Options include printer sharing, e-mail, remote PC dial-in, bridges and gateways.

ViP

See *Lotus Notes Visual Programmer*.

virtual

An adjective applied to almost anything today that expresses a condition without boundaries or constraints.

Virtual 8086 Mode

An operational mode in Intel 386s and up that allows it to perform as multiple 8086 CPUs. Under direction of a control program, each virtual machine runs as a stand-alone 8086 running its own operating system and applications, thus DOS, UNIX and other operating systems can be running simultaneously. All virtual machines are multitasked together.

This mode divides up the computer into multiple address spaces and maintains virtual registers for each virtual machine. This is not the same as the 386's virtual memory mode, which extends main memory to disk.

virtual circuit

(1) The communications path created between devices in a switched communications system. For example, a message from New York to Los Angeles may actually be routed through Atlanta and St. Louis. Within a smaller geography, such as a building or campus, the virtual circuit traverses some number of switches, hubs and other network devices.

(2) A shared circuit that appears private to the users that are communicating with each other. See *PVC* and *SVC*.

virtual company, virtual corporation

An organization that uses computer and telecommunications technologies to extend its capabilities by working routinely with employees or contractors located throughout the country or the world. Using faxes, modems, data and videoconferencing, it implies a high degree of telecommuting as well as remote workgroups and facilities.

The extreme virtual company is one that hires only temporary help and whose office facilities are little more than a post office box and answering machine.

virtual desktop

An infinitely-large desktop, which is provided either by a virtual screen capability or a shell program that enhances the user interface.

virtual device, virtual device driver

See *virtual peripheral* and *VxD*.

virtual disk

See *volume set* and *RAM disk*.

virtual function

In object-oriented programming, a function that has a default operation for a base class, but which can be overridden and perform a different operation by a derived class. A derived class inherits the attributes (data) and methods (processing) of a higher-level class.

virtual image

In graphics, the complete graphic image stored in memory, not just the part of it that is displayed at the current time.

virtualize

(1) To activate a program in virtual memory.
(2) To create a virtual screen.

virtual LAN

A logical subgroup within a local area network. It is used to establish a "logical workgroup" within the network without having to alter physical cabling. It also allows users to be easily added to and deleted from the network. Hubs and switches are increasingly offering this capability, which allows a virtual LAN to span multiple LAN segments. See *virtual network*.

virtual library

The worldwide collection of online books, journals and articles available on the Internet.

virtual machine

(1) A computer that runs an operating system that can host other operating systems or multiple copies of itself. Each operating system runs its own set of applications timeshared equally or in some priority with all the other operating systems. Computers can be built with hardware circuits that support a virtual machine environment; for example, the Virtual 8086 Mode in the PC starting with the 386. See *VM* and *Virtual 8086 Mode*.
(2)A computer that has built-in virtual memory capability.

virtual memory

Simulating more memory than actually exists, allowing the computer to run larger programs or more programs concurrently. It breaks up the program into small segments, called *pages*, and brings as many pages into memory that fit into a reserved area for that program. When additional pages are required, it makes room for them by swapping them to disk. It keeps track of pages that have been modified, so that they can be retrieved when needed again.

If a program's logic points back and forth to opposite ends of the program, excessive disk accesses, or *thrashing*, can slow down execution.

Virtual memory can be implemented in software only, but efficient operation requires virtual memory hardware. Programs sometimes claim virtual memory capability by bringing additional parts of the program in as needed; however, true virtual memory is a hardware and operating system implementation that works with all applications. See *Windows swap file*.

virtual monitor

In the Macintosh, the ability to dynamically configure to any monitor type and to use multiple monitors of different types including displaying the same object across two or more screens.

Programmers Like to Write
Today's programs take thousands of lines of source code. Virtual memory lets large programs run in computers that do not have as much memory as the program would normally require.

virtual network

An interconnected group of networks (an internet) that appear as one large network to the user. Optionally, or perhaps ideally, a virtual network can be centrally managed and controlled.

Banyan Systems, creator of VINES, which stands for VIrtual NEtworking System, defines virtual networking as "the ability for users to transparently communicate locally and remotely across similar and dissimilar networks through a simple and consistent user interface." See *virtual LAN*.

virtual operating system

An operating system that can host other operating systems. See *virtual machine*.

virtual peripheral

A peripheral device simulated by the operating system.

virtual printer

A simulated printer. If a program is ready to print, but all printers are busy, the operating system will transfer the printer output to disk and keep it there until a printer becomes available.

virtual processing

A parallel processing technique that simulates a processor for applications that require a processor for each data element. It creates processors for data elements above and beyond the number of processors available.

virtual processor

A simulated processor in a virtual processing system.

virtual reality

An artificial reality that projects the user into a 3-D space generated by the computer. It requires the use of a unique kind of glove, called a *data glove*, and stereoscopic goggles, which are both wired to the computer. The glove lets users point to and manipulate computer-generated objects that are displayed on tiny monitors inside the goggles.

Virtual reality, or VR, can be used to create any illusion of reality or imagined reality and is used both for entertainment and training. Virtual reality has been around for some time now. For example, flight simulators, used to train airplane pilots and astronauts, have provided a very realistic simulation of the environment, albeit extremely expensive.

A relatively new variation of virtual reality, known as unencumbered virtual reality or computer automatic virtual environment (CAVE), is becoming popular for entertainment. For example, using a glove, but not goggles, you can play a simulated ballgame such as volley ball or basketball. A video camera captures your movements while you watch yourself on a large screen. You hit a simulated ball that is passed to you by your on-screen opponent and play the game as if it were real. See *HMD, CAVE, 6DOF* and *cyberspace*.

virtual route

Same as *virtual circuit*.

virtual screen

A viewing area that is larger than the physical borders of the screen. It allows the user to scroll very large documents or multiple documents side by side by moving the mouse pointer beyond the edge of the screen. For example, you might look through an 800x600 screen resolution into a 2048x2048 virtual screen.

virtual storage

Same as *virtual memory*.

virtual terminal

Terminal emulation that allows access to a foreign system. Often refers to a personal computer gaining access to a mini or mainframe.

virtual toolkit

Development software that creates programs for several computer environments. Its output may require additional conversions or translations to produce executable programs.

virus

Software used to infect a computer. After the virus code is written, it is buried within an existing program. Once that program is executed, the virus code is activated and attaches copies of itself to other programs in the system. Infected programs copy the virus to other programs.

The effect of the virus may be a simple prank that pops up a message on screen out of the blue or the actual destruction of programs and data.

A virus cannot be attached to data. It must be attached to a runnable program that is downloaded into or installed in the computer. The virus-attached program must be executed in order to activate the virus. See *polymorphic virus, stealth virus* and *worm.*

Be Careful Out There!
Before you run a shareware, public domain or freeware program, check it with a virus detection program first!

Medicine for the 1990s
An example of one of the first virus protection programs for personal computers. *(Illustration courtesy of InterPath.)*

INTERPATH

C-4

ANTI-VIRAL SHIELD

Safeguards computer systems against the proliferation of hazardous computer viruses by providing a reliable barrier to contamination and by inhibiting viral reproduction and propagation. Contains the copyrighted viral blocking agent - Cylene- 4™.

FOR IBM PC/XT/AT PS/2 (DOS) AND COMPATIBLES

virus signature

The binary pattern of the machine code of a particular virus. Antivirus programs use virus signatures for fast detection of known viruses.

VIS

(Voice Information Service) A variety of voice processing service applications.

visa

See *VESA.*

ViSCA

(VIdeo System Control Architecture) A Sony protocol for synchronized control of multiple video peripherals. A ViSCA-compatible VCR can be controlled very precisely by the computer. ViSCA is the software interface. Control-L is the hardware plug and socket.

VisiCalc

The first electronic spreadsheet. It was introduced in 1978 for the Apple II. Conceived by Dan Bricklin, a Harvard student, and programmed by a friend, Bob Frankston, it became a major success. It launched an industry and was almost entirely responsible for the Apple II being used in business. Thousands of $3,000 Apples were bought to run the $150 VisiCalc.

VisiCalc was a command-driven program that was followed by SuperCalc, MultiPlan, Lotus 1-2-3 and a host of others, each improving the user interface. Spreadsheets have also been implemented on minis and mainframes. It all started with VisiCalc.

Visio

A drawing and diagramming program for Windows from Visio Corporation (formerly Shapeware), Seattle, WA, that includes a variety of pre-drawn shapes and picture elements that can be dragged and dropped onto the illustration. Users can define their own elements and place them onto the Visio palette. Visio Home is a version of Visio designed for personal use and includes elements for landscaping, family trees, decorating, etc.

Visual AppBuilder

See *AppWare*.

Visual Basic

A version of BASIC from Microsoft specialized for developing Windows applications. It is similar to Microsoft's QuickBASIC, but is not 100% compatible with it. User interfaces are developed by dragging objects from the Visual Basic Toolbox onto the application form.

Visual Basic has become a very popular Windows programming language and is often used to write client front ends for client/server applications. Visual Basic for Applications (VBA), a subset of Visual Basic, is a common macro language that Microsoft includes with many of its applications.

Visual C++

A C and C++ development system for DOS and Windows applications from Microsoft. It includes Visual Workbench, an integrated Windows-based development environment and Version 2.0 of the Microsoft Foundation Class Library (MFC), which provide a basic framework of object-oriented code to build an application upon.

Introduced in 1993, the Standard Edition of Visual C++ replaces QuickC for Windows and the Professional Edition includes the Windows SDK and replaces Microsoft C/C++ 7.0.

Visual dBASE

Version 5.5 of dBASE for Windows was renamed Visual dBASE. See *dBASE*.

visualization

In computer graphics, the converting of numeric data into picture form to allow humans to recognize patterns that are difficult to identify in numeric form. It is used especially in research situations, both theoretical and practical.

Visual Objects

See *CA-Visual Objects*.

visual programming

Developing programs with tools that allow menus, buttons and other graphics elements to be selected from a palette and drawn and built on screen. It may include developing source code by creating and/or interacting with flow charts that graphically display the logic paths and associated code.

Visual Workbench

See *Visual C++*.

ISA

VKD

(Virtual Keyboard Device) In Windows, a built-in virtual device driver that manages the keyboard and allows keystrokes to be sent to the appropriate, active application.

EISA

VLB

See *VL-bus*.

PCI

VL-bus

(VESA Local-BUS) A local bus for PCs standardized by VESA that provides a high-speed data path between the CPU and peripherals (video, disk, network, etc.). Up to three VL-bus slots can be placed onto the motherboard. See *local bus*.

VL-bus

The VL-bus runs at speeds up to 40MHz or up to 66MHz for controllers built directly on the motherboard. It is currently a 32-bit bus with 64-bit capability forthcoming to handle the Pentium CPU. The VL-bus expansion slot uses one 32-bit Micro Channel slot placed adjacent to the standard ISA, EISA or Micro Channel slot, allowing vendors to design boards that use only the local bus or both buses at the same time. VL-bus also supports bus mastering.

Micro Channel

VLF

(Very Low Frequency) See *low radiation*.

VLSI

(1) (Very Large Scale Integration) Between 100,000 and one million transistors on a chip. See *SSI, MSI, LSI* and *ULSI*.
(2) (VLSI Technology, Inc., Tempe, AZ) A designer and manufacturer of custom chips.

VM

(1) (Virtual Machine) An IBM mainframe operating system, originally developed by its customers and eventually adopted as an IBM system product (VM/SP). It can run multiple operating systems within the computer at the same time, each one running its own programs. CMS (Conversational Monitor System) provides VM's interactive capability.
(2) (Virtual Machine) One instance of a virtual machine in a virtual machine environment. See *virtual machine*.

VM/386

(Virtual Machine/386) A multiuser operating system for 386s and up from IGC Corporation, San Jose, CA. It allows one PC to serve as a central computer to multiple workstations, each capable of running several DOS and Windows programs simultaneously.

v-mail

(Video mail) The ability to send video clips along with e-mail messages. This is not the same as videoconferencing, which requires realtime capabilities between sender and receiver, but it does require high-speed computers and networks.

VMC, VM Channel

See *VESA Media Channel*.

VMEbus

(VersaModule Eurocard bus) A 32-bit bus developed by Motorola, Signetics, Mostek and Thompson CSF. It is widely used in industrial, commercial and military applications with over 300 manufacturers of VMEbus products worldwide. VME64 is an expanded version that provides 64-bit data transfer and addressing.

VMM

(1) (Virtual Machine Manager) The underlying operating system component of Windows. It manages the computer's memory and virtual machines. The services in the VMM are not directly called by Windows applictions, but are accessible by virtual device drivers (VxDs).

(2) (Virtual Memory Manager) The software that manages virtual memory in a computer.

VMS

(1) (Virtual Memory System) A multiuser, multitasking, virtual memory operating system for the VAX series from Digital. VMS applications will run on any VAX from the MicroVAX to the largest VAX.

(2) (Voice Messaging System) See *voice mail.*

VM/SP

See *VM.*

VMTP

(Virtual Message Transaction Protocol) A datagram communications protocol that provides efficient and reliable transmission across networks.

VOD

See *video on demand.*

voice

See *MIDI voices.*

voice channel

A transmission channel or subchannel that carries human voice.

voice coil

A type of motor used to move the access arm of a disk drive in very small increments. Like the voice coil of a speaker, the amount of current determines the amount of movement. Contrast with *stepper motor,* which works in fixed increments.

voice grade

Refers to the bandwidth required to transmit human voice, which is usually about 4,000Hz.

voice mail

A computerized telephone answering system that digitizes incoming voice messages and stores them on disk. It usually provides auto attendant capability, which uses prerecorded messages to route the caller to the appropriate person, department or mail box.

voice menu

A series of options and the corresponding number to press that are announced to the listener in an audiotex or voice processing system.

voice messaging

Using voice mail as an alternative to electronic mail, in which voice messages are intentionally recorded, not because the recipient was not available.

voice processing

The computerized handling of voice, which includes voice store and forward, voice response, voice recognition and text to speech technologies.

voice recognition

The conversion of spoken words into computer text. Speech is first digitized and then matched against a dictionary of coded waveforms. The matches are converted into text as if the words were typed on the keyboard.

Speaker-dependent systems must be trained before using, by taking samples of actual words from the person who will use it. Speaker-independent systems can recognize limited vocabularies such as numeric digits and a handful of words. In the telephone companies, these systems will begin to replace the human operator for services, such as collect and credit card calls, for example.

In the future, voice recognition systems will be able to understand large vocabularies from just about anybody; however, it could be well past the turn of the century before voice recognition is part of every computer system.

voice response

The generation of voice output by computer. It provides pre-recorded information either with or without selection by the caller. Interactive voice response allows interactive manipulation of a database. See *audiotex*.

VoiceSpan

A modem technology for simultaneous voice and data transmission over the same line from AT&T. When the telephone handset is picked up, the modem changes to 4800 bps and modulates the voice over the data. A higher-rate burst mode is expected. See *SVD*.

voice store and forward

The technology behind voice mail and messaging systems. Human voice is digitized, stored in the computer, routed to the recipient's mailbox and retrieved by the user when required.

VoiceView

A modem technology for simultaneous voice and data transmission over the same line from Radish Communications, Boulder, CO. VoiceView works in different modes. One mode can transmit up to regular V.34 speeds for data only with up to an eight-second delay to change to voice. Another mode, suited for sending small amounts of data, uses 9600 bps for simultaneous voice and data. See *SVD*.

volatile memory

A memory that does not hold its contents without power. A computer's main memory, made up of dynamic RAM or static RAM chips, loses its content immediately upon loss of power.

volt

A unit of measurement of force, or pressure, in an electrical circuit. The common voltage of an AC power line is 120 volts of alternating current (alternating directions). Common voltages within a computer are from 5 to 12 volts of direct current (one direction only).

voltage regulator

A device used to maintain a level amount of voltage in the electrical line. Contrast with *surge suppressor*, which filters out excessive amounts of current, and contrast with *UPS*, which provides backup power in the event of a power failure.

volt-amps

The measurement of electrical usage that is computed by multiplying volts times amps. See *watt*.

volume

(1) A physical storage unit, such as a hard disk, floppy disk, disk cartridge or reel of tape.
(2) A logical storage unit, which is a part of one physical drive or one that spans several physical drives.

volume label

(1) A name assigned to a disk (usually optional).
(2) An identifying stick-on label attached to the outside of a tape reel or disk cartridge. The label is handwritten or printed for human viewing.
(3) See *header label*.

volume set

A logical storage unit that spans several physical drives. The operating system sees the volume set as a contiguous group of storage blocks, but the physical data resides on multiple drives, broken up by various methods. See *RAID* and *disk striping*.

von Neumann architecture

The sequential nature of computers: an instruction is analyzed, data is processed, the next instruction is analyzed, and so on. Hungarian-born John von Neumann (1903-1957), an internationally renowned mathematician, promoted the stored program concept in the 1940s.

VOS

An operating system used in Stratus computers. FTX is Stratus' UNIX operating system.

voxel

(VOlume piXEL) A three-dimensional pixel. A voxel represents a quantity of 3-D data just as a pixel represents a point or cluster of points in 2-D data. It is used in scientific and medical applications that process 3-D images.

VPC

(Virtual Processor Complex) An IBM mainframe multiprocessing that uses several computers under tight central control.

VP/ix

See *SCO VP/ix*.

VPN

(Virtual Private Network) A wide area communications network provided by a common carrier that provides what seems like dedicated lines when used, but backbone trunks are shared among all customers as in a public network. It allows a private network to be configured within a public network.
For years, X.25 and switched T1 services have provided VPN-like services. However, VPN refers to newer technologies such as frame relay and ATM, which offer more sophistication and power. See *PVC*.

VP ratio

(Virtual Processor ratio) The number of virtual processors that a physical processor is simulating.

VPS

(Vectors Per Second) The measurement of the speed of a vector or array processor.

VR

See *virtual reality*.

Vr4400

A CPU chip manufactured by NEC Technologies, Inc., that is based on the MIPS R4400 architecture. It is being used in PCs that run Windows NT. Initial models run at 150MHz internally.

VRAM

See *video RAM*.

VRC

(Vertical Redundancy Check) An error checking method that generates and tests a parity bit for each byte of data that is moved or transmitted.

VS

(1) (Virtual Storage) Same as *virtual memory*.
(2)(Virtual Storage) A family of minicomputers from Wang introduced in 1977, which use virtual memory techniques.

VSAM

(Virtual Storage Access Method) An IBM access method for storing data, widely used in IBM mainframes. It uses the B+tree method for organizing data.

VSAT

(Very Small Aperture satellite Terminal) A small earth station for satellite transmission that handles up to 56 Kbits/sec of digital transmission. VSATs that handle the T1 data rate (up to 1.544 Mbits/sec) are called *TSATs*.

VSE

(Disk Operating System/Virtual Storage Extended) An IBM multiuser, multitasking operating system that typically runs on IBM's 43xx series. It used to be called DOS, but due to the abundance of DOS PCs, it is now referred to as VSE.

V Series

A series of of small to medium-scale mainframes from Unisys that were the Burroughs B2500 and B3500 product lines, originally introduced in 1966.

VSHARE.386

See *SHARE.EXE*.

VSPA

(Extremely Small Peripheral Array) A surface mount chip housing from the Archistrat Technologies division of The Panda Project, Boca Raton, FL. VSPA offers a 60% reduction in size over the popular PQFP method while adding more lines.

VSX

(Verification Suite for X/Open) A testing procedure from X/Open that verifies compliance with their endorsed standards. VSX3 has over 5,500 tests for compliance with XPG3.

VT100, 200, 300, etc.

A series of asynchronous display terminals from Digital for its PDP and VAX computers. Available in text and graphics models in both monochrome and color.

VTAM

(Virtual Telecommunications Access Method) Also called ACF/VTAM (Advanced Communications Function/VTAM), software that controls communications in an IBM SNA environment. It usually resides in the mainframe under MVS or VM, but may be offloaded into a front end processor that is tightly coupled to the mainframe. It supports a wide variety of network protocols, including SDLC and Token Ring. VTAM can be thought of as the network operating system of SNA.

VTOC

(Volume Table Of Contents) A list of files on a disk. The VTOC is the mainframe counterpart to the FAT table on a PC.

VTR

(VideoTape Recorder) A video recording and playback machine that uses reels of magnetic tape. Contrast with *VCR*, which uses tape cassettes.

VUP

(VAX Unit of Performance) A unit of measurement equal to the performance of the VAX 11/780, the first VAX machine.

VxD

(Virtual Device Driver) A special type of Windows driver that allows Windows to perform functions that cannot be done by applications communicating with Windows in the normal manner. VxDs run at the most priviledged CPU mode (ring 0) and allow low-level interaction with the hardware and internal Windows functions, such as memory management.

Like DOS TSRs, poorly-written VxDs can conflict and lock up the system. WIN386.EXE (Win 3.1) and VMM32.VXD (Win 95) are the VxD files that provide the primary functions (kernel) in Windows.

W

Wabi

(Windows **ABI**) Software from SunSoft that emulates Windows applications under UNIX by converting the calls made by Windows applications into X Window calls. Since it executes native code, it runs Windows applications at the same or higher performance level than a Windows machine. Wabi is an option for Sun's Solaris environment as well as for OEM products.

wafer

(1) The base material in chip making. It is a slice (approximately 1/30" thick) from a salami-like silicon crystal from 3 to 8" in diameter. Larger-diameter wafers are expected in the 1996 timeframe. The wafer goes through a series of photomasking, etching and implantation steps. See *chip*.

(2)A small, continuous-loop magnetic tape cartridge that is used for the storage of data.

Wafers
On the left is a magnetic tape wafer. The silicon wafer on the right will be cut apart into the number of chips that have been created on it via a series of etching and implantation stages.

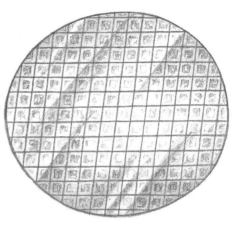

wafer scale integration

The evolution in semiconductor technology that builds a gigantic circuit on an entire wafer. Just as the integrated circuit eliminated cutting apart thousands of transistors from the wafer only to wire them back again on circuit boards, wafer scale integration eliminates cutting apart the chips. All the circuits for an entire computer are designed onto one super-sized chip.

Thus far, wafer scale integration has not come to fruition (see *Trilogy*); however, the multichip module (MCM), in which several chips are connected closely together in a single package, is expected to be widely used instead.

WAIS

(Wide Area Information Server) A database on the Internet that contains indexes to documents that reside on the Internet. Using the Z39.50 query language, text files can be searched based on key words.

Information resources on the Internet are called "sources." A directory of WAIS servers and sources is avalable from Thinking Machines Corporation, Cambridge, MA, at address **quake.think.com**. See *Archie* and *Gopher*.

wait state

The time spent waiting for an operation to take place. It may refer to a variable length of time a program has to wait before it can be processed, or to a fixed duration of time, such as a machine cycle.

When memory is too slow to respond to the CPU's request for it, wait states are introduced until the memory can catch up.

wallpaper

A pattern or picture used to represent the desktop surface (screen background) in a graphical user interface. GUIs comes with several wallpaper choices, and third-party wallpaper files are available. You can also scan in your favorite picture and make it wallpaper.

If you wonder why you cover a desktop with wallpaper, don't. Very little makes sense in this industry, why should this?

WAN

(Wide Area Network) A communications network that covers a wide geographic area, such as state or country. A LAN (local area network) is contained within a building or complex, and a MAN (metropolitan area network) generally covers a city or suburb. Following are the typical WAN networking technologies and services available.

Non-switched	**Switched**
Analog private line	Dial-up via modem
Digital private line (DDS)	ISDN
Fractional T1 private line	Packet switched (X.25)
T1 private line	Frame relay
T3 private line	SMDS
Frame relay	ATM
ATM	

WAN analyzer

See *network analyzer*.

wand

A hand-held optical reader used to read typewritten fonts, printed fonts, OCR fonts and bar codes. The wand is waved over each line of characters or codes in a single pass.

Wand

Wang Labs

(Wang Laboratories, Inc., Lowell, MA) A computer systems manufacturer and software and services company. Founded in 1951 by Dr. An Wang, the company specialized in electronic devices and became famous for its desktop calculator in the late 1960s.

In the 1970s, Wang introduced various systems that evolved into the WPS word processor and VS minicomputer lines. By 1978, it was North America's largest supplier of small business computers and the world's largest supplier of CRT-based word processors. There are still over 30,000 VS systems in use. Throughout the 1980s, Wang developed integrated voice and data networks and imaging systems. In August 1992, Wang declared Chapter 11, but came out of it in late 1993. In 1994, it acquired Groupe Bull's federal systems integration business, its European

Dr. An Wang
Dr. Wang's contribution to the development of computer memories helped advance the second generation of computers. *(Photo courtesy of Wang Laboratories.)*

imaging installations and its maintenance operations in the U.S., Canada, Mexico and Australia. Today, the company is structured into units that specialize in client/server software for open systems, software and systems integration primarily for the U.S. government and network integration and support services for new and existing customers worldwide.

Dr. Wang came from China in 1945 to study applied physics at Harvard. Six years later, he started Wang Labs. In 1988, two years before he died, he was inducted into the National Inventors Hall of Fame for his 1948 invention of a pulse transfer device that let magnetic cores be used for computer memory. The Hall of Fame has recognized an elite group including Edison, Pasteur and Bell.

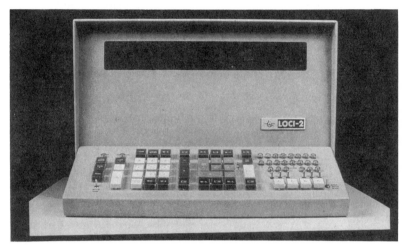

The Wang Calculator
This picture was taken in 1965. By the late 1960s, Wang calculators were an industry standard. *(Photo courtesy of Wang Laboratories.)*

warm boot, warm start
Restarting the computer by performing a reset operation (pressing reset, Ctrl-Alt-Del, etc.). See *boot, cold boot* and *clean boot.*

warm swap
To pull out a component from a system and plug in a new one without turning the power off. Although often used synonymously with *hot swap*, a unit that is warm swapped must not be functioning. For example, a hard disk cannot be reading or writing while it is pulled out. See *hot swap.*

Warnier-Orr diagram
A graphic charting technique used in software engineering for system analysis and design.

WARP
(1) See *OS/2 Warp.*
(2) A parallel processor developed at Carnegie-Mellon University that was the predecessor of iWARP.

Warp Server
The server version of OS/2 from IBM. Warp Server combines OS/2 and Lan Server into one package and is scheduled for early 1996. It is expected that Lotus Notes

and a suite of networking and database products will be bundled with Warp Server.

Watcom compilers

C and FORTRAN compilers for PCs from Watcom International Corporation, Waterloo, Ontario, noted for generating fast, compact code. WATCOM C/386 was the first 32-bit compiler for extended DOS, Windows, OS/2 2.0 and AutoCAD ADS and ADI applications. The corporate mission is to provide advanced compilers for x86 environments. Watcom is a subsidiary of Powersoft Corporation, makers of PowerBuilder.

Watcom SQL

A relational database management system (DBMS) for DOS, Windows, Windows NT, NetWare and OS/2 from Watcom International Corporation, Waterloo, Ontario. Watcom SQL is also packaged with Powersoft's PowerBuilder products.

watermark

See *digital watermark*.

watt

The measurement of electrical power. One watt is one ampere of current flowing at one volt. Watts are typically rated as AMPS x VOLTS; however, AMPS x VOLTS, or VOLT-AMP (V-A) ratings and watts are only equivalent when powering devices that absorb all the energy such as electric heating coils or incandescent light bulbs. With computer power supplies, the actual watt rating is only 60 to 70% of the VOLT-AMP rating.

WAV

A Windows sound file, which uses the .WAV extension. Wave files take up a lot of disk space. Depending on sampling frequency and rate, one minute of audio, without compression, can take from 644KB to 5MB. See *sound card.*

wave

The shape of radiated energy. All radio signals, light rays, x-rays, and cosmic rays radiate an energy that looks likes rippling waves. To visualize waves, take a piece of paper and start drawing an up and down line very fast while pulling the paper perpendicular to the line.

wave file

See *WAV.*

waveform

The pattern of a particular sound wave or other electronic signal in analog form.

waveform synthesis

Same as *wave table synthesis.*

waveguide

A rectangular, circular or elliptical tube through which radio waves are transmitted.

wavelength

The distance between crests of a wave, computed by speed divided by frequency (speed / Hz). Wavelength in meters of electromagnetic waves equals 300,000,000 / Hz. Wavelength in meters for sound travelling through the air equals 335 / Hz.

wavelets

A lossy compression method used for color images. It uses a transform, similar to

JPEG, but instead of applying it to small 8x8 pixel blocks, it applies it to the entire image and is capable of achieving excellent results at 100:1 ratios.

wave table synthesis

A MIDI technique for creating musical sounds by storing digitized samples of the actual instruments. It provides more realistic sound than the FM synthesis method, which generates the sound waves entirely via electronic circuits. The more notes sampled in the wave table method, the better the resulting sound recreation.

WDM

(Wavelength Division Multiplexing) A technology that transmits multiple signals simultaneosly over a single optical fiber. Each signal travels within its own unique color band, which is modulated by the data (text, voice, video, etc.). WDM works with the existing optical fiber infrastructure installed by the telephone companies. The ITU is expected to standardize 96-color WDM. Contrast with *TDM*. See also *FDM*.

weak typing

A programming language characteristic that allows different types of data to be moved freely among data structures, as is found in Smalltalk and other earlier object-oriented languages. Contrast with *strong typing*.

Web

See *World Wide Web*.

Web browser

A program used to view documents on the World Wide Web. See *World Wide Web*, *Mosaic* and *HTML*.

Webmaster

A person responsible for a Web page and/or site. Webmasters are the Web equivalents of system administrators.

Web page

A page in a World Wide Web document. See *World Wide Web* and *Webmaster*.

Web server

Same as *Web site*.

Web site

A server on the Internet that contains World Wide Web documents. See *World Wide Web* and *HTTP*.

webzine

A magazine published on the World Wide Web.

Weitek coprocessor

A high-performance math coprocessor from Weitek Corporation. Since 1981, Weitek has been making coprocessors for CAD and graphics workstations. In order to use a coprocessor, the software must be written to activate it.

well behaved

Refers to programs that do not deviate from a standard.

Wellfleet

See *Bay Networks*.

well mannered

Same as *well behaved.*

Western Digital

(Western Digital Corporation, Irvine, CA) Founded originally as a specialty semiconductor company under the name General Digital in 1970, its name was changed to Western Digital in 1971. In 1976, it introduced the first floppy disk controller, and later, hard disk controllers. In the late 1980s, it introduced a line of display adapters for the PC and also entered the disk drive business. Western Digital's line of award-winning Caviar drives, introduced in 1990, are widely used in PCs.

wetware

A biological system. It typically refers to the human brain and nervous system.

WFW

See *Windows for Workgroups.*

what if?

Using a spreadsheet as a planning tool. When new data is entered, results are calculated based upon the formulas. Assumptions can be plugged in that ripple through to the bottom line. For example, "what if hourly pay is increased $2?" "What if interest rates are lowered a half a point?"

Whetstones

A benchmark program that tests floating point operations. Results are expressed in Whetstones per second. Whetstone I tests 32-bit, and Whetstone II tests 64-bit operations. See *Dhrystones.*

WHIRLWIND

The first electronic digital computer with realtime capability and the first to use magnetic core memory. Developed at the Massachusetts Institute of Technology throughout the 1940s, it became operational in the early 1950s. The machine was continually enhanced, eventually using 12,000 vacuum tubes and 20,000 diodes and occupying two floors of an MIT campus building. It used 2K words of core memory and magnetic drum and tape for storage.

WHIRLWIND's circuit design, use of CRTs and realtime communications contributed towards the making of future computers. Project members later worked on IBM's 700 series. One in particular, Kenneth Olsen, founded Digital Equipment.

Whirlwind Computer
Imagine how impressive this computer room must have been in the 1950s. *(Photo courtesy of The MIT Museum.)*

whiteboard

The electronic equivalent of chalk and blackboard. Whiteboards allow participants across a network to simultaneously view one or more users drawing on the computer.

White Book

The documentation for the technical specification of Video CDs. See *Video CD*.

white noise

Same as *Gaussian noise*.

white pages

A directory list. See *DIB*.

white point

The measurement of "white" on a color monitor. It can be expressed in degrees Kelvin or as one of the standard illuminants or in x-y coordinates from the CIE Chromaticity Diagram. For example, the most neutral white point is 6500 degrees Kelvin or D65 or x=0.3127/y=0.3290.

WHOIS

An Internet utility used to query a host and find out if a certain user is registered on that system.

wide area network

See *WAN*.

wideband

In communications, transmission rates from 64 Kbps to 2 Mbps. Contrast with *narrowband* and *broadband*.

widget set

A group of screen structures (menu, button, scroll bar, etc.) provided in a graphical interface.

widow & orphan

A *widow* is the last line of a paragraph that appears alone at the top of the next page, and an *orphan* is the first line of a paragraph that appears alone at the bottom of a page. Widow and orphan settings are usually set for a minimum of two lines.

width table

A list of horizontal measurements for each character in a font, used by word processing and desktop publishing programs.

wild cards

Symbols used to represent any value when naming files. In DOS and UNIX, the asterisk (*) represents any name, and the question mark (?) represents any single character. See *DOS wild cards*.

wimp interface

(Windows, Icons, Menus and a Pointing device) Same as *GUI*.

Win16 application

An application written for Windows 3.x, which runs within the computer's 16-bit mode of operation. A Win32 application is written for Windows 95, Windows NT or the Win32s extensions to Windows 3.1. See *Win32* and *32-bit processing*.

Win32

The programming interface (API) for 32-bit mode supported in Windows NT and Windows 95. When applications are written to Win32, they are activating the PCs native and most efficient internal functions.

Many Win32 functions are also available in Windows 3.1, and Windows 3.1 applications can be written to the Win32 subset (Win32s) to gain improved performance. The Win32s capability within Windows 3.1 was not originally installed with Windows 3.1. If a Windows 3.1 application uses Win32s, it generally installs the Win32s software along with the application.

API	Supported by
Win16	Windows NT, Windows 95, Windows 3.x
Win32s	Windows NT, Windows 95, Windows 3.1
Win32c	Windows 95
Win32	Windows NT

Microsoft has combined all Win32 interfaces into one so that there are no supersets and subsets of the specification, except where there are functions not available in the other versions. For example, Windows NT provides security features that are not in Windows 95 or 3.1. A program written for those features in NT will not run under the other Windows versions. Most applications however written to the latest Win32 specification run under Windows NT, Windows 95 and Windows 3.1 with the Win32s extensions installed.

Win32 application

An application written for Windows 95, Windows NT or the Win32s extensions to Windows 3.1. See *Win32* and *32-bit processing*.

Winbench

A series of tests that analyze computer performance from Ziff-Davis' PC Labs. See *Winmark*.

Winchester disk

An early removable disk from IBM that put the heads and platters in a sealed unit for greater speed. Its dual 30MB modules, or 30-30 design, caught the "Winchester rifle" nickname. The term later referred to any fixed hard disk.

WinCIM

(WINdows CompuServe Information Manager) CompuServe's online access program for Windows. It allows subscribers to use all of CompuServe's forums and services. Without WinCIM, PC users can still log onto CompuServe with a generic communications program, but must interact via the command line rather than a Windows interface.

WinDisk

A driver from Future Domain Corporation that converts Windows 3.1 FastDisk accesses into the SCSI CAM standard supported on its SCSI host adapters.

window

(1) A scrollable viewing area on screen. Windows are generally rectangular, although round and polygonal windows are used in specialized applications. A window may refer to a part of the application, such as the scrollable index window or the text window in the electronic versions of this database, or it may refer to the entire application in a window. See *GUI* and *Windows 95 abc's*.

(2) A reserved area of memory.

(3) A time period.

windowing software

Same as *windows program*.

window manager

Software incorporated into all popular GUIs, which displays a window with accompanying menus, buttons and scroll bars. It allows the windows to be relocated, overlapped, resized, minimized and maximized. See *desktop manager*.

Windows

A graphics-based windows environment from Microsoft that integrates with and interacts with DOS. It provides a desktop environment similar to the Macintosh, in which applications are displayed in re-sizable, movable windows on screen.

In order to use all the features of Windows, applications must be written for it. However, Windows also runs DOS applications and is increasingly being used as the primary operating environment from which all programs are launched.

For fundamentals on how to work with Windows, see *Windows 95 abc's* and various "Windows 95" topics. Also see *Windows Resource Kit*.

Windows 95 Operating Modes

There are no operating modes in Windows 95 like there are in Windows 3.x. It functions similar to the Enhanced Mode but is more advanced.

Windows 3.x Operating Modes

Windows 3.x operates in different modes depending on memory and compatibility requirements.

386 Enhanced Mode (Windows 3.1 and Workgroups)

Uses the 386's virtual machine and virtual memory capabilities. This is the common mode for Windows 3.1 and the only mode for Windows for Workgroups. DOS applications can be multitasked in the background, and DOS applications can be run within a window. Text can be copied between DOS applications. Windows 3.0 can manage up to 16MB of memory and Windows 3.1 up to 256MB.

Standard Mode (Windows 3.0 and 3.1)

Used when running on a 286. Also used in Windows 3.0 on 386s because it ran faster. Provides access to extended memory and allows users to run full-screen DOS applications.

Real Mode (Windows 3.0)

For computers with less than 1MB memory. Provided compatibility with Windows 1.x and 2.x applications.

Windows Evolution

Windows 1.x, introduced in 1985, Windows 286 (2.x) and Windows/386 were the first versions of the product. However, it wasn't until Windows 3.0 in 1990 that Windows took off and created an industry due to its enhanced user interface and ability to break DOS' infamous 1MB memory barrier. Windows contains its own DOS extender, which allows it to manage extended memory.

Windows 3.1, introduced in 1992, is more stable and faster, supports multimedia, TrueType fonts and drag & drop commands. Compound documents (OLE) are added and Real Mode is eliminated.

Windows applications are 16-bit programs that run on all x86 CPUs. Windows applications can also be written that exploit the 386's native 32-bit instructions. These "Win32s" applications require Windows 3.1 and will also run under Windows 95 and Windows NT (see *Win32*).

Windows 95

Windows 95, code named Chicago, is a major upgrade of Windows introduced in August 1995. It is a 32-bit self-contained operating system that requires a 386 minimum. It has a different interface than 3.1 and a variety of new features. See *Windows 95.*

WIN.INI & SYSTEM.INI

WIN.INI and SYSTEM.INI are text files used to configure Windows. WIN.INI contains environment information (desktop, fonts, sounds, etc.) as well as individual applications. SYSTEM.INI contains hardware information.
Install programs and Windows' own SETUP.EXE program modify these files, but they can be edited manually in Notepad or any text editor. When an application is installed, it often adds text to WIN.INI, which it may modify from time to time. If the application is deleted by the user, the lines of text remain, but have no purpose. A useful utilty, called SYSEDIT.EXE, resides in the \WINDOWS\SYSTEM directory and opens all four files: WIN.INI, SYSTEM.INI, AUTOEXEC.BAT and CONFIG.SYS, for editing.

Advantages of Windows

The windowing capability is, of course, its major feature. Keeping multiple applications open is more productive than having to close one in order to use another. In addition, data can be copied between applications via the Windows clipboard.
Windows applications provide a measure of consistency. Users know how to select from menus and open, close, copy, move and paste data in all applications. Applications use the same help system, which provides help windows that can be left open to read the instructions while trying out an operation (see Windows help system).

Windows' centralized printer and font management is far better than DOS. DOS applications are invidually responsible for controlling the printer. When a DOS application is installed, it must be told what printer is connected. If a user changes printers, each DOS application must be notified of the change. When Windows is notified that a new printer is installed, that printer is made available to all Windows applications. The same goes for fonts. In DOS, fonts are often duplicated. The fonts that work for one application do not work in any other. In Windows, fonts are installed in one place and are available to all programs.

Windows DDE (dynamic data exchange) and OLE (object linking and embedding) allow for information in one database to automatically update information in another. Windows multimedia provides a consistent way to manage audio and video. Windows provides integration and standardization, which DOS does not.
Microsoft's Windows Open System Architecture (WOSA) provides standards between client applications and server software so that any WOSA-supported client program can access any WOSA-supported server program. This system-level interoperability is vitally needed in any environment as complex as the distributed, heterogeneous networks commonly implemented in today's organizations. See *WOSA.*
Microsoft had designed its future around Windows, and there is little doubt that Windows will be around for a long time.

Disadvantages of Windows

Windows, and especially Windows 95, is a complicated operating environment that has its roots in DOS, which was developed for the first PCs. Fine tuning Windows on a fully-loaded PC that is running a mix of DOS and Windows applications can be a daunting task, requiring knowledge of the CONFIG.SYS, AUTOEXEC.BAT, WIN.INI, SYSTEM.INI configuration files and with Windows 95, the Registry database. Windows applications can be just as intimidating as DOS applications ever were, in fact more so. The graphics-based environment allows for enormous creativity in the design of the user interface. Too often, the myriads of buttons with fancy symbols are more difficult to understand than simple menus with straightforward titles. There has been a rush to outdo each other with feature-rich applications providing so many functions that they can thoroughly confuse even the most experienced computer person.

Windows doesn't enforce its guidelines on the development community, and perhaps there is no way to really do that. Installation programs can overlay newer software modules with older ones and generally add tons of files that are never used. There is often no way to uninstall a program correctly. After a couple of years of using a Windows 3.1 system heavily, it becomes necessary to clean out the entire machine and reinstall what you really need.
Microsoft has addressed some of this with Windows 95, and the install/uninstall situation is expected to improve. Time will tell.
Windows is the clear winner on the desktop and its popularity tends to overshadow the fact that a Windows interface guarantees only a certain amount of consistency, not a well-designed application, which is what you work with hours on end.

Windows 1.0

The original version of Microsoft Windows introduced in late 1985, which provided a graphical interface and windowing environment under DOS. It displayed tiled windows (side by side) and was not popular. See *Windows*.

Windows 2.0

A major upgrade to Windows introduced in 1988. It supported overlapping and tiled windows and was later renamed Windows/286. Control of Windows was very DOS oriented with programs being launched from an "MS-DOS Executive" window that displayed directory lists not all that different than the DOS Dir command. All display elements (windows, scroll bars, etc.) were two dimensional. Windows 2.0 ran DOS applications full screen or in a window and supported expanded memory for internal use. Although popular in several circles and adopted by some large organizations, it was not widely used.

Windows 3.0

A complete overhaul of Microsoft Windows introduced in 1990. It was widely supported because of its improved interface and ability to manage large amounts of memory. Windows 3.0 runs 16-bit Windows and DOS applications on 286s and above. Windows 3.0 substituted the MS-DOS Executive with Program Manager and File Manager. Display elements (windows, scroll bars, etc.) were changed to a three-dimensional appearance. See *Windows*.

Windows 3.1

The first upgrade of Windows 3.0, introduced in 1992, which provided a more stable environment for running 16-bit Windows and DOS applications than did Windows 3.0. It supports multimedia, TrueType fonts, compound documents (OLE) and drag & drop capabilities. Windows 3.1 also runs 32-bit Win32s applications by translating them into 16-bit calls. See *Windows, Windows 95* and *Win32*.

Windows 3.11

An upgrade to and the final release of Windows 3.1.

Windows/386

An early version of Windows for the 386. Using the Virtual 8086 Mode, it was the forerunner of the 386 Enhanced Mode in Windows 3.x.

Windows 4.0

See *Windows 95*.

Windows 4GL

A client/server development tool for Windows and X terminals from Computer Associates. It was originally developed by Ingres Corporation, which was acquired by the Ask Group, and later CA. CA has enhanced and renamed the product CA-OpenRoad. See *CA-OpenRoad*.

Windows 95

A major upgrade of Windows 3.1 designed to replace Windows 3.11, Windows for Workgroups 3.11 and MS-DOS. Released in August 1995, it is an object-oriented 32-bit operating system that requires a 386 minimum and will not run in a 286. It is a self-contained operating system that includes a built-in and enhanced version of DOS.

Windows 95 runs Windows 95, Windows 3.x and DOS applications. The user interface provides a desktop and foldering capabilities similar to the Macintosh. The Windows 3.x Program Manager and File Manager are included, but are not the default interface.

Windows 95 includes Plug and Play capabilities and built-in networking for Windows, NetWare, VINES and UNIX networks. The Windows Resources memory limitation has been greatly expanded.

Additional features are the ability to use file names longer than eight characters and to make icons and buttons larger. The latter is a welcome addition for users that run large monitors at high resolutions, causing application windows and their controls to appear much smaller on screen.

Windows 95 was code named Chicago and was originally thought to become Windows 4.0. Microsoft announced the new name almost a year before its introduction.

Windows 95 abc's

The Windows 95 abc's and the Windows 95 entries that follow provide a brief overview of the Windows 95 operating system and how to perform basic operations. The remainder of this definition is intended for the first-time user of Windows. To learn more, Windows provides an online help system that covers most Windows operations (press F1 after loading Windows). However, a good book on the subject is also very worthwhile. If you want to become an accomplished Windows user, read "Windows 95 Secrets" by Brian Livingston & Davis Straub (IDG Books, ISBN 1-56884-453-0) or "Using Windows 95" by Ron Person (Que, ISBN 1-56529-921-3).

What's a Window? A window is a rectangular area on screen surrounded by a window frame with a title at the top. When you launch a Windows application, it is displayed in its own window. A major Windows feature is that you can have multiple windows active at the same time. The maximum number depends on how much memory you have in your computer. You get an "Out of memory" message when you try to launch another application, and there's no room for another window.

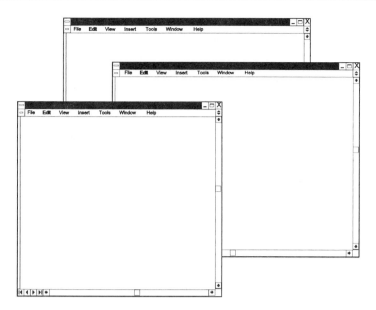

Windows

You can change the appearance of a window by making it smaller or larger. On large screens, you can keep them side by side. On smaller screens, you can overlap them or have one window take up the entire screen. The latter is called "maximizing" the window.

Windows 3.1 applications also run under Windows 95. They appear as they did under 3.1, except for slight differences in the title bar across the top and the fonts used in the menus.

DOS applications also run under Windows 95, and run either full screen or in a window side by side with Windows 95 and Windows 3.1 applications.

Desktop, Files and Folders

The Windows 95 desktop electronically simulates an office desktop. On screen, it appears as the underlying background below everything that is placed on top of it. In a new Windows 95 installation, the desktop contains only a few icons such as My Computer, Network Neighborhood and the Recycle Bin. Additional items are placed on the desktop by the user.

In DOS and Windows 3.1, the disk is divided into directories and subdirectories. In Windows 95, directories are called *folders*, and subdirectories are called *subfolders*, because they are represented by icons that look like open and closed manilla folders. Folders can be placed on the desktop, and, just like the paper variety you hold in your hand, folders can be inserted into other folders.

Program and document files are represented by a variety of icons. Files are initially stored in folders, but can also be moved to the desktop as a way to find often-used programs and documents more easily. Shortcuts (pointers) to files can also be created and placed on the desktop.

When files and folders are placed on the desktop, they remain there until moved elsewhere. When you start up the computer the next day, everything on the desktop is the same as you left it.

My Computer and Network Neighborhood

All the resources available to the computer are displayed from two icons that remain on the desktop. The My Computer icon displays all the local resources, including the disk drives and settings for the environment and all other hardware devices. Network Neighborhood displays the remote resources available on any networks the computer is connected to.

The Windows 95
Desktop

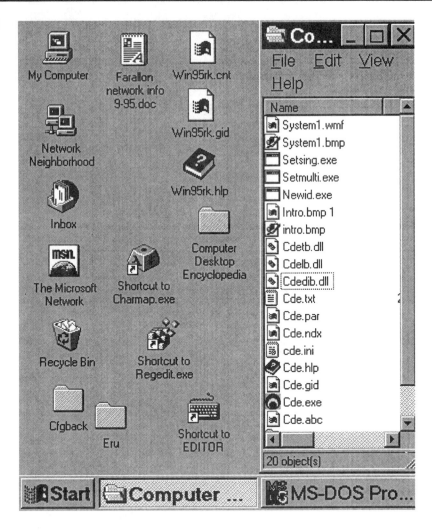

Start Menu

The Start menu, which is displayed by pressing the Start button at the bottom left side of the screen, is a major launching pad for applications. It takes the place of Program Manager in Windows 3.1, and new menu items are added to the Start menu when a new application is installed.

The Start menu can be rearranged and customized to a user's preference. Items can be added and removed directly from the menu. See *Windows 95 Start menu.*

Explorer

The Explorer takes the place of File Manager in Windows 3.1 and lets you copy, move, delete and rename files and folders. See *Windows 95 Explorer.*

The Registry and Properties

The Registry is a Windows 95 database that holds all the settings about your current system configuration. Many settings previously stored in the WIN.INI and SYSTEM.INI configuration files in Windows 3.1 are in the Registry.

Access to the Registry is normally done via the Control Panels and Properties option in the File menu. In addition, if you right click on almost any icon, you can select Properties. See *Windows 95 Properties.*

Summary

Most people use an operating system to launch applications and manage files. These tasks can be learned rather quickly in Windows 95, and you may never need to do much else. But, Windows 95 is a mixture of DOS, Windows 3.1 and the Macintosh, all rolled into one, which makes it rather complicated. In addition, there are often several ways to perform the same operation. Mastering Windows 95 will take effort and practice.

Windows 95 - Changing window appearance

In Windows, you can move, resize and overlap windows on screen.

How to change Window appearance

Move Window Around Screen
Point to window title bar (top of window) and drag.

Change One Side of a Window
Point to a side. When pointer changes to a double arrow, drag to new location.

Change Two Sides of a Window
Point to a corner. When pointer changes to an angled double arrow, drag to new location.

Turn Window into a Taskbar Button (Minimize)
Click the left most button at the top right side of the window (underscore character).

Turn Taskbar Icon back into a Window
Click the taskbar button icon.

Make Window Cover Entire Screen (Maximize)
Click the middle button at the top right side of the window (rectangle).

Restore Window to Previous Size
Click the middle button at the top right side of the window (double rectangles).

Windows 95 clipboard

See *Windows 95 - Copying between windows.*

Windows 95 - Copying between windows

To copy text or an image within a document and insert it into another, highlight the text or image and select COPY from the Edit menu. Your selected item will be copied into the clipboard. Then switch to the window that contains the destination document. Position the cursor where you want the text or image to appear and select PASTE from the Edit menu. To move the object instead of copying it, select CUT instead of COPY from the Edit menu.

To copy or move data from a DOS window, see *Windows 95 - Running DOS programs*

Windows 95 Device Manager

The Device Manger Property sheet shows the status of all the peripheral devices connected to your computer. To display it, Double click My Computer, Control Panel and System. Then click once on the DEVICE MANAGER tab. See *Windows 95 Properties.*

Windows 95 display settings

Settings such as desktop and window colors, screen saver and resolution are in the Display control panel. Right click on any uncovered area on the desktop and select PROPERTIES.

Configuration information about the display adapter is in Device Manager in the System control panel. Double click My Computer, Control Panel and System. Click on the DEVICE MANAGER tab.

Windows 95 Explorer

Explorer lets you create and delete folders and copy, move and delete files. In its left window, Explorer displays a hierarchical tree of folders. In its right window, the contents of the currently selected folder are displayed.

Explorer maintains the tree and contents windows independently. For example, you can display the contents of a folder on the right and then expand the tree on the left to display subfolders that you might want to copy or move files into.

Explorer has only one contents window on the right side. However, you can open up as many folders as you wish each into their own window. You can also launch multiple instances of Explorer.

How to do basic Explorer operations

Launch Explorer
Right click Start menu and select EXPLORE.

Display Contents of a Folder
Click once on the folder in the tree on the left. Its contents will be displayed in the right window.

To open a folder into its own window (not the right side of Explorer), click the folder in the tree and select OPEN.

Display Names of Subfolders "Expand the Tree"
If there is a + to the left of the folder, there are subfolders. To display the subfolder hierarchy, click the +. The + changes to a -. To compress the tree back again, click the -.

Display Contents of a Subfolder
Click once on the subfolder icon in the left side of the Explorer window, or double click on the subfolder icon in the right side of the window.

Create Folder
Click the drive or folder icon in which the new folder will be placed, and select NEW from the File menu. Then select FOLDER.

Delete Folder
Click the folder icon and select DELETE from the File menu.

Rename File or Folder
Click the icon. Select RENAME from the File menu. Or, click the icon name twice (but not so fast that it is picked up as a double click). Type in a new name and press Enter.

Switch Drives
Click the drive icon.

Copy or Move File or Folder
Right click, drag source icon and drop on destination icon. Select

COPY or MOVE from menu. Note that there is a default selection in the menu. If you remember what the defaults are, you can left click and drag and the operation will be performed automatically.

Type of file:	Left drag action taken:
Data file	Move
Program file	Shortcut created

Select Multiple Files
Hold Ctrl down and click icons. If the file names are contiguous, you can lasso them by clicking to the right of the file name on top or bottom and dragging to the diagonal corner.

Windows 95 Explorer

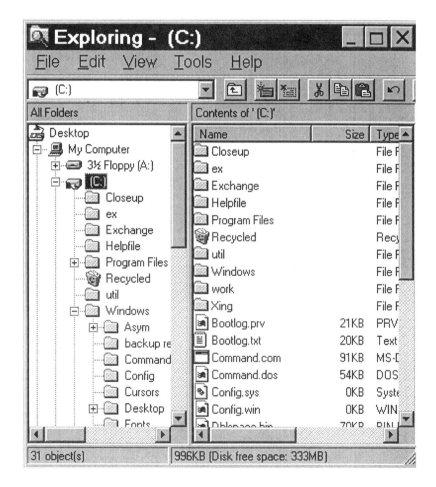

Windows 95 hardware configuration

See *Windows 95 Device Manager.*

Windows 95 keyboard commands

Following are the ways to command Windows without a mouse:

MENUS
All menus are selectable by pressing Alt and the UNDERLINED letter of the menu title. For example, Alt-F for File menu.

MENU OPTIONS
All menu options are selectable by pressing the UNDERLINED letter of thier name. Most of the time, it is the first letter. However, if two menu options start with the same letter, one of them will use a letter in the middle of the name as a keyboard command.

CANCEL MENU Esc
HELP MENU F1

<u>START/STOP</u>
DISPLAY START MENU Ctrl-Esc
LAUNCH APPLICATION FROM ICON Enter
CLOSE WINDOW Alt-F4 or Alt-spacebar, C.

<u>GO TO/CHANGE WINDOWS</u>
GO TO ALL WINDOWS Alt-Tab-Tab...
GO BETWEEN LAST TWO Alt-Tab
GO TO NEXT TABBED SHEET Ctrl-Tab
MOVE WINDOW Alt-spacebar, M. Cursor to new location and press Enter.
RESIZE WINDOW Alt-spacebar, S. Cursor to new size and press Enter.

<u>MINIMIZE/MAXIMIZE</u>
DISPLAY CONTROL MENU Alt-spacebar
MAXIMIZE Alt-spacebar X
MINIMIZE Alt-spacebar N

<u>CLIPBOARD</u>
COPY SELECTED ITEM INTO CLIPBOARD Ctrl-C
CUT SELECTED ITEM INTO CLIPBOARD Ctrl-X
PASTE FROM CLIPBOARD Ctrl-V
HIGHLIGHT TEXT Hold Shift down while moving the cursor keys.

<u>MISCELLANEOUS</u>
UNDO LAST OPERATION Ctrl-Z or Alt-backspace
TOGGLE DOS FULL SCREEN & WINDOW Alt-enter

Windows 95 long file names

Windows 95 supports file and folder names up to 255 characters in length. It also maintains the name in the 8.3 short form for compatibility with DOS and Windows 3.1 programs that cannot access long file names.
The valid characters are the same as in DOS:

A-Z, a-z, 0-9 ! @ # $ % & ( ) ' ` - { } ~ as well as:+ , ; = [ ] . space
File extensions are still used and are attached to the file name with a period as they are in DOS/Windows 3.1. However, you can place dots within the file name. The name **letters to friends.pat.sue.sam.doc** is valid in Windows 95. The DOC would be treated as an extension name.
The short name that Windows 95 creates can be confusing, because it takes the first

six letters of the long name and adds the Spanish tilde and a digit. For example, **MY LETTER TO FRIENDS** becomes **MYLETT~1**. Therefore, if you plan on using DOS and Windows 3.1 applications for a while, you will have to be careful how you name files and folders with Windows 95 applications. If you are not careful about keeping the first letters different (as you always did in the past), the resulting 8.3 names Windows 95 creates may all look similar or be too cryptic, so be careful out there among the old and new Windows!

The New DOS Handles Long Names

If you use the DOS prompt in Windows 95, it will handle the new names. Use quotes if you have spaces, for example:

copy oldbudgets newbudgets
copy oldbudgets "new budgets"
copy "old budgets" "new budgets"

Windows 95 - Minimizing windows

To remove some of the clutter of your open windows, you can "minimize" a window, turning it into a button on the Taskbar at the bottom of the screen.
To minimize your open window, click on the _ button at the top right corner of the window. The minimized application remains active but out of your way. To turn it back into a window, "maximize" it, click the appropriate Taskbar button or pressing Alt-Tab-Tab-etc.

MINIMIZE THEM ALL
You can minimize all your open windows at once by right clicking on an empty area of the Taskbar and selecting MINIMIZE ALL WINDOWS.

DON'T FORGET YOUR MINIMIZED APPLICATIONS
If you forget you have a minimized application, and you double click on the program icon back in the Start menu, on the desktop or in Explorer, you will launch another copy of the application.

Windows 95 My Computer

The My Computer icon on a Windows 95 desktop serves as a window into all of the resources on the computer. It includes the disk drives and system folders, which contain the control panels, print spoolers and dial-up networking. My Computer displays local resources. Its counterpart for remote resources on the network is the Network Neighborhood, which is also on the desktop.

Windows 95 My Computer
Windows 95 My Computer
The Control Panel folder is one of the main components of My Computer. Double clicking the Control Panel icon displays the Control Panel window and all the control panels available to the user.

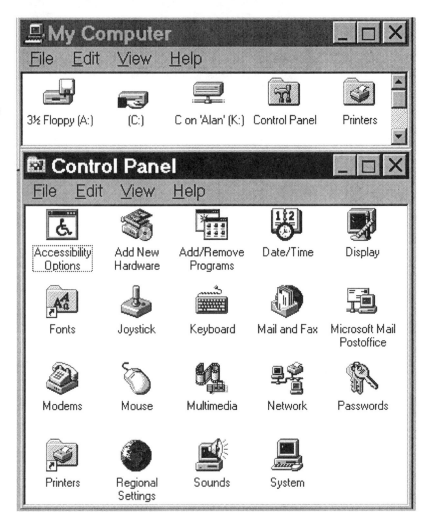

Windows 95 Network Neighborhood

The Network Neighborhood icon on a Windows 95 desktop serves as a window into all of the network resources available to the user. Network Neighborhood displays remote resources. Its counterpart for local resources is My Computer, which is also on the desktop.

Windows 95 - Printing the screen

To print your current Windows screen, you have to copy it to the clipboard, then paste the clipboard into a graphics or desktop publishing program and print it from there.

To copy the current window into the clipboard, press Alt-PrintScreen. To copy the entire screen with all the windows showing into the clipboard, press PrintScreen. Then, launch any application that you can paste an image into, such as a paint, drawing or desktop publishing program, and paste the clipboard image into a new document by selecting PASTE from the Edit menu. Print the screen capture from this application.

Windows 95 Network Neighborhood

Selecting Network Neighborhood displays the Network Neighborhood window which shows the available computers in the network. Double clicking a specific computer, in this case "Alan," displays the folders and printers that are sharable. By making the C: drive sharable ("c" folder), all files and folders on that drive are available to network users.

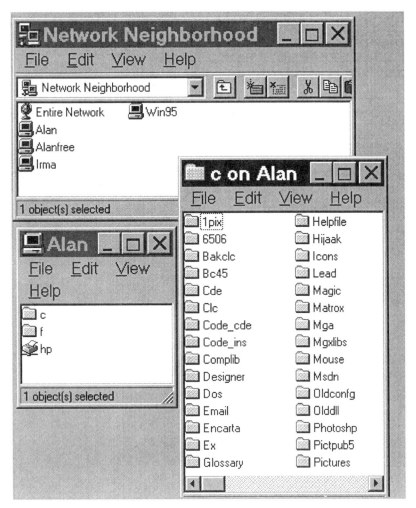

Windows 95 Properties

A Windows 95 Property sheet displays the current settings of a particular resource in the computer. It is also used to modify the settings and serves as a front end to the Registry, which is the database where these settings are stored (see *Windows 95 Registry*).

Property sheets are displayed by selecting the different Control Panels in My Computer as well as from the Properties option in the File menu. Right clicking on various objects also displays them. Following are ways to access some useful Property sheets.

Desktop and Window Colors and Screen Saver

Right click on any uncovered part of the desktop.

Hardware Configuration (CPU and Peripherals)

Double click My Computer, Control Panel and System. Select DEVICE MANAGER.

TaskBar (Hide or Restore, Show Clock)
Right click on any uncovered part of the Taskbar (in between the buttons).

Most All Properties Sheets
Double click My Computer and a Control Panel.

The Device Manager

The System Properties Device Manager shows what the computer's hardware components are all about. Windows 95 is considerably more aware of its peripheral resources than Windows 3.1. In fact, if you pull a hard drive out of one Win 95 machine and place it in another, Windows 95 may not work unless the system is identical. The version of Windows 95 on that hard disk is tightly configured to that specific PC.

Windows 95 Registry

The Registry is a Windows 95 database that holds configuration data about the hardware and environment of the PC it has been installed in. It is made up of the SYSTEM.DAT and USER.DAT files. Many settings that were previously stored in WIN.INI and SYSTEM.INI in Windows 3.1 are in the Registry.

The Registry can be edited directly, but that is usually only done for very technical enhancements or as a last resort. Routine access is done via the Control Panels in My Computer and the Properties menu option, which is on the File menu. In addition, right clicking on almost every icon brings you the option of selecting Properties. See *Windows 95 Properties*.

Registry Details

To get into the Registry itself, run the Registry Editor program (REGEDIT.EXE) in the \WINDOWS directory. The Registry contains six folders, each named with an HKEY prefix (stands for "Handle to a Key").

HKEY_CLASSES_ROOT

Contains file associations and OLE information. It shows exactly the same thing as the subsequent folder HKEY_LOCAL_MACHINE\Software\Classes.

HKEY_CURRENT_USER

The portion of HKEY_USERS that pertains to the current user. It contains the colors, fonts and attributes for the desktop environment as well as any network connections. If the current user is the only user of the system, HKEY_CURRENT_USER and HKEY_USERS are the same.

HKEY_USERS

Contains the above information for all users of the system. It is the USER.DAT file.

HKEY_LOCAL_MACHINE

Holds a large number of settings for the hardware, system software and applications. Install programs also create folders within this folder and place information in them, taking the place of the INI files commonly used in Windows 3.1.

HKEY_CURRENT_CONFIGURATION

Contains settings for the current display resolution and printers.

HKEY_DYN_DATA

Holds performance statistics which can be viewed with the Windows 95 System Monitor (SYSMON.EXE).

Windows 95 - Running DOS programs

In Windows, you can run and keep DOS programs active along with Windows programs. Pressing Alt-Tab will switch you between all active applications, whether Windows or DOS.

DOS programs are normally run in a window, but they can be run full screen as they normally would in DOS. To switch between a window and full screen, press Alt-Enter.

The advantage of running a DOS program in a window is that you can display a DOS window side by side or overlapped with a Windows windows. Also, you can copy text from a DOS window into the clipboard and paste text from the clipboard into the DOS window. You could even copy text from one DOS program to another.

If you have trouble running a DOS application in Windows, you may have to change its properties. To do that, right click on the DOS program icon and select PROPERTIES.

How to run DOS Programs

Start DOS Application by Name
Select RUN from the Start menu and type in the path to the program.

Start DOS Application from an Icon
Double click on the program icon in a folder, on the desktop or from Explorer.

Place a DOS Application in the Start Menu
1. Right click Start menu and select OPEN.
2. Drag the DOS program icon into the Start menu window.
A Shortcut to the program will be created.
3. Close the window, and a new menu item will be displayed the next

time **you click the Start menu.**

End DOS Application
End your DOS application as you normally would. If the window is still open, click the X button at the top right side of the window.

Run DOS Program in a Window
Press Alt-Enter to toggle between full screen and window modes.

Copy Text from a DOS Window
Click the Mark button (dashed rectangle) on the toolbar. Highlight the text and click the Copy button (double pages).

Copy Text to a DOS Window
Click the Paste button (clipboard) on the toolbar.

Quick Way to Get the DOS Prompt
Right click the Start menu and select MS-DOS PROMPT.

Windows 95 - Running Windows programs

How to run Windows 3.1 and Windows 95 Programs

From the Start Menu
Click PROGRAMS from the Start menu. Click the Program Group, then click the program name you want to launch.

From Explorer
Right click Start menu and select EXPLORE. Click on the desired folder icon, then the application icon.

From a Folder on the Desktop
Double click the folder on the desktop. Double click the application or document icon. In order for the document icon to launch the appropriate software, it must already be associated by extension name to the program. All popular documents have been associated.

From a Shortcut on the Desktop
Shortcuts have a small northeast-pointing arrow at the bottom left side of the icon. Double click the icon to launch the program.

By Name
Select RUN from the Start menu. Type in the path to the program name. To learn more about paths, see *DOS path name.*

End Windows Application
Click the rightmost button at the top right side of the window (X) or double click the application icon at the top left side.

Windows 95 Shortcuts

Windows 95 allows you to create pointers, or Shortcuts, to your program and data files. The Shortcut icons can be placed on the desktop or stored in other folders. Double clicking a Shortcut is the same as double clicking the original file. However, deleting a Shortcut does not remove the original. Shortcut icons have a small arrow in their lower left corner pointing northeast.

Create a Shortcut to a Program File

Drag the icon from a folder or Explorer window and drop it on the desktop or into another folder.

Create a Shortcut to a Data File

Right click and drag the icon from a folder or Explorer window and drop in on the desktop or into another folder. Select CREATE SHORTCUT.

Create a Shortcut to a Folder

Right click and drag the icon of a folder from within another folder window or from the Explorer window and drop in on the desktop or into another folder. Select CREATE SHORTCUT.

To find out how to add Shortcuts to the Start menu, see *Windows 95 Start menu.*

Windows 95 - Starting and stopping

Windows 95 is automatically loaded when you start the computer.

To end your Windows 95 session, save all the data in your active windows and select SHUT DOWN from the START menu. Wait until the message "It is now safe to turn off your computer" before you turn it off.

When you turn the computer back on, your screen will appear the way you left it.

Windows 95 Start menu

The Start menu is a launching pad for applications and takes the place of Program Manager in Windows 3.1. And, just like the Program Manager desktop, the Start menu can be customized.

What you generally do with the Start menu is to put a Shortcut to your application in it, not the actual application itself. You can add items to the main part of the Start menu or to the submenus.

Add a Shortcut to the Main Start Menu

Drop the icon directly over the Start menu button.

Add a Shortcut to a Start Submenu

Right click the Start menu and select OPEN. Open the submenu and drop icons into it.

Delete a Shortcut from the Start Menu

Right click the Start menu and select OPEN. Drag the icons you don't want into the Recycle Bin. If the item is in a submenu, open it and do the same thing.

Clear items from the Documents Menu

One of the Start menu options is Documents, which contains the last 15 documents worked on by a Windows 95 (not 3.1) application.

To clear the Documents list, right click the Taskbar, select   PROPERTIES, then the tab marked START MENU PROGRAMS and finally CLEAR.

Windows 95 Swap file

See *Windows swap file.*

Windows 95 - Switching windows

In Windows, it's easy to switch between active windows.

Toggle Between ALL Windows
Press Alt-Tab-Tab... Hold Alt down while pressing Tab. Release Alt when the title of the window you want is displayed.

Toggle Between LAST TWO Windows
Press Alt-Tab once.

You Can Click on Any Visible Part of the Window
You can switch to another window by clicking on any part of it. If any side or corner is visible, simply click on it to make it the current topmost window.

Your Window Did Not Go Away Forever!
When you switch windows, the other windows may be temporarily out of view. Just hold Alt down and press Tab several times. Look at the window titles as they appear one after the other. When you get to the one you want, let go of the Alt key.

Windows 95 Taskbar

The Windows 95 Taskbar is a row of buttons across the bottom of the screen. When an application is minimized (the _ button), it turns into a button on the Taskbar. When the button is clicked, it is restored to its previous position on screen.
The Taskbar can be moved to the top, right or left side of the screen by clicking any free space on the bar and dragging it there.
The Taskbar can also be hidden and made to appear when the cursor is moved to the edge of the screen. To hide the Taskbar, right click on any free space on the bar and select AUTO HIDE from the TASKBAR OPTIONS Properties sheet.

Windows 95 Tips

Following are a number of ways to help you use Windows 95 more easily.

Move TaskBar to Top, Left or Right of Screen
Click on any uncovered area on the Taskbar and move to any extreme side of the screen.

Make TaskBar Disappear
Right click on any uncovered area button on the Taskbar. Select PROPERTIES and AUTO HIDE.

Fast Way to Get Explorer or the DOS Prompt
Right click the Start menu and select EXPLORE or MS-DOS PROMPT.

Show Extensions with File Names
Windows 95 defaults to hiding the file extensions when file names are displayed. To display all extensions, open any folder and select OPTIONS/VIEW from the View menu. Deselect "Hide MS-DOS file extensions..." and select "Show all files."

Find a File that Contains Specific Text
Right click Start menu and select FIND. Define the location of the search with LOOK IN. Tab to ADVANCED and type in the specific text. If you want to confine the search to specific files, choose an option in OF TYPE.

Rename My Computer
If you prefer another name for My Computer, right click the icon and select RENAME. Type in the name you want and press Enter.

Put the Desktop on the Taskbar

Pressing Alt-Tab switches you between all active applications, but not to the desktop. You can however put the desktop onto the Taskbar by doing the following:

1. Double click My Computer.
2. If My Computer and its icon does not appear above the Name column, select TOOLBAR from the View menu to display it.
3. Click My Computer on the toolbar.
4. Scroll up and select DESKTOP. You now have a window to your desktop. Size it and arrange the icons to your preference.
5. Be sure that "Browse folders using a separate window" is active (select OPTIONS/FOLDER from the View menu).
6. Minimize the window. Your desktop is now on the Taskbar.

Switch Between the DOS Prompt and Explorer

When you right click on a folder in Explorer, you can have the DOS prompt as an option. If you select it, you are automatically set to the same folder (directory) at the command line. To attach the option, do this:

1. In Explorer, select OPTIONS/FILE TYPES from the View menu.
2. Double click the FOLDER icon and select NEW.
3. Type **DOS prompt** in the "Action" line.
4. Type **c:\windows\command.com /k cd** in the "Application used to perform action" line.
5. Select OK/CLOSE/CLOSE.

Create a Shortcut to the Device Manager

You can easily create a Shortcut to the System Control Panel by dragging it to the desktop. However, if you want to immediately display the second Properties sheet (Device Manager), you have to do the following:

1. Right click the desktop and select NEW/SHORTCUT.
2. Type in the following and select NEXT. **c:\windows\control.exe sysdm.cpl,system,1**
3. Type Device Manager and select FINISH.

Windows 95 - Typing special characters

In Windows, you can insert special characters into your document that are in the font, but have no corresponding keyboard keys. To see what characters are available in the current font, select the Character Map applet from the Accessories group in the Start menu.

All the characters are displayed on screen. Go to an individual character by clicking on it or using the Arrow keys. Note the keystroke numbers at the bottom right side of the window. For example, if Alt+0171 appears, you would enter that character by holding down the Alt key and pressing 0, 1, 7 and 1 on the numeric keypad on the right side of your keyboard. To change fonts, select a different font from the Font menu at the top left.

You can copy a series of characters from the Character Map to the clipboard and paste them into your document. Press SELECT button to add a character to the Characters to Copy input box. Press COPY to copy the characters to the clipboard. Go into your document, move the cursor to the appropriate location, and select PASTE from the Edit menu.

Windows 95 Undo

To undo a Windows 95 operation, press Ctrl-Z or Alt-Backspace to go back a step and start over.

Windows 95J

The Japanese version of Windows 95. It is expected to be released by Microsoft and NEC by the end of 1995.

Windows accelerator

A graphics accelerator with a driver for Windows. See *graphics accelerator*.

windows environment

(1) Any operating system, operating system extension or application program that provides multiple windows on screen. Windows, OS/2, Mac, Motif and X Windows are operating system examples.

(2) (Windows environment) Refers to computers run by and applications running under Windows 3.x, Windows 95 and/or Windows NT.

Windows for Workgroups

Also known as *WFW*, it is a version of Windows 3.1 that includes peer-to-peer networking and electronic mail. Users can share files and printers and send messages to WFW and Windows 95 users on the network. Microsoft's Workgroup Add-On for MS-DOS upgrades DOS and Windows 3.1 computers to connect to WFW and Windows 95 users.

WFW's network drivers use a small amount of conventional memory (4-15KB), which helps installation in fully-loaded PCs. WFW also includes 32-bit file access, which bypasses DOS and replaces SmartDrive with another disk cache for increased performance. This is not the same as Windows' 32-bit disk access, which drives the disk controller directly (see *FastDisk*).

Windows help system

Windows provides a help system that almost all software developers use to provide online help to customers. The help screens appear in windows so that instructions can be displayed side by side with the application itself. You can keep the help on screen as long as you need it. The help index is displayed by pressing F1 in all applications.

Help screens can be developed by technically-oriented users as well as programmers. The text is written in a word processor, such as Word for Windows, which can import and export RTF files. Common word processing formatting, such as underlined text, hidden text and footnotes, is used to create links from one item to another. The RFT file is compiled into final form by the Windows help compiler, which is part of the Windows SDK.

Windows memory limitation

No matter how much memory you have in your Windows 3.1 PC, you never seem to have enough. The more you get used to Windows, the more you want to keep all the applications open that you use during the day. Unfortunately, each one takes up a certain amount of memory.

If you get an "Out of Memory" message often, there are several things you can do as a routine.

Keep windows minimized rather than full screen.

Keep the clipboard empty.

Turn off the desktop wallpaper in Control Panel. Wallpaper uses memory.

Check your permanent swap file. The larger the swap file, the more applications can be "rolled out" to disk temporarily.

If all else fails, closing one or more applications should give you enough room to open up another application.

System Resources

No matter how much actual RAM or virtual memory (swap file) you have,

Windows 3.1 uses only two 64K regions of memory to keep track of its active applications. When an application is active in a window, each of the application's components (windows, dialog boxes, icons, buttons, etc.) uses up several bytes of this "System Resources" memory.

Windows will tell you there is "Not enough memory..." when either of the regions get close to full. There's nothing you can do but unload one or more applications.

In addition, when these memory regions are filled more than half way, strange things can occur. Select About from your Program Manager's Help menu and look at System Resources. When this number gets below 30%, watch out, anything can happen.

In Windows 95, the situation has improved greatly. Windows 95 uses much larger memory buffers to hold the resources it needs.

Windows Metafile

A Windows file format that holds vector graphics, bitmaps and text. It uses the .WMF file extension for 16-bit Windows and the .EMF extension for 32-bit Windows (see *EMF*). The Windows Metafile is Windows' preferred vector format, since it contains actual Windows commands (GDI calls) to draw the images. It is also used by programs to hold data between sessions, and, Windows sometimes uses it for temporary storage.

The Aldus Placeable Metafile is a PageMaker variation that contains a header indicating into what size rectangle the object will be rendered.

Windows network

Also called a *Microsoft network* or a *Microsoft Windows network*, it is a local area network made up of Windows for Workgroups, Windows 95 and Windows NT computers, which all have built-in networking capabilities.

Windows NT

(Windows New Technology) An advanced 32-bit operating system from Microsoft for 386s and up, MIPS, Alpha and PowerPC CPUs. Introduced in 1993, NT does not use DOS, it is a self-contained operating system. NT runs NT-specific applications as well as DOS and Windows applications.

Features include peer-to-peer networking, preemptive multitasking, multithreading, multiprocessing, fault tolerance and support for the Unicode character set. NT provides extensive security features and continually tests the validity of application requests even after the application has been opened.

Windows NT supports 2GB of virtual memory for applications and 2GB for its own use. Windows NT and Windows NT Workstation are the first and second releases of the client version. Windows NT Advanced Server (NTAS) and Windows NT Server (NTS) are first and second releases of the server version, which supports symmetric multiprocessing and provides transaction processing for hundreds of online users. NT supports a dual boot feature.

In its first year on the market, the client version of NT has not caught on, but the server versions are increasingly being used. It is expected that Windows NT will become a predominant server operating system in the future.

Windows on Windows

The module within Windows NT that emulates Windows 3.1 applications. When a Windows 3.1 application calls Windows, the calls are converted into their NT equivalents and run in 32-bit native mode.

Windows out of memory

See *Windows memory limitation*.

windows program
(1)Software that adds a windows capability to an existing operating system.
(2) An application program written to run under Windows.

Windows requirements
Windows places far more demands of a PC than does DOS. A fast display adapter is also as important as a fast CPU. Today, all VGA cards have built-in graphics acceleration for Windows; however, some are much faster than others. To get more utility and enjoyment from Windows, obtain the largest monitor you can afford. Following are the recommended requirements.

	Word processing, database, spreadsheets:	CAD, imaging, desktop publishing:
CPU:	486/25	Pentium/90
Bus:	ISA	ISA/PCI
RAM:	8-16MB	32MB+
Hard disk:	500MB	1GB
Monitor:	17"	21"
Resolution:	800x600	1024x768, 1280x1024

Multimedia for loading programs:	2x CD-ROM	
games/video/interaction:		4x CD-ROM, sound board and speakers

Windows Resource Kit
Windows technical documentation from Microsoft written for support personnel. It is a comprehensive document with over 500 pages of technical details that includes flow charts and a chapter on troubleshooting. The text has been licensed by WUGNET, the Windows Users Group Network, and compiled into a Windows help system with hypertext links. See *WUGNET.*

Windows Resources
See *Windows memory limitation.*

Windows SDK
A set of development utilities for writing Windows applications in Microsoft C. It provides tools for creating custom cursors, fonts and icons, bitmaps, menus and online help.

Windows shell
An add-on user interface for Windows. There are many Windows shells available that streamline the Windows interface by providing such features as foldering, customized toolbars and quick access to the DOS command line. Windows shells can replace Program Manager and File Manager or coexist with them side by side. They often come with a variety of utility programs.

Windows SNA APIs
Programming interfaces that allow Windows applications to communicate with SNA protocols and functions, such as HLLAPI and APPC.

Windows swap file
A disk file used by Windows for its virtual memory. A virtual memory system temporarily stores segments of the application on disk when there is not enough memory to hold all the programs called for.

Windows 3.1

By default, in 386 Enhanced Mode, Windows 3.1 creates a temporary swap file (WIN386.SWP), which it dynamically enlarges and reduces and then abandons at the end of each session. Creating a permanent swap file (hidden files SPART.PAR and 386SPART.PAR) improves speed because it guarantees an amount of contiguous virtual memory space.

To free up disk space, you can delete or reduce the size of the permanent swap file (select Control Panel/386 Enhanced/Virtual Memory/Change).

Windows 95

Windows 95 creates only a temporary swap file (WIN386.SWP) that is dynamically sized and abandoned. It can also reside on a compressed drive as long as it is under the control of the DRVSPACE.VXD Protected Mode driver. Windows 95 can use the permanent swap file created in Windows 3.1, but cannot reduce its size to less than the original file size.

To adjust the Windows 95 swap file, double click on the System Control Panel and select the Performance tab, then Virtual Memory.

Windows Telephony

See *TAPI.*

WINFILE.EXE

The program name for File Manager in Windows 3.x and Windows 95.

WinG

(WINdows Games) A programming interface (API) that lets Windows application developers access the video frame buffer directly. It allows game programs to be written to run as fast in Windows as they do under DOS.

WINGZ

A presentation-oriented Macintosh spreadsheet from Informix Software., Menlo Park, CA. Text, graphs and charts, scanned images, freehand illustration and spreadsheet data can be combined. When data is updated, related graphics and numerical references within the text are changed.

WIN.INI

(WINdows INItialization) A Windows configuration file that describes the current state of the Windows environment. It contains hundreds of entries and is read by Windows on startup. It tells Windows such things as which programs to load or run automatically, if any, what the various screen, keyboard and mouse settings are, what the desktop looks like (icon spacing, wallpaper, colors, etc.) and what fonts are used. Information in WIN.INI is grouped by section headers, which are names enclosed in brackets. For example, the [Colors] section contains the colors selected by the user for window borders, titles, backgrounds and so forth.

The information in WIN.INI is updated by Windows when you change various defaults; however, the file can also be edited with a text editor or a word processor that imports ASCII files. Sections in WIN.INI are added by many application install programs under their own section header and are used to inform the application about the current defaults. SYSTEM.INI is another major Windows configuration file that is read at startup. See *SYSTEM.INI.*

Winmark

A unit of performance based on Ziff-Davis' PC Labs Winbench tests. Graphics Winmarks rate Windows video performance as a weighted average of 12 benchmarks. Common VGA adapters are rated around two million Winmarks. Fast graphics accelerators using local buses can achieve 50 million Winmarks and more. Winbench Version 3.1 provides more accurate Winmark tests and avoids slanted

results from "benchmark-aware" drivers used in some graphics accelerator boards. It is necessary to know which Winmark version is being used for the test. Version 4.0 reports fewer Winmarks for the same performance than Version 3.1.
Disk Winmarks rate the speed of disks and disk caching. See *DOSmark*.

Win-OS/2

(WINdows-OS/2) The Windows functionality in OS/2 Version 2.x. OS/2 Version 2.x contains the original Windows source code.

WINS

(Windows Internet Naming Service) Software from Microsoft that lets users locate computers on remote networks automatically. It runs under Windows NT Server and maintains a database of computer names and their physical IP address. In inhouse TCP/IP networks as well as the Internet, every computer is identified by an IP address. WINS maps the host name to the IP address.
When a computer is moved to another subnet and a new IP address is assigned by DHCP, the WINS database is updated.

Winsock API

(WINdows SOCKets API) A common programming interface between a Windows application and the TCP/IP protocol. Most TCP/IP stacks designed to run under Windows and most Windows software that communicates via TCP/IP are Winsock compliant. The Winsock routines are implemented as a dynamic link library (DLL). The WINSOCK.DLL file is often included and installed with Internet utilities.

Winsock client

A Windows program that communicates to a TCP/IP-based communications network, such as UNIX or the Internet.

WinWord

See *Microsoft Word*.

wireframe modeling

In CAD, a technique for representing 3-D objects, in which all surfaces are visibly outlined in lines, including the opposite sides and all internal components that are normally hidden from view. Compared to surface and solid modeling, wireframe modeling is the least complex method for representing 3-D images.

A Wireframe Image
(Drawing courtesy of CADKEY, Inc.)

wireless

Radio transmission via the airwaves. Various communications techniques are used to provide wireless transmission including infrared line of sight, cellular, microwave, satellite. packet radio and spread spectrum. See *Ardis, Mobitex, FDMA, TDMA, CDMA* and *CDPD*.

wire wrap

An early method of wiring circuit boards. A tool strips the end of the wire and coils it. The coil is pressed onto a metal prong on the board.

wiring closet

The central distribution or servicing point for cables in a network.

wizard

Instructional help that guides the user through a series of steps to accomplish a task.

wizzy wig

See *WYSIWYG*.

WK1, WKS

Lotus 1-2-3 Version 2.0 and Version 1A file extensions.

WMF

See *Windows Metafile*.

WO

See *write once*.

wobby

See *Wabi*.

word

(1)The computer's internal storage unit. Refers to the amount of data it can hold in its registers and process at one time. A word is often 16 bits, in which case 32 bits is called a double word. Given the same clock rate, a 32-bit computer processes four bytes in the same time it takes a 16-bit machine to process two.
(2) The primary text element, identified by a word separator (blank space, comma, etc.) before and after a group of contiguous characters.
(3) See *Microsoft Word*.

word addressable

A computer that can address memory only on word boundaries. Contrast with *byte addressable*.

WordBASIC

A subset of Microsoft QuickBASIC with added word processing functions used to customize Microsoft Word word processors.

Word for Windows

See *Microsoft Word*.

WordPerfect

A full-featured word processing program from WordPerfect Corporation. Introduced in 1980 for the Data General mini, WordPerfect had once become the most widely used word processor in the world, running on all major personal computers and workstations.

Version 5.0 introduced significant improvements that included desktop publishing features and a WYSIWYG preview mode. Version 5.1 added menus.

A Windows version was introduced as Version 5.1 to keep it in sync with the DOS version. In 1993, Version 6.0 for DOS added significant features including new graphics modes, scalable fonts, and built-in fax, e-mail and spreadsheet functions. As of January 1994, WordPerfect indicated that, except for interim releases to keep it file compatible with the Windows version, WordPerfect for DOS will not be upgraded.

WordPerfect Corporation

(WordPerfect Corporation, Orem, UT) Founded in 1979 as Satellite Software International by Alan Ashton, Bruce Bastian and Don Owens. Its first product, SSI*WP, was a word processor for the Data General minicomputer. In 1980, W. E. Pete Peterson, Bastian's brother-in-law, joined the company as office manager and later became executive vice president.

In 1982, WordPerfect was introduced, a version of SSI*WP for the IBM PC. At the time, WordStar was number one, and there were several other word processors available for the PC. Yet, over time, WordPerfect outsold them all. In 1986, SSI was renamed WordPerfect Corporation.

For an interesting inside story by Pete Peterson on how the company got started and grew into a software giant without external financing, read his book, "AlmostPerfect," published by Prima Publishing, Rocklin, CA 95677, 916/786-0426, ISBN 1-55958-477-7.

In 1994, WordPerfect was acquired by Novell.

WordPerfect Office

See *Group Wise.*

Word Pro

A full-featured Windows word processing program from Lotus. The successor to Ami Pro, Word Pro provides groupware features that allow documents to be created and edited collaboratively. It also includes version control, which is used to track a document's updates. It is tightly integrated with Lotus Notes via the Notes F/X technology.

The original Ami Pro was developed by Samna Corporation and was one of the first full-featured word processors for Windows. It was later acquired by Lotus and then superseded by Word Pro.

word processing

The creation of text documents. Except for labels and envelopes, it has replaced the electric typewriter in most offices, because of the ease in which documents can be edited, searched and reprinted.

Advanced word processors function as elementary desktop publishing systems. Although there are still machines dedicated only to word processing, most word processing is performed on general-purpose computers using word processing software.

Functions of a Full-featured Word Processor	**Text editing** Text can be changed by deleting it, typing over it or by inserting additional text within it. **Word wrap and centering** Words that extend beyond the right margin are wrapped around to the next line. Text can be centered between left and right margins. **Search and replace, move and copy** Any occurrence of text can be replaced with another block of text. You can mark a

block of text and move it elsewhere in the document or copy it throughout the document.

Layout settings
Margins, tabs, line spacing, indents, font changes, underlining, boldface and italics can be set and reset anywhere within the document.

Headers, footers and page numbering
Headers and footers are common text printed on the top and bottom of every page. Headers, footers and page numbering can be set and reset anywhere within the doucment. Page numbering in optional Roman numerals or alphabetic letters is common.

Style sheets
After designing a document, its format can be used again. Layout codes (margins, tabs, fonts, etc.) can be stored in a style sheet file and applied to a new document.

Mail merge
Creates customized letters from a form letter and a list of names and addresses. The list can be created as a document or can be imported from popular database formats.

Math and sorting
Columns of numbers can be summed and simple arithmetic expressions can be computed. Lines of text can be reordered into ascending (A-Z) or descending (Z-A) sequence.

Preview, print and group print
A document can be previewed before it is printed to show any layout change that may not normally show on screen (page breaks, headers, footers, etc.). Documents can be printed individually or as a group with page numbers consecutively numbered from the first to the last document.

Footnotes
Footnote entries can be made at any place in the document, and the footnotes printed at the end of a page or document.

Spelling check and Thesauras
Spelling for an individual word, marked block of text or an entire document can be checked. When words are in doubt, possible corrections are suggested. Advanced systems can correct the misspellings automatically the next time. A thesaurus displays synonyms for the word at the current cursor location.

File management
Documents can be copied, renamed and deleted, and directories, or folders, can be created and deleted from within the program. Advanced systems set up a purge list of names or glimpses of document contents in order to allow a user to easily rid the disk of unwanted files.

Advanced Functions

Windows
Allows two or more documents to be worked on at the same time. Text can be moved or copied from one document to the other.

Columns
Columns can be created in all word processors by tabbing to a tab stop. However, true column capability wraps words to the next line within each column. Columns re required for writing resumes with employer information on the left and work history on the right. Script writing also requires column capability. Magazine-style columns flow words from the bottom of one column to the top of the next.

Tables of contents and indexes

Tables of contents and indexes can be generated from entries typed throughout the document.

Desktop publishing

Graphics can be merged into the text and either displayed on screen with the text or in a preview mode before printing. A graphic object can be resized (scaled), rotated and anchored so that it remains with a particular segment of text. Rules and borders can also be created within the text.

Graphics-based Vs Text-based

Graphics-based programs (Windows, Macintosh, etc.) show a close facsimile on screen of the typefaces that will be printed. Text-based programs always show the same type size on screen.

Graphics-based systems are far superior for preparing newsletters and brochures that contain a variety of font sizes. Text-based screens are fine for office typing or for documents with a simple format. They are also very responsive and good for creative writing.

Format Standards

Every major word processing program generates its own proprietary codes for layout settings. For example, in WordStar, ^PB turns on and off boldface. In WordPerfect 5.x, [BOLD] turns boldface on, and [bold] turns it off.

Conversion programs are used to translate documents from one format to another. If a conversion program doesn't exist for the two required formats, multiple search & replace commands can be performed on the original document. However, if the same code turns a mode on as well as off, as in the WordStar example above, the codes have to be changed manually one at a time.

The User Interface

Word processing programs run from the ridiculous to the sublime. Some of the most awkward programs have sold well. As a novice, it's difficult to tell a good one from a bad one. It takes time to explore the nuances. Also, what's acceptable for the slow typist can be horrendous for the fast typist.

Repetitive functions such as centering and changing display attributes (boldface, italics, etc.) should be a snap. Changing margins, tabs, indents and fonts should also be easy.

The most important components in word processing hardware are the keyboard and screen. The feel of a keyboard is personal, but proper key placement is critical. Display screens should have the highest resolution possible, and color screens are better than monochrome as long as the program allows the user to change colors.

word processing machine

A computer that is specialized for only word processing functions.

word processor

(1) Software that provides word processing functions on a computer.

(2) A computer specialized for word processing. Until the late 1970s, word processors were always dedicated machines. Today, personal computers have replaced almost all dedicated word processors.

word separator

A character that separates a word, such as a blank space, comma, period, -, ? and !.

WordStar

A full-featured PC word processing program from Corel Corporation, Ottawa, Ontario. Introduced in 1978 for CP/M machines, it was the first program to give full word processing capabilities to personal computer users at far less cost than the dedicated word processors of the time. Many WordStar keyboard commands have become de facto standards.

word wheel

A lookup method in which each character that is typed in moves the on-screen index to the closest match. By watching the index move character by character, you can easily tell if you have made a typo. In addition, you can get to the beginning of a word group quickly and then scroll to the word or phrase you are looking for. The DOS and Windows versions of this database use a word wheel.

word wrap

A word processing feature that moves words to the next line automatically as you type based on the current right margin setting. Some word processing programs allow word wrap to be turned off for writing source code.

workflow

The automatic routing of documents to the users responsible for working on them. Workflow is concerned with providing the information required to support each step of the business cycle. The documents may be physically moved over the network or maintained in a single database with the appropriate users given access to the data at the required times. Triggers can be implemented in the system to alert managers when operations are overdue.

Although there is overlap in terminology and functions, a workflow system is generally different than a workgroup, or groupware, system. Workgroup systems are concerned more with information sharing and threaded discussions, rather than step-by-step processes.

For an excellent book on the subject of workflow, read "The Workflow Imperative" by Thomas M. Koulopoulos, published by Van Nostrand Reinhold, ISBN 0-442-01975-0.

workflow automation

See *workflow*.

workgroup

Two or more individuals who share files and databases. LANs designed around workgroups provide electronic sharing of required data. See *groupware* and *workflow*.

Workgroups

See *Windows for Workgroups*.

workgroup system

Same as *groupware*.

working directory

See *current directory*.

Workplace

An earlier umbrella term from IBM for a set of strategies and system software technologies for developing future products. It included the use of a microkernel-based operating system, object technologies (SOM/DSOM) and voice and pen recognition. Only the term was dropped, not the technology development.

Workplace Shell

The primary component of the OS/2 2.x user interface, which provides the equivalent functionality of Program Manager and File Manager in Windows. The Workplace Shell is extensible and application developers may use Workplace Shell library functions when developing programs.

worksheet

Same as *spreadsheet*.

worksheet compiler

Same as *spreadsheet compiler*.

workstation

(1) A high-performance, single-user microcomputer or minicomputer that is used for graphics, CAD, CAE, simulation and scientific applications. It is typically a RISC-based computer that runs under some variation of UNIX. High-end PCs (Pentium, PowerPC, etc.) increasingly take market share from the low-end workstation models. According to Computer Reseller News, in 1994, approximately 780,000 workstations were sold worldwide, up from 622,000 in 1993. The breakdown of the largest vendors was 282,000 from Sun, 154,000 from HP and 101,000 from IBM. Digital and Silicon Graphics (SGI) were next in order of sales.
(2) A personal computer in a network. In this context, a workstation is the same as a client. Contrast with *server* and *host*.
(3) In the telecom industry, a combined telephone and computer.
(4) Any terminal or personal computer.

World Wide Web

An Internet service that links documents by providing hypertext links from server to server. It allows a user to jump from document to related document no matter where it is stored on the Internet. World Wide Web client programs, or Web browsers, such as Mosaic and NetScape, allow users to browse "the Web."
Developed at the European Center for Nuclear Research (CERN) in Geneva, it was created to link research information between different locations. WWW documents are structured with format codes and hypertext links using the HyperText Markup Language, or HTML. A home page is created for each server with links to other documents locally and throughout the Internet.
The Web has become a centerpiece of Internet activity, because its documents can contain both text and graphics, and it is quickly turning the Internet into an online shopping mall. In 1994, Web traffic increased more than 18 times that of the previous year.
For an index of Web sites, see *Yahoo*.

World Wide Web

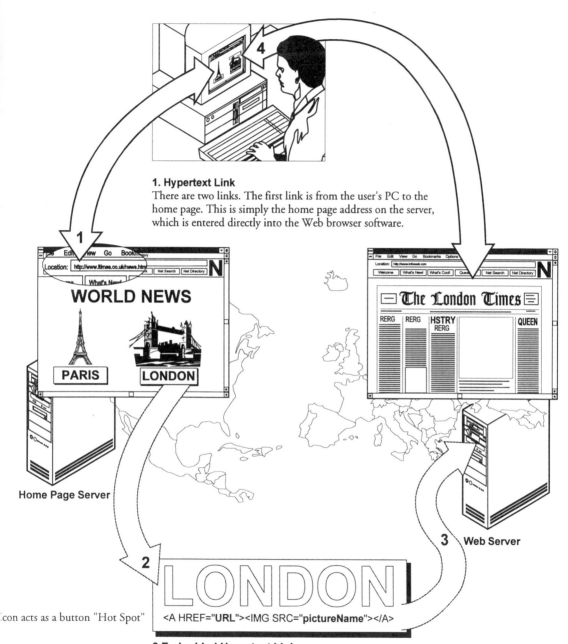

1. Hypertext Link
There are two links. The first link is from the user's PC to the home page. This is simply the home page address on the server, which is entered directly into the Web browser software.

WORLD NEWS

PARIS   LONDON

The London Times

| RERG | RERG | HSTRY RERG | | QUEEN |

Home Page Server

3 Web Server

con acts as a button "Hot Spot"

2 LONDON

`<A HREF="URL"><IMG SRC="pictureName"></A>`

2.Embedded Hypertext Link
The home page contains the links to documents on other servers(**3**). The syntax embedded within the home page for each link is shown above. The URL is the path to the file, and the picture is the icon that is pressed to activate the link; the syntax might read as follows:

`<A HREF="http://www.ltimes.co.uk/news.html"><IMG SRC="ltimes.gif"></A>`

WorldWorx

A multimedia network service from AT&T that provides point-to-point and multipoint connections between remote videoconferencing stations.

worm

(1) A destructive program that replicates itself throughout disk and memory, using up the computers resources and eventually putting the system down. See *virus* and *logic bomb*.

(2) A program that moves through a network and deposits information at each node for diagnostic purposes or causes idle computers to share some of the processing workload.

(3) (WORM) (Write Once Read Many) An optical disk that can be recorded only once. Updating requires destroying the existing data (all 0s made 1s), and writing new data to an unused part of the disk.

There are two kinds of WORM technologies. Ablative WORM is the traditional WORM technology that makes a permanent change in the optical material. Continuous composite write (CCW) WORM is an optional mode in 5.25" magneto-optic drives that emulates a WORM drive. The data is not permanently changed, but the drive contains firmware that ensures that recorded areas are not rewritten.

WOSA

(Windows Open System Architecture) An umbrella term for a variety of programming interfaces from Microsoft that are designed to provide application interoperability across the Windows environment. It provides standards between Windows clients and servers, allowing Windows applications to access services on the network from any software provider (database manager, document manager, network services, etc.) that supports a WOSA standard.

WOSA provides a common denominator for front-end Windows applications to access back-end services from different vendors. For example, any WOSA-compliant query program from one vendor can gain access to any WOSA-compliant DBMS from any another vendor. WOSA-compliant word processors can store documents in WOSA-compliant document management system. Different mail programs can send messages to each other and so on. See *SPI*.

WOSA Interface	Provides access to
ODBC	Databases (DBMSs)
MAPI	Messaging systems
TAPI	Telephone network services
LASPI	Software licensing
Windows SNA	IBM SNA networks
Windows Sockets	Internet, TCP/IP networks
Microsoft RPC	Run remote procedures
Financial Services	Banking services
WOSA/XRT	News, stock market, etc.

WOW

See *Windows on Windows*.

WP

See *word processing* and *WordPerfect*.

WPcom

See *write precompensation*.

WPS

(1) See *Workplace Shell.*
(2) (Windows Printing System) A printing system for Windows and the LaserJet II and III from Microsoft. It includes a cartridge for the printer and an enhanced printer driver, which collectively improve performance and provide more feedback on the status of the printer.
(3) (Word Processing System) A Chinese word processor developed by Jinshan. It was originally developed for DOS and later for Windows.

WRAM

(Window **RAM**) A type of RAM developed by Samsung Electronics that is optimized for display adapters. Although faster than VRAM, it uses the same type of dual-ported structure that simultaneously refreshes the screen while text and images are being drawn in the memory. See *video RAM.*

Wrist Pro

A wrist support from Wrist Pro, St. Louis, MO, that provides a multi-level platform that keeps the wrist in a neutral wrist position.

wrist rest

A platform used to raise the wrist to keyboard level for typing.

wrist support

A product that prevents and provides a therapy for carpal tunnel syndrome by keeping the hands in a neutral wrist position.

write

To store data in memory or record data onto a storage medium, such as disk and tape. Read and write is analogous to play and record on an audio tape recorder.

write access

Authorization to record or update data stored in the computer.

write back cache

A disk or memory cache that supports the caching of writing. Data normally written to memory or to disk by the CPU is first written into the cache. During idle machine cycles, the data is written from the cache into real memory or onto disk. Write back caches improve performance, because a write to the high-speed cache is faster than to normal RAM or disk.

A write back cache for disks adds a degree of risk, because the data stays in memory longer. Although it is generally no more than a few seconds until the data is written to disk, if the computer crashes or is shut down before then, the data is lost. A write back cache for memory is no more or less risky than normal memory, because all memory loses its data when the power is turned off. See *write through cache.*

write cycle

The operation of writing data into a memory or storage device.

write error

The inability to store into memory or record onto disk or tape. Malfunctioning memory cells or damaged portions of the disk or tape's surface will cause those areas to be unusable.

write once

Refers to storage media that can be written to but not erased. WORM and CD-R disks are examples. See *rewritable*.

write once CD

See *CD-R*.

write only code

Jokingly refers to source code that is difficult to understand.

write precompensation

Using a stronger magnetic field to write data in sectors that are closer to the center of the disk. In CAV recording, in which the disk spins at a constant speed, the sectors closest to the spindle are packed tighter than the outer sectors.
One of the hard disk parameters stored in a PC's CMOS RAM is the WPcom number, which is the track where precompensation begins.

write protect

A mode that restricts erasing or editing a disk file. See *file protection*.

Write protect error

A DOS error message that means the floppy disk has been protected and data cannot be recorded on it. Either unprotect it or use another disk. See *file protection*.

write protect notch

A small, square cutout on the side of a 5.25" floppy disk used to prevent it from being written and erased. To enable the protection, the notch is covered with self-sticking tape. See *file protection*.

write through cache

A disk or memory cache that supports the caching of writing. Data written by the CPU to memory or to disk is also written into the cache. Write performance is not improved with this method. However, if a subsequent read operation needs that same data, read performance is improved, because the data is already in the high-speed cache. See *write back cache*.

WSI

See *wafer scale integration*.

WUGNET

(Windows Users Group NETwork, 126 E. State St., Media, PA 19063, 215/565-1861) An organization of Windows users and developers founded in 1988. It provides technical information, software resources and tools, CompuServe forums and newsletters.

WWW

See *World Wide Web*.

WXmodem

(Window Xmodem) A faster version of the Xmodem protocol that allows the sending system to transmit data without waiting for the receiving system to acknowledge the transfer.

WYSIWYG

(What You See Is What You Get) Pronounced "wizzy-wig." Refers to text and graphics appearing on screen the same as they print. To have WYSIWYG text, a screen font must be installed that matches each printer font. Otherwise, a 24-point font may display in correct size relationship to a 10-point font, but it won't look like the printed typeface.

It is almost impossible to get 100% identical representation, because screen and printer resolutions rarely match. Even a 300 dpi printer has a higher resolution than almost every monitor.

WYSIWYG

WYSIWYG MOL

(WYSIWYG More Or Less) Quite often what you get, when what you want is WYSIWYG!

X

x

In programming, symbol used to identify a hexadecimal number. For example, 0x0A and \x0A specify the hex number 0A. See *X Window*.

X.3

An ITU standard (1977) for a PAD (packet assembler/disassembler), which divides a data message into packets for transmission over a packet-switched network and reassembles them at the receiving side.

X11

The current version of the X Window System. X11R5 (Version 11, Release 5, Sept. 1991) provides a stable and feature-rich environment.

X12

An ANSI standard protocol for EDI. See *Tradacoms* and *EDIFACT.*

X.21

An ITU standard protocol for a circuit switching network.

X.25

An ITU standard (1976) for packet switching networks. Public X.25 communications networks have been available worldwide for many years, but they are typically limited to 56 Kbps and less. New packet-switched networks employ frame relay and SMDS technologies rather than X.25. See *packet switching.*

X.28

An ITU standard (1977) for exchange of information between a DTE and a PAD; commonly known as PAD commands.

X.29

An ITU standard (1977) for exchange of information between a local PAD and a remote PAD; procedures for interworking between PADs.

X.32

An ITU standard (1984) for connecting to an X.25 network by dial up. It defines how the network identifies the terminal for billing and security purposes and how default parameters are negotiated for the connection.

X.400

An OSI and ITU standard messaging protocol. It is an application layer protocol (layer 7 in the OSI model). X.400 has been defined to run over various network transports including Ethernet, X.25, TCP/IP and dial-up lines. See *messaging protocol* and *CMC.*
The format of an X.400 address is:

```
c=   /admd=   /prmd=   /o=   /s=   /g=
```

```
c       country
admd    administrative management domain
        (public e-mail service)
prmd    private management domain
        (inhouse e-mail)
o       organization
s       surname
g       given name
```

See *X.400 API Association* and *messaging protocol.*

X.400 API Association

Known as the *XAPIA*, it is a consortium dedicated to standardizing X.400 and other specifications, such as the CMC messaging API. For information, contact Leslie Schroeder Press Relations, 10151 Western Drive, Cupertino, CA 95014, 408/446-9158.

X.445

An ITU standard for sending X.400 traffic over standard telephone lines. It is also known as the Asynchronous Protocol Specification (APS).

X.500

An OSI protocol for managing online directories of users and resources. X.500 can be used to support X.400 and other messaging systems, but it is not restricted to e-mail usage. It provides a hierarchical structure that fits the world's classification system: countries, states, cities, streets, houses, families, etc. The goal is to have a directory that can be used globally.

An X.500 directory is called a Directory Information Base (DIB) or white pages. The program that maintains the DIBs is called a Directory Server Agent (DSA). A Directory Client Agent (DCA) is used to search DSA sites for names and addresses. The X.500 specification was published in 1988, and the 1993 edition is interoperable with it. The 1993 edition includes replication and access control. Using the Directory Information Shadowing Protocol (DISP), replication allows a portion of the Directory Information Tree (DIT) to be copied between nodes. Access control provides a method to allow or deny access to a particular attribute of a directory entry based on the identity of the requesting user.

X.75

An ITU standard for connecting X.25 networks.

x86

Refers to the Intel 8086 CPU family (8086, 8088, 80186, 80286, 386, 486, Pentium). Starting with the 386, Intel has dropped the "80" prefix in its reference manuals. The x86 designation is also referenced as 80x86. The following list contains the members of the x86 family of CPUs.

	CPU #	Clock Speed (MHz)	Bus Size (bits)	Max RAM (———	Floppy Disk Bytes———)	Typical Hard disk (MB)	OS
16-bit CPUs	8088	5	8	1M	5.25" 360K	10-20	DOS, DR DOS
	8086	5-10	16	1M			
	286	6-12	16	16M	5.25" 1.2M	20-80	DOS, DR DOS OS/2 1.x
32-bit CPUs	386DX	16-40	32	4G	5.25" 1.2M	80-200	DOS, DR DOS
	386SX	16-33	16	16M	3.5" 1.44M	60-100	OS/2 1.x, 2.x
	386SL	20-25	16	32M		60-100	Windows NT
	486DX	25-100	32	4G		340-1GB	Windows 95
	486SX	20-40	32	4G		200-500	UNIX
	Pentium	60-150	64	4G		500-5GB	
	Pentium Pro	150-200	64	4G		1GB-20GB	

x86 clone

A CPU chip that is compatible with various models of the Intel x86 family. Companies such as AMD, Cyrix and NexGen make x86 clones.

XA

See *CD-ROM XA* and *370/XA*.

XAPIA

See *X.400 API Association*.

x-axis

See *x-y matrix*.

Xbase

Refers to dBASE-like languages such as Clipper and FoxPro. Originally almost identical to dBASE, new commands and features over the years have made Xbase languages only partially dBASE compatible.

X-based

See *X Window* and *Xbase*.

X Bitmap

A black and white raster graphics format used in the UNIX environment. It uses the .XBM extension and is often used as a hypertext icon on a Web page. Many Web browsers treat the white parts of the image as transparent, or background, which takes on the color of the underlying window.

XBM

The file extension used by an X Bitmap image. See *X Bitmap*.

XCMD

(eXternal CoMmanD) A user-developed HyperCard command written in a language such as C or Pascal. See *XFCN*.

Xcopy

A DOS and OS/2 utility that copies files and subdirectories.

XDB Enterprise Server

A relational database management system (DBMS) for DOS, Windows, Windows NT and OS/2 from XDB Systems, Inc., Laurel, MD. XDB is fully compatible with IBM's DB2 database.

XDOS

Software from Hunter Systems, Inc., Mountain View, CA, that converts Intel x86 executable code into Motorola 68020 code ready to run under UNIX. A PC program can be translated into a running program on a UNIX-based 68020 computer.

XDR

(EXternal Data Representation) A data format developed by Sun that is part of its networking standards. It deals with integer size, byte ordering, data representation, etc. and is used as an interchange format. Different systems convert to XDR for sending and from XDR upon receipt.

XENIX

See *SCO XENIX*.

xerography

See *electrophotographic*.

XFCN

(eXternal FunCtioN) A user-developed HyperCard function that is written in a language, such as C or Pascal. XFCNs usually return a value. See *XCMD*.

xfr

Often used as an abbreviation for "transfer" in may electronic and communications terms and phrases.

XGA

(EXtended Graphics Array) An IBM video display standard (1990) optimized for graphical user interfaces. It adds 132 column text to VGA, plus additional resolutions up to 1024x768 with 256 colors interlaced. XGA-2 (1992) provides non-interlaced 1024x768x64K.

XGML

A family of text manipulation software for PCs, Macs, IBM mainframes, UNIX and others from Software Exoterica Corporation, Ottawa, Ontario. With strong support for SGML, it includes XTRAN, a language that translates, matches and links text.

x-height

In typography, the height of the letter x in lower case. Point size includes the x-height, the height of the ascender and the height of the descender. See *typeface*.

XIE

(XImage Extension) Extensions to the X Window system that enhance its graphics capability. It allows the desktop terminal or PC (the server) to retrieve various types of compressed images from the client and be able to manipulate them.
Remember, in X, the client and server are the opposite of what they are in client/server. See *X Window*.

XIP

(Execute In Place) The ability to execute a program directly from a memory card.

XL

See *Excel*.

Xlib

(X LIBrary) Functions in the X Window System. See *X toolkit*.

XLISP

A microcomputer version of the LISP programming language that has been in the public domain for a number of years.

XMI

A high-speed bus from Digital used in large VAX machines.

Xmodem

The first widely-used file transfer protocol for personal computers, developed by Ward Christensen for CP/M machines. Early versions used a checksum to detect errors. Later versions use the more effective CRC method (Xmodem-CRC). Programs typically include both methods and drop back to checksum if CRC is not present at the other end.

Xmodem transmits 128-byte blocks. Xmodem-1K improves speed by transmitting 1,024-byte blocks. Xmodem-1K-G transmits without acknowledgment (for error-free channels or when modems are self correcting), but transmission is cancelled upon any error.

XMP

(X/Open Management Protocol) A high-level network management protocol governed by X/Open. Network management software written to the XMP interface is shielded from the details of the underlying SNMP or CMIP protocols.

XMS

(eXtended Memory Specification) A programming interface that allows DOS programs to use extended memory in 286s and up. It provides a set of functions for reserving, releasing and transferring data to and from extended memory without conflict, including the high memory area (HMA). See *HIMEM.SYS* and *DOS extender*.

XMS Versus VCPI/DPMI

XMS, VCPI and DPMI all deal with extended memory. However, XMS allows data and programs to be stored in and retrieved from extended memory, whereas the VCPI and DPMI interfaces allow programs to "run" in extended memory.

XMT

In communications, an abbreviation for transmit.

XNS

(Xerox Network Services) An early networking protocol suite developed at Xerox's Palo Alto Research Center (PARC). XNS has been the basis for many popular network architectures including Novell's NetWare, Banyan's VINES and 3Com's 3+.

XNS Layer	XNSProtocols	OSI Layers	NetWare Protocols
4 Application		7	
3 Control		5 & 6	
2 Transport	SPP, PEP	4	SPX
1 Internet	IDP	3	IPX
0 Transmission	Ethernet	1 & 2	

xon-xoff

In communications, a simple asynchronous protocol that keeps the receiving device in synchronization with the sender. When the buffer in the receiving device is full, it sends an *x-off* signal (transmit off) to the sending device, telling it to stop transmitting. When the receiving device is ready to accept more, it sends the sending device an *x-on* signal (transmit on) to start again.

X/Open

A consortium of international computer vendors founded in 1984 to resolve standards issues. Incorporated in 1987 and based in London, North American offices are in San Francisco. Its purpose is to integrate evolving de facto and international standards in order to achieve an open environment, or CAE (Common Application Environent). XPG defines X/Open's specification, and VSX defines its testing and verification procedure.

In late 1993, Spec 1170 was announced, a specification that contains over 1,100 APIs. Spec 1170 was designed to provide a unified programming interface for UNIX.

X/Open is also responsible for governing the CDE graphical interface, yet one more attempt to provide a standard for UNIX. The first CDE products were introduced in early 1995. For information about X/Open, call 415/323-7992; in the U.K. 44-734-508311.

X/Open Portability Guide

Known as the *XPG*, it is a set of standards that specify compliance with X/Open's Common Application Environment (CAE). XPG3 (Release 3), introduced in 1989, specifies standards for UNIX System V Release 4.0.

X.PC

A communications protocol developed by McDonnell Douglas for connecting a PC to its Tymnet packet-switched public data network.

XPG

See *X/Open Portability Guide*.

X Pixelmap

An 8-bit raster graphics format used in the UNIX environment. It uses the .XPM extension and is similar to the X Bitmap format, but provides 256 colors. X Pixelmaps are often used for X Window icons and hypertext icons on Web pages.

X Pixmap

See *X Pixelmap*.

XPM

The file extension used by an X Pixelmap image. See *X Pixelmap*.

X protocol

The message format of the X Window System.

X server

The receiving computer in an X Window system. The X server displays the application that is running on a remote machine, which is the X client. See *X Window*.

X standard

See *X Window* and *X.400*.

XT

(1) (EXtended Technology) The first IBM PC with a hard disk, introduced in 1983. It still used the same 8088 CPU as the original PC and included 128KB of RAM and a 10MB hard drive. See *PC*.
(2) (Xt) See *X toolkit*.

XT bus

See *PC bus*.

XT class

Refers to first-generation PCs, which includes the first floppy-disk PC, the actual "XT" PC with a hard disk and all compatibles that use the 8088 or 8086 or compatible CPU and an 8-bit bus.

X terminal

A terminal with built-in X server capability.

The XT
In 1983, the 10MB hard disk and 1MBof memory on the XT was considered serious state-of-the-art.

X toolkit

Development software for building X Window applications. Typically includes a widget set, X Toolkit Intrinsics (Xt) libraries for managing the widget set and the X Library (Xlib).

XTP

(Xpress Transfer Protocol) A research transport protocol designed by Greg Chesson of Silicon Graphics. It is a type of lightweight protocol designed for high-speed networks and provides services at layers 3 and 4 of the OSI model.

XTP is flexible and can select rate and flow control. In order to handle different traffic; for example, transactions versus realtime video, XTP's "universal receiver" has the transmitting station tell the receiver when to acknowledge. ANSI's version is called HSTP (High Speed Transport Protocol).

XTRAN

See *XGML*.

XTreeGold

File manager programs for DOS and Windows from Symantec (originally Central Point Software). Introduced in 1985 for DOS by the Xtree Co., Xtree was the first program to help users manage hard disks by providing a hierarchical display of directories. Along with its file management functions, XtreeGold includes file viewers for over 100 formats.

Xtrieve

A menu-driven query and report language from Novell that accesses Btrieve files.

XVT

(EXtensible Virtual Toolkit) A developers toolkit for creating user interfaces across multiple environments from XVT Software, Inc., Boulder, CO. Programmers design the user interface by calling XVT functions, which are then translated to Windows, OS/2, Motif or the Mac.

X Window, X Windows

Formally "X Window System," also called "X Windows" and "X," it is a windowing system developed at MIT, which runs under UNIX and all major operating systems. X lets users run applications on other computers in the network and view the output on their own screen.

X generates a rudimentary window that can be enhanced with GUIs, such as Open Look and Motif, but does not require applications to conform to a GUI standard. The window manager component of the GUI allows multiple resizable, relocatable X windows to be viewed on screen at the same time.

X client software resides in the computer that performs the processing and X server software resides in the computer that displays it. Both components can also be in the same machine. This seems opposite to today's client/server terminology, but the concept is that the server is "serving up" the image. See *XIE*.

x-y matrix

A group of rows and columns. The x-axis is the horizontal row, and the y-axis is the vertical column. An x-y matrix is the reference framework for two-dimensional structures, such as mathematical tables, display screens, digitizer tablets, dot matrix printers and 2-D graphics images.

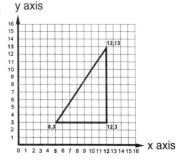

x-y monitor

In graphics, the display screen of a vector display terminal. The entire vector display comprises the monitor and vector graphics controller.

x-y plotter

Same as *plotter*.

XyWrite

Pronounced "zy-write." PC word processing programs from The Technology Group (XYQUEST division), Baltimore, MD. XyWrite word processors, including XyWrite III and XyWrite III Plus, have been used extensively by major newspapers and magazines throughout the country. XyWrite was noted for its typesetting orientation long before it was common to have the variety of fonts found in today's software.

XyWrite differs from most word processors in that it generates a pure ASCII file like a text editor. Format commands are embedded within the extended ASCII double left and right arrow characters, which can be revealed or kept hidden. When hidden, the command is displayed as a single triangle character in the text. XyWrite is also noted for its complete customizability. Using a programmer-oriented macro language, you can cause XyWrite to perform almost any text processing task. Menus and keyboard commands can also be customized. Up to nine document windows can be displayed on screen at the same time.

Signature, a version jointly developed by XYQUEST (Billerica, MA) and IBM, was designed to be the successor to XyWrite III Plus and IBM's DisplayWrite. It recognized XyWrite, DisplayWrite and DCA documents directly. XyWrite 4.0 for DOS and XyWrite for Windows, which also have this ability, are successors to both XyWrite III Plus and Signature.

Nota Bene, originally developed by Dragonfly Software, adds indexed text retrieval, bibliographic and citation management to XyWrite. It is a self-contained product using the XyWrite engine and is available separately. In 1992, The Technology Group acquired all of these products and created the XYQUEST division.

x-y-z matrix

A three-dimensional structure. The x and y axes represent the first two dimensions; the z axis, the third dimension. In a graphic image, the x and y denote width and height; the z denotes depth.

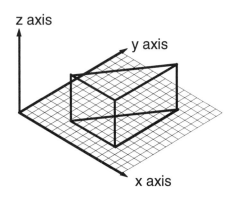

Y

yacc

(Yet Another Compiler Compiler) A UNIX compiler that is used to create C compilers. Part of its code is included in the generated compiler. See *bison*.

Yahoo

A World Wide Web site that maintains a directory of Web sites around the world. The URL for Yahoo is **http://www.yahoo.com**

y-axis

See *x-y matrix*.

Yellow Book

The standard for the physical format of a CD-ROM disk. The ISO 9660 standard defines the logical format for the disk. See *CD*.

Yellow Pages

See *NIS* and *naming service*.

YIQ

The color model used for color TV. The Y stands for luminosity or lightness, which was the original black and white TV signal. The I and Q were added to make color TV backward compatible with the black and white standard. Known as chromacity, the I and Q signals are the color differences that are derived from the difference between red, blue and the luminosity (I=red-Y, Q=blue-Y).

Ymodem

A file transfer protocol identical to Xmodem-1K plus batch file transfer (also called Ymodem Batch). It is faster than standard Xmodem and sends the file name before sending the data. Ymodem-G transmits without acknowledgment for error-free channels or when modems are self correcting, but transmission is cancelled upon any error.

YUV

The native signal format of video. When video is digitized and compressed (MPEG, Indeo, etc.), it is kept in YUV format, because it takes less storage than the RGB equivalent. In order to display YUV data on a monitor, it must be converted into RGB, which is known as *color space conversion*.

Z

Z

A mathematical language used for developing the functional specification of a software program. Developed in the late 1970s at Oxford University, IBM's CICS software is specified in Z.

Z39.50

An ANSI standard query language that is a simplified version of SQL. It is used on the Internet to search for documents. See *WAIS*.

Z80

An 8-bit microprocessor from Zilog Corporation that was the successor to the Intel 8080. The Z80 was widely used in first-generation personal computers that used the CP/M operating system. Subsequent Z180 and Z280 chips have also been widely used in embedded systems with more than a half billion shipped as of late 1994.

Z8000

A 16-bit microprocessor from Zilog Corporation that was the successor to the Z80. It was not widely used.

zap

A command that typically deletes the data within a file but leaves the file structure intact so that new data can be entered.

z-axis

The third dimension in a graphics image. The width is the x-axis and the height is the y-axis.

ZBR

(Zone Bit Recording) A technique for recording more bits on a disk. On a standard disk, each track contains the same number of bits even though the physical circumference of each track differs in length from the innermost shortest track to the outermost longest track. The disk rotates at a constant speed (CAV), and the clock, which governs the recording rate, is also constant. This results in denser bits in the center tracks while the outer tracks have more space between them.

In zone bit recording, also called zoned constant angular velocity (ZCAV), the disk is divided into a number of concentric zones with higher recording densities toward the outer tracks. The clock rate changes as the read/write head moves from zone to zone.

ZCAV

See *ZBR.*

ZD Net

Formerly ZiffNet, ZD Net is an online information service for PC users from Ziff-Davis Interactive, a division of Ziff-Davis Publishing Company. It provides a wide of variety of shareware and public domain software as well as technical forums and information. ZD Net can be accessed via PRODIGY and CompuServe. Address: One Athenaeum St., Cambridge, MA 02142. See *online services* and *shareware awards.*

zenix

See *SCO XENIX.*

zero-slot LAN

Refers to transmitting between computers over a serial or parallel port, thus freeing up an expansion slot normally used by LAN cards (NICs).

zero wait state

Refers to a high-speed memory that transfers its data immediately upon being accessed without waiting one or more machine cycles to respond.

ZiffNet

See *ZD Net*.

ZIF socket

(Zero Insertion Force socket) A chip socket that is easy to plug a chip into. Intel has popularized this type of socket with its OverDrive upgrades. The chip is dropped into the socket's holes and a small lever is turned to lock them in.

zinc air

A rechargeable battery technology that provides more charge per pound than nickel cadmium or nickel hydride and does not suffer from the memory effect. It uses a carbon membrane that absorbs oxygen, a zinc plate and potassium hydroxide as the electrolyte. AER Energy Systems, Smyrna, GA, is the pioneer in this emerging battery technology.

zip

(1) To compress a file with PKZIP. See *PK software*.
(2) (ZIP) (Zig-Zag Inline Package) Similar to a DIP, but smaller and tilted on its side for mounting on boards with limited space.
(3) (ZIP) A proprietary messaging protocol from IBM. PROFS uses ZIP for its e-mail transport.

Zip disk

A 3.5" removable disk drive from Iomega Corporation, Roy, UT. It uses design concepts from Iomega's Bernoulli technology as well as hard disks to provide 25MB and 100MB removable cartridges that are expected to have street prices of $10 and $20. Software bundled with the drive catalogs Zip disks to help users find the disk they need. A security utility can lock the files on the disk.

Zmodem

A file transfer protocol that has become very popular because it handles noisy and changing line conditions very well, including satellite transmission. It sends file name, date and size first, uses variable length blocks and CRC error correction. If a transmission is interrupted using Zmodem or Ymodem, Zmodem will transmit only the remainder of the file on the next try. This feature is extremely valuable when sending large files over noisy lines.

zoned constant angular velocity

See *ZBR*.

Zoo

A freeware compression program, including source code, used in UNIX, DOS and other environments.

zoom

To change from a distant view to a more close-up view (zoom in) and vice versa (zoom out). An application may provide fixed or variable levels of zoom. A video display board (graphics adapter) may also have built-in zoom, which provides zoom capability for everything that is displayed independent of and in addition to the application's zoom levels.

Zortech compilers

A series of C and C++ compilers from Zortech Inc., which was acquired by Symantec in 1991. Zortech compilers are now called Symantec compilers.

ZyIMAGE

Document management software for Windows from ZyLAB Inc., Gaithersburg, MD, that provides storage and retrieval for text documents, dBASE files and TIFF images. It provides full indexing on text, spreadsheet and data files and allows key words to be appended to TIFF files. ZyIMAGE includes the ZyINDEX system.

ZyINDEX

Text management software for DOS and Windows from ZyLAB Inc., Gaithersburg, MD. It indexes the full text of word processing documents, spreadsheets and dBASE files. ZyINDEX works with Calera Recognition Systems WordScan OCR program to provide integrated scanning, optical character recognition and indexing. See *ZyIMAGE*.

zywrite

See *XyWrite*.

0-9

0K

(Zero Kilobytes) Typically references motherboards that do not include memory as priced.

0x

In programming, the symbol for a hexadecimal number. See *x*.

1-bit DAC

(1-bit Digtal to Analog Converter) A serial method of converting digital samples back into analog form for amplification. Each bit of the sample is converted into its analog weight rather than all bits of the sample converted in parallel. See *ladder DAC*.

1.2M

Refers to the 1.2MB high-density 5.25" floppy disk used in PCs.

1.44M

Refers to the 1.44MB high-density 3.5" disk used in PCs.

10Base2

An Ethernet standard that uses a thin coaxial cable. It attaches to the network nodes via BNC connectors in the adapter cards. Also called *thin Ethernet, ThinWire* and *ThinNet*. See *Ethernet*.

10Base5

The original Ethernet standard that uses a thick coaxial cable. It attaches to the network nodes via transceivers that tap into the cable and provide a line to a 15-pin plug in the adapter card called an *AUI connector*. Also called *thick Ethernet, ThickWire* and *ThickNet*.

10BaseF

An Ethernet standard that uses optical fibers. All stations connect in a star configuration to a repeater or to a central concentrator. Connections are made via ST or SMA fiberoptic connectors. Adapter cards with AUI connectors are connected to 10BaseF networks via a fiber optic transceiver.
The 10BaseFL standard defines the link between the concentrator and a station; 10BaseFP defines a star-coupled network; 10BaseFB defines a fiber backbone. See *Ethernet*.

10BaseT

An Ethernet standard that uses twisted wire pairs (telephone wire). All stations connect in a star configuration to a central hub, also known as a *multiport repeater*. 10BaseT is widely used due to the lower cost and flexibility of installing twisted pair. See *Ethernet*.

16-bit

See *bit specifications*.

16-bit driver

A driver written for a 16-bit environment. See *Real Mode driver*.

16-bit sample

A sample of a sound wave based on measuring the wave on a scale of 65,536 increments. A "16-bit sound card" should mean that it takes 16-bit samples; however, it could also mean that it generates 8-bit samples, but fits into a 16-bit slot. See *8-bit sample*.

100BaseVG, 100VG-AnyLAN

A high-speed version of Ethernet (IEEE 802.12) developed by HP that supports Token Ring as well as 10BaseT networks. It is a shared media LAN like regular Ethernet, but transmits at 100 Mbps rather than 10 Mbps. It employs the Demand Priority access method rather than the original CSMA/CD method used in 10Base and 100BaseT Ethernets. Demand Priority is suited to videoconferencing, because it allows realtime voice and video packets to be given a higher priority than data. In the past, 100VG-AnyLAN has also been called *100BaseVG*. It is also called *Fast Ethernet*, although Fast Ethernet generally refers to 100BaseT.

100BaseT

A high-speed version of Ethernet (IEEE 802.3). Also called *Fast Ethernet*. 100BaseT transmits at 100 Mbps rather than 10 Mbps. Like regular Ethernet, Fast Ethernet is a shared media LAN. All nodes share the 100 Mbps bandwidth. 100BaseT uses the same CSMA/CD access method as regular Ethernet with some modification. Two cabling variations are provided. 100BaseTX uses two pairs of Category 5 UTP, and 100BaseT4 uses four pairs of Category 3 and above. Contrast with *100VG-AnyLAN*.

123, 1-2-3

See *Lotus 1-2-3*.

128-bit

See *bit specifications*.

128-bit graphics accelerator

A display adapter that has a pathway 128 bits wide between its on-board graphics processor and memory (video RAM).

1024x768

Standard super VGA resolution of 1,024 columns by 768 rows (lines). In the specification 1024x768x64K, the 64K is the number of colors. See *resolution*.

1280x1024

Standard super VGA resolution of 1,280 columns by 1,024 rows (lines). In the specification 1280x1024x64K, the 64K is the number of colors. See *resolution*.

1284

See *IEEE 1284*.

IBM 1401
The 1401 was extremely sophisticated for its time. The author was a programmer on the 1401 for the Pennsylvania Department of Revenue. Throughout the 1960s and with a paltry 12K of memory, the machine routinely processed all six million drivers in the state.

1401

A second-generation IBM computer introduced in 1959 and used until the late 1960s. It had 16K of core memory, six tape drives and used punched cards for input. It was an outstanding success due to its reliability (18,000 installed). For migration to IBM's third-generation computer, 1401 emulators were built into various System/360 models.

16450, 16550
See *UART.*

2B+D
See *ISDN.*

2B1Q
(2Binary 1Quaternary) An encoding method used in ISDN in which each pair of binary digits represents four discrete amplitude and polarity values.

2e
See *Apple II.*

23B+D
See *ISDN.*

24-bit color
Also called *true color*, it refers to using 24 bits, or three bytes, per pixel to represent a color image in a computer. The 24 bits allows up to 16,777,216 colors to be stored and displayed. See *bit depth* and *bit specifications.*

256-bit
See *bit specifications.*

286
The successor to the 8088 CPU used in the first PC (XT-class). Refers to the Intel 80286 CPU chip or to a PC (AT class) that uses it. It is more responsive than an XT and isn't limited to its infamous one-megabyte barrier, but is still sluggish for Windows and graphics-intensive applications. See *PC* and *x86.*

286 CPU Technical Specs

A 16-bit multitasking microprocessor in a 68-pin PGA, PLCC or LCC package. Has 15 16-bit registers including eight general-purpose. Operational modes: "Real Mode" performs as a fast 8086 CPU and addresses 1MB memory. "Protected Mode" addresses 16MB physical and 1GB virtual memory and provides access to memory protection capabilities. Contains 130,000 transistors.

286/12, 286/16...
The designation of CPU speed for a 286. The second number is the clock rate: 286/12 means 12MHz.

2000 time problem
The year 2000 presents a problem for many legacy systems whose databases were designed with two-byte year fields. Years ago, saving two bytes in a record meant alot more than it does today. A "00" in the year field is assumed to mean the year 1900, and financial calculations that deal with aging will be incorrect.
There are consultants that specialize in this and software than analyzes and patches systems to eliminate the problem. However, older information systems are often programmed by people that are no longer around and in languages that are difficult to support. Thus, many legacy systems are ticking time bombs, literally.

2780, 3780
Standard communications protocols for transmitting batch data. The numbers originated with early IBM remote job entry (RJE) terminals that included a card reader and a printer.

3Com

(3Com Corporation, Santa Clara, CA) Founded in 1979 by Bob Metcalfe, 3Com is a leading communications hardware vendor, offering a wide variety of network adapters, hubs and related products.

3Com used to develop and support a line of network operating systems, which it discontinued in 1993. 3+Share was a DOS-based network operating system for PC and Mac clients. 3+Open was OS/2 based and supported DOS, OS/2 and Mac clients.

3-D audio

Audio reproduction that simulates sounds coming from all directions. Using signal processing techniques as well as multiple speakers, 3-D audio is used in virtual reality and home theater systems.

3D Fax

A file transfer program for Windows from InfoImaging Technologies, Inc., Palo Alto, CA, that allows binary files to be transmitted via fax. The sending software encodes and converts the file into a printed image that is sent to the recipient's fax machine. Software on the receiving side, which is freely distributable, decodes the image into the original file format after it has been scanned into the computer.

3DO

A multimedia and video game technology from 3DO Company, Mountain View, CA. It is licensed to manufacturers and developers. The first 3DO player is Panasonic's REAL (Realistic Entertainment Active Learning) Multiplayer, which plays audio CDs and can be fitted for Video CDs.

3DO developers are able to create games from a large library of royalty-free sound effects, music, stills, clip art and film. The technology provides very high speeds for animation and can also provide a 3-D capability that is viewed through glasses.

3DO was founded by Trip Hawkins, one of Apple's earliest employees and founder of Electronic Arts software company. In 1990, Hawkins left Electronic Arts to start 3DO.

3DOF

See *6DOF*.

3-D sound

See *3-D audio*.

3D Studio

A 3-D modeling and animation program for DOS from AutoDesk, Inc., Sausalito, CA. It was the first program to bring professional animation and 3-D rendering from high-end workstations to the PC. Its 2D Shaper module lets you create 2-D shapes that become the cross sections of the 3-D models. 3D Lofter creates the underlying framework of the 3-D model, and 3D Editor is used to prepare the scene for rendering. In Release 4, the Keyframer animation module includes Inverse Kinematics, which links components so that they move together.

3GL

See *third-generation language*.

3.3v

(3.3 Volts) Refers to the amount of voltage required by the chips on newer personal computer motherboards. See *5v*.

3.5"

(1) Refers to the common 3 1/2 inch microfloppy disk used in personal computers.
(2) Refers to disk drives and other devices with a 3 1/2 inch wide form factor.

32-bit color

Using 24 bits per pixel to represent a color image in a computer, plus an additional eight bits for an alpha channel. See *24-bit color, alpha channel, bit depth* and *bit specifications*.

32-bit disk access

See *FastDisk*.

32-bit driver

A driver written for a 32-bit environment. See *Protected Mode driver*.

32-bit file access

See *Windows for Workgroups*.

32-bit processing

In a PC with a 386 or higher CPU, this refers to programs written for the 386's 32-bit mode, which is its fastest mode of operation. Starting with the 386, Intel CPUs have a split personality in order to maintain backward compatibility with previous CPUs. They can process 16-bits, or two bytes at a time, or process 32-bits, or four bytes at a time.

In the 386's Real Mode, a program can execute 16-bit instructions. In Protected Mode, a program has access to both 16-bit and 32-bit instructions, the maximum amount of RAM, virtual memory and virtual machine capabilities as well as memory protection, which keeps one program from crashing another.

DOS applications run in Real Mode, while Windows switches back and forth between Real Mode and Protected Mode. OS/2, UNIX, Windows NT, Windows 95 and other 32-bit operating systems run in the machine's Protected Mode to take advantage of the CPU's advanced capabilities.

32-bit Windows

Refers to Windows NT and Windows 95, which use the 32-bit native mode of the CPU (386 and above). See *Win32*.

360

See *System/360*.

360K

May refer to the 360K 5.25" minifloppy disk used with PCs.

370

See *System/370*.

370 architecture

Refers to a computer that will run IBM mainframe applications. See *System/370* and *IBM mainframes*.

370/XA

(370 EXtended Architecture) A major enhancement (1981) to System/370 architecture which improved multiprocessing, introduced a new I/O system and increased addressing from 24 to 31 bits (16MB to 2GB).

386

The successor to the 286. Also known as the 386DX, it refers to the Intel 386 CPU chip or to a PC that uses it. The 386 is faster than the 286 and provides a more sophisticated method for running multiple DOS programs. It is more responsive than the 286, but is still relatively slow for Windows and graphics-based applications. The 386 architecture has been followed in all of Intel's subsequent CPUs (486, Pentium, etc.).

The 386 addresses more memory than the 286, and provides enhanced memory management by allowing both extended and expanded (EMS) memory to be allocated on demand. See *PC* and *x86*.

**386 CPU
Technical Specs**

A 32-bit multitasking microprocessor in a 132-pin PGA package. Supports 8, 16 and 32-bit data types. Has 32 32-bit registers including eight general-purpose. Operational modes: "Real Mode" performs as a fast 8086 CPU and addresses 1MB memory. "Protected Mode" addresses 4GB physical and 64TB virtual memory and provides access to memory management, paging and memory protection capabilities (see *32-bit processing*). "Virtual 8086 Mode" is a Protected Mode subset that runs tasks as if each were in an individual 8086 CPU. See **Virtual 8086 mode**. The 386 uses 1.5 micron technology (transistor elements are as small as 1.5 microns).

386/25, 386/33...

The designation of CPU speed for a 386. The second number is the clock rate: 386/25 means 25MHz.

386DX

See *386*.

386 Enhanced Mode

An operational mode in Windows. See *Windows*.

386MAX

A DOS memory manager for 386s and up from Qualitas, Inc., Bethesda, MD, noted for its advanced capabilities. BlueMAX is a version for PS/2 models.

386SL

A version of the 386SX designed for laptops. It has built in power management, and its variable clock rate allows it to idle for long suspend and resume periods. Except for memory and video controller, the 386SL and the 82360SL chip make up almost the entire computer. See *x86*.

386SLC

An IBM version of the 386SX that includes an internal 8KB memory cache. It includes power management capabilities and runs as fast as a 386DX.

386SX

A version of the 386 from Intel that runs at slower speeds than the 386DX, addresses only 16MB of memory (not 4GB) and supports only a 16-bit data bus (not 32). It uses less power and dispells less heat than the 386DX. See *386SL* and *x86*.

387

Math coprocessor for the 386.

390

See *System/390*.

303x

A series of medium to large-scale IBM mainframes introduced in 1977, which includes the 3031, 3032 and 3033. See *IBM mainframes.*

308x

A series of large-scale IBM mainframes introduced in 1980, which includes the 3081, 3083 and 3084. See *IBM mainframes.*

3090

A series of large-scale IBM mainframes introduced in 1986. Before the ES/9000 models (System/390), 3090s were the largest mainframes in the System/370 line. Models 120, 150 and 180 are single CPUs. Models 200 through 600 are multiprocessor systems (first digit indicates the number of CPUs). The E, S and J models represent increased speed respectively. See *IBM mainframes.*

3270

A family of IBM mainframe terminals and related protocols (includes 3278 mono and 3279 color terminal). See *3270 emulator.*

3270 Data Stream

The format for transmitting data from an application to a 3270-type terminal.

3270 emulator

A plug-in board that converts a personal computer or workstation into an IBM mainframe terminal. The first 3270 emulator was the Irma board from Attachmate Corporation.

3480, 3490

Two series of half-inch magnetic tape cartridge drives from IBM that are used with mainframes and AS/400s. The 3480 units store two bytes from top to bottom on 18 parallel tracks at 38000 bpi. The 3490s store two or four bytes on 18 or 36 parallel tracks at 38000 bpi.

3770

The standard communications protocol for batch transmission in an IBM SNA environment.

3780

See *2780, 3780.*

37xx

IBM communications controllers that includes the 3704, 3705, 3720, 3725 and 3745 models. The 3704 and 3705 are early units, and the 3745 models are newer and more versatile. The 3745 includes a cluster controller that can connect 512 terminals, eight token ring networks and 16 T1 lines.

34010, 34020

General-purpose microprocessors from TI that are optimized for graphics and conform to the TIGA interface.

4DOS

A popular DOS command processor from JP Software Inc., East Arlington, MA, that replaces DOS' COMMAND.COM file. It includes enhanced commands that allow multiple files to be referenced with a single command. For example, you can copy several files with different names with one copy statement, which would require a copy statement for each file in DOS.

4GL

See *fourth-generation language*.

4mm tape

See *DAT*.

486

Also known as the *486DX*, it refers to the Intel 486 CPU chip or to a PC that uses it. It is the successor to the 386 and has become the entry-level machine in the Intel x86 line. Depending on clock rates, it runs from two to five times as fast as a 386 and provides the minimum speed necessary for Windows, CAD and other graphics-intensive applications. Its built-in math coprocessor is often required by CAD applications.

Intel has improved the performance of the 486 by offering versions with double and triple the internal speed while maintaining the same external speeds and connections (see *DX2* and *DX4*). See *OverDrive chip, PC* and *x86*.

486 CPU Technical Specs

A 32-bit multitasking microprocessor in a 168-pin PGA package. It uses the same registers and operational modes as the 386 (see *386* and *32-bit processing*). It obtains its speed from an internal 8KB memory cache that it quickly fills in burst mode.

The 486DX chip contains 1.2 million transistors; the 486SX contains 1.1 million. Both use 1.0 micron technology (transistor elements are as small as one micron).

486/25, 486/33...

The designation of CPU speed for a 486. The second number is the clock rate: 486/25 means 25MHz. CPUs beyond 33MHz may have different internal and external speeds as noted in the following table. The internal clock speed is the rate at which the CPU processes (calculates, compares, etc.). The external clock speed is the rate at which it communicates with RAM and external bus.

486 Type	Internal	External
486/25	25MHz	25MHz
486/33	33MHz	33MHz
486/50	50MHz	50MHz
486/50DX2	50MHz	25MHz
486/66	66MHz	33MHz
DX4/75	75MHz	25MHz
DX4/100	100MHz	33MHz

486DLC

A 486SX-compatible CPU from Cyrix Corporation that is pin compatible with the 386DX. Designed for upgrading 386s, it comes in a variety of speeds including clock doubling versions.

486DX

See *486*.

486DX2

See *486*.

486SL

A version of the 486 from Intel designed for laptops. It runs on 3.3 volts (instead of 5) and includes power management features like the 386SL.

486SLC

(1) A 486SX-compatible CPU from Cyrix Corporation that is pin compatible with the 386SX, has a 1K cache and uses a 16-bit bus. It provides an upgrade path for 386SXs.
(2) The IBM version of the 486SX.

486SX

A version of the 486 from Intel that runs at slower clock speeds than the 486DX and does not include the math coprocessor. 486SXs can be upgraded to 486DX2s with Intel's OverDrive chip, which includes the coprocessor. The DX2 chip is plugged into the empty coprocessor socket, disabling the original CPU. See *486*.

487

The math coprocessor for the 486.

4004

The first microprocessor. Designed by Marcian E. "Ted" Hoff at Intel, it was a 4-bit, general-purpose CPU initially developed for the Japanese Busicom calculator.

43xx

A series of medium-scale IBM mainframes initially introduced in 1979, which include the 4300, 4321, 4331, 4341, 4361 and 4381.

5v

(5 Volts) Refers to the amount of DC electricity required by the chips on most personal computer motherboards. The power supply converts 120v alternating current (AC) into 5v direct current (DC). It also generates 12v for the disk drives. See *3.3v*.

5.1 channel

A digital audio recording and playback system for home theater. It includes five channels (left, right, center, rear/surround left and right) plus a subwoofer channel. The major 5.1 channel standards are Dolby AC-3 and Philips Musicam.

5.25"

(1) Refers to disk drives and other devices with a 5 1/4 inch wide form factor.
(2) Refers to the common 5 1/4 inch floppy disk that was widely used in personal computers. By late 1994, usage dwindled to nil.

586

See *Pentium*.

5100

The first IBM desktop computer (1974). It came with up to 64K of RAM, a built-in tape drive and used APL or BASIC. Eight inch floppy disks became available in 1976.

5250

A family of terminals and related protocols for IBM midrange computers (System 3x, AS/400).

5250 emulator

Same as *twinax card*.

6DOF

(6 Degrees Of Freedom) The amount of motion supported by a virtual reality

system. Six degrees provides forward/back, up/down, left/right, up/down pitch, left/right yaw and left/right rotation movement. Three degrees of freedom, or 3DOF, provides the first three movements only.

64-bit

See *bit specifications*.

64-bit graphics accelerator

A display adapter that has a pathway 64 bits wide between its on-board graphics processor and memory (video RAM).

68K

See *68000*.

601

The first model of the PowerPC chip. See *PowerPC*.

603

A low-power PowerPC chip designed for notebooks and portable applications. See *PowerPC*.

604

The second model of the PowerPC chip. Depending on clock speed, it runs applications from 50 to 100% faster than the 601. The 604e is a version of the 604 that has enhanced architecture for improving DOS and Windows emulation. See *PowerPC*.

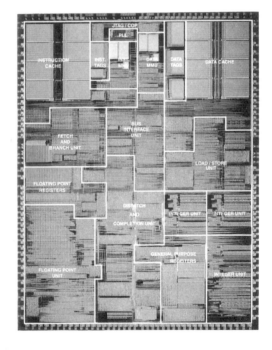

The PowerPC 604

A CPU chip such as the 604 contains many integrated, although individual, sections. Each one is responsible for a specific function. There are more than three million transistors on the 604. *(Photo courtesy of Motorola, Inc.)*

615

An IBM version of the PowerPC that provides x86 and PowerPC instruction execution on the chip itself. For example, on a CHRP-based machine, both the Mac OS and Windows 95 could run simultaneously. It is expected that when released in 1996, the 615 will run DOS/Windows applications at the rate of a 90MHz Pentium. See *CHRP*.

620

The third model of the PowerPC chip. It is expected that the 620 will run from two to three times as fast as the 601. See *PowerPC*.

640K

(640 Kilobytes) Typically refers to the first 640 kilobytes of memory in a PC, known as *conventional memory*. See *PC memory* and *PC memory map*.

640x480

Standard VGA resolution of 640 columns by 480 rows (lines). In the specification 640x480x16, the 16 is the number of colors. See *resolution*.

650

IBM's first major computer success. Introduced in 1954, it used magnetic drum memory, magnetic tape and punched cards. By the end of the 1950s, there were an estimated 1,800 units installed, making it the most widely used computer in the world.

IBM 650
The 650 put IBM in the lead early on in the computer game. The machines were mostly adjuncts to the tabulating equipment of the era by performing the more elaborate calculations. Although master records were maintained on magnetic tape, transaction input was created on punched cards.
(Photo courtesy of International Business Machines Corporation.)

686

See *P6.*

6502

An 8-bit microprocessor from Rockwell International Corporation used in the Apple II and earlier Atari and Commodore computers.

6800

An 8-bit microprocessor from Motorola. The 6801 is a computer-on-a-chip version.

68000

A family of 32-bit microprocessors from Motorola that are the CPUs in Macintoshes and a variety of workstations. It is also known as the 68K or 680x0 series.

Model	Bus Size	Max RAM
68000	16	16MB
68020	32	4GB
68030	32	4GB (built-in cache)
68040	32	4GB (2x fast as 68030)

680x0

Refers to the Motorola 68000 family of CPU chips or to applications that are written for that chip. See *68000*.

7-bit ASCII

Refers to transferring ASCII text in which an 8-bit byte holds the ASCII character plus a parity bit. Some PBXs allow only 7-bit transmission.

7-track

Refers to older magnetic tape formats that recorded 6-bit characters plus a parity bit on seven parallel tracks along the length of the tape. See *half-inch tape*.

720K

May refer to the 720K microfloppy disk used in PCs.

750

See *i750*.

786

See *P7*.

8-bit

See *bit specifications*.

8-bit sample

A sample of a sound wave based on measuring the wave on a scale of 256 increments. See *16-bit sample*.

8mm tape

A tape format used in high-capacity tape drives for backup. See *Exabyte*.

8-N-1

(8 bits, No parity, 1 stop bit) Common parameters for modem transmission.

8.3

Often refers to the method used to name files in DOS and Windows 3.x. The file name is up to eight characters long and the file extension is up to three characters long.

88K

See *88000*.

88Open

A consortium founded in 1988 that provides information and certification for the Motorola 88000-based platform. Companies such as Data General, Encore and Harris offer products using the 88K chips.

800x600

Standard super VGA resolution of 800 columns by 600 rows (lines). In the specification 800x600x256, the 256 is the number of colors. See *resolution*.

802.1

An IEEE standard for network management. See *IEEE 802*.

802.12

See *100VG-AnyLAN.*

802.2

An IEEE standard that specifies the data link layer for various media access methods. See *IEEE 802.*

802.3

An IEEE standard for a CSMA/CD local area network access method, which is widely implemented in Ethernet. See *IEEE 802.*

802.4

An IEEE standard for a token bus local area network access method, which is used in the MAP factory automation protocol. See *IEEE 802.*

802.5

An IEEE standard for a token ring local area network access method, which is widely implemented in Token Ring. See *IEEE 802.*

802.6

An IEEE standard for a DQDB metropolitan area network access method. See *IEEE 802.*

860

See *i860.*

8080

An Intel 8-bit CPU chip introduced in 1974. It was the successor to the first commercial 8-bit microprocessor (8008) and precursor to the x86 family. It contained 4,500 transistors and other electronic components.

8086, 80x86

Introduced in 1978, the CPU chip that defines the base architecture of Intel's x86 family (XT, AT, 386, 486, Pentium). 8086s are used in some XT-class machines. See *PC* and *x86.*

8086 CPU Technical Specs

A 16-bit microprocessor in a 40-pin CERDIP package. Has 14 16-bit registers including eight general-purpose. Addresses 1MB memory using base addresses contained in segment registers. Contains 29,000 transistors.

8087

The math coprocessor for the 8086/8088.

8088

The Intel CPU chip used in first-generation PCs (XT class). It is a slower version of the 8086, chosen for migration from CP/M programs, the predominate business applications of the early 1980s. See *PC* and *x86.*

8088 CPU Technical Specs

Same as the 8086 CPU except that is uses an 8-bit data bus instead of a 16-bit data bus. Designed to ease conversion from 8-bit, Z80-based CP/M programs. Contains 25,000 transistors.

8100

An IBM minicomputer introduced in 1978 that was designed for departmental computing and used the DPPX/SP operating system.

8250A
See *UART.*

8259A
Known as a Programmable Interrupt Controller, it is the interrupt controller chip used in a PC. It is superseded by the 82489DX chip. See *IRQ* and *PIC.*

8514
The IBM monitor used with its 8514/A display adapter.

8514/A
An IBM high-resolution display adapter that provides an interlaced display of 1024x768 with 256 colors or 64 shades of gray. It contains an on-board coprocessor for performing 2-D graphics and it is designed to coexist with VGA for dual monitor capability. Introduced on Micro Channel machines, third-party vendors provide non-interlaced versions for the ISA bus.

80186/80188
An integrated version of the 8086/8088 CPU that includes additional system components, such as the clock, DMA and interrupt controller, on the same chip.

80286, 80287
See *286.*

80386, 80386DX
See *386.*

80386SL, 80386SX
See *386SL* and *386SX.*

80387
See 386.

80486, 80486DX
See *486.*

80486SX, 80487
See *486SX.*

80860
See *860.*

82385
An Intel controller chip that manages the memory cache in 386 and 486 CPUs.

82489DX
Known as the Advanced Programmable Interrupt Controller, it is the successor to the 8259A interrupt controller. The 82489DX is enhanced for multiprocessing. See *IRQ* and *PIC.*

88000
A family of 32-bit RISC microprocessors from Motorola. The 88100 is the first processor in the 88000 family. Introduced in 1988, it incorporates four built-in execution units that allow up to five operations to be performed in parallel. Although the 88000 processors are very sophisticated chips, they never took off in the marketplace. See *88Open.*

9-track

Refers to magnetic tape that records 8-bit bytes plus parity on nine parallel tracks along the length of the tape. This is the common format for half-inch open reels of tape. See *half-inch tape*.

9370

A series of IBM entry-level mainframes introduced in 1986 that use the 370 architecture. In 1990, the Enterprise System models (ES/9370) were introduced, which use the Micro Channel bus and a 386 for I/O processing. The ES/9370 Model 14 biprocessor system adds a second 386 that can run DOS and OS/2 applications. A high-speed link is available between the 386 and 370 processors.

9660

See *ISO 9660*.

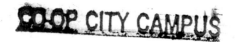